HANDBOOK OF
LATIN AMERICAN STUDIES:
No. 66

A Selective and Annotated Guide to Recent Publications in Art,
History, Literature, Music, and Philosophy

VOLUME 67 WILL BE DEVOTED TO THE SOCIAL SCIENCES:
ANTHROPOLOGY, GEOGRAPHY, GOVERNMENT AND POLITICS,
INTERNATIONAL RELATIONS, POLITICAL ECONOMY,
AND SOCIOLOGY

EDITORIAL NOTE: Comments concerning the *Handbook of Latin American
Studies* should be sent directly to the Humanities or Social Sciences Editor,
Handbook of Latin American Studies, Hispanic Division, Library of
Congress, Washington, D.C. 20540-4851.

HANDBOOK OF LATIN AMERICAN STUDIES: NO. 66

HUMANITIES

Prepared by a Number of Scholars
for the Hispanic Division of The Library of Congress

KATHERINE D. McCANN, *Humanities Editor*
TRACY NORTH, *Social Sciences Editor*

2011

UNIVERSITY OF TEXAS PRESS   *Austin*

International Standard Book Number: 978-0-292-72643-7
International Standard Serial Number: 0072-9833
Library of Congress Catalog Card Number: 36-32633
Copyright ©2011 by the University of Texas Press.
Printed in the United States of America.

First Edition, 2011

∞ The paper used in the publication meets the minimum requirements of
American National Standard for Information Sciences—Permanence of Paper
for Printed Library Materials,

ANSI Z39.48-1984.

CONTRIBUTING EDITORS

HUMANITIES

Maureen Ahern, *Ohio State University*, TRANSLATIONS
Diana Alvarez-Amell, *Seton Hall University*, LITERATURE
Severino J. Albuquerque, *University of Wisconsin-Madison*, LITERATURE
Félix Ángel, *Inter-American Development Bank*, ART
Leslie Bayers, *St. Mary's College of Maryland*, LITERATURE
Dain Borges, *University of Chicago*, HISTORY
Dário Borim, *University of Massachusetts, Dartmouth*, LITERATURE
John Britton, *Francis Marion University*, HISTORY
Francisco Cabanillas, *Bowling Green State University*, LITERATURE
José Cardona-López, *Texas A&M International University*, LITERATURE
Matt Childs, *University of South Carolina*, HISTORY
Don M. Coerver, *Texas Christian University*, HISTORY
Jerry W. Cooney, *Professor Emeritus, University of Louisville*, HISTORY
Édgar Cota-Torres, *University of Colorado, Colorado Springs*, LITERATURE
Edward L. Cox, *Rice University*, HISTORY
Sandra Cypess, *University of Maryland, College Park*, LITERATURE
Paula De Vos, *San Diego State University*, HISTORY
Juan Duschesne-Winter, *Pittsburgh University*, LITERATURE
César Ferreira, *University of Wisconsin-Milwaukee*, LITERATURE
Myrna García-Calderón, *Syracuse University*, LITERATURE
John D. Garrigus, *University of Texas at Arlington*, HISTORY
Janet Gold, *University of New Hampshire*, LITERATURE
Luis A. González, *Indiana University, Bloomington*, HISTORY
Lolita Gutiérrez Brockington, *North Carolina Central University*, HISTORY
Paola Hernández, *University of Wisconsin-Madison*, LITERATURE
Regina Igel, *University of Maryland, College Park*, LITERATURE
Clara Jalif de Bertranou, *Universidad Nacional de Cuyo, Mendoza, Argentina*,
    PHILOSOPHY
Héctor Jaimes, *North Carolina State University*, LITERATURE
Jill S. Kuhnheim, *University of Kansas*, LITERATURE
Erick D. Langer, *Georgetown University*, HISTORY
Hal Langfur, *The State University of New York at Buffalo*, HISTORY
Dana Leibsohn, *Smith College*, ART
Alfred E. Lemmon, *Historic New Orleans Collection*, MUSIC
Peter S. Linder, *New Mexico Highlands University*, HISTORY
Maria Angélica Guimarães Lopes, *Professor Emerita, University of South Carolina*,
    LITERATURE
Laura Loustau, *Chapman University*, LITERATURE
Cristina Magaldi, *Towson University*, MUSIC

Charles D. Brockett *Sewanee: The University of the South*, GOVERNMENT AND POLITICS
Luis René Cáceres, *Inter-American Development Bank*, ECONOMICS
Roderic A. Camp, *Claremont-McKenna College*, GOVERNMENT AND POLITICS
María Esperanza Casullo, *Universidad de Río Negro, Argentina*, SOCIOLOGY
César N. Caviedes, *University of Florida, Gainesville*, GEOGRAPHY
Thomaz Guedes Da Costa, *National Defense University*, INTERNATIONAL RELATIONS
María Amparo Cruz-Saco, *Connecticut College*, ECONOMICS
Bartholomew Dean, *University of Kansas*, ANTHROPOLOGY
David W. Dent, *Towson University*, GOVERNMENT AND POLITICS
Duncan Earle, *Wake Forest University*, ANTHROPOLOGY
Scott M. Fitzpatrick, *North Carolina State University*, ANTHROPOLOGY
Michael Fleet, *Marquette University*, GOVERNMENT AND POLITICS
Daniel W. Gade, *The University of Vermont*, GEOGRAPHY
Mario A. González-Corzo, *The City University of New York (CUNY)*, ECONOMICS
Clifford E. Griffin, *North Carolina State University*, GOVERNMENT AND POLITICS
Daniel Hellinger, *Webster University*, POLITICAL ECONOMY
John Henderson, *Cornell University*, ANTHROPOLOGY
Peter H. Herlihy, *University of Kansas*, GEOGRAPHY
Eric Hershberg, *American University*, POLITICAL ECONOMY
Joan F. Higbee, *Hispanic Division, Library of Congress*, GOVERNMENT AND POLITICS
Daniel Hilliard, *Georgetown University*, SOCIOLOGY
Silvia María Hirsch, *FLACSO Argentina*, ANTHROPOLOGY
Jonathan Hiskey, *Vanderbilt University*, POLITICAL ECONOMY
Keith Jamtgaard, *University of Missouri*, SOCIOLOGY
Arthur A. Joyce, *University of Colorado at Boulder*, ANTHROPOLOGY
Barbara Kotschwar, *Georgetown University*, POLITICAL ECONOMY
José Antonio Lucero, *University of Washington, Seattle*, GOVERNMENT AND POLITICS
Markos J. Mamalakis, *University of Wisconsin-Milwaukee*, ECONOMICS
Ana Margheritis, *University of Florida, Gainesville*, POLITICAL ECONOMY
Daniel Masís-Iverson, *American University*, POLITICAL ECONOMY
Kent Mathewson, *Louisiana State University*, GEOGRAPHY
Philip Mauceri, *University of Northern Iowa*, GOVERNMENT AND POLITICS
Betty J. Meggers, *Smithsonian Institution*, ANTHROPOLOGY
Mary K. Meyer McAleese, *Eckerd College*, INTERNATIONAL RELATIONS
Frank O. Mora, *National War College*, INTERNATIONAL RELATIONS
Donna J. Nash, *University of Illinois at Chicago*, ANTHROPOLOGY
Andrew Orta, *University of Illinois at Urbana-Champaign*, ANTHROPOLOGY
Jason Pribilsky, *Whitman College*, SOCIOLOGY
René Salgado, *Independent Consultant*, GOVERNMENT AND POLITICS
Joseph Leonard Scarpaci, Jr. *Virginia Military Institute*, GEOGRAPHY
David W. Schodt, *St. Olaf College*, ECONOMICS
Jörn Seeman, *Universidade Regional do Cariri, Brazil*, GEOGRAPHY
Andrew D. Selee, *Woodrow Wilson International Center for Scholars*, INTERNATIONAL RELATIONS
Peter M. Siavelis, *Wake Forest University*, POLITICAL ECONOMY
Russell E. Smith, *Washburn University*, ECONOMICS
Anthony Peter Spanakos, *Montclair State University*, POLITICAL ECONOMY
Pamela K. Starr, *University of Southern California*, POLITICAL ECONOMY

Steven L. Taylor, *Troy University*, GOVERNMENT AND POLITICS
Brian Turner, *Randolph-Macon College*, GOVERNMENT AND POLITICS
Antonio Ugalde, *The University of Texas at Austin*, SOCIOLOGY
Aldo C. Vacs, *Skidmore College*, INTERNATIONAL RELATIONS
Hannah Wittman, *Simon Fraser University*, SOCIOLOGY
Robin M. Wright, *University of Florida, Gainesville* ANTHROPOLOGY

Special Contributing Editors

Georgette M. Dorn, *Library of Congress*, HUNGARIAN LANGUAGE
Vincent C. Peloso, *Howard University*, ITALIAN LANGUAGE
Juan Manuel Pérez, *Library of Congress*, GALICIAN LANGUAGE
Iêda Siqueira Wiarda, *Library of Congress*, SPECIAL MATERIALS IN PORTUGUESE
   LANGUAGE

CONTENTS

HISTORY

LITERATURE

SPANISH AMERICA

NDEX

EDITOR'S NOTE

I. GENERAL AND REGIONAL TRENDS

With 2010 marking the bicentennial and centennial anniversaries of Latin American independence movements and the Mexican Revolution respectively, it is not surprising that publications revisiting these events are a major trend in *HLAS* 66. A new cycle of publications on Bolívar, Miranda, and San Martín; the long and short-term causes of the conflicts; and the social, cultural, political, and economic opportunities and changes wrought by the end of colonial rule made their appearance. These scholarly treatments of the wars look not only at the major events and activities of the well-known heroes, but also attempt to parse the hopes and aspirations that propelled individuals into action. As one work reviewed by the philosophy specialist indicated, the European revolutionary ideas of freedom and equality could not have taken hold in Latin America were it not for the existence of a local creole mentality (item **3649**). Recent publications on the independence movements bring to light the important role played by actors left out of earlier renditions, and many examine events from a broader perspective, thanks to the influence of Atlantic Studies, or shift their focus away from the center to areas previously regarded as peripheral. While Brazil followed a different course to independence, it too has begun the commemoration and scholarly examination of the long bicentennial from the 1808 transfer of the monarchy to Rio de Janeiro to the declaration of independence in 1822.

The lives of the elite and members of the court, Crown efforts to maintain political control, and the ideas that ultimately helped loosen those ties captured the attention of those working on Portuguese America. A new biography of Don João VI, who as prince regent established the court in exile in Rio de Janeiro, "clarifies the complex relations among Portugal, Brazil, Spain, France, and England during the ruler's 13 years in Brazil" (item **1943**). A collection of 315 letters from his daughter-in-law, the Empress Leopoldina, to her family and other significant figures of the era, sheds light on the times and on the rather poignant personal life of a young woman who bore witness to Brazil's transformation to independent nation (item **1935**). Notable among the biographies of the Spanish American heroes was a "thoughtful and readable" biography of San Martín by John Lynch praised here as "an example of how history should be written" (item **1544**). A wealth of works on the history of ideas in Latin America looks at Bolivaran thought, in particular his political and military ideas, and even the influence of his ideas on contemporary international law (see, among others, items **3602, 3607,** and **3614**). A "brilliant biography of long-neglected Manuela Sáenz," the friend, lover, and trusted confidant of Bolívar is a most welcome study of a woman who played a key role in the events of the time (item **1660**). Sáenz also drew the attention of novelists, so one can read this archival-based work in tandem with a fictional version of the lives of these two charismatic figures (item **2417**).

The confluence of Atlantic Studies and Latin American Studies, while not brand new, is now indisputable. Works with a transatlantic perspective reviewed in this volume are far too numerous to offer a complete list here, but a sampling will demonstrate the influence of this outlook on current writing. Those looking for an introduction to Atlantic Studies tipped toward Latin America should consult the "seminal" article by Alison Games in the *American Historical Review* (item **419**) and a book by Jeremy Adelman surveying the colonial and independence periods (item **390**). Among the works on independence, Wim Klooster provides a "stimulating, comparative study of the four revolutions that dominated North America, Europe, the Caribbean, and Spanish America from 1775 to the 1820s" (item **544**) and from Jane Landers, a fascinating and exhaustively researched account of the Afro-Caribbeans or Atlantic Creoles who "contributed decisively to the revolutions and independence movements in the circum-Caribbean" (item **1163**). Reaching back to an earlier colonial period, *Chasing Empire* by Kenneth Banks focuses on the challenges faced by the French state in managing its Canadian and Caribbean colonies (item **1176**). Other works reflecting the Atlantic perspective range from studies of the cultural complexity of majolica (item **28**) to the role of gender in the Spanish and Portuguese empires (item **515**), from the significance of intermediaries in the Angola-Rio de Janeiro slave trade (item **1910**) to the connection between *limpieza de sangre* (purity of blood) and the *sistema de castas* (caste system) (item **743**) and the impact of the British colonies, especially plantation life, on English culture (item **1175**).

Atlantic Studies offers a framework that deemphasizes national boundaries and seeks connections among "trade, transportation, communication, immigration, slavery, the environment, politics and empire" (p. 96). Studying slavery and the slave trade from within this context has allowed a broader understanding of the institution to emerge. In the Francophone Caribbean, the rise of Atlantic Studies has been "particularly useful in describing the impact of the French and Haitian Revolutions on slave societies throughout the Americas" (p. 211) and coincides with a new interest in Caribbean history among French academics who seek to understand and explain contemporary racial strife in their own country. Jeremy Popkin's works exploring the connections between the French and Haitian Revolutions are especially notable in this regard (see items **1242** and **1243**). In a more focused study that is revealing of the impacts of the Haitian Revolution, Rebecca Scott and Jean Hébrard trace the story of a Saint-Domingue slave and her children and grandchildren's escape to Mexico, New Orleans, and eventually Europe (item **1251**).

As shown above, Atlantic Studies can be credited with helping to illuminate the historical experiences of Afro-Latins. These works are joined by a wealth of studies published in recent years that together offer a more detailed and nuanced understanding of this population. An article on the African diaspora by Ben Vinson offers a useful overview of recent historiographical trends (item **465**). A trilingual reader edited by McKnight and Garofalo gives voice to the Afro-Latin population by presenting original letters, court testimony, petitions to the Crown, and other documents with contextual essays. Two works, an anthology of essays edited by Vinson and Matthew Restall, and a monograph by Restall, look at how the Afro-Mexican population integrated into Mexican society and the relationships among blacks, indigenous peoples, and Spaniards (items **681** and **769**). Other country-specific studies range from Jean-Pierre Tardieu's "benchmark book" on blacks in colonial Ecuador (item **1398**) to George Reid Andrew's survey of Afro-Uruguayan history, *Blackness in the White Nation* (item **1901**). The cultural contributions of black Uruguayans are further explored in a work on the country's musical traditions, particularly the tango (item **3427**). Three other works use music and the lives of musicians to explore race relations and racial identity in Brazil and Cuba (items **3445** and **3351**). With his work on race and slavery in the Ancien Régime, Pierre H. Boulle offers new information on the social history of Caribbean people of color in France and asserts that racial prejudice among the working class was a post-revolutionary construct (item **1179**). The distinguished Honduran author, Julio Escoto, "re-creates Afro-Caribbean history through an assemblage of characters of mythical proportions" in his "magnum opus" *El génesis en Santa Cariba* (item **2247**). A photographic essay documenting five years in the life of high priest Santiago Castañeda Vera provides a visual exploration of the African spiritual traditions of Santeria, Palo Monte, and Espritisimo in Cuba (item **99**).

With some exceptions, gender studies ceded space to studies of the migration experience and new examinations of indigenous peoples. The works on the history and culture of indigenous populations show a subtle shift toward more sophisticated renderings of ethnic identity and cultural continuity. Through the use of archival documents and archeological evidence, scholars are increasingly able to demonstrate that indigenous/non-indigenous interactions have been characterized by a high degree of cultural complexity. Indigenous peoples from the colonial era to the 20th century used colonial, and later, state institutions to defend individual and group interests, and to gain or maintain control over their own lives. Yanna Yannakakis' work on colonial "native intermediaries" shows how the indigenous elite both enforced and resisted Spanish authority and thus influenced the development of colonial institutions (item **800**). Indigenous engagement with the state is ongoing as shown in a book of essays on modern Ecuador, which examines indigenous attempts to gain control over state formation (item **1704**). In her book tracing land disputes in Chiapas from the colonial era to the present day, Shannon Speed demonstrates how the deep connection between indigenous identity and communal property rights can drive resistance to state control into violent action (item **265**). And, as Laura Gotkowitz shows in her "brilliant book" on Bolivia, despite intense state pressure to relinquish community land, indigenous groups remain determined to show that landownership laws favor indigenous ownership (item **1772**).

Equally significant are a growing body of studies that demonstrate the early and continued mingling of indigenous and European practices. In her article and book on chocolate, Marcy Norton shows that the delicacy was not prepared to appeal to Europeans, but instead, Europeans "sought to emulate and approximate Mesoamerican preparations of chocolate, preferring its traditional red color and flower spices" (items **502** and **754**). And Gimmel's interpretation of the *Cruz Badiano Codex* sees indigenous medicinal practices, not as a result of European hegemony as previously argued, but instead as a melding of Nahua and European ideas (item **711**).

Various migrant groups also receive their due attention this biennium. The improbable story of French immigrants from the city of Bordeaux plunked down in the Chaco wilderness as a result of an ill-advised Paraguayan colonization scheme is one of the lesser-known chapters of Latin American migration history brought to light here (item **1899**). Perhaps most notable are the numbers of works on Middle Eastern migrants and Muslims. The topics cover a wide range, giving the reader a sense of the long and varied history of "los árabes" in Latin America: from a work tracing Arab presence in Peru since the late 16th century (item **1719**) to "an exhaustively researched account" of Lebanese identity and social mobility in Mexico (item **899**), from a work describing the sale of the Koran in 19th-century Rio de Janeiro (item **2115**) to three works on the impact and integration of Middle

Easterners in Colombia (items **1639**, **1653**, and **1686**). The contentious and some-times tragic history of seasonal and permanent Mexican migration to the US is also recounted in a variety of works. Two timely studies explore the Bracero Program. One focuses on the transformative impact of the program on the city of Cerritos in San Luis Potosí (item **965**), while the other offers first-hand perspectives of US and Mexican witnesses and participants in "an excellent mix of official, academic, and journalistic accounts and analyses from the era" (item **912**).

Latin American Studies has long been known for its interdisciplinary nature (see Editor's Note, *HLAS 62*, p. xvi) and works reviewed this biennium prove to be no exception. In an issue of the *Hispanic American Historical Review*, the con-clusions drawn from an econometric analysis of the Spanish Empire and its fiscal policies led to a serious written debate on the centralizing power of the empire and the formation of nation-state in the region (see items **433**, **434**, **443**, and **462**). Musicologists are applying archival research, literary analysis, and field interviews to create a more complete picture of composers, dances, and musical forms. In his " groundbreaking" study of musical life in colonial Cuzco, Geoffrey Baker eschewed the more typical examination of musical scores, focusing instead on archival documents describing urban and rural parishes, monasteries and convents, and individual musicians (item **3369**). Carroll Edward Mace uses both literary and musical analysis in his historical study of Quiche drama as practiced by the Achi Indians of Guatemala (item **3339**). Recent works slide over to the hard sciences, borrowing their methods to help explore evidence. A study of precolumbian and colonial health analyzes skeletal and dental remains in an attempt to determine the demographic impact of epidemics (item **741**). Arnold Dean and his cohorts combine chemistry, archeology, and ethnography to understand the "chemical and ritual aspects" of the production of the bright azure pigment known as "Maya blue" (item **1**). Georgina Endfield's "meticulously documented and highly sugges-tive book" details climatic history in Mexico, looking at the biophysical implica-tions of climatic events and the social responses to them (item **700**). Her work is particularly interesting in light of current scientific inquiries about the pace and future repercussions of climate change.

In a recent issue of *Forum*, the Latin American Studies Association publica-tion, the editor of the *Latin American Research Review* announced that LASA members residing in Latin America will have free, full-text access to the journal. This will be welcome news to Latin Americans. Contributing Editors to this vol-ume applauded the increased access to scholarly research resources made available through digitization, web sites, and newly published transcriptions of primary documents. The contributor for Venezuelan history, for example, notes that two archives, the Acervo Histórico del Estado Zulia and the Registro Principal del Estado Zulia are currently digitizing their holdings. And the contributor for Puerto Rican history describes the important contributions of two e-journal providers, Scielo and Redalyc. Offering free access to their full-text content, both began by, and still emphasize, provision of digital scientific, technological, and medical jour-nals. However, with increasing numbers of humanities and social science journals listed among their electronic offerings, Scielo and Redalyc are at the forefront in providing free electronic access to Latin American Studies journals. In the US, two not-for-profit services, JSTOR and Project MUSE, lead the way in offering fee-based access to digitized versions of scholarly journals. Both of the US-based subscription services offer access to *LARR*, among other Latin American studies journals.

JSTOR and Project MUSE recently announced separate plans to partner with scholarly presses to provide e-books to their subscribers. With e-book readers finally taking hold in the US marketplace, several US scholarly presses have announced efforts to head into e-book publishing, either through on-demand provision of backlist and out-of-print titles, or through simultaneous publication of paper and e-book versions of new titles. Libraries have benefitted from a growing number of readers eager for the ease of downloading books from home or work, and one hopes that the recent moves by commercial publishers to change the pricing structure of e-books sold to libraries, limiting the numbers of borrowers per book,[1] will not squash the e-book revolution before it has truly begun. US publishers are certainly not the only ones to recognize the benefit of e-publishing. In Brazil, government support of the arts has allowed São Paulo state's official printing house, Imprensa Oficial, to provide free online access to a series of books on theater (p. 593).

The literary field has embraced the swiftness, dynamism, and interactivity of web publishing—both web sites and blogs—as a space for sharing everything from original poetry to newly translated short stories, from literary criticism to announcements of conferences, book fairs, and readings.[2] Thanks in part to web sites like *Words Without Borders*, which publishes original translations, and publisher Chad Post's blog *Three Percent*, the publicity arm of the literary translation press, Open Letter, translators and works in translation have become increasingly visible—and viable—in the book marketplace (p. 603 and p. 607). In Brazil, the steampunk community aptly uses the most revolutionary technology of our age to share their fantastical visions of a world still enchanted with Victorian-era dress, inventions, and steam-powered contraptions (p. 609–610). The literary community also recognizes and makes use of the internet's power to inform and encourage political action: writers in Nicaragua used social media to voice their opposition to censorship by the Ortega administration, and in Honduras the internet offered a vehicle for sharing creative reactions to political upheaval (p. 425).

Access to materials does not always require entering the digital realm, however. Nor would one want to overstate the electronic availability of primary, or even secondary, source material when much remains to be discovered through patient, but no less exhilarating, hours in archives and libraries. A great number of recently updated versions of classic works and transcriptions of primary sources will make those hours even more pleasurable. Several publications singled out by Contributing Editors make available a rich selection of resources for the study of indigenous peoples. The publication of a collection of "primordial titles" or writings produced within indigenous communities that are "purported to show continuous possession of lands from 'time immemorial'" will aid considerably in studying the history of indigenous land rights, (item **270**). A work containing Spanish transcriptions of 14th–15th-century Inca *quipus* (item **351**) and a "monumental, important, and long-awaited book" on the Charka (item **355**) together provide a wealth of material on the South American indigenous society. A new edition of the *Virtues of the Indian* offers "a transcription and side-by-side translation of the treatise written by Juan de Palafox y Mendoza, the famous 17th-century Bishop of Puebla and Visitor-General of New Spain" (item **760**).

Among the many new editions and new compilations reviewed in this volume, the following works deserve mention in the hope that they will stimulate

[1]Bosman, Julie. "Publisher Limits Shelf Life for Library E-Books," *New York Times*, March 14, 2011 or http://www.nytimes.com/2011/03/15/business/media/15libraries.html.
[2]For descriptions of specific digital projects recently undertaken by literature departments in US universities, see: Cohen, Patricia. "Giving Literature Virtual Life," *New York Times*, March 21, 2011 or http://www.nytimes.com/2011/03/22/books/digital-humanities-boots-up-on-some-campuses.html.

further research and inspire more fine writing in a variety of fields: first, a "sumptuous, annotated edition" of *A historia do Brazil de Frei Vicente do Salvador* which contains stunning illustrations and meticulously written essays contextualizing the Bahian-born friar's 17th-century account of Portuguese America (p. 356 and item **1942**); second, the "definitive version" of the diary of José Santos Vargas, the independence war guerrilla, in a newly republished edition with notes by Gunnar Mendoza, the long-time director of the Biblioteca y Archivo Nacional in Sucre (item **1795**); and third, *Estudios sobre el arte y la architectura coloniales en Colombia*, a compilation of important works by art historian Santiago Sebastián which are "models of scholarly research and classics in the field" (p. 4).

II. OBITUARY

DAVID BUSHNELL (1923–2010)
    Latin Americanists from around the world mourn the passing of David Bushnell at the age of 87. He shines as of one of great historians of the independence period in South America, and is particularly known for his groundbreaking work on the history of Colombia. In addition to his many seminal works, David was a staunch supporter of libraries.
    David was a close associate of Howard F. Cline, who was director of the Hispanic Division from 1953 until his untimely death in 1971. David was also a valued advisor to the Hispanic Division and more recently to me. He served as a Contributing Editor to the *Handbook of Latin American Studies*, for the history of the Independence Period from 1957–90. He was a member of its advisory board from 1981–92. His unstinting support for 50 years, and his insight in selecting the best publications for inclusion, helped to make the *Handbook* into the scholarly bibliography of record.
    David was active in the profession until the very end. Last March he was the first person I invited to present a paper at an all-day international conference on "Creating Freedom in the Americas: 1776–1826," sponsored by the Department of State's Western Hemisphere Affairs and the Library of Congress and held on November 19, 2010. We exchanged email messages for six months and David suggested scholars from both sides of the Atlantic. Then on August 8, he wrote to me that his health had taken a turn for the worse and that he would not be able participate in an event which he had been ". . . eagerly anticipating."
    We remember David with gratitude for his many years of advice and we will miss his friendship. [G. Dorn]

III. CLOSING DATE

    With some exceptions, the closing date for works annotated in this volume was 2010. Publications received and cataloged at the Library of Congress after that date will be annotated in the next humanities volume, *HLAS 68*. In consultation with the *HLAS* Advisory Board, in recent years the *Handbook* has begun to pay closer attention to publication dates of materials considered for review. We are more stringent about including works from only the previous five years.

IV. ELECTRONIC ACCESS TO THE HANDBOOK

HLAS Online
    The *Handbook's* web site, *HLAS Online*, continues to offer, free of charge, all bibliographic records corresponding to *HLAS* volumes 1–66. Records that did

not appear in a print volume may or may not be annotated, and newer records are in a preliminary editorial stage. The web site also includes a list of *HLAS* subject headings, a list of journal titles and the corresponding journal abbreviations found in *HLAS* records, tables of contents for volumes 50–59 and linked introductory essays for volumes 50–57 (*http://www.loc.gov/hlas/contents.html*), as well as introductory essays for volumes 1–49, which are searchable in the database by using the phrase "general statement." The web address for *HLAS Online* is *http://www.loc.gov/hlas/*. The site is updated weekly. *HLAS Online* is an Open-URL source, allowing seamless linking from *HLAS* entries to related electronic resources available at your institution. One major improvement to the *HLAS* citations is the inclusion of the full journal title for article records. We hope this additional piece of information helps patrons and librarians alike in locating materials.

HLAS Web

HLAS records from volumes 50 onward may also be searched through *HLAS Web*. Searches may be limited by language, publication date, place of publication, and type of material (book or journal article). The address for *HLAS Web* is *http://hlasopac.loc.gov/*. In addition, selected bibliographic records in the Library of Congress online catalog (*http://catalog.loc.gov/*) now contain *HLAS* annotations.

CD-ROM

Volumes 1–55 (1935–96) of the *Handbook* are also available on the *Handbook of Latin American Studies: CD-ROM: HLAS/CD (v. 2.0)*. This retrospective version is produced by the Fundación Histórica TAVERA (Madrid) and distributed for them by DIGIBIS. For ordering information, contact DIGIBIS:

DIGIBIS Producciones Digitales
Calle Claudio Coello, 123, 4a planta
28006 Madrid SPAIN
Tel. 00 34 91 581 20 01
Fax. 00 34 91 581 47 36
http://www.digibis.com/colecciones_cd_referencia.html/.

V. CHANGES FROM THE PREVIOUS HUMANITIES VOLUME

History

Lisa Sousa of Occidental College and Kevin Terraciano of UCLA began coverage of works on the ethnohistory of Mesoamerica. In addition to her ongoing review of works on post-revolutionary Mexican history with collaborator Don Coerver, Suzanne B. Pasztor of Humboldt State University stepped in to examine general works on Mexican history, while Contributing Editor Jürgen Buchenau took a hiatus from *HLAS*. Peter Szok of Texas Christian University collaborated on the Central American history section, annotating works on the 19th and 20th century. Two new Contributing Editors joined the roster of Caribbean historians: Matt Childs of the University of South Carolina canvassed works on the history of Cuba from the colonial era to the 20th century, while Luis A. González of Indiana University, Bloomington reviewed materials on Puerto Rico. The section on colonial South America likewise gained new members. Lolita Guitérrez Brockington, professor emerita of North Carolina Central University, prepared comments on the history of Charcas (colonial Bolivia), while Bianca Premo of Florida International University annotated the literature on Quito and Peru, and María Marsilli of John Carroll University reviewed works on Venezuela, Nueva Granada, and Chile. Daniel Masterson of the United States Naval Academy returned to *HLAS* to compile the section on 19th- and 20th-century Peruvian history.

Literature

Édgar Cota-Torres of the University of Colorado, Colorado Springs reviewed works of Mexican fiction, while Janet Gold of the University of New Hampshire began canvassing the prose fiction of Central America. Myrna García-Calderón of Syracuse University commented on the prose fiction of Puerto Rico. Laura Loustau of Chapman University joined Claire Martin to prepare annotations on the literature of Argentina. The poetry section welcomed Leslie Bayers of St. Mary's College of Maryland, who examined works of Peruvian poetry and Juan Duchesne-Winter of the University of Pittsburgh, who reviewed poetry from Central America. Jill Kuhnheim of the University of Kansas, who formerly commented on works of Peruvian poetry, took over responsibility for the poetry of the Rio de la Plata region. Paola Hernández of the University of Wisconsin, Madison examined South American plays and other works related to the theater. Dario Borim of the University of Massachusetts, Dartmouth began annotating the crônicas of Brazil, while Charles A. Perrone of the University of Florida turned his attention to the poetry of the same country.

Katherine D. McCann, *Humanities Editor*

ART

SPANISH AMERICA
Precolumbian and Colonial

DANA LEIBSOHN, *Professor of Art, Smith College*
HUMBERTO RODRÍGUEZ-CAMILLONI, *Professor of Architecture and Director, Henry H. Wiss Center for Theory and History of Art and Architecture, Virginia Polytechnic Institute and State University*

MESOAMERICA AND THE CARIBBEAN

AS HAS LONG BEEN THE CASE, recent scholarship on the art and architecture of precolumbian Mesoamerica and colonial New Spain privileges the study of specific sites and objects. Alongside this interest a significant number of scholars are turning to questions, sites, and themes that have not yet received their due. The intellectual commitments that now define the field include the desire to produce deeper and more nuanced studies of canonical settings and artworks, and an equally strong push to study unfamiliar subjects. Within this context, three broad intellectual projects are notable. First, comparative work represents an increasingly dominant mode of inquiry. Monographic studies of specific archeological sites, iconographic traditions, and indigenous manuscripts—genres of study that have long anchored scholarship in the field—continue, yet research that highlights comparative perspectives is becoming more common. In the case of prehispanic scholarship, relationships between polities, or across political and cultural boundaries is now an important theme in the field; for the colonial period, the most interesting comparative work highlights transatlantic and transpacific patterns of lived experience (items **22** and **41**). Second, scholars of colonial visual culture are more frequently writing about objects and practices created in, and for the northern regions of the New Spain, places long considered "peripheral" to the metropolitan centers of Mexico City, Oaxaca and Puebla. Third, studies of materials and materiality are gaining ground. Many of these projects are interdisciplinary, wedding archeology, art history, and chemistry. And as a group, they are leading to sharper understandings of both the techniques used to fashion artworks in the past and the meanings of materials in prehispanic and colonial settings.

In studies of the prehispanic period, comparative research highlights cultural commensurability across Mesoamerica. For instance, the writings of Rex Koontz and William Ringle, on El Tajín and Chichén Itzá (items **8** and **11**), interpret buildings and decorative programs through the lens of wide-ranging Mesoamerican practices of image-making and ritual observance. This kind of transregional work—as opposed to that which is hemispheric or transcontinental—emphasizes the distinctive aspects of Mesoamerican visual culture and belief. Although less frequent, some comparative work engages cross-cultural topics not bound strictly to the Americas, including themes such as "antiquity" or "legacies of the antique." By situating Aztec imperial traditions vis-à-vis those of classical antiquity and their humanist legacies, the exhibition catalog from the Getty Museum represents one example (item 10). Work in this vein, which is often collaborative, opens opportunities to address a diversity of readers, from specialists in the field to those whose expertise lies elsewhere; it also throws into question what is unique to Mesoamerica and the implications of studying these traditions as such.

Of all the cultures that comprise the Mesoamerican world, from the perspective of art and architecture, scholarship still consistently focuses upon the Aztec, Maya, and Teotihuacan. And within this triad, Teotihuacan stands out. More than any other single site, this metropolis fuels vibrant research in archeology, art history, and anthropology, largely (although not exclusively) by scholars based in Mexico (items 4, 3, and 14). Scholarship on the Aztec and Maya seems increasingly concerned with interpretive and cultural complexity. For instance, questions of style and heterogeneity across the Aztec empire have occupied Catherine Umberger (item 13), and Sarah Jackson enlists anthropological theories on the power of objects to explain Maya court practices and their representation (item 7). Working along different methodological avenues, but still keenly attuned to the visual experiences of the classic Maya, Stephen Houston and his colleagues have written a groundbreaking book on color—its chemistry, perception, and connotative meanings (item 15).

Mexican scholars, as opposed to those based in Europe and the US, seem more engaged by iconographic questions, which continue to hold a prominent place in the field (items 6 and 9). Less expected are the interdisciplinary studies that conjoin archeology and scientific analyses. If Houston et al., working on Maya color, represent one example, the studies by Dean Arnold and his colleagues (item 1) and Margaret Sax and hers (item 12) are no less ambitious methodologically. Both groups of scholars work across several registers, studying objects long held in museum collections, in conjunction with ethnohistoric writings, and chemical and material forms. Through this work, they present new understandings of prehispanic practices and, as well, shed light on complex histories of ownership of precolumbian objects or, in the case of Sax et al., their forgery. Moving to studies of New Spain, one sees relatively little work marked by an explicit engagement with cultural criticism: Carlos Rincón's essay, on what it means to look at colonial art today, stands out in this regard (item 23). Instead, as with much art and architectural history of the early modern period, research on New Spain is more positivist in its leanings. Several manuscript studies, for instance, explore the lived realities and prehispanic memories evoked by colonial representations, with significant interest in central Mexico (items 2, 5, and 32). The close readings of María Castañeda de la Paz (Mapa de Sigüenza), Catherine DiCesare (Ochpaniztli festival), and Jean-François Genotte (Mapa de Otumba) make clear two points: strategies of analysis well honed in the field of manuscript studies have not been exhausted; and, current knowledge of the connections and breaks between prehispanic and colonial image making is not yet as refined as it could (or should) be.

The history of collecting, while a vital topic of research among early modernists, currently plays a less prominent role in scholarship on New Spain. Museum collections and archival documents are becoming ever more accessible, however. Several Mexican museums have produced important reference works, with useful essays and exceptional bibliographies and/or DVDs of high-quality images of artworks not often on exhibit. Striking examples include the exhibition on Lorenzo Boturini, the publication of the Museo Nacional del Virreinato's sculpture collection, and the catalog of ceramics excavated from the ex-convento of Santo Domingo in Oaxaca (items **26**, **38**, and **33**). The publication and analysis of primary documents represent another fundamental mode of scholarship. By and large, this work emphasizes painting over other expressive forms: excerpts of artists' contracts from Mexico compiled by Carmen Sotos Serrano and Pedro Angeles Jiménz represent one good example; and the study of painting supplies shipped to the Americas in the 17th century, by José María Sánchez and María Dolores Quiñones, binds archival research to an interest in the materials of art-making (items **40** and **29**). The republication of the writings of Fray Andrés de San Miguel deserves mention in this context, both for its biographical content and interest in architecture (item **25**). It is unfortunate, but nevertheless true: it continues to be the case that too few primary documents related to the architectural history of New Spain see their way into print.

In spite of this fact, architectural history represents a dynamic part of the field, with impressive new research on buildings north of the urban centers of New Spain, from Nayar to Texas, Arizona, and California. Religious architecture forms a primary focus, yet the questions posed range broadly, from histories of patronage, to studies of building materials, and the symbolic meanings of architectural forms (items **31**, **34**, and **35**). Studies of architectural decorative programs—murals, ceiling paintings, and sculpture—also characterize the field. Much of this work highlights the relationship between foreign, imported imagery and that which was locally made. The studies of Martín Olmedo Muñoz's on Meztitlán (item **39**), Emily Umberger on San Xavier del Bac (item **43**), and Clara Bargellini on Santa María de Cuevas (item **27**) all stand as fine examples. In many instances, these architectural research projects also bring to light excellent new images, itself no small contribution to the field.

Studies of the sacred continue to infuse research on New Spain, especially through research that is thematic in orientation (items **36**, **37**, and **42**). While this work confirms how important are the connections between religious practice and visual culture, several scholars are pressing the boundaries of colonial art history to consider the meaning of objects, as material things, not strictly (or even primarily) as bearers of iconography. Kelly Donahue-Wallace's essay on prints, which considers the connotative meanings of printed media, provides one example (item **30**), while the exhibition catalog on mayolica, edited by Robin Farwell Gavin, Donna Pierce, and Alfonso Pleguezuelo, offers another (item **28**). In the latter case, the daily use of colonial ceramics, and their relationships to both early modern Spanish models and later, 19th- and 20th-century Mexican traditions take center stage. In suggesting how the connotative meanings of materials shape colonial art, these projects align with the intellectual turn to materiality as a subject of study in the humanities more generally. This work, along with that which is more explicitly transoceanic—such as Michael Schreffler's essay on evocations of the conquest of Mexico or the Mayer symposium essays on the trade between Spanish America and Asia (items **41** and **22**)—is also among the most explicit about methodological concerns.

Turning to the Caribbean, certain long-standing patterns persist, including a relative sparseness of new research, particularly on individual sites and collections. On a more positive note, interdisciplinary work has a long history in the Caribbean field, and continues to shape current research. For example, to explain social contexts and lived experiences in the Caribbean, Alice Samson and Bridget

Waller suggest how insights from psychology and social anthropology might be brought to bear on artifacts from the Greater Antilles (item 16). Looking from the colonial period into the present, and drawing examples from English- and Spanish-speaking islands, Patricia Mohammed explores the imaginary worlds created and sustained by the circulation of Caribbean imagery (item 44). Her work draws colonial images into conversation with those that are modern, suggesting the importance of comparative work that stretches across time, not strictly geography. [DL]

SOUTH AMERICA

Items reviewed for this biennium include a wide range of topics, with a major emphasis on architecture, painting, and sculpture. In contrast, references to the decorative arts are few; and civil, vernacular, and rural architecture do not receive enough attention. Important advances in scholarship are perhaps best reflected in multi-authored volumes (items 17 and 54) that allow for side-by-side comparisons of different research methods.

Anthologies of classic studies by distinguished scholars (item 47) are most welcome as they make available to a new generation of students and scholars in the field invaluable sources that were often originally published in journals that are now out of print and/or difficult to find. Publications of proceedings from symposia held in conjunction with museum exhibitions (item 21) have today also become dissemination opportunities for state-of-the-art research on particular areas of study.

Religious art and architecture are well represented with several titles of exceptional merit. Héctor Schenone's *Santa María* (item 24) completes the trilogy of encyclopedic volumes devoted to religious iconography in Spanish colonial art that began with *Iconografía del arte colonial: los santos*, 1992 (see *HLAS 56:64*) and *Iconografía del arte colonial: Jesucristo*, 1998 (see *HLAS 60:5*). *Escultura colonial quiteña* by Ximena Escudero-Albornoz (item 48) is a deluxe edition illustrated with spectacular full-color plates which offers the most comprehensive overview of the development of Spanish colonial sculpture in Quito published to date. Special attention is given to religious art consisting of figural sculpture, ornamental forms from gilded altarpieces, pulpits, and wooden ceilings (*artesonados*), which represent a magnificent artistic corpus by the finest artists associated with the Quito School, such as Manuel Chili "Caspicara," Bernardo Legarda, and Miguel Samaniego Jaramillo.

Santiago Sebastián's *Estudios sobre el arte y la arquitectura coloniales en Colombia* (item 47) deserves to be singled out as a major contribution to the field. Carefully compiled here in a single volume are several of the most important works by the late distinguished Spanish art historian Sebastián (d. 1995), who championed the iconographic studies of art and architecture of the Spanish colonial New Kingdom of Granada (today Colombia). Widely recognized as models of scholarly research and classics in the field, this edition makes them again available to academicians and the general public alike. A more recent complementary study dealing with painting from the New Kingdom of Granada is Vivian Marcela Carrión Barrero's *Pintura colonial y la educación de la mirada* (item 46) that analyzes this art in general terms as a reflection of the new society that the Spanish conquest created in South America. From a useful sociopolitical perspective, the author shows how the recurrent representations of *castas* (different ethnic groups) were viewed as reminders of class distinctions and the position of power enjoyed by the privileged Spanish population. The Jesuit mission towns built during the

17th and 18th centuries in the land of the Guaraní Indians in Argentina, Bolivia, Brazil, and Paraguay are discussed in Horacio Bollini's *Imágenes y símbolos del mundo jesuítico-guaraní* (item 45) and Vladimir Rodríguez Trujillo's "Architectural and structural comparison of South American and European Timber Frame Structures" (item 53). The visual and written documentation on the architectural remains of these sites (now mostly in ruins and on UNESCO's World Heritage List) is of vital importance for their conservation. Bollini's well-documented iconographic study provides a general historical background addressing the different challenges faced by the missionaries engaged in the evangelization process that included all aspects considered essential for the full and intellectual development of the Guaraní Indians. The excerpts from contemporary descriptions and inventories of the Spanish colonial period of the mission churches of San Ignacio Miní, San Miguel, Trinidad, and Jesús permit a better appreciation of their original splendor. Relying on morphological analysis, Rodríguez Trujillo compares extant timber frame Jesuit mission churches from Bolivia with similar structures from Belgium, Switzerland, and France.

Two new deluxe volumes added to the *Colección Arte y Tesoros del Perú* published under the auspices of Banco de Crédito del Perú follow the high standard of that series. Beautifully illustrated with stunning color photographs and carefully crafted contributions by leading scholars, they are examples of the best contemporary research in the field. Jorge A. Flores Ochoa's *Cuzco: del mito a la historia* (item 17) is a monumental work covering multiple aspects of the legendary city of Cuzco, tracing in detail the origins of the Inca civilization and its development during the 14th and 15th centuries, with an emphasis on the ideology that defined its worldview. Of special interest for the Spanish colonial period is the chapter "El Cuzco que vieron los españoles" (p. 219–323), which provides a synthesis of some of the earliest accounts handed down by the 16th-century cronistas who were witnesses to the first years of the encounter between the European and indigenous civilizations that gave birth to the new Spanish colonial society. Ramón Mujica Pinilla's *Visión y símbolos del virreinato criollo a la República Peruana* (item 54) celebrates the 200th anniversary of independence movements in Latin America dating from 1808, covering several important topics that focus on the critical historical period of transition from colonization to independence.

An outstanding publication dealing with the precolumbian period is Margaret Young-Sánchez's *Tiwanaku: Ancestors of the Inca* (item 21), which collects the proceedings from the January 2005 Mayer Center for Pre-Columbian & Spanish Colonial Art symposium held in conjunction with the exhibition with the same title at the Denver Art Museum. This was the first major international exhibition devoted to the Tiwanaku pre-Inca culture which developed on the southern shore of Lake Titicaca (today Bolivia) during the Middle Horizon Period (circa AD 500–1000). With only one omission, full texts of 11 papers presented at the symposium are included here. The papers reflect the most recent research on the Tiwanaku civilization, including urban planning, architecture, sculpture and calendrics. It should prove indispensable for future studies. Although not specifically focused on the Tiwanaku, Tom D. Dillehay and Ramiro Matos' essay "History, Memory and Knowledge in Andean Visual Imagery: The Intersection of Art, Architecture, and Landscape" (item 18) is of far-reaching importance for the contribution it makes to present and future precolumbian Andean studies. While reviewing the historiography of South American precolumbian art and architecture, the authors point out that "traditionally, most Andeanists have looked to diffusion, migration, innovation, structuralism, and cognition to explain the transmission of symbols and the continuity and change in their various forms" (p. 317). In contrast to these methodologies, which have often been limited to a single aspect, a new more holistic contextual approach involving art, architecture, and landscape is proposed.

One study which addresses the important topic of botanical illustrations is Víctor Peralta Ruiz and Charles F. Walker's chapter "Viajeros naturalistas, científicos y dibujantes" in item **54** mentioned above. While expeditions from Europe and the Americas have been studied from the point of view of their scientific relevance, little attention has been given to the study of the production of their visual imagery from the perspective of art history. Of related interest is the 2010 publication by José María Moreno Martin *et al.*, *The Malaspina Expedition*, which provides a wealth of visual material for an excellent comparative study. This publication brings together the visual legacy of the 1789–1794 expedition led by Italian born naval officer Alejandro Malaspina (1754–1810), consisting of maps and scientific and artistic illustrations documenting the flora, fauna, seas, people, and land of the Spanish American colonies.

National and international conferences of note included the session on "Late Gothic and Neo-Gothic in Latin America" chaired by Richardt Sundt, University of Oregon, at the 63rd Annual Meeting of the Society of Architectural Historians held in Chicago, IL between April 21–25, 2010, featuring the presentation of the paper "Late Gothic Architecture at Guadalupe and Saña on the Northern Peruvian Coast" by Humberto Rodríguez-Camilloni; and the First International Conference on Structures and Architecture held at Guimarães, Portugal between July 21–23, 2010, featuring the presentation of the papers "Architectural and Structural Comparison of South American and European Timber Frame Structures" by Vladimir Rodríguez Trujillo (item **53**) and "Constantino de Vasconcelos and Quincha Architecture in Spanish Colonial Peru" by Humberto Rodríguez-Camilloni (item **52**). The splendid 2005 Tiwanaku symposium sponsored by the Mayer Center for Pre-Columbian and Spanish Colonial Art at the Denver Art Museum is fully documented in the review of item **21**.

Finally, it is with deep sorrow that I report on the passing of distinguished Bolivian architect and art historian José de Mesa Figueroa, colleague and personal friend, on July 24, 2010. Born in La Paz, Bolivia, March 30, 1925, Mesa graduated in 1950 with a professional degree in architecture and urbanism from the Universidad Mayor de San Andrés, La Paz; and continued advanced studies in Spanish colonial art and architecture in Seville (1952–53) and Madrid (1958). Through a lifetime of scholarly work, together with his wife Teresa Gisbert, Mesa was one of the preeminent authorities on Andean Spanish colonial art and architecture. He is perhaps best known for the monumental work *Historia de la pintura cusqueña* which he co-authored with Gisbert in 1962, but he also published alone or in collaboration with Gisbert many other books and articles considered to be standard works in the field. Several of these, I had the honor and privilege to review for *HLAS* across the years and, most recently, for *HLAS 60:3, 73,* and *78.* His academic memberships included the Academia Nacional de Ciencias de Bolivia, Academia Chilena de la Historia, Academia de la Historia del Perú, Real Academia de la Historia de Madrid, Academia de Bellas Artes de Sevilla, and honorary membership to the Colegio de Arquitectos del Perú. He was the recipient of several awards, including the prestigious José de la Riva-Agüero y Osma Medal from the Peruvian Pontífica Universidad Católica; Orden de Isabel la Católica and Medal of Merit from the Spanish government; Gold Medal from the municipal government of Trujillo, Peru; and the Orden del Sol, the highest honor from the Peruvian government. With sincere appreciation and gratitude, I dedicate this section to his memory. [HRC]

PRECOLUMBIAN

Mesoamerica

1   Arnold, Dean *et al.* The first direct evidence for the production of Maya blue: rediscovery of a technology. (*Antiquity/Cambridge*, 82, 2008, p. 151–164)

Focusing on a vessel from the cenote at Chichén Itzá (now in the Field Museum of Natural History, Chicago), this essay examines chemical and ritual aspects involved in the production of the pigment known today as "Maya blue." The analysis links the pigment to the production of copal; the authors also demonstrate how new questions can be asked of older museum collections, in part by wedding chemical analysis with archeological and ethnographic studies. [DL]

Boone, Elizabeth Hill. Marriage almanacs in the Mexican divinatory codices. See item **198**.

2   Castañeda de la Paz, María. Pintura de la peregrinación de los Culhuaque-Mexitin, mapa de Sigüenza: Análisis de un documento de origen tenocha. Zinacantepec, Mexico: El Colegio Mexiquense: Consejo Nacional para la Cultura y las Artes: Instituto Nacional de Antropología e Historia, 2006. 177 p. : bibl., ill., maps.

This book, which draws upon Castañeda de la Paz's doctoral dissertation, offers a close reading of the Mapa de Sigüenza. Its discussion covers style, the use of color, the depiction of human and architectural forms, and an analysis of toponymic elements. Known copies of the Mapa de Sigüenza, as well as its collection and publication history receive substantial discussion, making this volume useful for those interested in the afterlives of colonial manuscripts. The book also includes a good color foldout of the map. [DL]

Chinchilla-Mazariegos, Oswaldo. The stars of the Palenque sarcophagus. See item **207**.

3   De la Fuente, Beatriz *et al.* Museo de murales teotihuacanos: Beatriz de la Fuente. Traducción de textos de Carole Castelli *et al.* México: UNAM, Instituto de Investigaciones Estéticas: INAH, 2007. 238 p.: bibl., col. ill., ports.

This volume, a well-illustrated collection of recent scholarship on Teotihuacan, presents a tribute to the Mexican scholar, Beatriz de la Fuente (1929–2005) and her contributions to the fields of prehispanic art history and archeology. Along with an essay on de la Fuente's research and career, the volume includes studies of the ball game and primary iconographies of Teotihuacan paintings, the materials and techniques used to create murals at the site, and a report on excavations from 1997. Many of the essays have been revised from earlier publications, and texts are bilingual (English/Spanish). [DL]

4   Díaz Alvarez, Ana Guadalupe. Huella de un cronogénesis: propuesta de identificación de los murales teotihuacanos conocidos como "estructuras arquitectónicas". (*An. Inst. Invest. Estét.*, 30:93, otoño 2008, p. 5–32)

An analysis of early murals from Teotihuacan, which argues that concepts of, and rites associated with renewal and period-ending—akin to those practiced by the Aztec—have deep roots in central Mexico. Díaz Alvarez contends that iconographic elements previously labeled "estructuras arquitectónicas" are not indigenous buildings, but abstracted glyphic elements linked to calendrical concepts, including cyclical period endings. Comparisons with the *Codex Borbonicus* help suggest that renewal rituals, not unlike those of the New Fire Ceremonies described in 16th-century codices, were also known and practiced at Teotihuacan. [DL]

5   **DiCesare, Catherine R.** Sweeping the way: divine transformation in the Aztec festival of Ochpaniztli. Boulder: Univ. Press of Colorado, 2009. 208 p.: bibl., ills., index, photos (Mesoamerican worlds: from the Olmecs to the danzantes)

An analysis of Aztec sacrality, through the lens of Ochpaniztli ("Sweeping"). Examining a variety of pictorial scenes from 16th-century central Mexican codices, including well-known Ochpaniztli pages from *Codex Borbonicus*, DiCesare explores how memories and reconstructions of Aztec ritual were forged in the first years after the Spanish conquest. Of central concern are the recasting of prehispanic ritual images and early colonial possibilities of Nahua agency. The book contributes to current discussions of both Aztec engagements with the sacred and their colonial evocation. [DL]

Diel, Lori Boornazian. Women and political power: the inclusion and exclusion of noblewomen in Aztec pictorial histories. See item **216**.

6   **Iconografía mexicana V: vida, muerte y transfiguración.** Coordinación de Beatriz Barba de Piña Chán. México: Instituto Nacional de Antropología e Historia, 2004. 235 p. (Col. Científica. serie antropología social; 447)

A collection of essays on the iconography of transfiguration and death, which grows out of a conference held in 2000. Several essays study prehispanic materials, others colonial topics. While some of the papers, such as that by Piña Chán, range widely across Mesoamerica, most highlight a specific site or iconographic theme. Emphasis rests on archeological and ethnohistorical interpretive methodologies. All of the papers were written by scholars working in Mexico; the volume therefore gives a good sense of iconographic research being done under the auspices of INAH in the 2000s. [DL]

7   **Jackson, Sarah.** Imagining courtly communities: an exploration of Classic Maya experiences of status and identity through painted ceramic vessels. (*Anc. Mesoam.*, 20:1, Spring 2009, p. 71–85)

An analysis of courtly communities based upon the iconography of Classic Maya vase painting and anthropological writings on social performance and identity formation. Jackson emphasizes particular aspects of courtly depiction that extend across Classic Maya sites, including representations of "mixed courts"—images of humans and super-naturals depicted on vases. She also explores ceramic vases as objects that shape and create Maya experiences and subjectivity; here her work owes much to that of Alfred Gell and others who have written about the power of objects and the ways things create meaning in the world. [DL]

8   **Koontz, Rex.** Lightning gods and feathered serpents: the public sculpture of El Tajín. Austin: Univ. of Texas Press, 2009. 152 p.: bibl., ill., index, photos, maps. (The Linda Schele series in Maya and pre-Columbian studies)

Koontz focuses on the ballcourts of El Tajín, the Pyramid of the Niches, and the Mound of the Building Columns. By comparing El Tajín's relief sculptures to iconographic elements in other prehispanic settings, including Teotihuacan, Las Higueras, and the Gulf Coast, as well as paintings from Maya vessels and central Mexican manuscripts, Koontz argues that wide-reaching exchange networks among elites were fundamental to the formation of El Tajín (and other sites of the Epi-classic). The book includes an excellent bibliography. [DL]

9   **Navarijo Ornelas, María de Lourdes.** La naturaleza alada en el lenguaje pictórico. (*Estud. Cult. Maya*, 28, 2006, p. 83–100, bibl., photo, tables)

This essay surveys murals at several Maya sites—including Bonampak, Xelhá, Calakmul, Xuelén, Mulchi and Chichén Itzá—to better understand Maya ecological knowledge. Navarjio Ornelas has intentionally chosen images from different regions and time periods, and she identifies paintings of several birds, including falcons, parrots, pelicans and vultures. Ultimately, the essay argues that Maya avian depictions, while mimetic in many regards, have symbolic implications and did not simply represent local environments. [DL]

Navarrete, Federico. The hidden codes of the Codex Azcatitlan. See item **240**.

10 Pohl, John M. D. Lyons, Claire L. The Aztec pantheon and the art of empire. Los Angeles, Calif.: J. Paul Getty Museum, 2010. 98 p.: bibl., ill. (some col.), index, maps (some col.)

A catalog published in conjunction with an exhibition of art from classical antiquity and the Aztec empire. Short essays address Aztec political and religious history and the Greco-Roman traditions that intellectually anchored friars and others involved in the conquest and settlement of New Spain. The images, all reproduced via excellent photographs, range from well-known Aztec sculptures (largely from the collection of the Museo Nacional de Antropología) to engravings from books printed in Europe in the 17th and 18th centuries (many owned by the J. Paul Getty Museum). Discussion of individual objects highlights iconography and how European knowledge of Greco-Roman antiquity shaped Creole and European understandings of the prehispanic Aztecs. [DL]

11 Ringle, William. The art of war: imagery of the Upper Temple of the Jaguars, Chichén Itzá. (*Anc. Mesoam.*, 20:1, Spring 2009, p. 15–44)

Working from copies of paintings made in the early 20th century by Adela Breton, Ringle discusses the iconography and composition of murals at the Upper Temple of the Jaguars. He interprets the scenes as a series of historical conquests and, comparing the paintings to other Mesoamerican imagery, he suggests the Temple may have been associated with rites of investiture that were widely known across Mesoamerica and of long standing antiquity. [DL]

12 Sax, Margaret *et al.* The origins of two purportedly precolumbian Mexican crystal skulls. (*J. Archaeol. Sci.*, 35:10, Oct. 2008, p. 2751–2760)

A study of the authenticity of two well-known crystal skulls linked to the collector Eugène Boban. Drawing upon mineralogical and physical analysis of the skulls (today in the British Museum and Smithsonian Institution), comparative ethnohistoric work, and research on precolumbian artifacts from other cultures—including a Mixtec quartz goblet—, Sax *et al.* demonstrate that neither skull is prehispanic. Among the more interesting aspects of the essay: the authors distinguish 19th-century carving techniques (British Museum) from those of the 20th century (Smithsonian). Methodologically, a good example of interdisciplinary work on museum collections. [DL]

Staines Cicero, Leticia. Testimonios de pintura mural prehispánica: dibujos de Agustín Villagra Caleti. See item **266**.

13 Umberger, Emily. Historia del arte e Imperio Azteca: la evidencia de las esculturas. (*Rev. Esp. Antropol. Am.*, 37:2, 2007, p. 165–202)

A comparative study of Aztec sculpture from the Toluca Valley and the Gulf Coast. At issue is the extent and form of Aztec influence outside the Valley of Mexico. Focusing on sculptures from Castillo de Teayo and Calixtlahuaca, both of which experienced imperial intrusions after 1450, Umberger shows how the imperial style exhibits consistent elements yet is marked by local contributions. In addition to its focus on Aztec imperium (and especially its internal complexity), the essay includes a useful discussion of style as a category of art historical analysis. [DL]

14 Valdez Bubnova, Tatiana. El valor en la imagen gráfica teotihuacana: reflexiones desde la Ventilla. (*An. Inst. Invest. Estét.*, 30:92, primavera 2008, p. 5–47)

An interpretation of the glyphic elements discovered at the "Patio de los Glifos" during the La Ventilla excavations of 1992–94 at Teotihuacan. Valdez Bubnova argues these images cannot be interpreted as isolated elements, but should instead be read within a broad context formed by physical relationships, other graphic representations from Teotihuacan, and traditions of early writing known from Mesoamerica, Mesopotamia and Asia. Through comparative analysis, Valdez Bubnova refutes the hypothesis that the images at Patio de los Glifos represent intrusive, foreign elements at Teotihuacan. [DL]

15 Houston, Stephen D. *et al.* Veiled brightness: a history of ancient Maya color. Austin: Univ. of Texas Press, 2009. 148 p.: bibl., col. ill., index, maps. (The William & Bettye Nowlin series in art, history, and culture of the western hemisphere)

A collaborative study of color—its terminology, production, perception, and symbolic meanings—in the ancient Maya world. Because the history of Maya color use, which shows increasing complexity over time, forms the primary concern of the book, the sweep of the text is broad, although careful attention is given to temporal and regional divisions. The analysis is interdisciplinary, building upon the work and methodologies of archeologists, art historians, chemists, and linguists. Examples come primarily from Maya vases, but also architectural sculpture, murals, and relief carvings. Overall, the book offers an interesting model for future research, with a wide-ranging and impressive bibliography that stretches traditional Maya scholarship in new directions. [DL]

The Caribbean

16   **Samson Alice** and **Bridget Waller.** Not growling but smiling: new interpretations of the bared-teeth motif in the precolumbian Caribbean. (*Curr. Anthropol.*, 51, June 2010, p. 425–433)

Focusing on artifacts from the Greater Antilles, this essay draws upon the scholarship of archeology, psychology, and ethnohistory. Working from studies of facial expression in human and nonhuman primates, Samson and Waller propose the Taíno bared-teeth motif, known from sculptures, may have been integral to the development of social cohesion. This interpretation challenges older analyses of the motif, which draw more heavily on 16th-century European accounts of the Caribbean, and highlight the interpretive themes of death, shamanic trance, and aggression. [DL]

South America

17   **Cuzco: del mito a la historia.** Textos de Jorge A. Flores Ochoa *et al.* Lima: Banco de Crédito, 2007. 345 p.: bibl., ill. (Col. Arte y tesoros del Perú)

Splendid multi-authored edition by distinguished art historians Flores Ochoa, Elizabeth Kuon Arce, Roberto Samanez Argumedo, Luis Federico Barreda Murillo, and Catherine Julien is another important contribution to the *Colección Arte y tesoros*

del Perú published under the sponsorship of the Banco de Crédito del Perú. Spectacular color plates reveal the beauty of the city of Cuzco and its surrounding countryside which rose to become the imperial capital of the Tawantinsuyo during Inca times. Aerial photographs, panoramic views, and close-up details complemented with full-color reproductions of works of art and historic documents comprise an impressive corpus of visual material. The well-documented text traces in detail the origins of the Inca civilization and its development during the 14th and 15th centuries, with an emphasis on the ideology that defined its worldview. A comprehensive discussion of Inca administration, demographic distribution, and social and economic milieu provides an excellent background for the presentation of the Incas' greatest achievements in urbanism, architecture, and engineering in the city of Cuzco and such satellite royal estates as Machu Picchu, Ollantaytambo, and Pisac. Of special interest for the Spanish colonial period is the chapter "El Cuzco que vieron los españoles" (p. 219–323), which provides a synthesis of some of the earliest accounts handed down by 16th-century *cronistas* who witnessed the first years of the encounter between the European and indigenous civilizations that gave birth to the new Spanish colonial society. As a result of this encounter, the city of Cuzco underwent a major change in the physiognomy of its buildings, streets, and plazas, a topic which is discussed with beautifully illustrated examples in the section "El Cuzco español," "Reparto de solares," and "Las dos repúblicas" (p. 293–303). Extensive notes for each chapter (p. 325–327) and a comprehensive bibliography including historic and contemporary sources (p. 329–333) add significant value to this publication as an indispensable source for future research. [HRC]

18   **Dillehay, Tom D.** and **Ramiro Matos.** History, memory and knowledge in Andean visual imagery: the intersection of art, architecture, and landscape. (*in* Pre-Columbian world. Edited by Jeffrey Quilter and Mary Miller. Washington: Dumbarton Oaks Research Library and Collection, 2006, p. 313–341, bibl., ill., photos)

This chapter by distinguished scholars is of exceptional importance for the contribution it makes to present and future precolumbian Andean studies. While reviewing the historiography of South American precolumbian art and architecture, the authors point out that, "traditionally, most Andeanists have looked to diffusion, migration, innovation, structuralism, and cognition to explain the transmissions of symbols and the continuity and change in their various forms" (p. 317). In contrast to these methodologies, which have often been limited to a single aspect, a new more holistic contextual approach involving art, architecture, and landscape is proposed. Even though at the end the authors concede that the intent of their study was not "to provide new data and to formulate a new methodology to study [the cultural heritage of ancient America]" (p. 335), it is clear that future archeological and artistic studies of visual imagery would benefit greatly from this intelligent suggestion. For ethnohistorian's comment, see item **310**. [HRC]

19 Madrid de Zito Fontán, Liliana and Zulma Palermo. Cuentan las culturas, los objetos dicen—. Con la colaboración de Diego Outes Coll. Salta, Argentina: Ediciones Fundación Pajcha, 2008. 101 p.: bibl., ill. (some col.).

This handsome publication from the Fundación Pajcha in the province of Salta, Argentina, seeks to promote the study and conservation of indigenous material culture of the Americas from precolumbian times to the present day. Described more as a literary voyage rather than an art historical narrative, the seven short chapters of the book present a variety of topics ranging from religious art during the Spanish colonial period (CH. 4: "El mundo de las creencias: impacto de la conquista") to examples of 19th- and 20th-century folk art from Peru, Bolivia, and Argentina (CH. 3: "El heterogéneo mundo andino"). Fine quality b/w and color illustrations accompany the text, but some of the small size reproductions do not permit a full appreciation of the works. The selected bibliography provides useful references for further reading. [HRC]

20 Mason, Peter. Siete maneras de ser moai. (*Bol. Mus. Chil. Arte Precolomb.*, 10:2, 2005, p. 9–27, bibl., maps, photos)

Using the well-known "Mapamundi surrealista" geographic map originally published in *Variétés* in 1929 prominently locating Easter Island in Chile as a starting point, author offers a literary narrative discussing the different ways the famous *moai* or colossal anthropomorphic carved stones on the island have been depicted across time. Not an archeological or art historical study per se, the study sheds no new light on the meaning of these enigmatic sculptures, but instead examines the effects that various ways of representing the *moai* have produced on their viewers. It makes the assumption that these perceptions are conditioned by an emphasis on either the natural or the cultural aspect of the *moai*. For a more scientific approach to the subject, the reader should refer to the essential bibliography at the end of the article. [HRC]

21 Young-Sánchez, Margaret. Tiwanaku: ancestors of the Inca. Denver, Colo.: Denver Art Museum, 2009. 215 p.: bibl., ill. (some col.), index, maps (some col.).

This handsome volume makes available the proceedings from the Jan. 2005 Mayer Center for Pre-Columbian & Spanish Colonial Art symposium at the Denver Art Museum held in conjunction with the exhibition "Tiwanaku: Ancestors of the Inca" which opened the year before in the same museum. It was the first major international exhibition devoted to the Tiwanaku pre-Inca culture which developed on the southern shore of Lake Titicaca (today Bolivia) during the Middle Horizon Period (c. AD 500–1000). The show brought together Tiwanaku-style works of art in stone, ceramics, gold, wood, bone, and textiles currently dispersed among South American, North American, and European collections, which could also be compared with objects produced by other earlier cultures such as Wankarani, Chiripa, Pucara, and the Wari, a contemporary and most closely related civilization to Tiwanaku. The 11 papers presented at the symposium by distinguished scholars reflect the most recent research on the Tiwanaku civilization, including extensive fieldwork, analysis, and interpretation. Topics such as urban planning, architecture, sculpture, and calendrics at the Tiwanaku site are frequently discussed. The fine quality visual material includes color, b/w photographs, line drawings, and virtual reconstructions. Extensive notes and bibliographies follow each of the chapters. For archeologist's review of 1st ed., see *HLAS 63:352.* [HRC]

COLONIAL

General

22   Mayer Center Symposium, *Denver Art Museum, 2006.* Asia & Spanish America: trans-Pacific artistic and cultural exchange, 1500–1850: papers from the 2006 Mayer Center Symposium at the Denver Art Museum. Edited by Donna Pierce and Ronald Otsuka. Denver, Colo.: Denver Art Museum 2009. 200 p.: bibl., ill. (chiefly col.), col. maps (some folded). (Symposium series/ Mayer Center for Pre-Columbian and Spanish Colonial Art; 2006)

This volume presents diverse perspectives on Pacific trade and its influence on objects made and used in Latin America and Asia in early modernity. As a whole, the studies highlight works from public museum collections, with essays on porcelain, biombos, paintings, textiles, lacquer boxes and furniture, and ivory carvings. Many of the essays were originally presented at the symposium of the Frederick and Jan Mayer Center for Pre-Columbian and Spanish Colonial Art at the Denver Art Museum in 2006. Some of the authors are specialists on Latin America, some on Asia, all present useful new information about specific objects, many of which are not well known. [DL]

23   Rincón, Carlos. De la guerra de las imágenes a la mezcla barroca de los imaginarios en el mundo colonial americano. Bogotá: Univ. Nacional de (Colombia, Facultad de Artes, 2007. 82 p.: bibl., ill. Col. sin condición; 12)

In this extended essay on colonial images and their cultural legacies, Rincón ranges across Spanish America, considering concepts of the sacred, of presence and *ixiptla,* and of mixing (and remixing). His analysis is inspired by a broad range of authors, from Serge Gruzinski and Teresa Gisbert to Jean Baudrillard and Paul Virilio. The essay touches upon many kinds of colonial objects—including casta paintings and church facades—but Rincón's primary interests align more closely with art criticism than art history, provoking interesting questions about what it means to look at (or study) colonial images today. [DL]

24   Schenone, Héctor H. Santa María. Buenos Aires: Editorial de la Univ. Católica Argentina, 2008. 636 p.: bibl., ill. (some col.).

Monumental work by leading Argentinian art historian Schenone offers an encyclopedic compendium of Marian iconography during the Spanish colonial period. Following closely the methodology of the classic studies by Louis Réau, *Iconographie de l'art Chrétien* (1957) and A. Pigler, *Barockthemen* (1956), the text describes in detail every episode in the life of the Virgin Mary illustrated with representative examples of Spanish colonial paintings and sculptures. Also reproduced are a number of European prints that were used as sources of inspiration by the artists working in the Spanish American colonies. Useful lists of works of art with information as to their whereabouts are provided at the end of each of the iconographic themes discussed. All in all, an excellent contribution to the field that complements the author's previous major reference works, *Iconografía del arte colonial: los santos,* Vol. 1–2, 1992 (see *HLAS 56:64*) and *Iconografía del arte colonial: Jesucristo,* Vol. 3, 1998 (see *HLAS 60:5*). [HRC]

Mesoamerica

25   Andrés de San Miguel, fray. Obras de fray Andrés de San Miguel. Introducción, notas y versión paleográfica de Eduardo Báez Macías. 2. ed. México: UNAM, Instituto de Investigaciones Estéticas, 2007. 524 p.: bibl., ill., index, facsims, plans.

This book, an updated version of the author's 1969 publication, provides access to the architectural writings of Fray Andrés de San Miguel (1557–1652). In addition to a biography of Fray Andrés, Baez Macias discusses the 17th-century projects in which the friar was involved (including the desagüe, Valley of Mexico) and the role of the Discalced Carmelites in New Spain (the order to which Fray Andrés belonged). The prose of Fray Andrés offers a good window into the working knowledge of architecture, mathematics, and hydrology in the 17th century. [DL]

26   **Antei, Giorgio.** El caballero andante: vida, obra y desventuras de Lorenzo Boturini Benaduci, 1698–1755. México: Museo de la Basílica de Guadalupe, 2007. 334 p.: bibl., col. ill., col. maps

This catalog was produced in conjunction with an exhibition at the Museo de la Basílica de Guadalupe (Mexico City). The text, which is extensive, explores Boturini's biography, drawing particular attention to his travels and writings. The images are varied in media and theme, ranging from indigenous codices and handwritten manuscripts to European paintings and prints. While the volume says relatively little about how, specifically, Boturini collected the objects he did, it offers much on the world of ideas and cultural ambitions in which Boturini circulated. [DL]

27   **Bargellini, Clara.** El entablado jesuita de Santa María de Cuevas: sobrevivencia y desarrollo de una tradición. (*An. Inst. Invest. Estét.*, 29:91, otoño 2007, p. 9–30)

This essay sketches the history of the church of Santa María de Cuevas (Chihuahua), although Bargellini's central interests rest upon the ceiling painting, particularly its visual similarities to works from Michoacan, the Baja Tarahumara, and Europe. Through comparative analysis, Bargellini recognizes new patterns of artistic exchange and production in Nueva Vizcaya and, more broadly, New Spain. The study is distinctive, in large part, for the range of visual associations it explores. [DL]

28   **Cerámica y cultura: the story of Spanish and Mexican mayólica.** Edited by Robin Farwell Gavin, Donna Pierce, and Alfonso Pleguezuelo Hernández. Translations by Kenny Fitzgerald. Albuquerque: Univ. of New Mexico Press, 2003. 356 p.: bibl., ill. (chiefly col.), index, maps.

Published in conjunction with an exhibition held at the International Museum of International Folk Art (Santa Fe, New Mexico), this catalog explores the history of mayolica, emphasizing connections between Spain and New Spain. This transatlantic lens brings out the cultural complexity of ceramic traditions in Europe and the Americas, making it clear that Mexican ceramics were never simply derivatives of Spanish models. Most essays discuss the production and daily use of mayolica in early modernity, although some address the 20th century and living ceramicists. Color images throughout make the volume very useful as reference work, as does the bibliography, which features recent research. [DL]

29   **Cuerpo de documentos y bibliografía para el estudio de la pintura en la Nueva España, 1543–1623.** Compilación de Carmen Soto Serrano y Pedro Angeles Jiménez. México: UNAM, Instituto de Investigaciones Estéticas, 2007. 195 p.: bibl, index.

This volume is comprised of transcriptions of archival documents related to the practice and commerce of painting in New Spain, primarily excerpts of contracts. The book also includes lists of expenses for fiesta preparations, inventories, documents concerning indigenous painters in central Mexico, and several documents involving Simón Peyrens. The excerpts have been drawn from the Archivo General de Indias and the Archivo General de la Nación, as well as notarial and other archives in Mexico City, Puebla, and Tlaxcala. Very useful as a primary source on the early colonial period and the history of painting in New Spain. [DL]

30   **Donahue-Wallace, Kelly.** Picturing prints in early modern New Spain. (*Americas/Washington*, 64:3, Jan. 2008, p. 325–349, ill.)

In this analysis, Donahue-Wallace explores the connotative meanings of prints. The essay includes a brief history of prints in New Spain and discusses examples of paintings of prints, particularly in portraits of clerics and casta paintings. In contrast to earlier literature, which viewed collecting and the display of prints largely as markers of relative poverty, Donahue-Wallace argues that prints held wider associations in New Spain, signaling social and economic statues, devotional commitment, and corporate identity. For colonial historian's comment, see item **699**. [DL]

31   **Ettinger, Catherine.** Images of order: descriptions of domestic architecture in mission-era California. (*An. Inst. Invest. Estét.*, 29:91, otoño 2007, p. 155–182)

This essay discusses changes in indigenous domestic architecture in the wake of Franciscan mission building in Alta California in the late 18th and early 19th centuries. Ettinger's analysis centers upon European ideas about how spatial order could create and foster the kind of "civilized" life sought for indigenous converts to Catholicism. The evidence she draws upon features friars' written descriptions of mission housing, as well as the accounts of travelers and colonial officials. [DL]

32   Genotte, Jean-François. El método de Galarza aplicado al *Mapa de Otumba*: un documento pictográfico poco conocido del México colonial. (*Desacatos*, 22, sept./ dic. 2006, p. 119–134, bibl., ill.)

This case study of the *Mapa de Otumba* works from multiple kinds of evidence: excavations in the region of Otumba, the topography of the area, and painted elements of the map itself. Genotte's primary interpretive method follows that of Joaquín Galarza, a Mexican scholar who argued that detailed analyses of pictographic elements were fundamental to any correct understanding of indigenous paintings from 16th-century central Mexico. The essay ultimately provides a close reading of an early colonial document, and suggests how sociopolitical and religious shifts were experienced by indigenous communities in the first generations after the Spanish conquest. For comment by ethnohistorians, see item 221. [DL]

33   Gómez Serafín, Susana and Enrique Fernández Dávila. Catálogo de los objetos cerámicos de la orden dominicana del ex convento de Santo Domingo de Oaxaca. México: Instituto Nacional de Antropología e Historia, 2007. 228 p.: bibl., ill. (Col. Científica; 503. Serie Arqueología)

A catalog of ceramics excavated from the monastic complex of Santo Domingo (today held in the Museo de las Culturas de Oaxaca). The ceramics range in date from the late 16th century to the late 20th century, and the catalog describes locally made wares as well as imports from Europe and Asia. The volume includes black and white images, and brief descriptions of physical features and general find site of each ceramic example. A companion CD provides color images. For a more extensive interpretive work on this material see, *Las cerámicas coloniales del ex convento de Santo Domingo de Oaxaca, Pasado y presente de una tradición* (2007), which draws upon the same 1990s excavations. [DL]

34   Gutíerrez Arriola, Cecelia. Misiones del Nayar: la postrera obra de los jesuitas en la Nueva España. (*An. Inst. Invest. Estét.*, 29:91, otoño 2007, p. 31–68)

A survey of Jesuit missions constructed in the province of San Joseph de Toledo del Gran Nayar (northwest Mexico). Gutíerrez Arriola draws upon both documentary and structural evidence to establish basic chronologies and describe the architectural features of several Jesuit projects of the 18th century; the essay also discusses the importance of musical instruments in mission inventories. In addition to providing useful images of buildings, Gutíerrez Arriola offers new insight into the architectural history of a region that was decidedly nonurban and remains, as yet, poorly studied. [DL]

35   Ivey, James E. The completion of the church roof of San Antonio de Valero. (*An. Inst. Invest. Estét.*, 29:91, otoño 2007, p. 125–153)

A sophisticated architectural analysis that explores the thinking of builders and their patrons in Northern New Spain in the late 18th and early 19th centuries. At the center of the essay is a rare drawing of a proposed roof for the church at the Alamo (Texas). Ivey explores the image, but also local choices for building materials and the history of architectural traditions in the region. Of particular interest is the distinction he draws between Franciscan and military ideas about architecture. [DL]

36   Lara, Jaime. Christian texts for Aztecs: art and liturgy in colonial Mexico. Notre Dame, Ind.: Univ. of Notre Dame Press, 2008. 372 p.: bibl., ill. (chiefly col.), index, map, music.

A study of native liturgical worship in central Mexico, with an emphasis on outward (as opposed to inward, spiritual) aspects of Christian practice. Lara's work covers much ground: from medieval traditions in Europe to missionary texts in New Spain; it also discusses Corpus Christi and other feast day processions and material objects associated with worship. Central to Lara's analyses is his idea that Aztec religion was not so much destroyed as "recycled" through the Christianization of its verbal and visual metaphors. The book includes many useful images, especially of indigenous codices and murals in monastic complexes, and English translations of relevant liturgical texts. [DL]

Luján Muñoz, Jorge. Nueva antología de artículos de historia del arte, arquitectura y urbanismo. See item **1053**.

37   Merlo Juárez, Eduardo and **Evelin Flores Rueda.** Quién como Dios: San Miguel Arcangel: catálogo de la exposición temporal, abril 9-julio 31, 2005. Puebla, Mexico: Museo de Arte Popular Religioso: CONACULTA-INAH: UPAEP, 2005. 114 p.: bibl., col. ill.

This exhibition catalogue from the Museo de Arte Popular Religioso (Puebla) features 18th-century paintings and sculptures of San Miguel, largely drawn from public and private collections in Mexico, especially churches and other religious institutions in Puebla and nearby towns. Catalog texts focus on iconography, the role of San Miguel in Christian writings, and his importance to the history of Puebla de los Angeles. While some 19th- and 20th-century images of San Miguel appear, it is the relationship among religion, visual images, and Novohispanic history in the 18th century that comes through most clearly. [DL]

38   Museo Nacional del Virreinato (Mexico). Escultura: Museo Nacional del Virreinato. Coordinación general de Miguel Fernández Félix. Toluca, Mexico: Gobierno del Estado de México; Tepotzotlán, Mexico: Museo Nacional del Virreinato; México: Asociación de Amigos del Museo Nacional del Virreinato: Instituto Nacional de Antropología e Historia: Consejo Nacional para la Cultura y las Artes, 2007. 205 p.: bibl., col. ill.

A suite of scholarly essays and exceptional photographs of the sculpture collection of the Museo Nacional del Virreinato. The essays provide an introduction to sculptural traditions in New Spain, discuss the use of materials and techniques preferred by Novohispanic carvers (including work with pasta de caña, wood, wax, stone, and ivory), and examine the transatlantic trade of images and objects in the 17th cen-

tury. A companion CD allows one to study and sort works by title, material, or century, and provides full catalog information. Overall, an excellent resource for scholars, with useful diagrams, x-ray photographs of selected images, glossary, and short bibliography. [DL]

39   Olmedo Muñoz, Martín. La vision del mundo agustino en Meztitlán. (*An. Inst. Invest. Estét.*, 31:94, primavera 2009, p. 27–58)

A reconstruction of the visual features and religious context of mural paintings in the refectory and stairwell of the Augustinian convent of Meztitlán (Hidalgo). Olmedo Muñoz compares the refectory wall paintings to the map of Meztitlan from the Relaciones Geograficas, and discusses how space and topography are depicted in each. He also argues that the stairwell images, in contrast, rework a series of Dutch prints, and highlight the theme of *Triunfo de la Castidad* and *Triunfo de la Paciencia.* The essay includes excellent images of the murals by the author. [DL]

40   Sánchez, José María and **María Dolores Quiñones.** Materiales pictóricos enviados a América en el siglo XVI. (*An. Inst. Invest. Estét.*, 31:94, primavera 2009, p. 45–67)

This essay offers excerpts of transatlantic flotilla records that identify artists' supplies sent to New Spain. It singles out several of the most common pigments and varnishes—white, greens, reds, yellows, and blues—and explains their features, sources, and uses. Sánchez and Quiñones also provide a good sense of relative demand for, and value of each color and its variants. Overall, a clear and concise view into the vocabularies and valued material properties of paint in both Spain and New Spain. [DL]

41   Schreffler, Michael. "Their Cortés and our Cortés": Spanish colonialism and Aztec representation. (*Art Bull.*, 91:4, Dec. 2009, p. 407–425)

This essay asks how Aztec representation took form in, and was shaped by the writings of Spanish authors, including Bernal Díaz del Castillo, Francisco López de Gómara and Antonio de Solís. Schreffler considers indigenous images as well as Spanish pictorial practices, in order to suggest how early modern notions of cultural difference were forged. The work of Manuel González, in shell and paint, figures prominently in Schreffler's analysis. Overall, the essay stands as a good example of current transatlantic interpretive work that moves beyond traditional questions of influence and syncretism. [DL]

42   Shean, Julie. "From his roots a branch will bear fruit": the development of missionary iconography in late-18th-century cult images of Sebastián de Aparaicio, 1502–1600. (*Colon. Lat. Am. Rev.*, 18:1, April 2009, p. 17–50)
        This essay examines representations of the life works of Sebastián de Aparicio, a Franciscan active in Puebla de los Angeles. Focusing on a 1789 publication that commemorated his beatification, Shean discusses the iconography of printed images, paintings in the Chapel de la Conquistadora in Puebla that were inspired by the publication, and how both sought to align Sebastián de Aparicio with the broad program of early Franciscan work in New Spain. For colonial historian's comment, see item **785**. [DL]

43   Umberger, Emily. Bac on the border. (*An. Inst. Invest. Estét.*, 29:91, otoño 2007, p. 68–123)
        Umberger focuses on the Franciscan period (late 18th/early 19th century) of San Xavier del Bac's history (Arizona), especially Franciscan transformations to the earlier Jesuit structure. A proposed reconstruction of the sculptures in the Franciscan main retablo forms the center of the essay. Umberger also considers local contributions to the production of sculptures and paintings, and indigenous readings of this imagery. This essay is useful both for its discussion of a specific (and complex) building in northern New Spain, and because it situates a major set of religious projects from the late colonial period within the broader context of Spanish and Novohispanic religious art. [DL]

The Caribbean

44   Mohammed, Patricia. Imaging the Caribbean: culture and visual translation. Oxford, England: Macmillan, 2009. 387 p.: bibl., ill. (some col.), index, maps.

        A history of representation, focused on the West Indies. Mohammed is interested in the visual metaphors produced in, and about the Caribbean, and her examples come from the 16th century to the present, both "high art" and popular culture. Spanish American material appears throughout, but is most fully discussed in chapters on antiquity and cartography. Other thematic chapters center on European perspectives of the Caribbean and its residents, national imagery and imaginaries, and practices developed out of African and Asian traditions. The range of images discussed—including posters, paintings, maps, altars, temples, and markets—distinguishes this book, as does the range of references, which are equally diverse. [DL]

Chile, Argentina, Paraguay, and Uruguay

45   Bollini, Horacio. Imágenes y símbolos del mundo jesuítico-guaraní. Corrientes, Argentina: Moglia Ediciones; Argentina: Fundación Tierra Sin Mal, 2006. 182 p.: bibl., ill. (some col.).
        Useful art historical iconographic study of a selection of architectural remains and religious art from the Jesuit mission towns founded in Argentina, Brazil, and Paraguay during the 17th and 18th centuries to protect Guarani Indians from the Portuguese slave trade, abuses of Spanish colonists, and to teach them the doctrine of the Christian faith. The well-documented text provides a general historical background addressing the different challenges faced by the missionaries engaged in the evangelization process that included all aspects considered essential for the full spiritual and intellectual development of the Guarani. The fine religious art produced in such missions as San Ignacio Miní, San Miguel, Trinidad and Jésus, is highlighted as eloquent testimony of the skill of the indigenous American artists who created them. Excerpts from contemporary descriptions and inventories dating from the Spanish colonial period included in the appendix permit a better appreciation of the original splendor of several mission churches now lost or preserved only as ruins. [HRC]

Madrid de Zito Fontán, Liliana and **Zulma Palermo.** Cuentan las culturas, los objetos dicen—. See item **19**.

Colombia

46 Carrión Barrero, Vivian Marcela.
Pintura colonial y la educación de la mirada: conformación de identidades y de la otredad. (*Tabula Rasa*, 4, enero/junio 2006, p. 241–265, bibl., photos)

Colonial painting from the New Kingdom of Granada (today Colombia) is analyzed in general terms as a reflection of the new society that the Spanish conquest created in South America. Selecting pictorial representation as one of the means by which a policy of "otherness" was constructed and produced in the context of 17th-century colonial society, the author seeks to show how a discourse was elaborated and appropriated through images in which a policy of segregation was founded that implied the difference and the recognition of "another one" as different. From a sociopolitical perspective, recurrent representations of *castas* (different ethnic groups) are viewed as reminders of class distinctions and the position of power enjoyed by the Spanish population. [HRC]

47 Sebastián, Santiago. Estudios sobre el arte y la arquitectura coloniales en Colombia. Bogotá: Corporación La Candelaria: Convenio Andrés Bello, 2006. 495 p.: bibl., ill., index.

Published under the auspices of the municipal government of Bogotá, Corporación La Candelaria, and Convenio Andrés Bello, this most welcome publication pays tribute to the late Spanish art historian Santiago Sebastián, whose death in 1995 brought to a close a life-long career of distinguished scholarship and teaching. A sensitive introduction by Jorge Sebastián Lozano and Pablo Sebastián Lozano, "Cautivo por Colombia: Santiago Sebastián, muchas páginas después" (p. 25–39); and prologue by Ramón Gutiérrez, "La vocación americanista de Santiago Sebastián" (p. 41–49), recognize Sebastián's important contributions to the historiography of the field. Carefully compiled here in a single volume are Sebastián's major studies dealing with the art and architecture of Spanish colonial Colombia, which was his primary area of expertise. Using a variety of methodological approaches, including morphological and iconographic analysis, these studies are widely recognized as classics in the field. Representing some 40 years of scholarship and now dispersed in various no-longer-extant or out-of-print publications, this edition makes them again readily available to academicians and the general public alike. Included here are Sebastián's model survey of Spanish colonial architecture in Colombia, "Itinerarios artísticos de la Nueva Granada" (p. 57–179); his indispensable studies on architectural iconography, "La ornamentación arquitectónica en la Nueva Granada" (p. 189–291); and selected articles dealing with urbanism, architecture, painting, and graphic arts in Nueva Granada (p. 295–377). The general bibliography includes a comprehensive list of Sebastián's publications; and the book concludes with an album of high-quality color photographs of works referenced in the text. [HRC]

Bolivia, Ecuador, Peru

Cuzco: del mito a la historia. See item **17**.

48 Escudero-Albornoz, Ximena. Escultura colonial quiteña: arte y oficio. Quito: Trama, 2007. 368 p.: bibl., col. ill.

Deluxe edition illustrated with spectacular full-color plates throughout offers the most comprehensive overview of the development of Spanish colonial sculpture in Quito published to date. Exhaustive research using both primary and secondary sources presents a selection of major works by well-known artists of the period such as Manuel Chili "Caspicara," Bernardo Legarda, and Manuel Samaniego y Jaramillo, and comparative analysis includes other high-quality anonymous works from public and private collections often not readily available to scholars. Pride of place is given to religious art consisting of figural sculpture, ornamental forms from gilded altarpieces, pulpits, and painted wooden ceilings (*artesonados*), which represent a magnificent artistic corpus created by the finest artists associated with the Quito School. The main text covers essential historical data complemented by critical analysis and useful information on materials and tools of the trade. Plate captions give full description of the works, their state of conservation and date when they were photographed. A complete listing of archival and bibliographic sources should prove invaluable for future studies. [HRC]

49 Grupp Castello, Franz. Arte y *mundo andino*: teatralidad del arte barroco andino. (*Allpanchis/Cuzco*, 38:69, primer semestre 2008, p. 147–163, bibl., photos)

Brief essay discusses Baroque art from the point of view of its theatrical impact and its important propagandistic role for the Roman Catholic Counterreformation movement during the 16th and 17th centuries. A few Spanish colonial works of art from Cuzco and Arequipa are mentioned only in passing as examples of *barroco andino*; but the claim of the originality of this art as distinct from European Baroque lacks sufficient development. [HRC]

50 Holland, Augusta Emilia. Nueva coronica: tradiciones artísticas europeas en el virreynato del Perú. Cuzco, Peru: Centro Bartolomé de Las Casas, 2008. 229 p.: bibl., ill., maps. (Archivos de historia andina; 42)

Original research on the famous chronicle *Nueva corónica i buen gobierno* (1615) by Felipe Guamán Poma y Ayala adds significantly to our understanding of this unique work from the Spanish colonial period and its author. Close analysis of the drawings in the *Nueva corónica* shows that their composition bears a striking resemblance with the pictorial tradition of mural paintings in medieval European churches and Spanish colonial churches around Cuzco and Titicaca Lake region. Convincing visual comparisons of some of the original 399 drawings in the *Nueva corónica* with other drawings that have been attributed to Guamán Poma either confirm or refute their authorship. Technical issues of execution and iconography are also carefully considered. The well-documented text concludes with a comprehensive bibliography of primary and secondary sources. Without a doubt, this is a major contribution to the field and an indispensable reference for future studies on Guamán Poma and his work. For colonial historian's comment, see item **1418**. [HRC]

51 Nair, Stella E. Localizing sacredness, difference, and *Yachacuscamcani* in a colonial Andean painting. (*Art Bull.*, 89:2, June 2007, p. 211–238, bibl., ill., photos)

A model of scholarly research, this study focuses on close analysis and interpretation of the 1693 painting *Virgin of Monserrat* by the indigenous artist Francisco Chivantito honoring the titular saint of the church of Chinchero in the outskirts of Cuzco, Peru. This important work, representative of the Cuzco School of painting, depicts an Iberian holy image and landscape, along with Inca elites and architecture, weaving Andean symbolic and spatial understanding with European painting conventions to create a multivalent image that encompassed both Roman Catholic teachings and indigenous understandings of sacredness and history. As Nair explains, the Quechua word *Yachacuscamcani* refers to knowing the traditions of the Andean past. In Chivantito's painting, it appears the indigenous women at Chinchero used *Yachacuscamcani* as a local strategy to claim their ancestral Inca status and authority. In addition to Chivantito's multilayered painted narrative, his work is identified as one of the few known examples of a local landscape illustration in a Spanish colonial Andean painting. Well documented with a wealth of visual material and fully annotated literary sources. [HRC]

52 Rodríguez-Camilloni, Humberto. Constantino de Vasconcelos and *quincha* architecture in Spanish colonial Peru. (*in* International Conference on Structures & Architecture, 1st, Guimarães, Portugal, 2010. Structures & architecture: ICSA—1st International Conference on Structures and Architecture, July 21–23 2010 in Guimarães, Portugal. Edited by Paulo J. da Sousa Cruz. Boca Raton, Fla.: CRC; London: Taylor & Francis, 2010, p. 311–312, abstract and full-text in CD-ROM, ill., photos)

With the inception of *quincha* architecture in the City of Kings or Lima during the 17th century, a definitive solution was found to the earthquake problem that for over a century had affected the stability of Spanish colonial buildings. This study argues that largely responsible for this innovative antiseismic system of construction was the Portuguese architect Constantino de Vasconcelos (d. 1668) in collaboration with the limeño architect Manuel de Escobar (1639–93), and that it consisted in the ingenious adaptation of precolumbian *quincha* construction for the complex forms of different types of vaults that large scale interiors of Spanish colonial buildings required.

The basic building materials for Vasconcelos' improved *quincha* superstructures consisted of wood for the structural frames and cane or bamboo for the fill-in webs. The use of *quincha* construction in the church of San Francisco in Lima commissioned to Vasconcelos following the collapse of an earlier structure in 1656 is examined in detail and a number of European models dealing with wooden structures that may have informed Vasconcelos are discussed. The acceptance of *quincha* architecture and its dissemination during the 17th and 18th centuries along the Peruvian coast is further illustrated with a number of urban and rural buildings that demonstrated the flexibility of *quincha* to accommodate the most varied shapes, including retablo façades. [HRC]

53   Rodríguez Trujillo, Vladimir *et al.*
Architectural and structural comparison of South American and European timber frame structures. (*in* International Conference on Structures & Architecture, 1st, Guimarães, Portugal, 2010. Structures & architecture: ICSA—1st International Conference on Structures and Architecture, July 21–23 2010 in Guimarães, Portugal. Edited by Paulo J. da Sousa Cruz. Boca Raton, Fla.: CRC; London: Taylor & Francis, 2010, p. 309, abstract and full-text in CD-ROM, ill., photos)
Well-documented study compares extant timber frame Jesuit mission churches in Bolivia (which were once part of the domain of the Jesuit missions in Paraguay during the 18th century) with similar structures from Belgium, Switzerland, and France. Morphological analysis reveals that the typical Jesuit mission church plan is a rectangular interior space subdivided into three bays by two rows of carved timber columns. The entrance hall or narthex is protected by a gable roof extending from the interior to form an exterior portico that connects to open galleries of free-standing wooden colonnades flanking the nave and lateral aisles. In Europe, this technology appears to correspond to a tradition of vernacular wooden structures such as barns, market halls, and even rural churches. Examples are the barns of Ter Doest in Flanders, Belgium, and Meslay in Indre, France; the French market halls of Crémieu in Isère and Mereville in Essone; and the timber

frame churches of Meiringen in Bern, Switzerland; Honfleur in Calvados, France; and Outines in Marne, France. [HRC]

Sociedad y gobierno episcopal: las visitas del obispo Manuel de Mollinedo y Angulo: Cuzco, 1674–1694. See item **1451.**

54   Visión y símbolos del virreinato criollo a la República Peruana. Textos de Ramón Mujica Pinilla *et al.* Lima: Banco de Crédito, 2006. 367 p.: bibl., ill. (chiefly col.), index. (Col. Arte y tesoros del Perú)
Multi-authored volume by distinguished scholars is another splendid addition to the series *Colección Arte y tesoros del Perú* published under the sponsorship of the Banco de Crédito in Lima. Anticipating the celebration of the 200th anniversary of independence movements in Latin America dating from 1808, this 2006 publication is devoted to several important topics focusing on the critical historical period of transition from colonialism to independence. The original research often providing revisionist perspectives is presented in fine chapters beautifully illustrated with excellent full-color reproductions of archival documents and works of art and architecture, many covering the entire page. Chapters include: "Patria e historia: tríptico peruano," by David A. Brading (p. 1–41); "Indios nobles o mestizos reales?: memoriales, legitimidad y liderazgo entre la Colonia y la Independencia," by Scarlett O'Phelan Godoy (p. 42–83); "El Visitador General Areche y su campaña iconoclasta contra la cultura andina," by David Cahill (p. 84–111); "Avatares del 'bello ideal': modernismo clasicista versus tradiciones barrocas en Lima, 1750–1825," by Luis Eduardo Wuffarden (p. 112–159); "Iconografía mitológica y masónica a fines del virreinato e inicios de la República," by Teresa Gisbert (p. 160–201); "Los fabricantes de emblemas: los símbolos nacionales en la transición republicana: Perú, 1820–1825," by Natalia Majluf (p. 202–241); "Viajeros naturalistas, científicos y dibujantes: de la ilustración al costumbrismo en las artes (siglos XVIII y XIX)," by Víctor Peralta Ruiz and Charles F. Walker (p. 242–273); and "La rebelión de los lápices: la caricatura política peruana en el siglo XIX," by Ramón Mujica Pinilla (p. 274–349). The fully annotated chapters are complemented by a comprehensive general bibliography. [HRC]

19th and 20th Centuries

FÉLIX ÁNGEL, *Curator, Cultural Center, Inter-American Development Bank*

AFTER A DECADE in which the world has not come to grips with the effects of globalization and the information overload created by the banality of information dissemination, for the sake of nothing less than economic productivity based on financial speculation and out of control consumerism, the arts appear to have lost the human component. Everyone knows that the arts can be controversial at times, but they have allowed people, in the not so distant past, to connect genuinely with creativity, and through the latter, with the array of life issues which continue to challenge common sense, prosperity and opportunity.

The panorama of the arts in Latin America and the Caribbean today is far from satisfactory. Many scholars can barely follow the never-ending succession of recycled fads and trends inspired by previous periods and presented as new developments with the simple addition of technological devices. No matter how refined those developments can be, or how often they are curated over and over again by institutions, both galleries and artists alike offer them as if in a competition to capture attention (and ticket sales) at the expense of an obligation to the public to contribute to public enlighenment, rather than mere entertainment or amazement.

The capacity of the scholar to research and express a voice of equanimity in the arts (as well in other areas, one would imagine), is needed now more than ever, despite—or because of—the fact that so few spectators appear to be paying attention to whatever may be artistically significant or substantial. Instead, the collective frenzy is more inclined to embrace the trivialization of life, as if life is designed by casual fact, the uncontrolled use of technology, and the traps created by promotion and advertisement, backed, of course, by money and the agenda of a few.

As important as it is to look forward, it is always important to look back, not to *go* back but to be able to reference the present, and avoid the perils of meaningless repetition that may hamper the future, foolishly thinking that, what one has chosen to ignore may represent novelty, regardless of how astutely something—including the frivolous and worthless—is repackaged and served for collective consumption.

In this line of thought, the current biennial selection for *HLAS* as far as art publications are concerned, brings a number of uplifting books and articles that, under the circumstances, are not only welcome but necessary.

A good number of publications are concerned with looking at what has happened in the 20th century. These publications come from across the region, including some from countries that have rarely shown interest, willingness, or capacity with regard to examination of their immediate past, save for precolumbian or colonial art.

Argentina continues to be one country within a group of two or three that have by far the most diverse and high quality publications. *Fuera de Campo: literatura y arte argentinos después de Duchamp*, is an imaginative essay that explores possible relations between Marcel Duchamp and Argentine literature and art, departing from the nine-month sojourn the French artist spent in Buenos Aires between 1918–19 (item **112**). *Vanguardia, internacionalismo y política: arte* *argentino en los años sesenta* (reviewed in previous years), an expanded re-edition of the original 2001 book, is a pivotal reference to understanding the cultural attitude developed by Argentina's community in the 1960s (item **110**). In the same context, *Del Di Tella a "Tucuman arde": vanguardia artistica y política en el 68 argentino*, focuses on the situation affecting the arts, culture, and politics in the country by the end of the same decade (item **111**).

For a number of reasons, the best publications from Colombia are concerned with Bogotá, paying little attention to developments in other parts of the country, and this biennium there is no difference. *Plástica dieciocho; Beatriz Daza: hace mucho tiempo, 1956–1968;* and *Lucy Tejada: años cincuenta,* are three pieces of research that represent a substantial advancement in art history concerning the transition between what can be considered modern and contemporary in the 20th century (items **120**, **118**, and **121**). The three volumes are dedicated to women artists, and their role in the transformation of the visual arts, from a centralist perspective. In the same spirit, also from Colombia, *Miguel Díaz Vargas: una modernidad invisible,* makes clear the tortuous trail and consequences an artist may assume when practicing his talents, immersed in a considerably backward society behind the progressive transformations that were shaping the modern world at the time (item **122**).

Mexico brings us this time an interesting approach to genre and sex in the history of art, with *Miradas disidentes: géneros y sexo en la historia del arte,* and its discussion of a subject seldom brought to the table as a phenomenon and still unresolved in the field of artistic research (item **71**). *Looking for Mexico: Modern Visual Culture and National Identity,* is a book with a quintessential Mexican theme, that of identity, which never seems to lose the interest of Mexicans themselves (item **80**).

From Nicaragua, *Arte en Centroamérica, 1980–2003: últimas tendencias* is a welcome endeavor, constructing a framework by which to examine recent artistic manifestations and the problems of isolation from the international scene which Central America has consistently suffered (item **95**).

Cuba: Art and History, From 1868 to Today, the catalog of the exhibition of the same name by the Montreal Museum of Art is a considerable endeavor. It attempts to clarify the place and role of Cuban artists in society, and tries to answer the elusive question of how to maintain individuality of expression, while still adhering to a collective political ideal (item **98**). Along the same lines, *Los 70: puente para la rupturas,* expresses some points of view about the generation that precedes the so-called Renaissance of the 1980s (item **101**).

Among the articles reviewed for this edition of *HLAS* and expanded into other topics, *Jose Gómez Sicre and the "Idea" of Latin American Art* summarizes the critic's agenda while dealing with the arts of the hemisphere during the 1950s and 1960s (item **55**). *Jorge Romero Brest and the Coordinates of Aesthetic Modernism in Latin America; Words for Mario Pedroza;* and *Marta Traba: Internationalism or Regional Resistance?,* serve as excellent contrasts to the variety of positions adopted by those who led, in some regard, the theoretical platforms that supported the promotion and international dissemination of the arts in the region during those years (items **59** and **116**).

Finally, three articles: *El financiamiento privado de las artes y la cultura en Argentina: entretelones de la Ley de Menenazgo; No, yo tampoco. El amor al arte, probablemente: notas sobre el coleccionismo de arte contemporáneo argentino;*

and *Sobre los inicios del coleccionismo y los museos de arte en la Argentina*, shed light on how to incentivize the beneficial effects that the arts have on a society, and the passion of collecting, a cultural attitude at which Argentina has always excelled, despite the many challenges posed by unpredictable legislation and political upheaval (items **107**, **108** and **106**).

These are some of the many exciting publications that, in spite of the reigning confusion and the "new world disorder," are worth rescuing for the sake of understanding what has happened in the past and what is happening currently in the arts of Latin America and the Caribbean.

GENERAL

55   Anreus, Alejandro. José Gómez Sicre and the "idea" of Latin American art. (*Art J.*, 64:4, Winter 2005, p. 83–84, photo)

Anreus summarizes Gómez Sicrés agenda when dealing with the arts of the hemisphere during the 1950s and 1960s as part of his political position in the context of the Cold War, which implicitly opposed the ideological and nationalistic folklore of post-revolutionary Mexican art. Gómez Sicrés also condemned communism, particularly after the takeover of his own homeland in 1958 by Fidel Castro. Anreus indicates the many contradictions of Gómez Sicre when mixing in his vision of the region—perhaps to counterbalance the cohesive, artistic weight of the US or Europe—the complex historical traditions, colonial influences, and the modern desire to move forward. Gómez Sicre was one of the first Latin American art critics truly concerned with the need to differentiate and recognize the contributions to modern art produced in the region. While acknowledging his pioneering role, Anreus shows that Gomez Sicrés' personality and preferences led him to ignore other facts, which in turn led to isolation within his own created stereotype.

56   Barriendos Rodríguez, Joaquín. El arte público, las ciudades-laboratorio y los imaginarios urbanos de Latinoamérica. (*Aisthesis/Santiago*, 41, julio 2007, p. 57–67, photos)

This is an ambitious paper in which the author attempts to enhance the interdisciplinary discussion at the crossroads of urban imagery and the artistic practices taking place in the contemporary Latin American city. The article is chiefly examing the idea of "contextualizing the capacity of art...in the

redefinition of public space." To implement his analysis, Barriendos Rodríguez uses two case studies, different in scale and operational mode. The first is the 9th Havana Biennial, which had a main theme on the dynamics of urban culture; the second is Mexican artist Héctor Zamorás intervention on the façade of the Carillo Gil Museum, named Paracaidista. Av. Revolución No. 1608 (Parachuter: Revolution Avenue No. 1608). The disparity of the examples underscores the authors intention to juxtapose the intimacy of the micro politics of art, the legitimization of the division between "public" and "private," and the macro urban dimension of the realms in which art undertakes its development. As expected, Barriendos seems to dismiss in his conclusion the possibility of being able to comprehend the intersubjectivity of esthetics. He considers the tools for evaluating the social life unfolding in the contemporary Latin American city, such as traditional sociology, urbanism, or art anthropology, as "close" disciplines. Given the complexity of the current urban reality, he calls it "the global market of subjectivity." He suggests it is necessary to concentrate in the multifocal dynamic of urban space which is what defines the new Latin American reality.

57   Cerveira Pinto, António. En las fronteras = In borderlines: arte latinoamericano en la colección del MEIAC. Textos por António Cerveira Pinto, Carlos Jiménez y Omar Pascual Castillo. Madrid: Instituto Cervantes; Badajoz: Junta de Extremadura, Consejería de Cultura, 2005. 93 p.: ill. (some col.).

Catalog of the 2006 exhibition with works from the collection of Spain's Museo Extremeño e Iberoamericano de Arte Contemporáneo (MEIAC), held in Prague on occasion of the inauguration of the Instituto Cervantes. According to Antonio Franco Domínguez, Director of MEIAC, the exhibition presents itself as a brief sojourn through two or three different generational moments, with a selection of artists represented at the MEIAC collection that help to define the current state of Latin American art today, a fragmented expression of a reality in constant change. Original text in Spanish, with illustrations. Includes a separate non-illustrated booklet in Czech.

58   City/art : the urban scene in Latin America. Edited by Rebecca E. Biron. Durham, N.C.: Duke Univ. Press, 2009. 274 p.: bibl., ill., index.

The collection of essays assembled by Biron strives to provide students and scholars of urban cultural studies with a range of models for approaching Latin American cities as sites of creativity. These cities are defined by the editor as "nodal points in a cultural tapestry" that provide strength and structure, as well as problems. Each Latin American city has its own unique components that cannot be generalized or simplified at the peril of rendering the tapestry illegible. The book is structured in three parts: Urban Designs, Street Signs, and Traffic, and the 10 contributors include such well-known names as Néstor García Canclini, Nelly Richard, and Hugo Achugar. Complemented by b/w illustrations and a bibliography.

59   Giunta, Andrea. Jorge Romero Brest and the coordinates of aesthetic modernism in Latin America. (*Art J.*, 64:4, Winter 2005, p. 89–91, photo)

For those unfamiliar with the tremendous contributions made toward understanding modern Latin American art during the last 60 years of the 20th century, and in particular the evolution of the visual arts in Argentina, the encapsulated profile of Romero Brest (1905–88) by Giunta will be an accurate and precise introduction. The article takes the reader by the hand following the physicist and lawyer turned critic and philosopher as he tried to define a path for modern art in the region. Brest's perspective was never disconnected from European culture (from which Argentina intelligentsia has always felt was de-

scended). He aggressively defended geometric abstraction as the highest expression in the arts (vindicating the Argentine artists of the 1940s), and during the 1960s turned his attention to pop art. His own activism in Latin America's unevenly populated field of art criticism led him to become one of the most influential art theoreticians, in his own country and abroad. Once he became director of the Center for the Visual Arts of the Torcuatto Di Tella Institute in Buenos Aires, Brest became the standard-bearer of Argentina's artistic agenda; he strongly believed it had achieved enough originality by the mid 1960s to be recognized within the international artistic community.

60   Gorelik, Adrián. Las metrópolis latinoamericanas, el arte y la vida: arte y ciudad en tiempos de globalización. (*Aisthesis/Santiago*, 41, julio 2007, p. 36–56)

The premise of Gorelik's analysis departs from a 19th-century tradition that in Latin America describes "art and life" as an urban, metropolitan experience. Added to that is the contemporary, globalized idea of urban marketing which, in the current environment, is necessary to compete for the "global market of cities," while coexisting in the public space with old avant-garde models and politicized expressions struggling to survive by reinventing themselves. Gorelik dedicates some time to explaining the symptoms that characterize the "activation of the globalized context," such as the displacement of artistic circuits from the museum and the traditional art gallery to the city, the role of design and advertisement, and urban marketing as theory and methodology for promotion. He suggests that in many Latin American cities, with few exceptions, globalization is not yet real, but is instead a "desire" that sublimates the absence of real mechanisms to develop an urban cultural economy similar to the globalized economy of more advanced countries. The examples Gorelik presents, Puerto Madero in Buenos Aires and Arte/Cidade in São Paulo make sense of the authors viewpoints.

61   Greeley, Robin Adèle. Modernism: what *El Norte* can learn from Latin America. (*Art J.*, 64:4, Winter 2005, p. 82–83)

In her overview of the essays analyzing six contemporary Latin American and Chicano/a critics (Marta Traba, Jorge Romero Brest, José Gómez Sicre, etc.) and their contribution to understanding modernism's developments at the regional, national, and international levels in Latin America art, Greeley explores the diversity of views among them and their interpretations of modernism, modernity, and modernization, in light of the predominant currents of art criticism in the US and Europe. In her view, Latin American critics take a radically different stance, but she concedes that their ideas are indeed essential perspectives on the development of modernism in the western hemisphere. The essays were originally presented at a forum on Latin American modernism.

Madrid de Zito Fontán, Liliana and **Zulma Palermo.** Cuentan las culturas, los objetos dicen—. See item **19**.

62   Religion as art: Guadalupe, Orishas, and Sufi. Edited by Steven Loza. Albuquerque, NM: Univ. of New Mexico Press, 2009. 353 p.: bibl., index.

The examples included here are as dissimilar as the Virgen de Guadalupe, the Orishas system of the West African Yoruba, and the musical/textual practices of devotional ecstasy to God of Islam's Sufi sect. Originally presented at the University of New Mexico in 2004, this collection of essays explores how visual-made religion transcends symbolism to the point of creating a reinterpretation of itself, history, and esthetics.

63   Ruiz, Iván. Piedra de sol: ¿afinidades entre pintura y poesía? (*An. Inst. Invest. Estét.*, 27:87, otoño 2005, p. 145–173)

The article focuses on the analysis of a painting by Peruvian artist Fernando de Szyszlo which takes its title from an homonymous poem by Octavio Paz. Ruiz establishes that the relationship between poetry and painting is at the core of the issue of "modern tradition" in Latin America because of, first, the fashion in which specific aspects of precolumbian art and culture are incorporated in the creative discourse; second, the poetic and plastic tension that such an association produces, creating the set for the exploration of a number of issues that

art history has systematically brought up since the formalization of art history in the 18th century (namely the comparisons between poetry and painting, the assumption of art criticism by poets—which has been crucial for the understanding of modern art); and finally, the intercorrespondence—or interdependency, of all arts, a fundamental theme in European symbolist esthetic.

64   Spitta, Silvia. Misplaced objects: migrating collections and recollections in Europe and the Americas. Austin: Univ. of Texas Press, 2009. 288 p.: bibl., photos (b/w and color), index. (Joe R. and Teresa Lozano Long series in Latin American and Latino art and culture)

The intention behind this lengthy study appears to be the theoretical differences between trans-culturation and mestizaje, focused on objects, not on subjects. That things appear to have a life of their own is a popular assertion by most people, including Garcia Márquez and Jorge Luis Borges, which coincide with Spitta and becomes the springboard for coming to terms with the premise that: "When things move, things change." The title of the book may lead to confusion, however. Things, including objects, move for many reasons, but are not always carelessly misplaced. Be that as it may, the force driving the book is an "attempt to highlight those moments when objects enter a new cultural context." Object, by definition, does not refer here exclusively to an "artistic object," but rather an anthropological entity. The result is an engaging discussion of culture in the broadest sense, and within that context, the capacity of objects to impact space, and individual and collective behavior. Beautifully illustrated and meticulously researched.

MEXICO

65   Alfonso de Lara Gallardo: pintor. Edición y coordinación de Arabella González Huezo. Guadalajara, Mexico: Secretaría de Cultura Jalisco, 2007. 184 p.: bibl., ill. (some col.), ports. (Creadores artísticos de Jalisco)

Monograph on the watercolorist, illustrator, mural painter, teacher, and stained-glass artist from Guadalajara, from the Series Creadores Artísticos de

Jalisco, produced by the Jalisco Secretariat of Culture. Guillermo García Oropeza calls González Huezo "the last religious artist of Mexico" due to the artist's many Catholic, religious commissions executed for a number of churches in Mexico. González, a family man, considered nature an expression of God, and in his work he treated it accordingly, making his journey through the arts "an expression of my Faith." Very well illustrated, the semblance of the artist is entertaining, and the generous reproductions leave no doubts about González Huezo's proficiency for illustration which characterizes all his pictorial work, and may lead one to think that he left his most enduring legacy in that particular field.

66 Arte joven: 40 años, 1967–2007. Textos de Marel de Lara. Fotografía de Joel Torres Romero. Diseño de Niurka Bali. Aguascalientes, Mexico: Instituto Cultural de Aguascalientes, 2007. 139 p.: ill.

Commemorative publication that summarizes and celebrates the 40th anniversary of the Concurso Nacional de Estudiantes de Artes Plásticas (National Contest of Fine Arts Students), held in Aguascalientes sponsored by the state's Cultural Institute, as part of the annual cultural festival; in 1981 it was renamed the Encuentro Nacional de Arte Joven. Othón Téllez has written the narrative explaining the genesis and evolution of the event. Illustrated in chronological order, with biographical profiles of the outstanding artists that the contest helped to bring to the public's attention over four decades.

67 Artistas en México. v. 13, José Luis Cuevas. v. 14, Marina Láscaris. v. 15, Fernando González Gortázar. v. 16, Roberto Rébora. Mexico City: Impronta Editores: Taller Gráfica Bordes: Casa Verde, 2006–2008. 4 v.: bibl., ill.

Bilingual-pocket size booklets dedicated to individual Mexican artists (two sculptors, Láscaris and González Gortázar; one painter, Roberto Rébora; and a draftsman and sculptor, José Luis Cuevas), written by various authors. Includes a short critical commentary and biography, and color and black and white plates of selected works.

68 Auguste Rodin, Javier Marín: encuentros y divergencias. Dirección editorial de Lupina Lara Elizondo. Textos de Lupina Lara Elizondo *et al.* México: Quálitas Compañía de Seguros: Promoción de Arte Mexicano, 2008. 277 p.: bibl., col. ill.

Well-designed, beautifully illustrated, and well-produced volume intent on establishing homology between the work of French sculptor August Rodin and Mexican sculptor Javier Marín, emphasizing those aspects in which they may share a common interest or divergence, as the title suggests. Most of the essays are dedicated to the history of classical sculpture (ancient Greece, Rome, and the Renaissance, in particular Michelangelo), building the case that the work of Rodin and Marín may be inserted within these same traditions. Ultimately, the book is aimed at securing a place for Marín as a universal, "virtuoso" artist in the realm of sculpture. Without doubting his technical proficiency or and the powerful drama that the work of Mexican exudes, the reader must decide if such an attempt to secure a place for the artist in modern history comes across a little too hard.

69 Azuela de la Cueva, Alicia. *Peace by revolution*: una aproximación léxico-visual al México revolucionario. (*Hist. Mex./México*, 56:4, abril/junio 2007, p. 1263–1307, bibl., ill., map, photo)

The article focuses on the book of the same name by Frank Tannenbaum, written in 1933 and illustrated by Miguel Covarrubias, as an example of Mexican history—written by foreigners utilizing methodologies prior to the professionalization of the social sciences—that is an interpretation of the past with an eye to understanding the present. Azuela de la Cueva suggests that similar books, often illustrated by both Mexican nationals and foreigners, were destined for an "extraterritorial audience," mostly English-speaking. Nonetheless their analysis is important to understand the different facets of the Mexican Revolution and afterwards. That said, it is not strange that Tannenbaum attributed many problems of post-revolutionary Mexican society—race, politics, social classes, economic differences, and cultural dichotomy—to the Spanish conquest and the colonial system. When analyzing the illustrations by Covarrubias—which is the core purpose of the article—Azuela de la Cueva points out how the artist adapted to Tannenbaum's vision of history and personal opinion about events and people (including many leading figures of Mexican history). Most of the themes and visual elements present in the illustrations are familiar traditions and syncretized expressions that evolved even before the Revolution, such as the "Deer Dance," "The Moors and the Christians," as well some byproducts of the conflict, for instance, the "Soldaderas," or women soldiers. For historian's comment, see item 903.

70 Barajas, Rafael. Posada: mito y mitote: la caricatura política de José Guadalupe Posada y Manuel Alfonso Manila. México: Fondo de Cultura Economica, 2009. 548 p.: bibl., ill., index. (Col. Tezontle)

Posada represents the pluralism of the Porfirio Díaz regime, according to Barajas who, appropriately indicates that although the people of Mexico cultivate the myth of Posada, it was through Dr. Atl, Diego Rivera, and the muralist artists, that he acquired his high status during post-revolutionary Mexico. Barajas Durán attempts to clarify important aspects of Posada's life, his talents and creativity, his ideological and political positions, and his journalistic trajectory. In one chapter, Barajas establishes the relationship between and parallel lives of Posada and Alfonso Manilla, a character not so well known outside Mexico, and his relationship with another important publisher, Vanegas Arroyo. Very well illustrated, this study helps to advance and shed light on Posada's life and work, about whom Cardozo y Aragón once said, people have written so much, but said very little.

71 Coloquio Internacional de Historia del Arte, *29th*, *Puebla de Zaragoza*, *Mexico*, *2005*. Miradas disidentes: géneros y sexo en la historia del arte. XXIX Coloquio Internacional de Historia del Arte. Edición a cargo de Alberto Dallal. México: UNAM, Instituto de Investigaciones Estéticas, 2007. 406 p.: bibl., ill.

Choosing to unite in one volume a selection of essays on gender and sex in the arts emphasizes the unresolved nature of this topic within traditional art criticism,

despite, according to Dallal (the editor and also a contributor), its constant presence in the history of art. Three chapters organize an equal number of subdivisions of the main theme, summarized in: 1) contradiction to norms, hegemonic practices, marginal cases and deviations; 2) anatomy as a device to elaborate genre differences; and 3) analysis of theoretical, curatorial, and historiographical practices derived from policies of genre. Subthemes are much more varied and approaches differ. All of them burrow into areas still blurred by traditional art criticism, spanning many centuries.

72 Eckmann, Teresa. Javier de la Garza and Alejandro Arango: reevaluating signs of identity. (*An. Inst. Invest. Estét.*, 27:86, primavera 2005, p. 55–93)

The November 1986 Alejandro Arango exhibition, "The Conquest," at Galería OMR in Mexico City, and the presentation three months later of Javier de la Garza's "Lost Innocence" at the same place, is the departure for Eckmann's close analysis of the neo-Mexican movement which has been almost uniformly criticized as being too blind in its self-gratifying and glorified nationalism, to the point of being unintentionally kitsch. Some important points are made here; one is that most critics lost sight of the skepticism that seeks to separate myth from reality, and at the same time, illustrates the reality of myth through form and strident color. The themes of machismo, mestizaje, and indigenismo run through a critique inspired by and poking fun at a trivialized discourse of *mexicanidad*. The article is not shy in detailing the exhibition's components, and is complemented with several illustrations.

73 Gallo, Rubén. New tendencies in Mexican art: the 1990s. New York: Palgrave Macmillan, 2004. 183 p.: bibl., ill., index. (New directions in Latino American cultures)

Gallo presents the sociopolitical and economic context of the 1990s in his introduction, and the following five chapters—Orientalism, Voyeurism, Radiophonism, Urbanism, and Institutionalism. He describes the dominant trends that in his view were able to radically transform contemporary Mexican arts. The author establishes his own perspective on the 1990s, a decade he calls "one of the most turbulent periods in recent Mexican history" which started with the presidency of Carlos Salinas de Gortari after the apparent defeat of Cuauhtémoc Cárdenas. Such a beginning found its expression in the work of the "neo-Mexicanists," whose mere "art of simulacrum," as Gallo borrows Hal Foster's term to describe a repertoire of empty images, did not have references to "the historical context in which they were produced." Then he examines Temístocles' house group who worked in the dilapidated mansion in the district of Polanco. Artists such as Francis Alys and Melanie Smith were able to rally a younger generation who 1) rejected traditional painting by favoring installation, video, photography, ready-made, and performance; 2) adopted globalized symbols from mass media; and 3) renounced the commercialism that characterized the neo-Mexicans. According to Gallo, Mexican art went from object-base practice to action-base experiments. Without attempting to be comprehensive, the dozen or so artists selected by Gallo to prove his thesis create a stimulating approach to Mexican art at the end of the millennium.

74 González Mello, Renato. Manuel Gamio, Diego Rivera, and the politics of Mexican anthropology. (*Res/Cambridge*, 45, Spring 2004, p. 161–185, bibl., ill.)

Mello affirms that Manuel Gamio ("the founding figure of 20th-century Mexican anthropology"), and his role in the development of the cultural agenda of post-revolutionary Mexico, has been neglected in favor of José Vasconcelos, who is credited with the artistic renaissance and the mural projects initiated with Diego Rivera. Gamio was "a student of the German professor Franz Boas at Columbia University, who proposed esthetic integration as an evolutionary alternative to traditional notions of race." The article is very detailed about Gamio's work as a scientist: he was able to renew his relationship with science, power, and social evolution while distancing himself from 19th-century evolutionary Positivism. In this regard, Mello points out that Gamio and Rivera were "analogous in their paradoxical alternatives." Both of them were "realists," "revolutionary," modernists,

boulevardiers, criollos, visionaries, utopian dreamers, nationalists, and "the most enduring consequence of their work is the celebration of Mexican parochial life."

75 La identidad nacional mexicana en las expresiones artísticas: estudios históricos y contemporáneos. Coordinación de Raúl Béjar y Héctor Rosales. México: UNAM: Plaza y Valdés, 2008. 338 p.: bibl., col. ill.

In the prologue of this collection of essays by 19 authors, Lourdes Arizpe states that in Mexico, the arts have always been a public matter, even today, when the arts are more self-sustaining. The statement anticipates the concern for identity implicit in the array of artistic expressions at which Mexico has excelled, from craftmaking to filmmaking, and the diversity of historical moments the essays examine, while also recognizing the realities and challenges brought about by the 21st century.

76 Krippner-Martínez, James. Traces, images, and fictions: Paul Strand in Mexico, 1932–34. (*Americas/Washington*, 63:3, Jan. 2007, p. 359–383, photo)

The author analyzes, from different angles, the photographer and filmmaker Paul Strand during his stay in Mexico between 1932–34, years in which the Mexican government intended to consolidate the achievements of the Revolution. In this context, and as a result of the invitation extended to him by Carlos Chávez—then Director of the Fine Arts Department of the Secretariat of Public Education (while at the same time being director of the National Symphony Orchestra)—Strand attempted to create a visual record documenting Mexico's unique character, emphasizing its revolutionary transformation. In so doing, Strand set the foundation for a visual social history of Mexico through photography, a pattern he would later follow in other countries. The techniques and concepts utilized by Strand for his photography were often called to question due to what Krippner-Martínez calls "cultural distance and power imbalance." There was also the anticlerical sentiment against the peasantry, which was sponsored by the state to the extent of becoming a civil conflict, and entangled Strand's religious-themed photography when related to the common people. The article is detailed and well documented. It offers a vision of Mexico rarely seen from the window of a genuine and passionate foreign artist who happened to be an extraordinary witness of its transformation.

77   Martínez, Jesús. Historia del grabado. v. 1, Grabado prehispánico. El grabado en la Colonia. v. 2, Manilla y Posada. Grabadores de calaveras. Grabado contemporáneo. Guanajuato, Mexico: Ediciones La Rana, 2006. 2 v.: ill. (some col.). (Artes y oficios)

The first volume of this history of printmaking (in Mexico, one may add since the specification is missing in the title), focuses on the precolumbian and colonial eras, while the second volume covers Manuel Manilla and José Guadalupe Posada ("skull printmakers" the author calls them), and the most modern and contemporary periods, starting with Julio Ruelas. The narrative prose is uncomplicated, making it an unpretentious treatise particularly appropriate for art students, young collectors, and printmaking practitioners who wish to learn the basic development of Mexican printmaking. The hardcover, well-bound volumes are generously illustrated, mostly b/w.

78   Mexico and modern printmaking: a revolution in the graphic arts, 1920 to 1950. Edited by John Ittmann with contributions by Innis Howe Shoemaker, James M. Wechsler, and Lyle W. Williams. Philadelphia: Philadelphia Museum of Art, 2006. 289 p.:

This book claims to be the "first to undertake an in-depth examination of these (Mexican) prints, the vital contributions made by Mexico's printmaking to international modern art, and their influence on coming generations of artists." The volume is indeed comprehensive; some 300 prints are reproduced, many previously unpublished (Dr. Atl's "pochoirs" or stencils, are superb). The discussion on the printmaking practices (and techniques) of Orozco, Rivera, Siqueiros, Tamayo, and others is intertwined with essays by scholars who participated in the project. Reference are also made to the roles played by scores of non-Mexican artists, such as Jean Charlot, and by Mexicans who went abroad, like Emilio Armero. The Taller de Gráfica Popular was crucial

for the dissemination of graphics inside and outside of Mexico. The Weyhe Gallery in New York was responsible for producing many Rivera prints in the 1930s. All these factors gathered together allow the reader to understand the important position Mexican printmaking achieved, not only as a companion of ideological and artistic considerations ingrained in the concept of Mexican identity and as a countercurrent against European art in particular, but also as a pivotal expression that continues to be influential in American art and US Southwestern and Western art. A first class publication.

79   Molina, Carlos. Fernando Gamboa y su particular versión de México. (*An. Inst. Invest. Estét.*, 27:87, otoño 2005, p. 117–143)

Molina begins comparing Gamboa's work as a "museographer" in 1950 with that of Miguel Covarrubias, which he had developed at least 10 years earlier at The Museum of Modern Art (New York), implying that both of them had curatorial visions in common long before the distinction between curator and museographer was established. That is just one among many reasons why Gamboa's merit and contribution as "the father of Mexican museography" requires a better examination. The author juxtaposes both curatorial strategies—Cobarrubias' New York exhibition (1940) with Gamboa's European Mexican traveling exhibition (1950–53)—characterizing Cobarrubias' as ethnographic (regional), and Gamboa's as more esthetic (universalist) while at the same time deeply nationalistic, hence the title of Molina's article. What makes Molina's article interesting is the context in which he places both characters: inseparable from the Mexican cultural-political agenda that the state leadership had in mind for the "cultural patrimony of the Mexican people." In light of the government's urgent need to position Mexico before the eyes of the rest of the world with impressive exhibitions, the weak theoretical foundation that accompanied them was ignored. Molina also examines the role of German photographer Gisèle Freund, who Gamboa utilized to document the exhibitions and provide the sociological framework for the art exhibited. Molina concludes that Covarrubias and Gamboa were the first to take advantage of the legislation issued in Mexico in 1942 to advance the concept of Mexicanism through art exhibitions and establish museography as a career within the school of anthropology.

80 **Mraz, John.** Looking for Mexico: modern visual culture and national identity. Durham, N.C.: Duke Univ. Press, 2009. 343 p.: bibl., ill., index

Sections of these essays were published earlier (the oldest in 1984) in different publications. The author warns that it is a "subjective book" and the result of his experience of Mexican visual culture and his own interests and opinions. The focus is identity which, according to Mraz, "has been used as the ideological justification for one of the world's longest-lasting party dictatorships" (the PRI, which ended in 2000). The statement may be difficult to contradict and speaks for itself about the author's perspective. Topics such as war, revolution, culture, cinema and celebrities, photojournalism, and the struggle between the old and the new are organized in five chronological chapters. With generous notes, bibliography, and some b/w illustrations.

81 **Pappe, Silvia.** Estridentópolis: urbanización y montaje. México: Univ. Autónoma Metropolitana, Unidad Azcapotzalco, 2006. 143 p.: bibl., ill. (some col.). (Col. Ensayos; 14)

An interesting essay that forms part of a research project at the Division of Social Sciences and Humanities of the Universidad Autónoma Metropolitana in Mexico. The subject is the 1920s Estridentópolis movement, a "literary city" built mostly within Mexico City (including Puebla, Jalapa, and Zacatecas, and an imaginary metropolis), by a group of young poets and graphic artists. The group aimed to create an alternative to the post-revolutionary Mexico which, according to the author, did little politically to demolish the old order. One characteristic of the Estridentópolis movement is its dissonant and subversive, at times belligerent, "strategic" reason for being. Manuel Maples Arce defined it as "a gesture, an eruption." From an intellectual perspective, it may be seen as an avant-garde attitude taken by a segment of the younger generation. At that time, the Mexican post-revolutionary ap-

paratus was institutionalizing a cultural agenda anchored in the traditions and values of the majority. Estridentópolis offered a more radical approach for the cultural life of the nation.

82 **Pérez Gavilán, Ana Isabel.** Chávez Morado, destructor de mitos: silencios y aniquilaciones de La ciudad, 1949. (An. Inst. Invest. Estét., 27:87, otoño 2005, p. 65–115)

In 1949, Mexico City's newspaper Excélsior sponsored a contest under the theme "The City of México Interpreted by its Painters." José Chávez Morado participated with two canvases, "Río Revuelto" and "La ciudad," representing in both the relationship among economic, religious, and political powers, and the crumbling of national history in an out-of-control urban context. "Río Revuelto" received Third Prize, but "La Ciudad" was ignored, intentionally perhaps, due to the shocking character of its imagery (a decaying landscape in the form of a naked woman). The painting fell into oblivion for generations. It was even believed and publicized that the author had destroyed it, but he kept it in his personal collection until his death in 2002. Pérez Gavilán vindicates the painting, analyzing at length the circumstances surrounding the artist's ideological and esthetic position, the historical crossroads of Mexico at midcentury, the power schemes that Mexican art history wove around the painting, and the complex dimensions that converge in the artist's narrative.

83 **Proyecto cívico = Civic project: Gabriel Acevedo V., Francis Alÿs, Shoja Azari.** Edición de Ruth Estévez y Lucia Sanromán. Contribuciones de Lucia Sanromán et al. Tijuana, Mexico: Centro Cultural Tijuana: CONACULTA, 2008. 123 p.: bibl., ill. (some col.)

Color-illustrated catalog of the inaugural exhibition at El Cubo (The Cube), an international exhibition space newly added to the Tijuana Cultural Center. The center is part of the Mexican government's focus on a policy of co-responsibility and co-participation to facilitate access to cultural spaces in the northwest of Mexico. The group exhibition included 18 names familiar within the Mexico contemporary art scene. The common denominator of their work is collective concerns, such as individual rights, urban violence, identity, social fragmentation, and marginalization.

84 Ramírez, Fausto. Modernización y modernismo en el arte mexicano. México: UNAM, Instituto de Investigaciones Estéticas, 2008. 477 p.: bibl., ill. (some col.), index.

The term *modernism*, coined to characterize the transformation of Hispano-American letters at the end of the 19th century and the beginning of the 20th century is applied in this book by Ramírez to similarities in the evolution of the visual arts in Mexico during the same period of time. The 1870s are considered by some historians as the beginning of the second industrial revolution; the period coincides with the installation of the Porfiriato, connecting modernism to the changes associated with aggressive industrial exploitation, technological invention, and scientific discovery, as well as Mexico's opening to foreign investment and its subsequent economic dependence on the centers of world capitalism. In this context, Ramírez analyzes the visual artistic production before the development of the Mural School, gathering together previously published articles on key figures such as Jesús Contreras, Julio Ruelas, Gerardo Murillo, Ángel Zárraga, Saturnino Herrán, José Guadalupe Posada, and the then younger José Clemente Orozco. The essays demonstrate the transformation of Mexico's art, evolving from a cosmopolitan aspiration to a proud nationalism. Interesting book about the arts in Mexico during a time that has received little attention.

85 Ramírez Godoy, Guillermo. Historia abreviada de la pintura del siglo XX en Guadalajara. Guadalajara, Mexico: Seminario de Cultura Mexicana; Zapopan, Mexico: Colegio de Jalisco; Guadalajara, Mexico: Promoción Cultural de Jalisco, 2008. 336 p.: bibl., ill. (some col.)

Three hundred sixteen artists born in Jalisco (mostly in Guadalajara), plus 85 born elsewhere but established in Jalisco, are included in this 20th-century abridged version of the history of painting in that region of Mexico. The work attempts to contextualize

painting beyond a regional expression of the facts, situations, characters, and institutions that influenced the evolution of the city and the country up to the present. The narrative is chronological, not restricted to the main trends and ruptures. Illustrated in color and complemented with a bibliography.

86 *Resumen: pintores y pintura mexicana.* No. 73, enero/febrero 2005: Francisco Castro Leñero. Armando Zesatti. No. 74, marzo/abril 2005: Rocio Caballero. No. 75, mayo/junio 2005: Phil Kelly. Ismael Guardado. México: Promoción de Arte Mexicano.

Color illustrated bimonthly booklet dedicated to highlighting the works of individual Mexican artists, paired in each of the booklets. Some artists are better known than others. The series, directed and written by Lupina Lara de Elizondo, celebrated its 10th anniversary in 2005. The texts are simple and clear, and aimed to comprise a synthetic monograph on selected artists. The selection appears to be a prerogative of Ms. Lara de Elizondo and gives an opportunity to both the well-known and the lesser-known artists to be noted. The printing quality as well as the reproductions are excellent.

87 Rivera, Diego. Homenaje a Diego Rivera: retratos = A tribute to Diego Rivera: portraits. México: "Fiduciario" Museo Dolores Olmedo Patiño: Consejo Nacional para la Cultura y las Artes: Instituto Nacional de Bellas Artes, 2007. 173 p.: ill. (chiefly col.).

Color-illustrated, bilingual catalog of the very complete exhibition of Rivera's portraits at the Dolores Olmedo Museum of Mexico City in memory of the 50th anniversary of his death. Also includes essays by various authors, among them Carlos Monsiváis and Elisa García Barragán. Portraiture was one Rivera's most singular and prolific genres even before he became a household name among Hollywood stars and socialites. The exhibit begins with Rivera's pencil portrait of his mother María Barrientos de Rivera, and ends with those of Dolores' siblings in the same technique. Portraits of Russian children in oil and watercolor prove that his health may have hampered his stamina, but to the end his capacity to observe and penetrate the psychology of his subjects, including himself, remained undiminished. A wonderful summary of Rivera's artistic interpretation of his contemporaries, characters who amused and entertained him, adding more color to a never dull career.

88 Rodríguez Bolufé, Olga María. Las artes plásticas en el Caribe que nos une: el paradigma de México. (*Rev. Antropol./São Paulo,* 47:2, julho/dez. 2004, p. 149–167, bibl.)

This article hopes to contribute to the recognition and analysis of the connection between Mexican art produced during the first half of the 20th century and Hispanic Caribbean art produced between 1920–1950, a period which coincides with the definition of esthetic modernization for many countries in the region and the formation of a nationalistic perspective. The work addresses social themes, a vindication of marginalized segments of society, a re-evaluation of history, a need to communicate messages, and an abandonment of European-inspired academic models. The author cites examples to illustrate her points: in the Dominican Republic, artist Jaime Colson and Darío Suro; in Puerto Rico, the "Generation of the 1940s"; and in Cuba, the many articles about Mexican art that were published after 1920, Vansconcelos' visit to Havana in 1925, as well as the visit of several Cuban artists to Mexico before going to Europe. The author concludes that the Mexican model installed itself as a paradigm that suited the needs of the Caribbean artists.

89 Soriano, Juan. Juan Soriano: la rebelión y la libertad: exposición. Museo Amparo, del 26 de noviembre de 2005 al 27 de febrero de 2006. Puebla, Mexico: Fundación Amparo, 2005. 32 p., 74 p. of plates: chiefly col. ill.

Generous color-illustrated catalog of the exhibition (2005–06) organized by El Museo Amparo, in Puebla, to celebrate the 85th birthday of the artist, with works from several private collections. Includes a brief presentation by curator Miguel Cervantes. The exhibit was put together in the form of a small retrospective allowing the viewer to follow the several facets of Soriano's work, including his early fantastic, almost surreal compositions, the significant change

in style after his trip to Greece in 1954, and his portraiture, which Nobel Prize winner Octavio Paz celebrated so frequently, crediting Soriano for the genre's renewal in Mexico.

90 Topete del Valle, Alejandro. José Guadalupe Posada: prócer de la gráfica popular mexicana. Aguascalientes, Mexico: Univ. Autónoma de Aguascalientes, 2007. 114 p.: ill.

Previously unreleased material from Topete del Valle's daughter appears to have been added to a facsimile edition reprinted in Aguascalientes in 1980, crediting the author with having rescued from oblivion the memory of Posada, converting the artist into a symbol not only of Aguascalientes— the artist's place of birth—but of Mexico as a whole. Illustrated, including the 11 lithographs that Posada made for the political weekly *El Jicote,* which are considered the earliest work of the artist.

91 Verdín Saldaña, J. de Jesús. Descubriendo a Bustos. Prólogo de Berta Taracena. Guanajuato, Mexico: Ediciones La Rana, 2007. 131 p.: bibl., ill. (some col.). (Artistas de Guanajuato)

Hermenegildo Bustos was really "discovered" in the early 1920s by Carlos Orozco Romero and Roberto Montenegro, as part of the wave of nationalism that engulfed Mexico after the Revolution, along with the ambitious cultural program initiated by then minister of culture José Vasconcelos. This work complements previous studies on Bustos by Pascual Aceves Barajas and Francisco Orozco Muñoz. The most valuable addition is the historic compilation of the artist's paintings and documents, some unknown until now, in particular the religious paintings. Complementing the images are the author's personal appreciations of individual works of this important representative of "independent" popular art in Mexico during the second half of the 19th century.

92 Zavala, Adriana. Un arte nuevo: el aporte de María Izquierdo. Traducción y presentaciones de James Oles y Mónica Mayer. Textos de Adriana Zavala = A new art: the contribution of María Izquierdo. Translations and forewords by James Oles and Mónica Mayer. Texts by Adriana Zavala. Mexico: UNAM, 2008. 93 p.: bibl., col. ill., port.

Color-illustrated catalog of an exhibition dedicated to Maria Izquierdo, which emphasizes the personal vision of the artist: her inward, intimate world; her inclination toward memories associated with her solitary childhood, maternity, landscape, popular culture, and her own dreams. This was the inaugural exhibition of the temporary exhibit hall of the Blaisten Collection, dedicated to increasing the understanding of the history of modern Mexican art and history. Most of the catalog illustrations are nicely annotated, adding to the overall usefulness of the publication. Zavala's texts give a good semblance of the artist and her life, allowing the reader to gain a better understanding of Izquierdo's work.

93 Zúñiga, Ariel. Emilio Amero: un modernista liminal = a liminal modernist. Traducción al inglés de Sophia Vackimes. Mexico: Albedrío, 2008. 247 p.: bibl., ill. (some col.), ports

The author's perspective on Amero is clear. Between reality and the "official story," in this case, the story of Mexican art during the years that the mural school reigned supreme, there are many omissions, and Amero is one of them. Having committed the "sin" of leaving Mexico in 1925, Amero became a sort of self-exile in the US. His countrymen responded by excluding him from most written accounts of the period and eventually banished him from history. Zúñiga's recollection is unique, fascinating, and insightful, however unassuming. This well-illustrated and bilingual volume sheds light on one of the most polyfaceted, low-profile figures of the Mexican renaissance. Includes plenty of annotations and a chronology.

CENTRAL AMERICA

94 Landings nine. Edited by Joan Duran. Belize City: Five-o-one Art Projects, 2008. 125 p.: chiefly col. ill.

Over 50 artists from Belize, Central America, and the Caribbean have been exhibiting around the world to critical acclaim in a series of exhibitions titled "Landings." Twenty of those artists met in Belize in

August of 2008 to share ideas and take stock of what they had accomplished, and what more was left to be done. The result is a book that captures the ideas, quotations, essays, and thoughts of the Ideas of Landings Nine forum about the purpose, execution, and ultimately, the value of the project.

95 Torres, María Dolores G. Arte en Centroamérica, 1980–2003: últimas tendencias. María Dolores G. Torres y Werner Mackenbach. San José: Univ. de Costa Rica, Vicerrectoría de Acción Social, 2004. 77 p.: bibl., ill. (some col.). (Revista herencia, vol. 16, no. 1–2)

Edited version of the lecture presented at the University of Costa Rica in 2003 which summarizes the artistic activity in the visual arts and literature in Guatemala, El Salvador, Honduras, Belize, Nicaragua, Costa Rica, and Panamá, indicating the main trends and some notorious individual proposals, in the context of Central American art. Both the Introduction and the Conclusion point out circumstances that have made the recognition of Central American cultural contributions difficult in the past, but also point out that the current globalized world is putting an end to that traditional isolation. Includes illustrations in color and black and white, and a succinct bibliography.

THE CARIBBEAN

96 Acosta de Arriba, Rafael. Caminos de la mirada. Ciudad de la Habana: Ediciones Unión, 2007. 266 p.: bibl.

This small volume of art criticism gathers a number of essays written over a span of eight years, and for that reason may be considered an overview of issues related to recent developments in Cuban art, including photography and filmmaking. The author explains that the essays respond to his subjective point of view—the pleasure of looking at art. Acosta de Arriba opted for organizing the text in three chapters: Diálogos, Visiones Puntuales, and La Otra Mirada. Most subjects, but not all, are related to Cuban art and artists. As Rufo Caballero indicates in his introduction, the book is also about the character and the meaning of art criticism, an undercurrent that articulates the whole book.

97   Bettelheim, Judith. Caribbean espiritismo (spiritist) altars: the Indian and the Congo. (*Art Bull.*, 87:2, June 2005, p. 312–330, bibl., ill., photos)

The article centers around Espiritismo (Spiritism), one of the least researched visual aspects of African diaspora and Caribbean culture. The author traveled to Guyama in Puerto Rico to visit the Spiritism Center of Don Miguel Flores. The altar gives testimony, according to Bettelheim, to the intriguing complexity of Caribbean religious art. In her article, she relies on formal and stylistic attributes for her analysis, and Puerto Rico and Cuba are her main interests. Her thesis is that similarities suggest that some images may derive from Central Africa (Congo), filtered through the Cuban-based Palo Monte Mayombe. The appropriation of the Indian (Native American) corresponds with an ideology, a faith, or a personally developed belief system already in place. That is why she concludes that there is the possibility of a Pan-Caribbean style that connects Cuba, Puerto Rico, and New Orleans. The article is very specialized, and well documented, so it is not strange that the author included 93 footnotes to clarify and sustain her assertions.

98   Cuba: art and history, from 1868 to today. Edited by Nathalie Bondil. Translation by Timothy Bernard *et al.* Montréal, Canada: Montreal Museum of Fine Arts, 2008. 424 p.: bibl., ill. (chiefly col.), col. map

This well-produced volume accompanied the 2008 exhibition of the same name at the Montreal Museum of Fine Arts. Bondil (Director and Chief Curator of the museum, and editor of the publication) claimed the exhibition was to be "the first of its kind to showcase 150 years of Cuban art." Institutions in Cuba and Canada, collections and individuals from Dominican Republic, France, Germany, Italy, Switzerland, and the US all added to the effort. Twenty experts of various nationalities contributed essays to the book, which also contains more than 400 reproductions of all types of works, including examples from a large selection of photographers (in the Fototeca de Cuba) which were previously unseen. Together they reconstruct the major chapters in the history of Cuban art starting with the country's 19th-century wars

of independence. It appears that the exhibition and resulting publication lean heavily towards clarification of the place and role of Cuban artists in society, facing—or perhaps giving its own answer to—the dilemma of how to be part of a collective political action while maintaining an expression of individuality.

99   Garoutte, Claire and **Anneke Wambaugh.** Crossing the water: a photographic path to the Afro-Cuban spirit world. Durham, N.C.: Duke Univ. Press, 2007. 258 p.: bibl., index.

The book chronicles the work of Santiago Castañeda Vera, high priest of Espiritismo, Santería, and Palo Monte, three important spiritual traditions in Cuba, and in this case, of the fascinating cultural dimensions of Santiago de Cuba. Espiritismo is based in European spiritism; Santería derives from the Yoruba peoples of Africa; and Palo Monte comes from the Bantu-speaking communities of Kongo and Angola. All of them combine more than one religion and, in the case of Castañeda Vera, he adds his own independent approach which is not unusual among practitioners. With more than 150 photographs in b/w, and some in color, Garouttea and Wambaugh's account of their five-year experience in Cuba with Santiago and his family circle offers a fascinating insight into the Afro-Cuban realm of the spirits and their socioreligious implications. Equally rewarding is the text (including several songs translated into English) which aids in understanding the many sources and not-so-conventional behaviors, as well the abilities implicit in such a fascinating interaction.

100   Harris, Alex. The idea of Cuba. Photographs and text by Alex Harris with an essay by Lillian Guerra. Albuquerque: Univ. of New Mexico Press in association with the Center for Documentary Studies at Duke University at Durham, NC, 2007. 136 p.: bibl.

The title of this book, which gathers a collection of photographs about Cuba, is inspired by Marti's utopian vision of a country and his view of Cuba's relations with the US. Harris, a student of photographer Walker Evans who published his seminal and acclaimed book *The Crime of Cuba*, in the 1930s, offers an unapologetic, non-political vision of a culture and a people in the waning years of Fidel Castro's persona. Harris first visited Cuba in the late 1980s and writes eloquently of the country. He looks at the issues of family and community and recalls his own childhood: a privileged, suburban, and oddly ephemeral life in Georgia. An essay by Cuban-American Lillian Guerra complements Harris' vision of the country as a former tropical paradise with an imaginative population now isolated by Castro's communism. The photographs are organized thematically (e.g., Martí, Panoramas, Portraits, etc). Particularly interesting are the views of the city of Havana taken from old cars.

101   Montero Méndez, Hortensia. Los 70: puente para las rupturas. La Habana, Cuba: Centro de Investigación y Desarrollo de la Cultura Cubana Juan Marinello, 2006. 169 p.: bibl., ill.

Overview about the Cuban arts scene that started to develop during the mid-1960s and evolved during the 1970s (from 1967 to 1981, to be more precise), shaping the "generation of true hope," in the words of Juan Marinello. That generation was the prelude to the so-called "Renaissance" of the Cuban arts of the 1980s. The work is set against the backdrop of work done by the Museo Nacional de Bellas Artes (MNBA), where the author has worked as a specialist of Cuban art since 1975. The work is a reasonable effort to analyze Cuban art and art criticism during the period. Montero attempts to interpret the visual and other elements of expression that characterized 1970s artistic production, and to set the work within the broader context of the mission of the Museo. The publication is complemented with a bibliography, appendix, photos of several works, and catalogs of exhibitions.

102   National Art Gallery of the Bahamas. Third national exhibition, 2006: ne3. Curated and with a text by Krista A. Thompson. Nassau: National Art Gallery of the Bahamas, 2006. 44 p.: col. ill.

For many years a group of citizens and artists has been pushing for the creation of a National Gallery of The Bahamas. The Inter-American Development Bank Cultural Center, in Washington DC,

gave the NAGB Committee a grant many years ago to study the creation of such an institution. Many claim it is needed to preserve the country's fragile national identity through the arts, and to encourage creativity and highlight diversity in a country where "culture" is usually defined by consumerism, gambling, and tourism. The present (illustrated) publication documents the third exhibition of 23 artists and 35 works: "the only time that many artists entered the doors of the National Art Gallery." The exhibit is curated by Krista A. Thompson, Ph.D. Her accompanying essay emphasizes the importance of such an event in a place traditionally dominated by "popular photorealist representations of picturesque and idyllic island scenes." Selected artists include veterans such as John Beadle, Maxwell Taylor, Stan Burnside, along with newcomers, the youngest being Jonathan Murray (b. 1986).

103   Price, Sally and Richard Price. Romare Bearden: the Caribbean dimension. Philadelphia: Univ. of Pennsylvania Press, 2006. 189 p.: bibl., ill (chiefly col.).

The authors claim in the preface that the "American difficulty with accepting the Caribbean as a site of serious culture has created a void in the art world's vision of Romare Bearden," the Charlotte-born, North Carolina native artist and famous son. The purpose of this book is to introduce Bearden's little-known, mostly watercolor Caribbean paintings to a wider public, and the impact his Caribbean experience (the couple owned a house in Saint Martin's, birth place of his wife) had on his artistic vision in the last 15 years of his life. Aimed at proving both premises, the Prices have documented a wealth of Bearden's work that has been little known or exhibited elsewhere. They passionately make the point of indicating its conspicuous absence from almost every major show, including the 2003 retrospective at Washington's National Gallery of Art (which included only half a dozen of such works), and the minimal attention given to them in the accompanying catalog. The book appears to be well documented, and the selected visual material is convincing.

104 Weiss, Rachel. Visions, valves, and vestiges: the curdled victories of the Bienal de La Habana. (*Art J.*, 66:1, Spring 2007, p. 10–26, photos)

The Bienal de La Habana started in 1984 and, as Weiss points out, has always been a governmental project (organized, administered, and funded), although the form of government intervention "has not been static." The biennial is organized by the Centro Wifredo Lam, a subsidiary of the Consejo Nacional de las Artes Plásticas (CNAP), a subdivision of the Ministry of Culture. Weiss's article, with its panoramic overview of the history of the biennial through different phases, offers some important criticism that most international art magazines never dare to mention, and instead celebrate the event enthusiastically and unconditionally. Weiss states that directors and curators are directly intertwined with the national project of the Cuban state. No outsiders are brought in for short-term appointments; yet the number of reviews written by Europeans or North Americans with little or no prior experience or knowledge of the island is surprising (Weiss calls it the most notorious phase in the history of the biennial). Equally remarkable is the lack of discussion of the censorship that clouds the event. Weiss asserts that the biennial has reinforced the outside perception of Cuba as a place of authoritarian limits on expression: that is debatable. Judging by the generous coverage the biennial receives, the enormous market that it has generated for many Cuban and Latin American artists, and the collective disregard of the political controversies, Weiss may be wrong in her assertion. She is right in saying that the biennial's power is as much to certify, as to ban, and its decline is related to "a personal verdict on socialism, Castro, and utopianism."

SOUTH AMERICA

Argentina

105 Arte en revistas: publicaciones culturales en la Argentina 1900–1950. Direccion del volumen de Patricia M. Artundo. Rosario, Argentina: Beatriz Viterbo Editora, 2008. 205 p.: bibl., ill. (Ensayos críticos; 41)

The articles that make up this volume analyze the visual discourse contained in five Argentine magazines: *Athinae*, *Revista de la Sociedad Central de Arquitectos*, *La Campana de Palo*, *Correo Literario*, and *Saber Vivir*. The ideas of the individuals and groups that were in charge of the periodicals, and the contributors that they enlisted shared a similar outlook and discourse. This is the reason why, according to Artundo, the magazines achieved a coherence that persisted during the time they were published. To those interested in the art and culture of Argentina, the book may be valuable because the magazines were thought to be outside the institutional establishment, and frequently assumed ideological opposition and confrontation. The publication pays tribute to the role that magazines have played in the development of Argentine culture since the early 1900s.

106 Baldasarre, Maria Isabel. Sobre los inicios del coleccionismo y los museos de arte en la Argentina. (*An. Mus. Paul.*, 14:1, jan./junho 2006, p. 293–321, bibl., photos)

Among Latin American countries, there are only a few specialists who show sustained and systematic interest in researching and analyzing the origins of art collecting in their respective countries; that is why the Argentine case is outstanding. In the present article, Baldasarre digs into the practice of collecting, reconstructing some of the selection mechanisms utilized by collectors as they build their collections—of which the National Museum of Fine Art is the best example. Strongly linked to the implementation of the NMBA were the esthetic decisions made by Eduardo Schiaffino—its mentor and first director who set the course for the museum, which was then maintained for many years. The article analyzes other museums created after the MNBA in provinces outside Buenos Aires, the strong participation of the private collector in their development in contrast with the NMBA, the diversity of economic and stylistic paradigms (especially after the WWI), and the orientation toward national, rather than international, artistic production.

107 Bayardo, Rubens. El financiamiento privado de las artes y la cultura en Argentina: entretelones de la Ley de Mecenazgo. (*in* Congreso Argentino de Americanistas Año 2004. Buenos Aires: Sociedad Argentina de Americanistas, 2005, p. 23–52, bibl.)

In the last few years in Latin America, many experts have recommended allocating 1 percent of each country's budget to support cultural development at the national level. In Argentina, however (according to Bayardo), it merely reaches a fifth of that figure or 0.19 percent, not counting cuts and redirected monies originally intended for culture. No matter how well local economies have performed in the last few years or weathered the world economic crisis, politicians always seem to have "other priorities." As a result, several groups have proposed private financing to foment and stimulate culture. Consensus has been difficult. Argentina's Ley de Mecenazgo (philanthropy, or law for the stimulus of culture), attempts to create tax incentives for those who participate in the effort to support the sector. Departing from the experience provided by the two classic models, the French and the Anglo-Saxon, Bayardo recounts the various experiments and attempts implemented in Argentina, as well examples provided by other countries such as Spain and Chile, to guarantee the sustainability of cultural activity and support its many participants and contributors.

108 Cerviño, Mariana. No, yo tampoco. El amor al arte, probablemente: notas sobre el coleccionismo de arte contemporáneo argentino. (*Apunt. Invest. CECYP*, 11:12, julio 2007, p. 183–198, bibl.)

In her introduction, Cerviño establishes the differences between "symbolic" and "economic" values as two different logics that in the arts do not necessarily harmonize in terms of marketing. The "symbolic capital" usually distances itself from the market, but eventually, according to Bourdieu, both the symbolic and economic capitals will coincide. The digression is important for Cerviño before she tackles particular aspects of collecting art in Argentina, and the incidence of the socioeconomic, political, and cultural issues viewed

from a 19th-century historical perspective. In turn, such a perspective places in context the radical changes that took place as the 20th century advanced, citing as outstanding examples the cases of Eduardo F. Constantini and Mauro Herlitzka, the rise of private collecting over the traditional state, public and institutional collecting, and other trends visible today.

109 Cuadros de viaje: artistas argentinos en Europa y Estados Unidos, 1880–1910. Selección y prólogo de Laura Malosetti Costa. Contribuciones de Ernesto de la Cárcova *et al.* Buenos Aires: Fondo de Cultura Económica, 2008. 383 p.: bibl., ill. (Col. Tierra firme)

Malosetti examines a time when it was difficult for artists from Buenos Aires, or for that matter from Latin America, to travel abroad to study and appreciate the world's great works of art, especially the European masterpieces. The author points out that in 1880 (when Buenos Aires was officially declared the Federal Capital of Argentina) it was rare to find photographic reproductions of art in printed media. Magazine and newspaper descriptions of places and specific works of art and exhibitions tried to compensate for the public's lack of access to museums and sites. In Argentina, such descriptions made by the fortunate artists who enjoyed the privilege of traveling, such as Eduardo Schiaffino, Martín A. Malharro, Eduardo Sívori, and Fernando Fader, to mention just a few. They became, according the Malosetti, the intermediaries between world art and the public of Buenos Aires. The artists' accounts are captivating and help to build the context in which Argentine society developed its artistic taste, trying to reconnect through the arts with a European cultural perspective.

Giunta, Andrea. Jorge Romero Brest and the coordinates of aesthetic modernism in Latin America. See item **59.**

110 Giunta, Andrea. Vanguardia, internacionalismo y política: arte argentino en los años sesenta. Ed. ampliada y corr. Buenos Aires: Siglo Veintiuno Editores, 2008. 391 p.: bibl., ill. (Sociología y política)

Expanded and revised version of the original text published in 2001. The author had two reasons for revising the book: 1) to return to the years in which Argentinean art was celebrated with high expectations; 2) to review the original approach in the light of new material, new ideas, and the experiences derived from contact with individuals during the intervening years. The meticulous research shows the relevance of the leading artistic figures of the time. As with the first edition, the new version is a pivotal reference for understanding the cultural attitude developed by Argentine art in the convoluted scenario of the 1960s, supported by a pro-active, "official" international agenda, strategic showings, intense theoretical and institutional activity, and eagerness to recover historical, contemporary relevance in the context of artistic progress along ideological and political positions. Divided in seven chapters, with 70 pages of notations, excellent bibliography and a few b/w reproductions of archival photographs.

111 Longoni, Ana and **Mariano Mestman.** Del Di Tella a "Tucumán Arde": vanguardia artística y política en el 68 argentino. Buenos Aires: Eudeba, 2008. 485 p.: bibl., ill., index. (Lectores)

Nineteen sixty-eight is an important year in the history of the 20th century for many reasons, and it is no less significant in Argentina. The date serves as the focal point for Longoni and Mestman's study of the country's arts, culture, and politics. A good portion of the book is dedicated to 18 interviews with Argentine artists, intellectuals, union leaders, and activists involved in some of the events of 1968. The November declaration of the Artistic Commission of the Argentine CGT (Argentina's Workers Confederation) in Buenos Aires and the exhibition "Tucumán Arde" in Rosario, among other events, represent the peak of the tensions and complexities experienced by the Argentine avant-garde. Many artists abandoned their purely artistic positions and aligned themselves with the "new left," burning bridges with the leading artistic institutions, like the Institute Di Tella, which had engaged in an agenda to "internationalize" Argentine art. Good analysis of the moment's multidimension-

ality and diversification of artistic trends, which together characterize one of the most dynamic moments of 20th-century art in Argentina.

112 Speranza, Graciela. Fuera de campo: literatura y arte argentinos después de Duchamp. Barcelona: Editorial Anagrama, 2006. 426 p.: ill., maps. (Argumentos; 351)

Imaginative essay that explores the possible relationship between Marcel Duchamp and Argentine literature and art, from the nine-month sojourn the French artist made to Buenos Aires between 1918–19 through the visit that the author made to the Duchamp rooms at the Philadelphia Museum of Art in 2004. According to the author, the "effect" Duchamp, which spread throughout 20th-century art in the West (including Latin America, of course), may be summarized in three creative attitudes: The institutionalization in the 20th century of mass-produced items as art object themselves—a consequence of Duchamps' categorization of the "ready-made" as such; the eclectic interaction and interconnection of techniques and expressions for the sake of the development of new forms; and the prominence of the idea over the technical (as in conceptual art). Writers such as Borges, Cortázar, and Puig, and a number of other artists serve as cases in point for Speranzas' hypothetical sequels.

Chile

113 Neira, Edgardo. El desorejado: padre fundacional de Chile. Chile: Museo Nacional Bellas Artes; Univ. de Concepción, 2005. 1 v. (unpaged): col. ill.

Color-illustrated catalog of Edgardo Neira's exhibition at the Museo Nacional de Bellas Artes, in Santiago, Chile (between March–April, 2005), with essays by Dr. Gilberto Triviños and critic Justo Pastor Mellado. Triviños explains the genesis of the exhibition as the outcome of Neira's research project developed at the University of Concepción. The artist is attempting to bring together the plastic arts, history, literature, and geography of Chile through the 500-year old legend of El Desorejado: a soldier who is believed to have been part of Don Diego de Almagro's forces and who, after being punished with the loss of his ears, went into exile in the Atacama desert, rejecting his Spanish and Catholic past. Neira uses this anecdote as the conceptual platform for his exhibition, and to reflect on the country's character and evolution in light of the celebration of 200 years of Chilean independence in 2010.

Subercaseaux, Bernardo. Historia de las ideas y de la cultura en Chile. See item **1850**.

114 Transformer: exposición curada por Mario Navarro. Santiago: Centro Cultural Matucana, 2005. 143 p.: bibl., ill. (some col.).

Catalog of the group exhibition in Santiago of 15 artists, put together in the form of a document that depicts the art produced in Chile from just before democratization to the present. One premise for the exhibition is an exploration of how art survives in a state that has lost touch with the majority of its population, thanks to the post-Pinochet, liberal economic policies, the increasingly visual nature of mass media, and the fragile, personal environments of the participating artists. For 30 days, each artist modified his/her artwork every day. The result was 30 different exhibitions, each observed by an equal number of people. In the end, the most important goal was to question the current direction of contemporary art and the connection that art may have with everyday life, while at the same time mirroring the inconclusive process of democratic stability in Chile.

Colombia

115 Ángel, Félix. Nosotros, vosotros, ellos: memoria del arte en Medellín durante los años setenta. Prólogo de Álvaro Tirado Mejía. Medellín, Colombia: Tragaluz Editores, 2008. 300 p.: col. ill., ports.

In 2005, Ángel interviewed artists, architects, curators, professors of art, critics, poets, and dramatists, all of whom were active in Medellín, and most of whom were born in the 1920s, 1930s and 1940s. The interview texts and examples of each person's artistic work (primarily from the 1970s) form the core of the volume. Personal experiences and meditations on the making of art in Medellín come through with clar-

ity and poignancy; among those included are Dora Ramírez, Aníbal Vallejo, and Alberto Uribe. High-quality photographs provide examples of Colombian contemporary art that is not well published, especially for English-speaking audiences. [D. Leibsohn]

116 Bazzano-Nelson, Florencia. Marta Traba: internationalism or regional resistance? (*Art J.*, 64:4, Winter 2005, p. 87–89, photo)

Marta Traba's shift from an Eurocentric view of the arts during the 1940 and 1950s (the years she collaborated with Jorge Romero Brest, took specialized art history courses in Paris, and married a Colombian intellectual), to a regionalized perspective influenced by Marxists ideas starting in the 1960s, is the focus of the article. In her most important book of the 1960s *Dos décadas vulnerables en las artes plásticas latinoamericanas*, Traba lays the foundation of her theory of an art of "resistance" in Latin America that needed to oppose the homogenization of the dominant cultures, mainly that of the US. Bazzano-Nelson points out that the "mistakes" (in quotation marks), one may find in her work over 40 years of active art criticism are more interesting than "many critics' truths." To that one may add that the contradictions one may detect in Traba correspond to her reformulation of ideas when trying to understand certain phenomenon outside the experience of her adopted country, Colombia. The text recognizes the great input given to the arts of Latin America by one of its most influential and colorful theoreticians of the 20th century.

117 Bonnett, Piedad. Arte del siglo XX: lo mágico y lo maravilloso en Alejo Carpentier y Wifredo Lam. Bogotá: Univ. Nacional de Colombia, Sede Bogotá, Maestría en Historia y Teoría del Arte y la Arquitectura, Facultad de Artes, 2004. 84, 51 p.: bibl., ill. (Textos: documentos de historia y teoria; 11)

This publication includes two separate essays on different artists and by individual Master of Arts graduates at the School of Fine Arts of Colombia's National University. The first concerns Luis Caballero (Malagón) whose title is extracted from a text apparently written by Caballero himself in 1990, in which he defines a great work of art as a "necessary image," differentiating *image* from *picture*. The essay identifies the main concerns of Caballero's work—emotion, sentiment, experience—as defined by the artist himself in an interview at the end of the 1980s, rejecting the 1960s "avant-garde" incursions that won him noteriety, before moving to Paris. The text contains many statements made by Caballero during his successful career, in which he insisted upon the highly sensual and spiritual connotations of his nudes, a recurrent theme until his death in 1995. The second essay (Bonnett) relates to the author's interest in Carpentier's literary production and its parallels with the work of fellow Cuban painter Wifredo Lam. The coincidences relate to the personal experiences of both the writer and the painter: their self-imposed exiles, their returns to Cuba, their many journeys through the Europe, Asia, Africa, and the Caribbean, and the appropriation of inherited and foreign cultural codes, which in turn translates into a Baroque, profuse, deliberately artificial language full of hues. Good attempt by both prospects in dissecting the particularities of two well-known artists.

118 Daza, Beatriz. Beatriz Daza: hace mucho tiempo, 1956–1968. Bogotá: Fundación Gilberto Alzate Avendaño, 2008. 249 p.: bibl., ill. (some col.)

The book accompanies an anthological exhibition of more than 50 pieces created over a 12-year period by Beatriz Daza. The collection of collages, paintings, prints, ceramic vases, and pots inspired by ancient mythologies includes the ceramic piece "Crisol para Prometeo," which won first prize in the XV Salón de Artistas Colombianos in 1963. With texts by Germán Rubiano, Marta Traba, and others.

119 Garay Celeita, Alejandro. El campo artístico colombiano en el Salón de Arte de 1910. (*Hist. Crít./Bogotá*, 32, julio/dic. 2006, p. 302–333, bibl., photos)

Pierre Bourdieu's theory about "fields" is utilized by Garay Celeita to structure his analysis of Colombia's 1910 art salon, which took place as part of the celebrations of the first centennial of the Republic, in a period dominated by the hegemony of the Conservative Party. Despite previous artistic exhibitions and the creation of the School of Fine Arts in 1886 (which was in great part responsible for the outcome of the Salon), Garay's thesis proposes that the 1910 exhibition, under the direction of Andres de Santa Maria, boasting its own art pavilion specifically built for that purpose, was the first time Colombian art was able to define its own artistic nature. In such a space, the coexistence and interaction of artists, commentators, collectors, and critics made it possible for the field to be established. By then, the "academic" orientation of the School of Fine Arts was not as orthodox as one may think. The presence of Santa Maria allowed for the introduction of some ideas that eventually helped determine some of the directions Colombian art adopted during the early part of the 20th century, mainly the practice of landscape painting, as opposed to the traditional biblical and religious themes, and portraiture.

120 Grupo de Investigación "En un Lugar de la Plástica" (Firm). Plástica dieciocho. Concepción editorial, diseño y diagramación de Nicolás Gómez et al. Presentación de Carolina Franco. Bogotá: Fundación Gilberto Alzate Avendaño: Univ. de los Andes, Facultad de Artes y Humanidades: Ediciones Uniandes, 2007. 293 p.: bibl., facsims., ill., index, maps.

Remarkable piece of research, representing an unusual effort for Colombia, in its attempt to preserve the contributions of artist Judith Marquez (1925–94) to the national arts, and the dissemination of artistic ideas during the 1950s through the magazine *Plástica*, which she founded and directed between 1956–60. This unpretentious volume represents a step forward in the advancement of art history research in Colombia. The work includes an introduction, four essays by various authors, an anthology of the 17 *Plástica* issues published in four years, a few reproductions of Judith Márquez' work, a chronology of her life (in context) with an emphasis on the period between 1954 (when she returned to Colombia from Tenessee, US) and 1960 (after which she moved to Mexico City), and an addemdum with interviews and letters. The anthology is of particular interest because of the number of articles written by the most prominent figures in the avant-garde of art criticism in Latin America at the time, such as Marta Traba (Argentina), José Gómez Sicre (Cuba), Walter Engel (Colombia), and Aristides Meneghetti (Uruguay), to name a few. The publication constitutes a fascinating microcosm of the arts environment that pervaded the capital of the country, Bogotá, in the years following "La Violencia," the presidency of General Gustavo Rojas Pinilla and his eventual ousting (1953–57), the creation of the bipartisan National Front (1958), and restitution of democratic governability.

121 Lucy Tejada: años cincuenta. Compilación e investigación de Nicolás Gómez Echeverri. Bogotá: Fundación Gilberto Alzate Avendaño: Alcaldía Mayor de Bogotá D.C., Cultura, Recreación y Deporte, 2008. 214 p.: bibl., ill. (some col.)

Illustrated catalog of the retrospective exhibition of Beatriz Daza is part of the efforts of the Gilberto Alzate Avendaño Foundation to pay tribute to a number of women artists who were crucial to the development of Colombian art during the mid-20th century. Daza's 1965–66 work with ceramics may be considered the most relevant part of her career. Her inclusion of chinaware and broken pottery in compositions eventually lead her to a kind of informal abstraction, years before internationally well known artists such as the North American Julian Schnabel did the same. Her last paintings indicate a departure from her previous interest and it is difficult to know in which direction she was heading. Due to her relatively early death, Daza's oeuvre may be considered inconclusive. However, she was a significant presence within the active Bogotá art scene of the 1950s and 1960s, and in the more ample context of Latin American art, including the important transformation which coincided with the Cold War. The publication reproduces a number of articles written on Daza's work through the years by well-known Colombian art critics and historians, such as Walter Engel, Eugenio Barney, Marta Traba, and Germán Rubiano Caballero. Accompanied by a chronology and succinct bibliography.

122 Miguel Díaz Vargas: una modernidad invisible. Grupo de Investigación: Taller Historia Crítica del Arte. Proyecto curatorial de William Alfonso López Rosas.

Bogotá: Fundación Gilberto Alzate Avendaño, 2008. 377 p.: bibl., ill. (some col.)

The book, which accompanied the 2008 exhibition in Bogotá, is the first comprehensive attempt to reconstruct the historical and artistic context within which Díaz Vargas (1886–1956) developed his talent as a painter and practiced his craft despite living in a society whose visual and intellectual education was considerably behind that of some other Latin American countries and Europe. By the time Díaz Vargas was able to travel to Spain to study at the Royal Academy of San Fernando he was 40 years old. The influence of the Catalonian school on his work thereafter is palpable. For traits inherent to his style, Díaz Vargas may be considered a (late) naturalist, a neocostumbrista, or a realist academician, terms practically contradictory but symptomatic of the hybrid, conservative taste, and shortsighted vision that prevailed in Bogotá circles (and much of the rest of Colombia) at the time, in matters of art. Six essays by different authors examine the artist's work from diverse angles. The book is well researched, and a notable feature is a compilation of articles originally published during the artist's lifetime by nearly every art authority in the country. Nicely illustrated in color and b/w.

123 Quinche Ramírez, Victor Alberto. La crítica de arte en Colombia: los primeros años. (*Hist. Crít./Bogotá,* 32, julio/dic. 2006, p. 274–301, bibl.)

Quinche Ramírez traces the beginnings of art criticism in Colombia to the middle of the 19th century, mostly in the capital, Bogota. The article introduces the notion of "art criticism," and how this practice acquired a standard procedure that followed the models of academic art produced in Colombia (in the manner of French Academism). The procedure came to a breaking point with the exhibition in Bogota of the work of Andres de Santa Maria (at the end of the 19th century). In the context of the historic and political situation of the times, the author concludes that the disfavor with which Santa Maria's work was received eventually helped reformulate the character and vision of art criticism in the country. This is a reasonably well done, substantiated, informative, and educational attempt to explain the origins of art criticism in Colombia, which offers a counterpoint to some of the opinions of other individuals (not necessarily art critics, or trained as such). The work makes a distinction among news and information, analysis, and critical essay, and the theoretical traditions in which the last two may be inscribed. It also establishes the difference between "art historians" and "sociologists," the "literaturization" and anecdotal character of much criticism, and the scarcity of philosophical perspective, all of which abound in this still unorganized and not-so-rigorous area of the Colombian arts.

124   La tras escena del museo: nación y objetos en el Museo Nacional de Colombia. Edicion académica de Gabriel Andrés Eljaiek Rodríguez. Bogotá: Editorial Pontificia Univ. Javeriana, 2006. 134 p.: ill. (some col.). (Cuadernos pensar en público; 1)

Three essays are gathered in this probing, but simple volume, the first in a series planned by PENSAR (the Institute of Social and Cultural Studies) of Javeriana University in Bogotá, in cooperation with the curators of the National Museum of Colombia. The basis of the essays are objects and artifacts found in the collections of the museum which, despite their unorthodox nature (for instance, the trophy of the 1959 Miss Universe, Colombian Luz Marina Zuluaga), have a social and cultural significance that allows for different readings when juxtaposed with other more "relevant" items. They also help expand the discussion of issues (such as genre, in the case of "queen" Luz Marina) in light of other achievements by Colombian women. The other two essays concern the cranium of an assassin and the lyrics of the national anthem as an expression of nationalism.

125   Vélez, Marta Elena. La obra de Marta Elena Vélez. Curaduría de Alberto Sierra Maya y María del Rosario Esobar. Medellín: Fondo Editorial Universidad EAFIT, 2008. 147 p.: ill. (chiefly col.)

The former School of Business Administration, known now as EAFIT University, in Medellín, has undertaken a commendable editorial initiative in the last few years, producing books dedicated to highlighting significant local artists and staging exhibitions that accompany the publications. The task comes from the realization that the two main local museums had not been able to perform this role satisfactorily. Although the methodology and research utilized by EAFIT in its art publications leaves room for substantial improvement and is far from the rigor that demanding scholars are accustomed to, some of the publications such as the present one dedicated to Vélez fill a void given the traditional lack of interest in historical analysis and criticism of the city as artistic phenomena. Miguel González gives perhaps the best description of Marta Elena Vélez' contribution when he concludes that her work reveals the reiteration of her obsessions—such as love—and the emotion of being alive, while measuring the pulse of the visual and conceptual preoccupations of her lifetime.

Ecuador

126   Colvin, Jean. Arte de Tigua: a reflection of indigenous culture in Ecuador = una reflexión de la cultura indígena en Ecuador. Quito: Ediciones ABYA-YALA, 2004. 160 p.: col. ill.

The Tiguas Indians are believed to have occupied the highlands of the central/ western region of the Ecuadorian Andes since antiquity, and are just one among many ethnic groups whose existence is closely associated with the extraordinary biodiversity of the country. Currently the Tiguas comprise eight communities in the Páramo de Cotopaxi province. For centuries they were subjected to the control of landowners, and only in the last 30 years have they enjoyed relative independence, according to Hernán Crespo Toral, the former UNESCO vice-director for culture, who writes the prologue. The Kichwa peoples, who decorate their festival drums and masks with geometric designs have further developed their skills on canvas—a means of sustaining their community—and their repertoire has expanded to themes related to history, politics, folk legends, and other traditions. Colvin's work explains the expressions used by the Tiguas in both visual and narrative modes, which allows for an understanding of the peoples' cosmovision mixed with the reality of globalization. Well illustrated in color, with texts in both English and Spanish.

Paraguay

127 **Escobar, Ticio.** Una interpretación
de las artes visuales en el Paraguay.
2. ed. Asunción: Servilibro, 2007. 630 p.:
bibl., ill.

Reedition in single book of the original two-volume history of the visual arts in
Paraguay as interpreted by the author and
initially published in 1982 and 1984 respectively. Corrections have been made, but
no new material has been added. The new
volume is divided in two parts (corresponding with the original, separate volumes),
the first dedicated to indigenous peoples
(Guarani), colonial and 19th century arts;
and the second dedicated exclusively to the
20th century. Illustrated in b/w, and bibliographies concerning each part.

Peru

128 **Taller 72: muestra antológica, 1972–
2007.** Textos de Manuel Munive.
Lima: ICPNA, Instituto Cultural Peruano
Norteamericano, 2008. 94 p.: bibl., chiefly
ill. (chiefly col.).

Color and b/w illustrated catalog of
the exhibition presented at the Peruvian-
American Cultural Institute (ICPNA) in
Lima, to mark the 36th anniversary of the
creation of the Taller 72, the oldest privately
owned workshop in the country dedicated
exclusively to the practice and development
of graphics arts in Peru. Munive acted as
curator of the anthological exhibition, and
wrote a brief history of the workshop giving credit to the founders, Eulalia Orsero
Zunino, Jorge Ara Manchego and Miguel
Gutiérrez, and to other artists that joined
through the years such as Cristina Dueñas,
Alberto Agapito, and Gabriela de Bernardi,
among many others. The Krausse printing
press is the emblem for the workshop. Five
information bulletins issued by the Taller
72 between 1981 and 1984 are included as an
Annex.

Uruguay

129 **Matto, Francisco.** Matto: el misterio de la forma. Texto de Alicia
Haber y Cecilia de Torres. Montevideo:
Galería Oscar Prato, 2007. 192 p.: ill.
(chiefly col.)

Monograph on the Uruguayan artist
intended to revive and make better known
the body of work developed by the artist in
painting and sculpture. Francisco Matto was
a founder and active member of the Taller,
the Joaquín Torres-García Workshop set
up in 1943 by the geometric abstractionist
master in Montevideo to advance his ideas
about universal constructivism. Matto is
not as well known as other members of
the workshop, such as Gonzalo Fonseca,
although he considered Matto the greatest
member of the group. Illustrated in color
and b/w.

130 **Montani, Andrés.** Andrés Montani,
pinturas, 1960–1992. Montevideo:
Galería de las Misiones; Miami: Latin
America & Contemporary Art, 2006. 49 p.:
ill. (some col.).

Catalog of the exhibition honoring
the artist (1918–2002), organized four years
after his death, at the Galería de las Misiones in Montevideo and Punta del Este,
and Sammer Gallery in Coral Gables, US.
The selection of works is from 1960–92
and, as Alfredo Torres points out in his
introductory essay, it allows for a reading
of Montani's abstract style, which derives
without apology from Spanish informalism;
this includes the lyrical abstraction of Pierre
Soulages, the German Hans Hartung and
the Italian Alberto Burri, and the program-
matic methods for performing a painting
characteristic of the US abstract expression-
ists, and the brutal character of the COBRA
group. His work aspires to both freedom
and synthesis. Chronologically, the surge
of "free" abstraction coincides in Uruguay
with the collapse of the "immaculate democracy" of the Uruguayan republic and
the settlement of new political and social
realities that eventually left the country
deeply scarred. Uruguay has never boasted a
strong abstract expressionistic current, and
those like Montani who practiced it belong
to a minority group. Thus, this booklet with
its short text, small number of historical
photographs of the artist and his friends or
in his studio, and the color reproductions of
his paintings is an interesting homage to an
artist who seldom receives as much attention of other paradigmatic figures in the
River Plate basin.

BRAZIL

JOSÉ M. NEISTEIN, *Independent Consultant, Washington, DC*

OF THE 55 WORKS ANNOTATED FOR *HLAS 66*, almost one third deal with the modern era. If we include works of architecture, city planning, and photography in their 20th and 21st century manifestations, modernity encompasses about 80 percent of the bibliography ranged here. The vast majority of the scholars reviewed focus their efforts on the artistic and creative power of Brazil's modern era. Notwithstanding, this thematic emphasis, the remaining subdivisions also offer relevant items.

Concerning theoretical and reference works, *Os tempos da fotografia: o efêmero e o perpétuo* is a noted contribution to the knowledge of the epistemological nature of photography and its historical importance (item **131**). On the colonial period, and the first years of independence, the publication of Jean-Baptiste Debret's complete iconography on Brazil is an event of magnitude (item **132**). Also the study on the contribution of the Guarani to colonial imagery is to be mentioned. An overall view of the artistic output of the 19th century published in Italian in succinct form deserves to be translated for the benefit of larger audiences (item **138**). The book on Debret as a historian offers new perspectives on the 19th century (item **137**).

Among the works on the 20th century, Portinari continues to be the object of new studies and new approaches as a social artist (items **151**, **152**, and **155**). The classic artists of modernism, Cícero Dias (item **149**) and Tarsila do Amaral (item **140**), were each examined in monograph-length works. Beyond Portinari, the classic artists of the second modernism, Livio Abramo (item **142**) and Antônio Bandeira (item **143**), are represented by one study each. The avant-garde is represented in several excellent monographs: Mira Schendel (item **150**), neo-concretism in Rio de Janeiro (item **157**), recent art in São Paulo (item **158**), Anna Bella Geiger (item **154**), and Elisa Bracher (item **145**). Various modern artists were celebrated: Maria Bonomi on the 50th anniversary of her professional life, Iberê Camargo, Emanoel Araújos' autobiography, the 60th anniversary of the São Paulo Museum of Modern Art, Francisco Brennand's life output, and Bonfanti's 40 years in art (items **141**, **144**, **146**, **147**, **148**, and **159**).

The topics of architecture and city planning is well represented in a variety of works: 19th-century São Paulo (item **176**), Vitória do Espírito Santo (item **181**), Goiânia (item **178**), problems and issues of big cities (item **177**) and smaller cities (item **182**), and monographs on Rosa Kliass (item **184**)and Carlos Bratke (item **175**).

The section on photography offers new contributions on the 19th century (items **168**, **164**, and **165**), 20th century (items **166**, **170**, and **171**), and photography and political power (item **162**). Folklore and crafts are covered by *Mestres de ofícios de Minas Gerais: resgate cultural do artesanato mineiro and Pernambuco popular: um toque de mestre* (items **161** and **160**). Afro-Brazilian traditions are represented by two excellent items: the discussion of the concept of Afro-Brazilian art (item **185**) and the remapping of the cultural history of Afro-Brazilians art (item **186**). And finally the two relevant items of miscellaneous: the iconographical holdings of the National Archives and the papers of the 25th conference of the Brazilian Committee of art history (items **188** and **187**).

With few exceptions, all the items annotated here were published in the past five years.

REFERENCE AND THEORETICAL WORKS

131 Kossoy, Boris. Os tempos da fotografia: o efêmero e o perpétuo. Cotia, Brazil: Ateliê Editorial, 2007. 174 p.: bibl., ill.

Together with *Fotografia e Historia* (1989) and *Realidades e ficções na trama fotográfica* (1999), this annotated title rounds out the theoretical trilogy of Boris Kossoy on the epistemological nature of photography and its historical and sociocultural impact and meaning. Several essays set together discuss the medium's "power to inform and disinform, its ability to stir and transform emotions, and to denounce and manipulate." For that matter the author dismantles information in order to explain the supporting pillars of photography's theoretical principles and the formal codes that permeate images and their substance. An original contribution.

COLONIAL PERIOD

132 Bandeira, Júlio; and **Pedro Corrêa do Lago.** Debret e o Brasil: obra completa, 1816–1831. Prefácio de José Murilo de Carvalho. Rio de Janeiro: Capivara, 2007. 705 p.: bibl., ill. (chiefly col.), index.

Part of the celebration of the 200th anniversary of the arrival of Prince Regent D. João VI, the royal family, and the Portuguese court in Rio de Janeiro, this book assembles, clarifies, and analyzes the complete output of Jean-Baptiste Debret in and about Brazil. Over 1060 works are included and reproduced; including virtually all works known in Brazil and abroad, which belong to both public and private collections. Debret (1768–1848) is the creator of the largest body of art works produced during the first half of the 19th century, and his work was related to all aspects of life in Brazil during that period. His oil paintings, watercolors, lithographs, sketches, and drawings provide an encompassing view of Brazil's social life on all strata of society.

133 Boff, Claudete. A imaginária Guarani: o acervo do Museu das Missões. Santo Ângelo, Brazil: Centro de Cultura Missioneira: EDIURI, 2005. 171 p.: bibl., col. ill.

Originally a master's degree thesis, the main topic of this book is the esthetics and cultural evaluation of the carved images in the collection of the Rio Grande do Sul Museum of the Missions in the southern area of the state, where the Jesuits attempted to Christianize the Guarani population in the 17th and 18th centuries. Baroque images were brought from Europe, and later the Jesuits taught indigenous peoples how to make them. The images were used in the evangelization process. Author pinpoints native features mixed with Western art, and analyzes the original style that was created. Working with European modern art historical theories, the author tries to convey the contributions of a New World perspective.

Bollini, Horacio. Imágenes y símbolos del mundo jesuítico-guaraní. See item **45**.

134 Daum, Denise. Albert Eckhouts "gemalte Kolonie": Bild- und Wissensproduktion über Niederländisch-Brasilien um 1640 [Albert Eckhout's "painted colony": knowledge and image-production in Dutch Brazil around 1640]. Marburg, Germany: Jonas, 2009. 198 p.: bibl., ill. (some col.).

Albert Eckhout, a painter in Dutch Brazil during the administration of Count Maurice of Nassau-Siegen in Pernambuco (1637–44), not only painted the first oil portraits of Brazilian Indians (and two Africans), most probably after his return in Europe, but also produced important sketches about natural history and thus contributed to Dutch scientific interest in the country. This work focuses on the symbolic value of the portraits (now in Copenhagen): even though European colonists are not portrayed, the depiction of other peoples refers to the European as model so far as color, ethnicity, and gender are concerned. [F. Obermeier]

135 Talento, Biaggio; and **Helenita Hollanda.** Basílicas & capelinhas: história, arte e arquitetura de 42 igrejas de Salvador. Salvador, Brazil: Edição dos Autores, 2006. 215 p.: bibl., ill.

Preceded by a historical account of the Catholic Church in Bahia and its relationship to black African slaves and freed slaves, the book discusses circumstances and building features of 42 churches and chapels in Salvador, Bahia, built from 1540 to 1850 and beyond, including interior carving details, sculptures, and ceiling paintings. An array of artists are introduced and briefly studied. Includes annotated bibliography and poor b/w photos. Addresses of the churches and chapels provided.

19TH CENTURY

Bandeira, Júlio; and **Pedro Corrêa do Lago.** Debret e o Brasil: obra completa, 1816–1831. See item **132.**

136 Brasilien: von Österreich zur Neuen Welt. [Brazil: from Austria to the New World.] Herausgegeben von Tayfun Belgin. Krems an der Donau, Austria: Kunstmeile Kunsthalle Krems, 2007. 128 p.: bibl., ill. (chiefly col.)

Exhibition catalog from a show presented at the Kunsthalle Krems in Krems an der Donau, Austria (Sept. 16, 2007– Feb.17, 2008) about the 19th-century presence of Austrian artists in Brazil (Thomas Ender among them). The exhibit also included a selection of works by Brazilian artists. [F. Obermeier]

137 Lima, Valéria. J.B. Debret, historiador e pintor: a viagem pitoresca e histórica ao Brasil, 1816–1839. Campinas, Brazil: Editora Unicamp, 2007. 325 p.: bibl., ill. Col. Várias histórias; 25)

Originally presented as the author's doctoral thesis, the principle that runs through this exhaustive research is the strong correlation between social history and image. In the specific case of Jean Baptiste Debret, who lived and worked in Brazil from 1816–31, produced hundreds of drawings and watercolors, and who later became famous after converting these works into lithographs in Paris, his work can only be fully understood and appraised if in association with his notes, remarks, descriptions, commentaries, and log books. Together this material forms a primary source for the knowledge and understanding of the socioeconomical and political history of Brazil and the country's transformations in the passage from colony to independence. Reproductions, quotations, and bibliography enhance this relevant contribution.

138 Migliaccio, Luciano. Arte brasiliana del secolo XIX. Udine, Italy: Forum, 2007. 102 p.: bibl., ill. (some col.). (Testi e saggi latinoamericani; 2)

Leaning on the best Brazilian bibliography available on this topic, Luciano Migliaccio is able to offer a concise overview of painting and sculpture in Brazil from the late 18th century to 1905 in a mere 100 pages. Designed for an Italian readership, the text is historically divided in three blocks: from colony to independence, the Dom Pedro I era, and the Dom Pedro II empire. The book touches upon topics ranging from Portuguese, French, and Italian influences, to the awareness of a national identity, and the gradual coming of age of a distinctive Brazilian visual vernacular. The roles of royalty, aristocracy, bourgeoisie, and immigrants are clearly pointed out in their sociopolitical contexts. Richly illustrated albeit poor printing.

20TH CENTURY

139 Alambert, Francisco. 1001 words for Mário Pedrosa. (*Art J.*, 64:4, Winter 2005, p. 85–86, photo)

In his tribute to Brazilian Mário Pedrosa, Alambert characterizes the critic as an individual for whom "the combination of political and critical radicalism was especially meaningful," and his "aesthetic ideas indistinguishable from his political trajectory." Pedrosa did not conceive of modern art without revolutionary politics, and vice versa. Alambert goes on to say that for Pedrosa, the liberating potential of art came from the possibility of making freely an action that dislocated the reification of alienated subjectivity. Alambert connects Pedrosa with Clement Greenberg, not through the issues of bi-dimensionality and abstraction, but rather through the importance of concept and ideology. His disenchantment with the forms of interventions that art could provide to transform society, and his conclusion about the incapacity of art to impose quality over ambiguity, led Pedrosa to abandon art criticism and work toward the goal of saving the socialist utopia. [F. Ángel]

140 Amaral, Tarsila do. Tarsila por Tarsila. São Paulo: Celebris, 2004. 189 p.: bibl., ill. (some col.).

The author is a grandniece of the great artist from whom she inherited her name, and whose biography she now writes. Filled with personal reminiscenses, the book offers a sensitive study of Tarsila, the beautiful, intelligent, cultural woman, her personal growth and the development of her art. One of the finest among Brazilian early modernists, Tarsila had many friends among the intellectual, artistic, social, and political elite of Brazil and France. Her story is told against the background of her times, a broad mural of Paris, São Paulo, and Rio de Janeiro in the effervescence of modernism. Bibliography, reproductions, memorabilia, and photos.

141 Araújo, Emanoel. Emanoel Araújo: autobiografia do gesto. São Paulo: Imprensa Oficial: Instituto Tomie Ohtake, 2008. 271 p.: ill. (chiefly col.).

A descendant of three generations of goldsmiths, Emanoel Araújo (Bahia, 1940) became an apprentice at an early age, learning book printing and woodcarving crafts. This intimacy with techniques of precision was to be of crucial importance in the making and stylistic development of the sculptor, printmaker, draftsman, and book, poster, and stage set designer. This catalog registers the dozens of artworks that made up this retrospective of almost 50 years of creativity. The essay combines biography and critical appraisal. The title refers to the artist's personal way of drawing lines and folding forms. Chronology and list of works. No bibliography. Richly illustrated.

142 Araújo, Olívio Tavares de. Livio Abramo. São Paulo: Instituto Tomie Ohtake, 2007. 175 p.: bibl., ill. (some col.).

This exhibition catalog turns out to be the first, long overdue, study of the artist who, alongside Oswaldo Goeldi, historically legitimized printmaking as an autonomous and superior art form within early Brazilian modernism. A son of Italian immigrants, Livio Abramo (1903–92) entered art through political action. As a militant Trotzkyist, he aligned himself with working class people, who became the subject of his woodblock prints. His highly personal, artistic, and uncompromising ethical standards made him a highly respected and influential personality in Brazil as well as in Paraguay, his adopted country during the three last decades of his life. The author contextualizes the life and output of Abramo as a genuine expressionist of nonaffiliation. Updated bibliography, chronology, and excellent illustrations.

143 Bandeira, Antônio. Antônio Bandeira: desconfigurações. Curadoria de Roberto Galvão e José Guedes. São Paulo: USP MAC, 2008. 156 p.: chiefly ill. (chiefly col.).

Catalog of an exhibition of select works by Antônio Bandeira (1922–67) belonging to the collection of the Pinacoteca do Estado do Ceará. The show offered an overall view of the esthetic itinerary of Bandeira, including works representative of the artist's different artistic periods, such as his figurative works of the 1940s, his informal abstractions while living in Paris, and his mature output of the 1960s, all of which provide a comprehensive approach to his creative process and the relevance of his contribution to Brazilian art. Bandeira regarded himself as a recreator of the impressionistic view of art rather than of an abstractionist one. He once said: "they call me abstract in Paris, but when I start a painting, I never think of this supposed abstractionism. I want simply to paint, starting with the image or ideas of human beings, cities, etc, i.e. things that I have already seen spontaneously." His vision is lyrical poetic.

144 Bonomi, Maria. De viés. Curadoria de Francisco Bosco. Curitiba, Brazil: Museu Oscar Niemeyer, 2007. 109 p.: ill. (chiefly col.).

To celebrate the 50 years of Maria Bonomi's artistry, the Oscar Niemeyer Museum in Curitiba presented an exhibition of the distinguished contemporary printmaker, sculptor, and installation artist. In a comprehensive overview of her output, Bonomi explains that the guideline for her art is Nietzsche's statement that anything great is born from the conciliation of opposites. Hence, Bonomi's work is all-inclusive from the poster-like prints of the 1960s to the large panels of public art—including objects and sculpture—to recent installation performances. As a critic points out, she "politicizes the abstract." A detailed CV completes the publication. Lavishly illustrated.

145 Bracher, Elisa. Maneira branca: gravuras de Elisa Bracher. São Paulo: Cosac Naify, 2006. 127 p.: bibl., ill. (some col.).

This book was published in conjunction with the artist's exhibition at the São Paulo Pinacoteca. Departing from Goya's prints early in her youth, Elisa Bracher (1965) evolved into printmaking of a minimalist nature and monumental sizes that were unfolded over several sheets of paper. Her technique, the "manière blanche" expresses "the plenitude of the whites and the abyss of the blacks, (and) contains an existential intensity that is not possible with other media. This might explain why all prints, without exception, are melancholic." (L. Mammì). Bracher is also known for her monumental sculptures in wood and marble, most of them displayed in Brazilian cities. Additional texts by Sonia Salzstein and José Bento Ferreira. CV, chronology and English version of the original Portuguese texts.

146 Bueno, Guilherme. Bonfanti: através do espelho. Rio de Janeiro: Contracapa, 2009. 191 p.: bibl., ill. (chiefly col.).

Published on the occasion of the retrospective exhibit of Gianguido Bonfanti (1948) and his 40 years of art production at the Paço Imperial in Rio, book includes analytical chronology by Marisa Scharger Maia, chronological lists of exhibitions, and bibliographical references. Reminiscent of Goya's drawings and etchings, and of the paintings by Munch, Kandinsky, and the Fauves, Bonfanti's statements are highly personal. Texts point out and discuss his expressionistic perspective that also encompasses surreal themes, eroticism and eschatology, alternated by geometric and abstract periods. His noted self-portraits are autobiographical and convey existential multidimensions.

147 Camargo, Iberê. Iberê Camargo: um ensaio visual. Porto Alegre, Brazil: Fundação Iberê Camargo, 2009. 115 p.: bibl., ill. (some col.).

This essay accompanied a major exhibition of the renowned Brazilian artist. The exhibit displayed selected works in a wide array of media, belonging to the foundation that bears his name. Iberê Camargo's (1914–94) art echoes the impact of Van Gogh, Cézanne, concretism, and abstract expressionism. Both essays and illustrations give an account that draws upon his representational beginnings to his late abstraction, reminiscent of action painting. He excelled in a wide array of media, but painting bears his deepest mark.

148 Cover = reencenação + repetição. Coordenação editorial de Magnólia Costa. Curadoria de Fernando Oliva. São Paulo: Museu de Arte Moderna MAM São Paulo, 2008. 88 p.: ill. (some col.).

In celebration of the 60th anniversary of the São Paulo Museum of Modern Art, an avant-garde show was organized with works by several young artists to reflect the reenactment conditions through the practice of initiating extant bands of music, assuming that music imitation is a stage artifice. The original performers supply material for satire, the works presented drawings from performances recorded with cheap technologies. Makes the point that contemporary art is constantly aware of technological intermediation in image use. A critique of global culture was implicit in the exhibit. Additional texts by Chirstopher Kihm and Marcelo Rezende, in Portuguese and English, with French quotations.

149 Dias, Cícero. Cícero Dias: oito décadas de pintura. Projeto, curadoria e coordenação de Waldir Simões de Assis Filho. Curitiba, Brazil: Museu Oscar Niemeyer, 2006. 322 p.: ill. (chiefly col.), photos.

Catalog of the most comprehensive exhibition yet of this classic artist of Brazilian modernism, covering representative works from his early career in the 1920s, his abstract paintings once integrated in the School of Paris, and his latest canvasses where he resumed figurativism. Texts by Mário de Andrade, Manuel Bandeira, Oswald de Andrade, Sêrgio Milliet, Léon Degand, Antonio Bento, Mário Pedrosa, Pierre Restany, Murilo Mendes, Mário Hélio Gomes de Lima, Gilberto Freyre, João Cabral de Melo Neto, and more. Chronology of Cícero (1907–2003) by Raymonde Dias. Photographs, documents, and many reproductions. No bibliography

150 Dias, Geraldo de Souza. Mira Schendel: do espiritual à corporeidade. Prefácio de Andreas Haus. São Paulo: Cosac Naify, 2009. 347 p.: bibl., ill. (chiefly col.), index.

The Portuguese translation of the author's doctoral thesis, originally published in Berlin in 2000 in the German language. To date, this is the most comprehensive study of the life and work of the internationally acclaimed Zürich-born artist who settled in Brazil in 1950, and who, over the years, became one of the most distinguished and original among Brazil's avant-garde artists. Author handles with competence a large amount of biographical and theoretical-critical materials and conveys a full portrait of the artist, her rich European heritage, her assimilation to Brazil, and her creative process and results. Mira (1919–88) was an artist-thinker, and the spiritual nature of her work, close to and independent from concretism and minimalism, is nourished by deep philosophical and theological concerns. Rich bibliography and name index. Lavishly illustrated. A most welcome publication.

151 Fabris, Annateresa. Portinari e a arte social. (*Estud. Ibero-Am./Porto Alegre*, 31:2, dez. 2005, p. 79–103, photos)

Since his first series of government paintings at the Ministério de Educação e Saúde Pública was commissioned by Gustavo Capanema, Cândido Portinari has been accused, mostly by left-wing critics and artists, of being an "official painter." The accusation has persisted since 1936–38. Using strong arguments to affirm that Portinari was an artist firmly engaged in Brazil's social issues—focusing on black workers who he frequently portrayed in his work—Fabris affirms the opposite, conceding that the artist was not politically minded. The background of the essay is the polemic on realism in art, which started in France with Léger, Aragon, Breton and continued in Brazil with Pedrosa, Afonso Arinos, and others.

152 Guerra e Paz, Portinari. Produced by the Portinari Project. Rio de Janeiro: Projeto Portinari, 2007. 231 p.: bibl., ill. (some col.).

"A gift from Brazil to the United Nations and to the cause of world peace," and published in commemoration of the 50th anniversary of the "War and Peace" panels installation at the UN headquarters in New York. Includes seven original texts written by Enrico Bianco, Israel Pedrosa, and others, supplemented by an illustrated chronobiography of Portinari, and the reproductions of 119 of the 180 studies that Portinari drew and painted as he created the panels. Published simultaneously in Portuguese and English. Errata slip inserted. Includes bibliographical references.

153 Inhotim Centro de Arte Contemporânea. Inhotim Centro de Arte Contemporânea. Brumadinho, Brazil: Inhotim Centro de Arte Contemporânea, 2008. 398 p.: bibl., ill. (chiefly col.).

When art collector Bernardo de Mello Bar turned visionary in the late 1960s, he decided to assemble a collection of Brazilian contemporary art. Now, 40 years later, his project has become not only a major center for younger generations of Brazilian artists, but also an irresistible attraction for artists all over the world. Located in a huge landscaped rural property in Minas Gerais, scattered outdoors and indoors with several buildings, this international collection serves an educational purpose to visitors from many countries, and is committed to the local community of Brumadinho. Artists are given ideal conditions of experimentation without boundaries, and are engaged in an ongoing dialogue of the most diverse esthetic manifestations, of which this catalog gives an excellent account through 11 critical texts and dozens of color illustrations.

154 Jaremtchuk, Dária. Anna Bella Geiger: passagens conceituais. Belo Horizonte, Brazil: Editora C/Arte; São Paulo, Brazil: Edusp: FAPESP, 2007. 179 p.: bibl., ill. (some col.). (História & arte)

Study describes and discusses the itinerary of Anna Bella Geiger from figurative and abstract printmaking to pioneering conceptual art in Brazil in the 1970's, in Brazilian terms at that. This scholarly approach shows how the artist investigated questions regarding the nature of art, cultural, social, and political contexts, her reactions against sheer visuality, and how she expanded the use of a variety of materials including photography, Xerox, artist's books, super-8, videos, postcards, and installations. She fought for the transformative function of the artistic object and for the artist's responsibility toward the human condition through the consciousness of their actions. Extensive bibliographical references and illustrations exemplify the author's points.

155 Klintowitz, Jacob. Museu Casa de Portinari. Brodowski, Brazil: Museu Casa de Portinari, 2007. 131 p.: ill. (chiefly col.).

The house where Cândido Portinari spent his childhood and early youth in Brodowski, São Paulo, has been converted into a museum. The museum houses frescoes, paintings, and drawings, including the celebrated series of drawings "Meninos de Brodowski." The house is the site of Portinari's grandmother's chapel, designed and decorated by the artist, and also contains documents, memorabilia, photos, personal belongings, the artist's tools and colors, family furniture, and more. A good part of this inventory is reproduced and illustrated. Text covers some biography, testimonies and a brief, generalized evaluation of Portinari (1903–62) as "the most important 20th century Brazilian artist, who like nobody else, portrayed Brazilians, their social, economical, and cultural, and religious history."

156 Magalhães, Roberto. Roberto Magalhães. São Paulo: J.J. Carol Editora, 2009. 96 p.: chiefly col. ill. (Portfolio Brasil. Artes plásticas)

A personal statement and a few excerpts by various art critics introduce a selection from 50 years of artworks by Roberto Magalhães (1940). Included are reproductions of drawings, woodblock prints, paintings, and painted objects created by the leading artist of the "Nova Figuração," who became active in Rio de Janeiro after the historical avant-garde exhibition "Opinião 65." Known for his esoteric drawings produced in the 1970s, he later concentrated on paintings of visionary and fantastic themes, which were produced in minute detail. Additional CV and English translation of the texts.

157 Marques Parracho Sant'Anna, Sabrina. O Museu de Arte Moderna e a trajetória do concretismo carioca. (Estud. Hist./Rio de Janeiro, 38, 2006, p. 33–48, bibl.)

Essay discusses the beginnings of concretism (or neoconcretism) in the visual arts in Rio de Janeiro stemming from Grupo Frente in the 1950s and the role that the Museum of Modern Art played in modernizing

the art movements of that period. Also discusses how friendships and affinities helped artists develop a collective, objective view of both modernity and of Brazil, as opposed to the subjective, nationalistic view of art and "Brazility" as represented by figurative artists like Portinari and di Cavalcanti, who were identified with social art and remote historical roots. The concretists envisioned an urban, industrial, updated Brazil, expressed in an abstract, geometrical, impersonal esthetic with their own idiosyncrasies against Paulista concretism and against their own rivals in Rio amalgamated in other groups. Footnotes and bibliography.

158 Museu de Arte Moderna de São Paulo. MAM 60. Curadoria de Annateresa Fabris e Luiz Camillo Osorio. São Paulo: Museu de Arte Moderna de São Paulo-MAM, 2008. 235 p.: ill (some col.).

Catalog of an exhibition that celebrated the 60th anniversary of the foundation of the São Paulo Museum of Modern Art. The authors wrote one essay each on the modern and contemporary segments of the collection, which today account for 5,000 holdings. The 500 works selected for this exhibition offer an idea of the scope of the collection, as well as an idea of the development of modern and contemporary art in Brazil. All items exhibited are reproduced mainly in small format. No bibliography, but additional documents and interviews are included.

159 Tavares, Júlio. Brennand: arte e sonho na construção de um novo mundo. São Paulo: Terra das Artes Editora, 2007. 184 p.: bibl., col. ill.

An essay enriched with poems and prose excerpts written by Brazilian and international authors about the painter, sculptor, potter, printmaker, muralist, and writer Francisco Brennand (1927). Known mainly for his poetic, surrealistic, and monumental ceramic sculptures, Brennand has been experimenting with clays, colors, and forms of strong, daring emotions for decades. His totemic works of ancestral shapes and contemporary humor, rich in sexual overtones, both naïf and passionate, are concentrated in his factory-sanctuary in Pernambuco, a Brazilian landmark. Chronology and bibliography. Lavishly illustrated.

FOLK ART

160 Lody, Raul Giovanni da Motta;
Pernambuco popular: um toque de
mestre. Recife, Brazil: Relicário Produções
Culturais e Editoriais, 2005. 143 p.: bibl.,
col. ill., map.

This introduction to the folk crafts
of Pernambuco describes and illustrates the
production, uses, and cultural context of
crafted objects such as hand puppets, prow
figures, rural and urban toys made out of
wood and metal scraps, clay figures, em-
broidered garments, chapbooks, and musical
instruments. Each category is represented
by a noted master. In addition to Iberian
and African cultural influences, Muslim
Maghreb traditions are also emphasized.
Bibliography and rich color illustrations.

161 Sampaio, Márcio. Mestres de ofícios
de Minas Gerais: resgate cultural do
artesanato mineiro. Brasília: SEBRAE NA;
Belo Horizonte, Brazil: SEBRAE MG: Secretaria de Estado de Cultura de Minas Gerais,
2003. 135 p.: bibl., col. ill.

Of the many crafts that have been
practiced in Minas Gerais since the 18th
century, fewer than 30 are still alive. Several state government agencies are making
an effort to maintain these cultural and
traditional practices, both for their socioeconomic and cultural significance. This
book points out which ones still exist and
where the communities that practice them
are to be found. Examples are described and
illustrated. Bibliography.

PHOTOGRAPHY

162 Andermann, Jens. The optic of the
state: visuality and power in Argentina and Brazil. Pittsburgh, Pa.: Univ.
of Pittsburgh Press, 2007. 256 p.: bibl., ill.,
index, maps. (Illuminations)

Of special interest here is the state's
use of visual material—particularly photography—to produce images as artifices
that enhance power. Author discusses how
in Argentina and Brazil, toward the end of
the 19th century, a special correlation between politics and esthetics was established
to orchestrate a new way of seeing, and to
impose this perspective on the masses. The
emergence of new forms of power consolidated the modern state with the help of vi-

sual mechanisms in museums, educational
institutions, and the media. Themes, such
as favors from European imperial powers,
political agendas, and violence are scrutinized. An original contribution enriched
with bibliography.

163 Andrade, Alecio de. Alécio de Andrade. Concepção, coordenação e
curadoria do Instituto Moreira Salles. São
Paulo: IMS-Instituto Moreira Salles, 2008.
207 p.: bibl., chiefly ill.

Starting as a poet, Alécio de Andrade
(1938–2003) became a photographer in his
native Rio de Janeiro, later settling in Paris
in 1965, where he would live for the rest of
his life. Under the impact of Henri Cartier
Bresson, he perfected his photojournalist
skills, becoming the internationally acclaimed "master of the instant." He travelled and photographed extensively in Europe, the US, and Brazil, and his photographs
appeared in top magazines around the
world. He was mostly noted for his photos of
children, everyday life in Paris, and portraits
of world-renowned intellectuals and artists.
He left behind 4,000 b/w and 3,000 color
photographs. This catalog of an exhibition
includes texts of great empathy and approximately 150 photographs. Bibliography, biography, chronology, and documents.

164 Carrilho, Marcos José. Fazendas de
café oitocentistas no Vale do Paraíba.
(*An. Mus. Paul.*, 14:1, jan./junho 2006,
p. 59–80, bibl., maps, photos)

Study focuses on the rural architecture of the old coffee plantation estates
in São Paulo's Paraíba Valley. Details and
structural characteristics of these buildings
are analyzed with photographs both current
and from the period, 19th-century literature,
owners' deeds, etc. Only a few bibliographical references.

165 Dias, Elaine. A representação da
realeza no Brasil: uma análise dos
retratos de D. João VI e D. Pedro I, de Jean-
Baptiste Debret. (*An. Mus. Paul.*, 14:1, jan./
junho 2006, p. 243–261, bibl., photos)

French history painter, Jean-Baptiste
Debret worked for King D. João VI of Brazil
and Prince D. Pedro I, who was later to become emperor. The painter produced several
portraits of both figures. The essay studies
the images made of the king and prince, their

physical attributes, and political representation, and also compares them to European and American models. Political changes are also documented in the portraits.

166   **Fontes, Antonio Augusto** *et al.* Brasil sem fronteiras. Rio de Janeiro: Tempo d'Imagem, 2001. 215 p.: chiefly ill., map.

Designed to celebrate the 500th anniversary of the discovery of Brazil, this collaboration between writers and photographers portrays the ethnic richness, remote landscapes, and realities of the country. Instead of representing these themes in the context of Brazil's Portuguese roots, this publication attempts to draw a picture of a country that shares geography and social conditions with its Spanish-speaking neighbors. Vast rivers and endless territories are captured, along with adults and children, thus conveying a portrait of "piled up solitudes" within a wide number of ecosystems. Text and image explore a Brazil without borders, native illuminations, collective experience, diplomacy, diversity, and more. Glossary.

167   **Lago, Bia Corrêa do** and **Pedro Corrêa do Lago.** Os fotógrafos do Império: a fotografia brasileira do século XIX. Rio de Janeiro: Capivara, 2005. 239 p.: bibl., chiefly ill., index, map.

Originally published in French by Gallimard (Paris, 2005) under the title *Brésil: Les premiers photographes d'un empire sous les Tropiques*, this Portuguese translation by Lucía Jahn conveys basic information on the subject, and introduces a selection of 320 reproductions of the best images of the period. This publication offers an overall view of 19th-century Brazilian photography. Fourteen photographers are represented. Their material includes portraits, cityscapes, landscapes, images of architecture, street life, ethnic varieties, social spectrum, and more. A broad glimpse of this land and a major contribution to the history of 19th-century world photography.

168   **Lima Vailati, Luiz.** As fotografias "anjos" no Brasil do século XIX. (*An. Mus. Paul.,* 14:2, julho/dez. 2006, p. 51–71, bibl., photos)

Essay discusses a special chapter in the social history and photographic history of Brazil, namely the photographing of dead children, the *anjos* (angels), a custom also described by 19th-century travelers. In evidence are the practices and representations related to deceased children of middle and upper-middle classes in Brazil in the period studied. The well-known photographer Militão Augusto de Azevedo was active in this field. Extensive bibliographical references and many photos.

169   **Manzon, Jean.** Jean Manzon: retrato vivo da grande aventura. Rio de Janeiro: Aprazível Edições; São Paulo: Cepar Consultoria, 2006. 239 p.: chiefly ill.

French photographer Jean Manzon (1915–90) pioneered photojournalism in Brazil in the 1940s and 1950s working for the weekly *O Cruzeiro.* He captured all possible aspects of life in Brazil, as well as a variety of landscapes in 17,000 negatives, unveiling Brazil for Brazilians and the world. This book shows a selection of 200 images. It includes portraits of top personalities such as Presidents Vargas and Kubitschek, composer Villa Lobos, as well as photos of anonymous sailors, fishermen, gauchos, movie stars, pin up girls, soldiers, Indians, and more. He was criticized for his impeccably beautiful b/w frames and also because he used to say that he was paid to show the good side of Brazil. Ultimately, he photographed the modernization of the country as few others have done.

170   **Possamai, Zita Rosane.** O circuito social da fotografia em Porto Alegre, 1922 e 1935. (*An. Mus. Paul.,* 14:1, jan./junho 2006, p. 263–289, bibl.)

Historians have been studying photography in Brazil under various criteria, including that of a social circuit vantage. As such, photography is looked upon as an artifact that finds its place in people's lives in a variety of contexts. In this study, author analyzes the life of the various social classes in Porto Alegre during the 1920s and 1930s, and concludes that the massification of photography, through its profuse reproduction in magazines dealing with urban life and city improvements, contributed to the modernization of the mind. Also examines cameras as objects of prestige.

171   **Seminário Fotografia e Novas Mídias,** *Rio de Janeiro, Brazil, 2007.* Fotografia e novas mídias. Coordenação geral de Milton Guran. Rio de Janeiro:

ContraCapa: Oi Futuro, 2008. 178 p. (Col.
Arte e tecnologia)
   Papers presented at the Seminário
Fotografia e Novas Mídias, held in August
6–9, 2007 at the Centro Cultural Oi Futuro,
in Rio de Janeiro. The topics covered in the
seminar included: "Photography and Contemporary Art," "New Images and Other
Imaginaries," "The Eye Reconfigured—New
Apparatuses," and "Instant Landscapes."
The seminar focused on the digital and me-
chanical processes of current photography
and the "resulting profound changes in the
structural production of imagery in the 21st
century, adding new layers of meaning to
today's concept of image."

172   Silva, Áurea Pereira da. Engenhos e
         fazendas de café em Campinas, séc.
XVIII– séc. XX. (*An. Mus. Paul.*, 14:1, jan./
junho 2006, p. 81–119, bibl., maps, photos)
   Study of the sugarcane and coffee
fazendas in rural Campinas. The publication focuses on the fazendas' architecture
in a historical context. Old documents and
modern photos.

173   Thiesen, Beatriz Valladão. Significa-
         dos nas representações escultóricas da
fachada da Cervejaria Bopp & Irmãos, Porto
Alegre. (*An. Mus. Paul.*, 14:1, jan./junho
2006, p. 167–194, bibl., photos)
   A study in urban archeology that
focuses on the symbology found on the
façade of a beer brewery of the early 20th
century, Porto Alegre. The book analyzed
the meaning of these symbols in the context
of the society of the time and its values.
Many features are reminiscent of equiva-
lents in Germany. Illustrated by modern
photographers.

CITY PLANNING, ARCHITECTURE, AND LANDSCAPE ARCHITECTURE

174   Alex, Sun. Projeto da praça: convívio
         e exclusão no espaço público. São
Paulo: Senac, 2008. 291 p.: bibl., ill., plans.
   Originally author's doctoral thesis,
this book introduces the concept of piazza,
plaza, and square in Western history as
public spaces designed for convivial purposes. In recent decades, however, under the
influence of American city planning and

landscaping, the praças have lost their original purpose and have become nonintegrated
urban spaces. Chinese-born Brazilian architect of international experience discusses
six praças in São Paulo and the obstacles
that prevent their proper use. Author also
points to solution for their recuperation and
legitimate use of these spaces. Good variety
of photos and plans. Updated bibliography.
An original contribution.

175   Bratke, Carlos. Carlos Bratke. São
         Paulo: J.J. Carol Editora, 2009. 130 p.:
ill. (some col.), photos. (*Portfolio Brasil.
Arquitetura*)
   The architectural ideas and solutions
of this contemporary São Paulo architect
are exemplified in this solo anthology of
eight completed projects, and one under
construction. Each of these buildings was
designed for a unique purpose; they include
an art gallery, a country house, a car dealer-
ship, an apartment building, an office building, and more. Sketches, drawings, photos,
plans, and an extensive list of published
works, most of them illustrated by photos.
Short biography.

176   Campos, Eudes. A cidade de São Paulo
         e a era dos *melhoramentos materiaes*.:
obras públicas e arquitetura vistas por meio
de fotografias de autoria de Militão Augusto
de Azevedo, datadas do período 1862–1863.
(*An. Mus. Paul.*, 15:1, jan./junho 2007,
p. 11–114, bibl., ill., photos)
   The photographs in question are often
referred to as a document of São Paulo's
backwardness even in the 19th century. The
author's view contradicts the references
based on primary sources from the same period, which state that architecture and city
planning were already showing modernization at the time. Campos sketches a history
of material improvements and anticipation
of progress in São Paulo, departing from
Azevedo's "Album comparativo da cidade
de São Paulo, 1862–1887." Many photo reproductions, varied primary resources, and
extensive bibliography.

177   Cidade: impasses e perspectivas.
         Organização de Maria Lúcia Caira
Gitahy e José Tavares Correia de Lira. São
Paulo: Annablume: FUPAM, 2007. 319 p.:
bibl., ill., maps. (Arquiteses; 2)

Volume 2 of the "Arquiteses" project, developed by the school of Architecture and Urbanism of the University of São Paulo. The volume gathers 19 selected postgraduate papers covering a wide spectrum of topics, including space production in Latin American and Brazilian cities today, urban legislation, planning of working class residential neighborhoods, urban-rural interrelation, and other various city planning initiatives throughout Brazil. A valuable updated discussion and resource for professionals and architecture historians. Richly illustrated. Substantial bibliography.

178   Formas e tempos da cidade. Organização de Manuel Ferreira Lima Filho e Laís Aparecida Machado. Goiânia, Brazil: Cânone Editorial: Editora da UCG, 2007. 280 p.: bibl., ill. (some col.), maps, photos.

This collection of essays written by different authors draws a broad picture of the city of Goiânia, capital of the State of Goiás. Planned in the 1930s and inaugurated in 1942, Goiânia replaced colonial Goiás Velho, which had been the state capital for almost two centuries. Most essays deal with city planning and architecture themes, while others are historical analyses. Over 20 residents, between the ages of 70 and mid-90s, were interviewed about their memories of the development and changes the city has undergone. Archeology, geology, immigrants' contributions, children's views in drawing, furniture, and decoration are also included. Bibliography, comparative statistics, photos, and maps round out this publication.

179   Lara, Fernando Luiz. The rise of popular modernist architecture in Brazil. Gainesville: Univ. Press of Florida, 2008. 149 p.: bibl., ill., index.

Book discusses how architecture is seen and practiced by the population at large in Brazil as opposed to the modern, paradigmatic architecture created by professionals and discussed by critics, scholars, and architects themselves. Lara tries to legitimize the unique and unknown dissemination of modernism in Brazil as well as the popular appropriation of learned modernism, interpreting its features in daily life through ordinary buildings that shape our relationship to the built environment by way of the local vernacular. An original contribution enriched by extensive bibliography.

180   Martins D'Elboux, Roseli Maria. Uma *promenade* nos trópicos: os barões do café sob as palmeiras-imperiais, entre o Rio de Janeiro e São Paulo. (*An. Mus. Paul.*, 14:2, julho/dez. 2006, p. 193–250, bibl., photos)

This uncommon essay discusses the transformation of the urban landscape in the Paraíba River Valley due to the role that the coffee-growing elite played in the development of the Brazilian economy. Although the paper covers a time span from 1808 to 1911, special attention is given to the period of transition from monarchy to the republic in the 1880s and 1890s. The discussion focuses on the prominent use of the imperial palm trees (Roystonea oleracea) as a symbol of nobility, its use in public spaces, and the way the tree defined the cityscapes of Rio, São Paulo, Lorena, Taubaté, and other places. Many noted photographers registered the topic. Bibliography.

181   Monteiro, Peter Ribon. Vitória: cidade e presépio—os vazios visíveis da capital capixaba. São Paulo: Annablume, 2008. 217 p.: bibl., ill. (some col.), maps (some col.).

Originally a master's thesis, this broad study of the state capital of Espírito Santo describes the development of the city over the centuries both from a local and a national perspective. The built environment and empty spaces, which have emerged in the specific geographic features of the region, determine the city's topography. The theme is analyzed from the ocean's vantage point, but from aerial and land perspectives as well. Other than city planning and landscaping, architecture is also studied. Many buildings are described and photographed. Plans, maps, and bibliography offer much information on the uniqueness of Vitória.

182   Moro Junior, Enio. A redenção inexistente nos planos urbanísticos municipais: o caso do Projeto Eixo Tamanduatehy. São Paulo: Annablume, 2007. 114 p.: bibl.

Starting with an analysis of a single municipal urban project in Santo André in São Paulo, author discusses the realities of projects of equal pretense and brings up the specifics of Brazilian society. Moro Junior also touches upon economical and political models in order to understand the developmental factors. Book focuses on the role of the municipal sphere in minimizing social inequalities, looks at urban projects and analyzes how they help to promote local development. A political vision of urban planning.

183   Pires, Mário Jorge. Sobrados e barões da velha São Paulo. Barueri, Brazil: Manole, 2006. 169 p.: bibl., ill.

As soon as the first railroad system was built, coffee planters moved to the city of São Paulo, while their fazendas were in the interior of the state. Also, the Law School founded in 1828 attracted students from several states. Soon the sleepy capital became a metropolis. The prevailing Portuguese colonial modes of construction were replaced by large one-family dwellings in the European cosmopolitan styles of France, Germany, and Italy, and the arrival of eventually successful immigrants stimulated the architectural variety. Resorting to unusual sources like old telephone directories and 19th-century almanacs, author answers many questions related to this new elite. Residential status, for instance, was reflected in the size of construction rather than by location. Later on, prestigious neighborhoods represented a social mix of old and new money. A new approach to architecture and society in 19th-century São Paulo.

184   Zein, Ruth Verde. Rosa Kliass: desenhando paisagens, moldando uma profissão. São Paulo: Editora SENAC São Paulo, 2006. 221 p.: bibl., ill. (chiefly col.), index, col. maps, photos.

This publication celebrates 50 years of activity of Rosa Kliass as a landscape architect. Based in São Paulo, she is the creator of a wide array of projects in public and private spaces of São Paulo and other Brazilian cities, as well as one of the pioneers of the second generation of Brazilian landscape architects. A major concern in Kliass' professional activity has been achieving harmony between the urban and the natural systems. With this framework, she has been paying special attention to geographical, ecological, urbanistic, and sociopolitical problems. All her main projects are included in this publication, which also includes plans, color photos, and descriptions. Texts in Portuguese and English.

AFRO-BRAZILIAN AND INDIAN TRADITIONS

185   Conduru, Roberto. Arte afro-brasileira. Belo Horizonte, Brazil: Editora C/Arte, 2007. 126 p.: bibl., ill. (chiefly col.). (Col. Didática. Historiando a arte brasileira; 2)

Author devotes considerable space to the discussion of the controversial theme of Afro-Brazilian art as a preamble for the description, analysis, and evaluation of art created by this sector of the population. The publication also analyzes Afro-Brazilian art that has permeated the Brazilian art scene at large since the beginnings of black African slavery in the former Portuguese colony. This analysis covers topics such as ethnicity, religion, syncretism, politics, and sociocultural history from the perspective of anthropology, history, and esthetics. The study exemplifies the many representations of "negritude" in Brazilian art and architecture in contemporary creativity, and in all of Brazilian art. Book opens paths for future in-depth research. Bibliography, pedagogical orientations, and many illustrations.

186   Sansi-Roca, Roger. Fetishes and monuments: Afro-Brazilian art and culture in the 20th century. New York: Berghahn Books, 2007. 213 p.: bibl., ill. (Remapping cultural history; 6)

Successful attempt to remap the cultural history of Afro-Brazilian art. This study encompasses the broad spectrum of this intricate, complex field of scholarly research ranging from the concept of the field itself to its sociopolitical and historical implications, reviewing and reconsidering anthropological, esthetic, art historical, religious, and sociological research. The practice of candomblé is at the heart of the study with an emphasis on the objectification of Afro-Brazilian culture, and on candomblé as national heritage, public art, and as the reappropriations of Afro-Brazilian culture on modern and contemporary Brazilian art at large. Extensive bibliography. A relevant contribution.

MISCELLANEOUS

**187   Comitê Brasileiro de História da
    Arte. Colóquio.** *25th, Tiradentes,
Minas Gerais, Brazil, 2005. Anais. Organi-
zação de Marília Andrés Ribeiro e Denise
da Silva Gonçalves. Belo Horizonte, Brazil:
C/Arte: Comitê Brasileiro de História da
Arte, 2006. 318 p.: bibl., ill.

This edition includes the research
work of members of the Brazilian Committee of Art History (CBHA). The papers
examine the "second period" of art history:
colonial, 18th century, modern, and contemporary art, with a particular emphasis on
art and the city, art and museums, and art
and the public. Papers on international, art
historical, and theoretical issues have also
been included.

188   Heynemann, Cláudia B. and **Maria
    do Carmo Teixeira Rainho.** Uma
história das imagens: o acervo iconográfico
do Arquivo Nacional. (*Estud. Hist./Rio de
Janeiro*, 38, 2006, p. 105–115, bibl.)

Brief overall view of the iconographic
collections of the National Archive, mostly
related to the history of Brazil, including engravings and photographs—of special interest here—but also maps, documents, manuscripts, etc. Article also mentions thematic
exhibitions organized by the Archive, some
which display precious information on the
arts of Brazil. Some notes. Poor bibliography.

HISTORY

ETHNOHISTORY
Mesoamerica

LISA SOUSA, *Associate Professor of History, Occidental College*
KEVIN TERRACIANO, *Professor of History, University of California, Los Angeles*

AS WE EASE INTO THE FORMIDABLE (if not daunting) role of surveying works in this rich field of study, we would like to acknowledge the fine work of our predecessors, Stephanie Wood and Robert Haskett, who have contributed so much to the *Handbook* for many years. In this volume we will focus on works published before 2008, overlapping with the period covered in *HLAS 64*; we look forward to addressing works published from 2008 to 2011 in *HLAS 68*.

Mesoamerican writing systems continue to captivate scholars in several disciplines who examine the form, iconography, and function of preconquest and colonial pictorial texts and maps. As usual, solid studies abound for central Mexico. Federico Navarrete examines strategic graphic conventions in the *Codex Azcatitlan* and demonstrates the manuscript's Tlatelolcan perspective and provenance (item **240**). Elizabeth Boone outlines the importance of marriage prognostications in the Borgia Group codices (item **198**). Cecilia Rossell analyzes the meaning of symbols and their relation to the Nahuatl language in the *Historia Tolteca-Chichimeca* (item **253**). Lori Boornazian Diel considers the inclusion and omission of women in pictorial manuscripts (item **216**). Justyna Olko defines the specific markers of royal attributes among the Mexica and then looks at manuscripts from peripheral regions of central Mexico for evidence of Mexica influence on other regions of Mesoamerica (item **241**). Susan Schroeder examines the adoption of alphabetic writing by nobles to preserve genealogies and local histories (item **260**). In two separate articles, Michel Oudijk and María Castañeda de la Paz interpret the function of 16th-century pictographic texts from Xochimilco (items **204** and **242**), and Miguel Ángel Ruz Barrio analyzes a similar type of document that was submitted in a lawsuit between Tepexpan and Temaxcalapa (item **255**). Angélica Galicia Gordillo and Sergio Sánchez Vásquez survey various colonial-era and early independence maps from Tulancingo (item **218**).

Paula López Caballero has published one of the first books on the colonial-era genre of writing known as "primordial titles," synthesizing much of the scholarship on these documents and presenting transcriptions of 26 Spanish-language titles from central Mexico (item **270**). This is a valuable collection of transcribed texts that were produced within indigenous communities in the second half of the colonial period. David Wright, a pioneer in the study of the Otomí language, makes a valuable contribution to native-language studies by providing a preliminary description and analysis of more than a dozen colonial-era Otomí-language manuscripts and texts owned by the Newberry and Princeton Libraries (item 273). The Otomí are a major culture and language group in central Mexico that have not received the scholarly attention they deserve. Rosa Brambila Paz reveals the little known, pioneering work of Ángel María Garibay on the Otomí language of central Mexico (item 199). Garibay is much better known, of course, for his work on the older Nahuatl language. The most interesting study of Nahuatl that we have read for this review is Mark Morris' examination of Nahuatl-language broadsides that were produced by the Spanish crown to promote support for the colonial government in 1810; this is a fascinating lengthy article that propels the study of Nahuatl texts into the independence period (item 238).

Moving south from central Mexico toward Oaxaca, Maarten Jansen reads several Mixtec or Ñudzaui codices against central Mexican and Mayan manuscripts to present an interpretation of early postclassic history that connects Tula, Cholula, the Mixteca, and Yucatán (item 226). A thick volume edited by Sebastián van Doesburg showcases trends in the study of Mixtec, Zapotec, Chocho, Chontal, and Ixcatec writings of Oaxaca, focusing especially on pictorial texts (item 246). For the Maya area, the Consejo Nacional de Educación Maya of Guatemala has produced an excellent, affordable facsimile of the *Codex Madrid* (item 209). This is the Maya codex that Maricela Ayala Falcón compares with another famous preconquest-style manuscript, the *Codex Dresden*, looking especially at the central deities featured in the two texts (item 192).

Two works consider methods of interpretation, a study called *codicológico* in Spanish; Luz María Mohar Betancourt and Rita Fernández Díaz demonstrate the usefulness of the "Galarza method" of analyzing pictorial writings, named after Joaquín Galarza (item 235), whereas Jean-François Genotte applies the Galarza method to a colonial manuscript known as the *Mapa de Otumba* (item 221). Baltazar Brito Guadarrama reproduces an unpublished manuscript by the famous scholar, Francisco del Paso y Troncoso, on the authenticity of the so-called *Codex Ciclográfico* (item 200).

Numerous studies of pictorial writings and other sources focus on sacred beliefs and rituals. Indeed, this area of inquiry continues to flourish. Víctor de la Cruz uses historical, archeological, and ethnographic evidence to present an informed and lengthy discussion of the cosmovision, cosmogony, calendar, and sacred beliefs and practices of the Binnigula'sa' (Zapotecs) in the classic and postclassic periods (item 211). Karl Taube contemplates concepts of life, beauty, and paradise among the classic Maya (item 268). Manuel Alberto Morales Damián mulls over Maya-language metaphors to understand Maya concepts of human nature (item 237), and in a separate article interprets contemporary Maya practices in Mexico from the perspective of beliefs associated with the ancient sacred tree (item 236). Mónica Chávez Guzmán interrogates ideological concepts concerning illness and healing among the colonial Yucatec Maya (item 206).

Some scholars use both historical and ethnographic evidence to approach sacred practices and beliefs that are rooted in the past but can be observed best in the lived present. Ethnographic fieldwork offers fascinating insights into sacred practices in Mesoamerica and northern Mexico. In general, Mexican scholars play a leading role in this type of versatile scholarship. Johanna Broda and Catharine Good Eshelman present a 500-page anthology on indigenous agrarian rituals throughout Mexico, with a preliminary study by Broda on the relevance of the data for understanding prehispanic rituals (item 224). Roberto Martínez González employs historical and ethnographic evidence to consider the role and social function of the *nahualli* (item **230**). Danièle Dehouve examines precise and complex Tlapanec ritual offerings in the state of Guerrero (item **214**). Carlo Bonfiglioli, Arturo Gutiérrez, and María Eugenia Olavarría introduce five essays on inter-ethnic relations in the prehispanic and colonial periods, and 10 ethnographic studies on cosmology and symbolism in northeast Mexico among the Hopi, Huichol, Cora, Tarahumara, Yaqui, and Tepehuan (item **272**). Blas Román Castellón Huerta has edited a collection of ethnographic studies that consider indigenous cosmology, symbolism, and mythology among nine ethnic groups from Mexico, including the Yaqui, Huichol, Cora, Tepehuan, Nahua, Purépecha, Mixe, and Mixtec (item **249**).

The evolution of indigenous spirituality in contact with Christianity and the development of local religious beliefs and practices is another rich area of research. Félix Báez-Jorge's classic work, *Entre los naguales y los santos*, is now reprinted with commentaries by Johanna Broda and Alessandro Lupo (item **194**). Báez-Jorge turns his attention to the devil in Mesoamerica in *Los disfraces del diablo*, a massive 700-page work that complements historical research with ethnographic data (item **193**). Mario Humberto Ruz offers an anthology of 14 essays on saints and demons and other sacred phenomena among the contemporary Maya of Yucatán and Guatemala (item **213**). Druzo Maldonado Jiménez examines sacred practices, especially agrarian rituals, in the Nahua pueblo of Coatetelco, Morelos (item **228**). Dora Sierra Carrillo uses historical and ethnographic sources to analyze the ritual power that people of Morelos attribute to flowers called *yauhtli* in Nahuatl or *pericón* in Spanish, and the long roots of this tradition, which merges Mesoamerican and Christian beliefs and practices (item **262**). Saúl Millán illuminates the importance of the secular-religious cargo system among the Huave of Tehuantepec (item **233**). R. Jon McGee follows three generations of a Lacandon family in Nahá (Chan K'in Viejo) observing religious traditions and healing practices (among other things) (item **231**).

Moving from the sacred to the more profane, we encounter stacks of readings on a wide variety of topics. Patricia Hernández presents a population profile of three Mesoamerican settlements in the preclassic, classic, and postclassic periods (item **223**). The political and military expansion of the Aztec empire is a topic that continues to generate discussion and debate. José Fernando Robles Castellanos bemoans the conceptual limits of the "triple alliance" or "Aztec" empire and digs into the ethnohistorical and archeological records for evidence of a deeper "Culhua Mexico" expansion in the late postclassic period (item **250**). Isabel Bueno Bravo emphasizes the importance of warfare in a book and a related article on Mexica expansion (items **201** and **202**). On the other hand, Frances Berdan considers how the Mexica made certain exceptional arrangements with tribute-paying provinces on the frontier of Mexica expansion (item **197**). Alonso Barros demonstrates how the Spanish-led conquest of the Oaxaca region and colonial processes of the 16th century impacted the Mixe, a major ethnic group whose contacts and territories extended into the Isthmus of Tehuantepec in the late postclassic period (item **195**). Agustín García Márquez imagines Veracruz before and after the Mexica entered the region (item **220**). Carlos Santamarina Novillo sets his sights on the origin of a Mexica group, the Tepaneca, and the strategic importance of Azcapotzalco, a Tepaneca center of power in the basin of Mexico, for the rise of Mexica power (item **258**). Two studies use archeological evidence to shed light on preconquest Maya rituals that marked the consolidation of political power and ideologies that governed relations between rulers and nobles (items **207** and **219**).

Mesoamerican social history has advanced considerably in the last few decades. In general, native elites continue to command the most attention. Several works focus on the rise to power of indigenous caciques in the colonial period, such as Patricia Cruz Pazos' profile of Juan de Moctezuma y Cortés, the cacique of Tepexi de la Seda (item **212**). Humberto Ávila Márquez relates the fascinating story of a Zacateco cacique of Jalisco, don Francisco Tenamaztle, who was enslaved and shipped to Spain, where he appealed to the Council of Indies—with the support of Bartolomé de las Casas (item **269**). José Rubén Romero Galván analyzes the writings of the Nahua chronicler, Hernando Alvarado Tezozómoc, especially his *Crónica mexicana*, in terms of his reflections on the decline and the loss of traditional privileges among the indigenous nobility (item **252**). Miguel Ángel Ruz Barrio uses a rich collection of private documents from the Chimaltecuhtli-Casco family of Cholula for the 16th and 17th centuries (item **255**). Sergio Eduardo Carrera Quezada examines the structure and organization of an indigenous community in the Huasteca region of Mexico in the 18th and early 19th centuries, focusing on Xochiatipan's *cabildo* (municipal council) and *cofradías* (lay sodalities) (item **203**).

A number of good books and articles attend to the roles and status of women in preconquest, colonial, and contemporary Mesoamerican communities. Boornazian Diel's study of women in pictorial manuscripts from central Mexico, mentioned above, deserves another mention here for both its merit and relevance (item **216**). María J. Rodríguez-Shadow has edited an interdisciplinary volume on women in preconquest Mexico, dividing 12 essays into the Maya, Oaxacan, and Mexica areas (item **232**). Gladys Ilarregui presents five essays on women in colonial Mexico (item **225**). Stacy Schaefer demonstrates the social and sacred significance of weaving among women in the Sierra Madre Occidental of western Mexico, people who call themselves *Wixárika* (most often called Huichol) (item **259**). Paola Peniche offers a major study of Yucatec Mayan kinship from the 16th to the early 19th centuries, which pays ample attention to women and gender relations at the household level (item **245**). Some studies of gender and sexuality focus on men. Pete Sigal uses the *Florentine Codex* and other Church-sponsored, Nahuatl-language materials of the early colonial period to explore homosexuality in Nahua society in two separate but complementary research articles (items **263** and **264**). John Chuchiak uses Maya petitions, confessional manuals, and dictionaries to explore the politics of the sexual conquest of the Maya, focusing on the exploits of priests (item **208**).

Speaking of conquest, the military conquest is being revisited from new and not-so-new perspectives, including popular treatments of major figures, such as Moctezuma and Malinche, and more scholarly works that examine the conquest as it spread to the northern and southern regions of New Spain. Two monographs reviewed here reproduce primary documents: Rodrigo Martínez Baracs' reconstruction of the lost account of conquistador Juan Cano de Saavedra (item **229**); and Ruud van Akkeren's analysis of indigenous pictorial texts from Guatemala (item **190**).

Some notable works address the intertwined questions of identity, ethnicity, and language in particular regions, such as Michoacán and Oaxaca. Scholars and activists in Michoacán debate the origins and semantic range of the terms "Tarascan" and "Purépecha." The proceedings of the 4th *Semana de la Cultura* Zapoteca take up this issue for the Isthmus of Tehuantepec (item **261**). Likewise, the proceedings of the *Semana de la Cultura Mixteca* cover several broad themes that apply to the Mixteca region of Oaxaca, including archeology, language, codices, and migration (item **243**).

Colonial and contemporary rebellion and violence is another major theme in the literature. Carlos Rubén Ruiz Medrano examines an indigenous riot in 1757 against forced labor in mines (item **254**). Shannon Speed studies the history of a community named Nicolás Ruiz in central Chiapas, where violent disputes over land broke out in the 1990s, in the wake of the Zapatista rebellion, demonstrating how disputes over land in this community of Tzeltal origin are rooted in the colonial period (item **265**).

Finally, we refer here to a few works that do not fit neatly into any of the categories above, but that deserve inclusion here for their contributions to the field. For example, two works examine native peoples on the southernmost edge of Mesoamerica, in Costa Rica: Francisco Corrales Ulloa uses ethnohistorical and archeological (site survey) data to reconstruct the territorial divisions, social organization, and population of indigenous groups in southeast Costa Rica in the early 16th century (item **210**); Roberto Castillo Vásquez employs similar data to project a mid-19th-century population estimate for an indigenous group in the north called the Maleku (item **205**). In the opposite direction, on the far northern frontier of Mesoamerica, Rosa Elba Rodríguez Tomp provides a panoramic view of the indigenous peoples of Baja California and their environment from preconquest times to the early 20th century (item **251**). Our final reference is to a fascinating collection of sketches and paintings by Agustín Villagra Caleti, one of the first sketch artists employed by the Instituto Nacional de Antropología e Historia, in the Dept. of Prehispanic Monuments, in the 1930s (item **266**). In her article on the artist, Leticia Staines Cicero provides a preliminary overview of Villagra's corpus, which was donated to the Instituto de Investigaciones Estéticas in 2006.

189   Ahumada González, Abelardo. Mitos y realidades de la conquista y fundación de Colima. Colima, Mexico: Univ. de Colima, 2006. 135 p.: ill., maps.

A general treatment of the conquest of Colima by Spanish-led forces in the early 1520s.

190   Akkeren, Ruud van. La visión indígena de la conquista. Guatemala: Serviprensa, 2007. 147 p.: bibl., ill. (some col.).

Van Akkeren has produced a lavishly illustrated (with many color photos) treatment of the Spanish-led invasion of Guatemala, emphasizing indigenous points of view as seen through a variety of pictorial sources, especially the *Lienzo de Quauhquechollan*. In fact, the book comes with 24 × 17 in. facsimile of the *lienzo* (painting on cloth). This careful study complements Florine Asselbergs's analysis of the same wonderful *lienzo*.

191   Arroyo Arámbul, Rubén. Ahuacatlán 2: por la señal de la Santa Cruz—. Nayarit, Mexico: CONACULTA, Culturas Populares, Dirección Estatal Nayarit, 2007. 340 p.: bibl., ill. (some col), indexes, maps.

A local history of Ahuacatlán, Jalisco, treating the colonial period to the 19th century, written for a popular audience.

192   Ayala Falcón, Maricela. De la procedencia y el uso del *Códice Madrid* (Tro-Cortesiano). *Estud. Cult. Maya*, 27, 2006, p. 15–41, bibl., ill.

The author argues that the *Codex Madrid* is based on certain passages in the *Codex Dresden*, and suggests that differences in the central deities featured in the two codices indicate that they had different uses.

193   Báez-Jorge, Félix. Los disfraces del diablo: ensayo sobre la reinterpretación de la noción cristiana del mal en Mesoamérica. Xalapa, Mexico: Univ. Veracruzana, 2003. 689 p.: bibl., ill. (some col.). (Biblioteca)

A major, sophisticated study of evil from the perspectives of the Christian and Mesoamerican cosmovisions, the arrival of the concept of the Devil in Mesoamerica, Christian attempts to "satanize" Mesoamerican deities, resistance to those attempts, and the syncretic results of this process. The author combines historical and ethnographic research to demonstrate the relevance of ideas about good and evil in the colonial period to specific indigenous beliefs and practices today.

194   Báez-Jorge, Félix. Entre los naguales y los santos. Con comentarios críticos de Johanna Broda y Alessandro Lupo. 2. ed. corr. y aum. Xalapa, Mexico: Dirección Editorial, Univ. Veracruzana, 2008. 295 p.: bibl., ill. (Biblioteca)

This is the second edition of Báez-Jorge's acclaimed study of popular religion in Guatemala and Mexico, almost a decade after its first publication. Johanna Broda and Alessandro Lupo comment on the new edition. For comment on 1st edition, see *HLAS 60:1213*.

195   Barros van Hövell tot Westerflier, Alonso. Cien años de guerras mixes: territorialidades prehispánicas, expansión burocrática y zapotequización en el Istmo de Tehuantepec durante el siglo XVI. (*Hist. Mex./México*, 57:2, oct./dic. 2007, p. 325–403, bibl., maps, photos)

Barros demonstrates how the Spanish-led conquest of the Oaxaca region and colonial processes of the 16th century impacted the Mixe, a major ethnic group whose contacts and territories extended from the northern sierra of Oaxaca to the Isthmus of Tehuantepec in the late postclassic period. Barros' treatment of this period sheds light on how the Spaniards manipulated preexisting ethnic rivalries, to the special detriment of certain groups that failed to form alliances with colonial authorities. The Mixe, in particular, exemplify this process, which Barros reconstructs through a careful analysis of early colonial texts and archival records.

196   Batalla Rosado, Juan José. Estudio codicológico de la sección del xiuhpohualli del *Códice Telleriano-Remensis*. (*Rev. Esp. Antropol. Am.*, 36:2, 2006, p. 69–87, bibl., ill., photos)

This article considers the composition of the *Codex Telleriano-Remensis*, revealing evidence that the *xiuhpohualli* information was probably added after the original composition of the work, that folio 7r., which refers to the *nemontemi* days, was not originally included in the *xiuhpohualli* count, and that the *Codex Vaticanus A* is not a translation of the Telleriano, but that both manuscripts were copied from another, now lost, original.

Batalla Rosado, Juan José. The scribes who painted the Matrícula de Tributos and the Codex Mendoza. See *HLAS 65:224*.

197   Berdan, Frances F. En la periferia del imperio: provincias tributarias aztecas en la frontera imperial. (*Rev. Esp. Antropol. Am.*, 37:2, 2007, p. 119–138, bibl., map)

This article contributes to the scholarship on Aztec empire-building by explaining how and why exceptional arrangements of tribute-paying provinces on the imperial periphery were established.

198   Boone, Elizabeth Hill. Marriage almanacs in the Mexican divinatory codices. (*An. Inst. Invest. Estét.*, 28:89, otoño 2006, p. 71–92, ill., photos, tables)

Boone examines the importance of marriage as a subject treated in divinatory codices such as the *Códices Borgia, Laud*, and *Vaticanus B*, and considers the importance of a couple's day signs and numbers for a good Mesoamerican marriage, among other things.

199   Brambila Paz, Rosa. Los otomíes en la mirada de Ángel María Garibay. Toluca, Mexico: Instituto Mexiquense de Cultura, 2006. 428 p.: bibl. (Biblioteca de los pueblos indígenas)

The great Ángel María Garibay, known especially for his translations of colonial-era Nahuatl texts, also turned his prodigious talents to the study of Otomi. In his many years as a priest, Garibay lived in Otomi-speaking communities of central Mexico such as Jilotepec and Huizquilucan learning about the language, collecting stories, and publishing pieces on Otomi culture and language. This volume brings together much of his work on the Otomi, including a manuscript that Garibay copied and analyzed, called the *Anales de Jilotepec*, various legends and stories attributed to the Otomís, and several other essays and notes. Rosa Brambila Paz collected, edited, and introduced the texts; Ana María Crespo and María Elena Villagas M. contributed complementary studies of the language.

200 Brito Guadarrama, Baltazar. Un manuscrito de Francisco del Paso y Troncoso sobre el *Códice Ciclográfico*. *Estud. Cult. Náhuatl*, 37, 2006, p. 275–291, bibl., ill., photos)

This article revisits a debate between two great Mexican scholars, Alfredo Chavero and Francisco del Paso y Troncoso, over the authenticity of a pictographic manuscript known as the *Códice Ciclográfico*, which refers to three cyclical Nahua feasts: *teoxihuitl, atamalcualiztli,* and *xiuhmolilli*. In particular, the author reproduces an unpublished manuscript by Paso y Troncoso on the codex.

201 Bueno Bravo, Isabel. La guerra en el imperio azteca: expansión, ideología y arte. Madrid: Editorial Complutense, 2007. 371 p.: bibl., ill. (La mirada de la historia)

This study covers well-traversed terrain in its attempt to answer the oft-asked question: how did a small group of Mexica rise to such prominence and power in such a brief period? The author addresses the mechanisms of political and military expansion and the tactics of warfare that led to the rise and fall of the Aztec empire.

202 Bueno Bravo, Isabel. Mesoamérica: territorio en guerra. *(Rev. Hist. Mil.,* 1:101, 2007, p. 11–40, bibl.)

This article argues that Mesoamerican military traditions merit further consideration due to the significance of war and conquest in the region.

203 Carrera Quezada, Sergio Eduardo. A son de campana: la fragua de Xochiatipan. México: CIESAS; San Luis Potosí, Mexico: Colegio de San Luis; Pachuca, Mexico: Univ. Autónoma del Estado de Hidalgo, 2007. 323 p.: bibl., ill. (some col.), tables. (Col. Huasteca)

Study of the structure and organization of an indigenous community in the Huasteca region of Mexico called Xochiatipan. The author focuses especially on the *cabildo* (municipal council) and *cofradías* (lay sodalities) of the community in the 18th and early 19th centuries. The work includes seven appendices and numerous tables.

204 Castañeda de la Paz, María and **Michel R. Oudijk.** La lucha por la herencia en una familia de Xochimilco del siglo XVI. *(Rev. Esp. Antropol. Am.,* 36:2, 2006, p. 125–137, bibl., ill., photos)

Analysis of a legal case from the Archivo General de la Nación in Mexico City, from the section Tierras, that includes rich pictorial and alphabetic texts to document a dispute between a mother-in-law and a daughter-in-law over the property of their deceased son and husband, respectively.

205 Castillo Vásquez, Roberto. Población indígena Maleku en Costa Rica. *(Anu. Estud. Centroam.,* 31, 2005, p. 115–136, bibl., graphs, maps, tables)

The author posits a reconstruction of the population of a northern Costa Rican indigenous group called the Maleku, in the mid-19th century, based on ethnohistoric sources and field research (site surveys).

206 Chávez Guzmán, Mónica. El sol como fundamento curativo de las terapias mayas yucatecas en el período colonial. *(Estud. Cult. Maya,* 28, 2006, p. 121–139, bibl., ill., photo)

This article uses colonial Maya documents to examine concepts of illness and belief in solar heat in medicinal plants. Considers adoption and adaptation of some European concepts and practices in Yucatec Maya healing therapies.

207 Chinchilla-Mazariegos, Oswaldo. The stars of the Palenque sarcophagus. *(Res/Cambridge,* 49/50, Spring/Autumn 2006, p. 40–58, bibl., ill.)

The author draws upon archeological evidence, colonial sources, and modern ethnography to offer a new interpretation of the sarcophagus lid of Palenque. Argues that stars on the sarcophagus represent the transformation of lesser nobles into celestial bodies that accompany the ruler, the sun's equivalent, in the afterlife.

208 Chuchiak, John F. The sins of the fathers: Franciscan friars, parish priests, and the sexual conquest of the Yucatec Maya, 1545–1808. (*Ethnohistory/Columbus*, 54:1, Winter 2007, p. 69–127, ill., map, tables)

This is a richly detailed study based on Maya petitions, confessional manuals, and dictionaries of the politics of the sexual conquest of the Maya. The author argues that the Maya used the imposed Christian morality against Spanish priests to maintain their own sexual concepts and practices. For colonial historian's comment, see item **688**.

209 Códice de Madrid = tz'ib' rech Madrid: codex Tro-Cortesianus. Reproducción comentada por Daniel Matul y Federico Fahsen. Fotografías de Ernesto Sierra. Coordinación de Ana Victoria Guerrero. Traducción al K'iche' de Manuel Roxulew. Guatemala: Consejo Nacional de Educación Maya (CNEM): Amanuense Editorial: Nojib'sa Editorial, 2007. 140 p.: col. ill.

This handsome, oversized color facsimile of the famous Maya screenfold codex includes little analysis, but it does feature a bilingual Quiché Maya/Spanish introduction.

210 Corrales Ulloa, Francisco. Arqueología y etnohistoria de los grupos indígenas del sureste de Costa Rica. (*Rev. Arch. Nac./San José*, 70:1/12, 2006, p. 147–188, bibl., ill., maps, tables)

A comparison of the ethnohistorical (Spanish-language reports) and archeological records of southeast Costa Rica in the early 16th century. The essay considers the evidence for indigenous territorial divisions, social organization, and population.

211 Cruz, Víctor de la. El pensamiento de los binnigula'sa': cosmovisión, religión y calendario con especial referencia a los binnizá. México: Instituto Nacional de Antropología e Historia: Centro de Investigaciones y Estudios Superiores en Antropología Social (CIESAS): Casa Juan Pablos; Santa María Ixcotel, Mexico: Instituto Estatal de Educación Pública de Oaxaca, 2007. 544 p.: bibl., ill. (Publicaciones de la Casa Chata)

The Binnizá or Binnigula'sa' refers to the people of Oaxaca, Mexico, who are called in Spanish the Zapotecos, based on the Nahuatl name that was applied to them. This big, ambitious book uses linguistic, historical, archeological, and ethnographic evidence to present an informed discussion of the cosmovision, cosmogony, calendar, and sacred beliefs and practices of the Binnigula'sa' in the classic and postclassic periods. For archeologist's comment, see *HLAS 65:32*.

212 Cruz Pazos, Patricia. Juan de Moctezuma y Cortés: el ascenso al poder de un cacique indígena, Tepexi de la Seda, 1703–1778. (*Rev. Esp. Antropol. Am.*, 38:1, 2007, p. 31–50, bibl.)

This article examines the rise to power of Juan de Moctezuma y Cortés, the cacique of Tepexi de la Seda in the 18th century, and argues that Moctezuma y Cortés emphasized his hereditary status as well as nonverbal expressions of power, including the adoption of Spanish dress, riding a horse, and living in an elaborate residence, to assert his local authority.

213 De la mano de lo sacro: santos y demonios en el mundo Maya. Coordinación de Mario Humberto Ruz. México: UNAM, Instituto de Investigaciones Filológicos, Centro de Estudios Mayas, 2006. 366 p.: bibl., ill. (some col.). (Antologías; 1)

A collection of 14 essays on various aspects of sacred beliefs and practices in the modern Maya world of southern Mexico and Guatemala, focusing on images of Christian saints and demons in their local, popular contexts.

214 Dehouve, Danièle. La ofrenda sacrificial entre los tlapanecos de Guerrero. México: Univ. Autónoma de Guerrero: Plaza y Valdés: Centro de Estudios Mexicanos y Centroamericanos, 2007. 325 p.: bibl., ill. (Antropología e Historia)

A fascinating, detailed examination of ritual offerings and sacrifices among the Tlapanecos or indigenous inhabitants of the state of Guerrero, and reflections on the continuities of indigenous practices that are rooted in the preconquest past. Dehouve focuses especially on one type of offering: the "depósito ritual," which consists of the burial of various ceremonial objects, carefully counted and arranged in vertical levels, often topped by a sacrificed being such as a bird or cat. This practice, Dehouve argues, defies the false distinction that friars made between *sacrificios* and *ofrendas*.

Desmond, Lawrence Gustave. Yucatán through her eyes: Alice Dixon Le Plongeon: writer and expeditionary photographer. See item **822**.

215 Díaz, José Luis. El revuelo de la serpiente: Quetzalcóatl resucitado. México: Herder, 2006. 182 p.: bibl., ill.

A scientist known more for his work on psychotropic plants and cognitive neuroscience, Díaz is the *pensador* who considers how the legend and image of Quetzalcoatl has continued to resurface and resonate among Mexican thinkers until the present day.

Diel, Lori Boornazian. Till death do us part. See *HLAS 65:33*.

216 Diel, Lori Boornazian. Women and political power: the inclusion and exclusion of noblewomen in Aztec pictorial histories. (*Res/Cambridge*, 47, Spring 2005, p. 83–106, bibl., ill., photos)

Diel takes up the very significant question of why Nahua pictorial histories included or excluded women, using the *Tira de Tepechpan* and other codices to illustrate the range of important roles attributed to noblewomen, distinguishing differences between Mexica representations of women and those of other communities in central Mexico.

217 Dreiss, Meredith L. and **Sharon Greenhill.** Chocolate: pathway to the gods. Tucson: Univ. of Arizona Press, 2008. 195 p.: bibl., ill. (chiefly col.), col. map, index, DVD.

This lavishly illustrated volume discusses chocolate (cacao) as a ritual and economic item ("the money that grows on trees"). Just as chocolate continues to be beloved as a food, authors continue to examine its use in ceremonies and as a cureall. Ends by emphasizing chocolate's role in rainforest ecology. [B. Tenenbaum]

218 Galicia Gordillo, Angélica and **Sergio Sánchez Vázquez.** Cartografía histórica de Tulancingo, siglos XVI al XIX.

Hidalgo, Mexico: Univ. Autónoma del Estado de Hidalgo, 2007. 101 p., 16 p. of plates: bibl., ill., maps (some col.). (Patrimonio cultural hidalguense; 5)

An examination of various colonialera and early independence maps from Tulancingo, a Nahua *altepetl* in Hidalgo, from the Archivo General de la Nación and the Archivo Histórico de la Catedral de Tulancingo. The volume includes an appendix of 16 maps in color.

219 García Barrios, Ana and **Rogelio Valencia Rivera.** El uso político del baile en el Clásico maya: el baile de K'awiil. (*Rev. Esp. Antropol. Am.*, 37:2, 2007, p. 23–38, bibl., photos, table)

Examines the significance of the use of ceremonial dance among the classic period Maya to signify political relationships and mark the change of government. The author argues that the depiction of some Maya rulers holding the k'awiil scepter and dancing, whose claims to the rulership were not clear, indicates that this ritual served to consolidate authority.

220 García Márquez, Agustín. Los aztecas en el centro de Veracruz. México: UNAM, 2005. 213 p.: bibl., ill., maps.

This book considers the three provinces of Cotaxtla, Cuauhtochco, and Cempoala in Veracruz before and after the Mexica entered the region around the middle of the 15th century, until the arrival of the Spaniards.

221 Genotte, Jean-François. El método de Galarza aplicado al *Mapa de Otumba*: un documento pictográfico poco conocido del México colonial. (*Desacatos*, 22, sept./dic. 2006, p. 119–134, bibl., ill.)

Explanation of how the methods of analysis used by Joaquín Galarza allowed the author to read the *Mapa de Otumba* to better understand resource management, sociopolitical organization, and the introduction of Christianity in the first five decades of Spanish rule, as well as the geography of the region. For art historian's comment, see item **32**.

Gimmel, Millie. Reading medicine in the Codex de la Cruz Badiano. See item **711**.

222 Gómez Mata, Carlos. Lagos indio. Lagos de Moreno, Mexico: Univ. de Guadalajara, Centro Universitario de los Lagos, 2006. 189 p.: bibl.

This book attempts to recover the indigenous history of a region in the highlands of Jalisco, in Lagos de Moreno, which fell under the jurisdiction of Nueva Galicia in the colonial period. The author traces the documented existence of many indigenous communities from the 16th century to the early 19th century, demonstrating the region's indigenous roots to those who may have not known, forgotten, or underappreciated that part of the past.

223 Hernández, Patricia. La regulación del crecimiento de la población en el México prehispánico. México: Instituto Nacional de Antropología e Historia, 2006. 180 p.: bibl., ill. (Divulgación)

A paleodemographic study of the population profile and reproductive capacity of three Mesoamerican settlements: Tlatilco (located in the present day Estado de Mexico) in the preclassic period, an elite sector of Palenque (Chiapas) in the classic, and San Gregorio Atlapulco (Xochimilco) in the postclassic. An earlier version of this study won INAH's Javier Romero Prize in 2003 for its theoretical and methodological sophistication.

224 Historia y vida ceremonial en las comunidades mesoamericanas: los ritos agrícolas. Coordinación de Johanna Broda y Catharine Good Eshelman. Prólogo de Félix Báez-Jorge. México: Instituto Nacional de Antropología e Historia: UNAM, 2004. 498 p.: bibl., ill. (Col. Etnografía de los pueblos indígenas de México. Serie Estudios monográficos)

Johanna Broda and Catharine Good Eshelman have organized 21 chapters on the ceremonial rituals of indigenous communities throughout Mesoamerica, including studies in northern and southern Puebla, Guerrero, the Huasteca, Veracruz, Tepoztlán, Hidalgo, Morelos, the Valley of Ixtlahuaca, Michoacán, and the state of Mexico. The studies result from the authors' collaboration with El Proyecto Nacional de Etnografía de las Regiones Indígenas en México, supported by INAH. Most of the studies focus on agricultural rituals and cos-

movision. Broda lends the ethnographies a historical context by opening with a concise essay on prehispanic rituals that resonate with findings presented in the subsequent 20 chapters. This is a major contribution to Mesoamerican ethnography by Mexican scholars.

225 Ilarregui, Gladys M. Las mujeres de la conquista: antes y después de Cortés. Puebla, Mexico: Benemerita Univ. Autónoma de Puebla, Dirección de Fomento Editorial, 2007. 218 p.: bibl., ill.

This book presents five separate and seemingly unrelated essays on women in Mexico, beginning with Catalina Xuárez, Cortés' wife whom he allegedly murdered, followed by a general discussion of Nahua women, especially as seen in the *Florentine Codex*. Isabel Moctezuma is the protagonist of the third essay. The fourth and fifth essays consider the sacred roles of female deities and indigenous women before and after the conquest, and Malinche, and the types of work women performed in the colonial period.

226 Jansen, Maarten E.R.G.N. Los señoríos de Ñuu Dzaui y la expansión tolteca. (*Rev. Esp. Antropol. Am.*, 36:2, 2006, p. 175–208, bibl., ill., photos)

This article examines scenes in preconquest-style Mixtec or Ñuudzaui codices that depict a relationship between Lord 8 Deer "Jaguar Claw" and a leader of the Toltecs named Lord 4 Jaguar. Jansen then compares these scenes with representations of the Toltecs in central Mexican and Maya codices. The Toltec capital referred to in the Mixtec codices is Cholula. Jansen argues that this ruler of Cholula, known as Nacxitl Topiltzin Quetzalcoatl or Kukulcan, connected the Toltec and Maya realms in the early postclassic period.

227 Loera y Chávez de Esteinou, Margarita. Memoria india en templos cristianos: historia político-territorial y cosmovisión en San Antonio la Isla, San Lucás Tepemaxalco y Amecameca: el Valle de Toluca y el Valle de México en el virreinato. México: Instituto Nacional de Antropología e Historia, 2006. 129 p.: bibl., ill., maps. (Col. científica; 501. Serie Historia)

This work looks for signs of a palpable indigenous presence in the colonial architecture, historical record, and photographs of three churches in the state of Mexico.

228 Maldonado Jiménez, Druzo. Religiosidad indígena: historia y etnografía: Coatetelco, Morelos. México: Instituto Nacional de Antropología e Historia, 2005. 166 p.: bibl., ill., maps. (Col. científica)

A consideration of the spectrum of Mesoamerican and Christian sacred practices in the Nahua *altepetl* or community of Coatetelco, in the state of Morelos, using both historical and ethnographical findings—especially the latter. Special attention is given to agrarian rituals.

229 Martínez Baracs, Rodrigo. La perdida *Relación de la Nueva España* y su conquista de Juan Cano. México: Instituto Nacional de Antropología e Historia, 2006. 181 p.: bibl. (Col. científica; 497. Serie Historia)

Juan Cano de Saavedra (ca. 1502–72), a Spanish conquistador who married a daughter of Moteuczoma, wrote a history of the conquest of Mexico, which is now lost. Alonso de Zorita, an acquaintance of Cano, used Cano's manuscript in his own history of the conquest in the third part of his *Relación de la Nueva España*. In this volume, Martínez Baracs provides a biographical sketch of Cano and then reconstructs part of his history by searching, transcribing, and analyzing Zorita's many references to Cano's original manuscript. The author's careful study makes it possible to read yet another valuable text on the conquest, written by one of its participants.

230 Martínez González, Roberto. Sobre la función social del buen *nahualli*. (*Rev. Esp. Antropol. Am.*, 36:2, 2006, p. 39–63, bibl.)

This article uses an array of historical (colonial) and ethnographic sources to consider the role and social function of the *nahualli* (a shape-shifting being) within the Mesoamerican cosmovision, beginning with references to the good *nahualli*.

231 McGee, R. Jon. Watching Lacandon Maya lives. Boston, Mass.: Allyn and Bacon, 2002. 194 p.: bibl., ill., index, maps.

The author follows three generations of a Lacandon family in Nahá (Chan K'in Viejo) observing work, marriage, parent-

hood, religious traditions, healing practices, and many other aspects of Lacandon culture. The work also considers three centuries of change.

232 Mesa de Estudios de Género, *3rd*, Mexico City, 2003. Las mujeres en Mesoamérica prehispánica. Coordinación de María J. Rodríguez-Shadow. Toluca, Mexico: Univ. Autónoma del Estado de México, 2007. 278 p.: ill.

This interdisciplinary volume, edited by Rodríguez-Shadow, presents the proceedings of the third roundtable on gender held in Mexico City in 2003. Twelve authors discuss various aspects of Mesomerican women in the preconquest period, dividing their studies into the Maya, Oaxacan, and Mexica areas. Topics include female Quiché deities, Zapotec funerary urns, Mexica femininity and masculinity, and Coatlicue's skirt.

233 Millán, Saúl. El cuerpo de la nube: jerarquía y simbolismo ritual en la cosmovisión de un pueblo huave. México: Instituto Nacional de Antropología e Historia, 2007. 272 p.: bibl., ill. (Col. Etnografía de los pueblos indígenas de México. Serie Estudios monográficos)

This book resulted from Millán's doctoral dissertation in Anthropology at the Univ. Autónoma Metropolitana, which in 2005 won INAH's Fray Bernardino de Sahagún award for the best doctoral thesis in social anthropology and ethnology. The book examines how the cargo system among the Huaves of the Isthmus of Tehuantepec, especially in San Mateo del Mar, governs social relations, regulates productive activities, defines the territorial organization of the community, and conserves the sacred practices and symbolic rituals that are rooted in the past. Millán observes how one key Huave cultural concept, called *ombas*, embodies Huave principles of social and sacred relations. This is an informed, sophisticated, and well-organized study of an extremely important institution—the secular-religious cargo system—that unifies people within indigenous communities.

234 Miralles Ostos, Juan. La Malinche: raíz de México. México: Tusquets, 2004. 384 p.: bibl.

A readable reconsideration of Malinche's role in the conquest of Mexico, within a narrative of the conquest itself, aimed at a more popular audience, but with ample notes and appendices.

235 Mohar Betancourt, Luz María and Rita Fernández Díaz. El estudio de los códices. (*Desacatos*, 22, sept./dic. 2006, p. 9–36, bibl., ill.)

Two Mexican scholars present a general overview of how we "read" or interpret Mesoamerican pictorial writings, called codices, elaborating on the "Galarzan method" proposed by Joaquín Galarza.

236 Morales Damián, Manuel Alberto. Árbol sagrado: origen y estructura del universo en el pensamiento maya. Pachuca, Mexico: Univ. Autónoma del Estado de Hidalgo; Tuxtla Gutiérrez, Mexico: Univ. Autónoma de Chiapas, 2006. 233 p.: bibl., ill. (Col. social y humanística)

This book considers the symbolic and sacred importance of the tree in the ancient Maya cosmovision, with references to continuing practices in the Maya zone of Mexico.

237 Morales Damián, Manuel Alberto. *Uinicil te Uinicil tun*: la naturaleza humana en el pensamiento maya. (*Estud. Cult. Maya*, 29, 2007, p. 83–102, bibl., photos)

Examines Maya-language metaphors and symbolism to shed light on the Maya conception of humans as part of the larger physical world.

238 Morris, Mark. Language in service of the state: the Nahuatl counterinsurgency broadsides of 1810. (*HAHR*, 87:3, Aug. 2007, p. 433–470)

Morris offers an excellent description and analysis of Nahuatl-language broadsides printed and circulated in 1810, in response to the uprising in the Bajío, to promote Nahua loyalty to the Spanish Crown. Careful comparison between Spanish and Nahuatl-language broadsides shows that the Crown manipulated its message to appeal to indigenous traditions of political authority. For Mexican historian's comment, see item **854**.

239 Nájera Coronado, Martha Ilia. El rito del palo volador: encuentro de significados. (*Rev. Esp. Antropol. Am.*, 38:1, 2007, p. 51–73, bibl., ill., photos)

Article uses comparative, synchronic, and diachronic analysis to argue that the ritual of the *palo volador* represents a reconciliation of forces of the masculine/celestial and feminine/underworld realms and a revitalization of the cosmic tree and forces of nature.

240 Navarrete, Federico. The hidden codes of the *Codex Azcatitlan*. (*Res/Cambridge*, 45, Spring 2004, p. 144–160, bibl., ill.)

Argues that the painters of the *Codex Azcatitlan* strategically chose to use certain motifs and conventions to present a multilayered narrative that would address interests and concerns of Spanish, Tenochca, and Tlatelolcan audiences.

New world, first nations: native peoples of Mesoamerica and the Andes under colonial rule. See item **1432**.

241 Olko, Justyna. ¿Imitación, patrimonio pan-regional o distorsión colonial?: influencia mexica en manuscritos pictográficos del centro de México. (*Rev. Esp. Antropol. Am.*, 36:2, 2006, p. 139–174, bibl., ill., photos)

This lengthy essay considers evidence in numerous pictorial manuscripts from colonial central Mexico in order to distinguish possible imperial loans from local or regional conventions, focusing on the specific markers of royal attributes. Olko defines the characteristic markers of royalty among the Mexica and then considers manuscripts from peripheral regions of central Mexico, in Tlaxcala, Guerrero, Hidalgo, Morelos, Puebla, Oaxaca, and Veracruz.

242 Oudijk, Michel R. and María Castañeda de la Paz. Un testamento pictográfico de Xochimilco. (*Rev. Esp. Antropol. Am.*, 36:2, 2006, p. 111–123, bibl., ill., photos)

This article examines two pictorial documents that were submitted to the Royal Audiencia in Mexico City to support claims to land. The images were separated at some point from the accompanying alphabetic text, which is now lost; one of the images ended up in the National Library of France in Paris, and the other in the Newberry Library in Chicago. The authors argue that the pictorial writings serve the same purposes as a colonial last will and testament by delineating the heirs and properties of a Nahua noble from Xochimilco named don Miguel Damián.

243 Pasado y presente de la cultura mixteca. Recopilación de Reina Ortiz Escamilla y Ignacio Ortiz Castro. Huajuapan de León, Mexico: Univ. Tecnológica de la Mixteca, 2005. 321 p.: bibl., ill. (some col.), maps.

This anthology presents the proceedings of the *Semana de la Cultura Mixteca* in Huajuapan de León, in the Mixteca Baja region of Oaxaca. The essays by Mexican scholars cover four broad themes: archeology and the preconquest-style codices; religion and culture; migration; and gender.

244 Peck, Douglas T. Re-examination of Spanish colonial period documents related to prehistoric Maya history and mythology. (*Rev. Hist. Am./México*, 136, 2005, p. 21–35)

Peck examines the problematic corpus of early colonial writings on the Maya, including Spanish and indigenous texts, highlighting their many limitations for our understanding of the preconquest Maya and their contribution to several enduring misunderstandings and inaccuracies.

245 Peniche, Paola. Ambitos del parentesco: la sociedad maya en tiempos de la Colonia. Mexico: CIESAS: Miguel Ángel Porrúa, 2007. 378 p.: bibl., ill., maps. (Col. Peninsular. Serie Estudios) (Antropología)

A major study of kinship among the Yucatec Maya in the colonial period, based on ample published and unpublished sources. The book addresses naming systems, marriage, residence and inheritance patterns, and political organization and succession in Yucatán from the 16th to the early 19th centuries. The study is relevant for anyone interested in gender relations and the household, and possesses great potential for systematic comparisons with ethnographic studies of the same region.

246 Pictografía y escritura alfabética en Oaxaca. Coordinación de Sebastián van Doesburg. Oaxaca, Mexico: Instituto Estatal de Educación Publica de Oaxaca, 2008. 387 p.: bibl., ill.

This handsome volume, expertly edited by Sebastián van Doesburg, is another example of the type of outstanding work being done with indigenous writings in Oaxaca by scholars from Mexico, Europe, and the US. With the exception of two chapters on colonial-era Zapotec and 20th-century Ixcatec (surprisingly) alphabetic writings, the other 11 chapters focus on preconquest-style pictorial writings from the Mixtec, Zapotec, Chocho, and Chontal regions of Oaxaca in the classic and mainly postclassic periods.

247 A pre-Columbian world. Edited by Jeffrey Quilter and Mary Miller. Washington, D.C.: Dumbarton Oaks Research Library & Collection: Harvard Univ. Press, 2006. 395 p.: bibl., ill., index.

Quilter and Miller have organized a solid, handsome anthology with contributions from Elizabeth Hill Boone, Enrique Florescano, and other well-known scholars. Most—but not all—of the essays focus on Mesoamerica; a particularly fascinating contribution is the long piece by Polly Schaafsma and Karl Taube which presents convincing evidence that rain ceremonies and symbolism among Mesoamerican and Pueblo communities are nearly identical.

248 Prufer, Keith M. and **W. Jeffrey Hurst.** Chocolate in the underworld space of death: cacao seeds from an early classic mortuary cave. (*Ethnohistory/Columbus*, 54:2, Spring 2007, p. 273–301, bibl., ill., map, photo)

Examines the sacred, social, and economic significance of cacao using archeological, historical, and ethnographic data. Shows that cacao was used in a broad range of life cycle rituals and argues that its inclusion in a mortuary offering demonstrates that it was an important possession that the deceased needed on their journey to the afterworld.

249 Relatos ocultos en la niebla y el tiempo: selección de mitos y estudios. Coordinación de Blas Román Castellón Huerta. México: Instituto Nacional de Antropología e Historia, 2007. 448 p.: bibl., map. (Col. Etnografía de los pueblos indígenas de México. Serie Estudios monográficos)

A collection of fascinating indigenous legends and stories from various regions and ethnic groups of Mexico, including the Yaquis, Huicholes, Coras, Tepehuanes, Nahuas, Purépechas, Mixes, and Mixtecs. Each of the six essays combines transcriptions of the stories with analysis of their cosmological significance.

250 Robles Castellanos, José Fernando. Culhua México: una revisión arqueoetnohistórica del imperio de los mexica tenochca. México: Instituto Nacional de Antropología e Historia, 2007. 431 p.: bibl., ill., maps. (Obra diversa)

Unsatisfied with the concept of the tribute-collecting "Triple Alliance" or "Aztec empire," the author uses a variety of ethnohistorical sources and archeological data to project a deeper understanding of the nature of the "Culhua Mexico empire," seeking to identify the processes by which the Culhua lords engineered the military and political expansion of Mexico Tenochtitlán. There is much food for thought in this dense, mature work.

251 Rodríguez Tomp, Rosa Elba. Los límites de la identidad: los grupos indígenas de Baja California ante el cambio cultural. La Paz, Mexico: Gobierno del Estado de Baja California Sur, Instituto Sudcaliforniano de Cultura, 2006. 325 p.: bibl., ill., maps. (Col. Sociedad y cultura)

A broad treatment of the indigenous peoples of Baja California and their environment in preconquest times, the colonial period, and into the 19th and early 20th centuries, based mainly on published sources.

252 Romero Galván, José Rubén. Los privilegios perdidos: Hernando Alvarado Tezozómoc, su tiempo, su nobleza y su crónica mexicana. México: UNAM, Instituto de Investigaciones Históricas, 2003. 168 p.: bibl. (Serie Teoría e historia de la historiografía; 1)

At the turn of the 16th and 17th centuries, the Nahua writer named Tezozómoc lamented the decline of the indigenous population, especially in his *Crónica mexicana*. The first part of this book outlines the indigenous nobility at the time of the conquest; the second part analyzes Tezozómoc's writings and reveals the sense of loss, nostalgia, and decline that they convey.

253 Rossell, Cecilia. Estilo y escritura en la *Historia Tolteca-Chichimeca*. (*Desacatos*, 22, sept./dic. 2006, p. 65–92, bibl., ill.)

An examination of the meaning of many symbols in Nahua pictographic writing, and the relation of pictorial signs to the Nahuatl language, focusing on the *Historia Tolteca-Chichimeca*.

254 Ruiz Medrano, Carlos Rubén. El tumulto de abril de 1757 en Actopan: coerción laboral y las formas de movilización y resistencia social de las comunidades indígenas. (*Estud. Hist. Novohisp.*, 36 enero/junio 2007, p. 101–129)

Examines an indigenous riot in 1757 against forced labor in mines. Argues that the uprising reveals the use of collective violence to pressure colonial authorities to recognize labor demands and address unresolved social conflicts.

255 Ruz Barrio, Miguel Ángel. Cholula durante el siglo XVI: la familia Chimaltecuhtli-Casco. (*Rev. Esp. Antropol. Am.*, 38:1, 2007, p. 7–29, bibl., graph, map)

Uses a rich collection of documents from the Chimaltecuhtli-Casco family, including lawsuits, testaments, and bills of land sales dating from the mid-16th through the mid-17th centuries, now held in a private collection, to shed light on the social, political, and economic history of Cholula and this prominent family.

256 Ruz Barrio, Miguel Ángel. *Pintura del pleito entre Tepexpan y Temaxcalapa*, estudio preliminar. (*Rev. Esp. Antropol. Am.*, 36:2, 2006, p. 89–109, bibl., ill., photos)

This article examines a pictorial document in the Archivo General de las Indias submitted as evidence in a lawsuit between Tepexpan and Temaxcalapa in terms of its dating, authorship, and contents.

257 Santamarina Novillo, Carlos. Azcapotzalco antes que Tenochtitlan: reflexiones en torno a un modelo azteca de imperio. (*Rev. Esp. Antropol. Am.*, 37:2, 2007, p. 99–118, bibl., graph)

This article considers the strategic and hegemonic importance of Azcapotzalco a Tepaneca polity in the Basin of Mexico that provided a foundation for subsequent

Mexica dominance and expansion in the late postclassic period, especially after the so-called Tepanec War.

258 Santamarina Novillo, Carlos. Los *azteca-tepaneca*: en torno a sus orígenes y gentilicio. (*Rev. Esp. Antropol. Am.*, 36:1, 2006, p. 63–83, bibl., photos, tables)

This essay considers the origins of the Tepanecs, a Mexica group that migrated from Aztlan, based on etymological evidence and pictorial representations in early colonial sources.

259 Schaefer, Stacy B. To think with a good heart: Wixárika women, weavers, and shamans. Salt Lake City: Univ. of Utah Press, 2002. 355 p., 8 p. of plates: bibl., ill. (some col.), index.

A full-length ethnographic study of the multifaceted importance of weaving among women of a distinct indigenous group in the remote Sierra Madre Occidental in western Mexico, often called the *Huichol* by Spaniards in the colonial period and to the present day, people who call themselves *Wixárika* or *téwi* (people) and distinguish themselves from nearby *Náyari* (Cora) and Tepehuan peoples.

260 Schroeder, Susan. Writing two cultures: the meaning of "amoxtli" (book) in Nahua New Spain. (*in* New world, first nations: native peoples of Mesoamerica and the Andes under colonial rule. Edited by David Cahill and Blanca Tovías. Brighton, England; Portland, Ore.: Sussex Academic Press, 2006, p.13–35, bibl.)

Discusses the role of dynastic nobles in preserving local history, recording royal genealogies, and promoting *altepetl* patriotism in Nahuatl-language writings. Argues for continuity in function and content between pictorial and alphabetic writing, despite changes in form.

261 Semana de la Cultura Zapoteca, 4th, Universidad del Istmo, 2005. Un recorrido por el Istmo. Recopilación de Eva E. Ramírez Gasga. Tehuantepec, Mexico: Univ. del Istmo, 2006. 224 p.: bibl., col. maps.

This anthology presents the proceedings of the 4th Semana de la Cultura Zapoteca, sponsored by the Univ. del Istmo in Tehuantepec and Ixtepec. Six essays address various Isthmus Zapotec cultural and historical topics, including three essays on women. Language and identity is another concern. The final, seventh essay offers a selection of Zapotec-language poems and their translation into Spanish.

262 Sierra Carrillo, Dora. El demonio anda suelto: el poder de la Cruz de Pericón. México: Instituto Nacional de Antropología e Historia, 2007. 168 p.: bibl., ill., map. (Col. Fuentes)

On Sept. 28, many campesinos in central Mexico, especially in the state of Morelos, collect yellow flowers called *yauhtli* in Nahuatl or *pericón* in Spanish. People decorate crosses with the flowers in order to protect them from bad winds which can damage people, crops, and houses, and to protect the first harvest of the season. The author uses historical and ethnographic sources to analyze the ritual power that people attribute to these flowers, and the long roots of this tradition, which merges Mesoamerican and Christian beliefs and practices.

263 Sigal, Peter Herman. The *cuiloni*, the *patlache*, and the abominable sin: homosexualities in early colonial Nahua society. (*HAHR*, 85:4, Nov. 2005, p. 555–593, photos)

Sigal uses the *Florentine Codex* and other Church-sponsored Nahuatl-language materials of the early colonial period to explore homosexuality in Nahua society and its convergence and divergence with European notions of sexuality.

264 Sigal, Peter Herman. Queer Nahuatl: Sahagún's faggots and sodomites, lesbians and hermaphrodites. (*Ethnohistory/ Columbus*, 54:1, Winter 2007, p. 9–34, ill.)

This piece with the provocative and seemingly "presentist" title provides a method for interpreting the place of sexuality in texts such as the *Florentine Codex*, a 16th-century bilingual Nahuatl-Spanish encyclopedia, written by Nahua men in central Mexico, who were working under the auspices of the Franciscans. Sigal uses this text (especially book 10 of the 12-book work, titled "The People") to examine cross-dressing individuals, homosexualities, and gender inversions in Nahua society in the 16th century.

265 Speed, Shannon. Bajo la lanza: lucha
por la tierra e identidad comunitaria
en Nicolás Ruiz. Tuxtla Gutiérrez, Mexico:
Gobierno del Estado de Chiapas, 2006. 96 p.:
bibl., ill., geneal. table. (Biblioteca popular
de Chiapas; 121. Estudios etnohistoria)

Nicolás Ruiz, a community in central
Chiapas characterized by violent disputes
over land in the 1990s, in the wake of the
Zapatista rebellion, is the focus of this
study. The author shows how disputes over
land in this community of Tzeltal origin are
rooted in the colonial period; since the late
17th century, hacendados and caciques employed a variety of fraudulent and manipula-
tive measures to divest the community of
important landholdings. The longue-durée
view of landholding reveals how the history
of this community is a struggle to maintain,
defend, and recover primordial lands. This
brief but concise work also considers how
the recent discourse on indigenous rights
has affected the collective identity of the
residents of Nicolás Ruiz.

266 Staines Cicero, Leticia. Testimonios
de pintura mural prehispánica: dibujos de Agustín Villagra Caleti. (An. Inst.
Invest. Estét., 28:89, otoño 2006, p. 185–196,
bibl., photos)

Agustín Villagra Caleti began his
career as a painter in the 1920s and was
one of the first sketch artists employed by
the Instituto Nacional de Antropología e
Historia, in the Department of Prehispanic
Monuments. He became a professor of illustration in the National School of Anthropology in 1939. In his career, he copied numerous paintings and reliefs, from the tombs of
Monte Albán to the murals of Bonampak.
This article describes the impressive corpus
that Villagra left behind, which in 2006 was
donated to the Instituto de Investigaciones
Estéticas.

**267 ¿Tarascos o purepecha?: voces sobre
antiguas y nuevas discusiones en
torno al gentilicio michoacano.** Recopilación de Pedro Márquez Joaquín. Morelia,
Mexico: Univ. Michoacana de San Nicolás
de Hidalgo, Instituto de Investigaciones
Históricas: Colegio de Michoacán: Gobierno del Estado de Michoacán: Univ.
Intercultural Indígena de Michoacán:

Grupo Kw'anískuyarhani de Estudiosos
del Pueblo Purépecha: Fondo Editorial
Morevallado, 2007. 255 p.: bibl., ill. (Col.
Kw'anískuyarhani; 2)

At conferences in Pátzcuaro and the
Colegio de Michoacán (2002), numerous
estudiosos from various backgrounds and
disciplines took up the semantic and cultural topic of how to refer to the indigenous
people of Michoacán, from both modern
and historical perspectives. This anthology,
edited by Márquez Joaquín, summarizes
those discussions and presents a collection
of relevant writings on the topic of indigenous identity, ethnicity, and nomenclature
in Michoacán since the 19th century. The
resulting mixture of multiple indigenous
and scholarly perspectives and the attention
given to language makes the book a must
read for anyone interested in the indigenous
peoples of Michoacán.

268 Taube, Karl A. Flower Mountain:
concepts of life, beauty, and paradise
among the Classic Maya. (Res/Cambridge,
45, Spring 2004, p. 69–98, bibl., ill.)

Taube follows Jane Hill's study ("The
Flower World of Old Uto-Aztecan," in Journal of Anthropological Research, Vol. 48,
No. 2, 1992, p. 117–144) of the concept of a
floral paradise among indigenous peoples of
Mesoamerica and the Uto-Aztecan north,
and the concept's associations with the
sun, heat, music, and brilliant colors. He
focuses on the classic-era Maya, arguing
in support of one of Hill's hypotheses that
the Flower World complex was introduced
from southern Mesoamerica, rather than
from the north, introducing evidence for the
existence of such a complex as early as the
Middle Formative Olmec and the late preclassic and classic Maya periods.

**269 Tenamaztle: defensor pionero de los
derechos humanos.** Estudio preliminar y transcripción de Humberto Ávila
Márquez. Zacatecas, Mexico: Gobierno del
Estado de Zacatecas: Instituto Zacatecano
de Cultura, 2006. 187 p.: bibl., ill. (some
col.).

Transcription and analysis of a document in the Archivo General de las Indias
in Seville in which a Zacateco cacique of
Jalisco, don Francisco Tenamaztle, appealed

to the king in 1555 for redress of grievances and crimes attributed to the conquistador of the region, Nuño de Guzmán. Tenamaztle is the indigenous hero who resisted invasion, was captured, enslaved and brought to Spain, and ended up in a Dominican *convento* in Valladolid. There in Spain, with the assistance of none other than fray Bartolomé de las Casas, he made his petition to the Council of Indies and Crown, and died in 1558.

270 Los títulos primordiales del centro de México. Estudio introductorio, compilación y paleografía de Paula López Caballero. México: Consejo Nacional para la Cultura y las Artes, Fondo Editorial Tierra Adentro: Dirección General de Publicaciones, Consejo Nacional para la Cultura y las Artes, 2003. 351 p.: bibl., maps. (Cien de México)

Paula López Caballero has produced one of the first books published in Mexico on the genre of colonial-era documentation known as the "primordial titles," writings produced within indigenous communities, written in Spanish or indigenous languages, that purported to show continuous possession of lands from "time immemorial." These late colonial texts often inscribed and recorded native oral traditions and origin legends and were often accompanied by maps that marked the boundaries of the local community. In this volume, the author summarizes much of the existing scholarship on the primordial titles (until around 2000), adds her own observations, and presents transcriptions of 26 Spanish-language titles from central Mexico, providing a corpus for subsequent studies.

271 Vázquez, Germán. Moctezuma. Madrid; San Juan, P.R.: Algaba Ediciones, 2006. 309 p., 16 p. of plates: bibl., col. ill., maps. (Historia; 20)

A lively study of the famous Mexica ruler's life, based on the usual canon of colonial texts, especially those in Spanish, written for a general audience.

272 Las vías del noroeste I: una macrorregión indígena americana. Recopilación de Carlo Bonfiglioli, Arturo Gutiérrez, y María Eugenia Olavarría. México: UNAM: Instituto de Investigaciones Antropológicas, 2006. 346 p.: bibl., ill., maps.

This anthology of essays on northeastern Mexico, edited by Carlo Bonfiglioli, Arturo Gutiérrez, and María Eugenia Olavarría, consists of five essays on interethnic relations in the prehispanic and colonial periods, and 10 essays of a more ethnographic nature on cosmology and symbolism. The Northeast, as defined here, includes numerous culture groups, from the Hopi, Huichol, and Cora to the Tarahumara, Yaqui, and Tepehuanes.

273 Wright, David. Manuscritos otomíes en la Biblioteca Newberry y la Biblioteca de la Universidad de Princeton. Guanajuata, Mexico: Ediciones La Rana, 2006. 159, 47 p.: bibl. (Nuestra cultura)

A description and brief analysis, with copious notes, of more than a dozen colonial-era Otomi-language manuscripts and texts owned by the Newberry Library of Chicago and the Princeton University Library.

South America

SUSAN E. RAMÍREZ, *Professor of History and Neville G. Penrose Chair of History and Latin American Studies, Texas Christian University*

RECENT PUBLICATIONS on the anthropological history of South America show steady progress toward understanding past peoples and their cultures. As this brief overview will show, scholars from various disciplines contributed to current syntheses and debates. Archeologists and anthropologists with their long tradition of pioneering in this endeavor, for example, have written detailed and sometimes beautifully illustrated studies on the material culture of early Americans. Studies on Mochica *huacos retratos* (effigy jars) (item **387**), ethnobotony (item **379**), wooden beakers (item **359**), and the *quipu* (items **351** and **358**) are complementary to two volumes on the Inca kings (items **304** and **382**), a study of the peoples of the Cauca Valley (item **363**), and articles on Vilcabamba (items **341** and **348**). Related to these are a slim book on *amautas* (philosophers) and another on prehispanic navigation (item **340**). A somewhat broader overview of economic systems begins with the prehispanic and continues to the eve of the colonial era (item **296**).

Transcribed primary sources from the colonial era balance these. Among these are new editions and re-editions of the accounts of the classical Spanish and mestizo chroniclers, such as Pedro de Cieza de León (item **294**), Garcilaso de la Vega (items **384** and **385**), Felipe Guamán Poma de Ayala (item **322**), and the anonymous "Costumbres" (item **277**). Researchers also published newly transcribed manuscripts—many from local archives— such as the 17th-century *mita* distribution records from Cajamarca (item **278**); the wills from the native peoples around Bogotá (item **377**); the extirpation records from Trujillo (item **334**); testimonies on early Spanish-Inca and native interactions in the initial contact era (item **324**); and others covering the Mapuches (item **281**) and the peoples of Maynas, Chachapoyas, and Pará (items **329** and **315**). Of special note are the thick, long-awaited volume on Charcas (item **355**) and the equally important texts on Inca and colonial *quipus* from as early as 1535 (item **351**). These primary sources are usually introduced by background material and a critical analysis. Guamán Poma de Ayala's text stands out in this regard with four separate studies on his writings (items **275**, **305**, **356**, and **368**). Such analyses (in the tradition of Sabine MacCormack's 2007 book *On the Wings of Time: Rome, the Incas, Spain and Peru*) of the mental paradigms of manuscript creators help investigators to become conscious of the author's filters and thus better able to interpret the writings.

Editions and compilations of secondary sources also facilitate research by bringing together sometimes difficult to find materials. Compilations of essays and monographs by some of the most noteworthy and long-time contributors in the field include those by María Rostworowski (item **365** and **366**); Edmundo Guillén Guillén (item **324**); Luis Millones (item **344**); Abraham Valencia Espinoza (item **383**); Martha Bechis (item **280**), and Carlos Radicati di Primeglio (item **358**). (See also items **329**, **350**, and **364**.) Paralleling these tomes are the collected essays of multiple authors, long a staple in the field. These, likewise, disseminate work—often formerly presented at conferences— that might otherwise escape the attention of many readers (items **291**, **297**, **298**, **325**, **330**, and **378**). Although the themes, styles, and quality of the individual chapters vary, interesting papers may be buried in these volumes. Here, I am referring to pieces on indigenous memory in the proceedings of a broader Ecuadorian conference (item **297**) and David Cahill's analysis of Cuzco elites, published in a tome that he helped to edit (item **288**). They serve to exemplify the need to review such volumes.

As in past years, most of the remaining items are based on one or more specific ethnic groups or places. Books and articles on the Mapuche and Araucanians (See *HLAS 64:322* and item **364**), Cañari (item **287**), Calchaquí (item **362**), Quijos (item **381**), Palikur (item **352**), Pilagá (item **328**), Guarayo (item **318**), Pocoata (item **372**), Angaraes (item **292**), Shuar (item **300**), and the Chiriguano (item **295**) mark a developing trend toward focusing on a group no matter where they lived, thus taking into account dispersed settlement patterns, verticality, and horizontality, instead of defining the work strictly by place, e.g., Mendoza (item **367**), Jujuy (item **302**), La Rioja (item **361**), Córdoba (item **345**), the Yucay and Cauca Valleys (items **301** and **363**), Sechura and Catacaos (item **309**), Amazonia (items **378** and **381**), Cuenca (items **346** and **354**), southern Ecuador (item **299**), Riobamba and

Otavalo (item **285**), Calí (item **303**), Darién (item **307**), Bahia (item **320**), and Santa Catarina (item **343**). Of course, studies of colonial times, especially after the *reducciones*, and the fixating dislocation such a colonial policy caused by destroying prehispanic settlement patterns and seasonal migrations, plus the necessity of restricting a topic to a manageable and affordable size, justify the traditional regional focus.

The predominant and recurring themes in this literature are definition, representation, and identity (items **287**, **291**, **297**, **325**, and **376**). They cluster around such key and overlapping words as memory, religion (broadly defined), cosmology, imagination, and how these changed (see for example, item **290**, among others). Underlying the approaches is the question of who will define and represent the people studied. The texts that include some elements of ethnography (items **282** and **314**) allow subjects to help portray themselves. The edited volume, entitled *Time and Memory in Indigenous Amazonia: Anthropological Perspectives*, explores the historicities of Lowland South American Indians and the concepts of time, memory, and change from the native point of view (item **378**). Those of us who rely more narrowly on artifacts or the written word cannot return to interrogate our subjects. The goal of determining how they represented themselves is more difficult, but not impossible as Cahill's study of the "liminal" Cuzco elites (item **288**) makes clear. Some texts trace how different groups changed their identities as they began to accept elements of Catholicism and/or attended mission schools (items **318** and **373**). Additional studies outline how intellectuals and other writers have used the "other" over the years (item **332**). Illustrative in this regard are books by Manuel Burga on the Inca and Manuel Andrés García on Peruvians and Indians. The elusive goal is writing the story from an emic point of view. The danger is the use of sources uncritically and out of context, thus allowing our own filters and imaginative interpretations to dominate to the extent that the native perspective remains submerged (item **349**).

274 Alva Mariñas, Pedro. Don Víctor Huamán Reyes: el "cacique moral" de Cañaris. (*Bull. Inst. fr. étud. andin.*, 37:1, 2008, p. 257–270, bibl.)

A biographical portrait of Don Víctor Huamán Reyes, recognized as the "cacique of [the] Cañaris." The author, an anthropologist with many years of research in the north, shows how Huamán Reyes acted as leader for "his people."

275 Amaya Farías, Fernando. Indio y cristiano en condiciones coloniales: lectura teológica de la obra de Felipe Guamán Poma de Ayala, *Nueva crónica y buen gobierno*. Quito: Abya-Yala, 2008. 359 p.: bibl., ill.

A revised doctoral thesis, this publication examines Felipe Guamán Poma de Ayala's long letter to the king from a theological perspective. The analysis focuses on the contradiction between Christian salvation and the violence and exploitation sometimes practiced by Catholic priests during the colonial era, and on how natives could accept Christianity, while continuing to worship their own ancestral deities. A final section deals with the letter's relevance to more modern times.

276 Andrés García, Manuel. De peruanos e indios: la figura del indígena en la intelectualidad y política criollas: Perú, siglos XVIII—XIX. Spain: Univ. Internacional de Andalucía, 2007. 382 p.: bibl. (Col. Encuentros iberoamericanos; 10)

A serious monograph that traces the image and use of "the Indian" among intellectuals and politicians in 18th- and 19th-century Peru. Some argued for integration and others for subordination. The author traces thoughts on the subject back to the Tupac Amaru rebellion that raised fear of a racial war against "whites," and to the scientific racism that served as a basis for claiming that the Indian was inferior.

The book includes sections on the Cortes of Cádiz, José de San Martín and Simón Bolívar, Bartolomé Herrera, Civilismo, the rebellion of Huancané, the War of the Pacific, the rebellion of Huanta, indigenismo, Social Darwinism, and Clorinda Matto de Turner. A similar book with a wider focus is Rebecca Earle's recent book, *Return of the Native: Indians and Myth-Making in Spanish America, 1810–1930* (see item **412**).

277 Anónimo. De las costumbres antiguas de los naturales del Pirú. Edición de Chiara Albertin. Madrid: Iberoamericana; Frankfurt am Main: Vervuert, 2008. 91 p.: bibl., ill. (Textos y documentos españoles y americanos; 5)

Another edition of the late-16th or early-17th-century chronicle by an unknown author on the ancient customs of the natives of Peru. The editor not only offers a new paleographic transcription, but a detailed study of the authorship of the document (Padre Blas Valera or Luis López) and of the debate on the veracity of the information it contains (e.g., on human sacrifice). The book concludes with a glossary of Quechua and Aymará terms prepared by the noted linguist Rodolfo Cerrón-Palomino.

278 Argouse, Aude. "¿Son todos caciques?": curacas, principales e indios urbanos en Cajamarca, siglo XVII. (*Bull. Inst. fr. étud. andin.*, 37:1, 2008, p. 163–184, bibl.)

An interesting article on Cajamarca (northern highlands of Peru) which, despite being a pueblo de indios, had a significant non-notive population. Native authorities shared public spaces with representatives of the Spanish king. The author discusses two families of local lords, one that assumed the role of caciques and the other that became tribute collectors.

279 Argouse, Aude. Transcription d'un document inédit: répartition de *mita* en 1666, rationalisation de l'économie et main d'œuvre indienne dans le *Corregimiento* de Cajamarca. (*Bull. Inst. fr. étud. andin.*, 33:1, 2004, p. 97–134, bibl., table)

A valuable addition to the corpus of published documents, this one from Cajamarca in 1666. The manuscript provides information on the distribution of mita labor, the names of estate owners, and an indication of where the estates were and what they produced.

280 Bechis, Martha. Piezas de etnohistoria del sur sudamericano. Madrid: Consejo Superior de Investigaciones Científicas, 2008. 440 p.: bibl., ill., maps (Col. América; 10)

A book that unites key studies of Martha Bechis, a pioneer in the history of indigenous peoples in what is now Argentina. Of the three parts, the first (consisting of eight works) is on inter-ethnic conflict from the end of the 17th century into the late 19th century. Included here are articles on conflicts over cattle (the so-called "guerra de las vacas"), the peace treaty between the Gobernación of Buenos Aires and the cacique Tehuelche-Serrano Cangapo, and the origins of the "nación pehuenche." The second section deals with the political organization of native society, especially native leaders and their basis for legitimate rule. The last section centers on methodological issues. The texts include primary documents, maps, and diagrams. This is a must read for ethnohistorians of South America.

281 Bengoa, José. El Tratado de Quilín: documentos adicionales a la *Historia de los antiguos mapuches del sur*. Santiago: Catalonia, 2007. 131 p.: bibl., ill., map (Dos siglos)

The volume presents the transcription of the Peace Treaty of Quilín, negotiated by the Mapuches and the Spanish and signed on 5 and 6 January 1641. It is an Appendix to the volume *Historia de los antiguos mapuches del sur* by the same author. This treaty divided the territory that became Chile at the Bío Bío River. This partition allowed the Mapuche to live independently and in peace for 240 years.

282 Bernand, Carmen. Cerros, nevados y páramos: un intento de arqueología etnográfica. (*Rev. Esp. Antropol. Am.*, 38:1, 2007, p. 167–189, bibl.)

An ethnographic study of Pindilig and Taday (Province of Cañar), and Sigchos in the northern sierra (Province of Cotopaxi). The author discusses surviving elements of mountain worship and ancestor cults in these three settlements against a historical overview of the same in early colonial times (mostly the 17th century) based on extirpation documents from Peru and other sources

283 Beyersdorff, Margot. Covering the earth: mapping the walkabout in Andean *pueblos de indios*. (*LARR*, 42:3, 2007, p. 129–160, bibl., maps, photos)

An interesting article that poses a possible explanation for the lack of maps in early colonial documents. The author emphasizes the importance of "performative-based knowledge" of landholdings by discussing the "Relaciones geográficas," especially that of Yauyos; the muyuriy or circular path; "memory mapping"; boundary markers and marking, and the nature of toponyms. Of special interest are the two appendices, one of which is in Quechua with its English translation.

284 Bonilla, Víctor Daniel. Siervos de Dios y amos de indios: el estado y la misión capuchina en el Putumayo. Textos introductorios de Jesús Adalberto Carlosama, *et al.* Edición a cargo de Cristóbal Gnecco. Colombia: Editorial Universidad del Cauca: Univ. del Valle, Facultad de Humanidades, 2006. 413 p.: bibl., ill., maps. (Biblioteca del Gran Cauca)

A revised re-edition of the first Spanish edition published in 1968. The book contains the history of the Sibundoy Valley (Department of Putumayo in southwest Colombia) and the rapid transformation of the lives of the Inga and Kamentsás inhabitants. The author recounts how priests and settlers arrived and took control, sometimes through abuses and violence. Under the pretext of evangelizing and civilizing the Indians, both groups imposed their religion and introduced European concepts and techniques that replaced and discredited ancestral knowledge, opening the way to the abandonment of native cultural values.

285 Borchart de Moreno, Christiana Renate. Otavalo: el proceso de formación de un corregimiento de indios en la Audiencia de Quito, 1535–1623. (*Bull. Inst. fr. étud. andin.*, 35:2, 2006, p. 187–206, map, tables)

An information-filled article that analyzes the different aspects of a political process that started with the first encomienda concessions and was followed, after the civil wars, by attempts to organize the local administration, leading to the establishment of the corregimientos de indios of Riobamba and Otavalo. The consolidation of the new jurisdictions in 1575 is examined together with the multiplication of duties

entrusted to the corregidor, especially after the foundation of Ibarra, and, finally, in 1623, the division of the northern part of the Ecuadorian highlands into the corregimientos de Otavalo and Ibarra. Many of the early encomenderos and corregidores are named.

286 Burga, Manuel. Nacimiento de una utopía: muerte y resurrección de los incas. 2. ed., corr. Lima: Univ. Nacional Mayor de San Marcos: Universidad de Guadalajara, 2005. 449 p.: bibl., ill. (some col.) (Serie Coediciones)

A new edition of the 1988 book written by one of Peru's important historians. He traces the idea of the "Andean utopia" back to its roots in the 16th and 17th centuries and its furtive continuity in the culture of many Peruvian communities. His chapters focus on folklore, ritual, myth, and the imaginations of chroniclers like Juan de Santacruz Pachacuti, Felipe Guamán Poma de Ayala, and the Inca Garcilaso de la Vega.

287 Burgos Guevara, Hugo. La identidad del pueblo cañari: de-construcción de una nación etnica. Quito: Abya-Yala, 2003. 91 p.: bibl., ill. (Serie Cuadernos de antropología "Hugo Burgos"; 1)

A synthesis of the history of the Cañaris of Ecuador first dominated by legions of the Inca, then conquered by the Spanish, and finally subjected to the internal colonialism of a republican regime. The author shows that throughout this history a portion of the Cañaris nation has maintained its culture and language, while another portion has changed and been subject to a profound mestizaje.

288 Cahill, David Patrick. A liminal nobility: the Incas in the middle ground of late colonial Peru. (*in* New world, first nations: native peoples of Mesoamerica and the Andes under colonial rule. Edited by David Cahill and Blanca Tovías. Brighton, England; Portland, Or.: Sussex Academic Press, 2006, p.169–194, bibl.)

An excellent chapter on the Cuzco elites that shows that the Inca elites were tightly entwined with the Creole upper class. The author's detailed and nuanced analysis of the connections and overlap within the elite focuses on Juan Bustamante Carlos Inca, Diego Felipe Betancur, and Mateo García Pumacahua. The author concludes that failure to take such cross-racial networks and collaborations into account has obscured the key role played by Incan nobles in the sovereignty crisis of 1808–14 and the related constitutional struggles of 1812–14. He also proposes the use of "Incan Creoles" or "Creole Incas" or "Liminal Incas" rather than continuing to insist on the present sharp demarcation between Creole and Inca.

289 Caillavet, Chantal. "Como caçica y señora desta tierra mando . . .": insignias, funciones y poderes de las soberanas del norte andino, siglos XV–XVI. (*Bull. Inst. fr. étud. andin.*, 37:1, 2008, p. 57–80, bibl.)

A study of ethnic female authorities between 1530 and 1560 in the northern Andes. The author, a leading authority on Ecuadorian ethnohistory, studies emblematic objects tied to possession and exercise of command. She concludes that the necessary condition of a sovereign was the possession of "native servants" who were transferable to others. This finding reconfirms the importance of a following as the underpinning of authority in the Andes.

290 Cajavilca Navarro, Luis. Metamorfosis de los dioses y las sacerdotisas andinos en Huamantanga, Canta, siglo XVII. (*Investig. Soc./San Marcos*, 18, junio 2007, p. 221–242, bibl.)

This article is a short, sometimes repetitive description of the survival of native religion in the mid-17th century in Huamantanga, based (in part) on documents from the Archivo Arzobispal of Lima. The author includes discussions of ancestral gods, sacrifices, religious practitioners, and persecution by Spanish officials determined to destroy such practices.

291 Cambio y continuidad en Bolivia: etnicidad, cultura e identidad. Edición de Nicholas A. Robins. La Paz: Plural Editores: Asociación de Estudios Bolivianos, 2005. 150 p.: bibl. (Estudios bolivianos; 2)

The studies included in this edited volume analyze the changing ethnic identity of Bolivia. One contribution discusses the Aymará within the colonial context; others analyze the rebellion of Tomás Katari, the struggle of the Lecos to build identity and community, the identity-building festival of the Virgin of Urkupiña of Quillacollo, and indigenous education.

292 Carrasco, Tulio. Angaraes: la nación de las águilas reales: mitos, tradiciones e historias: homenaje al pueblo chanca. Lima: Editorial San Marcos, 2007. 382 p.: ill.

A minimally referenced textbook on the Angaraes, which begins with myth, continues with archeological findings on prehispanic times, and finishes with excerpts from the chroniclers (e.g., Pedro Cieza de León and others) and modern historians (e.g., Federico Kauffman Doig). A short bibliography completes the book. The tome contains basic information filtered through Western lenses.

293 Chassin, Joëlle. El rol de los alcaldes de indios en las insurrecciones andinas: Perú a inicios del siglo XIX. (*Bull. Inst. fr. étud. andin.*, 37:1, 2008, p. 227–242, bibl.)

An analysis of the role of the elected officials or native councilmen with whom the Bourbons replaced caciques after the Tupac Amaru rebellion. The author focuses on these power brokers during the 1812 insurrection of Huánuco, which is famous for being led by the councilmen, who mobilized various parties, constituting, according to Viceroy Abascal, the "most critical point of my Viceroyalty."

294 Cieza de León, Pedro de. Crónica del Perú: el señorío de los Incas. Selección, prólogo, notas, modernización del texto, cronología y bibliografía de Franklin Pease G.Y. Caracas: Fundación Biblioteca Ayacucho, 2005. 497 p.: bibl. (Biblioteca Ayacucho; 226)

Cieza de León, the "príncipe de los cronistas," is considered one of the most accurate of the chroniclers of the era, having traveled from Nueva Granada to Peru. He joined the forces of President Pedro de la Gasca in 1547 and returned to Spain in 1550 or 1551. Thus, he was an eyewitness to the civil wars and other important events. His work is the first to convey an integral conception of the history of Peru from its remote origins to the middle of the 16th century. Note that the orthography has been modernized; explicative notes have been added; and some references to the third and fourth part of the Chronicle have been omitted from the Proemio.

295 **Combès, Isabelle** and **Kathleen Lowrey.** Slaves without masters?: Arawakan dynasties among the Chiriguano, Boliviano Chaco, sixteenth to twentieth centuries. (*Ethnohistory/Columbus*, 53:3, Summer 2006, p. 689–714, bibl.)

An article that offers an understanding of Chiriguano society as a product of the conquest of an Arawak population by Tupi-Guarani migrants. The authors suggest that the assimilation of the Chiriguano to Tupi-Guarani sociopolitical models demonstrates a process of "Guaranization." By analyzing the Chiriguano political system, the authors recover the Arawakan heritage of this mestizo society in which different cultural traditions are both counterposed and combined. An in-depth case study of the Izozog region of the Bolivian Chaco highlights the piece.

296 **Compendio de historia económica del Perú.** t. 1, Economía prehispánica. Edición de Carlos Contreras. Lima: Banco Central de Reserva del Perú: IEP Instituto de Estudios Peruanos, 2008. 1 v.: bibl., ill. (chiefly col.), maps (some col.) (Histórica económica, 1)

A handsome volume that summarizes the research on the prehispanic economies of various Andean civilizations, starting with hunters and gatherers. Archeologist Luis Guillermo Lumbreras provides an overview of the economic origins of Andean societies with sections on hunters, gatherers, and fishermen; domestication; and ecological diversity. Peter Kaulicke describes the formative period economies on the North and Central Coasts and at Chavín de Huántar. Julián Santillana offers an overview of the coastal and highland populations from circa 200 B.C.E. to 1476. Finally, historian Waldemar Espinoza Soriano surveys the structure of the economy under the Incas with sections on land tenure, the work force, and exchange.

297 **Congreso Ecuatoriano de Antropología y Arqueología, 2nd, Quito, Ecuador, 2006.** Balance de la última década: aportes, retos y nuevos temas. Compilación de Fernando García Serrano. Quito: Abya Yala: Banco Mundial Ecuador, 2007. 2 v.: bibl., ill.

Papers from a meeting of Ecuadorian anthropologists and archeologists. Some of the topics include gender, maternity, sacrifice, caciques (of Otavalo), memory, food, the informal economy, and identity. The papers from the symposiums on ethnohistory and culture and religiousity are especially relevant and good.

298 **Construcción de la memoria indígena.** Compilación de Betty Osorio Garcés. Bogotá: Siglo del Hombre Editores: Univ. de Los Andes, 2007. 346 p.: bibl., ill. (Biblioteca José Martí. Serie Razón y fábula)

An edited volume of the papers first presented at a symposium entitled "La construcción de la memoria indígena: perspectivas multi-disciplinarias." Themes covered include indigenous myths; the construction of an image of the "prehispánico" during the 19th century; conquest and colonization; mestizaje; and Felipe Guaman Poma de Ayala, among others.

299 **Cordero Iñiguez, Juan.** Historia de la región austral del Ecuador desde su poblamiento hasta el siglo XVI. 1, Nuestra primera historia: tiempos indígenas o los Sigsales. 2, El imperio andino del sol en el sur ecuatoriano. 3, Historia de Cuenca y su región, siglo XVI: choques y reajustes culturales. Cuenca, Ecuador: Municipalidad de Cuenca: Fundación Cultural Cordero, 2007. 3 v.: bibl., ill. (some col.), indexes, col. maps.

A beautifully illustrated set of three volumes on the southern part of Ecuador. One book is an archeological survey of the region, which covers geological, climatic, and demographic overviews from the lithic period into immediate precolonial times. Of special interest is a chapter on the Cañaris and the Paltas. Another volume surveys the Inca presence in the region from approximately 1450 to the Spanish conquest in 1532. The Paltas and the Cañaris under Inca domination, the city of Tomebamba, and other prehispanic sites such as Ingapirca are discussed in detail. The third tome is on the colonial history of the city of Cuenca, Ecuador with chapters on the Cañaris in the 16th century, the region before the city's founding, and its founding in 1571. The mita, encomienda, caciques, tribute, reducciones, haciendas, mining, the Church, and ethnic relations are some of the topics covered. The original order to found the city and the act of foundation are transcribed and included in the text.

300 Costales, Piedad Peñaherrera de. Historia de la nación shuar. Quito: Abya Yala: IEAG, 2006. 2 v.

A two-volume history of the Shuar peoples, which includes a significant selection of primary texts. The historical analysis covers the Yaguarzongos and Bracamoros, peoples of the Paroacica and the Chinchipe, and their language, customs, and arms. Transcribed documents that date from the late 17th century to the late 18th century reflect colonial interests and the search for such valuable commodities as cascarilla (for quinine), cinnamon, and gold.

301 Covey, R. Alan and **Christina M. Elson.** Ethnicity, demography, and estate management in sixteenth-century Yucay. (*Ethnohistory/Columbus*, 54:2, Spring 2007, p. 303–335, bibl., graph, maps, tables)

This essay outlines how the management of the Yucay "estate" system (not to be confused with a Spanish farm or ranch), constructed to serve Guayna Capac, evolved in the early colonial period. The population of permanent retainers (yanacona) was eventually resettled in four Spanish-style towns (reducciones). The article also presents an ethnic and demographic overview of the retainer population identified in primary documents.

302 Cruz, Enrique Normando. Historia de Jujuy. Vol. 1, Período indígena. Jujuy, Argentina: Centro de Estudios Indígenas y Coloniales, Univ. Nacional de Jujuy, 2006. 1 v.: bibl., ill., maps.

A regional history of the Jujuy of Argentina with an additional discussion of its interaction with the Inca empire, based on secondary sources.

303 Cuevas Arenas, Héctor Manuel. La república de indios: un acercamiento a las encomiendas, mitas, pueblos de indios y relaciones interestamentales en Cali, siglo XVII. Cali, Colombia: Archivo Histórico de Cali, 2005. 117 p.: bibl., map.

A contribution to the regional history of Cali (Colombia), based, in part, on unpublished primary sources. The text covers demographic collapse, encomiendas, tribute, mitas, and mestizaje. Much of the demographic data is summarized in tables. Table 5 lists native towns from 1559 to 1716.

304 Cummins, Thomas B.F. et al. Los incas, reyes del Perú. Lima: Banco de Crédito, 2005. 337 p.: bibl., ill. (chiefly col.) (Col. Arte y tesoros del Perú)

Another of the beautiful annual coffee-table books commissioned and published by the Banco de Crédito del Perú to give to their best clients. As in the past, this volume includes abundant color illustrations and chapters written by well-known and serious scholars in accessible styles. A unifying theme is how the Incas were portrayed and how memories of the same were constructed from the conquest to 1900.

305 De la Puente, José Carlos. Cuando el "punto de vista nativo" no es el punto de vista de los nativos: Felipe Guamán Poma de Ayala y la apropiación de tierras. (*Bull. Inst. fr. étud. andin.*, 37:1, 2008, p. 123–149, bibl.)

An article based on new information on Felipe Guamán Poma de Ayala who served as an assistant to the *visita de tierras* of the 1590s. As a result, he became involved in a law suit over some lands near the city of Huamanga. The author concludes that, as native lords of the town and Valley of Chupas, Guamán Poma's alleged ancestors and then their heirs participated in a typical process of appropriation of previously open common lands and pastures.

306 Decoster, Jean-Jacques. Identidad étnica y manipulación cultural: la indumentaria inca en la época colonial. (*Estud. Atacameños*, 29, 2005, p. 163–170)

An article on precolonial Andean dress and especially the *uncu*, the *liclla* and the *acso*. These pieces served to express ethnic identity and the status or condition of the individual. The author uses dress as a semiotic expression of identity and addresses its manipulation in various contexts

**307 El diablo vestido de negro y los cunas del Darién en el siglo XVIII: Jacobo Walburger y su *Breve noticia de la provincia del Darién, de la ley y costumbres de los yndios, de la poca esperanza de plantar nuestra fé, y del número de sus naturales, 1748.* Edición de Carl Henrik Langebaek. Bogotá: Univ. de Los Andes, Facultad de Ciencias Sociales, Departamento de Ciencia Política, Centro de Estudios Socioculturales e Internacionales, 2006. 115 p.: bibl. (Biblioteca banco popular)

The highlight of this book is the publication of a 1748 description of the natives of the Darien, written by a Jesuit named Jacobo Walburger, with the purpose of establishing the state of the missions. Walburger's text shows the traditional power of the leres (religious specialists) and illustrates the failure of Spanish policies to strengthen the power of caciques. Langebaek's Introduction, emphasizing ethnographic elements of the text, discusses the social organization of the Cuna Indians, their culture, and the impact of colonial pressures.

308 Díaz, Alberto and **Germán Morong.**
El desierto y la miseria: indios y tributación en el sur peruano, Sibaya, 1822. (*Anthropol. Dep. Cienc. Soc.*, 24:24, 2006, p. 129–152, bibl., tables)

An article discussing the local context associated with taxes and tributes in the Andean communities of the Peruvian south, particularly the community of Sibaya. Documents describing the social and economic conditions in which Sibaya inhabitants lived are analyzed in connection with the problem of tax collection and the inability of the community to pay taxes and tributes due to the death of community members, the territorial dispersion of its inhabitants, and the precarious condition of the land. Integral to the analysis is a document from 1822 describing the local crisis situation.

309 Diez, Alejandro. Los problemas del poder: política local y gobierno en las reducciones de la costa de Piura, siglo XVII. (*Anthropol. Dep. Cienc. Soc.*, 24:24, 2006, p. 107–127, tables)

An article by a well-published anthropologist with a long history of writings on the far north coast on the native towns of San Juan de Catacaos and San Martín de Sechura under Spanish colonial rule. The author focuses on the colonial caciques and their mechanisms of acquiring power and legitimacy and the two-faced role that they were forced to play as they mediated between their followers and the colonial state.

310 Dillehay, Tom D. and **Ramiro Matos.**
History, memory and knowledge in Andean visual imagery: the intersection of art, architecture, and landscape. (*in* Pre-Columbian world. Edited by Jeffrey Quilter and Mary Miller. Washington: Dumbarton Oaks Research Library and Collection, 2006, p. 313–341, bibl., ill., photos)

An article by two leading scholars contending that precolumbian societies were fundamentally memorial to the same degree that modern industrial societies are documentary. The authors examine the intersection of meaning and context across technology, art, architecture, cultural landscapes, and skyscapes of different societies, observing that each served as a mechanism for handing down traditions, rituals, cosmologies, power and authority, and knowledge. Further, the authors show that stylistic differences in art, iconography, architecture, and landscape may have resulted from historical conditions and the influence of marginalized groups, disputing the notion that only elites and overarching political institutions controlled the artistic and physical scene. For art historian's comment, see item **18**.

311 Dueñas, Alcira. Fronteras culturales difusas: autonomía étnica e identidad en textos andinos del siglo XVII. (*Bull. Inst. fr. étud. andin.*, 37:1, 2008, p. 187–197, bibl.)

An essay examining notions of ethnic power and the discursive constructions of identity in two important Andean texts written after the age of Guamán Poma de Ayala and Garcilaso de la Vega. Reinterpreting scholastic medieval notions of "natural law," "common good," and "good government," these writings sought to legitimize the right of Andean peoples to rule their own political bodies given that Spanish rule in Peru transgressed basic notions of legitimacy. These manuscripts criticized the abuses and racism of Spanish rule and the contradictions of colonialism.

312 Durston, Alan. Native-language literacy in colonial Peru: the question of mundane Quechua writing revisited. (*HAHR*, 88:1, Feb. 2008, p. 41–70)

A study of nine Quechua documents and the extent, functions, and channels of mundane Quechua literacy in the jurisdiction of the Audiencia of Lima. The author argues that Quechua literacy was widespread among the indigenous elite, but that the institutions of colonial indigenous self-rule did not make use of alphabetic record-keeping to the extent that their Mesoamerican counterparts did.

313 Eeckhout, Peter. Relatos míticos y prácticas rituales en Pachacamac. (*Bull. Inst. fr. étud. andin.*, 33:1, 2004, p. 1–54, bibl., ill.)

A good article on the cult of Ychsma, an important prehispanic deity whose sanctuary is in the Pachacamac complex near Lima. Ethnohistorical, ethnographical, and archeological methods confirm the coastal origin of the god and show how the cult and its myths were manipulated by the Inca. Special attention is given to human and animal sacrifice, offerings, pilgrimage, divination, and the cult of the ancestors.

314 Escolar, Diego. Los dones étnicos de la nación: identidades huarpe y modos de producción de soberanía en Argentina. Buenos Aires: Prometeo, 2007. 249 p.: bibl., ill. (Col. miradas antropológicas)

A serious text on the Huarpe peoples of the province of Cuyo, Argentina, who disappeared at the beginning of the 17th century from extinction, acculturation, and biological miscegenation. The author explains why and how the ethnic identity was revived in the 1990s, based on ethnographic fieldwork in the province since 1994. He states that this revival contradicts the myth of a white and culturally European Argentina.

315 Espinoza Soriano, Waldemar. Amazonía del Perú: historia de la gobernación y comandancia general de Maynas (hoy regiones de Loreto, San Martín, Ucayali y Provincia de Concorcanqui): del siglo XV a la primera mitad del siglo XIX. Lima: Fondo Editorial del Congreso del Peru: Banco Central de Reserva del Perú, 2006. 598 p.: bibl., ill., maps.

A history of the gobernación of Maynas (today the region of Loreto, San Martín, Ucayali and the province of Condorcanqui (Peru)) from the 15th to the first half of the 19th century, based on both primary and secondary sources. After introductory remarks on the climate, flora and fauna, and inhabitants, the author—one of the most prolific in Peru—discusses expeditions, the founding of towns and native resistance in the 16th century; the establishment of missions and reducciones in the 17th; the age of rebellions and science in the 18th; and Independence and its consequences in the 19th. Besides such basic information on the Jesuit foundation of Iquitos in 1750, Espinoza Soriano includes the origins of dozens of other towns, which still dot the Amazonian region.

Espinoza Soriano, Waldemar. La etnia Guayacundo en Ayabaca, Huancabamba y Caxas, (siglos XV–XVI). See item **1412**.

316 Espinoza Soriano, Waldemar. Las lenguas nativas del Altiplano peruano-boliviano en el sigo XVI. (*Investig. Soc./San Marcos*, 14, mayo 2005, p. 121–153, bibl.)

A good article that provides an overview on the languages spoken in ancient Peru. The author reiterates that the origin of Quechua is on the Central Coast. He also outlines the geographical distribution of several Andean languages and explains the persistence of the Puquina language until the 19th century in the Bishoprics of La Plata, La Paz, Cuzco, and Arequipa. The article is based on chronicles, dictionaries, and grammars of the 16th century as well as manuscript sources from Peru and Spain. In an appendix, he publishes a 1605 anonymous manuscript source that lists the parishes of the Bishopric of Charcas and the language that each priest used during mass.

317 Flores Quelopana, Gustavo. Los amautas filósofos: un ensayo de filosofía prehispánica. Lima: IIPCIAL, Fondo Editorial, 2006. 116 p.: bibl. (Biblioteca IIPCIAL de filosofía)

A book that answers the question of why Garcilaso de la Vega translated the Quechua word "amautas" as "philosophers." The author also discusses the philosophical repercussions of translating "Pachacamac" as "animator" instead of "creator." The author bases his interpretive study on published chronicles and secondary sources.

318 García Jordán, Pilar. "Yo soy libre y no indio, soy guarayo": para una historia de Guarayos, 1790–1948. Lima: Instituto Francés de Estudios Andinos, 2006.

611 p.: bibl., ill., index, charts, facsims., maps (Travaux de l'Institut français d'études andines, 219)

A long book, based on abundant primary sources in archives in Bolivia and Argentina, on the Franciscan missionaries to the Guarayo peoples from the late 18th century to the middle of the twentieth. The author recounts the failure of the Franciscans to "civilize" the natives who lived in Asunsión, Nuestra Señora de los Ángeles de Urubichá, San Francisco de Yotaú, Santa Cruz de Yaguarú, and San Pablo. Once the Franciscan "tutelage" disappeared, the natives lost lands and were reduced to laboring for agricultural enterprises. The text also includes 24 transcribed documents and photos, dating from as early as 1898. For Bolivian historian's comment, see *HLAS 64:1361.*

319   Gareis, Iris. Los rituales del estado colonial y las élites andinas. (*Bull. Inst. fr. étud. andin.,* 37:1, 2008, p. 97–109, bibl.)

An article analyzing the staging and use of rituals under Spanish colonial rule. The author argues that local ethnic elites used these rituals to highlight their social standing and to consolidate their own political power within the colonial state.

Garrett, David T. Sombras del imperio: la nobleza indígena del Cuzco, 1750–1825. See item **1415.**

Gato Castaño, Purificación. Aproximación al mundo chiriguano: a través del diario de la expedición a las Salinas, 1785–1790. See item **1464.**

320   Giménez, Célia Beatriz. Bahia indígena: encontro de dois mundos. Verdade do descobrimento do Brasil by Raimundo dos Santos Coelho. Rio de Janeiro: Topbooks, 2005. 239 p.: bibl., ill., maps.

The results of an investigation on the natives of Brazil at the time of its European "discovery." The first chapters provide a panoramic view of the Brazilian natives. The second half of the book revises the history of the encounter. This work is lightly footnoted and is based on secondary sources; therefore, it should be considered as a text for a general audience.

Gómez, Gérard. Entre las bellas palabras y las palabras sagradas: el sincretismo lingüístico-religioso en las reducciones jesuíticas del Paraguay. See item **1529.**

321   Graubart, Karen B. De qadis y caciques. (*Bull. Inst. fr. étud. andin.,* 37:1, 2008, p. 83–95, bibl.)

An essay that proposes a connection between the limited autonomy granted to indigenous communities under a cacique in the colonized New World and that previously granted to mudejar or Muslim communities under a *qadi* in late medieval Iberia. The author finds that the relationship between these two structures is evident in terms of law, theoretical spatial organization, and the failure of the structures to "contain" their populations.

322   Guamán Poma de Ayala, Felipe. Nueva corónica y buen gobierno. Edición y prólogo de Franklin Pease G.Y. Vocabulario y traducciones de Jan Szemiński. 2. reimpresión. Lima: Fondo de Cultura Económica, 2008. 3 v.: bibl., ill., indexes. (Sección de obras de historia)

An important 3-volume reedition of a standard early-17th-century chronicle. Two of the leading scholars of the Andes contribute a forward, original and corrected pagination, a section of Quechua to Spanish translations, and onomastic, toponymic, and ethnonymic indexes. Because of the untimely passing of Franklin Pease, the forward does not reference some of the latest research, showing Guamán Poma de Ayala to be a Hispanized native. This undermines the claim that Guamán Poma de Ayala is an "authentic" native voice that reflects the prehispanic past.

323   Guide to documentary sources for Andean studies, 1530–1900. Edited by Joanne Pillsbury. Norman: Univ. of Oklahoma Press, 2008. 3 v.: bibl., ill., indexes, maps.

A definitive resource for early works on indigenous cultures. This three-volume reference work, written with the contributions of over 122 scholars in nineteen countries, offers updated information on key sources. Volume I reviews the origin and nature of the sources, focusing on recent research and interpretations. Volumes II and

III analyze the work of specific authors and their texts with added information on the location of the manuscripts, publication history, translations, and references to secondary literature.

324 Guillén Guillén, Edmundo. Ensayos de historia andina. 1, Los Incas y el inicio de la guerra de reconquista. 2, Los Incas y el trágico final del Tawantinsuyo. Lima: Univ. Alas Peruanas: Academia de Historia del Perú Andino, 2005. 2 v.: bibl., ill. (some col.)

A valuable and convenient compilation of the writings of a well-known Peruvian historian who has contributed to our general knowledge on the Incas and early colonial South America. The first volume contains 24 chapters, grouped into two parts: Inca civilization and structure; and the Inca resistance against the Spanish invaders. The second volume contains transcribed testimonies dealing with Inca resistance to Spanish aggression. This set is a "must read" for all serious students of the early colonial period.

325 Guzmán Palomino, Luis *et al.* Nación e identidad en la historia del Perú. Compilación, edición y prólogo de Germán Calderón Ticse. San Luis, Lima: Academia de la Historia del Perú Andino, 2006. 212 p.: bibl., ill.

An edited anthology on identity and nation in Peru from the prehispanic period to the present, written by such well-known historians as Juan José Vega and Edmundo Guillén Guillén. Among the presented perspectives are a critique of capitalism and the "republica criolla" and a romanticized image of the Andean community.

326 Hernández Astete, Francisco. Las panacas y el poder en el Tahuantinsuyo. (*Bull. Inst. fr. étud. andin.*, 37:1, 2008, p. 29–45, bibl.)

A penetrating analysis of the word and category *panaca* as used in the standard Inca sources. The traditional division of the Cuzqueño elite into 10 or 12 panacas is questioned. The author proposes, instead, that the Cuzco elite was divided into Cápac Aillu and Hatun Aillu and concludes that the so-called panacas were *aillus* made up of the descendants of the noble women identified as *pana*.

Holland, Augusta Emilia. Nueva coronica: tradiciones artísticas europeas en el virreynato del Perú. See item **1418**.

327 Huertas Vallejos, Lorenzo. Los oráculos en la historia andina. Lima: Universidad Ricardo Palma, Editorial Universitaria, 2006. 50 p.: bibl. (Col. Realidad nacional; 3)

A short book by a well-known historian of Peru's north and central regions. The text includes a discussion of the function of the oracles and their attendants in relation to periodic crises during Inca times and their revitalization in the 17th century.

328 Idoyaga Molina, Anatilde. El mito y las uniones imposibles: análisis de la trama de un relato de los indígenas pilagá, Chaco Central. (*Rev. Esp. Antropol. Am.*, 38:1, 2007, p. 91–104, bibl.)

An analysis of a myth of the Pilagá Indians of the central Chaco of Argentina. The myth relates the impossible union between a female star and a homely common man. The myth, based on original materials, and its interpretation warns against breaking moral codes and the social and cosmic order of society.

329 Ijurra, Manuel. Viajes a las montañas de Maynas, Chachapoyas y Pará: vía de Amazonas, 1841–1843. Estudio preliminar de Nanda Leonardini. Lima: Seminario de Historia Rural Andina, Universidad Nacional Mayor de San Marcos, 2007. 126 p. : ill.

The re-edition of accounts of two mid-19th-century expeditions taken by entrepreneur Manuel Ijurra to Amazonia, first published in *El Peruano*. In the first account, Ijurra describes the Brazilian province of Pará, the Kuelap site, the Chachapoyas, mining, and the flora and fauna of the region. His route took him from Lima, during the government of General Agustin Gamarra, through Cerro de Pasco and Huánuco to Chiguangala. He encountered Cocamas, Huambisas, Paturas, Ticunas, Yaguas, Atacuaris, and many other indigenous groups. In his second account, Ijurra advocates the exportation of raw materials from the Amazon using the Brazilian port of Pará to the Atlantic and Europe. Ijurra himself became an exporter of cascarilla (quinine) and later in life attempted to found an agricultural colony in Alto-Amazon.

330 International Congress of Americanists, 51st, Santiago, Chile, 2003. De la etnohistoria a la historia en los Andes. Edición de John Fisher y David Cahill con la colaboración de Blanca Tovías. Quito: Abya Yala, 2008. 309 p.: bibl.

An edited book with contributions written by excellent historians, some with long publication histories, that touches on central themes of Andean history, such as the last days of Inca domination, visitation records as sources for early colonial history, the urban life of natives, the colonial Inca of Cuzco, the monarchical movement of the 19th century, the impact of liberalism on native communities, and native tribute to the end of the 19th century. Such themes contribute to the effort to rewrite a more integrated national history.

331 Julien, Catherine. Kandire in real time and space: sixteenth-century expeditions from the Pantanal to the Andes. (Ethnohistory/Columbus, 54:2, Spring 2007, p. 245–272, bibl., map)

A rereading of the historical record on the 16th-century expeditions from the Pantanal west to the Andes. The author suggests that testimonies from or about the expeditions of 1542–43, 1543–44, and 1557–59 show that in addition to migration in search of a "land-without-evil" (which she glosses as a land of virgin soil and forest), native people moved west to trade for metals and to free captives taken on previous trips. The text also discusses dispersal and settlement of native peoples and the meaning of the word Candire/Camire/Canire.

332 Langebaek, Carl Henrik. Los herederos del pasado: indígenas y pensamiento en Colombia y Venezuela. Bogotá: Univ. de los Andes: Ediciones Uniandes, 2009. 1 v.: bibl., ill. (some col.), index

Volume 2 of a large-format, well-illustrated set with chapters on education, race, ecology, and colonialism. Specifically mentioned are the Muiscas and the Caribes. A common theme is the creoles' ongoing construction of an idealized vision of the native and native history in order to legitimize their own presence and create a sense of identity.

333 Langebaek, Carl Henrik. Indios y españoles en la antigua provincia de Santa Marta, Colombia: documentos de los siglos XVI y XVII. Bogotá: Facultad de Ciencias Sociales, Universidad de Los Andes, 2007. 251 p.: bibl., maps.

A welcome contribution to the history of the province of Santa Marta (Colombia), best known to the general public through the novel by Gabriel García Márquez, One Hundred Years of Solitude (see HLAS 30:3299 and HLAS 40:7898). The volume consists of 10 transcriptions of 16th- and 17th-century documents with short introductions. Of particular note are a report on the city of Santa Marta, dated 1538; information on the people of Tairona in 1571; a "relación geográfica" on the city of Nueva Salamanca de La Ramada in 1578; information on Santa Marta and Rio de la Hacha in 1580; native resistance in 1599; encomiendas and tribute in 1625; and idolatry in the 17th century, among others.

334 Larco, Laura. Más allá de los encantos: documentos históricos y etnografía contemporánea sobre extirpación de idolatrías en Trujillo: siglos XVIII–XX. Prólogo por Luis Millones. Lima: Fondo Editorial, UNMSM; Instituto Francés de Estudios Andinos, UMIFRE 17, CNRS-MAEE, 2008. 402 p.: bibl., maps (Serie Coediciones)

An exciting new edition of extirpation of idolatry documents from a region long known for its herbalists and "maestros" (healers). The author, whose family has a long history in the area, transcribed 19 legajos (bundles) of idolatry trials (of a total of 25). They range in date from 1752–1818 and 1824–1924. Accusations of witchcraft occurred in Mansiche, Huamán, Huanchaco, Moche, Paiján, Santiago de Cao, Guadalupe, Chepén, Puebo Nuevo, San Pedro de Lloc, Otuzco, Lucma, Marmot, and Huamachuco. These and others published by Ana Sánchez, Mario Polia Meconi, and Pierre Duviols form a rich documentary corpus for a more general history of popular religiousity and thinking that awaits an author.

335 Latin American Indian Literatures Association. Symposium. 17th, Columbus, Ohio, 2006. Ensayos de cultura virreinal latinoamericana. Edición de Juan Zevallos-Aguilar y Takahiro Kato y Luis Millones. Lima: Fondo Editorial de la

Facultad de Ciencias Sociales, UNMSM, 2006. 218 p.: bibl., ill. (chiefly col.).

An edited book with interesting chapters on native uses and understanding of Catholicism and its practices on a Mexican frontier; the resistance to Catholic conversion in the *Anales* of Juan Bautista Muñoz, a tribute collector in the zone of Moyotlán (Mexico); the significance of green stone in Amazonia, Colombia, and Mesoamerica; Titu Cusi Yupanqui as seen through a previously unpublished letter; the political and ideological meaning of the play *Apu Ollantay*; the drawings of Bishop Baltazar Jaime Martínez Compañón; the chronicle of Garcilaso de la Vega; and the adaptation of writing and its consequences by Nahua speakers of Mexico as epitomized by José Alvarado Tezozómoc and Domingo Francisco de San Antón Muñón Chimalpahin.

336 Lequernaqué, Jorge Pável Elías. Don Sebastián de Colán y Pariñas y sus ancestros: caciques de dos pueblos indígenas de la costa del corregimiento de Piura, siglos XVI–XVII. (*Bull. Inst. fr. étud. andin.*, 37:1, 2008, p. 151–161, bibl.)

An essay on the social and economic behavior of the caciques of the population of Colan (Department of Piura) during the 16th and 17th centuries. The author focuses on the dual role that the cacique played in viceregal society, mediating between his followers and Crown officials.

337 Lozada Pereira, Blithz. Cosmovisión, historia y política en los Andes. La Paz: Producciones CIMA, 2007. 320 p.: bibl., ill., maps (Col. de la Maestría en historias andinas y amazónicas; 8)

A study of the worldview of Andeans as a reflection of culture from its origins to the present with particular reference to Bolivia. The author discusses representations of territory, concepts of ethnicity, political thought, reciprocity, verticality, Andean deities, and ritual. Notable are his ideas on cyclical time and history as a "pachacuti" (great change or reform, crisis, or renewal). The election of President Evo Morales is explained as part of a trajectory of social conflicts that started in colonial times.

338 Mandrini, Raúl J. La Argentina aborigen: de los primeros pobladores a 1910. Buenos Aires: Siglo Veintiuno Editores, 2008. 287 p.: bibl., ill., maps (Biblioteca básica de historia)

A basic, unfootnoted textbook on the original populations of what is today Argentina from circa 12,000 B.C.E. with chapters on hunters and gatherers, the agricultural revolution, pottery, specialization, chieftancies, the Inca conquest, the Spanish colonial era, the rise of the state, and native reactions. The bibliography is short and fundamental.

339 Mantha, Alexis. Territoriality, social boundaries and ancestry veneration in the Central Andes of Peru. (*J. Anthropol. Archaeol.*, 28:2, June 2009, p. 158–176)

The author argues that the distribution of various types of above-ground mortuary structures across the landscape was a powerful mechanism of social control that not only served to assess territorial rights, but also to confine or exclude people by the delimiting social boundaries. Furthermore, above-ground structures reflected a growing concern for territorial behaviors during the late intermediate period that allowed household members, kinship groups, and/or political units to draw social boundaries between insiders and outsiders by reifying identity and social solidarity through ancestor worship. This argument overlooks much recent research on *ocupación salpicada*; status ranking as a reflection of numbers of followers; population movements through time and space (sometimes carrying their ancestors or their representations); and the meaning of the terms *marcayoc* and *llactayoc*, and *chullpas* as genealogical markers (not territorial ones).

340 Marcos, Jorge G. Los pueblos navegantes del Ecuador prehispánico. Quito: Abya-Yala: ESPOL, 2005. 206 p.: ill., maps (some col.)

A book on prehispanic mariners of Ecuador. The first part reviews the historiography on the "discovery" of America with special focus on the Andean coast, citing such chroniclers as Pedro Cieza de León, Agustín Zárate, and Francisco de Xerez. In the second part, the author reviews the history of settlement. In the third section, the author discusses the Spondylus Princeps and Strombus Peruvianus as offerings for rain, beginning with the Valdivia culture of coastal Ecuador and spreading toward the Central Andes and north into Mesoamerica.

341 Martín Rubio, María del Carmen. Buscando a un Inca: la cripta de Topa Amaro. (*Investig. Soc./San Marcos*, 15, dic. 2005, p. 77–108, bibl.)

An article based on documentary sources that suggest the resting place of Topa Amaro, the last ruler of Vilcabamba. The author summarizes the architectural history of the Qorikancha (Temple of the Sun) where the remains of the Inca were buried. She discusses the excavations (that date from John Rowe's dig of 1942) and other efforts to find the tomb of this important ruler. Four documents (the earliest dating to 1572) are included in an Appendix. The key piece of evidence is a 1645 petition and testimony that the Inca was buried in the Convento of Santo Domingo that was built atop the Qorikancha.

342 Mathis, Sophia. Vicente Mora Chimo, de "indio principal" a "Procurador General de los Indios del Perú": cambio de legitimidad del poder autóctono a principios del siglo XVIII. (*Bull. Inst. fr. étud. andin.*, 37:1, 2008, p. 199–215, bibl.)

An analysis of the life of Vicente Mora Chimo, descendant of caciques settled in the Chicama Valley (Trujillo, Peru) that shows how the natives' autochthonous power acquired new bases of legitimacy in the first half of the 18th century. The author follows the native leader from "principal" from the community of Santiago de Cao to becoming Attorney General who could exert power from Spain. He assimilated the rules of colonial justice to defend the Indians and thus gain their trust and recognition. He presented a "Manifesto of the offences damages, prejudices, humiliations, evils, and troubles suffered by the Indians of Peru" to the Council of the Indies in 1732. He thus helped reformulate power at an imperial level.

343 Mello, Amílcar d'Avila de. Expedições: Santa Catarina na era dos descobrimentos geográficos. v. 1, Exploração e conquista, 1501–1542. v. 2, Colonização e abandono, 1550–1658. v. 3, Crônicas das origens. Florianópolis: Editora Expressão, 2005. 3 v.: bibl., ill. (chiefly col.), maps (some col.), facsims.

The first volume of a handsome, beautifully illustrated three-tome boxed set on the exploration and conquest of Santa Catarina from 1501–42 by an author who has published on the naval history of Brazil. Based on primary sources, it contributes to knowledge about relations between the newly arrived Europeans and native peoples. The first chapters deal with peninsular history, European maritime expansion, and maritime technology, followed by texts on colonial administration, natives, and the expeditions of Américo Vespúcio, Binot Paulmier de Gonneville, João de Lisboa, João Dias de Solis, Cristóvão Jaques, Garcia Maratya, Frei Francisco Gracía Jofre de Loaysa, Sebastián Caboto, Diego Garcia de Moguer, and Martim Afonso de Sousa. The second volume reviews colonization efforts in the middle of the 16th century against a backdrop of jurisdictional disputes between Spain and Portugal and the ascendance of British power. The exploits of dom Diego de Sanabria (1500–56), Jaime Rasquín (1559), Juan Ortiz de Zárate (1572–73), Diego Flores de Valdés and Pedro Sarmiento de Gamboa (1582–90), Edward Fenton (1582–83), Richard Hawkins (1593–94), and dom Diego Rodríguez Valdés y de la Banda (1598) are summarized. Of special interest for scholars is a list defining measures and measurements used in the 16th century, a discussion introducing currencies used, and the names of passengers who arrived between 1550–1600. The third and last of the volumes features a chapter on toponyms and lengthy overviews of the writings of chroniclers who describe the area, including Binot Paulmier de Gonneville, Antonio de Herrera y Tordesillas, Martín Fernández de Enciso, dom Rodrigo de Acuña, Francisco Dávila, Martín Méndez, Sebastião Caboto, Luis Ramírez, Roger Barlow, Francisco López de Gómara, Alvar Núñez Cabeza de Vaca, Gonzalo F. de Oviedo y Valdés, Padre Manuel da Nóbrega, Hans Staden, Theodore de Bry, Juan López de Velasco, Luke Ward, João Pinto, Pedro Sarmiento de Gamboa, and Richard Hakluyt, among others.

344 Millones, Luis. Perú indígena: poder y religión en los Andes centrales. Lima: Fondo Editorial del Congreso del Perú, 2008. 207 p.: bibl., col. ill., col. map.

A panoramic overview of native Peru by Luis Millones, an established anthropologist and historian. In trying to define "native" and write about ethnic identity, he writes about prehispanic religion and Catholic evangelization, as well as the perception and description of native societies by Spanish and Creole conquerors, priests, and bureaucrats. He also explores how European travelers, Jorge Juan and Antonio de Ulloa, Alexander von Humboldt, and Juan Jacobo von Tschudi among them, described the indigenous populations that they encountered. Elsewhere, he compares the vision of native chroniclers to that of indigenista intellectuals in the early 20th century and explores indigenous relations with the nation-state, highlighting the construction of stereotypes and prejudices. In so doing, this book underscores the richness of native cultures and traditions over the centuries.

345 Montes, Aníbal. Indígenas y conquistadores de Córdoba. Compilación de Carlos J. Freytag. Buenos Aires: Ediciones Isquitipe, 2008. 669 p.: maps.

A valuable book on the conquest of the peoples of what is today Córdoba Province (Argentina) written by a military man and topographer and put together after his death from typed originals with the help of an index dated 1952. The author aimed to correct historical errors regarding the native inhabitants by publishing documents from the Archivo Histórico de Córdoba and the Archivo de Catastro, especially court cases involving land ownership disputes between Indians and conquerors, and surveys of Spanish haciendas. The author describes the native inhabitants, the founding of Córdoba, the conquerors and encomenderos, the reducciones, and the establishment of haciendas. Throughout, he quotes from and transcribes primary documents to support his statements. Of value to future investigators is his list of Mercedes (Chapter 44), his register of encomiendas, and a huge list of native toponyms found in the documents he reviewed.

346 Moscoso, Martha. El sistema de autoridad indígena en el corregimiento de Cuenca. (*Procesos/Quito*, 25, primer semestre 2007, p. 159–162)

A summary of the book on colonial Cuenca, *Mosaico indígena* by Jacques Poloni-Simard. The attention here is on native authorities and how they changed during three centuries of colonial rule. The author concludes that native lords adopt and use colonial institutions to protect their interests until the 18th century when native cabildos often rob the lords of their power and influence.

347 Mukerjee, Anil. La negociación de un compromiso: la mita de las minas de plata de San Agustín de Huantajaya, Tarapacá, Perú, 1756–1766. (*Bull. Inst. fr. étud. andin.*, 37:1, 2008, p. 217–225, bibl.)

A valuable analysis of the mining mita in Huantajaya, the only mining area in the viceroyalty that was not located in the Andes. The author finds that the efforts of the curacas of Tarapacá prevented the mining mita from being implemented. The work is based on a mine owner's registry that recorded the sometimes daily exchange of letters between the mine owner and the native lords.

Murúa, Martín de. Historia general del Piru: facsimile of J. Paul Getty Museum Ms. Ludwig XIII 16. See item **1431.**

New world, first nations: native peoples of Mesoamerica and the Andes under colonial rule. See item **1432.**

348 Nowack, Kerstin. Las mercedes que pedía para su salida: the Vilcabamba Inca and the Spanish state, 1539–1572. (*in* New world, first nations: native peoples of Mesoamerica and the Andes under colonial rule. Edited by David Cahill and Blanca Tovías. Brighton, England; Portland, Or.: Sussex Academic Press, 2006, p.57–91, bibl.)

A perceptive and detailed article, characteristic of this author, on the negotiations and circumstances surrounding the end of Inca rule over the Vilcabamba alternative state in the Andes of the 16th century. The author discusses Manco Inca, Sayri Tupac (Manco Inca's son), Titu Cusi, and Tupac Amaru. Viceroy Francisco Toledo proved ruthless, authoritarian, and cynical in his dealings with the Inca, but respected the treaty concluded by Garia de Castro and ratified by the King. The author concludes that Inca independence in Vilcabamba was inevitable. The Inca refuge fell victim to a changing Realpolitik and the Incas' short-sightedness and inability to control their own followers.

349 Ogburn, Dennis Edward. Becoming Saraguro: ethnogenesis in the context of Inca and Spanish colonialism. (*Ethnohistory/Columbus*, 55:2, Spring 2008, p. 287–319, bibl., ill.)

An article that hypothesizes that the Incas reinforced ethnic identity and vertical relations with the state to prevent unity and resistance, while the Spanish downplayed ethnic identity to create a homogeneous underclass of "Indians" to serve them. The research suffers from too literal a reading of the chronicles and reliance on dated secondary sources. Furthermore, the author's definition of *doctrina* overlooks the fact that Viceroy Francisco de Toledo defined it as a rural parish made up of 400 native household heads, i.e., it was not geographically defined. Finally, his discussion of territoriality (even porous territoriality) contradicts the multi-ethnicity of the local populations.

350 Ogburn, Dennis Edward. Power in stone: the long-distance movement of building block in the Inca Empire. (*Ethnohistory/Columbus*, 51:1, Winter 2004, p. 101–135, bibl., ill.)

An article that analyzes the objectives and implications of the long-distance transport of building blocks in the Inca Empire based on both archeology and Spanish and native reports. Chronicles relate that the Incas transported building stones over great distances, e.g., from a major southern stone quarry to Ecuador. These stones and their movement embodied the sanctity and power of the ruler and demonstrated publicly the momentous state control over labor. For ethnographer's comment, see *HLAS 63:330*.

Pachacamac. See *HLAS 65:458*.

351 Pärssinen, Martti and Jukka Kivi-harju. Textos andinos. t. 1, Corpus de textos "khipu" incaicos y coloniales. Madrid: Instituto Iberoamericano de Finlandia: Departamento de Filología, Univ. Complutense de Madrid, 2004. 1 v.: ill. (Acta Ibero-americana Fennica. Series Hispano-americano; 6)

A wonderful book of primary sources all connected to the *quipu* (or *khipu*) and early accounting methods in the Andes. This system of knotted and colorful strings served to convey inventories, population counts, and tribute. The book contains transcriptions of Inca *quipus* that were orally transmitted to Spanish notaries for inclusion and transcribed in Spanish texts dated between 1535 and 1653. The texts include petitions, census counts, tribute lists, encomienda grants, and reports. A second volume of specialized papers on the *quipu*, more transcribed texts, and an index to both volumes is forthcoming.

352 Passes, Alan. The gathering of the clans: the making of the Palikur naoné. (*Ethnohistory/Columbus*, 51:2, Spring 2004, p. 257–291, bibl., maps)

An article concerned with the historical creation, composition, and renewal of the Palikur nation or ethnicity from the beginning of the 16th century onward. It describes how various clans combined with other ethnic entities to create, at its height (c. 1800), a dominant regional polity, linked to wider cross-ethnic macro-polities under a single leader. These confederations were a response to new circumstances and the renewal of a preconquest sociopolitical strategy. The author also writes of the chief's skills as a peacemaker and a warmonger.

353 Pérez Galán, Beatriz. Alcaldes y kurakas: origen y significado cultural de la fila de autoridades indígenas en Pisac—Calca, Cuzco. (*Bull. Inst. fr. étud. andin.*, 37:1, 2008, p. 245–255, bibl.)

An article that discusses the origin and social-cultural meaning of the system of traditional authorities present in the indigenous communities of the district of Pisac. The author explores the revalidating historical process experienced by these Andean authorities and its relationship to the hereditary system of *curacazgos* that was commonplace during the colonial period. The author uses the Corpus celebration to illustrate her points.

Pineda Camacho, Roberto. Historia, metamorfosis y poder en la orfebrería prehispánica de Colombia. See *HLAS 65:420*.

354 Poloni-Simard, Jacques. El oficio del historiador y la sociedad colonial. (*Procesos/Quito*, 25, primer semestre 2007, p. 163–166)

The printed version of a speech that the author gave on the occasion of the presentation of his book, *El mosaico indígena*. He notes that it began as his dissertation and is based on two years of residence and research in the archives of Quito and Cuenca. His object was to give voice and agency to natives and understand and explain the complexity of their lives under Spanish colonial rule.

355 Qaraqara-Charka: mallku, inka y rey en la provincia de Charcas, siglos XV–XVII: historia antropológica de una confederación aymara. Edición documental y ensayos interpretativos de Tristán Platt, Thérèse Bouysse-Cassagne y Olivia Harris con el aliento de Thierra Saignes. Lima: Instituto Francés de Estudios Andinos (IFEA); La Paz: Plural editores, 2006. 1088 p.: bibl., ill. (some col.), indexes.

A monumental, important, and long-awaited book on the Quarqura and the Charka, two large Aymará-speaking chieftainships. The analyses and primary documents presented here refer to the period before Inca domination and are organized around such mega-themes as the cult, encomienda, tribute, land tenure, and native authorities. The book is enriched with tables, figures, maps, pictures, and extensive bibliography. For those unable to study all of the over thousand pages, the editors provide indexes to units of native organization (*ayllus, parcialidades*), as well as the more familiar indexes by name, theme, and geographical location.

356 Quispe-Agnoli, Rocío. La fe andina en la escritura: resistencia e identidad en la obra de Guamán Poma de Ayala. Presentación de Carmen Arellano Hoffmann. Lima: Univ. Nacional Mayor de San Marcos, 2006. 333 p.: bibl., ill. (Serie Coediciones)

A literary analysis of the early-17th century chronicle. The author concludes that Guamán Poma de Ayala used the dominant Spanish ideology and forms of expression to present "lo andino" and to remedy the pain that colonialism caused native peoples. Finds that there existed native forms of communication and recorded expression that are equivalent to alphabetic writing.

357 Radding Murrieta, Cynthia. Landscapes of power and identity: comparative histories in the Sonoran desert and the forests of Amazonia from colony to republic. Durham: Duke University Press, 2005. 431 p.: bibl., index.

An innovative comparative history of two societies on the frontiers of the Spanish empire—the Sonora region of northwestern Mexico and the Chiquitos region of eastern Bolivia's lowlands from the late colonial period through the middle of the 19th century. This environmental and cultural history considers the relationships between human societies and the geographical landscapes they inhabit and create. The author demonstrates how colonial encounters were conditioned by both landscape and cultural expectations: how the colonizers and colonized understood notions of territory and property; how religion influenced culture and memories; and how conflict between indigenous inhabitants and Creole societies evolved.

358 Radicati di Primeglio, Carlos. Estudios sobre los quipus. Compilación y estudio introductorio de Gary Urton. Lima: Fondo Editorial Univ. Nacional Mayor de San Marcos, 2006. 408 p.: bibl., ill. (Clásicos sanmarquinos.)

A book of the collected work and essays by a student of the Andean past and especially of the *quipu* (*khipu*). Included are an introduction to the study of the *quipu* (1951); an essay on "seriation," the presence of groupings or series of strings and knots of different colors, that he believes to be a key to understanding the *quipu* "ideográfico" (1964); a work on the accounting system of the *quipu* (1979); and another on the *quilca* (or *quelca*) (1984). This book should be read before reading Gary Urton's book *Signs of the Inka Khipu* (see *HLAS 62:372*). Such an ordering will help appreciate how *quipu* studies have evolved over the last 50 years or so.

Ramírez, Susan E. The cosmological bases of local power in the Andes during the sixteenth and seventeenth centuries. See item **1443**.

359   Ramos Gómez, Luis Javier. Las vasijas de madera ornamentadas con laca utilizadas por los dirigentes andinos de la época colonial: función y tipología de sus formas. (*Rev. Esp. Antropol. Am.*, 36:1, 2006, p. 85–119, bibl., photos)

An illustrated article that discusses the wooden beakers or vessels used during colonial times. After a discussion of the types of vessels (vasos, pajchas) based on a review of the literature, the author proposes an additional type.

360   Ravi Mumford, Jeremy. Litigation as ethnography in sixteenth-century Peru: Polo de Ondegardo and the Mitimaes. (*HAHR*, 88:1, Feb. 2008, p. 5–40, maps)

A deep analysis of two 16th-century Peruvian cases illustrates the use of court records as ethnographic evidence. The author is interested less in Andean social and legal ideas for their own sake than in how colonial lawsuits engaged or did not engage those ideas. The cases he investigates involve the Andean concepts of duality and complementarity, and the special status of people called *mitimaes*. He concludes that "litigation was not in general a field for ethnography" (p. 38). Spanish colonial institutions were not able to consistently apply indigenous law and concepts to native Andean peoples. Yet, when the circumstances were right, the adversarial context of litigation could be a strong stimulus for ethnography, though it was often self-interested, tentative, and partial. In the end, certain Andean legal concepts that Spaniards considered alien to their own law and that opposed some of their most dearly held political ideas became firmly lodged in colonial legal thought.

Río, María de las Mercedes del. Etnicidad, territorialidad y colonialismo en los Andes: tradición y cambio entre los Soras de los siglos XVI y XVII (Bolivia). See item **1467**.

361   Robledo, Víctor Hugo. La Rioja indígena: origen, conquista y persistencia. La Rioja, Argentina: Nexo Ediciones, 2007. 551 p.: bibl., ill. (Nueva historia de La Rioja)

The first of a projected multi-volume history of La Rioja, Argentina. The volume begins with hunters and gathers and ends in the early 19th century. Some of the cultures and peoples mentioned are the Ampajango,

Aycimpitín, Saujil, Condorhuasi, Cienaga, Diaguitas, Olongasta, Araucos, and Incas. The colonial era begins with the invasion of the Spanish. Land tenure, tribute, ritual, resistance, and the rebellion of Tupac Amaru are discussed with detailed examinations of specific towns, fields, and ranches. This work is based on both primary and secondary sources. The former come from local as well as overseas archives.

362   Rodríguez, Lorena. Después de las desnaturalizaciones: transformaciones socio-económicas y étnicas al sur del valle Calchaquí, Santa María, fines del siglo XVII—fines del XVIII. Buenos Aires: Editorial Antropofagia, 2008. 253 p.: bibl., ill., maps.

A serious book that retells the history of the native population of the Santa María Valley (Argentina) from the late 17th-century Calchaquíes War to the last years of the 18th century. The story of compulsory relocation and the consequent social, economic, and ethnic reconfiguration of the native population touches on the subjects of land tenure, economic production, and ethnic classification.

363   Rodríguez Cuenca, José Vicente. Pueblos, rituales y condiciones de vida prehispánicas en el Valle del Cauca. Con la colaboración de Sonia Blanco y Alexander Clavijo. Bogotá: Univ. Nacional de Colombia, 2005. 212 p.: bibl., ill. (some col.), maps (1 col.)

An archeological study of the peoples of the Cauca Valley. The author finds that they developed ingenious adaptive strategies to balance their needs with the available resources. Separate chapters review the people, their customs—especially in regard to burial, prehispanic diseases, and demographic trends.

364   Rossignol, Jacques. Chilenos y mapuches a mediados del siglo XIX: una situación colonial: estudios históricos. Compilación de Raúl Guerrero. Concepción, Chile: Centro de Estudios Urbanos Regionales, Univ. del Bío-Bío: Ediciones Universidad del Bío-Bío, 2007. 246 p.: bibl., ill., maps.

The publication of articles and parts of a thesis of Jacques Rossigual (1931–97) who resided in Chile from 1966–71. The selection includes interdisciplinary writings on methodology, Araucanian Indians in the middle of the 19th century, and a social history of the borderlands that expands to treat native Pehuenches, Abajinas, Arribanas, and Huilliches. The valuable Appendices include census data from as early as 1812 and a table with the names of caciques and reducciones.

365 Rostworowski de Diez Canseco, María. Ensayos de historia andina. Vol. 2, Pampas de Nasca, género, hechicería. 2. ed. Lima: IEP, 2006. 1 v.: ill., maps (Obras completas de María Rostworowski; 6) (Serie Historia andina, 34)

Another volume of the complete works of the noted Peruvian ethnohistorian María Rostworowski. This volume includes nine studies on such diverse topics as the Nazca lines, idolatry, migration, irrigation systems, ritual, and a critical analysis of the data in Inca Garcilaso de la Vegas' 17th-century chronicle. The studies are based solidly on primary sources. For comment on Vol. 1, *Elites, etnías, recursos*, see *HLAS 56:640.* Also see by the same author, item **366.**

366 Rostworowski de Diez Canseco, María. Pachacamac y el Señor de los Milagros: una trayectoria melenaria; Señorios indígenas de Lima y Canta. Lima: Instituto de Estudios Peruanos, 2002. 404 p.: bibl., col. ill., maps (Historia andina; 25) (Obras completas; 2)

The second volume of the *Obras completas* [Complete Works] of the Peruvian ethnohistorian María Rostworowski. The book includes three studies of chieftainships in what is now the Department of Lima during the late prehispanic and early colonial times. The three formed a large ethnic group around the chieftainship of Ichsma. The three studies are: Pachacamac and the Señor de los Milagros; the Señorío de Pachacamac; and the Señoríos of Lima and Canta.

367 Roulet, Florencia. Con la pluma y la palabra: el lado oscuro de las negociaciones de paz entre españoles e indígenas. (*Rev. Indias*, 64:231, mayo/agosto 2004, p. 313–348, bibl.)

A thoughtful article dealing with the diplomatic negotiations between indigenous peoples and the Spanish colonial state in the last two decades of the 18th century in the southern frontier of Mendoza (Argentina). The author shows that peace treaties do not accurately reflect the negotiations, accords, and understandings of the two parties. Records of the oral discussions between the parties prove that treaties must be kept in context to fully understand the interests of the contenders.

368 Rueda Enciso, José Eduardo. La representación pública de América en las crónicas de Indias. Colombia: Escuela Superior de Administración Pública, Instituto de Investigaciones, 2004. 57 p.: bibl. (Serie de documentos. Pensamiento administrativo público, 2)

A brief and unique effort to reread the colonial chronicles on Colombia from a public administration perspective, focusing on native populations and the environment. Among the chronicles analyzed are those of Bartolomé de las Casas, Juan de Castellanos, Pedro de Cieza de León, Fray Pedro de Aguado, and Juan Rodríguez Freyle.

Salazar-Soler, Carmen. La presencia de la antropología francesca en los Andes peruanos. See *HLAS 65:461.*

369 Salles, Estela Cristina and Héctor Omar Noejovich Ch. La herencia femenina andina prehispánica y su transformación en el mundo colonial. (*Bull. Inst. fr. étud. andin.*, 35:1, 2006, p. 37–53)

A thoughtful, short essay on female inheritance of power and goods in the prehispanic and Spanish colonial Andes, respectively. The authors discuss *capullanas* of the north coast, female cacicas, the *collana-payan-cayao* tripartition, and positional inheritance. Viewpoint—native or Spanish—is important to their analysis.

370 Schjellerup, Inge. Sacando a los caciques de la oscuridad del olvido: étnias chachapoya y chilcho. (*Bull. Inst. fr. étud. andin.*, 37:1, 2008, p. 111–122, bibl.)

An article that highlights specific 16th-century examples of ethnic groups in the Chachapoyas and Huallaga regions, based on anthropological and archeological fieldwork as well as research in Peruvian historical archives. Alonso de Alvarado and Juan Pérez de Guevara are two actors discussed.

371 Schroedl, Annette. La capacocha como ritual político: negociaciones en torno al poder entre Cuzco y los curacas. (*Bull. Inst. fr. étud. andin.*, 37:1, 2008, p. 19–27, bibl.)

An article on the function of political rituals in the Inca state through the analysis of the Capacocha ritual cycle. The author's analysis of this ritual highlights the establishment or reaffirmation of relations between the Inca and local elites, especially with the curacas.

372 Serulnikov, Sergio. The politics of intracommunity land conflict in the late colonial Andes. (*Ethnohistory/Columbus*, 55:1, Winter 2008, p. 119–152, tables)

A well-documented article that explores the causes, ideological underpinnings, and political consequences of conflict over land among the Pocoata, an ethnic group in the southern Andes, during the 18th century. The competing native concepts of land tenure; the legal and extralegal means of solving disputes; and the key roles of caciques are discussed. The author argues that the inability of caciques to handle demographic pressure and intra-ethnic strife led to a disruption of rural authority.

373 Sotomayor, María Lucía. Cofradías, caciques y mayordomos: reconstrucción social y reorganización política en los pueblos de indios, siglo XVIII. Bogotá: Instituto Colombiano de Antropología e Historia, 2004. 227 p.: bibl., ill., map. (Col. Cuadernos coloniales; 12)

A study of the *cofradía* as a religious institution in *pueblos de indios* (Indian towns) in the region of Sogamoso (Boyacá), and especially in the native centers of Cuítiva, Iza, and Pesca. The author argues that the *cofradía* (religious brotherhood) became a mechanism that both represented its members and allowed them to participate in colonial society. The *cofradía*, she concludes, functioned to restructure the *pueblos de indios* religiously, politically, economically, and socially. The research is based solidly on material in parish and national archives and published primary and secondary sources.

374 Stavig, Will. Túpac Amaru, the body politic, and the embodiment of hope: Inca heritage and social justice in the Andes. (*in* Death, dismemberment, and memory: body politics in Latin America. Edited by Lyman L. Johnson. Albuquerque: Univ. of New Mexico Press, 2004, p. 27–62, ill., photos)

An interesting article that relates the history of the first Tupac Amaru with that of the second, the (in)famous leader of a massive rebellion in the 1780s, and their legacy down to the election of President Alejandro Toledo. The Inkarrí and resurrection are discussed. This paper is based mostly on secondary sources and is interpretive, rather than strictly original research.

375 Tarragó, Rafael Emilio. Los kurakas: una bibliografía anotada (1609–2005) de fuentes impresas sobre los señores andinos en Perú y Alto Perú entre 1533 y 1825. Madrid: Instituto de Cultura, Fundación Mapfre, 2006. 68 p.: indexes. (Documentos Tavera; 21)

An indispensable research tool for investigators of native authority in the precolumbian and colonial Andes. Fifty-four publications are reviewed for studies of the curaca. Helpful indices are included.

376 Teijeiro, José. La rebelión permanente: crisis de identidad y persistencia étnico-cultural aymara en Bolivia. La Paz: PIEB: Plural, 2007. 310 p.: bibl., ill., maps.

The author analyzes Aymara resistance since colonial times to elaborate a sense of ethnic identity ("etnicidad hacia adentro") based on cultural and religious practices in an effort to reconfirm "lo propio" and "lo aymará." Open rebellions (Tupac Katari and Zarate Willka), the author argues, are just the most obvious forms of resistance.

377 Testamentos indígenas de Santafé de Bogotá, siglos XVI–XVII. Edición y prólogo de Pablo Rodríguez Jiménez. Bogotá: Alcaldía Mayor de Bogotá: Instituto Distrital Cultura y Turismo: Observatorio de Cultura Urbana, 2002. 326 p.: bibl., ill. (some col.), index, map.

A compilation of native wills from 16th- and 17th-century Bogota of testators who came from Tunja, Chivatá, Suba, Ibagué, Riobamba, Cartago, Quito, and other places. Most are of commoners; a few are of caciques or gobernadores. As a corpus, they give silent testimony to notions of religiousity, migration, family life, values, and the interdependence that characterized colonial life.

378 Time and memory in indigenous Amazonia: anthropological perspectives. Edited by Carlos Fausto and Michael Heckenberger. Gainesville, FL: Univ. Press of Florida, 2007. 322 p.: bibl., ill., indexes, maps.

This book is about Lowland South American Indians and their sense of history. Various chapters deal with different indigenous historicities, on the meaning and connotations of such concepts as time, memory, and change from the native point of view. Overall it destroys the stereotype of the unchanging "Indian" who lives constantly in the present, reproducing himself identically over and over again through the generations. The methodology, conclusions, and research quality of the book merits a wide audience not limited to those studying South American Indians.

379 Towle, Margaret Ashley. The ethnobotany of pre-Columbian Peru. New Brunswick, N.J.: AldineTransaction, 2007. 180 p., 15 p. of plates: bib., ill., index, map.

A useful volume that categorizes plant material by region (e.g., North Coast, Central Coast, Highlands) and by era (e.g., epoch of pre-agriculture; incipient agriculture; formative; kingdoms and confederacies, etc.). It includes plates showing some plant remains and effigy jars depicting the same.

380 Ullán de la Rosa, Francisco Javier. La construcción del *indio domesticado* como categoría social y cognitiva entre los ticuna: para una psicología social de las relaciones de dominación en el alto Amazonas. (*Rev. Esp. Antropol. Am.,* 36:1, 2006, p. 183–504, bibl.)

An article that explores the reciprocal perceptions of "the other" that natives and Westerners developed during the process of colonial domination. The author contends that the Ticuna accepted domination and internalized the stereotypical image, created by Europeans, of the native as an inferior, adapting it to their own worldview. This generated a native complex of subordination that in turn made Europeans superior. This attitude functioned as a mechanism of indirect social control, allowing a small elite of colonial masters to govern a great number of natives without resorting constantly to physical coercion. Subordination and deliverance were reinterpreted in

terms of the supernatural. Thus, political and military resistance movements did not occur, although Ticuna history is sprinkled with millenarianist movements.

381 Uzendoski, Michael A. The horizontal archipelago: the Quijos/Upper Napo regional system. (*Ethnohistory/Columbus,* 51:2, Spring 2004, p. 317–357, bibl., ill., map)

An article that examines long-distance exchange, markets, and horizontality (a horizontal archipelago vis-à-vis a vertical one as described by John V. Murra) as significant aspects of social organization in the Quijos/Upper Napo region of the western Amazonian frontier at or just after the time of contact. The author argues that local and regional exchanges followed a social logic where human transactions such as marriage, adoption, and/or co-parenthood occupied the highest tier of value in the circulation process. Marriage and exchange, in particular, are examined as a way of "making kin." These principles are explored through an analysis of ethnohistorical sources and data from fieldwork in contemporary Upper Napo communities.

382 Valdivia Carrasco, Julio C. Los reyes inkas del Perú. Lambayeque, Peru: Univ. Nacional Pedro Ruiz Gallo, Facultad de Ciencias Histórico Sociales y Educación; Lima: Hermeneia Editores, 2008. 467 p.: bibl.

A straightforward, traditional history of the Incas, based on Spanish chronicles and secondary sources. The author offers a literal and chronological account of the development of the Inca state, divided into two eras: pre-imperial and imperial. The story is told through the biographies of the Inca kings. No systematic acknowledgment of inconsistencies and contradictions in the sources is included.

383 Valencia Espinoza, Abraham. Cuzco religioso. Cusco: Instituto Nacional de Cultura, Dirección Regional de Cultura de Cusco, 2007. 746 p.: bibl., ill.

A volume that unites 10 of the author's previously published works, centering on religiosity in Cuzco. "Taytacha Temblores" (1991) touches on the crisis of the clergy, the loss of jewels and relics from local churches, and the impact of tourism on convents and monasteries. The "Niño Compadrito" cult is contextualized and explained as an expression of popular religiousity. Other studies focus on Saqsaywaman, the "wak'a de suyu" and its multiple representations; the god Wiraqocha; the site of Ollantaytambo, the Qanchi Dance, the coca used in Chiaraqhe rituals, and the Rumitaqe battles of 1921 in Canas.

384 Vega, Garcilaso de la. Comentarios reales de los incas. Prólogo y cronología de Ricardo González Vigil. Cuidado de la edición de Daniel Dillon Alvarez. Lima: Univ. Inca Garcilaso de la Vega, 2007. 885 p.: bibl. (Serie Clásicos)

Another edition of the *Comentarios Reales* of Garcilaso de la Vega, the early 17th-century chronicler of Peru. This is a chronicle that has both historical and literary merit. The author was the son of a Spanish nobleman and a native woman. This work presents the Incas in a sympathetic light.

385 Vega, Garcilaso de la. Royal commentaries of the Incas and general history of Peru. Translated by Harold V. Livermore. Edited, with an introduction by Karen Spalding. Abridged. Indianapolis: Hackett Pub. Co., 2006. 232 p.: bibl., maps.

An abridged and translated version of the Royal Commentaries by the famed mestizo chronicler Garcilaso de la Vega. The sections are well-selected and the book as a whole is particularly well-suited for classroom use. Karen Spalding wrote an introduction that situates the work in its intellectual, historical, and cultural contexts.

386 Villarías-Robles, Juan J. R. La antropología posmoderna: una reflexión desde la etnohistoria peruanista. (*Rev. Dialectolog. Tradic. Pop.*, 63:1, enero/junio 2008, p. 37–74, bibl.)

A thoughtful article on post-modernism as applied to ethnohistory, using some examples from chronicles. The author argues that the post-modern perspective is not entirely new, but can be traced back to the beginning of the field itself.

387 Wołoszyn, Janusz Z. Los rostros silenciosos: los huacos retrato de la cultura moche. Traducción de Francisco Javier Villaverde González. Lima: Fondo Editorial, Pontificia Univ. Católica del Perú, 2008. 367 p.: ill. (some col.) (Col. Estudios andinos; 4)

An invaluable addition to knowledge on the Moche culture through a detailed study of pottery portrait jars. Included in this volume is a discussion of previous research on the topic and notions of adornment. The text and photographs reveal facial features, headdresses, face-painting, and jewelry of women, prisoners, children, priests, men of Recuay, and Moche warriors. Some vessels are related to drawings showing quotidian activities.

Wright, Robin M. História indígena e do indigenismo no Alto Rio Negro. See *HLAS* 65:579.

388 Zuidema, R. Tom. El Inca y sus curacas: poliginia real y construcción del poder. (*Bull. Inst. fr. étud. andin.*, 37:1, 2008, p. 47–55, bibl.)

A study on the matrimonial, political, calendrical, ritual, and mythical relations that the descendants of the curacas—known as the "Incas-by-privilege"—had with the Inca. The author finds that the wives or sisters of these authorities, the señoras Iñaca, played an important role in these relations.

GENERAL HISTORY

JOHN BRITTON, *Gasque Professor of History, Francis Marion University*

AS WE MOVE THROUGH THE DECADE that marks the 200th anniversary of the Latin American revolutions for independence, the history of nations and nation-states continues to be an important theme. In this biennium, Forment's article emphasizes the role of Catholic values in the independence movements and 19th-century civic culture (item 416). Earle evaluates the role of the Native American image in elite nationalism from the independence era to the early 20th century (item 412). There are several edited volumes that follow this thematic trend. Editor Alonso's work (item 408) underscores the importance of the press in the formation of nation-states during the first century of independence. Palacios (item 535) and Mc Evoy and Stuven (item 555) edit collections on the social and cultural dimensions of nation-building in the 19th century. Vázquez and Miño Grijalva assemble a collection (item 540) that traces the roots of nation-states across the independence and early national periods. Editors Casaús Arzú and Pérez Ledesma (item 453) concentrate the essays in their volume on the development of governments during the 1890–1940 period while the contributors to Jáuregui's book (item 530) examine the crucial topic of government finances in the 19th century. The May 2008 issue of the *Hispanic American Historical Review* contains a stimulating exchange on the possible roots of some Spanish-American nation-states in the colonial era in an article by Irigoin and Grafe (item 433), commentary by Marichal (item 443) and Summerhill (item 462) with a rejoinder by Irigoin and Grafe (item 434). König (item 438) examines the complex nature of national identity, and González Manrique (item 421) authored a well-organized textbook structured around the evolution of nation-states in the region.

In recent years Atlantic history has taken its place as a distinctive field of study. Comparable to Braudel's conception of Mediterranean history, this approach emphasizes trade, transportation, communication, immigration, slavery, the environment, politics, and empire, and posits South America, the Caribbean, North America, Europe, and Africa as components of the Atlantic region. For several generations Latin American historians have studied the three and one-third centuries of interactions between and among Spain and Portugal and their empires in the Americas which constitute a very large slice of what is now termed Atlantic history. Perhaps it is appropriate to regard Atlantic history and Latin American history as complementary and overlapping fields that can benefit from scholarly cooperation and exchange. The following are some examples of the many intriguing studies that appeared in Atlantic history in this biennium. Games set the parameters for the field in an article in the *American Historical Review* in 2006 (item 419). Adelman's synthesis (item 390) emphasizes the transatlantic essence of the Spanish and Portuguese empires. Klooster's comparative study of revolutions (item 544) encompasses Haiti, Spanish America, North America, and France. Gould's article probes the interconnections of the Spanish and British colonial systems (item 423), while Guasco offers a comparative study of English and Spanish racial attitudes (item 490). The transatlantic character of slavery is a central theme in the recent study by Davis (item 411). Norton (item 502) expands upon the importance of tobacco and chocolate in her book. The growth of sugarcane cultivation on the Canary Islands and in the Americas is covered in a book edited by de Luxán Meléndez and Viña Brito (item 405), and Moya examines the changes in economic conditions and in transportation and communications technology that help explain immigration in the postcolonial era (item 448).

Latin America has played a large role in geopolitical rivalries and conflicts as several of the publications annotated in this volume attest. Subrahmanyam's article (item 516) examines the interactions of the Spanish and Portuguese empires in the early colonial era. The title of Blaufarb's article, "The Western Question: The Geopolitics of Latin American Independence" (item **523**), identifies a crucial period that is also discussed by Diego García (item **533**) and Delgado Ribas (item **532**). The place of the US in the Latin American geopolitical landscape is the subject of contributions by Armillas Vicente on Spanish-US relations in the independence era (item **521**) and Stagg's examination of the policies devised by James Madison in the borderlands (item **565**). Cassinello Pérez offers a survey of Spain's continued military presence in the 19th century (item **526**). O'Brien's text (item **449**) serves as a commentary on the role of the US in the hemisphere since independence. Rood's article (item **560**) discusses the British reformulation of the mechanics of imperialism in the mid-19th century. Editor Brown's collection of articles explores the informal imperialism of Great Britain that rivaled the influence of the US in the 19th century. Vargas Garcia (item **568**) and Knight (item **437**) annotated separately from Brown's edited volume, item **430**) discuss conceptual frameworks for understanding informal imperialism. Whitehead analyzes (item **549**) the imperial assumptions behind a sampling of 19th-century travel writing. The international intrigues surrounding the Spanish American War are documented in the book by Torruella (item **566**). Geopolitical conflicts were also prominent in 20th-century Latin America. Leonard's edited volume covers World War II (item **590**). Several scholars delve into the Cold War rivalries including the article by Pettinà (item **593**) and the books edited by Camacho Navarro (item **595**) and Joseph and Spenser (item **587**).

GENERAL

389 **Actores, representaciones e imaginarios: homenaje a François-Xavier Guerra.** Compilación de Jaime Peire. Tres de Febrero, Argentina: Editorial de la Univ. Nacional de Tres de Febrero, 2007. 282 p.: bibl. (Col. de estudios de historia cultural)

A productive combination of historiography, political theory, and specialized studies. Peire and DiCione's survey of Guerra's contributions to political history and Gonzalo Bernaldo de Quiros' essay on the role of "sociabilidad" in politics complement the four detailed examinations of early 19th-century Argentina and Chile.

390 **Adelman, Jeremy.** Sovereignty and revolution in the Iberian Atlantic. Princeton, N.J.: Princeton Univ. Press, 2006. 409 p.: bibl., index.

A well-conceived, nicely written synthesis of colonial and independence periods that goes beyond the provision of a convenient survey to explore the broader dimensions of the transatlantic nature of the Iberian empires. Of value to Latin Americanists and also to their cousins in the field of Atlantic or transatlantic studies. Strengthened by informative footnotes.

391 **Aftershocks: earthquakes and popular politics in Latin America.** Edited by Jürgen Buchenau and Lyman L. Johnson. Albuquerque: Univ. of New Mexico Press, 2009. 230 p.: bibl., ill., index, photos. (Diálogos)

This group of seven scholarly articles explores not only the earthquakes themselves but also their political, social, and economic consequences. Ranges chronologically from 1746 (Peru) to 1985 (Mexico). The contributions are written in a clear, direct style suitable for undergraduates but the research content has depth that will inform scholars as well. The editors' introduction provides insightful perspective.

392 **Aguirre, Carlos.** Prisons and prisoners in modernising Latin America, 1800–1940. (*in* Cultures of confinement: a history of the prison in Africa, Asia and Latin America. Edited by Frank Dikötter and Ian Brown. Ithaca, N.Y.: Cornell Univ. Press, 2007, p.14–54, bibl.)

Well-organized overview of the dismal, punitive nature of imprisonment in the 19th century and the emergence of prison reform in the early 20th century. Places prisons within their political and cultural environments.

393 Andrews, George Reid. Workers, soldiers, activists: black mobilization in Brazil and Spanish America, 1800–2000. (*Estud. Interdiscipl. Am. Lat. Carib.*, 19:1, enero/junio 2008)

Probing comparative examination of surges of mobilization and activism among blacks from the independence era through the late 20th century.

394 O anti-semitismo nas Américas: memória e história. Organização de Maria Luiza Tucci Carneiro. São Paulo: EDUSP, 2007. 737 p.: bibl., ill.

This collection of scholarly studies contains four articles on the colonial era and 20 essays on the 20th century, with an emphasis on Brazil. The studies are based on a mix of published material and archival sources. Two commendable comparative studies deal with anti-Semitism and populism in Argentina and Brazil and with Peru and Bolivia as countries of refuge during the Nazi period.

395 Aprendiendo de Latinoamérica: el museo como protagonista. Edición de María Luisa Bellido Gant. Asturias, Spain: Ediciones Trea, 2007. 381 p.: bibl., ill, photos. (Biblioteconomía y administración cultural; 161)

Fifteen informative essays discuss the role of museums in history and the presentation of history in museums. B/w photographs are helpful.

396 Árabes y judíos en América Latina: historia, representaciones y desafíos. Compilación de Ignacio Klich. Buenos Aires: Siglo XXI, 2006. 409 p.: bibl.

Countervailing tendencies of community building and social/cultural conflict are among the main themes in this well-researched volume of 16 scholarly essays. Broad coverage of late 19th and 20th centuries with concentrations on Argentina, Brazil, Mexico, and Chile.

397 Árabes y judíos en Iberoamérica: similitudes, diferencias y tensiones. Coordinación de Raanan Rein. Sevilla, Spain: Fundación Tres Culturas del Mediterráneo, 2008. 460 p. (Ánfora; 4)

Perceptive scholarly examinations of these two important minorities form the bases for this collection of 17 articles. Eight focus on Argentina, but Brazil, Mexico, and Cuba are also included. Rein's introductory essay provides a helpful orientation for the generalist.

398 Asociación Española de Americanistas. Simposio Internacional. *Santiago de Compostela, Spain, 2005.* De ida y vuelta: América y España: los caminos de la cultura. Edición a cargo de Pilar Cagiao Vila y Eduardo Rey Tristán. Santiago de Compostela, Spain: Univ. de Santiago de Compostela, 2007. 477 p.: bibl., ill. (Cursos e congresos da Universidade de Santiago de Compostela; 175)

An exceptionally wide range of articles comprises this collection that reaches from the colonial period to the 20th century, but manages to adhere to the central theme in the title.

399 Asociación Latinoamérica de Estudios de la Religión. Congreso Internacional. *Lima, 2003.* Angeli novi: prácticas evangelizadoras, representaciones artísticas y construcciones del catolicismo en América (siglos XVII–XX). Edición de Fernando Armas Asin. Lima: Pontificia Univ. Católica del Perú, Fondo Editorial, 2004. 230 p., 9 p. of plates: bibl., ill.

Images, ideals, pedagogy, and evangelization form important elements in the history of the Catholic Church over the four centuries covered in this collection of 14 essays. Particularly useful for its examination of the interactions of religion and popular culture.

400 Beidian, Lion and Dong Jingsheng. Lading Meixhou Shi [Latin American history]. Beijing: Renmin Chubanshe [People's Press], 2010. 633 p.: bibl., index, maps, tables.

A new general history of Latin America written by Chinese scholars after the first one was published half a century ago. Consists of 12 chapters, examining five periods: ancient time, colonial rule, early development of Latin American nations, the road to independent development, and post-1980s adjustment and reform. Includes a special table with a chronological comparison between ancient America and ancient China. Extensively absorbs new materials from domestic and foreign sources and employs new methods of study. This profound work represents the current level of Latin American studies in China. Authors are professors at the Beijing University of China. [M. Xianglin]

401 Caleidoscopio de alternativas: estudios culturales desde la antropología y la historia. Coordinación de Ana María Crespo y Rosa Brambila Paz. México: Instituto Nacional de Antropología e Historia, 2006. 116 p.: bibl., charts, ill., maps. (Col. Científica; 485. Serie Antropología)

A worthwhile synthesis of these two disciplines emerges in these seven articles. Concentrations on colonial Mexico and Paraguay, and on Brazil in the modern era.

402 Ching, Erik Kristofer. Reframing Latin America: a cultural theory reading of the nineteenth and twentieth centuries. Austin: Univ. of Texas Press, 2007. 349 p.: bibl., ill., index.

An instructive university reader designed to explain cultural theory and postmodernism as applied to five major trends: 19th-century liberalism, nationalism, socialism, magical realism, and personal testimonials on immigrant life and poverty.

403 Coatsworth, John H. Structures, endowments, and institution in the economic history of Latin America. (*LARR*, 40:3, 2005, p. 126–144, bibl.)

A well-written examination of recent trends in economic history that encompasses the healthy growth in the accumulation of basic statistical information and various macroeconomic studies that attempt to explain the lags in Latin American development in the early 19th and late 20th centuries.

404 Coello de la Rosa, Alexandre. Historias naturales y colonialismo: Gonzalo Fernández de Oviedo y José de Acosta. (*Illes Imp.*, 8, primavera 2006, p. 45–67, bibl., photos)

The "discovery" of the Americas by Europeans demonstrated their limited knowledge of the world. The author re-examines the writings of Oviedo (1478–1557) and Acosta (1540–1600) to show two attempts at making sense of this "new world." He observed that Oviedo's objective was to hide the contradictions in Spain's colonial expansion. The obvious contradictions were the depopulation of the Caribbean convert-

ing it into a tabula rasa and the conflicts among the different factions of conquistadors. Oviedo described all aspects of natural life, while Acosta's counter-reformation orthodoxy led him to see the natural world as part of a divine plan. Consequently he presented the new and unknown as a more awe-inspiring cultural dimension. But Acosta did not think of the New World in terms of paradise or the marvelous, but rather in terms of civil and moral projects that would form the bases of a new Spanish colonial order. [F. McCann]

405 Coloquio de Historia Canario-Americana, *16th, Las Palmas, Canary Islands, 2004*. El azúcar el mundo atlántico: economía y hacienda: patrimonio cultural y geobotánico. Coordinación de Santiago de Luxán Meléndez y Ana Viña Brito. Las Palmas de Gran Canaria, Spain: Cabildo de Gran Canaria, Casa de Colón, 2006. 478 p.: bibl., ill.

An insightful set of 19 essays that covers economic, technological, cultural, and biological factors in the growth of sugar cultivation on the Canary Islands and throughout Latin America from the early colonial period into the 20th century.

406 Coloquio Los Historiadores y la Historia para el Siglo XXI, *Mexico City, 2004*. Memorias del Coloquio Los Historiadores y la Historia para el Siglo XXI. Coordinación de Gumersindo Vera Hernández. México: Escuela Nacional de Antropología e Historia, 2006. 401 p.: bibl.

Collection of essays that examines several challenges in the field of historiography including the perennial problems of anachronism and presentism, the value of interdisciplinary studies, and the impact of personal experience, as well as biographical approaches to historical writing.

407 A companion to Latin American history. Edited by Thomas H. Holloway. Malden, Mass.; Oxford: Blackwell Pub., 2008. 530 p.: bibl., ill., index, maps. (Blackwell companions to world history)

This thoughtfully edited compendium of 28 essays offers the general reader trenchant summaries of key topics from preconquest Native American societies to the environmentalism and neoliberalism of recent decades.

408 Construcciones impresas: panfletos, diarios y revistas en la formación de los estados nacionales en América Latina, 1820–1920. Compilación de Paula Alonso. México: Fondo de Cultura Económica, 2004. 344 p.: bibl. (Sección de obras de historia)

This volume concentrates on the role of the printed word in the early development of nation-states and the emergence of controversial issues within national politics as expressed in the print media. The first four articles deal with the immediate aftermath of independence; the next five discuss the national press as an institution in Chile, Mexico, Colombia, and Argentina; and the last four examine specific controversies.

409 Cuestiones agrarias en Argentina y Brasil: conflictos sociales, educación y medio ambiente. Coordinación de Noemí M. Girbal-Blacha y Sonia Regina de Mendonça. Buenos Aires: Prometeo Libros, 2007. 380 p.: bibl., ill.

The editors assembled an unusually comprehensive set of scholarly articles that cover three important themes: social/class conflicts from the time of the gaucho to the contemporary era, the role of education in agriculture in the 20th century, and technical innovations and business practices in the recent past. The 18 contributors combine primary research with a firm grasp of published studies.

410 Culturas en movimiento: contribuciones a la transformación de identidades étnicas y culturas en América. Edición de Wiltrud Dresler, Bernd Fahmel y Karoline Noack. México: UNAM, Instituto de Investigaciones Antropológicas; Berlin: Ibero-Amerikanisches Institut Preussischer Kulturbesitz, 2007. 462 p.: bibl., ill., maps.

Mexico and South America are the main subjects in this collection of 19 articles that has value for both historians and anthropologists. Supported by extensive bibliographies and footnotes.

411 Davis, David Brion. Inhuman bondage: the rise and fall of slavery in the New World. Oxford, England; New York: Oxford Univ. Press, 2006. 440 p.: bibl., ill., index, maps.

This outstanding synthesis considers slavery in its global context, placing the Latin American-Caribbean experience within the larger setting that includes African, European, and US history. Although trained as a US historian, Davis carefully examines the relevant events in Haiti, Brazil, and the circum-Caribbean.

412 Earle, Rebecca. The return of the native: Indians and myth-making in Spanish America, 1810–1930. Durham, N.C.: Duke Univ. Press, 2007. 367 p.: bibl., ill., index.

A sharply focused examination of the role of the Native American image in elite nationalism in Mexico, Guatemala, Colombia, Peru, Chile, and Ecuador. A significant contribution to the analysis of myth construction and its role in nation-building. Integrates social science concepts, archival research, and the contemporary popular press.

413 Entre continuidades y cambios: las Américas en la transición (s. XVIII a XIX). Edición de Eduardo Cavieres Figueroa. Valparaíso, Chile: Vice Rectoría de Investigación y Estudios Avanzados, Pontificia Univ. Católica de Valparaíso: Ediciones Universitarias de Valparaíso, 2006. 323 p.: bibl.

This edited volume contains unusual breadth and depth in the contributions including commentary on the work of Simon Collier and Eduard Said as well as historical analyses of the writings of Camilo Henríquez and Juan Ignacio Molina. Also offers contributions to the study of economic and social history, modernity, and state formation.

414 Formaciones de indianidad: articulaciones raciales, mestizaje y nación en América Latina. Edición de Marisol de la Cadena. Colombia: Envión, 2007. 402 p.: bibl., ill.

History, anthropology, and sociology intermingle in this exceptionally valuable collection of 13 essays exploring the often elusive concepts that arise in discussions of race and racial categorization. The contributions range from the South American Andes to the highlands of Guatemala and Oaxaca.

415 Formas de historia cultural. Edición de Sandra Gayol y Marta Madero. Buenos Aires: Prometeo Libros; Univ. Nacional de General Sarmiento, 2007. 396 p.: bibl., ill. (Col. Historia extramuros)

This collection features a wide variety of approaches to cultural history, including manifestations of honor, literary creativity, violence, criminality, theatrical entertainment, and other forms of popular culture. These 16 contributions tend to concentrate on the 19th and 20th centuries.

416 Forment, Carlos A. Selfhood and nationhood in Latin America: from colonial subject to democratic citizen. (*in* Empire to nation: historical perspectives on the making of the modern world. Edited by Joseph W. Esherick, Hasan Kayali, and Eric Van Young. Lanham, Md.: Rowman & Littlefield, 2006, p. 106–133, ill.)

Forment examines the importance of Catholic values and ideas in the independence movements and the development of civic culture in 19th-century Mexico and Peru. A convincing reassessment of the interaction of religion and politics in these two nations and, by implication, other nations in Spanish America.

417 Gallego, Marisa. Historia latinoamericana, 1700–2005: sociedades, culturas, procesos políticos y económicos. Ituzaingó, Argentina: Editorial Maipue, 2006. 508 p.: bibl., ill.

The authors of this university textbook stress the social and cultural factors underlying political and economic development. The chronological balance is on the 20th century with considerable attention to US influence.

418 Gallini, Stefania. El siglo decimonónico latinoamericano en la Red. (*Hist. Crít./Bogotá*, 34, julio/dic. 2007, p. 148–158, bibl.)

This essay describes internet sources useful for the study of 19th-century Latin American history. One of the author's goals is to provoke discussion of the problems that the internet produces for historians and for the production of writing and publishing historical accounts. [F.D. McCann]

419 Games, Alison F. Atlantic history: definitions, challenges, and opportunities. (*Am. Hist. Rev.*, 111:3, June 2006, p. 741–757, bibl.)

A seminal discussion of the historiographical background, the conceptual framework, and scholarly challenges in the relatively new field of Atlantic history. Topics include slavery, immigration, and tropical exports (chocolate and sugar). The author points to many opportunities for research in the south—especially Latin America and Africa.

420 González, Ondina E. Christianity in Latin America: a history. Cambridge, England; New York: Cambridge Univ. Press, 2008. 331 p.: bibl., index.

A much-needed single volume synthesis on this vital topic. The authors examine the history of the Catholic Church in some detail from the conquest to the contemporary era and also the rise of various forms of Protestantism in the 20th century. The writing style is exceptionally clear and is suitable for undergraduate students.

421 González Manrique, Luis Esteban. De la conquista a la globalización: estados, naciones y nacionalismos en América Latina. Madrid: Biblioteca Nueva: Estudios de Política Exterior, 2006. 525 p.: bibl., map.

This survey text extends from the origins of the Iberian colonies to the early 21st century. The author places the evolution of the nation-state and nationalism within an ideological/policy framework that includes populism (Juan Perón, Argentina), left-wing nationalism (Lázaro Cárdenas, Mexico), the national security state and neoliberalism (Augusto Pinochet, Chile), and the revival of the left (Hugo Chávez, Venezuela).

422 Gootenberg, Paul. Andean cocaine: the making of a global drug. Chapel Hill: Univ. of North Carolina Press, 2008. 442 p.: bibl., ill., index.

An impressive synthesis on an important topic. Gootenberg gives much attention to the formative 1850–1950 period and balances coverage of the evolution of cocaine processing, the emergence of smuggling networks, and governmental (especially US) efforts to combat the illicit trade. Thoroughly documented including much statistical information.

423 Gould, Eliga H. Entangled histories, entangled worlds: the English-speaking Atlantic as a Spanish periphery. (*Am. Hist. Rev.*, 112:3, June 2007, p. 764–785, bibl.)

By "entangled," Gould means interconnected history as contrasted with

comparative history. This essay synthesizes recent works that trace the political,
military, commercial, legal, and ideological interactions of the British and Spanish
Empires.

424 Günther, Falk-Thoralf. Afrika- und
Lateinamerikaforschung in Deutsch-
land zwischen Kaiserreich und Drittem
Reich [Academic research in Germany
about Africa and Latin America from the
Kaiserreich to the Third Reich]. Leipzig,
Germany: Meine Verlag, 2008. 417 p.: bibl.,
ill. (Thematische Schriften-reihe "Historische studien"; 2)

Overview about research concerning
Latin America and Africa from the foundation of the German Reich in 1871 to the end
of the national-socialist dictatorship in 1945.
The first Latin American research institutes
in Germany were founded in 1912 in the
cities of Bonn and Cologne. From 1917 onwards, the Ibero-Amerikanische Institut in
Hamburg became the most important, later
the Ibero-Amerikanisches Institut in Berlin founded in 1929 assumed this role. The
institutes not only assure rigorous research
standards, but also help to establish economic and political connections with Latin
American countries. [F. Obermeier]

425 Hagedorn, Dan. Conquistadors of
the sky: a history of aviation in Latin
America. Washington, D.C.: Smithsonian
National Air and Space Museum; Gainesville: Univ. Press of Florida, 2008. 587 p.,
8 p. of plates: bibl., ill. (some col.), index,
col. maps.

This general compendium covers the
history of flight in most of Latin America
from ballooning of the late 19th century to
the jet aircraft of the early 21st century. The
organization is based on chronologically
arranged chapters with country-by-country
accounts within these chapters. Includes
both civilian and military aviation. There
is much attention on the 1920s and 1930s,
WWII, and some aspects of the Cold War,
but little or no discussion of Cuban aviation
after 1959, air operations during the Bay of
Pigs invasion and the Cuban missile crisis,
and the Falklands/Malvinas War.

Heredia, Edmundo A. Relaciones internacionales latinoamericanas. See *HLAS 65:1965.*

**426 Historia de la infancia en América
Latina.** Coordinación de Pablo Rodríguez Jiménez y María Emma Manarelli.
Bogotá: Univ. Externado de Colombia, 2007.
673 p., 10 p. of plates: bibl., ill. (some col.).

A collection of much-needed articles
on an often neglected topic in social/cultural
history. The coverage extends from the prehispanic period to the present and features a
section on "Trauma y Infancia" that includes
the dirty war in Argentina and other cases of
social conflicts.

**427 Historias sumergidas: hacia la pro-
tección del patrimonio cultural sub-
acuático en Latinoamérica.** Compilación de
Carlos Del Cairo Hurtado y María Catalina
García Chaves. Bogotá: Univ. Externado de
Colombia, 2006. 316 p.: bibl., facsims., ill.
(some col.), maps, photos.

This volume serves as an informative introduction to a new field: submarine
archeology. The 15 essays include Colombia,
Mexico, Brazil, and Chile. Several of the
authors deal with events and topics from
the colonial era.

428 Hoffman, Richard C. et al. Environmental historians and environmental
crisis. (*Am. Hist. Rev.*, 113:5, Dec. 2008,
p. 1431–1465)

The five participants in this AHR
interview include Latin Americanist Lise
Sedrez. Prominent topics are the relationship between "historical time" and "natural
time," the need for interdisciplinary approaches to the study of the environment,
and the propensity for activism among
environmental historians.

**429 La iglesia hispanoamericana: de la
colonia a la república.** Coordinación
de Rodolfo Aguirre y Lucrecia Enríquez.
México: Instituto de Investigaciones sobre la
Universidad y la Educación: UNAM: Pontificia Univ. Católica de Chile: Plaza y Valdés,
2008. 384 p.: bibl., maps.

These 13 scholarly articles deal with
the 18th and early 19th centuries and tend
to concentrate on Church-government
relations. Considerable archival research is
included in these contributions.

**430 Informal empire in Latin America:
culture, commerce and capital.** Edited by Matthew Brown. Oxford, England:
Blackwell Pub., 2008. 274 p.: bibl., ill., index

A collection of essays that covers the gamut of informal empire from railways and finance to Bible sales, travel writing, and fiction. Five contributions concentrate on Argentina, but the volume as a whole presents an informative overview of a topic of importance for all of Latin America. Editor Matthew Brown's introduction provides a clear conceptual framework for understanding the sometimes slippery term "informal imperialism." For the contribution by Alan Knight, see item **437**.

431 **Instituciones y procesos políticos en América Latina: siglos XIX y XX.** Coordinación de María del Rosario Rodríguez Díaz. Morelia, Mexico: Univ. Michoacana de San Nicolás de Hidalgo: Instituto de Investigaciones Históricas: Univ. Autónoma del Estado de México, 2008. 357 p.: bibl., ill.

This varied collection covers themes ranging from politics and ideologies to diplomacy and propaganda. Half of the 14 contributions deal with Latin American-US relations. Most of the contributions draw from archives and newspapers.

432 **Interpreting Spanish colonialism: empires, nations, and legends.** Edited by Christopher Schmidt-Nowara and John M. Nieto-Phillips. Albuquerque: Univ. of New Mexico Press, 2005. 269 p.: bibl., ill., index, maps.

These essays constitute a uniquely rewarding exercise in historiographical analysis. The authors examine the attempts of historians in the 19th and 20th centuries to understand the Spanish colonial past. Notable historians under scrutiny include José Manuel Restrepo, Bartolomé Mitre, and Herbert Eugene Bolton.

433 **Irigoin, Alejandra** and **Regina Grafe.** Bargaining for absolutism: a Spanish path to nation-state and empire building. (*HAHR*, 88:2, May 2008, p. 173–209, appendix, graph, table)

Poses a revisionist view of the Spanish empire. The authors argue that previous emphasis on centralization and uniformity should be revised to stress the regionalist, fragmented character of what was a "component state." Authors cite examples involving local initiatives that came out of issues involving boundaries, taxation, legislation, and imperial redistribution of revenue,

and that these often conflicting initiatives carried over into the national period. For two articles that respond to this argument, see items **443** and **462**. And for Irigoin and Grafe's follow-up piece, see item **434**.

434 **Irigoin, Alejandra** and **Regina Grafe.** Response to Carlos Marichal and William Summerhill. (*HAHR*, 88:2, May 2008, p. 235–245)

The authors' rejoinder emphasizes the importance of "mass intercolonial transfers" of revenue and the need to explain the interplay of local initiative and imperial controls in this process. They also reiterate their point that these colonial local elites' struggles over the disposition of revenue continued into the national era and contributed to the political as well as economic instability of much of Spanish America. For comment on Marichal's article, see item **443** and for Summerhill's article, see item **462**.

435 **Jáuregui, Carlos A.** Canibalia: canibalismo, calibanismo, antropofagia cultural y consumo en América Latina. Madrid: Iberoamericana; Frankfurt am Main: Vervuert, 2008. 724 p., 32 p. of plates: bibl., ill., indexes. (Ensayos de teoría cultural; 1)

This thought-provoking study elaborates on the theme of cannibalism in literature with an appreciation for its philosophical and political ramifications. Jáuregui reveals a thorough understanding of a wide variety of themes and historical periods from the conquest and the colonial era to the Ariel/Caliban discussions of the modern age to postmodern issues. A seminal work of importance for students of literature, history, anthropology, and art.

436 **Klaiber, Jeffrey L.** Los Jesuitas en América Latina, 1549–2000: 450 años de inculturación, defensa de los derechos humanos y testimonio profético. Lima: Fondo Editorial de la Univ. Antonio Ruiz de Montoya, Jesuitas, 2007. 508 p.: bibl., index. (Serie Humanidades)

Chronologically balanced, sweeping survey of Jesuit history based on a broad reading of published works and selected archival material. While sympathetic to the order, the text places the crucial events in historical context. A useful synthesis.

437 Knight, Alan. Rethinking British informal empire in Latin America (especially Argentina). (*in* Informal empire in Latin America: culture, commerce and capital. Edited by Matthew Brown. Oxford, England: Blackwell Pub., 2008, p. 23–48)

Thoughtfully provocative interpretation of British informal empire within a global framework. Knight gives economic factors the highest rank among imperial motives and finds that the informal relationships between metropole and colony were often consensual and, in the case of Argentina and Britain, mutually beneficial. For comment on entire book, see item **430**.

438 König, Hans-Joachim. Discursos de identidad, estado-nación y ciudadanía en América Latina: viejos problemas, nuevo enfoques y dimensiones. (*Hist. Soc./Medellín*, 11, sept. 2005, p. 9–31)

Interesting essay on national identity that reflects the changing social science conceptual frameworks that emerged in the 1990s preoccupation with and enthusiasm for globalization.

439 Lamei Yanjiu: Zhuixun Lishide Guiji [Studies on Latin America: pursuing the historical locus]. Edited by Zhongguo Shehui Kexueyuan Lading Meixhou Yanjiusuo. Beijing: Shijie Zhishi Chubanshe [World Affairs Press], 2006. 374 p.

On the occasion of the 45th anniversary of its founding, the Institute of Latin American Studies (ILAS) at the Chinese Academy of Social Sciences published an edited collection of selected articles by all its retired researchers (one article from each person). The volume contains 34 articles by 35 researchers, with a brief biography of each author preceding his/her article. The original dates of publication for the articles span from 1961 to 2006. As ILAS is the primary national force for Latin American studies, this book represents the development of the field in China. [Mao Xianglin]

440 Lesser, Jeffrey H. and Raanan Rein. Challenging particularity: Jews as a lens on Latin American ethnicity. (*Lat. Am. Caribb. Ethn. Stud.*, 1:2, Sept. 2006, p. 249–263, bibl.)

An impressive review of the writing on the Jewish role in Latin America followed by some penetrating observations

that point to a general approach to minority studies that emphasizes the relative position of minority groups in various national contexts.

441 Lipsett-Rivera, Sonya. Latin America and the Caribbean. (*in* Companion to gender history. Edited by Teresa A. Meade and Merry E. Wiesner-Hanks. Malden, Mass.: Blackwell Publishing, 2004, p. 477–491, bibl.)

A sophisticated, clearly written synthesis of recent publications on the gradually expanding role of women from the 1700s to the early 20th century. The author emphasizes the enlargement of the functions of motherhood within the family and also the entry of women into the workforce outside the family.

442 Maíz, Claudio. Constelaciones unamunianas: enlaces entre España y América, 1898–1920. Salamanca, Spain: Ediciones Univ. de Salamanca, 2009. 209 p.: bibl. (Biblioteca unamuno; 36)

Suggestive discussion of the intellectual community that arose in the wake of Spain's defeat by the US. Unamuno's correspondence with Dario, Palma, and Ugarte form much of the foundation for this group.

443 Marichal, Carlos. Rethinking negotiation and coercion in an imperial state. (*HAHR*, 88:2, May 2008, p. 211–218)

Marichal's response to the Irigoin-Grafe revisionist article (see item **433**). Marichal cites evidence on the centralist nature of the Spanish Empire as exemplified by the Gálvez reforms in New Spain and the overall imperial consistencies in tax policies and government expenditures. He contends that while there were local initiatives, they were outweighed by the imperial power structure. For a comment on the response by Irigoin and Grafe, see item **434**.

444 Martínez Montiel, Luz María. Afroamérica I: la ruta del esclavo. México: UNAM, 2006. 299 p.: bibl. (Col. La pluralidad cultural en México; 13)

Convenient synthesis that traces the evolution of the slave trade over eight centuries to the 1800s. Includes helpful bibliography. Useful for undergraduates and graduate students.

445 Mazín Gómez, Oscar. Iberoamérica: del descubrimiento a la independencia. Traducción de Víctor Gayol Romo de Vivar y Óscar Mazín. México: Colegio de México, 2007. 332 p.: bibl., ill., indexes, maps. (Col. Tramas)

Nicely organized, well-illustrated textbook that is a convenient tool for the classroom and also a useful work of synthesis for scholars.

446 Milanich, Nara. Whither family history?: a road map from Latin America. (*Am. Hist. Rev.*, 112:2, April 2007, p. 439–458)

A timely historiographical assessment of this burgeoning field. The author uses the multivolume *The History of the European Family* as a source for comparative commentary in the extensive survey of the literature in the field.

447 Monsiváis, Carlos. De los intelectuales en América Latina. (*Am. Lat. Hoy/Salamanca*, 47, dic. 2007, p. 15–38, bibl.)

A fast-paced, sweeping survey of intellectual history ranging across the liberal-conservative debates of the late 19th century, the emergence of nationalism and cultural criticism of the early 20th century, the controversies of the Cold War years, and the rise of the public universities and "la industria académica" of recent decades. For philosophy specialist's comment, see item 3523.

448 Moya, José C. A continent of immigrants: postcolonial shifts in the Western hemisphere. (*HAHR*, 86:1, Feb. 2006, p. 1–28)

A clearly written introduction to a complex subject. Moya breaks with the nation-centered approach to employ an international, largely transatlantic perspective. He places immigration to the Americas in this context by including economic conditions that motivated migrants and technological innovations in transportation and communication that made migration easier.

449 O'Brien, Thomas F. Making the Americas: the United States and Latin America from the age of revolutions to the era of globalization. Albuquerque: Univ. of New Mexico Press, 2007. 390 p.: bibl., ill., index. (Diálogos)

This history of US-Latin American relations gives considerable attention to the roles of business interests—especially corporations—in setting and sometimes dominating the environment for diplomacy. The pioneering missions of early 19th-century merchants set a pattern similar to the neoliberal enthusiasts' promotion of globalization in the late 20th century. O'Brien deftly integrates cultural, political, and philanthropic initiatives into this synthesis.

450 Patiño, Víctor Manuel. Aproximación a la historia agropecuaria del Neotrópico: épocas prehispánica y colonial. Cali, Colombia: Univ. del Valle, Facultad de Humanidades, Biblioteca Departamental Jorge Barcés Borrero, 2007. 648 p.: bibl.

Encyclopedic, science-based volume that focuses on colonial agricultural history. The author employs a system of parenthetical citations that connect with a 62-p. bibliography.

451 Políticas y estéticas del cuerpo en América Latina. Complición de Zandra Pedraza Gómez. Bogotá: Univ. de Los Andes, Facultad de Ciencias Sociales-Ceso, Depto. de Antropología, 2007. 422 p.: bibl.

This unusual collection offers discussions of physical education, dress codes, public policy, and state formation in the 19th and 20th centuries. As a group, the 14 contributions suggest interesting connections between and among these themes.

452 Powell, Philip Wayne. Tree of hate: propaganda and prejudices affecting United States relations with the Hispanic world. Introduction by Robert Himmerich y Valencia. Albuquerque: Univ. of New Mexico Press, 2008. 210 p.: ill.

Reissue of classic study of anti-Hispanic bias in historical writing and teaching in Europe, the US, and Latin America (see *HLAS 34:1288*). New introduction by Robert Himmerich y Valencia adds valuable depth and context.

453 Redes intelectuales y formación de naciones en España y América Latina, 1890–1940. Edición de Marta Elena Casaús Arzú y Manuel Pérez Ledesma. Madrid: Ediciones Univ. Autónoma de Madrid, 2005. 450 p.: bibl. (Col. de estudios; 101)

A useful collection of 22 scholarly articles dealing with a crucial half-century in the evolution of nation-states in Latin America as well as Spain. Themes include intellectual history, the role of education, the formation of social networks, and gender roles.

454 Región, frontera y prácticas culturales en la historia de América Latina y el Caribe. Coordinación de María Teresa Cortés Zavala, Olga Cabrera y José Alfredo Uribe Salas. Morelia, Mexico: Univ. Michoacana de San Nicolás de Hidalgo, Facultad de Historia; Goiás, Brazil: Univ. Federal de Goiás, Centro de Estudos do Caribe no Brasil, 2002. 279 p.: ill., maps. (Col. Historia regional continental; 1)

This book of a dozen articles encompasses a wide range of topics and areas from architecture in colonial New Spain to nation-building in Puerto Rico and Suriname to railroad and highway construction in Michoacán, Mexico.

455 Reséndez, Andrés and Brian M. Kemp. Genetics and the history of Latin America. (*HAHR*, 85:2, May 2005, p. 283–298, graph, tables)

Science and history come together in this provocative assessment of the interdisciplinary potential in the use of DNA testing involving racial, ethnic, and national groupings in Latin America and southwest North America. The authors give much attention to work on Native Americans, but also include long-term trends within the general population regarding migration patterns, disease, and social change.

456 Responsabilidad histórica: preguntas del nuevo al viejo mundo. Edición de Juan Manuel Almarza y Gustavo Gutiérrez. Barcelona: Anthropos, 2007. 398 p.: bibl. (Pensamiento crítico/pensamiento utópico; 162)

Well-organized volume of 17 essays that confront the long-term issues surrounding the conquest of the Americas, including commentary based on the perspective of human rights. Bartolomé de las Casas figures prominently. A mix of thought pieces with scholarly work.

457 Revoluções de independências e nacionalismos nas Américas: região do Prata e Chile. Contribuções de João Paulo G. Pimenta *et al.* Organização de Marco A.

Pamplona e Maria Elisa Mäder. São Paulo: Paz e Terra, 2007. 299 p.: bibl., ill., maps. (Col. Margens. América Latina; 1)

This book is part of a series on the comparative history of Latin America that seeks to explore the region's diversity. It analyzes the struggles for independence and the creation of national identities. The provocative essays emphasized the consequences of the French invasion of Iberia, and the changes resulting from the Constitution of 1812 as key to undermining control over the Americas. The constitution extended political rights to the majority of the adult males of the region. Civil wars resulted from such extension between those wanting to preserve the old order and those supporting the constitutional changes. In 1814, Fernando VII's return and move to restore absolutism led to successful repression nearly everywhere, except in the Rio de la Plata. Argentina did not exist as a nation before political independence, but at that moment was a grouping of settlements, cities, and provinces. [F. McCann]

458 Rojas-Mix, Miguel. El dios de Pinochet: fisonomía del fascismo iberoamericano. Prólogo de Juan Carlos Rodríguez Ibarra. Madrid: Taller de Mario Muchnik, 2007. 278 p.: bibl., ill.

Rojas-Mix examines the historical bases of Iberoamerican fascism in Hispanic political traditions, Catholic theology, and various European ideologies. Written in a direct, popular style. A challenging polemic.

459 Roux López, Rodolfo de. El largo camino de "naciones católicas" a "repúblicas pluriculturales" en América Latina. (*Anu. IEHS*, 20, 2005, p. 63–86)

Broad survey of the evolution of the place of the Catholic Church in the histories of the nations of Latin America. Such a large topic requires concentration on some focal points and some omissions. The author emphasizes Vatican policies and the challenges of Protestantism and secular values.

460 Sonhos e pesadelos na história. Organização de Fernando Tadeu de Miranda Borges e Maria Adenir Peraro. Cuiabá, Brazil: EdUFMT: Carlini & Caniato Editorial, 2006. 352 p.: bibl., ill.

This collection of essays spans many historical periods examining what the

editors describe as "enchantment and disenchantment." They use dreams and nightmares as a way of classifying opposites and
contradictions: dreams of equality, democracy, liberty, life, peace, as against nightmares of exclusion, dictatorship, slavery,
death, and war. The range of topics is impressive: Spanish images of the modern age; colonial Portuguese policies in the 18th century;
new social spaces for German and French
immigrants; obtaining drinking water for
urban areas; the difficulties of living with
war; slaves' struggles for liberty; defense
of the republic; missionary activity among
Amazonian natives; 20th-century dictatorships in the Southern Cone; women's dreams
in central-west Brazil; votos and ex-votos
among Chilean Catholics; and proposals for
how to use dreams in historical research and
literature. The essays are well-written and
based on interesting research. [F.D. McCann]

461 Suárez Bosa, Miguel and Pablo Ojeda
Déniz. Los trabajadores canarios en
Latinoamérica. (Cuad. Am./México, 117:3,
julio/sept. 2006, p. 11–46, bibl.)
Synthesis on Canary Islander migration in the 19th and 20th centuries
with particular attention on the motives
for migration and the patterns of employment. Thoroughly footnoted with extensive
bibliography.

462 Summerhill, William Roderick. Fiscal bargains, political institutions,
and economic performance. (HAHR, 88:2,
May 2008, p. 219–233)
Summerhill's response to the Irigoin-
Grafe revisionist article (see item 433). He
praises their use of recent detailed studies
of Spanish imperial policies at the local and
regional levels, but he also points out that
these apparent lower-level initiatives must
be more thoroughly analyzed in the larger
central framework of the empire. Summerhill concludes that issues raised by Irigoin
and Grafe are helpful in understanding
the operations of the imperial system and
in making comparisons with the British
empire. For a comment on the response by
Irigoin and Grafe, see item 434.

463 Tinsman, Heidi. A paradigm of our
own: Joan Scott in Latin American
history. (Am. Hist. Rev., 113:5, Dec. 2008,
p. 1357–1374)

Comprehensive examination of
Scott's impact that utilizes three general
topics: gender and the state, the role of
women in labor history, and the history of
sexuality. Tinsman includes the development of her personal appreciation of Scott's
writing in the 1980s and 1990s.

464 Viales Hurtado, Ronny. Historia de
la pobreza, de los regímenes de bienestar y del estado del bienestar en occidente:
aportes para la construcción de un modelo
conceptual de análisis. (Rev. Hist. Am./
México, 138, 2007, p. 107–157)
Important and ambitious attempt
to create a conceptual framework for the
analysis of welfare states, poverty, and the
nature of inequality in Latin America.
Draws heavily from social theory and social
science literature including the works of
Simmel, Hong, and Ochando.

465 Vinson, Ben. African (black) diaspora
history, Latin American history.
(Americas/Washington, 63:1, July 2006,
p. 1–18)
A much-needed, thoughtful review
of historiographical trends in recent publications on the African diaspora in Latin
America.

466 Von fernen Frauen: Beiträge zur latei-
namerikanischen Frauen- und Gesch-
lechtergeschichte. [Women at a distance:
contributions to Latin American women
and gender history.] Herausgegeben von
Delia Gonzales [i.e. Gonzalez] de Reufels.
Stuttgart, Germany: Heinz, 2009. 256 p.: ill.
(Historamericana; 21)
Collection of various contributions to gender history in South America.
[F. Obermeier]

The Yoruba diaspora in the Atlantic world.
See item 1912.

467 Zárate Botía, Carlos Gilberto. Silvíco-
las, siringueros y agentes estatales: el
surgimiento de una sociedad transfronteriza
en la Amazonía de Brasil, Perú y Colombia
1880–1932. Leticia, Colombia: Univ. Nacional de Colombia, Sede Amazonia: Instituto
Amazónico de Investigaciones-Imani: Saber
y Gestión Ambiental, 2008. 428 p.: bibl., ill.,
maps.

Impressive multidimensional study of the rapid, unbalanced development of the frontiers of the Amazon basin. Zárate incorporates the roles of the nation-states, private corporations, missionaries, and indigenous peoples of the region. Based on archival research and a firm grasp of relevant social science methodology and theory.

COLONIAL

468 Afro-Latino voices: narratives from the early modern Ibero-Atlantic world, 1550–1812. Edited by Kathryn Joy McKnight and Leo J. Garofalo. Indianapolis, Ind.: Hackett Pub., 2009. 377 p.: bibl., index.

The 18 contributions consist of a scholarly introduction followed by original documents in Spanish or Portuguese with their English translation. The introduction is helpful for students and instructors.

469 La América Española: temas y fuentes. Coordinación de Nidia R. Areces. Rosario, Argentina: Editorial de la Univ. Nacional de Rosario, Secretaría de Extensión Universitaria, 2007. 307 p.: bibl. (Col. Académica)

These seven interpretive essays present some carefully considered generalizations about crucial episodes from the conquest through the Bourbon reforms, accompanied by selected documents. Appropriate for the university classroom.

470 Andrés Gallego, José. El motín de Esquilache, América y Europa. Madrid: Fundación Mapfre Tavera: Consejo Superior de Investigaciones Científicas, 2003. 799 p.: bibl., index, maps. (Biblioteca de historia; 53)

Wide-ranging, detailed account of the controversial Bourbon official emphasizing the repercussions of his policies in the American colonies. Based on extensive archival research and thoroughly footnoted.

471 Avonto, Luigi. Blancos salvajes: rebeldía y utopía popular en la América de la conquista. Mérida, Venezuela: Siembraviva Ediciones, 2003. 300 p.: bibl., ill., maps.

The author takes up an unusual theme: Europeans who lived among Native Americans for extended periods in the early colonial period. The book examines this

variation on the typical relationships of the conquest era in some biographical and sociological depth.

472 Blanchard, Peter. Under the flags of freedom: slave soldiers and the wars of independence in Spanish South America. Pittsburgh, Pa.: Univ. of Pittsburgh Press, 2008. 242 p.: bibl., index, maps. (Pitt Latin American series)

Details the diverse and contradictory ways in which independence affected the institution of slavery and slaves themselves Regionally themed chapters cover slaves who defended royal authority, forced recruits, and patriotic militia members. Conclusions concern the fragility of freedom for soldiers who had brought an end to colonialism, but not necessarily to human bondage. [B. Premo]

473 Calderón de Cuervo, Elena María. Nuevas tendencias críticas en los estudios coloniales. (*Rev. Hist. Am. Argent.* 26:41, 2006, p. 87–105, bibl.)

Review of recent intellectual trends in the consideration of colonial Hispano-American history. Emphasis has now changed to more focus upon cultural studies, as well as multidisciplinary efforts. Short, but provocative. [J. Cooney]

474 Cañizares-Esguerra, Jorge. Entangled histories: borderland historiographies in new clothes? (*Am. Hist. Rev.*, 112:3, June 2007, p. 787–799, bibl., ill.)

Short but provocative essay makes a case of viewing the history of the colonial Americas within transatlantic frameworks that offer more than comparisons of traditional imperial histories. Instead, Cañizares-Esguerra seeks an Atlantic history that "carves out a distinctly transnational space" crossing national and confessional boundaries. Author models a new approach—entangled histories—by following the influence of Spanish narratives of Amerindian satanic election on Puritan thought. [K. Melvin]

475 Colón en el mundo que le tocó vivir. Coordinación de Guillermo Céspedes del Castillo. Madrid: Real Academia de la Historia, 2007. 143 p.: bibl., ill. (Serie Estudios; 20)

This slender volume brings together five interpretive essays on Columbus and the environment in which he lived. Topics include Columbus' relationship with Queen Isabel, the culture of the mariners, and navigation.

476 Coloquio de Historia Canario-Americana, 16th, Las Palmas, Canary Islands, 2004. Isabel la Católica y el Atlántico: V Centenario de su muerte: XVI Coloquio de Historia Canario-Americana, 2004. Coordinación de Elisa Torres Santana. Las Palmas de Gran Canaria, Spain: Casa de Colón, 2006. 238 p.: bibl.

Essays representing recent interpretations on Queen Isabella and her expansionist reign, including reconquista soldiers' reactions to the New World, Africa's perspectives on colonization, vacillations and discrepancies in colonial policy, and a gender analysis of her ability to rule. [L.G. Brockington]

477 Coloquio Internacional Mezclado y Sospechoso: Movilidad e Identidades, España y América (siglos XVI–XVIII), 1st, Madrid, 2000. Coloquio internacional (29–31 de mayo de 2000). Actas reunidas y presentadas por Gregorio Salinero. Madrid: Casa de Velázquez, 2005. 270 p.: bibl., ill. (Coll. de la Casa de Velázquez; 90)

Compilation of conference papers exploring the influence of books on European and New World peoples' perceptions of each other, fueling a growing mistrust among social groups, particularly of mixed European and indigenous gene pools. [L.G. Brockington]

478 Congreso Internacional sobre los Dominicos y el Nuevo Mundo, 8th, Managua, 2004. Influencia lascasiana en el siglo XVI. Coordinación de José Luis Burguet Huerta, José Barrado Barquilla y Bernardo Fueyo Suárez. Salamanca, Spain: Editorial San Esteban, 2006. 356 p.: bibl., indexes. (Monumenta histórica iberoamericana de la Orden de Predicadores; 29)

These 21 original essays concentrate on two overarching themes: the role of Las Casas' ideas and the importance of institutions and individuals in the implementation of his ideas. Based on published sources with some archival research.

479 Delgado Ribas, Josep Maria. Dinámicas imperiales, 1650–1796: España, América y Europa en el cambio institucional del sistema colonial español. Prólogo de Josep Fontana. Barcelona: Edicions Bellaterra, 2007. 662 p.: bibl., index. (Serie General universitaria; 63)

A well-researched examination of the opening of the Spanish Empire to external commerce. Although attuned to the basic statistics on trade, the author's focus also includes changes in policy during times of peace and war. Thoroughly footnoted with an extensive bibliography. Based on a healthy combination of archival research and a broad reading of leading published monographs in American and European history.

480 Dote matrimonial y redes de poder en el antiguo régimen en España e Hispanoamérica. Coordinación de Nora Siegrist y Edda O. Samudio A. Mérida, Venezuela: Talleres Gráficos Universitarios, Univ. de los Andes, 2006. 416 p.: bibl., ill. (some col.), maps.

Collection of 13 essays on marriage and the dowry follow these institutions from 16th-century Spain (the opening essay) to 17th- and 18th-century Spanish Americas, tracking regional cases and giving special emphasis to Rio de la Plata (6 essays). Among the topics covered are material culture, the composition of dowries, and the creation of political-economic alliances and maintainence of familial prestige through marriage and dowries. [K. Melvin]

Earle, Rebecca. Consumption and excess in colonial and early-independent Spanish America. See item **1411**.

481 Escobar Quevedo, Ricardo. Inquisición y judaizantes en América española, siglos XVI–XVII. Prólogo de Charles Amiel. Bogotá: Editorial Univ. del Rosario, 2008. 438 p.: bibl., ill., tables. (Col. Textos de ciencias humanas)

Well-organized history of a crypto-Jewish community that originated in Portugal and spread throughout the New World from Lima to Cartagena to Curaçao generally through commerce. The author covers business, religious, and political history. Based on archival sources including records of the Inquisition.

482 La formación de la cultura virreinal. v. 3, El siglo XVIII. Recopilación de Karl Kohut y Sonia V. Rose. Frankfurt: Vervuert; Madrid: Iberoamericana, 2006. 1 v. (589 p.): bibl., index, ill. (Textos y estudios coloniales y de la independencia)

This collection provides both scholarly depth and topical range. Concentrations include elite-directed reform, regionalism, and intellectual history. Bibliographies are helpful.

483 Francis in the Americas: essays on the Franciscan family in North and South America. Edited by John F. Schwaller. Berkeley, Calif.: Academy of American Franciscan History, 2005. 399 p.: bibl., ill., maps, tables.

A variety of historical approaches characterize this collection that covers Franciscan missions from Brazil to the borderlands (New Mexico and California). Two of the essays deal with archeological research in California.

484 Gambín García, Mariano. En nombre del rey: los primeros gobernadores de Canarias y América, 1480–1526. Las Palmas de Gran Canaria, Spain: Cabildo Insular de Gran Canaria, 2006. 487 p.: bibl. (Historia/Cabildo de Gran Canaria)

Juxtaposition of the history of the Canary Islands with the initial phase of the Spanish Empire in the Caribbean. Confirms the importance of the Canary Islands in the development of the larger empire. Based on archival research.

485 Garavaglia, Juan Carlos. América Latina de los orígenes a la Independencia. Barcelona: Crítica, 2005. 2 v.: bibl., ill., indexes, maps. (Serie mayor)

A broad synthesis of precolumbian Native American history, the European invasion of the Americas, and the establishment of the Iberian empires. Emphasis on economic and social structures with perceptive comments on social stratification.

486 Gender, race and religion in the colonization of the Americas. Edited by Nora E. Jaffary. Aldershot, England; Burlington, Vt.: Ashgate, 2007. 206 p.: bibl., ill., index. (Women and gender in the early modern world)

This collection redresses the neglect of gender analysis in the recent spate of publications adopting the Atlantic paradigm. Original essays spanning English, Portuguese, French, and especially Spanish contexts in Europe and the New World are grouped by themes of frontiers, religiosity and race, and networks. Notable are the offerings that revise traditional depictions of contrasts between empires in terms of race-mixing and sexuality, and a brief final comment on the "separate destinies" of some women in the Atlantic.

487 Gil, Juan. Columbiana: estudios sobre Cristóbal Colón, 1984–2006. Santo Domingo: Academia dominicana de la historia, 2007. 641 p.: bibl., ill. (Academia Dominicana de la Historia; 76)

An impressive compilation of biographical details drawn from archival sources, this study devotes nearly half of its text to Columbus' life before the first voyage. Also gives coverage of his relations with religious orders after 1492.

488 Glüsenkamp, Uwe. Das Schicksal der Jesuiten aus der Oberdeutschen und den beiden Rheinischen Ordensprovinzen nach ihrer Vertreibung aus den Missionsgebieten des portugiesischen und spanischen Patronats, 1755–1809 [The destiny of the Jesuits from the Upper-German and Rhenanian provinces after their expulsion from missionary regions under Portuguese and Spanish patronage, 1755–1809]. Münster, Germany: Aschendorff, 2008. 295 p.: ill. (Spanische Forschungen der Görresgesellschaft. Zweite Reihe, 40)

After their expulsion from the Spanish and Portuguese colonies in Latin America, some Jesuits were imprisoned for several years before being allowed to return to their homelands. This work examines closely the individual destinies of the Jesuits from German Jesuit "provinces" after their return to Europe. The work gives an overview of their later activities and their publications concerning their imprisonment and, in some cases, their experiences in Latin America. [F. Obermeier]

489 González Cruz, David. La muerte en el discurso propagandístico de los conflictos bélicos del siglo XVIII en España y en la América Hispana. (*CLAHR*, 14:1, Winter 2005, p. 25–48)

An interesting examination of the development and deployment of propaganda in the War of the Spanish Succession and the decades thereafter. An important contribution on an often underrated subject.

490 Guasco, Michael. "Free from the tyrannous Spanyard"?: Englishmen and Africans in Spain's Atlantic world. (*Slavery Abolit.*, 29:1, Jan. 2008, p. 1–22)

A study of Englishmen's attitudes towards Africans in the Spanish colonies. Guasco concludes that Englishmen, like Spaniards, accepted slavery and the exploitation of Africans throughout the colonial era.

491 Historia general de América Latina. Vol. 3, Pts. 1 and 2. Consolidación del orden colonial. Dirección de Alfredo Castillero Calvo y Allan Kuethe. Madrid: Editorial Trotta; Paris: Ediciones UNESCO, 2007. 2 v.: bibl., ill., indexes, maps. (Historia general de América Latina; 3)

This collection of essays examines aspects of immigration, social structure, imperial defense, the Catholic Church, and colonial culture. Useful overviews drawn from recent scholarship.

492 Imperial subjects: race and identity in colonial Latin America. Edited by Andrew B. Fisher and Matthew D. O'Hara. Foreword by Irene Silverblatt. Durham, N.C.: Duke Univ. Press, 2009. 303 p.: bibl., index. (Latin America otherwise)

This edited volume includes nine essays that are essentially case studies from different parts of Latin America—and that range over the entire colonial period—brought together to examine the construction of race and identity in that period. Despite the wide variety of examples and contexts, the essays together contribute to a long debate over the reality of race as a meaningful category and a means of domination in the colonial system. The cases depicted not only highlight the complexity of the colonization process and the need to question simple assumptions about domination and resistance, but also focus on the multiple ways in which subalterns identified themselves and the ways in which ideas about identity and race changed according to period, place, and person. [P. De Vos]

493 International Interdisciplinary Symposium of the Colonial Americas Studies Association, 1st, Georgetown University, 2003. Repensando el pasado, recuperando el futuro: nuevos aportes interdisciplinarios para el estudio de la América colonial = Remembering the past, retrieving the future: new interdisciplinary contributions to the study of colonial Latin America. Edición de Verónica Salles-Reese. Bogotá: Editorial Pontificia Univ. Javeriana, 2005. 422 p.: bibl., ill., index. (Colonia)

History, literature, and philosophy come together in this thoughtfully assembled volume on the society and cultures of colonial Latin America.

494 Juan de Solórzano y Pereira: pensar la colonia desde la colonia. Recopilación de Diana Bonnett y Felipe Castañeda. Textos de Heraclio Bonilla *et al.* Bogotá: Univ. de los Andes, 2006. 270 p.: bibl. (Estudios interdisciplinarios sobre la conquista y la colonia de América; 2)

Edited collection of sophisticated reflections on how the colonial experience shaped the political and legal philosophy of this renowned 17th-century Andean jurist. Nine authors write on topics ranging from Spanish legitimacy to fiscal policy, with special focus on how indigenous peoples and customs shaped imperial jurisprudence. [B. Premo]

495 Klein, Herbert S. The Atlantic slave trade. 2nd ed. New York: Cambridge Univ. Press, 2010. 242 p.: bibl., index. (New approaches to the Americas)

This updated edition of a work on the Atlantic slave trade is based on research over the last decade in Europe, Latin America, the US, and Africa. For review of 1st ed., see *HLAS 60:897.*

496 Livi-Bacci, Massimo. Conquest: the destruction of the American Indios. Malden, Mass.: Polity, 2008. 317 p.: bibl., ill., index.

Livi-Bacci uses the tools of demography and historical research to reassess the causes of the decline of the Native American population in the wake of the conquest and its recovery later in the colonial era. A demographer by training, he insists that traditional historical sources are necessary in understanding the causative factors implicit in the statistics. Livi-Bacci concludes that biological, environmental, economic, and political factors all played important roles in the decline of the population. This work is an English translation of the original Italian publication (2005).

497 Livi-Bacci, Massimo. The depopulation of Hispanic America after the conquest. (*Popul. Dev. Rev.*, 32:2, June 2006, p. 199–232, bibl., maps, tables)

Studies in historical demography drawn from the following regions: the Caribbean, the coastal areas of New Spain, and Peru during the conquest and the exceptional experience of the Jesuit-led Paraguayan missions from the 1640s to the 1730s (see also item 1541). Valuable comparative insights. The author identifies epidemic diseases as one of several causative factors. For geography specialist's review, see *HLAS 65:946*.

498 Luque Alcaide, Elisa. Iglesia en América Latina, siglos XVI–XVIII: continuidad y renovación. Barañáin (Navarra), Spain: Ediciones Univ. de Navarra (EUNSA), 2008. 395 p.: bibl., index. (Col. Historia de la Iglesia; 38)

An institutional history of the Catholic Church that draws heavily from church documents to portray the intentions and practices of the hierarchy over three centuries. The last section of the book concentrates on the role of church education in the lives of the indigenous peoples of New Spain.

499 McFarlane, Anthony. Pre-columbian and colonial Latin America. (*in* Cambridge companion to modern Latin American culture. Edited by John King. Cambridge, U.K.; New York: Cambridge Univ. Press, 2004, p. 9–28, bibl.)

Thoughtful, incisive synthesis of Latin American history up to the independence era with emphasis on the interactions of Spanish and Portuguese settlers and indigenous peoples and the cultural ramifications of these interactions. McFarlane also discusses the impact of geographical isolation of urban centers and the influence of regional values.

Milanich, Jerald T. Laboring in the fields of the Lord: Spanish missions and southeastern Indians. See *HLAS 65:277*.

500 Mó Romero, Esperanza and **Margarita Eva Rodríguez García.** Educar: ¿a quien y para qué? (*in* Historia de las mujeres en España y América Latina: El mundo moderno. Coordinación de Margarita Ortega, Asunción Lavrin y Pilar Pérez Cantó. Madrid: Cátedra, 2005, v. 2, p. 729–756, photos)

Overview of women's education in the colonial era based on published works. Concludes that in spite of some expansion beyond narrowly religious content, the primary purpose of schooling continued to be the reinforcement of traditional roles for women.

501 Newson, Linda A. Medical practice in early colonial Spanish America: a prospectus. (*Bull. Lat. Am. Res.*, 25:3, July 2006, p. 367–391)

An examination of the archival sources for the history of medicine. The author includes some useful observations on the roles of the state and the Catholic Church in colonial medicine and also gives considerable attention to the importance of Native American and African practices. Cartagena de Indias provides a case study.

502 Norton, Marcy. Sacred gifts, profane pleasures: a history of tobacco and chocolate in the Atlantic world. Ithaca, N.Y.: Cornell Univ. Press, 2008. 334 p.: bibl., ill., index, maps.

In-depth research undergirds this scholarly examination of the spread of tobacco and chocolate from Spanish America to Europe over the course of the two centuries. The author is sensitive to the Native American origins of these products and to their commercialization by Europeans. A good combination of social and economic history.

503 Otazu, Alfonso and **José Ramón Díaz de Durana.** El espíritu emprendedor de los vascos. Madrid: Sílex, 2008. 715 p.: bibl., index. (Sílex universidad)

This well-researched book focuses on colonial-era Basque entrepreneurs and their commercial and financial activities outside of the Basque country, in other parts of Spain, Europe, and Latin America. It is divided into 10 chapters, three of which deal primarily with Latin America: "Los vascos en América. Entre México y Perú"; "Los vascos en Potosí"; and "Los vascos de Cádiz y la

Real Compañía Guipuzcoana de Caracas." Includes a comprehensive 32-p. bibliography. [J.M. Pérez]

504 Paquette, Gabriel B. Enlightenment, governance and reform in Spain and its empire 1759–1808. New York: Plagrave Macmillan, 2008. 244 p.: bibl., index.

Caught between international rivalries and declining economies on the peninsula and in the Americas, the Bourbon kings of the late 18th century embarked on a reform program to bolster the empire. Paquette explores the strategic, political, and economic dimensions of their policies and places them within the intellectual framework of the Enlightenment and the context of transatlantic rivalries. This study contains a balanced combination of archival research and well-structured generalizations.

505 Paquette, Gabriel B. State-civil society cooperation and conflict in the Spanish Empire: the intellectual and political activities of the ultramarine *consulados* and economic societies, c. 1780–1810. (*J. Lat. Am. Stud.*, 39:2, May 2007, p. 263–298)

A close examination of the actions of colonial elites through the *consulados* during this crucial period. The author's archival research indicates that these institutions were a stable, mildly reformist component of the Empire.

506 Pérez, Joseph. Mitos y tópicos de la historia de España y América. Madrid: Algaba Ediciones, 2006. 240 p.: bibl., index. (Historia)

A convenient compilation of scholarly articles published by Pérez from the 1970s to the present. Outstanding themes include the evolution of political power in Spain of the conquest era, Spanish literature of the 16th and 17th centuries, and Spanish colonial policy from Columbus through the Bourbons.

507 Raising an empire: children in early modern Iberia and colonial Latin America. Edited by Ondina E. González and Bianca Premo. Albuquerque: Univ. of New Mexico Press, 2007. 258 p.: bibl., index. (Diálogos)

Contributions cover a diverse range of social and cultural environments from the lives of Indians in Lima, Peru, to the famil-

ial circumstances of an aristocratic girl in Santiago, Chile, to childhood experiences of slaves in Brazil. Articles are based on thorough scholarship.

508 Redes sociales e instituciones comerciales en el imperio español, siglos XVII a XIX. Coordinación de Antonio Ibarra y Guillermina del Valle Pavón. México: UNAM, Facultad de Economía: Instituto Mora, 2007. 340 p.: bibl., ill., index, maps. (Historia económica)

An essay collection on the building of business networks between Spain and its colonies (17th to 19th century). Presents some very well documented studies for the history of commerce in the Spanish empire. [M. Marsilli]

509 Religión y conflictos bélicos en Iberoamérica. Edición de David González Cruz. Sevilla, Spain: Univ. Internacional de Andalucía, 2008. 203 p.: bibl., ill.

These six well-researched essays explore the role of religion in violent social and political upheavals throughout the colonial era. Although this work provides no major synthesis on religion as a causative factor, the archival research here constitutes significant steps in understanding the larger issues.

510 Revisiting the colonial question in Latin America. Edited by Mabel Moraña and Carlos A. Jáuregui. Madrid: Iberoamericana; Frankfurt am Main: Vervuert, 2008. 296 p.

Offers a set of theoretical and critical reflections on colonial Latin American topics, such as the importance of historical accounts, cultural practices, and symbolic representations. All combined, the chapters offer an outlook of the views held by the colonizers regarding the colonized. [M. Marsilli]

511 Saavedra Inaraja, María. La forja del Nuevo Mundo: huellas de la iglesia en la América española. Madrid: Sekotia, 2008. 222 p.: bibl., ill. (Grafite. Biblioteca de la historia)

The author focuses on the role of the Catholic Church in the formation of an American identity during the colonial era. Main themes include church organizational structure, religious orders, culture and education, and artistic expression.

512 Sanfuentes Echeverría, Olaya. Europa
y su percepción del Nuevo Mundo a
través de las especies comestibles y los espacios americanos en el siglo XVI. (*Historia/
Santiago*, 39:2, julio/dic. 2006, p. 531–556,
ill., photo)
A perceptive examination of European descriptions of the foods and natural
environments of the Americas. The author
points out that although these observations
were initially disdainful, the content of the
descriptions contained the basis for more
positive points of view.

513 Schwartz, Stuart B. All can be saved:
religious tolerance and salvation in
the Iberian Atlantic world. New Haven,
Conn.: Yale Univ. Press, 2008. 336 p.: bibl.,
ill., index, map.
Written in an engaging and compelling style, this volume explores a tendency
rarely covered in Iberian and Latin American history: religious tolerance among common folk. Schwartz looks at the notorious
Inquisition alongside the lives of dissidents
and the experiences of Jews, Native Americans, and slaves. Based on the author's decades of primary research and maturity of
judgment.

**514 Slaves, subjects, and subversives:
blacks in colonial Latin America.**
Edited by Jane G. Landers and Barry M. Robinson. Albuquerque: Univ. of New Mexico
Press, 2006. 318 p.: bibl., ill., index, maps.
(Diálogos)
A collection of nine well-researched,
original articles based on primary documents. The introduction by Jane Landers
provides a perceptive overview. The chronological framework extends from the 1500s to
the early 19th century.

515 Stolcke, Verena. A new world en-
gendered: the making of the Iberian
transatlantic empires. (*in* Companion to
gender history. Edited by Teresa A. Meade
and Merry E. Wiesner-Hanks. Malden,
Mass.: Blackwell Publishing, 2004, p. 371–
389, bibl.)
A thoughtful survey of the varied and
complex roles of gender in the early Spanish
and Portuguese empires. Topics include race
mixture, sexual morality, and marriage.

516 Subrahmanyam, Sanjay. Holding
the world in balance: the connected
histories of the Iberian overseas empires,
1500–1640. (*Am. Hist. Rev.*, 112:5, Dec.
2007, p. 1359–1385, ill., map, table)
The author argues persuasively that
the traditional historical notion of a sharp
separation of the Spanish and Portuguese
empires is overstated. The two empires were
"entangled" in a sociocultural sense and, to
some extent, in economic terms. The article
includes Asian as well as Latin American
examples.

517 Valdés Lakowsky, Vera. La plata en
la historia: del albo brillo a la pureza
y perfección. México: Plaza y Valdés, 2008.
647 p.: bibl., ill., maps. (Historia)
Broadly based synthesis on the mining, processing, and trading of silver that
ranges across Asia, Europe, and Africa
with substantial coverage of the Americas.
Drawn from secondary sources and based on
author's PhD dissertation (UNAM, 1997).

518 Vargas Machuca, Bernardo de. The
Indian militia and description of the
Indies: an English translation of the original
Spanish edition published in Madrid, 1599.
Edited by Kris Lane. Translated by Timothy
Johnson. Durham, N.C.: Duke Univ. Press,
2008. 341 p.: bibl., index. (The cultures and
practice of violence series)
Translation of a 1599 "training manual for conquistadors." An engaging introduction situates the Spanish author in the
milieu of early colonial New Granada. Original text, framed by editors' illuminating
choices of illustrations and photos, contains
diverse commentary on indigenous warfare
techniques, medicine, and on-the-ground
advice on how to conquer people. [B. Premo]

INDEPENDENCE
AND 19TH CENTURY

**519 Alejandro de Humboldt: una nueva
visión del mundo: en conmemoración
al bicentenario de la llegada de Humboldt a
México.** México: UNAM, 2003. 205 p.: bibl.,
ill. (some col.).
This recent addition to the crowded
field of Humboldt scholarship contains important original essays—especially Walther

Bernecker's incisive contribution on Humboldt as propagandist for Mexican economic development. The quality of the illustrations is exceptional.

520   Los americanistas del siglo XIX: la construcción de una comunidad científica internacional. Edición de Leoncio López-Ocón, Jean-Pierre Chaumeil y Ana Verde Casanova. Madrid: Iberoamericana; Frankfurt am Main: Vervuert, 2005. 355 p.: bibl., ill.

A group of wide-ranging, well-informed essays on the formative century of modern anthropological and historical studies. This volume focuses on European contributions: especially Spanish, British, French, and German. Featured scholars are Marcos Jiménez de la Espada and Clements Markham.

521   Armillas Vicente, José A. Relaciones diplomáticas entre España y los Estados Unidos de América desde el Tratado de San Lorenzo, 1795, al de Adams-Onís, 1819. (*Rev. Hist. Mil.*, 51, número extraordinario 2, 2007, p. 159–200)

A detailed examination of relations between Spain and the US based on archival sources. The article covers signal events—the Louisiana Purchase and the US acquisition of Florida. Much biographical detail on Spanish diplomats.

522   Balzan, Luigi. A carretón y canoa: la aventura científica de Luigi Balzan por Sudamérica, 1885–1893. Edición, estudio, notas y traducción del italiano de Clara López Beltrán. Lima: Institut de recherche pour le développement: Instituto Francés de Estudios Andinos: Ambasciata d'Italia in Bolivia: Plural Editores, 2008. 419 p.: bibl., ill., indexes, maps. (Col. "Travaux de l'Institut Français d'Études Andines"; 269)

Editor López Beltrán's introduction and informative footnotes add depth and perspective to the Italian naturalist and explorer Balzán's account of his travels. For review by Bolivian historian, see item **1759**.

523   Blaufarb, Rafe. The Western question: the geopolitics of Latin American independence. (*Am. Hist. Rev.*, 112:3, June 2007, p. 742–762, bibl.)

An impressive reconsideration of the era of Latin American independence from a geopolitical perspective. The collapse of the Spanish empire opened the way for competition between Britain and France with the newly formed US also a factor in this struggle. Blaufarb sees the US acquisition of Florida as a crucial event.

524   Breña, Roberto. El liberalismo hispánico a debate: aspectos de la relación entre el primer liberalismo español y la emancipación americana. (*Hist. Contemp.*, 33, 2006, p. 463–494)

Breña sees the movements for independence in Spanish America as the culmination of the gradual spread of Spanish liberalism in the American colonies. The author uses a broad and inclusive definition of the term liberal. Based on published sources and previous scholarly studies.

525   Un cambio de siglo, 1898: España, Cuba, Puerto Rico, Filipinas y Estados Unidos. Edición de José Girón Garrote. Spain: Univ. de Oviedo, 2008. 418 p.: bibl., ill.

This collection of 53 compact essays deals with the causes, course, and legacy of the War of 1898. Contributors examine the political, military, diplomatic, and cultural history of the war. Eighteen of the essays are on Spanish history and an equal number on Cuba. Excellent photographs and other illustrations on glossy pages. Morales Moya's bibliographical essay describes recent books published in Spanish on this topic.

526   Cassinello Pérez, Andrés. El ejército español en Indias ante el siglo XIX. (*Rev. Hist. Mil.*, 51, número extraordinario 2, 2007, p. 15–38, bibl., map, tables)

Straightforward description of the Spanish forces including the navy, coastal fortifications, the regular army, and militias. Based on published sources and some archival research.

527   Centeno, Miguel Angel. Critical debates: Latin American independence and the double dilemma. (*Lat. Am. Polit. Soc.*, 50:3, Fall 2008, p. 147–161, bibl.)

The double dilemma in this book review essay consists of reflections on the attempts to create central governments in the newly independent countries and the simultaneous efforts to build national communities and a sense of national unity. The author's discussion of the need for a comprehensive, pragmatic theoretical framework for historical analysis includes commentary on the ideas of Benedict Anderson.

528 Chirinos, Juan Carlos. Miranda, el nómada sentimental. Caracas: Editorial Norma, 2006. 335 p., 16 p. of plates: bibl., ill., index, maps, ports. (Col. Biografías y documentos)

Sympathetic biography that emphasizes Miranda's sojourns in the US, Britain, and continental Europe. Chirinos deepens his portrait of Miranda with discussions of the international contexts through which he moved.

529 Congreso das Academias da História Ibero-Americanas, 9th, Madrid, 2004. La América hispana en los albores de la emancipación. Presentaciones de Gonzalo Anes y Álvarez de Castrillón and Rafael del Pino y Moreno. Madrid: Real Academia de la Historia: Fundación Rafael del Pino: Marcial Pons, Ediciones Jurídicas y Sociales, 2005. 702 p.: bibl. (Col. Historia; 5)

Well-researched collection of essays that treats the early stages of the independence movements in 16 regions of the Spanish empire and Brazil. Also includes general studies of Portugal and Spain.

530 De riqueza e inequidad: el problema de las contribuciones directas en América Latina, siglo XIX. Coordinación de Luis Jáuregui. México: Instituto Mora, 2006. 294 p.: bibl., graphs, ill., index, tables. (Historia económica.)

The formative era in governmental finances is the central topic in this collection of eight scholarly articles that focus on Argentina, Bolivia, Mexico, and Peru. The authors use a mix of statistics and analytical essays. Footnotes and bibliography are helpful.

531 Deere, Carmen Diana and **Magdalena León.** Liberalism and married women's property rights in nineteenth-century Latin America. (*HAHR*, 85:4, Nov. 2005, p. 627–677, tables)

The authors explore the regional variations in spousal property rights in the context of 19th-century liberalism. In general, Mexico and the Central American nations established a separation of property regime while most of South America retained male primacy of the colonial system. A complex analysis of legal, intellectual, and religious influences. Based on extensive primary research.

532 Delgado Ribas, Josep Maria. La desintegración del Imperio español: un caso de descolonización frustrada, 1797–1837. (*Illes Imp.*, 8, primavera 2006, p. 5–44, bibl.)

Interpretive account of Spanish policy that emphasizes the unrealistic efforts to hold and later to recover the American colonies. Includes some primary documentation

533 Diego García, Emilio de. El significado estratégico de la América Hispana en la Guerra de 1808–1814. (*Rev. Hist. Mil.*, 51, número extraordinario 2, 2007, p. 201–221)

The author places Spain's imperial policies and the Spanish American struggles for independence in the context of the British-French conflict for dominance of the transatlantic world. Explores some of the larger multidimensional strategic issues.

534 Encuentro Internacional "Revolución e Insurgencia en América del Sur", Salta, Argentina, 2007. Entre la Colonia y la República: insurgencias, rebeliones y cultura política en América del Sur. Compilación de Elsa Beatriz Bragon y Sara E. Mata Buenos Aires: Prometeo Libros, 2008. 357 p.: bibl. (Prometeo Bicentenario)

This carefully focused collection of 13 scholarly articles provides new depth on various revolutionary movements from La Plata to the high Andes to Nueva Granada. In general, these articles are based on primary research, and the editors have included an impressive 24-p. bibliography.

535 Ensayos sobre la nueva historia política de América Latina, siglo XIX. Coordinación de Guillermo Palacios. México: Centro de Estudios Históricos, Colegio de México, 2007. 314 p.: bibl., ill.

This collection of essays is exceptionally well edited. Concentration on the often neglected 19th century results in some valuable insights into the social and cultural aspects of nation-building. The 14 contributors and editor Palacios reveal a firm grasp of the historiography as the starting point for their innovative forays into understanding the fragile process of building the institutions of representative government.

536 Entre discursos y prácticas: América Latina en el siglo XIX. Edited by Eduardo Cavieres F. Valparaíso, Chile: Vice Rectoría de Investigación y Estudios Avanzados, Ediciones Universitarias de Valparaíso, Pontifiicia Univ. Católica de Valparaíso, 2003. 283 p.: bibl., ill.

Contains a well-researched group of articles on several themes in social/cultural history including the history of prisons, relations between literature and economic liberalism, and medical history. Several contributions on literature and literary criticism.

537 Fleury, Georges. El capitan Bouchard: corsaire de la liberté. Grenoble, France: Glénat, 2010. 363 p.: ill. (some col.), map. (Hommes et océans)

Fast-paced biographical approach that carries Bouchard from the Caribbean and North America to Buenos Aires, the western Pacific, and back to Peru. Unfortunately lacks documentation, footnotes, and other scholarly apparatus.

538 Geschichte Lateinamerikas vom 19. bis zum 21. Jahrhundert: Quellenband. Herausgegeben von Stefan Rinke, Georg Fischer und Frederik Schulze. Stuttgart, Germany: Verlag J.B. Metzler, 2009. 378 p.: bibl., ill., index.

Collection of sources for Latin American history from the 19th century onwards in German translation. Includes not only political documents, but also a few well-chosen documents about cultural history and indigenous peoples. [F. Obermeier]

539 González Deluca, María Elena. Dinámica espacial y representación del espacio en la historia de América Latina. (*Tierra Firme/Caracas*, 24:94, abril/junio 2006, p. 165–182)

Concise examination of the importance of the interplay between regionalism and centralization mainly in the 19th century.

540 Historia general de América Latina. Vol. 6, La construcción de las naciones latinoamericanas, 1820–1870. Dirección del volumen de Josefina Z. Vázquez y Manuel Miño Grijalva. Madrid: Editorial Trotta;

París: Ediciones UNESCO, 2004. 728 p.: bibl., ill., indexes, maps.

An impressive collection of 27 interpretive scholarly essays that span the last phases of independence and the critical early period of nation-building. The essays are topical and include a broad sampling of the histories of the new nations.

541 Jacobsen, Nils. "Liberalismo tropical": cómo explicar el auge de una doctrina económica europea en América Latina, 1780–1885. (*Hist. Crít./Bogotá*, 34, julio/dic. 2007, p. 118–147, bibl.)

An insightful explanation of the arrival and eventual domination of European liberalism among the elites of the new Latin American nations through commerce, immigration, and political discourse. A major contribution to transatlantic history.

542 Jornadas de Historia y Religión, 6th, Caracas, 2006. Miranda, Bolívar y Bello: tres tiempos del pensar latinoamericano: memoria de las VI Jornadas de Historia y Religión en homenaje a los doscientos años de la expedición libertadora de Francisco de Miranda. Caracas: Fundación Konrad Adenauer Stiftung: Univ. Católica Andrés Bello, 2007. 339 p.: bibl.

Intellectual and political history are combined in this collection of 18 essays that are focused on the ideas of this trio of figures from the early 19th century. Based largely on published sources.

543 Jornadas Nacionales de Historia Militar, 12th, Seville, Spain, 2004. Las guerras en el primer tercio del siglo XIX en España y América. Actas XII Jornadas Nacionales de Historia Militar, Sevilla, 8–12 de noviembre de 2004. Coordinación de Paulino Castañeda Delgado. Madrid: Deimos, 2005. 2 v.: bibl., ill., maps, ports.

This very large collection includes 79 articles that deal with military history in the broadest sense. Themes include government policy, mentalities, military medicine and science, as well as accounts of battles. The research is generally sound and the scholarly citations are informative.

544 Klooster, Wim. Revolutions in the Atlantic world: a comparative history. New York: New York Univ. Press, 2009. 239 p.: bibl., index, ill., maps.

Stimulating comparative study of the four revolutions that dominated North America, Europe, the Caribbean, and Spanish America from 1775 to the 1820s. Klooster synthesizes the findings of specialists in Spanish American, Haitian, US, and European history in his examination of the social, economic, political, and cultural factors in these epic revolutions. The author emphasizes international politics as important in all four revolutions. The concluding chapter presents a succinct summary of Klooster's findings.

545 Krebs, Ricardo. La iglesia de América Latina en el siglo XIX. Santiago: Ediciones Univ. Católica de Chile, 2002. 341 p.: bibl., ill., index. (Investigaciones)

A well-organized synthesis on the struggle and ultimate failure of the Catholic Church to maintain its advantaged position in the emerging nations of Latin America. Krebs discusses the rising influence of the secular state and the Church's concentration on its spiritual and educational missions. Impressive bibliography.

546 Martín-Merás, Luisa. La expedición hidrográfica del atlas de la América septentrional, 1792–1805. (*J. Lat. Am. Geogr.*, 7:1, 2008, p. 203–217, bibl., maps, photos)

Archival research supports this account of the multiphased expedition to map navigation routes, gather scientific information, and survey defensive fortifications during these tumultuous years in the Caribbean and Gulf of Mexico.

547 Menniti, Adonay. San Martín, libertador de Argentina, Chile y Perú: reivindicación histórica. 2. ed., corr. y aum. Mendoza, Argentina: Memphis Investigadores, 2007–2008. 3 v.: bibl., ill., maps.

Biographical and geographical details combined with frequent quotations from primary documents give a close-up view of San Martín's crossing of the Andes and his campaigns in Chile and Peru. Vol. 3 contains a collection of his correspondence after 1823.

548 Miller, Nicola. The "immoral" educator: race, gender and citizenship in Simón Rodríguez's programme for popular education. (*Hisp. Res. J.*, 7:1, Feb. 2006, p. 3–10, map)

Detailed exploration of the ideas and ideals of Simón Bolívar's tutor. Adds valuable insights to understanding Bolívar and Spanish American society and politics of the early 19th century.

Nineteenth-century nation building and the Latin American intellectual tradition: a reader. See item 3529.

549 Nineteenth-century travels, explorations, and empires: writings from the era of imperial consolidation, 1835–1910. Vol. 8, South America. Series edited by Peter J. Kitson. Volume edited by Neil L. Whitehead. London; Brookfield, Vt.: Pickering & Chatto, 2004. 1 v.: bibl., ill.

A useful perspective on the rise of informal imperialism. These selections and the editor's perceptive introduction emphasize that travel writing in this period reflected imperialistic assumptions and goals by providing commentary on travel, resources, and commercial expansion. This volume concentrates on British Guyana, Venezuela, and Brazil.

550 Ocampo, Emilio. La última campaña del emperador: Napoleón y la independencia de América. Buenos Aires: Claridad, 2007. 506 p., 8 p. of plates: bibl., ill., index, map.

Grand and somewhat popularized vision of empire, political intrigue, and international conspiracy are the dominant themes in this provocative examination of Napoleon after Waterloo. Drawn from multiple archives and extensively footnoted.

551 Pons, André. Blanco White y América. Oviedo, Spain: Instituto Feijoo de Estudios del Siglo XVIII, Univ. de Oviedo, 2006. 402 p.: bibl. (Textos y estudios del siglo XVIII; 25)

Thorough research supports this well-rounded combination of biography and political/intellectual history that places editor Blanco White in the context of the independence movements. The focus is on Venezuela, and the author draws much of his research from the records of the British Foreign Office.

552 Quijada, Mónica. Una constitución singular: la Carta Gaditana en perspectiva comparada. (*Rev. Indias*, 68:242, enero/abril 2008, p. 15–38, bibl.)

Insightful comparative study of the Spanish constitution of 1812 alongside the French constitutional experiments from 1789 to 1812 and the US Constitution of 1787.

553 Quintero Saravia, Gonzalo M. Pablo Morillo: general de dos mundos. Bogotá: Planeta, 2005. 640 p.: bibl., ill., maps. Serie Biografía)

Well-researched biography of the Spanish general including archival material as well as a wide array of published monographs on the Americas and Europe in the independence period. About one-third of the text concerns Morillo's campaigns in northern South America.

554 Rebok, Sandra. La expedición americana de Alexander von Humboldt y su contribución a la ciencia del siglo XIX. *Bull. Inst. fr. étud. andin.*, 32:3, 2003, p. 441–458, bibl.)

A broad overview of Humboldt's publications with emphasis on his holistic approach.

555 La república peregrina: hombres de armas y letras en América del Sur, 1800–1884. Edición de Carmen Mc Evoy y Ana María Stuven. Lima: Instituto Francés de Estudios Andinos: IEP, Instituto de Estudios Peruanos, 2007. 562 p.: bibl., ill. (Serie Estudios históricos; 46) (Actes & mémoires de l'Institut français d'études andines; 14)

This well-conceived collection of articles concentrates on the formation and early history of nation-states in South America. Topics examined include representative democracy, public education, and foreign influences.

556 Reza, Germán A. de la. El Congreso de Panamá de 1826 y otros ensayos de integración latinoamericana. México: Ediciones y Gráficos EÓN: Univ. Autónoma Metropolitana—Azcapotzalco, 2006. 286 p.: bibl.

Brief, balanced introductory essay accompanied by 32 selected documents, 23 of which deal with the Panama Congress. The remainder concern later conferences concluding with the second conference in Lima (1864–65).

557 Rinke, Stefan H. Revolutionen in Lateinamerika: Wege in die Unabhängigkeit 1760–1830 [Revolutions in Latin America: the path to independence

1760–1830]. München, Germany: Beck, 2010. 392 p.: bibl., ill., maps.

General presentation of independence movements in Latin America within the historical context of 1760 to 1830. Although it is difficult to generalize the rather heterogeneous developments of different regions and their social and political implications, the study offers a balanced judgement about the achievements and failures of nation-building in Latin America. [F. Obermeier]

558 Rodríguez León, Mario A. El obispo Juan Alejo de Arizmendi ante el proceso revolucionario y el inicio de la emancipación de América Latina y el Caribe. Prólogo del Ricardo E. Alegría. Bayamón, P.R.: Instituto de Estudios Históricos Juan Alejo de Arizmendi, Univ. Central de Bayamón, Centro de Estudios de los Dominicos del Caribe, 2003. 1005 p.: bibl., ill. (some col.), indexes, maps.

Lengthy biographical study of Arizmendi that provides insights into the role of the Catholic Church in the circum-Caribbean during the tumultuous events of the independence period.

559 Rodríguez O., Jaime E. El nacimiento de Hispanoamérica: Vicente Rocafuerte y el hispanoamericanismo, 1808–1832. 2. ed. corr. Quito: Univ. Andina Simón Bolívar: Corporación Editora Nacional, 2007. 322 p.: bibl., index, map. (Biblioteca de historia; 22)

Extensive archival research, a solid grasp of relevant published works, and a clear writing style make this an impressive biographical study. Rodríguez gives attention to intellectual and political factors. The footnotes and bibliography are thorough.

560 Rood, Daniel. Herman Merivale's Black Legend: rethinking the intellectual history of free trade imperialism. (*NWIG*, 80:3/4, 2006, p. 163–189, bibl.)

A nuanced examination of the ideas of Merivale, a political economist and British colonial official. Rood sees Merivale as a transitional figure between the older British empire that relied on slave labor and the new empire of free trade and inexpensive free labor combined with a species of political authoritarianism. For comment by historian of the British Caribbean, see item **1293.**

561 Rosas Ledezma, Enrique. Simón Bolívar, el monroismo y la independencia de Cuba. Panamá: Editorial Universitaria Carlos Manuel Gasteazoro, 2009. 143 p.: bibl., ill., maps.

Interesting thought piece on the confluence of Bolivar's ideas and the Monroe Doctrine as applied to the Spanish-American War. Author's conclusions invite controversy.

562 Los rostros de la modernidad: vías de transición al capitalismo: Europa y América Latina, siglos XIX–XX. Coordinación de Andrea Reguera. Rosario, Argentina: Prohistoria Ediciones, 2006. 172 p.: bibl., ill. (Col. Actas; 3)

This nicely edited volume of six scholarly case studies of the early stages of capitalism concentrates on political, legal, ideological, and cultural factors rather than the statistical approach usually employed in economic history. The introduction by editor Andrea Reguera is a balanced essay in comparative history, based on broad reading in this field.

563 Rupke, Nicolaas A. Alexander von Humboldt: a metabiography. Chicago: Univ. of Chicago Press, 2008. 316 p.: bibl., ill., index.

Wide-ranging, deeply researched, and well-written. This biography examines the many aspects of Humboldt's varied career including his lasting influences in Latin America. One chapter is devoted to Humboldt as a "pioneer of globalization." Extensive bibliography.

564 Sánchez Andrés, Agustín. Una diplomacia defensiva: la política exterior española en el Caribe y el golfo de México entre 1865 y 1878. (*Hispania/Madrid*, 67:226, mayo/agosto 2007, p. 487–516)

Studies Spanish counterbalancing techniques vis-à-vis the US in the years following the US Civil War and the close of the first war against Spain when Spain was trying hard to hold on to Cuba. Traces Spain's attempt to reestablish relations with the Dominican Republic and Haiti and its successes in its relations with Colombia and Mexico. [B. Tenenbaum]

565 Stagg, John Charles Anderson. Borderlines in borderlands: James Madison and the Spanish-American frontier, 1776–1821. New Haven, Conn.: Yale Univ.

Press, 2009. 307 p.: bibl., index, maps. (The Lamar series in western history)

Stagg explains the strategic analyses that underlay Madison's role in the complex history of the Florida-Louisiana-Texas borderlands. This extensively researched study adds important depth on the negotiations between Spain and the US that culminated in the Adams-Onís or Transcontinental Treaty

566 Torruella, Juan R. Global intrigues: the era of the Spanish-American War and the rise of the United States to world power. San Juan: La Editorial, Univ. de Puerto Rico, 2007. 224 p., 30 p. of plates: bibl., ill., index, maps, ports.

The author adeptly documents the multiple "intrigues" carried out by world powers—Britain, Germany, Japan, and France—during the Spanish-American War. This publication also contains a convenient synthesis of recent publications on these episodes that constituted a turning point of the history of the western hemisphere and global power politics.

567 Urquijo Torres, Pedro Sergio. Humboldt y el Jorullo: historia de una exploración. México: UNAM: Centro de Investigaciones en Geografía Ambiental, Coordinación de Estudios de Pogrado, Instituto de Geografía: Secretaría de Medio Ambiente y Recursos Naturales: Instituto Nacional de Ecología, 2008. 103 p.: bibl., ill., maps.

Succinct, well-illustrated study of Humboldt's examination of the Michoacán volcano.

568 Vargas Garcia, Eugênio. ¿Imperio informal?: la política británica hacia América Latina en el siglo XIX. (*Foro Int./ México*, 46:2, abril/junio 2006, p. 353–385)

A useful survey of recent publication on the British presence in Latin America. Vargas Garcia concludes that after some military/naval interventions in the first half of the century, London abandoned the tactic and relied on bankers, merchants, and engineers to expand their enterprises. The author places Britain's Latin American policies within a global framework.

569 Violencia y legitimidad: política y revoluciones en España y América Latina, 1840–1910. Edición de Carlos Malamud y Carlos Dardé. Santander, Spain: Univ. de Cantabria, 2004. 227 p.: bibl., ill., maps.

The authors of this collection of articles explore the complex relationship between violent grassroots revolutions and the electoral process. This volume benefits from a consistent editorial focus on this theme. The Latin American portion includes Central America, Bolivia, Peru, and Argentina.

570 Weil, François. Las migraciones de Francia hacia las Américas: un objeto de saberes en el siglo XIX. (*Estud. Migr. Latinoam.*, 20:61, dic. 2006, p. 473–487)

Concise examination of the French analysis of and promotion of immigration to Latin America. Utilizes government and press sources.

571 Zermeño P., Guillermo. Los usos políticos de América/americanos: México, 1750–1850. (*Rev. Estud. Polít.*, 134, dic. 2006, p. 71–95, bibl.)

Well-informed discussion of the origins and semantic evolution of the terms "América" and "americanos" that emphasizes the political debates of the early 19th century.

20TH CENTURY

572 Actores y dimensión religiosa en los movimientos sociales latinoamericanos, 1960–1992. Coordinación de María Alicia Puente Lutteroth. Mexico: Univ. Autónoma del Estado del Morelos, Facultad de Humanidades: Miguel Ángel Porrúa, 2006. 320 p.: bibl.

The dynamics of the history of the Catholic Church reached an exceptional level of intensity in the last decades of the 20th century. This volume contains a stimulating aggregation of scholarly articles and opinion pieces by a mix of sociologists, theologians, historians, and priests who discuss liberation theology, *communidades de base*, and the actions of Archbishops Oscar Arnulfo Romero and Dom Helder Câmara.

573 Altamira y Crevea, Rafael. Mi viaje a América: libro de documentos. Oviedo, Spain: Univ. de Oviedo, 2007. 358 p.

A collection of documents that detail the visits of Altamira y Crevea to universities in Argentina, Uruguay, Chile, Peru, Mexico, and Cuba in 1909–10. He was a pioneer in inter-university relations.

574 América hispánica en el siglo XX: identidades, culturas y sociedades. Coordinación de Jean-Marie Lemogodeuc. Caracas: Univ. Católica Andrés Bello: Banco Industrial, 2002. 406 p.: bibl., index, maps.

Multi-authored volume that explores questions surrounding the nature of social/cultural identity in the complexity of Latin American society. The authors examine rural and urban dichotomies, the role of politics, and the growth of globalization.

575 Ameringer, Charles D. The socialist impulse: Latin America in the twentieth century. Gainesville: Univ. Press of Florida, 2009. 333 p.: bibl., index.

This carefully considered, nonpolemical study of the promises, struggles, and frustrations of socialist movements in the region will benefit leftists, moderates, and rightists. Ameringer brings the maturity of a lifetime of study to this country-by-country survey. He concludes that while socialist movements have not succeeded, the causes of such movements are embedded in the unequal distribution of material wealth and the persistent poverty that continue to plague Latin America. Therefore, socialist movements are likely to continue to play some role on the political landscape.

576 Barros, Maria Cândida Drumond Mendes. A missão Summer Institute of Linguistics e o indigenismo latino-americano: história de uma aliança (décadas de 1930 a 1970). (*Rev. Antropol./São Paulo*, 47:1, jan./junho 2004, p. 45–85, bibl.)

A general study of this organization's linguistic and political projects in Mexico, Peru, and Brazil. Founded as the Wycliff Bible translators by William Cameron Townsend.

577 Besse, Susan K. Engendering reform and revolution in twentieth-century Latin America and the Caribbean. (*in* Companion to gender history. Edited by Teresa A. Meade and Merry E. Wiesner-Hanks. Malden, Mass.: Blackwell Publishing, 2004, p. 568–585, bibl.)

A perceptive synthesis of recent publications on the growing participation of women in liberal and leftist movements in the 20th century, including populism in the early decades, revolutions in the Castro era, and resistance to military dictatorships in the 1970s and 1980s.

578 Cappelli, Vittorio. Entre inmigrantes, socialistas y masones: (*Estud. Migr. Latinoam.*, 19:57, agosto 2005, p. 335–366, bibl.)

Covers a previously neglected topic in considerable depth. The author effectively combines immigration history and political history. Based on archival work and published sources.

579 Crítica y teoría en el pensamiento social latinoamericano. Buenos Aires: CLACSO, 2006. 437 p.: bibl., ill. (Col. Becas de investigación)

The disciplines of sociology, economics, and anthropology are well represented in these seven essays. The authors question some of the basic neoconservative principles used to justify the process of globalization under the aegis of capitalism. Cogent presentations of a critical perspective.

580 Entre historias y memorias: los desafíos metodológicos del legado reciente de América Latina. Coordinación de Maria Rosaria Stabili. Netherlands: Asociación de Historiadores Latinoamericanistas Europeos; Madrid: Iberoamericana; Frankfurt am Main: Vervuert, 2007. 246 p.: bibl. (Estudios AHILA de historia latinoamericana; 2)

The interaction of memory and history is an important subject—especially when the subject matter involves sensitive and controversial issues such as human rights violations, dictatorial government, and secret intelligence work. This book concentrates on the recent past in Argentina, Chile, Brazil, and Guatemala.

581 Los estudios sobre América Latina y el Caribe: nuevos temas y perspectivas. México: UNAM, Centro Coordinador y Difusor de Estudios Latinoamericanos, 2005. 585 p.: bibl. (Serie Coloquios; 1)

Immigration, multiculturalism, and democratization are three themes that give these 32 essays some coherence. Six of the essays are in literary criticism.

582 Ferrer, Carlos. De Ernesto al Che: el segundo y último viaje de Guevara por Latinoamérica. Prólogo de Alberto Granado. Buenos Aires: Marea Editorial, 2005. 217 p.: bibl., ill., photos. (Col. Historia urgente)

First-person account by Che Guevara's companion on his 1953 trip from Argentina through Bolivia, Peru, and Ecuador. Ferrer balances a story of youthful adventure with an explanation of intellectual discovery. Includes photographs.

583 Giraudo, Laura. Historia de AHILA: perfil de la Asociación de Historiadores Latinoamericanistas Europeos, 1969–2008. Con textos de Magnus Mörner, Ádám Anderle y John Fisher, y entrevista a Francisco Morales Padrón. Madrid: Iberoamericana: Frankfurt am Main: Vervuert, 2008. 210 p.: bibl. (Estudios AHILA de Historia Latinoamericana; 5)

Succinct, thoroughly documented study of the origins and early decades of AHILA including the correspondence of Magnus Mörner and Marcello Carmangani. Supplemented by over 100 pages of documents.

584 Gootenberg, Paul. The "pre-Colombian" era of drug trafficking in the Americas: cocaine, 1945–1965. (*Americas/ Washington*, 64:2, Oct. 2007, p. 133–176)

An exceptionally well-researched account of the early decades of cocaine smuggling that focuses on the Peruvian town of Huánuco and includes operations in Chile, Castro's Cuba, and Brazil, all placed in the framework of prohibitionist law enforcement in the US. Essential in understanding the little-studied initial methods in what became a huge illicit export business.

585 Gould, Jeffrey L. Solidarity under siege: the Latin American Left, 1968. (*Am. Hist. Rev.*, 114:2, April 2009, p. 348–375, bibl., facsims., photos)

Gould adroitly combines original sources from interviews and journalistic accounts with social and political theory to explain the significance of the student-inspired uprisings in Uruguay, Brazil, and Mexico. The article also includes an assessment of the long-term influences of these movements and the responses of right-wing military regimes.

586 Guerra, Sergio. Laberintos de la integración latinoamericana: historia, mito y realidad de una utopía. Caracas: Comala.com, 2006. 93 p.: bibl. (Col. Nuestra América)

Succinct essay on the promises and pitfalls of Latin American integration with appropriate attention to the threatening presence of the US.

587 In from the cold: Latin America's new encounter with the Cold War. Edited by Gilbert M. Joseph and Daniela Spenser. Durham, N.C.; London: Duke Univ. Press, 2007. 439 p.: bibl., index. (American encounters/global interactions)

This edited volume explores Latin America's experience with the Cold War in terms of the politics, cultures, and ideologies of the Latin American nations thereby avoiding the all too frequent approach of thrusting all of these nations into an artificial dichotomous world-encompassing mold. Joseph's introduction, Spencer's conclusion, and the individual contributions emphasize the variety of leftist movements and national policies and the unfortunate consequences of the responses of the US. Excellent bibliography.

588 Joly, Allain. Fiefs et entreprises en Amérique Latine. Québec: Les Presses de l'Université Laval, 2004. 145 p.: bibl. (Col. Sciences de l'administration)

Joly addresses the issues surrounding Latin America's troubled economic record in the last decades of the 20th century and finds some examples of success that ran contrary to the larger trends. He employs an unusually broad range of conceptual frameworks from Fernand Braudel to Max Weber to Jeffrey Sachs.

589 Kuntz Ficker, Sandra. From structuralism to the new institutional economics: the impact of theory on the study of foreign trade in Latin America. (*LARR*, 40:3, 2005, p. 145–162, bibl.)

A thought-provoking assessment of the long-term strengths and weaknesses of structuralism and the emergence of the Washington consensus version of neoliberalism with attention to commentary by John Coatsworth, John Williamson, Joseph Love, and Paul Krugman.

590 Latin America during World War II. Edited by Thomas M. Leonard and John F. Bratzel. Lanham, Md.: Rowman & Littlefield, 2007. 226 p., 12 p. of plates: bibl., ill., index, map. (Jaguar books on Latin America series)

Ten scholarly articles cover the domestic politics, economic developments, and international relations of Spanish America and Brazil. The five nations of Central America are covered in Leonard's trenchant survey while strategically important Panama receives an article unto itself by Orlando Pérez. Most of the contributors give appropriate attention to espionage. Editor Bratzel's introduction provides a helpful overview.

591 Love, Joseph L. The rise and decline of economic structuralism in Latin America: new dimensions. (*LARR*, 40:3, 2005, p. 100–125, bibl.)

This exceptionally clear, well-written study of the history of structuralism concentrates on import substitution-industrialization, the informal economic sector, and a discussion of structuralism as a movement. Avoids excessive technical jargon and is suitable for the general reader.

592 Movimientos universitarios: América Latina siglo XX. Edición de Olmedo Vargas Hernández. Bogotá: RUDECOLOMBIA: Doctorado en Ciencias de la Educación, 2005. 271 p.: bibl., ill.

This collection of essays and thought pieces offers several perspectives on student movements from the Argentine Univ. de Córdoba in the early decades of the century to Chilean, Argentine, and Uruguayan universities under the military governments of the 1970s. Much attention to Colombia and the role of Germán Arcienegas.

593 Pettinà, Vanni. Del anticomunismo al antinacionalismo: la presidencia Eisenhower y el giro autoritario en la América Latina de los años 50. (*Rev. Indias*, 67:240, mayo/agosto 2007, p. 573–606, bibl.)

This nicely honed interpretive article traces the change in US policy towards Latin America from reconciliation with nationalist/reformist governments in the 1930s and 1940s to the anti-communist, anti-reformist approach of the 1950s. Pinpoints the role of C.P. Cabell in the Washington establishment. Sources include a good mix of published works and archival sources.

594 La radio en Iberoamérica: evolución, diagnóstico, prospectiva. Coordinación de Arturo Merayo Pérez. Sevilla, Spain: Comunicación Social, 2007. 461 p.: bibl., ill. (Col. periodística; 21)

The authors tend to emphasize the technical and business aspects of radio. Most of the articles are footnoted and some have extensive bibliographies. Most of the sources are monographs and published documents with some internet sites.

595 El rebelde contemporáneo en el Circuncaribe: imágenes y representaciones. Coordinación de Enrique Camacho Navarro. México: UNAM, Centro Coordinador Difusor de Estudios Latinoamericanos: Edere, 2006. 431 p.: bibl., ill., maps.

This volume contains 13 scholarly essays that explore social unrest and political upheaval in the circum-Caribbean of the 20th century. Among the topics covered are the Cold War revolutions in Cuba, Nicaragua, and Guatemala, and lesser-known movements in Mexico and Colombia. These contributions have a mix of literary, sociological, and historical approaches.

Reid, Michael. Forgotten continent: the battle for Latin America's soul. See *HLAS 65:1434.*

596 Rethinking Jewish-Latin Americans. Edited by Jeffrey Lesser and Raanan Rein. Albuquerque: Univ. of New Mexico Press, 2008. 294 p.: bibl., ill., index. (Diálogos)

This collection of well-researched scholarly articles strikes a balance between the general and the particular. The editors' introduction and the second chapter give social and political overviews, and the 10 specialized contributions deal with a variety of case studies from ethnic/political stereotyping to the role of ideology, and from Jewish orphanages and a Buenos Aires Yiddish chorus to prostitution.

597 Sabsay, Fernando L. Protagonistas de América Latina. v. 2. Buenos Aires: Editorial El Ateneo, 2006. 1 v. (365 p.): bibl., photos.

Biographical sketches of well-known historical figures from Ramón Castilla to Emiliano Zapata to Eva Perón. Intended for a general readership. Lacks scholarly apparatus.

598 Sosa Fuentes, Samuel. Modernización, dependencia y sistema-mundo: los paradigmas del desarrollo latinoamericano y los desafíos del siglo XXI. (*Relac. Int./México,* 96, sept./dic. 2006, p. 87–121)

A low key, yet provocative recapitulation of four of the major schools of thought on Latin American economic history: modernization theory, CEPAL's center-periphery concept, dependency theory, and the world-systems framework. The author sees some vitality and continued relevance in Marxist critical perspectives.

599 Tur Donatti, Carlos M. La utopía del regreso: la cultura del nacionalismo hispanista en América Latina. México: Instituto Nacional de Antropología e Historia, 2006. 119 p.: bibl. (Col. Científica; 504. Serie Historia)

The author identifies an important theme frequently overlooked by historians who study Mexico, Peru, and Argentina of the first half of the 20th century. Sometimes overshadowed by the surges of interest in Native American culture in Mexico and Peru, the resilience of Spanish cultural influences—especially in architecture and literature—gain attention in this volume. Tur Donatti also traces similar Spanish influences in the context of Argentina of the Perón era.

600 Urquidi, Víctor L. Otro siglo perdido: las políticas de desarrollo en América Latina, 1930–2005. México: Colegio de México, Fideicomiso Historia de las Américas: Fondo de Cultura Económica, 2005. 568 p.: bibl. (Sección de Obras de Historia)

Respected veteran economist Urquidi takes on the challenge of explaining Latin America's difficulties in the recent past. He probes several weaknesses including import-substitution industrialization, monetary problems, foreign debt, and the uncertainties of globalization since 1990. The last chapter is his formula for a sustainable future.

MEXICO
General

SUZANNE B. PASZTOR, *Associate Professor of History, Humboldt State University*

A HEALTHY NUMBER of state, local, and regional studies continue to be published in Mexico. Among the more notable works produced in the last biennium are collections on Baja California by Cariño Olvera and Castorena Davis (item 666) and González Cruz and Altable (item 632), as well as a study of Tecate by Santiago Guerrero (item 662). Northeastern Mexico is explored in Ortega Ridaura (item 654), Cavazos Garza and Morado Macías (item 613), and in a volume commemorating the centenary of the city of Torreón, Coahuila (item 640). The state of Mexico is explored in a collection by Zamudio Espinosa and Camacho Pichardo (item 624) and in studies of individual municipalities by Hernández Rodríguez and Sánchez Blas (item 673 and 661). Mendoza Muñoz and Moreno Pérez examine the history of specific areas in Querétaro (item 646 and 652), and Rionda Arreguín provides a sketch of one of Guanajuato's original settlements (item 658). Southern Mexico is represented in studies by Guzmán Flores (item 631) and Carpio Penagos and Whiting (item 633). Ojeda and Alcocer provide an interesting look at an Afro-American community in the Yucatán (item 670).

A handful of notable works on cultural and social history appeared in the last biennium. Carmen Collado offers an edited volume on Mexico City during the 19th and 20th centuries (item 651), while Gonzalbo Aizpuru and Zárate Toscano provide a fascinating look at the evolution of *mentalités* in colonial and modern Mexico (item 629). Vázquez Parada and Muñoz Pini include essays on a variety of topics related to religion, society, and culture from the precolumbian to the modern era (item 617), and the variety of ways in which Mexicans and Spaniards have represented one another is the topic of a collection by Miquel (item 635).

Although neither topic attracted many scholars in the last biennium, a few notable works of economic and immigration history appeared. Mexico's important mining industry is examined in Burnes Ortiz who presents a comprehensive view of the scope and implications of this economic sector (item 610), and Flores Clair brings together essays on credit and financing in the mining economy (item 616). Barragán Maldonado traces the history of a German family during the 19th century (item 606), Domínguez Martín and Cerutti present a history of Cantabrian immigrants (item 618), and Villaverde García examines Galicians in Mexico (item 672).

Several individual works of note also appeared in this cycle. The bicentennial of independence and the centennial of the Mexican Revolution inspire an excellent volume edited by Mayer and including a variety of topics that span the scope of Mexico's history (item 648). Palacio Montiel provides a collection on the history of print media focused on several regions of the country (item 664), and García, Galván, and Moctezuma explore the messages contained in school textbooks utilized from the colonial era forward (item 639). Rangel Silva and Ruiz Medrano present a volume on the history of popular resistance (item 621), and Melgar brings together essays that reveal the state of scholarship on women in Mexico (item 656). Finally, Buchenau presents a volume that explores Mexico through foreign eyes (item 649), and Acuña examines Mexican migrants and their activism (item 602).

GENERAL

601 Abundis Canales, Jaime Antonio. La huella carmelita en San Ángel. México: Instituto Nacional de Antropología e Historia, 2007. 2 v. (1585 p.): bibl., ill.

This study is an extensive treatment of the Carmelite order in Mexico, with a focus on its presence in the southwestern section of Mexico City. The author, an architect, traces the development of the order in the context of the city's history while exploring the architecture of the Carmelites and of the more contemporary neighborhood of San Ángel.

602 Acuña, Rodolfo F. Corridors of migration: the odyssey of Mexican laborers, 1600–1933. Tucson: Univ. of Arizona Press, 2007. 408 p.: bibl., index.

This is an excellent and sweeping exploration of Mexican migration, Mexican labor, and Mexican activism. The author is particularly focused on the history that culminated in the 1933 cotton strike in San Joaquín County, California. He challenges the notion of a leaderless and apathetic Mexican labor force.

603 Anti-Americanism in Latin America and the Caribbean. Edited by Alan McPherson. New York: Berghahn Books, 2006. 301 p.: bibl., index. (Explorations in culture and international history; 3)

This impressive volume explores several contexts of anti-Americanism, with a focus on the 20th and early 21st centuries. John Britton's essay on Mexico traces the evolution of anti-American thought in the post-revolutionary era, particularly with regard to the oil expropriation of 1938. Britton demonstrates that Mexican anti-Americanism included a pointed criticism of US dominance of the global financial system.

604 Ayala Anguiano, Armando. La epopeya de México. México: Fondo de Cultura Económica, 2005. 2 v.: indexes. (Col. popular; 656)

The author, a journalist, provides a sweeping account of Mexico's history from precolumbian times to approximately 2000. The focus of these volumes is political change, with much attention paid to the "great men" of Mexico's past. Suitable for a general reader, this work draws upon major secondary sources.

605 Banko, Catalina. La industria azucarera en Venezuela y México: un estudio comparativo. (*Bol. Acad. Nac. Hist./ Caracas,* 88:352, oct./dic. 2005, p. 157–179, bibl.)

The author provides a comprehensive analysis of the differences between the sugar industries in both countries, from the colonial era to the age of neoliberal reforms. While Mexico developed a viable and modern industry earlier, both countries experienced impressive state-sponsored growth during the middle of the 20th century. After the 1970s, however, both countries experienced a slowing of growth, as well as a turn toward privatization of the sugar industry.

606 Barragán Maldonado, Leopoldo. Las migraciones alemanas en Colima, 1848–1890: un estudio de caso: familia Schulte Vogel. Colima, Mexico: Gobierno del Estado de Colima, Secretaría de Cultura, Fondo Estatal para la Cultura y las Artes de Colima; Mexico: CONACULTA, 2007. 152 p.: bibl., ill., maps.

This study utilizes state, local, and family archives, as well as interviews to trace the fortunes of Carlos Schulte, who immigrated to Colima during the Porfirian era, and to analyze the family's loss of its German identity. The author also provides the historical contexts that encouraged emigration from Germany and immigration to Mexico during the presidencies of Benito Juárez and Porfirio Díaz.

607 Beltrán Dengra, Joaquín. Visión desde España del México revolucionario: viajeros, diplomacia, y prensa. México: Centro de Estudios Filosóficos, Políticos y Sociales Vincente Lombardo Toledano, 2007. 186 p.: bibl. (Col. Tópicos sobre problemas políticos y sociales de nuestro tiempo)

A brief analysis of the ideas of 10 Spanish intellectuals who experienced the revolutionary era and recorded their impressions. The author explores Spanish opinions about the country, its people and leaders (from Porfirio Díaz to Plutarco Elías Calles), and the phenomena of Hispanophobia, indigenismo, and pan-Hispanism.

608 Breve historia de Baja California. Coordinación de Marco Antonio Samaniego López. México: 2007 año del Cincuentenario de la UABC; Mexicali, Mexico:

Univ. Autónoma de Baja California; México: M. A. Porrúa, 2006. 241 p.: bibl., ill., maps. (Serie conmemorativa 50 aniversario UABC)

Part of a series commemorating 50 years of the University of Baja California, this short work is specifically intended for a general audience, and particularly for use in secondary schools. The authors, all professional academics, focus on the broadest political, economic, and social trends.

609 Buchenau, Jürgen. Mexican mosaic: a brief history of Mexico. Wheeling, Ill.: Harlan Davidson, Inc., 2008. 164 p., 16 p. of plates: bibl., ill., index, maps. (Global history series)

Concise introduction to Mexican history for students or travelers. The author's focus is on the last 200 years, up to the election of President Felipe Calderón in 2006. Relatively little space is given to the indigenous past. Includes well-chosen illustrations. [B. Tenenbaum]

610 Burnes Ortiz, Arturo. El drama de la minería mexicana: del pacto colonial a la globalización contemporánea. Zacatecas, Mexico: Univ. Autónoma de Zacatecas, 2006. 395 p.: bibl., maps.

Based on the extensive existing scholarship, as well as on primary sources, this study takes a long view of Mexico's mining industry and the many ways in which this economic sector has affected and been affected by local, national, and international forces. The author places particular emphasis on the relationship between mining and the global economy, underscoring the failure of this extractive industry to bring comprehensive economic development to Mexico.

611 Calderón Viedas, Carlos. Huellas de modernidad en Sinaloa. México: Fontamara: Gobierno del Estado de Sinaloa, Coordinación General de Asesoría y Políticas Públicas, 2007. 241 p.: bibl. (ABC de Sinaloa; 7)

This brief volume is primarily a reflection on the issue of modernity in Mexico's past. The author searches for traces of modernity in the political, economic, and cultural histories of Mexico and of Sinaloa.

612 Catrina y sepulcro: cultura y espacios funerarios en México. Compilación de Carlos Alberto Mercado Limones y Luz de Lourdes Serna Cerrillo. México: Univ.

Autonoma Metropolitana, Unidad Xochimilco, 2006. 261 p.: bibl., ill., maps.

This book, suitable for a general audience, resulted from papers presented at an international congress on cemeteries and funeral art. The authors intend to encourage the preservation of this part of Mexico's heritage. The volume explores Mesoamerican cosmogony and the Día de los Muertos tradition, epitaphs and vegetation contained in cemeteries, and the Museo de las Momias of Guanajuato. The authors also profile the histories of five Mexican cemeteries.

613 Cavazos Garza, Israel and **César Morado Macías.** Fábrica de la frontera: Monterrey, capital de Nuevo León, 1596–2006. Monterrey, México: Ayuntamiento de Monterrey, 2006. 241 p.: bibl., index.

Intended for a popular audience, this book gathers together the work of both authors in a survey of Monterrey's history. Organized thematically, the book contains sections on political, economic, and social history that explore the city's evolution from an era of colonization to a global, cosmopolitan era.

614 Coloquio Internacional del Noreste Mexicano y Texas, 1st, Saltillo, Coahuila, Mexico, 2003. Memoria del Primer Coloquio Internacional del Noreste Mexicano y Texas. Coordinación de Juana Gabriela Román Jáquez. México: Instituto Nacional de Antropología e Historia, 2008. 358 p.: bibl., ill., maps. (Regiones de México)

Set of interdisciplinary essays considers Northern Mexico and Texas as one region with a common history. Essays cover from prehispanic to contemporary times. [K. Melvin]

615 Contribuciones a la historia económica, social y cultural de Sinaloa. Coordinación de Arturo Carrillo Rojas; Mayra Lizzete Vidales Quintero; y Rigoberto Rodríguez Benítez. Culiacán, Mexico: Editorial UAS, 2007. 296 p.: bibl.

The first part of this collection is the most useful and deals primarily with the state's economic history, including brief essays on the agricultural industry, local entrepreneurs, and the effect of revolutionary activity and agrarian reform on local economic realities. The second section is more wide-ranging, and includes a rather puzzling array of political, cultural, and historiographical topics.

616 Crédito y financiamiento a la industria minera: siglos XVI–XX. Coordinación de Eduardo Flores Clair. México: Plaza y Valdés, 2006. 292 p.: bibl., ill.

Six essays that examine the strategies involved in securing capital and credit for Mexico's mining industry. The authors explore examples from San Luis Potosí, Guanajuato, Zacatecas, Michoacán, and the northern tier of Mexican states. A valuable addition to the history of an important economic sector.

617 Cultura, religión, y sociedad. Coordinación de Lourdes Celina Vázquez Parada y Laura María Muñoz Pini. Guadalajara, Mexico: U DE G-Centro Universitario de Ciencias Sociales y Humanidades, 2007. 304 p.: bibl., ill.

This selection of essays by authors from a variety of disciplines takes a broad view of religion and culture and treats themes from the precolumbian to the modern era. Missions and missionary groups in northwestern New Spain, religious themes in the writing of Alfonso Junco, 19th-century Mexican sermons, and Church-state relations in post-revolutionary Mexico are among the religious topics explored. The search for *lo mexicano*, the issue of "culture" in post-revolutionary Mexico, and the experience of Italians as immigrants to Porfirian Mexico, are among the cultural themes examined.

618 De la colonia a la globalización: empresarios cántabros en México. Edición de Rafael Domínguez Martín y Mario Cerutti Pignat. Santander, Mexico: Servicio de Publicaciones de la Univ. de Cantabria, 2006. 321 p.: bibl., ill., index, maps.

This series of 10 essays focuses on the economic success that Cantabrian immigrants have historically enjoyed in Mexico. What emerges is a clear sense of Cantabrian business acumen, which finds contemporary manifestation in global enterprises such as the Gigante supermarket chain.

619 De la Guadalajara de ayer —y de antier. Compilación de J. Jesús Gómez Fregoso. Guadalajara, Mexico: Univ. de Guadalajara, 2006. 298 p.: bibl.

A collection of brief essays, most by recent history graduates of the Universidad de Guadalajara. Topics include the history of theater, food, amusements, local government and economy, crime, education, and religion. Most selections deal with the colonial and 19th centuries and attempt to utilize both primary and secondary sources.

620 Desacatos. Vol. 26, enero/abril 2008, Archivos públicos en México: organización versus transparencia. Mexico: CIESAS.

This volume includes six essays that probe the state of several Mexican archives including the Archivo General de la Nación, the Archivo Histórico de Migración, and local archives in Jalisco, Hidalgo, and Chiapas. The articles offer commentary on the effect of recent Mexican laws promoting transparency and access to public documents. Also included is an explanation of the successful attempt to preserve the integrity of the state archive of Coahuila.

621 Discursos públicos, negociaciones y estrategias de lucha colectiva: aportaciones al estudio de las movilizaciones sociales en México, siglos XVIII y XIX. Coordinación de José Alfredo Rangel Silva y Carlos Rubén Ruiz Medrano. San Luis Potosí, Mexico: El Colegio de San Luis; Archivo Histórico del Estado de San Luis Potosí, 2006. 178 p.: bibl., maps. (Col. Investigaciones)

This is an excellent series of five detailed essays (all but one on the 19th century) that shed new light on the phenomenon of resistance and collective action. The authors probe movements in the Huasteca, the Mexico-Veracruz corridor, and Oaxaca. The essays underscore the complexity of such movements, and the different ways in which local populations defended their interests.

622 Una docena de visiones de la historia: entrevistas con historiadores americanistas. Entrevistas por Verónica Zárate Toscano; transcripción de Ignacio Hernández García. México: Instituto Mora, 2004. 174 p.: bibl., index. (Historia social y cultural)

A collection of 12 transcribed interviews that examine the interests and perspectives of scholars not from Mexico. The interviews are especially concerned with the issue of "foreigners" interpreting Mexican and Latin American history. Christon Archer, François-Xavier Guerra, Brian Hamnett, Annick Lempériére, and Jaime Rodríguez O. are among the interview subjects.

623 Encuentro Internacional de Historia de la Educación, 9th, Universidad de Colima, 2004. Miradas a la historia regional de la educación. Coordinación de Lucía Martínez Moctezuma y Antonio Padilla Arroyo. México: Univ. Autónoma del Estado de Morelos: M.A. Porrúa, 2006. 335 p.: bibl., ill., maps.

This volume, the result of an international symposium on the history of education, brings together a variety of studies that contribute to a decentered view of this topic. Most essays deal explicitly with the methodological issues involved in this type of regional history. Morelos, Tlaxcala, Puebla, Quintana Roo, Chiapas, and Oaxaca are among the states studied, and most essays deal with the late 19th and early 20th centuries.

624 Estado de México: experiencias de investigación histórica. Coordinación de Guadalupe Yolanda Zamudio Espinosa y Gloria Camacho Pichardo. Toluca, Mexico: Universidad Autónoma del Estado de México, 2005. 311 p.: bibl., ill. (Col. Humanidades. Serie Historia)

The authors, primarily historians and anthropologists, present a series of brief studies on the state of Mexico. Selections on the colonial era include explorations of Mexica uses of history, the indigenous economy, changes in land tenure, and demographic and cultural transformations among indigenous peoples. Essays on the 19th and 20th centuries explore political, economic, and cultural themes with a focus on methodological approaches.

625 Figueiras Tapia, Leonardo. Del gremialismo al antisindicalismo en la UNAM: una historia de las asociaciones autónomas del personal académico de la UNAM. México: Editorial comunicación y política, 2003. 306 p.: bibl.

An exploration of the professional associations which emerged in the 1970s as the preferred alternative to an all-encompassing union. The author details the discussions and debates that took place

among university personnel and between the university and President José López-Portillo. Although the university rector's anti-union stance encouraged the triumph of this model, other considerations were at work, including the belief of full-time professors that the method of the strike had no place in a university.

626 García Fernández, Estrellita. Colima, el fruto de sus fieles patrimonio y devoción en el occidente de México. Zapopan, Mexico: El Colegio de Jalisco, 2007. 159 p.: bibl., ill.

This is a brief study of the historical process by which major religious structures, including Colima's basilica, were erected, restored, and renovated. The author outlines the context in which Colima's faithful attended to these religious buildings, and provides three case studies of the renovation of such structures.

627 Gómez Peralta, Héctor. La Iglesia católica en México como institución de derecha. (Rev. Mex. Cienc. Polít. Soc., 49:199, enero/abril 2007, p. 63–78, bibl.)

The author provides an analysis of the church from the colonial times to the contemporary era. He argues against the view of this institution as the ideological arm of the "bourgeois" state. Instead, for most of its history, the Mexican Church has assumed an intransigent stance against the modernizing tendencies of governments, no matter their ideological orientation.

628 González Gómez, Francisco. Del porfirismo al neoliberalismo. 2. ed., corr. México: Ediciones Quinto Sol, 2007. 391 p.: bibl.

Originally published in 1990, this book revises and expands upon a general political history of modern Mexico from the Porfirian era to the contested presidential election of 2006. The authors are critical of official neoliberal policies, and they identify in Mexico's contemporary political system continuing anti-democratic tendencies.

629 Gozos y sufrimientos en la historia de México. Coordinación de Pilar Gonzalbo Aizpuru y Verónica Zárate Toscano. México: El Colegio de México, Centro de Estudios Históricos: Instituto de

Investigaciones Dr. José María Mora, 2007. 315 p.: bibl., ill.

A fascinating collection of essays that delve into the *mentalité* of colonial and modern Mexico through an exploration of the various ways in which sentiments were expressed. In three distinct sections, authors consider the role of the colonial Church in regulating manifestations of emotion, the importance of social pressures and public censure in the late colonial era, and the meaning of diversions and punishments in the 19th century.

630 Gutiérrez Gutiérrez, José Antonio.
Historia de la Iglesia Católica en Aguascalientes. Aguascalientes, Mexico: Univ. Autónoma de Aguascalientes: Obispado de Aguascalientes; Guadalajara: Univ. de Guadalajara, 2007. 3 v.: bibl., ill. (some col.)

This is the third volume in a series on the church in Aguascalientes. The author traces the history of the state's diocese from its creation in 1899 to approximately 2000. He places the term of each bishop in its historical context, and discusses the activities of the local church in areas such as education and social services.

631 Guzmán Flores, René Enedina.
Raigambre púrpura: imágenes de Pinotepa de Don Luis. Oaxaca, Mexico: Fondo Editorial IEEPO, 2005. 257 p.: bibl., ill. (some col.) (Col. Voces del fondo. Serie Molinos de viento)

This is a somewhat nostalgic profile of an indigenous municipality located on Oaxaca's coast. The author, a native, includes a brief historical overview and focuses primarily on providing a profile of the culture, structure, and characteristics of the contemporary community.

Higgins, Nicholas P. Understanding the Chiapas rebellion: modernist visions and the invisible Indian. See *HLAS 65:508.*

632 Historia general de Baja California Sur. México: Plaza y Valdés, 2002–2004. 3 v.: bibl., ill., maps.

Under the broad categories of region, society, and culture, the authors of this volume present essays on various aspects of the region's history. Studies of several specific population centers, including La Paz and

Los Cabos, are included in the first category, while Baja's society is examined through demographic trends, ecological history, education, politics, unionism, public health, the Catholic Church, and the media. Part three contains studies of the peninsula's history of cultural expression, including art, music, dance, literature, theater, and indigenous cultural expressions.

633 Historia, sociedad y ambiente en la cuenca del Río Negro, frontera Chiapas-Oaxaca. Edición de Carlos Uriel del Carpio Penagos y Thomas Lee Whiting. Tuxtla Gutiérrez, Mexico: Univ. de Ciencias y Artes de Chiapas, 2007. 370 p.: bibl., ill., maps.

A multidisciplinary volume inspired by the issues of agrarian conflict and sustainable development in one corner of Mexico. The authors examine the archeology, history, and natural environment of this part of the Rio Negro basin. Essays on the evolution of land tenure and land disputes will be the most useful to historians.

634 El historiador frente a la historia: perfiles y rumbos de la historia. Sesenta años de investigación histórica en México. Coordinación de Virginia Guedea. México: UNAM, 2007. 216 p.: bibl. (Serie Divulgación/Instituto de Investigaciones Históricas; 7)

This volume commemorates 60 years of the Instituto de Investigaciones Históricas at the National Autonomous University. Eight authors examine historical and historiographical production and trends, primarily in the published work of the Institute. The essays treat precolumbian, colonial, and post-independence Mexican history, as well as the more specific subfields of political, economic, cultural, and regional history.

635 Imágenes cruzadas México y España: siglos XIX y XX. Compilación de Ángel Miquel. Cuernavaca, Mexico: Univ. Autónoma del Estado de Morelos, 2005. 298 p: bibl., ill.

A diverse collection of essays, most of which treat Spanish images of Mexico and Mexican images of Spain. The authors examine literary, cinematic, journalistic, and pictographic images. Selections include Mexican images of Spain and Spaniards in the aftermath of Mexican Independence,

19th-century pictographic representations of Mexico and Spain, Spanish representations of colonial style architecture in Mexico, Mexican cinematic depictions of the society of New Spain, and writings of Spanish republican exiles in Mexico.

636 Imágenes e imaginarios sobre España en México, siglos XIX y XX. Coordinación de Agustín Sánchez Andrés, Tomás Pérez Vejo y Marco Antonio Landavazo. Mexico: Porrúa: Instituto de Investigaciones Históricas, Univ. Michoacana de San Nicolás de Hidalgo: Consejo Nacional de Ciencia y Tecnología, 2007. 659 p.: bibl., ill.

The authors of this volume examine the complex relationship that Mexico and Mexicans have had with Spain and things Spanish. Hispanophobia is explored in several historical contexts, including the independence era and the Mexican Revolution. Authors also examine the representation of Spain in Mexican literature, theater, film, and the visual arts.

637 Knight, Alan. Patterns and prescriptions in Mexican historiography. (*Bull. Lat. Am. Res.*, 25:3, July 2006, p. 340–366)

The author provides a sweeping assessment of the field, paying particular attention to cultural history and to the call by some historians to "reclaim the political." Recent histories on the early republic, the economics of the Porfiriato, and the regional history of the Mexican Revolution are identified by Knight as the most original and useful in the field.

638 Lafaye, Jacques. En el traspatio de la historia. Zapopán, Mexico: Colegio de Jalisco, 2005–2008. v. 1–3: bibl., ill., indexes.

This collection brings together several writings and addresses by Lafaye. Most selections deal broadly with the Americas and the historical and historiographical legacies of discovery and conquest. Two essays deal more specifically with Mexico, exploring the issue of identity and indigenismo and reflecting on the 1968 Tlalelolco massacre 20 years after its occurrence.

639 Lecturas y lectores en la historia de México. Coordinación de Carmen Castañeda García, Luz Elena Galván Lafarga y Lucía Martínez Moctezuma. México:

CIESAS; Cuernavaca, Morelos: Univ. Autónoma del Estado de Morelos; Zamora, Michoacán: Colegio de Michoacán, 2004. 372 p.: bibl., ill. (Historias CIESAS)

This book represents an interesting attempt at analyzing the historical use of textbooks in Mexico, and how those texts were received, or intended to be received, by their readers. The authors probe texts used during the colonial era, 19th century, revolutionary period, and the 1990s. The focus is mostly on primary school texts, including those used to teach reading, although the volume also includes studies of books intended to shape the lives of women, campesinos, and indigenous peoples in the context of Mexico's revolutionary change.

640 Llanura sin fin: ensayos de historiografía lagunera. Comisión de Historia del Consejo para la Celebración del Centenario de Torreón. Coordinación de Sergio Antonio Corona Páez. Torreón, Mexico: Dirección Municipal de Cultura, 2005. 189 p.: bibl., ill., maps. (Col. Centenario; t. 33)

The last in a series of 33 volumes published in celebration of Torreón's centenary. Of particular merit are selections on the city's economic history, including the history of the railroad and of the Mercado Juárez.

641 Luna Sánchez, Patricia. Molino de San Antonio antes Molino de Cortés: inversionistas en la molinería, Queretana, 1608–1942. México: Fondo Editorial de Querétaro, 2005. 230 p.: bibl., ill., maps. (Documentos de Querétaro)

The author traces the history of a single flour mill in north-central Mexico, with considerations of the organization and evolution of the enterprise. Technological innovations, the background and context of the mill's various owners, and financing strategies are examined.

642 Malvido, Elsa. La población, siglos XVI al XX. México: UNAM; Editorial Océano de México, 2006. 248 p.: bibl., ill., maps. (Historia económica de México; 7)

Part of a larger series on the economic history of Mexico, this well researched study contributes to an understanding of the dynamics behind attempts to count people, and reveals the contexts of census numbers. The author examines how and why individuals were counted from the colonial to contemporary eras.

643 Las maravillas del agua. Coordinación de Sonia Butze y Carlos Viramontes. Querétaro, Mexico: Instituto Nacional de Antropología e Historia, 2006. 303 p.: bibl., ill. (some col.), maps.

A series of 15 essays resulting from an interdisciplinary seminar. The authors explore the issue of water in different historical and social contexts. Includes studies of archeological, artistic, and religious representations of water throughout Mexico's history. Six essays focus specifically on Querétaro.

644 Martínez Assad, Carlos R. El Grijalva, un río que fluye en la historia. (*Signos Hist.*, 14, julio/dic. 2005, p. 140–161, bibl.)

This is a brief description of the role of the Grijalva in the histories of Mexico and Tabasco. The author demonstrates the river's role in the conquest era, during the 19th century, and into the revolutionary era. He concludes with a description of some of the contemporary threats to the river system.

645 Medrano de Luna, Gabriel. La morena y sus chorriados: los ferrocarriles en Aguascalientes. Aguascalientes, Mexico: Univ. Autónoma de Aguascalientes, 2006. 171 p.: bibl., ill.

In this brief study, the author examines the central place occupied by the railroad and the railroad industry in the growth and development of the city of Aguascalientes, and the society that grew around it. The study includes a focus on union activity among railroad workers. Extensively illustrated and incorporating numerous quotations from primary sources.

646 Mendoza Muñoz, Jesús. Cadereyta, cuatro siglos de gobierno: siglos XVII–XVIII–XIX y XX. Cadereyta de Montes, Mexico: Fomento Histórico y Cultural de Cadereyta, 2005. 403 p.: bibl., map. (Serie de historia; 4)

This is an extensively researched account of a Querétaro municipality that was formally established during the 17th century. The first third of the study explores the political evolution of Cadereyta and how that evolution was affected by historical events and trends, such as the Intendancy

period, the French Intervention, and the Mexican Revolution. The second and third sections provide a complete list of local authorities throughout Cadereyta's history, and a collection of 20 documents.

647 Menes Llaguno, Juan Manuel. Historia mínima del estado de Hidalgo. México: M.A. Porrúa, 2006. 254 p.: bibl., ill., maps.

The author, who is extensively published on local history, provides a summary of the state's history from precolumbian times to the present. Based on primary and secondary sources, this volume is suitable for a general reader.

648 México en tres momentos, 1810–1910–2010: hacia la conmemoración del bicentenario de la Independencia y del centenario de la Revolución Mexicana: retos y perspectivas. Coordinación de Alicia Mayer; prólogo de Juan Ramón de la Fuente. México: UNAM, Instituto de Investigaciones Históricas, 2007. 2 v.: bibl., ill., maps, ports.

An excellent collection of essays providing a fresh look at the broad sweep of Mexico's history, as well as historiographical perspectives on independence and the revolution. The authors, including several nonhistorians, explore a variety of social, cultural, political, and economic themes, including the history of illness and medicine, Mexico's changing geographical landscape, and Mexico's relations with the world.

649 Mexico otherwise: modern Mexico in the eyes of foreign observers. Edited and translated by Jürgen Buchenau. Albuquerque: Univ. of New Mexico Press, 2005. 285 p.: bibl., map. (Diálogos)

This volume brings together an impressive array of North American and European writings on Mexico since 1800. The commentaries on nation-building, modernization, the Mexican Revolution, and the post-WWII economic boom and collapse invite the student and general reader to contextualize and discover topical links among the selections.

650 Mexiko heute: Politik, Wirtschaft, Kultur. 3., vollständig neu bearbeitete Aufl. Frankfurt am Main: Vervuert, 2004. 826 p.: bibl., ill., indexes. (Bibliotheca Ibero-Americana, Bd. 98)

A diverse collection of essays on themes related to contemporary Mexico. The primarily German authors explore politics, economics, culture, and literature. German-Mexican relations, human rights and corruption, the 1994 Zapatista uprising, and trends in Mexican film, art, architecture and literature are among the topics discussed.

651 Miradas recurrentes: la ciudad de México en los siglos XIX y XX. Coordinación de María del Carmen Collado. México: Instituto Mora: Univ. Autónoma Metropolitana, 2004. v. 2: ill., maps. (Historia urbana y regional)

An excellent collection of essays that probe various topics related to Mexico City's cultural and social history. Topics include popular art and literary images of 19th-century Mexico City, the role of city shopkeepers in a revolt against the viceroy, city workers and the Casa del Obrero Mundial, bathhouses and homosexual behavior in the late Porfirian era, and contemporary urbanization and changes in religious affiliation.

652 Moreno Pérez, Edgardo. Vuelo y andanzas por los barrios de Santiago de Querétaro. Santiago de Querétaro, Mexico: Gobierno del Estado de Querétaro, Oficialía Mayor, Archivo Histórico de Querétaro, 2005. 404 p.: bibl., col. ill., col. map. (Historiografía queretana; 16)

This book is an exploration of the history of several neighborhoods, most located in the historic center of Querétaro. The author examines the physical and cultural history of several barrios, with a particular emphasis on traditional celebrations and fiestas. Extensively illustrated and with an appendix containing statistical information on the barrios.

653 El mundo ranchero. Coordinación de Rodolfo Fernández y Daria Deraga. Guadalajara, Mexico: Univ. de Guadalajara, 2006. 227 p.: ill. (Col. Estudios del hombre. Serie Antropologia; 21)

This collection examines one aspect of rural Mexico, with a focus on Jalisco. In five brief microhistories, the authors probe changes in landholding patterns during the colonial era, profile the social and ethnic makeup of the rural population, comment on the role of those professionals who sup-

port the contemporary ranching industry, and detail the historical evolution of the ranchero class. Three supplements, including a travel narrative by a Jalisco ranchero, and three book reviews of recent works on rural history, are also included.

654 El noreste: reflexiones. Coordinación de Isabel Ortega Ridaura et al. Monterrey, Mexico: Fondo Editorial, 2006. 336 p.: bibl., ill.

This is an outstanding collection of articles on the Coahuila-Nuevo León-Tamaulipas zone. Mexican and North American authors examine the historical development of this area, analyze the transnational nature of its social evolution, search for commonalities in the cultural expression of the northeast, and explore the economic aspects of the region's contemporary integration with the US.

655 Palou, Pedro Ángel. Intelectuales y poder en México. (Am. Lat. Hoy/Salamanca, 47, dic. 2007, p. 77–85, bibl.)

This is a general survey of the role of intellectuals in Mexico, with a focus on the 20th century. The author identifies key influences on Mexican thinkers, and analyzes the relationship between intellectuals and the state.

656 Persistencia y cambio: acercamientos a la historia de las mujeres en México. Compilación de Lucía Melgar. México: El Colegio de México, 2008. 253 p.: bibl., ill.

This is an excellent series of essays that reveals the state of historical scholarship on women and that suggests future directions. The authors present historiographical commentary, as well as original research on topics ranging from the gendered effects of the demographic disaster of the conquest to 19th and 20th century views of women in official and popular publications.

Poblaciones y culturas de origen africano en México. See *HLAS 65:2527.*

657 La prensa como fuente para la historia. Coordinación de Celia del Palacio Montiel. Guadalajara, Mexico: Univ. de Guadalajara: Consejo Nacional de Ciencia y Tecnología: Miguel Angel Porrúa, 2006. 228 p.: bibl.

An interesting illustration of the many ways in which newspapers can be used to approach a variety of historical topics related to 19th- and 20th-century Mexican history. The relationship between the press and politics, media coverage of mental illness and crime, and newspaper depictions of zapatismo and of the "Indian" are among the topics explored.

658 Rionda Arreguín, Isauro. El barrio de Pastita de la ciudad de Guanajuato. Guanajuato, Mexico: Presidencia Municipal de Guanajuato, Dirección Municipal de Cultura, 2006. 110 p.: bibl. (Col. Barrios de Guanajuato; 2)

A brief sketch of one of Guanajuato's original settlements by the city's chronicler, based on research in local, national, and Spanish colonial archives. The focus is primarily on economic development related to mining activities.

659 Rosas, Alejandro. Mitos de la historia de México: de Hidalgo a Zedillo. México: Planeta, 2006. 324 p.: bibl.

A popular exploration of the people, symbols, institutional images, and cultural practices that constitute an "official" history of Mexico. The author examines a variety of specific anecdotes and myths, including those about Mexico's heroes (including Juárez and Madero), holidays (such as 16 de septiembre), icons (Obregón's arm), and events (the great flood of 1629).

660 Salomón Meráz, Liliana. Historia de los menonitas radicados en Durango. Durango, Mexico: Programa de Apoyo a Comunidades Municipales y Comunitarias, 2004. 130 p.: bibl., ill.

The author provides a basic history including the context of Mennonite immigration to Mexico and Durango, and the social, economic, political, and cultural characteristics of contemporary Mennonite communities. Based in part on a series of interviews with Mennonite leaders.

661 Sánchez Blas, Joaquín. Estudio histórico de la zona mazahua. Toluca, Estado de México: Instituto Mexiquense de Cultura, 2007. 466 p.: bibl., ill., maps. (Documentos y testimonios) (Biblioteca mexiquense del bicentenario)

This is a well-researched study of the municipality of Ixtlahuaca. One chapter surveys the colonial and post-independence history of the region, with extensive quotations from historical documents. The rest of the volume is a profile of contemporary Ixtlahuaca.

662 Santiago Guerrero, L. Bibiana. La gente al pie del Cuchumá: memoria histórica de Tecate. Mexicali, Mexico: Univ. Autónoma de Baja California, Instituto de Investigaciones Históricas: Fundación La Puerta, 2005. 526 p.: bibl., ill., index, maps.

This is an extensive and well-researched volume on what eventually became the urban center of Tecate. The author utilizes archival materials, as well as oral histories of residents and descendants of those who founded the original colony. She details the rural development which characterized colonial and 19th century growth, and explains the process by which urban Tecate developed and evolved.

663 Señor Juárez. Oaxaca de Juárez, Mexico: Almadía, 2007. 125 p.: bibl. (Archipiélago antologías)

Four essays that explore the legacy of Benito Juárez and 19th century Mexican liberalism. Authors include a political activist, an historian of feminism, a Zapotec scholar and anthropologist, and an essayist and poet. All selections attempt to relate their theme to current events, including the contested presidential elections of 2006.

664 Siete regiones de la prensa en México, 1792–1950. Coordinación de Celia del Palacio Montiel. Guadalajara, Mexico: Univ. de Guadalajara: Consejo Nacional de Ciencia y Tecnología: Miguel Angel Porrúa, 2006. 428 p.: bibl., map.

This volume departs from the typical focus on the Mexico City press, with essays on Veracruz, Jalisco, Oaxaca, Zacatecas, Sinaloa, Chiapas, and Michoacán. The authors focus primarily on elaborating a periodization for the evolution of print media in each region, while suggesting directions for further research. A valuable resource for those interested in the history of these regions, and in the comparative history of periodicals in Mexico.

665 Simposio de Antropología e Historia Contemporánea de América Latina y el Caribe, *1st, Mexico City, Mexico, 2005.* Itinerarios: cultura, memoria e identidades en América Latina y el Caribe. Coordinación de José Luis González y Franco Savarino. México: CONACULTA-INAH, Escuela Nacional de Antropología e Historia, 2006. 216 p.: bibl.

All but two of these wide-ranging essays, derived from a symposium on contemporary Latin American and Caribbean history, deal with Mexican topics. The authors explore Italian images of Mexican nationalism between the world wars, modernization in Ciudad Juárez, banditry, Christian Base Communities and public health, Mexican historiography, cultural identity among children in Quintana Roo and among the inhabitants of the Quintana Roo-Belize frontier zone, and the role of the middle classes in the PRI.

666 Sudcalifornia: de sus orígenes a nuestros días. Edición de Micheline Cariño Olvera y Lorella Castorena Davis. La Paz, Mexico: Univ. Autónoma de Baja California Sur; Gobierno del Estado de Baja California Sur, Instituto Sudcaliforniano de Cultura, 2007. 324 p., 8 p. of plates: bibl., ill.

This volume is intended for a general audience and includes eight essays on the peninsula's history, from prehispanic times to approximately 2000. The last two chapters provide especially good commentary on regionalism in Baja California (a product of insularity, isolation, and aridity), and on the peninsula's distinct experience with modernization.

667 Tiempo y región: estudios históricos y sociales. Coordinación de Ricardo Jarillo Hernández. Querétaro, Mexico: Municipio de Querétaro: Univ. Autónoma de Querétaro; México: Instituto Nacional de Antropología e Historia, 2007. 1 v.: bibl., ill. (some col.), maps.

A scattered collection of essays which examine diverse aspects of Querétaro's history. Includes studies of precolumbian archeological sites, an examination the colonial Catholic Church, and four essays on the 19th century, including an exploration of agrarian rebellion and anti-Protestant activity in the state.

668 Los últimos cien años: los próximos cien. Coordinación de Ariel Rodríguez Kuri y Sergio Tamayo Flores-Alatorre. México: Univ. Autónoma Metropolitana, 2004. 319 p.: bibl., ill., maps (Cultura universitaria; 76. Serie Ensayo)

The authors probe themes related to the long and short term history of the capital city. The first half of the volume treats the topics of crime and the police, academic portrayals of Mexico City, the disappearance of streetcars, and the concept of citizenship. The second half treats more contemporary topics, including the preservation of public spaces, democratization, the revival of the historic district in the context of globalization, and the Zócalo as a cultural and discursive space. Two concluding commentaries look ahead, suggesting challenges and possibilities for the city of the future.

669 Universidad de Guadalajara. Centro Universitario de Los Altos. Seminario de Estudios Regionales. Anuario 2005: Seminario de estudios regionales. Edición de Federico de la Torre de la Torre *et al.* Tepatitlán de Morelos, Mexico: Univ. de Guadalajara, Centro Universitario de Los Altos, 2007. 230 p.: bibl., ill.

Most of the essays in this collection are by historians and social scientists and touch on various aspects of Jalisco's history. Perhaps most notable are three essays dealing with immigration and emigration, and three essays on cultural history, including explorations of suicide and public opinion, and abortion and infanticide in the 19th century.

670 Victoria Ojeda, Jorge. San Fernando Aké: microhistoria de una comunidad afroamericana en Yucatán. Mérida, México: Ediciones de la Univ. Autónoma de Yucatán, 2006. 142 p.: bibl., ill., maps. (Tratados; 24)

This relatively short volume combines the archeological record with extensive research in Spanish, Caribbean, Central American, South American, and Yucatecan archives. The authors examine the origins, and social and economic structure of San Fernando Aké, a colony established in the 18th century for African auxiliary troops from the Spanish Caribbean. The settlement was abandoned by its inhabitants during the Caste War of the Yucatan.

671 **Villalpando César, José Manuel.**
Muertes históricas. México: Planeta
Mexicana, 2008. 203 p.: ill., index.

This is a brief and popular treatment
of the deaths—mostly violent—of several
historical figures. Victims of the independence era (Miguel Hidalgo, José María Morelos), key players in 19th century politics
(Benito Juárez, Porfirio Díaz), and martyrs of
the revolution (Francisco Madero, Emiliano
Zapata) are among those covered.

672 **Villaverde García, Elixio.** Galegos
en México, 1878–1936: inmigración e
sociedade no alén mar. Santiago de Compostela: Sotelo Blanco, 2003. 302 p.: bibl., maps.
(Col. Estudios e investigacións)

This well-researched study utilizes
Mexican, Spanish, and Galician archives
to analyze the migration of Galician immigrants, which was initially encouraged by
the stability and economic opportunities of
the Porfirian era. The author provides detailed demographic information, including
data related to the socioeconomic characteristics of immigrants and patterns of settlement in Mexico.

673 **Zinacantepec.** Coordinación de
Rosaura Hernández Rodríguez. Zinacantepec, Mexico: Colegio Mexiquense:
H. Ayuntamiento de Zinacantepec, 2005.
152 p.: bibl., ill., maps. (Serie Cuadernos
municipales; 20)

Part of a series on the municipalities
of the state of Mexico, this volume contains
brief treatments of the history and archeology of the area. In addition to considerations
of the indigenous heritage of Zinacantepec,
the authors also examine missionary work,
land tenure, and demographic changes during the colonial era, as well as the relationship between haciendas and pueblos during
the Porfiriato.

Colonial Period

PAULA DE VOS, *Associate Professor of History, San Diego State University*
KAREN MELVIN, *Assistant Professor of History, Bates College*

OUR INTRODUCTION TO *HLAS 64* began with Eric Van Young's useful survey of Anglophone publications in colonial Mexican history during the previous
20 years. In that article, Van Young noted the ascendancy of cultural history and
the corresponding diminution of conventional economic history, findings largely
supported by our survey of literature published between 2002 and 2006. Now the
field appears to be undergoing some significant shifts, and the formerly divergent
trajectories of economic and cultural historiographies seem to be converging in
exciting ways as they, along with social and political history, move beyond their
traditional forms. Works are defying easy categorization by merging disciplinary
approaches, localizing the general, bridging distances, and rethinking temporal
boundaries. For example, a number of impressive new works embrace themes
usually associated with cultural history—religion, race and ethnicity—but are
firmly grounded in particular social, political, and economic contexts (see items
687, 731, 743, 769, and **776**). In addition, Georgina Endfield's multi-faceted environmental history of Mexico, *Climate and Society: A Study in Vulnerability* (item
700), employs methods and arguments from geography, environmental studies,
and history to examine climactic conditions in colonial Mexico. Endfield examines communities' methods of social adaptation to climactic calamity in order to
help identify the most vulnerable areas today in light of the impact and effects of
global warming.

In terms of time and space, the works surveyed continue to be wide-ranging, although not without clusters of emphasis. Central Mexico and Mexico City remain favorite areas of study, but more "peripheral" areas of colonization, particularly Guatemala, Yucatán, Oaxaca, and especially the borderlands of northern Mexico were also well represented (see items **769** and **800**). Translocal histories continue to push at established frameworks, suggesting webs of connections over geographic distance. Transatlantic approaches continue to be the most prominent among these works, offering examples of informal networks, shared identities, and ideological influences that ran in multiple directions throughout the Hispanic world (see items **718**, **725**, **743**, **747**, and **765**). In his essay for the *American Historical Review*, Cañizares-Esguerra (item **474**) advocates taking transatlantic histories beyond such national or confessional limits and, as the next step, finding ways to connect histories of the colonial Americas, creating what he terms "entangled histories."

Our survey also noted innovation with regard to time period, particularly in Anglophone literature. In contrast to the previous concentration on the 18th century, works published in the last four years have given more attention to earlier periods, bridging the pre- and postcontact period, focusing on the conquest and initial decades of colonization, and, most notably, examining the once "forgotten" 17th century, carving out a "long 17th century" running anywhere from the 1570s to the 1730s. Certainly, ideas of a colonial period bookended by conquest and independence with an empty or stagnant middle are long dead, but recent works have accomplished a great deal in defining this middle as crucial to the maturation of a highly complex colonial society. This society was comprised of people of mixed ancestry, ethnicity, custom, and belief who negotiated their identity and place within colonial society, participating in the formation of a system that was ultimately hegemonic, but never monolithic (items **492** and **800**). The 18th century has by no means been neglected, however. Scholars, especially those outside of the US or interested in the borderlands, continue to take advantage of the period's bounty of documents to investigate transformations in the wake of Bourbon reforms, new ideas about family and social status, and changing circumstances in the Northern missions (see items **701**, **713**, **714**, **740**, **752**, **768**, **770**, and **792**).

The majority of works included in this volume are archivally based, and many incorporate different types of documents that highlight both "bottom up" and imperial, "top-down" practices and views. Several works on indigenous worldview—including Nahua, Zapotec, and Maya—utilize both pictorial and alphabetic writing produced by indigenous communities (items **688**, **746**, **769**, and **788**). For works tracing colonial processes, cases from civil, criminal, ecclesiastical, and Indian courts make up the basis of primary source documentation. Historians appear to be taking better advantage of these documents and correcting what Brian Owensby refers to as "the mismatch between the volume of legal documentation involving Indians and the attention historians have paid to the processes they represent" (item **759**, p. 3; see also items **698**, **795**, and **800**).

Having established the broader methodological, spatial, and temporal outlines of recent historiography in the field, we now turn to constellations of individual themes, including new interpretations of conquest. Two primary-source readers, a newly abridged edition of Bernal Díaz's account edited by David Carrasco (item **697**), and Restall and Asselberg's *Invading Guatemala* (see *HLAS 64:232*) provide excellent information about the historical context in which the sources were produced, and bring to light hitherto unpublished letters and excerpts of the original writings. Another edited volume, *Invasion and*

Transformation (item **721**) examines paintings of Cortes' conquest, challenging the heroic imagery included in them, particularly the iconic figures of Cortes, Malinche, and Montezuma. Most innovative, however, are several volumes focusing on "native intermediaries" in the conquest. Camille Townsend's *Malintzin's Choices* seeks to uncover the "real young woman" by thoughtfully studying and revealing the indigenous thought patterns and context in which she lived (see *HLAS 64:308*). Matthew and Oudijk's collection of essays, *Indian Conquistadors*, offers a new paradigm for conquest, arguing that the multiple layers of native groups who allied with the Spanish and each other in a complex and shifting system are what ultimately allowed the Spanish to gain hegemony over the region. This work, which delves heavily into the native context, ought to serve as a new basis for understanding conquest (see *HLAS 64:231*)

Several works, as noted above, connect the pre- and postcontact eras, seeking in-depth understanding of how indigenous cosmology and worldview prior to their encounters with Europeans were transformed (or not) in the ensuing years. Articles by Caso Barrera and Aliphat Fernández (item **685**) and by Garraty (item **709**) employ anthropological methods to judge the political and economic consequences of both precolonial indigenous and later Spanish colonization. Megged (item **746**), Chuchiak (item **688**) and Távarez (item **788**) examine the continuity of cosmological, sexual, and religious worlds of the Nahua, Maya, and Zapotecs respectively. Gimmel (item **711**) offers a new interpretation of the *Cruz-Badiano Codex*, viewing indigenous medicine as a bicultural product of Nahua and European ideas and textual practices, rather than as an example of European hegemony. As late as the independence period, Morris finds the Crown publishing broadsides and pamphlets in Nahuatl in order to appeal to the indigenous populace and refer back to the multilingualism that characterized much of colonial society prior to the Bourbons (see items **238** and **854**).

Another set of works serves to explain how Spanish colonial society and institutions formed and took hold. Building on scholarship that has eschewed simple models of imposition or domination, these works continue to illuminate variations and complexities in the processes that shaped early colonial society. Holler's suggestive essay examines the reimagining of space during the transition from Tenochtitlán to Mexico City (item **720**). Ruiz Medrano's *Reshaping New Spain* (item **782**), a much-needed study of the Second Audiencia and the reign of Viceroy Antonio de Mendoza, highlights the methods by which the Crown was able to establish successful and profitable colonial rule despite the manipulations of colonial officials. Marcy Norton's innovative article "Tasting Empire," suggests the ways in which Europeans were also colonized in certain ways, adopting Mesoamerican taste and esthetics in the drinking of chocolate (item **754**). The role of native intermediaries is also coming increasingly to light, not only through the work of Matthew and Oudijk and the contributors to their volume, but through such works as Yannakakis' *The Art of Being In-Between*, a masterful treatment of the role of the native nobility in 17th-century Oaxaca (item **800**). Similarly, Restall's *The Black Middle* (item **769**), argues that Afro-Yucatecans played a significant role mediating the interstices between indigenous and Spanish society. On a microhistorical level, Lopes Don (item **698**) follows the testimonies in Don Carlos' 1539 trial to examine how doubts about the legitimacy of his rule and new moral codes promoted by Franciscans exacerbated tensions within native society.

Several studies highlight the importance of the court system in establishing Spanish hegemony. Drawing on the earlier arguments of Woodrow Borah, Susan

Kellogg, and Steve Stern that a strong litigious tradition developed among indigenous peoples, Brian Owensby presents the justice system as perhaps the most important source of Spanish authority in Mexico (item 759). Other scholars, including Yannakakis, Kanter, Uribe Uran, Lopes Don, Kessell, Cáceres Menéndez, and Robert Patch have drawn upon the richness of court cases to highlight diverse aspects of colonial society, including indigenous-Spanish relations in rural, peripheral, and urban areas, and systems of punishment in place for different groups in society, from those who committed spousal homicide to the "incorrigible sons" of the elite. The courts and the ways of Spanish justice did not go uncontested, however. Osvaldo Pardo demonstrates in his article "How to Punish Indians," that there was significant debate and tension between civil and ecclesiastical authorities over who ought to have jurisdiction over native peoples (item 761).

The themes of race and ethnicity continue to attract attention, most commonly as one category of analysis in works with a wider focus. Some scholars have taken those very conceptions of race and historicized them, most notably in the work of María Elena Martínez who traces the development of New Spain's *sistema de castas* from peninsular ideas about purity of blood defined by religious heritage (item 743). Placed in a racially mixed society, these ideas evolved over the 17th and 18th centuries to define purity by the absence of non-Spanish blood. Janine Gasco reconceptualizes the terms Ladino and Indian as part of a continuum by examining the case of Soconusco, Chiapas where 18th-century transformations in landholding patterns led more Indians to enter the wage labor force and declare themselves Ladino (item 710). These themes also play out in the cases described by Althouse and included in Fisher and O'Hara's edited volume *Imperial Subjects,* which highlights the contested and shifting nature of racial identity throughout the colonial period (item 492). Within the topic of race is also a valuable and growing focus on Afro-Mexicans. Building on the pioneering work of Gonzalo Aguirre Beltrán, Colin Palmer, Ben Vinson, and Herman Benentt, recent works have continued to highlight the significant presence of Africans and African culture in New Spain. Matthew Restall's *The Black Middle,* discussed earlier, stands out in particular as the first major work on Afro-Yucatecans in the colonial period (item 769). Essays in Restall and Vinson's *Black Mexico* (item 681) present a variety of case studies of the ways in which blacks integrated into Mexican society, while Herman Bennett's *Colonial Blackness* examined ecclesiastical documents to trace the formation of black communities in the 17th century (item 680). Finally, of note is Frank Proctor's article on manumission that emphasizes the importance of considering gender within that process (item 766).

Another group of works focus on themes of medicine, science, and health, from the biological and anthropological work of Márquez Morfín and Hernández Espinoza to historical work on disease, medical practitioners, and the methods of imperial science (item 741). In medicine, Fields' *Pestilence and Headcolds* (item 703) provides work that complements earlier histories of medical institutions and epidemics by focusing on everyday diseases and the way that people experienced and interpreted them. Rodríguez-Sala has continued to publish works on the enumeration of surgeons working in and connected to various institutions in New Spain (see for example, item 774). Rubial García found that inquisitors in six cases against nuns from the 18th century were more likely than their 17th-century predecessors to attribute the nuns' "sins against the faith" to medical reasons (illness or insanity) than theological ones (demonic possession) (item 779). And finally, articles by Barrera and De Vos bring New Spain into a wider conversation about the relationship between science and empire, arguing that the Spanish Empire played an important role in the development of the Scientific Revolution as evident in the Crown's empirical practices with respect to information—and specimen—gathering in the Americas (items **677** and **694**).

Finally, there are a series of works on colonial evangelization that provide new directions to the field. Kenneth Mills (item **750**) noted that recent investigations of colonial religion have called into question a convenient three-part story told as a burst of Franciscan evangelization followed by a flourishing Baroque and ending with religion's marginalization in the face of growing secularism. Our survey bears out his proposition. For example, Matthew O'Hara's "Stone, Mortar, and Memory" grounds secularization efforts in the concrete structures of the regular clergy, using debates over ownership of these structures to demonstrate continued parochialism and corporate identity among parishioners despite Bourbon efforts to the contrary (item **756**). One particular beneficiary of new approaches or questions has been the study of colonial nuns. Asunción Lavrin's magisterial *Brides of Christ*, handles the subject with both breadth and depth, tracing nuns' material and spiritual concerns and illuminating the overall experience of being a nun in one of New Spain's 57 convents (item **731**). In addition to Lavrin's comprehensive work, Margaret Chowning has taken the case of a troubled convent and contextualized its change-over-time story to illuminate a series of themes related to women and the Church during the 18th and 19th centuries (item **687**). See also Kirk's work that contrasts nuns' lived experiences with rigid male prescriptions for convent life (item **729**). Churchmen have yet to receive the same level of attention as nuns, but Lavrin's "Masculine and Feminine" article lays out some possibilities for using religious life to compare models of masculine and feminine behavior (item **733**).

Also prominent are works that highlight local contexts of religious ideas and practices, particularly those featuring shrines. William Taylor's 2008 CLAH Luncheon Address contextualizes devotion to the Virgin of Guadalupe within New Spain's collection of many local shrines, a devotion that reinforced "the importance of locality—of many localities—and many images, more than centralizing a vast spiritual geography" (p. 6–7). Osowski's examination of the shrine of Holy Sepulcher of Christ near Amecameca demonstrates different groups could promote devotions for different reasons (item **758**), and Pescador tracks the movement and evolution of current immigrant favorite Santo Niño de Atocha over five centuries from its peninsular origins to colonial Zacatecas and into its northern migrations (item **765**). Finally, studies of Church structures and institutions have received coverage mostly in Spanish-language literature. In particular, several solid collections of essays cover topics ranging from bishops, parish priests, missions, credit, and sermons (see items **692**, **768**, **776**, and **783**).

COLONIAL

General

Aguilar-Robledo, Miguel. Archival, ethno-historical, and cartographic reconstruction of the environmental history of the Valles jurisdiction, eastern New Spain, mid-16th to early 19th century. See *HLAS 65:1029.*

674 Althouse, Aaron P. Writing by caste, counting the past: alphabetic literacy and age consciousness in the colonial Pátzcuaro Region, 1680–1750. (*Americas/Washington*, 65:3, Jan. 2009, p. 297–319)

Examines over 2000 criminal lawsuits in 17th- and 18th-century Patzcuaro to investigate how people identified themselves and correlates that finding with two key pieces of information—if they were literate and if they knew their age. Althouse finds that caste was a significant marker of social rank and identity in colonial society, but that identity formation and its effects were not monolithic. Rather, life experience and social context blended so that caste "remained open to manipulation and negotiation by people descending from innumerable combinations of cultural backgrounds" (p. 319). [PDV]

675 Andrade Muñoz, Germán Luis. Un mar de intereses: la producción de pertrechos navales en Nueva España, siglo XVIII. México: Instituto Mora, 2006. 210 p.: bibl., ill., index, maps. (Historia internacional)

Examines the provisioning and materials needed to maintain the Spanish navy and army in 18th-century New Spain. [KM]

676 Assadourian, Carlos Sempat. Zacatecas, conquista y transformacion de la frontera en el siglo XVI: minas de plata, guerra y evangelización. México: Colegio de México, Centro de Estudios Históricos, 2008. 558 p.: bibl.

Essays, supplemented by a lengthy section of transcribed documents, explain the protracted military conquest of northern New Spain and the region's subsequent development centered around mining and agriculture. [KM]

677 Barrera, Antonio. Empire and knowledge: reporting from the new world. (*Colon. Lat. Am. Rev.*, 15:1, June 2006, p. 39–54, bibl.)

This article traces the "institutionalization of empirical practices" in the Spanish Empire's efforts to gather, organize, and codify information about the Americas. Barrera examines several steps in this process, from the establishment of early institutions to support empirical efforts to the production of books, questionnaires, and reports, culminating in the expeditions of Francisco Hernandez and Jaime Juan in the late 16th century. These efforts served to alter the epistemological basis of knowledge, taking personal experience as a basis for scientific knowledge, and shows that "early modern empires and science were born together." [PDV]

678 Beleña, Eusebio Buenaventura. Manifiesto de Eusebio Bentura Beleña. Edición, introducción y notas por Ignacio Almada Bay *et al.* Zamora, Mexico: El Colegio de Michoacán; Guadalajara, Mexico: Univ. de Guadalajara, 2006. 245 p.: bibl., indexes, maps (some col.). (Col. Fuentes)

Important contribution about the jurist, confidant of José de Galvez, and Bourbon official responsible for the expulsion of the Jesuits in Nueva Galicia, Eusebio Bentura Beleña. Useful background essays supplement the transcription of his *manifiesto*, written between 1768 and 1772 and which includes letters and decrees. [KM]

679 Béligand, Nadine. La muerte en la ciudad de México en el siglo XVIII. (*Hist. Mex./México*, 57:1, julio/sept. 2007, p. 5–52, bibl., ill., map)

Examines burial practices in Mexico City in the colonial period, arguing that these practices underwent changes in the 18th century due to changing ideas of disease. During epidemics, infected bodies were buried outside the city rather than in church cemeteries, for fear of contagion. Despite this rational, however, Baroque funerary practices continued, as Mexican society still clung to traditional ideas of the celebration and communion of the dead with the living, as evident in modern-day celebrations of the Days of the Dead/Días de los Muertos. [PDV]

680 Bennett, Herman Lee. Colonial blackness: a history of Afro-Mexico. Bloomington: Indiana Univ. Press, 2009. 227 p.: bibl., index. (Blacks in the diaspora)

This study employs ecclesiastical documentation from the archives of Mexico to examine the black experience in 17th-century Mexico—the formation of black identities, extended families, and central and regional communities. Bennett argues that canon law allowed Africans, blacks, and mulattos certain freedoms in their private lives that were not sanctioned by civil authorities' interpretation of slaves as property. The richness and extent of black communities, however, attest to the triumph of the former and allow Bennett to trace colonial blacks as historical subjects in their own right, with their own history apart from the overdetermined narratives of slavery and the slave consciousness that developed from it. This study overcomes and goes beyond what Bennett refers to as a static "black structuralism." [PDV]

681 Black Mexico: race and society from colonial to modern times. Edited by Ben Vinson III and Matthew Restall. Albuquerque: Univ. of New Mexico Press, 2009. 278 p.: bibl., index. (Diálogos)

Vinson and Restall's anthology brings together a series of essays devoted to history and development of the Afro-Mexican population that span the colonial and modern periods. This volume "comes at a particular historical juncture" (p. 3) of rising interest in and awareness of this population coupled with increasingly sophisticated historical studies of the caste, class, and power in colonial Mexico. In its attention to the ways in which blacks integrated into Mexican society, *Black Mexico* builds on the tradition established by Gonzalo Aguirre Beltrán, whose 1946 publication of *La población negra de México* established the foundation for this growing field. The colonial essays focus on slave rebellions, relations between blacks, native Americans, and Spaniards as manifested through labor, confraternity membership, and ritual and love-magic. [PDV]

682 Cáceres Menéndez, Beatriz and **Robert W. Patch.** Gente de mal vivir: families and incorrigible sons in New Spain, 1721–1729. (*Rev. Indias*, 66:237, mayo/agosto 2006, p. 363–392, tables)

Examines a registry of 220 men who were deported to the Philippines or Marianas Islands from New Spain between 1722–28. The Spanish Crown had employed this tactic from 1626 through independence to deal with incorrigible or undesirable subjects, but this registry is the only existing documentation found on the policy and the exiles to date. The authors found that exiles were exclusively male, consisting mainly of American-born Spaniards and men of mixed blood, who had committed a variety of crimes from stealing property to violent acts. There were also those who were deemed "undesirable" due to habitual drunkenness, gambling, or refusal of gainful employment. Oftentimes, parents used deportation to rid themselves of sons who were dishonoring families, thus revealing that honor code and punishments existed for men as well as women, the usual target for such studies. [PDV]

683 Carter, William B. Indian alliances and the Spanish in the Southwest, 750–1750. Norman: Univ. of Oklahoma Press, 2009. 308 p.: bibl., index.

Broadly accessible ethnohistory offers a narrative of the transformations among Pueblo Indians and Southern Athapaskans (Apaches and Navajos) in the Southwest over a 1000-year period. Carter presents these two groups as more closely linked through economies, kinship, and shared ideologies than usually supposed. The book's first half addresses the prehispanic period, including migrations, urbanization, and the effects of environmental changes. The second half turns to early Spanish entradas and missions, and concludes with a chapter on the Pueblo Revolt of 1680. [KM]

684 Carvajal López, David. Una corporación ante las revoluciones hispánicas: el convento carmelita de San Juan de la Cruz de Orizaba, 1794–1834. (*Secuencia/México*, 69, sept./dic. 2007, p. 13–35, bibl.)

This study of the (male) Carmelite convent in Orizaba tests conventional wisdom regarding religious corporations during the late colony/early republic in its findings that the convent adjusted to changing circumstances, if not easily, than at least better than expected. [KM]

685 Caso Barrera, Laura and **Mario Aliphat Fernández.** Cacao, vanilla and annatto: three production and exchange systems in the Southern Maya lowlands, XVI–XVII centuries. (*J. Lat. Am. Geogr.*, 5:2, 2006, p. 29–52, bibl., maps)

Discusses the cultivation of three crops important to ceremonial power of the Itza through the drinking of chocolate. Given the importance of the crops, the Itza tried to take over production of them in the southern Maya lowlands, as did the Spanish as well in the 17th century. This article illustrates the competition over natural resources in this area even though production declines greatly after Spanish conquest. [PDV]

686 Chevalier, François. Orígenes y elaboración de *La formación de los grandes latifundios en México*: tierra y sociedad en los siglos XVI y XVII. (*Signos Hist.*, 17, enero/junio. 2007, p. 33–43)

Distinguished historian traces his intellectual roots and the trajectory of his classic work on haciendas. For citation of Spanish language translation of Chevalier's classic work, see *HLAS 23:3158*. For review of the 1952 original work in French, see *HLAS 18:1747a*. [KM]

687 Chowning, Margaret. Rebellious nuns: the troubled history of a Mexican convent, 1752–1863. Oxford, England; New York: Oxford Univ. Press, 2006. 296 p.: bibl., ill., index.

Engaging tale centers on the rebellions of nuns in San Miguel's La Purísima Concepción convent who resisted attempts to force them to follow stricter interpretations of their vows. Rich documentation provides an unusually sharp picture of a convent's inner-workings and illuminates the personalities of individual nuns. Chowning contextualizes the convent's history within late 18th-century reform efforts, the insurgency, and 19th-century state hostility. A significant contribution to the history of women and the Church, the politics of religion, and Mexico during the late colony and early republic. [KM]

688 Chuchiak, John F. The sins of the fathers: Franciscan friars, parish priests, and the sexual conquest of the Yucatec Maya, 1545–1808. (*Ethnohistory/Columbus,* 54:1, Winter 2007, p. 69–127, ill., map, tables)

This article examines Spanish attempts to regulate and control Maya sexuality in a "complete conquest" that reveals much about the formation of early colonial society in Yucatan. Spaniards brought with them "two worlds" of sexuality—chastity and virginity on the one hand, and lasciviousness on the other. Both worlds collided with a third Maya world of sexual mores and practices. The Maya were able to exploit the contradiction between the two Spanish worlds in order to defend their own practices, largely through accusations of misconduct of Franciscan friars. In doing so their sexual world was also altered, but it served as a way of having some power and protection in their exploited society. For ethnohistorian's comment, see item **208**. [PDV]

689 Connell, William F. "Because I was drunk and the devil had tricked me": pulque, *pulquerías,* and violence in the Mexico City uprising of 1692. (*CLAHR,* 14:4, Fall 2005, p. 369–401)

Argues that Spanish elites' explanations that Indian drunkenness caused the uprising of 1692 are not supported by trial records. See also item **715**. [KM]

690 Cueva, Juan de la and **Diego de la Cueva.** Entre Castro del Río y México: correspondencia privada de Diego de la Cueva y su hermano Juan, emigrante en Indias, 1601–1641. Edición de Patricio Hidalgo Nuchera. Córdoba, Spain: Servicio de Publicaciones, Univ. de Córdoba: Caja-Sur Publicaciones, 2006. 290 p.: bibl., ill., indexes, maps. (Serie Estudios de historia moderna. Col. Documental; 2)

Noteworthy correspondence between a 17th-century immigrant to New Spain and his brother in Andalusia illuminates their lives and circumstances. Includes a helpful introductory essay. [KM]

691 De la Iglesia indiana: homenaje a Elsa Cecilia Frost. Coordinación de Patricia Escandón. México: UNAM, 2006. 157 p.: bibl., ill. (some col.).

Six essays written in homage to Elsa Cecilia Frost cover: Alonso de Molina's writings as emblems of early 16th-century Franciscan notions of political society; Spanish identity in *Fr. Gerónimo de Mendieta's History*; 16th-century Maya of the Yucatan; the development of the cult of Our Lady of Antigua in Mexico City; Juan de Palafox's promotion of prodigious images and nuns; and Franciscan missionary colleges as a partnership between Church and state. [KM]

692 De sendas, brechas y atajos: contexto y crítica de las fuentes eclesiásticas, siglos XVI–XVIII. Coordinación de Doris Bieñko de Peralta y Berenise Bravo Rubio. México: Escuela Nacional de Antropología e Historia: Instituto Nacional de Antropología e Historia, 2008. 253 p.: bibl.

Interesting collection of 13 essays examines the theme of Church and religion in colonial Mexico through primary source documents and the people, institutions, and practices that produced them. [KM]

693 De Vos, Paula. Natural history and the pursuit of empire in eighteenth-century Spain. (*Eighteenth-Century Stud.*, 40:2, Jan. 2007, p. 209–239)

Examines the natural history specimens brought to Spain from the Americas though the bureaucratic networks of natural history collecting, arguing that the vast majority of these specimens were useful items meant to improve Spain's economy. These efforts were part of the political economy embraced by prominent enlightened statesmen who believed that natural history offered the key to reviving the fortunes of the Spanish Empire. [KM]

694 De Vos, Paula. Research, development, and empire: state support of science in the later Spanish empire. (*Colon. Lat. Am. Rev.*, 15:1, June 2006, p. 55–79, bibl.)

Examines the Spanish Crown's significant efforts to support scientific research, especially in the 18th century, evident through collection of natural history specimens by bureaucrats in the Americas. De Vos makes the case that these efforts have been largely neglected in the historiography which tends to emphasize British and French efforts in this area. [KM]

695 De Vos, Paula. The science of spices: empiricism and economic botany in the early Spanish empire. (*J. World Hist.*, 17:4, Dec. 2006, p. 399–427, bibl.)

Traces the transplantation of spices from the Spice Islands and the Philippines to Mexico, then to Hispaniola and finally to botanical gardens established in Spain. De Vos argues that these early efforts in economic botany precede the British Empire's endeavors in this area and demonstrate the emphasis on empirical approaches to nature—a crucial step in the Scientific Revolution—that took place under the Spanish Crown. [KM]

696 Delgado, Jessica. *Sin temor de Dios*: women and ecclesiastical justice in eighteenth-century Toluca. (*Colon. Lat. Am. Rev.*, 18:1, April 2009, p. 99–121, bibl.)

Cases from Toluca's ecclesiastical court demonstrate that women looked to Church courts for protection or redress in instances of rape, virginity theft, and broken promises to marry by appealing to Church concerns about marriage and sexuality and beseeching judges to protect the social order and sanctity of sacraments. [PDV]

697 Díaz del Castillo, Bernal. The history of the conquest of New Spain. Edited and with an introduction by Davíd Carrasco with additional essays by Rolena Adorno, Davíd Carrasco, Sandra Cypess, and Karen Vieira Powers. Albuquerque: Univ. of New Mexico Press, 2008. 473 p.: ill., maps.

This new abridged version of Díaz del Castillo's classic account of the conquest of Tenochtitlán presents a number of much-needed correctives to former English-language editions. In Davíd Carrasco's insightful introductory essay, he points to the deficiencies of previous editions in their telling of an account that has almost iconic status among students of Spanish colonialism. In the first place, earlier editions do not adequately or effectively problematize the validity of Díaz's account, and in fact emphasize his disinterestedness and reliability. Second, these editions end with the surrender of the Aztecs in Tenochtitlán, leaving an impression of Spanish triumph without including Díaz's own accounts of the difficulties and infighting that followed. The present edition seeks to correct these deficiencies by first including a series of interpretive essays by premier scholars that contextualize various aspects of the conquest and thus allow students to do their own interpreting of Díaz's words; and second, by including several passages on events following the surrender not found in earlier abridgments. It also includes a number of valuable maps of the places Díaz discusses. [PDV]

698 Don, Patricia Lopes. The 1539 inquisition and trial of Don Carlos of Texcoco in early Mexico. (*HAHR*, 88:4, Nov. 2008, p. 573–606)

Novel interpretation of Don Carlos' trial considered in terms of pressures and fissures within indigenous society during a period of intense change. Rather than questioning his guilt, Lopes Don explains why he was denounced: doubts about the legitimacy of his rule along with tensions over new moral codes promoted by Franciscans. [KM]

699 Donahue-Wallace, Kelly. Picturing prints in early modern New Spain. (*Americas/Washington*, 64:3, Jan. 2008, p. 325–349, ill.)

This article examines prints in secular portraits and paintings in New Spain and explains what they signified for colonial society. Scholars usually argue that they represent lack of wealth on the part of the owners; prints were produced and bought because they were easy to transport and usually associated with poverty and a didactic role in conversion. But Donahue-Wallace argues that they had importance beyond pragmatism and poverty. In religious portraits, they served as an important marker of community, humility, and devotion, and in casta paintings they signified esthetic sensibility among certain castas and a desire for upward social mobility. For art historian's comment, see item **30**. [PDV]

700 Endfield, Georgina H. Climate and society in colonial Mexico: a study in vulnerability. Malden, Mass.: Blackwell Pub., 2008. 235 p.: bibl., ill., index, maps. (RGS-IBG book series)

Endfield presents here a meticulously documented and highly suggestive book that will interest environmentalists, geographers, and historians alike. Utilizing historical documents from the Archivo Nacional in Mexico City along with a number of regional archives, both civil and ecclesiastical, Endfield has woven together the history of climate and climactic events—rainfall, frosts, drought, floods, and storms—in three different regions of Mexico, including the arid Conchos basin in Chihuana, the fertile Bajío region, and the Oaxaca Valley where indigenous modes of production remained relatively constant throughout the colonial period. In doing so, Endfield has sought to uncover not only the biophysical threats posed by extreme weather events, but also the social response to and interpretation of these events. Such a "double-sided" approach allows her to determine each society's vulnerability to climactic change and may also help researchers "identify the most vulnerable societies and places" in Mexico today. This finding is especially important given both the wide climactic variation throughout Mexican history and the growing threats and dislocations brought on by global warming in the present day. [PDV]

701 Esteinou, Rosario. El surgimiento de la familia nuclear en Mexico. (*Estud. Hist. Novohisp.*, 31, julio/dic. 2004, p. 99–136, bibl.)

Anthropologist Rosario Esteinou, employing Marzio Barbagli's model of the family, concludes that family structure, internal dynamics, and extended relations in colonial Mexico demonstrate a move toward the model of the nuclear family, even if this model did not predominate until the second half of the 19th century. [KM]

702 Fedewa, Marilyn H. María of Ágreda: mystical lady in blue. Albuquerque: Univ. of New Mexico Press, 2009. 337 p.: bibl., index.

Expansive and document-based account of the famous bilocating Franciscan nun that follows "an empathetic yet reportorial approach" and seeks to reconstruct her voice rather than offer a scholarly treatise. [KM]

703 Fields, Sherry Lee. Pestilence and headcolds: encountering illness in colonial Mexico. New York: Columbia Univ. Press, 2008. 188 p.: bibl. (Gutenberg (e))

This work on the history of medicine in colonial Mexico offers a unique and pathbreaking approach to the historiography. The author seeks to describe and understand everyday illness and the way it was experienced, understood, and interpreted by people in New Spain. Unlike most histories of medicine in New Spain (of which there are few), Fields does not focus on epidemics or medical institutions, but rather on everyday diseases which, while they did not kill, certainly brought on significant hardship and disability to the diseased. Using a variety of documentation, including ex-votos, personal letters, *receptarios* (prescription books), and even the *Relaciones geográficas*, Fields is able to illustrate a side of medical history not often depicted or even investigated by historians. The book first outlines the main diseases in colonial Mexican society, European and indigenous interpretations of those diseases, and the wide array of medical practitioners who dealt with them. [PDV]

704 Flagler, Edward K. Comercio y ferias de trueque: España y los indios de Nuevo México. (*Rev. Esp. Antropol. Am.*, 37:1, 2007, p. 51–65, bibl., map, photos)

Covers trade and economic inter-actions between Spaniards and indigenous peoples in New Mexico between the 17th and 19th centuries. [KM]

705 Flint, Richard. No settlement, no conquest: a history of the Coronado Entrada. Albuquerque: Univ. of New Mexico Press, 2008. 358 p.: bibl., index, maps.

Well-documented account of the Coronado expedition (1539–42) from central New Spain into what is now the Southwestern US reassesses common misconceptions about the expedition, particularly for a general audience. [KM]

706 Flores Farfán, José Antonio. La Malinche: portavoz de dos mundos. (*Estud. Cult. Náhuatl*, 37, 2006, p. 117–137, facsim., ill.)

Reconstruction of the historical Malinche from her origins to her roles on the Cortés expedition. Includes a discussion of contemporary depictions of her. For comment by ethnohistorian, see *HLAS 64:219.* [KM]

707 Foro de las Misiones del Noroeste de México, 3rd, Hermosillo, Mexico, 2005. Misiones del noroeste de México: origen y destino 2005. Recopilación de José Rómulo Félix Gastélum y Raquel Padilla Ramos. Hermosillo, Mexico: CONACULTA: Fondo Regional para la Cultura y las Artes del Noroeste, 2007. 366 p.: bibl., ill., maps.

Twenty-four short essays provide an interdisciplinary perspective on the Franciscan and Jesuit missions of Northern Mexico. [KM]

708 Galván Mirafuentes, José Luis. Tradición y cambio sociocultural: los indios del noroeste de México ante el dominio español, siglo XVIII. (*Estud. Hist. Novohisp.*, 35, julio/dic. 2006, p. 71–115)

Indians in Northeastern New Spain fled Jesuit missions, and most went to Spanish mining towns or to places remote enough to be removed from Spanish control. Both types of places offered Indians new freedoms by allowing them to control their own labor and to interact with more types of people. [KM]

709 Garraty, Christopher P. Aztec Teotihuacán: political processes at a postclassic and early colonial city-state in the Basin of Mexico. (*Lat. Am. Antiq.*, 17:4, Dec. 2006, p. 363–387, bibl., graphs, maps, tables)

This article examines pottery sherds of the Teotihuacan Mapping Project to learn more about the internal development of Teotihuacán under Aztec domination. Studies have often focused on Tenochtitlán and its relations with the 50 or so city-states in the Mexico basin, but the internal organization and development of these altepetl are often neglected in the literature. Garraty is able to analyze, using various sophisticated methods, Aztec-period pottery sherds to determine first that a major relocation of Teotihuacán's center took place in the late 14th/early 15th century, and second, that Teotihuacán trended toward decentralization under the Aztecs. For archeologist's comment, see *HLAS 63:50.* [PDV]

710 Gasco, Janine. Beyond the Indian/Ladino dichotomy: shifting identities in colonial and contemporary Chiapas, Mexico. (*in* New world, first nations: native peoples of Mesoamerica and the Andes under colonial rule. Edited by David Cahill and Blanca Tovías. Brighton, England; Portland, Ore.: Sussex Academic Press, 2006, p. 115–128, bibl., map)

Author uses the case of Soconusco, Chiapas, to argue that the terms *Indian* and *ladino* should been seen as part of a continuum rather than as a dichotomy. Most people identified as Indians during the early 18th century, but as the economic stresses of the Bourbon reforms transformed landownership patterns, more indigenous people entered the wage labor force and declared themselves ladino to avoid paying tribute. [KM]

711 Gimmel, Millie. Reading medicine in the *Codex de la Cruz Badiano*. (*J. Hist. Ideas*, 69:2, April 2008, p. 169–192)

This article examines the *Codex de la Cruz Badiano* and finds that it was a product of both Nahua and early modern European textual practices, techniques, ideas, and theories of medicine. Previous scholars have interpreted the *Codex* as a product of European cultural hegemony, through its alphabetized Nahuatl, use of Latin, imitation of the European herbal tradition, and embrace of European medical theories of humoralism. A closer look, however, reveals Nahua glyphs and pictoral, nonlinear reading, all examples of indigenous literary styles, and indigenous ideas of the balances of hot and cold life forces that appear to be humoralism. In this way, the *Codex* is a product of bicultural, hybrid mestizaje, with indigenous writers taking advantage of European writing techniques as much as the viceregal, colonial officials were taking advantage of indigenous natural resources. Scholars need to keep in mind that things that appear to be European on the surface are not necessarily so, but may still contain indigenous elements—otherwise they are in danger of "colonizing the colonial." [PDV]

712 Gómez Álvarez, Cristina. Comercio y comerciantes del libro en la Carrera de Indias: Cádiz-Veracruz, 1750–1778. (*Hist. Mex./México*, 57:3, enero/marzo 2008, p. 621–667)

This article examines 135 legajos from the Archivo General de Indias of the Registros de Navíos for ships going from Cádiz to Veracruz between 1750 and 1778. The author finds that the 244 ships making the voyage during that time carried 4,896 boxes of books, each containing an average of 108 books for a total of 472,824 volumes that crossed the Atlantic to New Spain, the vast majority of which remained there. These books were published throughout Europe and were traded mainly by Spanish merchants who dominated the trade at the expense of booksellers (*libreros*) and publishers in New Spain. These findings thus indicate the great appetite and market for books in 18th-century New Spain, and the fact that printing and publishing there remained relatively weak, dominated by metropolitan production. [PDV]

713 Gonzalbo Aizpuru, Pilar. Afectos e intereses en los matrimonios en la ciudad de México a fines de la colonia. (*Hist. Mex./México*, 56:4, abril/junio 2007, p. 1117–1161, bibl., tables)

Data analysis of Mexico City's parochial marriage registers over a decade (1760–70) indicates that marriage was usually contracted between people of the same group and that ecclesiastical authorities demonstrated little concern for maintaining purity of blood (outside of minor aristocracy). Author also suggests that economic interests were a more significant factor in marriage choice than in earlier periods. [KM]

714 Gonzalbo Aizpuru, Pilar. Del decoro a la ostentación: los límites del lujo en la ciudad de México en el siglo XVIII. (*Colon. Lat. Am. Rev.*, 16:1, June 2007, p. 3–22, bibl., graph, tables)

Notarial records including dowries and wills are the basis of this examination of the place of clothing in people's lives. Attire was important, the author concludes, but people were not as extravagant with their clothing as some contemporaries claimed. [KM]

715 Gonzalbo Aizpuru, Pilar. El nacimiento del miedo, 1692: indios y españoles en la ciudad de México. (*Rev. Indias*, 68:244, sept./dic. 2008, p. 9–34, bibl.)

After the riot of 1692, fearful authorities blamed a hostile Indian population even though the participants included a wider range of the city's racially mixed population. See also item **689**. [KM]

716 Gordon, Richard A. Following Estevanico: the influential presence of an African slave in sixteenth-century new world historiography. (*Colon. Lat. Am. Rev.*, 15:2, Dec. 2006, p. 183–206, bibl.)

Examines the range with which some texts from the mid-16th to early-17th century depicted Estevanico, the Moroccan-born Spanish slave who, after surviving the Cabeza de Vaca journey, became an important source of information on the Marcos de Niza expedition. [KM]

717 Gosner, Kevin. Indigenous production and consumption of cotton in eighteenth-century Chiapas: re-evaluating the coercive practices of the *Reparto de Efectos*. (*in* New world, first nations: native peoples of Mesoamerica and the Andes under colonial rule. Edited by David Cahill and Blanca Tovías. Brighton, England; Portland, Ore.: Sussex Academic Press, 2006, p. 129–143, tables)

Gosner's examination of cotton production in Chiapas reassesses the effects of *repartimientos de mercancías*. He argues that the costs and benefits varied according to the products being exchanged since different crops had different modes of productions. *Repartimientos* could thus be both empowering and alienating to indigenous groups. [KM]

718 Hausberger, Bernd. La conquista del empleo público en la Nueva España: el comerciante gaditano Tomás Ruiz de Apodaca y sus amigos, siglo XVIII. (*Hist. Mex./México*, 56:3, enero/marzo 2007, p. 725–778, bibl.)

This detailed reconstruction of an 18th-century businessman's transatlantic connections serves as an example of how the Spanish commercial system functioned. Hausberger convincingly argues that this web of flexible associations among family, friends, and countrymen was of such importance to its collective membership (past, present, and future) that its welfare could override individual interests, explaining why members engaged in projects that assisted other members, even if those projects did not benefit themselves directly. [KM]

719 Historia de la vida cotidiana en México. v. 1, Mesoamérica y los ámbitos indígenas de la Nueva España. Coordinación de Pablo Escalante Gonzalbo. Dirección de Pilar Gonzalbo Aizpuru. México: El Colegio de México; Fondo de Cultura Económica, 2004. 1 v.: bibl., index. (Sección de obras de historia)

This is a monumental and wide-ranging collection of social history essays on "daily life" in colonial Mexico. As Gonzalbo contends in the introduction, eating, drinking, sleeping, living, and dying are universal, but are not done or perceived in uniform ways. They are, rather, historically contingent, and when studied as such, give us valuable insight into society. The volume is divided into two main themes: essays concerning material culture, and essays highlighting personal relations. Together they form a unique and detailed picture of colonial Mexican society, both its traditional elements and the growing spirit of enlightened reform in the 18th-century

which emphasized material and spiritual well-being. This was the case, however, in a society in which, as the essays in the volume illustrate, there were major discrepancies of wealth and standard of living. For review of vol. 4 on the 19th century, see *HLAS 64:674*. [PDV]

720 Holler, Jacqueline. Conquered spaces, colonial skirmishes: spatial contestation in sixteenth-century Mexico City. (*Radic. Hist. Rev.*, 99, Fall 2007, p. 107–120, map)

Four cases between 1540 and 1580 illustrate how indigenous spaces of Tenochtitlán were reimagined as colonial spaces of Mexico City, shifts that took place through a process of negotiation rather than Spanish domination. Useful contribution that links ideas about racial identity and physical space. [KM]

721 Invasion and transformation: interdisciplinary perspectives on the conquest of Mexico. Edited by Rebecca P. Brienen and Margaret A. Jackson. Boulder: Univ. Press of Colorado, 2007. 231 p.: bibl., index. (Mesoamerican worlds)

This edited volume developed out of an international symposium by the same name that was held in conjunction with the opening of an art exhibition on paintings of the conquest of Mexico entitled "Visions of Empire: Picturing the Conquest in Colonial Mexico." The essays by an impressive group of invited scholars presented in this volume revisit the major figures and consequences of conquest and use the paintings to decipher particular moments of the conquest that have often gained iconic status. [PDV]

722 Irigoyen López, Antonio. Un obispado para la familia: Francisco Verdín Molina, prelado de Guadalajara y Valladolid en la segunda mitad del siglo XVII. (*Hist. Mex./México*, 58:2, oct./dic. 2008, p. 557–594, bibl.)

Rich reconstruction of Francisco Verdín Molina's webs of family connections illuminates the parallel ascendancy of the bishop and his family. The author argues individuals "desarrollaba en, por, y para la familia" (p. 559) and that families were the primary motor of social mobility. [KM]

723 Jiménez Gómez, Juan Ricardo. La república de indios en Querétaro, 1550–1820: gobierno, elecciones y bienes de comunidad. Querétaro, Mexico: Instituto de Estudios Constitucionales, 2006. 910 p.: bibl., col. ill., index, col. maps.

Substantial volume brings together archival documents to describe and explain the structure, composition, and functioning of Indian government in the district of Querétaro from the creation of the first organizations in 1550 to the promulgation of the Constitución de Cádiz in 1820. Covers the roles of different offices, election results, tribute payments, community property, administrative responsibilities, struggles with outsiders, and public functions such as running hospitals and celebrating feast days. Includes transcriptions of many documents, some with facsimiles of the original. [KM]

724 Johnson, Lyman L. Digging up Cuauhtémoc. (in Death, dismemberment, and memory: body politics in Latin America. Edited by Lyman L. Johnson. Albuquerque: Univ. of New Mexico Press, 2004, p. 207–244, photos)

Highly readable account of the controversies associated with the 1949 unearthing of the purported grave of Cuauhtémoc in Ixcateopan, Guerrero, places the cult of the last Aztec leader in the context of 19th- and 20th-century politics. [KM]

725 Jordán, Maria V. Desde los campos de León a Nueva España: espiritualidad transatlántica en una obra de Juan Suárez de Gamboa, 1625. (Colon. Lat. Am. Rev., 18:1, April 2009, p. 123–139, bibl.)

Jordan explores the transatlantic spirituality of Suárez de Gamboa through his 1625 published account of La labradora, a rustic laywoman from León, Spain, who he, a pious layman from Vizcaya living in Puebla, presented as a saintly but accessible model for New Spain's residents to emulate. [PDV]

726 Kanter, Deborah Ellen. Hijos del pueblo: gender, family, and community in rural Mexico, 1730–1850. Austin: Univ. of Texas Press, 2008. 151 p.: bibl., index, maps.

This book provides a rich, in-depth examination of rural life in the Tenango

Valley of Toluca from 1730 to 1850. The history of the valley, which was composed largely of indigenous villages and a large hacienda, provides a microcosm of ethnic, gender, and social relations from the period of Bourbon reforms through Independence to the dissolution of indigenous communal lands in the 19th century. Using mainly court cases, Kanter provides a rich portrait of the patriarchal relations that governed social interactions and brought order to late colonial and early national Mexico. [PDV]

727 Kessell, John L. Death delayed: the sad case of the two Marías, 1773–1779. (N.M. Hist. Rev., 83:2, Spring 2008, p. 157–170, ill.)

Recounts the extraordinary case of Maria Francisca and her mother who conspired to murder Maria's new husband, apparently because he was forcing her to move to his neighboring New Mexico pueblo. [KM]

728 Kessell, John L. Pueblos, Spaniards, and the kingdom of New Mexico. Norman: Univ. of Oklahoma Press, 2008. 225 p.: bibl., ill., index, maps.

Brief, readable history of 17th-century New Mexico that foregrounds people and events and that presents Pueblo Indians and Spaniards as groups preoccupied with their own internal struggles so that outbreaks of violence between them, as in the Pueblo Revolt of 1680, were exceptional. [KM]

729 Kirk, Stephanie L. Convent life in colonial Mexico: a tale of two communities. Gainesville: Univ. Press of Florida, 2007. 241 p.: bibl., index.

In this book, Kirk traces the history of convent life in colonial Mexico using a variety of published and archival sources, including religious tracts, poetry, and religious biographies as well as Inquisition documents, personal letters, sermons, and legal decrees. Her focus is to trace the dualistic nature of the convents: on the one hand, they constituted a way for the Catholic Church to institute and ensure female chastity through cloistering, particularly in the context of the Counter-Reformation. On the other hand, however, the emphasis on female morality and the effort to control convent life down to minute detail belie a deep-seated anxiety among church officials that the women in the convent did possess and indeed practiced agency. Kirk outlines the types of friendships and alliances that formed within convent walls and the opportunities available for women within these institutions, thus highlighting the fact that "the lived experiences of women . . . belie the rigid controls male clerics mandated in their prescriptive texts" (p. 8). [PDV]

730 Kuri Camacho, Ramón. *Libertad divina y humana* en algunos jesuitas novohispanos: Pedro de Abarca, Miguel de Castilla y Antonio de Figueroa Valdés. (*Estud. Hist. Novohisp.*, 37, julio/dic. 2007, p. 91–122)

Author provides a detailed examination of the writings of three Jesuit theologians in New Spain who engaged questions about divine grace and free will (Molina's *scientia media*). [KM]

731 Lavrin, Asunción. Brides of Christ: conventual life in colonial Mexico. Stanford, Calif.: Stanford Univ. Press, 2007. 496 p.: bibl., index.

Impressive exploration of nunneries in colonial Mexico vividly recreates convent life and describes what it meant to become a bride of Christ. Based on years of archival research and integrating a wide range of secondary sources, this is the definitive work on colonial nuns. The book is organized topically, covering the process of becoming a nun, spiritual practices, convent governance, daily life, attitudes toward death and disease in the convent, maintaining chastity, the creation of convents for Indian women, disputes over the *vida común* (common life), and nuns' writings. [KM]

732 Lavrin, Asunción. Las esposas de cristo en Hispanoamérica. (*in* Historia de las mujeres en España y América Latina: el mundo moderno. Coordinación de Margarita Ortega, Asunción Lavrin y Pilar Pérez Cantó. Madrid: Cátedra, 2005, v. 2, p. 667–693, bibl., photos)

Good succinct overview of nuns and their worlds that covers foundations and expansion of convents throughout the Spanish Americas as well as their social hierarchies, financial workings, governance, and cultural and spiritual life. [KM]

733 Lavrin, Asunción. Masculine and feminine: the construction of gender roles in the regular orders in early modern Mexico. (*Explor. Renaissance Cult.*, 34:1, Summer 2008, p. 3–26)

Originally the keynote address at the South-Central Renaissance Conference, this article uses prescriptive literature on nuns and friars to pose intriguing questions about models of masculinity and femininity specific to 17th- and 18th-century Mexico. Masculine valor and boldness in evangelization efforts, including the use of soldier metaphors, may have contrasted with feminine virtues of modesty and seclusion, but Lavrin shuns a polarized model for one that includes grey areas and overlap around issues such as virginity and contemplation. [KM]

734 León-Portilla, Ascensión H. de. Fray Alonso de Molina y el proyecto indigenista de la Orden Seráfica. (*Estud. Hist. Novohisp.*, 36, enero/junio 2007, p. 63–81, bibl.)

Tracks the reasoning behind early Franciscan interest in learning indigenous languages. Author argues that the Franciscans' linguistic efforts were intended not only as a means to communicate but also to construct a common space between two cultures, a project the author labels as indigenista. [KM]

735 Levy, Buddy. Conquistador: Hernán Cortés, King Montezuma, and the last stand of the Aztecs. New York: Bantam Books, 2008. 429 p., 8 p. of plates: bibl., ill. (chiefly col.), index, col. map.

This history of the conquest, written in an engaging and accessible style, has appeal for a popular as well as a scholarly audience. The account is based upon the usual sources employed for conquest histories, both Spanish and Nahua, and follows in the tradition of authors Hugh Thomas and Ross Hassig, upon whose interpretation, the author, by his own omission, relies heavily. [PDV]

736 Lewis, Laura A. From sodomy to superstition: the active pathic and bodily transgressions in New Spain. (*Ethnohistory/Columbus*, 54:1, Winter 2007, p. 129–157)

This suggestive article argues that women, Indians, and men who cross-dressed or committed the *pecado nefando"* were linked through ideologies that viewed them as weak and easily corrupted by the devil. [KM]

737 **López de la Cámara Alta, Agustín.** Descripción general de la colonia de Nuevo Santander. Estudio preliminar, transcripción y notas de Patricia Osante. Presentación de J. Omar Moncada Maya. México: UNAM, 2006. 193 p.: ill. (some col.), maps. (Serie Documental; 27)

Transcription of Agustín López de la Cámara Alta's *relación* of 1757 includes information on the towns of Nuevo Santander. [KM]

738 **López Sarrelangue, Delfina Esmeralda.** Una villa mexicana en el siglo XVIII: Nuestra Señora de Guadalupe. 2. ed. México: Instituto de Investigaciones Históricas: Miguel Ángel Porrúa, 2005. 297 p.: bibl., ill., map.

Reworking, with additional archival material, of the original 1957 edition of this history of the town that is home to Mexico's most famous Marian image. Tracks the origins of the town, jurisdictional disputes, economic conditions, and Guadalupe's role in the daily life of its residents. For review of 1st ed., see *HLAS 23:3171.* [KM]

739 **Malvido, Elsa.** Some avatars of death in New Spain's Southeast. (*in* New world, first nations: native peoples of Mesoamerica and the Andes under colonial rule. Edited by David Cahill and Blanca Tovías. Brighton, England; Portland, Ore.: Sussex Academic Press, 2006, p. 92–111)

Examines beliefs about death in colonial Yucatan, focusing on what the author refers to as the Triumph of Death (the ubiquity of death after the conquest demonstrated God's wrath and death's democratic view), the Bad Death (accidents which did not allow people time to prepare their souls), and the Good Death (when the soul could be prepared with Last Rites). [KM]

740 **Marichal, Carlos.** Bankruptcy of empire: Mexican silver and the wars between Spain, Britain, and France, 1760–1810. New York: Cambridge Univ. Press, 2007. 318 p.: bibl., ill., index. (Cambridge Latin American studies; 91)

Rigorous examination of New Spain's fiscal income structure, including taxes, donations, and forced loans, in the context of empire. During the second half of the 18th century the Bourbon monarchy created a highly successful tax regime that Marichal characterizes as "pure financial colonialism." New Spain was the empire's richest tax colony and shouldered a disproportionate amount of the state's debts. The crown's need to pay for wars led to a debt explosion in the 1790s and the Mexican government's indebtedness continued to grow as "astonishing" amounts of money flowed back to Spain, even after 1808. [KM]

741 **Márquez Morfín, Lourdes** and **Patricia Hernández Espinoza.** Salud y sociedad en el México prehispánico y colonial. México: Conaculta-INAH: Promep, 2006. 439 p.: bibl., ill.

This work is a compilation of studies from students and researchers at the Escuela Nacional de Antropología e Historia (ENAH) who use a "biocultural" anthropological approach to the study of indigenous health in prehispanic and colonial Mexico. The majority of studies focus on the prehispanic period, using methods of paleopathology to study skeletal and dental remains in order to determine the state of indigenous health and how it differed with the transition from hunger-gatherer to intensive agricultural societies. The work also examines health differentials according to social hierarchy, increasing urbanization, and changes in diet and nutrition. Although the editors state that it is difficult to draw broad conclusions and the focus here is on individual situations, the authors do see a broad increase in epidemics with increasing urbanization and the increase in complexity of classic and post-classic societies. [PDV]

742 **Martín Flores, José de Jesús.** Fray Miguel de Bolonia: el guardián de los indios. Guadalajara, Mexico: Entre Amigos, 2006. 159 p.: bibl., ill.

Biographical study of a 16th-century Franciscan missionary to Michoacán includes a transcription of an Inquisition case against him (for heretical propositions). [KM]

743 Martínez, María Elena. Genealogical
fictions: limpieza de sangre, religion,
and gender in colonial Mexico. Stanford,
Calif.: Stanford Univ. Press, 2008. 407 p.:
bibl., ill., index.

Innovative and thought-provoking
study historicizes ideas about race by connecting concepts of *limpieza de sangre*
(purity of blood) to the development of New
Spain's *sistema de castas* (caste system).
Spanish ideas about *limpieza* defined by
religion and demarcated by Christian, rather
than Jewish or Muslim, ancestors transformed in the Americas where the mixing
of Spanish, Indian, and African populations
added racial dimensions. The author sees
the 17th century as crucial to the crystal-
lization of a Christian, Spanish, white identity set apart from "impure" African, racially mixed, and, more ambiguously, native
ancestry. By the late colonial period and as
expressed in casta paintings, the concept of
purity had been secularized to be associated
with Spanishness. The author's arguments
also highlight the role of gender in the development of ideas about *limpieza*. [KM]

744 Materiales para la historia de Sonora.
Textos de Rafael Pérez-Taylor A. y
Miguel Ángel Paz Frayre. México: UNAM,
Instituto de Investigaciones Antropológicas;
Jalisco, Mexico: Colegio de Jalisco, 2007.
467 p.: bibl., col. maps. (Col. Fuentes para
el estudio del norte de México; 1)

Collection of documents related to
the history of the Jesuits in Sonora. [KM]

745 McFarlane, Anthony. Los ejércitos
coloniales y la crisis del imperio español, 1808–1810. (*Hist. Mex./México*, 58:1,
julio/sept. 2008, p. 229–285)

Well-conceived article examines the
impact of Bourbon reforms on the colonial
military, the military's responses to the crisis of 1808–10, and how regional variations
in those responses affected Spain's ability to
defend its colonies. [KM]

746 Megged, Amos. Social memory in
ancient and colonial Mesoamerica.
Cambridge, England; New York: Cambridge
Univ. Press, 2010. 342 p.: bibl., index.

Megged examines Nahua ways of
remembering the past and commemorating it from the late post-classic period (ca.
1430) and the mid-18th century. He uses

ancient and colonial Nahua sources, both
pictoral and alphabetic, to uncover early
Nahua conceptions of time, space, and
cosmology and the way these factors served
to construct their social memory and, as
such, their identity. Unlike other historians
and ethnographers—most notably Serge
Gruzinski and Enrique Florescano—Megged
finds significant continuity between pre-
contact and colonial Nahua representations
of history. He finds that Nahuas "did in fact
retain a very vivid memory of their sense of
belonging to their former ethnic state . . .
[and] . . . were far from having lost their
long-term memory. . . ." [PDV]

747 Melvin, Karen. Charity without
borders: alms-giving in New Spain for
captives in North Africa. (*Colon. Lat. Am.
Rev.*, 18:1, April 2009, p. 75–97, bibl., tables)

Residents of New Spain sent enormous sums of money back to Europe in
order to redeem Christians held captive in
North Africa. They did so in response to
appeals from members of the Mercedarian
Order that focused on the need to defend the
Church from a dangerous, Muslim enemy,
suggesting that people saw themselves as
part of a Catholic community united across
great distances. [PDV]

748 Mendieta, Eva. In search of Catalina
de Erauso: the national and sexual
identity of the lieutenant nun. Translated
by Angeles Prado. Reno: Center for Basque
Studies, Univ. of Nevada, Reno, 2009. 243 p.:
bibl., ill., index. (Occasional papers series/
Center for Basque Studies; 16)

In this study of the famous "lieutenant nun" Catalina de Erauso, a Basque
woman who escaped from her convent at the
age of 15 and went on to live a tumultuous
life of adventure in the Americas disguised
as a man, Mendieta brings new elements
that have not been treated in depth in earlier studies. First, Mendieta emphasizes
Erauso's Basque origins, arguing that the
unique solidarity and unity of the Basque
community provided her with many opportunities in the Americas and at times
even saved her life. Second, Mendieta delves
deeply into Erauso's sexuality, exploring
contemporary views of women's social roles
and modern studies of transvestitism and
transgender identity to argue in the end
that Erauso identified as a man trapped in

a woman's body rather than a woman masquerading as a man. [PDV]

749 Mendoza Muñoz, Jesús. Secularización de la Parroquia de Santiago de Querétaro en el siglo XVlll. Cadereyta, Mexico: Fomento Histórico y Cultural de Cadereyta, 2008. 140 p.: bibl., ill. (Serie de historia; 9)

This book examines the establishment of the Franciscan Order in the city of Querétaro in the 16th century and its eventual secularization in the 18th. The Franciscan ecclesiastical establishment was one of the main influences in the development of Querétaro, which became an important economic, administrative, and religious center from which were launched missions and evangelization campaigns to the north. A number of other convents and institutions were also set up, but their influence was gradually diminished as the Enlightenment led to increasing secularization. In 1759 the Parroquia was shut down and religious authority in Querétaro shifted to the secular church. [PDV]

750 Mills, Kenneth. Introduction: Religious life in New Spain: novel approaches. (*Colon. Lat. Am. Rev.*, 18:1, April 2009, p. 3–15, bibl., ill.)

Insightful essay introduces this special journal issue with thoughts on reimagining colonial religious history outside the "seductive" boundaries of a three-stage tale: a frenzy of early Franciscan evangelization, a hybrid Baroque middle, and a secularizing finish. [PDV]

751 Miranda Ojeda, Pedro. Las comisarías del Santo Oficio: funciones y funcionarios en la estructura inquisitorial de Yucatán, 1571–1820. (*Desacatos*, 25, sept./dic. 2007, p. 163–190, bibl., ill., tables)

Examines the roles of local officials of the Inquisition—comisarios, notarios, and familiares—in the Yucatan. [KM]

New world, first nations: native peoples of Mesoamerica and the Andes under colonial rule. See item 1432.

752 Newell, Quincy D. Constructing lives at Mission San Francisco: native Californians and Hispanic colonists, 1776–1821. Albuquerque: Univ. of New Mexico Press, 2009. 267 p.: bibl., index.

Author uses mission registers to reconstruct the life histories and social worlds of Bay Area Indians, covering religious life, labor, family, marriage, and godparenthood. Argues that Indians preserved key elements of their culture and opportunistically combined Catholicism and their religious traditions to best suit their needs. [KM]

753 Newell, Quincy D. The varieties of religious experience: baptized Indians at Mission San Francisco de Asís, 1776–1821. (*Am. Indian Q.*, 32:4, Fall 2008, p. 412–442, ill., map)

Where Indians of the San Francisco mission chose to give birth and die provides evidence of varying levels of acceptance of Catholicism. [KM]

754 Norton, Marcy. Tasting empire: chocolate and the European internalization of Mesoamerican aesthetics. (*Am. Hist. Rev.*, 111:3, June 2006, p. 660–691, ill., photo)

This article examines the European taste for chocolate, making the case that the formation of taste was also part of the Columbian Exchange between Europe and the Americas. Norton argues that the European adoption of chocolate did not proceed along the lines that historians have generally charted for it—that it was adopted and made to fit European tastes through the addition of copious amounts of sugar. Rather, she finds that Europeans sought to emulate and approximate Mesoamerican preparations of chocolate, preferring its traditional red color and flower spices, and using the same drinking vessels and rituals as the Mayas. Through this study of European adoption of chocolate, it is possible to see the impact of Mesoamerican esthetics on Europeans. The Columbian Exchange, then, involved a "cross-cultural transmission of tastes." [PDV]

755 Offutt, Leslie Scott. Defending corporate identity on New Spain's northeastern frontier: San Esteban de Nueva Tlaxcala, 1780–1810. (*Americas/Washington*, 64:3, Jan. 2008, p. 351–375)

San Esteban's conflicts with the neighboring Spanish town of Saltillo during a "crisis" period marked by drought, disease, and Indian depredations demonstrate a pueblo trying to defend its corporate identity and existence as well as ensure the survival of its residents. [KM]

756 O'Hara, Matthew D. Stone, mortar, and memory: church construction and communities in late colonial Mexico City. (*HAHR*, 86:4, Nov. 2006, p. 647–680)

Examines the 18th-century secularization of parishes that occurred with the Bourbon Reforms. Secularization and the reorganization that accompanied it often led to disputes over who would control the buildings and possessions within the secularized parishes. Mendicants agreed that it was the property of the universal church, while indigenous communities saw the buildings as local possessions, reminders of the time and labor that their ancestors had put into building and acquiring them. The physical remains were thus reminders of the past that reinforced indigenous identity, and in this way, O'Hara argues that parochialism and corporate identities persisted despite efforts to dismantle them in the late colonial period. [PDV]

757 Ortelli, Sara. Trama de una guerra conveniente: Nueva Vizcaya y la sombra de los apaches, 1748–1790. México: Centro de Estudios Históricos, El Colegio de México, 2007. 259 p.: bibl., ill., indexes, maps.

Well-argued study of New Vizcaya during the second half of the 18th century reassesses the idea of an Apache war and looks instead to new intrusions of royal authority, especially in the form of Bourbon reforms. [KM]

758 Osowski, Edward W. Passion miracles and indigenous historical memory in New Spain. (*HAHR*, 88:4, Nov. 2008, p. 607–638)

Argues indigenous and Franciscan accounts of the miraculous image of the Holy Sepulcher of Christ near Amecameca offer different reasons for supporting the shrine: the triumph of Christianity versus proof of autonomous political authority. [KM]

759 Owensby, Brian Philip. Empire of law and Indian justice in colonial Mexico. Stanford, Calif.: Stanford Univ. Press, 2008. 379 p.: bibl., index.

In this work, Owensby examines court cases from the archives of Mexico and Spain that involve indigenous litigants. Although there is a rich mine of such sources, Owensby points out the fact that they have been underutilized by colonial historians, and scholars that do focus on legal matters have either examined the laws themselves—in the tradition of *derecho indiano*—or their inability to protect indigenous peoples from exploitation. Owensby joins a more recent set of historians in examining the role of legal justice within indigenous peoples lives in concrete situations "on the ground." He focuses specifically on a long 17th century (from 1590–1700) in order to trace the growing entrenchment of and familiarity with Spanish law in indigenous understanding. [PDV]

760 Palafox y Mendoza, Juan de. Virtues of the Indian = Virtudes del Indio. Edited and with general introduction, biographical essay, and annotated translation by Nancy H. Fee. Introduction to the text by Alejandro Cañeque. Lanham, Md.: Rowman & Littlefield Publishers, 2009. 243 p.: bibl., index.

This work includes a transcription and side-by-side translation of a treatise written by Juan de Palafox y Mendoza, the famous 17th-century Bishop of Puebla and Visitor-General of New Spain. As one of Palafox's many writings, *Virtues of the Indian* is significant for the insight it provides into elite Spanish images of indigenous peoples in the mid-17th century, a period that was witnessing increasing miscegenation and the development of a Creole identity in the Americas, and a growing disillusionment regarding the supposed success of the "spiritual conquest." In a treatise that differs from the earlier ethnographic treatments of Bartolomé de Las Casas and José de Acosta, Palafox treats indigenous peoples as homogenous. He defends indigenous character, emphasizing their humility, innocence, freedom from vice, and complete acceptance of both Spanish rule and Catholicism to emphasize the need for the Crown to defend and protect them from exploitation in the colonial system, which continually placed excessive demands upon them. With royal protection, indigenous peoples of the Americas would be excellent Christians and excellent subjects, and as such would lead to the salvation of the Spanish Empire. [PDV]

761 Pardo, Osvaldo F. How to punish Indians: law and cultural change in early colonial Mexico. (*Comp. Stud. Soc. Hist.*, 48:1, 2006, p. 79–109)

Examines tensions between civil and ecclesiastical authorities over the punishment of indigenous peoples from the 1540s through the early 17th century. Ecclesiastic officials, especially friars, wished to control civil and criminal justice and punishment in New Spain. They argued that they were closer to indigenous peoples and understood their rites and customs and how to best correct unwanted behavior. The author examines arguments concerning the practice of shaming through the shaving of hair, an Aztec ritual of removing one's *tonalli*, to illustrate his argument that ecclesiastical influence on judicial proceedings was declining and increasingly unable to challenge secular authority. [PDV]

762 Parroquia del Sagrario Metropolitano (Mexico City, Mexico). Los "padrones" de confesión y comunión de la Parroquia del Sagrario Metropolitano de la Ciudad de México. Coordinación de Óscar Mazín y Esteban Sánchez de Tagle. México: Colegio de México, Centro de Estudios Históricos; Murcia, Spain: Red Columnaria, 2009. 87 p.: bibl., ill., 1 CD-ROM.

Six essays suggest uses for the rich census information found in a series of registers (1670–1825) from Mexico City's central parish. Essays cover the registers as a form of social control; an excursion through city streets; a record of the parish's social boundaries; a promising if challenging source for tracking a mobile, urban population; a source for history of the city's urbs. Includes a helpful introduction. [KM]

763 Pearce, Adrian J. Rescates and Anglo-Spanish trade in the Caribbean during the French Revolutionary Wars, ca. 1797–1804. (*J. Lat. Am. Stud.*, 38:3, Aug. 2006, p. 607–624, table)

This article examines the practice of "rescate," or the ransom of Spanish ships captured by British forces during the French Revolutionary wars. These ships and their cargo could be repurchased from the British by Spanish and Spanish American merchants who applied for and often received permits or licenses to enter British ports.

Although they ostensibly were meant to recoup losses only, the licenses allowed legal transactions with British merchants and in this way served to promote continued Anglo-Spanish trade despite the war. Thus they constituted one strategy for minimizing the effect of blockades and warfare on intercolonial commerce and demonstrate the little-known fact that Anglo-Spanish trade was flowering at the end of the 18th century. [PDV]

764 Pérez Canto, Pilar. Las españolas en la vida colonial. (*in* Historia de las mujeres en España y América Latina: El mundo moderno. Coordinación de Margarita Ortega, Asunción Lavrin y Pilar Pérez Cantó. Madrid: Cátedra, 2005, v. 2, p. 525–553, bibl., ill.)

Synopsis of elite Creole and peninsular women in the Spanish Americas focuses on "exceptional" women, such as those who participated in the conquest of Chile, the wives of royal officials who exercised unofficial power, and owners of properties including haciendas. [KM]

765 Pescador, Juan Javier. Crossing borders with the Santo Niño de Atocha. Albuquerque: Univ. of New Mexico Press, 2009. 256 p.: bibl., index.

Well-conceived history traces the evolution of the cult of Santo Niño de Atocha from Spain to Zacatecas, its 19th- and 20th-century journeys northward, and its thriving role in contemporary US immigrant communities. Aptly described as a "shapeshifter," the Holy Child transformed along with his constituencies and changing social conditions. [KM]

766 Proctor, Frank T. Gender and the manumission of slaves in New Spain. (*HAHR*, 86:2, May 2006, p. 309–336, bibl.)

This article examines patterns of manumission in New Spain between the 1640s and the 1760s and argues that it was a thoroughly gendered process and must be understood as such in order to understand manumission patterns overall. Historians have pointed out the predominance of women and children in manumission records and often attribute it to sexual relations between slave women and masters, the with master freeing the children resulting from their union. However, female masters freed slaves at higher overall rates than did male masters, and they tended to free women and children slaves in particular, often citing child-rearing, mother-daughter type relations as the reason, with female slaves often acting as nannies and wet-nurses to white children. This pattern indicates that increasing chance for manumission was often associated with closeness and intimacy between slaves and masters in the domestic sphere, but it was not of a sexual nature. The pattern continues after the end of the slave trade, even though the value (prices of manumission) of female slaves increased due to their reproductive capacity. Understanding these patterns thus requires an understanding of gender and gender relations in the manumission process. [PDV]

767 La proeza histórica de un pueblo: San Mateo Atenco en el valle de Toluca (siglos VIII al XIX). Textos de Yoko Sigiura Yamamoto *et al.* Coordinación de René García Castro y María Teresa Jarquín Ortega. Toluca, Mexico: El Colegio Mexiquense: Univ. Autónoma del Estado de México, 2006. 222 p.: bibl., maps.

Scholars from multiple disciplines offer essays that, together, offer a multi-century history of the pueblo of San Mateo Atenco. [KM]

768 Religión, poder y autoridad en la Nueva España. Recopilación de Alicia Mayer y Ernesto de la Torre Villar. México: UNAM, 2004. 444 p.: bibl., ill. (Serie Historia novohispana; 72)

Well-documented collection of essays centered on the relationships between religion, power, and authority during the 16th to 18th centuries. Essays cover a wide range of topics, including bishops, sermons, missions, elites, confession guides, and credit. [KM]

769 Restall, Matthew. The Black middle: Africans, Mayas, and Spaniards in colonial Yucatan. Stanford, Calif.: Stanford Univ. Press, 2009. 433 p.: bibl., ill., index, maps.

In this pioneering work, the second in a trilogy on Yucatan's colonial Mayans, Africans, and Spaniards, respectively, Restall focuses on the African—or what he terms the "Afro-Yucatecan"—presence in colonial Yucatan, a topic that has received almost no

attention thus far in the scholarly literature. In his work Restall asserts that the lack of literature by no means indicates a lack of significance of the Afro-Yucatecans. Rather, a rich—albeit somewhat hidden—archival store of documents delineating the African presence in colonial Yucatán gives testament to the demographic, economic, and sociocultural importance of that population to the development of the history of Yucatan. Restall argues that, although Yucatan did not constitute a "slave society," the importation of African slaves to Yucatan and their free and mixed-blood descendants permanently changed the area by acting as a "black middle" intermediary between Spaniards and Mayans, playing an "interstitial role" in colonial society and managed "to build complex and varied lives" within an exploitative system. [PDV]

770 Río, Ignacio del. Comercio, libranzas de Real Hacienda y circulación monetaria en el norte de la Nueva España, 1773–1810. (*Estud. Hist. Novohisp.*, 35, julio/dic. 2006, p. 117–131)

Although chronic currency shortages plagued New Spain, peripheral areas were particularly hard hit. Giving special attention to Sinaloa and Sonora, Río follows a predominantly one-way flow of currency out of northern mining areas. Beginning with José de Gálvez, a series of late 18th-century efforts to combat the outflow had mixed results at best. [KM]

771 Rocher Salas, Adriana Delfina. Religiosidad e identidad en San Francisco de Campeche: siglos XVI y XVII. (*Anu. Estud. Am.*, 63:2, 2006, p. 27–47)

Examines local devotions and patron saints in an effort to define local identity in Campeche. [KM]

772 Rodríguez-Sala, María Luisa. Los cirujanos de hospitales de la Nueva España (1700–1833): miembros de un estamento profesional o de una comunidad científica? Colaboración de Verónica Ramírez *et al.* México: UNAM, Instituto de Investigaciones Sociales: Academia Mexicana de Cirugía: Patronato del Hospital de Jesús, 2006. 275 p.: bibl., ill., index, maps. (Serie Los Cirujanos en la Nueva España: miembros de un estamento profesional o de una comunidad científica?; 5)

This is the fifth volume of a series that seeks to provide an exhaustive and comprehensive listing and study of surgeons in colonial Mexico. Using a variety of archives in Mexico and Spain, the author has enumerated now over 1,200 surgeons practicing in a variety of institutions in Mexico. In this volume, she investigates those surgeons employed in or involved with the hospitals of New Spain in the late colonial period, both those of lay origins and those founded by religious. For review of the fourth volume in the series, see *HLAS 64:592*. Also see items **773** and **774**. [PDV]

773 Rodríguez-Sala, María Luisa. Los cirujanos en los colegios novohispanos de la Ciudad de México (1567–1838). Colaboración con Verónica Ramírez *et al.* México: UNAM, Instituto de Investigaciones Sociales: Academia Mexicana de Cirugía: Patronato del Hospital de Jesús, 2006. 360 p.: bibl., ill., index. (Serie Los Cirujanos en la Nueva España; 6)

This is the sixth volume of a series that seeks to provide an exhaustive and comprehensive listing and study of surgeons in colonial Mexico. In this volume, the author investigates those surgeons employed in or involved with a variety of educational institutions of ecclesiastical, civil, and *hospicio* foundations that educated a wide variety of students, rich and poor, male and female, and of Spanish, indigenous, or mixed ancestry. This volume includes valuable information on surgeons as an emerging professional group, but also sheds valuable light on the variety of educational institutions in colonial Mexico. Also see items **772** and **774**. [PDV]

774 Rodríguez-Sala, María Luisa. Los cirujanos en los conventos de la ciudad de México (siglos XVI–XIX). Colaboración de Verónica Ramírez *et al.* México: UNAM, Instituto de Investigaciones Sociales: Academia Mexicana de Cirugía, Patronato del Hospital de Jesús, 2008. 328 p.: bibl., ill., index. (Serie Los cirujanos en la Nueva España; 7)

This is the seventh volume of a series that seeks to provide an exhaustive and comprehensive listing and study of surgeons in colonial Mexico. In this volume, the author investigates those surgeons employed

in or involved with both male and female convents in Mexico City from the 16th to the 19th centuries. Also see items **772** and **773**. [PDV]

775 Rojas, Beatriz. Las ciudades novohispanas ante la crisis: entre la antigua y la nueva constitución, 1808–1814. (*Hist. Mex./México*, 58:1, julio/sept. 2008, p. 287–324, bibl., table)

The crisis of 1808–14 provided opportunities for cities to assert themselves over other corporate bodies as the primary representatives of New Spain's political body. [KM]

776 Roselló Soberón, Estela. Así en la tierra como en el cielo: manifestaciones cotidianas de la culpa y el perdón en la Nueva España de los siglos XVI y XVII. México: El Colegio de México, Centro de Estudios Históricos, 2006. 267 p.: bibl.

Author examines the process of Christianization on the individual conscience in New Spain and how ideas about sin and pardon guided people's daily activities during the 16th and a long 17th century. [KM]

777 Rosenmüller, Christoph. Friends, followers, countrymen: viceregal patronage in mid-eighteenth century New Spain. (*Estud. Hist. Novohisp.*, 34, enero/junio 2006, p. 47–72, bibl., table)

This article examines the social networks built and utilized by the Viceroy of Mexico Juan Francisco de Guemes y Horcasitas in the mid-18th century. These social networks were based upon ties of kinship, "spiritual kinship" (i.e., *compadrazgo* and *padrinazgo*), friendship, and shared local origins, but encompassed a wide-ranging, transatlantic network that extended from elites to minor alcaldes. This study thus brings the issue of patronage into focus for the colonial period and points out the importance of local ties and local cooperation needed by Viceroys to implement reform. [PDV]

778 Rosenmüller, Christoph. Patrons, partisans, and palace intrigues: the court society of colonial Mexico, 1702–1710. Calgary, Canada: Univ. of Calgary Press, 2008. 278 p.: bibl., ill., index, map. (Latin American and Caribbean series; 6)

In this work, Rosenmuller examines colonial Mexican politics during the reign of the tenth Duke of Albuquerque as Viceroy of New Spain from 1702–10. Coinciding with the transfer of power from Hapsburg to Bourbon during the War of Spanish Succession, Albuquerque's rule in some ways anticipates the effectiveness—or lack thereof—of later Bourbon reforming policies, and demonstrates the ways in which the colonial state asserted its power. Rosenmüller emphasizes the use of patronage and the establishment of social networks within the viceregal court as an important strategy of royal power, and the various ways in which nativist sentiment and actions sought to limit that power. [PDV]

779 Rubial García, Antonio. ¿Herejes en el claustro?: monjas ante la Inquisición novohispana de siglo XVIII. (*Estud. Hist. Novohisp.*, 31, julio/dic. 2004, p. 19–38, bibl.)

Using the cases of six nuns accused of "delitos contra la fe" during the 18th century, Rubial García argues that inquisitors during this time were more willing than their predecessors to attribute the women's actions to illness or insanity rather than demonic influence. [KM]

780 Ruiz Medrano, Carlos Rubén. "*Alevosos, ingratos y traidores: ¿queréis sacudir el yugo del monarca más católico?*": el discurso de la contrainsurgencia en la Nueva España durante el siglo XVIII. (*HAHR*, 87:3, Aug. 2007, p. 471–497)

Article applies Ranajit Guha's "prose of the counter-insurgency" to 18th-century responses to popular resistance in order to explain a culture of dominance that naturalized the subordination of the masses. [KM]

781 Ruiz Medrano, Carlos Rubén. La resistencia indígena en la sierra de Tututepeque, Nueva España, durante la segunda mitad del siglo XVIII. (*Mesoamérica/Antigua*, 26:47, 2005, p. 23–46, bibl., maps)

In this region that is now part of the state of Hidalgo, indigenous strategies of resistance during the period of Bourbon reforms included protests and legal challenges and sought the restitution of traditionally accepted terms and practices. [KM]

782 Ruiz Medrano, Ethelia. Reshaping New Spain: government and private interests in the colonial bureaucracy, 1531–1550. Translated by Julia Constantino and Pauline Marmasse. Boulder: Univ. Press of Colorado, 2006. 320 p.: bibl., index.

This book, an English translation of the 1991 original, examines the establishment of early colonial government in New Spain during the time of the Second Audiencia from 1531 to 1535 and the subsequent rule of the Viceroy Antonio de Mendoza from 1535 to 1550. The author seeks to understand the aims and methods of the early bureaucracy by examining the records of visitas, residencies, and the correspondence between Audiencia members and the viceroy in order to gain an in-depth understanding of the actions and motivations of early Audiencia members. Finds that many early colonial administrators, granted wide powers by the Crown, manipulated laws to their own economic favor in order to take advantage of the growing potential for wealth in the colony, and in that way also helped to encourage New Spain's internal economic development. A particular case in point was the actions of the *Oidor* Lorenzo de Tejada, who exploited Spanish law and indigenous workers for entrepreneurial purposes during his tenure in office. Despite cases such as these, however, Ruiz Medrano concludes that the Second Audiencia did succeed in establishing entrenched Spanish rule of law and colonial dominion over New Spain, and turning a profit for the Crown as well. For commentary on Spanish-language version, see *HLAS 54:1267.* [PDV]

783 Salazar Andreu, Juan Pablo. Obispos de Puebla de los Ángeles en el periodo de los Austria (1521–1700): algunos aspectos políticos y jurídicos. Prólogo de Rafael Sánchez Vázquez. México: Editorial Porrúa, 2005. 377 p.: bibl., ill.

Compilation of information on each of the 13 bishops of Puebla during Hapsburg rule also includes bibliographies and transcriptions of documents. [KM]

784 Serrano Álvarez, José Manuel and Allan J. Kuethe. La Texas colonial entre Pedro de Rivera y el marqués de Rubí, 1729–1772: aportaciones económicas al sistema presidial. (*CLAHR*, 14:3, Summer 2005, p. 281–311, tables)

Authors' attempt to fill a gap in the historiography of colonial Texas through this examination of the economic administration of the military in 18th-century presidios. [KM]

785 Shean, Julie. "From his roots a branch will bear fruit": the development of missionary iconography in late 18th-century cult images of Sebastián de Aparaicio, 1502–1600. (*Colon. Lat. Am. Rev.*, 18:1, April 2009, p. 17–50)

Iconography of Sebastián de Aparicio demonstrates Franciscan efforts to remodel his story in order to help him "make the leap from popular local figure to internationally recognized saint." His transformation into emblem of Franciscan missionary charity reflected the Franciscans' late 18th-century anxieties over their missionary program. For art historian's comment, see item **42**. [PDV]

786 Simpson, Lesley Byrd. The encomienda in New Spain: the beginning of Spanish Mexico. Berkeley: Univ. of California Press, 2008. 263 p.: ill., index. (California library reprint series) <http://hdl.handle.net/2027/heb.02789>

Simpson's classic work on the encomienda in New Spain, newly published by the Univ. of California Press, is now available online as an ACLS Humanities E-Book. [PDV]

787 Solís Robleda, Gabriela. Entre la tierra y el cielo: religión y sociedad en los pueblos mayas del Yucatán colonial. México: Centro de Investigaciones y Estudios Superiores en Antropología Social: Instituto de Cultura de Yucatán: Miguel Angel Porrúa, 2005. 382 p.: bibl. (Col. Peninsular)

Uses financial data of alms and confraternities to examine the role of religion in the social order of colonial Maya towns in the Yucatan. [KM]

788 Távarez, David Eduardo. The passion according to the wooden drum: the Christian appropriation of a Zapotec ritual genre in New Spain. (*Americas/Washington*, 62:3, Jan. 2006, p. 413–444)

Examines booklets of Zapotec ritual songs surrendered by Zapotec leaders in 1704–06 as part of an innovative extirpation campaign. Along with Maya books of Chi-

lam Balam and some Nahua writings, these Zapotec booklets constitute some of the most significant accounts of native ritual practice written down and practiced outside Spanish colonial authority in New Spain. Fifteen of the songs are discussed here for the first time, as part of a larger, long-term, multidisciplinary study of the booklets. An analysis of their content finds Christian themes, vocabulary, and cosmology interwoven with Zapotec beliefs. The booklets are arguably part of a new Dominican strategy in the 18th century to attract and keep Christian followers through accommodation rather than displacement of indigenous ritual belief and practice. For ethnohistorian's comment, see *HLAS 64:303*. [PDV]

789 Taylor, William B. 2008 CLAH luncheon address: Dos palabras on Mexican shrines and contagiousness of the sacred. (*Americas/Washington*, 65:1, July 2008, p. 1–7)

This address begins with Taylor's reflections on a long and distinguished career that include his dedication to teaching and his efforts as a teacher-scholar. It ends with a discussion of the localized worship of the Virgin of Guadalupe, in which the colonial period tended not to see long, protracted pilgrimages to Tepeyac. Rather, worship of the Virgin often occurred more locally, and she was identified with private altars and many local shrines. Thus devotion to the Virgin of Guadalupe in colonial Mexico reinforced "the importance of locality—of many localities—and many images, more than centralizing a vast spiritual geography." [PDV]

790 Torales Pacheco, María Cristina. Tierras de indios, tierras de españoles: confirmación y composición de tierras y aguas en la jurisdicción de Cholula (siglos XVI–XVIII). México: Univ. Iberoamericana, Depto. de Historia, 2005. 126 p.: bibl.

Study of the legal process of granting agricultural properties (royal *confirmaciones* and *composiciones*) in the jurisdiction of Cholula includes a CD with an additional six charts and 15 maps. [KM]

791 Torre Curiel, José Refugio de la. Comerciantes, precios y salarios en Sonora en el periodo colonial tardío: caracterización de un circuito comercial cautivo.

(*Hist. Mex./México*, 58:2, oct./dic. 2008, p. 595–656, tables)
This article examines the commercial system in place in the province of Sonora in the late colonial period, arguing that it was a "captive" system of trade managed by merchants from Mexico City. At the same time, however, local intermediaries also manipulated the system by paying salaries in specie and perpetuating a system of debt peonage. [PDV]

792 Torre Curiel, José Refugio de la.
Decline and renaissance amidst the crisis: the transformation of Sonora's mission structures in the late colonial period. (*Colon. Lat. Am. Rev.*, 18:1, April 2009, p. 51–73, bibl., map)
The dynamism of missions run by the Franciscan College at Querétaro contrasts with the more troubled system run by the Province of Xalisco and demonstrates that the order's Northern missions should not be indiscriminately labeled as in "decline." The author effectively argues these were maturing rather than dying institutions, transformed in the face of new social organizations. [PDV]

793 Tortorici, Zeb. "Heran todos putos": sodomitical subcultures and disordered desire in early colonial Mexico. (*Ethnohistory/Columbus*, 54:1, Winter 2007, p. 35–67, tables)
Author uses a 1604 case of 13 indigenous men accused of sodomy to argue for the existence of colonial sodomitical subcultures even in rural areas. While Spanish authorities viewed sodomy as a perversion of male/active and female/passive dichotomies and treated the crime harshly, community members might have ignored or even tolerated it. [KM]

794 Tortorici, Zeb. Masturbation, salvation, and desire: connecting sexuality and religiosity in colonial Mexico. (*J. Hist. Sex.*, 16:3, 2007, p. 355–372)
This article discusses an Inquisition case brought against Augustina Ruiz in 1621 for her confession of masturbation while fantasizing about sexual acts with religious figures such as Jesus and the Virgin Mary. It brings to light a rare case of female erotic behavior and demonstrates the disjuncture between Catholic prescriptions and actual behaviors. This article also sets the case in the context of recent secondary works, including historiography on women, sexuality, and desire in colonial Mexico. [PDV]

795 Uribe-Uran, Victor M. Innocent infants or abusive patriarchs?: spousal homicides, the punishment of Indians and the law in colonial Mexico, 1740s–1820s. (*J. Lat. Am. Stud.*, 38:4, Nov. 2006, p. 793–828, tables)
This article examines cases of spousal homicide throughout central Mexico (the Audiencias of Mexico and Nueva Galicia) in the late colonial period, and finds a decided pattern of leniency for offenders, particularly if they were indigenous and claimed drunkenness as a contributing factor. Uribe-Uran finds that indigenous people received generally lighter sentences than did mixed blood peoples, particularly those of African descent. He attributes this phenomenon not to the absence of judicial or legal frameworks, but to the patriarchal attitude toward indigenous husbands which was complementary to that of the king. The author compares his results to the work of William Taylor and Steve Stern and finds many similarities. [PDV]

796 Valdés, Carlos Manuel. Ataque a la Misión de Nadadores: dos versiones documentales sobre un indio cuechale. Introducción y notas de Carlos Manuel Valdés. Paleografía de Sergio Antonio Corona Páez. Torreón, Mexico: Univ. Iberoamericana, 2002. 76 p.: bibl., ill., maps. (Col. Lobo rampante; 6)
Two 18th-century documents offer contrasting accounts of Diego de Valdés, an Indian from Coahuila, and "Ataque a la Misión" uses source analysis to make sense of those contrasts. Includes transcripts of the two documents. [KM]

797 Vázquez Mantecón, María del Carmen. La palabra del poder: vida pública de José María Tornel, 1795–1853. 2. ed. rev. México: UNAM, 2008. 266 p.: bibl., ill. (some col.), index, col. map. (Serie Historia moderna y contemporánea/Instituto de Investigaciones Históricas; 28)
Second edition adds additional archival research and footnotes to the original 1997 edition reviewed in Vol. 60 (see *HLAS* 60:1201). [KM]

798 Victoria Moreno, Dionisio. La Guerra de Independencia en el Estado de México. Toluca de Lerdo, Mexico: Gobierno del Estado de México, 2007. 205 p.: bibl., indexes. (Biblioteca Mexiquense del Bicentenario. Col. Mayor. Historia y Sociedad; 1)

Transcription of 133 documents (the majority from 1810–13) related to the wars of independence in what is now the state of Mexico. [KM]

799 La visita de Gómez Nieto a Huasteca, 1532–1533. Paleografía, introducción y notas de Juan Manuel Pérez Zevallos. México: Centro de Investigaciones y Estudios Superiores en Antropología Social: Centro de Estudios Mexicanos y Centroamericanos: Archivo General de la Nación; San Luis Potosí, Mexico: El Colegio de San Luis, 2001. 223 p.: bibl., index, map. (Col. Huasteca)

Transcription of the Visita of the Huasteca made during the years 1532–33 with supplemental information on the region. [KM]

800 Yannakakis, Yanna P. The art of being in-between: native intermediaries, Indian identity, and local rule in colonial Oaxaca. Durham, N.C.: Duke Univ. Press, 2008. 290 p.: bibl., ill., index, maps.

This work traces the history of Oaxaca's Sierra Norte, a "peripheral" region that serves to highlight the complex dynamics involved in the development of the colonial order. Yannakakis focuses on those dynamics by studying the actions and discourse of "native intermediaries," or those peoples, mainly men and derived largely from the indigenous nobility, who sought to enforce the demands of the Spanish colonial order on the local level but who also answered to their local constituency in seeking to modify these demands or resist them altogether when deemed overly exploitative. Yannakakis combines methods of cultural and social history to trace the workings of power in the colonial system on a day-to-day level, and uses a variety of archival documentation from Oaxaca, Mexico City, and Seville to show how native intermediaries influenced the colonization of the Sierra Norte from the 1660s through independence. Their influence provides valuable insight into how hegemony is established and functions within a colonial order. [PDV]

801 Yannakakis, Yanna P. Witnesses, spatial practices and a land dispute in colonial Oaxaca. (*Americas/Washington,* 65:2, Oct. 2008, p. 161–192)

This article is a microhistorical analysis of a land dispute case in 18th-century Oaxaca, a region that was enduring significant demographic, economic, and religious pressures. The dispute occurred between two villages who both presented written documents to prove their case, but whose validity was questioned and thus supplemented by oral testimony, mainly from elite indigenous witnesses. These witnesses used various practices to manipulate the meaning and use of indigenous space as it was adjudicated according to Spanish concepts of land ownership. Their testimonies demonstrate that these witnesses were able to mediate between local/vernacular and official/colonial systems and could advocate within the Spanish legal system for local interests. This article problematizes monolithic categories like "Indian," "Spanish," "prehispanic," and "Hispanized." [PDV]

Independence, Revolution, and Post-Revolution

DON M. COERVER, *Professor of History, Texas Christian University*
SUZANNE B. PASZTOR, *Associate Professor of History, Humboldt State University*
BARBARA A. TENENBAUM, *Mexican Specialist and Curator of the Jay I. Kislak Collection, Library of Congress*

INDEPENDENCE TO REVOLUTION

SURPRISINGLY, MANY FEWER MAGISTERIAL WORKS appeared in this biennium than in the last, which is happy news that allows libraries to restore their budgets. 2010 was an anniversary year as Mexico celebrated 200 years since its proclamation of independence from Spain, and 100 years after it called for an overthrow of the regime of Porfirio Díaz. Although political history far outweighed any other genre, economic history produced two important book-length studies, those by Salvucci on the history of the British debt (item **874**), and Kuntz Ficker on foreign trade (item **844**), while Rugeley contributed to political history with his summary of the epic Caste War of Yucatán (item **873**).

A worrisome trend noted in the last two biennia continues. Thanks to proximity, scholars in the US write more about Mexico than about any other Latin American nation. However, there appear to be few Spanish-speakers reading work not published in that language. At the recent XIII meeting of US, Canadian, and Mexican historians of Mexico held in Querétaro in October 2010, the vast majority of papers were given in Spanish as were all of the plenary sessions. Organizers of the forthcoming meeting scheduled for 2013 in Chicago, Illinois seem intent on insisting that all papers be in Spanish. It would be tragic if important work published only in English is slighted by a favoring of Spanish, since not everything can appear in that language. Currently, however, many articles of interest continue to appear in English, as this series of annotations attests.

For example, Passananti's article on the government's handling of the economy during the Porfiriato disagrees with the current received interpretation of that period (item **860**), Chassen's article on Juana Catarina Romero (item **817**) contributes to a bolder look at gender roles, while DeLay brings an understanding of frontier Indians into the 19th century (item **821**). Hart looks at the origins of Zapatismo (item **839**), and Piccato studies honor and pragmatism (item **863**), which brings an understanding of trends previously discussed by Bertram Wyatt-Brown in the 1980s for antebellum America. All of these works are in English.

That's not to say that English-language writers had anything like a monopoly on new and provocative additions to the literature. Certainly Palacio Montiel provided a fascinating discussion of newspapers throughout the country (item **871**), while Serrano Ortega gave us a very thoughtful and thorough look at taxes in the early republic (item **882**). There were quite a few works on women in both languages including Levy on the economic ramifications of marriage in Yucatán (item **845**), Núñez Becerra on lesbianism (item **856**), Sloan on romantic relations between the sexes (item **884**), Cortés Rocca on the concept of the "punitive portrait" of sex workers (item **819**), and Serrano Barquín on finding gender through photography (item **881**).

There were even new works on the writing of history itself with Ortiz Monasterio taking another look at Vicente Riva Palacio (item **859**), and Díaz Maldonado examining the work of Manuel Orozco y Berra (item **823**).

The next biennium looks particularly exciting with many, many new studies on the independence and the Revolution subsidized by the Mexican government just waiting to be purchased and the appearance of new books of which the articles discussed here are only a part. [BT]

REVOLUTION AND POST-REVOLUTION

INTEREST IN POST-REVOLUTIONARY insurgencies and popular movements was strong in the last biennium. Henck provides a biography of Subcomandante Marcos (item **946**), and probes the indigenous aspect of the Zapatista movement in Chiapas. Works by Swords (item **1010**), Estrada Saavedra (item **931**) and Andrews (item **900**) examine support for this movement, while Stahler-Sholk (item **1007**) analyzes obstacles to the movement's sustainability, and Mora (item **966**) describes Zapatista activism during Mexico's 2006 election. The *Jaramillista* insurgency in Morelos is the subject of two works by Padilla (items **972** and **973**), while Ayala Guevara provides an interpretation of the popular movement in Guerrero that gave rise to the Partido de los Pobres (item **902**). The 1970s guerrilla movement in Aguascalientes is examined by García (item **934**), Esteva chronicles the emergence of Oaxaca's Asamblea Popular de los Pueblos de Oaxaca (APPO) (item **930**), and Poniatowska provides a first-hand account of the protest movement emerging out of Mexico's 2006 presidential election (item **977**). Finally, Oikión Solano and García Ugarte provide three volumes on armed movements of the 20th century (item **968**), and Pérez Arce examines various types of opposition movements from 1968 to 1998 (item **975**).

Cultural and social history continues to attract numerous scholars. Significant studies on women and gender in a revolutionary context include the volume edited by Olcott, Vaughan, and Cano (item **996**) and Smith (item **1004**). Vaughan and Lewis edit a collection of essays on nation-building and identity during the 1920s and 1930s (item **927**), while collections by Sacristán and Piccato (item **994**) and Hernández (item **998**) apply the methodologies of social and cultural history to a variety of topics. Following earlier scholars who have focused on specific attempts of the postrevolutionary state to transform its citizens, Aguilar Rodríguez examines government-sponsored dining halls for the working class (item **898**), while Agostoni and Aréchiga analyzes state efforts to promote health and hygiene (items **897** and **901**, respectively). The influence of cinema is explored by Sosenski (item **1006**). A study by Ervin suggests the importance of statistics and maps in nation-building (item **929**). Finally, scholars continued work on education. Rockwell demonstrates resistance to centralized educational policies (item **984**) and Sigüenza Orozco explores the role of public education and national identity (item **997**).

Scholars maintained an active interest in Church-state relations. *The Americas* devoted an entire issue to anticlericalism (Vol. 65, No. 4, April 2009), featuring articles by Adrian Bantjes (item **904**), Matthew Butler (item **915**), Robert Curley (item **923**), Ben Fallaw (item **932**), and Benjamin Smith (item **999**). Lisbona Guillén looks at early efforts by the Constitutionalists to introduce anticlerical sentiments in Chiapas (item **955**). Ramón del Llano Ibañez (item **956**) and Jean Meyer (item **964**) provide state-level examinations of the Cristero revolt, concluding that the faithful resisted, but not violently. Ramírez Rancaño describes efforts under Calles to establish a national Mexican Catholic Church (item **978**) while Yves Solis demonstrates that there were major disagreements within the Church about how to deal with the Church-state crisis (item **1005**). Roderic Camp examines the role of the Church in the presidential elections of 2006 (item **916**).

As in the last biennium, the impact of immigration on Mexico's history continued to attract scholars. Savarino examines Italian immigrants (item **992**), Alfaro-Velcamp continues her work on Middle Eastern immigrants (item **899**), and Rangel Treviño probes the roots of anti-Chinese sentiment in Mexico (item **980**). Dávila Valdés and Suárez Plata provide different approaches to the experience of Spanish Republican exiles (items **924** and **1008**), while Weis focuses on the fate of one group of Spaniards during the Mexican Revolution (item **1019**), and Yankelevich identifies patterns in Mexico's treatment of US Americans in a revolutionary context (item **1023**). Mexican emigration also continues to be a popular theme. Ochoa Alvarez (item **970**) and Valdéz Gardea suggest current trends in emigration (item **1017**), Montoya studies migration from San Luis Potosí to the US during the *Bracero* era (item **965**), and Enríquez Acosta describes the impact of migration on border cities (item **928**). Finally, Martínez (item **961**) and Lybecker (item **959**) identify impacts of US border policy on emigration.

Several notable works that are not easily categorized appeared during the latest period. Samuel Brunk (item **914**) follows up on his earlier political biography of Zapata with a look at the uses and abuses of the Zapata cult. Two veteran researchers of the US-Mexico border region, Charles H. Harris III and Louis R. Sadler, discuss the impact of the Revolution on the Texas Rangers and the city of El Paso (items **944** and **945**). [DC and SP]

INDEPENDENCE
TO REVOLUTION

802 Abbondanza, Ermanno. La Cuestión Yaqui en el segundo Porfiriato, 1890–1909: una revisión de la historia oficial. (*Signos Hist.*, 19, enero/junio 2008, p. 94–126, bibl.)
Focuses on the role of Bernardo Reyes in this conflict. Blames him for the continuation of the war on the Yaqui indigenous group. Author contends that it was a conflict of two different cosmos with their inherent difficulties.

Aguirre, Robert D. Informal empire: Mexico and Central America in Victorian culture. See *HLAS 65:2005.*

Alejandro de Humboldt: una nueva visión del mundo: en conmemoración al bicentenario de la llegada de Humboldt a México. See item **519**.

803 Ávila, Alfredo. Para la libertad: los republicanos en tiempos del imperio 1821–1823. México: UNAM, 2004. 346 p.: bibl. (Serie de historia moderna y contemporánea; 41)
Major work describes the struggle of republicans to overthrow the short-lived empire of Agustín I (1821–23) following his success in liberating Mexico from Spain. Beautifully written and thoroughly researched, author challenges much of perceived wisdom from past histories. Highly recommended.

804 Ayala Flores, Hubonor. Salvaguardar el orden social: el manicomio del estado de Veracruz, 1883–1920. Zamora, Mexico: El Colegio de Michoacán, A.C., 2007. 245 p.: bibl., indexes.

Sees efforts at providing mental health services as covers for maintaining control and watchfulness. Also discusses the intrusion of medicine into mental health and other "illnesses."

805 Barrera Enderle, Alberto. La invención de la identidad de Nuevo León, siglo XIX. Monterrey, Mexico: Fondo Editorial de Nuevo León: Archivo General del Estado de Nuevo León, 2008. 168 p.: bibl., ill. (Historia del nordeste mexicano/anuario del Archivo General del Estado de Nuevo León; 6)
Shows how the national debate over Mexico's past played out in Nuevo León. Although the title indicates coverage of the entire 19th century, the text stops before 1867, and hardly mentions economic factors

806 Beezley, William H. Mexican national identity: memory, innuendo, and popular culture. Tucson, Ariz.: Univ. of Arizona Press, 2008. 206 p.: bibl., ill., index.
Continues author's attempt in *Judas at the Jockey Club and other episodes of Porfirian Mexico* (see *HLAS 50:1139*) and his work on puppets to find a way into the popular psyche of 19th-century Mexicans. Sections are too compact to provide much more than anecdotal inferences.

807 Bello Gomez, Felipe de Jesús. Inmigración y capacidad empresarial en los albores de la industrialización de México. (*Secuencia/México*, 68, mayo/agosto 2007, p. 9–54, bibl.)
Analyzes Spanish, French, and Lebanese immigrations from many aspects including, but not exclusively, their previous history, their entrepreneurial capacity, and sociocultural factors. Not surprisingly, the

Barcelonettes availed themselves of a wide array of communal links, while the Lebanese had to depend on their own individual resources.

808 Bringas Nostti, Raúl. La regeneración de un pueblo pestilente: la anexión de México a Estados Unidos, 1846–1848. México: Miguel Ángel Porrúa, 2008. 300 p.: bibl., map.

Discussion of political ideology using US newspaper sources from the US perspective. Describes how annexationism failed, thereby allowing Mexico to develop on its own.

809 Briseño Senosiain, Lillian. Candil de la calle, oscuridad de su casa: la iluminación en la Ciudad de México durante el porfiriato. México: Tecnológico de Monterrey: Instituto Mora; Miguel Ángel Porrúa, 2008. 221 p.: bibl.

Fascinating look at the meaning of the electrification of Mexico City during the Porfiriato. Details both public and private transformation thanks to the new technology. Recommended.

810 Calvo, Vicente. Descripción política, física, moral y comercial del departamento de Sonora en la República Mexicana por Vicente Calvo en 1843. Compilación de Eduardo Flores Clair y Edgar O. Gutiérrez López. México: INAH, 2006. 277 p.: bibl., index. (Regiones de Mexico)

Fascinating discussion of an obscure manuscript found in the Biblioteca Nacional de Madrid, including lengthy speculation on the identity of Vicente Calvo. Excellent portrait of Sonora in the 1840s. Recommended.

811 Caplan, Karen Deborah. Indigenous citizens: local liberalism in early national Oaxaca and Yucatán. Stanford, Calif.: Stanford Univ. Press, 2009. 289 p.: bibl., index.

Emphasizes the local component in the elaboration of liberalism throughout Mexico. Through two exemplary, but hugely differing political entities, the author shows that both suffered because of the consolidation of national liberalism at the expense of the local variety. Recommended, but reference apparatus eschews straightforward bibliography.

812 Carbajal López, David. La política eclesiástica del estado de Veracruz, 1824–1834. México: CONACULTA-INAH: Miguel Ángel Porrúa, 2006. 148 p.: bibl.

Outlines the deep ties of the Church in civil society, which protected it from the onslaught of radical politics. Explains indirectly the behavior of Santa Anna of Veracruz in this period.

813 Carregha Lamadrid, Luz. 1876: la revuelta de Tuxtepec en el estado de San Luis Potosí. San Luis Potosí, Mexico: El Colegio de San Luis: Archivo Histórico del Estado de San Luis Potosí, 2007. 177 p.: bibl., maps. (Col. Investigaciones)

Interesting portrait of choices presented by continuing with Lerdo or going with the forces of Porfirio Díaz in a state far from Tuxtepec, Oaxaca. The state soon went over to Díaz, who ruled in total contradiction to his promises.

814 Castillo, Manuel Angel; Mónica Toussaint Ribot; and Mario Vázquez Olivera. Espacios diversos, historia en común: México, Guatemala y Belice: la construcción de una frontera. México: Secretaría de Relaciones Exteriores, 2006. 284 p.: bibl., ill., index, maps., ports. (Col. México y sus fronteras. Frontera sur) (Las fronteras de México)

Thorough discussion of the making of Mexico's southern frontier and its relations with Guatemala and Belize up to the present time. Focuses on important figures like Matías Romero, Ignacio Mariscal, Rafael Carrera of Guatemala, etc. Recommended.

815 Cázares Puente, Eduardo. Nuevo León durante la guerra México-Estados Unidos, 1846–1848. San Pedro Garza García, Mexico: Centro de Estudios Históricos UDEM, 2009. 133 p.: bibl., ill., maps.

Although the Mexican-American War led to spiritual depression in Mexico City, it provided immense opportunities in Nuevo León. While the taking of Monterrey was a terrible defeat for the Mexicans, it enabled that city to become the trading and military center of the area.

816 Ceja Andrade, Claudia. Al amparo del imperio: ideas y creencias sobre la justicia y el buen gobierno durante el Segundo Imperio mexicano. Ciudad Juárez, Mexico: Univ. Autónoma de Ciudad Juárez, 2007. 193 p.: maps.

Riveting addition to the growing body of literature of popular ideas about politics. Detailed study of letters and petitions to Maximilian to obtain justice and good government.

817 Chassen de López, Francie R. A patron of progress: Juana Catarina Romero, the nineteenth-century cacica of Tehuantepec. (*HAHR*, 88:3, Aug. 2008, p. 393–426, port.)

Tells the story of Juana Catarina Romero, who started out as an illiterate cigarette vendor in Tehuantepec and rose to become the modernizing *cacica* of her area and its number one philanthropist. Impressive study of both social and economic mobility and successful blend of erudite and popular sources. Recommended.

Chowning, Margaret. Rebellious nuns: the troubled history of a Mexican convent, 1752–1863. See item **687.**

818 Contribuciones a la historia social y cultural de Guadalajara, 1770–1926. Coordinación de Águeda Jiménez Pelayo. Guadalajara, Mexico: Univ. de Guadalajara, 2007. 205 p.: bibl., ill.

Collection of five essays about divorce, love, prostitution, death, and modern agriculture in the second largest city in the republic. Curious information surfaces here such as the fact that in 1885 "el rapto," so often a pretext for marriage when there is parental opposition, was made illegal in the penal code.

819 Cortés Rocca, Paola. Subjectivities and techniques of control in late nineteenth-century Mexico: Emperor Maximilian's *Registro de Mujeres Públicas.* (*J. Lat. Am. Cult. Stud.,* 14:2, Aug. 2005, p. 211–222, bibl., photos)

Brief discussion of what the author refers to as the "punitive portrait," in this case, she is referring to prostitutes. While the author speculates on the relationship between photography and criminology, photography of sex workers would continue as a trend (see Monsiváis' introduction to *La casa de citas* in HLAS 54:1346) .

820 Culturas de pobreza y resistencia: estudios de marginados, proscritos y descontentos: México, 1804–1910. Coordinación de Romana Falcón. México: El Colegio de México A.C., Centro de Estudios Históricos; Santiago de Querétaro, Mexico; Univ. Autónoma de Querétaro, Centro Universitario, 2005. 358 p.: bibl., ill., index.

Fascinating collection of articles on local social history emphasizing the lowest groups—slaves, street people, and rebels in the countryside. Shows challenges to state authority on many different levels. Recommended.

821 DeLay, Brian. Independent Indians and the U.S.-Mexican War. (*Am. Hist. Rev.,* 112:1, Feb. 2007, p. 35–68, ill., map)

Finally puts Indian raids on the frontier in proper perspective and indicates their role in the outcome of the war with the US. Provides a bulk of information to spur greater research. Recommended.

822 Desmond, Lawrence Gustave. Yucatán through her eyes: Alice Dixon Le Plongeon: writer and expeditionary photographer. Albuquerque, N.M.: Univ. of New Mexico Press, 2009. 221 p.: bibl., index, map, tables.

Tells the vivid story of Alice Dixon Le Plongeon, talented photographer and writer who accompanied her archeologist husband on research trips to the Yucatan. Offers an interesting recounting of what it was like to do archeology in such an inhospitable locale. Recommended.

823 Díaz Maldonado, Rodrigo. Manuel Orozco y Berra, o, La historia como reconciliación de los opuestos. México: UNAM, 2010. 96 p.: bibl. (Serie Teoría e historia de la historiografía/Instituto de Investigaciones Históricas; 10)

Examination of where Orozco y Berra fits into Western historiography and its influence on him. Important contribution to intellectual history.

824 Dobado González, Rafael; Aurora Gómez Galvarriato; and Jeffrey G. Williamson. Mexican exceptionalism: globalization and de-industrialization, 1750–1877. (*J. Econ. Hist.,* 68:3, Sept. 2008, p. 758–811, bibl., graphs, tables)

Essay compares Mexico with the rest of the "poor periphery" to help scholars understand how the republic fared better because of some tariff protection of manufactures and the worldwide revolution in cheap food. Important for students of the 1800s, but authors could have been more helpful by adding explanatory terms.

825 **12 ensayos sobre política y sociedad potosina durante la Independencia y la Revolución.** Coordinación de Flor de María Salazar Mendoza. San Luis Potosí, Mexico: Univ. Autónoma de San Luis Potosí: LVIII Legislatura San Luis Potosí; Archivo Histórico del Estado San Luis Potosí, 2009. 130 p.: bibl., map.

Brings together a dozen essays on traditional themes from 18th- and 19th-century Mexico—America septentrional, *pronunciamientos*, and revolutionary moments with new looks at food supply, the role of women, and *pulquerías*. Good look at how national trends played out on a local level.

826 **Dugard, Martin.** The training ground: Grant, Lee, Sherman, and Davis in the Mexican War, 1846–1848. Lincoln: Univ. of Nebraska Press, 2009. 446 p.: bibl., index.

Places important figures from the US during the 1846–48 period in biographical context while showing the war from their perspective. No scholarly apparatus, but a good read nonetheless.

827 **Elizondo Elizondo, Ricardo.** Pliegues en la membrana del tiempo: fotografía y correspondencia en la frontera norte 1840–1870. Monterrey, Mexico: Fondo Editorial de Nuevo León, 2006. 203 p.: bibl., ill., maps, ports. (La historia en la ciudad del conocimiento)

Interesting compilation of photos of the elite of the northeast. Includes details about the lives of certain photographers and lists those active at the time.

828 **Empresas y modernización en México desde las reformas borbónicas hasta el Porfiriato.** Edición de Reinhard Liehr. Madrid: Iberoamericana; Frankfurt am Main: Vervuert, 2006. 180 p.: bibl., ill. (Bibliotheca Ibero-Americana; 108)

Collection of four essays on various economic subjects ranging from methodological questions concerning industrialization in the west to an empresarial biography of Iñigo Noriega Lazo, an agricultural promoter. Article by Meyer Cosío on British interests in Mexico in general and Ewan MacKintosh in particular is vital for understanding government finance. Recommended.

829 **Fernández Ruiz, Jorge.** Juárez y sus contemporáneos. 2. ed. México: UNAM, 2006. 410 p.: bibl., ill. (Serie Doctrina jurídica; 284)

Argues for a re-evaluation of the life of Benito Juárez by putting him in the context of his times. Based solely on secondary material, nevertheless this book is a basic, solid addition to the scholarly literature.

830 **Frasquet, Ivana.** Las caras del águila: del liberalismo gaditano a la República Federal Mexicana, 1820–1824. Castellón de la Plana, Spain: Univ. Jaume I, 2008. 382 p.: bibl. (Col. Amèrica; 11)

Volume looks at how Mexico transcended the politics of the Cádiz cortes in 1820 to create federal republicanism. Shows conclusively why centralism was not an option in this period.

831 **Galante, Mirian.** Debates en torno al liberalismo: representación e instituciones en el congreso constituyente mexicano, 1824. (*Rev. Indias*, 68:242, enero/abril 2008, p. 123–152, bibl.)

Looks at the Spanish concept of liberalism as seen in the Cádiz cortes and in the 1824 debates. For example, "liberty" was defined as freedom from foreign domination, but not from to home-grown tyranny.

832 **García Jacales, María.** Apuntes sobre los orígenes de la ciudadanía mexicana: derechos civiles y políticos en la construcción de una sociedad laica. (*Estud. Polít./México*, 8, mayo/agosto 2004, p. 171–218)

Posits the historical evolution of citizenship in Mexico from Cádiz onward. Yet the structures and corporations still managed to hang on in part due to the necessity of dealing with lower groups in society.

833 **El Golfo-Caribe y sus puertos.** t. 2, 1850–1930. Coordinación de Johanna von Grafenstein Gareis. México: Instituto Mora, 2006. 522 p.: bibl., ill., indexes, maps. (Historia internacional)

Collection of 13 interesting essays on ports, two on Puerto Rico, one concerning Trinidad, two on Cuba, and the rest about Yucatán, Tehuantepec, Tuxpan, Tampico (2) and Veracruz (2). Would have benefitted greatly from an introduction and a conclusion tying the essays together.

834 Gómez Villanueva, Augusto. Nacionalismo revolucionario: orígenes socioeconómicos de la doctrina internacional de la Revolución mexicana. México: Cámara de Diputados, LX Legislatura: M.A. Porrúa, 2009. 244 p.: bibl. (La serie Historia) (Conocer para decidir)

Essay argues commonplace that economic sovereignty dictates all others. Tries to show that the entire struggle of the Mexican nation since independence was to attain that power.

835 González, Gerardo Palomo. La inestabilidad político-militar durante la primera república central, 1835–1839: la lógica del pronunciamiento en la figura del General José Urrea. (*Estud. Hist. Mod. Contemp. Méx.*, 36, julio/dic. 2008, p. 85–126)

Crucial shift from federalism to centralism (1835–39) produced overwhelming numbers of revolts throughout the country. Puts French blockade of ports squarely in the narrative, claiming that Mexicans became more supportive of the government in Mexico City than they otherwise would have been as a result. Recommended.

836 Gorbach, Frida. Los caprichos de la histeria: cuadros para una identidad. (*Hist. Graf./México*, 31, 2008, p. 77–101)

Outlines four possible "frames" for understanding the medical behavior of 19th-century females in Mexico. Shows how Mexican debates were similar to those in Europe and the US.

837 Guerra e imaginarios políticos en la época de las independencias. Coordinación de Moisés Guzmán Pérez. Morelia, Mexico: Instituto de Investigaciones Históricas: Univ. Michoacana de San Nicolás de Hidalgo, 2007. 286 p.: bibl., maps. (Col. Bicentenario de la independencia; 2)

Brings together seven essays and a solid introduction on details surrounding the initial insurgency leading up to 1810. Should be read in tandem with Van Young (item **893**) for a well-rounded picture of these events.

838 Hart, John Mason. The silver of the Sierra Madre: John Robinson, Boss Shepherd, and the people of the canyons. Tucson, Ariz.: Univ. of Arizona Press, 2008. 237 p.: bibl., ill., index, maps.

Presents the story of mining and exploitation in the Batopilas area of Chihuahua as mined by US capitalists including the last governor of Washington, DC, Boss Shepherd. Provides a good explanation for the willingness of the workers to join Pascual Orozco's revolution.

839 Hart, Paul. Bitter harvest: the social transformation of Morelos, Mexico, and the origins of the Zapatista revolution, 1840–1910. Albuquerque, N.M.: Univ. of New Mexico Press, 2005. 291 p.: bibl., ill., index, map.

Points out the crucial role of the displaced peasant villagers who became a rural working class. When the sugar industry experienced a major crisis in the mid-19th century, the conditions existed to propel a revolutionary movement throughout the country, demanding a more equitable distribution of land. Recommended.

840 Henderson, Timothy J. The Mexican wars for independence. New York, N.Y.: Hill and Wang, 2009. 246 p.: bibl., ill., index, map.

Probably designed for a student audience, this book displays little regular scholarly apparatus. Study ignores economics and seems particularly anti-Iturbide.

841 La independencia de México: temas e interpretaciones recientes. Coordinación de Alfredo Ávila y Virgina Guedea. Textos de Christon Archer *et al.* 1. reimpresión México: UNAM, 2010. 256 p.: bibl. (Serie historia moderna y contemporánea / Instituto de Investigaciones Históricas; 48)

Based on the papers given at a conference in 2003, these articles represent the most recent summaries of the historiography of Mexican independence, written by many of the foremost scholars in the field. Especially noteworthy are Ávila on intellectual history, von Grafenstein on foreign views, and Breña on how Spain understood the process. Highly recommended.

842 Irwin, Robert McKee. Lola Casanova: la Malinche invertida en la cultura nacional mexicana. (*Lit. Mex.*, 18:1, 2007, p. 59–87, bibl., ill.)

In Feb. 1850, Dolores Casanova traveled by a *diligencia* that was assaulted by indigenous peoples who killed everyone except her, who they raped. She decided not to return to Guaymas because she had fallen in love with Coyote Iguana, the tribal chief, whom she married and with whom she had a son. Turns positivism on its head.

843 Juárez: bajo el pincel de la oposición. Oaxaca, Mexico: Univ. Autónoma Benito Juárez de Oaxaca: Instituto Estatal de Educación Pública de Oaxaca: Recinto de Homenaje a Don Benito Juárez, Secretaría de Hacienda y Crédito Público, 2007. 229 p.: ill., 1 CD-ROM.

Benito Juárez before he became saintly is the focus of this beautiful book. A terrific addition to our knowledge of political contentiousness, printing, cartooning, etc. A must read for researchers of this period. Highly recommended.

844 Kuntz Ficker, Sandra. El comercio exterior de México en la era del capitalismo liberal, 1870–1929. México: El Colegio de México, Centro de Estudios Históricos, 2007. 531 p.: bibl., ill., maps.

Major work on Mexico's foreign trade. Notes importantly the role of commerce in politics and vice versa. Fundamental contribution and highly recommended.

845 Levy, Juliette. The marriage penalty: women, property rights, and credit markets in Yucatán, 1850–1900. (*HAHR*, 88:3, Aug. 2008, p. 427–454, graph, tables)

Indicates that married women paid higher interest for loans than did their husbands in Yucatan because it was assumed that females taking out loans were doing so for their husband's benefit. Article also suggests that most scholars should be wary of statistics about women.

846 López Cancelada, Juan. Sucesos de Nueva España hasta la coronación de Iturbide. Estudio introductorio y notas de Verónica Zárate Toscano. México: Instituto Mora, 2008. 710 p.: bibl., ill., index. (Col. Pensadores)

Presents commentary on the concluding events of the independence wars penned by the editor of the *Gazeta de México* following his return to Spain. Fresh perspective on pre- and post-Emperor Iturbide conditions in Mexico.

847 Macías-González, Víctor Manuel. Las amistades apasionadas y la homosociabilidad en la primera mitad del siglo XIX. (*Hist. Graf./México*, 31, 2008, p. 19–48)

Opens up a new way of looking at passionate friendships between males of higher and lesser rank and equivalent statures. Hints at the importance and perhaps homosexual aspect of those unions. Recommended.

848 McNamara, Patrick J. Sons of the Sierra: Juárez, Díaz, and the people of Ixtlán, Oaxaca, 1855–1920. Chapel Hill, N.C.: Univ. of North Carolina Press, 2007. 282 p.: bibl., index.

Tells the story of the presidencies of Benito Juárez and Porfirio Díaz from the vantage point of the region that nurtured them both (Ixtlán, Oaxaca). Soldiers from the area used their military service as a way to establish relationships with higher-ups. Recommended.

849 Mecánica política: para una relectura del siglo XIX mexicano: antología de correspondencia política. Coordinación de Beatriz Rojas. Guadalajara, Mexico: Univ. de Guadalajara; México: Instituto Mora, 2006. 385 p. (Historia política)

Continuing at long last a long-abandoned trend, this volume contains eight essays on the letters of famous and semi-famous Mexican political figures. Sheds much light on politics in the 19th century, particularly by looking at more minor figures like Aguilar y Marocho.

850 Meyer Cosío, Francisco Javier. Del acero de las armas al acero del riel. Querétaro, Mexico: Instituto de Estudios Constitucionales, 2006. 171 p.: bibl., ill., maps. (Ensayos de historia de Querétaro)

Examines how the military government made way for civilian rule by looking at a shift in its priorities. Shows how important using steel for railroads came to be and how Querétaro participated in expositions.

851 Miranda Arrieta, Eduardo. Entre armas y tradiciones: los indígenas de Guerrero en el siglo XIX. México: Centro de Investigaciones y Estudios Superiores en Antropología Social: Comisión Nacional para el Desarrollo de los Pueblos Indígenas: Univ. Michoacana de San Nicolás de Hidalgo, 2006. 304 p.: bibl., ill. (some col.). (Historia de los Pueblos Indígenas de México)

Emphasizes the importance of the indigenous peoples, who made up the majority of the population of the state of Guerrero in 1892, and their determination to resist outside threats. Gives appropriate weight to individual charisma in determining who would lead these people in their struggle to maintain their rights.

852 Miranda Ojeda, Pedro. Sociedad y trabajo durante el siglo XIX: la utilidad social como problema económico. (*Estud. Sociol./México*, 25:74, mayo/agosto 2007, p. 369–397, bibl.)

Linking practicing productive work with citizenship, this article tries to indicate how vagrancy and other social ills were perceived and addressed in 19th-century Mexico. The state used repression, then laws, and then finally the most successful approaches: jail time, impressment into the army, or forced employment.

853 Morales Moreno, Humberto. Los franceses en México: 1890–1910; nueva revisión histórica (agentes comerciales, residentes e imperialismo informal). (*Signos Hist.*, 17, enero/junio 2007, p. 174–223, graphs, tables)

Revisionist article based on an 1892 registry of 523 French businesspeople in Mexico. Signals that the French had their greatest impact internally in central Mexico rather than in the international arena.

854 Morris, Mark. Language in service of the state: the Nahuatl counterinsurgency broadsides of 1810. (*HAHR*, 87:3, Aug. 2007, p. 433–470)

Analyzes two broadsides that the new Viceroy Francisco Javier Venegas de Saavedra had printed to distribute to the local population. In point of fact, the publication presents a depiction of indigenous life prior to the conquest. Highly recommended. For comment by ethnohistorians, see item **238**.

855 Navajas, María José. El voto y el fusil: una interpretación del discurso Maderista en la coyuntura política de 1909–1910. (*Hist. Mex./México*, 57:4, abril/junio 2008, p. 1107–1153, bibl.)

Francisco Madero's political party was to avoid two unwanted results during the years of the Porfiriato—anarchy or the possibility of complete repression and perhaps foreign conquest. Seen in this context, armed insurrection seemed the much better alternative.

856 Núñez Becerra, Fernanda. El agridulce beso de Safo: discursos sobre las lesbianas a fines del siglo XIX mexicano. (*Hist. Graf./México*, 31, 2008, p. 49–75)

Article seeks to find evidence of lesbian practices through the passage of laws against them. Should women, however, practice this "vice," there were many punishments for love that dared to exist without reference to men.

857 Los obispados de México frente a la reforma liberal. Coordinación de Jaime Olveda. Zapopan, Mexico: Colegio de Jalisco; México: Univ. Autónoma Metropolitana; Oaxaca de Juárez, Mexico: Univ. Autónoma "Benito Juárez" de Oaxaca, 2007. 397 p.: bibl., ill. (some col.). (Col. del bicentenario del natalicio de Benito Juárez, 1806–2006)

Collection of 10 essays concerning Mexico City, Michoacán, Guadalajara, Zacatecas, Puebla, San Luis Potosí, Oaxaca, Durango, Coahuila and the north, and Sonora. Presents much more subtle readings of what used to be the seen as the most vociferous defenders of the Church. Recommended.

858 Ojeda Gastélum, Samuel Octavio. El mezcal en Sinaloa: una fuente de riqueza durante el Porfiriato. Prólogo y coordinación de la edición de José Gaxiola López. Culiacán, Mexico: Colegio de Sinaloa, 2006. 171 p.: bibl.

Part of the increase in attention in Sinaloa on Porfirian studies in the 1980s, this book traces the history of the mescal plant starting in prehispanic times. Ultimately, thanks to the railroad, it became an important export crop.

859 Ortiz Monasterio, José. México eternamente: Vicente Riva Palacio ante la escritura de la historia. México: Instituto Mora: Fondo de Cultura Económica, 2004. 407 p.: bibl. (Sección de obras de historia)

Thorough examination of how Mexican history came to be written in the 19th century and Riva Palacio's role in it. Regrettably, his participation in the creation of the Paseo de la Reforma is hardly mentioned or discussed in this otherwise admirable addition to the literature.

860 Passananti, Thomas P. "Nada de Papeluchos!": managing globalization in early Porfirian Mexico. (*LARR*, 42:3, 2007, p. 101–128)

Argues that Porfirian officials followed a deft strategy using sequencing and pacing to grow the economy before the settling of the foreign debt. Claims that Haber, Maurer, and Razo (see *HLAS 62:730*) are too narrow in their insistence on a vertical integration pattern of development. Recommended.

861 Pérez de Sarmiento, Marisa. Las razones de la "alternancia": el relevo de los gobernadores de Yucatán. México: Instituto de Investigaciones Dr. José María Luis Mora, 2008. 259 p.: bibl., ill., indexes, maps. (Historia política)

Examines a case in which the state of Yucatan, the only one in Mexico to do so, refused to follow the prescribed order of reelection so cherished nationally and in the rest of the country. This policy continued until 1902 when henequen baron Olegario Molina was simply too strong to resist.

862 Pérez Siller, Javier. Los franceses desde el silencio: la población del panteón francés de la ciudad de México: 1865–1910. (*Estud. Migr. Latinoam.*, 20:61, dic. 2006, p. 527–555, graph, tables)

Looks at a French cemetery in Mexico City as a way of perceiving French influence in the country. Even in the very populating of this cemetery itself, Mexicans always outnumbered the French.

Pescador, Juan Javier. Crossing borders with the Santo Niño de Atocha. See item **765**.

863 Piccato, Pablo. The tyranny of opinion: honor in the construction of the Mexican public sphere. Durham, N.C.: Duke Univ. Press, 2010. 388 p.: bibl., index.

Careful, though opinionated study of a previously overlooked tension in Mexican political society between honor and prag-

matism (here defined as positivism). A must read for understanding the early and later Porfiriato. Very highly recommended.

864 Priego Martínez, Natalia. Ciencia, historia y modernidad: la microbiología en México durante el Porfiriato. Madrid: Consejo Superior de Investigaciones Científicas, 2009. 208 p.: bibl. (Difusión y Estudio. Escuela de Estudios Hispanoamericanos)

By examining the effect of a new concern with bacteriology in Mexico, author adds another dimension to our understanding of the evolution of the nation. Also shows how these scientists fared during the post-Revolution period. Recommended.

865 Rajchenberg S., Enrique and **Catherine Héau-Lambert.** La frontera en la comunidad imaginada del siglo XIX. (*Front. Norte*, 19:38, julio/dic. 2007, p. 37–61, bibl.)

Makes the argument that the frontier is what distinguished Mexico from other areas in 19th-century Spanish America. The concept that the frontier is viewed differently in other places is somewhat contentious.

866 Razo Oliva, Juan Diego. De cuando San Carlos ganó la lotería y hasta casa compró: e, Informe sobre ciegos. México: UNAM, Escuela Nacional de Artes Plásticas, 2008. 171 p.: bibl., ill. (Col. Ensayos)

Two very interesting essays on the Academia de San Carlos, the government-sponsored art school whose teachers and students produced much of the official art of the period. First essay explains how San Carlos received its funding, while the second looks at its lighting. Provides insight on the economy, budgeting, technology, and, of course, art.

867 La reforma bancaria de 1908: una discusión entre Toribio Esquivel Obregón y Joaquín Casasús. México: Dirección General de Asuntos del Personal Académico, UNAM: Facultad de Economía, UNAM, 2008. 309 p.: bibl. (Col. de documentos para el estudio de la historia del pensamiento económico de México)

Extremely important collection of newspaper articles shows splits in the ruling class on basic issues such as the fiscal economy. One of the few times historians can view such quarrels up close.

868 **Relaciones de poder, procesos sociales y conflictos políticos en Zacatecas: de la colonia a la etapa porfirista.** Coordinación de René Amaro Peñaflores. Zacatecas, Mexico: Univ. Autónoma de Zacatecas, Unidad Académica de Historia, Maestría-Doctorado en Historia: México: Consejo Nacional de Ciencia y Tecnología, 2008. 211 p.: bibl., maps.

Important collection of five essays on Zacatecas attempts to add social history to the largely political analyses thus far available for that state. Fascinating look at the creation of the myth of Tata Pachito (aka Francisco García Salinas) and bandits who worked on common causes with caudillos.

869 **Robinson, Amy.** Mexican banditry and discourses of class: the case of Chucho el Roto. (*LARR*, 44:1, 2009, p. 5–31, photo)

Studies various depictions of the Robin Hood-style bandit to show how society's views changed from the 1880s to the revolution. For example, society endowed Chucho el Roto with some of the trappings of elite privilege to make him seem less threatening personally as he battled the inequities of his world.

870 **Rodríguez O., Jaime E.** Nosotros somos ahora los verdaderos españoles: la transición de la Nueva España de un reino de la monarquía española a la República Federal Mexicana, 1808–1824. Zamora, Mexico: Colegio de Michoacán; México: Instituto Mora, 2009. 799 p.: bibl., ill., indexes, maps.

Long-awaited magnum opus outlines how the independence struggle consists of two movements—one to transform the Spanish monarchy into a modern nation-state and the other to create self-governance in its former colonies. Details how each intertwined to create post-colonial Mexico. Highly recommended and provocative.

871 **Rompecabezas de papel: la prensa y el periodismo desde las regiones de México, siglos XIX y XX.** Coordinación de Celia del Palacio Montiel. México: Univ. de Guadalajara: Consejo Nacional de Ciencia y Tecnología: Miguel Angel Porrúa, 2006. 266 p.: bibl.

Collection of 16 essays discussing newspapers from *El Despertador Americano*

(by Fregoso Gennis) of the independence years to 1945 and publishing in Aguascalientes (by Luévano Díaz). Especially notable is the discussion of the illustrations found in Oaxaca by Ruiz Cervantes and Sánchez Silva.

872 **Rosado, Georgina Rosado** and **Landy Santana Rivas.** María Uicab: reina, sacerdotisa y jefa militar de los mayas rebeldes de Yucatán, 1863–1875. (*Mesoamérica/Antigua*, 29:50, 2008, p. 112–139, bibl. photos)

Examines the role of queen and priestess María Uicab, who was a priestess of the Speaking Cross. She held power for a long period during the 1860s until at least 1875.

873 **Rugeley, Terry.** Rebellion now and forever: Mayas, Hispanics, and Caste War violence in Yucatán, 1800–1880. Stanford, Calif.: Stanford Univ. Press, 2009. 464 p.: bibl., ill., index, maps.

First monumental account of the Maya rebellion in Yucatán since the publication of Nelson Reed's *The Caste War of Yucatán* in 1964 (see *HLAS 26:568*). Shows both the singularity of Yucatan and its similarities to the rest of Mexico. Highly recommended.

874 **Salvucci, Richard J.** Politics, markets and Mexico's "London debt," 1823–1887. New York, N.Y.: Cambridge Univ. Press, 2009. 326 p.: bibl., ill., index. (Cambridge Latin American studies; 93)

Only modern major study of the most important debt owed by the Mexican republic in the 19th century. Author contends that federalism made fiscal collection impossible, but as studies in this volume show, centralism was equally impossible because of poor communications, transportation, and local political formations. Recommended.

875 **Sánchez Arteche, Alfonso.** Estudios sobre la Constitución Federal de los Estados Unidos Mexicanos, 1857. Toluca, Mexico: Univ. Autónoma del Estado de México, 2008. 81 p.: ill.

Even in the heady times of 2010, some places, in this case, Mexico State, still look at the times in between. Sánchez Arteche and the images of the Constitution of 1857 are particularly interesting.

876 Sánchez Santiró, Ernest. Las alcaba-
las mexicanas, 1821–1857: los dilemas
en la construcción de la hacienda nacional.
México: Instituto Mora, 2009. 367 p.: bibl.,
ill., indexes, maps. (Historia económica)
Extremely important study of fledg-
ing tax structure of the early republic.
Shows how, given that direct taxes were
not an option, indirect levies were one of
the only possibilities of raising revenue, but
were wildly unpopular. Recommended.

877 Sánchez Silva, Carlos. "No todo
empezó en Cádiz": simbiosis política
en Oaxaca entre colonia y república. (Signos
Hist., 19, enero/junio 2008, p. 8–35, bibl.)
Studies local elections throughout the
colony and then contends that Oaxaca had
representative institutions even before Cádiz
supposedly imposed them on the populace.

878 Sánchez Tagle, Héctor. Insurgencia y
contrainsurgencia en Zacatecas,
1810–1813. Zacatecas, Mexico: Univ. Autónoma de Zacatecas: LIX Legislatura del
Estado de Zacatecas: SPAUZ 2008–2011,
2009. 301 p.: bibl.
Interesting look at the insurgency
and its defeat in what would become one of
the most progressive states of the republic.
Despite the rise of the counterinsurgency,
the insurgents managed to leave permanent
scars on the body politic, setting up future
conflict in the state and the nation.

**879 Santos Carrera, Moisés; Natividad de
Jesús Alvarez Hernández; and Angel
Crespo Acevedo.** Hacienda de Chichihualco:
historia del despojo de tierras a los indígenas de Xochipala, siglo XIX. Chilpancingo
Guerrero, Mexico: Univ. Autónoma de Guerrero, 2009. 254 p.: bibl., ill.
Hacienda study that shows how indigenous land in Guerrero became part of the
Hacienda de Chichihualco that was owned
by the Bravo family. Outlines the legal and
violent struggle to retake the land and return it to its original tillers.

880 Schell, Patience Alexandra. Entre la
libertad y el control política educativa
mexicana y reacciones desde el Porfiriato
hasta la revolución. (in Instituciones y
formas de control social en América Latina,
1840–1940: una revisión. Edición de Johna-
than Ablard et al. Buenos Aires: Prometeo
Libros, 2005, p. 73–91, bibl.)

Primary education controlled by
municipalities always felt the pull of two
forces—control and liberty. In the 1880s
Joaquín Baranda, Minister of Justicia e Instrucción Pública, fought for and instituted
free, obligatory, and unified public education throughout Mexico. He also enacted
into law, in 1888, the beginning of what
would ultimately become the Secretaría de
Educación Pública (SEP).

881 Serrano Barquín, Héctor P. Miradas fotográficas en el México decimonónico: las simbolizaciones de género.
Toluca, Mexico: Instituto Mexiquense de
Cultura, 2008. 268 p.: bibl., ill. (Biblioteca
mexiquense del bicentenario)
Important analysis of 19th-century
photography, focusing on the construction
of gender through photographs. Highly theoretical, the last part of the volume finally
gets down to systematizing photographs and
their content.

882 Serrano Ortega, José Antonio. Igualdad, uniformidad, proporcionalidad:
contribuciones directas y reformas fiscales
en México, 1810–1846. México: Instituto
Mora; Zamora, Mexico: Colegio de Michoacán, 2007. 214 p.: bibl., indexes. (Historia
económica)
Serious study of some of the major
problems of the fiscal economy in the early
19th century. Adds the issue of equality in
regional, personal, and business aspects to
the analytical mix, probably as part of the
current tax debate. Recommended.

883 Shelton, Laura Marie. For tranquility and order: family and community
on Mexico's northern frontier, 1800–1850.
Tucson, Ariz.: Univ. of Arizona Press, 2010.
206 p.: bibl., index.
Study uses gender predominately to
show how the colonial order evolved into a
republican one. Nevertheless, even though
suppression of both Apaches and Yaquis led
to new opportunities for growth, nothing is
made of the vecino to the north and the pull
of its customs and economy.

884 Sloan, Kathryn A. Runaway daughters: seduction, elopement, and honor
in nineteenth-century Mexico. Albuquerque, N.M.: Univ. of New Mexico Press,
2008. 244 p.: bibl., ill., index, maps.

Looks at 212 *rapto* cases and other romantic relations between the sexes in Oaxaca. Title misleads since the book concerns mainly Oaxaca and mostly the poor. Extends arguments made earlier by William French in his contribution to *The Human Tradition in Mexico* (see *HLAS 62:600*).

885 Solís Robleda, Gabriela. Las primeras letras en Yucatán: la instrucción básica entre la Conquista y el Segundo Imperio. México: CIESAS: M.Á. Porrúa, 2008. 319 p.: bibl. (Col. Peninsular)

Study reiterates the painful shift in educational policy that came from the Bourbon Reforms. Education in Yucatán then faced an insurmountable challenge from the Caste Wars. Recommended.

886 Teitelbaum, Vanesa E. and **Florencia Gutiérrez.** Sociedades de artesanos y poder público: Ciudad de México, segunda mitad del siglo XIX. (*Estud. Hist. Mod. Contemp. Méx.*, 36, julio/dic. 2008, p. 127–158, bibl.)

Sheds light on the relationship between mutual societies developed by workers to protect themselves from the vicissitudes of industrialization and government power starting in the 1850s. These organizations were sanctioned by the Constitution of 1857 and Código Civil of 1871 and institutionalized during the Porfiriato.

887 Terán Fuentes, Mariana. Haciendo patria: cultura cívica en Zacatecas, siglo XIX. México: CONACYT; Zacatecas, Mexico: Univ. Autónoma de Zacatecas, Coordinación de Investigación y Posgrado, 2006. 203 p.: bibl. (Serie Fuentes para el estudio del federalismo en Zacatecas)

Shows the formation of a civic culture in Zacatecas prior to the suppression of federalism there in 1834. Demonstrates the impact of the US model for the area.

888 Tirado Villegas, Gloria. Los efectos sociales del ferrocarril interoceánico: Puebla en el porfiriato. Puebla, Mexico: Benemérita Univ. Autónoma de Puebla Instituto de Ciencias Sociales y Humanidades "Alfonso Vélez Pliego," Dirección de Fomento Editorial, 2007. 359 p.: bibl., ill., maps.

Outlines the changes in population figures and personalities that came to the fore in Puebla as a result of the new rail-road. Stresses how railroad concessions produced a group of people close to both Mexico City and the governor of Puebla. Recommended.

889 Tortolero, Alejandro. Notarios y agricultores: crecimiento y atraso en el campo mexicano, 1780–1920: propiedad, crédito, irrigación y conflictos sociales en el agro mexicano. México: Univ. Autónoma Metropolitana, Iztapalapa: Siglo Veintiuno Editores, 2008. 328 p.: bibl., ill., maps. (Historia)

Discusses the reasons why Mexican agriculture fell behind during the long 19th century. Cites the lack of circulating capital, ecology, and paucity of water systems that provoked both active and passive conflict. Recommended.

890 Toulet Abasolo, Lucina M. La vida cotidiana en las escuelas tlaxcaltecas del siglo XIX. Tlaxcala, Mexico: Gobierno del Estado de Tlaxcala: Fideicomiso Colegio de Historia de Tlaxcala, 2009. 246 p.: bibl., ill. (Biblioteca Tlaxcalteca. Estudios Regionales)

Following the pattern set by El Colegio de México, this study attempts to piece together scholastic life in Tlaxcala. The book is filled with pieces of information valuable to scholars of the area.

891 Trejo, Zulema. Estructura administrativa del segundo imperio: el caso de la administración imperial sonorense. (*Hist. Mex./México*, 57:4, abril/junio 2008, p. 1013–1044, maps, tables)

Close study of regime changes made by the second empire on the frontier state of Sonora, which contested against liberals, Yaquis, Mayos, Apache, and factional struggles as well. Finds that the system functioned smoothly, due to the flexibility of officials *in situ*.

892 Treviño, Mario. Entre caciques y caudillos: Nuevo León, siglo XIX. Monterrey, Mexico: Univ. Autónoma de Nuevo León, 2009. 423 p.: bibl. (Ancla de tiempo)

Straight-forward account of political events in a state with substantial archival documents. Also contains biographical information on important figures.

Uhthoff López, Luz María. Hacia la modernización de la política presupuestaria en México: los impuestos exteriores e interiores, 1870–1930. See item **1015.**

893 Van Young, Eric. The limits of Atlantic-world nationalism in a revolutionary age: imagined communities and lived communities in Mexico, 1810–1821. (*in* Empire to nation: historical perspectives on the making of the modern world. Edited by Joseph W. Esherick, Hasan Kayal, and Eric Van Young. Lanham, Md.: Rowman & Littlefield, 2006, p. 34–67, map)

Explains massacres of Spaniards as a way to locate and destroy a cultural "other" whose elimination would, in some way, serve as expiation for the colonial regime. Doubts that the vast majority of Mexicans who fought against Spaniards did so out of a sense of nationalism. Recommended.

894 Vázquez Mantecón, María del Carmen. Las fiestas para el libertador y monarca de México Agustín de Iturbide, 1821–1823. (*Estud. Hist. Mod. Contemp. Méx.,* 36, julio/dic. 2008, p. 45–83, ill.)

Indicates the power of ceremony ("*arquitectura efímera*") for a country having survived war for 11 years. Includes detailed descriptions of these fêtes and their categories. Author stresses the difficulties in maintaining the empire given that it was so reminiscent of the one before.

895 Washbrook, Sarah. *Enganche* and exports in Chiapas, Mexico: a comparison of plantation labour in the districts of Soconusco and Palenque, 1876–1911. (*J. Lat. Am. Stud.,* 39:4, Nov. 2007, p. 797–825, map, tables)

Compares the situation of workers in Palenque and Soconusco, Chiapas. Shows that Palenque, where workers were drawn from the local indigenous population, fared worse than the transients in Soconusco.

896 Wright-Rios, Edward Newport. Revolutions in Mexican Catholicism: reform and revelation in Oaxaca, 1887–1934. Durham, N.C.: Duke Univ. Press, 2009. 361 p.: bibl., ill., index, map.

Fascinating analysis of the trajectory of Catholicism in local rural communities. Indicates that colonial society persisted

despite all attempts at modernization. Recommended.

REVOLUTION AND POST-REVOLUTION

897 Agostoni, Claudia. Las mensajeras de la salud: enfermeras visitadoras en la Ciudad de México durante la década de los 1920. (*Estud. Hist. Mod. Contemp. Méx.,* 33, enero/junio 2007, p. 89–120, bibl.)

This brief study examines the central role played by a newly created group of nurses in an official campaign to promote maternal and infant health. Mexico City's "visiting nurses" brought modern ideas of health and hygiene into the homes of the poor, advancing the cause of preventative medicine.

898 Aguilar Rodríguez, Sandra. Cooking modernity: nutrition policies, class and gender in 1940s and 1950s Mexico. (*Americas/Washington,* 64:2, Oct. 2007, p. 177–205, photos, tables)

The author examines government attempts to modernize the Mexican working class through public dining halls that promoted particular ideas of nutrition, hygiene, and behavior. In this attempt to transform the masses into respectable citizens, working-class women were considered an especially important audience. At the same time, the middle class reformers that staffed these dining halls assumed these women incapable of adequately feeding or shaping their own families.

Aguirre, Gabriela. La iglesia católica y la revolución mexicana, 1913–1920. See item **3561.**

899 Alfaro-Velcamp, Theresa. So far from Allah, so close to Mexico: Middle Eastern immigrants in modern Mexico. Austin: Univ. of Texas Press, 2007. 272 p.: bibl., ill., index, maps.

This is an exhaustively researched account by a descendant of Lebanese immigrants. The author places Middle Eastern immigrants in the context of Porfirian, revolutionary, and post-revolutionary Mexico, while also addressing the broader transnational backdrop that encouraged emigration. While the more upwardly mobile migrants maintained a Lebanese identity, those of more modest means drew closer to Mexicanidad.

900 Andrews, Abigail. Constructing mutuality: the Zapatistas transformation of transnational activist power dynamics. (*Lat. Am. Polit. Soc.*, 52:1, Spring 2010, p. 89–120, bibl.)

Study of the international solidarity support network of the Zapatista movement between 1994 and 2008. The Zapatistas determined who would be included in their support network, set terms for their partnerships, and asserted their autonomy from donors. While the Zapatistas were able to maintain control of their movement, their defiance of Northern Hemisphere NGOs may have placed their long-term viability at risk.

901 Aréchiga Córdoba, Ernesto. Educación, propaganda o "dictadura sanitaria": estrategias discursivas de higiene y salubridad públicas en el México posrevolucionario, 1917–1945. (*Estud. Hist. Mod. Contemp. Méx.*, 33, enero/junio 2007, p. 57–88)

The author discusses the development of a structure through which the revolutionary state attempted to implement its public health initiatives throughout the country. Through both the Depto. de Salud and the Secretaría de Educación Pública, the central government sought to impose its view of a modern, hygienic nation on all citizens.

Astorga Almanza, Luis Alejandro. El siglo de las drogas: el narcotráfico, del Porfiriato al nuevo milenio. See *HLAS 65:2460.*

902 Ayala Guevara, Leopoldo. La guerra sucia en Guerrero: impunidad, terrorismo y abuso de poder. Chilpancingo, Mexico: Editorial Ayalacenter, 2005. 296 p.

This is a strident account that ties the state's history of violence and political repression to the growth of the PRI. The author finds the roots of Guerrero's troubles in the corruption of the 1950s, which encouraged students to organize, and eventually gave rise to the Partido de los Pobres. With the Aguas Blancas massacre of 1988, state-sponsored terrorism continued.

903 Azuela de la Cueva, Alicia. *Peace by revolution*: una aproximación léxico-visual al México revolucionario. (*Hist. Mex./México*, 56:4, abril/junio 2007, p. 1263–1307, bibl., ill., map, photo)

The author examines a 1933 version of this well-known text in which Tannenbaum's study was paired with illustrations by Mexican artist Miguel Covarrubias. She analyzes both the textual and visual interpretations of Mexico and of the Revolution, and argues that these were mostly similar in what they sought to convey. For art specialist's comment, see item **69.**

904 Bantjes, Adrian A. Mexican revolutionary anticlericalism: concepts and typologies. (*Americas/Washington*, 65:4, April 2009, p. 467–480)

This essay introduces an entire volume of work on a relatively new area of research. Bantjes conceptualizes anticlericalism, highlights major approaches to the topic contained in the volume, and suggests avenues for further research.

905 Beezley, William H. and Colin M. MacLachlan. Mexicans in revolution, 1910–1946: an introduction. Lincoln: Univ. of Nebraska Press, 2009. 189 p.: bibl., index. (The Mexican experience)

Two widely published scholars of Mexican history offer an introduction to the early decades of the Revolution in connection with the centennial of the Revolution. Intended for a general audience.

906 Beltrán Dengra, Joaquín. La Revolución mexicana a través de la prensa española, 1911–1924. Monterrey, Mexico: Consejo para la Cultura y las Artes de Nuevo León, 2008. 237 p.: bibl. (Investigación / Consejo para la Cultura y las Artes de Nuevo León)

Drawing on newspapers primarily from Barcelona and Madrid, the author analyzes the response of the Spanish press to revolutionary events. The newspapers represent a wide spectrum of political tendencies from monarchist to anarchist. In addition to political affiliations, the responses of the papers depended on such factors as eurocentrism, ethnic prejudice, a desire for new markets for Spain, and an anti-US sentiment.

907 *Boletín del Fideicomiso Archivos Plutarco Elías Calles y Fernando Torreblanca.* No. 55, mayo/agosto 2007. El espionaje mexicano al servicio del anti-imperialismo. México: Fideicomiso Archivos Plutarco Elías Calles y Fernando Torreblanca.

Analysis of the possibility of the use of force by the US as relations with the Calles administration deteriorated. Based on documents taken by Mexican secret agents from the office of the US military attaché at the embassy in Mexico City. Agents operated under orders from Luis Morones, union boss and secretary of industry, commerce, and labor under Calles.

908 *Boletín del Fideicomiso Archivos Plutarco Elías Calles y Fernando Torreblanca.* No. 56, sept./dic. 2007. Legislación e intereses extranjeros: el caso de petróleo durante el gobierno de Alvaro Obregón. México: Fideicomiso Archivos Plutarco Elías Calles y Fernando Torreblanca.

Examination of the relations between the Obregón administration and the foreign-owned oil companies, with particular emphasis on Obregón's desire for recognition by the US. Internal and external problems prevented Obregón from taking a revolutionary, nationalistic position in regard to petroleum.

909 *Boletín del Fideicomiso Archivos Plutarco Elías Calles y Fernando Torreblanca.* No. 60, enero/abril 2009. Fotografía cristera. México: Fideicomiso Archivos Plutarco Elías Calles y Fernando Torreblanca.

Discussion of the photography of the Cristero Rebellion. Photos of the rebellion have had a limited circulation compared to those of the Revolution. Article has 24 photos taken from the Archivo de Joaquín Amaro which is held by the Calles/Torreblanca Archives.

910 **Borbolla, Carlos.** La guerra sucia: hechos y testimonios. Colima, México: Univ. de Colima; México: Club Primera Plana, 2007. 369 p.

Long-time reporter examines the "dirty war" of the 1960s, 1970s, and early 1980s. Some of the work appeared originally in 2001 and 2002 as a series of reports in the newspaper *Excelsior.* Work is divided into three parts: the facts of the dirty war, the disappeared guerrilla fighters, and the first investigations and accusations.

911 **Boyer, Christopher R.** Revolución y paternalismo ecológico: Miguel Ángel de Quevedo y la política forestal en México, 1926–1940. (*Hist. Mex./México,* 57:1, julio/sept. 2007, p. 91–138, bibl.)

This article details the efforts of Quevedo and other Mexican scientists to conserve Mexico's forests. Quevedo and his colleagues exhibited a "scientific paternalism," in which campesinos were seen as the biggest threat to conservation, and in need of a firm hand from the newly interventionist Mexican state.

912 **Braceros: las miradas mexicana y estadounidense: antología (1945–1964).** Introducción, compilación y notas de Jorge Durand. México: Senado de la República, LX Legislatura: Univ. Autónoma de Zacatecas: Miguel Ángel Porrúa, 2007. 527 p.: bibl. (América Latina y el nuevo orden mundial)

Inspired by the contemporary debate over Mexican immigration to the US, this volume provides a variety of perspectives on the Bracero Program from those who witnessed the program in operation. This is an excellent mix of official, academic, and journalistic accounts and analyses from the era.

913 **Brunk, Samuel.** The mortal remains of Emiliano Zapata. (*in* Death, dismemberment, and memory: body politics in Latin America. Edited by Lyman L. Johnson. Albuquerque, N.M.: Univ. of New Mexico Press, 2004, p. 141–178, photos)

Brunk examines Mexico's political culture through uses of and conflicts over Zapata's body. The hero cult surrounding Zapata arose almost immediately after his death, but so too did debates over his remains and what they meant: were these indeed his remains, where should they be buried, and who should control them and the messages associated with their commemoration? [K. Melvin]

914 **Brunk, Samuel.** The posthumous career of Emiliano Zapata: myth, memory, and Mexico's twentieth century. Austin: Univ. of Texas Press, 2008. 353 p.: bibl., ill., index, photos. (Joe R. and Teresa

Lozano Long Series in Latin American and Latino Art and Culture)

Following up on his political biography of Zapata published in 1995 (see *HLAS 58:1401*), the author examines the uses and abuses of the Zapata cult and its relation to political culture after the Revolution. In the interest of political hegemony, the state made Zapata a "founding father" but had difficulty controlling his posthumous career.

915 Butler, Matthew. Sotanas Rojinegras: Catholic anticlericalism and Mexico's revolutionary schism. (*Americas/Washington,* 65:4, April 2009, p. 535–558)

The author argues that the schismatic Mexican Catholic and Apostolic Church (ICAM) represented a genuine form of religious anticlericalism, not merely a political pawn of the Revolution's leaders. ICAM offered a broad reform of Roman Catholicism; one that embraced nationalism, the social goals of the Revolution, and a purer form of Christianity.

916 Camp, Roderic Ai. Exercising political influence: religion, democracy, and the Mexican 2006 presidential race. (*J. Church State,* 50:1, Winter 2008, p. 49–72)

Using surveys, the author does not detect any pattern of the Church attempting to persuade people to vote one way or the other. The Church did "influence" the election by encouraging electoral participation, by urging candidates to run a clean campaign, and by supporting the legitimacy of the Federal Electoral Tribunal in its decision about the election results.

917 Camp, Roderic Ai. The metamorphosis of leadership in a democratic Mexico. New York, N.Y.: Oxford Univ. Press, 2010. 312 p.: bibl., index.

Author, the dean of studies of Mexican political leadership, captures the evolution of Mexico's political system from the 1930s to 2010. Contends that the nation is undergoing process of democratic consolidation, but is not there yet. Many of his results are either counterintuitive—party militancy generally greater among Panistas than Priistas—or unexpected. A must-read for anyone who hopes to know Mexico.

918 Cárdenas García, Nicolás. La incómoda herencia de Gruening a México (*Secuencia/México,* 69, sept./dic. 2007, p. 63–84, bibl.)

Author examines the main points of Ernest Gruening's *Mexico and Its Heritage,* originally published in New York and London in 1928. Author classifies Gruening as a "progressive liberal" whose criticisms of the revolutionary process do not represent hostility toward the Revolution but rather a disappointment with its limited accomplishments.

919 Castañeda López, Gabriela and Ana Cecilia Rodríguez de Romo. Henry Sigerist y José Joaquín Izquierdo: dos actitudes frente a la historia de la medicina en el siglo XX. (*Hist. Mex./México,* 57:1, julio/ sept. 2007, p. 139–191, bibl.)

This article examines the relationship between a Swiss-born historian of medicine and a Mexican doctor. Sigerist, who helped advance the historical study of medicine in the US, carried on a long correspondence with Izquierdo, who produced seminal works on the history of medicine in his own country.

920 Castro Martínez, Pedro Fernando. El asesinato del general Álvaro Obregón: las caras de un imaginario dividido. (*Iztapalapa/México,* 27:61, julio/dic. 2006, p. 143–168, bibl.)

Author rounds up the usual suspects, plus a few others, in the assassination of Obregón. Opposition to Obregón's reelection, the conflict with the Church, disagreements among the main political actors, and deficient police investigations converged to form a "fragmented imaginary."

921 Cedillo, Juan Alberto. Los nazis en México. México: Debate, 2007. 156 p., 8 p. of plates: bibl., ill.

Journalist describes the variety of Nazi espionage activities in Mexico by assembling a colorful cast of characters: a Hollywood star (Errol Flynn), a general with presidential ambitions (Juan Almazán), the current president's brother (Maximino Avila Camacho), a future president (Miguel Alemán), a wealthy US businessman (Jean Paul Getty), and the founder of Mexico's first major drug cartel (Gen. Francisco Javie

Aguilar González). Lengthy discussion of Trotsky's assassination.

922 Cerutti, Mario. La construcción de una agrociudad en el noroeste de México, Ciudad Obregón, 1925–1960. (*Secuencia/México*, 64, enero/abril 2006, p. 113–143, bibl., graphs, maps, photos, tables)

Focusing on southern Sonora and northern Sinaloa, the author analyzes the development process that led to Ciudad Obregón becoming one of Mexico's best examples of an "agrociudad"—an urban, centralizing nucleus created by the agricultural development of the area around it. Presidential connections, irrigation, and an entrepreneurial spirit were key components of the process.

Cordero Olivero, Immaculada. El espejo desenterrado: España en México, 1975–1982. See *HLAS 65:2011.*

923 Curley, Robert. Anticlericalism and public space in revolutionary Jalisco. (*Americas/Washington*, 65:4, April 2009, p. 511–533)

The author compares the policies of two governors in an attempt to reveal different modes of anticlericalism. While Manuel M. Diéguez's anticlerical actions were tactical, occurring in the context of the civil war, José Guadalupe Zuno presided over an era of rebuilding, and thus exhibited a strategic anticlericalism, executed with the more long-term goal of eliminating the "political Catholicism" that allowed for opposition to the revolutionary state.

924 Dávila Valdés, Claudia. El tratamiento jurídico-administrativo a los refugiados de la guerra civil española en Francia y México: un estudio comparativo. (*Secuencia/México*, 69, sept./dic. 2007, p. 117–136, bibl.)

The author examines the contexts in which both France and Mexico accepted Republican refugees. For France, the economic and political pressures of the 1930s, as well as the exigencies of WWII, encouraged a marginalization of the refugees. By contrast, Mexico's era of relative prosperity resulted in a policy focused on a swift and complete integration of these new immigrants.

925 Diez, Jordi. Legislative oversight of the armed forces in Mexico. (*Mex. Stud.*, 24:1, Winter 2008, p. 113–145)

Study of the role played by the Mexican Congress in controlling the armed forces as Mexico transitions to greater democracy. The corporatist structure employed under PRI rule resulted in considerable autonomy for the armed forces. After examining the role of Congress in civil-military relations since 2000, the author concludes that congressional oversight of the military generally remains weak.

926 Dwyer, John Joseph. The agrarian dispute: the expropriation of American-owned rural land in postrevolutionary Mexico. Durham, N.C.: Duke Univ. Press, 2008. 387 p.: bibl., ill., index, map. (American encounters/global interactions)

Examination of the "land dispute" growing out of Cárdenas' expropriation of land in the mid- to late 1930s, focusing on the states of Sonora and Baja California. The author uses the dispute to highlight the relationship between domestic and international affairs and concludes that the land dispute—not the oil expropriation of 1938—was the first major test of the Good Neighbor Policy, with the Mexican government negotiating a favorable settlement of the controversy.

927 The eagle and the virgin: nation and cultural revolution in Mexico, 1920–1940. Edited by Mary Kay Vaughan and Stephen E. Lewis. Durham, N.C.: Duke Univ. Press, 2006. 363 p., 20 p. of plates: bibl., ill., index.

This is an important collection that makes a case for the varied and often-inconsistent nature of nation-building and identity formation in the aftermath of the Mexican Revolution. The authors explore several themes, including the esthetics of the revolutionary era, attempts at social and behavioral transformation, and efforts to promote a national identity among Mexicans.

928 Enríquez Acosta, Jesús Angel. Migration and urbanization in Northwest Mexico's border cities. (*J. Southwest*, 51:4, Winter 2009, p. 445–455)

Examination of the impact of migration on Northwest Mexico's major cities, primarily Tijuana, Nogales, and Juárez.

Post-WWII development in the US Southwest played a key role in the migration, with migrants coming to the Mexican border for jobs or to cross into the US. Lack of public services and income inequality are major problems in the region, but workers' earnings are considerably above the national minimum wage.

929 Ervin, Michael A. The 1930 agrarian census in Mexico: agronomists, middle politics, and the negotiation of data collection. (*HAHR*, 87:3, Aug. 2007, p. 537–570, table)

This impressive study demonstrates the role of a new professional middle class in shaping revolutionary politics. The agronomists of the Depto. de Estadísticas Nacionales played a key role in reviving land redistribution as a political goal, even as they stressed the duty of campesinos to participate in the revolutionary project.

930 Esteva, Gustavo. The Asamblea Popular de los Pueblos de Oaxaca: a chronicle of radical democracy. (*Lat. Am. Perspect.*, 34:1, Jan. 2007, p. 129–144, photos)

A participant's view of the growing discontent with the state and federal governments, leading to the formation of the APPO in 2006. Striking teachers merged with other social groups to resist growing repression by state authorities.

931 Estrada Saavedra, Marco. La comunidad armada rebelde y el EZLN: un estudio histórico y sociológico sobre las bases de apoyo zapatistas en las cañadas tojolabales de la Selva Lacandona, 1930–2005. México: El Colegio de México, 2007. 625 p.: bibl., ill., maps.

Focusing on the Chiapan municipality of Las Margaritas, the author provides a wide-ranging comparative study between rebel groups and groups that chose to continue the struggle politically, rather than militarily. Study includes the support groups' formation, organization, and interactions with other regional actors such as religious organizations and the government bureaucracy, as well as internal splits.

932 Fallaw, Ben W. Varieties of Mexican revolutionary anticlericalism: radicalism, iconoclasm, and otherwise, 1914–1935. (*Americas/Washington*, 65:4, April 2009, p. 481–509)

The author probes the varieties of anticlericalism in Mexico. Radical iconoclasts sought to destroy the Catholic Church, while moderate reformists envisioned alternatives to a strong Catholic Church. Both camps harbored ideas for positive change in this aspect of Mexican society.

933 Favret Tondato, Rita. Arteaga, tierra de manzanos: configuración de una región agrícola de Coahuila (1940–1990). Mexico: Univ. Autónoma Agraria Antonio Narro: Plaza y Valdéz, 2006. 337 p.: bibl., ill., maps.

This is a meticulously researched account of the region of Arteaga's economic and social history, with a focus on the region's dominant apple industry. The author examines the factors involved in the growth of this sector, which received a boost after 1940 from a central government determined to substitute local products for US imports. The 1980s brought more change, with Mexico's neoliberal opening challenging Arteaga growers with competition and lower prices.

934 García, Daniel Carlos. Fulgor rebelde: la guerrilla en Aguascalientes. Aguascalientes, Mexico: Filo de Agua, 2006. 164 p.: bibl. (Col. Fuego fresco) (Ensayo)

This is a brief treatment of the state's guerrilla movement during the 1970s. The author traces the history of the Frente Revolucionario de Acción Socialista and places it in the context of national and international protest movements.

935 Garciadiego Dantan, Javier. Cultura y política en el México posrevolucionario. México: Instituto Nacional de Estudios Históricos de las Revoluciones de México, 2006. 644 p.: bibl. (Biblioteca INEHRM)

Collection of essays—most of them previously published—on a variety of topics: UNAM, Manuel Gómez Morin, Alfonso Reyes, and historiography.

936 Genocidio: la verdadera noche de Tlatelolco. Recopilación de Norberto Moreno. México: N. Moreno, 2008. 1 v. (various pagings): bibl.

This volume is part of the effort by Mexico's Human Rights Commission to gather and bring to light evidence on the government's response to the student movement, which culminated in the Tlatelolco massacre. In addition to detailing the events of 1968, this publication also includes a consideration of the government's reaction to the growth of guerrilla movements during the 1960s and 1970s. The editor includes the names of those killed and disappeared during this era of Mexico's history.

937 Gonzales, Michael J. Imagining Mexico in 1910: visions of the *Patria* in the centennial celebration in Mexico City. (*J. Lat. Am. Stud.*, 39:3, Aug. 2007, p. 495–533, photos, tables)

This article provides a detailed description of the various components of the centennial celebration in Mexico City in 1910. The author focuses especially on the historical parade, through which Porfirian elites sought to promote a particular view of their nation. That view revealed many of the contradictions of Porfirian Mexico.

938 González Jácome, Alba. Humedales en el suroeste de Tlaxcala: agua y agricultura en el siglo XX. México: Univ. Iberoamericana, 2008. 317 p.: bibl., ill., maps.

Extensively researched and illustrated study of a wetlands area in Tlaxcala on the border with the state of Puebla. The wetlands have been negatively affected by a variety of forces: agrarian reform, modernization, the creation of an irrigation district, and NAFTA. The struggle over the wetlands has focused on the land rather than the water. The water extracted from the area goes to Puebla.

939 Grammont, Hubert Carton de and **Horacio Mackinlay.** Campesino and indigenous social organizations facing democratic transition in Mexico, 1938–2006. (*Lat. Am. Perspect.*, 36:4, July 2009, p. 21–40)

Authors emphasize the role played by social rather than political organizations in the transition to democracy and see rural Mexican political society as having gone through three stages: 1938–1988 (PRI domination), 1988–2000 (democratic transition), and the period since 2000. Authors identify the growing importance of social organizations but believe that rejection of the political process weakens the campesino and indigenous organizations.

940 Guerra Manzo, Enrique. Caciquismo y orden público en Michoacán: 1920–1940. México: El Colegio de México, 2002. 311 p.: bibl.

This study of post-revolutionary power dynamics underscores the extent to which local figures, including rural teachers, *agraristas*, and priests continued to play a crucial role, even in the face of political centralization. The author focuses on two specific regions, and utilizes national, local, and private archives.

941 Guerra Manzo, Enrique. Pensar la revolución mexicana: tres horizontes de interpretación. (*Secuencia/México*, 64, enero/abril 2006, p. 51–78, bibl., photos)

Review of the three generations of studies of the Mexican Revolution: 1910–40, 1940–68, and 1968 to the present. The studies have been bogged down with the third generation, the "revisionist" phase. To break the stalemate reached by revisionist literature, it will be necessary to combine the methodological perspective of the first and second generations ("commitment") with that of the third generation ("distancing").

942 Guerra Manzo, Enrique. The resistance of the marginalised: Catholics in eastern Michoacán and the Mexican state, 1920–40. (*J. Lat. Am. Stud.*, 40:1, Feb. 2008, p. 109–133)

The author examines the extent to which resistance to revolutionary anticlericalism was shaped by preexisting power dynamics. His focus is primarily on the district of Zitácuaro, where liberalism and Protestantism had made inroads during the late 19th century. Because of the pragmatic approach of the Church and its adherents in the face of liberal and *agrarista* challenges, Catholicism as both a political and cultural force survived.

943 Harris, Charles H. and **Louis R. Sadler.** The archaeologist was a spy: Sylvanus G. Morley and the Office of Naval Intelligence. Albuquerque, N.M.: Univ. of New Mexico Press, 2003. 450 p.: bibl., ill., index, 1 map.

Authors trace the WWI intelligence career of the man who was the most influential Mayanist of his generation. The Office of Naval Intelligence recruited Morley to engage in intelligence activities in Mexico and Central America. Morley in turn recruited his own network of spies. Morley's career highlights the problem of scholars as spies and demonstrates the organizational problems experienced by the early intelligence community.

944 Harris, Charles H. and **Louis R. Sadler.** The secret war in El Paso: Mexican revolutionary intrigue, 1906–1920. Albuquerque, N.M.: Univ. of New Mexico Press, 2009. 488 p.: bibl., ill., index.

Examination of the importance of access to the US border in determining which revolutionary faction triumphed, focusing on the largest and most important city on the border, EI Paso. The Revolution played a key role in the development of EI Paso just as EI Paso played a key role in the development of the Revolution. The authors assemble a wide variety of revolutionary characters, many of whom were "more interested in the cash than in the cause" (p. 378). Extensively illustrated and thoroughly researched.

945 Harris, Charles H. and **Louis R. Sadler.** The Texas Rangers and the Mexican Revolution: the bloodiest decade, 1910–1920. Albuquerque, N.M.: Univ. of New Mexico Press, 2004. 673 p.: bibl., ill., index, maps.

Veteran border researchers explore an important phase in the evolution of Texas Rangers and a largely neglected aspect of the Mexican Revolution. Work is organized around the administrations of the three governors who held office during the period. Authors conclude that the Ranger force during the period was "under-strength, underpaid, and living on its reputation" (p. 502).

946 Henck, Nick. Laying a ghost to rest: Subcommander Marcos' playing of the indigenous card. (*Mex. Stud.*, 25:1, Winter 2009, p. 155–170)

Author seeks to refute the assertion that subcomandante Marcos was originally a socialist unconcerned with the Indian who played the indigenous card to win support for the Zapatistas after realizing that the indigenous aspect of the uprising had caught the world's attention. Author maintains that Marcos embraced the indigenous cause as early as 1992.

947 Hernández García de León, Héctor. Historia política del sinarquismo, 1934–1944. México: Univ. Iberoamericana; M.A. Porrúa, 2004. 458 p.: bibl., index.

Translation of the work first published in English (London, 1999) with the title *The Sinarquista Movement: With Special Reference to the Period 1934–1944*.

948 Hidalgo, Dennis R. The evolution of history and the informed empire: La Decena Trágica in the British Press. (*Mex. Stud.*, 23:2, Summer 2007, p. 317–354)

Author examines seven British newspapers' handling of the Decena Trágica of February 1913. The papers were interested in the treatment of foreigners, the role that the US played in the Revolution, and the issue of what type of government Mexico needed. The articles displayed a widespread conviction of Mexican inferiority and lack of preparedness for democracy.

949 Holiday in Mexico: critical reflections on tourism and tourist encounters. Edited by Dina Berger and Andrew Grant Wood. Durham, N.C.: Duke Univ. Press, 2009. 393 p.: bibl., index. (American encounters/global interactions)

Excellent collection of essays dealing with the cultural, diplomatic, economic, and social aspects of tourism. Essays reflect a variety of locations—Acapulco, Cancun, Los Cabos, San Miguel de Allende—as well as topics: the politics of tourist development, the exploitation of the indigenous past, border vice, carnival. Work makes a good case that tourism research is not "social sciences light" (p. 6).

950 Huberman, Elizabeth L. Historia del movimiento obrero. México: Univ. Obrera de México, 2006. 217 p.: bibl., ill.

Presents a translation of a study completed in the 1950s. The focus is on the worker's movement during the Lázaro Cárdenas years and on the leadership of the movement under Vicente Lombardo Toledano. The author demonstrates the movement's complexity and importance.

951 La huelga del Río Blanco. Recopilación de Bernardo García Díaz. Jalapa Enríquez, Mexico: Veracruz, Gobierno del Estado, 2007. 298 p.: bibl., ill., ports.

This volume is a commemorative collection of works published since 1957 on the famous textile strike. Mexican authors, including Moises González Navarro, and non-Mexican scholars, including Rodney Anderson, shed light on the social, political, and economic aspects of this event. The collection is supplemented by eight brief primary documents.

Johnson, Lyman L. Digging up Cuauhtémoc. See item **724.**

952 Ledesma-Mateos, Ismael. De Balderas a la Casa del Lago: la institucionalización de la biología en México. Benito Juárez, Mexico: Univ. Autónoma de la Ciudad de México, 2007. 351 p., 5 p. of plates: bibl., ill., ports. (Ciencia y sociedad)

This volume traces the development of the field of biology through the lives and thought of Alfonso L. Herrera and Isaac Ochoterena. Because of his links to power, particularly within the medical community, Ochoterena's view of biology as descriptive and taxonomic, won out over Herrera's vision of a more general science tied to evolutionary theory.

953 Lewis, Daniel. Iron horse imperialism: the Southern Pacific of Mexico, 1880–1951. Tucson, Ariz.: Univ. of Arizona Press, 2007. 179 p.: bibl., index, map, table.

The author provides a well-researched account of the development of the Southern Pacific of Mexico—a Southern Pacific subsidiary whose lines ran from Nogales to Guadalajara—and its eventual sale to the Mexican government. Despite its continuing lack of profitability, railroad officials clung to the line as a symbol of American power. Corporate leaders were not able to adjust to the increasingly effective regulation and control exercised by the Mexican government. In the end, Mexico's determination to assert itself as a sovereign nation triumphed. Well researched, including use of corporate records.

954 El libro rojo: continuación. Vol. 1, 1868–1928. Idea y coordinación general de Gerardo Villadelángel Viñas. Curaduría artística de Edgardo Ganado Kim. México: Fondo de Cultura Económica, 2008. 941 p.: bibl., ill. (some col.). (Tezontle)

"Continuation" of *El libro rojo, 1520–1867*, published in 1870. The work is a collection of essays dealing with high-profile crimes, murders, assassinations, and executions, covering the period from 1868 to 1928. Most of the work is devoted to the 1901–1928 period and includes a number of revolutionary figures: Reyes, Madero, Angeles, Zapata, Villa, and Obregon.

955 Lisbona Guillén, Miguel. Los inicios de la política anticlerical en Chiapas durante el periodo de la Revolución, 1910–1920. (*Hist. Mex./México*, 57:2, oct./dic. 2007, p. 491–530, bibl.)

The author examines the extent to which the anticlericalism of the Revolution injected itself into Chiapas, particularly during the occupation of Constitutionalist forces. Constitutionalist leaders met with some success in their attempts to impose anticlerical laws and to promote anticlerical sentiments. Meanwhile, the small number of clergy in the state made for a tepid response by the Church.

956 Llano Ibáñez, Ramón del. Lucha por el cielo: religión y política en el estado de Querétaro, 1910–1929. México: Miguel Ángel Porrúa, 2006. 340 p.: bibl., ill.

Study of Church-state relations from the outbreak of the Madero revolution until the end of the Cristero revolt in a state that was traditionally conservative. Author believes that a culture of intransigence—but not violence—prevailed. Most of the faithful did not join in the Cristero revolt, as a pacifist attitude dominated.

957 Lopes, Maria Aparecida de S. Revolución y ganadería en el norte de México. (*Hist. Mex./México*, 57:3, enero/marzo 2008, p. 863–910, graphs)

The author provides a detailed examination, including statistical data, of the fate of the cattle industry in Sonora and Chihuahua. Due to the economy of the Revolution, cattle disappeared in large number from both states. Sonora, whose leaders played a prominent role in post-revolutionary Mexico, revived its industry with greater ease, perhaps in part because of the less radical nature of agrarian reform in that state.

958 Lorenzo, María Dolores. "Ayúdame que yo te ayudaré": la política laboral en el Banco Oriental de México, 1900–1915. (*Secuencia/México*, 64, enero/abril 2006, p. 31–48, bibl., graph)

Analysis of the development of the Banco Oriental de México, directed by a group of Spaniards. The Banco became one of Mexico's most important banks of emission, drawing its employees from fellow Spaniards. The Revolution was the undoing of the bank which was seized by the Carranza administration in 1915.

959 Lybecker, Donna L. The policy of border fencing between the United States and Mexico: permeability and shifting functions. (*J. Southwest*, 50:3, Autumn 2008, p. 335–352)

Study of the effect of US border policy upon the environment, specifically southwestern Arizona. US border policy has caused the movement of illegal immigration to less-protected, rural areas, resulting in unintended ecological damage.

960 Maldonado Sández, Braulio. Baja California: comentarios políticos y otras obras selectas. Selección de textos, investigación documental e iconográfica de Aidé Grijalva. Estudio introductorio de Gabriel Trujillo Muñoz. Tijuana, Mexico: Univ. Autónoma de Baja California, Instituto de Investigaciones Históricas, 2006. 491 p.: bibl., ill., index. (Baja California: Nuestra Historia; 4)

This is a collection of six works, initially published between 1960 and 1986, by the first governor of Baja California, a left-leaning member of the PRI and personal friend of Adolfo Ruiz Cortines. Maldonado reflects upon his governorship and political views, and defends himself against more traditional members of the PRI who criticized him and who smeared his government after he left office. An interesting look at post-revolutionary politics. For political scientist's review of earlier edition, see *HLAS 57:3076.*

961 Martínez, Oscar Jáquez. Border conflict, border fences, and the "Tortilla Curtain" incident of 1978–1979. (*J. Southwest*, 50:3, Autumn 2008, p. 263–278)

Study of the controversial US proposal to erect a barbed wire and razor fence in the vicinities of Tijuana and Juárez. Under heavy criticism, the US government scaled back the proposal, eliminating the razor part. Author also explains why many in El Paso did not support the Curtain while many in San Diego did.

962 Medina Vidal, D. Xavier et al. Partisan attachment and democracy in Mexico: some cautionary observations. (*Lat. Am. Polit. Soc.*, 52:1, Spring 2010, p. 63–87)

Many scholars assume that party identification promotes the growth of stable democracies. This study indicates that party identification in the democratization process in Mexico partially supports this view but that the Mexican experience, historically, also has some examples where party identification has not supported democratic politics.

Merrill, Dennis. Negotiating paradise: U.S. tourism and empire in twentieth-century Latin America. See item **1333**.

963 México, País refugio: la experiencia de los exilios en el siglo XX. Coordinación de Pablo Yankelevich. México: Plaza y Valdés: Concultura, INAH, 2002. 338 p.: bibl. (Historia)

This is an intriguing collection of essays, some by descendants of immigrants. Three distinct sections examine immigrants from Europe, the US, and Latin America. The authors include considerations of German, French, and Jewish immigrants, as well as McCarthy-era exiles from the US and exiles from South America's "dirty wars."

964 Meyer, Jean A. El conflicto religioso en Oaxaca, 1926–1937. México: Centro de Investigaciones y Estudios Superiores en Antropología Social (Mexico): Univ. Autónoma "Benito Juárez" de Oaxaca: Instituto de Artes Gráficas de Oaxaca, 2006. 90 p., 20 pages of plates: bibl., ill.

The author examines the evidence for Oaxaca's peaceful coexistence with the Catholic Church during the Cristero era. The majority of the state's Catholics followed the line of peaceful resistance, while the local government tempered its anticlericalism. An important step toward a more nuanced view of the Cristero years.

965 Montoya, Ramón Alejandro. La migración potosina hacia Estados Unidos de Norteamérica antes y durante el Programa Bracero: el caso de Cerritos, San Luis Potosí. San Luis Potosí, Mexico: Ponciano Arriaga, 2006. 272 p.: bibl., ill., maps.

The author uses archives and interviews with former braceros to reconstruct the migrant experience, with a focus on a single municipality. From the early 1900s through the years of the Bracero Program, Cerritos and its people were transformed socially, economically, and culturally. Migration connections established between Cerritos and the US continue.

966 Mora, Mariana. Zapatista anticapitalist politics and the "Other Campaign": learning from the struggle for indigenous rights and autonomy. (*Lat. Am. Perspect.*, 34:2, March 2007, p. 64–77)

Author examines the "Other Campaign" created by the Zapatistas in 2005 in preparation for the presidential campaign of 2006. The Zapatistas hoped to link their movement with other anticapitalist liberation groups around the nation.

967 Mottier, Nicole. Drug gangs and politics in Ciudad Juárez: 1928–1936. (*Mex. Stud.*, 25:1, Winter 2009, p. 19–46)

Examination of the rise of the Fernández and Quevedo drug gangs in Juárez beginning in the late 1920s. Both gangs had their origins in gambling, and both depended on political connections, with one of the Quevedo brothers even serving as governor of Chihuahua. Politics also proved their undoing, with the growing power of President Cárdenas and his supporters in the state.

968 Movimientos armados en México, siglo XX. Recopilación de Verónica Oikión Solano y María Eugenia García Ugarte. Zamora, Mexico: Colegio de Michoacán; México: CIESAS, 2006. 3 v. (846 p.): bibl., ill., indexes, maps. (Col. Debates)

Multivolume collection of essays dealing with topics ranging from the original Zapatistas of the Revolution to the "neozapatistas" of the 1990s. Good regional balance in the coverage of the movements.

969 Niblo, Stephen R. and **Diane M. Niblo.** Acapulco in dreams and reality. (*Mex. Stud.*, 24:1, Winter 2008, p. 31–51)

Authors examine the rise of tourism in Acapulco and its importance to the Mexican model of development. Tourism became important as early as the 1920s, received considerable public funding in the 1940s, but went into decline in the late 1960s in the face of environmental problems and growing indigenous resistance to land encroachments.

970 Ochoa Alvarez, Carmen. Immigration from the inside out: understanding Mexico's job(less) situation through the views of middle-class Mexicans. (*Lat. Am. Perspect.*, 35:1, Jan. 2008, p. 120–134)

Author examines the immigration issue by focusing on the views and experiences of those who chose not to migrate, in this case the middle class. Middle-class Mexicans tend to be employed in small businesses or self employed, often in the volatile service sector. Feeling strong cultural and social ties to Mexico, most middle-class Mexicans remain in Mexico rather than leaving in hopes of finding better opportunities in the US.

971 Ozler, S. Ilgu. Out of the plaza and into the office: social movement leaders in the PRD. (*Mex. Stud.*, 25:1, Winter 2009, p. 125–154)

Author uses the PRD (Party of the Democratic Revolution) as a case study in how social movement leaders adapt to organizational politics. Former social movement leaders comprise about one-third of PRD leadership. Despite problems with ideology and strategy, the former social-movement leaders believe that party membership has allowed them to better achieve their goals.

972 Padilla, Tanalís. From agraristas to guerrilleros: the Jaramillista Movement in Morelos. (*HAHR*, 87:2, May 2007, p. 255–292)

The author analyzes the agrarian movement of Rubén Jaramillo, which grew out of Zapatismo and was inspired by the policies of President Lázaro Cárdenas (1934–40). By 1959, Jaramillo's followers embraced a more militant approach, encouraged by the success of the Cuban Revolution and necessitated by the Mexican government's repression of their demands for an agrarian colony in western Morelos.

973 Padilla, Tanalís. Rural resistance in the land of Zapata: the Jaramillista Movement and the myth of the Pax Priísta, 1940–1962. Durham, N.C.: Duke Univ. Press, 2008. 285 p.: bibl., ill., index, map.

Well-documented "post revisionist study" (p. 14) of the resistance movement led by Rubén Jaramillo, who was murdered by government forces in 1962. The Jaramillistas fluctuated between armed resistance and political action. The movement helped to destroy the image of the "Pax Priísta," the postwar period of supposed development, modernization, and social stability. The movement suffered from its localized nature, its over-reliance on Jaramillo's leadership, and its emphasis on economic concessions.

974 Penyak, Lee M. and **Pilar García Fabregat.** El General Manuel D. Asúnsolo y su paso por la revolución mexicana. (*Rev. Hist. Am./México*, 136, 2005, p. 77–101)

Asúnsolo, who was a mine owner and Madero supporter, had military training which won him quick promotion to revolutionary general with the forces of the Figueroa brothers of Guerrero. Asúnsolo achieved passing fame as the general who captured Cuernavaca in May 1911, ahead of Zapata. Asúnsolo abandoned the Figueroa family to side with Zapata, with whom he fell out of favor. Asúnsolo misjudged the Revolution and his revolutionary alliances.

975 Pérez Arce, Francisco. El principio: 1968–1998, años de rebeldía. México: Ítaca, 2007. 203 p.: bibl. (Memorias del porvenir)

Author traces opposition movements—student, worker, guerrilla, popular—from Tlatelolco to the "civic rebellion" of the 1988 elections. Author sees the cumulative impact of the two decades as the beginning of the end of the PRI regime.

976 Pérez Montfort, Ricardo. Expresiones populares y estereotipos culturales en México, siglos XIX y XX: diez ensayos. México: CIESAS, 2007. 321 p.: bibl., ill.

These selections analyze the creation of "typical" images of Mexico in the context of the history of the 19th and 20th centuries. The author considers forms of entertainment, including dance, song, and celebrations, and well as images, such as the *china poblana* and the *jarocho.*

977 Poniatowska, Elena. Amanecer en el Zócalo: los 50 días que confrontaron a México. México: Planeta, 2007. 394 p., 24 p. of plates: ill.

This is a first-hand chronicle of the protest movement that surrounded the election of Felipe Calderón in 2006. The author participated in the protests in Mexico City on behalf of Andrés Manuel Lopez Obrador, the challenger. She details activities from July to September.

978 Ramírez Rancaño, Mario. El patriarca Pérez: la iglesia católica apostólica mexicana. México: UNAM, Instituto de Investigaciones Sociales, 2006. 388 p.: bibl.

Analysis of efforts by reform-minded priest with a checkered past, José Joaquín Pérez Budar, to establish a national Mexican Catholic Church with the support of President Calles and labor boss Luis Morones. Pérez Budar's movement enjoyed some success but rapidly declined after the 1929 agreement between the Mexican government and the Catholic Church.

979 Ramos Escobar, Norma. El trabajo y la vida de las maestras nuevoleonesas: un estudio histórico de finales del siglo XIX y principios del siglo XX. Monterrey, Mexico: Consejo para la Cultura y las Artes de Nuevo León, 2007. 249 p.: bibl., ill. (Investigación)

This study utilizes archives and oral histories to reconstruct the lives of female public school teachers. The author analyzes the evolution of females in the teaching profession, teachers' roles in post-revolutionary educational projects, and conditions of work. She also profiles two rural teachers in southern Nuevo León.

980 Rangel Treviño, Javier. Los "hijos del cielo" en el infierno: un reporte sobre el racismo hacia las comunidades chinas en México, 1880–1930. (*Foro Int./México*, 45:3, julio/sept. 2005, p. 409–444, bibl.)

This excellent study details the history of Mexico's dealings with Chinese immigrants during the Porfirian and revolutionary eras. The author challenges the usual view of anti-Chinese actions as motivated primarily by economic considerations.

Instead, Mexico's anti-Chinese sentiment resulted from a long history of racism, in which things "Western" were deemed superior, and in which the Chinese became a symbol of "the other."

981 Religión y sociedad en México durante el siglo XX. Coordinación de María Martha Pacheco. México: Instituto Nacional de Estudios Históricos de las Revoluciónes de México, 2007. 513 p.: bibl. (Col. Biblioteca INEHRM)

This collection focuses primarily on the Catholic Church, but also examines the Methodist, Mormon, and Protestant traditions in Mexico. The "daily practices" of these religious traditions, religious thought, and Church-state relations are among the themes explored.

Reyes de la Maza, Luis. El teatro en México durante la Revolución, 1911–1913. See item **2960.**

982 Ríos-Figueroa, Julio. Fragmentation of power and the emergence of an effective judiciary in Mexico, 1994–2002. (*Lat. Am. Polit. Soc.*, 49:1, Spring 2007, p. 31–57, bibl., tables)

Author starts with the 1994 judicial reforms that were designed to make the Mexican judiciary an equal partner in power with the legislative and executive branches of government. The subsequent political fragmentation of the executive and legislative branches (control by different political parties) creates the opportunity for a more powerful and active judicial branch of government.

983 Rivas Ontiveros, René. La izquierda estudiantil en la UNAM: organizaciones, movilizaciones y liderazgos (1958–1972). Prólogo de Sergio Zermeño. México: UNAM, Facultad de Estudios Superiores Aragón: Miguel Ángel Porrúa, 2007. 913 p.: bibl., index.

After defining some "fundamental concepts" and outlining the basic political, social, and economic context of the period, the author examines the 1958–1972 period when the leftist "tendency" prevailed at UNAM, replacing the earlier conservative and "oficialist" (pro-PRI) tendencies. Author maintains that the process of politicizing students and developing a leftist student

leadership began in the late 1950s rather than in the late 1960s, as suggested in many of the accounts of the student movement of 1968.

984 Rockwell, Elsie. Hacer escuela, hacer estado: la educación posrevolucionaria vista desde Tlaxcala. Zamora, Mexico: Colegio de Michoacán; México: CIESAS: Cinvestav-Sede Sur, Depto. de Investigaciones Educativas, 2007. 406 p.: bibl., ill., indexes. (Col. Investigaciones)

Author examines connection—or lack of it—between educational policy and state formation. The people of Tlaxcala were not always quick to embrace the new educational policies of the central government such as "the new Mexican school" and "socialist eductation." Author rejects the idea of an "educational revolution" carried out from the national capital (p. 23).

985 Rodríguez Kuri, Ariel. La proscripción del aura: arquitectura y política en la restauración de la catedral de México, 1967–1971. (*Hist. Mex./México*, 56:4, abril/junio 2007, p. 1309–1392)

In the aftermath of a 1967 fire that destroyed a section of the national cathedral, a "culture war" broke out, pitting "restorationists" (those wishing to restore the cathedral to its original Baroque form) against "modernists" (those wishing to remodel the cathedral so as to accentuate its spaciousness and to respond to the call for a more "open" church via Vatican II). The author examines the debate, which was won by the restorationists.

986 Romero de Solís, José Miguel. El aguijón del Espíritu: historia contemporánea de la Iglesia en México, 1892–1992. 2. ed. México: Instituto Mexicano de Doctrina Social Cristiana: El Colegio de Michoacán: Archivo Historico del Municipio de Colima: Univ. de Colima, 2006. 750 p.: bibl., index.

Second edition of work first published in 1994 by the Instituto Mexicano de Doctrina Social Cristiana.

987 Salmerón, Pedro. La división del norte: los hombres, las razones y la historia de un ejército del pueblo. México: Planeta, 2006. 529 p.: bibl., maps.

More than a standard military history of Villa's famed División del Norte, the author explores the composition of the division, the geographical connections of its brigades, and the grievances and demands that motivated its members. The author sees the division as the "most powerful, heterogeneous, and contradictory of the popular movements" (p. 13).

988 Salmerón Sanginés, Pedro. Lucha agraria y revolución en el oriente de Durango, 1900–1929. (*Hist. Mex./México*, 56:1, julio/sept. 2006, p. 117–173, bibl.)

This article details the fight for land in the district of Cuencamé, an area characterized by tremendous land concentration. Calixto Contreras was the central figure in this fight, leading local *magonistas, maderistas,* and *villistas.* The result was a significant change in Cuencamé's system of land tenure.

989 Samaniego López, Marco Antonio. Nacionalismo y revolución: los acontecimientos de 1911 en Baja California. Mexicali, Mexico: Instituto de Investigaciones Históricas, Univ. Autónoma de Baja California; Tijuana, Mexico: Centro Cultural Tijuana, 2008. 648 p.: bibl., map.

Author examines traditional views of whether those involved in the armed movement in Baja California in 1911 were revolutionaries or filibusters. Stresses the diversity of those involved in the fighting and the shifting or nonexistent political ideologies that influenced some of them. Many of the residents of Baja thought that they were resisting a filibustering effort.

990 Samaniego López, Marco Antonio. La revolución mexicana en Baja California: maderismo, magonismo, filibusterismo y la pequeña revuelta local. (*Hist. Mex./México*, 56:4, abril/junio 2007, p. 1201–1262, bibl.)

The author attempts to discover the true nature of the armed movement that emerged in northern Baja California in 1911. He outlines the broader issue of water rights in the Mexicali and Imperial Valleys, which shaped the actions of many insurgents, and examines the varied and sometimes contradictory interests of the factions that participated in the movement.

991 San Pedro López, Patricia. Desde el otro lado del río: la mirada histórica norteamericana sobre el conflicto rural mexicano. México: Univ. Autónoma Metropolitana, Unidad Azcapotzalco: Instituto Nacional de Antropología e Historia: Consejo Nacional para la Cultura y las Artes, 2008. 320 p.: bibl. (Col. Ensayos; 18)

Analysis of works by North American academics on peasant revolutions written between the decades of the 1960s and the 1980s. These academicians dominated quantitatively the historiography of Mexican rural conflict, with the writings reflecting a larger boom in Latin American Studies.

992 Savarino Roggero, Franco. Bajo el signo del *Littorio:* la comunidad italiana en México y el fascismo, 1924–1941. (*Rev. Mex. Sociol.*, 64:2, abril/junio 2002, p. 113–139, bibl.)

Analysis of the impact of the rise of fascism in Italy on the Italian community in Mexico. Fascism gave Italian-Mexicans a way to affirm their identity in the face of growing Mexican nationalism. Support for fascism came to be identified with patriotism but faced an increasingly hostile climate in Mexico from 1936 due to Italian intervention in Spain, Mussolini's ties to Hitler, and the anti-fascist position of the Cárdenas administration.

993 Scherer García, Julio and **Carlos Monsiváis.** Parte de guerra II: los rostros del 68. 2. ed. México: Aguilar: UNAM, 2002. 302 p.: ill., maps. (Nuevo siglo)

Revised edition of *Parte de guerra: Tlatelolco 1968* published in 1999 (see *HLAS 58:3508* and *HLAS 61:2033*). Emphasis here is on new photographic evidence and the correspondence of Gen. Marcelino García Barragán, minister of defense at the time.

994 Seminario Internacional La Experiencia Institucional en la Ciudad de México: Esfera Pública y Elites Intelectuales, 4th, Mexico City, 2002. Actores, espacios y debates en la historia de la esfera pública en la ciudad de México. Coordinación de Cristina Sacristán y Pablo Piccato. México: Instituto de Investigaciones Históricas: Instituto Mora, 2005. 283 p.: bibl., index, 1 map. (Historia política)

These eight works of cultural history are inspired by the work of Jurgen Habermas and his ideas of "public reason" and "communicative action." The authors investigate various 19th- and 20th-century topics, including public opinion and discourse about liberalism, honor, the medical profession, and mental illness.

995 Servín Massieu, Manuel. Tras las huellas de Urrutia: médico eminente o político represor? México: Plaza y Valdés Editores, 2005. 223 p.: bibl., ill., maps. (Historia)

A brief treatment of a physician who served as minister of gobernación under Victoriano Huerta, and who led efforts to eliminate Huerta's enemies. The author probes Urrutia's reputation for repression, which is posited against his reputation as an outstanding physician.

996 Sex in revolution: gender, politics, and power in modern Mexico. Edited by Jocelyn Olcott, Mary Kay Vaughan, and Gabriela Cano. Foreword by Carlos Monsiváis. Durham, N.C.: Duke Univ. Press, 2006. 320 p.: bibl., ill., index.

This is an important collection of essays that focuses on various forms of activism among women during the revolutionary era. The authors probe a variety of topics, including gender identities and body politics, changes in divorce and adoption policies, and efforts of women workers and political activists to assert themselves within the context of the Mexican Revolution.

997 Sigüenza Orozco, Salvador. Héroes y escuelas: la educación en la Sierra Norte de Oaxaca (1927–1972). México: Instituto Nacional de Antropología e Historia; Oaxaca, Mexico: Instituto Estatal de Educación Pública de Oaxaca, 2007. 316 p.: bibl., ill.

Examination of the role of public basic education as an homogenizing factor in the construction of a national identity. The area examined is a complex one of high illiteracy, ethnic diversity, isolated communities, and limited schools.

998 Simposio Diálogos entre la Historia Social y la Historia Cultural, Mexico City, 2004. Memorias. Coordinación de Gumersindo Vera Hernández et al. México:

CONACULTA-INAH, Escuela Nacional de Antropología e Historia, 2005. 570 p.: bibl., ill.

This series of largely theoretical essays seeks to employ the methods of social and cultural history. Topics are as disparate as the assassination of Álvaro Obregón, the Revolution and cultural nationalism, the Mexican Communist Party, armed movements in Michoacán during the second half of the 20th century, and religious expression among emigrants to the US. Approximately half of the essays deal with the 19th century; the rest with topics pertinent to the 20th century and contemporary Mexico.

999 Smith, Benjamin T. Anticlericalism, politics, and freemasonry in Mexico, 1920–1940. (Americas/Washington, 65:4, April 2009, p. 559–588)

This study utilizes archives from the Grand Lodge of Oaxaca to examine the reaction of Masonic lodges to revolutionary change. Mexico's lodges broadened their membership to include representatives of revolutionary groups, and they tended to embrace the state's anticlericalism, as well as its other revolutionary initiatives.

1000 Smith, Benjamin T. Defending our beautiful freedom: state formation and local autonomy in Oaxaca, 1930–1940. (Mex. Stud., 23:1, Winter 2007, p. 125–153)

Analysis of the 1936 election for governor in Oaxaca and the role played by President Cárdenas in the election. Cárdenas wanted to avoid the election of a governor with strong local ties as had been the case with the governor serving from 1928 to 1936. The president succeeded in imposing his candidate but later had to try to pacify the local interests by allowing greater choice in local and educational officials.

1001 Smith, Benjamin T. Inventing tradition at gunpoint: culture, caciquismo and state formation in the Región Mixe, Oaxaca, 1930–1959. (Bull. Lat. Am. Res., 27:2, April 2008, p. 215–234)

Excellent case study of the development and maintenance of a cacicazgo by Luis Rodríguez, who used a blend of both modern and traditional methods to gain and keep control. Rodríguez used the central government's own programs—ranging from indigenismo to promotion of basketball—to fend off outside interference while using traditional methods of intimidation and violence to maintain control within his region.

1002 Smith, Benjamin T. Pistoleros and popular movements: the politics of state formation in postrevolutionary Oaxaca. Lincoln: Univ. of Nebraska Press, 2009. 273 p.: bibl., ill., index, photos. (The Mexican experience)

After discussing the historiographical issues and methodological approaches involved, the author examines the differential impact of state-building efforts of the central government in the diverse state of Oaxaca down to 1952. A variety of interest groups ignored, bypassed, modified and opposed federal programs with violence a regular part of the political scene.

1003 Smith, Michael M. Andrés G. García: Venustiano Carranza's eyes, ears, and voice on the border. (*Mex. Stud.*, 23:2, Summer 2007, p. 355–386)

García provided important services to the Carranza cause as a combination of intelligence agent, consul, publicist, and contraband dealer along the border. García tried to promote good relations between the US government and Carranza and cooperated with US officials in the pursuit of Pancho Villa.

1004 Smith, Stephanie J. Gender and the Mexican Revolution: Yucatán women and the realities of patriarchy. Chapel Hill, N.C.: Univ. of North Carolina Press, 2009. 257 p.: bibl., index, map.

Focusing on issues such as divorce and prostitution, the author demonstrates both women's agency and the persistence of restrictive social norms. The volume also includes a careful consideration of Maya women and the factor of ethnicity in the context of attempts of state authorities to modernize society. This is an important challenge to the image of a "radical" Yucatan that prevails in the historiography.

1005 Solis, Yves. Divorcio a la italiana: la ruptura entre el delegado apostólico de los Estados Unidos y el delegado apostólico de México durante la segunda Cristiada. (*Rev. Humanid./Monterrey*, 24, 2008, p. 121–176, bibl.)

Examination of the antagonistic relationship between the apostolic delegate for the US, Amleto Cicognani, and the apostolic delegate for Mexico, Leopoldo Ruiz y Flores, from 1933 to 1937. The two disagreed over how to deal with the religious crisis in Mexico. The disagreement eventually led to the removal of Leopoldo Ruiz y Flores. Based on documents from the Secret Vatican Archive.

1006 Sosenski, Susana. Diversiones malsanas: el cine y la infancia en la ciudad de México en la década de 1920. (*Secuencia/México*, 66, sept./dic. 2006, p. 37–64, bibl.)

This article examines the attraction of the cinema for Mexican children and adolescents, and surveys the debate that ensued about proper entertainment for Mexico's youth. The 1920s witnessed an increase in cinema attendance among Mexican youth, and generated the beginning of a movement to provide films that would be both age-appropriate and didactic.

1007 Stahler-Sholk, Richard. Resisting neoliberal homogenization: the Zapatista Autonomy Movement. (*Lat. Am. Perspect.*, 34:2, March 2007, p. 48–63)

Author sees three dilemmas influencing the sustainability of the Zapatista movement: territorially based autonomy, resource allocation, and multiculturalism. The movement is in its fourth phase which began in August 2003 with the creation of the Juntas de Buen Gobierno.

1008 Suárez Plata, Pilar. Huellas, memoria y sensibilidad: los hijos de los exiliados españoles en Puebla. Puebla, Mexico: Instituto de Ciencias Sociales y Humanidades, Benemérita Univ. Autónoma de Puebla, 2006. 267 p.: bibl., ill.

Insight into the lives of Spanish Republican exiles and their children in Puebla, featuring extensive interviews with the children. Many of the exiles came to Puebla as their second stop in Mexico. The exiles found themselves in a mostly conservative society that had mistaken views about them.

1009 Suarez-Potts, William J. The Mexican Supreme Court and the *Juntas de Conciliación y Arbitraje*, 1917–1924: the judicialisation of labour relations after the Revolution. (*J. Lat. Am. Stud.*, 41:4, Nov. 2009, p. 723–755)

The author examines the process by which Mexico's highest court reversed its opinion about the authority of state labor boards created in the Constitution of 1917. Between 1917 and 1924, changes in the makeup of the court, as well as the court's shifting opinions about adjudication, resulted in an endorsement of the power of the labor boards.

1010 Swords, Alicia C.S. Neo-Zapatista network politics: transforming democracy and development. (*Lat. Am. Perspect.*, 34:2, March 2007, p. 78–93)

Case studies of three organizations that support Zapatista demands but are not recognized by the Zapatistas as part of their bases of support. The three organizations include a coffee producers' network, an indigenous women's collective, and a pro-democracy organization run by a small staff of mostly mestizo urban dwellers.

1011 Swords, Alicia C.S. and Ronald L. Mize. Beyond tourist gazes and performances: U.S. consumption of land and labor in Puerto Rican and Mexican destinations. (*Lat. Am. Perspect.*, 35:3, May 2008, p. 53–69)

Comparative study of the impact of US tourism on land and labor in Puerto Rico and Mexico. Authors conclude that US tourism has negatively affected both areas due to the "fundamentally opposed interests" (p. 54) of laborers, tourists, and multinational companies.

1012 Taylor Hansen, Lawrence Douglas. Los orígenes de la Fuerza Aérea Mexicana, 1913–1915. (*Hist. Mex./México*, 56:1, julio/sept. 2006, p. 175–230, bibl.)

This is a well-researched exploration of the use of aviation by the Constitutionalist forces. The successful use of airplanes for reconnaissance, and the psychological advantage provided by aircraft, encouraged Venustiano Carranza to establish Mexico's first department of aviation.

1013 True stories of crime in modern Mexico. Compiled by Robert Buffington and Pablo Piccato. Albuquerque, N.M.: Univ. of New Mexico Press, 2009. 276 p.: bibl., ill., index. (Dialogos series)

Authors use eight essays—mostly about the 20th century—to illustrate changes in society and gender roles. Excellent for classroom use and highly provocative.

1014 Uhthoff López, Luz María. El Departamento de Contraloría y la búsqueda del control del presupuesto en México, 1917–1932: una aproximación. (*Secuencia/México*, 74, mayo/agosto 2009, p. 81–101, bibl.)

As part of the centralization process, post-revolutionary governments faced the problem of reorganizing the public treasury. Part of this reorganization involved the establishment of the Treasury Inspector's Office in 1917 to supervise collection of taxes and the handling of public resources. The Office came into conflict with the Ministry of the Treasury, resulting in the Office's dissolution and the absorption of its functions by the Treasury in 1934.

1015 Uhthoff López, Luz María. Hacia la modernización de la política presupuestaria en México: los impuestos exteriores e interiores, 1870–1930. (*Signos Hist.*, 18, julio/dic. 2007, p. 59–78, tables)

Analysis of the incomes of the federal government with an emphasis on the reforms of Matías Romero in the 1870s and Alberto Pani in the 1920s. Concern about the dependency on taxes on external commerce led to a long-term trend from 1870 to 1918 to reduce those taxes in favor of greater emphasis on internal taxes. Pani's major reform was the introduction of an income tax in 1924.

1016 Valadés, José C. La revolución y los revolucionarios. Tomo 2, parte 1, La revolución constitucionalista. Artículos, entrevistas y reportajes de José C. Valadés. México: Instituto Nacional de Estudios Históricos de las Revolucónes de México, 2007. 1 v.: bibl. (Memorias y testimonios)

One installment in three-volume, seven-part work. The work is a collection of articles and interviews first published in the newspapers *La Opinión* (Los Angeles) and *La Prensa* (San Antonio) by Valadés, a well-known journalist and historian. This volume deals with the Constitutionalist phase of the Revolution (1913–17) and includes diverse figures such as Joaquín Amaro, Jesús Carranza, and Francisco Murguía.

1017 Valdéz Gardea, Gloria Ciria. Current trends in Mexican migration. (*J. Southwest*, 51:4, Winter 2009, p. 563–583)

Analysis of migration trends indicates increasing diversity in migrant populations, both in terms of gender and socioeconomic background. More migrants are coming from nontraditional areas in Mexico such as Veracruz and are crossing at different points due to tighter security at traditional crossing-points. Emphasis on Arizona-Sonora border area.

1018 Velázquez Flores, Rafael. La política exterior de México durante la Segunda Guerra Mundial. Oaxaca, Mexico: Univ. del Mar; México: Plaza y Valdés Editores, 2007. 205 p.: bibl., index.

Analysis of the factors which determined Mexico's foreign policy during WWII. The author sees a combination of internal factors (political, social, and economic stability) combining with external factors (the US promotion of hemispheric solidarity) to give Mexico an unprecedented position in international negotiations.

1019 Weis, Robert. Immigrant entrepreneurs, bread, and class negotiations in postrevolutionary Mexico City. (*Mex. Stud.*, 25:1, Winter 2009, p. 71–100)

Author refutes traditional view that Spanish bakery owners suffered during the 1920s and 1930s. Despite the widespread Hispanophobia, many Spanish bakery owners were able to maintain both their social and economic positions by keeping the population fed and the work force in line. For the government's part, it was more concerned with the interests of the owners and the consumers than with the interests of the workers.

1020 Welsome, Eileen. The general and the jaguar: Pershing's hunt for Pancho Villa: a true story of revolution and revenge. New York, N.Y.: Little, Brown and Co., 2006. 403 p., 16 p. of plates: bibl., ill., index, maps.

A Pulitzer Prize-winning journalist provides a detailed account of the events leading to the attack on Pancho Villa in Columbus, N.M., the attack itself, the punitive expedition, and the little-examined aftermath of the raid.

1021 Wilson, Tamar Diana. Economic and social impacts of tourism in Mexico. (*Lat. Am. Perspect.*, 35:3, May 2008, p. 37–52)

Examination of the social and economic effects of state-led tourism. Author focuses on five resort areas connected with the Fondo Nacional de Fomento al Turismo (FONATUR). The federal government was relatively successful in achieving its tourism goals of earning foreign exchange, creating employment, and redirecting internal migration. On the negative side, Mexico increased its dependency on foreign loans, foreign capital, and foreign patronage.

1022 Work, David K. Enforcing neutrality: the Tenth U.S. Cavalry on the Mexican Border, 1913–1919. (*West. Hist. Q.*, 40:2, Summer 2009, p. 179–200)

Author chronicles the activities of an African-American cavalry regiment patrolling the border between Nogales and Yuma. The Tenth was poorly trained and supplied and had served the previous three years in Vermont. Action picked up after the removal of restrictions on military crossings of the border in 1916, but the Tenth's main accomplishment was to provide a reassuring presence for fearful Americans in border towns.

1023 Yankelevich, Pablo. Explotadores, truhanes, agitadores y negros, deportaciones y restricciones a estadounidenses en el México revolucionario. (*Hist. Mex./ México*, 57:4, abril/junio 2008, p. 1155–1199, bibl.)

The author examines the application of anti-foreign nationalism to US Americans from the outbreak of the Revolution to approximately 1930. Mexican governments expelled numerous Americans during the revolutionary era, accusing some of political meddling, others of vice, and still others of threatening to bring an unwelcome "negro" element into the country.

CENTRAL AMERICA

PETER SZOK, Associate Professor of History, Texas Christian University
STEPHEN WEBRE, W.Y. Thompson Endowed Professor of History, Louisiana Tech University

SCHOLARLY PRODUCTION IN CENTRAL AMERICAN HISTORY continues to increase in quality and quantity. Costa Rica is still home to the most advanced and sophisticated community of historians, but increased professionalism is evident throughout the isthmus, as reflected in the continuing vitality of the biennial Central American Historical Congresses. At the most recent congress, held in Managua in July, 2010, the program included more than 340 papers.

The field of colonial history recently celebrated the reappearance of two foundational works, a new edition of MacLeod's classic *Spanish Central America* (item **1055**) and the first English translation of Martínez Peláez's *La patria del criollo* (item **1058**). With her new studies on the development of colonial medicine (items **1049** and **1050**) and the subversive qualities of chocolate (item **1048**), Martha Few remains one of the most innovative historians working in the field. Frequently neglected by colonial specialists, Nicaragua is the subject of important new works by Tous Mata (item **1069**) and Werner (item **1071**). The African experience both on the Atlantic coast and in the interior continues to draw interest, as seen in works by Euraque (item **1033**), Claudia García (item **1051**), Pike (item **1060**), and Tompson (item **1067**). New works by Bertrand (item **1045**), Gutiérrez Cruz (item **1052**), and Patch (item **1059**) continue to explore the importance of family and other networks for understanding colonial society. Finally, although ongoing bicentennial observances of Latin American independence have yet to show much impact on Central American historiography, there are welcome new works by Dym (item **1047**) and Pollack (item **1061**).

For the modern period, Ana Patricia Rodríguez (item **1135**) and Molina Jiménez (see *HLAS 64:922*) deliberately attempt a transnational focus, but most work still focuses on individual countries. For Guatemala, for example, the pervasive violence of the last half century continues to attract researchers, as seen in works by Prudencio García (item **1104**), Luján Muñoz (see *HLAS 64:916*), and Santos (item **1143**). A two-volume rightist retelling of Guatemala's 20th-century history by Argentine sociologist Sabino (items **1139** and **1140**) has provoked much controversy and is the object of a critical assault by Cambranes (item **1086**). Meanwhile, El Salvador's own history of violence is also represented. In particular, the bloody 1932 wave of repressive violence known as the *Matanza* and its place in Salvadoran memory are the subjects of new studies by Ching, López Bernal, and Tilley (item **1089**); Gould and Lauria-Santiago (item **1106**); Lindo-Fuentes (item **1114**); and Lindo-Fuentes, Ching, and Lara-Martínez (item **1115**).

For scholars of Nicaraguan history, the figures of Augusto C. Sandino and the later revolutionary movement bearing his name remain central. On Sandino himself, recent new contributions include those of Bendaña (item **1080**) and Schroeder (item **1144**), whose new website featuring Sandino documents has great promise (item **1142**). The overthrow of Somoza rule, the rise to power of the Sandinista Front, and the relevance of these events for the present are explored, often quite critically, in studies by Barbosa (item **1078**), Cortés Domínguez (item **1092**), Carlos Ernesto García (item **1103**), Kinzer (item **1112**), Ortega Saavedra (item **1128**), Reyes (item **1133**), and Wingartz Plata (item **1154**).

Once regarded as unfashionable in Costa Rica, political history is enjoying a revival, and is, as always, seeking clues to the origins of the country's democratic and welfarist traditions. Particularly important is a series of works by Molina Jiménez, including three on the role of the country's Communist Party (items **1119, 1121**, and **1122**). Even so, Costa Rican scholars have not abandoned their well-established interest in cultural history. Solano examines local festivals, or *turnos* (item **1098**), while Fumero focuses on urbanization, the print media, and the emergence of mass culture (item **1101**). Palmer's work on the professionalization of medicine is a major contribution (item **1039**), while Flores González (item **1100**) and Gamboa Barboza (item **1102**) both break new ground by exploiting the records of psychiatric institutions.

Finally, in Panama, the 100th anniversary of independence from Colombia inspired the magnificent multi-volume *Historia general de Panamá* (items **1034**). There are also useful new biographies of Panamanian politicians by Rivera Forero (item **1134**) and Salamín C. (item **1141**). McGuinness (item **1117**) examines the impact of the California gold rush and the construction of the Panama railroad, while the story of the building of the Panama Canal itself remains in vogue, as evidenced by new works by Greene (item **1107**), Pérez (item **1129**), and Sutter (item **1148**), all of which represent refreshing departures from previous heroic accounts that privileged the engineering and public health achievements of North American elites.

GENERAL

1024 Araúz, Celestino Andrés; Argelia Tello Burgos; and Alfredo Figueroa Navarro. Manual de historia de Panamá. Bethania, Panamá: Litho Editorial Chen, 2006. 2 v., 972 p.: bibl., ill., maps.

Useful synthesis by recognized national historians. Extensive bibliographies.

1025 Benavides Barquero, Manuel. Relación entre estado e iglesia en Costa Rica a través de su historia. (*Rev. Hist. Am./ México*, 136, 2005, p. 103–128, bibl.)

Examination of Costa Rica's confessional state. Traces roots back to colonial period and argues that close Church-state ties survived even the Liberal era and reflect the cultural importance of Catholicism.

1026 Braulio Carrillo. t. 3, Episodios de su vida pública y privada. Edición de José Hilario Villalobos Rodríguez y Luz Alba Chacón de Umaña. San José: [s.n.], 2006. 1 v.: bibl., ill.

Biographical study of Braulio Carrillo (1800–45), from his birth in Cartago to his assassination in El Salvador. Focuses on the Costa Rican statesman's personal life, leaving politics to second volume in series.

1027 Cabrera, Roberto P. Tierra y ganadería en Guanacaste. Cartago, Costa Rica: Editorial Tecnológica de Costa Rica, 2007. 857 p.: bibl., ill., maps.

Historical and anthropological study of Guanacaste's cattle industry from the 18th century to 1990s. Relies heavily on oral history and includes massive transcript of interviews with cattleman Virgilio Angulo Reyes (1899–1990).

1028 Cambranes, J.C. 500 años de lucha por la tierra: estudios sobre propiedad rural y reforma agraria en Guatemala = Ruch'ojinem qalewal. Guatemala: CHOLSAMAJ, 2004. 430 p.: bibl. (Serie Entre líneas)

Guatemala's history seen through centuries-long struggle for land. Republication with corrections of Cambranes's own chapters originally published in 1992 multi-author volume with similar title (see *HLAS 55:4656*). Author's transition since end of Cold War from Marxism to indigenism requires little more than new editorial packaging, nor has much changed in countryside since original version appeared.

1029 Casaús Arzú, Marta Elena. La genealogía del racismo y del discurso racial en las élites de poder en Guatemala, siglos

XIX y XX]. (*Cuad. Am./México*, 117:3, julio/ sept. 2006, p. 85–126, maps)

Racism is seen as a constant theme in Guatemalan history, manifesting itself down to the present in discriminatory and even genocidal behavior. Good introduction to ideological dimension of ethnic relations.

1030 Casaús Arzú, Marta Elena. Guatemala: linaje y racismo. 3. ed., rev. y ampliada. Guatemala: F&G Editores, 2007. 339 p.: bibl, ill., index.

Revised and expanded edition of influential work, first published in 1992 (*HLAS 54:1624*).

1031 The Costa Rica reader: history, culture, politics. Edited by Steven Paul Palmer and Iván Jiménez Molina. Durham, N.C.: Duke Univ. Press, 2004. 383 p.: bibl., ill., index, map (The Latin America readers)

Collection of primary documents representing a variety of social sectors and historical periods, ranging from colony to recent years. Excellent text for advanced undergraduate classes. Informative essays contextualize documents.

1032 Esgueva Gómez, Antonio. Las fronteras de Nicaragua y Costa Rica en los documentos históricos. Managua: IHNCA-UCA, 2007. 464 p.: bibl., maps.

Comprehensive collection of documents related to territorial limits between Nicaragua and Costa Rica. Selections stretch from conquest to 1900, when borders were definitively established by the Alexander Commission.

1033 Euraque, Darío A. Free *pardos* and mulattoes vanquish indians: cultural civility as conquest and modernity in Honduras. (*in* Beyond slavery: the multilayered legacy of Africans in Latin America and the Caribbean. Edited by Darién J. Davis. Lanham, Md.: Rowman & Littlefield Publishers, Inc., 2007, p. 81–105, table)

Focusing on experience of heavily pardo Olanchito in Yoro department, argues for regionally based history of mestizaje as ideological process. Beginning in 18th century and continuing to present, racialized discourse emerged that assimilated Hondurans of African descent to broader mestizo identity, excluding blackness from national identity by restricting it to Atlantic Coast immigrant populations, such as Garifuna.

1034 Historia general de Panamá. v. 1, t. 1, Las sociedades originarias. v. 1, t. 2, El orden colonial. v. 2, El siglo XIX. v. 3, t. 1, El siglo XX. v. 3, t. 2, El siglo XX. Dirección de Alfredo Castillero Calvo. Panamá: Comité Nacional del Centenario de la República, 2004. 3 v. in 5: bibl., ill., maps.

Monumental synthesis overseen by Panama's most distinguished living historian, who personally wrote the vast majority of the chapters on the colonial period. Detailed analyses and broad thematic reach set a high standard for similar projects elsewhere.

1035 Kühl Aráuz, Eddy. Nicaragua: historia de inmigrantes. Managua: Editorial HISPAMER, 2007. 426 p.: bibl., ill., index, 1 map.

Descriptive account of immigration from colonial times to early 20th century. Especially strong on the Liberal period with dozens of biographies of European immigrants

1036 Lovell, W. George and **Christopher H. Lutz.** Historia sin máscara: vida y obra de Severo Martínez Peláez. Guatemala: Centro de Estudios Urbanos y Regionales (CEUR), Univ. de San Carlos, 2009. 63 p.

Brief, informative biography of central figure in recent Guatemalan historiography, published to coincide with appearance of first English edition of his best-known work, *La patria del criollo* (see item **1058**).

1037 Marín Hernández, Juan José. La tierra del pecado, entre la quimera y el anhelo: historia de la prostitución en Costa Rica, 1750–2005. San José: Librería Alma Mater: Sociedad Nueva Cultura, 2006. 181 p.: bibl., ill.

History of prostitution, from colonial times to present, directed toward general public. Seeks to explain phenomenon through broad examination of its economic, cultural, social, commercial, and moral context.

1038 Mauleón Isla, Mercedes. La población de Nicaragua, 1748–1867: de la época final de la colonia hasta las primeras décadas del período independiente. Managua: Fundación Uno, 2008. 267 p.: ill.

Impressive collection of population data, accompanied by informative commentary on meaning and nature of sources. Excellent reference and starting point for social and demographic studies.

1039 Palmer, Steven Paul. From popular medicine to medical populism: doctors, healers, and public power in Costa Rica, 1800–1940. Durham, N.C.: Duke Univ. Press, 2003. 329 p.: bibl., ill., index.

Impressive work on history of Costa Rican medicine from late colonial period to mid-20th century. Demonstrates that heterogeneous forms of popular medicine remained vital to country's health care system, even as it became more professionalized and hierarchical.

1040 Peláez Almengor, Oscar Guillermo. La ciudad ilustrada. [Guatemala]: Universidad de San Carlos de Guatemala, Centro de Estudios Urbanos y Regionales, 2008. 235 p.: bibl., ill. (some col.), maps.

Collection of three studies on the history of Guatemala City from the destruction of Antigua in 1773 to the early national period. Topics covered are the role of the Enlightenment and the Bourbon Reforms in determining the establishment of the new city, organization and supervision of the city's food supply, and impressions of foreign visitors.

1041 Pobreza e historia en Costa Rica: determinantes estructurales y representantes sociales del siglo XVII a 1950. Edición de Ronny J. Viales Hurtado. San José: Editorial de la Univ. de Costa Rica: Centro de Investigaciones Históricas de América Central: Posgrado Centroamericano en Historia, Univ. de Costa Rica, 2005. 328 p.: bibl., ill. (Col. Nueva historia)

Collection of papers from a 2003 symposium. Poverty in Costa Rica is seen not as a recent aberration attributable to neoliberal economic policies, but rather as an enduring phenomenon with deep historical roots. Essays cover both multiple material dimensions of poverty and its place in systems of social representation.

1042 Seminario "Entre Dos Siglos" Alajuela, Costa Rica, 2002. Entre dos siglos: la investigación histórica costarricense, 1992–2002. Edición de Iván Molina Jiménez, Francisco José Enríquez Solano y José Manuel Cerdas Albertazzi. Alajuela, Costa Rica: Museo Histórico Cultural Juan Santamaría, 2003. 336 p.: bibl., ill.

Papers delivered at 2002 conference on the development of Costa Rican historiography between 1992 and 2002. Essays cover colonial and modern periods and include discussions of social, economic, political, and ethnic history, as well as archeology, gender, and regional and local perspectives.

1043 Tierra ardiente: el occidente de Nicaragua a través de su historia. Coordinación de Jilma Romero. Managua: Departamento de Historia de la Univ. Nacional Autónoma de Nicaragua (UNAN-Nicaragua), 2005. 260 p.: bibl., ill., maps (some col.)

Collaborative and multidisciplinary text tracing León and Chinandega's history from prehispanic times to the present. Intended for use in primary and secondary schools. Part of series devoted to country's various regions.

1044 White, Christopher M. The history of El Salvador. Westport, Conn.: Greenwood Press, 2009. 147 p.: bibl., index, map. (The Greenwood histories of the modern nations, 1096–2905)

Straightforward history of El Salvador from prehispanic times to the present. Includes informative chapter on "El Salvador today" and extensive bibliographic essay.

COLONIAL

1045 Bertrand, Michel. Poder, negocios y familia en Guatemala a principios del siglo XIX. (*Hist. Mex./México*, 56:3, enero/marzo 2007, p. 863–917, bibl.)

Study of Juan Bautista Yrizarri and his efforts to maintain trade privileges in the wake of the 1799 destitution of José Domás y Valle as captain general. Case reveals that family loyalties divided the elite but so too did professional, ideological, and other more "modern" concerns.

1046 Black, Nancy Johnson. Los Mercedarios y la evangelización de los Lencas en Santa Bárbara de Tencoa, Honduras. (*Yaxkin/Tegucigalpa*, 24:2, 2008, p. 9–27, map, photo)

Brief sketch of missionary activities from arrival of Spanish to middle of 17th century. Summarizes points made in greater detail in author's book-length work, published in English in 1995 (see *HLAS 58:1627*). Important because of scarcity of work on this topic for Honduras.

1047 Dym, Jordana. "Our pueblos, fractions with no central unity": municipal sovereignty in Central America, 1801–1821. (*HAHR*, 86:3, Aug. 2006, p. 431–466)

Between 1801 and 1821, scholastic conceptions and introduction of constitutional monarchy served to revive municipal councils and divide Central America on eve of independence. Deemphasizing ideological and regional divisions, argues that municipal sovereignty was important factor contributing to instability after independence.

1048 Few, Martha. Chocolate, sex, and disorderly women in late-seventeenth- and early-eighteenth-century Guatemala. (*Ethnohistory/Columbus*, 52:4, Fall 2005, p. 673–687, bibl.)

Based largely on Inquisition records, innovative study examines chocolate's ambiguous place in colonial society. Popular and widely accessible, consumer product also had threatening gendered associations, including witchcraft, poisoning, and disorderly conduct in general.

1049 Few, Martha. Medical *mestizaje* and the politics of pregnancy in colonial Guatemala, 1660–1730. (*in* Science in the Spanish and Portuguese empires, 1500–1800. Edited by Daniela Bleichmar et al. Stanford, Calif.: Stanford University Press, 2008, p. 132–146)

Based on recorded cases of problem pregnancies, author proposes concept of "medical mestizaje," in which Mesoamerican and European traditions of explaining and curing illnesses competed, but also influenced one another. Also suggests future directions for exploring gendered implications of authority claims in various realms of health and healing.

1050 Few, Martha. "That monster of nature": gender, sexuality, and the medicalization of a "hermaphrodite" in late colonial Guatemala. (*Ethnohistory/Columbus*, 54:1, Winter 2007, p. 159–176)

Analysis of prominent physician Narciso Esparragosa's report in celebrated Juana Aguilar case. Focuses on Enlightenment values, emergence of professional medical authority, and evolving understandings of sexual identity and behavior.

1051 García, Claudia. Ambivalencia de las representaciones coloniales: líderes indios y zambos de la Costa de Mosquitos a fines del siglo XVIII. (*Rev. Indias*, 67:241, sept./dic. 2007, p. 673–694, bibl.)

Ethnic, political, and economic organization of the Mosquito kingdom from its emergence in the 17th century, with extensive consideration of its relationship to both British and Spanish colonial empires. Special attention to reasons for Spain's inability to establish effective dominion on the Honduran and Nicaraguan coasts even when Britain was willing to step aside and Mosquito authorities were receptive to new order.

1052 Gutiérrez Cruz, Sergio Nicolás. Casa, crisol y altar: de la hidalguía vasconavarra a la hacienda chiapaneca: los Esponda y Olaechea, 1731–1821. Tuxtla Gutiérrez, Mexico: Univ. de Ciencias y Artes de Chiapas, 2009. 386 p.: bibl., ill., index, maps. (Col. Selva Negra)

Social and economic history of 18th-century Chiapas as reflected in experience of single family of aristocratic Basque immigrants. Thoroughly documented.

1053 Luján Muñoz, Jorge. Nueva antología de artículos de historia del arte, arquitectura y urbanismo. Guatemala: El Autor, 2009. 269 p.: bibl., ill., index.

Valuable collection of studies by Guatemala's most distinguished living historian, some previously unpublished, others available only in hard-to-find versions. Topics covered include Central America's earliest town foundations, Guatemala's cathedrals, Baroque design elements (see item **1054**, a similar work by author's late brother), silverwork, engraving, altarpieces and ephemeral architecture, social and economic history of the building trades, and the impact of Enlightenment ideas on late 18th-century urban planning.

1054 Luján Muñoz, Luis. La pilastra abalaustrada serliana en el Reino de Guatemala, 1730–1790. Guatemala: Editorial Universitaria, 2007. 183 p.: bibl., ill. (Col. Monografías)

Focusing on a single decorative element, author probes both the Baroque esthetic and the social history of 18th-century Guatemala.

1055 MacLeod, Murdo J. Spanish Central America: a socioeconomic history, 1520–1720. With a new introduction. 1st Univ. of Texas Press ed. Austin: Univ. of Texas Press: Teresa Lozano Long Institute of Latin American Studies, 2008. 554 p.: bibl., ill., index, maps (LLILAS special publications)

Welcome reprinting of classic work, originally noted in *HLAS 36:2186*. Author's new introduction provides valuable overview of historiographical developments in field since book first appeared in 1973.

1056 Marín Araya, Giselle. La población de Bocas del Toro y la Comarca Ngöbe-Buglé hasta inicios del siglo XIX. (*Anu. Estud. Centroam.*, 30:1/2, 2004, p. 119–162, map, table)

Substantial study of western Panama's Caribbean coastal region. In contrast with existing accounts that pay little attention to region prior to arrival of Afro-Caribbeans and mestizos from interior in early 19th century, author highlights earlier protagonism of native peoples, along with region's strategic importance in colonial period as node in Caribbean trade network.

1057 Martínez, Mario Felipe. Temas históricos inéditos de Honduras. Tegucigalpa: Fundación para el Museo del Hombre Hondureño, 2009. 107 p. (Col. Centro histórico; 4)

Eclectic assemblage of short pieces focusing mostly on colonial topics, among them origins of Tegucigalpa, transatlantic travels in 16th century, colonial education, militia units, early history of silver mining, and a 1774 earthquake in the western district of Santa Rosa de Copán. Abundant references to primary documents from Spanish and Central American archives.

1058 Martínez Peláez, Severo. La patria del criollo: an interpretation of colonial Guatemala. Translated by Susan M. Neve and W. George Lovell. Edited and introduced by W. George Lovell and Christopher H. Lutz. Durham, N.C.: Duke Univ. Press, 2009. 330 p.: bibl., index, map.

Long-awaited English translation of classic work, first published in Spanish in 1970. Abridged but undiminished. For original, see *HLAS 34:1918*.

1059 Patch, Robert W. Cura y empresario: los préstamos financieros de Mateo Cornejo y la producción de añil en El Salvador, 1764–1780. (*Mesoamérica/Antigua*, 27:48, 2006, p. 47–67, map, tables)

Analysis of money-lending activities of parish priest of San Vicente, business partner of famed Guatemala merchant Juan Fermín de Aycinena. Major indigo grower in his own right, credit extended by Cornejo played important role in financing dye industry's expansion during 18th-century export boom.

1060 Pike, Ruth. Black rebels: The cimarrons of sixteenth-century Panama. (*Americas/Washington*, 64:2, Oct. 2007, p. 243–266)

Rise and fall of independent Maroon communities, with attention to Spanish political and military response. Perceived threats to colonial order included alliances with foreign pirates, notably Sir Francis Drake. Engaging narrative based chiefly on printed sources.

1061 Pollack, Aaron. Levantamiento k'iche en Totonicapán, 1820: los lugares de las políticas subalternas. Ciudad de Guatemala: Instituto AVANCSO, 2008. 252 p.: bibl., ill., maps. (Autores invitados; 18)

New interpretation of frequently discussed Independence-era episode stresses importance of understanding K'iche' political agency in terms of historically specific facts of geography, mobility, internal community factionalism, and external contacts and influences, all seen in context of a revolutionary moment that made what occurred in Totonicapán in 1820 qualitatively different than earlier Indian revolts.

1062 Pompejano, Daniele. Popoyá-Petapa: historia de un poblado maya, siglos XVI–XIX. Ciudad de Guatemala: Editorial Universitaria, Univ. de San Carlos de Guatemala, 2009. 379 p.: bibl., ill., maps. (Col. Monografías/Editorial Universitaria, Univ. de San Carlos de Guatemala)

Extensively documented community study focuses on complexity of social and ethnic relations in colonial period. Suggestive conclusions regarding local impact of Bourbon Reforms and roots of violent resistance in early republican period.

1063 *Revista de Historia,* 57/58, 2008. Univ. Nacional: Heredia, Costa Rica. Special number of respected Costa Rican journal dedicated to memory of colonial history specialist Claudia Quirós Vargas (1931–2006). Contributors include Elizet Payne Iglesias on Quirós' legacy; Christophe Belaubre on relocation of Guatemala City, 1773–1779; Carmela Velázquez Bonilla on cathedral chapter of León, Nicaragua; Eduardo Madrigal Muñoz on Costa Rican elites; Madrigal Muñoz and María Clara Vargas Cullell on colonial music in Costa Rica; and María de los Angeles Acuña León on slave women in 18th-century Costa Rica.

1064 **Sacor Q., Hugo Fidel.** El Cacao: producción y comercio durante las épocas prehispánica e hispánica en Guatemala. (*Antropol. Hist. Guatem.,* 3:6, 2007, p. 97–125, bibl., ill., photo, tables)
  Broader in scope than title suggests, synthetic overview of prehispanic and colonial economies, with some special attention to cacao. Based largely on familiar secondary sources.

1065 **Santana Pérez, Juan Manuel** and **José Antonio Sánchez Suárez.** Repoblación de Costa de Mosquitos en el último cuarto del siglo XVIII. (*Rev. Indias,* 67:241, sept./dic. 2007, p. 695–712, bibl., graphs, map, tables)
  Against backdrop of war with Great Britain, examines Spanish efforts under Charles III to repopulate Mosquito Coast with Spanish families, noting problems and hardships that led to failure.

1066 **Solórzano, Juan Carlos** and **Claudia Quirós Vargas.** Costa Rica en el siglo XVI: descubrimiento, exploración y conquista. San José: Editorial de la Universidad de Costa Rica, 2006. 266 p.: bibl., maps (some col.) (Col. Historia de Costa Rica; 10)
  Sophisticated synthesis appropriate for scholarly audience, but accessible to general readers as well. Focus is on exploration, conquest, and early settlement.

1067 **Tompson, Doug.** Refugiados libertos y esclavos asalariados: entre esclavitud y libertad en la costa atlántica de Honduras, ca. 1800. (*Mesoamérica/Antigua,* 29:50, 2008, p. 96–111, bibl., map)

Empasizes the diversity of Afro-Honduran experience on Caribbean coast in late colonial period. Because of chronic labor shortages, escaped slaves from British islands in Caribbean received their freedom as an incentive to remain and work, while for their services, royal slaves at the fortress at Omoa received wages at the prevailing rate.

1068 **Tous Mata, Meritxell.** Caciques y cabildos: organización socio-política de los pueblos de indios en la alcaldía mayor de Sonsonate, s. XVI. (*Rev. Indias,* 69:247, sept./dic. 2009, p. 63–82, bibl.)
  Imposition of Castilian model of municipal government provided sufficient autonomy for native elites of western El Salvador to preserve essential components of prehispanic structures of authority, hierarchy, and even land tenure.

1069 **Tous Mata, Meritxell.** De protagonistas a desaparecidos: las sociedades indígenas de la Gran Nicoya, siglos XIV a XVII. Managua: Lea Grupo Editorial, 2008. 608 p.: bibl., ill., maps.
  First-rate account of origins of colonial society in Gran Nicoya (Pacific coastal Nicaragua and Nicoya peninsula). Detailed treatment of preconquest era followed by study of Spanish conquest and settlement. Author estimates 92 percent population decline after contact, providing other evidence regarding "disappearance" of native cultures. Resistance to colonialism noted and examined, including origin of traditional dance known as *El güegüense,* or *Macho ratón.*

1070 **Velázquez, Carmela.** La Diócesis de Nicaragua y Costa Rica: su conformación y sus conflictos, 1531–1850. (*Rev. Hist./ Heredia,* 49/50, 2004, p. 245–286, map, table)
  Detailed institutional history. Organization and operation of ecclesiastical administration, from establishment of first bishopric in Nicaragua to creation of separate diocese for Costa Rica in decades following Independence.

1071 **Werner, Patrick S.** Etnohistoria de la Nicaragua temprana: demografía y encomiendas de las comunidades indígenas. Traducción del inglés al español de Adolfo Bonilla. Managua: Lea Grupo Editorial: Alcaldía de Managua, 2009. 564 p.: bibl., maps.

Valuable reference. Extended analysis and informed commentary on Nicaragua portion of record of 1548 tributary count ordered by Audiencia president Alonso López de Cerrato. In addition to providing population data, the work attempts to locate all communities referred to, including many since disappeared, and to classify them ethnically and linguistically.

NATIONAL

1072 Acosta, Antonio. Municipio, estado y crisis económica, El Salvador, 1870–1880: una contribución al análisis desde las haciendas municipales. (*Rev. Indias*, 67:240, mayo/agosto 2007, p. 367–402, bibl., table)

Examination of municipal finances in 1870s, revealing the weakness of local and national governments, the regressive nature of taxation, and the disparities between services for coffee and noncoffee producing areas.

Aguirre, Robert D. Informal empire: Mexico and Central America in Victorian culture. See *HLAS 65:2005.*

1073 Alda Mejías, Sonia. La resistencia de los pueblos a la tiranía en Centroamérica (siglo XIX). (*Mesoamérica/Antigua*, 26:47, 2005, p. 47–79, bibl., photos)

Challenging traditional analysis of 19th-century uprisings, article suggests that revolts in the region were more than consequence of tumultuous political life. Revolts occurred when rulers violated highly diffused concept of popular sovereignty, based on new Liberal principles and older Spanish political thought.

1074 Alvarenga Venutolo, Patricia. Comunidades y agentes del estado en la construcción de formas cotidianas de negociación: Costa Rica, 1850–1914. (*Rev. Hist./Heredia*, 49/50, 2004, p. 13–57)

Examination of Central Valley during period of coffee expansion. Hegemonic practices related to infrastructure and collectivization of work arose from complex interactions between state agents and peasant communities.

1075 Arellano, Jorge Eduardo. La Pax americana en Nicaragua: 1910–1932. Managua: Academia de Geografía e Historia de Nicaragua: Fondo Editorial CIRA, 2004. 280 p.: bibl., ill., map, ports.

Connects US tutelage of Nicaragua to North American messianic thought and earlier interventions in Latin America. Suggests that Nicaraguan political divisions also encouraged US entry and that Somoza's rise was ultimate consequence.

1076 Arias Sánchez, Raúl Francisco. Los soldados de la Campaña Nacional, 1856–1857. San José: EUNED, 2007. 398 p.: bibl., ill., maps (Biblioteca del cincuenta y seis; 2)

Encyclopedic study of struggle against William Walker's occupation of Nicaragua. Offers analysis of major battles and demographic statistics on communities that contributed soldiers. Final chapter lists names of 3,785 combatants.

1077 Asturias, Miguel Angel. Sociología guatemalteca: el problema social del indio. Edición e introducción de Julio César Pinto Soria. Guatemala: Editorial Universitaria, Univ. de San Carlos de Guatemala, 2007. 112 p.: bibl.

First Guatemalan edition of Nobel prizewinner in literature's 1923 thesis for law degree at national university. Asturias later disowned controversial eugenicist recommendations as products of "youthful enthusiasm." Pinto's excellent introduction sets work in specific historial and intellectual context. For earlier editions in France and US, see *HLAS 42:5283* and *HLAS 43:8139.*

1078 Barbosa, Francisco J. July 23, 1959: student protest and state violence as myth and memory in León, Nicaragua. (*HAHR*, 85:2, May 2005, p. 187–221, photos)

Analysis of 1959 León protest and its repression by the Guardia Nacional. Students used popular culture traditions to launch a critique of the Somoza regime. The Sandinistas, Somocistas, and people of León subsequently created competing interpretations of the tragedy.

1079 Belaubre, Christophe. La construcción de una identidad centroamericana a principios del siglo XIX: interpretación micro-histórica de un fracaso. (*Anu. IEHS*, 20, 2005, p. 87–119)

Examination of social and political networks in Guatemala and El Salvador and how these contributed to division after independence. Underscores the importance of monarchy and Catholicism during the colony and how abandoning the Crown while retaining religion heightened the conflict between regions.

1080 Bendaña, Alejandro. Sandino: mística, libertad y socialismo. Managua: Centro de Estudios Internacionales, 2007. 192 p.: bibl., ill.

Analysis of Sandino's ideological perspective through various stages of his life. Although not an intellectual, Sandino fashioned cohesive political perspective as spiritualist, socialist, and defender of liberty.

1081 Botey, Ana María. Costa Rica entre guerras, 1914–1940. San José: Editorial de la Universidad de Costa Rica, 2005. 124 p.: bibl. (Serie Cuadernos de historia de las instituciones de Costa Rica; 6)

Discusses the period seen as key to understanding of Costa Rica's modern agricultural export economy and characteristic political institutions. Emphasis on conjunctures presented by WWI, 1929 crash and Great Depression, and outbreak of WWII

1082 Boza Villareal, Alejandra. Política en la Talamanca indígena: el estado nacional y los caciques, Costa Rica, 1840–1922. (Anu. Estud. Centroam., 29:1/2, 2003, p. 113–145, bibl., ills., map, photos)

Examination of relations between Costa Rican state and indigenous groups in Talamanca. State repeatedly failed to establish control of Talamanca, leading to early political rights for the region's inhabitants and to the rise of "kings" or indigenous intermediaries.

1083 Brenes Tencio, Guillermo. La nación costarricense en duelo: los funerales del expresidente Jesús Jiménez Zamora, Cartago, 1897. (Rev. Arch. Nac./San José, 70:1/12, 2006, p. 115–146, bibl., map, photos, tables)

Interpretation of 1897 funeral of Jesús Jiménez Zamora as a means of sanctifying the Liberal state, conveying its ideals, and reinforcing social hierarchy.

1084 Cabrales de Wahn, Alicia. Prisioneros de una guerra ajena. Santa Tecla, El Salvador: Clásicos Roxsil, 2002. 117 p.: bibl., ill., maps (Col. Testimonio; 1002)

Short testimonial by wife of German immigrant, narrating her family's arrest in Guatemala during WWII and subsequent deportation to the US and then Germany. After years in Europe and Brazil, the Wahn-Cabrales family returned to El Salvador and opened one of country's important book stores.

1085 Cal Montoya, José Edgardo. El discurso historiográfico de la Sociedad Económica de Amigos del Estado de Guatemala en la primera mitad del siglo XIX: primeros acercamientos desde la historia cultural. (Anu. Estud. Centroam., 30:1/2, 2004, p. 87–118)

Analysis of José del Valle's Historia (1830), published by Amigos del Estado de Guatemala. Author sees text as fundamental to the region's liberal political thought and notes that del Valle's ideas appear in many subsequent works, such as Alejandro Marure Villavicencio's Historia del Estado de Guatemala (1833).

1086 Cambranes, J.C. Guatemala: sobre la recuperación de la memoria histórica (entrevista a dos voces). Guatemala: Editora Cultural de Centroamérica, 2008. 348 p.

Presented in interview style, prominent Guatemalan historian reflects on his own life and career and on Guatemalan politics and historiography in the 20th century. Intended largely as a critical response to Carlos A. Sabino's Guatemala: la historia silenciada, 1944–1989, see items **1139** and **1140**.

1087 Casaús Arzú, Marta Elena. De la incógnita del indio al indio como sombra: el debate de la antropología guatemalteca en torno al indio y la nación, 1921–1938. (Rev. Indias, 65:234, mayo/agosto 2005, p. 375–404, bibl., graphs)

Study of elite ideas surrounding position of Indians in the nation. Positivists and "spiritualists" debated issue, with former eventually imposing their ideas and excluding indigenous peoples from conceptions of Guatemala.

1088 Charlip, Julie A. Cultivating coffee: the farmers of Carazo, Nicaragua, 1880–1930. Athens: Ohio Univ. Press, 2003. 288 p.: bibl., maps. (Ohio University research in international studies. Latin America series; 39)

Small and medium-size landowners thrived in Nicaragua's most important coffee-producing region between 1880 and 1930. Study undermines the widespread notion that the introduction of coffee created enormous social disparities, suggesting these emerged only later under Somoza.

1089 Ching, Erik Kristofer; Carlos Gregorio López Bernal; and Virginia Tilley. Las masas, la matanza y el martinato en El Salvador: ensayos sobre 1932. San Salvador: Univ. Centroamericana, 2007. 230 p.: bibl., ill., index.

Study of 1932 massacre, including impact of Communist Party and ethnicity and causes of extreme violence. Investigation also examines Maximiliano Hernández Martínez regime (1931–44) and how Salvadorans have remembered events of 1932.

1090 Colombia y Panamá: Geopolítica, Identidad, Memoria e Historia, *Univ. Nacional de Colombia, 2002–2003.* Colombia y Panamá: la metamorfosis de la nación en el siglo XX. Edición de Heraclio Bonilla y Gustavo Montañez. Bogotá: Univ. Nacional de Colombia, 2004. 463 p.: ill. (Espacio y territorio)

Series of essays by mostly Colombian and Panamanian scholars on antecedents and consequences of Panama's separation from Colombia. Essays also touch on US-Panama relations and historiographical and popular memories of secession in both countries.

1091 Corrales Ulloa, Francisco and Guillermo Cubero Barrantes. De cuarteles a museos: los museos y el discurso de la civilidad costarricense. (*Maguaré/Bogotá*, 19, 2005, p. 11–23, bibl., photos)

Conversion of Cuartel Bellavista into Museo Nacional in 1948 coincided with abolition of Costa Rican army. Event began tradition of transforming forts into museums, exhibiting *civilista* theme of Costa Rican nationalism.

1092 Cortés Domínguez, Guillermo. De León al Búnker. Managua: Editarte, 2003. 391 p.: bibl., index

"Multiple testimony" of Somoza regime's fall, utilizing interviews with FSLN commanders and members of Guardia Nacional. Relates role of León's popular barrios in final offensive of June-July, 1979.

1093 Craft, Renée Alexander. "Una raza, dos etnias": the politics of be(com)ing/performing "Afropanemeño." (*Lat. Am. Caribb. Ethn. Stud.*, 3:2, July 2008, p. 123–147, bibl.)

Examination of Afro-Panamanian identity in 20th century. Seen as divided through much of the period, Afro-Antillean and Afro-colonial populations experienced convergence of interests after 1989 US invasion and later transfer of Panama Canal.

1094 Crónicas de la guerra nacional, 1856–1857. Compilación de Elías Zeledón Cartín. San José: Editorial Costa Rica, 2006. 377 p.: bibl., ill.

Thirty-five documents and essays dealing with the National War against William Walker.

1095 Díaz Arias, David. Construcción de un estado moderno: política, estado e identidad nacional en Costa Rica, 1821–1914. San José: Univ. de Costa Rica, Escuela de Historia, Cátedra de Historia de las Instituciones de Costa Rica; Editorial de la Universidad de Costa Rica, 2005. 86 p.: bibl. (Serie Cuadernos de historia de las instituciones de Costa Rica; 18)

Early political stability of Costa Rica helped to foment a sense of national identity, which was tied to the rise of the state and to notions of a racially homogenous, egalitarian nation. First apparent among Central Valley's elite, these ideas later spread out among the popular classes.

1096 Díaz Vázquez, María del Carmen. Centroamérica en la política exterior del México posrevolucionario: la búsqueda de acercamiento. (*Cuad. Am./México*, 118:4, oct./dic. 2006, p. 145–160, bibl.)

In 1920s, Mexico sought strengthened ties with Central America to counterbalance US hostility over new constitutional restrictions on foreign property. Article emphasizes cultural diplomacy and role of education minister José Vasconcelos.

1097 Dym, Jordana. Citizen of which republic?: foreigners and the construction of national citizenship in Central America, 1823–1845. (*Americas/Washington*, 64:4, April 2008, p. 477–510)

Analysis of evolving conceptions of citizenship through status of British and French residents. Influenced by European and US examples and growing difficulties of dealing with foreigners, Central Americans abandoned idea of "incorporating inhabitants into the nation," developing more restrictive and demanding sense of citizenship.

1098 Enríquez Solano, Francisco José. El turno, un espacio de diversión en Costa Rica, 1890–1930. (*Rev. Hist./Heredia*, 49/50, 2004, p. 155–181, tables)

Study traces *turno* celebrations back to colonial *cofradías*. From 1890 to 1930, the Church primarily organized these community festivals in order to raise money for the construction of temples. Activities included games, raffles, and the sale of meals.

Euraque, Darío A. Conversaciones históricas con el mestizaje y su identidad nacional en Honduras. See *HLAS 65:495*.

1099 Extranjeros hacia Tegucigalpa: 1857–1928. Prólogo de Juan Ramón Martínez. Compilación y traducción de Ramón Rosa Izaguirre. Tegucigalpa: [s.n.], 2007. 239 p.: bibl., ill.

Collected excerpts from foreign travelers' accounts of Honduras, presented in Spanish translation. Featured writers are Carl Scherzer, Cecil Charles, Frank Vincent, Richard Harding Davis, Frederick Palmer, Harry Franck, Wallace Thompson, and Arthur Ruhl.

1100 Flores González, Mercedes. La construcción cultural de la locura femenina en Costa Rica, 1890–1910. San José: Editorial UCR, 2007. 195 p.: bibl.

Complex study of feminine insanity based on extensive research in Costa Rican psychiatric institutions. Explores construction of notions of insanity, diagnoses, treatments, and experiences of interned women, as well as popular conceptions of mental health.

1101 Fumero, Patricia. Cultura y sociedad en Costa Rica, 1914–1950. San José: Univ. de Costa Rica, Escuela de Historia, Cátedra de Historia de las Instituciones de Costa Rica; Editorial de la Universidad de Costa Rica, 2005. 58 p.: bibl. (Serie Cuadernos de historia de las instituciones de Costa Rica; 16)

New mass culture, closely connected to press, arose with urbanization and redefined San José's public and private spaces, while distancing spheres of work and recreation. State efforts to regulate mass culture were often ineffective, allowing women and popular sectors to participate with greater freedom.

1102 Gamboa Barboza, Isabel. En el hospital psiquiátrico: el sexo como lo cura. San José: Univ. de Costa Rica, 2009. 299 p.: bibl., ill.

Play on words in title (*lo cura* for *locura*) suggests innovative nature of work. Examines patient records and other appropriate sources to demonstrate role of psychiatry in defining and reinforcing sexual norms in late 20th-century Costa Rica. Medicalization seen as mechanism for repressing behaviors classified as "deviant."

1103 García, Carlos Ernesto. Bajo la sombre de Sandino: historia de una revolución inconclusa. Barcelona, Spain: La Ínsula de los Libros, 2007. 216 p.: ports. (Memoria del tiempo)

Interviews with eight former Sandinista commanders, including Edén Pastora. Testimonials reveal the background and growth of the Sandinista movement, as well as its tensions, contradictions, and failures.

1104 García, Prudencio. El genocidio de Guatemala: a la luz de la sociología militar. Madrid: Sepha Edición y Diseño, 2005. 514 p.: bibl. (Libros abiertos; 1)

Innovative treatise by retired Spanish military officer and former UN human rights official in Central America. Documents massive human rights violations by Guatemalan army between 1962 and 1996 and analyzes these through Imperative-Moral (I-M) model.

1105 Goebel M., Anthony. La política económica liberal y su rol en el consumo de bienes "monopolizados": el caso del monopolio del tabaco en Costa Rica, 1880–1907. (*Anu. Estud. Centroam.*, 29:1/2, 2003, p. 147–169, bibl., tables)

State intervened forcefully to promote cultivation and sale of tobacco. Although these efforts failed to preserve government monopoly, they contradict image of laissez-faire economy and help provide nuanced understanding of Liberal period.

1106 Gould, Jeffrey L. and **Aldo Lauria-Santiago.** To rise in darkness: revolution, repression, and memory in El Salvador, 1920–1932. Durham: Duke Univ. Press, 2007. 368 p.: bibl., index.

Relying on oral history, as well as new archival material, study examines 1932 Matanza. Focusing on ethnicity, authors argue western El Salvador had fluid ethnic conceptions and that Indians participated in design of Communist rebellion. Communists and Indians not as divided as previously thought.

1107 Greene, Julie. The canal builders: making America's empire at the Panama Canal. New York: Penguin Press, 2009. 475 p.: bibl., ill., index, maps, photographs (The Penguin history of American life)

Major contribution and model of transnational labor history. Building of Panama Canal told from workers' point of view. Unlike previous heroic accounts of technical mastery in engineering and public health, focus is on efficient management of large multinational, multiracial labor force. Questions of social control, law, gender, domestic relations, and other topics help illuminate early US experience as colonial power.

Harris, Charles H. and **Louis R. Sadler.** The archaeologist was a spy: Sylvanus G. Morley and the Office of Naval Intelligence. See item **943.**

1108 Harrison, Benjamin T. Woodrow Wilson and Nicaragua. (*Caribb. Q./Mona,* 51:1, March 2005, p. 25–36, bibl.)

Contests notion that Wilson's involvement in Nicaragua served US corporate interests. Instead, Wilson hoped to spread democracy and encourage ethical investment in country. However, errors of predecessors thwarted his agenda.

1109 Heine, Wilhelm. Impresiones de un pintor alemán en Nicaragua, 1851–1852. Alajuela, Costa Rica: Museo Histórico Cultural Juan Santamaría, 2005. 190 p.: ill.

Translation of German painter's narrative of 1851–52 visit to Nicaragua, during which he interacted with various military leaders and traveled to country's northern mining region. Includes several illustrations by author that previously appeared in

Ephraim G. Squier's *The States of Central America* (1858).

1110 Herrera, José Iván. La venta de la cofradía de Nuestra Señora de Concepción de Colama. (*Rev. Centroam. Econ.,* 11:67/68, 2006, p. 67–91, bibl.)

Although the transaction benefited the Honduran government financially, this study demonstrates that the 1853 sale of *cofradía* lands arose out of conflicts among clergy, brotherhood members, and local residents.

1111 Herrera, Sajid Alfredo. La invención liberal de la identidad estatal salvadoreña, 1824–1839. (*J. Lat. Am. Cult. Stud.,* 15:3, Dec. 2006, p. 913–936, bibl.)

A Salvadoran state identity preceded the rise of a national project, resting on Liberal-federal ideas and fear of Guatemalan impositions. Despite essentially modern nature, efforts never overcame colonial legacies to create sense of unified pueblo.

1112 Kinzer, Stephen. Blood of brothers: life and war in Nicaragua. 1st edition David Rockefeller Center for Latin American Studies. Cambridge, Mass.; London, England: David Rockefeller Center for Latin American Studies, Harvard Univ., 2007. 460 p., 16 p. of plates: bibl., ill., index, maps.

Reprint of 1991 journalistic account by former *New York Times* bureau chief in Managua. Traces background and course of 1979 revolution, Contra War, and Sandinistas' achievements and failures. New afterword by author paints pessimistic vision of country, emphasizing corrupt nature of political leadership.

1113 Kodrich, Kris. The role of state advertising in Latin American newspapers: was the demise of Nicaragua's *Barricada* newspaper political sabotage? (*Bull. Lat. Am. Res.,* 27:1, Jan. 2008, p. 61–82, tables)

Case study of 1998 closure of pro-Sandinista newspaper. Apportionment of state advertising money seen as subtle but effective means to control media.

1114 Lindo-Fuentes, Héctor. Políticas de la memoria: el levantamiento de 1932 en El Salvador. (*Rev. Hist./Heredia,* 49/50, 2004, p. 287–316)

Review of popular histories of 1932 uprising. Memories of *La Matanza* have varied over time, corresponding to political twists and turns. Changing views help to illuminate 20th-century history.

1115 Lindo-Fuentes, Héctor; Erik Ching; and Rafael Lara-Martínez. Remembering a massacre in El Salvador: the insurrection of 1932, Roque Dalton, and the politics of historical memory. Albuquerque: Univ. of New Mexico Press, 2007. 411 p.: bibl., index. (Diálogos)

Complex examination of 1932 Matanza and fluid historical debates surrounding its meanings, with especially detailed analysis of Roque Dalton's classic *Miguel Mármol* (see *HLAS 38:2799* [Spanish] and *HLAS 50:7994* [English]). Left and right-wing interpretations of massacre responded to changing political circumstances, while tending to emphasize influence of communism, versus ethnicity and other competing factors.

1116 Martínez B., Juan Ramón. Oficio de caníbales: militares y guerrilleros en El Patuca. Tegucigalpa: Ediciones 18 Conejo, 2006. 252 p.: bibl.

Account of failed 1983 guerrilla movement headed by José María Reyes Mata and active in La Mosquitia of Honduras. Delves into wide range of topics, including US policy in Central America, Catholic Church, and military-civilian relations, as well as interactions with Nicaragua and Cuba.

1117 McGuinness, Aims. Path of empire: Panama and the California Gold Rush. Ithaca: Cornell Univ. Press, 2008. 249 p.: bibl., ill., maps (The United States in the world)

Transnational history of Panama during California Gold Rush. US construction of Panama Railroad dramatically disrupted Panamanian society, sparking elite and popular debates on sovereignty. Especially good treatment of black Liberal politics and 1856 Watermelon Riot.

1118 Menjívar Ochoa, Rafael. Tiempos de locura: El Salvador 1979–1981. 2. ed. ampliada. San Salvador: FLACSO, 2006. 306 p.: bibl.

Creative journalistic account of Salvadoran history, from coup of October 15, 1979, to guerrilla "final offensive" of January 10, 1981. Relying heavily on interviews with key actors, reveals tensions and contradictions dividing major factions.

Milla Reyes, Jorge. Costa Rica y Nicaragua: historias de un arreglo de fronteras. See *HLAS 65:2045.*

1119 Molina Jiménez, Iván. Anticomunismo reformista: competencia electoral y cuestión social en Costa Rica, 1931–1948. San José: Editorial Costa Rica, 2007. 222 p.: bibl., ill., index (Ensayo)

Founded in 1931, the Communist Party played a key role in forcing acceptance of social reform during presidency of Rafael Ángel Calderón Guardia (1940–44). The world economic crisis and the country's competitive electoral system gave Communists an unprecedented influence, convincing Church and political adversaries to adopt elements of party's agenda.

1120 Molina Jiménez, Iván. Demoperfectocracia: la democracia pre-reformada en Costa Rica, 1885–1948. Heredia, Costa Rica: EUNA, 2005. 484 p.: bibl., ill.

Analysis of Costa Rican electoral politics from 1885–1948, challenging "black myth" of traditional historiography. Demonstrates transition to more open and competitive system, which gradually responded to popular demands.

1121 Molina Jiménez, Iván. La participación del Partido Comunista de Costa Rica en la década de 1930: el caso de los comicios de 1934. (*Hist. Polít.,* 13, 2005, p. 175–199, tables)

Proportional representation and abstentionism combined to create Communist electoral victories in 1934. Policies of President Ricardo Jiménez Oreamuno (1932–36) also encouraged party's integration into electoral politics. Exceptional in Central America, the process led other parties to consider social reform.

1122 Molina Jiménez, Iván. Presidencia de la república y legalización del partido comunista de Costa Rica en la década de los treinta: una revaloración de los factores institucionales. (*Politeia/Caracas,* 34/35, 2005, p. 3–19, bibl.)

Examines function of political institutions in legalization of Costa Rican Communist Party. Presidencies, as opposed to economic or social factors, played important role in establishing party's legitimacy and helping to spread its reform agenda.

1123 Muñoz Pinzón, Armando and **María Rosa B. de Muñoz.** La huelga de los conductores del servicio públicio de 1932. (*Tareas,* 123, mayo/agosto 2006, p. 103–119, bibl.)

Although occurring during the presidential campaign, the successful 1932 Panama City drivers' strike lacked any political or ideological nature. Supported by local merchants, the strikers limited themselves to eliminating a recent ban on bus transit along Avenida Central.

1124 Nicaragua en el siglo XIX: testimonio de funcionarios, diplomáticos y viajeros. Compilación y presentaciones de Jorge Eduardo Arellano. Managua: Colección Cultural de Centro América, 2005. 482 p.: bibl., ill., index (Serie Viajeros; 6)

Collection of 15 testimonials by foreigners who visited Nicaragua between 1823 and 1900. Editor provides introduction and bibliography for each text. Contributions include writings by John Lloyd Stephens, Mark Twain, and the last Spanish governor.

1125 Norori Gutiérrez, Róger. Crisis económica, bancos y reforma monetaria en Nicaragua, 1870–1926. Managua: Academia de Geografía e Historia de Nicaragua, 2008. 199 p.: bibl., ill.

Monetary reform of 1912 analyzed in broader context of national and international economic trends, with special attention to displacement of British by US interests.

1126 Oertzen, Eleonore von. Protestantism and ethnic identity: Moravian missionaries on the Nicaraguan Atlantic Coast in the 19th century. (*Cuad. Antropol./San José,* 15, dic. 2005, p. 45–52, bibl., maps, photos)

Short article on the success of Moravian missionaries among the Miskito Indians of Nicaragua's Atlantic Coast. The Moravians exploited a moment of crisis in the Miskito society, disrupted by previous European penetrations. In the long term, missionaries helped to strengthen Miskito identity, even as they insisted on important cultural changes.

1127 Opie, Frederick Douglass. Black Americans and the state in turn-of-the-century Guatemala. (*Americas/Washington,* 64:4, April 2008, p. 583–609)

A revealing essay on African-Americans who migrated to Guatemala to work on railroad projects. US racism and the need for labor encouraged migration, with an estimated 7,000 arriving in 1890s alone. Author focuses on resistance to poor labor conditions and notes how some immigrants used US citizenship to advantage.

1128 Ortega Saavedra, Humberto. La epopeya de la insurrección: Nicaragua siglo XX: pensamiento y acción, análisis histórico, narración inédita. Managua: Lea Grupo Editorial, 2004. 510 p.: bibl., ill., 1 map.

History of 20th-century Nicaragua, written from the perspective of a top Sandinista commander. Includes extensive sections on the anti-Somoza struggle and the development of Sandinista revolutionary theory. Concludes with an eccentric outline of human history and a "Mural for a Better World."

1129 Pérez, Juan Manuel. Pro mundi beneficio: los trabajadores gallegos en la construcción del Canal del Panamá, 1904–1914. Spain: Fundación Pedro Barrié de la Maza, 2007. 237 p.: bibl., ill., maps (Col. Galicia exterior)

Richly documented study of 10,000 Galician workers who participated in construction of Panama Canal. Author focuses on recruitment of Galicians, working and living conditions, and participation in labor conflicts.

1130 Pérez Chávez, Porfirio. Santos Guardiola, política y guerra filibustera. Tegucigalpa: Univ. Nacional Autónoma de Honduras, Editorial Universitaria, 2006. 430 p.: bibl.

Archival based work on the Santos Guardiola presidency (1856–62), focusing on his participation in National War against William Walker, his efforts to recover Bay Islands, and his relations with Church and other political opponents.

1131 Peters Solórzano, Gertrud. Exportadores y consignatarios del café costarricense a finales del siglo XIX. (*Rev. Hist./Heredia,* 49/50, 2004, p. 59–109, photo, tables)

Study of Costa Rican coffee exports at end of 19th century. Focuses on trading companies' strategies to increase participation in international market as well as impact of falling coffee prices.

1132 Quesada Camacho, Juan Rafael. *Clarín patriótico*: la guerra contra los filibusteros y la nacionalidad costarricense. Alajuela, Costa Rica: Museo Histórico Cultural Juan Santamaría; Costa Rica: Ministerio de Cultura Juventud y Deportes: Colegio de Licenciados y Profesores en Letras, Filosofía, Ciencias y Artes, 2006. 288 p.: bibl., ill.

Investigation of Costa Rican nationalism through an analysis of Tadeo Nadeo Gómez's *Clarín patriótico o Colección de canciones y otras poesías compuestas en Costa Rica en la guerra contra los filibusteros invasores de Centro-América* (1857). Posits that nationalism is a product of colonial culture integrated with new Liberal political values.

1133 Reyes, Nahem. La alteración de las relaciones civiles-militares nicaragüenses durante la Revolución Sandinista, 1979–1984. (*Tierra Firme/Caracas*, 22:88, oct./dic. 2004, p. 487–512, bibl., table)

Despite title, essay covers period from 1930–84. Author sees continuities between Somoza and Sandinista periods, suggesting that the military dominated civilians in both regimes.

1134 Rivera Forero, Franklin. Ricardo J. Alfaro: vida diplomática. Panamá : Editorial Universitaria "Carlos Manuel Gasteazoro", 1999. 187 p.: bibl., ill.

An account of the career of Panamanian diplomat Alfaro (1882–1971) and his long career in public service. He served briefly as president (1931–32) and represented the country in some of most contentious negotiations with US from 1920s through 1960s.

1135 Rodríguez, Ana Patricia. Dividing the Isthmus: Central American transnational histories, literatures, and cultures. Austin: Univ. of Texas Press, 2009. 291 p.: bibl., ills., index.

An ambitious examination of 20th-century "grand narratives of (anti)imperialism, revolution, subalterity, globalization, and tran-national migration." The work seeks to move beyond old national analysis and approach Central America as transnational whole.

1136 Rodríguez Rosales, Isolda. Historia de la educación en Nicaragua: 50 años en el sistema educativo, 1929–1979. Managua: Hispamer, 2007. 274 p.: bibl., ill.

The third work by this author on Nicaraguan education. In the 1930s, Liberals again dominated education, and instruction became increasingly technocratic, utilitarian, and open to experimentation, despite rise of Somoza regime. US aid and Central American integration later contributed to same tendencies.

1137 Rodríguez Rosales, Isolda. Historia de la educación en Nicaragua: restauración conservadora, 1910–1930. Managua: Hispamer, 2005. 294 p.: bibl., ill.

Follow-up to author's earlier study of Liberal educational reform between 1893 and 1901. Conservative governments reversed Liberal ideas and returned educational system to Church control. Political and economic turmoil impeded growth of education.

1138 Royo Aspa, Antoni. La reforma agraria en Costa Rica, 1962–2002: balance de las intervenciones estatales en el cantón de Osa. (*Rev. Hist./Heredia*, 48, julio/dic. 2003, p. 227–269, bibl., graphs, tables)

Analysis of agrarian reform, focusing on Osa. Land reform efforts responded more to political concerns than to economic realities. Most campesinos were unable to support themselves on plots due to poor quality of soil and lack of credit and technical assistance.

1139 Sabino, Carlos A. Guatemala: la historia silenciada, 1944–1989. t. 1, Revolución y liberación. Ciudad de Guatemala: Fondo de Cultura Económica de Guatemala, 2007–2008. 1 v.: bibl., ill., index, maps (Historia)

Conservative reinterpretation of Guatemalan history from 1944–63. Author suggests that the Arévalo and Arbenz regimes represented Communist threats and that military governments were the only means to block the path of the extreme left, particularly in the wake of Cuban Revolution. (For critical response by historian J.C. Cambranes, see item **1086**.)

1140 Sabino, Carlos A. Guatemala: la historia silenciada, 1944–1989. t. 2, El dominó que no cayó. Ciudad de Guatemala: Fondo de Cultura Económica de Guatemala, 2007–2008. 1 v.: bibl., ill., index, maps (Historia)

Conservative treatment of recent Guatemalan history from 1963–96 peace accords. Emphasizes polarization of political elements, ideological weakness of left, and its resort to armed conflict.

1141 Salamín C., Marcel A. Pancho Arias y su época: ensayo crítico para una biografía de la patria. Venezuela: [s.n.], 2005 435 p.: bibl.

Biography of a leading Panamanian politician in the first half of the 20th century. Pancho Arias never reached the presidency; however the author credits him for his progressive ideas and for helping steer the country away from authoritarian tendencies and toward the social democratic constitution of 1946.

1142 The Sandino Rebellion: Nicaragua, 1927–1934. A documentary history. Annville, PA: Lebanon Valley College, 2010. <http://www.sandinorebellion.com>

Project by historian Michael J. Schroeder to create digital archive of primary materials on Sandino and struggle against US occupation of Nicaragua. Currently offers access to more than 1,000 documents and photographic images, about five percent of ultimate goal.

1143 Santos, Carlos. Guatemala, el silencio del gallo: un misionero español en la guerra más cruenta de América. Barcelona, Spain: Debate, 2007. 382 p.: ill., index.

Biography of Spanish missionary Luis Gurriarán and his work among the Maya in war-torn Guatemala. Excellent insights into impact of conflict and liberation theology on elements of clergy.

1144 Schroeder, Michael J. Social memory and tactical doctrine: the air war in Nicaragua during the Sandino Rebellion, 1927–1932. (*Int. Hist. Rev./Burnaby*, 29:3, Sept. 2007, p. 508–549, ill., map)

Analysis of US air war against Sandino and how the campaign became an enduring theme of Latin American anti-imperialist literature. Racism and poor training led to large civilian casualties, while tactics themselves were seen as cowardly and dishonorable.

1145 Sibaja Chacón, Luis Fernando. Del Cañas-Jerez al Chamorro-Bryan: las relaciones limítrofes entre Costa Rica y Nicaragua en la perspectiva histórica, 1858–1916. Alajuela, Costa Rica: Museo Histórico Cultural Juan Santamaría, Ministerio de Cultura, Juventud y Deportes, 2006. 291 p.: bibl., col. maps.

Based largely on Costa Rican sources, descriptive survey of territorial disputes between Costa Rica and Nicaragua. Emphasizes the role of interoceanic transit and rising US influence as most important factors affecting relations between countries.

1146 Sinclair, David. Sir Gregor MacGregor and the land that never was: the extraordinary story of the most audacious fraud in history. London: Review, 2003. 358 p., 8 p. of plates: ill., ports.

Readable, popular account that draws on some primary sources. Declaring himself the "cazique" (sic) of Poyais, an imaginary country on Honduras's Atlantic Coast, soldier of fortune and confidence artist MacGregor (1786–1845) took advantage of the European enthusiasm for imagined economic potential of the newly independent Latin America to sell shares and recruit settlers for an ultimately disastrous scheme.

1147 Squier, Ephraim George. Nicaragua de océano a océano; Cinco semblanzas de Squier. Contribuciones de Francisco Xavier Aguirre Sacasa *et al.* Managua: Colección Cultural de Centro América, 2005. 292 p.: ill., maps. (Serie Viajeros; 7)

Translation of Squier's 1855 articles published in Harper's *New Monthly Magazine*, describing an 1853 trip to Nicaragua. The volume includes the original English-language version, along with five essays analyzing Squier's life and observations.

1148 Sutter, Paul. El control de los zancudos en Panamá: los entomólogos y el cambio ambiental durante la construcción del Canal. (*Hist. Crít./Bogotá*, 30, julio/dic. 2005, p. 67–90, bibl.)

In contrast to traditional heroic narratives, this essay suggests that the US construction of the Canal actually increased habitats of disease-carrying mosquitoes. Advancements in scientific knowledge helped reveal contradiction, weakening imperialist conception of nature.

1149 Tropical travel: the representation of Central America in the nineteenth century: facsimiles of illustrated texts, 1854–1895. Edited and with an introduction by Juan Carlos Vargas. San José: Editorial UCR, 2008. 570 p.: bibl., ill.

Collection of 21 articles published between 1854 and 1895 in prominent US magazines. The introduction emphasizes the importance of illustrations, framing both images and texts in the context of 19th-century racial theories.

1150 Urbina Gaitán, Chester. Exclusión social, desarticulación cultural y teatro en El Salvador, 1875–1944. (*Anu. Estud. Centroam.*, 29:1/2, 2003, p. 101–111, bibl.)

Study of theater and nationalism in Liberal-era El Salvador. Drama failed to convey sense of unity due to divisions between eastern and western regions of country and lack of nationalist vision among coffee elite.

1151 Vargas, Armando. El doctor Zambrana. San José: EUNED, 2006. 552 p.: bibl.

Sympathetic biography of Cuban Antonio Zambrana and his work in Costa Rica in the late 19th and early 20th centuries as journalist, educator, and legal scholar. Presents Zambrana as an important architect of Costa Rican democracy.

1152 Vega Cantor, Renán; Sandra Jáuregui González; and **Luis Carlos Ortiz Vásquez.** El Panamá colombiano en la repartición imperialista. Bogotá: Ediciones Pensamiento Crítico: Alejandría Libros, 2003. 302 p.: bibl., ill., maps.

Interpretation of Panama's 1903 independence, written from Colombian perspective and based largely on French archival materials. Covering Panamanian history from mid-19th century forward, authors suggest that country's independence was consequence of US imperialism and isthmus' insertion into global capitalist system.

1153 Vega Jiménez, Patricia. Los responsables de los impresos en Costa Rica, 1900–1930. (*Rev. Hist./Heredia*, 49/50, 2004, p. 183–220, tables)

Biographic analysis of 247 journalists, editors, and others associated with publication of Costa Rican newspapers. Comparisons reveal that the industry was overwhelmingly male and highly concentrated. Creators of Costa Rica's "public sphere" tended to be lawyers, educators, and some of country's leading literary figures.

1154 Wingartz Plata, Oscar. Nicaragua ante su historia: esperanza o frustración? Querétaro, Mexico: Univ. Autónoma de Querétaro, Facultad de Filosofía; Ediciones UAQ, 2003. 227 p.: bibl. (Serie Humanidades)

Reflections on Sandinista Revolution from 1981 to electoral defeat of 1990, to "conservative restoration" of 1996. Author discusses weaknesses and errors of Sandinista program and the necessity for a renewed commitment to ethics and social justice.

THE CARIBBEAN, THE GUIANAS AND THE SPANISH BORDERLANDS

MATT D. CHILDS, *Associate Professor of History, University of South Carolina*
EDWARD L. COX, *Associate Professor of History, Rice University, Houston*
JOHN D. GARRIGUS, *Associate Professor of History, University of Texas at Arlington*
LUIS A. GONZÁLEZ, *Librarian for Latin American Studies, Spanish and Portuguese, Chicano-Riqueño and Latino Studies Indiana University, Bloomington*
VALENTINA PEGUERO, *Professor of History, University of Wisconsin, Stevens-Point*

THE BRITISH CARIBBEAN

THIS CYCLE HAS WITNESSED the appearance of a number of highly important publications that, taken together, reflect the vibrancy of scholarly interest in the

British Caribbean. While the publications do not constitute a trend, it is heartening to note that women and gender issues and slavery have maintained their position as areas meriting scholarly attention.

S.D. Smith's important study of the Lascelles family in Barbados illuminates the challenges, joys, and frustrations of a prominent British family that was heavily involved in the business of slave ownership, plantation management, and commercial activity (item **1201**). Linda Heywood's fascinating and well-researched study of the charter generation of Africans arriving in the Americas indicates their Central African origins while simultaneously demonstrating the severity of slavery that existed even in these early years (item **1191**). Engaging the current debate over the writings of Eric Williams regarding the role of economic factors in slave trade abolition and slave emancipation, David Beck Ryden argues quite persuasively that events within the slave plantation economies of the British Caribbean, particularly Jamaica, more than political and economic forces within England, sharply influenced the British decision to abolish the Atlantic slave trade (item **1246**).

Women and gender studies on the British Caribbean have benefitted from the appearance of a number of highly significant works. James Delle's insightful study based on an estate journal during slavery demonstrates how women were able to overcome some of the disadvantages they faced on the estate and use their gender to protest and to further their own interests (item **1270**). Rhoda Reddock argues that the high disproportion between women and men who arrived from India during the indentureship period ushered in a new form of slavery that ultimately led to efforts to promote reproduction among the migrants, but which was viewed as "the prostitution of women" (item **1291**). The forms of entertainment that women of varying classes in St. Vincent engaged in to define themselves is the subject of a fine publication by Sheena Boa, who persuasively argues that race, class, and gender were successfully intertwined at multiple levels in women's public behavior (item **1261**). Bridget Brereton's examination of the reasons why women withdrew from plantation wage labor in the period after emancipation suggests that their determination to help in taking care of their families, especially in the raising of their children, profoundly influenced their decisions, which planters wrongly viewed as an aversion to wage labor (item **1262**). Finally, focusing on the pro-slavery debates in the late 18th and early 19th centuries, Henrice Altink reminds us that the long debate in Jamaica over enslaved women's sexuality and interracial sex actually prolonged slavery in the British Caribbean (item **1204**).

Two authors devote much-needed attention to the legacies of slavery on contemporary society. Concentrating on attempts to focus national awareness on efforts to preserve that legacy, Alvin Thompson asserts that the excesses of Forbes Burnham's race-based political party and government have caused the other major ethnic group in Guyana to feel that its Indian heritage is unimportant and that its members were left out of the conversation regarding the meaning of slavery in Guyana (item **1174**). Bridget Brereton's careful evaluation of the main themes undergirding historical writing on Trinidad and Tobago indicates that ethnicity continues to play a crucial role in how the groups view the nation's past, particularly from slavery to the present (item **1155**).

Military history has benefitted from the appearance of two highly important and timely publications. Richard Smith's well-researched and cogently argued study on Jamaican volunteers who served in the British Regiments during World War I indicates a high level of unease on the part of the British to use these volunteers in combat (item **1350**). Used mostly as drudge workers, the volunteers embraced and exhibited masculine rhetoric that later contributed to the rise of nationalism. Arlene Munro shows that Guyana contributed significantly towards the British war efforts both in terms of volunteers and financial donations, as well as a settler location for displaced European Jews seeking to avoid Hitler's attempts to eliminate them (item **1335**).

Three well-crafted and significant autobiographies of Trinidadians in the late 19th and early 20th centuries deserve special mention because of the considerable contribution they make toward understanding the society of which they were a part. A long-standing civil servant, Percy Fraser provides an important perspective into the workings of the island's major correctional institution where he worked in the first half of the 20th century (item **1316**). A first generation Trinidadian whose parents came from India, Ramnarine Binda provides an extremely useful perspective of 20th-century Trinidadian society and politics through his interactions with different political and trade union leaders in the middle and late 20th centuries (item **1302**). Lionel Frank Seukeran's masterful and reflective autobiography shows how this largely self-made man interacted with the major players as Trinidad moved from Crown Colony government to eventual independence (item **1348**). [ELC]

THE FRENCH CARIBBEAN AND FRENCH GUIANA

An important scholarly development for the Francophone Caribbean has been the rise of the field of Atlantic Studies, which views the Atlantic as a realm of connections and activities that cross or avoid imperial and national boundaries. In recent years, this Atlantic perspective has been particularly useful in describing the impact of the French and Haitian revolutions on slave societies throughout the Americas. Although historians of the French Revolution have long ignored events in Saint-Domingue/Haiti, this is now changing. Historians of the US and France increasingly recognize that events in Haiti shaped the way those nations defined citizenship within their own boundaries.

The growing popularity of Atlantic Studies is one reason why so many of the publications in this biennial period focused on the revolutionary era. Another reason is the publication of a number of anthologies commemorating the bicentennial of Haitian independence in 2004. A further important development has been the publication of new collections of documents from the revolutionary era and the slave period that preceded it.

In France the field of post-slavery studies has been stimulated by a series of sustained general strikes in Martinique and Guadeloupe in 2009. Though triggered by economic conditions, these protests are part of an ongoing debate in metropolitan and overseas France about immigration, national identity, and France's slave-trading past. As Cécile Vidal (item **1356**) explains in a 2006 article, political forces and intellectual fashions in French academia have historically provided little support for scholars interested in Caribbean history. Scholars working in the Anglophone world have been the primary practitioners of Atlantic history. But the contemporary importance of issues like racism, citizenship, cultural integration have brought the slave trade and Caribbean plantation slavery into French public attention.

The major event in the study of France's early attempts to colonize the Antilles is the publication of Boucher's *France and the American Tropics to 1700* (item **1178**), which surveys French colonization efforts in the 17th century, including the role of the state, and French attitudes towards indigenous people and the Caribbean environment, as well as the slow turn towards plantation agriculture. His portrait of this early world is echoed in another work that places even more emphasis on the Caribbean environment. In *La forêt antillaise* the botanist Hatzenberger describes the very different ways that Native Americans, Europeans, and Africans experienced the aboriginal forests of the Antilles (item **1189**). A different approach to the Caribbean environment comes in a handful of works on the history of science in the Caribbean. Examining the 18th and 19th centuries, McClellan (item **1237**) and Kimber (item **1327**) describe the efforts of French botanists and royal officials to explore, domesticate, and exploit the environment and flora of Saint-Domingue and Martinique, respectively. In a closely related piece, François Regourd examines how scientific expeditions and military engineers transmitted technical knowledge to colonial elites, especially in Saint-Domingue (item **1200**).

Scholars have written much of French Caribbean historiography around the actions of the imperial state, in large part because of the records it generated. Kenneth Banks investigates the workings of that state in his *Chasing Empire Across the Sea* (item **1176**). The book reveals how royal officials managed information, royal ceremonies, and troublesome colonial populations in the very different societies of Martinique, Québec, and French Louisiana.

It has been left to Anglophone historians to describe the Atlantic movements of French-speaking people who were not, strictly speaking, under the control of the French state. The best example of this during this biennial period is Christopher Hodson's (item **1192**) article on Acadians sent to Saint-Domingue after the failed attempt to establish a new colony in French Guyana. Like Bank's book, Hodson's article, part of a forthcoming book on the Acadian diaspora, illustrates how the new Atlantic scholarship does not ignore the French state but illuminates its actions in new ways.

Since the 2005 riots over police violence in the suburbs of Paris, the question of whether people of color have been able to integrate into French metropolitan society has sparked scholarship on the history of racism and civil rights in France. This biennial saw the publication of four books dealing with this question. Erick Noël offers a social history of the some 5,000 people of African descent living in 18th-century France, the vast majority of whom were from the Antilles (item **1240**). Pierre Boulle, whose articles have been illuminating such questions for decades, combines his older work on the intellectual and cultural roots of French racism, with new social historical work on the black experience (item **1179**). Florence Gauthier carries this scholarship into the revolutionary era with a book about the political activity of free men of color in revolutionary Paris (item **1225**). And Bernard Gainot follows the careers of soldiers, especially officers, of color in France during the Revolutionary decade to show how rhetoric of universal rights often had little practical impact on these Caribbean men serving in the metropole (item **1220**). Following a set of similar questions about the importance of racial difference in 18th-century France, Dominique Rogers (item **1245**) argues that racial discrimination and segregation among whites and free coloreds in Saint-Domingue was not becoming stronger on the eve of the French and Haitian Revolutions, as nearly all historians have maintained.

Emphasis on such cultural issues has not completely overshadowed the plantation studies that for so long were the mainstay of scholarship on the French Antilles. Natacha Bonnet's article examines the work load and demographic conditions on three plantations in Saint-Domingue's northern plain (item **1196**). She describes how estate records about acres planted, hogsheads of sugar produced, and numbers of enslaved workers born or buried, can mislead historians trying to understand the phenomenon of overwork. Similarly Bernard Foubert continues to publish elements of his thesis on the massive Laborde estates in Saint-Domingue; here he studies the African origins of the nearly 1,000 workers on these three adjoining properties (item **1235**).

But in this biennial, at least, publications have focused more on culture than on traditional estate studies. One example is Jacques de Cauna's article surveying the French colonial ruins that still litter the Haitian countryside (item **1209**). Even greater testament to a growing popular interest in these topics is the collection of documents and images from French slave societies collected by Evelyne Camara, Isabelle Dion, and Jacques Dion of the French National Archives (item **1156**). A number of the images they present have not been widely reproduced and this is especially true of their textual sources, which cover the slave trade, slave plantation era, and the revolutionary decade.

Another important publication of primary sources is Jeremy Popkin's *Facing Racial Revolution*, a well-edited collection of 24 documents from survivors of the revolutionary era in Saint-Domingue (item **1219**). This is only one of two major publications by this historian best known up to the present as a French Revolutionary specialist. Popkin's *You are All Free* offers a deeply researched narrative of the events surrounding Sonthonax's 1793 declaration of emancipation in Saint-Domingue (item **1243**).

The concept of an "Atlantic" world is beautifully illustrated in an article by Rebecca Scott and Jean Hébrard (item **1251**). They trace the life of an African woman enslaved in Saint-Domingue during the Haitian Revolution and reveal the travels and achievements of her children and grandchildren. In the same volume, John Garrigus presents new information on one of the most "Atlantic" of the free colored leaders of the Revolutionary era, Vincent Ogé *le jeune* (item **1223**). With their analysis of an extraordinary document from revolutionary Saint-Domingue, Laurent Dubois and Bernard Camier argue that people of color in the French Caribbean appropriated and reworked Enlightenment texts like Voltaire's popular play *Zaïre* (item **1217**).

Gender is another cultural element of the French Caribbean experience that is receiving more attention from scholars than before, especially during the revolutionary era. An innovative article by Elizabeth Colwill (item **1214**) on the marriage policy of white and black leaders in revolutionary Saint-Domingue is perhaps the most important of a group of valuable analyses and syntheses by Gautier, Cottias, Fabella, Girard, and Peabody. All of these works examine the way gender shaped women's access to citizenship and freedom in the 18th and 19th century. Changing definitions of freedom and French identity in 19th-century Martinique are the main subjects of Rebecca Schloss' important book about the end of slavery in 1848 (item **1250**). But what makes Schloss' account especially distinctive is her emphasis on the importance of gender and sexuality during this pivotal period. In the historically masculine domain of military service, a similar group of articles treats the ways in which Caribbean men of color experienced freedom or were denied equality in Saint-Domingue (item **1195**) Guadeloupe (items **1216** and **1244**), and France (item **1220**).

Finally, Miranda Spieler's important article argues forcefully that the French Revolutionary state consistently rejected the citizenship of people of color in the

Caribbean, even in the much celebrated Constitution of 1795 that appeared to abolish the distinction between colonial and metropolitan territory (item **1252**).

Although historians of the 19th century did not generate the volume of articles that appeared in this biennial for the revolutionary era, they did produce a number of important books. Nelly Schmidt, writing about the many social injustices that lasted long after France's second abolition of slavery in 1848, reflects the current dissatisfaction of many Antilleans with their relationship with the metropole. Similarly the French Guyanese historian Serge Mam-Lam-Fouck writes the history of assimilationism as if to remind his readers that for two centuries up to the 1950s, people of color in the Antilles wanted nothing more than to erase the distinctions between themselves and metropolitan French people (item **1165**). Today intellectuals and others put greater emphasis on the cultural distinctiveness of the Antilles.

Finally, two major works on Haiti appeared in this biennial. Jean-François Brière's narrative of the relationship between Haiti and France in the first half-century of independence covers this familiar ground in new detail, with a critical eye on French demands, especially (item **1264**). And in the 20th century, where scholars have been fascinated by the long US occupation of Haiti and the rise of the Duvalier dictatorship, Matthew Smith fills in the intervening years with a rich and nuanced account of the rise of urban politics in the 1940s and early 1950s (item **1349**).

It seems likely that the revolutionary era will continue to dominate the historiography of the Francophone Caribbean. Scholarly recognition of the importance of the Haitian Revolution in particular continues to grow, among historians, other scholars, and even the public at large. New narrative histories and documentary collections make it easier to teach the Haitian Revolution as one of the canonical events of world history, and this attention, still quite new in the academy, will hopefully continue to draw new researchers into the field. [JG]

PUERTO RICO

The works selected for this issue of *HLAS* represent a robust field of historical scholarship. Applying a variety of theoretical approaches, methodologies, and sources, these works investigate key themes such as slavery, gender, sexuality, and colonialism. From microhistory to comparative history, from cultural studies to oral history, the theoretical and methodological repertoire informing current research challenges us to reconsider much of the conventional wisdom about Puerto Rican culture, society, and history.

Slavery continues to be a predominant theme in the historiography of 19th-century Puerto Rico. Drawing on slave census data, parish registers, judicial, criminal, and notarial records, researchers have scrutinized key aspects of slavery as a social and labor institution, advancing our understanding of the slave experience within Puerto Rico and the larger Caribbean region. Chinea probes the discourse supporting chattel slavery, the distinctively racialized coerced labor regime that took root in the Americas (item **1211**). The harsh slave codes, penal servitude, and antivagrancy laws introduced by Spain during the first half of the 1800s are the subjects of a piece by Santiago-Valles (item **1248**). These penal policies impinged heavily on both slaves and the free racially mixed subordinate classes. Labor power was in great demand in the colony's expanding agroexport economy, and the penal policies pursued by Spain linked race to punishment as a method of labor-power extraction. Despite these state-led efforts to seek additional forms of labor, slavery continued to thrive in Puerto Rico until its definitive abolition in 1873. In their analysis of the 1872 *Registro Central de Esclavos*, Negrón-Portillo and Mayo Santana demonstrate that slavery was widespread throughout the island, including the central highlands, a nonexport region (item **1285**). Furthermore, the pattern of slaveholding in Puerto Rico was characterized by ownership of small lots of slaves. This suggests that many people were involved in slavery, if only as holders of a few bond servants each. A similar pattern occurred in Brazil, Cuba, and the US, where a low ratio of slaves to masters was also the norm. Together with Negrón-Portillo and Mayo Santana, Picó expands on the theme of slave agency by studying family structures, extended kinship networks, and community ties among slaves and between slaves and the free population (item **1167**). These dynamics enabled enslaved people to better withstand the oppression and constraints of life in bondage.

Influenced by postmodern and cultural studies approaches, a growing body of literature centers on women, gender, and sexuality. Significantly, this trend has made prostitution a focal point of scholarly interest. Political, medical, legal, and religious entities spared no effort dealing with the practice of female commercial sex in Puerto Rico, originally legalized in 1876 but suppressed in the late 1910s. This theme is addressed by Flores Ramos (item **1274**) and Vázquez Lazo (item **1298**) in their detailed monographic studies of prostitution in San Juan and Ponce, respectively. Flores Ramos' book is the revised version of a master's thesis in history originally presented at the Universidad de Puerto Rico in 1995. This seminal work established prostitution and sexuality as historical problems worthy of scholarly inquiry in Puerto Rican historiography, paving the way for later research by Eileen Findlay (*HLAS 60:1954*) and Laura Briggs (*HLAS 64:1090*). In each of these works, the practices and discourses related to sexuality and prostitution serve as the lens through which larger issues in modern Puerto Rican history (gender, sexuality, class, race, citizenship, and nation) are brought into sharper focus.

Similarly, cultural studies has shed new light on central issues in the century-old history of US-Puerto Rico relations. The conventional focus on the structural dimensions of US domination (economic, military, and strategic) has given way to more nuanced analyses of colonial processes that highlight instances of contestation and negotiation. Arguing that the colonial interaction shapes both colonizer and colonized, Go demonstrates how Philippine and Puerto Rican political elites actively engaged the educational, electoral, and administrative policies introduced by the US (item **1320**), sometimes accommodating, sometimes transforming these policies. Merrill, in an innovative study, presents tourism as a space for negotiating power relations, one that allows both insular government officials and non-state actors to define the parameters of American influence (item **1333**). The rigorous comparative framework employed by these two authors is a welcome contribution, situating the island's colonial experience in a larger international perspective beyond the customary Caribbean context. Furthermore, Merrill's use of photographs points to the richness that visual sources offer the cultural historian.

Since the early 1970s, Puerto Rican historiography has developed in close dialogue with regional and international paradigms in historical research and writing. During the 1970s and 1980s practitioners of the so-called New History, or *nueva historia*, renovated the field with their works on economic, labor, social, and women's history issues. Since the 1990s, the shift toward cultural history has yielded revisionist interpretations of the Puerto Rican historical experience.

In more ways than one, the general histories written by Fernando Picó, *Historia general de Puerto Rico* (item **1168**), and César J. Ayala and Rafael Bernabe, *Puerto Rico in the American Century* (item **1299**), exemplify the development of the historical discipline in Puerto Rico over the last several decades. A key figure in the New History generation, Picó originally published his *Historia general* in 1986, incorporating the contributions of the social and economic historiography then in vogue. The work's 20th-anniversary commemorative edition constitutes a milestone in the development of the field. For their part, Ayala and Bernabe have undertaken the challenge of incorporating current theories and methodologies of cultural analysis into a provocative new synthesis. In one of their central contributions, they engage directly with the history of the Puerto Rican diaspora, introducing innovative ways of thinking about transnational relationships.

In concluding this overview of current trends in historical research on Puerto Rico, encouraging developments in the publishing landscape should also be noted. In comparison to the 1970s and 1980s, a greater number of local, independent small presses have become actively involved in disseminating historical scholarship on Puerto Rico. Besides the well-regarded Ediciones Huracán—which exerted such a pivotal influence on the development of the New History—several new small publishers are supporting the work of both established and junior researchers. These include Ediciones Callejón and Publicaciones Puertorriqueñas, two of the most prominent publishers to appear in recent years. In tandem with these local efforts, several leading North American university presses have developed a strong interest in the Caribbean in general and Puerto Rico in particular. The lists of Duke University Press, the University of North Carolina Press, and the University Press of Florida (with its own distinctive "Directions in Puerto Rican Studies" monographic series) abound in invaluable scholarly contributions focused on Puerto Rico.

A noteworthy development in the field is the electronic dissemination of research content. Academic and cultural institutions have begun to explore electronic access as an alternative mode of disseminating scholarship. Three prominent academic journals in the field have successfully adopted electronic publishing: *Caribbean Studies* (ISSN 0008–6533) and *Op. Cit.: Revista del Centro de Investigaciones Históricas* (ISSN 1526–5323), published by the Universidad de Puerto Rico, and *Centro Journal* (ISSN 1538–6279), issued by the Centro de Estudios Puertorriqueños at the City University of New York (CUNY). Their publishing strategies vary, however. While *Caribbean Studies* and *Centro Journal* have both joined the open-access international initiative known as the *Red de Revistas Científicas de América Latina y el Caribe, España y Portugal* or *Redalyc* (http://redalyc.uaemex.mx/), the history journal *Op. Cit.* is available only through *Informe!*, a fee-based full-text collection of Spanish-language periodicals created by the commercial vendor Gale Cengage. For its part, the Fundación Puertorriqueña de las Humanidades has broken new ground by launching the fully searchable *Enciclopedia de Puerto Rico/Encyclopedia of Puerto Rico* (item **1159**) (http://www.enciclopediapr.org/). Featuring contributions by prominent scholars, this free bilingual reference resource provides both textual and multimedia content, including images, audio, and video from archival collections. [LG]

CUBA

Over the past five years, work on Cuban history has shown more methodological and topical innovations than at perhaps any other time since the Cuban Revolution of 1959. For most of the second half of the 20th century, the primary goal of Cuban historiography was to explain the origins, course, and trajectory of the Cuban Revolution. This effort resulted in privileging late 19th- and 20th-century Cuban history at the expense of Cuba's first 350 years as a Spanish colony. During the first decade of the 21st century, with Fidel Castro sidelined since 2006 and the Cuban Revolution moving into its "geriatric" stage, new topics of historical study are being debated. Scholars are no longer focused solely on economic and social history viewed through a dependency lens. Works on class conflict and structural analysis now compete with, and have recently been overtaken by, titles on nationalism and racial identity. Cultural history, religion, and slavery are currently being studied with a vigor that places authors in dynamic dialogue with historians inside and outside of the field of Cuban studies.

In *Isla en la Historia* (item **1358**), Oscar Zanetti offers a succinct summary of Cuban historiography as it developed and evolved over the course of the 20th century. In particular, Zanetti traces prerevolutionary historiography from the 1900s to the 1950s with its emphasis on forming the nation-state, to revolutionary historiography from 1959 to the 1990s with its focus on class conflict as a means of explaining the Marxist nature of the revolution. He then offers a critique and appreciation of the "Special Period" in the 1990s with its turn toward studies of nationalism and identity. For a quick bibliographic assessment of these changing patterns in historical investigations, *Cuban Studies* remains the authoritative journal for the field. As with past issues of the journal, the annual bibliography under the title "Recent Work in Cuban Studies," which indexes Volumes 38–40 (2007–09) is the single best place to start a bibliographic inquiry for recent titles in Cuban history.

Scholarly developments over the past five years have shifted both the temporal and thematic focus away from an exclusive emphasis on the Revolution. This trend can be seen in new titles covering the 16th to 18th centuries: Alejandro de la Fuente's *Havana and the Atlantic in the Sixteenth Century* (item **1185**) provides a detailed social and cultural history based on archival sources that finally does justice to the important role Havana played in Spain's 16th-century imperial system. Likewise, Clune's *Cuban Convents in the Age of Enlightened Reform* (item **1212**) examines developments in the historiography of the Bourbon Reforms in continental Latin America to explain how they impacted Cuba's religious life.

With the turn to identity, race, and ethnicity as part of a new interest in cultural history, migrants, once pushed to the margins of Cuban history, are now in the historical spotlight thanks to studies of their role in shaping the development of Cuban society. Miriam Herrera Jerez and Mario Castillo Santana analyze the role of the Chinese in Cuba during the 20th century complementing previous scholarship focused on the 19th century (item **1323**). Spanish historians of Cuba continue to display a keen interest in Spanish migrants to the island in the late 19th and first half of the 20th century. Antonio M. Moral Roncal analyzes diplomatic relations during the Spanish Civil War (item **1334**), Juan Andrés Blanco Rodríguez examines the role of migrants from Castile and Leon during the 19th and 20th century (item **1303**), and Julio Antonio Yanes Mesa focuses on the specific migration of Canary islanders to Cuba from 1902–35 (item **1357**).

Studies of slavery continue to produce a burgeoning and ever-growing list of titles. Several scholars are adopting "Atlantic," "transnational" and "comparative" frameworks to place Cuban slave studies in multiple contexts. Rebecca Scott's *Degrees of Freedom* skillfully compares Cuba and Louisiana in the second half of the 19th century to show the important convergences and divergences of the two societies in the aftermath of slavery (item **1296**). Manuel Barcia's study of resistance among enslaved Africans emphasizes their "African" background in terms of military and religious ideas that influenced plans to rebel, and thereby forces scholar to consider African history much more seriously when studying Cuban slavery (item **1259**). Continuing the Atlantic/Transnational trend are the 16 chapters in the book edited by Spanish historian José Piqueras that examine Cuba from social, cultural, economic, and political perspectives during the Age of Revolution from the 1780s to 1830s (item **1213**)

In addition to these innovations, the Cuban Wars for Independence and the Cuban Revolution of 1959 continue to produce numerous and noteworthy studies. José Miguel Abreu Cardet provides a penetrating cultural and social history of the ideas behind the Ten Years' War by focusing on the conflicting roles of *caudillismo* and *regionalimso* (item **1257**). Fernando Fernández Rodríguez's study of Ángel Guerra Porra examines a lesser-known military leader of the Wars for Independence (item **1271**). Studies of the 1959 Revolution in the forms of document compilations and biographical studies appear every year. Such publications issued this biennium include versions of diaries by Raul Castro, Che Guevera, and other military leaders edited by Heinz Dieterich, Pedro Álvarez Tabío, Paco Ignacio Taibo (item **1312**), and Benito Estrada Fernández (item **1314**).

As 2009 marked the 50th anniversary of the Cuban Revolution, reassessments of the event began to appear in advance of the commemorations. Memoirs by former supporters such as Carlos Franqui (item **1315**), biographies of Castro by Norberto Fuentes (item **1317**), and interviews with Fidel Castro (item **1307**) have shown new insights into previously understudied topics. One of the major areas of growth in Cuban historiography in the near future will undoubtedly be revisionist studies that "decenter" Fidel and other well-known leaders from their central role in shaping Cuban history. The next volume of *HLAS* will certainly have more annotations on the Cuban Revolution that take stock of the 50th anniversary and its accompanying scholarly output. [MDC]

DOMINICAN REPUBLIC

Stemming from both scholarly and public interest, during the first decade of the 21st century, authors have generated a substantive quantity of historical studies. Thoughtfully exploring a variety of issues, the material refers to local, national, and global events that have affected the development of the Dominican Republic, the Caribbean, Latin America, and the world, during the last 200 years.

In particular, reflective economic and political analysis has strengthened traditional narrative. From a political perspective, Dominican scholarship continues to emphasize the role and impact of Trujillo's government. Although overlapping of material is inevitable, the authors examine different aspects of the regime and each offers riveting and distinctive references. Four monographs (5 volumes) on Trujillo *La Era de Trujillo: Cronología histórica, 1930–1961* by Fernando Infante (item **1326**); *Mujeres dominicanas, 1930–1961: antitrujillistas y exiliadas en Puerto Rico* by Myrna Herrera Mora (item **1324**); *Trujillo: el tiranicidio de 1961* by Juan Daniel Balcácer (item **1300**); and *Radio Caribe: en la era de Trujillo* by Lipe Collado (item **1308**) illustrate this trend. Similarly, the Revolution of April 1965 and the subsequent intervention of the US are two other topics that continue to receive critical analysis. Among other works, *El peligro comunista en la revolución de abril: ¿mito o realidad?* by Bernardo Vega (item **1355**) and *La Revolución* *de abril de 1965: siete días de guerra civil* by Jesús de la Rosa (item **1344**) are excellent contributions that depict the thematic importance of these two topics.

Beyond works on Trujillo and the events of 1965, studies of influential political figures remain a solid contribution to the literature. An updated and revised version of the ideological program of Juan Pablo Duarte, one of the founders of the Dominican nation (item **1267**), a collection of documents by former President Juan Bosch (item **1304**), and a collection of speeches by Alberto Caamaño, leader of the 14 de Junio movement (item **1305**), indicate the relevance of political discourse. From a different perspective, Yolanda Ricardo's *Magisterio y creación: los Henríquez Ureña* is worth noting (item **1292**). This compressive monograph, which discusses the cultural and intellectual development of the Dominican society, fills an important gap in cultural study.

Ranging from historical accounts to fascinating anecdotes, a substantial number of publications show an interest in provincial and local history. The works of Arturo Bueno, Constancio Cassá, and Rafael Darío Herrera, for example, highlight the contribution of Santiago (item **1265**), Constanza (item **1306**), and Montecristi (item **1325**) to the country's cultural, socioeconomic, and political development. The strengths of these texts are the authors' engagement of academic and non-academic readers who learn about specific characteristics of several regions of the country.

Graphic illustrations and photographic images are included in almost all publications. The impressive photographs of the revolution and the US military intervention of April 1965, for example, vividly show the complexity and brutality of the confrontation. These images help readers to visualize the textual conceptualization.

The reference publications in this section are clear signs for confirming the strength of Dominican historiography. Wide-ranging, thoughtful historical analyses appear in critical works. However, while fruitful work has been done in gender and cultural studies, there is room for more research in these and other areas. Nonetheless, the different topics included in this annotated bibliography reveal the broad scope of the authors' social and political thought and illuminate the culture of politics in the realm of global events and socioeconomic developments. [VP]

GENERAL

1155 Brereton, Bridget. Contesting the past: narratives of Trinidad and Tobago history. (*NWIG*, 81:3/4, 2007, p. 169–196, bibl.)

In this important article, the author, a recognized authority on the history of Trinidad and Tobago, discusses the four main narratives of the nation's historical writings from the colonial period to the present. Makes a compelling argument for viewing each of the major ethnic groups as seeking to ensure that its voice is adequately heard and that it obtains adequate space in the canonical national history. Expresses concern that these current efforts might diminish the emergence of a truly national perspective. [ELC]

1156 Camara, Evelyne; Isabelle Dion; and **Jacques Dion.** Esclaves: regards de blancs 1672–1913. Aix-en-Provence, France: Archives nationales d'outre-mer; Marseille: Images en manoeuvres, 2008. 272 p.: bibl., col. ill. (Histoires d'outre-mer)

Collection of primary sources on French Caribbean slavery and the slave trade extending from the late 17th century to the early 20th century. Organized thematically rather than chronologically or geographically. Besides its valuable collection of archival texts on the trade, slave resistance, and everyday life, the volume contains dozens of high-quality color photographs of images and artifacts from French archives and national museums. [JDG]

1157 Cottias, Myriam. Gender and republican citizenship in the French West Indies, 1848–1945. (*Slavery Abolit.*, 26:2, Aug. 2005, p. 233–245)

Drawing on the author's social and demographic history of the town of Trois Ilets (1985), this article exposes the way in which French 19th-century bourgeois values imposed marriage as a central republican value for ex-slaves after emancipation in 1848. Many ex-slave women did not marry, while those who did were able to attain a measure of respectability. Voluntary associations open only to "respectable" married women allowed some women of color to have a voice in public affairs. This was important because women were not eligible to vote in France until 1944. [JDG]

1158 Denis, Watson R. Orígenes y manifestaciones de la francofilia haitiana: nacionalismo y política exterior en Haití, 1880–1915. (*Secuencia/México*, 67, enero/ abril 2007, p. 93–139, bibl.)

Examines the ways that Haitian diplomats and men of letters in the late 19th and early 20th centuries emphasized their Francophone culture as a way of rejecting racial prejudice and asserting the unique identity of their nation. Denis sees this as one additional factor isolating the nation within the Caribbean. [JDG]

1159 Enciclopedia de Puerto Rico/Encyclopedia of Puerto Rico. San Juan: Fundación Puertorriqueña de las Humanidades, 2008. <http://www.enciclopediapr.org/>

Fully bilingual, innovative online reference work covering a wide range of topics, from history to literature to popular culture, including material on the Puerto Rican diaspora. Features contributions by prominent scholars. Text of many entries is enhanced with multimedia content such as images, audio, and video from archival collections. Though designed for a precollege audience, its authoritative content will be of great use to university students as well as seasoned specialists. Sponsored by the Fundación Puertorriqueña de las Humanidades, a well-established nonprofit cultural heritage organization, affiliated with the prestigious National Endowment for the Humanities. [LAG]

1160 Funes Monzote, Reinaldo. From rainforest to cane field in Cuba: an environmental history since 1492. Translated by Alex Martin. Chapel Hill: Univ. of North Carolina Press, 2008. 357 p.: bibl., ill., index, maps. (Envisioning Cuba)

Pioneering contribution to the nascent field of Cuban environmental history. Interesting analysis of the linked relationship between deforestation to fuel cane mills and the sugar boom of the 19th century. Specific focus is on the devastating century-long ecological consequences of an 1815 decree allowing plantation owners the freedom to exploit and clear the forest for monocrop agriculture that continued until the 20th century. [MC]

1161 Goldish, Josette C. Once Jews: stories of Caribbean Sephardim. Princeton, N.J.: Markus Wiener Publishers, 2009. 334 p.: bibl., ill., index, map.

This books provides a "history from the top" by focusing on elite Sephardic Jews of Curaçao and their 19th-century migrations to four sites in the Caribbean—St. Thomas, Coro, Santo Domingo, and Barranquilla. Through casual interviews with present-day, financially successful, mostly male descendants, most of whom are no longer Jews, at least in terms of religious affiliation, and many of whom left a public imprint on broader civic culture. [C.E. Griffin]

1162 Inniss, Probyn, Sir. Methodism in St. Kitts, 1787–2006. S.l.: s.n., 2006. 126 p.: bibl., ill.

Written by a Methodist lay preacher and former vice president of the Methodist Church in the Caribbean and the Americas, this book provides extremely useful information on the 200-year fortunes of the Methodist Church in St. Kitts and questions concerning the future of the church in St. Kitts and the Caribbean as a whole. Provides names of various ministers who served from 1900 onwards. Also contains important information on the island's early history. [ELC

1163 Landers, Jane. Atlantic Creoles in the age of revolutions. Cambridge, Mass.: Harvard Univ. Press, 2010. 340 p.: bibl., ill., index, maps.

Based on exhaustive archival research, Professor Landers analyzes the impact of remarkable Afro-Caribbeans or Atlantic Creoles who, after shedding the shackles of slavery, contributed decisively to the revolutions and independence movements in the circum-Caribbean. Of diverse ethnic origins, they fought and played important political roles throughout the French, Spanish, and English colonies from the mid-18th century to the 1850. Landers concentrates on the counter-revolution in Saint Domingue, on the Afro-Caribbean rebels in Havana, and includes an insightful chapter on the African-descended Seminoles in the US. This is a major contribution to Afro-Latin studies and will be indispensable as a teaching tool. [G.M. Dorn]

1164 Latimer, Jon. Buccaneers of the Caribbean: Cambridge, MA: Harvard Univ. Press, 2009 368 p.: illus.

This book charts the exploits of 17th-century sea raiders—privateers licensed to attack the Spanish by the governments of England, France and Holland—who followed few rules as they forged new empires by drawing on letters, diaries, and memoirs of such figures as William Dampier, Sieur Raveneau de Lussan, Alexander Oliver Exquemelin, and Basil Ringrose [C.E. Griffin].

1165 Mam-Lam-Fouck, Serge. L'histoire de l'assimilation: des "vieilles colonies" françaises aux départements d'outre-mer: la culture politique de l'assimilation en Guyane et aux Antilles françaises, XIXe et XXe siècles. Matoury, French Guiana: Ibis Rouge Editions, 2006. 258 p.: bibl. (Espace outre-mer)

A leading historian of French Guyana returns to the archive to trace the rhetoric of "assimilationism" in the French Caribbean, and especially in his home region. Though deeply discredited in the French Caribbean today, the notion that colonial people would be best served by policies that would render them politically and culturally indistinct from the European French was a central tenant of colonial culture until 1946, when these former colonies voted to become full-fledged departments of France. [JDG]

1166 Peabody, Sue. Négresse, mulâtresse, citoyenne: gender and emancipation in the French Caribbean, 1650–1848. (in Gender and emancipation in the Atlantic world, 1650–1848. Edited by Pamela Scully and Diana Paton. Raleigh, NC: Duke Univ. Press, 2005, p. 57–78.)

Useful and well-written overview of the distinctive French mechanisms for slave manumission as they applied to women. Peabody not only synthesizes the emerging French and English-language scholarship on this question, but she illustrates these conclusions with original archival examples from 18th- and 19th-century Martinique. [JDG]

1167 Picó, Fernando. Cayeyanos: familias y solidaridades en la historia de Cayey. San Juan: Ediciones Huracán, 2007. 183 p.: bibl., ill.

Stimulating microhistory of a mountain town in central Puerto Rico from its foundation in the late 18th century through the year 2000. Focuses on the everyday life of both prominent and common people and shows the critical role of slave labor in the region's economy. Slaves' marriage and ritual kinship practices demonstrate a degree of agency, calling into question the prevailing notion of passivity. Abundantly documented research in church, notarial, police, and government records. [LAG]

1168 Picó, Fernando. Historia general de Puerto Rico. 3. ed., conmemorativa. San Juan: Ediciones Huracán, 2006. 320 p.: bibl., ill., index, maps. (Col. Huracán academia)

Commemorative edition marking the 20th anniversary of Picó's *Historia general de Puerto Rico*. When originally published in 1986, this work filled a void in Puerto Rican studies. Tapping the historiographical contributions of the so-called New History, Picó wrote a comprehensive interpretation of the country's past. Departing from the conventional emphasis on great leaders, political events and institutions, the book focused instead on common people, everyday life, and economic processes, as well as cultural developments. Also noteworthy is the author's effort to situate Puerto Rican history within the larger Caribbean experience. Includes an updated selected bibliography. For review of earlier ed., see *HLAS 48:2375*. [LAG]

1169 Picó, Fernando. History of Puerto
Rico: a panorama of its people. Princ-
eton, N.J.: Markus Wiener Publishers., 2006.
351 p.: bibl., ill., maps.
First English translation of the au-
thor's celebrated *Historia general de Puerto
Rico.* Features a new chapter covering re-
cent social, cultural, and political events.
See also *HLAS 48:2375* and item **1168.**
[LAG]

1170 Ramos Méndez, Mario. Posesión del
ayer: la nacionalidad cultural en la es-
tadidad. San Juan: Isla Negra Editores, 2007.
209 p.: bibl. (Col. Visiones y cegueras)
This book attempts to demonstrate
that since 1898, the Puerto Rican statehood
movement has been a culturally nationalist
movement that sees a permanent annexation to the US as a solution to the colonial
problem without forfeiting a sense of Puerto
Rican culture and personality. Contains
analysis, public pronouncements, and
public actions by major statehood leaders.
[M. García-Calderón]

**1171 Regional footprints: the travels and
travails of early Caribbean migrants.**
Edited by Annette Insanally, Mark Clifford,
and Sean Sheriff. Kingston: Latin American-
Caribbean Centre, Univ. of the West Indies/
SALISES, 2006. 482 p.: bibl., ill., index, map.
Based on a series of seminar papers
presented at the Mona Campus of the Univ.
of the West Indies, this book highlights
Anglophone Caribbean migration to Cuba,
Panama, Costa Rica, Colombia, Haiti, Nicaragua, and Belize. Together the essays
demonstrate that the migrants maintained
a West Indian identity and inculcated into
the younger generation West Indian values
like strict parental guidance, insistence on
religious instruction, and a strong focus on
formal education. [ELC]

1172 Rogers, Dominique. Les Antilles à
l'époque moderne: tendances et perspectives d'un demi-siècle de recherches
francophones et anglophones en histoire
sociale. (*in* Société, colonisation et esclavage
dans le monde atlantique. Historiographies
des sociétés coloniales américaines, 1492–
1898. Édition de François-Joseph Ruggiu and
Cécile Vidal. Rennes: Les Perséides, 2008,
p. 243–281.

Perceptive synthesis of 50 years of
French- and English-language historiography on Caribbean slave societies, with special attention to France's plantation colonie
in the region. [JDG]

1173 Silva Gotay, Samuel. Catolicismo y
política en Puerto Rico: bajo España y
Estados Unidos, siglos XIX y XX. San Juan:
Editorial Univ. de Puerto Rico, 2005. 503 p.:
bibl.
The second installment of a projected trilogy on the politics of the Catholic
Church in Puerto Rico under both Spanish
and US domination. In the sociology-of-
religion vein, the author explores both insti
tutional and popular religion for evidence o
Catholicism's political dimension vis-à-vis
doctrine and practice. Documents from the
Secret Vatican Archive in Rome shed new
light on the Vatican-led diplomacy leading
up to the Spanish-Cuban-American War of
1898. [LAG]

1174 Thompson, Alvin O. Symbolic legacies of slavery in Guyana. (*NWIG*,
80:3/4, 2006, p. 191–220, bibl., photos)
Contends that divisions in the multi-
ethnic nation of Guyana, fostered in part
during Forbes Burnham's administration,
have made it difficult to promote a successful national conversation about preserving
slavery's legacy on Guyana. Although East
Indians "have no real problem with those
slaves who have been elevated to national
hero status," they nonetheless feel that
they had long been neglected by the almost
predominantly black government which
failed to "give due respect to Indians whose
ancestors deserved a place in the national
pantheon of 'gods'" (p. 217). [ELC]

EARLY COLONIAL

1175 Amussen, Susan Dwyer. Caribbean
exchanges: slavery and the transformation of English society, 1640–1700.
Chapel Hill: Univ. of North Carolina Press,
2007. 302 p.: bibl., index.
In considering the impact on English
society of its Caribbean colonies and slavery, the author contends that slavery left no
institution in England untouched because
of the transatlantic movement of peoples
and slaves. Suggests that important aspects
of the details of plantation life—like race,

gender, law, punishment, labor, and class—made their way back to England and were incorporated into English life and culture. [ELC]

1176 Banks, Kenneth J. Chasing empire across the sea: communications and the state in the French Atlantic, 1713–1763. Montreal; Ithaca: McGill-Queen's Univ. Press, 2002. 319 p.: bibl., index, maps.

Innovative study examines Martinique's place in France's New World Empire alongside Canada in the first half of the 18th century. For those interested in the Francophone Caribbean this is an important work in the still emerging field of "Atlantic Studies." Banks focuses on the challenges faced by the French state: difficulties of communication, gathering information, controlling marginal populations, and adapting royal rituals to local conditions. [JDG]

1177 Beckles, Hilary. Kalinago (Carib) resistance to European colonisation of the Caribbean. (*Caribb. Q./Mona*, 54:4, Dec. 2008, p. 77–94, bibl.)

In specifying "some of the political and military responses" of the Kalinago people to the European intrusion in the Caribbean primarily between 1624 and 1700, the author demonstrates the protracted wars of resistance they waged against colonization and slavery. More successful in the Lesser Antilles in resisting first the Spanish and later the French and English, the Kalinagos eventually faced major efforts at extermination by the English that resulted in their effective depopulation. [ELC]

1178 Boucher, Philip P. France and the American tropics to 1700: tropics of discontent? Baltimore: Johns Hopkins Univ. Press, 2008. 372 p.: bibl, index.

Valuable survey of early French Caribbean colonization, by the leading English-language scholar of the period. This highly readable text is based on primary sources and concerned with social, cultural, and environmental themes. Boucher joins the rising number of scholars who temper the idea of a rapid "sugar revolution" by stressing that the sugar plantation complex in France's possessions arose only in the early decades of the 18th century, more than 50 years after the introduction of sugar processing techniques. [JDG]

1179 Boulle, Pierre H. Race et esclavage dans la France de l'Ancien Régime. Paris: Perrin, 2007. 286 p.: bibl., index.

Important publication by the senior scholar in this field. Boulle's book contains many of his earlier articles on the history of the concept of race in France. But the book also contains new work on the social history of Caribbean, African, and Asian people of color in 18th-century France. Perhaps most interesting is his contention that prejudice against blacks before the Revolution was primarily confined to the French upper classes and was not observable among the working class. [JDG]

1180 Burnard, Trevor. "Do thou in gentle Phibia smile": scenes from an interracial marriage, Jamaica, 1754–86. (*in* Beyond bondage: free women of color in the Americas. Edited by David Barry Gaspar and Darlene Clark Hine. Chicago: Univ. of Illinois Press, 2004, p. 82–105, bibl.)

Author sees Phibbah, the long-standing slave mistress of Thomas Thistlewood, as an accommodater with apparently real emotional attachment to Thistlewood. Neither victim nor heroine, she transcended herself to slavery in a more metaphysical way until her eventual freedom after Thistlewood's death. Contends that her activities "blurred the distinctions that whites believed naturally existed between whites and blacks." [ELC]

1181 Crow Via, Vicki. A comparison of the colonial laws of Jamaica under governor Thomas Lynch 1681–1684 with those enumerated in the John Taylor manuscript of 1688. (*J. Caribb. Hist.*, 39:2, 2005, p. 236–248, bibl.)

Asserts that the Crown's growing interest in maintaining social order and increasing revenue in Jamaica in the second half of the 18th century is reflected in the number and quality of laws passed during that time. Jamaican planters resisted many of these laws, particularly those aimed at producing revenue at their expense. [ELC]

1182 Documentos históricos de Puerto Rico. Recopilación de Ricardo E. Alegría. San Juan: Centro de Estudios Avanzados de Puerto Rico y el Caribe, 2009. 5 v.: bibl., ill., index.

Invaluable collection of archival sources covering key aspects of 16th-century Puerto Rico, including indigenous groups, slavery, the government and economy, military fortifications, and religion. Drawn mainly from the holdings of the Archivo General de Indias in Sevilla, Spain, these documents have been transcribed by professional paleographers and historians. Use of the set is facilitated by its chronological organization and comprehensive indexes for subjects, personal names, and places. [LAG]

1183 Dubois, Laurent. The French Atlantic. (in Atlantic History: a critical appraisal. Edited by Jack P. Greene and Philip D. Morgan. Cambridge, England: Oxford Univ. Press, 2009, p. 137–162)

Valuable overview of France's 18th-century Atlantic holdings, and their historiography. The article by a major historian of this region focuses largely, though not exclusively, on the Francophone Caribbean. [JDG]

1184 Epstein, James. Politics of colonial sensation: the trial of Thomas Picton and the cause of Louisa Calderon. (Am. Hist. Rev., 112:3, June 2007, p. 712–741, bibl., ill.)

Gripping evaluation of the political intrigue and implications of the trial of a governor of colonial Trinidad who was accused of the torture of a young mulatto girl. The case and the article portray the problems of administration in a recently acquired British colony where Spanish laws prevailed. [ELC]

1185 Fuente, Alejandro de la. Havana and the Atlantic in the sixteenth century. With the collaboration of César García del Pino and Bernardo Iglesias Delgado. Chapel Hill: Univ. of North Carolina Press, 2008. 287 p.: bibl., index. (Envisioning Cuba)

Provides the most detailed account to date of Havana in the 1500s. Displays a thorough command of the extant published and archival sources, most notably notarial, cabildo, and ecclesiastical records. Especially innovative is the argument on the need to analyze Havana as created by the fleet system, but also to understand that its residents had much more dynamic lives than simply created by trade at the port. [MC]

1186 García Fernández, Nélida. Interacciones mercantiles entre los imperios del Atlántico: el comercio directo del añil colonial español hacia Bristol, vía Jamaica. (Caribb. Stud., 34:2, July/Dec. 2006, p. 47–98, bibl., graph, map, tables)

Useful review of Spanish commerce in Central America carried on by the British who were interested in Spanish dye for their textile industry. Hence Jamaica was an important entrepôt in the route between Central America and Bristol at a time when Jewish merchants were familiar with the Spanish language and had connections in Spanish America. [ELC]

1187 Giordini, Jean-Pierre. La création urbaine à Saint-Domingue (Haïti): processus planificateur et modèle urbaine au XVIIIe siècle. Misères et destinée d'une gestion. (in Techniques et colonies (XVIe–XXe siècles). Edité par Sylviane Llinares and Philippe Hrodĕj. Paris: Publications de la Société française d'Histoire d'Outre Mer et de l'Université de Bretagne Sud—SOLITO, 2005, p. 127–162.

Detailed survey of the creation of cities in Saint-Domingue based on primary sources, particularly on the correspondence of engineers and administrators. Analyzes urban construction in the context of both French and Caribbean condition. The notes constitute an excellent bibliography of French-language scholarship on this neglected topic. [JDG]

1188 Green, Cecilia A. Hierarchies of whiteness in the geographies of empire: Thomas Thistlewood and the Barretts of Jamaica. (NWIG, 80:1/2, 2006, p. 5–43)

Insightful article that centers on evidence taken from the lives of Thomas Thistlewood and the Barrett family that lived in Jamaica from 1655. Argues that Trevor Burnard overstates the degree of white egalitarianism, glosses over important differences among nonelite whites, and "ignores critical evidence of the sociostructural factors separating the socioeconomic or class niche of respected, socially mobile lesser-white settlers like Thistlewood and that of the upper plantocracy." [ELC]

1189 Hatzenberger, Françoise. La forêt antillaise, lieu de souffrance et d'espérance. (in L'esclave et les plantations:

de l'établissement de la servitude à son abolition: un hommage à Pierre Pluchon. Édition de Philippe Hrodĕj. Rennes: Presses universitaires de Rennes, 2008, p. 25–58.

Hatzenberger is an expert on Caribbean botany. Here she draws on a variety of primary and secondary sources to depict life in the forests of Hispaniola under Spanish and French colonial control. Notable because it is one of the few attempts to write an environmental history of Saint-Domingue/Haiti and because of its focus on enslaved Tainos and blacks. [JDG]

1190 Haudrère, Philippe. Les tribulations de Paul Jean-François Le Mercier De La Rivière, Ancien ordonnateur de la marine, devenue habitant de Saint-Domingue, 1787–1791. (in Esclave et les plantations: de l'établissement de la servitude à son abolition: un hommage à Pierre Pluchon. Edité par Philippe Hrodĕj. Rennes: Presses universitaires de Rennes, 2008, p. 187–208)

Haudrère reproduces 15 years of correspondence of Paul-Jean François Le Mercier de la Rivière. French-born, but a member of a famous colonial family, Paul-Jean failed in his ambitious attempt to build a prosperous coffee plantation in Saint-Domingue from the 1770s to 1792. The letters, largely uncommented, provide an excellent example of the diverse preoccupations of a French colonial planter on the eve of the Haitian Revolution. [JDG]

1191 Heywood, Linda Marinda and John K. Thornton. Central Africans, Atlantic Creoles, and the foundation of the Americas, 1585–1660. New York: Cambridge Univ. Press, 2007. 370 p.: bibl., ill., index, maps.

Exploring the specific origins of the charter generation of Africans coming to English and Dutch America, authors conclude that their Central African origins where they had successfully interacted with Europeans for more than 150 years enhanced their role as founders and shapers of African American culture. Wonderfully researched and compellingly argued, the book engages current historiography and shows the brutality of slavery even in these early years. Excellent. [ELC]

1192 Hodson, Christopher. "A bondage so harsh": Acadian labor in the French Caribbean, 1763–1766. (Early Amer. Stud., 5:1, 2007, p. 95–131)

This highly accessible article traces the fate of Acadian refugees to make an important point about the French empire in the aftermath of defeat in the Seven Years War. Pulling together a wide range of primary sources, Hodson argues that physiocratic ideas popular in France became a new imperial ideology. Dismayed by planters' lack of loyalty during the war, Versailles tried, but failed, to establish white farming communities in Cayenne as well as in Saint-Domingue in place of slave labor. [JDG]

1193 Hrodĕj, Philippe. Les esclaves à Saint-Domingue aux temps pionniers, 1630–1700: la rafle, la traite et l'interlope. (in L'esclave et les plantations: de l'établissement de la servitude à son abolition: un hommage à Pierre Pluchon. Edité par Philippe Hrodĕj. Rennes: Presses universitaires de Rennes, 2008, p. 59–84.)

Hrodĕj, the author of a 1999 dissertation on the life of Saint-Domingue's governor Du Casse, describes the beginnings of the transition of this colony from settler to slave society based on primary sources. His emphasis is not on the sugar industry but instead on the military issues of colonial defense, raids on neighboring colonies, and the balance of incoming African captives and indentured servants. [JDG]

1194 Hrodĕj, Philippe. Et le sucre fut: l'apparition de l'or blanc dans la partie française de Saint-Domingue. (in Techniques et colonies (XVIe–XXe siècles). Edité par Sylviane Llinares et Philippe Hrodĕj. Paris: Publications de la Société française d'Histoire d'Outre Mer et de l'Université de Bretagne Sud—SOLITO, 2005, p. 203–233)

Hrodĕj, the author of a 1999 dissertation on Saint-Domingue's governor Du Casse, narrates the slow emergence of sugar planting in that colony up to 1710. Excellent detail drawn from French archival sources. [JDG]

1195 Lesueur, Boris. Les troupes coloniales aux Antilles sous l'Ancien Régime. (Hist. écon. soc., 28:4, 2009, p, 3–19)

Useful overview of French colonial troops in the Antilles in the 18th century, based on archival sources. Lesueur provides information on troop mortality, describes recruiting practices, and narrates policy changes up to the Revolution. He concludeds there was an evolution that gradually opened colonial forces to greater cooperation between the Navy and Army, and to a wider array of recruits. [JDG]

1196 Bonnet, Natacha. L'organisation du travail servile sur la sucrerie domingoise au XVIIIe siècle. (in L'esclave et les plantations: de l'établissement de la servitude à son abolition: un hommage à Pierre Pluchon. Edité par Philippe Hrodĕj. Rennes: Presses universitaires de Rennes, 2008, p. 125–160)

Important detailed study of productivity and demography on four medium-sized sugar plantations in Saint-Domingue. Excellent use of historiography and new sources to show that some estates invested in more land while others invested heavily in more slaves. Furthermore, suggests that the question of slave overwork cannot simply be calculated based on ratios of slaves to surface area. The comparison suggests that slaves on all plantations were worked to their maximum. [JDG]

Mandelblatt, Bertie. A transatlantic commodity: Irish salt beef in the French Atlantic world. See HLAS 65:984.

1197 Pichardo Viñals, Hortensia. Temas históricos del oriente cubano. Selección, liminar y notas de Fernando Carr Parúas. La Habana: Editorial de Ciencias Sociales, 2006. 300 p.: bibl., ill., ports. (Col. Premio nacional de ciencias sociales)

Collection of narrative history essays dealing with Oriente in the colonial era united by a focus on the era of the conquest, founding of the first cities in the region, and an examination of the life of Carlos Manuel de Céspedes. A lengthy interview provides a biography of Pichardo and sheds insights into the Cuban historical profession during the 20th century. [MC]

1198 Portuondo Zúñiga, Olga. Entre esclavos y libres de Cuba colonial. Santiago, Cuba: Editorial Oriente, 2003. 273 p.: bibl., ill.

Diverse collection of short and lengthy chapters tied together by a thematic unity illustrating the cultural history of Eastern Cuba during the colonial period. Thoroughly documented with regional and national archival sources, the book explores the experience of slaves, free people of color, immigrants, and the urban working poor. [MC]

1199 Régent, Frédéric. Les blancs métissés en Guadeloupe au XVIIIe siècle. (Ultramarines/Aix-en-Provence, 24, 2004, p. 25–28)

This brief article presents evidence from 18th-century parish registers that in at least several Guadeloupe districts, priests recategorized people of mixed racial descent as "white." Regent calls for a more detailed colony-wide survey of this phenomenon which shows the subjectivity of racial labels. In one parish 40 percent of the "whites" had at least one African ancestor. [JDG]

1200 Regourd, François. Diffusion et assimilation des techniques académiques de collete et d'expertise dans l'espace caraïbe, xviie–xviiie siècles. (in Techniques et colonies (XVIe–XXe siècles). Edité par Sylviane Llinares and Philippe Hrodĕj. Paris: Publications de la Société française d'Histoire d'Outre Mer et de l'Université de Bretagne Sud—SOLITO, 2005, p. 33–47)

Deeply researched article about the scientific interests of elite colonists in the 18th-century French Caribbean, especially in Saint-Domingue. Regourd examines the ways in which these colonists were exposed to techniques and instruments by visiting scientific expeditions, as well as military cartographers and engineers. [JDG]

1201 Smith, Simon David. Slavery, family, and gentry capitalism in the British Atlantic: the world of the Lascelles,1648–1834. Cambridge, England; New York: Cambridge Univ. Press, 2006. 380 p.: bibl., ill., index, maps. (Cambridge studies in economic history. Second series)

This well-researched case study of a British family that was intricately involved in plantation agriculture and slavery in Barbados casts new light on the commercial and cultural networks the Lascelles created between the mid-17th century and the 1830s. The author also examines the challenges of managing Barbadian sugar estates and the dehumanizing aspects of slavery and slave life on the plantations owned by the Lascelles family. Very useful. [ELC]

1202 Waters, Anita M. Planning the past: heritage tourism and post-colonial politics at Port Royal. Lanham, Md.: Lexington Books, 2006. 125 p.: bibl., index.

Very useful though short study of a 17th-century Jamaican town, once the haunt of pirates and admirals and well-known for its licentious lifestyle, which was eventually destroyed by earthquakes. Contends that the various plans developed over time to promote heritage tourism at Port Royal reflect the changing post-colonial values, assumptions, and attitudes about pirates and maritime history. [ELC]

1203 Widmer, Rudolf. Désastres 'naturels' et sécurité alimentaire: La Martinique et Santiago de Cap-Vert au XVIIIe siècle. (*in* Sur les chemins de l'histoire antillaise: mélanges offerts à Lucien Abénon. Edité par Jean Bernabé et Serge Mam Lam Fouck. Matoury, French Guiana: Ibis rouge, 2006, p. 181–200)

Innovative comparison of the ways in which natural disasters and food shortages were handled by authorities and elites in French Martinique and Portuguese Cape Verde. Using 18th-century government documents from the two empires, Widmer shows how in both societies elites' concern with maximizing commercial exports led to a lack of local food production and preventable famines. [JDG]

LATE COLONIAL AND FRENCH REVOLUTIONARY PERIOD

1204 Altink, Henrice. Forbidden fruit: proslavery attitudes towards enslaved women's sexuality and interracial sex. (*J. Caribb. Hist.*, 39:2, 2005, p. 201–235, bibl.)

Analysis of the pro-slavery debate about the sexuality of Jamaica's enslaved women between 1770 and 1834. Arguing that many of the pro-slavery writers viewed the sexuality of enslaved women as deviant, while the pro-slavery rhetoric on interracial sex actually contradicted the behavior of white Jamaicans men. Suggests that debate about enslaved Jamaican women's sexuality and interracial sex acted together to sustain or prolong slavery in the British Caribbean. [ELC]

1205 Benot, Yves. The insurgents of 1791: their leaders and the concept of independence. (*in* World of the Haitian Revolution. Edited by David P. Geggus and Norman Fiering. Bloomington: Indiana Univ. Press, 2009, p. 99–110)

Benot closely examines the events surrounding the Haitian uprising of August 1791. He offers evidence that specific free men of color and a handful of royalists supported and encouraged rebel slave leaders to move to outright revolt. He suggests that the rebels always had some idea of wresting the colony from white control. But he argues that this was often hidden by their royalist rhetoric and by the actions of leaders, including Toussaint Louverture, who were willing to negotiate with the whites. [JDG]

1206 Buck-Morss, Susan. Hegel, Haiti and Universal history. Pittsburgh, Pa.: Univ. of Pittsburgh Press, 2009. 164 p.: bibl., ill. (Illuminations)

This is an expanded edition of Buck-Morss's celebrated essay "Hegel and Haiti," which first appeared in Critical Inquiry (2000). Using historical research into press accounts of the Haitian Revolution appearing in Germany, including the German masonic publication, *Minerva*, the essay provides considerable evidence that Hegel was inspired by recent events in Haiti when he first presented his deeply influential reflections on the dialectic relationship between master and slave in 1805–06. The second half of this volume consists of an essay on the concept of universal history that draws on the historiography of the Haitian Revolution. [JDG]

1207 Cauna, Jacques de. Autour de la thèse du complot: Franc-maçonnerie, révolution et contre-révolution à Saint-Domingue, 1789–1791. (*in* Franc-maçonnerie et religions dans l'Europe des lumières. Edité par Charles Porset et Cécile Révauger. Paris: Champion, 2006, p. 289–310)

Cauna connects his theory that white royalists planned a slave revolt in Saint-Domingue with the importance of free masons in the colony. He outlines the some possible connections between royalist and masonic social networks. Ultimately the argument is not convincing, but Cauna knows this archival material well and the article may be useful to researchers. [JDG]

1208 Cauna, Jacques de. Toussaint Louverture et le déclenchement de l'insurrection des esclaves du Nord en 1791: un retour aux sources. (*in* Haiti, regards croisés. Édition de Nathalie Dessens and Jean-Pierre Le Glaunec. Paris: Éditions le Manuscrit, 2007, p. 35–68)

Densely argued article supporting the idea that the slave revolt of 1791 was orchestrated secretly by Toussaint Louverture, working for moderate royalists who hoped an uprising would unite ultra conservatives and white pro-revolutionary colonists. While not convincing, Cauna assembles evidence for the location of the Bois Caiman ceremony and the plantation origins of the black leaders of the initial uprising. [JDG]

1209 Cauna, Jacques de. Vestiges of the built landscape of pre-revolutionary Saint-Domingue. (*in* World of the Haitian Revolution. Edited by David P. Geggus and Norman Fiering Bloomington, IN: Indiana Univ. Press, 2009, p. 23–48.)

One of the leading French scholars of the Haitian Revolution, Cauna lived and worked in Haiti for 13 years. This illustrated article provides an unprecedented view of the archeological remains of Saint-Domingue's sugar and coffee plantations and irrigation works, buttressed by the author's deep familiarity with colonial archives. [JDG]

1210 Chauleau, Liliane. La Martinique et le guerre d'indépendance américaine. (*in* Sur les chemins de l'histoire antillaise: mélanges offerts à Lucien Abénon. Edité par Jean Bernabé and Serge Mam Lam Fouck. Matoury, French Guiana: Ibis rouge, 2006, p. 115–128)

Uses the memoir of the Marquis de Bouillé and other diplomatic sources to describe the important role played by Martinique as a center of commerce and information during the war of American independence. [JDG]

1211 Chinea, Jorge L. Un discurso esclavista de la Ilustración: la trata negrera en el proyecto plantocrático de Louis Balbes des Berton, duque de Crillón y Mahón. (*Rev. Complut. Hist. Am.*, 34, 2008, p. 257–268, bibl.)

Discusses the Duke of Crillón y Mahón's failed initiative to promote and control the transatlantic slave trade in late 18th-century Puerto Rico. Although the plan resonated with the Bourbon Reforms' goal of economically revitalizing Spain's overseas possessions, it was opposed by the Consejo de Indias, which feared potential French penetration of the slave trade. The Duke of Crillón's correspondence offers a unique window into the racist discourse underpinning his proslavery proposals. [LAG]

1212 Clune, John James. Cuban convents in the age of Enlightened Reform, 1761–1807. Gainesville: Univ. Press of Florida, 2008. 131 p.: bibl., index.

Important addition to Cuban religious history and the cultural impact of the Bourbon reforms on the island. Specifically, the book focuses on the female religious orders with special attention on the Clares to demonstrate their declining prestige in the larger Cuban society as a result of secular pressure to offer more public services such as education and not cater exclusively to the elite. [MC]

1213 Coloquio Internacional de Historia Social, 3rd, Castellón de la Plana, Spain, 2002. Las Antillas en la era de las luces y la revolución. Recopilación de José A. Piqueras. Madrid: Siglo XXI, 2005. 391 p.: bibl., ill., index, map.

Brings together 16 conference papers analyzing the Spanish Caribbean from the 1780s to 1830s with a particular focus on Cuba. Collectively the different authors contribute to the literature explaining Cuban loyalty to Spain during the era of Latin American independence by emphasizing the mechanisms for Creole inclusion in the empire, expansion of the plantation economy, and the increased reliance on slave labor. [MC]

1214 Colwill, Elizabeth. "Fêtes de l'hymen, fêtes de la liberté": marriage, manhood and emancipation in revolutionary Saint-Domingue. (*in* World of the Haitian Revolution. Edited by David P. Geggus and Norman Fiering Bloomington, IN: Indiana Univ. Press, 2009, p. 125–155)

Colwill provides an innovative reading of the roles of gender, sexuality, and marriage in the events of 1793, when slavery formally ended in Saint-Domingue. She contrasts the attempts of French Republican commissioners to erase racial distinctions, through highly masculine military rituals and Republican marriages, with a counter-revolutionary's account that described participation of women of color as evidence of the commissioners' moral corruption. She finishes by considering the very diverse experiences of enslaved women to the insurrection and the republican proclamation of emancipation. [JDG]

1215 Dubois, Laurent. Avenging America: the politics of violence in the Haitan revolution. (*in* World of the Haitian Revolution. Edited by David P. Geggus and Norman Fiering. Bloomington: Indiana Univ. Press, 2009, p. 111–124)

Though its historical material is drawn largely from his *Avengers . . .* (see *HLAS 62:1089*), this essay fills a gap in the literature by addressing the ways that Haitian revolutionaries, as well as their allies and enemies, manipulated violence and representations of violence. [JDG]

1216 Dubois, Laurent. Citizen-Soldiers: emancipation and military service in the revolutionary French Caribbean. (*in* The arming of slaves from the classical era to the Civil War. Edited by Christopher Leslie Brown and Philip D. Morgan. New Haven: Yale Univ. Press, p. 233–255.)

This article offers a meaty summary of the military events in revolutionary Guadeloupe where black and mixed race men were integrated into the French army after 1794, and then in 1802 had to chose between accepting the return of slavery or fighting against the revolution that had temporarily made them citizen-soldiers. Good survey of events in nearby Saint Lucia, as well. [JDG]

1217 Dubois, Laurent and Bernard Camier. Voltaire, *Zaïre*, Dessalines: le théâtre des lumières dans l'atlantique français. (*Rev. hist. mod. contemp.*, 54:4, déc. 2007, p. 39–69)

Deeply researched article on the importance of theater as a vehicle for the communication of ideas in Saint-Domingue. Using a document published in 1793, Dubois and Camier show that a free black [and perhaps African-born] man in Saint-Domingue used key phrases from Voltaire's play *Zaïre* in describing the unjust enslavement of

specific African woman in the colony. The overarching importance of this case lies in the way it supports Dubois's contention that black Saint-Dominguans used and extended Enlightenment ideas during the Haitian Revolution. [JDG]

1218 Fabella, Yvonne. "An empire founded on libertinage": the *Mulâtresse* and colonial anxiety in Saint Domingue. (*in* Gender, race and religion in the colonization of the Americas. Edited by Nora E Jaffary. Aldershot, England: Ashgate, 2007, p. 109–124)

A close reading of Hilliard d'Aubteuil's controversial *Considérations sur Saint-Domingue* (1776) is at the heart of this article. Fabella deploys recent scholarship on the cultural history of Saint-Domingue to reveal why d'Aubteuil believed free women of color were a destabilizing infuence on Saint-Domingue's free society. For review of entire book, see item **486**. [JDG]

1219 Facing racial revolution: eyewitness accounts of the Haitian insurrection. Edited by Jeremy D. Popkin. Chicago: Univ. of Chicago Press, 2007. 400 p.: bibl, ill., index.

This important contribution to the historiography of the Haitian Revolution is valuable first of all for reproducing in English substantial selections from two dozen eyewitness testimonies from survivors of the events, almost all of them white colonists. Nearly as important, however, is Popkin's painstaking contextualization and an opening essay in which he notes that many of these "victims" of revolutionary violence were also, before 1791, "perpetrators" of violence against their own enslaved workers. [JDG]

1220 Gainot, Bernard. Les officiers de couleur dans les armées de la République et de l'Empire, 1792–1815: de l'esclavage à la condition militaire dans les Antilles françaises. Paris: Karthala, 2007. 232 p., 8 p. of plates: bibl., ill. (some col.). (Hommes et sociétés)

Important study of the careers of close to 600 soldiers of color in the armies of the French Revolution in Europe, with special attention to their officers. Gainot shows how these men who found themselves in Europe were not made part of the regular French army and were repeatedly segregated and used for the most difficult duties. [JDG]

1221 Garrigus, John D. Opportunist or patriot?: Julien Raimond (1744–1801) and the Haitian Revolution. (*Slavery Abolit.*, 28:1, April 2007, p. 1–21)

A biographical sketch of this free man of color who was the pivotal figure in the debate over whether race would be a criteria for citizenship during the early years of the Haitian Revolution. Though a socially conservative planter and large slaveowner, Raimond came to embrace the Revolution and even advocated extending its benefits to Saint-Domingue's slaves. By the end of his life he became a major supporter of Toussaint Louverture, turning his back on Bonaparte's France. [JDG]

1222 Garrigus, John D. Saint-Domingue's free people of color and the tools of revolution. (*in* World of the Haitian Revolution. Edited by David P. Geggus and Norman Fiering. Bloomington: Indiana Univ. Press, 2009, p. 49–64)

Summarizes the political tools and cultural perspectives of Saint-Domingue's wealthiest free people of color on the eve of the French Revolution. These planters and merchants used events in France to raise an anti-racist agenda in the colony that ultimately destabilized the plantation regime. [JDG]

1223 Garrigus, John D. "Thy Coming Fame, Ogé! Is Sure": new evidence on Ogé's 1790 revolt and the beginnings of the Haitian Revolution. (*in* Assumed identities: the meanings of race in the Atlantic world. Edited by John D. Garrigus and Christopher Morris. College Station, Tex.: Texas A&M Univ. Press, 2010, p. 19–45)

Presents new information on the so-called "Ogé revolt," a critical event in the coming of the Haitian Revolution in 1791. Reveals that Ogé had planned to return to Saint-Domingue from France long before he actually did. Describes his attempt to create a political movement in the colony based on the new militia imagery from revolutionary Paris. [JDG]

1224 Garrigus, John D. "To establish a community of property: marriage and race before and during the Haitian Revolution. (*Hist. Fam.*, 12:2, 2007, p. 142–152)

This study of 1000 marriage contracts among wealthy free people of color in the Haitian Revolution finds that the slave rebellion, general emancipation, and Haitian independence from France did not break the pattern of endogamous unions observed in data from the 1760s and 1780s. Rather the social instability appears to have strengthened this tendancy. [JDG]

1225 Gauthier, Florence. L'aristocratie de l'épiderme: le combat de la Société des citoyens de couleur, 1789–1791. Paris: CNRS éditions, 2007. 446 p.: bibl., ill., index. (Histoires pour aujourd'hui)

A senior French scholar examines the political impact of Caribbean men of color in revolutionary France. Though deeply researched, the book is flawed by Gauthier's insistence that Julien Raimond, the leading free-colored political figure, was an idealist who was opposed to slavery from the beginning of the revolution. Though valuable for the author's familiarity with the archives of the period, researchers should balance her account with other interpretations of these events. [JDG]

1226 Gautier, Arlette. Genre et esclavage aux Antilles françaises: Bilan de l'historiographie. (*in* L'esclave et les plantations: de l'établissement de la servitude à son abolition: hommage à Pierre Pluchon. Edité par Philippe Hrodéj. Rennes: Presses universitaires de Rennes, 2008, p. 161–186.)

Gautier, the most important French writer on the subject of enslaved women, conducts a survey of the field and concludes that women are still omitted from many representations of French Caribbean slavery or are reduced to the stereotype of the planter's mulatto mistress. While describing the state of historiography, the article also provides a valuable overview of what is currently know about the demography and life experiences of enslaved women in the Antilles. [JDG]

1227 Geggus, David Patrick. The Caribbean in the age of revolution. (*in* "Age of revolutions" or "world crisis"?: global causation, connections, and comparison.

Edited by David Armitage and Sanjay Suramanyam. England: Palgrave Macmillan, 2009, p. 83–100)

Geggus, the leading historian of the Haitian Revolution, examines the impact of that event on the Caribbean in the context of the "Age of Revolutions." He examines the historiography of British abolitionism, as well as that of the Haitian Revolution. Geggus provides his case against the ideological interpretation of the Haitian Revolution advanced by Laurent Dubois. [JDG]

1228 Geggus, David Patrick. Print culture and the Haitian Revolution: the written and the spoken word. (*in* Liberty, egalité, independencia: print culture and enlightenment, and revolution in the Americas, 1776–1838. Worcester, Mass.: American Antiquarian Society, 2007, p. 79–96)

Important tool for researchers; Geggus knows the archives of the Haitian Revolution better than anyone and here he lays out a guide to the most important texts produced by colonists, free people of color, and rebel slaves, and the controversies surrounding them. [JDG]

1229 Geggus, Patrick D. Saint-Domingue on the eve of the Haitian Revolution. (*in* World of the Haitian Revolution. Edited by David P. Geggus and Norman Fiering Bloomington: Indiana Univ. Press, 2009, p. 3–20)

A nuanced but accessible overview of conditions in Saint-Domingue on the eve of the Haitian Revolution. The article serves as a valuable summary of the author's deep investigation of material and cultural conditions among Saint-Domingue's slaves. Geggus concludes that there was no clear evidence of either mounting stress or overriding stability among the enslaved population. [JDG]

1230 Girard, Philippe R. Black Talleyrand: Toussaint Louverture's diplomacy, 1798–1802. (*William Mary Q.*, 66:1, Jan. 2009, p. 119–138, tables)

Deeply researched article pulls together recent findings on Toussaint's foreign policy with perspectives from French, US, Spanish, and British archives. The article includes a thorough review of the historiography. Its contention that most historians have presented only partial views of Tous-

saint appears overstated; nevertheless, this offers a wideranging review of primary and secondary literature. [JDG]

1231 Girard, Philippe R. Napoléon Bonaparte and the emancipation issue in Saint-Domingue: 1799–1803. (*Fr. Hist. Stud.*, 32:4, Fall 2009, p. 587–618)

Well-researched article argues for the revision of two central themes of Haitian Revolutionary historiography: that the Leclerc expedition of 1802 was guided by the wishes of colonial planters and that Napoleon had a clear plan of restoring slavery. Though clear evidence is lacking, Girard stresses that Bonaparte was above all a pragmatist and that the French invasion of 1802 was guided primarily by military and strategic considerations. [JDG]

1232 Girard, Philippe R. Rebelles with a cause: women in the Haitian War of Independence, 1802–1804. (*Gend. Hist.*, 21:1, 2009, p. 60–85)

Combing through the military and political archives of the Haitian Revolution, Girard assembles a portrait of the role of women—white, black and of mixed ancestry—in these events. Pushing against recent historiography that sees sexuality as a tool used by men against women, Girard emphasizes how some women gained access to unusual power during the revolutionary chaos. He provides examples of the the ways women contributed to the revolution and counterrevolution as spies, fighters, and provisioners. Violence is a central theme for Girard. [JDG]

1233 Huygues-Belrose, Vincent. Avant le fruit à pain: la cuisine martiniquise au XVIIIe siècle. (*in* Sur les chemins de l'histoire antillaise: mélanges offerts à Lucien Abénon. Edité par Jean Bernabé et Serge Mam Lam Fouck. Matoury, French Guiana: Ibis rouge, 2006, p. 201–214.)

Uses memoires and travel accounts from the 17th and 18th centuries to describe key elements of the cuisine of the daily food as well as gastronomic specialties of the planter class. [JDG]

1234 Llinares, Sylviane. Marine, colonies et innovations techniques: quelques exemples de transferts (XVIIIe et première moitié du XIXe siècles). (*in* Techniques et colonies (XVIe–XXe siècles). Edité par

Sylviane Llinares and Philippe Hrodĕj. Paris: Publications de la Société française d'Histoire d'Outre Mer et de l'Université de Bretagne Sud—SOLITO, 2005, p. 163–181.)

Well-documented examination of the technologies and products from the Antilles adopted by the French navy in the 18th and 19th centuries. The most notable is the two-masted schooner or *goelette*, a ship that was first used for Caribbean smuggling and only gradually adopted by the French navy after 1766. [JDG]

1235 Foubert, Bernard. L'origine des esclaves des habitations Laborde (in L'esclave et les plantations: de l'établissement de la servitude à son abolition: un hommage à Pierre Pluchon. Edité par Philippe Hrodĕj. Rennes: Presses universitaires de Rennes, p. 103–124.)

Foubert continues his decades long study of the three Laborde sugar plantations in southern Saint-Domingue. Laborde was a one-time court banker and real estate investor in Paris who had made his first fortune in Atlantic trade. He continued to invest in the slave trade after acquiring three adjoining colonial plantations in the years between 1768 and 1771. This access to African captives allowed Laborde's managers to acquire 2,273 enslaved workers in this colonial region that was infrequently visited by slave traders. [JDG]

1236 Marshall, Bernard A. Maronnage in slave plantation societies: a case study of Dominica, 1785–1815. (*Caribb. Q./ Mona*, 54:4, Dec. 2008, p. 103–110, bibl.)

Examines Maroon activity on the island of Dominica in the late 18th and early 19th centuries when British sugar plantation agriculture replaced the coffee, cocoa, and other spices grown on small farms by original French settlers. Enslaved Africans retreated to the hills after British occupation started, and tirelessly and successfully resisted government efforts either to sue for peace or to exterminate them. But flailing economic fortunes of the planter class through Maroon presence and activity necessitated the determination by the planter class to eliminate the Maroons. Starting in 1798, a number of enhanced and strategic military incursions by the British led to the defeat and final suppression of the Maroons in 1814. [ELC]

1237 McClellan III, James E. Gardens and forests in colonial Saint Domingue. (in Gardens and forests in the Caribbean. Edited by Robert Anderson, Karis Hiebert, and Richard H. Grove. Oxford: MacMillan, 2006, p. 65–86.)

The leading historian of science in the French colonial Caribbean describes the network of botanical gardens in the colony. Although Saint-Domingue was the site of major environmental projects, like irrigation and flood control, the colony was decades behind other French possessions in getting its own botanical gardens in the 1770s and 1780s. [JDG]

1238 Mentor, Gaétan. Dessalines: l'esclave devenu empereur. Pétionville, Haïti: Gaétan Mentor, 2003, 96 p., 24 p. of plates: ill. (some col.).

Historians will find the primary interest of this small volume to be the photographic reproductions of documents from Dessalines's career. Most appear to be from the Mangonès collection housed in Port-au-Prince in the Bibliothèque Haitien des Pères de Saint-Esprit, but also several from unnamed private collections, presumably also in Haiti. [JDG]

1239 Meyering, Anne. Marriage and Creole identity: an example from the French West Indies, 1789–1841. (in Sur les chemins de l'histoire antillaise: mélanges offerts à Lucien Abénon. Edité par Jean Bernabé and Serge Mam Lam Fouck. Matoury, French Guiana: Ibis rouge, 2006, p. 139–166.)

Uses the 1790 marriage between the colonial official Auguste Benoist and the Guadeloupe-born planter's daughter Caroline Vidal to investigate the nature of Creole identity and colonial marriage. [JDG]

1240 Noël, Erick. Etre noir en France au XVIIIe siècle. Paris: Tallandier, 2006. 320 p.: bibl., ill. (some col.), index, maps.

A solid contribution to the emerging literature on racial diversity in 18th-century France. Most of the people of color who Noël studies came to Europe from the Antilles, and he makes good use of admiralty records as well as the archives of port cities. One third of the book is devoted to the revolutionary period, when racial categories and laws were in flux, often as a response to events in the Caribbean. [JDG]

1241 Ogle, Gene E. The Trans-Atlantic king and imperial public spheres: everyday politics in pre-revolutionary Saint-Domingue. (*in* World of the Haitian Revolution. Edited by David P. Geggus and Norman Fiering. Bloomington: Indiana Univ. Press, 2009, p. 79–96.)

Ogle provides an elaborate description of the ways in which colonial political culture was changing in the 1780s. He focuses on how the reduced status of the king and the rise of the public sphere raised controversy about nearly all social divisions within free colonial society. [JDG]

1242 Popkin, Jeremy D. The French Revolution's other island. (*in* World of the Haitian Revolution. Edited by David P. Geggus and Norman Fiering. Bloomington: Indiana Univ. Press, 2009, p. 199–222)

Armed with powerful examples, Popkin argues convincingly that news from Saint-Domingue played a important role in French Revolutionary politics, although historians have ignored this connection. Policies and events in the colonies served both right and left as propaganda for their cause from 1789 to 1802. Popkin's article is required reading for those seeking a more Atlantic understanding of the French Revolution. [JDG]

1243 Popkin, Jeremy D. You are all free: the Haitian revolution and the abolition of slavery. New York: Cambridge Univ. Press, 2011. 440 p.: bibl., index.

Popkin is the first major historian of the French Revolution to also beome an important figure in the historiography of the Haitian Revolution. In this deeply researched but very readable volume, he narrates the events leading up to the abolition of slavery in Saint-Domingue in 1793. A major contribution to the literature. [JDG]

1244 Régent, Frédéric. Armement des hommes de couleur et liberté aux Antilles: le cas de la Guadeloupe pendant l'ancien régime et la révolution. (*Ann. hist. Révolut. fr.*, 348, 2007, p. 7–24)

Valuable account of history of armed men of color in Guadeloupe that traces this phenomenon back to the 17th century, based almost entirely on primary sources. Régent pays most attention to the 18th century, especially to the revolutionary period and the gradual evolution of the practice until Victor Hugues expanded it. In the Revolution, Régent sees white colonists as aware of Sonthonax's alliance with black rebels in St. Domingue and therefore unwilling to arm black slaves to fight the English in 1794. Ends on a triumphant note with emissaries from Guadeloupe arming the ex-slaves of neighboring Saint-Lucia. [JDG]

1245 Rogers, Dominique. On the road to citizenship: the complex route to integration of the free people of color in the two capitals of Saint-Domingue. (*in* World of the Haitian Revolution. Edited by David P. Geggus and Norman Fiering. Bloomington: Indiana Univ. Press, 2009, p. 65–78.)

Using a corpus of 7,000 legal documents, Rogers argues against the accepted notion that racial discrimination was increasingly harsh in Saint-Domingue on the eve of the French and Haitian revolutions. Her detailed evidence allows her to show that important regional differences existed within the colony regarding the way that whites treated free people of color. [JDG]

1246 Ryden, David B. West Indian slavery and British abolition, 1783–1807. Cambridge, England; New York: Cambridge Univ. Press, 2009. 332 p.: bibl., ill., index.

Very valuable work that addresses the long-standing debate concerning the role of economic factors in the West Indies in the decision of British policymakers to abolish the slave trade in the British West Indies. Author has mined carefully the minutes of the Society of West India Planters and Merchants and British Parliamentary Papers to reevaluate contentions made about economic conditions in the British West Indies and how they influenced and were influenced by political decisions made in England at the end of the 18th century. Enormously useful. [ELC]

1247 Saint-Domingue espagnol et la révolution nègre d'Haïti, 1790–1822: commémoration du bicentenaire de la naissance de l'état d'Haïti 1804–2004. Sous la direction de Alain Yacou. Paris: Karthala; Pointe-à-Pitre: CERC, 2007. 683 p.: bibl., ill., maps. (Hommes et sociétés)

This anthology of the work of 16 historians, 7 of them from Spain or the Dominican Republic, provides an overview of relations between Saint-Domingue/Haiti and Santo Domingo during the revolutionary period. The scholarly quality of the contributions is uneven, but the volume is valuable because this topic has received very limited attention in the French and English historiography. [JDG]

1248 Santiago-Valles, Kelvin A. Bloody legislations, "Entombment," and race making in the Spanish Atlantic: differentiated spaces of general(ized) confinement in Spain and Puerto Rico, 1750–1840. (*Radic. Hist. Rev.*, 96, Fall 2006, p. 33–57)

Perceptive examination of transformations in the penal policies pursued by Spain to regulate subaltern populations (the poor, peasants, vagrants, and slaves) by controlling their labor power. Whereas the metropolis managed to abolish penal servitude and establish a modern prison system on its own territory, the Caribbean outpost, in contrast, experienced the expansion of coerced labor regimes—from chattel slavery to peonage—precisely as a result of developing greater linkages to the world economy during the early 19th century. [LAG]

1249 Schloss, Rebecca Hartkopf. The February 1831 slave uprising in Martinique and the policing of white identity. (*Fr. Hist. Stud.*, 30:2, Spring 2007, p. 203–236)

Reactions to the brief 1831 slave revolt in St Pierre Martinique allow Schloss to illustrate the anxiety of colonial elites about the identity of the white class. She argues that planters blamed the degeneracy of poor whites, rather than admit that racial and social intermixing was occurring at all levels in society. She draws special attention to elites' worries about the behavior of the island's white working women. [JDG]

1250 Schloss, Rebecca Hartkopf. Sweet liberty: the final days of slavery in Martinique. Philadelphia: Univ. of Pennsylvania Press, 2009. 300 p.: bibl., ill., index, maps. (Early American studies)

Deeply researched social and political history of Martinique from the end of the Napoleonic Wars through the end of slavery. Drawing on a wealth of primary material from the colony and metropole, Schloss argues that the end of slavery and the enfranchisement of people of color were important moments in the ongoing definition of French identity. She portrays how

the island's planters fought to delay these events, manipulating the courts, educational institutions, and stereotypes of race, gender, and sexual danger. [JDG]

1251 Scott, Rebecca J. and **Jean M. Hébrard.** Rosalie of the Poulard nation: freedom, law, and dignity in the era of the Haitian Revolution. (*in* Assumed identities: the meanings of race in the Atlantic World. Edited by John D. Garrigus and Christopher Morris. College Station, TX: Texas A&M Univ. Press, 2010. p. 19–45)

A remarkable microhistory of an African woman enslaved in Saint-Domingue whose children and grandchildren were able to escape to Cuba, New Orleans, and eventually to Mexico and Europe. A powerful example of Atlantic history and the impact of the Haitian Revolution over time. Deserves to be widely read. [JDG]

1252 Spieler, Miranda. The legal structure of colonial rule during the French Revolution. (*William Mary Q.*, 66:2, Jan. 2009, p. 365–409)

Important well-researched article describing the reluctance of French Revolutionary officials to extend constitutional rights to the colonies. Examining the years from 1789 to 1799, Spieler convincingly argues that key members of the Committee of Public Safety were opposed to emancipation in 1794 and that the Constitution of 1795 did not apply to the colonies, reversing historians' long-standing assumptions on this last point. [JDG]

1253 Victoria Ojeda, Jorge. Jean François y Biassou: dos líderes olvidados de la historia de la revolución haitiana (y de España). (*Caribb. Stud.*, 34:2, July/Dec. 2006, p. 163–204)

While it is not true that these two leaders have been "forgotten" by historians, Victoria Ojeda does use Spanish archives to tell their stories. English- and French-language historians have often bypassed these sources, which reveal the royalism of these two leaders as well as the rivalry that divided them. [JDG]

1254 Victoria Ojeda, Jorge. Rebeldes de la revolución haitiana en las naves reales de don Gabriel de Aristizábal. (*Rev. Hist. Nav.*, 24:95, 2006, p. 53–70, photo)

Narrates the history of Spain's alliance with the rebel slave leaders Jean-François and Georges Biassou from the perspective of the Spanish naval commander Gabriel de Aristizábal, who was in charge of transporting these rebels out of Santo Domingo to Cuba and Spain in 1796. Based on Spanish archives. [JDG]

1255 Welch, Pedro L.V. Puerta de las Antillas: la ciudad Puerto de Bridgetown, Barbados, 1714–1834. (*in* Golfo-Caribe y sus puertos: tomo I, 1600–1850. Coordinación de Johanna von Grafenstein Gareis. México: Instituto Mora, 2006, p. 127–157, bibl., ill., maps, tables)

Argues that in the 18th and early 19th centuries, Bridgetown was an important seaport town that was the center of a multifaceted commercial Caribbean system. Its importance also lay in its contributions to the island's economic and social structures. Contends that further studies of other New World cities would help us in understanding the peculiarities of New World societies. [ELC]

SPANISH BORDERLANDS

1256 Dessens, Nathalie. From Saint-Domingue to New Orleans: migration and influences. Foreword by Stanley Harrold and Randall M. Miller. Gainesville: Univ. Press of Florida, 2007. 257 p.: bibl., ill., index. (Southern dissent)

Provides a valuable overview of the influence of Saint-Domingue refugees in 19th-century Louisiana. Dessens's survey is based on primary sources like Church records and notarial documents as well as a thorough reading of the secondary literature in both French and English. Unlike earlier authors, she looks at white, free colored, and enslaved refugees from Saint-Domingue, underlining their economic and cultural impact and their role in maintaining the distinctive Francophone culture of Louisiana well into the 19th century. [JDG]

19TH CENTURY

1257 Abreu Cardet, José Miguel. Introducción a las armas: la guerra de 1868 en Cuba. La Habana: Editorial de Ciencias Sociales, 2005. 226 p. (Historia)

Succinct analysis of the ideas and loyalties that shaped the beginning years of the struggle for independence in Cuba. Author analyzes how the dynamics of *caudillismo* and *regionalismo* both catalyzed armed action and limited its expansion to other geographic areas. Important new insights to understanding why the Ten Years' War reached an early stalemate. [MC]

1258 African Americans and the Haitian revolution: selected essays and historical documents. Edited by Maurice Jackson and Jacqueline Bacon. New York: Routledge, 2009. 259 p.: bibl., index

Contains nine essays on the importance of the Haitian Revolution within African American culture in the 19th century, including Matthew Clavin on the ways black US soldiers invoked Toussaint Louverture and Julius Scott, a black US sailor who visited Haiti in 1793. The second half of the volume includes documents about Haiti from 19th- and 20th-century authors, including William Wells Brown, Frederick Douglass, Langston Hughes, and Ralph Ellison. [JDG]

1259 Barcia, Manuel. Revolts among enslaved Africans in nineteenth-century Cuba: a new look to an old problem. (*J. Caribb. Hist.*, 39:2, 2005, p. 173–200)

Thematic survey of slave revolts in the first half of the 19th-century in Cuba through sources from Cuban national and regional archives. Especially noteworthy is the author's analysis of what he labels "African Elements" in the uprising, stressing the religious, military, and associational ties that manifested themselves during insurrections. [MC]

1260 Berloquin-Chassany, Pascale. Un fossé à dimension variable: la vision française des relations haïtiano-allemandes, 1890–1910. (*in* Haïti 1804: lumières et ténèbres: impact et résonances d'une révolution. Edité par by Léon-François Hoffmann. Madrid: Iberoamericana, 2008, p. 143–159)

Using primary sources in French diplomatic archives, this article describes French perceptions of the growing influence of German businessmen in late-19th century and early-20th century Haiti. By 1909, the four largest import firms in Haiti were German. But the hostility of President Nord

Alexis (1902–08) to foreign influence halted French and German commercial rivalry in Haiti. [JDG]

1261 Boa, Sheena. Young ladies and dissolute women: conflicting views of culture and gender in public entertainment, Kingstown, St. Vincent, 1838–88. (*in* Gender and slave emancipation in the Atlantic world. Edited by Pamela Scully and Diana Paton. Durham, N.C.: Duke Univ. Press, 2005, p. 247–266)

Exploration of how women used a variety of types of entertainment to define themselves. Members of elite society embraced politeness and respectability to highlight their position, while the mostly brown-skinned middle-class women used dress styles, religious affiliations, and social pursuits. Many of the poorest, however, often used entertainment in the streets to show their rejection of race, class, and gender prescriptions. [ELC]

1262 Brereton, Bridget. Family strategies, gender, and the shift to wage labor in the British Caribbean. (*in* Gender and slave emancipation in the Atlantic world. Edited by Pamela Scully and Diana Paton. Durham, N.C.: Duke Univ. Press, 2005, p. 143–161)

Based on evidence regarding the extent and timing of women's withdrawal from estate labor in the British Caribbean, author examines how women used their family time to secure a degree of autonomy and economic independence in order to consider the role of gender ideologies in women's removal from the labor force. Concludes that women decided to withdraw from the labor force because they pursued rational family strategies aimed at securing the survival and welfare of their kin groups . . . "and at carving out lives which would not be wholly dependent on the plantation" (p. 157). [ELC]

1263 Brereton, Bridget. Post-emancipation protest in the Caribbean: the "Belmanna Riots" in Tobago, 1876. (*Caribb. Q./Mona*, 54:4, Dec. 2008, p. 111–128, bibl.)

Argues that Barbadian immigrants played an important role in the outbreak of this 19th-century labor disturbance on Tobago's Windward districts that facilitated the island's conversion into a pure Crown colony. Native Tobagonians eventually joined the disturbances in an effort to rectify long-standing grievances. [ELC]

1264 Brière, Jean-François. Haïti et la France, 1804–1848: le rêve brisé. Paris: Karthala, 2008. 354 p, [16] p. of plates: bibl., ill., ports., facsims.

Well-researched scholarly narrative of French/Haitian diplomatic and political relations during the first four decades of Haitian independence. Based primarily on French archives but maintains a critical stance towards French policies, which Brière ultimately describes as impoverishing the new nation. [JDG]

1265 Bueno, Arturo. Santiago: quien te vio y quien te ve. 2da. ed. Santo Domingo: Sociedad Dominicana de Bibliófilos, 2006. 2 v.: bibl., ill., indexes. (Col. Bibliófilos 2000; 16)

The two volumes offer a fascinating, vivid, and revealing portrait of Santiago de los Caballeros, the second largest city in the Dominican Republic, during the 19th century and the first quarter of the 20th century. The content is a mix of anecdotes, accounts of oral traditions, historical facts, relevant descriptions of personalities, picturesque figures, and epic and real adventures. First published in 1961 and republished here, as indicated by the author, the material took 22 years to compile. Entertaining and informative are over 80 reprinted pages of commercial ads promoting business and products in Santiago and its surrounding areas. The book also relates the author's firsthand experience with some personalities and his familiarity with Santiago's lifestyle. [VP]

1266 Castillo Téllez, Calixto. La iglesia protestante en las luchas por la independencia de Cuba, 1868–1898. La Habana: Editorial de Ciencias Sociales, 2003. 108 p.: bibl., indexes. (Historia)

Brief narrative of the role of Cuban and American Protestants in the Wars for Independence. Analysis emphasizes the contribution and sacrifices to free Cuba from Spanish control. Nearly one-third of the book consists of documents and appendices. [MC]

1267 Castro Ventura, Santiago. Duarte en la proa de la historia. Santo Domingo: Editora Manatí, 2005. 317 p.: bibl.

This portrait of Juan Pablo Duarte, ideologue and founder of the Dominican state, highlights the personality and political activities of this unquestioned leader. The material, in opposition to other depictions of Duarte as an idealistic young man with fanciful plans, presents a vigorous and combative man who organized the resistance against Haitian domination and built the road toward independence. The author also discusses the weaknesses and mistakes of Duarte's political project. The notes are superb and strengthen the content significantly. The work is helpful to general readers and students. [VP]

1268 Cottias, Myriam. Droit, justice et dépendance dans les Antilles françaises, 1848–1852. (*Ann. hist. sci. soc.*, 59:3, mai/juin 2004, p. 547–567)

A survey of the new system of local juries that was set in place in Martinique after the abolition of slavery in 1848. Using archival sources, Cottias describes how the juries refused to acknowledge the validity of former slaves' complaints. Rather than create a new public social identity for workers, the jury system taught ex-slaves to be skeptical about the law. Freedmen forged new social identities by entering into sharecropping-style contracts with former masters, prolonging some aspects of the dependent relations that characterized slavery. [JDG]

1269 Delisle, Philippe. Catholicisme, esclavage et acculturation dans la Caraïbe francophone et en Guyane au XIXe siècle. Matoury, French Guiana: Ibis Rouge Editions, 2006. 103 p.: bibl., maps. (Espace outre-mer)

Deslisle is the leading historian of Catholicism in the Francophone Caribbean. In this slim volume, brief but scholarly chapters describe the state of research on the stance of Catholic clergy regarding slavery, especially in the early 1800s, the degree to which either French Caribbean Catholicism and a countervailing anti-clericalism were local phenomena or were transplanted from Europe, and the nature of religious belief and practice in this region. [JDG]

1270 Delle, James A. Women's lives and labour on Radnor: a Jamaican coffee plantation, 1822–1826. (*Caribb. Q./Mona*, 54:4, Dec. 2008, p. 7–23, bibl., tables)

Making excellent use of material from an estate journal that documents the day-to-day workings of the Radnor Plantation between Jan. 1822 and March 1826, author shows how enslaved women were able to negotiate gender identities amidst the harsh labor and production regimens under which they operated. Concludes that though women constituted the majority of the estate's enslaved population, they were limited from operating in estate's first gang. Women nevertheless exploited the expanding cash economy by successfully producing castor oil. Despite the threat of apprehension and violent oppression, more women than men chose flight and absences from the plantation as strategies of resistance. Finally, evidence suggests that women were actively engaged in various forms of contraception spurred either by delayed lactation or by taking advantage of post-natal taboos on sexual intercourse. [ELC]

1271 Fernández Rodríguez, Fernando. El ángel armífero. Holguín, Cuba: Ediciones Holguín, 2005. 138 p.: bibl., ill. (Col. Comunidad)

Biographical study of Ángel Guerra Porra, who served as a military leader in the Cuban Wars for Independence. Thoroughly researched in local, regional, and national archives. Important contribution to a growing literature that focuses on important but less known "heroes" of the independence struggle. The appendix includes over a dozen documents detailing Ángel Guerra Porra's life. [MC]

1272 Ferrer, Ada. Armed slaves and anti-colonial insurgency in late nineteenth-century Cuba. (*in* Arming slaves from classical times to the modern age. Edited by Christopher Leslie Brown and Philip D. Morgan. New Haven: Yale Univ. Press, 2006, p. 304–329)

Innovative study on the role of slaves in Cuba's Wars for Independence. Especially noteworthy is the analysis of the lived experiences of the enslaved who freed themselves by joining the rebel army and how they discursively figured into the ideas that justified political independence. [MC]

1273 Ferrer Carbonell, Oscar. Néstor Leonelo Carbonell: como el grito del águila. La Habana: Editorial de Ciencias Sociales, 2005. 268 p.: bibl., ill.

238 / **Handbook of Latin American Studies v. 66**

Biographical study of Néstor Leonelo Carbonell, a revolutionary who played a crucial leadership role among tobacco workers in Tampa during the War for Independence. This study joins a growing body of literature providing biographies of lesser-known leaders of the independence struggle. Authored by a family relative who discovered and had access to family papers, many of which are appended as documents. [MC]

1274 Flores Ramos, José Enrique. Eugenesia, higiene pública y alcanfor para las pasiones: la prostitución en San Juan de Puerto Rico, 1876–1919. Hato Rey, P.R.: Publicaciones Puertorriqueñas, 2006. 249 p.: bibl., ill.

Explores the shift in state policy from regulation to prosecution of prostitution in San Juan in light of the city's dual role as site of government and military garrison. Inspired by cultural studies, the author dissects contemporary medical, intellectual, and political discourse on women, gender, and sexuality. Describing the everyday life of women who practiced prostitution in the capital, the author provides a rich profile of a population group that actively contested state intervention into the realm of private life. Includes a historiographical essay about research on prostitution in Latin America and the Caribbean. [LAG]

1275 Gaffield, Julia. Complexities of imagining Haiti: a study of national constitutions, 1801–1807. (*J. Soc. Hist.*, 41:1, Fall 2007, p. 81–103)

Uses Benedict Anderson's concept of "imagined community" to analyze the Haitian constitutions of 1801, 1805, 1806, and 1807. The article turns away from the tendancy of scholars in the 1970s and 1980s to emphasize the centrality of racial and social divisions within post-colonial Haiti. [JDG]

1276 Goin, Linda. Fort Charlotte's graffiti: 19th century Bahamian military life: the spaces, textures, and memories. (*J. Bahamas Hist. Soc.*, 27, Oct. 2005, p. 23–32, bibl., photo)

In this preliminary investigation of a sample of the various symbols and drawings on the fort built by Lord Dunsmore in the late 18th century, the author asserts that they demonstrate that the soldiers of the West India Regiments, who presumably made the symbols and drawings, used them as their own memorials "as girders to frame their thought processes as they adapted to a foreign culture." Hopes further research and discussions would shed additional light on Bahamas' military history as well as the process of creolization in the colony. [ELC]

El Golfo-Caribe y sus puertos. See item **833.**

1277 Gómez, Máximo. Máximo Gómez: tras las huellas del Zanjón: selección de documentos. Compilación de Yoel Cordoví Núñez. Santiago, Cuba: Editorial Oriente, 2005. 197 p.: bibl. (Bronce) (Col. Historia)

Reproduction of documents authored by Máximo Gómez detailing the Ten Years' War (1868–78). Most documents have been reproduced in other collections. Introduction provides historical context and setting for understanding the documents. [MC]

1278 Hoffmann, Léon-François. Faustin Soulouque d'Haïti: dans l'histoire et la littérature. Avec la collaboration de Carl Hermann Middelanis. Paris: L'Harmattan, 2007. 267 p.: bibl., ill. (Collection Autrement mêmes)

This history of perceptions of the Haitian Emperor Soulouque (1847–59) emphasizes how the rise of Emperor Napoleon III in France shaped depictions of the Haitian leader. Beyond the analysis, this volume will be important to researchers because it reproduces 16 political caricatures and the same number of French literary texts about Souloque and Haiti during his reign. [JDG]

1279 Horrego Estuch, Leopoldo. Juan Gualberto Gómez: un gran inconforme. Ed. homenaje por el 150 aniversario del natalicio de Juan Gualberto Gómez. La Habana: Editorial de Ciencias Sociales, 2004. 314 p.: bibl. (Biografía)

Republication of 1954 biography of Afro-Cuban leader of the independence struggle and early republic to mark the 150th anniversary of his birth. Remains one of the most complete biographies of Juan Gualberto Gómez in print, but as a commemorative edition of his birth tends toward hagiography and does not include recent insights from the last 20 years of historiography. [MC]

1280 Los ingenios: colección de vistas de los principales ingenios de azúcar de la Isla de Cuba. Texto redactado por Justo G. Cantero con láminas dibujadas del natural y litografiadas por Eduardo Laplante. Recopilación de Luís Miguel García Mora y Antonio Santamaría García. Madrid: Centro Estudios y Experimentación de Obras Públicas, 2005. 451 p.: bibl., ill. (some col.), indexes, maps (some col.), plans.

Lavish oversized reproduction of a classic 1857 study of the Cuban sugar industry with detailed descriptions of the major mills on the island. Original drawings by Laplante provide the most detailed visual representations of the interior workings of *ingenios* for the mid-19th century. Excellent introduction by the editors provides a concise overview of the Cuban sugar economy of the 19th century. [MC]

1281 Johnson, Howard. From pariah to patriot: the posthumous career of George William Gordon. (*NWIG*, 81:3/4, 2007, p. 197–218, bibl.)

Traces efforts to rehabilitate the image of Gordon, who was executed in 1865 for his supposed role in political disturbances that year in Jamaica. Contends that his elevation as one of Jamaica's national heroes in the post-colonial era reflects how images of Gordon have changed in the 19th and 20th centuries. [ELC]

1282 Kennedy, Fred W. Daddy Sharpe: a narrative of the life and adventures of Samuel Sharpe, a West Indian slave, written by himself, 1832. Kingston; Miami: Ian Randle Publishers, 2008. 411 p.: bibl., ill., maps (some folded).

Fictionalized artistic representation of the life of Sharpe, the leader of a slave rebellion on Jamaica in 1831 who later was named a national hero. Author based his account on historical documents relating to the period to portray a gripping story of what might have been Sam Sharpe's experiences and motivation for crafting the revolt. [ELC]

1283 Lazo, Rodrigo. Writing to Cuba: filibustering and Cuban exiles in the United States. Chapel Hill: Univ. of North Carolina Press, 2005. 252 p.: bibl., index. (Envisioning Cuba)

Important analysis of the proliferation of Cuban writings produced in exile through newspapers published in the US during the 19th century. Provides a nuanced approach to the concept of a *filibustero* emphasizing the degree to which Cuban writers helped craft the image to support annexation, rather than the usual depiction of a filibuster as a mechanism of support for American imperial claims to the island. [MC]

1284 Leti, Geneviève. L'empoisonnement aux Antilles françaises à l'époque de l'esclavage, 1724–1848. (*in* L'esclave et les plantations: de l'établissement de la servitude à son abolition: un hommage à Pierre Pluchon. Edité par Philippe Hrodĕj. Rennes: Presses universitaires de Rennes, 2008, p. 209–228.)

Survey of the theme of slave poisoning, focusing mostly on 19th-century Martinique. Leti offers no new conclusions here but does point to an evolution of poisoning fears, from animals, to slaves, to masters. She closes with a discussion of contemporary Martinican folk beliefs and practices associated with poisoning. [JDG]

1285 Negrón-Portillo, Mariano and **Raúl Mayo Santana.** La esclavitud menor: la esclavitud en los municipios del interior de Puerto Rico en el siglo XIX. San Juan: Centro de Investigaciones Sociales, Univ. de Puerto Rico, Recinto de Río Piedras, 2007. 152 p.: bibl., facsims. (Estudio del Registro de esclavos de 1872; 2)

Drawing on a unique source of slave census data—the Registro Central de Esclavos de 1872, recorded the year before slavery was abolished in Puerto Rico—the authors analyze slavery in the central highlands, a region characterized until that time by small-scale, nonexport agriculture, small production units, and small slave-holding patterns. Comparison with three sugar-producing municipalities in the southern and southwestern lowlands shows variations in slave labor regimes, slave family structure, and race relations. Complements two previous studies by the same researchers examining urban slavery in 19th-century San Juan (see *HLAS 54:2065* and *HLAS 58:1997*). [LAG]

1286 Oudin-Bastide, Caroline. Des nègres et des juges: la scandaleuse affaire Spoutourne, 1831–1834. Bruxelles, Belgium;

Paris: Éd. Complexe, 2008. 1 vol. (197 p., 4 p. de pl.): bibl., ill. (b/w and col.). (De source sûre)

The Spoutourne Affaire began when close to 100 enslaved plantation workers in Martinique lodged a complaint of abuse against their white plantation manager in 1831. Newly appointed European legal officials resisted pressure from white Creole elites to turn a blind eye to these events, creating a legal archive that reveals the attitudes of enslaved and free people during the final two decades of French slavery. Writing in a style accessible to nonspecialists, Oudin-Bastide provides context and extensive selections from primary documents. [JDG]

1287 Perera Díaz, Aisnara and **María de los A. Meriño Fuentes.** Esclavitud, familia y parroquia en Cuba: otra mirada desde la microhistoria. Santiago, Cuba: Instituto Cubano del Libro, Editorial Oriente, 2006. 274 p.: bibl., ill.

Important addition to social and gender history of slavery in the 19th century. Through detailed investigation of Church and notarial records dealing with small town of Bejucal (outside of Havana), provides an enlightening analysis of the strength and vitality of the family unit under slavery. [MC]

1288 Portuondo Zúñiga, Olga. José Antonio Saco: eternamente polémico. Santiago, Cuba: Editorial Oriente, 2005. 229 p.: bibl., ill. (Bronce. Col. Historia)

Critical biography of one of Cuba's most influential 19th-century writers on slavery and politics. Important revision to previous biographies with its detailed analysis of how family and economic relations in Bayamo and Santiago influenced Saco's writings. Thoroughly documented from local, regional, national, and imperial archives, as well as Saco's voluminous publications. [MC]

1289 Quintana García, José Antonio. Venezuela y la independencia de Cuba, 1868–1898. Havana: P. de la Torriente Editorial, 2005. 223 p.: bibl., ill.

Analysis of the relations between Cuban insurgents and Venezuela during the struggle for independence. Book is structured in two parts: the first is a narrative of relations between Cuban patriots and Venezuelan politicians who aided the independence struggle, and the second includes biographical chapters on Venezuelans who joined the Cuban independence army. Important analysis of various pro-independent Cuban clubs in existence in Venezuela. [MC]

1290 Ramsey, Kate. Legislating "civilization" in postrevolutionary Haiti. (*in* Race, nation, and religion in the Americas. Edited by Henry Goldschmidt and Elizabeth McAlister. New York: Oxford Univ. Press, 2004, p. 231–258)

A sophisticated study of the persecution of Haitian spiritual traditions in the 19th century, especially after the reintroduction of Catholic clergy in 1860. Ramsey points to the importance for Haitian elites of judicial law and the suppression of "superstition" as emblematic of Haiti's claims to nationhood. [JDG]

1291 Reddock, Rhoda. Indian women and indentureship in Trinidad and Tobago, 1845–1917: freedom denied. (*Caribb. Q./Mona,* 54:4, Dec. 2008, p. 41–68, bibl.)

Author contends that the Anti-Slavery Society's opposition to the "new form of slavery" occasioned by the small number of women included among the initial Indian migrants induced the prohibition of migration and eventually a policy by the Indian government that women should constitute at least 12 percent of ships' cargoes. Examines recruitment policy and efforts to promote reproduction in migrants' labor force and use of women's labor in plantation and peasant production. Indian nationalists' campaign against what they viewed as "the slavery of men and the prostitution of women" eventually led to the abolition of apprenticeship. [ELC]

1292 Ricardo, Yolanda. Magisterio y creación: los Henríquez Ureña: en homenaje al sesquicentenario del natalicio de José Martí y por el centenario de fallecimiento de Eugenio María de Hostos. Santo Domingo: Academia de Ciencias de la República Dominicana, 2003. 380 p.: bibl., ill.

This well-rounded study focuses on the remarkable humanistic and intellectual legacy of Salome Ureña, her husband Francisco Henríquez y Cavajal, their children Pedro, Max, and Camila, and other relatives.

Ricardo's comprehensive work explains how this family of intellectuals, educators, and artists contributed to the establishment of the educational and cultural foundation of modern Dominican society. The analysis and incorporation of a wide range of documents shed light not only on the accomplishments of the family, but also on the triangular connection and solidarity among Cuban, Dominican, and Puerto Rican thinkers and political figures, such as Eugenio María de Hostos, José Martí, and Máximo Gómez. The work enriches the understanding of the contribution of one of the most influential Dominican families and the flowering of the intellectual life of the country. This study will be very useful to researchers and readers in general. [VP]

Rodríguez León, Mario A. El obispo Juan Alejo de Arizmendi ante el proceso revolucionario y el inicio de la emancipación de América Latina y el Caribe. See item **558**.

1293 Rood, Daniel. Herman Merivale's Black Legend: rethinking the intellectual history of free trade imperialism. (*NWIG*, 80:3/4, 2006, p. 163–189, bibl.)

Drawing heavily on Merivale's *Lectures on Colonization*, the author contends that although Merivale cast aspersions on "the distant past of the now decrepit Spanish Empire," Cuba's "transformation in slavery" in the 19th century had nonetheless witnessed a coupling of slavery with high powered capital accumulation. Asserts that Merivale's quest for social hierarchy and political control of a free market utopia become evident in his Lectures, "complicating oppositions between the pre- and postabolition British empires, as well as between the free trade empire and the Cuban, Brazilian, and southern United States slave societies of the period." For additional comment, see item **560**. [ELC]

1294 Santamaría García, Antonio. Nuevos temas de historia económica y social de Cuba, siglo XIX: diversificación y economías externas. (*CLAHR*, 14:2, Spring 2005, p. 153–190)

Excellent overview of Cuban economic history with a particular emphasis on industries other than sugar, which remain understudied. Especially useful is the reference to many hard-to-find publications

in edited collections produced during and in the wake of Cuba's centennial celebrations. [MC]

1295 Schmidt, Nelly. La France, a-t-elle aboli l'esclavage: Guadeloupe-Martinique-Guyane, 1830–1935. Paris: Perrin, 2009. 361 p.: bibl, index.

Written by the foremost scholar of French abolitionism in the 19th century, this volume continues the history of the major Caribbean colonies until 1935. Using archival research, Schmidt argues that the end of slavery in 1848 was only one step in the struggle for social justice in these territories. She describes how the slow process of political reform, metropolitan subsidies for the sugar industry, and the informal maintenance of color prejudice, all contributed to maintain the power of the colonial planter class. [JDG]

Schnakenbourg, Christian. Histoire de l'industrie sucrière en Guadeloupe aux XIXe et XXe siècles. See item **1346**.

1296 Scott, Rebecca J. Degrees of freedom: Louisiana and Cuba after slavery. Cambridge, Mass.: Belknap Press of Harvard Univ. Press, 2005. 365 p.: bibl., ill., index, maps.

Innovative study of the political, social, and cultural battles to define citizenship in post-emancipation Louisiana and Cuba through exhaustive archival research. Skillfully examines the individual actions of emancipated slaves against the larger social and political changes of the time period. Concludes that the dynamics of fighting for independence in Cuba by people of African descent provided political and social rights unavailable to African-Americas in the US in the era after Reconstruction. [MC]

1297 Sheller, Mimi. Acting as free men: subaltern masculinities and citizenship in postslavery Jamaica. (*in* Gender and slave emancipation in the Atlantic world. Edited by Pamela Scully and Diana Paton. Durham, N.C.: Duke Univ. Press, 2005, p. 79–98)

An examination of the relationship between gender, racial formations, and ethnic and national identities in popular political contention over freedom, citizenship, and manhood in post-slavery Jamaica. Contends that the complex intersection of race and gender in political struggles have affected freedom, citizenship, and political inclusion and exclusion in the Atlantic world. [ELC]

1298 Vázquez Lazo, Nieve de los Ángeles. Meretrices: la prostitución en Puerto Rico de 1876 a 1917. Hato Rey, P.R.: Publicaciones Puertorriqueñas, 2008. 293 p.: bibl., ill.

Examines the interaction between women and the state, particularly lower-class women in the southern municipality of Ponce, through the lens of state policies—and the attendant medical, religious, and media discourse—on prostitution. This well-documented study demonstrates how state regulation of prostitution introduced controls over women's sexuality and effectively curtailed their status as equal citizens at a time when women were demanding greater rights, from access to education to suffrage. Appendix provides a chronology of legal policies and regulations on prostitution from the early colonial period to the present. [LAG]

20TH CENTURY

1299 Ayala, César J. and Rafael Bernabe. Puerto Rico in the American century: a history since 1898. Chapel Hill: Univ. of North Carolina Press, 2007. 428 p.: bibl., index.

A groundbreaking interpretation of 20th-century Puerto Rican history that interweaves intellectual, literary, and cultural perspectives with historical and political-economic analysis. Especially significant are the authors' engagement with the history of the Puerto Rican diaspora on the US mainland, their discussion of the interaction between insular developments and global trends, and their insightful exploration of Puerto Rican identity. Combines primary source material (contemporary newspapers, cultural periodicals, and memoirs) with systematic use of secondary literature. Includes a useful bibliographical essay. [LAG]

1300 Balcácer, Juan Daniel. Trujillo: el tiranicidio de 1961. 2. ed. Santo Domingo: Taurus, Grupo Santillana, 2007. 540 p.: bibl., ill., index. (Taurus historia)

Insightful and well-documented book provides an encompassing appraisal of Trujillo's death. Beginning with the last day of Trujillo's life and continuing to the end of the dictatorship, the material guides readers to the resistance, agenda, objectives, and plan of action of the conspirators. The text includes valuable bibliographical data on each conspirator and also makes reference to each spouse. The author emphasizes the role, somewhat neglected in other studies, of the wives, mothers, daughters, sisters, and other women who directly or indirectly were part of the plot. Chronologically organized and graphically illustrated, the book offers a powerful vision of the many events that took place on May 30, 1961. Discussing a wide variety of issues, the author backs up factual statements with documents and photos which add strength to the material. Balcácer's work is innovative and offers a good model for students of social political history and good information to all readers. [VP]

1301 Bégot, Danielle. Aux origines de la patrimonialisation de la culture antillaise: la revue *Parallèles*, Martinique, Guadeloupe, 1964–1971. (*in* Sur les chemins de l'histoire antillaise: mélanges offerts à Lucien Abénon. Edité par Jean Bernabé and Serge Mam Lam Fouck. Matoury, French Guiana: Ibis rouge, 2006, p. 31–46)

Reviews the origins and content of this locally produced journal of the 1960s, which Bégot describes as the first self-conscious expression of the "originality and coherence" of French Antillean culture in Martinique and Guadeloupe. It was the work of Anca Bertrand née Ionesco, a Romanian survivor of WWII who married a Martiniquan painter and moved to Martinique in 1950. [JDG]

1302 Binda, Ramnarine. Courage in Caroni: the autobiography of Ramnarine Binda. Forward by Brinsley Samaroo. Arima Trinidad & Tobago: Saffire Books, 2008. 273 p.: ill., index.

Autobiography of first-generation Indo-Trinidadian whose parents came from northern India as indentured workers. His leadership skills became apparent at multiple levels, and he was involved with activists and leading politicians in the middle and late 20th century. Binda's astute commentary on his interaction with leaders, as well as his reflection on their actions, help us understand Trinidad's society and politi-

cal culture. Book contains a useful introduction by Brinsley Samaroo, a historian
currently working at the Univ. of Trinidad
and Tobago. [ELC]

1303 Blanco Rodríguez, Juan Andrés. Castellanos y leoneses en Cuba: el sueño
de tantos. Valladolid, Spain: Ámbito, 2005.
328 p.: bibl.

Account of the influence of Spaniards
from Castile and León in Cuba from the War
of Independence through the 20th century.
The major focus is biographical portraits of
the Spanish associational clubs that thrived
in the 20th century to illustrate the strong
ties to Spain after colonialism ended. [MC]

1304 Bosch, Juan. Temas internacionales:
ensayos y artículos. Compilación de
Miguel Collado. Santo Domingo: Fundación
Juan Bosch, 2006. 633 p.: bibl.

A noteworthy contribution to international relations, the text is a compilation
of selected articles and essays by the distinguished writer and former president of
the Dominican Republic. The articles and
essays were published between 1975–93 in
the magazine *Politica: Teoria y Acción* and
in the newspaper *Vanguardia del Pueblo*,
both official publications of the Partido de
la Liberación Dominicana (PLD), a major
political party founded by Bosch after he
separated from the Partido Revolucionario
Domininicano (PRD) in 1973. The content of
the articles is educational, multidisciplinary,
and international. On international events,
Bosch expresses his opinion and applies his
analytical skills to many issues, including
the French, Russian, and Cuban revolutions.
Bosch also offers his point of view on the
Cold War, atomic weapons, the US political
and economic interference in Latin America,
Africa, and Korea. Other topics include the
wars in Iraq and Iran and the US war against
drugs (cocaine). An article on the history of
Haiti is quite interesting. Analyzing events
from the Haitian Revolution and the liberation of the slaves, at the end of the 18th
century, to the dictatorships of François
Duvalier (1957–71) and his son Jean Claude
Duvalier (1971–86), Bosch emphasizes the
resilience and determination of the Haitian
people, who, struggling against all the odds,
have resisted domination and exploitation
for more than two centuries. The article,
published in 1986, depicts a distressing

socioeconomic reality that is even more
evident after the earthquake that struck
Haiti on Jan. 12, 2010. From the educational
point of view, Bosch offers a clear distinction
between a Latin American and a Hispanic
American person. The explanation might appear simplistic, but it is useful for those who
might be confused about the meaning of
both terms. Thus, while expressing his opinion and making analytical remarks, Bosch
also tries to inform some sectors of society
about historical terminology. [VP]

Burgos, Elizabeth. Cuba en Bolivia. See
item **1760**.

1305 Caamaño Deñó, Francisco Alberto.
El Presidente Caamaño: discursos
y documentos. Selección de textos y fo-
tos de Edgar Valenzuela. Santo Domingo:
CPEP, Comisión Permanente de Efemérides
Patrias, 2006. 330 p.: bibl., ill. (Col. de la
Comisión Permanente de Efemérides Pa-
trias; 13)

Presents a compilation of speeches
and documents that traces the military
advancement and political transformation of
Francisco Alberto Caamaño Deñó, who was
a colonel in the army at the beginning the
revolution that exploded on April 24, 1965,
and became the Constitutionalist president on May 4, 1965. Caamaño's speeches
are valuable for researchers and constitute
about one-third of the material. The remainder of the book brings together documented
accounts related to the event. Combining
historical data with an excellent selection of
photos by Juan Pérez Terrero, known as the
photographer of revolution and a Pulitzer
Prize winner, and by Milvio Pérez Pérez,
another famous photographer, Valenzuela
offers a graphic revelation of the upheaval
that abruptly changed Caamaño's life and
polarized the nation. [VP]

Cancio Isla, Wilfredo. Crónicas de la impaciencia: el periodismo de Alejo Carpentier.
See item **2346**.

1306 Cassá, Constancio. Más relatos sobre
Constanza. Constanza, Dominican
Republic: Ayuntamiento municipal de Con-
stanza, 2007. 273 p.: bibl., ill., index.

This work provides an informative
and interesting description of the town of
Constanza. The historical narrative, statistical data, geographical information, and

anthropological background reinforce the content of the author's previous work, *Relatos y crónicas de Constanza*, published in 2003 (see *HLAS 64:936*). This volume, however, reveals more vividly the multinational and multicultural composition of the population. As Cassá explains, mostly as a result of Trujillo's migratory policy, Constanza is the home of Hungarian, Japanese, and Spanish settlers who came in the mid-1950s. Marriages between immigrants of different nationalities—and with Dominicans—have resulted in the formation of a multiracial society. The study explains how these connections have added cultural diversity to the region. An enjoyable read. [VP]

1307 Castro, Fidel. Cien horas con Fidel. Conversaciones con Ignacio Ramonet. 2a. ed., rev. y enriquecida con nuevos datos. La Habana: Oficina de Publicaciones del Consejo de Estado, 2006. 798 p.: bibl., ill., index.

Transcriptions of interviews conducted by Spanish-born, French journalist Ignacio Ramonet with Fidel Castro during 2003–2005. Especially noteworthy is that almost one-half of the interviews cover the time period since the fall of the Soviet Union, with special attention on the Ochoa affair, ex-president Jimmy Carter's visit, and the arrest of dissidents. Nearly identical to *Fidel Castro, biografía a dos voces* (item **1342**). [MC]

1308 Collado, Lipe. Radio Caribe: en la era de Trujillo. Santo Domingo: Editora Collado, 2008. 318 p.: bibl., ill., index.

Drawn principally from editorials and articles published in *La Nación* and transmitted by Radio Caribe (Trujillo's official means of communication), the author brings to light the origin, development, and impact of this radio channel that came on the air in 1959. Based on the objectives and transmitted programs, Collado explains in detail how Radio Caribe became a powerful tool of control and propaganda, used by the Servicio de Inteligencia Militar (SIM), and other agencies, to spy on citizens and to denounce opposition. Framed within the political and cultural environment of the second half of the 20th century, the material is easily accessible to a new generation of readers who may have no knowledge of the negative role played by this broadcasting instrument. The study will be of interest for those familiar with such a practice as well. [VP]

1309 Constenla, Julia. Che Guevara: la vida en juego. Buenos Aires: Edhasa, 2006. 287 p.: bibl., ill.

Synthetic and sympathetic biography drawn from secondary sources and Che Guevara's published writing. Lavishly illustrated, with nearly every page containing photos documenting his life. [MC]

1310 Corse, Theron Edward. Protestants, revolution, and the Cuba-U.S. bond. Gainesville: Univ. Press of Florida, 2007. 194 p.: bibl., index. (Contemporary Cuba)

Pioneering study of the conflicts and continuing persistence of Protestant churches in post-1959 revolutionary Cuba. Especially well detailed for the turbulent Church-state conflicts of the 1960s and based upon impressive research in Protestant archives. Nicely complements studies of Afro-Cuban and Catholic religious traditions to join a growing body of religious literature on post-revolutionary Cuba. [MC]

1311 DePalma, Anthony. The man who invented Fidel: Cuba, Castro, and Herbert L. Matthews of *The New York Times*. New York: Public Affairs, 2006. 308 p., 8 p. of plates: bibl., ill., index.

Study of print journalist who introduced many Americans to Fidel Castro and the Cuban Revolution through his writings. Despite the title, this book analyzes the achievements and stresses the limitations and failure of Matthews in shaping popular opinion and US policy toward Cuba. [MC]

1312 Dieterich, Heinz; Paco Ignacio Taibo II; and **Pedro Álvarez Tabío.** Diarios de guerra: Raúl Castro y Che Guevara. Madrid: Fábrica, 2006. 289 p.: ill. (Biblioteca BlowUp. Memorias)

Transcription of Raúl Castro's and Che Guevara's diaries during the opening months of the guerrilla struggle from Dec. 1956 through Feb. 1957. [MC]

1313 Documentos de la revolución cubana, 1959. Recopilación de José Bell, Delia Luisa López, y Tania Caram. La Habana: Ciencias Sociales, 2006. 329 p.

Collection of documents chronicling the first year of the Cuban Revolution, 1959. Most documents are public pronouncements of revolutionary laws and Fidel Castro's speeches and policy statements. Useful collection for assessing how fast the Revolution radicalized during the first year in power. [MC]

Dupuy, Alex. The prophet and power: Jean-Bertrand Aristide, the international community, and Haiti. See *HLAS 65:1560.*

1314 Estrada Fernández, Benito. Combatientes del mayor. Camagüey, Cuba: Editorial Ácana, 2006. 163, 23 p.: bibl. (Suma y reflejo)

Collection of personal diaries and narratives by Cubans who participated in the Angolan Revolution. Provides a valuable perspective on the experiences of soldiers and medical doctors who served Cuba's foreign policy with their service in Africa. [MC]

1315 Franqui, Carlos. Cuba, la revolución: mito o realidad?: memorias de un fantasma socialista. Barcelona: Ediciones Península, 2006. 460 p.: bibl., ill., index. (Atalaya; 235)

Collection of short writings and memoir-like reminiscences by one time revolutionary intellectual-turned-exile Carlos Franqui. Provides important insights to both the vibrant intellectual production the Cuban revolution generated, but also the political and creative limits on that scholarship. [MC]

1316 Fraser, Percy L. Looking over my shoulder: forty-seven years a public servant, 1885–1932. Introduction and endnotes by Bridget Brereton. San Juan, Trinidad and Tobago: Lexicon: Adrian Camps-Campins, 2007. 230 p.: bibl., ill.

Published posthumously, this book contains reminiscences by a long-standing Trinidadian civil servant of his life and experiences. Opens an important window into Trinidad's society in late 19th and early 20th centuries. Author's service for many years in the island's prison system permitted him to provide close-up account of the inner workings of this correctional facility. Includes a useful introduction and annotations by Bridget Brereton, a renowned historian of Trinidad. [ELC]

1317 Fuentes, Norberto. La autobiografía de Fidel Castro. Barcelona: Ediciones Destino, 2004–2007. 2 v.: bibl., ill. (some col.), index, maps. (Col. Imago mundi; v. 47, 62)

Extensive biography of Fidel Castro numbering more than 1400 pages, largely drawn from printed sources and interviews. [MC]

1318 García Álvarez, Alejandro and **Antonio Santamaría García.** El azúcar y la historiografía cubana. (*in* Açúcar e o quotidiano. Coordenação de Alberto Vieira. Funchal, Portugal: CEHA, 2004, p. 489–528)

Authoritative overview of the voluminous scholarship on Cuban sugar over the last century with particular focus on economic history. Well-balanced coverage of pre- and post-revolutionary literature with assessment of recent trends and future avenues of research. [MC]

1319 García Oliveras, Julio A. Contra Batista. La Habana: Instituto Cubano del Libro, Editorial de Ciencias Sociales, 2006. 509 p.: bibl., ill. (Memorias)

Personal memoir of one-time leader of the Student Revolutionary Directoriate of the 1950s who participated in the 1957 assault on the Presidential Palace with José Antonio Echeverria and was later a member of the Central Committee. Most of the memoir deals with the student struggle against Batista during the 1950s. [MC]

1320 Go, Julian. American empire and the politics of meaning: elite political cultures in the Philippines and Puerto Rico during U.S. colonialism. Durham, N.C.: Duke Univ. Press, 2008. 377 p.: bibl., ill., index. (Politics, history, and culture)

Rigorous comparative study of the impact of US colonialism on the political cultures of ruling elites in both Puerto Rico and the Philippines during the first decade of American occupation following the Spanish-Cuban-American War of 1898. Sheds light on US foreign intervention from the perspective of local elites, showing how ruling groups in both countries actively negotiated the terms of their new political relationships with the US. Abundantly documented with sources gathered at archival and library collections in Puerto Rico, the Philippines, and the US. [LAG]

1321 Gómez Abad, José. Cómo el Che burló a la CIA. Sevilla, Spain: RD Editores, 2007. 462 p.: bibl.

A sympathetic account of Che Guevara's last years with particular emphasis on espionage and how Che confounded repeated attempts by the CIA to track him down. The author served for more than 30 years in the Cuban Ministry of the Interior and he employs that knowledge to clarify debated issues regarding Che's clandestine and secret activities during the last years of his life. [MC]

1322 Hart, Richard. The end of empire: transition to independence in Jamaica and other Caribbean region colonies. Kingston: Arawak, 2006. 411 p.: bibl., ill., indexes, ports. (The Hart memoirs)

An insider's account of the struggle for labor, political-constitutional, and economic development in Jamaica and other former British colonies as they moved toward independence. The author, a trade union and party activist, was a participant in many of the events he describes. Book is thus doubly important for the light it casts on the struggle toward decolonization in the British Caribbean. Indispensable. [ELC]

1323 Herrera Jerez, Miriam and **Mario Castillo Santana.** De la memoria a la vida pública: identidades, espacios y jerarquías de los chinos en La Habana republicana, 1902–1968. La Habana: Centro de Investigación y Desarrollo de la Cultura Cubana Juan Marinello, 2003. 182 p.: bibl.

Important analysis of the 20th-century Chinese community in Cuba. Fills an important historiographical gap as most of the existing literature focuses on the labor of indentured servants in the 19th century. This study shows ongoing migration to Cuba in the 20th century, the vibrancy of immigrant associations, and how both the Chinese and Cuban Revolutions influenced the Chinese community in Cuba. [MC]

1324 Herrera Mora, Myrna. Mujeres dominicanas, 1930–1961: antitrujillistas y exiliadas en Puerto Rico. San Juan: Isla Negra, 2008. 250 p.: bibl., ill.

Deep and concise, this book, based on the author's PhD thesis, offers a fresh area of research on women's studies and female opposition to oppressive regimes. Describing mostly the struggle of Dominican women exiled in Puerto Rico, the author selects gender as a perspective for her study of the era of Trujillo. The work discusses women's resistance inside the country and the consequences women suffered because of their political stance. Four well-organized chapters help readers to better assess women's activism against the dictatorship and to better understand the close relationship between the Dominican Republic and Puerto Rico. Focusing on these connections, Herrera points out the mutual migratory currents that have contributed to historical developments in both islands. The interviews of 14 women and men, who relate their experience and/or knowledge of events, add tremendously to the text. The interviewers offer insights that no other sources provide. Similarly, the selection of documents (newspaper clippings, letters, poems, etc.) is very valuable. Although some references cited in the notes do not appear in the bibliography, the work is well-documented. [VP]

1325 Herrera Rodríguez, Rafael Darío. Montecristi entre campeches y bananos. Santo Domingo: Academia Dominicana de la Historia, 2006. 174 p.: bibl., ill. (Academia Dominicana de la Historia; 72)

The book documents and analyzes the natural resources, origins, development, and life in the city and province of Montecristi, once an economic and political powerhouse and today one of the most economically neglected Dominican cities. The study discusses mainly the period from the end of the 19th century to the end of the 20th century. Among other events are the changes caused by the economic transformation that took place from 1870 to 1930 and the Haitian massacre of 1937. Relevant also is the data about the role of many local personalities who contributed to the development of the city and a wide variety of immigrants who, at some point, represented a microcosm of transnational immigration in the Caribbean. Valuable statistics, worthy interviews, and rare photos enrich the text. Informative and rich in details, the text will be useful for anyone doing research on this region or on the topic of migration in the early 20th century. [VP]

1326 Infante, Fernando A. La era de Trujillo: cronología histórica, 1930–1961. Dominican Republic: Editora Collado, 2007. 2 v. (875 p.): ill., indexes.

These two volumes provide readers with detailed information about the modus operandi of the Trujillo regime. The first volume covers the period from 1930–45 and the second volume covers from 1945–61. The author uses primarily publications of the most important newspapers of this period, among them *Diario del Comercio, El Caribe, El Nuevo Diario, La Información, La Nación, La Opinión,* and *Listín Diario* to compile the entries. In the introduction, Infante warns readers to be aware that some reports did not correspond to reality. He explains that because of censorship, the newspapers could not publish information about crimes and acts of violence committed by the regime, and many crimes were disguised as accidents, personal confrontations, suicides, or other actions. Beyond the chronology, the material also includes photos illustrative of the political atmosphere and the popular culture. This voluminous and laborious work is a good reference source for the socioeconomic and political life of Dominican society during these 31 years. [VP]

1327 Kimber, Clarissa Thérèse. Le Jardin Colonial des Plantes of Martinique. (*in* Gardens and forests in the Caribbean. Edited by Robert Anderson, Karis Hiebert, and Richard H. Grove. Oxford: MacMillan, 2006. p. 87–121.)

Well-researched article focuses on the 99-year history of the Jardin Colonial de Saint-Pierre, destroyed in 1902 by a volcanic eruption. Kimber's emphasis is on the role of the Jardin in the exchange of species throughout the French empire, but the article also serves as a quick sketch of French ideas about Martinique's environment, all the way to the beginnings of a national parks movement in the 1970s. [JDG]

1328 Klepak, Hal P. Cuba's military, 1990–2005: revolutionary soldiers during counter-revolutionary times. New York: Palgrave MacMillan, 2005. 340 p.: bibl., index. (Studies of the Americas)

Insightful analysis of Cuba's military since the Special Period. Correctly assesses that above all institutions the military has provided a sense of security and stability in Cuban politics, even while their role in society has radically changed with involvement in certain sectors of the economy. Emphasizes that Cuba's Revolutionary Army will be one of the key factors in any transition situation. [MC]

1329 López Das Eiras, Horacio. Ernestito Guevara antes de ser el Che. Córdoba, Argentina: Ediciones del Boulevard, 2006. 328 p.: ill.

Detailed analysis of Che Guevara's adolescence and rearing in Argentina. Draws upon secondary sources, printed primary sources and interviews with people who knew Che and his family while living in Argentina. [MC]

1330 Mam-Lam-Fouck, Serge. Lutte nationaliste, maintien de l'ordre et culture politique dans les départements français d'Amérique: les arrestations de 1974 en Guyane. (*in* Sur les chemins de l'histoire antillaise: mélanges offerts à Lucien Abénon. Edité par Jean Bernabé et Serge Mam Lam Fouck. Matoury, French Guiana: Ibis rouge, 2006. p. 73–94.)

Mam Lam Fouck uses interviews, as well as private sources and newspaper archives to describe the nationalist movements in French Guyana in the 1970s and the events of 1974. The author argues that nationalism was an important force in 1946 when the territory became a French department, but that the metropolitan state effectively repressed this movement in the 1950s, only to have it re-emerge in the early 1970s. [JDG]

1331 Masetti, Jorge Ricardo. Los que luchan y los que lloran: el Fidel Castro que yo vi y otros escritos inéditos. Prólogo de Graciela Masetti de Morado. Buenos Aires: Nuestra América, 2006. 286 p.: ill., 1 sound disc.

Reprints the passionate and spirited account of Argentine journalist Jorge Masetti, who covered the Cuban Revolution and interviewed Fidel Castro and Che Guevara during the guerrilla war. Masetti later became an important journalist in Cuba working for *Prensa Latina*. His chronicle of the Cuban Revolution and his other writings provide an important account of the revolutionary struggle and the consolidation of power. [MC]

1332 Mencía, Mario. El Moncada: la respuesta necesaria. La Habana: Oficina de Publicaciones del Consejo de Estado, 2006. 463 p.: bibl., ill., index, maps.

Extremely detailed analysis of the preparation, assault, and consequences of the attack on the Moncada Barracks on 26 July 1953. Author draws from his previous work on the topic, supplemented by hundreds of additional interviews, as well as biographical and statistical data on many of the participants. Encyclopedic in its coverage. [MC]

1333 Merrill, Dennis. Negotiating paradise: U.S. tourism and empire in twentieth-century Latin America. Chapel Hill: Univ. of North Carolina Press, 2009. 327 p.: bibl., ill., index.

Taking interwar Mexico and Cold War-era Cuba and Puerto Rico as case studies, the author explores the intersections of tourism and power to provide a textured understanding of US foreign relations with Latin America. Tourism served not only as a form of soft power that facilitated American hemispheric dominance but equally as a space of negotiation. Host nations—from government planners to service workers—actively used this space to challenge or negotiate American influence. Innovative application of cultural theory to the study of US foreign relations and diplomacy. [LAG]

1334 Moral Roncal, Antonio Manuel. Cuba ante la Guerra Civil española: la acción diplomática de Ramón Estalella. Prólogo de Juan P. Fusi. Madrid: Biblioteca Nueva, 2003. 267 p.: bibl., ill. (Col. Historia Biblioteca Nueva)

Biographical study of the role of Cuban diplomat Ramón Estalella, who aided over 500 Republican exiles fleeing Spain for Cuba during the Spanish Civil War. Chapters cover the politics of aiding Republican exiles, the experience of refugees in Cuba, and the role of Cuba as a Latin American leader to end the conflict and provide humanitarian assistance. [MC]

1335 Munro, Arlene. British Guiana's contribution to the British war effort, 1939–1945. (J. Caribb. Hist., 39:2, 2005, p. 249–261, bibl.)

In demonstrating useful participation of volunteers from British Guiana to Britain's war effort, author examines reasons why young men volunteered and discusses their fate during and after the war. Makes a compelling case for appreciating the small but important financial contributions by Guyanese citizens at a time when the country's economic plight was severe. Also portrays Guyana's role as a settler location for Eastern European Jews threatened by the Germans. [ELC]

1336 Pamphile, Léon Dénius. Clash of cultures: America's educational strategies in occupied Haiti, 1915–1934. Lanham, MD: Univ. Press of America, 2008. 177 p.: bibl.

A history of US educational reforms during the occupation of Haiti (1919–34). Based on US and Haitian diplomatic and newspaper archives. Pamphile describes the clash of US vocational goals for the Haitian educational system with the country's elite tradition of classical studies, culminating in the student strike of 1929. [JDG]

1337 Patsides, Nicholas. Marcus Gravey, race uplift and his vision of Jamaican self-government. (Caribb. Q./Mona, 51:1, March 2005, p. 37–52, bibl.)

Contends that Garvey's attention to race globalism has been overstated, though his rhetoric remains universal in scope because it applied simultaneously to a large number of persons of African descent. Yet his race rhetoric facilitated Jamaican self-rule because of its appeal to Jamaica's needs and its national consciousness. [ELC]

1338 Payano-Safadit, Pedro N. El otro abril: crisis político-social de 1984. Santo Domingo: Editorial Búho, 2004. 204 p.: bibl.

Based on publications from several newspapers and about a dozen other sources, the book highlights political and social tensions that the Dominican people confronted in April 1965 and in April 1984. About half of the text describes the background to the calamity of the 1980s, particularly the socioeconomic crisis that took place between 1982–84. Contrasting the events, Payano brings to the forefront several developments. He looks at parallel occurrences during the administration of two leaders of the Partido

Revolucionario Dominicano (PRD). Juan Bosch, the first elected president after the Trujillo era, lasted only seven months in power. On Sept. 25, 1963, he was overthrown and replaced by a three-man military junta. Two years later, a civil-military confrontation, which aimed to return Juan Bosch to power, led to the second US military intervention in the Dominican Republic and intensified the armed confrontation in April 1965. Similarly, between 1982–84, Dominicans faced another sociopolitical crisis. The author describes how, during these two years, the peso lost its value and prices of many food staples nearly doubled. In addition, with an aim to produce economic stabilization, as mandated by the International Monetary Fund (IMF), President Jorge Blanco (1982–86) announced a short-term program of economic austerity. Payano points out that, as in 1965, in 1984 foreign intervention accelerated economic and political tensions and produced violent disturbances, including the deaths of more than 100 people. Payano's work is an important addition to the ongoing debates on the Dominican economic and social problems. [VP]

Péan, Leslie Jean-Robert. Haïti: économie politique de la corruption. See *HLAS 65:1564.*

1339 Pedraza, Silvia. Political disaffection in Cuba's revolution and exodus. New York: Cambridge Univ. Press, 2007. 359 p.: bibl., ill., index, map. (Cambridge studies in contentious politics)

Sociological analysis of the "four waves" of migration out of Cuba and mainly to the US since the 1959 Revolution. Employs a mixture of quantitative and qualitative sources with an analysis on political ideas and opinions derived from 120 interviews. [MC]

1340 Perfiles de la nación. Compilación e introducción de María del Pilar Díaz Castañón. La Habana: Editorial de Ciencias Sociales, 2004–2006. 2 v.: bibl., ill. (Pensar en Cuba)

Collection of 14 essays that deal with different aspects of Cuban nationalism through cultural categories from the second half of the 19th century to the 1959 Revolution. Chapters cover such topics as sports,

religion, civic organizations, migration, and education. Adds to the literature on Cuban nationalism by focusing on topics other than politics and founding figures. [MC]

1341 Raful, Tony. Movimiento 14 de Junio: historia y documentos. 3. ed. Santo Domingo: Búho, 2007. 780 p.: bibl., ill., index.

An important contribution to the study of the political evolution of a group that, organized by a large number of young middle-class Dominicans, opposed the Trujillo regime and paid the consequences. After Trujillo's death in 1961, under the leadership of its first president, Manuel Tavares Justo (Manolo), the group continued its political struggle, fighting oppression ideologically and militarily. Along with an intriguing examination of the tumultuous life of Manolo, Raful's narrative shows how applying theoretical principles to combative action, in Nov. 1963, Manolo led an armed insurrection, known as "Frente Guerrillero de Manaclas," at the Central Mountain region, where he was captured and killed in Dec. 1963. Well-documented and fully illustrated, the material offers good insight into the complexities of the Dominican nation during the second half of the 20th century. The information obtained through interviews is very helpful. The text is of interest to those who want to study modern Dominican political history. For review of 1st ed., see *HLAS 48:2599.* [VP]

1342 Ramonet, Ignacio. Fidel Castro, biografía a dos voces. Ed. ampliada y revisada. Barcelona: Debate, 2007. 759 p.: bibl., ill. (some col.), index.

"Biography" which offers transcriptions of interviews conducted by Spanish born, French journalist Ignacio Ramonet with Fidel Castro during 2003–2005. Especially noteworthy is that almost one-half of the interviews cover the time period since the fall of the Soviet Union, with special attention on the Ochoa affair, ex-president Jimmy Carter's visit, and the arrest of dissidents. Nearly identical to item **1307**. [MC]

Rojas, Rafael. Anatomía del entusiasmo: la revolución como espectáculo de ideas. See item **3598**.

1343 **Román, Reinaldo L.** Governing spirits: religion, miracles, and spectacles in Cuba and Puerto Rico, 1898–1956. Chapel Hill: Univ. of North Carolina Press, 2007. 273 p.: bibl., ill., index.

Provocative study of the interplay among popular religious practices, the state, the media, and religious institutions in Cuba and Puerto Rico during the first half of the 20th century. Argues that superstition, certain African-derived religious practices, and popular Catholicism raised key issues of race, class, and religion-issues that underpinned broader debates about civil and political freedoms in neocolonial states concerned largely with maintaining moral and political order. Based on rich archival and oral-history research. [LAG]

1344 **Rosa, Jesús de la.** La revolución de abril de 1965: siete días de guerra civil. Santo Domingo: Secretaría de Estado de Cultura, Editora Nacional, 2005. 188 p.: bibl., ill. (Col. Premios nacionales)

This well-known scholar, winner of the Premio Nacional de Historia (2005), utilizes a descriptive approach to reveal important details of the civil-military confrontation of 1965, known as the Dominican Constitutionalist Revolution of 1965. Aimed at returning Juan Bosch to power, elected in Dec. 1962 and deposed in Sept. 1963, the turmoil was representative of the crisis that usually develops during the transition from dictatorship to democracy. The work relies on De la Rosa's own experience during the revolutionary upheaval. He was a high-ranking naval officer, fought on the rebels' side, and was the only military officer, among 83 other persons, labeled as a Communist by the US government. Six appendices, including the list of the 83 Communists that was published on May 5, 1965, photos of the main leaders on both sides of the struggle, vivid illustrations of several episodes, and other relevant documents, enrich the text. [VP]

1345 **Saunier, Annie.** Les orphelins de la Pelée entre 1912 et 1916. (*in* Sur les chemins de l'histoire antillaise: mélanges offerts à Lucien Abénon. Edité par Jean Bernabé and Serge Mam Lam Fouck. Matoury, French Guiana: Ibis rouge, 2006, p. 47–72.)

Uses the register of 260 children orphaned by the 1902 volcanic eruption of Mount Pelée to trace the lives of this cross-section of Martiniquan society. Concludes that a strong element of family cohesion meant that most of them remained on the island, most frequently in the Fort-de-France urban area. Many eventually returned as adults to live in the northern part of the island where the disaster occurred. [JDG]

Schmidt, Nelly. La France, a-t-elle aboli l'esclavage: Guadeloupe-Martinique-Guyane, 1830–1935. See item **1295.**

1346 **Schnakenbourg, Christian.** Histoire de l'industrie sucrière en Guadeloupe aux XIXe et XXe siècles. Tome III, Fluctuations et dépendance 1884–1946. Paris: L'Harmattan, 2008. 1 vol. (240 p.): bibliogr., cartes, couv. ill.

In this continuation of his history of Guadeloupe's sugar industry, Schnakenbourg describes the near total elimination of locally owned sugar refiners during the collapse of world sugar prices at the end of the 1800s. Although somewhat buoyed by the popularity of rum in Europe during the post-WWI years, Guadeloupe's sugar-dependent economy was deeply scarred by the Great Depression. Conditions during this era further concentrated the sugar processing industry, which was already exclusively owned by metropolitan firms. [JDG]

1347 **Serra, Ana.** The "new man" in Cuba: culture and identity in the Revolution. Gainesville: Univ. Press of Florida, 2007. 210 p.: bibl., ill., index. (Contemporary Cuba)

Cultural analysis of the Cuban Revolution with a critical assessment of the achievements and limitations of the literacy campaign, the changing role of intellectuals, the 10 million ton harvest of 1970, gender relations, and childhood. For literary specialist's comment, see item **2358.** [MC]

1348 **Seukeran, Lionel Frank.** Mr. Speaker, sir: an autobiography of Lionel Frank Seukeran, the silver-tongued orator. Edited and abridged by Ken Ramchand. San Fernando, Trinidad and Tobago: Chandrabose Publications, 2006. 488 p.: ill. (some col.), maps.

Enormously reflective autobiography of this largely self-made man who was involved in various aspects of Trinidad's political history throughout most of the 20th century. Recounts his interactions with and thoughts of some of the major political players as Trinidad moved steadily from Crown Colony government to representative colonial government and finally to independent nation. [ELC]

1349 Smith, Matthew J. Red and black in Haiti: radicalism, conflict, and political change, 1934–1957. Chapel Hill, NC: Univ. of North Carolina Press, 2009. 278 p.: bibl., index, photos.

This well-researched political history fills an important gap in the historiography of modern Haiti. Smith uses Haitian and US archives, as well as interviews, to reconstruct what he argues was the critical period between the end of the long US occupation (1915–34) and the election of François Duvalier as president in 1957. He focuses on the events of 1946, when a revolt toppled the pro-US president, illustrating the new power of the black urban middle and working classes, as well as leftist radicals associated with the cultural elite. [JDG]

1350 Smith, Richard. Jamaican volunteers in the First World War: race, masculinity and the development of national consciousness. Manchester, England; New York: Manchester Univ. Press; New York: Palgrave, 2004. 180 p.: bibl., ill., index.

Concentrating on Jamaicans who served in the British Regiments during WWI, this important study shows how despite the initial hesitancy to accept West Indian volunteers because of race, their use as ordinary laborers, and exclusion from the front lines, the war provided a major impetus for masculine rhetoric, imagery, and material experiences that contributed to the rise of nationalism in the 1930s. [ELC]

1351 Symmes, Patrick. Thirty days as a Cuban: pinching pesos and dropping pounds in Havana. (*Harper's*, Oct. 2010, p. 43–57.)

Journalistic account of the current economic shortages and political transitions occurring in Cuba based upon trying to live on the equivalent of a Cuban salary of $20 for 30 days. Insightful and revealing of the day-to-day "lucha" that marks average Cubans lives during the special period. [MC]

1352 Toro, Carlos del. La alta burguesía cubana, 1920–1958. La Habana: Editorial de Ciencias Sociales, 2003. 301 p.: bibl. (Historia)

Marxist analysis of the rise and role of "New Bourgeoise" in the decades leading up to the 1959 Revolution. In addition to studying the role of economic influence of the bourgeoise, this book also examines their cultural influence through clubs, societies, and associations. Well-documented analysis of the interconnections between politics, economics, and culture of Cuba's ruling class. [MC]

1353 Valdés Sánchez, Servando. Cuba: ejército y reformismo, 1933–1940. Santiago, Cuba: Instituto Cubano del Libro, Editorial Oriente, 2006. 114 p.: bibl.

Important analysis of the role of the Cuban military beyond politics alone in the 1930s and singular focus of Fulgencio Batista. Emphasis is placed on the professionalization of the military, educational training, and reforms. Based largely upon printed primary sources and use of military regulations and codes. [MC]

Valdés Sánchez, Servando. Cuba y Estados Unidos: relaciones militares, 1933–1958. See *HLAS 65:2077.*

1354 Vázquez García, Humberto. El gobierno de la kubanidad. Santiago, Cuba: Editorial Oriente, 2005. 575 p.: bibl., index.

Political analysis of the presidency of Ramón Grau San Martín (1944–48). Drawing largely from printed primary and secondary sources, the author emphasizes the corruption that marked the Grau presidency, ties with the US, and directly and indirectly the conditions that gave rise to the 1959 Revolution. The appendix includes useful short biographies of political figures of the era and a detailed chronology of the Grau presidency. [MC]

1355 Vega, Bernardo. El peligro comunista en la revolución de abril: ¿mito o realidad? Santo Domingo: Fundación Cultural Dominicana, 2006. 373 p.: bibl., ill., index.

This remarkable historical source provides meticulous analysis and a new perspective on the revolution that drastically divided Dominican society in April 1965; as the author points out, this event is one the most turbulent periods of the Dominican political history of the 20th century. Through interviews, testimonies, and conflicting reports, Vega argues that although communists participated in the struggle, they did not control the movement. The supposed communist leadership was the justification of President Lyndon Johnson to send, at first, the Army's 82nd Airborne Division to the Dominican Republic at the end of April 1965. Ultimately, 42,000 soldiers and marines were ordered to the Dominican Republic. Analyzing the relevance of the incident, the author relies on a wealth of unpublished documents to provide essential facts not only about the US military intervention in the Dominican Republic, but also about the intricacies of international relations that developed during the Cold War. Within the context of international relations, as Vega shows, President Lyndon Johnson's decision to send troops to the Dominican Republic was influenced by fear of communism. The President received continuous reports that communists were taking control of the country. Thus, in order to prevent "a second Cuba" in the Caribbean, the US invaded the Dominican Republic and sided with the conservatives. With this publication, Vega, a well-known writer and winner of numerous recognitions, who has published more than 20 volumes on Dominican history, offers to scholars and the general public very solid archival research to deepen information available on the topic. The text includes transcripts of the communications between President Johnson, the CIA, the US Dept. of State, and Dominican military officers, and other US and Dominican reports, as well as international reports. Vivid photographic images and revealing information obtained from interviews strengthen the content. The new data, sharp-witted comments, and previously unknown details enrich the existing bibliography on the topic. Scholarly, Vega's contribution is both quantitatively and qualitatively impressive. [VP]

1356 Vidal, Cécile. The reluctance of French historians to address Atlantic history. (*South. Q.*, 43:4, 2006, p. 153–189)

This important article by French scholar of North America places the historiography of the Caribbean in the French political and cultural context of the years from 1930 to 2006. She describes the controversies over French colonial history and the slave trade, and analyzes how the structure of French academia has worked against the integration of French Caribbean and Atlantic history into the history of metropolitan France. Notes offer a deep survey of recent French and U.S. historiography and commentary on Atlantic studies. [JDG]

1357 Yanes Mesa, Julio Antonio. El ocaso de la emigración canaria a Cuba, 1920–1935. Tegueste, Cuba: Ediciones Baile del Sol, 2006. 281 p.: bibl., indexes. (Textos del desorden; 11)

Detailed sociohistorical analysis of Canary Islander migration to Cuba from 1920–35. Emphasis is placed on traditional migratory tools of analysis emphasizing push-pull factors, but also personal and familial connections that facilitated migration. Well-documented with statistical evidence on size and flow of migratory patterns. [MC]

1358 Zanetti Lecuona, Oscar. Isla en la historia: la historiografía de Cuba en el siglo XX. La Habana: Ediciones Unión, 2005. 124 p.: bibl. (Col. Clio)

Succinct overview of Cuba historiography emphasizing methodological orientations and thematic changes prompted by political circumstances before and after the 1959 Revolution. Reserved but poignant criticism of some literature produced during the 1970s and 1980s as dictated by Revolutionary politics. Argues that scholarship in the 1990s emphasized more nationalism and identity and less economics and structuralism in response to the fall of the Soviet Union and the centennial commemorations of independence. [MC]

SPANISH SOUTH AMERICA
Colonial Period

LOLITA GUTIÉRREZ BROCKINGTON, *Professor Emerita of History, North Carolina Central University, Durham, and Senior Scholar Institute of African-American Research, University of North Carolina, Chapel Hill*
JERRY W. COONEY, *Professor Emeritus of History, University of Louisville*
MARÍA N. MARSILLI, *Associate Professor of History, John Carroll University*
BIANCA PREMO, *Associate Professor of History, Florida International University*

VENEZUELA AND NUEVA GRANADA

THE INCREASING PROFESSIONALIZATION OF HISTORICAL RESEARCH in Colombia and Venezuela and a growing international interest in the area have resulted in an engaging, diverse scholarly production about colonial New Granada. Studies focusing on the national period had already made this trend clear in previous years. The good news is that colonial studies are now producing interesting, innovative works offering bright prospects for continued research and publication in the future.

Simón Bolívar and his times and deeds were the focus of two attention-grabbing studies that explore aspects of the subject so far overlooked. Matthew Brown's book details the lives of over 7,000 British and Irish mercenaries that joined Bolívar's troops and adds a fascinating international dimension to our understanding of South America's war for independence (item **1368**). Pedro Hoyos explains Bolívar's ideas regarding people of African heritage in the organization of the new republic (item **1373**).

African slavery, an important component of the colony's society, garnered the attention of several authors. María Cristina Navarrete explores the complexities of the illegal means used to smuggle African slaves into New Granada (item **1377**). Sherwin Bryant explains the importance of slavery to Popayán's 17th-century gold mining and suggests that this economic activity created in the area the prototype of a Spanish America slave society (item **1369**). María Angélica Suaza convincingly details the daily lives of African slaves in the landed estates of the Nieva province by supplementing archival information with archeological data (item **1387**). Ernesto Mora illustrates the religious assimilation of by blacks in Venezuela during the 18th century (item **1363**). Finally, María Cristina Navarrete explains the development, collapse, and legacy of fugitive African slave communities in colonial Colombia (item **1378**).

Groups located on opposite sides of the colonial social spectrum were the focus of some studies that deserve mention. The formation of an urban low class is the subject of Marta Zambrano's research on Indian-European relations in early colonial Bogotá (item **1390**). Orián Jiménez's study of popular festivals and folk celebrations in Antioquía details colorful popular culture traditions (item **1374**). Local upper classes also received scholarly attention. Yuleida Artigas used family reconstruction techniques (paying particular attention to marriages and dowries) to map the power networks built by Mérida's local elite during the 17th century (item **1360**). María Teresa Ripoll details the increasing social, political, and economic power of Cartagena's merchant elite during the late colonial period (item **1382**). Finally, in a study that nicely intersects social and intellectual history,

Diana Soto describes the activities of botanist and educator Celestino Mutis and his influence on 18th-century Colombian elite using as overarching paradigm the influence of the Enlightenment in colonial Spanish America (item **1386**).

Some works stand as excellent models of interdisciplinary analysis. In particular, María Piedad Quevedo's study of the role that the body and sensory input played in the mystical experience of a set of *granadinas* nuns provides an engaging research window into a pathbreaking topic (item **1381**). The use of archeological information in addition to historical data also produced remarkable results, such as Suaza's study on rural African slavery (item **1387**). We would also like to note an earlier publication that scholars may wish to consult for similar methodolgies: Mario Sanoja's well-documented explanation of the role that access to water played in the urban organization of early colonial Caracas (see *HLAS 61:470*).

Research focusing on colonial printing constitutes a most welcome contribution, and two studies stand as inspiring venues of future research. Mauricio Nieto's book on the 1808–10 coverage of *El Semanario del Reyno de Nueva Granada* sheds light on the relationship between science, natural history, and the Enlightenment and its impact on local elites' ideas about social and political power (item **1380**). Also, Álvaro Garzón's meticulously annotated catalog of Colombian colonial printings (1738 to 1810) provides a valuable source for future research on the topic (item **1371**).

The much anticipated boom in commemorative research due to the bicentennial celebration of Latin American independence has not yet made its full impact on studies focusing on colonial New Granada. Topics such as the effects of Bourbon imperial reforms, the increasing development of local political awareness, and the vicissitudes of the war of independence should appear more prominently in coming years. Even so, there are some fine recent studies that should be noted. Adriana Alzate details the Bourbon efforts to modernize public sanitation and health in New Granada (item **1367**). Jaime Rodríguez O.'s piece on late colonial Quito explains the political dynamics at work during the war of independence (item **1397**). Justo Cuño explores the effects of the 1815–21 reestablishment of imperial control over the city of Cartagena (item **1370**). Finally, Steinar Saether clarifies the impact that the war for independence had in the provinces of Santa Marta and Riohacha (item **1384**). [MNM]

QUITO AND PERU

This essay considers scholarship on both colonial Ecuador (Quito) and Peru, in part because of the relatively small, if growing, body of scholarship on the former, and in part because of the obvious historical and historiographical connections between the countries. Whether considered separately or together, both regions continue to inspire vibrant histories in both English and Spanish. If clear thematic trends exist within this diverse and rich collection of works, they would include a galvanized interest in "communication," and new attention to material and visual culture. There is also a slow but steady insistence that we consider regions outside the capitals and away from the central Andes and, indeed, that we question the very concepts of "regions" and "frontiers." And, finally, there is a sustained scholarly attraction to the 18th century and late colonial themes.

A number of works examine what might be broadly construed as communication. These publications range from studies of colonial language politics (item **1407**) to works that follow networks of information (items **1416** and **1454**) to a number of works that highlight the importance of the press in the late colonial period (items **1426**, **1428**, **1448**, and **1454**).

Communication is conceived of materially, as well. There are the talking books discussed by Lamana (item **1421**) and the *quipus* in Charles' article (item **1408**), with both authors undertaking methodological exercises to recover native epistemologies. Peralta's study looks at *papel sellado*, the very paper on which much colonial writing took place (item **1437**). In addition to paper, items such as luxury goods (item **1411**)and tobacco (item **1455**), as well as cloth (item **1437**) and artisanal tools (item **1442**), play protagonists in histories of diverse types. In addition, some notable works provide novel considerations of art. Among these are O'Phelan's examination of the French clothing used in saintly iconography (item **1433**), Holland's iconoclastic argument that Guamán Poma did not draw the illustrations in his famous chronicle (item **1418**), and the pairing of history and art history in Guibovich and Wuffraden's book on Church politics and Church adornments and architecture in the bishopric of Cuzco (item **1451**).

It is striking that, despite the increasing incursion of race and gender scholars into the "Atlantic" paradigm (items **486** and **1458**), it seems there are fewer monographic works tightly focused on the history of peoples of African descent or women than in the past years. In fact, one of the few exceptions to this notion is an English translation of a previously published book that fast became a "classic": Mannarelli's 1994 study of sex and illegitimacy in Lima (item **1424**; for review of Spanish original, see *HLAS 56:2434*). Some other exceptions are worth mentioning since (perhaps not coincidentally), they offer quite original analysis or thematics: the study of late colonial Andean cacicas by Garrett (item **1414**); Blanchard's book on independence and peoples of African decent (item **472**); and Tardieu's benchmark study of peoples of African descent in the Audiencia of Quito (item **1398**).

Regionally, capital cities and the central Andes seem to be bottomless repositories for new arguments, such those advanced by Osorio about 17th-century Lima as a modern yet Baroque South Seas "hub" (item **1434**), and new themes, such as Lima's 1746 earthquake (items **1456** and **1457**). But regional historians are persistently edging inward from the peripheries, with works on regional history in Peru (item **1434**). Some studies of frontiers, cities, or voyages consider space not only geographically but also conceptually, challenging the concept of nation, peripheries, and centers (items **1393**, **1420**, **1434**, and **1449**). Especially notable is burgeoning scholarship on Northern Peru, where O'Toole (item **1435**) and Espinoza (item **1412**) are bringing attention to complex ethnic histories on the coast, and where Ramírez (item **1444**) and Berquist (item **1401**) put Trujillo on the broader Enlightenment map with studies of Bishop Martínez Campañón.

The final two works also showcase scholars' continued fascination with the rapid changes of the late colonial period, despite the significant offerings—many already mentioned—on the 17th century. Deeper attention to the social aspects of the Bourbon Reforms inspired Milton's article on the legal privileges of "poverty" in Quito (item **1396**). In addition, late colonial events and sources once considered the stuff of traditional "political" history are inspiring renewed interest, as is the case with Rosas Lauro's consideration of the French Revolution in Peru and several investigations into events in Peru during the Napoleonic crisis and establishment of the Cortes of Cádiz (items **1438** and **1439**). The mid-18th century also seems to be attracting deeper attention, and only in part because scholars have begun to highlight the transformations wrought by Lima's 1746 earthquake. A renewed interest in intellectual history has drawn scholars back to the first half of the century, as showcased in Thurner's reconsideration of Barnuevo Peralta's early 18th-century histories (item **1452**) and in Hernández Asensio's delightful study of La Condamine's geographic exploration to Ecuador in the 1730s (item **1394**). Mid-century bureaucrats and intellectuals also appear as subjects in Rodríguez García's study of Creole patriotism (item **1445**) and studies of politics during the reign of Felipe V (items **1429** and **1430**).

Finally, in terms of broader publishing trends, the ever-growing accessibility of published versions of primary documents is worth mentioning. A substantial number of transcribed primary documents have appeared, and quite a few are regional visitas or other genres of writing that illuminate Church-indigenous relations (items **1406**, **1440**, **1441**, and **1446**). In addition, many monographic studies include key primary documents in appendices. [BP]

CHARCAS

Most of the works on the colonial history of Charcas break new ground or offer fresh insights into earlier studies. The majority discuss resistance prior to Bolivia's independence from Spain or the wars of independence themselves, some in geographic regions overlooked or understudied until now, and often casting entirely new light on the many forms and complexities of Andean rebellion. Robins' work, for example, among other important issues focuses on the lesser-known history of ongoing abuse of indigenous villagers by some parish priests and other members of the clergy (item **1468**). Supported by ample documentation from villager complaints throughout the region, patterns of economic exploitation, forced labor, physical abuse including female sexual violations, and forced marriages clearly emerge. Risking retaliation, indigenous peoples formalized their grievances within the legal system. Clergy abuse contributed additional burdens to the existing layers of exploitation imposed from above, further fueling indigenous participation in the massive armed rebellion of 1781.

Roca, on the other hand, examines Charcas' weakening ties with Spain and the many internal and external alliances and conflicts involved in the break, further complicated by Argentina and Peru and their respective attempts to control the Audiencia and its still-productive Potosí silver mines (item **1469**). He explains the considerable political and military influence of internal local actors, as well as the influence of the more widely recognized José de San Martín and Simón Bolívar, throughout the region. Further, the switching of these alliances played a crucial role in the success and failure of political and military advances toward full independence from Spain as well as from Argentina and Peru. This informed work is valuable for scholars of Latin American independence movements, their origins, complicities, and complexities.

Serulnikov adopts yet another well-documented, illuminating slant on the Andean uprisings culminating in the Rebellion of 1780–81 (item **1472**). Focusing on the Aymara-speaking ethnic groups in the Chayanta province north of Potosí, he concludes that struggles in that region followed a distinct, more slowly evolving, less-ruptured path than the more well-known Tupac Amaru uprising in Cuzco. In this case, ongoing arbitration and accommodation starting in the 1740s resulted in a successful culmination of processes, rather than the sporadic bursts of aggression experienced elsewhere and resolving little. This notion is best illustrated in the prolonged disputes between ethnic *ayllus*, caciques, and local officials, and particularly in the actions of strong local leaders such as Tomás Katari. These arguments add further support to the recent scholarship on rural commun ties, collective conscience, and solidarity serving as a break from colonial rule and a reaffirmation of the corporate nature of rural communities no longer in need of administration intermediaries.

Other recently published works look to semi-Altiplano and non-Altiplano regions, and often to earlier time periods as well. Tonelli Justiniano, for example, covers an impressive time span and array of subjects in Bolivia's far eastern province of Chiquitos (item **1473**). The many chapters of his book cover the ethnography of local indigenous groups; European and Brazilian conquests and ongoing invasions; and the extensive and intensive Jesuit missionary activities, their expulsion and its aftermath. The area served as a constant war zone during the 15 years of war for independence, and endured often difficult, hostile relations with Brazil.

Río examines another region in an exemplary revisionist ethnohistory of the Sora people who dwelled in the province of Oruro, a region favorably situated geographically to provide the benefits of at least two ecological niches which the Sora used to their considerable advantage (item **1467**). This work provides yet another model of an indigenous peoples' successful resistance and adaptations to colonial and other threatening forces, "recreating" themselves in the process, considerably aided economically by an ongoing pious fund established by their generous encomendero-cum-benefactor Lorenzo de Aldaña.

From still another region, the cloud forests of the northern Beni province, Santamaría provides persuasive arguments to question the more traditional explanations of conquest history, particularly the mutually beneficial alliances between ethnic groups and the Catholic missionaries, due in large measure to the significant social and religious status of each group's "shaman" (item **1470**).

Finally, further contributing to the scholarship on indigenous autonomy and ongoing resistance to conquest and colonial subjugation is Gato Castaño's slender but important volume on a major Spanish peace expedition into the Tarija-Pilcomayo territory of the aggressive Chiriguano people in the far southeastern limits of Charcas (item **1464**). The terms of the agreement were of considerable significance to both the Spaniards and the Chiriguano, with both sides agreeing to accommodate the needs and concerns of the other. Not surprisingly, the treaty lasted two years. [LGB]

CHILE

There are several relevant trends and dry spells in the latest scholarly production on colonial Chile. First and foremost, it is worth noting that traditional strengths in Chilean historiography, like rural and Indian history, have kept and even expanded their prominence. In particular, the works by Pablo Lacoste on the agrarian life in the province of Cuyo (items **1480**, **1481**, and **1482**) open new research avenues into agrarian entrepreneurship as it influenced and was affected by colonial social and gender structure. Significant studies on the colonial provinces located across the Andean mountains indicates the expansion of our understanding of Chilean colonial rural life. In this regard, José Vera's study on salt mining (item **1491**) sheds light on the importance of mapping colonial rural space as it was defined by the economic and social interactions that it hosted.

Indians, traditionally an important topic, also garnered attention. In particular, Francis Goicovich's study on the set of control mechanisms implemented by the Spanish administration to bring the Arauco War to an end (item **1477**) gives a clear idea of the importance that the Spanish empire attached to the pacification of colonial Chile. Along these lines, Margarita Gascón's research on the reality and perceptions of the struggle to pacify the Mapuche Indians (item **1476**) provides a good overview of the importance of the Arauco War from an imperial perspective. Finally, Indian activities in colonial urban environments, a topic so far scarcely studied, received some attention in Jaime Valenzuela's research on the role assigned to natives in colonial celebrations of political power (item **1490**).

Some attempts to advance innovative research agendas are worth mentioning. In particular, studies on gender, violence, and masculinity constitute a most welcome contribution to the area's scholarly production. Verónica Undurraga explores the culture of the duel in colonial Santiago, using as framework the socially and legally constructed tools that men used to defend their honor (item **1489**). Teresa Pereira's research on emotions and affections in family life (item **1487**) shows an attempt to take colonial studies into a groundbreaking arena. Along the same lines, Paulina Zamorano details the nature of urban violence against women in colonial Santiago and indicates that such crimes were embedded in social and family networks (item **1492**).

Natural disasters constitute another subject so far insufficiently studied in the area, in spite of the importance that recent, tragic events have conferred on these occurrences. Manuel Fernández's study on the 1868 earthquake and tsunami is, therefore, a most welcome contribution (item **1812**). Although not strictly dated in colonial times, the tragedy that took place in Arica is convincingly detailed in a social and economic setting that retains its colonial character. Fernández correctly points out the need to historically document natural disasters in Chile and the social, legal, and political issues that have influenced the outcomes of these tragedies.

Two areas deserve additional scholarly attention. The first is the study and publication of primary sources. The annotated transcript of over 60 colonial wills (item **1488**), the new edition of a time-honored study of Gerónimo de Bibar's colonial chronicle (item **1485**), and the publication of Dominican nun Sor Josefa de los Dolores Peña y Lillo's correspondence (item **1486**) constitute a timid effort to fill a large void. Studies centered on Chile's political culture on the eve of independence from the Spanish empire also are surprisingly scarce, particularly in view of the bicentennial celebration of the event. Alfredo Jocelyn-Holt's provocative reflective essay on the 1808–09 conjuncture (item **1478**) and Leonardo León's well-documented piece on the Chilean elite's prevalent prejudices about lower classes (item **1483**) cannot alone fulfill the need for more work in this area.

In spite of these gaps, the quality of recent historical research on colonial Chile is gratifying. It includes some accomplished studies that are not part of the traditional historical corpus and deserve to receive the attention of the coming generations of historians of Chile. [MNM]

RÍO DE LA PLATA

Social history of the colonial Río de la Plata continues to be of high quality. Noteworthy is the collaborative treatise on death and religion in Montevideo (item **1500**) and the impact of Bourbon Reforms upon social order in Córdoba (item **1519**) Sonia Tell's study of rural Córdoba in the late 1700s is also excellent (item **1569**), as is the work on a rural partido of Buenos Aires of the same period (item **1548**). Jeffrey Shumway's account of trials and tribulations when love encountered the state in the late colonial and early national era is good social history on the personal level (item **1565**). The analysis of women who fell afoul of the imposition of greater social control in Córdoba in the late 1700s contributes much to this field for the colonial period (item **1571**).

Interest in the Jesuits remains high. Guillermo Wilde's revisionist work merits attention (item **1572**), as does the ecclesiastical career of a Bishop of Buenos Aires greatly involved in the political debate in the l760s over that order's activities since the 1750s (item **1494**). There is an excellent review of the complex problem of the demography of the Jesuit missions (item **1541**) and a good work on the little known aspect of the Jesuits' efforts in the Banda Oriental (item **1536**).

The history of the frontiers of the Río de la Plata is attracting greater attention. The viceregal policy of encouraging settlements on the frontiers of the Banda Oriental and Entre Rios is handled well by Julio Djenderedjian (item **1518**) while Nidia R. Areces' detailed study of the region of Concepción in the late colonial and early national era throws light upon the problems Paraguay's northern frontier (item **1496**). In Córdoba in the late 1700s "undesirables" encountered a forced frontier relocation to bolster defenses against nomadic Indians (item **1563**).

The rise of the contraband traffic in the Río de la Plata in the early 1600s through the 1700s continues to interest historians. That activity is explored well by Macarena Perusset (item **1557**) and by a short, but succinct, account of how the British *asiento* of the early 1700s aggravated the problem (item **1547**).

The approach of the bicentennial of Spanish American independence has prompted a production of works on the British invasions of Buenos Aires in 1806–1807 and the revolt of Buenos Aires a few years after. As one would expect, their quality varies greatly. A new biography of Admiral William Brown of the Buenos Aires navy deserves attention (item **1549**). John Lynch has contributed a biography of José de San Martín of very high quality (item **1544**). A study of the province of Corrientes in 1810–1812 sheds light on the reception of the Buenos Aires revolt in the far periphery of the viceroyalty (item **1559**). In addition, the very detailed account of the British invasions by Guillermo Palombo is useful as reference (item **1553**). A contribution to the field of intellectual history is a collection of essays on the evolution of political thought on revolution through 1810–1820 in the Río de la Plata (item **1560**).

There is now an excellent interdisciplinary study of the construction of the defenses of Montevideo in the late colonial era (item **1543**). And there are some general historical works of high quality from Paraguay. The first volume of Dr. Francia's papers, transcribed from the Doroteo Bareiro collection, is simply the best documentary collection ever published in that nation (item **1526**). Ignacio Telesca's demographic, territorial, and social study of Paraguay between the expulsion of the Jesuits and the onset of the Intendencia system is a groundbreaking work (item **1568**). Juan Bautista Rivarola Paoli has added a new volume to his ongoing study of the Paraguayan Real Hacienda (item **1561**). Finally, the translation into Spanish of Günter Kahle's doctoral dissertation on the growth of Paraguayan national consciousness is quite welcome (item **1533**). [JWC]

VENEZUELA

1359 Araque, Oneiver Arturo. Conventos coloniales de Mérida 1591–1886: catálogo. Mérida, Venezuela: Univ. de Los Andes, Rectorado-Secretaría, Archivo Histórico, 2004. 141 p.: bibl. (Col. La ULA y su historia; 3)

Presented here is a detailed catalog of the archival documents on the local colonial convents in the city of Mérida dated from 1591 to 1886 and held at the Fondo Conventos of the Archivo Histórico de la Univ. de Los Andes. Of interest for specialists. [MNM]

1360 Artigas Dugarte, Yuleida. Familia y poder en Mérida colonial: siglo XVII. (*Tierra Firme/Caracas*, 25:97, enero/marzo 2007, p. 18–36)
Uses family reconstruction to map out power networks built by the local elite in the city of Mérida during the 17th century. Pays particular attention to the use that these families made of marriages and dowries to secure access to the local colonial bureaucracy. [MNM]

1361 Hernández González, Manuel. Los canarios en la Venezuela colonial, 1670–1810. Presentación de Tomás Straka. Ed. revisada y ampliada. Venezuela: Bid & Co., 2008. 601 p.: bibl., index. (Col. histórica; 6)
Extensively details the role of immigrants from the Canary Islands in colonial Venezuela. Substantial, well-documented research. For review of 1st ed., see *HLAS 60:2128.* [MNM]

1362 Hutten, Philipp von. Cartas: los documentos del conquistador de los Welser y capitán general de Venezuela. Edición de Eberhard Schmitt y Friedrich Karl von Hutten. Maracaibo, Venezuela: Univ. Católica Cecilio Acosta, 2005. 191 p.: bibl., col. ill., 1 col. map. (El nombre secreto)
Reproduces the correspondence (1534–41) of Philipp von Hutten, German explorer of early colonial Venezuela. A primary source of interest for studies of exploration and early descriptions of the New World. [MNM]

1363 Mora Queipo, Ernesto. Los esclavos de Dios: religión, esclavitud e identidades en la Venezuela del siglo XVIII. Venezuela: Univ. del Zulia, Ediciones del Vice Rectorado Académico, 2007. 202 p.: bibl., ill. (Col. Textos universitarios)
Illustrates the Catholic religious assimilations worked by black slaves in colonial Venezuela during the 18th century. [MNM]

1364 Rey Fajardo, José del. Los Jesuitas en Venezuela. Caracas: Univ. Católica Andrés Bello, Pontificia Univ. Javeriana, 2006. 2 v.: bibl., index.
The first 2 vols. of this multivolume collection, titled *Las fuentes* and *Los hombres*, present the biographies of all known Jesuits at work in colonial Venezuela, from the 16th to the late 18th century. Sources are carefully annotated. A good primary source for studies on colonial evangelization. [MNM]

1365 Rey Fajardo, José del. Un sueño educativo frustrado: los Jesuitas en el coro colonial. Caracas: Univ. Católica Andrés Bello; Valencia, Venezuela: Univ. Arturo Michelena, 2005. 386 p.: bibl., index.
Documents the activities of the Society of Jesus in the education in the colonial city of Coro. [MNM]

1366 Samudio Azpúrua, Edda O. De la Ermita de Nuestra Señora del Pilar de Zaragoza al Convento de San Francisco de Mérida. Caracas: Academia Nacional de la Historia, 2007. 206 p.: bibl., ill. (Biblioteca de la Academia Nacional de la Historia; 261. Fuentes para la historia colonial de Venezuela)
Explains the foundation of the Convento de San Francisco in the city of Mérida, in colonial Venezuela, during the 17th century. Presents selected primary sources adequately contextualized to understand the urban social dynamics at work behind religious devotion. [MNM]

NUEVA GRANADA

1367 Alzate Echeverri, Adriana María. Sociedad y orden: reformas sanitarias borbónicas en la Nueva Granada 1760–1810. Bogotá: Escuela de Ciencias Humanas: Univ. Colegio Mayor de Nuestra Señora del Rosario: Editorial Univ. del Rosario: Facultad de Ciencias Sociales y Humanas, Univ. de Antioquia: Instituto Colombiano de Antropología e Historia, 2007. 316 p.: bibl., ill., index. (Col. Textos de ciencias humanas)
Details the efforts by the Bourbon administration to modernize public sanitation and health in Nueva Granada in the late colonial period. Explains the reactions that these measures induced and the written records that were left as a result. An interesting work for urban history topics. [MNM]

1368 Brown, Matthew. Adventuring through Spanish colonies: Simón Bolívar, foreign mercenaries and the birth of new nations. Liverpool, England: Liverpool Univ. Press, 2006. 266 p.: ill., maps. (Liverpool Latin American studies; 8)

Documents the deeds and challenges of nearly 7,000 British and Irish mercenaries who travelled to Gran Colombia and joined Simón Bolívar's army to fight against Spanish rule. Using extensive archival material, this study shows how these men were important protagonists in South America's war for independence. [MNM]

1369 Bryant, Sherwin K. Finding gold, forming slavery: the creation of a classic slave society, Popayán, 1600–1700. (*Americas/Washington*, 63:1, July 2006, p. 81–112, maps)

Details the intricate connection between slave import and gold mining in 17th-century Popayán, New Granada. Proposes that both variables turned local society into the prototype of a Spanish American slave society. [MNM]

1370 Cuño, Justo. El retorno del rey: el restablecimiento del régimen colonial en Cartagena de Indias, 1815–1821. Castellón de la Plana, Spain: Univ. Jaume I, 2008. 481 p.: bibl. (Amèrica / Universitat Jaume I; 9)

Examines the different ideas and motivations among the protagonists of the war for independence in the city of Cartagena de Indias. Uses as setting the arrival of the Spanish army sent to bring the region back to Spanish control. [MNM]

1371 Garzón Marthá, Álvaro. Historia y catálogo descriptivo de la imprenta en Colombia, 1738–1810. Bogotá: Nomos Impresores, 2008. 617 p.: bibl., ill., index, maps.

A detailed, annotated catalog of colonial printings in Colombia (1738–1810) with meticulous indexes. A useful source for colonial studies in the region. [MNM]

Herrera Angel, Marta. Las bases prehispánicas de la configuración territorial de la provincia de Popayán en el período colonial. See HLAS 65:1105.

1372 Herrera Ángel, Marta. Ordenar para controlar: ordenamiento espacial y control político en las llanuras del Caribe y en los Andes Centrales Neogranadinos, siglo XVIII. 3. ed. Medellín, Colombia: La Carreta Editores: CESO, Univ. de los Andes, 2007. 385 p.: bibl., ill., maps. (La Carreta histórica)

Details the human geography, land settlement, and social structure of the colonial provinces of Cartagena and Santa Marta and Santafé, in Colombia, during the 18th century. Extensively detailed; makes abundant use of archival material. For reviews of earlier edition, see HLAS 61:1685 and HLAS 62:1296. [MNM]

1373 Hoyos Körbel, Pedro Felipe. Las negritudes y Bolívar: momentos históricos de una minoría étnica en la Gran Colombia. Bogotá: Hoyos Editores, 2007. 394 p.: bibl.

Provides an introduction to the study of black slavery in the area and details Simón Bolívar's stance regarding the role of this ethnic group in the organization of the new nation. [M. Marsilli]

1374 Jiménez Meneses, Orián. El frenesí del vulgo: fiestas, juegos y bailes en la sociedad colonial. Medellín, Colombia: Univ. de Antioquia, 2007. 157 p.: bibl. (Col. Premios nacionales de cultura Universidad de Antioquia)

Presents an overview of religious festivals, folk dancing, rites, and ceremonies in the province of Antioquía, in colonial Colombia. Makes extensive use of archival material to produce colorful descriptions of religious life and customs. [MNM]

1375 Morales Guinaldo, Lucía. El indio y el indiano según la visión de un conquistador español de finales del siglo XVI, Bernardo de Vargas Machuca, 1555–1622. Bogotá: Univ. de los Andes, Facultad de Ciencias Sociales, Depto. de Historia, 2008. 152 p.: bibl. (Col. Prometeo)

Analyzes the writings of Spanish conqueror of New Granada and bureaucrat Bernardo de Vargas Machuca (1555–1622). Pays particular attention to the author's viewpoints on social relations in the colony. [MNM]

1376 Moreno Sandoval, Armando. Minería y sociedad en la jurisdicción de Mariquita: reales de minas de Las Lajas y Santa Ana: 1543–1651. Ibagué, Colombia: Univ. del Tolima, 2006. 184 p.: bibl., ill., map. (Col. Universidad del Tolima 50 años; 8)

Details the mining activities in the Mariquita region (Colombia) during the 16th and 17th centuries. Pays close attention to the extraction process, as well as to the social and administrative matters involved. A good source for colonial mining history. [MNM]

1377 Navarrete Peláez, María Cristina. De las "malas entradas" y las estrategias del "buen pasaje": el contrabando de esclavos en el Caribe neogranadino, 1550–1690. (*Hist. Crít./Bogotá*, 34, julio/dic. 2007, p. 160–183, bibl.)

Details illegal slave trade mechanisms at work in New Granada during the 16th and 17th centuries. Documents two main venues of slave contraband: pirates and Portuguese slave providers. Both illegal trades benefited from rampant Spanish administrative corruption in the area. [MNM]

1378 Navarrete Peláez, María Cristina. San Basilio de Palenque, memoria y tradición: surgimiento y avatares de las gestas cimarronas en el Caribe colombiano. Cali, Colombia: Programa Editorial, Univ. del Valle, 2008. 178 p.: bibl., ill., maps. (Col. Libros de investigación)

Explains the development, composition, and collapse of a community of fugitive African slaves in 17th-century Colombia. Uses abundant archival information and an updated bibliography on the topic. [MNM]

1379 Nebgen, Christoph. Jesuiten aus Zentraleuropa in Portugiesisch- und Spanisch-Amerika: ein bio-bibliographisches Handbuch mit einem Überblick über das aussereuropäische Wirken der Gesellschaft Jesu in der frühen Neuzeit. 3, Neugranada: 1618–1771. Herausgegeben von Johannes Meier. Münster, Germany: Aschendorff, 2008. 244 p.: ill.

Another volume publishing the results of a research project done at Mainz University about Jesuits from German-speaking central European provinces in colonial South America. This volume is dedicated to the Jesuits in Nueva Granada (founded in 1696) comprising the territory of the contemporary states Colombia, Panama, and Venezuela, and, until the mid-17th century, Hispaniola (Santo Domingo), when the island was divided between the French and the Spanish. [F. Obermeier]

Nieto Olarte, Mauricio. La obra cartográfica de Francisco José de Caldas. See *HLAS* 65:1109.

1380 Nieto Olarte, Mauricio. Orden natural y orden social: ciencia y política en el *Semanario del nuevo reyno de Granada*. Bogotá: Univ. de los Andes, Facultad de Ciencias Sociales-CESO, Depto. de Historia, 2009. 420 p.: bibl., ill., maps.

Explores the topics covered by the newspaper *El Semanario del nuevo reyno de Granada*, published between 1808–10. Pays close attention to the relationship between science, natural history, and Enlightenment. Also details the relationship between these sets of ideas and local social and political power. [MNM]

1381 Quevedo Alvarado, María Piedad. Un cuerpo para el espíritu: mística en la Nueva Granada, el cuerpo, el gusto y el asco, 1680–1750. Bogotá: Instituto Colombiano de Antropología e Historia, 2007. 253 p.: bibl., ill. (Col. Cuadernos coloniales; 13)

Uses the biographies of four colonial New Granada nuns (late 17th to mid-18th century) to analyze the role of the human body in their mystical experience. Female mysticism is studied in relation to socially sanctioned sensory input. An engaging, well-developed topic. [MNM]

1382 Ripoll de Lemaitre, María Teresa. La elite en Cartagena y su tránsito a la República: revolución política sin renovación social. Bogotá: Univ. de los Andes, Facultad de Ciencias Sociales—CESO, Depto. de Historia: Ediciones Uniandes, 2006. 174 p.: bibl., ill., map. (Col. Prometeo)

Explains the increasing social, political, and economic power of Cartagena's merchant elite during the late 18th and early 19th centuries. Makes extensive use of local archives. [MNM]

1383 Rubio Hernández, Alfonso. La escritura en el archivo: mecanismo de dominio y control en el Nuevo Reino de Granada. (*Procesos/Quito*, 26, segundo semestre 2007, p. 6–28, bibl.)

Traces the path of the oral testimony of indigenous peoples to be captured in written, legal documentation and filed under colonial Spanish rule. Though the destination—that indigenous peoples began to effectively utilize legal mechanisms, and that Spanish-speaking indigenous elites played a crucial role in native history—is well-known, the author takes a new path through more recent theory about writing and royal authority. [B. Premo]

1384 Saether, Steinar A. Identidades e
independencia en Santa Marta y Riohacha, 1750–1850. Traducción de Claudia Ríos
Echeverry. Bogotá: ICANH, Instituto Colombiano de Antropología e Historia, 2005.
300 p.: bibl., ill., maps. (Col. Año 200)

Details the social composition of and
the impact that the war of independence had
in the colonial provinces of Santa Marta and
Riohacha. [MNM]

Sánchez Cabra, Efraín. Las ideas de progreso
en Colombia en el siglo XIX. See item **3623**.

1385 Serrano Álvarez, José Manuel.
Economía, rentas y situados en Carta-
gena de Indias, 1761–1800. (*Anu. Estud.
Am.*, 63:2, 2006, p. 75–96, graphs, tables)

Documents the impact of the *situado*
(financial assistance assigned for military
purposes) given to the Cartagena military
garrison in the local economy during the
late 18th century. Makes extensive use of
colonial financial records to determine that,
by that time, the local garrison was actually
supported by locally collected taxes. [MNM]

1386 Soto Arango, Diana. Mutis: educador
de la élite neogranadina. Colombia:
Rudecolombia: Univ. Pedagógica y Tecnológica de Colombia, 2005. 304 p.: bibl., ill.

Explains the activities of botanist and
educator José Celestino Mutis (1732–1808)
in 18th-century Colombia. Provides a robust
contextualization of the scholar's activities
using as background the influence of Enlightenment in the Spanish colonies. A good
source for late colonial intellectual history.
[MNM]

1387 Suaza Español, María Angélica.
Los esclavos en las haciendas de la
provincia de Neiva durante el siglo XVIII:
arqueología histórica de la Nueva Granada.
Neiva, Colombia: Gobernación del Huila,
Secretaría de Cultura y Turismo, Fondo de
Autores Huilenses, 2007. 266 p.: bibl., ill.,
maps.

Details the activities carried out by
black slaves in the landed estates of the
province of Neiva, colonial Colombia, during the 18th century. Complements archival
primary sources with archeological data.
[MNM]

1388 Urueña Cervera, Jaime. Nariño,
Torres y la revolución francesa. Colombia: Ediciones Aurora, 2007. 262 p.: bibl.,
ill.

Traces the influence of the French
Revolution in the ideas of Camilo Torres
(1766–1816) and Antonio Nariño (1760–1823),
two main figures of Colombia's war for
independence. [MNM]

1389 Wiesner Gracia, Luis Eduardo. Tunja,
ciudad y poder en el siglo XVII. Tunja,
Colombia: Univ. Pedagógica y Tecnológica
de Colombia, 2008. 307 p., 4 leaves of plates:
bibl., geneal. table, ill., map. (Col. Educación
UPTC 70 años)

Details the social structure and
economic activities of the city of Tunja, in
colonial Colombia, during the 17th century.
Extensively documented using archival
material. [MNM]

1390 Zambrano, Marta. Trabajadores, vil-
lanos y amantes: encuentros entre
indígenas y españoles en la ciudad letrada,
Santa Fe de Bogotá, 1550–1650. Bogotá:
Instituto Colombiano de Antropología e
Historia, 2008. 271 p.: bibl., index. (Col.
Antropología en la modernidad)

Details the role that Muisca Indians
played in the colonial city of Santa Fe de
Bogotá, from the mid-16th to the mid-17th
century, using judicial cases. Explains the
creation of an urban lower class as the result
of the race relations that indigenous peoples and Europeans established in the city.
[MNM]

QUITO

**1391 Actas del Cabildo colonial de
Guayaquil.** v. 10, 1708 a 1712. v. 11,
1715 y 1716. Ezio Garay Arellano basada
en la de J. Gabriel Pino Roca. Revisada por
Rafael E. Silva. Guayaquil: Publicaciones
del Archivo Histórico del Guayas, 2004. 2 v.:
ill., indexes.

Vols. 10 (1708–12) and 11 (1715–16)
of the valuable series of transcribed acts of
the Cabildo of Guayaquil. For annotation
of Vol. 1, see *HLAS 36:2553*. For annotation
of Vols. 2, 3, and 4, see *HLAS 38:3086*. For
annotation of Vol. 8, see *HLAS 62:1315*. For
annotation of Vol. 9, see *HLAS 62:1316*. [BP]

1392 Donoso, Sebastián I. Piratas en Guayaquil: historia del asalto de 1687. Guayaquil, Ecuador: Universo, 2006. 536 p.: bibl., ill., indexes, maps.

Narrative recounting of the colonial assault on the coastal Ecuadorian town that draws from some archival material. Written for a popular audience. [BP]

1393 Hernández Asensio, Raúl. La frontera occidental de la Audiencia de Quito: viajeros y relatos de viajes, 1595–1630. Lima: IFEA: IEP, 2004. 214 p.: bibl., 1 map. (Travaux de l'Institut français d'études andines; 203) (Col. Popular; 1)

Offers a perspective on the western border area of the Audiencia of Quito from a "Spanish"—i.e., Creole and peninsular— vantage point, with special attention to the internal conflicts among the elites that informed their understanding of the frontier region. After an introduction to the theme of borders, the book follows the Mercederians, expeditionary forces under the auspices of the Real Audiencia, and private merchants into Esmeraldas in the 17th century. [BP]

1394 Hernández Asensio, Raúl. El matemático impaciente: La Condamine, las pirámides de Quito y la ciencia ilustrada (1740–1751). Lima: Instituto Francés de Estudios Andinos; Quito: Univ. Andina Simón Bolívar, Ecuador; Lima: Instituto de Estudios Peruanos, 2008. 316 p.: bibl., ill., maps. (Serie Estudios históricos; 50)

Lively study of Charles-Marie de La Condamine's exploratory mission to Quito in the 1730s to make longitudinal measures of the earth and erect a monument in celebration of French science. Accompanied by Spanish officials Antonio Juan and Jorge Juan, La Condamine's project ignited political and epistemological debates that galvanized Spanish science and exploration. [BP]

1395 Mejía, portavoz de América, 1775–1813. Coordinación de Jorge Núñez Sánchez. Quito: FONSAL, 2008. 510 p.: bibl., facsim., ill. (some col.), maps, ports. (Biblioteca del bicentenario de la independencia; 8) (Biblioteca básica de Quito; 16)

Edited collection on the celebrated colonial Ecuadorian intellectual and statesman who served as an American representative to the Corte de Cádiz. Each chapter examines a different aspect of his public life, such as his work as a poet and botanist. [BP]

1396 Milton, Cynthia E. Poverty and the politics of colonialism: "poor Spaniards," their petitions, and the erosion of privilege in late colonial Quito. (*HAHR*, 85:4, Nov. 2005, p. 525–626, photo, tables)

Deeply researched study of Quiteños' petitions for *pobre de solemnidad* status during the Bourbon reforms. Whites continued to seek the privilege of legal exemption that *pobre de solemnidad* conferred, as they had in the past. But the author argues that the colonial state, which had once granted the status in order to buttress the elite through hard times, increasingly frowned on their efforts in favor of a newer "poor": the "wretched" Indians, castas, and blacks who increasingly sought the status. For book-length treatment (2002) of this topic by the same author, see *HLAS 62:1353*. [BP]

1397 Rodríguez O., Jaime E. La revolución política durante la época de la independencia: el reino de Quito, 1808–1822. Quito: Univ. Andina Simón Bolívar: Corporación Editora Nacional, 2006. 238 p.: bibl. (Biblioteca de historia; 20)

Analyzes the political dynamics at work in the kingdom of Quito during the war of independence from Spain (1809–30). A well-documented study that makes extensive use of primary and secondary sources. [MNM]

1398 Tardieu, Jean-Pierre. El negro en la Real Audiencia de Quito (Ecuador): ss. XVI–XVIII. Quito: Abya-Yala; Lima: Instituto Francés de Estudios Andinos; Quito: Cooperazione Internazionale, 2006. 384 p.: bibl., ill., map. (Travaux de l'Institut français d'études andines; 183)

Benchmark book by a historian who has written foundational studies of the black population in Peru and elsewhere in Spanish America. Seven of the eight chapters are divided regionally and proceed chronologically, from the "tyranny" of the population of African descent in early colonial Esmeraldas to the 18th-century slave population in Cuenca. The final chapter looks at legal struggles against the cruelty of owners and for liberty, as well as flight and maroonage. [BP]

PERU

1399 Alaperrine-Bouyer, Monique. La educación de las elites indígenas en el Perú colonial. Lima: Instituto Francés de Estudios Andinos: Instituto Riva-Agüero, Pontificia Univ. Católica del Perú: Instituto de Estudios Peruanos, 2007. 345 p.: bibl., ill. (some col.), maps. (Travaux de l'Institut français d'études andines; 238) (Educación y sociedad; 4)

Analysis of the multiple Spanish colonial projects to educate and Hispanicize indigenous elites in the Andes, from early projects in Quito, to Lima and Cuzco, and through to the failed plan to bring noble youths to study in Granada. Focus is as much on social context and pedagogy as on institutions. Includes an appendix of select documents spanning the colonial period. [BP]

1400 Andazabal, Rosaura. Criminalística peruana en el siglo XVIII: ensayo de interpretación estadística en torno a la causal de homicidio. Lima: Seminario de Historia Rural Andina, Univ. Nacional Mayor de San Marcos, 2007. 214 p.: bibl., ill.

Working paper-style publication on homicide statistics and patterns in 18th-century Peru, drawing from 173 cases. Special attention is given to the occupations and biographical profiles of the accused and the victims, as well as to the social milieu in which the crimes occurred. [BP]

1401 Berquist, Emily. Bishop Martínez Compañón's pratical utopia in Enlightenment Peru. (*Americas/Washington*, 64:3, Jan. 2008, p. 377–408, ill.)

Thoroughly researched study of the Enlightened bishop's visions of a reformed northern Peru. Arguing that his ideas advanced a particularly Bourbon version of the ideal subject, this article explores his suggestions for sartorial and cultural reforms (he was a proponent of card playing since it would promote the royal monopoly), as well as of educational and economic reforms centered on the mining industry at Hualgayoc. [BP]

1402 La botánica al servicio de la corona: la expedición de Ruiz, Pavón y Dombey al virreinato del Perú (1777–1831). Barcelona: Lunwerg Editores, 2003. 220 p.: bibl., col. ill.

Lavishly illustrated history of the science and politics of the botanical expedition to Peru, a late 18th-century endeavor that resulted in the addition of Andean flora and fauna to the Spanish royal Botanical Gardens. Chapters by various authors explore the French antecedents to the Spanish expedition, the expedition itself, and its administration. [BP]

1403 Brown, Kendall W. Borbones y aguardiente: la reforma imperial en el sur peruano: Arequipa en vísperas de la Independencia. Traducción de María Vásquez. Revisión histórica de Marina Zuloaga. Lima: Banco Central de Reserva del Perú: Instituto de Estudios Peruanos, 2008. 320 p.: bibl., ill., maps. (Serie historia económica; 2)

Spanish-language translation of a 1986 study (see *HLAS 48:2729*) of late colonial administrative and fiscal reform in the Southern Andes. [BP]

1404 Busto Duthurburu, José Antonio del. Marchas y navegaciones en la conquista del Perú. Lima: Instituto Riva-Agüero, Pontificia Univ. Católica del Perú, 2006. 379 p.: bibl. (Publicación del Instituto Riva-Agüero; 231)

New and previously published essays on conquest expeditions, written by a Peruvian historian and present-day expeditionary chronicler. Two principal sections cover land and water, with chapters further divided by conqueror and route. Mostly drawn from chronicles, some cross-checked against other sources, documenting famous Spanish conquerors such as the Pizarros and de Soto. [BP]

1405 Cajavilca Navarro, Luis. Gentilicios africanos en la costa central del Perú, siglo XVII. (*Investig. Soc./San Marcos*, 15, dic. 2005, p. 371–386, bibl.)

Intended to contribute to the study of African populations and languages in the Americas. The most interesting section investigates the various African ethnic groups that corresponded to the last names given to slaves in the ecclesiastical records of the 17th-century bishopric of Lima. [BP]

1406 Cañedo-Argüelles Fabrega, Teresa. La visita de Juan Gutiérrez Flores al Colesuyo y Pleitos por los cacicazgos de Torata y Moquegua. Lima: Pontificia Univ. Católica del Perú, Fondo Editorial, 2005. 228 p.: bibl. (Col. Clásicos peruanos)

Analytical study and reproduction of a *visita* and litigation from early colonial Moquegua Valley in southern Peru, which served as outpost for Aymaras from Titicaca Basin. The previously unstudied 1573 *visita*, discovered by the author in the Lilly Library (Indiana Univ., Bloomington), was contained within a dispute over native leadership in Moquegua and Torata in the 1590s, and both documents reveal how Spanish conquest brought to the surface the political tensions and historical revisionism at play in the Inca rule of these Aymara communities. [BP]

1407 Charles, John. "More Ladino than necessary": indigenous litigants and the language policy debate in mid-colonial Peru. (*Colon. Lat. Am. Rev.*, 16:1, June 2007, p. 23–47, bibl.)

Examines how native Andeans contributed to imperial language polemics by following the complaint of one cacique about his local priest's failure to instruct indigenous parishioners in Quechua. The incident serves as a springboard for a larger discussion of cultural power in the 17th-century Andes, as well as of the political position of Spanish-speaking "*indios ladinos*" who utilized the court system. [BP]

1408 Charles, John. Unreliable confessions: *khipus* in the colonial parish. (*Americas/Washington*, 64:1, July 2007, p. 11–33)

Focuses on the enduring use, at the local level, of Andean *quipus*, the knotted cord used for recording history and administrative matters, including accounting and legal testimony. Underscores the "semiotic hybridity" of these nonalphabetic writing devices by showing that *quipus* were instruments in part utilized by priests in Catholic missionizing and in part wielded by Andean communities to record testimony against priests, for example at the Third Provincial Council of Lima in the late 16th century. [BP]

1409 Congreso Pueblos, Provincias y Regiones en la Historia del Perú, *Peru,* *2005.* Pueblos, provincias y regiones en la historia del Perú. Lima: Academia Nacional de la Historia, 2006. 982 p.: bibl., ill.

A massive edited collection of works presented at a 2005 Congress of the Academia Nacional de la Historia. Sections range from helpful updates and studies of

the sources available at various regional archives to diverse monographic chapters based in regional history, with local historians from beyond Lima featured prominently. [BP]

1410 Dargent-Chamot, Eduardo. La cocina monacal en la Lima virreinal. Lima: Univ. de San Martín de Porres, Fondo Editorial, 2009. 132 p.: bibl.

Working paper-style publication on the food served in colonial convents. Utilizes archival documentation from the ecclesiastical archives as well as chronicles and contemporary literature to detail ingredients and recipes, which combined Andean and European fare. [BP]

1411 Earle, Rebecca. Consumption and excess in colonial and early-independent Spanish America. (*in* Imported modernity in post-colonial state formation: the appropriation of political, educational, and cultural models in nineteenth-century Latin America. Edited by Eugenia Roldán Vera & Marcelo Caruso. Frankfurt am Main: Peter Lang, 2007, p. 341–361)

Engagingly written exploration of the ambivalence in 18th-century Spanish and Spanish American concepts of "luxurious consumption." Follows that ambivalence into debates about trade in the early republican period, when the identification of European luxury goods as civilizing items seized both patriotic imagination and policy. [BP]

1412 Espinoza Soriano, Waldemar. La etnia Guayacundo en Ayabaca, Huancabamba y Caxas, siglos XV–XVI. Lima: Instituto de Ciencias y Humanidades: Fondo Editorial del Pedagógico San Marcos, 2006. 307 p.: bibl., ill., maps. (Serie Historia)

A recuperation of the history of a northern Peruvian ethnic group with origins in regions with shifting names, caught up in the changing jurisdictions of early colonialism. Tightly focused on unveiling the social structure of the group; finds that they were well organized and integrated into the Inca empire. Second half of work reproduces key primary documents on the Guayacundo. [BP]

1413 Fisher, John Robert. Redes de poder en el Virreinato del Perú, 1776–1824: los burócratas. (*Rev. Indias*, 66:236, enero/abril 2006, p. 149–164)

A study of Peruvian high-ranking officials aimed at assessing the success of the reformist *visita* conducted in the 1770s through 1780 by Antonio Areche and Jorge Escobedo. Summarizes how the *visita* recommended personnel reforms at the highest bureaucratic levels; lists the key viceroys, intendants, and regents of the Audiencias of Lima and Cuzco in the post-*visita* period; and finally, briefly discusses independence. [BP]

1414 Garrett, David T. "In spite of her sex": the cacica and the politics of the pueblo in the late colonial Cusco. (*Americas/Washington*, 64:4, April 2008, p. 547–581, maps, tables)

An important study assessing the role and meanings of Andean female lordship in the late colonial period. Refines portraits of cacical authority as "patriarchal" by exposing the importance of the noble couple in Andean practice, as well as the crucial role of cacicas in preserving inherited noble status amidst growing tendency to democratize access to cabildo offices and increase community power. [BP]

1415 Garrett, David T. Sombras del imperio: la nobleza indígena del Cuzco, 1750–1825. Traducción de Javier Flores Espinoza. Lima: IEP, Instituto de Estudios Peruanos, 2009. 450 p.: bibl., maps. (Serie Estudios históricos; 52)

Spanish-language translation of 2005 work (see *HLAS 64:341*) on the indigenous elite of Cuzco. Discusses the effects of the Andean rebellions and reforms on the decline of the city. [BP]

1416 Glave Testino, Luis Miguel. Cultura política, participación indígena y redes de comunicación en la crisis colonial: el Virreinato peruano, 1809–1814. (*Hist. Mex./México*, 58:1, julio/sept. 2008, p. 369–426, bibl.)

Based on deep research in the Archivo de Indias, this article details various plots, suits, and seditions against the colonial government during Bonaparte's occupation of Spain. Pays particular attention to the way that written news was generated and passed to different parts of the viceroyalty. [BP]

1417 Guibovich Pérez, Pedro. Como güelfos y gibelinos: los colegios de San Bernardo y San Antonio Abad en el Cuzco durante el siglo XVII. (*Rev. Indias*, 66:236, enero/abril 2006, p. 107–132)

A "rereading" of the mid-17th-century clash between the Cuzco colleges of San Bernardo, run by the Jesuits, and San Antonio Abad, run by the secular clergy. Going beyond traditional institutional or class-based analyses, the author proposes that the conflict rested on the Jesuits' right to bestow the degrees necessary for political and economic advancement in colonial society. [BP]

1418 Holland, Augusta Emilia. Nueva corónica: tradiciones artísticas europeas en el virreynato del Perú. Cuzco, Peru: Centro Bartolomé de Las Casas, 2008. 229 p.: bibl., ill., maps. (Archivos de historia andina; 42)

Revisits Guamán Poma de Ayala's famous several hundred-page letter to the Spanish king by comparing the techniques and themes used in the document's many illustrations to church murals in late medieval Europe and early colonial Peru. Concludes that the illustrator of the early 17th-century document was not Guamán Poma, but rather a young man guided by European artistic conventions. For art historian's comment, see item **50**. [BP]

Hostnig, Rainer; Ciro Palomino Dongo; and Jean-Jacques Decoster. Proceso de composición y titulación de tierras en Apurímac-Perú, siglos XVI–XX. See *HLAS 65:1136*.

1419 Hurtado Ames, Carlos H. Curacas, industria y revuelta en el valle del Mantaro, siglo XVIII. San Borja, Lima: Consejo Nacional de Ciencia, Tecnología e Innovación Tecnológica, CONCYTEC, 2006. 166 p.: bibl.

Three-chapter examination of the river valley inhabited by Xauxa and Huanca indigenous groups in the colonial province of Jauja. In somewhat separate studies, the book details textile manufacturing of this region; examines indigenous elite who profited from textiles; and concludes with a consideration of a brief insurrection, led by the cacique Nicolás Dávila Astocuri, which coincided with the Andean rebellions of the 1780s. [BP]

1420 Iwasaki Cauti, Fernando. Extremo Oriente y el Perú en el siglo XVI. Lima: Pontificia Univ. Católica del Perú, Fondo Editorial, 2005. 340 p.: bibl., maps. (Col. Orientalia; 12)

Originally a 1992 PhD dissertation, this creative and original study of early colonial Peruvian engagement with the regions and the idea of the "Orient" recounts expeditions and missions—both trade and religious—to the Philippines, China, and Japan. The book also details silver and mercury trade and describes early Asian immigration to the Andes. [BP]

1421 Lamana, Gonzalo. Domination without dominance: Inca-Spanish encounters in early colonial Peru. Durham, N.C.: Duke Univ. Press, 2008. 287 p.: bibl., index. (Latin America otherwise)

An epistemological exercise in retelling the story of the conquest of the Incas and civil wars that followed in the Andes from a "decolonial" rather than "anticolonial" perspective. Revisiting now-canonical authors, such as Guamán Poma and Betanzos, the author explores themes that do not fit easily into resistance-based accounts that privilege narratives intelligible to Westerners, including the intervention of *huacas* and objects in events. [BP]

1422 Lazo García, Carlos. Obras escogidas de Carlos Lazo García. v. 1, Historia de la economía colonial. Lima: Instituto de Ciencias y Humanidades: Fondo Editorial del Pedagógico San Marcos, 2006. 1 v.: bibl., ill. (Serie Historia)

First of a three-part homage to a Peruvian economic historian. After Waldemar Espinoza places Lazo in biographical and historiographical context in an introduction, the volume reprints a general study of the colonial economy, based on strong empirical research with particular attention to mining. For review of vol. 2, see item **1423**. [BP]

1423 Lazo García, Carlos. Obras escogidas de Carlos Lazo García. v. 2, Historia de la economía colonial: hacienda, comercio, fiscalidad y luchas sociales (Perú colonial). Textos de Carlos Lazo García y Javier Tord Nicolini. Lima: Instituto de Ciencias y Humanidades: Fondo Editorial del Ped-

agógico San Marcos, 2008. 1 v.: bibl., ill. (Serie Historia)

Second of a three-part homage to a Peruvian economic historian. Reprints a study of the central Andes under Spanish colonial rule originally published in 1981. Focus is on lordship and the feudal character of the Spanish colonies. With a strong empirical base, the analysis is very revealing of the historiographical moment in which it was originally published. [BP]

1424 Mannarelli, María Emma. Private passions and public sins: men and women in seventeenth-century Lima. Translated by Sidney Evans and Meredith D. Dodge. Albuquerque: Univ. of New Mexico Press, 2007. 204 p.: bibl., index.

Long-awaited English translation of this pioneering social and gender history of sex and marriage in 17th-century Lima. For a review of the original Spanish-language book, see *HLAS 56:2434*. [BP]

1425 Marsilli, María N. Missing idolatry: mid-colonial interactions between parish priests and Indians in the Diocese of Arequipa. (*CLAHR*, 13:4, Fall 2004, p. 399–421, map)

Examines the persistence of native religion in the Southern Andes, where the great extirpation campaigns of the Andes did not reach. The author argues that parish priests in the region, unlike elsewhere, relied on good relations with local nobility in order to advance their careers and amass wealth, and this was a disincentive to root out native religious practice. [BP]

1426 Meléndez, Mariselle. Patria, *criollos* and blacks: imagining the nation in the *Mercurio peruano*, 1791–1795. (*Colon. Lat. Am. Rev.*, 15:2, Dec. 2006, p. 207–227, bibl.)

Study of how contributors to the Enlightened Lima newspaper tripped up in their efforts to advance the image of a "civilized" Peruvian nation when they confronted issues associated with the city's black and female population. Fretting over the inversion of "traditional" roles, Creole contributors viewed these subordinate populations as a drain on national progress. Particular attention is given to the newspaper's coverage of black religious organizations (*cofradías*) and gender deviance (*maricones*). [BP]

1427 El miedo en el Perú: siglos XVI al XX. Recopilación de Claudia Rosas Lauro. Lima: Pontificia Univ. Católica del Perú, Fondo Editorial: SIDEA, 2005. 285 p.: bibl.

Collection of innovative studies spanning Peru's history, each focused on a discrete manifestation of fear. Studies cover a wide range—from canonical precepts of fear of authority to fears of the APRA party members, from fears of piracy on the colonial coast to late 20th-century terrorism. [BP]

1428 Morán Ramos, Luis Daniel. Sociedad colonial y vida cotidiana en Lima a través de las páginas de *El Investigador* [del Perú], 1813–1814. Colaboración de María Isabel Aguirre Bello. Presentación de Waldemar Espinoza Soriano. Lima: s.n., 2007. 78 p.: bibl. (Col. Historia de la prensa peruana; 1)

Short study of a signal, if short-lived, Peruvian periodical born under the free press statute of the Spanish Constitution of 1812. Brief opening and closing chapters place the newspaper in its bibliographic context. The heart of the book is a chapter on the Enlightenment-inspired perspectives on "everyday life" that dominated most pieces in the paper: the creation of citizens and public opinion, alarms about crime, and anti-clericalism. [BP]

1429 Moreno Cebrián, Alfredo. La confusión entre lo público y lo privado en el reinado de Felipe V: en torno a la corrupción colonial en el Perú. (*Bol. Hist. Antig.*, 93:835, oct./dic. 2006, p. 837–855)

Using the case studies of two viceroys under Felipe V, argues that the Crown purposely "maintained confusion" over the boundaries of public and private, permitting functionaries to gain wealth outside "official" or "impartial" channels, as part of an early modern pattern of statecraft. [BP]

1430 Moreno Cebrián, Alfredo and Núria Sala i Vila. El "premio" de ser virrey: los intereses públicos y privados del gobierno virreinal en el Perú de Felipe V. Madrid: Consejo Superior de Investigaciones Científicas, Instituto de Historia, 2004. 335 p.: bibl., ill., index. (Col. Biblioteca de historia de América; 33)

A detailed, two-part study by two authors of the material benefits gained both licitly and illicitly by Peruvian viceroys under the Bourbon Spanish King Felipe V during the mid-1700s. Sala i Vila focuses on the tenure of the Marqués de Castelldusrios; Moreno Cebrián on the Marqués de Castelfuerte. [BP]

1431 Murúa, Martín de. Historia general del Piru: facsimile of J. Paul Getty Museum Ms. Ludwig XIII 16. Los Angeles, Calif.: Getty Research Institute, 2008. 187 p.

Beautiful, oversized collection of studies of the "making and reception" of the Mercedarian priest's *Historia general*, today known as the Getty Murúa. The book collects the work of leading scholars to trace the manuscript's history, travels, physical features, and relationship to textiles, as well as the connections between other contemporary histories and this early 17th-century recounting of Inca dynastic succession and experience during the first generation of Spanish rule. [BP]

1432 New world, first nations: native peoples of Mesoamerica and the Andes under colonial rule. Edited by David Cahill and Blanca Tovías. Brighton, England; Portland, Ore.: Sussex Academic Press, 2006. 265 p.: bibl., ill., index, maps.

Edited collection of studies by outstanding ethnohistorians from multiple countries. Several essays offer major reinterpretations of fundamental aspects of indigenous social and economic life, including the ideological bases of community authority in Peru, tribute and coercive credit systems in southern Mexico, and local identity during uprisings and independence movements. For review of a chapter on nationalism and community in early 19th-century Mexico, see *HLAS 64:716*. [BP]

1433 O'Phelan Godoy, Scarlett. La moda francesa y el terremoto de Lima de 1746. (*Bull. Inst. fr. étud. andin.*, 36:1, 2007, p. 19–38, bibl., ill.)

A fascinating history of how provocative French fashions, which were said to reveal too much womanly flesh, were blamed for the devastating 1746 earthquake and subsequent tsunami in Lima. Traces the importation of the fabrics and styles of French fashion, the manner in which the trends interlaced with saintly iconography, and how the sartorial styles outlasted the assault against them in the wake of the disaster to eventually adorn many paintings and female bodies in Lima. [BP]

1434 Osorio, Alejandra. Inventing Lima: Baroque modernity in Peru's south sea metropolis. New York: Palgrave Macmillan, 2008. 254 p.: bibl., ill., index, maps. (The Americas in the early modern Atlantic world)

Pushing against the historiographical current that holds that Lima was a conservative enclave or isolated "colonial" outpost, this book argues that the city was a thoroughly modern, Baroque commercial and literary hub connecting an imagined space of the South Seas. [BP]

1435 O'Toole, Rachel Sarah. "In a war against the Spanish": Andean protection and African resistance on the northern Peruvian coast. (*Americas/Washington,* 63:1, July 2006, p. 19–52)

Comprehensive study based on broad archival work of the interactions and strategies for economic survival among a shrinking but resilient indigenous population and people of African descent on Peru's north coast. Demonstrates that indigenous groups, along with enslaved and free people of African descent, had a shared history—but generally only in good times. In bad times, such as after agricultural crises, the two groups retreated into separate "locations" to protect their interests: Africans into diasporic and trade relations; indigenous peoples into a legal space of Crown and Church protections. [BP]

1436 Peralta, Luz. Indígenas, mestizos y criollos en Cusco y el Alto Perú, 1780–1815. Lima: Seminario de Historia Rural Andina, Univ. Nacional Mayor de San Marcos, 2008. 219 p.: bibl., ill.

Working paper-style publication of documents related to various uprisings and conspiracies in Cuzco and Chayanta, including the Túpac Amaru II uprising. The documents collected and transcribed are eclectic, treating topics ranging from noble status to confiscated books. Each set of documents is prefaced by a very short study. [BP]

1437 Peralta, Luz. El papel sellado en el Perú colonial, 1640–1824. Lima: Seminario de Historia Rural Andina, Univ. Nacional Mayor de San Marcos, 2007. 254 p.: bibl., ill.

Thorough material history of the official paper on which much of Spanish colonial history was recorded. Draws on notary, administrative, and judicial records in the Archivo Nacional to explore the cost and amount of paper imported to the viceroyalty, laws regulating its use, and its esthetic components. [BP]

1438 Peralta Ruiz, Víctor. Elecciones, autonomismos y sediciones: el virreinato del Perú en la época de la Junta Central, 1809–1810. (*Secuencia/México,* numero conmemorativo, 2008, p. 147–162, bibl.)

A reassessment of Peru's Supreme Governing Junta, which governed when King Ferdinand VII was a captive of the French from 1808–10. Special focus on Viceroy Abascal's reaction to the establishment of separate juntas in Chuquisaca and Quito, as well as the "seditious" salons that sprang up in Lima led by Fransciso Pérez Canosa and José Mateo Silva. [BP]

1439 Peralta Ruiz, Víctor. El impacto de las Cortes de Cádiz en el Perú: un balance historiográfico. (*Rev. Indias,* 68:242, enero/abril 2008, p. 67–96, bibl.)

A historiographical assessment of treatments of the importance of the years 1808–14 and Peru's first experiments with liberalism. Finds the most fruitful veins of study have involved the political cultural changes involved with electoral processes for sending representatives to the Cortes as well as studies of "the ethnic question"— that is, how the Constitution of 1812 dealt with the issues of race and citizenship. [BP]

1440 Pinto Huaracha, Miguel. Visitas eclesiásticas—Ancash, 1774–1820. Lima: Seminario de Historia Rural Andina, Univ. Nacional Mayor de San Marcos, 2006. 195 p., 1 folded leaf of plates: map.

Working paper-style publication of a selection of late colonial documents originally discovered in the ecclesiastical archives by historian Pablo Macera. Very brief opening study is followed by transcriptions of various elements of the *visitas,* or official Church inquiries, treating topics such as tithes, permission to construct churches, and demographic information. [BP]

1441 Procesos y visitas de idolatrías: Cajatambo, siglo XVII: con documentos anexos. Recopilación de Pierre Duviols. Revisión paleográfica de Laura Gutiérrez Arbulú y Luis Andrade Ciudad. Selección de los textos y estudios históricos de Pierre Duviols. Textos quechuas traducidos, editados y anotados de César Itier. Lima: Instituto Francés de Estudios Andinos: Pontificia Univ. Católica del Perú, 2003. 882 p., 1 leaf of folded plates: bibl., index, maps. (Col. Clásicos peruanos)

Half analysis, half transcription of rich documents related to idolatry investigations in the region during the mid-17th century. The study discusses the broader history of extirpation campaigns and introduces readers to the province of Cajatambo, Peru. Hundreds of pages of confessions and testimony reveal invaluable details on local Andean practices, memory, and interaction with instruments of Catholic colonialism. [BP]

1442 Quiroz, Francisco. Artesanos y manufactureros en Lima colonial. Lima: Banco Central de Reserva del Perú: Instituto de Estudios Peruanos, 2008. 267 p.: bibl., ill. (Serie Historia económica; 3)

Deeply researched monograph on artisanal production in 17th- and 18th-century Lima. Draws on diverse materials, especially notarial records, to detail the products, prices, and consumption of man-made goods in the city. Considers the trades and workers, including masters and apprentices of all castes. Concludes with a consideration of the impact of Bourbon-era "comercio libre." [BP]

1443 Ramírez, Susan E. The cosmological bases of local power in the Andes during the sixteenth and seventeenth centuries. (*in* New world, first nations: native peoples of Mesoamerica and the Andes under colonial rule. Edited by David Cahill and Blanca Tovías. Brighton, England; Portland, Ore.: Sussex Academic Press, 2006, p. 36–56, bibl., facsim.)

Curacas' responsibilities to their communities were not only administrative and material, as most scholars have emphasized, but also spiritual. Even as disease,

migration, and new social and economic pressures of colonial society transformed *curacas'* traditional roles, their ability to mediate between communities and the ancestors who exerted control over the world remained the basis of their power. [K. Melvin]

1444 Ramírez, Susan E. To serve God and king: the origins of public schools for native children in eighteenth-century northern Peru. (*Colon. Lat. Am. Rev.*, 17:1, June 2008, p. 73–99, appendix, bibl., map, table)

Drawing heavily on archival information in the Archivo General de Indias, this study reconstructs the Trujillo bishop's remarkable plans to provide a rational education to indigenous children. The plan, though tripped up by scant funding and other obstacles, provides a neat example of the local—and often Church-based—origins of Enlightenment projects in colonial Peru. [BP]

1445 Rodríguez García, Margarita Eva. Criollismo y patria en la Lima ilustrada (1732–1795). Buenos Aires: Miño y Dávila, 2006. 348 p.: bibl., ill.

Probes the intellectual roots of Creole patriotism in the Peruvian Enlightenment, reaching into the early part of the 18th century in the first half of the book. Examines well-known plays and periodicals such as *Mercurio peruano* as well as the writing of more obscure jurists such as Bravo de Lagunas y Castilla to argue that modern Creole identity was not a mere derivative of "European nationalism" or "Enlightenment" but rather an autocthonous movement marked by dynamism between traditionalists and modern notions of what served Creole interests. [BP]

1446 Rodríguez Tena, Fernando. Crónica de las misiones franciscanas del Perú, siglos XVII y XVIII. Introducción de Julián Heras. Iquitos, Peru: CETA, 2004. 1 v.: bibl., index. (Monumenta amazónica. B; 9)

First of a two-volume set of unpublished writings by a prolific 18th-century priest. A "convent chronicle," written inside the cloister, provides both natural history and religious history of Franciscan missions throughout the expansive Provincia de los Doce Apóstoles, drawing from contemporary Peruvian writers as well as traditional European authorities. [BP]

1447 Rosas Lauro, Claudia. Del trono a la guillotina: el impacto de la Revolución Francesa en el Perú, 1789–1808. Lima: IFEA, Instituto Francés de Estudios Andinos: Republique Française, Embajada de Francia: Fondo Editorial, Pontificia Univ. Católica del Perú, 2006. 287 p.: bibl., ill. (some col.). (Travaux de l'Institut français d'études andines; 220)

Creative analysis of how Peruvian historians and contemporaries represented the French Revolution. Begins at the end, with 19th- and 20th-century historiography, then focuses on archival materials from 1789–1809. Traces the circulation of news; investigates the use of "independence" as a concept among limeños; and follows state efforts to rally support for its war against France. [BP]

1448 Rosas Lauro, Claudia and José Ragas Rojas. Las revoluciones francesas en el Perú: una reinterpretación (1789–1848). (*Bull. Inst. fr. étud. andin.*, 36:1, 2007, p. 51–65, bibl.)

A comparison of the impact of the French revolutions of 1789 and 1848 on Peru, with special attention to how news of the occurrences spread through the region and how the news and concept of "revolution" shaped public opinion. Despite the negative connotations ascribed to the revolutions in the press, in both cases the events served to provide a lexicon for republican legitimacy. [BP]

1449 Rosas Moscoso, Fernando. Del Río de La Plata al Amazonas: el Perú y el Brasil, en la época de la dominación ibérica. Lima: Univ. Ricardo Palma, Editorial Universitaria, 2008. 496 p., 4 folded leaves: bibl., maps.

Monographic treatment of Peru's viceregal border with Brazil argues that the colonial history of border interactions between the two countries shaped the modern nations. Utilizes diplomatic and Jesuit records on the Amazon region, Mojos and Chiquitos and the colony of Sacramento, from the Treaty of Tordesillas to Bourbon territorial reform. Appendix includes key primary sources. [BP]

1450 Sarmiento Gutiérrez, Julio. El Perú y la dominación hispánica: Cajamarca, conquista y colonia. Cajamarca, Peru: Oficina General de Investigación, Univ. Nacional de Cajamarca, 2005. 180 p.: bibl., ill., maps.

Summary study of the colonial history of Cajamarca, with some archival material and data. [BP]

Scott, Heidi V. Rethinking landscape and colonialism in the context of early Spanish Peru. See *HLAS 65:1152.*

1451 Sociedad y gobierno episcopal: las visitas del obispo Manuel de Mollinedo y Angulo: Cuzco, 1674–1694. Edición de Pedro Guibovich Pérez y Luis Eduardo Wuffraden. Lima: Instituto Francés de Estudios Andinos, UMIFRE 17, CNRS-MAEE: Instituto Riva-Agüero, 2008. 243 p.: bibl., col. maps, indexes. (Col. "Travaux de l'Institut français d'études andines;" 264) (Publicación del Instituto Riva-Agüero; 243)

Transcription of a bishop's *visitas* throughout Cuzco, recounting the state of parish churches not only as institutions but also as buildings and repositories of holy art. Two introductory studies situate the *visitas* in administrative and artistic context. Of particular note is how the bishop's experiences in the art-soaked Spanish city of Toledo inspired him to implant Christianity using visual representation. [BP]

1452 Thurner, Mark. The as-if of the book of kings: Pedro de Peralta Barnuevo's colonial poetics of history. (*LARR*, 44:1, 2009, p. 32–57, bibl., fascims.)

Theoretically rich reassessment of Peralta Barnuevo's 18th-century histories. Argues that his "colonial dynastic histories" were not weak, groveling scholastic exercises but rather simultaneously colonial and postcolonial texts directed to the prince. In the histories, the concept of history itself imitated the prince to displace the king as the head of the nation. [BP]

1453 Vaccarella, Eric. Fábulas, letras, and razones historiales fidedignas: the praxis of renaissance historiography in Pedro Sarmiento de Gamboa's *Historia de los Incas.* (*Colon. Lat. Am. Rev.*, 16:1, June 2007, p. 93–107, bibl.)

Explores how Francisco de Toledo, Peru's fifth viceroy, commissioned Sarmiento's histories of Inca "tyrants" to justify Spanish rule. Proposes a reading of the histories in the Toledan context and with an eye for how Sarmiento's methods subsumed Inca oral history into the Renaissance concept of "*fábula*." [BP]

1454 Varillas Montenegro, Alberto. El periodismo en la historia del Perú: desde sus orígenes hasta 1850. Surquillo, Lima: Univ. de San Martín de Porres, Fondo Editorial, 2008. 456 p.: bibl., ill., index. (Serie Periodismo y literatura)

Factual and highly comprehensive study of various print publications during the colonial period and through the presidency of Ramón Castilla. Useful appendix lists early republican publications, some short-lived, for the period 1820–51. [BP]

1455 Vizcarra, Catalina. Bourbon intervention in the Peruvian tobacco industry, 1752–1813. (*J. Lat. Am. Stud.*, 39:3, Aug. 2007, p. 567–593, graphs, tables)

An economic study of the imposition of the tobacco monopoly in Peru. Finds that Bourbons were proficient managers of the production of tobacco, which reached its peak under José de Gálvez. However, the tobacco factories in Lima and Trujillo, a centerpiece of the reform, lasted only 11 years. Their brevity, the author contends, is owed to Carlos IV's reticence to follow through with reforms that threatened local interests, as well as Viceroy Gil de Toboaday y Lemos' belt-tightening of state expenses. [BP]

1456 Walker, Charles. Great balls of fire: premonitions and the destruction of Lima, 1746. (*in* Aftershocks: earthquakes and popular politics in Latin America. Edited by Jürgen Buchenau and Lyman L. Johnson. Univ. of New Mexico Press, 2009, p. 18–42)

Study of how nuns' reports of visions and premonitions of the massive 1746 earthquake that struck the city revealed increasing 18th-century anxiety about the shifting ground of the sacred and the secular. For historian's comment on entire book, see item **391**. [BP]

1457 Walker, Charles. Shaky colonialism: the 1746 earthquake-tsunami in Lima, Peru, and its long aftermath. Dur-

ham, N.C.: Duke Univ. Press, 2008. 260 p.: bibl., ill., index, maps.

Lively study of earthquake and tsunami that leveled Lima and divided the populace along the fault line of an older, Baroque political sensibility and newer, Bourbon plans for the city. Chapters treat urban planning, debates about rebuilding, and controversy about the reestablishment and role of monasteries, where anxiety about the place of women in the urban social order reverberated. [BP]

1458 Wood, Alice L. Religious women of color in seventeenth-century Lima: Estefania de San Ioseph and Ursula de Jesu Christo. (*in* Beyond bondage: free women of color in the Americas. Edited by David Barry Gaspar and Darlene Clark Hine. Chicago: Univ. of Illinois Press, 2004, p. 286–316, bibl.)

A study of the importance ascribed to two women of color in 17th-century Franciscan narratives. Although in broad form the hagiographic narratives of the lives of Estefania de San Ioseph (1561–1645) and Ursula de Jesu Christo (1604–?) were predetermined by the genre, the author argues that certain features of their life stories— such as Ursula's criticism of extreme mortification—reveal their unique position within their communities of other women of color, as well as within the dominant worlds of convent and elite households. [BP]

CHARCAS

1459 Beltrán Ávila, Marcos. Sucesos de la Guerra de Independencia del año 1810: Historia del Alto Perú en el año 1810 (obra documentada); Capítulos de la historia colonial de Oruro. Bio-bibliografía de Marcos Beltrán Ávila por Victor Varas Reyes. Lima: IFEA; La Paz: Instituto de Estudios Bolivianos, Facultad de Humanidades, Univ. Mayor de San Andrés; Bolivia: ASDI; Oruro, Bolivia: H. Alcaldía Municipal de Oruro, 2006. 354 p.: bibl., ill. (Travaux de l'Institut francais d'études andines; 228) (Col. Cuarto centenario de la fundación de Oruro)

Two volumes on the efforts of the population of Alto Perú (today Bolivia) to gain its independence, written nearly a century ago and recently rescued from obscurity. Libro 1 is a political, military, and intellectual analysis of the prevailing wisdom and actions in Spain at the time, and those occurring simultaneously in the Latin American regions of Charcas, Buenos Aires, and Lima. Libro 2 is similarly structured, but with a specific focus on Oruro, an important mining area in central Bolivia. [LGB]

1460 Berg, Hans van den. Con los yucarees (Bolivia): crónicas misionales, 1765–1825. Edición al cuidado de Andrés Eichmann Oehrli. Madrid: Iberoamericana; Frankfurt: Vervuert, 2010. 616 p.: bibl., map. (Biblioteca indiana; 23)

Source-based study about missionary efforts among the Yuracare Indians in Bolivian lowland near Cochabamba from 1765–1825. Repeated attempts by Franciscan missionaries to establish a settlement finally failed and no stable settlements were established. [BP]

1461 Bridikhina, Eugenia. Theatrum mundi: entramados del poder en Charcas colonial. La Paz: Plural Editores; Lima: IFEA, 2007. 384 p.: bibl., ill. (some col.). (Travaux de l'Institut francais d'études andines; 229)

This history of imperial mechanisms of power and control presents a new, fascinating analysis of royal politics originating in Spain, which deliberately imposed power struggles between Viceroyalties and Audiencias in Latin America, and used public religious and civil ceremonies of pomp and circumstance as well as symbolic reminders (portraits, coins, royal seals, etc.) to establish proper etiquette for the classes by engaging them in the "theaterization of power"—thus reinforcing the status quo. [LGB]

1462 Brockington, Lolita Gutiérrez. Blacks, Indians, and Spaniards in the Eastern Andes: reclaiming the forgotten in colonial Mizque, 1550–1782. Lincoln: Univ. of Nebraska Press, 2006. 342 p.: bibl., index, maps.

Deeply researched study of an often-overlooked region—the eastern Andes—and an often-overlooked group in Andean colonial history—African slaves. Details the political and economic connections between the Corregimiento de Mizque, in present-day Bolivia, and the rest of the Andes, as well as the unique features of the region that served as a home to dynamic interactions between peoples of diverse origins. [B. Premo]

1463 Ensayos históricos sobre Oruro. Recopilación de Ximena Medinaceli y María Luisa Soux. Textos de Magdalena Cajías de la Vega *et al.* La Paz: Instituto de Estudios Bolivianos: Asdi, 2006. 435 p.: bibl., ill., map. (Col. Cuarto centenario de la fundación de Oruro)

A commemorative compilation of essays on this key mining center examines a variety of topics including the history and folklore of the industry, and the participation of the region's indigenous and mestizo populations in the independence movements. [LGB]

1464 Gato Castaño, Purificación. Aproximación al mundo chiriguano: a través del diario de la expedición a las Salinas, 1785–1790. Sucre, Bolivia: Fundación Cultural del Banco Central de Bolivia: Archivo y Biblioteca Nacionales de Bolivia, 2007. 118 p.: bibl., ill., indexes, map.

Transcription and ethnohistorical analysis of a detailed account of a Spanish expedition into the heart of "Chiriguano territory" in an effort to negotiate a peace treaty with the "savage" Indians and the Archbishop and educator mastermind behind the process. Offers fresh insight into the lifestyles and worldview of this lowland autonomous ethnic group. [LGB]

1465 Lofstrom, William Lee. Tres familias de Charcas: fines del Virreinato, principios de la República. Sucre, Bolivia: Fundación Cultural del Banco Central de Bolivia: Archivo y Biblioteca Nacionales de Bolivia, 2005. 207 p.: bibl.

Historical genealogy based on extensive archival research in what is today Sucre, Bolivia. Traces the social and economic patterns of three extended families and their associates over several generations. Examines diverse patterns of interclass marriages and the related phenomena of upward and downward social mobility, with even the wealthiest of subjects growing increasingly impoverished over time. Discusses the related social and larger economic explanations. [LGB]

1466 Moreno, Gabriel René. Ultimos días coloniales en el Alto Perú. Prólogo, cronología y bibliografía de Luis H. Antezana y Josep M. Barnadas. Caracas: Biblioteca Ayacucho, 2003. 2 v.: bibl., ill. (Biblioteca Ayacucho; 208–209)

Detailed 2-volume history of Bolivia at the eve of independence offers a tripartite of perspectives and analyses that deserves to be treated as a whole. Author Moreno (1836–1908), historian and pioneer archivist, worked through unpublished documents—transcribed and reprinted here—to describe and explain the many events and actors involved in those final days. Equally useful are the historiographical contributions of present-day scholars Antezana and Barnadas. [LGB]

1467 Río, María de las Mercedes del. Etnicidad, territorialidad y colonialismo en los Andes: tradición y cambio entre los Soras de los siglos XVI y XVII (Bolivia). La Paz: Instituto de Estudios Bolivianos: ASDI; Lima: IFEA, 2005. 341 p.: bibl., ill. (Col. Cuarto centenario de la Fundación de Oruro) (Travaux de l'Institut francais d'études andines; 212)

Revisionist ethnohistory of the Aymara-speaking Sora of the central Altiplano of Bolivia who refused to submit to the Inca and later to the Spaniards. Based on their own terms of negotiation, they were further supported by economic aid via pious donations of their atypical encomendero. [LGB]

1468 Robins, Nicholas A. Priest-Indian conflict in upper Peru: the generation of rebellion, 1750–1780. Syracuse, N.Y.: Syracuse Univ. Press, 2007. 315 p.: bibl., index. (Religion and politics)

Detailed analysis of Church-state and interrelated economic policies based on meticulous archival research, demonstrating existing tensions in all sectors and levels of society which were further accelerated by the Bourbon Reforms. Most notable is the experience of indigenous villagers, who individually and collectively challenged clergy misbehavior through legal pursuit of court action. All events ultimately led to the Great Rebellion. [LGB]

1469 Roca, José Luis. Ni con Lima ni con Buenos Aires: la formación de un estado nacional en Charcas. La Paz: Plural Editores; Lima: IFEA, 2007. 771 p.: bibl., index. (Travaux de l'Institut français d'études andines; 248)

Impressive tome of this international scholar's provocative, often revisionist, essays written over the years on questions regarding state formation of the Audiencia (today Bolivia) and its independence movements as they relate to Bolivian national identity and the many shifting internal and external alliances. The work carries the reader from precolumbian Andean history, through the colonial period and beyond, to discuss the political and military influence of local Creole and royalist actors, as well as the more widely known José de San Martín and Simón Bolívar. [LGB]

1470 Santamaría, Daniel J. El rol de las alianzas entre misioneros e indígenas en la conquista de Apolobamba, siglos XVI–XVII. (*Rev. Indias*, 66:237, mayo/agosto 2006, p. 329–346)

Analysis of the lesser-known Leco, Chuncho, and other ethnicities of the northern high forests of the Beni province in what is now Bolivia provides new perspectives on the Spanish conquest. Indigenous groups experienced far more successful relations with the missionaries than with the colonial state or military due to mutually agreed on alliances that allowed each to maintain a desired autonomy from the royal apparatus. [LGB]

1471 Serulnikov, Sergio. "Las proezas de la ciudad y su ilustre ayuntamiento": simbolismo político y política urbana en Charcas a fines del siglo XVIII. (*LARR*, 43:3, 2008, p. 137–164)

Examines the repercussions of rumors in La Plata, seat of the Audiencia de Charcas (today Bolivia) of an alleged popular uprising in 1781. Author sees this event as an indication of an emerging new urban political culture diverging from its traditional "multi-secular" origins as upper and lower classes merged to resist the colonial order and soon the Bourbon Reforms and peninsular Spaniards as well. [LGB]

1472 Serulnikov, Sergio. Conflictos sociales e insurrección en el mundo colonial andino: el norte de Potosí en el siglo XVIII. México: Fondo de Cultura Económica, 2006. 468 p.: bibl.

A sociopolitical analysis of the complex Andean phenomenon of multiple regional uprisings during the second half of the 18th century, particularly in the Chayanta province north of Potosí. Explains local villager-cacique relations and conflicts with local officials which culminated over time in atypical accommodations. Also discusses the impact of the Bourbon Reforms and Creole fears of a caste war. [LGB]

1473 Tonelli Justiniano, Oscar. Reseña histórica, social y económica de la Chiquitania. Santa Cruz de la Sierra, Bolivia: Editorial El País, 2004. 405 p.: bibl., map.

Detailed history of Bolivia's eastern province of Chiquitanía (Chiquitos), covering a wide range of historiography and ethnohistory as well as religious, military, and economic history from preconquest to 2000 BC. [LGB]

1474 Urquidi U., Mario. Antecedentes revolucionarios en la Audiencia de Charcas. Cochabamba, Bolivia: Librería Editorial Los Amigos del Libro, 2006. 235 p.: bibl.

Synthesis of Bolivia's role in South American independence movements, looking first to events in Spain and placing Spain's activities in a European context, then moving on to its colonial activities in the larger context. Sees neither French nor North American Revolutions as influential. Based on excerpts of writings and proclamations of the many actors involved. [LGB]

CHILE

Dillehay, Tom D. Monuments, empires, and resistance: the Araucanian polity and ritual narratives. See *HLAS 65:405.*

1475 Enríquez Agrazar, Lucrecia Raquel. De colonial a nacional: la carrera eclesiástica del clero secular chileno entre 1650 y 1810. México: Instituto Panamericano de Geografía e Historia, 2006. 360 p.: bibl.

Describes the mechanisms of career advancement used by the Catholic secular clergy in Chile in the late colonial period. Uses as a framework the legal dispositions provided by colonial Church-state relations (Patronato). Makes extensive, diligent use of archival material. [MNM]

1476 Gascón, Margarita. "Los indios de Chile se mueren de risa": los enemigos de España en la frontera sur del virreinato del Perú en el siglo XVII. (*CLAHR*, 14:4, Fall 2005, p. 403–422)

Examines the difficulties faced by the colonial Spanish administration in attempting to keep southern Chile under control during the 17th century. Highlights how deficient military and economic support, Mapuche-Dutch alliances, and rampant administrative corruption jeopardized Spanish attempts to bring an end to the Arauco War. [MNM]

1477 Goicovich, Francis. Entre la conquista y la consolidación fronteriza: dispositivos de poder hispánico en los bosques meridionales del Reino de Chile durante la etapa de transición, 1598–1683. (*Historia/Santiago*, 40:2, julio/dic. 2007, p. 311–332)

Details the mid-colonial mechanisms of social and military control that the Spaniards put in place to end the war against the Mapuche Indians in southern Chile. [MNM]

1478 Jocelyn-Holt Letelier, Alfredo. Chile 1808–1809: la crisis a tiempo corto. (*Secuencia/México*, numero conmemorativo, 2008, p. 231–242, bibl.)

This article uses a short-term analysis to assess the complexities of the period 1808–09 as Chile moved towards independence from Spain. This time span traditionally has been viewed as a crisis because of its random, unpredictable nature. The author suggests that, in spite of its chaotic appearance, the period still shows a predominantly corporative colonial logic. [MNM]

1479 Lacoste, Pablo. Amor y esclavitud en la frontera sur del imperio español: la manumisión de Luis Suárez, 1762–1824. (*Estud. Ibero-Am./Porto Alegre*, 32:2, dez. 2006, p. 85–118)

Documents the judicial efforts of two slave parents to manumit their son in the province of Cuyo, Chile, in the late colonial period. Makes extensive use of archival documents. Although at times romantic, the article details the local society and its views on slavery and manumission. [MNM]

1480 Lacoste, Pablo. Complejidad de la industria vitivinícola colonial: crianza biológica de vino, Reino de Chile, siglo XVIII. (*LARR*, 42:2, 2007, p. 154–168)

Details the origins of the biological wine industry in the region of Cuyo, colonial Chile, during the 18th century. Concludes that the wine industry's success is indicative of the flexibility of the local social structure, which allowed small landholders to gain prominence. [MNM]

1481 Lacoste, Pablo. Vida y muerte de doña Melchora Lemos, empresaria vitivinícola y terciaria de la orden de predicadores: Mendoza, Reino de Chile, 1691–1741. (*Rev. Indias*, 66:237, mayo/agosto 2006, p. 425–452, table)

Documents the life of the only known female agrarian entrepreneur in the province of Cuyo, colonial Chile, in the 18th century. Uses archival records to illustrate local social and political power networks, as well as options that were instrumental to female agency in the colony. [MNM]

1482 Lacoste, Pablo. Viticultura y movilidad social: provincia de Cuyo, Reino de Chile, siglo XVIII. (*CLAHR*, 13:3, Summer 2004, p. 217–247, bibl., table)

Describes the impact of the wine industry on social mobility mechanisms in the province of Cuyo, colonial Chile, during the 18th century. Uses testaments and other notary records to document the social improvements that these agrarian entrepreneurs achieved. [MNM]

1483 León, Leonardo. "De muy malas intenciones y de perversas entrañas . . .": la imagen de la plebe en los preámbulos de la independencia de Chile, 1800–1810. (*CLAHR*, 14:4, Fall 2005, p. 337–368)

Analyzes the Chilean elite's prevalent views about their lower classes at the onset of independence from Spain. Presents opinions commonly accepted by the upper classes as stereotypes publicized by colonial chroniclers that can be identified in a set of selected contemporary judicial cases. [MNM]

1484 Moreno Jeria, Rodrigo. Misiones en Chile austral: los Jesuitas en Chiloé, 1608–1768. Sevilla, Spain: Consejo Superior de Investigaciones Científicas, Escuela de Estudios Hispano-Americanos: Univ. de Sevilla, 2007. 452 p.: bibl., index, maps. (Col. Americana. Serie: Nuestra América; 30)

Details the foundation and development of Jesuit missions in Chiloé (Southern Chile) from 1608 to 1768. Explains the functioning of the missions and the evangelical efforts to convert the local indigenous peoples. A well-documented study that makes extensive use of primary and secondary sources. [MNM]

1485 Orellana Rodríguez, Mario. La Crónica de Gerónimo de Bibar y los primeros años de la conquista de Chile. 2. ed. corr. y ampliada. Santiago: Librotecnia Editores, 2006. 279 p.: bibl., ill. (some col.), 1 col. map.

A new, expanded edition of the 1988 book of the same title. Dissects Gerónimo de Bibar's colonial chronicle on early colonial Chile, *Crónica y relación copiosa y verdadera de los reynos de Chile*. A classic text for the study of colonial Chile (to 1656) and its indigenous peoples. [MNM]

1486 Peña y Lillo, Josefa de los Dolores, Sor. Epistolario de sor Dolores Peña y Lillo, Chile, 1763–1769. Prólogo y edición crítica de Raïssa Kordic Riquelme. Madrid: Univ. de Navarra: Iberoamericana; Frankfurt am Main: Vervuert, 2008. 518 p.: bibl. (Biblioteca Indiana; 9) (Biblioteca Antigua Chilena; 7)

An annotated edition of Chilean Dominican nun Sor Josefa de los Dolores Peña y Lillo's correspondence (1763–69). Includes an engaging introductory essay. Interesting primary source for studies on colonial female spirituality. [MNM]

1487 Pereira Larraín, Teresa. Afectos e intimidades: el mundo familiar en los siglos XVII, XVIII y XIX. Santiago: Ediciones Univ. Católica de Chile, 2007. 397 p.: bibl., ill. (some col.), index. (Investigaciones)

Describes family life in colonial Chile, emphasizing the importance of emotions and affections in daily life. Interesting for social history topics. [MNM]

1488 Testamentos coloniales chilenos. Prólogo y edición crítica de Raïssa Kordić Riquelme. Estudio preliminar de Cedomil Goić. Pamplona, Spain: Univ. de Navarra; Madrid: Iberoamericana; Frankfurt am Main: Vervuert, 2005. 357 p.: bibl., index. (Biblioteca Indiana; 5) (Biblioteca Antigua chilena; 6)

Brings together more than 60 wills produced in colonial Chile during the 16th and 17th centuries. Offers a clear introduction to the documents. Interesting primary source for colonial social history. [MNM]

1489 Undurraga Schüler, Verónica. Cuando las afrentas se lavaban con sangre: honor, masculinidad y duelos de espadas en el siglo XVIII chileno. (*Historia/Santiago*, 41:1, enero/junio 2008, p. 165–188)

Explores the relationship between male honor, masculinity, and legal violence as expressed in the legally sanctioned practice of duel in Santiago, colonial Chile, during the 18th century. Uses archival records of a specific duel to reconstruct social and legal tools used to defend and restore male honor. [MNM]

1490 Valenzuela Márquez, Jaime. Poder y pirotecnia, artesanos y Mapuches: apogeo barroco de las proclamaciones reales en Santiago de Chile, 1760–1789. (*CLAHR*, 14:1, Winter 2005, p. 49–78, ill.)

Explores the changes and innovations officially introduced to public celebrations organized in Santiago, colonial Chile, during the 18th century. Pays special attention to the 1789 celebration of the coronation of Charles IV, when Mapuche Indians were first incorporated into the rituals. [MNM]

1491 Vera, José E. Tráfico de sal desde Las Salinas del Diamante por el Paso del Planchón. (*Rev. Chil. Hist. Geogr.*, 167, 2003, p. 113–132, bibl., graphs, ill., table)

Describes salt mining and the salt trade established between mines located across the Andean mountains and the provinces of Colchagua and Maule in southern colonial Chile during the 18th century. Based on official trade records and evidence of entrepreneurial initiatives of indigenous peoples. [MNM]

1492 Zamorano, Paulina. Mujeres, violencia y espacio público en el Santiago del siglo XVIII. (*Rev. Chil. Hist. Geogr.*, 169, 2006/2007, p. 101–117, bibl.)

Examines a set of 18th-century judicial cases involving violence against women in the colonial city of Santiago to explain the nature of urban violence and to reproduce the social and family networks in

which these transgressions were imbedded. [MNM]

RIO DE LA PLATA

1493 Acevedo, Alba María and **Sandra Pérez Stocco.** Concepción del tiempo, de la vida y de la muerte en la Mendoza colonial. (*Rev. Hist. Am. Argent.*, 26:41, 2006, p. 69–85, bibl.)

Everyday time was marked by the passing of the religious day. Death was a natural event brought about by God's will. Religiosity marked colonial life until the mid-1700s when a more humane view of existence began to be accepted. [JWC]

1494 Aguerre Core, Fernando. Una caída anunciada: el obispo Torre y los jesuitas del Río de la Plata, 1757–1773. Montevideo: Librería Linardi y Risso, 2007. 395 p.: bibl., ill.

Describes the ecclesiastical career of Manuel Antonio de la Torre in the Río de la Plata. This prelate served first as Bishop of Asunción, and then in the 1760s as Bishop of Buenos Aires. As such he reported diligently on the state of the Church in Paraguay, and in Buenos Aires he was deeply involved in Church politics relative to the "problem" of the Jesuits. He was an important figure in the prelude to the expulsion of the Jesuits as well as in opposition to Pedro de Cevallos, governor of Buenos Aires, in this matter. This book on Church politics in the Río de la Plata in the 1760s opens up a completely new window on the Jesuit expulsion. Excellent research. [JWC]

1495 Aguirre, Susana. Cruzando fronteras: relaciones interétnicas y mestizaje social en la campaña y la ciudad de Buenos Aires en el período colonial. La Plata, Argentina: Provincia de Buenos Aires, Instituto Cultural, Dirección Provincial de Patrimonio Cultural, Archivo Histórico "Dr. Ricardo Levene": Asociación Amigos del Archivo Histórico de la Provincia de Buenos Aires, 2005. 151 p.: bibl. (Estudios sobre la historia y la geografía histórica de la Provincia de Buenos Aires)

Short but useful study on the assimilation of the indigenous peoples of Buenos Aires province and those captives moved from the interior. Discusses their labor, prejudice against them, the position of *agregados* or dependents of the Spanish, and mestizaje both on the Pampas and in the city of Buenos Aires. [JWC]

1496 Areces, Nidia R. Estado y frontera en el Paraguay: Concepción durante el gobierno del Dr. Francia. Asunción: Univ. Católica Nuestra Señora de la Asunción, 2007. 496 p.: bibl., map. (Biblioteca de estudios paraguayos; 68) (Col. Bicentenario)

The Villa de Concepción in the far north of Paraguay, founded in 1773, became a bulwark against Portuguese expansion from Mato Grosso, as well as a new cattle frontier and the center of the yerba mate industry in the Intendencia era. This detailed book explores the geography of this region, the motives for this villa's foundation, land grants, the yerba industry, problems with indigenous peoples, and the work of administrators, settlers, and soldiers. It also describes the administration of this region under the dictator Dr. Francia, and its importance to the new republic of Paraguay. An excellent example of frontier history. [JWC]

1497 Arias Divito, Juan Carlos. Siembras de tabaco en el noroeste argentino, 1778–1812. Buenos Aires: Instituto Bibliográfico "Antonio Zinny", 2008. 156 p.: bibl.

Another fine work on this Bourbon monopoly in the Río de la Plata by the foremost specialist on the topic. The problems of dispersion of growing areas, transportation, crop failures, and vagaries of the contract system with growers are well handled. Excellent contribution to the economic history of northwest Argentina in the colonial period. [JWC]

1498 Barral, María Elena. De sotanas por la Pampa: religión y sociedad en el Buenos Aires rural tardocolonial. Buenos Aires: Prometeo, 2007. 234 p.: bibl.

The activities of priests in the scattered parishes of the Pampa of Buenos Aires in the 1700s were significant contributions to the civilization of this frontier region. This work discusses folk religion, the problems of distance and space, as well as the daily duties and difficulties faced by priests. [JWC]

1499 Barral, María Elena. Las parroquias rurales de Buenos Aires entre 1730 y 1820. (*ANDES Antropol. Hist.*, 15, 2004, p. 19–53, bibl., graphs, maps)

Discusses the growth of the frontier *parroquias* and *viceparroquias* of Buenos Aires during the Bourbon era. Describes the rural organization of the Church as well as the supply of clerics to these new parishes and the clerics' duties. Good maps. [JWC]

1500 Bentancor, Andrea; Arturo Bentancur; and Wilson González. Muerte y religiosidad en el Montevideo colonial: una historia de temores y esperanzas. Montevideo: Ediciones de la Banda Oriental, 2008. 332 p.: bibl., ill.

Excellent collaborative effort addressing all aspects of death and religiosity in colonial Montevideo. Topics from funerals to *capellanías* are discussed. Very well researched and a valuable contribution to the social history of Uruguay. [JWC]

1501 Bespali Machado, Yubarandt. La portuguesa "Santa" de Garzón. Montevideo: Del Sur Ediciones, 2008. 175 p.: bibl., ill., maps.

Describes the life of María Suárez, a Portuguese immigrant to the Banda Oriental from the Azores in the late 1700s. Good for a depiction of immigrants from those islands. Multi-archival research. [JWC]

1502 Borges, Leonardo. Artigas revelado: análisis crítico del ideario artiguista y sus influencias. Montevideo: Ediciones de la Plaza, 2009. 155 p.: bibl. (Col. Ensayos)

Presents the history and historiography of the ideology of José Artigas, and discusses the impact of his thought on the independence movement in the Banda Oriental. [JWC]

1503 Bravo Tedín, Miguel. Belgrano y su sombra. Rosario, Argentina: Homo Sapiens Ediciones, 2003. 142 p.: bibl.

Offers an account of Manuel Belgrano's early years as a poverty-stricken student at the Univ. de Salamanca in Spain in the early 1790s. Belgrano, later a great leader of the Buenos Aires revolution, was in a penurious state as his father then had a very expensive legal problem as a result of peripheral involvement in a famous scandal involving the theft of government monies by the administrator of customs in Buenos Aires. This case continued for several years and was a burden to the Belgrano family. [JWC]

1504 Brezzo, Liliana María. Imágenes de la periferia: las exploraciones de Juan Francisco de Aguirre y su *Historia y geografía de las prodvincias del Río de la Plata*. (*Temas Hist. Argent. Am.*, 6, enero/junio 2005, p. 13–44, bibl.)

Presents a brief introduction to the works of the chronicler Juan Francisco de Aguirre, Capitán de Fragata, who wrote expansively on the Upper Plata, particularly Paraguay, in the very late 1700s. [JWC]

1505 Bussu, Salvatore. Mártires sin altar: Padre Juan Antonio Solinas, Don Pedro Ortiz de Zárate y dieciocho cristianos laicos. Introducción del Giuseppe Pittau. Traducción de Miguel Antonio Barriola. 2a. ed. Salta, Argentina: Editorial Biblioteca de Textos Universitarios, 2003. 448 p.: bibl., ill., maps. (Col. Tercer milenio)

Massacre of two Jesuit missionaries and their Christian followers by Chaco Indians in the Río Bermejo region in 1688. Good description of the Chaco region in the colonial era. Rather hagiographical but useful for a depiction of the hazards that missionaries faced in this region. [JWC]

1506 Caballero Campos, Herib. El proceso de la independencia del Paraguay 1780–1813. Asunción: El Lector, 2010. 138 p.: graphs, ill., maps, tables. (Col. La gran historia del Paraguay; 4)

Overview of the origins of Paraguayan independence and the revolutionary period to 1813. A popular work but well done. Useful as an introduction to this era. [JWC]

1507 Campero, Rodolfo Martín. El marqués de Yavi: coronel del ejército de las provincias unidas del Río de la Plata. Buenos Aires: Catálogos, 2006. 195 p.: bibl.

Describes the military career of Juan José Feliciano Fernández Campero, fourth marqués del Valle de Tojo, a vast holding in the Puna of present northwest Argentina. This American-born holder of a Spanish title of nobility, because of a close relationship with Martín Guemes, opted for the revolutionary cause of the United Provinces and from 1813–16 served as a colonel in Belgrano's army of the north. Captured by Spanish forces in 1816, he then underwent a harsh imprisonment. [JWC]

1508 Carbonell, Rafael; Teresa Blumers; and Norberto Levinton. La reducción jesuítica de Santos Cosme y Damián: su historia, su economía y su arquitectura, 1633–1797. Asunción: Missionsprokur de la Compañia de Jesús de Nürnberg-Alemania, 2003. 287 p.: bibl., col. ill., maps.

Collaborative effort of historians and architects investigating the foundation, economy, and architectural heritage of this mission situated at present in the state of São Paulo, Brazil. Very thorough research. [JWC]

1509 Carrera, Julián. Los pulperos y la justicia rural bonaerense, 1770–1820. (*Anu. Inst. Hist. Argent.*, 5, 2005, p. 161–177, bibl., tables)

Pulperos, rural grocery store owners, occupied an ambiguous position in the society of the Pampas. They supplied a necessary function but their establishments often were the scenes of drunken violence and the purchase of stolen items, mainly hides. Authorities had to keep close control over *pulperos'* actions. [JWC]

1510 Clissa de Mendiolaza, Karina. Imágenes de honor mancillado en Córdoba del Tucumán, 1750–1797. (*CLAHR*, 14:3, Summer 2005, p. 245–280)

As Bourbon social control was strengthened, more attention was paid to the problems of insults to honor such as defamation, libel, and other injuries. Most actions were prompted by the anger of the moment in everyday life, with sex and money often involved. An interesting study with detailed definitions of the various injuries that fell under insults to honor. [JWC]

1511 Cooney, Jerry W. Commerce, contraband, and intrigue: Thomas O'Gorman in the Río de la Plata, 1797–1806. (*CLAHR*, 13:1, Winter 2004, p. 31–51)

A suggestive account of an Irish merchant and immigrant to the Rio de la Plata in the last years of colonial rule. Useful in understanding the illegal trade, in examining his role as a go-between for porteño contrabandistas and North American merchants, and in measuring British intelligence operations prior to the 1806 invasion. Founder of the O'Gorman clan in Argentina, Thomas departed Buenos Aires in 1806, leaving behind his wife, the notorious "Perichona," who became the mistress of Viceroy Santiago de Liniers. [T. Whigham]

1512 Cooney, Jerry W. El fin de la colonia: Paraguay 1810–1811. Asunción: Intercontinental Editora, 2010. 155 p. (Col. Independencia Nacional; 4)

Detailed account of the 18 months in 1810–11 that led to Paraguayan autonomy. Emphasizes the efforts of the Paraguayans and particularly the militia of the province. Multi-archival research. [JWC]

1513 Corcuera Ibáñez, Mario. Santiago Liniers: primera víctima de la violencia política argentina. Buenos Aires: Librería Editorial Histórica E.J. Perrot, 2006. 380 p.: ill. (Col. histórica; 16)

Popular account of Santiago Liniers, hero of the *reconquista* of Buenos Aires against the British in 1806, and then Viceroy of the Río de la Plata. Interesting account of his last days in Córdoba when he attempted to rally the interior against the revolutionaries of Buenos Aires in 1810. He then was subject to the "Jacobin terror" and executed by partisans of the revolution. [JWC]

1514 Correspondencia entre comerciantes: redes, negocios y familia en Córdoba. Selección y recopilación de Noelia Nieves Silvetti, Horacio Enrique Rodas y Carla Daniela Lemes Pedano. Córdoba, Argentina: Centro de Estudios Históricos "Prof. Carlos S.A. Segreti," 2008. 1 v. (Serie Documental/ Centro de Estudios Históricos; 15)

Private correspondence among merchants that dealt with business affairs as well as family matters, travel, and economic conditions. Most of this correspondence emanated from the Lozano family of Córdoba. Useful for business history of the late colonial era, and for the changed conditions of trade that came about with independence. Quite well done. [JWC]

1515 Cruz, Enrique Normando. Mujeres en la colonia: dominación colonial, diferencias étnicas y de género en cofradías y fiestas religiosas en Jujuy, Río de la Plata. (*Anthropol. Dep. Cienc. Soc.*, 23:23, 2005, p. 127–150, bibl.)

Indigenous women participated much more freely in religious festivals as compared to women of the more Hispanicized classes. For the latter, their conduct was more controlled by societal restrictions and by their men folk. Quite detailed depiction of ethnic and social status of women in these public events. [JWC]

1516 De Cristóforis, Nadia Andrea. Los migrantes del noroeste hispánico en el Buenos Aires tardo colonial: la construcción de un tejido relacional luego del traslado ultramarino. (*Anu. Inst. Hist. Argent.*, 6, 2007, p. 45–76, table)

Immigrants from the coastal regions of Galicia and Asturias were drawn to Buenos Aires in the late colonial era by opportunities for economic and social advancement. They retained contact with the peninsula, but immigrants, mainly men, did intermarry with criollas. At the same time, gallego newcomers were prone to intergenerational marriages with gallego-criolla daughters, thus retaining much of the gallego identity. [JWC]

1517 Desde San Juan hacia la historia de la región. Textos de Ana María J. García *et al.* Con la colaboración de María Julia Gnecco de Fernández *et al.* San Juan, Argentina: Instituto de Historia Regional y Argentina "Héctor Domingo Arias," EFFHA, Univ. Nacional de San Juan, 2006. 1 v.: bibl., ill. (some col.), maps.

Broad-reaching essays on the history of the region of Cuyo (San Juan and surroundings) from the early colonial period to the 20th century. Contributions address such topics as the geography of this region, viniculture, mining, religion, and the coming of the railroads. Regional history. [JWC]

1518 Djenderedjian, Julio. Roots of revolution: frontier settlement policy and the emergence of new spaces of power in the Río de la Plata borderlands, 1777–1810. (*HAHR*, 88:4, Nov. 2008, p. 639–668, map)

For defense against Portuguese expansion, viceregal policy in the Spanish Río de la Plata prompted the establishment of settlement of the frontiers of Entre Ríos and the Banda Oriental between the late 1770 and 1810. Resultant conflict over land between elites and more humble settlers are described, as well as the unexpected rural support for the 1810–11 revolution from the frontier. Excellent contribution to frontier history of this region. [JWC]

1519 Dominino Crespo, Darío. Escándalos y delitos de la gente plebe: Córdoba a fines del siglo XVIII. Córdoba, Argentina: Univ. Nacional de Córdoba, 2007. 333 p.: bibl., ill. (Serie Colecciones. Estudios históricos)

Study of the activities of the Alcaldes de Barrio as the Bourbon Reforms of the late 18th century imposed a greater social order upon the lower classes of the city. The powers and functions of these officials are well described, as are the different and often ambiguous misdeeds that attracted their attention. Well documented and a good contribution to urban history. [JWC]

Dote matrimonial y redes de poder en el antiguo régimen en España e Hispanoamérica. See item **480.**

1520 Durán Estragó, Margarita. Areguá: rescate histórico, 1576–1870. Asunción: Gobernación del Depto. Central, Secretaría de Educación y Cultura; Fondo Nacional de la Cultura y las Artes, 2005. 168 p.: bibl., ill., maps.

In the 1660s, after its settlement in the 1570s, the Paraguayan pueblo of Areguá passed into the hands of the Mercedarian order which possessed lands in that region. Areguá became a pueblo of freed blacks, under the control and guidance of the order. Utilizes primary sources from the Archivo Nacional de Asunción. Useful for local history and the description of the economy and society of that region. [JWC]

1521 Elissalde, Roberto L. Historias ignoradas de las invasiones inglesas. Buenos Aires: Aguilar, 2006. 214 p.: bibl., ill., 1 map.

Anecdotes—but supported by research—of the British invasions of Buenos Aires in 1806 and 1807. Some are useful in that they cast light upon personal reactions to the events. [JWC]

1522 Espínola, Julio César. La estrategia de la alianza y el primer mestizaje paraguayo. (*Estud. Parag.*, 22/23:1/2, dic. 2005, p. 9–27, bibl.)

Brief and clear analysis of the accommodation of the Guarani in Paraguay to Spanish conquerors in the 1540s and 1550s. *Parentesco* through polygamy, as well as seizure and enslavement of indigenous peoples, are discussed. [JWC]

1523 Farberman, Judith. Curacas, mandones, alcaldes y curas: legitimidad, autoridad y coerción en los pueblos de indios de Santiago del Estero, siglos XVII y XVIII. (*CLAHR*, 13:4, Fall 2004, p. 367–397, map, table)

Encomienda exactions weakened caciques' authority as the population looked upon them as "collaborators" with colonial officials. The result was a power struggle within Indian villages, often involving families, and leading eventually to an acceptance by government authorities of the leaders chosen within the communities. Good example of one type of Indian resistance to Spanish authority. [JWC]

1524 Farberman, Judith. Recolección, economía campesina y representaciones de los montaraces en Santiago del Estero, siglos XVI a XIX. (*Prohistoria/Rosario*, 10:10, primavera 2006, p. 11–26)

Describes the "gathering" of wild products such as honey, wax, and cochineal by peasants in the valleys of Santiago del Estero. An example of the survival of a "marginal" economy by a drifting population from the 1500s to the late 1800s. [JWC]

1525 Farberman, Judith and Roxana Boixadós. Sociedades indígenas y encomienda en el Tucumán colonial: un análisis comparado de la visita de Luján de Vargas. (*Rev. Indias*, 66:238, sept./dic. 2006, p. 601–628, table)

This *visita* by an oidor of the Charcas Audiencia found the encomienda in this region in a state of transition as Indian villages still possessed relative autonomy, but also were adapting to the colonial system of justice. The complexity of diverse indigenous groups in the encomienda system is discussed—as is the continuing practice of old religious customs. Still, for the most part, the indigenous population was developing into a mestizo or ladino culture. [JWC]

1526 Francia. Vol. 1, 1762–1817. Comentarios de Guido Rodríguez Alcalá, Margarita Durán Estragó y Martín Romano García. Ed. comentada, aum. y corr. de la colección Doroteo Bareiro del Archivo Nacional de Asunción. Asunción: Tiempo de Historia, 2009. 555 p.: index.

Edited transcript of documents related to Dr. José Gaspar Rodríguez de Francia found in the Colección Doroteo Bareiro, once director of the Archivo Nacional de Asunción. This document set covers the personal and political life of Dr. Francia—El Supremo. It promises to be the most important document set ever published on Paraguay, and is a great contribution to Paraguayan letters. Recourse to this volume is essential for anyone doing research on Dr. Francia and/or Paraguay's path to independence. The second volume covering the early years of the republic has already been published and the third and final volume on Francia is expected to be published soon. [JWC]

1527 Gascón, Margarita. Naturaleza e imperio: Araucanía, Patagonia, Pampas, 1598–1740. Buenos Aires: Editorial Dunken, 2007. 182 p.: ill., maps.

The southern frontier of Spanish settlement in the Río de la Plata was beset by violence from the late 1500s to the mid-1700s as Araucanian Indians raided Spanish settlements, stole cattle, and then took advantage of their control of Andean passes to send their booty to Chile. However, war often gave way to peaceful trade with the Spanish. At the same time, the situation was complicated by struggles among indigenous groups themselves on the southern frontier, creating a very fluid struggle. Good frontier history. [JWC]

1528 Gentile Lafaille, Margarita E. Testamentos de indios de la gobernación de Tucumán, 1579–1704. Prólogo de Alberto David Leiva. Buenos Aires: Cátedra Instituciones del Período Colonial e Independiente: Instituto Universitario Nacional del Arte: Área Transdepartamental de Folklore, 2008. 326 p.: bibl., ill., index.

Describes customs of the precolumbian and colonial eras in Tucumán in relation to society, religion, and economy. Describes how these customs were adapted to the Spanish legal system in the drafting of wills. Well researched. [JWC]

1529 Gómez, Gérard. Entre las bellas palabras y las palabras sagradas: el sincretismo lingüístico-religioso en las reducciones jesuíticas del Paraguay. Asunción: ServiLibro, 2006. 238 p.: bibl.

Various aspects of Guarani mythology aided the Jesuits in the Río de la Plata in the assimilation of Indians into Christian culture—the most important being the ideal of the Guarani of the "land without evil" as a stepping stone to that of Christian salvation. It was not an immediate process but it did promote a pervasive and all-encompassing mission culture. [JWC]

1530 Gorzalczany, Marisa Andrea and Alejandro Olmos Gaona. La biblioteca jesuítica de Asunción. Buenos Aires: M.A. Gorzalczany, A. Olmos Gaona, 2006. 463 p.: facsims.

Inventory of the library of the Colegio Jesuítico de Asunción compiled shortly after the expulsion of the order in 1767. Useful for an intellectual history of the order—and for bibliophiles. [JWC]

1531 La invasión de Inglaterra doscientos años después. Buenos Aires: Academia Argentina de la Historia, 2007. 295 p.: bibl., map.

A collection of essays on the invasions of Buenos Aires treating such topics as their origins, battles, mobilization of the resistance, and aftermath. For the general reader desiring to be better acquainted with the invasions of 1806 and 1807. [JWC]

1532 Jackson, Robert H. Demographic patterns in the Jesuit missions of the Río de la Plata region: the case of Corpus Christi Mission, 1622–1802. (*CLAHR*, 13:4, Fall 2004, p. 337–366, graphs, tables)

Intensive study of the demography of Corpus Christi Mission from 1622 to 1802. Contends that the impact of epidemics on population decadence in the Jesuit missions has been highly overrated as natural reproductive patterns after epidemics restored the population. An important study. See also item **1541**. [JWC]

1533 Kahle, Günter. Orígenes y fundamentos de la conciencia nacional paraguaya. Traducción de Rosalba Méndez Paiva R. Asunción: Instituto Cultural Paraguayo-Alemán Goethe Zentrum, 2005. 363 p.: bibl.

Günter Kahle's PhD dissertation at the Univ. of Köln, "Grundlagen und Anfänge des paraguayischen Nationalbewusstseins" (1962), was a significant step forward in German Studies of Paraguayan history. That work on the growth of

Paraguayan national consciousness surveyed the period from the conquest in the 1540s to the era of Dr. Francia in the early 1800s, treating such topics as relations with the Guarani Indians and resulting race mixture, the establishment of the encomienda system, the impact of the common use of the Guarani tongue, the impact of the Jesuits on Paraguay, Luso-Brazilian ambitions and Paraguay's response, the assimilation of Hispanic culture, and the independence era. While somewhat dated in light of recent historical advances, it remains a useful work, and stands out as a very worthwhile contribution to Paraguayan history. This translation is very much welcomed. [JWC]

1534 Lacoste, Pablo. The rise and secularization of viticulture in Mendoza: the Godoy family contribution, 1700–1831. (Americas/Washington, 63:3, Jan. 2007, p. 383–407, tables)

Good study of viniculture in Mendoza from the late 1600s to the mid-1800s as seen in the rise of the Godoy family's business. Describes the replacement of Church viniculture by private entrepreneurs with the latter introducing innovations to business and creating an integrated industry. Liberal reforms and secularization of society are emphasized in the politics of the family. [JWC]

1535 Lacoste, Pablo. Wine and women: grape growers and pulperas in Mendoza, 1561–1852. (HAHR, 88:3, Aug. 2008, p. 361–391, tables)

Viniculture as a small business enterprise gradually provided opportunities for women in the late colonial period, as did the operation of pulperías. Mendoza was an important trading center and the government severely controlled the operation of pulperías to ensure social order. Provides some good examples of women wine producers and pulpería owners. [JWC]

1536 Larguía, Alejandro. Misiones jesuíticas del Uruguay: la provincia perdida. Prólogo por R.P. Julián Zini. Buenos Aires: Corregidor, 2007. 1 vol. (316 p.): bibl., ill.

History of Jesuit missions in the Banda Oriental in the 18th century and their impact on political, social, and religious life. Multi-archival research in Brazil, Argentina, and Uruguay. [JWC]

1537 Laterza Rivarola, Gustavo. Historia de Lambaré: un pueblo, un nombre y un cacique ignotos: desde la Colonia hasta el Municipio. Asunción: Servilibro, 2009. 154 p.: ill.

Contends that the cacique Lambaré, chief of the Guarani in the Asunción region who in the early 1540s concluded a treaty with the conquistadors, never existed. Historians must find other reasons for the Spanish-Guarani cooperation in the conquest. [JWC]

1538 Lesser, Ricardo. La infancia de los próceres: Belgrano, Rivadavia, Moreno, Castelli, Azcuénaga. Buenos Aires: Editorial Biblos, 2004. 190 p.: bibl.

A laudable attempt of investigation of the infancy in late colonial Buenos Aires of five próceres of the revolution of 1810. However, the study is marred by the scarcity of information, even of these distinguished families and personages. Too often the author has to speculate on various aspects of the rearing of these children. [JWC]

1539 Lida, Miranda. Un clérigo ilustrado en la sociedad cordobesa: cohesión e identidad religiosa en la familia del Deán Gregorio Funes a fines del período colonial rioplatense. (Colon. Lat. Am. Rev., 14:2, Spring 2005, p. 105–133, photo)

Describes the family and early life of Deán Gregorio Funes in Córdoba. Funes was later prominent in the Buenos Aires revolution. The Funes family was close-knit, devout, active in commerce and local politics, and was prominent in the society of this city in the very late colonial era. [JWC]

1540 Lida, Miranda. Dos ciudades y un deán: biografía de Gregorio Funes, 1749–1829. Buenos Aires: Eudeba, 2006. 230 p. (Temas. Historia)

Well-researched biography of this important figure of the period of Argentine independence, with much attention paid to his formative years and ecclesiastic career in Córdoba. Also quite good on his changed views of Church and state as well as the culture of the Church in early 19th-century Argentina. [JWC]

1541 Livi-Bacci, Massimo and Ernesto J. Maeder. The missions of Paraguay: the demography of an experiment. (J. Inter-

discip. Hist., 35:2, Autumn 2004, p. 185–224, graphs, map, tables)

Excellent review of the demography of the Guarani missions in Paraguay. The authors conclude that disastrous epidemics were a major factor in mission demography, while marriage at an early age and rapid reproduction compensated for epidemic losses. Isolation from Europeans, as well as the social and economic strength of the missions, had a positive impact upon the demography. See also item **1532**. [JWC]

1542 Lorandi, Ana María. Poder central, poder local: funcionarios borbónicos en el Tucumán colonial: un estudio de antropología política. Buenos Aires: Prometeo Libros, 2008. 227 p.: bibl.

As Bourbon officials moved to assert greater imperial control over colonial Tucumán in the mid-1700s, they encountered resistance from the colonial elites— particularly in the matter of the expulsion of the Jesuit order. Discusses the various means of resistance employed by the elites and the imposition of royal authority. [JWC]

1543 Luque Azcona, Emilio José. Ciudad y poder: la construcción material y simbólica del Montevideo colonial, 1723–1810. Madrid: Consejo Superior de Investigaciones Científicas, Escuela de Estudios Hispano-Americanos; Sevilla: Univ. de Sevilla: Diputación de Sevilla, 2007. 356 p.: bibl., ill., maps. (Col. americana/Univ. de Sevilla; 31) (Serie Nuestra América; 22)

This work concentrates on the construction of the military defenses of Montevideo. Financial problems, planning, the lack of construction materials, labor relations and conditions, and political infighting are all discussed. Well researched and an excellent contribution to the urban history of Montevideo. For review of geography specialist's comment, see *HLAS 65:1271*. [JWC]

1544 Lynch, John. San Martín: Argentine soldier, American hero. New Haven, Conn.: Yale Univ. Press, 2009. 265 p.: bibl., ill., index, maps.

As one would expect from this distinguished expert on the Spanish American independence period, this is an outstanding English-language biography of the great Argentine soldier and liberator of the independence era. It is both thoughtful and readable as Lynch follows the career of this criollo from his early childhood on the frontier of the Viceroyalty of Buenos Aires, through his early military career in Europe, the return to his homeland, his triumphs in the struggle against the Spanish in southern South America, and the eventual self-imposed exile in Europe. The masterful concluding summation of the life of San Martín is an example of how history should be written. Highly recommended. [JWC]

1545 Martínez de Sánchez, Ana María. Cofradías y obras pías en Córdoba del Tucumán. Córdoba, Argentina: Editorial de la Univ. Católica de Córdoba, EDUCC, 2006. 353 p.: bibl.

Cofradías, a layman's group within the Church, was designed to promote Christian life and salvation. In Córdoba, as elsewhere in Hispanic America, these organizations, generally aligned on ethnic grounds, also provided social aid and expanded the social and economic horizons of their members. They were quite useful in time of troubles, as their close relation with the Church provided a measure of security. [JWC]

1546 Méndez Paz, Carlos A. Patricios y elites: el caso argentino, 1535–1943: ensayo. Buenos Aires: Instituto Ruy Díaz de Guzman, 2005. 505 p.

Discusses the creation of elites in Argentina from the colonial era through the 20th century; also describes their origins of power and the retention of elite status. Useful for elites on the local levels as well as the national scene. Family and kinship relations discussed and useful genealogical information is provided. [JWC]

1547 Mir, Lucio B. Ladrones de guante blanco: la corrupción porteña en tiempos de la South Sea Company, 1713–1752. Prólogo de Rodolfo González Lebrero. Buenos Aires: Editorial Biblos, 2008. 127 p.: bibl. (Historia)

Succinct observations on the massive contraband that flowed into Buenos Aires when, in the first part of the 18th century, the British South Sea company held the *asiento* for the importation of slaves into the Río de la Plata. Prohibited items were exchanged for silver as British employees of this company cooperated with porteño elite families and made a mockery of the policy of monopolistic control of trade. Well done. [JWC]

1548 Olivero, Sandra. Sociedad y economía en San Isidro colonial: Buenos Aires, siglo XVIII. Sevilla, Spain: Univ. de Sevilla, Secretariado de Publicaciones, 2006. 406 p.: bibl., charts, geneal. tables. (Serie Geografía e Historia/Universidad de Sevilla; 119)

Very complete analysis of a rural partido of the Pampas adjacent to Buenos Aires in the 1700s. Much attention is paid to the demographic growth of this region, particularly in the context of a mixed pastoral/agricultural economy. San Isidro was a source of wheat for Buenos Aires and independent cultivators of that crop found a respectable place in society. At the same time, cattle-raising, particularly for hides, was the pursuit of the landed elite. Social interrelationships, especially those attained by marriage, were an important factor for economic advancement for the cultivator class. Excellent research and a definite contribution to rural history of the 1700s. Useful tables. [JWC]

1549 Oyarzábal, Guillermo Andrés. Guillermo Brown. Buenos Aires: Librería-Editorial Histórica, 2006. 429 p.: bibl., ill. (Col. histórica; 21)

Biography of an Irish adventurer who became the first admiral of the navy of Buenos Aires during the revolution for independence, and then continued his naval career there in the post-independence era. Quite detailed and well researched. [JWC]

1550 Oyarzábal, Guillermo Andrés. Sobre marinos y funcionarios en el Río de la Plata: conflictos y necesidades, 1760–1800. (*Temas Hist. Argent. Am.*, 6, enero/junio 2005, p. 13–148, bibl.)

Deployment of the Spanish navy to Río de la Plata, particularly after creation of the Viceroyalty, was fraught with difficulties. Recruitment of crews was a challenge, and even frequent amnesties for deserters did not solve that problem. Montevideo was not a good port for naval vessels and there were serious problems of repair as well as supplies. [JWC]

1551 Page, Carlos A. El Colegio Máximo de Córdoba, Argentina según las Cartas Anuas de la Compañía de Jesús, 1609–1767. Córdoba, Argentina: BR Copias, 2004. 349

p. (Documentos para la historia de la Compañía de Jesús en Córdoba; 1)

Annual letters of the Compañía de Jesús concerning el Colegio de Córdoba from the difficulties of foundation in the very early 1600s to the expulsion of this order in 1767. Contains valuable information on the studies in the colegio, students, and faculty in the preparation of Jesuits for missionary work in the Río de la Plata. [JWC]

1552 Page, Carlos A. Los viajes de Europa a Buenos Aires según las crónicas de los jesuitas de los siglos XVII y XVIII. Córdoba, Argentina: Báez Ediciones, 2007. 325 p.: bibl., ill. (some col.)

Twelve accounts of voyages of Jesuits from Europe to the Río de la Plata in the 17th and 18th centuries, replete with observations on voyages, shipwrecks, storms, and the tedium of travel. [JWC]

1553 Palombo, Guillermo. Invasiones inglesas, 1806–1807: estudio documentado. Buenos Aires: Editorial Dunken, 2007. 230 p.: bibl.

Extremely well-detailed study of the British invasions and well documented. This work is really not for popular consumption as the details tend to overwhelm the reader. On the other hand, for a day-to-day account of this conflict and the organization of the British army and the criollo resistance, it is quite valuable. [JWC]

1554 Payró, Roberto Pablo. El Río de la Plata: de colonias a naciones independientes: de Solís a Rosas, 1516–1852. Buenos Aires: Alianza Editorial, 2006. 648 p.: bibl. (Alianza Singular; 16)

Broad, general history of the Río de la Plata from the early stages of colonization to mid-1800s. Strongest on era of late colonial period to 1850s, but in this section concentrates on the creation of the Argentine nation. [JWC]

1555 Peire, Jaime and Roberto Di Stefano. De la sociedad barroca a la ilustrada: aspectos económicos del proceso de secularización en el Río de la Plata. (*ANDES Antropol. Hist.*, 15, 2004, p. 117–148, bibl.)

By the mid-1700s the old order was breaking down among the religious orders in the Río de la Plata. Internal conflicts, litigation, and concern over material goods weakened them as Crown policy was to shift wealth and incomes to the poorer secular clergy. While the secular clergy benefitted from royal policy, the tension between orders and secular clergy was never clearly resolved. However, that conflict led to the Rivadavia reforms of the 1820s. [JWC]

1556 Perusset, Macarena. El contrabando en el Río de la Plata colonial temprano: redes, líderes y prácticas. (*Estud. Parag.*, 24:1/2, dic. 2006, p. 157–188, bibl.)

The closure of the port of Buenos Aires in the late 1500s led prominent families, government officials, and even Church figures to resort to contraband traffic— particularly with Portuguese smugglers. Personal contacts and *parentesco* were all important in this trade. Some of the mechanisms of smuggling are described. [JWC]

1557 Perusset, Macarena. Contrabando y sociedad en el Río de la Plata colonial. Buenos Aires: Editorial Dunken, 2006. 161 p.: bibl.

A culture of contraband among new commercial elites of Buenos Aires from 1610 to 1630, reinforced by kinship, advantageous marriages, corruption of royal officials, and even the cooperation of the Church, provided an opportunity for enrichment. Given the royal policy of the closure of the port of Buenos Aires, contraband trade was a natural entrepreneurial response. [JWC]

1558 El primer Sínodo del Paraguay y Río de la Plata en Asunción en el año de 1603. Introducción y notas de Bartomeu Meliá. Ed. facsimilar. Asunción: Centro de Estudios Paraguayos "Antonio Guasch": Missionsprokur Nürnberg, 2003. 91 p.: bibl.

Text and facsimile of the text of this document, which is held in the Archivo General de Indias in Seville, Spain. Important for Church history of colonial Paraguay and Christianization of Indians. [JWC]

1559 Ramírez Braschi, Dardo. Patriotas y sarracenos: la lucha revolucionaria en la provincia de Corrientes, 1810–1812. Corrientes, Argentina: Moglia Ediciones, 2009. 110 p.: bibl.

Discusses the adhesion of Corrientes Province to revolutionary Buenos Aires rather than to Asunción. Due to Corrientes' relative weak economic position and political dependence upon the port city, autonomy was no choice. Interfamily conflict was

important in this process. Excellent document section. [JWC]

1560 Revolución: política e ideas en el Río de la Plata durante la década de 1810. Compilación de Fabián Herrero. Textos de Klaus Gallo *et al.* Buenos Aires: Ediciones Cooperativas, 2004. 200 p.: bibl. (Col. Politeia de ciencias sociales)

Essays by various scholars on the evolution of political thought in the Río de la Plata region during the turbulent years of 1810–20. Some of the topics discussed include social conflict, elite views, militarization of society, and the rights of the people. [JWC]

1561 Rivarola Paoli, Juan Bautista. La contabilidad colonial y las Cajas Reales de Hacienda. Asunción: Intercontinental Editora, 2008. 567 p.: bibl., ill.

The foremost historian of the Real Hacienda del Paraguay continues his investigations into this institution with an analysis of the *contabilidad* of the Hacienda and its evolution from the 16th century onward. Very useful for any discussion of colonial Paraguay. [JWC]

1562 Romero de Vázquez, Natividad. Ypané—Guarambaré: fundamentos históricos de dos pueblos hermanados: textos y documentos. Asunción: Editora Litocolor, 2006. 372 p.: bibl., ill. (some col.), col. maps.

History of two Paraguayan reductions established by Franciscan missionaries in late 1500s that were moved to present location in 1670s after pressure from Portuguese *bandeirantes* and hostile Indians. The bulk of this work is the transcription of documents pertaining to these reductions—later villages—from their founding to the 1840s. Local history. [JWC]

1563 Rustán, María E. De perjudiciales a pobladores de la frontera: poblamiento de la frontera sur de la Gobernación Intendencia de Córdoba a fines del siglo XVIII. Córdoba, Argentina: Ferreyra, 2005. 138 p.

Describes the utilization of individuals prejudicial to social order as settlers on the frontier of the Intendencia of Córdoba. Describes types of offenses as well as problems of settlement. Problems with indigenous peoples were a prime motivation for such settlements. [JWC]

1564 San Martino, Laura. La administración Borbónica en el Río de la Plata. (*Rev. Hist. Mil.*, 51, número extraordinario 2, 2007, p. 95–122)

Overview of the Bourbon motives for reforms in the Río de la Plata in the 1700s. Defense from Portuguese aggression is discussed as are the new institutions of the Viceroyalty and Intendencias with their great impact upon political administration, law, and social control by the post-independence governments—both national and provincial. [JWC]

1565 Shumway, Jeffrey M. The case of the ugly suitor: & other histories of love, gender, & nation in Buenos Aires, 1776–1870. Lincoln: Univ. of Nebraska Press, 2005. 200 p.: bibl., ill., index. (Engendering Latin America)

Importance of the family as a social unit in late colonial and early national Buenos Aires and the problems of marriage when parental objections arose. Some good case studies dealing with social position, race, and familial differences in status. Points out that by the 1850s, old colonial rigidity in social views of marriage were breaking down. An interesting study, slightly marred only by the all too common confusion between *disenos* and appeals of *disensos* under the 1776 Pragmática that regularized dissents by parents or empowered officials to the marriage of minors or those of inappropriate race or social position. [JWC]

1566 Telesca, Ignacio. Población parda en Asunción a fines del siglo XVIII. (*Estud. Parag.*, 22/23:1/2, dic. 2005, p. 29–50, bibl., tables)

Well-researched study of numbers and condition of the black population of Asunción and an interesting case of the difficulties of a slave who legally attempted to gain his liberty. [JWC]

1567 Telesca, Ignacio. La Provincia del Paraguay, revolución y transformación 1680–1780. Asunción: El Lector, 2010. 140 p.: ill., tables. (Col. La gran historia del Paraguay; 3)

Brief, but good description of the province in the mid-colonial era. Covers the origin of the Comunero Revolt as well

after the aftermath; a good discussion of the Jesuit Colegio of Asunción; and the changes in demography and territorial control after the expulsion of the Jesuits. [JWC]

1568 Telesca, Ignacio. Tras los Expulsos: cambios demográficos y territoriales en el Paraguay después de la expulsión de los jesuitas. Asunción: Universidad Católica "Nuestra Señora de la Asunción". Centro de Estudios Antropológicos (CEADUC), 2009. 442 p.: ill., tables. (Biblioteca de estudios paraguayos. Col. Bicentenario; 76)

Most definitive account to date of the demography, society, and landholding in Paraguay after the expulsion of the Jesuits. Examines the period from 1760 to 1780 as a prelude to the rise of Paraguay's export economy during the Intendencia era. Very useful. Multi-archival research. [JWC]

1569 Tell, Sonia. Córdoba rural, una sociedad campesina, 1750–1850. Buenos Aires: Prometeo Libros: Asociación Argentina de Historia Económica, 2008. 451 p.: bibl., ill., maps.

Extensive study of the rural small landholders of Córdoba in the final years of the colonial period and first generation of independence. The majority of these small cultivators lived in small communities, and exploited by their labor different resources. Taxes on their agricultural production in the late colonial era were onerous burdens upon this humble population, and the forced labor and military requisitions in the independence and caudillo eras were no better. Detailed examination of population dynamics, items of production, local and long distance sale of their production, and cycles of the rural economy are well discussed. Very useful for the rural economy and society of this period. [JWC]

1570 Vassallo, Jaqueline. Delincuentes y pecadoras en la Córdoba tardo colonial. (*Anu. Estud. Am.*, 63:2, 2006, p. 97–116, table)

Crimes, punishments, and imprisonment of women, generally of the marginal classes, as social control were strengthened by Bourbon reformers. Crimes of violence by women were surprisingly high. [JWC]

1571 Vassallo, Jaqueline. Mujeres delincuentes: una mirada de género en la
Córdoba del siglo XVIII. Córdoba, Argentina: Centro de Estudios Avanzados, Univ.
Nacional de Córdoba, 2005. 598 p.: bibl.

Imposition of a stronger Bourbon
social order in Córdoba in the latter half of
the 18th century fell as heavy upon women
as men. This work narrates the "model" of
social comportment demanded by the new
policy as well as the various crimes committed by women and the punishments meted
out. This is a very thorough work, well
documented, excellent tables, and a definite
contribution to both women's history as
well as the urban history of Córdoba. [JWC]

1572 Wilde, Guillermo. Religión y poder
en las misiones de guaraníes. Buenos
Aires: Sb, 2009. 509 p.: bibl., ill., maps. (Paradigma indicial. Serie Historia americana)

A very important work in which the
author contends that the Guarani of the
Jesuit missions were not the passive individuals commonly portrayed. Rather they
became culturally informed, negotiating
with the Jesuits and outside agents, and
structuring views and new ideas within
the context of a mobile, ambiguous and
constantly changing environment. Highly
recommended. [JWC]

1573 Zorreguieta, Mariano. Apuntes
históricos de la Provincia de Salta
en la época del coloniaje. Salta, Argentina:
Univ. Católica de Salta: Eucasa, 2008. 439 p.:
port. (Col. Artes y ciencias. Serie Historia)

Reprint of the first edition of this
work published in the 1870s. Continues to
be a useful resource for the colonial history
of Salta. [JWC]

19th and 20th Centuries
Venezuela

PETER S. LINDER, *Associate Professor of History, New Mexico Highlands University*

AS VENEZUELA BEGINS THE CELEBRATION of the bicentennial of its independence, trends in the writing of its modern history observed in earlier volumes
continue to develop. Contemporary political issues and debates continue to cast
a long shadow, and to influence the production of historical works. Many recent
studies provide an increasingly critical scrutiny of Venezuela's past and some
reassessment of the myths and "received truths" of the independence era. Many
such works are explicitly influenced by contemporary disputes. At the same time,
the professionalization of the field continues apace; many of the innovative studies began as theses or dissertations written in Venezuelan university graduate
programs, or by Venezuelans studying abroad. A sizeable number of recent works
explore various aspects of the historical past with the present explicitly in mind.
Useful works have also emerged in social and cultural history, while regional
history continues to increase in quality, sophistication, and distribution. Works
of Venezuelan history, particularly regional studies, are also being disseminated
internationally.

Given that 2010 marks the bicentennial of the start of the independence
movement in Venezuela, it is unsurprising that a number of significant historical studies address that era. The initial phases of the independence process have
received considerable attention. Several recent works focus on the life and career

of Francisco de Miranda, including a two-volume collection of essays and documents dealing with the ill-fated Miranda expedition of 1806 (items **1581**). Michael Zeuske's brief work examines Miranda as an advocate and representative of liberalism and modernity in Venezuela (item **1584**). Walter Márquez's study analyzes the collapse of the First Republic as the result of a failed program of popular mobilization (item **1592**). Other recent studies reassess traditional historical views of independence. Angel Lombardi Boscán seeks to demythologize the wars of independence by examining the struggle from the royalist perspective (item **1589**). Lombardi Boscán has also analyzed an abortive uprising taking place in Maracaibo in 1799, an event commonly touted as a precursor of the independence movement. The author asserts that the 1799 event was in fact a minor incident bereft of political significance, used after the fact to counter accusations that Maracaibo's inhabitants lacked patriotic zeal (item **1590**).

The national state of the 19th and 20th centuries has also received considerable attention from historians. Elías Pino Iturrieta explores personalism in Venezuelan politics, and argues that the strongly leader-oriented politics of the 20th and 21st centuries can be traced back to elite failures to empower the lower classes during the early republic (item **1600**). In a similar vein, Diego B. Urbaneja provides an analysis of the little-studied Soublette administration as a period of tranquility and solid governmental achievement that contrasted with the personalist regimes of later leaders (item **1610**). Several studies of the 20th-century state explore the origins of contemporary Venezuelan politics. Two significant studies examine Juan Vicente Gómez and his era. Brian S. McBeth provides a detailed analysis of internal and international opposition to the Gómez regime, and argues that the Tachiran leader had substantial and widespread internal support, not merely the backing of foreign governments and oil companies (item **1596**). A lengthy work by the late Jorge Olavarría agrees that Gómez enjoyed significant domestic support that cut across class lines, and posits that most studies of the Gómez era have distorted reality to provide ideological support for later governments (item **1599**).

The governments that succeeded that of Juan Vicente Gómez have also received attention. Several works seek to reassess the "military presidents" of the 1930s and 1940s. Alirio Martínez characterizes the López Contreras administration as democratic and instrumental in the development of the nation's democratic institutions (item **1593**). Other works examine various aspects of the presidency of General Isías Medina Angarita; Eduardo Ramírez López asserts that Medina was a positive force in the modernization of Venezuela (item **1602**), while Carlos Alarico Gómez maintains that the democratic structures and practices characteristic of Venezuelan politics originated during the Medina Angarita administration (item **1585**). Nikolas Kozloff investigates the relationship between the Medina administration and the oil companies, and argues that Medina used public criticism of ecological disasters and press accounts of the oil companies' disregard for the environment to assert the state's right to control the industry (item **1587**). Leonardo Bracamonte's brief article examines efforts by the Acción Democrática government of 1945–48 to mobilize popular support for rapid political change (item **1614**). The Fourth Republic also receives some attention. Enrique Neira analyzes the politics of the Fourth Republic, and compares them favorably to the contemporary situation (item **1598**). Naudy Suárez Figueroa's brief study of the Pact of Punto Fijo challenges the new orthodoxy that damns the pact as a corrupt bargain (item **1608**). Alejandro Botia recounts the difficulties faced by Venezuela's print media to free itself from official censorship since 1958 (item **1577**). Pedro Pablo Linárez provides a sympathetic portrayal of the guerrillas who challenged the Venezuelan state in the 1960s and 1970s (item **1588**).

The period under review has seen a number of interesting studies exploring changes in Venezuelan institutions, society, and culture. Two books exploring the history of Venezuelan education deserve mention. Salomó Marquès Sureda and Juan José Martín Frechilla underline the important role played by Spanish Republican exiles in the development of education—particularly primary and secondary education—in Venezuela (item **1591**). Emma D. Martínez Vásquez investigates changing societal attitudes about the education of women in the 19th and early 20th centuries (item **1595**). Milton Jamail explores the connections between Venezuela's economic health and the export of Venezuelan players to Major League Baseball (item **1586**). Rosalba di Miele Milano has produced an arresting study of the evolution of divorce in Venezuela after independence, in which she asserts that ideological changes transformed marriage into a contractual arrangement (item **1582**). Cultural studies worthy of note include Miguel Tinker Salas' detailed examination of the social and cultural impact of the oil industry in 20th-century Venezuela (item **1609**). Luis Rincón Rubio's study of funerary practices in rural 19th-century Maracaibo Province demonstrates considerable continuity between the colonial and early independence periods (item **1604**).

Another development noted in previous volumes has been the growing sophistication of regional and local historical studies. Some traditional regional and local histories continue to appear. For example, Reynaldo Rojas' collection of essays on the history of Barquisimeto was written to commemorate 450 years since the city's founding (item **1605**). Nonetheless, sophisticated regional studies continue to proliferate. Graduate programs in history at many universities provide a growing output of innovative and illuminating works, particularly in the case of Maracaibo. Arlene Urdaneta's study of the Federalist era in Zulia illuminates the links between regional and national identity in the Maracaibo region (item **1612**). Nilda Bermúdez analyzes patriotic celebrations in fin-de-siècle Maracaibo, and argues that such nationalist observances represented a defense of the region's autonomy in the face of centralizing national governments (item **1576**). J.L. Monzant Gavidia discusses regional opposition to the dictatorship of Marcos Pérez Jiménez, and argues that Zulian opposition was independent of, and opposed to, the military revolt that toppled that regime (item **1597**).

A final development worthy of mention is the increasing role of digital technology in research and publication. There has been a proliferation of article-length historical studies being published electronically, including some cited here. A number of Venezuelan historians publish in refereed digital journals, including some originating in Colombia and Mexico. Their work is readily accessible internationally through systems such as the *Red de Revistas Científicas de América Latina y el Caribe, España y Portugal (Redalyc)*, operated by the Universidad Autónoma del Estado de México. In addition, a number of Venezuelan archives—including the Acervo Histórico del Estado Zulia and the Registro Principal del Estado Zulia—are in the process of digitizing their holdings. These trends will continue, and may result in easier access to documents and wider dissemination for research in 19th- and 20th-century Venezuelan history.

1574 Abreu Xavier, Antonio de. Con Portugal en la maleta: histórias de vida de los portugues en Venezuela, siglo XX. Caracas: Editorial Alfa, 2007. 253 p.: bibl., ill. (Col. tropicos; 7)

Entertaining and useful work detailing the experiences of Portuguese immigrants to Venezuela in the 20th century. The author asserts that the Portuguese immigrant experience evolved through four distinct periods. Based largely on interviews, this was originally the author's doctoral dissertation.

1575 Archivo del Registro Principal del Estado Zulia: catálogo y extractos de expedientes judiciales civiles y penales, 1780–1836. Edición de Luis Rincón Rubio et al. Maracaibo, Venezuela: Univ. Católica Cecilio Acosta, 2009. 470 p.: bibl., indexes. (Col. Investigación Mario Briceño Iragorry)

Funded by the Harvard University Program for Latin American Libraries and Archives, this catalog of judicial documents from the Maracaibo Registro Principal represents a continuation or companion of Augustín Millares Carlo's useful work of 1964 (see *HLAS 30:53*).

1576 Bermudez B., Nilda. Las fiestas centenarias de Bolivar y Urdaneta, 1833–1888: respuestas del colectivo zuliano en la lucha por el rescate de la autonomia política del estado. (*Tzintzun*, 48, julio/dic. 2008, p. 149–178., ill.)

Useful article examining patriotic celebrations in Maracaibo in the 19th century. The author argues that leading members of Maracaibo's elite and intelligencia organized and used such nationalist observances in order to demonstrate their patriotism and resist central government attacks on the autonomy of the state of Zulia. Based on regional archival and hemerographic research.

1577 Botía, Alejandro. Auge y crisis del cuarto poder: la prensa en democracia. Caracas: Debate, 2007. 327 p.: bibl., ill. (Col. Actualidad)

With a prologue written by perennial opposition politician and polemicist Teodoro Petkoff, an examination of the history and contemporary political role played by the Venezuelan print media, the "fourth power" of the title. The author presents the history of print journalism from 1958 to the present and maintains that the press has had to struggle since the end of the Pérez Jiménez regime to assert its independence of state censorship. Critical of recent attempts by the Chávez government to muzzle the press.

1578 Bracamonte, Leonard. La incorporación del pueblo a la nación venezolana, 1945–1948. (*Memorias*, 6:11, nov. 2009, p. 173–199, bibl.)

Exploration of the first government of Acción Democrática in 1945–48. The author reviews the party's efforts to mobilize the people in the service of political and social change, and argues that the coup that installed the military dictatorship resulted from the "immaturity" of the nation's conservatives.

1579 Carrera Damas, Germán et al. Mitos políticos en las sociedades andinas: orígenes, invenciones y ficciones. Caracas: Editorial Equinoccio, Univ. Simón Bolívar: Univ. de Marne la Valle: IFEA, 2006. 420 p.

Collection of essays exploring the development of political myths in the discourse of Venezuela and the other Andean republics emerging in the 19th and 20th centuries. Also making explicit reference to the political situation in contemporary Venezuela, and the "presencia abrumadora" of Hugo Chávez Frías. The editors note in the introduction that political myths have been used since the 19th century to convey legitimacy.

Chirinos, Juan Carlos. Miranda, el nómada sentimental. See item **528.**

1580 Coloquio de Historia y Sociedad, 2nd, Caracas, Venezuela, 2005. El problema de la soberanía: su historia ante el siglo XXI. Contribuciones de Claudio Alberto Briceño Monzón et al. Caracas: Editorial Equinoccio, Univ. Simón Bolívar: Univ. Católica Andrés Bello, 2007. 226 p.: bibl.

Collection of essays exploring national sovereignty in Venezuela from the beginning of the 19th century until the present. Originated as the proceedings of a colloquium held in 2005 at Universidad Católica Andres Bello.

1581 De Ocumare a Segovia: juicio militar a los expedicionarios mirandinos, 1806. Contribuciones de Gladys Arroyo *et al.* Caracas: Comisión Metropolitana para el Estudio de la Historia Regional, 2006. 2 v.: bibl. (Col. Caracas insurgente)

Two-volume study of the 1806 expedition of Francisco de Miranda, written in response to contemporary revolutionary ideas espoused by the current government. A series of introductory essays precede a lengthy transcript of testimony of members of the expedition, captured and interrogated by Spanish authorities. The editors seek to connect the popular struggle for Venezuela's independence from Spain with the movement headed by Hugo Chávez and popular resistance to the April 2002 coup d'etat.

1582 Di Miele Milano, Rosalba. El divorcio en el siglo XIX venezolano: tradición y liberalismo, 1830–1900. Caracas: Fundacion para la Cultura Urbana, 2006. 303 p.: bibl. (Fundación para la Cultura Urbana; 46)

Based on documents from the archives of the Archdiocese of Caracas, a study of divorce in the decades after Venezuelan independence. The author explores the impact of ideological changes— particularly the spread of liberalism—in changing understandings of marriage, from a sacred and indissoluble union to a legal contract susceptible of abrogation.

1583 Donis Ríos, Manuel Alberto. El báculo pastoral y la espada: relaciones entre la Iglesia Católica y el Estado en Venezuela, 1830–1964. Prólogo de Elías Pino Iturrieta. Caracas: bid&co.editor, 2007. 260 p.: bibl. (Col. histórica; 5)

Political history of relations between the Vatican and the Venezuelan state from the establishment of the republic in 1830 until the signing of a convenio in 1964. The author explores the Church's role in national politics, and argues that successive political regimes have sought to control the Church and limit its autonomy.

1584 Francisco de Miranda y la modernidad en América. Estudio de Michael Zeuske. = Francisco de Miranda e a modernidade na América. Estudo de Michael Zeuske. Madrid: Fundación Mapfre Tavera; Aranjuez, Spain: Ediciones Doce Calles; Madrid: SECIB, 2004. 223 p.: bibl., ill. (Prisma

histórico; 2) (Publicaciones del programa Iberoamérica; 4)

A collection of primary documents revealing the worldview of Francisco de Miranda, and his exemplary role as a modernizer and liberal. An informative introductory essay in Spanish and Portuguese is followed by reproductions in French and Spanish of the documents.

1585 Gómez, Carlos Alarico. El origen del estado democrático en Venezuela, 1941–1948. Caracas: Biblioteca de Autores y Temas Tachirenses, 2004. 217 p.: bibl., ill. (Biblioteca de Autores y Temas Tachirenses; 180)

A study of the transition to democracy in the 1940s, assessing General Isías Medina Angarita's administration. The author argues that the structures of Venezuelan democracy—including political parties, the press, and other institutions—developed precisely during the period. Based largely on interviews, newspaper accounts, and secondary sources.

1586 Jamail, Milton H. Venezuelan bust, baseball boom: Andrés Reiner and scouting on the new frontier. Lincoln: Univ. of Nebraska Press, 2008. 257 p.: bibl.

Journalistic account of the role of Andrés Reiner of the Houston Astros in bringing Venezuelan baseball players into Major League Baseball. Arguing that recent difficulties for the nation's petroleum industry have paradoxically facilitated the recruitment and preparation of Venezuelan players to make the transition to American teams' player development systems.

1587 Kozloff, Nikolas. Asserting state authority through environmental monitoring: Venezuela in the post-Gómez era, 1935–1945. (*Bull. Lat. Am. Res.*, 25:2, April 2006, p. 282–300)

Useful article exploring state-building through environmental advocacy. The author argues that President Isías Medina Angarita's administration used public statements and press accounts to pressure the oil companies about environmental contamination, thus asserting the power of the state to control the industry.

1588 Linárez, Pedro Pablo. La lucha armada en Venezuela: apuntes sobre guerra de guerrillas venezolanas en el

contexto de la Guerra Fría, 1959–1979 y
el rescate de los desaparecidos. Caracas:
Ediciones Universidad Bolivariana de
Venezuela, 2006. 215 p.: bibl., ill. (Col. Historia y pensamiento político venezolano
contemporáneo)

Positive portrayal of the leftist guerrillas challenging the Venezuelan government in the 1960s and 1970s. The author
asserts that the guerrillas represented a "heroic" response to the oppression of Rómulo
Betancourt and his successors.

1589 Lombardi, Ángel. Banderas del rey:
la visión realista de la independencia. Prólogo de Enrique Martínez Ruiz.
Venezuela: Ediciones del Rectorado, Univ.
Católica Cecilio Acosta y Univ. del Zulia,
2006. 348 p.: bibl. (Col. Ediciones del rectorado. Serie Estudios; 2)

Based on archival research in Spain
and originally the author's doctoral dissertation, this significant new study explores the
struggle for Venezuelan independence from
the perspective of the royalists. Maintains
that the existing histories of independence
have all been written in the interest of the
dominant classes, and have substituted
myth for vigorous research. Asserts also
that the struggle for independence was
more civil war than conflict of national
liberation.

1590 Lombardi, Ángel. Conspiración de
Maracaibo, 1799. Maracaibo, Venezuela: Univ. Católica Cecilio Acosta, 2009.
125 p.: bibl., ill. (Col. investigación "Mario
Briceño Iragorry")

Brief examination of a 1799 conspiracy in the western city of Maracaibo,
an event commonly cited as a significant
precursor to the Independence movement
of the early 19th century. The author argues
that the event was in fact minor, and the attention that it has received from historians
derives from a desire to counter questions
about the patriotism of the community,
given its conservatism and long support for
the royalist cause.

1591 Marquès Sureda, Salomó. La labor
educativa de los exiliados españoles
en Venezuela. Caracas: Fondo Editorial de
Humanidades y Educación, Universidad
Central de Venezuela, 2002. 250 p.: bibl., ill.,
maps. (Col. Estudios. Educación)

Interesting analysis of the roles
played by Spanish refugees from the Civil
War of 1936–39, in Venezuelan education,
particularly in primary and secondary education. The author observes that the exiles
had the most impact in newly urbanizing
areas lacking in educational infrastructure,
and that primary and secondary educators
from Spain often found themselves con-
strained to forgo their former political and
pedagogical approaches in order to adapt to
Venezuelan reality. Focused mainly in and
around Caracas.

1592 Márquez, Walter Enrique. La nación
en armas: Venezuela y la defensa de
su soberanía, 1810–1812. Caracas: Ministerio de la Cultura, Consejo Nacional de
la Cultura, 2005. 175 p.: bibl. (Col. Alfredo
Maneiro. Política y sociedad. Serie en la
historia)

Calling for a re-examination of the
history of the First Republic by professional
historians. Arguing that the First Republic
failed because the military and political
model that had been followed—that of a
people in arms—did not consolidate independence when faced by a concerted Spanish counterattack.

1593 Martínez, Alirio R. Autoritarismo y
democracia: Venezuela, 1936–1941.
Caracas: Academia Nacional de la Historia,
Fondo Editorial de Humanidades y Educación, Universidad Central de Venezuela,
2004. 212 p.: bibl. (Col. Estudios. Historia)

Inspired by contemporary political
controversies, this is a study of the López
Contreras administration and era. The
author characterizes the regime as transitional, and seeks to "describe and try to
explain the attributes and changes perceived
in the ideas of the politicians and intellectuals who molded democratic and modernizing thought during the five years that began
in 1936," arguing that López Contreras's era
was crucial in shaping and defining Venezuelan democracy.

1594 Martínez Carretero, Ismael. Desde
la Nueva Andalucía hasta las tierras
del Nuevo Reino de Granada: 50 años de la
provincia Bética en Venezuela y Colombia,
1954–2004. Mérida, Venezuela: Archivo Ar-
quidiocesano de Mérida, 2005. 2 v. (976 p.):

bibl., ill. (Fuentes para la historia eclesiástica de Venezuela; 11–12)

Detailed two-volume examination of the activities of the Carmelite order in Venezuela and Colombia from 1954 to 2004. A Carmelite himself, the author emphasizes the important "civilizing" role played by clerics from Spain in both republics.

1595 Martínez Vásquez, Emma D. La educación de las mujeres en Venezuela, 1840–1912. Caracas: Fondo Editorial de la Facultad de Humanidades y Educación, Univ. Central de Venezuela, 2006. 325 p.: ill. (Col. Estudios. Educación)

Pioneering study of the education of girls and women in Venezuela in the 19th and early 20th centuries. The author notes that women's opportunities for education in the 19th century were circumscribed by societal ideas and values about gender roles; those opportunities nonetheless expanded somewhat in the early 20th century as a result of economic changes and a national shortage of trained labor.

1596 McBeth, Brian Stuart. Dictatorship & politics: intrigue, betrayal, and survival in Venezuela, 1908–1935. Notre Dame, Ind.: Univ. of Notre Dame Press, 2008. 578 p.: appendices, bibl., index, tables.

A detailed, impeccably researched, reassessment of the Juan Vicente Gómez regime and political opposition to it. The author argues that, contrary to much of the historiography of the Gómez era, the caudillo did not rely solely upon repression in order to stay in power. He further asserts that opposition to the regime was more sophisticated and complex than traditionally portrayed, and received aid from foreign governments.

1597 Monzant Gavidia, J.L. Las trampas de la historiografía adeca: el antiperezjimenismo en el Zulia. Maracaibo: Univ. Católica Cecilio Acosta, 2006. 103 p.: bibl. (Col. Investigación Mario Briceño Iragorry)

Detailed examination of the 1948–58 era of military government in the western Venezuelan state of Zulia, which challenges orthodox views of the establishment of civilian government in 1958. The author argues that opposition to the Pérez Jiménez regime in Zulia was independent of—and

actually opposed to—the seizure of power by Acción Democrática militants and dissident military officers.

1598 Neira, Enrique. Venezuela: IVa y Va repúblicas, 1958–2006. Mérida, Venezuela: Publicaciones Vicerrectorado Académico y CDCHT, Univ. de los Andes, 2006. 341 p.: bibl., ill., 1 map (Col. Ciencias sociales y humanidades)

Analysis of the politics of the Fourth and Fifth Republics. Arguing that the political system has recently become seriously polarized and lacking in pluralism. The author advocates both political reconciliation and reform in order to restore stability. Based primarily on newspapers and secondary sources.

1599 Olavarría, Jorge. Gómez: un enigma histórico: una revisión al fenómeno histórico y político de Juan Vicente Gómez. Caracas: Fundación Olavarría, 2007. 955 p., [72] p. of plates: bibl., ill. (some col.), ports., geneal. table

A "revisionist" analysis of the life and regime of Juan Vicente Gómez, as well as an analysis of the treatment accorded him by historians. According to the author, traditional historiography about the era has been distorted and tainted by "fallacies" developed to legitimize later governments. Asserts that Gómez enjoyed significant support within Venezuela, and argues that he came to power in response to widespread discontent with the violence and conflicts of the preceding period. The author also draws explicit parallels between the rise of Gómez and the emergence a century later of Hugo Chávez Frías.

1600 Pino Iturrieta, Elías. Nada sino un hombre: los orígenes del personalismo en Venezuela. Caracas: Editorial Alfa, 2007. 350 p.: bibl. (Biblioteca Elías Pino Iturrieta; 3)

Analysis of the roots of Venezuelan personalism since independence. The author asserts that personalist regimes originated almost with the foundation of the republic, in part as a result of the unwillingness of elites to entrust the populace with an active role in the nation's political life, enabling charismatic personalist leaders to present themselves as defenders of plebeian interests.

1601 Pretorianismo venezolano del siglo XXI: ensayos sobre las relaciones civiles y militares venezolanas. Coordinación de Domingo Irwin, Hernán Castillo G. y Frédérique Langue. Caracas: Univ. Católica Andrés Bello: Univ. Pedagógica Experimental "Libertador," Vicerrectorado de Investigación y Postgrado, Centro de Investigaciones Históricas "Mario Briceño Iragorry," 2007. 393 p.: bibl.

Collection of essays exploring the military's roles in Venezuelan politics and society. Generally disapproving in tone, the essays in the volume link the Chávez administration with earlier episodes of military rule in Venezuela, and portray the administration as a pernicious return to praetorian traditions and approaches to government.

1602 Ramírez López, Eduardo and **Constantino Quero Morales.** Isaías Medina Angarita: presidente de la transformación. Caracas: Univ. Católica Andrés Bello, 2006. 325 p.: ill.

Portrayal of the life and career of President Isías Medina Angarita. The author characterizes him as a man of vision who sought to modernize and develop Venezuela. Seeking to redress a perceived lacuna in the historical record, the author argues that the Medina era represented a major transition in Venezuela toward modernity and democracy.

1603 Resonancias de la africanidad. Contribuciones de Irma Marina Mendoza *et al.* Caracas: Fondo Editorial Ipasme, 2005. 192 p.: bibl.

Collection of essays exploring the role of Afro-Venezuelans in the history, society, literature, and cultural identity of Venezuela. Uneven in quality.

1604 Rincón Rubio, Luis. Muerte: salvación del alma e inmortalidad del honor en una parroquia rural de la Provincia de Maracaibo, 1784–1834. (*Procesos Hist.*, 7:14, 2008)

Provocative article examining funerary practices in a rural parish in the Maracaibo region during the late colonial and early republican eras. The author indicates significant continuity in mortuary rituals from the colonial era to the early 19th century, resulting from both the persistence

of religious belief and as a means of demonstrating the enduring status and power of the local elite.

1605 Rojas, Reinaldo. De Variquecemeto a Barquisimeto: siete estudios históricos. Prólogo de Kaldone Nweihed. Barquisimeto, Venezuela: Fondo Editorial de la Fundación Buria, 2002. 395 p.: bibl.

Collection of seven essays focusing on the history of Barquisimeto, compiled to commemorate the 450th anniversary of the city's founding. Based largely on published sources, newspapers, and secondary sources.

1606 Sánchez García, Antonio. Dictadura o democracia: Venezuela en la encrucijada. Caracas: Editorial Altazor, 2003. 399 p.: bibl.

A collection of essays and polemical newspaper articles critical of the Chávez government from a conservative viewpoint. The author accuses the current government of seizing upon and distorting the image of Bolívar in the service of its political agenda.

1607 Sosa de León, Mireya. La crisis diplomática entre Venezuela y México, 1920–1935: visión histórica. Caracas: Facultad de Humanidades y Educación, Univ. Central de Venezuela: Fondo Editorial Tropykos, 2006. 393 p.: ill.

Originally the author's dissertation, an analysis of a diplomatic crisis arising between Venezuela and revolutionary Mexico and extending for the better part of a decade. Arguing that ideological differences with Mexico's revolutionary government led to friction and a severing of diplomatic ties between Mexico and Venezuela.

1608 Suárez Figueroa, Naudy. Punto Fijo y otros puntos: los grandes acuerdos políticos de 1958. Estudio preliminar de Naudy Suárez Figueroa. Prólogo y selección de Naudy Suárez Figueroa. Caracas: Fundación Rómulo Betancourt, 2006. 91 p.: bibl. (Serie Cuadernos de ideas políticas; 1)

Brief study of the "spririt of the 23rd of January" and the Pact of Punto Fijo. Maintaining that the pact represented a major point of departure for Venezuela, as it marked the emergence of a national consensus in favor of electoral democracy. Written in response to recent attacks on the pact and the Fourth Republic by critics who view the pact and the parties involved as corrupt and insufficiently revolutionary.

1609 Tinker Salas, Miguel. The enduring legacy: oil, culture, and society in Venezuela. Durham, N.C.: Duke Univ. Press, 2009. 324 p.: bibl., index (American encounters/global interactions)

Based on archival sources and interviews, an exploration of the transforming impact of oil boom in Venezuela. The author argues the oil boom beginning in the early 20th century fundamentally and profoundly transformed the country's social structure, national identity, and culture, and that extant historical literature fails to capture the complexities of oil's impact on Venezuelan society. "In a country in which the majority of the population was rural and depended on agriculture for subsistence, oil production fundamentally altered the sociocultural landscape."

1610 Urbaneja, Diego Bautista. El gobierno de Carlos Soublette, o, La importancia de lo normal. Caracas: Univ. Católica Andrés Bello, 2006. 247 p.: bibl. (Col. historica; 8)

Arguing that Venezuela's political history should be studied not only with reference to crises and upheavals, the author presents an account of the Soublette administration (1843–47). While Soublette is overshadowed by José Antonio Páez, the author argues that his administration was a period of solid achievement and the construction of key political institutions. He also focuses on the institutions of government, rather than on the figure and activity of the president, and maintains that personalist regimes and the decline in institutional function in 19th-century Venezuela were not inevitable.

1611 Urdaneta Quintero, Arlene. Separatismo y anexionismo en el Zulia, siglo XIX, Venezuela. (*Procesos Hist.*, 7:13, primer semestre 2008, p. 66–83)

Essay examining the complex relationships between various regions of western Venezuela in the 19th century. The author argues that declarations of autonomy by the government of Zulia, as well as efforts to unite the Venezuelan Andes with Maracaibo, represented political gambits and responses to a centralism inimical to regional and local interests rather than an active threat to national integrity. She notes also the central government's efforts to divide and disarticulate the regions of the west, in the service of its own supremacy.

1612 Urdaneta Quintero, Arlene. Tiempos de federación en el Zulia: construir la nación en Venezuela. Caracas: Academia Nacional de la Historia, 2008. 398 p.: bibl., map. (Biblioteca de la Academia Nacional de la Historia. Fuentes para la historia republicana de Venezuela; 92)

Published by the Academia Nacional de la Historia, an important new analysis of the era of federalism in 19th-century Zulia. Challenging traditional arguments portraying federalists as obstacles to national political integration, the author argues that Maracaibo's federalists supported Venezuelan unity while seeking to preserve a balance between national and local interests.

1613 Valery S., Rafael. La territorialidad de Venezuela: origen, formación, integración y cambios de nuestro patrimonio territorial. Prólogo por Aníbal R. Martínez. Caracas: Fundación Empresas Polar: Fundación Juan José Aguerrevere, Colegio de Ingenieros de Venezuela, 2006. 144 p.: bibl., maps.

Written by an architect, an historical study of the boundaries and territorial limits of Venezuela from the colonial era until the end of the 20th century. The author calls for education about Venezuela's territorial losses to its neighbors, in order to press for redress of land loss.

1614 Venezuela y Colombia: debates de la historia y retos del presente. Coordinación académico y edición de Socorro Ramírez y José María Cadenas. Caracas: Univ. Central de Venezuela; Colombia: IEPRI de la Universidad Nacional de Colombia, 2005. 293 p.: bibl., ill.

The product of a binational academic team, a collection of essays addressing the complex relationship between Venezuela and Colombia, from both historical and contemporary perspectives. Dealing with the history and present state of the complex and often tortured relationship between the two neighboring states.

1615 Virtuoso Arrieta, Francisco José.
Justicia social en Venezuela: la
preocupación social de la Compañía de
Jesús en Venezuela, 1968–1992. Caracas:
Univ. Católica Andrés Bello, 2004. 471 p.:
bibl.

Billed as an intellectual history of
Jesuit ideas about social justice, this is in
reality a study examining the promotion of
social justice by members of the Jesuit order
in Venezuela from 1968–92 through their
publication, *SIC*. The author asserts that the
Jesuit approach was to empower the poor
and enable them to liberate themselves,
and argues that current political turmoil in
Venezuela is in large part the result of social problems that went unaddressed by the
governments of previous decades.

Colombia and Ecuador

JANE M. RAUSCH, *Professor Emerita of History, University of Massachusetts-Amherst*

WELL-CRAFTED, INNOVATIVE HISTORICAL SCHOLARSHIP appears to be an
ever-expanding phenomenon in Colombia. The number of entries included in this
reporting period is nearly twice that selected for *HLAS 64*. Even more remarkable
is, that despite this increase, only two items concern La Violencia—a topic that
has dominated 20th-century political writing for almost two decades. Another
striking development is the number of new syntheses of national history, including Rodríguez Baquero's edited volume (item **1645**), updating the essential *Manual
de Historia de Colombia (1982)*. Finally, there are thoughtful reevaluations of the
contributions of 19th-century scholars, including José Manuel Restrepo, Miguel
Antonio Caro, and Francisco Vergara y Velasco. For the 20th century, not to be
missed is Jaramillo Uribe's autobiography, a fascinating memoir by the "padre de
la Nueva Historia" in Colombia (item **1649**).

Concerning the independence era, along with studies of the war's impact on
Cartagena and Pasto, Lasso, in an article published in the prestigious *American
Historical Review*, (item **1650**) explains why the anticolonial struggle in New
Granada generated nationalism embracing a myth of racial harmony, while the
North American Revolution solidified racial separation. Two well-researched
studies reexamine educational developments (items **1628** and **1640**), and Murray's
brilliant biography of long-neglected Manuela Sáenz fills a significant gap in our
understanding of Bolívar's career and the period in general (item **1660**).

For the 19th century, the Federation Era (1863–85) has attracted renewed
attention. Sparked by a 2006 Universidad Nacional seminar, 15 prominent historians have contributed essays on major figures in a volume edited by Sierra Mejía
(item **1670**), while three other books provide perspective into the Liberals' struggle
to reform primary education.

With regard to regional studies, Antioquia leads again with monographs
and articles concerning economic development and changing women's roles. Of
special note is Gärtner's chronicle of the department's struggle with neighboring
Cauca over the possession of the Cantón de Supía, a region that would become the
Department of Caldas in 1905. (item **1641**). There are three volumes dealing with
Tolima, and the Department of César sponsored its first academic conference in

2006, resulting in a collection of essays on varied aspects of Caribbean history (item **1618**).

Balancing books on regionalism are studies investigating the evolution of nationalism. Three books stress contributions of foreign immigrants to the Colombian nation, especially those of the so-called "árabes" or people from the Middle East, notwithstanding their small numbers (items **53, 1639, 1686**). Two other studies (items **1658** and **1688**) suggest that it was attitudes held by the highland elite that reduced the peripheral lowlands of Amazonia, the Llanos Orientales and the Pacific Coast to "frontiers," since they deliberately excluded mestizos and Afro-Colombians from their construction of national identity.

The thesis that Colombia embraced the 20th century during Rafael Reyes' controversial *quinquenio* (1904–09) receives support from Mazzuca and Robinson's *Hispanic American Historical Review* article. They show how the adoption of "the incomplete vote" system of 1905 helped to restore political peace after decades of civil war (item **1654**). Two novel topics are higher education and the role of the press. Regarding the first, Piñeres de la Ossa emphasizes the importance of the Universidad of Cartagena in the region's progress (item **1668**), while León Cáceres looks at the contribution of nonacademic employees in the development of the Universidad Nacional in Bogotá and Medellín (item **1652**). As for the media, Vera Zapata assesses the impact of Colombia's major newspapers in interpreting World War II events (item **1687**), Núñez Espinel investigates the relationship between periodicals and emerging class consciousness (item **1662**), Ayala Diago shows how *El Tiempo* deliberately misrepresented activities of opponents of the Frente Nacional (item **1617**), while Acevedo C. demonstrates how editorial cartoons can be analyzed as graphic indicators of political attitudes (item **1616**).

The 26 items concerning Ecuador likewise reflect a continuing emphasis on high quality scholarship. As in the case of Colombia, there are new comprehensive surveys of national history, but the standout contribution is surely Clark and Becker's edited volume, *Highland Indians and the State in Modern Ecuador* (item **1704**) a compilation of essays focusing on changing forms of indigenous engagement with the state from the early 19th century to the beginning of the 20th.

Prominent among entries on the 19th century is Henderson's revisionist biography of García Moreno (item **1702**). His conclusions are reinforced by Buriano's study of periodicals published between 1860–75, which challenges the image of conservatives as monolithic, political ideologues (item **1692**). Articles on the 20th century examine education and the evolution of the Socialist Party. There is a well-written monograph on the institutional history of the Banco Central, and a pioneering essay on the creation of the Forestry Department in 1948. Finally, and most intriguing is Lanázuri Camacho's history of the Hospital Psiquiátrico San Lázaro (item **1706**), a groundbreaking contribution since the study of the treatment of mental illness has received scant attention from Latin American scholars.

COLOMBIA

1616 Acevedo Carmona, Darío. Política y caudillos colombianos en la caricatura editorial, 1920–1950: estudio de los imaginarios políticos partidistas. Medellín, Colombia: Carreta Editores: Univ. Nacional de Colombia, 2009. 281 p.: bibl., ill., indexes. (La Carreta política)

By focusing on caricatures of leading political figures published in *El Tiempo, El Siglo, El Liberal, El Colombiano,* and *Revistas Semana y Cromos,* Acevedo Carmona offers unique insight into political partisanship in the 20th century. Meticulous research demonstrates that editorial cartoons are overlooked but valid historical documents in understanding political attitudes.

1617 Ayala Diago, César Augusto. Exclusión, discriminación y abuso de poder en *El Tiempo del Frente Nacional*: una aproximación desde el análisis crítico del discurso (ACD). Bogotá: Univ. Nacional de Colombia, Facultad de Ciencias Humanas, Departamento de Historia, Línea de Investigación en Historia Política y Social, 2008. 363 p.: bibl., ill., indexes. (Biblioteca abierta; 359. Col. general. Historia)

Examines *El Tiempo*'s editorial strategies to misrepresent activities of Alianza Nacional Popular (Anapo) and Movimiento Revolucionario Liberal (MRL) as eminent threats to the policies of Frente Nacional. Demonstrates that the newspaper consistently supported the "noble ideals" of National Front politicians as opposed to the anarchy espoused by the opposition.

Ayala Diago, César Augusto. El populismo atrapado, la memoria y el miedo: el caso de las elecciones de 1970. See *HLAS 65:1587*.

1618 Becas culturales en investigación sociocultural en historia regional y/o local del departamento del Cesar: resultados de la primera convo[ca]toria. Cartagena de Indias, Colombia: Observatorio del Caribe Colombiano, 2006. 390 p.: ill.

Seven papers presented at the first academic conference sponsored by the Department of Cesar's government and the Observatorio del Caribe Colombia in 2006. Two essays deal with the independence period; another concerns 19th-century agrarian structure. Twentieth-century topics include commerce, gender, and poetry. The volume reflects a growing interest in regional history.

1619 Betancourt Mendieta, Alexander. Historia y nación: tentativas de la escritura de la historia en Colombia. Medellín, Colombia: Carreta Editores: San Luis Potosí, Mexico: Univ. Autónoma San Luis Potosí, Coordinación de Ciencias Sociales y Humanidades, 2007. 293 p.: bibl. (La Carreta histórica)

Traces currents in the writing of Colombian history by Colombian scholars with a focus on 20th-century trends. Suggests that despite professionalization of investigations after the 1960s, historiography is still limited by the absence of debate and the need to include all segments of Colombian society. Unquestionably, an essential contribution to the field of historiography.

1620 Blanco B., José Agustín. El general Francisco Javier Vergara y Velasco y sus obras. Bogotá: Academia Colombiana de Historia, 2006. 219 p.: bibl., facsims., index, port. (Col. Germán Arciniegas; 3)

Vergara y Velasco (1860–1914) is best known for his *Nueva Geografía de Colombia* (1901–02), but he was also an engineer, educator, and general who helped to reform the military. Part I covers all aspects of his life. Part II contains analysis of his books. Part III includes periodical articles. Useful introduction to a seldom studied, multifaceted individual.

1621 Botero, María Mercedes. La ruta del oro: una economía primaria exportadora: Antioquia, 1850–1890. Medellín, Colombia: Fondo Editorial Univ. EAFIT, 2007. 289 p.: bibl., charts, ill., maps.

In-depth investigation into the exploitation of gold and changes that occurred in its internal circulation, different mining locations, network of export agents, and forms (i.e. dust, coins, bars). Shows importance of gold in domestic as well as export economy in second half of 19th century. Helpful charts and extensive bibliography.

1622 Botero Herrera, Fernando. Estado, nación y provincia de Antioquia: guerras civiles e invención de la región, 1829–1863. Medellín, Colombia: Hombre Nuevo Editores, 2003. 198 p.: bibl., maps. (Col. Historia)

Author challenges the prevailing notion that Antioquia achieved remarkable stability after 1864 because it was only marginally affected by civil wars in the first half of the 19th century. Argues instead that the "unity and cohesion" of the region were due to earlier military defeats that were fundamental in focusing Antioqueño attention on economic development. Helpful maps and bibliography.

1623 Bucheli, Marcelo. Enforcing business contracts in South America: the United Fruit Company and Colombian banana planters in the twentieth century. (*Bus. Hist. Rev./Boston*, 78:2, Summer 2004, p. 181–212, bibl., graphs)

Enlarging on a topic addressed in his book *Bananas and Business* (2006), Bucheli focuses on the local entrepeneurs who signed contracts with the United Fruit Company. Compares local private contractors in Magdalena and Urabá. Concludes UFCO investments initiated the banana industry, but eventually Magdalena entrepreneurs were able to develop a parallel operation.

1624 Buitrago Parra, José del Carmen. Guerrilleros, campesinos y política en el Sumapaz: El Frente Democratico de Liberación Nacional 1953–1956. Ibagué, Colombia: Univ. del Tolima, 2006. 204 p.: appendices, bibl., facsims., maps. (Col. Universidad del Tolima 50 años; 5)

Study of FDLN (1953–56), a guerrilla group located in the Sumapaz region that was eventually crushed by Rojas Pinilla's military government. Includes underlying conditions leading to group's formation, its political ideology, methods of finance, and defeat at the Battle of Villarrica. FDLN survivors fled to the Llanos. Helpful insight into the campesino aspect of La Violencia in the 1950s.

1625 Cardona Tobón, Alfredo. Los caudillos del desastre. Manizales, Colombia: Univ. Autónoma de Manizales, 2006. 326 p.: bibl., ill.

An engineer surveys 19th-century civil wars, emphasizing confrontations between Antioqueño and Caucano caudillos. Blames these men for bringing death and destruction to the Colombian countryside and delaying national unity, when they might have used their leadership talents for furthering the country's progress.

1626 Cardona Zuluaga, Patricia. La nación de papel: textos escolares, lectura, y política. Estados Unidos de Colombia, 1870–1876. Medellín, Colombia: Fondo Editorial, Universidad EAFIT, 2007. 180 p.: bibl., ill. (some col.) (Col. Académica)

Close analysis of elementary school texts introduced during the school reform (1870–76) reveals the authors' efforts to indoctrinate students with liberal principals. Emphasis on the Radical Era, but takes into account the impact of earlier 19th-century texts in shaping the conflict between liberal and conservative ideas. Important, ground-breaking contribution.

1627 Castro Carvajal, Beatriz. Caridad y beneficiencia, el tratamiento de la pobreza en Colombia 1870–1930. Bogotá: Univ. Externado de Colombia, 2007. 351 p.: bibl., map, tables.

Solidly researched monograph that describes two approaches to helping Colombia's poor between 1870 and 1930: institutional aid (i.e. shelters administered by religious orders), and home aid (i.e. building houses, schools and promoting savings accounts). The state increased its collaboration after 1910. By 1920, a network of institutions and societies to aid the poor had been created.

1628 Clark, Meri L. Conflictos entre el Estado y las elites locales sobre la educación colombiana durante las décadas de 1820 y 1830. (*Hist. Crít./Bogotá*, 34, julio/dic. 2007, p. 32–61, bibl.)

Provides new dimension to the 1820s educational campaign by examining conflicts between state and local elites over teaching methods, taxes, and curriculum. Case studies of Nemocón and Zipaquirá reveal indigenous leaders' reluctance to surrender *resguardo* lands to benefit schools, while leaders in Mompox preferred private charity over public support of education.

1629 Colombia: building peace in a time of war. Edited by Virginia M. Bouvier. Washington, DC: United States Institute of Peace, 2009. 488 p.: bibl., graphs, index, maps.

Compilation of essays by 30 authors, human rights activists, and peace practitioners from Colombia and abroad with the aim of analyzing peace initiatives proposed during the past two decades. The conclusion offers a spectrum of practical lessons for Colombia and those seeking to transform violent conflicts in other parts of the globe.

1630 Colpas Gutiérrez, Jaime. La formación del Departamento del Atlántico, 1905–1915: quinquenio y republicanismo en Colombia. Barranquilla, Colombia: Ediciones Barranquilla, 2005. 232 p.: bibl., ill., maps, ports.

Well-researched master's thesis investigates the creation of the Department of Atlántico, a project originating in 1905 during the Quinquenio. Places the question within the framework of national political struggles. Concludes that Atlántico's existence was a product of Rafael Reyes' political interests and not an initiative promoted by Barranquilla elites.

1631 Conde Calderón, Jorge. Buscando la nación: ciudadanía, clase y tensión racial en el Caribe colombiano, 1821–1855. Medellín, Colombia: La Carreta Editores: Univ. del Atlántico, 2009. 370 p.: bibl., ill. (La Carreta histórica)

Traces the definition during the first half of the 19th century of concepts of "citizen" and "nation" by Caribbean elites within a society dominated by pardos and blacks. Extensive use of archival and secondary sources.

1632 Correa Restrepo, Juan Santiago. Prensa de oposición: el radicalismo derrotado, 1880–1902. Bogotá: Univ. Externado de Colombia, 2007. 285 p. (Biblioteca de historia de las ideas; 7)

Collection of representative articles (for the most part unsigned) appearing in liberal journals opposing conservative rule after 1884. Taken as a group, they present a program rejecting violence in favor of a new political culture based on tolerance, democracy, and protection of civil liberties. Valuable insight into the Regeneration Era.

1633 David Bravo, Alba Inés. Mujer y trabajo en Medellín: condiciones laborales y significado social, 1850–1906. Medellín, Colombia: Instituto para el Desarrollo de Antioquia, IDEA, 2007. 159 p.: bibl., ill. (Col.; 6)

Prizewinning monograph charts the changing roles of women in Medellín in the second half of the 19th century. Topics cover the situations of elite and lower class women, marriage legislation, feminine ideals promoted in the press by liberals and conservatives, and the efforts made by women to seize work opportunities.

1634 Del Castillo, Lina. "Prefiriendo siempre a los agrimensores científicos": discriminación en la medición y el reparto de resguardos indígenas en el altiplano cundiboyacense, 1821–1854. (*Hist. Crít./Bo-*

gotá, 32, julio/dic. 2006, p. 68–93, bibl., map, table)

Explains how surveyors trained in the national military schools consolidated Bogotá's power over the privatization of *resguardos* and legitimated a process that fomented ethnic and gender discrimination. Study exposes flaws in the laws governing this process, permitting Bogotá to usurp powers of the Indian cabildos and provincial *jefes políticos*.

1635 Elías Caro, Jorge Enrique. La radiodifusión en Santa Marta, Colombia. (*Secuencia/México*, 72, sept./dic. 2008, p. 13–34, bibl.)

Combines oral tradition, newspapers and local archival material to trace the origins and development of broadcasting in Santa Marta with emphasis on early radio's cultural and social impact on Caribbean region. Good starting place for scholars interested in radio studies in Colombia.

1636 Froysland, Hayley. The regeneración de la raza in Colombia. (*in* Nationalism in the new world. Edited by Don H. Doyle and Marco Antonio Pamplona. Athens: Univ. of Georgia Press, 2006, p. 162–183)

Provides new insight on the Regeneration Era by suggesting that between 1880 and 1930, Colombian elites attempted to create a national consciousness based on charity and morality. Argues that although elites were "deeply pessimistic about the Colombian raza," they sought to incorporate the poor into their Catholic, moral, and personal world.

1637 Fuentes documentales para la historia empresarial. Siglo XIX en Antioquia. Compilación de Jairo Andrés Campuzan Hoyos. Medellín, Colombia: Fondo Editorial Universidad EAFIT, 2006. 1 v. (429 p.): bibl., facsims., ill., index.

First of a proposed series of volumes reproducing documents fundamental for the study of economic development in 19th-century Antioquia. Contains 42 documents transcribed from notarial manuscripts designed to provide a framework to trace economic growth from 1587 to 1897.

1638 Gálvez Abadía, Aída Cecilia. Por obligación de conciencia: los misioneros del Carmen Descalzo en Urabá, Colombia, 1918–1941. Bogotá: Escuela de

Ciencias Humanas: Univ. Colegio Mayor de Nuestra Señora del Rosario: Editorial Univ. del Rosario: Univ. de Antioquia, Facultad de Ciencias Sociales y Humanas: Instituto Colombiano de Antropología e Historia, 2006. 216 p.: bibl., ill., index. (Col. Textos de ciencias humanas)

Anthropologist provides a unique history of 20th-century missions in Urabá by focusing on narratives written by Prefect José Joaquín de la Virgen del Carmen and Brother Amando de la Virgen del Carmen. Narratives describe their very real suffering in obeying their duty to convert "savages" in a "hostile" environment.

1639 García Estrada, Rodrigo de J. Los extranjeros en Colombia: su aporte a la construcción de la nación, 1810–1920. Bogotá: Planeta, 2006. 240 p.: bibl.

Authoritative survey of the impact of immigration on the development of Colombia between 1810–1933. Demonstrates that government efforts to attract foreigners were largely failures, but despite their small numbers, Europeans, North Americans, and people from the Middle East made important contributions to the nation with their "blood, ideas, dreams and abilities."

1640 García Sánchez, Bárbara Yadira. De la educación doméstica a la educación pública en Colombia: transiciones de la colonia a la república. Bogotá: Fondo de Publicaciones, Univ. Distrital Francisco José de Caldas, 2007. 482 p.: bibl., ill.

Well-researched, revised dissertation compares education during the colonial era with changes legislated in the 1820s. As schooling moved out of homes and into public places, the government took over both the control and vigilance formerly wielded by parents. Parental resistance became one of the obstacles that complicated the state's plan to form new citizens.

1641 Gärtner, Álvaro. Guerras civiles en el antiguo Cantón de Supía: relatos de episodios armados acaecidos entre el siglo XVI y el XIX: luchas por las tierras del oro. Manizales, Colombia: Editorial Univ. de Caldas, 2006. 294 p.: bibl., index, map, photos. (Col. Ciencias jurídicas y sociales)

During the 19th century, Antioquia and Cauca fought for possession of the Cantón de Supía that separated the two provinces. Gärtner demonstrates that recurrent battles there reflected not only the widespread civil wars of 1860–63 and 1876–77, but also the struggle between rival provinces. The result was a compromise leading to the creation of the Department of Caldas in 1905. Excellent example of how little-known local history can provide insight into national developments.

1642 Giraldo Castaño, Germán Hislen. La colonización en la Orinoquia colombiana: Arauca, 1900–1980. Bogotá: G.H. Giraldo Castaño, 2006. 217 p.: bibl., ill., graphs, maps.

Groundbreaking history focusing on peasant colonization from the end of the 19th century through 1980. Discussions of the illegal feather trade and the impact of the Caja Agraria and INCORA on colonization are among other topics. Useful comparisons with other peripheral territories. Extensive bibliography, maps, and graphs. For historians of the Llanos, clearly a tour de force.

1643 Gutiérrez Ramos, Jairo. Los indios de Pasto contra la República, 1809–1824. Bogotá: Instituto Colombiano de Antropología e Historia, 2007. 274 p.: bibl. (Col. Año 200)

Draws material from Colombian, Spanish, and Ecuadorian archives to explain why Pastuso Indians supported Spanish colonialism and fought against the effort by patriot armies and their own elite leaders to establish independence. Argues that their struggle constituted a manifestation of regional identity and autonomy.

1644 Hernández García, José Ángel. La Guerra Civil Española y Colombia: influencia del principal conflicto de entreguerras en Colombia. Chía, Colombia: Univ. de La Sabana; Bogotá: Editorial Carrera 7a, 2006. 327 p.: bibl., ill.

Revisionist study suggests that day-to-day notices of the Spanish Civil War in *El Tiempo* and *El Siglo* simulated Colombian interest in international events for the first time. Liberals supported constitutionalists while conservatives championed Franco's forces. Data challenges popular belief that Colombians enthusiastically welcomed exiles from the conflict. Important addition to literature dealing with the Liberal Republic.

1645 Historia de Colombia: todo lo que hay que saber. Bogotá: Taurus, 2006. 366 p.: bibl. (Pensamiento)

Essays written by five prominent social scientists, arranged chronologically to provide an overview of Colombian history from precolumbian times to 1991. Basically, a one-volume update of the *Manual de Historia de Colombia* published in 1982 (see *HLAS 56:2307*). Contributors represent a new generation of historians who draw on materials produced since the 1980s. Useful compendium.

1646 Historia económica de Colombia. Compliación de José Antonio Ocampo Gaviria. 1st ed. revisada y actualizada. Bogotá: Planeta, 2007. 440 p.: bibl., graphs, tables.

Revised, updated collaborative text on economic history, first published in 1988. Reproduces the first six chapters of the 1988 volume that examine developments between 1500–1945. Chapter 7 (1945–80) has been shortened and revised. Most welcome is a new final chapter that carries the analysis up to 2006. Expanded bibliography. Essential reference that incorporates work of 11 distinguished scholars.

1647 Historia local: experiencias, métodos y enfoques. Compilación de Renzo Ramírez Bacca. Medellín, Colombia: La Carreta Editores; Facultad de Ciencias Sociales y Humanas, Univ. de Antioquia, 2005. 261 p.: bibl.

Proceedings of first Simposio Colombiano de Historia Local, sponsored by the Universidad de Antioquia in 2004, organized to promote debate and comparisons with other universities. Nine papers address the historical tendencies of local history in Colombia in recent years, examine their theoretical and methodological components, and provide some examples by Antioqueñan professors.

1648 Jaramillo Salgado, Diego. Satanización del socialismo y del comunismo en Colombia 1930–1953. Popayán, Colombia: Univ. del Cauca, Facultad de Ciencias Humanas y Sociales, Depto. de Filosofía, 2007. 311 p.: bibl. (Col. Cultura y política)

Revised doctoral dissertation explains how the Catholic Church and conservatives demonized socialism, communism, and even liberals, during the so-called Liberal Republic. Includes an extensive description of the socialist movement during this era. Shows how divisions between socialist leaders also served to weaken the movement.

1649 Jaramillo Uribe, Jaime. Memorias intelectuales. Bogotá: Taurus, 2007. 304 p.: ill., ports. (Memorias y biografías)

Autobiography written by one of Colombia's most distinguished historians. Born in 1917, Jaramillo reflects on Colombian history throughout the 20th century as he recalls his education, European experiences in the 1940s and 50s, academic and intellectual production, and ambassadorships. Fascinating memoir by the "padre de la Nueva Historia" in Colombia.

1650 Lasso, Marixa. Race war and nation in Caribbean Gran Colombia, Cartagena, 1810–1832. (*Am. Hist. Rev.*, 111:2, April 2006, p. 336–361, bibl., map)

Offers theory to explain differences between US and Latin American race relations. Suggests that the critical era was the emergence of nationalism during the revolutionary age. Argues that anticolonial movements in French and Spanish America endorsed a myth of racial harmony while the North American revolution only solidified racial separation.

1651 León, Claudia Leal. Un puerto en la selva: naturaleza y raza en la creación de la ciudad de Tumaco, 1860–1940. (*Hist. Crít./Bogotá*, 30, julio/dic. 2005, p. 39–65, bibl.)

Geographer looks at impact of tagua exploitation on the development of port of Tumaco. Suggests, among other conclusions, that tagua harvesting did not damage the forests, and that racial division of labor with Afro-Colombians as collectors and white elites as managers created tensions within the city, limiting its growth.

1652 León Cáceres, María Piedad. Servidores del saber: memoria histórica de los trabajadores de la Universidad Nacional de Colombia, 1940–1980. Medellín, Colombia: Univ. Nacional de Colombia, Sede Medellín, Facultad de Ciencias Humanas y

Económicas, Comité de Publicaciones, 2008. 236 p.: bibl., ill. (Col. humanista)

PhD thesis traces the role of nonacademic workers (i.e. administrators, service employees, manual laborers) in the development of the Universidad Nacional de Bogotá and Medellín. Noting that the contributions made by these employees are traditionally ignored, the author melds archival material, interviews with retired workers, laws, and a vast bibliography of secondary sources into an insightful narrative.

1653 Malvehy Ramírez, Daniel Enrique.
La actividad empresarial de los inmigrantes "árabes" en San Andrés, 1953–2000. Bogotá: Univ. de Los Andes, Facultad de Administración, 2005. 131 p.: appendices, bibl., graphs, ill., photos, tables. (Monografías de administración. Serie Mejores proyectos de grado, 89)

Tesis de grado examines the impact of "Arab" immigrants on the San Andres economy. Based on archival and published sources, as well as six interviews. Emphasizes the era when the island was a free port (1952–91). Provides insight into the history, society, and economy of a department often ignored in Colombian studies.

1654 Mazzuca, Sebastián and James A. Robinson. Political conflict and power sharing in the origins of modern Colombia. (*HAHR*, 89:2, May 2009, p. 285–321)

Two political scientists investigate the role of adoption in the "incomplete vote" system of 1905, which guaranteed the minority party one-third of seats in the national legislature. Reflects the revisionist view of Rafael Reyes' quinquenio by pointing out that this measure restored political peace to Colombia after decades of civil war.

1655 Mejía Macía, Sergio Andrés. La revolución en letras: la historia de la Revolución en Colombia de José Manuel Restrepo, 1781–1863. Bogotá: Univ. de Los Andes, Facultad de Ciencias Sociales, Departamento de Historia, Centro de Estudios Socioculturales e Internacionales; Medellín, Colombia: Fondo Editorial Univ. EAFIT, 2007. 294 p.: bibl., ill., index.

Ph.D. thesis analyzes Restrepo's history of the War of Independence, a work considered the "cornerstone" of Colombian historiography. Examines the book from a cultural, political, and nationalistic point of view. Provides a general discussion of Restrepo's ideas as well as his view of Bolívar's importance. Includes catalogs of titles in both Restrepo's and Antonio Nariño's libraries.

1656 Mejía P., Germán. Los años del cambio: historia urbana de Bogotá, 1820–1910. Santa Fe de Bogotá: Pontificia Univ. Javeriana, Facultad de Ciencias Sociales, Departamento de Historia: Instituto Colombiano de Cultura Hispanica, 1999. 498 p.: bibl., ill., maps. (Biblioteca personal)

Massive history of 19th-century Bogotá, challenges the assumption that the city's colonial nature did not change until after 1930 and the onset of industrialization. Uses archival materials to chart developments and argues that the 1870s mark the period when Bogotá became a bourgeois urban center. Major contribution to urban history.

1657 Mejía Restrepo, Isabela. La soberanía del 'pueblo' durante la época de la Independencia,1810–1815. (*Hist. Crít./Bogotá*, 29, enero/junio 2005, p. 101–123, map)

In 1810, following the collapse of the Spanish monarchy in 1808, New Granada provinces proclaimed their sovereignty and constituted provisional governments. Author uses various contemporary sources to review debates in Santafé, Cartagena, and Mompox over the process of claiming sovereignty. Shows how other towns claimed independence, complicating the emergence of political legitimacy.

1658 Múnera, Alfonso. Fronteras imaginadas: la construcción de las razas y de la geografía en el siglo XIX colombiano. Bogotá: Planeta, 2005. 225 p.: bibl.

Seven related essays examine how the intellectual elite constructed national identity in the 19th century by deliberately excluding mestizo and Afro-Colombians. This approach contributed to converting the lowland coastal regions, the Llanos, and Amazonia into frontier territories and branded their inhabitants as inferior and marginal to the nation.

1659 Muñoz Cordero, Lydia Inés. Todo por la patria!: el conflicto colombo-peruano y Clara E. Narváez, el cabo Pedro. San Juan de Pasto, Colombia: Ministerio de Cultura, República de Colombia: Fondo Mixto de Cultura Nariño, 2006. 233 p.: bibl., charts, facsims., ill., maps, ports. (Col. Sol de los pastos. Historia)

Unique view of the Colombian-Peruvian War of 1932. Author focuses on the participation of Clara Elisa Naváez Arteaga, who, spurred by patriotism, joined the army as the only woman soldier, and fought so valiantly that she received the name, "cabo Pedro." Also shows how the conflict impacted Nariño and Pasto.

1660 Murray, Pamela S. For glory and Bolívar: the remarkable life of Manuela Sáenz. Foreword by Fredrick B. Pike. Austin: Univ. of Texas Press, 2008. 222 p.: bibl., index, map, ports.

Definitive, comprehensive, archival based biography of Sáenz (1797–1856), who was Bolívar's friend, lover, and confidante. Exposes many myths about La Libertadora. Well-written narrative examines her role in the 1820s and her political activities while in exile in Paita, Peru. Murray balances recognition of Sáenz's uniqueness with awareness of the broader forces that shaped her.

1661 Niño Vargas, Juan Camilo. Hombres rojos pintados de rojo: observaciones sobre los viajes de Joseph de Brettes al Territorio Chimila en 1895–1896. (*Bol. Hist. Antig.*, 94:837, abril/mayo 2007, p. 237–284, bibl., photos)

Anthropologist assesses observations contained in two separate accounts by a French traveler to the Caribbean region in the 1890s. Concludes that while his information about the Chimila natives includes some errors, it remains a valuable source of information about this group for contemporary investigators.

1662 Núñez Espinel, Luz Ángela. El obrero ilustrado: prensa obrera y popular en Colombia 1909–1929. Bogotá: Univ. de Los Andes, Facultad de Ciencias Sociales-CESO, Departamento de Historia, 2006. 230 p.: bibl., ill. (Col. Prometeo)

Analysis of approximately 150 labor and popular periodicals published between 1900–30, emphasizing their relation to popular culture and national politics during conservative rule and the impact of capitalist modernization. Shows that the press played a key role in emerging class

consciousness. Essential study for labor and social historians.

1663 Ortiz Bernal, José Afranio. El Tolima en la historia nacional: ensayos. Bogotá: Editorial Códice, 2006. 224 p.: ill., maps. (Biblioteca libanense de cultura; 10)

Three essays offer insight into aspects of Tolima's history and suggest that this "geographical and spiritual heart of Colombia" has always played an important role in national development. Included are: "La cuestión agraria y el campesinado tolimense en la historia regional"; "'La Violencia'" en el Tolima (1948–1958)," and "La historia política del Tolima (1810–1958)."

1664 Ortiz Mesa, Luis Javier. Fusiles y plegarias: guerra de guerrillas en Cundinamarca, Boyacá y Santander, 1876–1877. Medellín, Colombia: Univ. Nacional de Colombia, Sede Medellín, Dirección de Investigaciones, 2004. 203 p.: bibl, ill., maps.

Investigation of the civil war of 1876–77, with emphasis on the activities of conservative guerrillas. Places conflict in the context of constant civil strife after independence. Shows how fighting affected life in the capital and center of republic. Provides insight into the Federation Era and conflict between lay and Catholic primary schools.

1665 Pachón Muñoz, Álvaro. La infraestructura de transporte en Colombia durante el siglo XX. Bogotá: Banco de la República: Ediciones Fondo de Cultura Economica, 2006. 548 p.: bibl., cd-rom (Anexo estadístico), charts, maps. (Sección de obras de economía)

Encyclopedic analysis of the evolution of transportation infrastructure and its impact on the economic development of Colombia. Part I, authored by Ramírez, covers 1900–1950. Part II, authored by Pachón, covers 1950–2000. Includes discussion of railroads, highways, ships, and airlines. Comes with CD-ROM packed with statistics for all transport types. Essential reference for transport research.

1666 Palacios, Marco. El café en Colombia, 1850–1970: una historia económica, social y política. 4a. edición corregida y actualizada. México: El Colegio de México; 2009. 575 p.: bibl., ill., index.

Fourth edition of classic work includes a new introduction with an interpretive synthesis of the development of coffee production in Colombia and the world, from its initiation to the beginning of the 19th century.

1667 Patiño Villa, Carlos Alberto. Las fortalezas de Colombia: ¿una contradicción? (*Actual/Mérida*, 59/60, mayo/dic. 2005, p. 97–123)

Interesting thesis challenges Colombia's ambivalent nationhood by demonstrating that recent decades of violence, in contrast to 19th-century civil wars, have affected all regions, bonding them together with a common identity. As a result, the state has become stronger in its efforts to "integrate the population and direct the society beyond political parties."

1668 Píneres de la Ossa, Dora. Modernidad, universidad y región: el caso de la Universidad de Cartagena, 1920–1946. Cartagena, Colombia: Univ. de Cartagena; Tunja: Univ. Pedagógica y Tecnológica de Colombia; San Juan de Pasto: Rudecolombia, 2008. 406 p.: bibl., ill. (Col. Tesis doctorales Rudecolombia)

A history of the Universidad de Cartagena that emphasizes important reforms introduced in the late 1920s to fight a national program to suppress departmental universities, which resulted in modernizing the institution. Topics include pedagogical practices, student movements, and the introduction of women to the university. Shows that the university played an important role in the region's progress.

1669 Quintero, Inés. El surgimiento de las historiografías nacionales: Venezuela y Colombia, una perspectiva comparada. (*Hist. Soc./Medellín*, 11, sept. 2005, p. 93–113)

Compares the key trends of Venezuelan and Colombian historiography, taking into account generations of historians and adopted methodologies. Concludes that emerging patterns are similar to those in other Latin American countries. Useful review and introduction to the intellectual histories of both countries.

1670 El radicalismo colombiano del siglo XIX. Edición de Rubén Sierra Mejía. Bogotá: Departamento de Filosofía, Facultad

de Ciencias Humanas, Univ. Nacional de Colombia, 2006. 398 p.: bibl., ill., photos. (Sapere aude!)

Fascinating collection of essays for scholars of the Radical Era (1863–85). Sparked by a Universidad Nacional seminar, 15 prominent historians have produced short essays focusing either on major figures (i.e. Samper, Camacho Roldán, Soledad Acosta de Samper) or on developments, such as the founding of Universidad Nacional. Includes working bibliographies and photographs.

1671 Ramírez Bacca, Renzo. Historia laboral de una hacienda cafetera: La Aurora, 1882–1982. Medellín, Colombia: Carrera Editores E.U.: Univ. Nacional de Colombia, Sede Medellín: Grupo de Investigación Historia, Trabajo, Sociedad y Cultura, 2008. 217 p.: bibl., ill., maps (La carrera histórica)

This interdisciplinary case study traces, over a period of 100 years, the history, evolution, labor organization, and management of "La Aurora," a coffee hacienda in El Líbano. Includes a summary in English. Important addition to Tolima's regional history and also to the study of Colombian agricultural development.

1672 Ramírez Bacca, Renzo and **Isaías Tobasura Acuña.** Migración boyacense en la cordillera central, 1876–1945: del antiplano cundiboyacense a los espacios de homogeneización antioqueña. (*Bull. Inst. fr. étud. andin.*, 33:2, 2004, p. 225–253, bibl., map, photo, tables)

Analysis of factors encouraging migration from Cundinamarca and Boyacá into Tolima and Caldas. Identifies local factors (lack of land, employment, violence) and external factors (the possibility of obtaining land and jobs), as well as personal motives to explain the distribution of *tierras baldíos* and coffee production in the Cordillera Central.

1673 Ramírez Bahamón, Jairo. Esplendor y ocaso del proyecto de Escuela Liberal: Huila, siglo XIX. Neiva, Colombia: Editorial Universidad Surcolombiana, 2007. 232 p.: bibl., maps. (Col. de Investigación)

Uses archival sources to trace the development of education in Huila during the 19th century. Emphasis placed on the contrast between liberal (radical) and Catholic (conservative) conceptions of primary education. Good insight from a provincial point of view on the impact of Federation Era (1863–85) and Regeneration (1886–1905) educational reforms. Includes some relevant documents.

1674 Restrepo Arango, María Luisa. En busca de un ideal: los intelectuales antioqueños en la formación de la vida cultural de una época, 1900–1915. (*Hist. Soc./ Medellín*, 11, sept. 2005, p. 115–132)

Surveys the importance of literary tertulias and journals in the intellectual and cultural development of Medellín between 1905–15. Emphasis is placed on two revistas: *Lectura y Arte* and *Alpha*. Suggests that a review of these and other journals offers insight into a little-known period of Antioqueñan history.

1675 Reyes Cárdenas, Ana Catalina. Mujeres y trabajo en Antioquia durante el siglo XX: formas de asociación y participación sindical. Medellín, Colombia: Ediciones Escuela Nacional Sindical, 2005. 188 p.: bibl., ill. (Ensayos laborales; 13)

Historical survey of the condition of women workers in 20th-century Antioquia. Stresses the mechanisms of association and forms of participation they developed, with a special emphasis on unions. The text is divided into two parts: 1900–50 and 1950–2000. Author uses a variety of sources and invites elaboration of similar studies in other departments for comparative purposes.

1676 Sáenz Rovner, Eduardo. La "prehistoria" de la marihuana en Colombia: consumo y cultivos entre los años 30 y 60. (*Cuad. Econ./Bogotá*, 26:47, segundo semestre 2007, p. 205–222, bibl.)

Demonstrates that Colombians knew, as early as the 1920s, that marijuana was good for something more than the fabrication of rope. Shows that marijuana was widely cultivated and consumed throughout the country long before the 1960s when North American demand encouraged a production boom.

1677 Sánchez, Efraín. Riqueza, trabajo y discriminación socioracial: algunos aspectos culturales del subdesarrollo colombiano en perspectiva histórica. (*Bol. Hist. Antig.*, 94:837, abril/mayo 2007, p. 201–236, photo)

Citing a lack of attention to the role of cultural variables in previous discussions of Colombian underdevelopment, this essay explores the impact of socioracial discrimination, ideas about wealth, and attitudes and values concerning work in retarding economic growth from colonial times to the present.

1678 Silva, Renán. A la sombra de Clío: diez ensayos sobre historia e historiografía. Medellín, Colombia: Carreta Editores, 2007. 314 p.: bibl. (Carreta histórica)

Ten brilliant essays by a renowned historian provide penetrating insight into the state of historiography in Colombia today. Topics range from the relationship between sociology and history to analyses of the scholarly values of such journals as *Historia Crítica* and *El Anuario Colombiano de Historia Social y de la Cultura*.

1679 Solano de las Aguas, Sergio Paolo and **Roicer Alberto Flórez Bolívar.** Resguardos indígenas, ganadería y conflictos sociales en el Bolívar Grande, 1850–1875. (*Hist. Crít./Bogotá*, 34, julio/dic. 2007, p. 92–117, bibl., maps, table)

Examines Indian efforts to protect communal land against expanding ranching economy. Despite their petitions, lawsuits, direct action and armed confrontations, they were unable to stop land expropriation and actions that contributed to the dissolution of their communities. By 1920, only one *resguardo* remained.

1680 Sourdis Nájera, Adelaida. El precio de la Independencia en la primera República: la población de Cartagena de Indias, 1814–1816. (*Bol. Hist. Antig.*, 94:836, enero/ marzo 2007, p. 59–80, map, photo, table)

Reviews the material and human devastation in Cartagena during the early struggle for independence and Spanish reconquest. Examination of fragmentary documents suggests that constant danger, hunger, the destruction of homes, and forced displacement of citizens reduced Cartagena's population by 10 percent and was responsible for the precipitous decline of its influence in the 19th century.

1681 Suárez Mayorga, Adriana María. La ciudad de los elegidos: crecimiento urbano, jerarquización social y poder político, Bogotá, 1910–1950. Bogotá: Adriana María

Suárez Mayorga, Editora Guadalupe, 2006. 229 p.: bibl., ill., maps.

Uses municipal archival documents to trace the development of Bogotá in the 20th century. Compares the city's growth with that of other Latin American metropolises. Argues that Bogotá's experience is an example of "modernization from above," typical of developing countries. Includes detailed maps, graphs, and figures.

1682 Toro Jaramillo, Iván Darío. El pensamiento de los católicos colombianos en el debate ideológico de la "crisis del medio siglo", 1850–1900. Medellín, Colombia: Fundación Univ. Luis Amigó, Fondo Editorial, 2005. 293 p.: bibl. (Col. profesores)

Innovative and much needed study of Catholic thought after 1850, with an emphasis on the role of Miguel Antonio Caro. Draws from manuscripts located in Vatican, Spanish, and Colombian archives. Shows how the participation of Catholic intellectuals helped determine fundamental concepts of Regeneration. Important contribution to political and intellectual history.

1683 Uribe de Hincapié, María Teresa. La guerra por las soberanías: memorias y relatos en la guerra civil de 1859–1862 en Colombia. Medellín, Colombia: Carreta Editores: Univ. de Antioquia, Instituto de Estudios Políticos, Grupo de Investigación Estudios Políticos, 2008. 272 p.: bibl., index.

Analysis of the 1859–62 civil war through investigation of moral, political, and legal justifications set out in historical narratives and memorials. Compares accounts before, during, and after the war. Sequel to an earlier monograph on the civil wars of 1839–42, 1851, and 1854 with the goal of demonstrating that each conflict had unique causes and outcomes.

1684 Uribe de Hincapié, María Teresa. Las palabras de la guerra: metáforas, narraciones y lenguajes políticos: un estudio sobre las memorias de las guerras civiles en Colombia. Medellín, Colombia: Carreta Editores; Colombia: Instituto de Estudios Políticos, Univ. de Antioquia: Corporación Región, 2006. 514 p.: bibl., index. (La Carreta histórica)

Innovative study of three 19th-century wars: the War of the Supremos (1839–42), the War of March 7, 1851, and the artisan-military war of 1854. For each case, authors compare the views of historians and the memories of protagonists with contemporary interpretations. Includes lists of principal actors and other data.

1685 Valencia Llano, Alonso. Dentro de la ley, fuera de la ley: resistencias sociales y políticas en el valle del río Cauca, 1830–1855. Cali, Colombia: Univ. de Valle, Facultad de Humanidades, Departamento de Historia, Centro de Estudios Regionales-Region, 2008. 257 p.: bibl., maps. (Valle y Colombia ayer hoy)

Between 1821 and 1854, Valle del Cauca elites repressed a series of revolts regarded as "race wars." Valencia Llano uses archival sources to show that the popular struggle included white and mestizo peasants determined to improve their economic situation, as well as African slaves who took advantage of the confusion to flee their masters. Well written. Extensive bibliography.

1686 Vargas Arana, Pilar. Los árabes en Colombia: del rechazo a la integración. Prólogo de Yamid Amat. Bogotá: Planeta, 2007. 229 p.: bibl., ill.

Exhaustive examination of periodicals published between 1880 and 1980 to ascertain numbers and locations of Syrians, Palestinians, and Lebanese in Colombia. Traces the history of Arab families once installed in the republic. Emphasizes that, despite being more accepted in the coastal departments and the Llanos, they were subject to social and legal discrimination.

1687 Vera Zapata, Wilmar. Entre el temor y la simpatía: la Segunda Guerra Mundial desde la prensa colombiana. Pereira, Colombia: El Arca Perdida Editores, 2007. 268 p.: bibl. (Col. Maestros; 4)

Journalism professor examines articles published in *El Tiempo*, *El Siglo*, and *El Colombiano* between 1939–45, to ascertain how they interpreted WWII events. Suggests that after the Allied triumph and Conservative victory in 1946, Colombian newspapers unconditionally supported the US against communism, despite earlier pro-fascist or pro-communist views.

1688 Villegas Vélez, Álvaro Andrés and Catalina Castrillón Gallego. Territorio, enfermedad y población en la producción de la geografía tropical colombiana, 1872–1934. (*Hist. Crít./Bogotá*, 32, julio/dic. 2006, p. 94–117, bibl.)

Fascinating essay that suggests that the Magdalena Valley, the Pacific Coast, and the Amazon jungle were converted to frontier territories in the 19th century because highland elites, in constructing the new nation, feared deadly diseases endemic to the Magdalena, the black population along the Pacific, and the Amazon tropical geography.

ECUADOR

1689 Albornoz Peralta, Osvaldo. Páginas de la historia ecuatoriana. Quito: Casa de la Cultura Ecuatoriana Benjamín Carrión, 2007. 2 v.: bibl. (Biblioteca mínima)

Published posthumously. A distinguished Marxist scholar's two-volume history of Ecuador from conquest to 1970s. Somewhat disjointed organization. Addressed to a popular audience, but interpretations of various developments may be of interest to investigators.

1690 Alou Forner, Gabriel. Diplomáticos, falangistas, emigrantes y exiliados españoles en Ecuador, 1936–1940. (*Cuad. Am./México*, 117:3, julio/sept. 2006, p. 63–82, bibl., tables)

Investigates response of members of small Spanish colony in Ecuador to the Civil War (1936–39). Argues that Ecuador's political instability tended to increase popular support for the Spanish Republic, but little material aid was given to the cause. Only about 50 Republican exiles sought sanctuary in Guayaquil after their defeat.

1691 Borrero Vega, Ana Luz. Cambios históricos en el paisaje de Cuenca, siglos XIX–XX. (*Procesos/Quito*, 24, segundo semestre 2006, p. 107–134, appendices, bibl., ill., maps, photos)

Uses methodologies of historical and landscape geography to analyze the growth and change in the urban landscape of Cuenca. Studies the perception that citizens control urban growth and land. Includes photographic register of principal buildings that make up Cuencan architectural patrimony. Unique contribution to Ecuadorian urban history.

1692 Buriano Castro, Ana. Tres momentos del discurso conservador ecuatoriano, 1860–1875. (*Procesos/Quito*, 21, segundo semestre 2004, p. 115–145, bibl.)

Analyzes materials published in "No oficial" section of the newspaper *El Nacional* to challenge the image of conservatism as a monolithic, unchanging political ideology. Concludes that by the 1880s the data suggests that at least some conservatives were flexible, "innovative, and capable of adaptation to the times and circumstances."

1693 Castro, Byron. El ferrocarril ecuatoriano: historia de la unidad de un pueblo. Quito: Banco Central del Ecuador, 2006. 419 p.: bibl., graphs, ill., index, maps, photos (Col. histórica; 29)

Traces history of Ecuador's railway from 1865–1948. Shows that the railroad was a determining factor in regional unification, made possible a new system of economic and social relations, and provided a new model of national unity. Includes photos, graphs, and index. Indispensable introduction to topic.

1694 Cepeda Astudillo, Franklin. Riobamba y el ferrocarril: nuevas dinámicas de intercambio regional en el primer cuarto del siglo XX. (*Procesos/Quito*, 24, segundo semestre 2006, p. 165–195, bibl., tables)

Analyzes the impact of the construction of the railroad linking Guayaquil and Quito via Riobamba. Underlines local conflicts taking into account the views of the government, the construction company, and the local press. Suggests that the railroad promoted expansion of internal market and development of settlements along its route.

1695 Clark, A. Kim. Feminismos estéticos y antiestéticos en el Ecuador de principios del siglo XX: un análisis de género y generaciones. (*Procesos/Quito*, 22, primer y segundo semestres 2005, p. 85–105, bibl.)

Valuable analysis of legal and social changes that women experienced as a result of the Liberal Revolution of 1895. Case studies of the only woman participant in the foundation of the Socialist Party in 1926 and the first licensed woman doctor (1910). Shows that women born in the 1880s were beneficiaries of government-promoted reforms.

1696 Coronel Feijóo, Rosario. Descalzos, "cocolos" y niñas de la caridad en Cuenca: cambios y continuidades en el régimen escolar, 1930–1945. (*Procesos/Quito*, 23, primer semestre 2006, p. 57–76)

Examination of impact of mandated liberal education on private Catholic primary schools. Concludes that thanks to cooperation between the Cabildo Municipal and the Church, female religious schools were able to assimilate ideals of "liberty and equality," and the poor could still opt to send their children to private schools.

1697 Cuvi, Nicolás. La institucionalización del conservacionismo en el Ecuador, 1949–1953: Misael Acosta Solis y el Departamento Forestal. (*Procesos/Quito*, 22, primer y segundo semestres 2005, p. 107–129, bibl.)

Pioneering essay documents antecedents and creation of the Forestry Department in 1948, as well as the influence of its first director, Misael Acosta Solís. Explores conservation concepts assumed by the state as well as the tensions between environmental discourse and practice. Despite conservation's increased visibility, environmental degradation continued unabated.

1698 Espinosa Apolo, Manuel. Mestizaje, cholificación y blanqueamiento en Quito: primera mitad del siglo XX. Quito: Univ. Andina Simón Bolívar, Ecuador: Abya-Yala: Corporación Editora Nacional, 2003. 94 p.: bibl. (Serie Magíster; 49)

Analysis of the impact of rural immigration on Quito in first half of 20th century. Discusses changes created by the new mix of diverse ethnic groups. Argues that newcomers contributed to city's modernization and brought "important elements to clarify fundamental problems of mestizaje: i.e., ethnogenesis, identity and mestizo culture."

1699 Esvertit Cobes, Natàlia. La incipiente provincia: Amazonía y estado ecuatoriano en el siglo XIX. Quito: Univ. Andina Simón Bolívar: Corporación Editora Nacional, 2008. 312 p.: bibl., maps. (Biblioteca de historia; 26)

Seminal study analyzes government efforts and regional initiatives undertaken in the 19th century to incorporate the Amazon region into the nation-state. Uses official sources as well as missionary and geographic accounts to reveal profound contradictions between the various groups in the region. Includes extensive bibliography and a set of excellent maps.

1700 Goetschel, Ana María. Educación de las mujeres, maestras y esferas públicas: Quito en la primera mitad del siglo XX. Quito: FLACSO Ecuador: Abya Yala, 2007. 328 p.: bibl., ill., photos, tables. (Atrio)

Revised dissertation examines a group of female teachers in Quito, who during the first half of the 20th century (1895–1946), took advantage of opportunities offered by lay education to promote the education of women in general and to open new possibilities for their participation in public life. Extensive bibliography.

1701 Hamerly, Michael T. Recuentos de dos ciudades: Guayaquil en 1899 y Quito en 1906. (*Procesos/Quito*, 24, segundo semestre 2006, p. 135–163, appendices, bibl., tables)

Careful review of census data gathered in Guayaquil in 1899 and in Quito in 1906 in order to compare the demographic evolution of the two cities. Considers the composition of both populations in terms of age groups, sex, occupation, marriage, birth rate, mortality, and education. Includes extensive bibliography.

1702 Henderson, Peter V.N. Gabriel García Moreno and conservative state formation in the Andes. Austin: Univ. of Texas Press; Teresa Lozano Long Institute of Latin American Studies, 2008. 310 p.: bibl., ill., index, map. (LLILAS new interpretations of Latin America series)

Definitive biography of García Moreno. Avoids polemics to place his career within the context of "state-formation theory and illustratrates why his life provides deeper understanding of critical issues facing 19th century Latin America." Argues that he used Catholic faith and patronage powers to shape Ecuador into a national model that other Conservative governments found exemplary. For comment by philosophy specialist, see item **3626**.

1703 Hidrovo Quiñónez, Tatiana. Manta: una ciudad-puerto en el siglo XIX; economía regional y mercado mundial. (*Procesos/Quito*, 24, segundo semestre 2006, p. 83–106, bibl., map, tables)

Discusses the surprising development of the port of Manta in the 19th century due first to the manufacturing boom of straw hats and later to the agro-export boom of vegetable ivory and cocao. Shows how global capitalism enabled the rise of local white-mestizo entrepreneurs who came to dominate the trade.

1704 Highland Indians and the state in modern Ecuador. Edited by A. Kim Clark and Marc Becker. Pittsburgh, Penn.: Univ. of Pittsburgh Press, 2007. 347 p.: bibl., index. (Pitt Latin American series)

Collection of 14 essays by 13 scholars reveal changing forms of indigenous engagement with the state from early 19th century to the beginning of 20th. Examines how indigenous people have attempted to claim control over state formation. Concludes with four comparative essays placing indigenous strategies in Ecuador within larger Latin American context.

1705 Kingman Garcés, Eduardo. La ciudad y los otros, Quito 1860–1940: higienismo, ornato y policía. Quito: FLACSO Ecuador: Universitat Rovira i Virgili, 2006. 431 p.: bibl., ill., maps (some col.). (Atrio)

Masterfully written monograph details the transition of feudal city to an early modern one. Investigates economic, social, cultural, and urban factors involved in the change. The author is especially interested in surveying a city where industry was undeveloped and power was held by a small elite. Important contribution to existing Quito studies.

1706 Landázuri Camacho, Mariana. Salir del encierro: medio siglo del Hospital Psiquiátrico San Lázaro. Quito: Banco Central del Ecuador, 2008. 452 p.: appendices, bibl., ill., index (Col. histórica; 30)

Well-written study of long ignored subject, treatment of mentally ill. Begins with 18th-century origins of the hospital but focuses on first half of the 20th century and the work of a "notable generation of Ecuadorian psychiatrists" who, with the help of the state, rehabilitated scores of patients. Appendices include statements written by patients and doctors.

1707 Marchán Romero, Carlos. Historia del Banco Central del Ecuador: de banco de gobierno a banco emisor y vuelta al pasado, 1927–2000. Quito: Banco Central del Ecuador, 2005. 333 p.: bibl., ill.

Analysis of the organizational structure and institutional history of the Banco Central (1927–2000). Reveals the erratic and contradictory character of monetary policy in Ecuador and the Banco's impact on national prices and the exchange rate. Well-researched monograph that makes a helpful contribution to the monetary history of Ecuador.

1708 O'Connor, Erin. Gender, Indian, nation: the contradictions of making Ecuador, 1830–1925. Tucson, Ariz.: Univ. of Arizona Press, 2007. 261 p.: bibl., index.

Reworked dissertation uses gender analysis to trace the links between Native American communities and the national state in the 19th century. Author "uncovers overlapping, conflicting, and ever-evolving patriarchies" in indigenous communities and official government institutions. Argues that gender mediated the interethnic struggles that ultimately created the modern nation. Extensive bibliography.

1709 Paz y Miño Cepeda, Juan José. Removiendo el presente: latinoamericanismo e historia en Ecuador. Quito: Pontificia Univ. Católica del Ecuador: THE, Taller de Historia Económica: ADHILAC, Asociación de Historiadores Latinoamericanos y del Caribe: Abya Yala, 2007. 221 p.: bibl.

Collection of nine papers previously presented by this distinguished professor of economic history. Organized chronologically, topics range from thought of Bolívar and Eloy Alfaro, to Ecuador-Peru border issues, to competing, contemporary economic development models. Perhaps of greatest interest is the final paper that examines the profound changes Ecuador experienced between 1979–2007.

1710 Rocafuerte, Vicente. Epistolario administrativo de don Vicente Rocafuerte, gobernador de la provincia de Guayaquil. t. 3, 1839–1843. Investigación de Alberto Cordero Aroca. Guayaquil, Ecuador: Publicación del Programa Editorial de la Biblioteca Municipal de Santiago de Guayaquil: Archivo Nacional: Fundación Casa de Rocafuerte: 2007. 1 v.: bibl., ill. (some col.), index, map.

Volume 3 in a series devoted to the publication of Vicente Rocafuerte's correspondence. Reprints 214 documents, located in the Archivo Nacional de Historia de Quito, composed by Rocafuerte between 1839–43 while he was governor of Provincia de Guayaquil. Includes index of topics covered. Important resource for recapturing early history of Guayaquil.

1711 Rodas Chaves, Germán. Socialismo casa adentro: aproximación a sus dos primeras décadas de vida. Quito: Ediciones La Tierra, 2006. 193 p.: bibl., ill. (Historia del socialismo en el Ecuador; 1)

History of the evolution of the Socialist Party (PSE) between 1926–46. Discusses international and internal influences and reviews developments emanating from 13 national Socialist congresses. Author wishes to demonstrate that PSE is one of the key institutions that forms Ecuadorian reality in the 20th and 21st centuries.

1712 Sevilla Flores, Alfonso. La intervención colombiana en el Ecuador: noviembre, 1877. Quito: [s.n.], 2002. 184 p.: bibl., ill., index. (Biblioteca 13 de mayo de 1830; 2)

Narration and documents highlight an often overlooked invasion of Ecuador by 3,000 Colombian troops in 1877 to support the Liberal government of General Ignacio de Veintemilla (1876–82) against a Conservative-backed revolt. The troops arrived after the Conservatives had been defeated, and their presence intensified Ecuadorian distrust of the Veintemilla government.

1713 Testigo del siglo: el Ecuador visto a través de diario *El Comercio*, 1906–2006. Edited by Fabián Corral Burbano de Lara *et al.* Quito: El Comercio, 2006. 568 p.: bibl., photos.

Substantial volume offers synopsis of Ecuadorian history from 1906–2006 as recorded by *El Comercio*, Quito's premier daily newspaper. Six chronological chapters survey eras ranging from 6 to 39 years. Each chapter summarizes key events and themes of the period. Includes biography of founder Carlos Mantilla Jácome (1897–1970), information on reporters, and numerous photographs. Essential resource for 20th-century scholars.

Peru

DANIEL MASTERSON, *Professor of History, United States Naval Academy, Annapolis*

PERUVIAN HISTORIOGRAPHY FOR THIS PERIOD, does not establish any new important trends. Rather, it reflects long-standing approaches in the fields of nationalism, ethnic identity and military conflict, biography, regional studies, labor, and urban and military history. This essay will mainly follow these categories in reviewing the work discussed in *HLAS 66*. One particular observation to note in the beginning is the high quality of the essays contained in the edited anthologies reviewed for this period. This is especially true of women's history and indigenismo.

The scarcity of monographs devoted to economic history that Hunefeldt noted in *HLAS 64* continues in this period of review. Attention to urban and even military history appears to have waned somewhat over the past few years. Still, some important studies of these two areas of scholarship will be reviewed in this essay. Although Peru was not a principal receiver nation of immigrants like Brazil or Argentina, immigration history has always been a strong point of its scholarship and this remains so. The interest in Japanese immigration to Peru has decidedly ebbed with the *denoument* of Fujimori, but very useful studies of smaller immigrant communities have appeared. Bartet (item **1719**) and Frey Bullón and Salazar Rodas (item **1729**) represent foundational studies for Arab and German immigrant and labor groups in Peru. In the broader context, political history still predominates, but younger Peruvian and non-Peruvian scholars have continued to enrich the already well-regarded body of social history scholarship produced by historians of Peru during the past three decades. Although an anthology and not a monograph, Meza and Hampe (item **1742**) compiled 15 informative essays on the history of Peruvian women from the 15th to the 20th century. Bazán and Zubieta Núñez (item **1735**) present an important addition to Peruvian historiography encompassed in 42 essays by both Peruvian and non-Peruvian scholars. This first section offers helpful general background essays by the likes of Braudel, Bloch, Hobsbawn, DeTocqueville, and Benedict Anderson. But at times the contextual significance of these essays is modest at best. Regarding general histories, Masterson's volume places a particular emphasis on environmental, social and urban history (item **1740**).

Concepts of nationalism and local identity are represented in a fine study by Skuban (item **1752**) who looks at coastal populations in Tacna and Arica after the War of the Pacific. His study is based upon careful work in national, regional, and local archives and offers useful new perspectives on the complexities of nationalism and local identity. The dire fate of Peru's indigenous Putumayos peoples during the rubber boom of the early 20th century is carefully examined in the context of a review of the brutal practices of the Peruvian Rubber Company (item **1750**). Richly illustrated and amply documented, this work, coauthored by Rey de Castro, Zumaeta, and Arana, is very useful for understanding a short-lived industry that exploited not only the indigenous population, but the newly arrived Asian immigrants as well. A valuable review article compiled by Ravines (item **1748**) and including most leading authorities on *indigenismo* presents a summary of the principal legislation and discussions of land questions and local communities among other important issues. Often linked to issues of identity are studies of education and educational reform. Yet the output on this topic is very sparse. Rios Burga's compilation of an anthology of 24 essays on the evolution of the Peruvian university in the 19th and 20th centuries makes a fine contribution to the scholarship on this topic.

Embedded in the fabric of Peruvian nationalism and identity is, of course, the War of the Pacific. The seemingly never-ending flow of scholarship on the War continues with this review period. Sater, a leading authority on the War of the Pacific offers perhaps the best military analysis of the war while remaining even-handed in his review of the conduct of the combatants (see *HLAS 64:1411*); Chaupis Torres and Rosario's collection of essays touches upon important social issues of the war such as the role of the subaltern classes, ethnicity, gender, and the fate of Chinese bonded workers (item **1731**); Castro Flores analyzes the important issue of the Lima press during the war (item **1724**); and for naval historians, Garrido-Lecca, M. presents a valuable insight into the mentality of the captain of the Peruvian Corvette *Union* with the publication of Nicholas del Portal's diary (item **1726**).

Any review of Peruvian biography must note the continuing stream of studies on the unquestioned icon of Peru's glorious heroes from the War of the Pacific, Miguel Grau, who is the subject of yet another multi-volume biography. In four volumes, Thorndike presents a sweeping history of Grau's era with the naval heroes of the War of the Pacific as the centerpiece (item **1754**). De la Puente Candamo's (item **1745**) one volume on Grau, published by the Peruvian Navy's Institute of Historical and Maritime Studies is strong on the Peruvian public's reaction to Grau heroics. The book is also nicely illustrated and represents well the continuing high quality of the Naval Institute's publications. Henry Meiggs, the flamboyant railroad entrepreneur in Peru and elsewhere, is the subject of a fine sociohistorical study by Salinas Sánchez (item **1751**). This work is, in essence, a biography with a strong economic, rather than social, emphasis. Carefully researched in Peruvian archives, the work will be helpful to students of 19th-century Peru. Also very helpful to 19th-century historians interested in the policies of Ramón Castilla is Nanda Leonardini's (item **1737**) "preliminary" study of the *Informes* of Peru's department prefects during the first government of military *caudillo* Ramón Castilla (1845–50). This useful volume could also fall into the category of regional history.

Notable by their scarcity in this cycle of publications are studies of *indigenismo* and Sendero Luminoso. One can point to the anthology edited by Rogger Ravines published in the *Boletín de Lima* on *indigenismo* as a good base line for research (item **1748**), but more primary studies are needed especially as the rural unrest during the last decades of the 20th century has subsided. Nevertheless, research on the Sendero Luminoso has waned. Always a topical subject for analysis over the course of the two decades after 1980, this is no longer the case. There is still much to be learned about the insurgency and particularly the *Rondas Campesinas* who were largely responsible for defeating it in the sierra. Sendero maintains a presence in the South Central sierra and the insurgency's imprisoned leader, Abimael Guzmán Reinoso, authored his autobiography in 2009 (item **1733**). The historical context of Sendero's rise to prominence can be found in Heilman's analysis of mobilization of the indigenous peoples by civilians "colonels" in Ayacucho during the 1920s (item **1734**).

Local, urban, and regional historians were active over the past half decade. Flores-Zúñiga (item **1728**) offers a comprehensive study of the Rimac Valley and its predominant haciendas. Raimondi's work on the Department of Ancash (item **1747**) will be valuable for students of mining and the geology of the region. Benito Rodríguez edited a volume of 16 essays on the northern districts of metropolitan Lima from the 16th century to the present (item **1725**). Soria Casaverde's (item **1753**) study of the colonization of the Peruvian Amazon in the decades after independence presents this process as a model for later Peruvian development. Falling into my rubric of local as well as labor history is García-Bryce Weinstein's study of the Lima's artisans in the 19th century (item **1730**). Quiroz's study of Lima's port city of Callao focuses on the years before the 20th century with special attention to the terrible earthquake and tsunami of 1746 (item **1746**).

A small study of peasant-based rebellions by Almonacid (item **1716**) on the Huamanga uprising of 1922 represents a relatively meager output of scholarship on rural based activism among the items reviewed. Beyond their relationship to counter-insurgency, studies of the Peruvian military are returning to familiar themes of civil military relations, institutional development, and the influence of the US on training and other issues. Toche's study in this vein is useful and up to date (item **1755**). Also helpful from the perspective of military history is Luqui-Lagleyze study of the military campaign's of the era of independence (item **1739**)

McEvoy's work (item **1741**) on Manuel Pardo goes beyond a biography of the Peruvian *Civilista* to present a comprehensive political and economic survey of the Pardo era. García Belaunde and Gonzales (item **1720**) offer a massive biography of Víctor Andres Belaúnde. Diplomatic relations between Peru and the US during the turbulent mid-20th century have been lightly studied. Walter's work (item **1756**) meets this important need through careful review of US ambassadorial papers, and some key interviews with Peruvian policy makers.

In sum, given Peru's sustained economic growth since the mid-1990s it is surprising that so little attention has been paid to the economic history of the past three decades. Peru has made a remarkable comeback from the dark days of terrorism and economic chaos before 1992. Peru's involvement with the US in a free trade agreement is historic and it needs historical context. An important exception to this trend is the Pinto Herrera study of Peru's gold mining industry since the early 1990s (item **1744**). Lastly, there are clear signs that Peru's indigenous peoples of the Amazon region are becoming quite active in the protection of their perceived rights. We look forward to seeing scholarly attention devoted to this issue in the future.

1714 Aguila Peralta, Alicia del. Los velos y las pieles: cuerpo, género y reordenamiento social en el Perú republicano, Lima, 1822–1872. Lima: Instituto de Estudios Peruanos, 2003. 169 p.: bibl., ill. (Serie Estudios históricos, 34)

This is a fine social history of Lima in the mid-19th century. The author explores issues such as perceptions of masculinity and femininity, the social functions of rituals, charlas, fiestas and paseos. One section of this study looks at the popular perfumes and cosmetics used liberally by women Limeños. Also reviewed are what the author refers to as "public" and "intimate" bath. There is a limited attempt to discuss Lima's social makeup by drawing on data from the census data of 1876 and 1891, but it is clear that Aguila is really most interested in portraying the private side of life in Lima. She does that well. As one would hope, this book is richly illustrated and the study is much the better for it. There are also extended references to these illustrations and they are very helpful.

1715 Aguirre, Carlos. Dénle duro que no siente: poder y transgresión en el Perú republicano. Lima: AFINED, Fondo de Investigadores y Editores, 2008. 318 p.: bibl. (Serie Historia)

A highly informative and wide-ranging analysis of urban slavery in Peru during the 19th century as well as the social implications of crime and delinquency among women and young people. In the final section of this study, Aguirre offers a valuable overview of Latin American prison systems. Again women and young people are featured in the study which also offers a useful discussion of "prison subcultures." The discussion of political prisons is somewhat limited and based more on the notorious practices of Machado in Cuba, Leguía in Peru, and others. This is an important socially based study on a topic which clearly merits continued inquiry.

1716 Almonacid, Gotardo. Gobierno local, gabelas y revuelta popular en Huamanga: 1922. Lima: Ediciones Altazor, 2007. 115 p.: bibl.

A short but helpful study of the background to the December 1922 uprising in Huanta during the first years of the Leguía dictatorship (1919–30). The author details the economic hardships of the two decades preceding the uprising and places particular blame on the tax policies of the Leguía administration. The value of this small book is the analysis of how the local government agencies responded to peasant unrest which would become more widespread as Leguía sought to further secure his leadership.

1717 Armas Asin, Fernando. Iglesia: bienes y rentas: secularización liberal y reorganización patrimonial en Lima, 1820–1950. Lima: Instituto Riva-Agüero, Pontificia Univ. Católica del Perú: IEP, Instituto de Estudios Peruanos, 2007. 205 p.: bibl. (Estudios históricos; 45)

This is a study of the legal and fiscal conditions of the Catholic Church in Lima during the formative years of the institution. The financial condition of Lima's monasteries and convents are given particular attention in this study. This work by Armas Asin is replete with informative graphs and tables which historians of the Catholic Church will find helpful in understanding the finances of the Church.

1718 Ayala, José Luis. El presidente Carlos Condorena Yujra. Lima: Editorial San Marcos, 2006. 467 p.

Biography of Aymara activist Carlos Condorena Yujra who was a product of the Popular University movement started by José Carlos Mariátegui in the early 1920's. His activism, in the face of fierce repression by the Leguía regime led him to become president of the visionary Republica Aymara Tawantinsuyana del Perú. Two of the principal initiatives of this movement were a program to build rural schools and the acquisition of legal sanction for the Aymara language as one of Peru's official languages. This important study is buttressed by informative interviews and photographs.

1719 Bartet, Leyla. Memorias de cedro y olivo: la inmigración árabe al Perú: 1885–1985. Lima: Fondo Editorial del Congreso del Perú, 2005. 186 p.: bibl., ill., maps.

Bartet, a leading authority on the Arab population in Peru approaches this analysis of Peru's Arabs with a classic discussion of the "push and pull" theories of immigration. Beginning as early as the late 16th century she defines "Arab identity." "Arab identity" in Peru is put in the context of the expansion of Islam and Ottoman Empire. Just as they had in Mexico, Argentina, and other Latin American nations, Peru's Arabs established themselves in the nation's commercial sector. Palestinian Arabs were particularly successful in Southern Peru. The number of these Arab immigrants was always small, but Lebanese, Syrians, Palestinians, and other groups were represented. With valuable family photographs of first generation Arab immigrants, this study with its broad introduction to the Arab diaspora is a useful contribution to understanding Peru's immigrant minorities.

1720 Belaúnde, Víctor Andrés. Víctor Andrés Belaúnde: peruanidad, contorno y confín (textos esenciales). Compilación de Domingo García Belaunde y Osmar Gonzales. Lima: Fondo Editorial del Congreso del Perú, 2007. 773 p.: bibl., ill.

A collection of the writings of the highly respected Peruvian intellectual, educator and statesman extending from his early student years to his presidency of the General Assembly of the UN. The writings reflect his support of social integration and stability rather than class struggle and violence. In essence, he was a nationalist trying to find a formula for social unity as a means of achieving Peru's untapped potential; an important addition to any Peruvian scholar's library.

1721 Benvenuto Murrieta, Pedro Manuel. Quince plazuelas, una alameda y un callejón: Lima en los años de 1884 a 1887. 3. ed. Perú: Univ. del Pacífico, 2003. 465 p.: ill., index.

This is a fascinating socioeconomic study of the various plazas and sectors of Lima through the lens of architecture. Richly illustrated with contemporary photographs and drawings, the text is also enhanced by poetry selections from the period of the 1880s that is the focus of this study.

1722 Briceño Berrú, José Enrique. Los límites del odio: el tramonto del amor. Lima: Editorial Milla Batres, 2008. 287 p.: bibl., ill.

This is an interesting book for its genre (polemical books on the War of the Pacific.) Informational footnotes are provided, but no bibliography. There are interesting period photographs and artwork depicting the battlefields. The author's prose is not standard by any means and resembles an extended free verse epic poem.

1723 Cándamo, Manuel. El Perú desde la intimidad: epistolario de Manuel Cándamo, 1873–1904. Investigación, estudio preliminar y notas de José A. de la Puente Cándamo y José de la Puente Brunke. Lima: Fondo Editorial de la Pontificia Univ. Católica del Perú, 2008. 807 p.: bibl., ill., index.

This volume is the compiled and edited collection of the very prominent 19th-century political leader, Manuel Cándamo. From one of the wealthiest families in Peru, Candamo was a founding member of the Civilista party. He was also a soldier in the defense of Lima during the War of the Pacific and a leader of the Peruvian legislature, Candamo twice held the presidency and died while holding that office in 1904. He was a prolific letter writer and most of the correspondence in this volume is to his wife Theresa. These letters are wide-ranging in topic and scope and they provide an important window into the thinking of Peru's ruling elite and the very challenging issues these leaders faced in the late 19th century. With the War of the Pacific and the Peru's civil war in the mid 1890; Cándamo's career bridges some of Peru's most difficult times in its republican history. This volume of letters might well be used in graduate programs to underscore the value of personal correspondence of a figure of the significance of Cándamo in Peruvian history.

1724 Castro Flores, Ángel Arturo. La prensa limeña en la Guerra del Pacífico: 1879–1884. Lima: Univ. Alas Peruanas, Fondo Editorial, 2008. 171 p.: bibl., ill. (some col.)

The book reviews the condition of Lima's main newspaper before, during, and after the War of the Pacific. Particular attention is devoted to the efforts of the Chilean occupiers of Lima to suppress or censor the city's press in order to present a favorable opinion of the occupiers. The author tends to digress a good deal from his main topic to review already very familiar topics such as General Cáceres' guerrilla campaign in the sierra. The book concludes with a review of the foreign press reaction to the Chilean occupation including *The Times* and *Morning Post* of London and *La Protesta* of Buenos Aires.

1725 Congreso de Historia de Lima Norte "Memoria, Identidad, Proyección," *1st, Lima, Peru, 2005.* Pasado, presente y futuro de Lima Norte: construyendo una identidad. Actas. Coordinación de José Antonio Benito Rodríguez. Lima: Univ. Católica Sedes Sapientiae, 2007. 290 p.: bibl.

These are valuable essays dealing with the regional history of the areas to Lima's north. Looking back to the early 16th century, the essays include discussion of the region's local archives, a look at Afro-Peruvian pastoralists in the region, and the formation of the barrios populares. The essays are indeed a bit scattered, over time if not over space, but the collection holds up well under the geographic theme that the editor Benito selected. This is one more example of how well Peruvian scholars are maintaining a continuing interest in regional and local history.

1726 Diario a bordo de la corbeta *Unión*: Guerra del Pacífico: testimonios inéditos. Edición de Hernán Garrido-Lecca M. Lima: La Casa del Libro Viejo, 2008. 230 p.: ill., index.

This book is primarily the personal log of the captain of one of the principal Peruvian warships in the War of the Pacific. Garrido Lecca's introduction to the *Unión's* role in the war is first rate as expected, the diary entries are cryptic and lacking in lengthy analysis, but they are very useful for understanding the mentality of the *Union's* captain and crew as well as the nature of the orders he was receiving from his superiors. This book is essential for naval historians seeking to understand the mentality of Peruvian naval officers in the thick of the fighting in one of Latin America's most pivotal conflicts.

1727 Díaz Paredes, María Luz. Las mujeres de Haya: ocho historias de pasión y rebeldía. Prólogo de Enrique Planas. 2. ed. Lima: Planeta, 2007. 207 p.: bibl., ill.

This journalistic exposé, as the title suggests, purports to place eight glamorous women in APRA leader Haya de la Torre's personal life during his most active and dangerous years before 1945. Díaz relies heavily on interviews to construct her narrative of Haya's purported liaisons. Some of these women, such as Ana Billinghurst, were from Peru's most powerful families. Beyond personal interviews, the sources for this intriguing study are slim. Interestingly, Frederick Pike's biography, which offered a conflicting view of Haya de la Torre's private life, is not listed.

1728 Flores-Zúñiga, Fernando. Haciendas y pueblos de Lima: historia del valle del Rímac de sus orígenes al siglo XX. 1, Valle de Huatica: Cercado, La Victoria, Lince y San Isidro. Lima Fondo Editorial del Congreso del Perú: Municipalidad Metropolitana de Lima, 2008. 1 v.: bibl., ill., col. maps

As the first volume of a multi-volume study, this is an important social and geographic analysis of the Rimac Valley from the early colonial period to the 20th century. It is well grounded in social history and offers a highly useful look at the development of the city of Lima and its environs over the course of three centuries. This work is a testament to the high quality of interdisciplinary studies that Peruvian scholars are producing with regard to local and regional history. Relying upon records from Peru's Archivo General de la Nación and other Lima archives, Flores-Zúñiga includes some seemingly timeless photographs, including one depicting a burgeoning Lima with paisanos appearing in the 1920s much the same as they do today.

1729 Frey Bullón, Herbert and **Sara Salazar Rodas.** Colonos alemanes fundadores de Oxapampa. Peru: s.n., 2007. 341 p.: bibl., ill., maps.

This work studies a colony of German-speaking immigrants from Prussia and Tirol who established communities in the Department of Pasco on the eastern slope of the Andes in Peru's high selva. The long trek from Lima depleted the original immigrant group of 300 by nearly half. But a remote community in the town of Pozuzo was eventually established. The authors had access to substantial documentation from the original immigrants and their descendents, but were not able to construct a reasonably useful social history of the colony or its relation to the broader German community in Peru. There is no indication, for example, whether this German-speaking community was included in the roundup of German immigrants by the Peruvian government during WWII. Much of the book is taken up with documentary material and genealogical studies of the colony's original inhabitants.

1730 García-Bryce, Iñigo Weinstein. República con ciudadanos: los artesanos de Lima, 1821–1879. Traducción de Javier Flores Espinoza. Lima: IEP, Instituto de Estudios Peruanos, 2008. 280 p.: bibl., ill., maps, facsims. (Estudios históricos; 51)

This is a revised translation of the author's earlier study on this topic published by the University of New Mexico Press in 2004. (See *HLAS 62:1662* for a comment on the English-language publication.) Drawing on the main archives in Lima and a broad range of Peruvian and North American scholars, the author systematically discusses the racial composition of Lima's

artisans as they increasingly self-identify with their work and place in Lima society throughout the 19th century. García-Bryce Weinstein could have strengthened this otherwise fine work by clearly defining Lima's artisans by occupation from the outset of this study.

Gootenberg, Paul. Andean cocaine: the making of a global drug. See item **422.**

1731 La Guerra del Pacífico: aportes para repensar su historia. Compilación de José Chaupis Torres y Emilio Rosario. Lima: Editorial Línea Andina: Univ. Nacional Mayor de San Marcos, 2007. 1 v.: bibl.

Excellent collection of essays on the War of the Pacific by some of Peru's leading historians. Rosario's essay on the banking elite's role in the lead up to the war is highly informative. In that same economic vein, Carmen McEvoy offers a highly informed essay on socioeconomic conditions in Peru during the Chilean occupation. Another useful discussion is Rodriquez Pastor's analysis of Chinese bonded labor and their fate during the conflict. This volume offers little for the student of military history, but is essential for a better understanding of the social and economic context of the War of the Pacific.

1732 Gutiérrez Samanez, José Carlos. La generación cusqueña de 1927. Lima: Editorial Horizonte, 2007. 158 p.: bibl., ill. (Arqueología e historia; 12)

A very satisfying study of the artists, primarily painters, social philosophers, and student activists, associated with what Gutiérrez refers to as the "The Generation of 27 and the Cultural movement of the southern region." Linked closely to the growing Indigenista movement in Peru, this cultural phenomenon broadly based in the arts, especially in the visual arts and theater, embraced the validation of Quechua as a principal language of Peru. Given that the 1920's were a vibrant time when many of Peru's principal political and social thinkers, such as Mariátegui, Haya de la Torre, Gonzales Prada, and Víctor Andrés Belaúnde, were maturing as the intellectual elite of Peru, this valuable little book establishes an important social and artistic context for new schools of thought and expression in southern Peru.

1733 Guzmán Reynoso, Abimael. De puño y letra. Los Olivos, Peru: Manoalzada, 2009. 407 p.: ill., facsims.

Abimael Guzmán Reinoso, the leader of the Sendero Luminoso, here presents his version of the so-called People's War against the Peruvian state from 1980 to his capture by a special police agency in 1992. Scholars hoping for fresh insights into the thinking of Guzmán will be disappointed with this book. It begins with a vague narration of his early life, all of which is well known. Much of the rest of the book is written in outline form accompanied by documents from Peru's Communist party and government decree's that the author deemed appropriate to his presentation. Sadly, this is not a book that will advance our knowledge of Sendero Luminoso in a fundamental way. Guzmán does not choose to address in a careful way his movement's methodology or it consequences. It is possible that he will be able to do this in the future, but it is difficult to imagine that his capability of introspection will improve in the future.

1734 Heilman, Jaymie Patricia. Under civilian colonels: indigenous political mobilization in the 1920's, Ayacucho, Peru. (*Americas/Washington*, 66:4, April 2010, p. 501–526)

This is an important article that is part of a larger study published by Stanford University Press in August 2010 entitled, *Before the Shining Path: Politics in Rural Ayacucho, 1895–1980*. This article pays particular attention to the role of peasant resistance leaders known a colonels, who during the 1920s in the Ayacucho region were able to create bonds across the usual community barriers and to create militarized resistance groups to struggle against unjust taxes, labor burdens imposed by the Leguía regime, and corruption. Peasant protesters called themselves *monteneros*, a term that harkens back to the campesino irregulars who fought with General Cáceres against invading Chilean troops during the last stages of the War of the Pacific. Heilman makes the important link between this type of peasant activism and the emergence of the *rondas campesinas* or self-defense brigades that battled Sendero Luminoso insurgents in the 1980s and 1990s.

1735 Historiografía general y del Perú: autores y obras del pensamiento histórico. Edición de Víctor Raúl Nomberto Bazán y Filomeno Zubieta Núñez. Prólogo de Lorenzo Huertas Vallejos. Lima: Univ. Ricardo Palma, Editorial Universitaria, 2007. 304 p.: bibl., index. (Col. Textos universitarios)

Highly informative reader with essays by many of the leading international historians and those of Peru. The first part of the anthology establishes the context of the discussion with essays from, among others, Benedict Anderson on nationalism, Edward Carr on the nature of history, and Michel Foucault on the "archeology of knowledge." The book's second part covers a broad range of historical issues from John Murra's classic on the organization of the Inca state to Alberto Flores Galindo "In Search of the Inca: Identity and Utopia in the Andes." These essays would be a very good place for the nonspecialist to begin gaining a grasp of the best of Peruvian historiography. The contextualizing effort presented in the first part may be unnecessary. Selections from Tocqueville on the end of the monarchy in France or Francis Fukuyama's selection on "The End of History and the Last Man" are not particularly relevant.

Hostnig, Rainer; Ciro Palomino Dongo; and Jean-Jacques Decoster. Proceso de composición y titulación de tierras en Apurímac-Perú, siglos XVI–XX. See *HLAS 65:1136.*

1736 Infante, Carlos. Canto Grande y las Dos Colinas: del exterminio de los pueblos al exterminio de comunistas en el penal Castro Castro, mayo 1992. Lima: Univ. Nacional de San Cristóbal de Huamanga: Univ. Nacional Mayor de San Marcos, Unidad de Post Grado de Ciencias Sociales: Manoalzada Editores, 2007. 343 p.: bibl., ill.

This study deals with the Fujimori government's suppression of prison protests at the Miguel Castro Castro Prison. Less well known than the massive military response to coordinated prison uprisings by Senderista during the first Alan García regime, this book goes beyond the study of the prison episode, which the author claims cost the lives of 41 prisoners, to a useful analysis of the highly committed nature of the Sendero's outlook inside and outside Peru's prisons.

1737 Informe de los prefectos durante el primer gobierno del Mariscal Ramón Castilla, 1845–1850. Compilación de Nanda Leonardini. Lima: Seminario de Historia Rural Andina, Univ. Nacional Mayor de San Marcos, 2007. 270 p.: bibl., ill.

This is a useful collection of documents issued by Peru's department prefects during the first administration (1845–51) of Peru's caudillo Ramón Castilla. The subjects of these reports, for example, deal with the condition of roads, bridges, police, jails, waterways, hospitals, commerce and agriculture. As one would imagine, some of these reports are quite cursory and others, such as the one from the Department of Ancash, quite detailed and useful to historians. Leonardina states in the preface that this is a preliminary work. The volume lacks a bibliography which would be a useful addition to further volumes. Additionally, information on the repositories used in compiling this volume would also be useful.

1738 Luna Pizarro, Francisco Javier de. Justicia sin crueldad: cartas inéditas (1813–1854) de Francisco Javier de Luna Pizarro, fundador de la República. Compilación, notas y estudio preliminar de Javier de Belaúnde Ruiz de Somocurcio. Lima: Fondo Editorial del Congreso del Perú, 2006. 454 p.: ill.

This volume contains a carefully edited selection of letters by one of the more prominent members of Peru's Independence generation. Remarkably broad ranging in their subject matter, these letters give insights into not only contemporary views of events in Peru but throughout South America and Spain as well. Discussion of the naval campaigns of the Independence War demonstrates the high level of sophistication of the correspondents.

1739 Luqui-Lagleyze, Julio M. Por el rey, la fe y la patria: el ejército realista del Perú en la independencia sudamericana, 1810–1825. Madrid: Ministerio de Defensa, Secretaría General Técnica, 2005. 425 p.: bibl. (Col. ADALID; 51)

This is a highly detailed and comprehensively researched analysis of Spanish and republican military operations in Peru

during the War of Independence. Both major and minor Peruvian archives are consulted as well as the Archivo General de Militar de Segovia, Archivo Palacio Real de Madrid and Archivo Servicio Histórico Militar del Ejército Español which are important repositories for this study. This is by no means strictly a traditional military narrative. The economics of funding the independence armies is discussed as are sanitation issues, recruitment, naval operations among other issues. This is a study that will advance our understanding of the Independence War in Peru even though the topic has already received significant scholarly attention.

1740 Masterson, Daniel M. The history of Peru. Westport, Conn.: Greenwood Press, 2009. 246 p., [4] p. of plates: bibl., ill., index, map. (The Greenwood histories of the modern nations, 1096–2905)

Part of the Greenwood Press History of Modern Nations Series, this volume was written as an introduction to the history of Peru from ancient times to the contemporary era. The volume stresses the great diversity of Peru's social and environmental landscape and the inherent strength and resilience of its people. In keeping with its introductory purpose, the volume contains a chronology of Peru's historical development and a listing of the nation's noteworthy individuals.

1741 Mc Evoy, Carmen. Homo politicus: Manuel Pardo, la política peruana y sus dilemas, 1871–1878. Lima: Instituto Riva-Agüero, Pontificia Univ. Católica del Perú: Instituto de Estudios Peruanos: Oficina Nacional de Procesos Electorales, 2007. 378 p.: bibl., ill., maps (No. 2 de la serie Coediciones; 2) (No. 242 de las Publicaciones del Instituto Riva-Agüero) (No. 47 de la Serie Estudios históricos; 47)

A thoroughly informed study of the formative period of Peruvian civilian politics by one of the leading historians of Peru, McEvoy situates the emergences of Civilista politics effectively against the backdrop of caudillismo following Peruvian independence. Most of all, McEvoy portrays the Pardo era as the real beginning of the modernization process in Peru but at the same time notes that these beginnings were accomplished in a climate of violence that would pervade Peruvian politics well into the 20th century. This is not a biography of Manuel Prado; other political contemporaries receive significant coverage as well. Readers looking for an insightful analysis of Peruvian politics in the decade before the War of the Pacific will be well satisfied with this study.

El miedo en el Perú: siglos XVI al XX. See item **1427.**

1742 La mujer en la historia del Perú: siglos XV al XX. Compilación de Carmen Meza y Teodoro Hampe. Lima: Fondo Editorial del Congreso del Perú; 2007. 645 p.: bibl.

Meza and Hampe have constructed a very important anthology encompassing the contributions of some of Peru's most esteemed scholars including Jorge Basadre and Maria Rostworowski. Covering the span from the 15th to the 20th century, this anthology is clearly intended to be the standard volume on Peruvian women for a good time to come. From that perspective, however, it falls short. There is no real discussion of the role of women in the post-WWII era, particularly in the urban context where they have played such an important role in community development. Still, each essay is accompanied by a useful bibliography and this volume is an important starting point for students interested in the history of Peruvian women. When you arrive at the 20th century, however, you are on your own.

1743 Ortíz Sotelo, Jorge. Acción y valor: historia de la Infantería de Marina del Peru. Lima: Securitas S.A.C./Forza S.A., 2010. 288 p.: ills.

This handsomely produced volume on the history of Peru's marine force, technically known at the naval infantry, by Ortíz Sotelo, a retired Peruvian marine and Peru's premier naval and maritime historian, does a fine job of balancing his study chronologically, but still gives sufficient emphasis to the naval infantry's operations against Sendero Luminoso in Peru's highlands. A subunit of Peru's navy, Peru's marines have struggled for an identity for most of the 20th century, and the counter-insurgency campaign in the late 20th century helped them to define that role. Like the navy, Peru's marines have held a close professional bond with their US Marine counterparts. For specialists studying Peru's armed forces, this volume will provide a wealth of information from training methods, institutional history and civil-military issues. In fact, this is the best up-to-date history of any Peruvian military institution now available.

1744 Pinto Herrera, Honorio Sabino. Gran minería aurífera en el Perú: el caso Barrick Misquichilca. Lima: Univ. Nacional Mayor de San Marcos, Seminario de Historia Rural Andina, 2009. 150 p.: bibl., ill., map.

A short, but carefully done, study of the Canadian-owned Barrick Gold Mining operation in Peru. Pinto Herrera places this extractive corporation's economic activities in the context of Peru's historically dynamic, but controversial, mining operations to include Cerro de Pasco, Marcona, and Southern Peru Copper Company. Now Peru's extractive industry is truly globalized with US, Chinese, Swiss, Australian, and Mexican investors dominating. Peru's export earnings have always been dominated by its extractive sector and its sustained economic growth since the mid-1990s is no different. Very much of a late comer to the Peruvian mining industry, Barrick Gold began operations in Peru in 1993. Pinto Herrera discusses at some length Barrick Gold's efforts to be "environmentally friendly" in Peru and the company's rise to one of the world's most productive mining operations. For students of Peru's mining industry especially during the rise of globalized mining ventures (1990 to the present), this is an important book.

Power, culture, and violence in the Andes. See item **1791.**

1745 Puente Candamo, José Agustín de la. Miguel Grau. Lima: Instituto de Estudios Histórico-Marítimos del Perú, 2003. 573 p.: bibl., ill. (some col.), index, 1 col. map.

This is a massive biography of Peru's leading naval hero and symbol of Peru's heroic but losing cause in the War of the Pacific. Grau and his Chilean counterpart Arturo Prat continue to be the subjects of a substantial percentage of the literature devoted to the naval history of both nations. De la Puente Candamo offers nothing new regarding Grau in this handsomely produced volume by Peru's Naval Institute.

In fact, previous works by noted Peruvian naval and maritime historian Jorge Ortiz Sotelo provide a good deal of the structure of this book. See for example, *HLAS 60:2617* for a comment on *El almirante Miguel Grau (1834–1879): una aproximación biográfica* by Ortiz Sotelo.

1746 Quiroz, Francisco. Historia del Callao: de puerto de Lima a provincia constitucional. Lima: Fondo Editorial del Pedagógico San Marcos: Gobierno Regional del Callao, 2007. 297 p.: bibl., ill., maps. (Serie Historia)

This is an excellent and multi-faceted history of Lima's port city of Callao from the Spanish settlement to the present day. Much of Quiroz' early attention in this work is rightly devoted to the development of the port of Callao. Significant attention is given to the impact of the disastrous earthquake and tsunami which devastated Callao in 1746. Still, the consistent environmental effects of El Niño are really not discussed to any degree. Neither is the 20th-century development of Callao as an extension of Lima's economy regarding transportation and many other facets of the capital city's economic life. This book continues in the vital tradition of Peruvian regional history that has been vibrant over the last decade. But much is left to be said regarding contemporary events of this vital Peruvian urban center.

1747 Raimondi, Antonio. El departamento de Ancachs y sus riquezas minerales, 1873. Compilación y estudio introductorio de Luis Felipe Villacorta Ostolaza. Lima: Fondo Editorial, Univ. Nacional Mayor de San Marcos: Asociación Educacional Antonio Raimondi: ANTAMINA: COFIDE, 2006. 591 p.: ill. (some col.) (Serie Clásicos sanmarquinos. Col. Estudios geológicos y mineros para la obra "El Perú"; 2)

This is the second volume of a study of Peru's minerals by the highly venerated naturalist, chemist, and geographer who played a very prominent role in promoting scientific inquiry in 19th-century Peru. Raimondi's field research in Ancash was conducted during four separate visits from 1859 to 1869. His research is meticulously organized by province and by the nature of the minerals itself. Considering that this work was published in the forefront of geo-logical field studies, these volumes rank as some of the most important early work in geology. An Italian immigrant who only arrived in Peru in 1850, Raimondi quickly made his mark as one of Peru's earliest and most prominent scientists.

1748 Ravines, Rogger. El indio, problema del indio: una antologia indigenista. (*Bol. Lima*, 19:107/110, 1997, p. 51–291, graph, ill., table)

A valuable collection of writings on the issue of indigenismo in Peru, the collection includes works by contemporary scholars such as Karen Spaulding, and some of the pioneers such as Manuel Gonzales Prada, Luis E. Valcárcel, and José Carlos Mariátegui. The selection is organized chronologically and by theme. Some sections, such as Chapter 5, "La tierra y la comunidad," would make excellent reading for graduate-level classes. Taken as a whole, this collection represents an accessible and highly informative overview of indigenismo in Peru from the colonial past to the contemporary period. It boasts selections from the leading commentators on this central issue of Peruvian national life.

1749 Rénique, José Luis. De la "traición aprista" al "gesto heroico": Luis de la Puente Uceda y la guerrilla del MIR. (*Ecuad. Debate*, 67, abril 2006, p. 77–98)

Describes activities of Luis de la Puente as the spark that created construction of a new militant and subversive political identity in Peru molded by the emergence of rural Peru on one hand and APRA's renunciation of fundamental aspects of its tradition of struggle on the other. [J. Rausch]

1750 Rey de Castro, Carlos *et al*. La defensa de los caucheros. Introducción de Andrew Gray. Presentación de Alberto Chirif. Iquitos, Perú: CETA; Copenhague, Dinamarca: IWGIA, 2005. 516 p.: bibl., ill. (Monumenta amazónica. E, Extractores; 2)

Carefully examines the dire fate of Peru's indigenous Putumayos peoples during the rubber boom of the early 20th century in the context of the brutal practices of the Peruvian Rubber Company. Richly illustrated and amply documented, this work is very useful for understanding a short-lived industry that exploited not only the indigenous population, but newly arrived Asian immigrants as well.

1751 Salinas Sánchez, Alejandro. Estudio socio-histórico del Epistolario Meiggs: 1866–1885. Lima: Seminario de Historia Rural Andina, Univ. Nacional Mayor de San Marcos, 2007. 316 p.: bibl., ill.

This is a valuable reference work and compilation of some of the letters of famed railroad builder and adventurer Henry Meiggs. The letters are introduced after Salinas presents a useful overview of Meiggs' career in Peru. The work is billed as a sociohistorical study and it largely meets the obligation of its title. A good deal of the correspondence deals strictly with business matters. Some letters, however, are Meiggs' exchanges with family members.

1752 Skuban, William E. Lines in the sand: nationalism and identity on the Peruvian-Chilean frontier. Albuquerque: Univ. of New Mexico Press, 2007. 314 p.: bibl., index.

Skuban looks at coastal populations in Tacna and Arica after the War of the Pacific. His study is based upon careful work in national, regional and local archives and offers useful new perspectives on the complexities of nationalism and local identity.

1753 Soria Casaverde, María Belén. El dorado republicano: visión oficial de la Amazonía peruana, 1821–1879. Lima: Seminario de Historia Rural Andina, Univ. Nacional Mayor de San Marcos, 2006. 148 p.: bibl., maps.

A beneficial overview of the European settlement and economic development of Peru's Amazon from the early missions in the 18th century. Soria does an admirable job of dealing effectively with such key topics as indigenous peoples, the ecology and geography of the region, the largely unsuccessful settlement schemes, and the role of the Peruvian navy in exploration and mapping. Useful bibliography for budding specialists to peruse.

1754 Thorndike, Guillermo. Grau. t. 1, Los hijos de los libertadores. t. 2, La traición y los héroes. t. 3, Caudillo, la ley. t. 4, La república caníbal. t. 5, 1878 crimen perfecto. Lima: Fondo Editorial del Congreso del Perú: Fondo Editorial del Banco de Crédito del Perú, 2006–2008. 5 v: bibl., ills., indexes.

Thorndike, one of Peru's most prominent journalist/historians, has written the most comprehensive biography of Peru's much studied and revered naval hero. Broadly contextualizing Grau's life and career, Thorndike has written a valuable history of Peru's mid-19th century political-military affairs, diplomacy, and technology. The reader must wait until Chapter five of the fourth volume to reach Thorndike's account of Grau's exploits on Peru's ill-fated flagship the *Huascar* as he engages the Chilean fleet in the War of the Pacific. His account is detailed, lively, and very much in the context of world naval affairs. As indicated, this is much more than a biography of Grau, it is an insightful history of the naval hero's era, At more than 1,400 pages in four volumes, the reader would expect this to be a comprehensive study, and it is.

1755 Toche, Eduardo. Guerra y democracia los militares peruanos y la construcción nacional. Lima: Consejo Latinoamericano de Ciencias Sociales, CLACSO: Centro de Estudios y Promoción del Desarrollo, DESCO, 2008. 308 p.: bibl., maps.

This is an excellent study of the Peruvian military over the course of the past six decades by a University of San Marcos historian and leading authority on the Peru's armed forces. The nation's modern military establishment is not a topic that Peruvian historians have taken up in any significant degree over the past half century. Toche's study addresses the institutional development and national defense perspective from the 1950s onward. The reformist military outlook of the Velasco administration (1968–75) is handled succinctly and effectively. The trauma of the Sendero Luminoso years (1980–95) is examined in a broad global context which is very useful. Toche's bibliography is an excellent guide for students of the Peruvian military who are looking to understand the armed forces' transformation in Peru, the arrogant reformists of the 1970s, to the chastened and more reflective institutions that transitioned to a far more limited role in the first decade of the 21st century. My one important caveat with this study is that Toche could have sharpened his analysis of the Peruvian military's professional outlook by reviewing contemporary armed forces journals.

1756 Walter, Richard J. Peru and the United States, 1960–1975: how their ambassadors managed foreign relations in a turbulent era. University Park: Pennsylvania State Univ. Press, 2010. 333 p.: bibl., index.

This book is a must read for students of modern Peru. It is based on an excellent foundation of primary materials including the papers of former US ambassadors to Peru, a wide array of US government documents, pertinent US and Peruvian newspapers, and interviews with some of the key actors in this story, including the aging retired army general Edgardo Mercado Jarrín who was the number two man in the Velasco administration. This book goes beyond its subtitle and looks at many important aspects of Peru's military and civilian policies during the dynamic period of the Alliance for Progress, the Vietnam War, the controversial reforms of the Velasco era and the troubled presidencies of the man many thought would be Peru's salvation, Fernando Belaúnde Terry. Too often, books on this time get mired in diplomatic nuance or are not balanced accounts from both countries' perspectives. Readers of Walter's study will certainly not be troubled by these difficulties as he presents a clear snapshot with a wide-angle lens of one of the most important periods in 20th-century Peruvian history.

Bolivia

ERICK D. LANGER, *Professor of History, Georgetown University*

THE ELECTION OF EVO MORALES, a president of indigenous origin who has helped destroy the political structures Bolivia built in the second half of the 20th century, has brought about a flowering of historical studies. Some scholars have tried to figure out the conditions that made it possible for such a figure to rise to political power and win an electoral majority. Others have argued against the simplistic version of history that members of the Morales administration, with the president himself prominently among them, have promulgated. Be that as it may, Bolivian history is in vogue in the country and elsewhere, bringing about a new vigor in historical studies in the past few years. This vigor includes Bolivian scholars as well as foreigners and, for the first time, a respectable number of studies addresses not just the Andean highlands, but also the eastern lowlands. The different wars, from the independence struggles to the Chaco War, have also attracted new analyses. In all, the indigenous perspective, more than any other, has gained even greater prominence.

With the anniversary of the independence wars upon us, a number of new publications, with some improved editions of old standbys, have made an important mark. A new authoritative edition of the classic diary of José Santos Vargas (item **1795**) provides a new transcription from the second, more complete manuscript, with an analytical introduction by Gunnar Mendoza, now with the footnotes included. Marie-Danielle Demélas' research has also seen fruit in her analysis of the diary and its author within the context of independence and the invention of modern-day guerrilla warfare (item **1764**). A republication of other independence-era diaries from the La Paz area (item **1765**), much shorter and but still useful, complement Vargas' work. In addition, the team led by Spanish historians Armando Martínez and Manuel Chust refocus Bolivian independence within the larger context of Europe and the Americas (item **1774**). In turn, Eduardo Trigo provides an excellent political narrative of Tarija, the province that elected to become part of Bolivia after independence rather than Argentina (item **1798**).

Scholars on Bolivia have participated in the important effort to understand how indigenous people became integrated into the nation-state, a topic that takes on even more importance in the current political climate. This is related to independence as well; Pilar Mendieta argues that elite indigenous families were able to maintain their privileges in the late colonial period by showing loyalty to the Spanish Crown, but after independence and the abolition of hereditary chieftainships, they were able to stay on top through intermarriage with Creoles, using commercial networks and their wide-ranging client networks (item **1786**). Marie-Danielle Demélas shows the plasticity of race after independence through the example of José Santos Vargas. His family evolved from mestizo to Creole status, and then, after the wars, Vargas married an Indian woman and became recognized as a community Indian (item **1763**). Javier Marion takes her concept one step further, arguing that the independence-era guerrillas had a new conception of race and ethnicity forged during their struggles against the royalists (item **1784**).

Forrest Hylton and Sinclair Thomson take a different tack, arguing that Bolivia's indigenous history since the 1780s contained a spirit of revolt that ultimately enabled Evo Morales to become president (item **1773**). In contrast, Marta Irurozqui asserts that Indians during the 19th century were not victims, but citizens who contributed much to building the nation-state (item **1776**). Similarly, Tristan Platt addresses the issue of indigenous citizenship through the payment of tribute and (the lack) of schools in Porco, Potosí (item **1790**), whereas Erick Langer provides evidence that community members around Oruro were active in state formation as merchants, teamsters, and miners, often siding with free traders. Pilar Mendieta shows that Indian leaders in the 19th century were already actively attempting to reclaim land through legal channels (item **1785**). Laura Gotkowitz takes this argument into the 20th century in a brilliant book, discussing how indigenous leaders reinterpreted government decisions in their own way, emerging victorious in the aftermath of the 1952 Revolution (item **1772**). Finally, two Argentine scholars, Raquel Gil (item **1770**) and Ana Teruel (item **1797**), respectively, provide analyses of 19th-century demographic and land tenure patterns in the southern-most parts of Andean Bolivia (and, in the case of Gil, in northern Argentina as well).

Relatively few topics on the 19th century did not concern indigenous history (quite rightfully), but Omar Chávez *et al.* tackle the electoral history of Bolivia from independence onward, arguing that Bolivia has now made the full transition to electoral autonomy (item **1758**). In turn, Marta Irurozqui examines the infamous Yañez massacre of 1861, showing that in its aftermath, armed civilian violence waned (item **1775**).

There is finally a substantial and growing bibliography on the Bolivian eastern lowlands, though it is heavily concentrated on the missions. Ferdy Langenbacher provides a useful administrative history of the Franciscan missions in the republican period, all of which were located in the eastern lowlands (item **1778**). Pilar García Jordán provides a compelling portrait of the Franciscan missions among the Guarayos in northern Santa Cruz, arguing that the missionaries did not provide their charges with the tools to become full citizens (*HLAS 64:1361* and item **318**). She follows up with an article on the failed secularization of the missions in the 1930s (item **1768**). Erick Langer, in his study of the Franciscan missions among the Chiriguanos on the border of the Chaco region, argues that the missionaries did have an idea of citizenship for their charges, but as working-class mestizos (item **1780**). In addition, he shows that until relatively late, power resided among the indigenous chiefs rather than with the friars. Isabelle Combès provides another perspective on the 1892 Chiriguano rebellion, debunking the historical conviction that the battle of Kuruyuki was one of white domination, since most of the combatants on both sides were Indians (item **1761**). Juan Víctor and Margarita Robertson provide information on the anticlerical Leocadio Trigo, who was the first National Delegate of the Chaco and an intrepid explorer (item **1792**). Ana María Lema elaborates on the labor history of the Chiquitano peoples in the 20th century with a good economic overview of the region (item **1782**).

The Chaco War (1932–35) has finally attracted attention from the indigenous perspective. Nicolas Richard is editor of a long-overdue volume on the fate (mostly tragic) of the indigenous people during the war (item **1783**), while Mario Parrón provides testimonies of Guaraní speakers, in this case only from the Bolivian point of view (item **1789**). Ricardo Scavone provides a diplomatic history of the many mistakes both Paraguay and Bolivia committed during their 19th-century relations, which eventually resulted in war (item **1796**). Cristián Garay reminds us that Bolivia's border troubles were related (item **1767**). He asserts that the loss of Acre (1903) to Brazil was related to the 1904 Treaty between Chile and Bolivia that officially ended the War of the Pacific (1879–84). He hypothesizes that Bolivia's attempt to bring in the US to mediate in these conflicts led Brazil and Chile to ally themselves against this danger and, in the end, achieved their goals of taking the territory.

As always, foreigners attract attention in Bolivia. Jean-Claude Roux attempts to show that Alcide d'Orbigny, the famous French traveler of the 1830s, was one of the first to bring human rights to the forefront (item **1794**). Clara López has translated and edited the travel diaries of an Italian naturalist who visited Bolivia in the late 19th century (item **1759**). Antonio Mitre addresses the difficult history of the Japanese before and during the World War II. He shows that the predominantly small-merchant Japanese population—and the German population—suffered expulsion from the country and internment in US concentration camps (item **1787**).

Political history of the last century is alive and well too. Robert Alexander's posthumous work on organized labor provides much information (item **1757**), but Sándor John's history of the Trotskyists in Bolivia is more impressive, sketching the movement from its beginnings to the recent past (item **1777**). He argues that the legacy of Trotskyism is vast in Bolivian politics and can be seen in the present government as well. Closely related are the inevitable histories of Che Guevara, such as that by William Gálvez, who counterposes the different diaries of the guerilla campaign (item **1766**). A truly novel and monumental work is that of Gustavo Rodríguez, who argues that the even more dismally failed Teoponte campaign (1970) in the aftermath of Guevara's death was really a continuation of that of Guevara (item **1793**). Elizabeth Burgos, who worked with the Cubans in the 1970s, has interesting views that largely corroborate Rodríguez (item **1760**). She also asserts that Evo Morales and many in his administration are a product of Cuba's concerted campaign to establish influence in Bolivia.

This leads us to more historical assessments of the Morales. In the edited volume by Christine Hunefeldt on power and violence in the Andes (item **1791**),

Herbert Klein examines the origins of indigenous power in Bolivia during the 20th century, whereas Nancy Postero shows the masterful use of historical symbols by Morales and his movement. In turn, *Unresolved Tensions*, a book edited by John Crabtree and Laurence Whitehead, is all about the Morales phenomenon (item **1762**). Although with few exceptions the book does not provide a long historical view (unlike the Hylton and Thomson volume above), the volume does provide the best perspectives on all the angles of the political situation, thanks to contributions from some of the most important (almost exclusively Bolivian) social scientists and historians. The only topic missing is the side of the NGOs, which Vera Gianotten provides in her history of CIPCA, one of the most significant NGOs working with indigenous peoples and some of whose leaders it has developed have important roles in the Morales government (item **1769**).

All in all, political turmoil within a largely democratic setting has been very good for the writing of Bolivian history. It is clear to all that history and its interpretations do matter, and thus more interpretations of history and a more complex understanding of the past (and thus the present), can only help in the serious debates going on in the country. Recent work has even included the more marginal areas and peoples, who, it is now seen, are not so marginal after all.

1757 Alexander, Robert Jackson. A history of organized labor in Bolivia. With the collaboration of Eldon M. Parker. Westport, Conn.: Praeger Publishers, 2005. 197 p.: bibl., index.

A good overview of labor history from the Chaco War (1932–35) to the end of the neoliberal regime of Víctor Paz Estenssoro (1989). Alexander uses secondary sources, newspapers, and interviews he conducted among labor leaders in the 1950s and 1970s. He relies on Guillermo Lora's Trotzkyist analysis, but the book is mainly a narrative that details Bolivian political history as seen through the lens of relations between the state and labor unions.

1758 La autonomía electoral: historia política e institucional del sistema electoral boliviano, 1825–2006. Textos de Omar Chávez Zamorano et al. La Paz: Konrad Adenauer Stiftung, 2007. 756 p.: bibl., ill.

A highly detailed history of Bolivian elections in their historical context. The authors use Ralph Goldman's concept of "critical transition" to democracy to break down Bolivian electoral history into four periods: the Bolivarian-Cádiz phase from 1825–80, the Oligarchic-Electoral phase from 1880–1920, the Constitutional-Electoral Autonomy phase from 1952–82, to the Full Electoral Autonomy phase from 1982 to the present.

1759 Balzan, Luigi. A carretón y canoa: la aventura científica de Luigi Balzan por Sudamérica, 1885–1893. Edición, estudio, notas y traducción del italiano de Clara López Beltrán. Lima: Institut de recherche pour le développement: Instituto Francés de Estudios Andinos: Ambasciata d'Italia in Bolivia: Plural Editores, 2008. 419 p.: bibl., ill., indexes, maps. (Col. "Travaux de l'Institut Français d'Études Andines"; 269)

An annotated travel diary of one of the most important Italian naturalists to visit Bolivia. Describes his travels through La Paz, Beni, and Santa Cruz, as well as in Paraguay. Contains a path-breaking study on pseudoscorpions, one of the results of this trip. Fine introduction by historian Clara López. For general review, see item **522.**

1760 Burgos, Elizabeth. Cuba en Bolivia. (*Encuentro Cult. Cuba.*, 44, primavera 2007, p. 129–143, photo)

The author, who was an official in the second Gen. Alfredo Ovando administration (1969–70), details the relationship that Cuba had with Bolivia since the 1959 Cuban Revolution. She shows that there were various phases and strategies. First, the Paz Estenssoro government (1960–64) permitted Cuba to use Bolivia as a launching pad for guerrilla movements in Peru and Argentina. She hypothesizes that Fidel Castro deliberately neglected Che Guevara, leading to his death during his ill-fated expedition to Bolivia. Cuba only halfway supported the guerrilla movement in Teoponte in 1970, leading to its demise. In the last phase, the author shows that Cuba has built up a cadre of individuals, such as Evo Morales, who have long been courted by Castro and for this reason have begun to create a Castro-like regime in Bolivia.

1761 Combès, Isabelle. Las batallas de Kuruyuki: variaciones sobre una derrota chiriguana. (*Bull. Inst. fr. étud. andin.*, 34:2, 2005, p. 221–233, bibl., photo)

An excellent analysis of the images of the Battle of Kuruyuki of 1892, in which some Chiriguano groups (now Ava-Guarani) lost in a big battle to Bolivian and allied Chiriguano forces. The author shows that, despite the historical record showing that Indians mostly fought against Indians, since the 1992 centenary the Ava-Guarani have taken this event to show their unity and the Santa Cruz separatists, the Nación Camba, have seen this as a federalist revolt.

1762 Crabtree, John and **Laurence White-head.** Unresolved tensions: Bolivia past and present. Pittsburgh, Pa.: Pittsburgh Press, 2008. 309 p.: bibl., graphs, index, maps, tables. (Pitt Latin American series)

An excellent compendium of some of the best social scientists' analyses of the situation in Bolivia after the election of Evo Morales. With 12 contributors, the volume ranges over the issues of ethnicity, regionalism, state-society relations, constitutionalism, economic development, and globalization. Presents the debates among scholars with differing views which provides for a fine summary of many of the main issues. For political scientist's comment, see *HLAS 65:1646.*

1763 Demélas, Marie-Danielle. José Santos Vargas y su familia: de cholos a criollos, de criollos a indios. (*Anu. Estud. Boliv. Arch. Bibliogr.*, 14, 2008, p. 173–188)

This study, based on the life of the author of the diary about the Independence War, shows that Vargas' father went from being a mestizo family in Oruro in the late colonial period to one that clawed its way up into the Creole elite. However, José Santos Vargas himself, despite his military glories for the new nation-state, decided to become a community Indian and settle in a small village in the valleys of La Paz. The article shows clearly the plasticity of race and how even Indian status was not necessarily seen as descending the social scale in the aftermath of independence.

1764 Demélas, Marie-Danielle. Nacimiento de la guerra de guerrilla: el diario de José Santos Vargas, 1810–1825. La Paz: Plural Editores; Lima: IFEA, 2007. 459 p.: bibl., ill. (some col.), index, col. maps, 1 DVD. (Travaux de l'Institut français d'études andines; 196)

An analysis of the famous diary of José Santos Vargas, who was a member of a patriot guerrilla band during the wars for independence. Demélas goes beyond the diary to examine the context of the manuscript, the places where Vargas fought, and the new type of guerrilla (ie., little war) warfare. She asserts that this type of warfare was new and an invention of the Spanish American world at the beginning of the 19th century.

1765 Diarios de la Revolución del 16 de julio de 1809. Textos de Crispín Diez de Medina *et al.* La Paz: Gobierno Municipal de La Paz, 2008. 169 p.: ill. (Biblioteca paceña. Col. Bicentenario)

A re-edition of a 1940 edition (first published in 1894), the book contains three diaries of individuals who wrote during the independence period about the region around La Paz. The contribution by Crispín Diez de Medina is the most detailed, whereas the writings by the priests José Cayetano Ortiz de Ariñez and Francisco Iturri Patiño mostly recount events and as such are less interesting. Lacks a contextualization of the authors of the diaries or notes to explain the events covered; thus not very useful for nonspecialists.

Dunkerley, James. Evo Morales, the "two Bolivias" and the third Bolivian revolution. See *HLAS 65:1649.*

1766 Gálvez Rodríguez, William. El guerrillero heroico: Che en Bolivia. Vizcaya, Spain: Status Ediciones, 2003. 750 p.: bibl., ill., maps.

The best feature of this book, despite its hagiographic introduction, is that it counterpoises the different diaries during Che Guevara's presence in Bolivia. This means that for each date, this book provides the different entries of each of the diaries, providing for different views of the failed campaign.

1767 Garay Vera, Cristián. El Acre y los "Asuntos del Pacífico": Bolivia, Brasil, Chile y Estados Unidos, 1898–1909. (*Historia/Santiago*, 41:2, julio/dic. 2008, p. 341–369, map)

Argues that the Acre conflict that led to the loss of the territory to Brazil (1903) and the loss of Antofagasta in the War of the Pacific against Chile were related. In the early 20th century, Bolivia attempted to have the US counterbalance its neighbors of Brazil and Chile so that it would not lose territory, but that this led to an alliance between Chile and Brazil that forced Bolivia to concede its territory to its neighbors.

1768 García Jordán, Pilar. Con la secularización "se abrió el campo; el que quería venía": la formación de un grupo dirigente en el ámbito local boliviano, 1938/39–1948. (*Rev. Indias*, 67:240, mayo/agosto 2007, p. 521–550, bibl., tables)

Shows the effects that secularization of the Franciscan missions among the Guarayos had on the indigenous population. The author analyzes how the new governors of the ex-missions despoiled the towns, taking much of the land for themselves and forcing the Guarayos to become laborers on estates often far from their original territory.

1769 Gianotten, Vera. CIPCA y poder campesino indígena: 35 años de historia. La Paz: CIPCA, 2006. 411 p.: bibl. (Cuadernos de investigación; 66)

A history of one of the largest and effective NGOs in Bolivia, focusing on institutional issues and also highlighting the turbulent history of Bolivia from 1970 to 2005. The study also provides an analysis of development projects and issues in summary form.

1770 Gil Montero, Raquel. La construcción de Argentina y Bolivia en los Andes meridionales: población, tierras y ambiente en el siglo XIX. Buenos Aires: Prometeo Libros, 2008. 282 p.: bibl., ill.

This important book on a muchneglected region examines the fate of indigenous peoples in the area straddling the border of Argentina and Bolivia during the "long nineteenth century." Based mainly on demographic records, the author shows that there were subsistence crises that affected reproduction of peasant households during the period. A good comparative study, she also shows how the Argentine policy of not recognizing indigenous land rights contrasted with that of Bolivia, though the liberal reforms at the end of the 19th century were detrimental to the Bolivian indigenous population as well.

1771 Gordillo, José M. Cochabamba's elites in ethnographic code. Translated by Sara Shields. (*T'inkazos*, 22, julio 2007, bibl., map, tables)

An interesting attempt at quantifying elite status in Cochabamba and how it changed during the 20th century. By correlating land tenure, company stock ownership, and social club adherence, the author shows that the Cochabamba elites disintegrated after the 1952 Revolution, in part because they lost their estates, but that subsequent generations have become more educated and many have left the region. Mostly intellectuals and artisans/workers have remained.

1772 Gotkowitz, Laura. A revolution for our rights: indigenous struggles for land and justice in Bolivia, 1880–1952. Durham, N.C.: Duke Univ. Press, 2007. 398 p.: bibl., ill., index, maps.

An essential study of indigenous political activity of the highlands in Bolivia mostly of the first half of the 20th century. Gotkowitz shows how the indigenous communities organized after the liberal onslaught against community lands at the turn of the century and how they persisted in interpreting the law in their own favor despite a state that, with few exceptions, tried to destroy the communities. The book shows how the Andean peoples, through their activism, contributed to Bolivian history and were able to achieve some of their aims in the 1952 Revolution.

1773 Hylton, Forrest and **Sinclair Thomson.** Revolutionary horizons: past and present in Bolivian politics. Prologue by Adolfo Gilly. London; New York: Verso, 2007. 177 p.: bibl., ill., index, maps.

This important book argues that the ascension of Evo Morales is part of a long historical process that goes back to the Túpac Katari rebellions of the 1780s. The authors assert that the mobilization of urban workers and peasants has been key to Bolivian revolutions, of which the most important were the ones in the 1780s, the 1952 Revolution spearheaded by the Movimiento Revolucionario Nacionalista, and the election of Evo Morales in 2005. For political scientist's comment, see *HLAS 65:1656.*

1774 Una independencia, muchos caminos: el caso de Bolivia (1808–1826). Recopilación de Armando Martínez y Manuel Chust. Textos de Braz A. Brancato *et al.* Castelló de la Plana, Spain: Univ. Jaume I, 2008. 243 p.: bibl. (Col. América; 10)

A nontraditional work that examines independence struggles of Bolivia from many different perspectives, taking into account the independence movements in the rest of Spanish America and the problems in Spain. In fact, little of the independence struggles in what was to become Bolivia are detailed. Written by a team of six historians, only one of whom (Soux) specializes on Bolivia. Written presumably for teachers, the book attempts to provide a larger context without nationalist prejudices.

1775 Irurozqui, Marta. Muerte en Loreto: ciudadanía armada y violence política en Bolivia, 1861–1862. (*Anu. Estud. Boliv. Arch. Bibliogr.,* 15, 2009, p. 183–214)

The author argues that political violence by armed civilians disappeared after the massacre perpetrated by Plácido Yañez in 1861, when he murdered a number of political opponents accused of conspiring against the government. Yañez himself was murdered by a crowd the following year, to revenge the massacre. This event brought about a change in political culture that, while it did not stop the military takeovers, did diminish political violence in the country.

1776 Irurozqui, Marta. Sobre indios, tópicos victimistas y maneras de ser ciudadano: Bolivia en el siglo XIX. (*Guaraguao/Barcelona,* 11:24, 2007, p. 50–73, bibl.)

A dense summary of her book "*A bala, piedra y palo*": la construcción de la ciudadanía política en Bolivia, 1826–1952 (see *HLAS 60:2662*) and other works, the author shows that the victimization of indigenous peoples and the black and white representation of centuries of exploitation and powerlessness of Indians is not validated by 19th-century history. She argues that Indians were useful citizens and made themselves essential members of Bolivian society until the late 19th century, when the Creoles began to marginalize them politically and conceptually.

1777 John, S. Sándor. Bolivia's radical tradition: permanent revolution in the Andes. Tucson: Univ. of Arizona Press, 2009. 317 p.: bibl., index.

This book is the first study of Bolivian Trotskyism in English. Based on a great variety of sources, the author details the movement from its origins in the 1930s until the present time. Weaker on the period after 1971, but does shows why Trotskyism became the dominant ideology of Bolivian labor.

1778 Langenbacher Jiménez, Ferdy. Origen, desarrollo e influjo de los Colegios de Propaganda Fide en la iglesia y sociedad de la recién fundada República Boliviana, 1834–1877. Introducción histórica de Francisco de Borja Medina. Grottaferrata, Italy: Frati editori di Quaracchi, 2005. 498 p.: bibl., index. (Analecta Franciscana; 15) (Nova series: Documenta et studia; 3)

A useful administrative history of the Franciscans in Bolivia. The author provides an overview of the colonial missions, then focuses on the history of the establishment of the *Colegios de Propaganda Fide* in Bolivia by Pope Leo IX in 1877, and then a short summary of convents and their missions after independence. Most valuable are the appendices, which list Franciscan leaders and important letters, decrees, and reports from the 18th to the 20th centuries. Best read as a supplement to other histories of the Franciscans.

1779 Langer, Erick D. Bringing the economic back in: Andean indians and the construction of the nation-state in 19th century Bolivia. (*J. Lat. Am. Stud.*, 41:3, Aug. 2009, p. 527–551)

Seminal article argues that in considering the construction of the nation-state, Indian peasants on the Bolivian Altiplano must be evaluated not only in terms of political interests, but economic ones as well. As this work shows, they supported free-trade regimes. Casts doubt on indigenous nationalism and reemphasizes the use of racial classifications because of tribute collections. Shows that hierarchies existed among indigenous population in the early republican period. The 1860s assault on landownership changed all this, and not for the better. [B. Tenenbaum]

1780 Langer, Erick D. Expecting pears from an elm tree: Franciscan missions on the Chiriguano frontier in the heart of South America, 1830–1949. Durham, N.C.: Duke Univ. Press, 2009. 375 p.: bibl., ill., index.

Thorough and excellent look at Franciscan missions to the Chiriguano villages in southeastern Bolivia established in the 1840s, and lasting until 1949. Evaluates the institution and the frontier it contributed to and gained from and its role in Bolivian state and society. Shows clearly the importance of both in the history of Latin America and takes special pains to examine the unique role of the mission as an institution as well. [B. Tenenbaum]

1781 Lavaud, Jean-Pierre. La dictadura minada: la huelga de hambre de las mujeres mineras, Bolivia, 1977–1978. Traducción de Luis H. Antezana. La Paz: IFEA: CESU-UMSS: Plural Editores, 2003. 284 p.: bibl. (Travaux de l'Institut français d'études andines; 168)

An intriguing analysis of the 1977 hunger strike of the wives of imprisoned miners in Bolivia from a social science perspective. Lavaud shows how these women were able to win and encourage over one thousand other hunger strikers to join them and end the Banzer dictatorship (1970–78).

1782 Lema, Ana María. El sentido del silencio: la mano de obra chiquitana en el oriente boliviano a principios del siglo XX. Santa Cruz de la Sierra, Bolivia: UPIEB:

Editorial El País, 2009. 221 p.: bibl. (Col. Ciencias sociales; 14)

An excellent historical study of the labor history of indigenous peoples in Velasco province, but in fact also a good economic history of Santa Cruz department at the turn of the 20th century. Also deals with the perceptions of labor relations and of indigenous peoples in Santa Cruz. A good start to understanding the post-independence history of the Bolivian lowlands.

1783 Mala guerra: los indígenas en la Guerra del Chaco, 1932–1935. Recopilación de Nicolas Richard. Asunción: ServiLibro: Museo del Barro; Paris: CoLibris, 2008. 421 p.: bibl., ill., maps.

This collection of essays details the relationships between the indigenous peoples of the Chaco and the Bolivian and Paraguayan militaries. The tragic story shows the death and destruction of a region claimed by two countries though it was inhabited by indigenous peoples. Broken down mostly by ethnic groups, each chapter describes the conflict from different sources, ranging from oral histories to manuscripts. Written mainly by eminent anthropologists, this is a much-needed new perspective of the war. For review by anthropologist, see *HLAS 65:624.*

1784 Marion, Javier F. *Indios blancos:* nascent polities and social convergence in the Ayopaya Rebellion, Alto Perú (Bolivia), 1814–1821. (*CLAHR*, 15:4, Fall 2006, p. 344–375, map)

An excellent discussion of the way in which the patriot forces conceived of ethnicity during the period of the *republiquetas* that emerged during the independence struggles in what is now Bolivia. Based largely on the independence-era diary of José Santos Vargas and other primary sources.

1785 Mendieta Parada, Pilar. Caminantes entre dos mundos: los apoderados indígenas en Bolivia, siglo XIX. (*Rev. Indias*, 66:238, sept./dic. 2006, p. 761–782)

The article shows the origins of the *apoderado* movement, which consisted of leaders of Andean communities organized to reclaim land rights based on colonial titles. The author shows that this movement goes back to 1871, in an alliance between Creoles and Indians who overthrew the

Mariano Melgarejo dictatorship. This alliance solidified after 1880, when the *apoderados* fell in with the Liberal Party, who used them to gain political advantage over the Conservatives. Shows the close relationship that indigenous leaders had with prominent Creoles during the 19th century.

1786 Mendieta Parada, Pilar. En defensa de sus privilegios: familias cacicales en el altiplano paceño, siglos XVIII–XIX. (*Anu. Estud. Boliv. Arch. Bibliogr.*, 15, 2009, p. 371–390)

An intriguing study, showing how the Cusicanqui and Siñani families were able to keep their power. After 1780, they were successful in maintaining some of their privileges by showing their loyalty to the Crown and continued to do so during the Wars for Independence. Only when it was clear that independence was imminent did they switch to the patriot side. After the abolition of hereditary chieftainships during the republic, these families used other strategies, such as intermarrying with Creoles, commercial activities, and using their networks of clients to keep their power and privileges.

1787 Mitre, Antonio. Náufragos en tierra firme: bloqueo comercial, despojo y confinamiento de japoneses de Bolivia durante la Segunda Guerra Mundial. Santa Cruz de la Sierra, Bolivia: Editorial El País, 2006. 202 p.: bibl., ill. (Col. Ciencias sociales; 6)

The first book that analyzes the Japanese presence in Bolivia from the turn of the century to 1945. The author shows that few of the Japanese who entered during this period were from the main islands and instead came from neighboring Peru, Brazil, or Chile. They mostly entered into commerce, establishing small merchant houses in La Paz, Cochabamba, Oruro, and in the lowland town of Riberalta. During WWII, like the Germans, many were deported and lost their businesses. Only the Japanese in the eastern lowlands remained, protected by distance from La Paz along with the support of local populations.

1788 Oporto, Luis. Historia de la archivística boliviana. La Paz: PIEB: Biblioteca y Archivo Histórico del H. Congreso Nacional: Colegio Nacional de Historiadores de Bolivia, 2006. 365 p.: bibl., ill. (Serie Investigaciones coeditadas)

A valuable guide to historical archives in Bolivia from one of the most knowledgeable Bolivian archivists. Goes back to European and Andean archives in a historical summary and provides histories of Bolivian archives. The major contributions are the often detailed descriptions of Bolivian archives, including ecclesiastical, departmental, and regional ones.

1789 Parrón, Mario Gustavo. Representaciones de la Guerra del Chaco en la memoria e identidad Guaraní. (*Anu. Estud. Boliv. Arch. Bibliogr.*, 15, 2009, p. 403–423)

A juxtaposition of indigenous testimonials and secondary literature on the Guarani in Bolivia provide a means to analyze the effect of the Chaco War on indigenous peoples, including not just the Guarani but also the Chulupí people. The author asserts that both Bolivian and Paraguayan troops were devastating to the indigenous groups and the latter had a difficult time reestablishing themselves in their ancestral lands.

La permanente construcción de lo cruceño: un estudio sobre la identidad en Santa Cruz de la Sierra. See *HLAS 65:1667.*

1790 Platt, Tristán. Tributo y ciudadanía en Potosí, Bolivia: consentimiento y libertad entre los ayllus de la provincial de Porco, 1830–1840. (*Anu. Estud. Boliv. Arch. Bibliogr.*, 14, 2008, p. 331–396)

The difficult topic of indigenous citizenship seen through local customs provides the theme of this expansive essay. The author shows that although no Indians were given the title of *ciudadano* nor were they permitted to join the militia, they did feel that they contributed to the state voluntarily through tribute payments and other informal mechanisms. In turn, the *curacas* of the communities were in an undefined position who saw themselves as citizens through tribute collection. However, the state did not provide the Indians with schools so that they could become citizens by learning to read and write.

1791 Power, culture, and violence in the Andes. Edited by Christine Hunefeldt and Misha Kokotovic. Brighton, England; Portland, Ore.: Sussex Academic Press,

2009. 202 p.: bibl., index. (New perspectives on Latin America: society, culture, and history)

An overall excellent collection of essays on violence, with most focused on Peru and Bolivia. The highlights are outstanding essays by Christine Hunefeldt on the role of violence in military recruitment in 19th-century Peru, Miguel La Serna on the intersection of community conflict with Sendero Luminoso guerrillas and military violence in Peru, Herbert Klein on the origins of indigenous power in Bolivia, and Nancy Postero on the use of symbolism behind Evo Morales' politics also in Bolivia.

Quispe Quispe, Ayar. Los tupakataristas revolucionarios. See *HLAS 65:1671*.

1792 Robertson Trigo, Juan Víctor and **Margarita Robertson Orozco.** Ese pedazo de tierra: el territorio de Manso. La Paz: Muela del Diablo, 2005. 178 p.: bibl., ill., maps.

An odd mixture of analysis of the Chaco region in Bolivia according to the secondary literature and published sources, plus tantalizing bits of primary documents that the authors have in their possession about the anticlerical Dr. Leocado Trigo, the founder of the Gran Delegación del Chaco in the early 20th century and expeditionary into the Gran Chaco.

1793 Rodríguez Ostria, Gustavo. Sin tiempo para las palabras: Teoponte, la otra guerrilla guevarista en Bolivia. Cochabamba, Bolivia: Grupo Editorial Kipus, 2006. 643 p.: bibl., ill. (some col.), col. map.

Definitive history of the guerrilla of Teoponte of 1970, showing its importance in 20th-century Latin American history. The author argues that the formation of the Ejército de Liberación Nacional was a continuation of the cycle of guerrilla warfare begun by Che Guevara. Exhaustive analysis and narrative of the actions of all participants from 1967 to 1970.

1794 Roux, Jean-Claude. La modernité de l'oeuvre d'Alcide d'Orbigny: un précurseur des droits de l'homme et de la géographie du développement en Bolivie. (*Outremers*, 92:344/345, 2004, p. 113–140, bibl.)

Analyzes the publications of the French scientist and traveler through Bolivia in the 1830s, arguing that D'Orbigny saw the relationship between the Bolivian state and indigenous peoples as an inherited colonial legacy. He urged a change to a more egalitarian system through economic development and public education.

1795 Santos Vargas, José. Diario histórico de todos los sucesos ocurridos en las provincias de Sicasica y Ayopaya durante la Guerra de la Independencia americana desde el añõ 1814 hasta el año 1825. Introducción y glosario de Gunnar Mendoza. La Paz: ABNB: Fundación Cultural BCB: Plural Editores, 2008. 512 p.: bibl., ill. (some col.), index, maps, 1 CD-ROM.

The definitive version of the famous diary of an independence war guerrilla in what is now Bolivia. This edition uses the second, more complete version of the diary and is based on a new transcription. The footnotes, left out of the 1982 edition, of Gunnar Mendoza's introduction, are incorporated. One of the most important primary documents of the independence struggle in Spanish America.

1796 Scavone Yegros, Ricardo. Las relaciones entre el Paraguay y Bolivia en el siglo XIX. Asunción: Servilibro, 2004. 584 p.: bibl., 1 map.

A very well documented diplomatic history of the relations between Bolivia and Paraguay, written by a Paraguayan and based on sources from both countries. The author's hypothesis is that a series of errors during the 19th century finally led to the Chaco War (1932–35). Most of the focus is on the period from 1879 to 1901.

1797 Teruel, Ana A. La desamortización de la propiedad comunal indígena: pervivencias y transformaciones en la estructura agraria de la Provincia de Sud Chichas. (*Anu. Estud. Boliv. Arch. Bibliogr.*, 13, 2007, p. 641–680)

Delineates the changes in land tenure and indigenous communities between the 19th century and the early 20th in one of the southern-most provinces of Bolivia, where mining was important. Although haciendas grew at the expense of Indian communities, resistance from community members made this process much less complete than the government had imagined.

1798 Trigo O'Connor d'Arlach, Eduardo. Tarija en la Independencia del Virreinato del Río de La Plata. La Paz: Plural Editores, 2009. 259 p.: bibl.

A very useful narrative political and military history of the independence struggles in the southern-most department of Tarija, which finally joined Bolivia rather than Argentina in 1826. Based mostly on published sources and secondary materials, the author adds appropriate context from Argentine sources as well.

Chile

WILLIAM F. SATER, *Professor Emeritus of History, California State University, Long Beach*

WHILE NOT NEGLECTING TRADITIONAL TOPICS, such as the Allende years, Chile's historians have expanded their horizons. Some, such as the contributors to the edited volume *Escucha Winka* (item **1810**), have tried to write about the nation's sad history of dealing with the Mapuche population. Crow (item **1806**) noted that Dr. Alejandro Lipschutz had encouraged the Allende regime to include the Indians in his agrarian reform, as well as try to ensure their culture's survival. Unfortunately, as León (item **1822**) and Almonacid Zapata (item **1800**) demonstrate, sometimes these best-intentioned Indian reforms misfired. Further, as Klubock (item **1831**) observes, for example, the government's attempt to develop the south's forest products industry grievously damaged Mapuche interests as well as the environment.

Perhaps it is a coincidence, but the 2007 publication of a translation into Spanish of *Urban Workers and Labor Unions in Chile, 1902–1927* (1983), Peter De Shazo's epic study on anarchists, seems to have precipitated a spate of other works on anarchism and its devotees. If, as Grez (item **1818**) demonstrates, the anarchist movement never became widely popular among the nation's workers, Massardo (item **1825**) shows that it, as well as other forces, influenced the leftist Luis Emilio Recabarren. Pinto Vallejos (item **1838**) carefully analyzes the various leftist ideologies that the nitrate miners espoused in their struggle with capitalism. One tragic manifestation of that conflict is explored in González's study of the infamous 1907 massacre at Iquiqué (item **1817**). Tarapacá remained a cockpit of unrest: the Moneda contributed to the chaos by backing the *Liga Patrióticas'* attempts to cleanse ethnically the province of Peruvians in anticipation of a plebiscite—never conducted—that would determine ownership of that contested area (item **1816**).

Scholarship on women's history has been advanced by Montecimos' edited volume (item **1835**) which contains numerous articles on women's activities and achievements in Chile. Others scholars concentrate on more specific subjects: Sánchez Manríquez's (item **1848**) article traces female attempts to gain entry into the University of Chile; Correa Gómez (item **1805**) writes on the role of female religious orders administering a woman's prison; while Mazzei de Grazia (item **1826**) explains female involvement in banking. Clearly the most significant volume on this topic is Zárate's (item **1858**) magisterial study on childbearing practices that culminated in the emergence of the medical speciality of obstetrics.

Thanks to Mooney (item **1833**), we have an all-encompassing and detailed study of the birth control movement in Chile.

If the Allende years still attract attention, the studies have become more specialized, focusing on topics such as UP policies toward the Mapuche. Two historians have concentrated on the collapse of the Allende government: Moniz Bandeira's work (item **1832**) looks at the role of the Chilean navy and is useful for explaining the role of the Brazilian government in fomenting the 1973 coup. A series of essays, edited by Albornoz, (item **1829**) describes specific facets of UP Chile prior to its overthrow; while Veneros (item **1854**) tries to explain the psychological forces that presumably shaped Allende's life and his regime. Medina (item **1827**) shows the UP's short-lived attempts to incorporate cybernetics.

Alejandro San Francisco's second volume further enhances his research on the military aspects of the 1891 Revolution (item **1847**). He also devoted attention to general military history by editing a book on Chile's *Academia de Guerra* and its impact on the evolution of the army (item **1799**). Magaich-Aerola's two-volume history of Chile's navy traces the fleet's post-1890 development; his second tome concentrates on the unsuccessful attempts of the lower deck to short circuit the naval officers' participation in the anti-Allende coup (item **1823**).

The Pinochet regime labored to eradicate its political opposition in Chile and abroad: Dinges concentrates on the Moneda's participation in an alliance of Latin American military regimes to quash guerrilla groups (item **1809**). Still, as Rivera Aravena (item **1842**) noted, opposition groups managed to function during Pinochet's regime, including the hostile radio stations. Wright chronicles the growth of opposition to the dictatorships in Argentina and Chile and their successful efforts to prosecute the dictatorship for human rights abuses (item **1856**).

Economic historians have been diligent: Millán catalogs various Chilean mines and their histories in the 20th century (item **1830**), while Méndez focuses solely on Anconcagua's mining families (item **1828**). The dean of the history of the province of Magallanes, Martinic Beros, (item **1824**) explains why railroads had a limited impact in developing the area's economy. Clearly the most significant contribution to economic history is Ortega's (item **1837**) epic and well-researched work chronicling the evolution of Chile's economy from the mid- to late-19th century. Anyone interested in this topic must begin his or her efforts by reading Ortega's study.

The government strained to reform various parts of Chilean life. As Yáñez Andrade describes, the Moneda (item **1857**) founded the *Oficina de Trabajo*, an organization initially chartered to collect statistical data, but which evolved into a force to regulate living and working conditions. The state, as Illanes (item **1821**) explains, also began to train social workers to help the desperate. Zárate's edited volume stresses various public health measures, including vaccination and family planning (item **1840**). Fernández Labbé (item **1813**) traces efforts to combat alcoholism by limiting the sale of spirits, an effort the nation's liquor lobby effectively squelched. State involvement did not preclude private efforts to improve living conditions. As Rodrigo Hidalgo (item **1819**) and others note, the Catholic Church attempted to improve housing. Rojas Flores (item **1844**) emphasizes the private efforts to protect children, a movement which failed due to the opposition of the Church and the wealthy. Some leftists also tried to improve the lot of the nation's youth by repudiating the government schools in favor of institutions that rejected capitalism and chauvinistic institutions (item **1841**).

Political history, long a staple of Chilean scholars, remains a favorite topic. Villalobos (item **1855**) as well as De Ramón (item **1807**) provide global views of the nation from the precolonial era to the present; Moulian concentrates on the period from Aguirre Cerda to Allende's election (item **1834**). Alejandro San Francisco and Angel Soto have edited a superb compilation of essays each one dealing with presidential elections beginning with Arturo Alessandri (item **1803**). Salazar (item **1846**) enhances our understanding of the early Republic while Brahm García (item **1802**) shows that Mariáno Egaña was not the éminence grise of conservatism. Thanks to Fernández Abara the oft-mentioned but little understood Ibáñez emerges a bit more clearly (item **1811**). Barría (item **1801**) concentrates on the reform of the late-19th-century public administration. Tomás Cornejo focuses on the articles and cartoons in *Topaze*, Chile's preeminent satirical journal which etched in acid the images of the country's politicians (item **1804**). Thankfully, Ulianova continues her efforts, enhancing our understanding of the relations of Chile's Communist Party and the Kremlin (item **1852**).

While Subercaseaux (item **1850**) provides an excellent study of social history, a particularly noteworthy contribution is Salazar Orellana's autobiography which traces his rise from *inquilino* to urban worker (item **1845**). His life stands in stark contrast to González's (item **1815**) description of the often profligate lifestyle of the late-19th-century Chilean colony in France and to Godoy's account of the raucous Carnival celebrations of Copiapós citizens (item **1814**).

A festschrift in honor of the late historian Armando Ramón (item **1820**) contains some innovative essays on Chile's urban development. Another singularly significant work is Serrano's book that focused on the travails of the Roman Catholic Church as it faced demands from in an increasingly militant and secular nation (item **1849**). Extremely well researched, it is one of the few works on this neglected topic.

The emphasis on different topics of investigation—the role of women, studies of modern political issues, questions of public health—as well as the continued interest in traditional subjects such as economic and political history auger well for the future. The happy confluence of new journals and newly minted doctoral students promises to open up new subjects for research while buttressing the old.

1799 La Academia de Guerra del Ejército de Chile, 1886–2006: ciento veinte años de historia. Edición de Alejandro San Francisco. Santiago: Centro de Estudios Bicentenario, 2006. 231 p.: bibl.

Essays written by civilian historians as well as serving officers, tracing the development and impact of the Academia de Guerra del Ejército plus a study of the Ensayo Militar. Excellent source for military historians.

1800 Almonacid Zapata, Fabián. La división de las comunidades indígenas del sur de Chile, 1925–1958: un proyecto inconcluso. (*Rev. Indias,* 68:243, mayo/agosto 2008, p. 115–150, bibl.)

Convinced that comunal landholding impoverished the Indians, the Chilean government reacted. In 1927, it passed a law to divide Mapuche communal land in the belief that private ownership would stimulate production. Although private interests favored this measure, resistance by the Indians forced the government to abandon it.

1801 Barría Traverso, Diego. Continuista o rupturista, radical o sencillísima: la reorganización de ministerios de 1887 y su discusión político-administrativa. (*Historia/Santiago,* 41:1, enero/junio 2008, p. 5–42, table)

The need for government reform led to the reorganization of the public administration and replacement of political appointees with trained career civil servants. Fearing that it would give the president too much power, conservatives initially opposed change. Later, politicans accepted it as part of a modernization program. Superbly researched; an important essay.

1802 Brahm García, Enrique I. Mariano Egaña: derecho y política en la fundación de la república conservadora. Santiago: Ediciones Centro de Estudios Bicentenario, 2007. 253 p.: bibl., index. (Col. América Latina)

Contrary to traditional beliefs, Maríano Egaña was not a conservative. Although not a democrat, he was a key aide to Portales, helping to implement laws that limited the power of the presidency, as well as other legislation and customs which guided Chile until 1925. A well-researched volume on an oft-neglected topic.

1803 Camino a La Moneda: las elecciones presidenciales en la historia de Chile, 1920–2000. Santiago: Instituto de Historia: Centro de Estudios Bicentenario, 2005. 520 p.: bibl., ill., index.

Fifteen authors have written essays on all of Chile's presidential elections beginning with Alessandri's 1920 triumph, and concluding with the 2000 contest. Of varying quality, these essays provide information on some of the least known contests. Well-researched, this book is essential for any historian of the modern period.

1804 Cornejo Cancino, Tomás. Una clase a medias: las representaciones satíricas de los grupos medios Chilenos en *Topaze*, 1931–1970. (*Historia/Santiago*, 40:2, julio/dic. 2007, p. 249–284, ill.)

Topaze, a Santiago satirical journal, relished lampooning the politicial class. Using a combination of sarcasm and cartoons, the magazine flayed all, particularly individuals believed to be betraying their supposed principles. Interesting insights that reveal political currents and middle class attitudes. Valuable for political and social historians for its comments on Chilean society.

1805 Correa Gómez, María José. Demandas penitenciarias: discusión y reforma de las cárceles de mujeres en Chile, 1930–1950. (*Historia/Santiago*, 38:1, enero/junio 2005, p. 9–30, bibl.)

The Chilean government entrusted the administration of womens' prisons to the Sister of the Good Shepard, who used prayer and silence to rehabilitate the criminals. As part of its attempt to secularize society, the state replaced the nuns with government agencies designed to educate the prisoners to deal with modern society.

1806 Crow, Joanna. Debates about ethnicity, class and nation in Allende's Chile, 1970–1973. (*Bull. Lat. Am. Res.*, 26:3, July 2007, p. 319–338)

The UP, encouraged by Alejandro Liptschutz, sought to improve the lot of the Mapuche. In addition to making them beneficiaries of the Agrarian Reform Program, it passed specific legislation encouraging bilingualism and cultivating a strong sense of identity among the heretofore neglected Indian population.

1807 De Ramón, Armando. Historia de Chile: desde la invasión incaica hasta nuestros dias, 1500–2000. Santiago: Catalonia, 2003. 316 p.: bibl., ill., index, maps.

A well-documented study of Chile's history from the colonial period to 2000. Author combines excellent research with a detailed analysis of the nation's history. Particularly perceptive for the later years, the author includes an excellent bibliography. Essential for historians of Chile.

1808 XIX: historias del siglo diecinueve chileno. Santiago: Vergara Grupo Zeta, 2006. 273 p.: bibl. (Biografía e historia)

Seven essays, authored by young historians, that revisit certain seminal events in Chile's history. (See also item **1853** for work on the 20th century.) Written with style and verve, each chapter will refresh the reader's memory while simultaneously providing new insights. A charming work which all 19th-century specialists can consult with profit.

1809 Dinges, John. The Condor years: how Pinochet and his allies brought terrorism to three continents. New York: New Press, 2004. 322 p.: bibl., index.

The intelligence services of the Southern Cone nations, plus Bolivia, created a network of agents to destroy what they perceived to be an alliance of leftist terrorists operating against right-wing governments. While containing an impressive bibliography, its highly partisan tone and the author's failure to use footnotes, limits the value of this research.

1810 **- Escucha, winka—!: cuatro ensayos de Historia Nacional Mapuche y un epílogo sobre el futuro.** Santiago: LOM Ediciones, 2006. 278 p.: bibl. (Col. Historia)

Four essays, each with different authors, describe precolumbian Mapuche society, their coexistence with Western culture, the destruction of indigenous society by those forces, and an essay on modern Indian culture. A necessary overview of the heretofore forgotten elements of Chilean society.

1811 **Fernández Abara, Joaquín.** El ibañismo, 1937–1952: un caso de populismo en la política chilena. Chile: Instituto de Historia, Pontificia Univ. Católica de Chile, 2007. 214 p.: bibl., ill. (Historia libros)

Carlos Ibañez overcame his fall from power, returning to seek the presidency in 1938, 1942, and 1952 when he finally triumphed. His election constituted a victory of a populism that cut across party and class lines and spoke to his ability to function without the structures of ideology. Important for the 1931–52 period, with an excellent bibliography and political charts.

1812 **Fernández Canque, Manuel A.** Arica 1868: un tsunami y un terremoto. Arica, Chile: Univ. de Tarapacá; Santiago: Centro de Investigación Diego Barros Arana, 2007. 332 p.: bibl., ill. (some col.), maps (some col.).

Presents a detailed study of the earthquake and tsunami that devastated the city of Arica in Aug. 1868. Reconstructs the events using several eyewitness accounts and offers an interesting view of 19th-century history of natural disasters. Unpublished photographs complement an in-depth description of the tragedy. [M. Marsilli]

1813 **Fernández Labbé, Marcos.** Los usos de la taberna: renta fiscal, combate al alcoholismo y cacicazgo político en Chile, 1870–1930. (Historia/Santiago, 39:2, julio/dic. 2006, p. 369–429, tables)

Domestic producers of wine enjoyed the political protection of the viticulturists in legislature. They opposed attempts to limit alcohol consumption as did local government which derived income from its sale, as well as select political interests which used free drink to suborn voters. Shows conflict between reformers and the powers that were.

1814 **Godoy Orellana, Milton.** "¡Cuándo el siglo se sacará la máscara!": fiesta, carnaval y disciplinamiento cultural en el Norte Chico, Copiapó, 1840–1900. (Historia/Santiago, 40:1, enero/junio 2007, p. 5–34, graph)

Copiapó's carnival activities—a traditional period of excess—unleashed raucous if not often illegal behavior. Eventually, political and economic considerations forced secular and parochial authorities to try and restore order. Based on primary materials, this investigation opens new areas for research.

1815 **González Errázuriz, Francisco Javier.** Aquellos años franceses, 1870–1900: Chile en la huella de París. Santiago: Taurus, 2003. 483 p.: bibl., ill. (Taurus historia)

France influenced Chile, particularly in the area of education and culture. During the Belle Époque and after the Balmaceda regime, a substantial number of Chileans resided in France, where they tended to live in the same neighborhoods, as they pursued a dissolute life. Interesting insights on the habits of the upper class.

1816 **González Miranda, Sergio.** El dios cautivo: las Ligas Patrióticas en la chilenización compulsiva de Tarapacá, 1910–1922. Santiago: LOM, 2004. 194 p.: bibl., ill. (Historia)

Employing a combination of fear and threats of violence, the extra-legal Ligas Patrióticas forced Peruvians either to flee Tacna and Arica or accept Chilean authority. Initially enjoying the tacit support of the Moneda, after 1922 the government became less hostile as it hoped to settle the border dispute with Peru. Uses interviews to some effect.

1817 **González Miranda, Sergio.** Ofrenda a una masacre: claves e indicios históricos de la emancipación pampina de 1907. Colaboración y prólogo de Pedro Bravo-Elizondo. Santiago: LOM Ediciones: CIHDE: Univ. Arturo Prat, 2007. 348 p.: bibl., ill., maps. (Historia)

The infamous 1907 massacre at the Santa María School in Iquique is a launching point for a discussion of the nitrate industry, as well as working conditions in the salitreras. Useful because it includes eyewitness accounts as well as references to literature of this event. Very helpful for social and economic historians.

1818 Grez Toso, Sergio. Los anarquistas y el movimiento obrero: la alborada de "la Idea" en Chile, 1893–1915. Santiago: LOM Ediciones, 2007. 435 p.: bibl., ill., index. (Historia)

Anarchists first appeared in the mid-1890s, an offshoot of various worker movements. Expanding from Valparaíso and Santiago, anarchism spread to the northern salitreras, playing a big role in fomenting labor unrest. Espousing pacificism, antimilitarism, and womens' rights, it repudiated the state, religion, and organized politics. An extremely well researched and necessary work.

1819 Hidalgo D., Rodrigo; Thomás Erráuriz Infante; and Rodrigo Booth Pinochet. Las viviendas de la beneficencia católica en Santiago: instituciones constructoras y efectos urbanos, 1890–1920. (*Historia/Santiago*, 38:2, julio/dic. 2005, p. 327–366, tables)

Migration from the countryside to Chile's cities, particularly Santiago, forced the lower class to inhabit substandard housing. Life in these conventillos was so wretched that Catholic charities began to work to provide decent housing. This effort anticipated and perhaps influenced the government to pass the 1906 law calling for adequate housing. Excellent for urban historians.

1820 Historias urbanas: homenaje a Armando de Ramón. Edición de Jaime Valenzuela Márquez. Santiago: Ediciones Univ. Catolica de Chile, 2007. 346 p.: bibl., ill. (some col.), index, maps.

Honoring the late Armando de Ramón, a Chilean urban historian, these essays concentrate on various aspects of urban life in Santiago or Valparaíso. The volume also provides some material on the colonial period. Focuses on Chile, but also explores Peru and Argentina. Contains a detailed bibliography of De Ramón's work. An excellent work.

Huneeus, Carlos. The Pinochet regime. See *HLAS 65:1744.*

1821 Illanes O., María Angélica. Cuerpo y sangre de la política: la construcción histórica de las visitadoras sociales, Chile, 1887–1940. Santiago: LOM, 2007. 497 p.: bibl., ill. (Historia)

Chilean authorities had to improve social conditions to prevent a revolution; authorities also wanted to protect the population for economic and strategic reasons. Building on private charities, the state created institutions, including schools of social welfare, to train social workers—the first in Latin America—to improve the lot of the lower classes. Excellent work with a great bibliography.

1822 León, Leonardo. La Araucanía: la violencia mestiza y el mito de la "pacificación," 1880–1900. Santiago: Univ. ARCIS, Escuela de Historia y Ciencias Sociales, 2005. 292 p.: bibl.

While it divided Araucanía among private owners and dismantled the Mapuche infrastructure, the Chilean state proved incapable of pacifying the newly integrated territory. The author largely blames mestizo groups for the violence that ravaged the new lands for the next 20 years. Interesting thesis; well-validated by use of the press and regional archives.

1823 Magasich-Airola, Jorge. Los que dijeron "no": historia del movimiento de los marinos antigolpistas de 1973. Santiago: LOM Ediciones, 2008. 2 v.: bibl., ill., indexes. (Historia)

Traces the navy's development culminating in the fleet officers' overthrow of Allende, the lower deck's efforts to abort the coup, as well as the punishment of those elements perceived as being loyal to the constitution. Highly partisan but interesting account that attacks the fleet officers' corps and its ties to the US and Brazilian navies.

1824 Martinic Beros, Mateo. Ferrocarriles en la zona austral de Chile,1869–1973. (*Historia/Santiago*, 38:2, julio/dic. 2005, p. 367–395, bibl., photos)

Magallanes could have used an extensive rail system but geographic conditions and the existence of maritime alternatives limited the application of the railway in the southern province. Providing a brief history of each rail line, this excellent work is written by the most prolific and accomplished scholar of Magallanes.

1825 Massardo, Jaime. La formación del imaginario político de Luis Emilio Recabarren: contribución al estudio crítico de la cultura política de las clases subalternas de la sociedad chilena. Santiago: LOM Ediciones, 2008. 345 p.: bibl. (Historia)

A variety of political influences, including service in the Partido Democratico, Argentine socialism, and anarchism, shaped Recabarren before his founding of the POS and, eventually, the Communist Party. Excellent bibliography, as well as description of post-1917 Chilean political events and Recabarren's difficult relations with the Soviets.

1826 Mazzei de Grazia, Leonardo. Participación femenina en el crédito en una sociedad en transcurso a la modernización: concepción a fines del siglo XIX. (*Historia/Santiago*, 40:1, enero/junio 2007, p. 69–90, maps, tables)

Thanks to the modernization of Chile, in particular the growth of credit institutions, women ceased playing as important a role in banking as they had in the colonial era. However, women still managed to borrow while their more affluent sisters, acting through the agency of their husbands, still made capital indirectly through borrowers.

1827 Medina, Eden. Designing freedom, regulating a nation: socialist cybernetics in Allende's Chile. (*J. Lat. Am. Stud.*, 38:3, Aug. 2006, p. 571–606)

The Allende government contracted with British academics to create a global computer program that would provide La Moneda with data that it could use to coordinate various sectors of the economy. The 1973 coup ended this program because the Pinochet administration, for ideological reasons, chose not to retain it.

1828 Méndez, Luz María. Los mineros de la Región de Aconcagua: familia y actividades económicas, 1818–1840. (*Rev. Chil. Hist. Geogr.*, 168, 2004/2005, p. 17–49, tables)

In Aconcagua, at least, the mining elites had diversified their economic activities. Many invested in agriculture, thereby

satisfying the needs of Valparaíso and helping create local industries. The agricultural-mining symbiosis made an impact on Chile's political development as well. Valuable for economic historians.

1829 1973: la vida cotidiana de un año crucial. Coordinación de Claudio Rolle. Santiago: Planeta, 2003. 354 p.: bibl., ill. (Historia y sociedad)

Nine essays focusing on various aspects of 1973 Chile. Of particular merit is that of Patricio Bernedo, who demonstrated how the press demonized its opposition, creating a climate of violence. Other studies deal with popular music and fashion. An enlightening work on heretofore ignored aspects of Allende's regime.

1830 Millán U., Augusto. La minería metálica en Chile en el siglo XX. Santiago: Editorial Universitaria, 2006. 178, [1] p.: bibl. (Imagen de Chile)

A history of each of Chile's mines, information on its output, and the type of technology employed, as well as an analysis of various government agencies which oversaw mining. Although it provides only a skimpy bibliography and no footnotes, this book is still useful for economic historians.

1831 Miller Klubock, Thomas. The politics of forests and forestry on Chile's southern frontier, 1880s–1940s. (*HAHR*, 86:3, Aug. 2006, p. 435–570)

Beginning in the 1930s, left-wing government encouraged the development of the forest industry in southern Chile. The rise of this economic sector, however, displaced the rural poor while depleting the soil, thus causing subsequent administrations to abandon earlier efforts to diversify the agrarian economy.

1832 Moniz Bandeira, Luis Alberto. Fórmula para el caos: la caída de Salvador Allende, 1970–1973. Santiago: Debate, 2008. 592 p.: bibl.

Although a traditional rehash of the last years of Allende's regime, this book also covers events in Bolivia, Peru, Argentina, and Uruguay. Utilizing Brazilian diplomatic dispatches, the author argues that Allende lacked the domestic resources to make important structural changes, particularly in face of US policies to disrupt the country.

1833 Mooney, Jadwiga E. Pieper. The politics of motherhood: maternity and women's rights in twentieth-century Chile. Pittsburgh, Pa.: Univ. of Pittsburgh Press, 2009. 301 p.: bibl., index. (Pitt Latin American series)

Appallingly high child mortality rates encouraged the Chilean government to become involved in improving womens' health. Conservative elements, however, prevented the medical profession from providing abortions and information on birth control. Eventually, birth control devices became available; abortions still remain illegal. Interesting work for gender issues.

1834 Moulian, Tomás. Fracturas: de Pedro Aguirre Cerda a Salvador Allende, 1938–1973. Santiago: LOM Ediciones, 2006. 274 p. (Historia)

Chile's right lost its power, but managed to protect its interests until 1938 when the Aguirre Cerda government moved to incorporate the middle class. This alliance retained the antiquated landholding system and the rhetoric of modernization until Allende's election shattered the calm. Well-documented analysis of post-1938 events.

1835 Mujeres chilenas: fragmentos de una historia. Compilación de Sonia Montecino Aguirre. Santiago: Editorial Catalonia: Cátedra Género UNESCO, CIEG, Facultad de Ciencias Sociales, Univ. de Chile, 2008. 625 p.: bibl., ill.

Some 53 articles, all written by experts in history and anthropology, explaining that women in Chile have played an important role from the prehistory of the nation to the present. Superb for social historians, as well as those who study the history of women.

1836 Nazer Ahumada, Ricardo. 110 años de energía para Magallanes: historia de EDELMAG S. A. 1897–2007. Santiago: Eds. Univ. Católica de Chile, 2009. 277 p.: bibl., ill., maps.

Traces the growth of Magallanes' electrical industry while revealing the area's economic and population growth within the context of Chilean development. Lavishly illustrated, it contains a wealth of statistical data. Essential for regional as well as economic historians.

1837 Ortega Martínez, Luis. Chile en ruta al capitalismo: cambio, euforia y depresión 1850–1880. Santiago: LOM Ediciones: Centro de Investigaciones Diego Barros Arana, 2005. 495 p.: bibl., ill. (Col. Sociedad y cultura; 38)

Extremely well documented and researched volume on Chile's economic development. Systematically traces the role of the nation's mineral and agricultural export sector, the growth of its industries, and the role of Chilean and British capitalists in this process. A lucid work based on a variety of primary sources which all scholars should consult.

Pereira Larraín, Teresa. Afectos e intimidades: el mundo familiar en los siglos XVII, XVIII y XIX. See item **1487**.

1838 Pinto Vallejos, Julio. Desgarros y utopías en la pampa salitrera: la consolidación de la identidad obrera en tiempos de la cuestión social, 1890–1923. Santiago: LOM Ediciones, 2007. 241 p.: bibl. (Historia)

The salitreras in Tarapacá and Antofagasta forged a sense of identify in northern miners. Politicized by the *manocomunals*, the IWW, socialism, and then communists, labor became more political. After living in fetid government hotels in Santiago, they would return to the salitreras where they voted for the left and Alessandri. Extremely well done by a preeminent historian.

1839 Alvarado P., Margarita and **Mariana Matthews.** Los Pioneros Valck: un siglo de fotografía en el sur de Chile. Santiago: Pehuén, 2005. 129 p.: ill. (some col.), photos (Biblioteca del bicentenario; 53) (Col. Relatos del ojo y la cámara. Fotografía patrimonial chilena; 1)

Charming study of Chile's south in the late 19th century, as well as individuals in Valparaíso and Santiago. Includes biographies of the various Valck family members, originally immigrants from Germany, who became photographers. A lovely work, which includes pictures of the south.

1840 Por la salud del cuerpo: historia y políticas sanitarias en Chile. Compilación de María Soledad Zárate C. Chile: Univ. Alberto Hurtado, 2008. 284 p.: bibl., ill. (Col. de historia)

Six excellent essays dealing with various aspects of public health: preventative medicine, vaccination programs, venereal disease, alcoholism, family planning, and abortion rights. A well-researched work and an essential starting place for those interested in health issues.

1841 Reyes-Jedlicki, Leonora. The crisis of the *Estado docente* and the critical education movement: the *Escuelas Obreras Federales Racionalistas* in Chile, 1921–1926. (*J. Lat. Am. Stud.*, 39:4, Nov. 2007, p. 827–855, tables)

Workers in 1920s Chile rejected the *Estado Docente*, the state's control of education. Instead, they created their own schools which rejected materialism, nationalism, and capitalism. Although successful in fostering education and practical skills, the legislature, charging that the communists controlled these schools, closed them.

1842 Rivera Aravena, Carla A. La verdad está en los hechos: una tensión entre objetividad y oposición, Radio Cooperativa en dictadura. (*Historia/Santiago*, 41:1, enero/junio 2008, p. 79–98)

Despite functioning during the Pinochet dictatorship, Radio Cooperativa used a variety of ways to send its listeners an anti-government message. Happily, the station's management managed to generate sufficient revenue which allowed it to spread its message to an increasingly large public. Interesting article on a rarely researched topic.

1843 Rojas, Mauricio F. Entre la legitimidad y la criminalidad: el caso del "aparaguayamiento" en Concepción, 1880–1850. (*Historia/Santiago*, 40:2, julio/dic. 2007, p. 419–444, bibl., graphs)

Concepción's political elites, both conservative and liberal, used "self help" to ensure their continued control of republican Chile, to protect their property from supposed malefactors, as well as to marginalize sectors of society. This adoption of their extra-legal methods eventually became part of the legal system.

1844 Rojas Flores, Jorge. Los derechos del niño en Chile: una aproximación histórica, 1910–1930. (*Historia/Santiago*, 40:1, enero/junio 2007, p. 129–164)

Beginning in 1900, leftist critics demanded that the state guarantee children certain rights: food, shelter, and education. The wealthy, however, never adopted the notion of helping poor orphans. And, thanks in part to this attitude, plus clerical opposition, the enforcement of the legislation remained moot, never embracing the notion of childrens' autonomy.

Rojas-Mix, Miguel. El dios de Pinochet: fisonomía del fascismo iberoamericano. See item **458**.

1845 Salazar Orellana, Benito. Memorias de un peón-gañán, 1892–1984. Edición de Gabriel Salazar Vergara. Santiago: LOM Ediciones, 2008. 273 p.: bibl., ill. (Memorias)

Superb diary of a self-taught *inquilino* and his life first on the *fundo*, and then in the city. An excellent study of the rural poor, their transition to the city, and their survival in 20th-century Santiago. A must for social and economic historians.

1846 Salazar Vergara, Gabriel. Construcción de estado en Chile, 1760–1860: democracia de "los pueblos," militarismo ciudadano, golpismo oligárquico. Santiago: Editorial Sudamericana, 2005. 550 p. (Biblioteca Todo es historia)

A welcome analysis of a largely overlooked period. Author describes the ideology and traditions which shaped Chile, including various important figures such as Ramón Freiré, whom he praises more than other traditional historians. A useful work, but flawed by its lack of dependence on primary sources.

1847 San Francisco, Alejandro. La deliberación política de los militares chilenos en el preludio de la guerra civil de 1891. (*Historia/Santiago*, 38:1, enero/junio 2005, p. 43–84, bibl.)

Based on a rich collection of primary sources, the author traces the growing gulf between various factions of the Chilean army. The gap became so great that when Balmaceda invoked the constitution to demand the military's loyalty, he had put himself outside the law. Insightful article written on a crucial event.

1848 Sánchez Manríquez, Karin. El ingreso de la mujer chilena a la universidad y los cambios en la costumbre por medio de la ley, 1872–1877. (*Historia/Santiago*, 39:2, julio/dic. 2006, p. 497–529, tables)

Women first gained admission to the Universidad de Chile in 1881. Their entry precipitated a widespread debate over the role of women in Chilean society, the notion that they were equals of men and that they eventually would achieve the rights of full citizenship, including the right to vote.

1849 Serrano, Sol. ¿Qué hacer con Dios en la república?: política y secularización en Chile, 1845–1885. Santiago: Fondo de Cultura Económico, 2008. 375 p.

Traces the evolution of Chile's Roman Catholic Church in a series of chapters, each of which deal with specific themes such as secular cemeteries. Written with style, each chapter is based upon extensive research largely taken from archives. An elegant work that includes extensive statistical information which 19th-century specialists must consult.

1850 Subercaseaux, Bernardo. Historia de las ideas y de la cultura en Chile. Vol. 3, El centenario y las vanguardias. Santiago: Editorial Universitaria, 2004. 1 v.: bibl., col. ill., index. (Col. Imagen de Chile)

Modernity in Chilean arts occurred with the arrival of a vanguard of men and women in 1910. These people, who began bitterly criticizing Chile's social and economic inequality, became a generation which altered the nation's literature, politics, and plastic arts. A superb study written with elegance and insight.

1851 Thomson, Ian. *La Nitrate Railways Co. Ltd.*: la pérdida de sus derechos exclusivos en el mercado del transporte de saltire y su respuesta a ella. (*Historia/Santiago*, 38:1, enero/junio 2005, p. 85–112, bibl.)

The Chilean government allowed the Peruvian chartered Railways Co. to function after the War of the Pacific, competition from other railroads forced the Railways Co. to reduce its charge. The decline of the nitrate industry and competition from state-owned rail lines forced the Nitrate Railways Co. to merge with its competition.

1852 Ulianova, Olga. Develando un mito: emisarios de la internacional comunista en Chile. (*Historia/Santiago*, 41:1, enero/junio 2008, p. 99–164)

Soviet professional spies or others in the employ of the USSR also acted as officials in the Chilean Communist Party. These men tried to guarantee that the local party toed the ideological line. A well-documented, fascinating study providing information on the various emissaries. A thorough exploration of a little known topic.

1853 XX: historias del siglo veinte chileno. Edición de Andrea Palet *et al.* Barcelona; Santiago: Vergara Grupo Zeta, 2008. 492 p.: bibl., ill. (Biografía e historia)

The same young historians have written another seven essays (see also item **1808**), each concentrating on certain moments of 20th-century Chile. Those interested in modern Chilean history should consult these works, particularly those describing the latter years, the Allende period, and reprisals which occurred after his fall. This work is a must for political historians.

1854 Veneros Ruiz-Tagle, Diana. Allende: un ensayo psicobiográfico. Santiago: Editorial Sudamericana, 2003. 463 p.: bibl. (Señales)

A partisan account which includes material on Allende's father and grandfather, Ramon Allende Padin. Praises the high living, check bouncing Socialist—whom the author claims never read Marx—while rarely admitting any of his flaws. Not an essential work.

1855 Villalobos R., Sergio. Chile y su historia. Santiago: Editorial Universitaria, 2005. 454 p.: bibl., ill., maps. (Col. Imagen de Chile)

A superbly organized, one-volume history of Chile by one of the nation's most respected historians. Containing ample statistics, as well as excellent illustrations, this is an extremely useful book that will appeal to generalists as well as scholars.

1856 Wright, Thomas C. State terrorism in Latin America: Chile, Argentina, and international human rights. Lanham, Md.: Rowman & Littlefield, 2007. 267 p.: bibl., index. (Latin American silhouettes)

Concentrating on Argentina and Chile, this volume explains the events that spawned the often draconian response of supposedly beleaguered right-wing states. Building upon earlier human rights laws, various organizations protested, leading to the demise of the authoritarian government and the creation of a human rights system. Well-researched and a balanced work.

1857 Yáñez Andrade, Juan Carlos. La intervención social en Chile y el nacimiento de la sociedad salarial, 1907–1932. Santiago: RIL Editores, 2008. 334 p.: bibl., ill. (Ensayo)

Created in 1907, the Oficina del Trabajo assisted the state to collect statistical data. Following the collapse of the salitreras, it became a government ministry dedicated to improving working and living conditions for Chileans. Contains a wealth of statistical information for specialists in the field.

1858 Zárate C., Maria Soledad. Dar a luz en Chile, siglo XIX: de la "ciencia de hembra" a la ciencia obstetrica. 2a ed. rev. Chile: Univ. Alberto Hurtado, 2008. 686 p.: bibl., ill. (Col. de historia)

Largely male obstetricians replaced the women who attended Chilean women during childbirth. While these doctors served their patients well, they displaced women from one of the few places that allowed them to work in Chilean society. Midwives, however, continued to work in the countryside. Superbly researched with a splendid bibliography.

Argentina, Paraguay, and Uruguay

THOMAS WHIGHAM, *Professor of History, University of Georgia*

ARGENTINE HISTORIOGRAPHY, as reflected in works published in the last several years, has grown appreciably in terms of depth, but has made fewer advances in terms of breadth. Traditional topics—or revisionist approaches that look new, but in fact are hackneyed—have thus dominated the scene, with only a few works standing out as particularly innovative or significant. Cavaleri's study of territorial nationalism in Argentina (item **1863**) sets a particularly timely tone in its analysis of the "Greater Argentina" idea, through which an irredentist version of manifest destiny was propagated and sustained. On a related aspect of Argentine identity and self-conception, we should note Shumway's examination of the repatriation of the bones of Juan Manuel de Rosas (item **1891**). Studies of the gaucho, practically a staple among Argentine scholars, have taken an interesting step forward with Ariel de la Fuente's account of rural uprisings in La Rioja (item **1866**), a work unequaled except in the studies of Richard Slatta and in the much earlier work of Emilio Coni. Regional history, another traditionally strong area, is here represented in José Antonio Sánchez Román's exceptional study of Tucumano sugar (item **1890**), and a short, but fascinating account of a mythical Patagonia by Pedro Floria Novarro et al. (item **1870**). Juan Carlos Garavaglia presents another excellent contribution in his long string of works on late colonial and early national period society, in this case focusing on public spaces and popular festivals (item **1872**). Jerry Cooney offers a work of similar weight and interest in his short biographical account of the Irish merchant Thomas O'Gorman (item **1511**). Another work on the abortive 1880 revolution in Buenos Aires, well-written and insightful, has enlivened the examination of 19th-century politics (item **1893**). Finally, the Academia Nacional de la Historia has done scholars a great service in providing an excellent three-volume, Spanish-language translation of Martin de Moussy's *Description Geographique et Statistique*, the classic and still very useful guide to Argentina in the 1850s (item **1879**).

Relatively speaking, Paraguayan historiography has made greater strides over the last two years than has Argentine, or for that matter, the Uruguayan. Paraguayan publishers deserve praise for highlighting long-lost memoirs and works focusing on the "underside" of society in the 1850s and1860s. In this respect, particular attention should be drawn to Falcón's *Escritos históricos* (item **1898**), a previously unpublished diary of Bonpland (item **1896**), and an excellent account of French colonization schemes in the Gran Chaco (item **1899**). Areces' poignant account of atrocities in Concepción during 1869 (item **1895**) provides an appropriate corrective to a somewhat stagnant historiography still dominated by the ghost of Juan O'Leary.

Unlike scholarly production for Paraguay, which has shown real signs of positive change, the situation in Uruguay has stood nearly still over the last several years. Other than several summary treatments of Uruguayan political history, perhaps the only significant study to appear has been that of Alvaro Cuenca on the British colony in Montevideo during World War I (item **1902**).

ARGENTINA

1859 Bonaudo, Marta. Aires gaditanos en el mundo rioplatense: la experiencia de los jefes políticos y el juicio por jurados en tierras santafesinas, segunda mitad del siglo XIX. (*Rev. Indias*, 68:242, enero/abril 2008, p. 255–280, bibl.)

A spotty investigation of the legal and political influences exercised by the 1812 Cadiz Constitution in the Argentine Litoral provinces. Author emphasizes two links—the system of political chiefs, which found ample reverberations in Santa Fe, and trials-by-jury, which likely did not.

1860 Bonaudo, Marta. Cuando las tuteladas tutelan y participan: la Sociedad Damas de Caridad, 1869–1894. (*Signos Hist.*, 15, enero/junio 2006, p. 70–97)

A brief but insightful look at a key ladies' charity in late 19th-century Argentina. Author sees the elaboration of this institution as being parallel to philanthropic lodges, which themselves mirror an oligarchic society in formation. Recommended.

1861 Buchbinder, Pablo. Estado, caudillismo y organización miliciana en la provincia de Corrientes en el siglo XIX: el caso de Nicanor Cáceres. (*Rev. Hist. Am./ México*, 136, 2005, p. 37–64)

A rather modest contribution to the analysis of *caudillismo* in the Argentine Northeast, largely dependent on the traditional studies of Manuel Mantilla and Valerio Bonastre. The author argues that Nicanor Cáceres's style of leadership had no choice but to yield to more modern forms of rural political organization by the end of the 1860s.

1862 Candioti, Magdalena. Caudillismo y reconstrucción del orden posrevolucionario en Santa Fe, 1815–1840. (*Td Temas Debates*, 7:6/7, nov. 2003, p. 44–64, bibl.)

A deft analysis of caudillismo in the Litoral provinces, focusing mainly on the Estanislao López regime of Santa Fe during the 1820s. Author sees the germ of modernity in what is usually viewed as a retrograde political process. The standard measure for López studies remains José Luis Busaniche.

1863 Cavaleri, Paulo. La restauración del Virreinato: orígenes del nacionalismo territorial argentino. Buenos Aires: Univ. Nacional de Quilmes Editorial, 2004. 211 p.: bibl. (Col. Convergencia. Entre memoria y sociedad)

Drawing from Benedict Anderson's concept of "imagined communities," Cavaleri examines the common myth of a "Greater Argentina" dispossessed of its rightful territories in Paraguay, Patagonia, and Upper Peru. That this mythic entity has found a place in every Argentine textbook since the time of Vicente Quesada and Gabriel Carrasco does not make the broader claim of a national birthright any more believable (even though, in the case of the Malvinas, it actually led to armed conflict). And yet, as Cavaleri demonstrates, an interpretation does not have to be valid in order to be persuasive, or dominate a large portion of the national historiography.

1864 De Cristóforis, Nadia Andrea. Movimientos migratorios de gallegos y asturianos hacia y desde Buenos Aires, 1810–1840. (*Estud. Migr. Latinoam.*, 18:55, dic. 2004, p. 427–462, bibl., tables)

Most studies of Argentine immigration—like those of Samuel Baily and Guido di Tella—focus on the late 19th century when huge numbers of Italians, Spaniards, and eastern Europeans arrived in Buenos Aires and radically changed the demographic composition of the country. De Cristóforis, by contrast, focuses on the period immediately after independence, and notes that the Gallegos and Asturians that appeared in the Plata had a very different set of challenges and expectations than did the later arrivals. The political struggles that followed in the wake of independence discouraged, but never entirely disrupted the flow of immigrants from Spain.

1865 De Cristóforis, Nadia Andrea. La revitalización de las migraciones de gallegos y asturianos a Buenos Aires, luego de las guerras de independencia: tendencias y problemas. (*Estud. Migr. Latinoam.*, 19:58, dic. 2005, p. 531–564, bibl., graphs, tables)

Traces factors favoring Spanish immigration to Argentina in the period after the independence wars. Part of a broader doctoral study on Asturian and Gallego immigration into the region.

1866 De la Fuente, Ariel. Children of Facundo: caudillo and gaucho insurgency during the Argentine state-formation process, La Rioja, 1853–1870. Durham, N.C.: Duke Univ. Press, 2000. 249 p.: bibl., index.

The Montonero uprisings of the 1860s have always presented thorny terrain for historians — little wonder, given that a large number of rebels were illiterate, and thus without "voices," while their opponents were polished proponents of an imperial and modernizing design in Argentina and anxious to depict the Montoneros as scarcely distinguishable from Indian "savages." The lack of any balance in the extant documentation, and the ponderings of a later generation of folklorists and mythologizers has clouded the historiography still further. Thus, it is a happy day when this topic gets its proper empirical attention, which is precisely what Ariel de la Fuente has achieved in this excellent study. Utilizing the documentation of a dozen regional archives in La Rioja, Cordoba, and Buenos Aires, he has stripped the gaucho rebels of all their mythic glitter, while leaving a core of hard facts that permit the reader to consider them as men (and women) of flesh and blood. But he also takes careful note of the role played by the Montoneros in the cultural tradition of the Northwest and how figures like "el Chacho" Peñaloza and Felipe Varela helped define the essence of caudillismo. He concludes that partisan identification explains more about their political beliefs and behavior than factors of class or mentalité.

1867 Debates de Mayo, 1st, Buenos Aires, Argentina, 2005. Nación, cultura y politicas. Compilación de José Nun con la colaboración de Alejandro Grimson. Buenos Aires: Secretaría de Cultura de la Nación; Barcelona, España: Editorial Gedisa, 2005. 317 p.: bibl., ill. (Libros del bicentenario)

An extremely useful compilation of papers originally presented in May 2005 at the Biblioteca Nacional in Buenos Aires. The Debates de Mayo conference, which preceded the bicentennial celebrations, took as its theme the the broad depiction of Argentine history and how it coincided or conflicted with the national identity. Given such parameters, the 18 scholars managed to produce some suggestive pieces. Of particular interest here is Margarita Guzmán's "1910. Nacion, ciudad y futuro," which examines how Porteños believed their city would develop in 100 years' time.

1868 Di Meglio, Gabriel. Ladrones: una aproximación a los robos en la ciudad de Buenos Aires, 1810–1830. (*ANDES Antropol. Hist.*, 17, 2006, p. 15–49, bibl., tables)

An examination of robbery in the city of Buenos Aires in the first two decades after independence. Di Meglio shows that, in contrast to other forms of urban criminality, robbery found its base almost exclusively from within the lower classes. The poor routinely sold purloined items to *pulperos* who resold them to the public within a parallel market of long historical prominence in Argentina. Based on documentation from the Archivo General de la Nación.

1869 Di Meglio, Gabriel. Viva el bajo pueblo!: la plebe urbana de Buenos Aires y la política entre la revolución de Mayo y el rosismo, 1810–1829. Buenos Aires: Prometeo Libros, 2006. 364 p.: ill.

Reconstructing the political attitudes and culture of "les classes dangereuses" in any place or period has always proven difficult for historians dependent on written records. The reason is simple enough: censal documentation and reports on vagrancy provide a certain sort of information, but they do not allow the poor to speak for themselves. Nor do travel accounts, no matter how sympathetic the authors may feel. This interesting study of plebeians in revolutionary Buenos Aires, while attractive in terms of its details (on public protests, the circulation of political gossip, etc.), provides mostly speculation in place of facts and figures. It may be, as di Meglio suggests, that the urban poor helped delineate the real character of political change in Buenos Aires, but even now the case is weak.

1870 Floria Navarro, Pedro; Leonardo Salgado; and Pablo Azar. La invención de los ancestros: el "patagón antiguo" y la construcción discursiva de un pasado nacional remoto para la Argentina, 1870–1915. (Rev. Indias, 64:231, mayo/agosto 2004, p. 405–424, bibl.)

Interesting examination of how the early (and largely mythical) notion of a race of Patagonian giants became integrated into Argentine anthropology, precisely because it responded to a nationalist impulse that demanded greatness even in the size of Indian crania.

1871 Fradkin, Raúl O. La historia de una montonera: bandolerismo y caudillismo en Buenos Aires, 1826. Buenos Aires: Siglo Veintiuno Editores, 2006. 220 p.: bibl. (Historia y cultura; 22)

In offering a detailed microstudy of the little-known Cipriano Benítez uprising of 1826, Fradkin posits some cogent interpretations about popular mobilization in the Argentine countryside during the 19th century. He rejects those analyses that seek to reduce the montoneras to atavistic reactions to pressures associated with a changing Atlantic economy. Instead, he sees the country people clearly pursuing their own ends as political actors.

1872 Garavaglia, Juan Carlos. Construir el estado, inventar la nación: el Río de la Plata, siglos XVIII–XIX. Buenos Aires: Prometeo Libros, 2007. 405 p.: bibl.

A masterly analysis of three overlapping tales: (1) How popular festivals were re-elaborated into public displays of support for political change from the late 1700s to the 1820s; (2) the evolution of public space as part of the broader construction of Argentine citizenship from 1806 to 1844; and (3) what an investigation of the Bonaerense state budget reveals about changing senses of nationalism in the Plata. Garavaglia never disappoints his readers, and this multifaceted study is one of his best efforts

1873 Garavaglia, Juan Carlos. Manifestaciones iniciales de la representación en el Rio de la Plata: la revolución en la laboriosa búsqueda de la *Autonomía de Individuo*, 1810–1812. (*Rev. Indias*, 64:231, mayo/agosto 2004, p.349–382, bibl., graphs)

A thoughtful examination of how Porteño elites succeeded in manipulating electoral processes in the first years of the revolutionary era, thus assuring their dominance of political power while simultaneously causing the plebeian classes to focus their hopes for change on leaders outside the "círculo rivadaviana."

1874 Geler, Lea. "Aquí . . . se habla de política": la participación de los afroporteños en las elecciones presidenciales de 1874. (*Rev. Indias*, 67:240, mayo/agosto 2007, p. 459–484, bibl.)

An examination of the role played by Afro-Argentine citizens of Buenos Aires in the election of 1874. Author argues that the support of this community was eagerly sought by both Mitre and Avellaneda through the instrument of newspapers, especially *La Igualdad* and *El Artesano*.

Gil Montero, Raquel. La construcción de Argentina y Bolivia en los Andes meridionales: población, tierras y ambiente en el siglo XIX. See item **1770.**

1875 Guy, Donna J. Women build the welfare state: performing charity and creating rights in Argentina, 1880–1955. Durham, N.C.: Duke Univ. Press, 2009. 252 p.: bibl., ill., index.

Donna Guy has written many path-breaking works, including *Sex and Danger in Buenos Aires: Prostitution, Family, and Nation in Argentina* (see *HLAS 54:2987*) and *White Slavery and Mothers Alive and Dead: The Troubled Meeting of Sex, Gender, Public Health and Progress in Latin America* (2000). The book under review here is a major contribution which presents an important historical analysis of women's philanthropic organizations and female volunteer activities in Argentina. Based on solid archival research and government documents, the author reviews the history of child welfare and the legal history of the country, starting with the various groups of *damas* who engaged in charitable activities in the 19th century, to the feminist physicians and social workers at the turn of the 20th century, through the Depression and finally to Eva Perón and the welfare state of the 1950s. An especially insightful chapter is devoted to juvenile delinquency and children within a framework of the prevailing patriarchy. Throughout, the book emphasizes that Argentine feminists and other professional women fought for the legal rights of biological mothers over their children. Their work culminated in successful child and family social and public health policies and the rise of the welfare state. [G.M. Dorn]

1876 Historia y bibliografía critica de las imprentas rioplatenses, 1830–1852. v. 1, 1830–1831. Contribuciones de Jorge C. Bohdziewicz *et al.* Buenos Aires: Edición del Instituto Bibliográfico "Antonio Zinny," 2008. 1 v.

First volume of a detailed and highly useful annotated bibliography of publications from the Platine states, 1830–31. The listing, which would appear to be exhaustive, covers government decrees, treaties, congressional hearings, almanacs, and funeral orations.

1877 Juarez-Dappe, Patricia. Cañeros and colonos: sugarcane planters in Tucumán, 1876–1895. (*J. Lat. Am. Stud.*, 38:1, Feb. 2006, p. 123–147, bibl.)

The unprecedented expansion of the Tucumán sugar industry in the late 1800s led to the incorporation of thousands of middle- and small-scale farmers into an industry that in other countries was domi-nated by large-scale enterprises. The author points out that despite mutual dependence, the relations between planters and mill owners were frequently antagonistic, with advantages not always accruing to the stronger group.

Knight, Alan. Rethinking British informal empire in Latin America (especially Argentina). See item **437.**

López Das Eiras, Horacio. Ernestito Guevara antes de ser el Che. See item **1329.**

1878 Luqui-Lagleyze, Julio M. El aporte extranjero a la conformación de las tripulaciones de las escuadras argentinas en las Guerras de Independencia y del Brasil, 1814–1830. (*Temas Hist. Argent. Am.*, 10, enero/junio 2007, p. 89–130, graphs)

Focused analysis of the national composition of crews in Argentine warships during the 1810s and 1820s. Author finds that the foreign composition of crews was well over 60 percent in the majority of cases.

1879 Martin de Moussy, Victor. Descripción geográfica y estadística de la Confederación Argentina. Edición a cargo de Beatriz Bosch. Buenos Aires: Academia Nacional de la Historia, 2005. 3 v.: bibl. (Col. Visiones de la Argentina; 2)

Martin de Moussy's *Description geographique* has long been considered a classic of mid-19th century Argentina, with something to say to every scholar of the Confederal period. By profession a medical doctor, the Frenchman Victor Martin de Moussy (1810–69) had already been living in Montevideo for a decade when the Urquiza government hired him to compose a scientific survey of Argentine resources that could serve as a definitive geographic guide to the new country. For four years he traveled throughout Argentina, from the Jesuit ruins of the northeast to the foothills of the Andes, and everywhere he was given full access to statistical information that had only been in local hands up to the point. He conducted meteorological research and made extensive investigations into the flora and fauna of even the most isolated locales. When he finally finished his labors, in 1859, Martin de Moussy had produced a study unequalled in its precision and depth that was used by successive Argentine governmental in planning economic strategies and attracting immigrants. Oddly, however, it is only with this edition that the full work finally appears in Spanish. The Academia Nacional de la Historia deserves extensive praise for this publication, which, though it was over 40 years in the making, still shines so brightly. A highly recommended work.

Méndez Paz, Carlos A. Patricios y elites: el caso argentino, 1535–1943: ensayo. See item **1546**.

1880 Mettauer, Philipp. Erzwungene Emigration nach Argentinien: österreichisch-jüdische Lebensgeschichten. Münster, Germany: Aschendorff, 2010. 230 p.: bibl., index. (Studien zur Geschichte und Kultur der iberischen und iberoamerikanischen Länder; 14 = Estudios sobre historia y cultura de los países ibéricos e iberoamericanos; 14)

This work, a contribution to the immigration history of Argentina, describes the situation for Austrian Jews who took refuge in Buenos Aires after 1938 (the date in which Austria became part of the German Reich under Nazi regime). The author collected personal histories of some of the immigrants in an oral history project, including contemporary letters. The 80 immigrants, interviewed between 2001–03, had emigrated primarily from the Vienna region. The complete interviews are not included, but extracts are integrated into chapters describing typical aspects of emigration, settling in the Buenos Aires area, and Argentine political reaction to the newly arrived. [F. Obermeier]

1881 Oteiza Gruss, Viviane Inés. *Le Courrier de la Plata:* diario republicano francés rioplatense. (*Estud. Migr. Latinoam.*, 20:61, dic. 2006, p. 557–580)

Summary analysis of the political trajectory of a Porteño newspaper whose influences went beyond service to the local French community; in its 81 years of operation (1865–1946) *Le Courrier* helped provide a key venue for the discussion of migration questions, high culture, and broad philosophy.

1882 Palermo, Silvana A. Elite técnica y estado liberal: la creación de una administración moderna en los Ferrocarriles del Estado, 1870–1910. (*Estud. Soc./Santa Fe,* 16:30, primer semestre 2006, p. 9–41, tables)

A careful and measured examination of the technical elite that grew concomitantly with the construction of Argentine railroads—both in terms of sophistication and as a symbol of a powerful oligarchy.

1883 Parada, Alejandro E. El orden y la memoria en la librería de Duportail Hermanos: un catálogo porteño de 1829. Buenos Aires: INIBI, Instituto de Investigaciones Bibliotecológicas, Facultad de Filosofía y Letras, Univ. de Buenos Aires, 2005. 192 p.: ill., indexes, facsims.

A transcription of a catalog of works offered for sale by a Porteño bookseller in the first year of the Rosas governorship. The catalog, which is offered here in facsimile, provides a window into the mind of the lettered portion of Buenos Aires society, whose tastes evidently turned to religious works, contemporary European politics, novels, and practical works on medicine and animal husbandry. Relatively few works on Latin American themes were included (a history of Puerto Rico and the Rengger and Longchamps essay on Paraguay being exceptions). Useful.

1884 Parolo, María Paula. Conflictividad, rebeldía y transgresión: los sectores populares de Tucumán en la primera mitad del siglo XIX. (*Estud. Soc./Santa Fe,* 15:29, segundo semestre 2005, p. 25–50, bibl., graphs, table)

Author contends that the province of Tucumán, which in the early 19th century was usually portrayed as a bastion of security and peace, in fact experienced daily manifestations of protest coming from the *classes dangereuses.* The true character of social relations in the province can only be understood, he maintains, by seeing official criminality as a form of resistance.

1885 Peard, Julyan G. Enchanted Edens and nation-making: Juana Manso, education, women and trans-American encounters in nineteenth-century Argentina. (*J. Lat. Am. Stud.,* 40:3, Aug. 2008, p. 453–476)

This article argues that the Argentine novelist Juana Manso de Noronha (1819–75) played a more crucial role in nation-building than is usually acknowledged. Having spent extensive time in Brazil, Uruguay, Cuba, and the US, she was in a unique position to transmit foreign ideas, especially about women, into the Argentine milieu. This notion is probably overstated given the undeniable influences of world travelers like Sarmiento and Alberdi, though no one can deny that, as a woman, Manso's viewpoints almost certainly drew from a different and perhaps more nuanced experience.

1886 Quijada, Mónica. Los límites del "pueblo soberano": territorio, nación y el tratamiento de la diversidad; Argentina, siglo XIX. (*Hist. Polít.*, 13, 2005, p. 143–174)

Quijada provides a thoughtful analysis of social and political integration in 19th-century Argentina. She argues that a diversity of ethnic identities ultimately gave way to a national character, not through a "melting pot" phenomenon, but rather through a hegemonic cohesion associated with the country's open spaces—an "alchemy of the land," as Quijada terms it.

1887 Reguera, Andrea. Entre la ley y el azar: la trama vincular del mundo político-empresarial de la frontera sur pampeana en el siglo XIX. (*Prohistoria/Rosario*, 10:10, primavera 2006, p. 47–72, map, tables)

A brief, occasionally insightful study of landownership in the south of Buenos Aires province during the course of the 1800s.

1888 Rosal, Miguel Á. Diversos aspectos atinentes a la situación de los afroporteños a principios del período postrevolucionario derivados del estudio de testamentos de morenos y pardos. (*Rev. Indias*, 66:237, mayo/agosto 2006, p. 393–424)

A suggestive examination of Afro-Porteño society in the years after independence based on testaments left by morenos and pardos. Occasionally useful.

1889 Sábato, Hilda. Buenos Aires en armas: la revolución de 1880. Buenos Aires: Siglo Veintiuno Editores Argentina, 2008. 333 p.: bibl., ill., maps (Historia y cultura; 35)

The noted historian of Porteño politics and electioneering here examines a very specific instance of challenges to the modernizing state. The 1880 "revolution," she explains, represented the last major impulse of Porteño particularism and ended with Buenos Aires having its status federalized as the national capital, and its militias placed under national authority. Sabato's analysis, which relies on the documents of eight different archives and a score of contemporary periodicals, provides a nuanced picture of a clash that was as subtle and contingent as it was violent.

1890 Sánchez Román, José Antonio. La dulce crisis: estado, empresarios e industria azucarera en Tucumán, Argentina, 1853–1914. Sevilla, Spain: Diputación de Sevilla: Univ. de Sevilla; Madrid: Consejo Superior de Investigaciones Científicas, Escuela de Estudios Hispano-Americanos, 2005. 383 p.: bibl., ill., maps (Col. Americana; 23) (Nuestra América; 8)

This finely-wrought analysis of Tucumano sugar politics both updates and expands upon the classic study of Donna Guy (see *HLAS 42:3360*). Sánchez Román specifically highlights the external financing of the sugar complex and particularly the impact of railroads on the expanding provincial industry. He credits state intervention as the moving force behind the subsequent success of the sugar promoters. Based on extensive archival research.

Shumway, Jeffrey M. The case of the ugly suitor: & other histories of love, gender, & nation in Buenos Aires, 1776–1870. See item **1565.**

1891 Shumway, Jeffrey M. "Sometimes knowing how to forget is also having memory": the repatriation on Juan Manuel de Rosas and the healing of Argentina. (*in* Death, dismemberment, and memory: body politics in Latin America. Edited by Lyman L. Johnson. Albuquerque: Univ. of New Mexico Press, 2004, p. 105–140, photos)

The mortal remains of Juan Manuel de Rosas, the "Restaurador de las Leyes" of the 1830s and 40s, and perhaps the most controversial Argentine of the 19th century, were finally returned from England and interred in La Recoleta in 1989. Shumway regards this event as part of a crucial process of reconciliation in Argentina wherein descendants of Rosas's supporters and of his victims sought finally to assert a common history. This helped pave the way for a greater political challenge for President Carlos Menem—his pardoning of some 300 military personnel convicted of atrocities during the *Guerra Sucia* (Dirty War).

1892 Ternavasio, Marcela. Correspondencia de Juan Manuel de Rosas. Buenos
Aires: EUDEBA, 2005. 233 p. (Historia
argentina)

A selected compilation of Rosas's
letters that demonstrates the Restaurador's
wide-ranging interests, his dedication to the
effective administration of the provinces, his
political acumen, and his private qualms.
More complete compilations exist, but this
selection is well-arranged as a sampling of
Rosas's thinking over a 40-year period.

Wright, Thomas C. State terrorism in Latin
America: Chile, Argentina, and international human rights. See item **1856**.

1893 Yablon, Ariel. Disciplined rebels: the
revolution of 1880 in Buenos Aires.
(*J. Lat. Am. Stud.*, 40:3, Aug. 2008, p. 483–507)

Yablon argues that the 1880 revolt
against the fraudulent election of General
Julio A. Roca, which is usually interpreted
as representing a shift in clientelistic patterns of political organization in the city of
Buenos Aires, had a more genuinely popular
character than is usually recognized. The
Porteño militias, it turns out, were composed of men dedicated to the principal of
clean suffrage and the right of the citizenry
to bear arms against illegitimate politicos.

1894 Zeballos, Estanislao Severo. Episo-
dios en los territorios del sur, 1879.
Estudio preliminar, edición y notas de Juan
Guillermo Durán. 1. ed. en El Elefante
Blanco. Buenos Aires: Elefante Blanco, 2004.
569 p.: bibl., ill., maps.

Zeballos (1854–1923) served as Argentine Foreign Minister during the period of
oligarchic ascendency in the late 19th century and fully reflected the Positivist orientation of that time. He was a talented writer
who churned out many thoughtful pieces
outlining his country's golden destiny. In
this compilation of articles that originally
appeared in the pages of *La Prensa*, Zeballos
turns his attention to the Patagonian frontier of 1879, focusing on both the natural
wonders and recent history of the territory.
He offers insights into the Indian uprising of
Calfucurá and provides biographical details
on the army officers who suppressed it.
Above all, he paints Patagonia as a land of
the future, fit for immigrants. The introduction by Juan Guillermo Durán, which sets
the work in broader historical context, is a
most welcome addition, as is the book itself.

PARAGUAY

1895 Areces, Nidia R. Terror y violencia
durante la guerra del Paraguay: "la
masacre de 1869" y las familias de Concepción. (*Rev. Eur. Estud. Latinoam. Caribe*, 81, oct. 2006, p. 43–63, bibl.)

A thoughtful study of a series of
terrible incidents during the final stages
of the Paraguayan War in which the army
of Francisco Solano López turned on civilians in Concepción, slaughtering upwards
of 100. Though the tone here is essentially
revisionist, Areces makes no excuse for the
massacre and instead speaks of the natural
consequences of paranoia in such a setting.

**1896 Contreras Roqué, Julio Rafael and Al-
fredo Boccia Romañach.** El Paraguay
en 1857: un viaje inédito de Aimé Bonpland.
Asunción: Univ. Nacional de Pilar: Servilibro, 2006. 222 p.: bibl., ill., maps.

The French explorer Aimé Bonpland
is usually associated with the early decades
of the 19th century, during which he accompanied Alexander von Humboldt to the
New World, and eventually fell prisoner to
the Paraguayan dictator, Dr. José Gaspar de
Francia. The publication of this 1857 diary,
however, proves how very active Bonpland
was in his later years as a proponent of
scientific research. The diary itself presented a rather limited record of Paraguayan
observations, but the notes and annotations
provided by Contreras Roquie and Boccia
offer a model of how interesting details can
enliven a somewhat dull text. This work
can be usefully compared with publications
on the same topic by Stephen Bell.

1897 Diaz, Ana Maria. El primer ciudadano: Paraguay, 1811–1814. (*Cah. Am.
lat.*, 46, 2004, p. 103–113, bibl.)

Diaz suggests that in opposing both
the Bourbon monarchists and the patriot
regime in Buenos Aires, the province of
Paraguay effectively crystallized a new
historical option for political actors: that
of the part-time citizen who occasionally
participated in electoral congresses but who
left all real decision-making to constituted
authorities like Dr. Francia.

1898 Falcón, José. Escritos históricos.
Edición y estudios preliminares de
Thomas L. Whigham y Ricardo Scavone
Yegros. Asunción: Servilibro, 2006. 245 p.

While known to certain 19th-century scholars, the memoirs of Jose Falcón went missing for decades during the course of the 20th century until uncovered in an improperly cataloged section of the Manuel Gondra Collection at the University of Texas Library. This discovery has proven very useful indeed, for Falcón was an eyewitness to many key events from the 1850s through the 1870s. He worked with the Paraguayan government as interim foreign minister and director of the National Archive and even participated in Francisco Solano López's "last stand" at Cerro Corã in March 1870. The memoir, which was clearly never finished, offers many details about life in wartime Paraguay, and is particularly helpful for those seeking to understand Paraguay's diplomatic history (especially the early land disputes with Bolivia).

Jara Goiris, Fabio Aníbal. Paraguay, ciclos adversos y cultura política. See *HLAS 65:1801.*

Mala guerra: los indígenas en la Guerra del Chaco, 1932–1935. See item **1783.**

1899 Rodríguez Alcalá, Guido and **Luc Capdevila.** Nueva Burdeos: colonización francesa en el Paraguay. Asunción: Embajada de Francia, 2005. 120 p.: ill.

A detailed and highly readable account of a project sponsored by the Carlos Antonio López government in the mid-1850s to settle French immigrants on unoccupied lands in the Paraguayan Chaco, just opposite Asunción. The project turned out to be a fiasco. The government failed to deliver needed assistance in the form of tools and seed, and the immigrants turned out to be city people from Bordeaux who had no sense of what faced them in the Chaco wilderness. The study discusses the place of Nueva Burdeos in the baleful historiography of Paraguayan colonization and includes 49 pages of correspondence between the Paraguayan and French foreign ministries of that era, as well of copies of archival documents.

1900 Salum-Flecha, Antonio. La política exterior del Paraguay: de 1811 hasta la Guerra de 1864–70. Asunción: Intercontinental Editora, 2006. 293 p.: bibl., maps.

Sixth edition of a standard work on Paraguayan diplomacy from the time of independence to the defeat of Marshal López in March 1870. Still useful despite its rather narrow focus and weak grasp of diplomatic complexities.

Scavone Yegros, Ricardo. Las relaciones entre el Paraguay y Bolivia en el siglo XIX. See item **1796.**

URUGUAY

1901 Andrews, George Reid. Blackness in the white nation: a history of Afro-Uruguay. Chapel Hill: Univ. of North Carolina Press, 2010. 241 p.: bibl., index.

In general Uruguay has been considered as a "white" nation. In this excellent pathbreaking and thorough work, the foremost scholar of people of African descent in Latin America demonstrates that the country is not really all that the white. He analyzes racial inequality, and more importantly, the history and cultural impact of Afro-Uruguayans from the colonial period to the present, especially on popular culture. Insightful chapters include "The New Negros, 1920–1960" and "Today Everyone Dances Candombe, 1950–2010" in which he highlights the impact of carnival. Excellent b/w illustrations enhance this book which is bound to become a standard for studying race relations in Latin America. [G.M. Dorn]

1902 Cuenca, Álvaro. La colonia británica de Montevideo y la Gran Guerra. Montevideo: Torre del Vigía Ediciones, 2006. 350 p.: bibl., ill., map.

A detailed examination of the British community in Montevideo, focusing on the patriotic reactions of Anglo-Uruguayans and expatriate Britons when faced with the challenges of WWI. Readable.

1903 Dotta, Mario. Caudillos, doctores y masones: protagonistas en la Gran Comarca Rioplatense, 1806–1865. 2da. ed. Montevideo: Ediciones de la Plaza, 2007. 386 p.: bibl., col. ill. (Col. Investigación histórica)

A well-written, but highly speculative account of Uruguayan Freemasonry in the formative period. The author argues that the prevalence of Masonic symbols in cemetery headstones and in public edifices demonstrates the centrality of lodges in the evolution of national politics.

BRAZIL

DAIN BORGES, *Associate Professor of History, University of Chicago*
HAL LANGFUR, *Associate Professor of History, The State University of New York at Buffalo*
FRANK D. McCANN, *Professor Emeritus of History, University of New Hampshire*

COLONIAL PERIOD

INTEREST IN TOPICS RELATED TO BRAZIL'S INDEPENDENCE ERA has become a dominant preoccupation among colonial scholars. The bicentenary commemoration of the 1808 transfer of the Portuguese court to Rio de Janeiro has captivated established scholars and newcomers, political and cultural historians, biographers and urban studies specialists alike. Their attention is likely to be sustained, given that the royal court remained in Brazil for 13 years, witness to a succession of dramatic developments that would finally lead to its departure in 1821 and national independence the following year. One need only review the chronology of this tropical sojourn to identify components of the larger research trend and anticipate forthcoming publications. Relevant events include the opening of the colony's ports to friendly nations; the establishment of its first printing press; the signing of a treaty enhancing British commercial power; the elevation of the colony to the status of a kingdom co-equal with Portugal; the military occupation and eventual annexation of the Banda Oriental; the death of Maria I and the succession to the throne of her son João VI; the court visit by the famed French artistic mission; the arrival of Princess Leopoldina of Austria, future empress of Brazil; the failed Republican Revolution in Pernambuco; Portugal's constitutionalist insurrections; and, finally, the return of João VI to Lisbon, leading to his son Pedro's declaration of independence and proclamation as emperor of Brazil. The recent crop of studies examines all of these developments and many others. Prominent are those works in which political history absorbs insights from social and especially cultural history. An unabashed emphasis on elites, however, means that there remains much to learn about the implications of the political traumas of the era for the populace at large, including poor whites, free persons of color, slaves, native peoples, and women. How these groups strove to shape, or found themselves further marginalized by, the transformation from colony to independent nation-state receives little attention.

Biographical and prosopographical research on the central historical figures of the independence era has produced a number of important studies. Pedreira's biography of João VI restores welcome interpretive balance to the monarch's life, which has been distorted by those who either exaggerate or underestimate his abilities as a leader (item **1943**). Sources documenting the exiled court's preoccupation with rituals marking key moments of royal family life allow Assunção to demonstrate how public spectacle helped consolidate the Crown's political power in the colony (item **1918**). Contributions to the age's intellectual effervescence and Enlightenment inheritance are traced in Silva's study of three prominent Luso-Brazilian statesmen (item **1949**) and in Raminelli's inquiry into the scientific and then administrative careers of a group of Brazilian-born, Coimbra-educated naturalist-voyagers (item **1944**). Relevant primary source collections include the edited letters of Princess and later Empress Leopoldina (item **1935**) and the transatlantic correspondence of members of the elite Pinto da França and Garcez families (item **1927**).

New modes of sociability and the changing political culture fostered by the Crown's residence in Rio de Janeiro inform Barata's examination of Freemasonry (item **1920**) and Slemian's history of urban ferment on the eve of independence (item **1955**). Cavalcanti's novel blend of architectural and urban history also culminates in the changes brought to the city and its denizens by the court's residency, although this study ranges over the entire preceding century (item **1925**). Revisionist approaches to the opening of Brazilian ports are best gauged in Oliveira and Ricupero's edited collection of essays evaluating this shock to the traditional mercantilist system (item **1913**). Ferreira contributes a valuable interdisciplinary perspective on the southern borderlands conflict, which only deepened after the achievement of independence (item **2032**).

To note that few works seriously explore race, color, and ethnicity as sources of individual and communal identities pertinent to independence-era politics is not to suggest that long-standing interest in Brazil's complex multiracial past is declining. Studies of native peoples continue to consolidate a place in the historiography secured only in recent decades. Works reviewed for this volume include Gonçalves on the Potiguara of the northeast (item **1929**), Caldeira and Langer on the Tupi-Guarani of the south (items **1924**, especially volume one; and **1933**), and Apolinário on the Akroá of central Brazil (item **1917**). Whitehead and Harbsmeier provide a new translation of Hans Staden's famed account of captivity among the coastal Tupinambá, with an incisive critical introduction and original illustrations (item **1957**).

Numerous works explore the social, cultural, and economic history of slavery, although remarkably little of it centers on captive labor in the colony's primary plantation zones. The transatlantic dimensions of slavery are central to a number of valuable contributions. Rodrigues concentrates on understudied intermediaries who facilitated the slave trade from Angola (item **1910**), while Chambouleyron highlights distinctive elements of the slave trade to Maranhão and Pará (item **1926**). Sweet argues subtly for a less rigid understanding of slaves' identities, allowing for greater expression of African cultural forms (item **1958**). The Yoruba diaspora in Brazil is the subject of several essays in a volume edited by Falola and Childs (item **1912**).

Kraay provides a model overview of the ubiquitous practice of arming slaves or, alternatively, freeing them in order to do so, when private owners or the state deemed their military services essential (item **1932**). Resistance to the slave system in its multiple forms is the subject of Silveira's study of manumission in Minas Gerais (item **1954**) and Gomes' expanded study of 19th-century runaway slave communities in rural Rio de Janeiro (item **2045**). Machado finds a constant state of social tension in rural São Paulo as slaves and their descendants struggled to emerge and then distance themselves from slavery (item **1937**).

While there has never been a shortage of scholarly interest in racial mixture in colonial Brazil, increasing sophistication characterizes recent studies of the origins, forms, and consequences of *mestiçagem*. Mattos emphasizes the legal regime of the 17th century as critical to understanding the social import of such categories as *mulato* and *pardo* (item **1940**). Viana follows these groups into the 18th century, locating in Rio de Janeiro's lay brotherhoods a social space in which some forged communal identities premised on being born in Brazil, no longer African, and no longer captive (item **1960**). Lara's revealing study of fast-growing urban populations of free and enslaved persons of color posits increasing racialization of the social hierarchy during the final decades of the 18th century (item **1934**). Free women of color, many of them of mixed racial descent, are the subject of essays by Barickman and Few, who focus on rural Bahia (item **1972**), and Karasch, who looks at Goiás (item **1931**).

Paralleling global trends, scholarship on colonial religious institutions and religiosity constitutes another dynamic area of research. Inquisition studies lead the way, as scholars continue to find new themes and elaborate on old ones. The wide range of this work can be sampled in a fine essay collection edited by Vainfas, Feitler, and Lima (item **1930**). Calainho follows the careers and social ascension of the administrative agents, as opposed to the victims, of the Inquisition (item **1922**). Wadsworth demonstrates the limitations of Inquisitorial power when it targeted heterodox Afro-Brazilian and indigenous practices (item **1961**). By contrast, Silva insists on the institution's coercive clout when it persecuted women for practicing Judaism (item **1951**). Employing records from Inquisition and state censors, Algranti's innovative inquiry into the history of print culture and popular piety, especially among women in convents, makes evident the authority exercised by the Church over the act of reading (item **1914**). Colonial religious sermons are the focus of Massimi's interdisciplinary study (item **1939**), while Santos examines popular processions associated with the annual Corpus Christi feast (item **1946**).

The accent on the independence period has resulted in an even greater preponderance than usual of studies focused on Rio de Janeiro; however, other regions, Minas Gerais chief among them, are the subject of notable scholarship, in addition to work already cited. Monographs by Andrade (item **1916**), Romeiro (item **1945**), and Caldeira (item **1924**, especially volume two) apply new approaches and sources to the study of the mining district's early development, yielding significant findings. Anastasia (item **1915**) and Silva (item **1950**) probe the origins of the region's notorious rural violence and criminality. Bahian-born Frei Vicente do Salvador, known as the "father of Brazilian history," attracts Oliveira's meticulous attention in her multi-essay study and sumptuous annotated edition of the friar's early 17th-century history of Portuguese America (item **1942**). The subsequent Dutch control of the Northeast forms the backdrop of two trenchant biographies, Mello's study of John Maurice of Nassau, the governor of Dutch-occupied territories (item **1941**), and Vainfas' excellent account of Manoel de Moraes, a mixed-race, Brazilian-born Jesuit missionary (item **1959**). Priore and Gomes have assembled an uncommonly coherent collection of essays focusing on the Amazon basin as a place alternately exoticized and forgotten by history (item **1911**). [HL]

EMPIRE TO FIRST REPUBLIC (1822–1930)

THE SELECTION OF BOOKS AND ARTICLES reviewed for this volume show that Brazilian scholars have replaced foreigners as the major contributors to the country's historical literature. This publication trend indicates that the Brazilian universities have successfully produced a generation of serious, well-prepared researchers and writers, and also raises questions about the health of Brazilian studies in the US. The breadth, depth, and high quality of the works are impressive. While the topics are familiar—formation of Brazil, growth of the state, the functioning of the empire, African slavery, European immigration, citizenship, railroads, state-sponsored internal exploration, the *Sertão*, Canudos, foreign relations, *cangaceiros*, women, labor, and race—these publications display imaginative, exciting, and stimulating new ways of looking at these themes. The articles by McPhee (item **2075**), Velasco e Cruz (item **2131**), Costa da Goulart (item **2046**), and Santos (item **2108**), and the books by Schettini Pereira (item **2094**), Cukierman (item **2011**), Dantas (item **2014**), Lucetti and Lucena (item **2064**) raise new questions and open new paths, while setting high standards that deserve to be emulated.

José Carlos Barreiro (item **1973**) looks at the beginnings of contemporary Brazilian society in *Imaginário e viajantes no Brasil do Século XIX* by setting the commentaries of foreign travelers against the actual lives of the people being described. This is truly a fascinating book whose closeness to primary sources lends texture and depth to the often superficial images of 19th-century Brazil. He shows that Brazil's lamented *"falta absoluta de braços"* (p. 38) was not so much a true lack of manpower as it was the inability of the landowning elite to control and discipline labor to their desires. Sadly, in this circumstance, the Church used its powerful influence to spread the idea of the Christian duty to work to motivate the poor and the slaves.

The combination of coffee fazendas, slavery, and family history is a staple of imperial era history. Here we have a family memoir *No tempo dos barões* by Maria Werneck de Castro (item item **1996**) that adds detail and intimacy to Stanley J. Stein's famous portrayal of the Lacerda Werneck family in his *Vassouras* (see *HLAS 22:3389*). She recounts her childhood on the Fazenda Abaíba in the Paraíba valley. This ethnographic portrait of family life on a fazenda in the first decades of the 20th century would be a useful source for the study of childhood and rural families of the era. The role of women on the decadent fazendas during the transition from slavery was fundamental in preserving the declining elite families. Many women administered fazendas when faced with their husbands' inaptitude or absence. The slaves of old had either left or had evolved into *"camaradas"* (salaried workers) or *"colonos"* (who had the right to cultivate a parcel of land). Werneck de Castro's sharp gaze captures the inter-ethnic relations of that time and place, and the pains of adjustment. She provides a useful series of historical sketches of the "traditional" *Fluminense* families, the Wernecks and the Avelars. Those interested in plantations, the details of master-slave relations, and particularly the landowning families of the Paraíba will find much of value here.

A fascinating question often left unanswered in studies of slavery is who were the slaves? The team of Barreto Farias, Líbano Soares, and Santos Gomes confront the question in *No labirinto das nações: africanos e identidades no Rio de Janeiro* (item **2027**) and won the 2003 Arquivo Nacional research prize for their efforts. Slaves arriving in Rio de Janeiro were from a mix of ethnic and linguistic groups from throughout Africa, each with their own identities, histories, and traditions. Although their old identities were kept and used in a variety of ways, as slaves they were pressed into a new social category, that of "African." The authors span the 19th century in their analysis of the legal and social processes involved in the imposition of this new identity. This is an important book that adds richness and detail to the history of slavery

Oddly, slavery may well have contributed to Brazil holding together while breaking from Portugal. Marcos de Carvalho (item **1993**) finds that runaway slaves in Pernambuco unintentionally made such a contribution. His deeply researched article shows that *quilombos* could have national importance. Elite fears of the inhabitants of the *quilombo* near Recife led slave masters to arm their slaves and to decide against attempts at independence. They came to believe that they needed imperial military forces to suppress the *quilombos* or risk a Haitian-style slave revolt. So they adhered to the royalist movement in Rio de Janeiro and strengthened Brazilian national unity.

Scholars seeking to understand how Brazil maintained its unity are naturally drawn to the study of the empire. Lilia Moritz Schwarcz makes a valuable contribution in that regard with her book *The Emperor's Beard* (1998 and 2004, see *HLAS 60:3331*). Researchers who have not digested that extensive study can read a summary version of her ideas in an article (item **2110**) on the creation of the empire's official image. The newly independent country needed a new history and in 1844 issued an international call for proposals. Karl von Martius won the competition, becoming the first of what we now call *Brazilianistas*. Schwarcz portrays Brazil as an "imagined community" creating a conscious self image "founded upon certain cultural roots that were . . . selected and delimited" (p. 26). In the process the image "conferred legitimacy" upon the new empire. She examines how Brazil in its initial official images characterized itself as "a mestizo and tropical monarchy." The survival of Brazilian unity was not a foregone conclusion, but the result of determined imperial policy and fierce suppression of secession movements.

Examining the creation and consolidation of the imperial order as seen from the city of Franca in São Paulo between 1824 and 1852 was the task of Antonio Marco Ventura Martins in *Um império a constituir, uma ordem a consolidar* (item **2072**). The author sees the great themes of Brazilian historiography as set against the background of a constant struggle between liberty and authority. Some historians, such as Oliveira Vianna and Richard Graham, argued that the hegemony and supremacy that rural landowners held over the imperial government turned it into the mere executor of their political interests. Others, such as Raymundo Faoro, disagreed, seeing the empire's bureaucracy as dominating Brazil's political life. He depicted the emperor as the grand manager of the political game; in short, Faoro saw the state as everything and the nation as almost nothing. But with 70 percent of the empire's revenue coming from taxes on exports and imports, the agricultural sector was Brazil's keystone. The book provides a quick analysis of the empire, its need to spread the state's presence over a vast territory, and it shows how the occupation of land left distinctive traces of the process. Martins uses Franca as a singular example. The book also examines the *município's* political elite particularly in their roles on the municipal council and in the *Guarda Nacional*. He concludes with an examination of the interaction between elites at the local and national levels in the process of formation and consolidation of the Brazilian national state.

The Instituto Histórico e Geográfico Brasileiro (IHGB), which organized the competition that von Martius won, also sponsored explorations into the country's largely unstudied, unmapped, and even, unknown interior. Scholars intrigued by Brazil's self-discovery and formation of identity will find much of interest in the *Diário de viagem de Francisco Freire Alemão* (item **1962**). It tells the story of an expedition by the Comissão Científica de Exploração, organized by the IHGB and composed exclusively of Brazilian naturalists and researchers, to study the geography, natural resources, and populations spread along the fringes of Brazilian territory. Behind the effort was a deliberate public policy to develop a discourse of knowledge that would secure a prominent international position for Brazil as a producer of scientific knowledge. The leader of the expedition was Francisco Freire Alemão, a medical doctor and naturalist, and long time member of the institute. He was to examine, describe, and classify new genus and species of Brazilian fauna. Each member had a specific assignment. The expedition spent nearly two and a half years in Ceará. This text is the diary that Freire Alemão kept. The reports and materials of the expedition are in the Biblioteca Nacional (Rio) and have been appropriately cataloged (1961). The life, place, and ambience of mid-19th century Ceará comes alive in these pages. The Cearenses harbored a suspicion of these men from the distant "court" of Rio de Janeiro. Some suspected them of seeking the supposed, and as yet undiscovered, mines of the province "to turn them over to the English, who [would] come to enslave all the people of Ceará" (p. 22). Freire Alemão observed that people with a certain level of education "showed themselves to be envious and cautious" (p. 33) regarding all from Rio de Janeiro. Contemporary critics unkindly called the expedition the Commission of the Butterflies.

An expedition with a similar intent was later sent to Amazonia. *Gonçalves Dias na Amazônia* (item **2018**) is the diary of that expedition on the Rio Negro. The Amazon region was the great unknown in Brazil and the empire was under pressure to open it to foreign commerce. António Gonçalves Dias was one of those sent to report on the region. He had participated in the earlier expedition to Ceará and was a grand poet favored by the emperor. He was a *mulato* with roots in São Luís, Maranhão. His collections of flora and fauna enriched the ethnographic holdings of the later *Museu Nacional*. His observations led him to assert that Brazilian Indians had an "elevated and complete culture before the discovery" (p. xiv). As an interpreter of Amazonas, some rank him with Euclides da Cunha.

Another interesting book that sheds light on the interior of Brazil is Teófilo Benedito Ottoni's mid-century reports on his efforts to open the Mucuri river area of northeastern Minas Gerais to settlement (item **2088**). He provided a surprisingly sympathetic description of the natives and horror at their treatment by military forces. The region's rich, dense forests, part of the great Atlantic Forest, had been, and continued to be devastated to create vast cattle fazendas. The native peoples, whose groups he referred to as *linguas*, suffered terrible privations and death. It was a disaster whose results still scar the land. The documents are given context by an excellent introductory essay by Regina Horta Duarte of the Universidade Federal de Minas Gerais.

The role of regional newspapers in an empire with a largely illiterate population is the subject of Fernandes' *A imprensa em pauta* (item **2029**) a study of three newspapers in Fortaleza, Ceará. Between the supposedly liberal (*Cearense*, 1846–91) and conservative papers (*Pedro II*, 1840–89 and *Constituição*, 1863–89) there were not great ideological differences. The editors of the last two saw themselves as liberals and believed that the Conservative Party was Brazil's truly liberal party. The author delves briefly into the business of newspapers in Fortaleza, including who printed them and their cost. Interestingly, they were subscription based, paid in advance. Provincial politics shaped content and influenced the language employed, which included using insults and virulent words and expressions to provoke their opponents. Reporting on the droughts and the influx of refugees and the government's attempts at relief was heated and politically slanted. The readership was decidedly small. In 1887 Fortaleza had 27,000 residents, of whom about 9,000 could read and had a profession. Ceará's political disputes could turn violent as exemplified by the destruction of the *Constituição* printing press in the early 1840s. The looters gathered the type in sacks and threw them into the sea. Researchers interested in urban development, politics, or social life will find leads here.

Slavery, wealth, and its distribution is the object of Zephyr Frank's important analysis in his *HAHR* article (item **2038**). He mined 1,220 estate inventories in Rio de Janeiro, São Paulo, São João del-Rei (Minas Gerais), and São José (Minas Gerais), and reached some interesting conclusions. In 1849 Rio de Janeiro had 33 percent of its households owning an average of 11 slaves. Rio also had the empire's highest levels of wealth. "Areas with dynamic and extensive urban-based financial networks (whether formal or informal witnessed higher levels of wealth and inequality" (p. 256). He noted that slaves were "much more important to middling and small wealth holders than [to] their wealthy cousins" (p. 256). Even more striking is his statement that "Brazil's slaveholder society was broadly based and that slavery was proportionally more important to middling and poorer wealth holders. Slavery thus had the perverse effect of lowering inequality among wealth holders even while it raised overall social inequality" (p. 257).

Modernization via expansion of railroads deepened the reach and power of slave-based coffee cultivation, but the results were not those expected. Two studies examine the history of railroads. The nicknamed "Inglesa," that opened the interior of São Paulo to the world by overcoming the escarpment that separates the Paulista plateau from the sea was begun by British engineers in 1867. The book (item 2074) is full of wonderful photos of people, equipment, bridges, documents, maps, and trains, trains, trains. William Summerhill (item 2123) uses railroads as a prime factor in his study of "social savings" in the 19th century. This jargon-laden article assesses the direct and indirect effects of railroads in Brazil. High transportation costs were a constant obstacle to economic growth. The absence of navigable rivers where they would have been most useful, and the difficult topography made railways appear attractive. In the 1850s the politically influential planter class demanded inexpensive transport and were able to secure government subsidies. By the 1870s the emphasis had shifted to foreign investment. But many concessions never left the drawing board. Subsidies became the rule and the government owned 61 percent of the railroads by 1914. Summerhill concludes that investment in rail contributed to the "lost opportunities in the late 19th century" (p. 95). The money, he concluded, would have had greater returns if it had been invested in education.

Related to the discussion of Brazilian economic development is the nature of São Paulo itself. Soares de Moura (item 2083) disagrees sharply with the views of Silva Bruno and Richard Morse, who she argues distorted the historiography. Her premise is that the mobility and tumultuousness of São Paulo existed before the "modernization promoted by the expansion of coffee production and export" (p. 15). The myth, in her view, of Paulista poverty in the late 18th and early 19th centuries has infected historical thinking. She sets herself against a deeply seated interpretation and carries the day.

Slavery is a theme or subtheme of many studies. Elaine Cancian's intriguing study asks what buildings can tell us about the people who lived in them and whether slavery can be studied from a city's architecture (item 1990). Gilberto Freyre certainly thought so (Casa Grande e Senzala 1933, and Sobrados e Mucambos, 1936). Brazilian historians have not been quick to follow his lead, and Cancian seeks to make a contribution in that direction. She uses the development of Cuiabá and Corumbá, Mato Grosso, to make her case. She studies the rich detail on daily life that the houses of the two cities' slaveholders provided. In Corumbá water carried via pipes from external sources did not exist until 1912, so every drop was brought in by slaves. Located in the distant rear of the houses, the kitchens were the slaves' special domain, not only for food preparation, they also slept there amidst utensils, stove fuel, tables, and supplies. Most houses were a single level and second floors were a sign of wealth. The streets were not paved and were dominated by animals and slaves on assignments. They were areas of "disorder and intranquility, at least for the slave owners" (p. 107). Paraguay held Corumbá for two years during the war of 1864–70. Only 20 ruined mud and wattle houses survived the occupation. By 1873 about 455 houses of stone had risen. They were concentrated on the principal streets and plaza. The outlying structures were the old style mud and wattle. There are some useful tables giving names of slaves, those of their owners and some comments about their abilities and locations. Interestingly some of the owners were black women (p. 145).

Rio de Janeiro was the largest slave city in the Americas in the 19th century. A group of scholars (item **2001**) focuses on Brazil's port cities studying how captives reshaped their lives, resurrecting and adapting African practices, ways, foods, music, dance, and language. Considering that Brazil received 38 to 43 percent of all the Africans shipped across the Atlantic, such studies are fundamentally important. The essays are well-written and based on solid research. The final chapter, "Recriando Africas" is especially praiseworthy.

Three articles provide surprising details regarding slavery. It is well known that after 1860 slaves shifted from the declining sugar plantations of the northeast to the expanding coffee areas of the southeast. Couceiro (item **2010**) examines the tensions and readjustments those importations caused among the slaves already there, the free farmers, local government, and fazenda administrators. Machado (item **2068**) looks at the history of Jabaquara, a runaway-slave encampment organized and supported by abolitionists within the city limits of Santos (SP). Was it really a *quilombo*? The question has present-day political implications, because the Constitution of 1988 guarantees land title to descendants of *quilombo* communities. Due to complex alliances and patronage arrangements residents of Jabaquara were drawn into the dock strike of 1891 as strike breakers. This is good social history with real life importance.

The current role of Muslim beliefs in the world provokes curiosity about African Muslims in Brazil. Costa e Silva (item **2115**) found that Korans were for sale in Rio de Janeiro bookstores. Into the early 20th century there was a Muslim community in the city, which included a Koranic (or Quranic) school. With the end of the slave trade and the decline in contacts with Africa, the community became isolated and gradually its descendants apparently converted to other faiths.

Discussions of slavery usually turn to abolition and the role of the royal family, especially Princess Isabel, in the termination of slavery. Robert Daibert (item **2013**) studies how the public image of Princess Isabel was constructed and resignified from her birth to her positioning among the civic heroes of Brazilian history. Dailbert carries his examination from her birth to the centenary celebrations (1988) of her signing the act of abolition. Among the strong points of the text is an enlightening discussion of African views of royalty that were carried to Brazil. He shows that the *"congados"* were not just entertainments, but reenactments of a hidden reality celebrating an African vision of kingship. He concludes that "the symbolic coronations of kings and queens in their religious festivals in the 19th century were part of an important process of constructing a Brazilian nationality on an African model . . . the conversion of everyone to Christianity was headed by an African leadership" (p. 219).

Slavery was also related to Brazil's major 19th-century war, that of the Triple Alliance against Paraguay. A fair number of Brazil's soldiers were slaves ceded to the government or were ex-slaves, and the war weakened the slave-labor system and contributed to its collapse. Pedrosa (item **2092**) labels it a "catastrophe of errors" in his richly annotated and calmly analytical study, which will appeal to military history and foreign relations specialists. Alfredo Taunay, whose *A retirada da Laguna* (1871) captured the sad withdrawal of defeated Brazilian forces from Mato Grosso, is the subject of Maria Lídia Lichtscheidl Maretti's study (item **2071**), which mixes biography and literary criticism. It adds an interesting dimension to the social history of late 19th-century Brazil. Some insight into Brazilian relations with the Rio de la Plata region can be obtained from the speeches in the imperial parliament of the Visconde do Rio Branco (father of the Baron) (item **2101**). His leadership, from 1850 to the 1870s was "fundamental in the construction of the thought process of Brazilian foreign policy" (p. 17). Students of the period should consult the discussions of the Council of State, which the foreign ministry has published (items **2006** and **2007**). The Council of State was the pinnacle of the imperial elite. Its members had lifetime tenure, checked only by political realities and the emperor's veto. Its foreign relations decisions can be studied in these volumes containing reports (*consultas*) submitted for its debate. These documents were preserved in the foreign ministry's archive bound together with critical reviews, opinions, and reports by ministry staff. They are a necessary source for the study of Brazilian foreign relations during the empire. The various *consultas* give a sense of the breadth and issues of the country's international relations.

Logistics played a huge role in the Triple Alliance War as Coralio Bragança Pardo Cabeda (item **1986**) demonstrates. Delays in operations, hunger among the troops, the loss of horses and mules, inability to open new fronts, and the prolongation of the war for five years were related to inadequate logistical support. This article provides a rapid overview of attempts to create a workable supply system based on contracted civilian suppliers. The system never worked effectively. After the war, the lessons were not absorbed and so the army suffered another logistical failure at Canudos.

One of the unintended consequences of the war was the growth of arrogance on the part of some army officers. Thomas Holloway's careful reconstruction (item **2053**) of the largely forgotten murder in 1883 of Apulco de Castro, a black newspaper publisher in Rio de Janeiro is a major contribution to our understanding of that turbulent decade.

The collapse of the empire and the onset of the republic continue to captivate. Maria Tereza Chaves de Mello's *República consentida* (item **2077**) probes the empire's last decades in her analysis of the strengthening of the republican idea. The author examines changing attitudes toward public space in Rio de Janeiro. In her telling, the republican idea slipped from the restricted conversations of republican clubs into the Carioca streets. With a population that was about 70 percent illiterate moving from the written word to ample public discourse was accomplished via speechmaking and reading aloud at news stands. Her description of this process led her into detailed analysis of the center of Rio de Janeiro, particularly the role of the popular Rua do Ouvidor. In one section she takes the reader through a typical day and night on Ouvidor, which will intrigue urban specialists. In that era "Rio de Janeiro monopolized national life" (p. 55), so what happened in Rio, especially on its principal street, had an outsized importance. This is a significant book.

An often mentioned symbol of the end of the empire was the grand ball at the *Ilha Fiscal* on November 9, 1889. Cláudio da Costa Braga's little book (item

1981) on this emblematic event is a useful reminder of the distance between the imperial government and the country it ruled. The *Ilha Fiscal* had been called Rat Island before its reconstruction (1881–89) as the intended customs house of Rio de Janeiro. The occasion for the ball was the visit of the Chilean warship *Almirante Cochrane*, named for the Scotsman who fathered both the Chilean and Brazilian navies. The intention was to show support for Chile, then threatened with a potentially hostile alliance of Peru, Bolivia, and Argentina. The location was selected for its drama and because the pro-monarchical navy controlled access, while possible sites on land were too easy for the restive and republican-inclined army to isolate and control. This well-illustrated book reviews the reasons for the event, the Rio elite's struggle to obtain invitations, the elaborate preparations, the obvious absence of army officers, the ostentatious presence of elaborately uniformed National Guard officers, and the opulent menu and decorations. It was all a wonderful façade that hid the reality of the moment, the imminent collapse of the Bragança monarchy.

The end of African slavery should not be separated from the study of immigration. Rogério Dezem (item **2017**) has written a very helpful study of the search for replacement Japanese labor. He sought out the origins of pro- and anti-Japanese sentiment. Basing his work on unpublished sources, he examines the development of a discourse that drew on popular images of the peoples and cultures of the Far East. *Fazendeiros* began with the idea of seeking European immigrants from Catholic cultures who would fit into Brazilian society. Dezem mined the images and texts produced by intellectuals, diplomats, state officials, and the agrarian elite. Exoticism ruled the day as *geishas* and *samurais* entered the cartoons of newspapers and magazines. With the Japanese victories in the Russo-Japanese War of 1905 and the arrival of Japanese immigrants in 1906, the imagined and the real confronted each other.

It is easy to imagine that the introduction of immigrants was a smooth process, but it was not. In an impressive piece of research and analysis, Karl Monsma (item **2079**) examines the every-day relations between Italian immigrants and Afro-Brazilians in western São Paulo between 1888 and 1914. Violence and intimidation generally had Italians attacking the dark skinned. There was "an atmosphere of intimidation" against people of color that eventually suggested hatred. The blacks and *mulatos* tried to protect themselves by strengthening patron-client bonds with *fazendeiros* and urban elites, "using one form of subordination to ward off another" (p. 1143). The racism did not develop into racial preference and segregation, because once the fear of black revolt faded, it was replaced with fear of immigrant violence and strikes. Monsma wisely concludes that "local elites did not need the support of poor whites, and much less that of foreigners, to maintain their political and economic power" (p. 1144).

The relationship between immigrants and local power holders is the subject of Isléia Rossler Streit's study (item **2121**) of local colonels in the north of Rio Grande do Sul and the immigrants who colonized the region. The question of how the politics of *coronelismo* dealt with the immigrants is an important one. The author highlights the role of colonization companies. She studies the land conflicts and political disputes in the region to explain the complex political game that involved public and private power in Rio Grande do Sul of the era. Oral histories and personal letters in regional and private archives stand out among her archival sources. Rio Grande do Sul's history is, seemingly, rich in insights. Mário José Maestri Filho's book (item **2070**) observes that positivism a la Augusto

Comte defended the idea of a society governed by elites based on positive principles that recognized "social necessities." Its key principle was "to conserve, while improving," at the same time opposing revolution and the democratic exercise of power" (p. 7–8). Oddly, the new social ideas of the late 19th century had developed in industrial Europe, but took root in the mostly pastoral province of Rio Grande do Sul. Its *gaúcho* leaders were young and from well-off landowning families. The positivists embraced republicanism in the 1880s and advocated immediate abolition of slavery without compensation for slave owners. They favored property taxes and elimination of contraband, which clashed with the views of *latifundiários*. The social situation in Rio Grande had been aggravated in 1870–75 when the open prairie had been fenced, causing a strong wave of unemployment. Curiously, a lot of the pastoral laborers were slaves, who were then sold to the coffee fazendas of the central-south. Beginning in 1884 there was widespread freeing of slaves on condition that they continue to work for seven years. With the coming of the republic, the social-economic tensions boiled into one of the most violent regional civil wars in Brazil's history. Maestri argues that the extreme violence had its origins in the weighty economic, political, and social questions then in play. This well-written book is based on extensive reading of secondary sources. Its clear language and skillful summary accounts will be useful for researchers seeking to understand the role of Rio Grande do Sul in the Old Republic.

Importing foreign labor was not the only solution to the need to replace the slaves. Olivia Maria Gomes da Cunha uncovered an effort in Petrópolis to train free replacements to do housework. She does several important things in this article (item **2012**). She examines the history of the domestic training school of *Nossa Senhora do Amparo* in Petrópolis, the ideology behind it, and how it was linked to ideas about domestic work. With slave emancipation, there was rising concern for preparing free labor to work in family homes. She also analyzes attempts to interpret, regulate, and organize such work. Along the way she discusses little-known feminist publications that had roles in the debates about domestic servants and educating young women.

The collapse of the empire did not bring the brilliant republic of which its proponents dreamed. Instead it was an economic disaster beset with violence. Discussions of the latter have often lacked tangible substance. The diaries of leaders of the Libertador rebels in Rio Grande do Sul (item **2125**) have been unknown until now so their publication is an important event. The Tavares brothers, Francisco and Joca, were born into a "traditional" family of the Rio Grandense frontier, members of the *Partido Conservador* during the empire, they joined the republican cause. But then they clashed with Julio de Castilhos' tight control of the *Partido Republicano* and formed the *Partido Federalista* in Bagé in 1892. During the so-called Revolution of 1893, Joca was the commanding general of the *Libertador* army and Francisco was one of the main civilian instigators of the revolt. The diaries constitute a small archive of the revolt and reproduce correspondence with leaders such as Gaspar Silveira Martins, Admiral Saldanha da Gama, and General Aparício Saraiva. Joca's diary focuses more on the military matters of the campaign, while that of Francisco deals with the political alliances and the struggle to finance the fighting. The details of waging a guerrilla war on the pampas will interest military specialists, and students of foreign relations will want to examine the ambiguous actions of the Argentine and Uruguayan authorities. The relations of the *gaúcho* forces and the rebellious navy get some clarification in these pages. The two volumes are a new source for the study of the tumultuous early years of the republic.

Ana Luiza Backes (item **1971**) examines the politics that resulted in the creation of a republican order by President Manuel Ferraz Campos Sales. His pact with the state-based oligarchies made the republican model functional *a la brasileira*. She reviews the tumultuous development of the republic in the 1890s, with a steady focus on how politics was reflected in the national congress. The role of amnesty in resolving violent disputes was notable. She rightly emphasizes that while regionalism was a major factor, national questions also defined politics and the fluid alliances of the era. By focusing on the relations between the president and the congress, she highlights the struggles that shaped the solutions that President Campos Sales crafted.

The opening decades of the 20th century were a highpoint for Brazilian diplomacy, which is odd given the state of the political system. If the elite had difficulty agreeing on politics, they seemingly united on foreign policy. Happily the diplomats kept good archives and so the literature seems destined to improve constantly. The foreign ministry has shown itself to be considerably introspective regarding its history. This tendency is exemplified by *Rio Branco, a América do Sul e a modernização do Brasil* (item **2102**). For students of Brazilian foreign relations this is a book not to be missed. It is a collection of 27 essays presented at a seminar held at the Itamaraty in Brasília in August 2002 to commemorate the centenary of the ministry of José Maria da Silva Paranhos Júnior, the Baron of Rio Branco. The baron's work is celebrated by examining how it influenced classic aspects of Brazilian diplomacy. The authors are a distinguished mix of diplomats and academic specialists. They studied, in carefully researched and clearly written analyses, the development of the intellectual bases, the traditions and methods, and the functioning of the republic's foreign relations. Various essays illuminate aspects of Rio Branco's complicated personal relations with Brazilian diplomats such as Oliveira Lima and Salvador de Mendonça, and his testy relationship with Argentine foreign minister Estanislau Zeballos.

The relationship between Rio Branco and Oliveira Lima was clarified from an unexpected angle in a collection of letters edited by Ângela de Castro Gomes (item **2023**). These letters between Manuel de Oliveira Lima and Gilberto Freyre are important in their own right and also shed light on their outlooks and their relationship. Though both were from Pernambuco, they were of very different generations: Oliveira Lima 1867–1928 and Freyre 1900–87. The letters run from April 1917 to June 1927 and total 100 from Freyre and 80 from Oliveira Lima. The two met in Recife in 1917 where Freyre was a student in the *Colégio Americano*. The slim teenager and the corpulent retired diplomat made a memorable pair. Oliveira Lima ended his diplomatic career under a cloud, having made an enemy of the Baron of Rio Branco and having supported Rui Barbosa against Hermes da Fonseca in the 1910 presidential election. He was an internationally known historian, whose writings, such as his *O Império brasileiro* (São Paulo, 1927), were highly praised. He was a regular contributor to newspapers such as Rio de Janeiro's *Jornal do Comércio* and *Jornal do Brasil*, São Paulo's *Estado de S. Paulo* and Recife's *Diário de Pernambuco*. Freyre soon joined him in the columns of the latter paper. In the annex of the edition under review, there are reprints of Freyre's newspaper and scholarly articles and various commentaries on Oliveira Lima's writings. During his years abroad, Oliveira Lima had collected, what was in the 1920s, perhaps the world's most valuable body of *Brasiliana*, which he donated to the Catholic University in Washington, DC. Because this correspondence took place while Oliveira Lima resided in Washington, it contains material of interest to students of Brazilian-American relations. Oliveira Lima saw the US as a good ally and as "a model republican nation, modern and industrial, that could serve as inspiration for a 'backward' Brazil" (p. 17). The letters show the development of a paternal friendship and provide information on Freyre's student years at Columbia University in New York.

The Itamaraty is publishing works on the stars of its diplomatic service. Two volumes on Joaquim Francisco de Assis Brasil (item **1970**) cover his years in Lisbon, Washington, and Buenos Aires. Assis Brasil was a leading figure in the Brazilian republic from its outset until the 1930s. His writings contributed to the formation of republican sentiments in the 1880s and to governmental theory in the 1890s. A *gaúcho*, he stood against *castilhismo* in Rio Grande do Sul and was an ardent defender of his home state. He advocated modernization of agriculture and practiced the latest methods on his properties in Rio Grande. In the early 1930s, as minister of agriculture, he influenced farming policies. This book, focused on his diplomatic career, is a collection of correspondence from the *Arquivo Histórico do Itamaraty* organized by the foreign ministry's *Centro de História e Documentação Diplomática*. The center's director, Alvaro da Costa Franco, introduces the volumes with a detailed and intriguing essay. Those interested in Brazilian relations with Argentina, Portugal, and the US will want to examine these letters. Of the three countries, most space was given to the latter. Assis Brasil's analysis of the situation early in the 1898 war with Spain emphasized Brazil's role as the only Latin American country to support the northern republic. The letters relative to Brazil's efforts to end the threat from the Bolivian Syndicate and to secure Acre add considerable insight into those tense events. Assis Brasil headed the Brazilian embassy in Buenos Aires in a period of sensitive relations when the two countries experienced a climate of competition mimicking, to some extent, the European scene. At the Pan American conference in Rio de Janeiro in 1906 he was the go-between with the Argentine delegation. He was in the middle of Rio Branco's difficult relations with Argentine foreign minister Zeballos. The correspondence in the second volume runs into mid-1933.

Another example of the foreign ministry's historical concerns is Geraldo Mesquita Júnior's edition of congressional documents on the Treaty of Petrópolis (1903) with Bolivia regarding Acre (item **2078**). Carlos Henrique Cardim's essay on the opposing views of Rio Branco and Rui Barbosa regarding the treaty adds a new page to the story.

The *Sertão* is attracting more scholarly interest and some of the studies are consciously looking for deeper explanations of the Canudos disaster of 1897. These naturally provide background for examinations of the Old Republic. The attitudes and culture of the *sertanejos* have long needed deep research. Martha S. Santos (item **2108**) has made a great contribution to the scholarly study of the 19th-century northeastern backlands with her article on honor, masculinity, survival, and conflict. Well-researched and cogently argued, this article sees assertions of honor by poor *sertanejos* as a mechanism used to defend their use of land, water, and livestock. From the early 1850s to 1877 the population of Ceará more than doubled from 350,000 to 816,556. *Sertanejos* from other provinces flooded into the *Cearense* backlands increasing competition for land and resources. Their large families were mostly defenseless partly because of the lack of land legislation between 1822 and 1850. The fragile landowning structure of Ceará and the inability of the empire to guarantee property boundaries encouraged a constant assertion of the honorable status of proprietor as a marker of respectability. Such declarations partly were aimed at fending off potential claims of large landowners on the *sertanejo's* labor. Honor, autonomy, and ability to support self and family were closely linked. This research weakens the idea that Mediterranean notions of honor can be applied easily to northeast Brazil.

Tyrone Cândido combines the study of railroad construction in Ceará during the drought in the *Sertão* with the impact it had on the *sertanejos* (item **1991**). Part of a series of small books published by Fortelaza's Museu do Ceará, *Trem da seca* tells how Cearense *sertanejos* fleeing the great drought of 1877–79 became railroad workers. In the process they escaped famine and learned new skills. Even before the drought, the small farmers of Ceará were struggling to survive in an economy of widespread poverty. In the first half of the century most of them were subsistence growers, but with the sharp rise in cotton prices during the Civil War in the US, they leapt into cotton culture leaving aside cultivation of family food. The sudden increase in Cearense cotton production abruptly ended when the American South recuperated its dominance of the world market after the war. Not having accumulated food stocks, the *sertanejos* were ill prepared as drought deepened. They swarmed into Fortaleza frightening the urban elite. An estimated 2,147,000 were set adrift by the crisis. The Baturité railroad project allowed thousands of them to be put to work, often under dreadful conditions. Cândido's well-researched study examines the formation of government policies that combined the railroad's need for labor with the desire to keep the rural-urban migration in check. Public works were to feed the starving.

In historical works the people fleeing the drought have often been merely nameless numbers. A research team funded by FAPESP (Fundação de Amparo à Pesquisa do Estado de São Paulo) have made available to researchers the names and personal data of drought refugees in *Os refugiados da seca: emigrantes cearenses, 1888–1889* (item **2098**). This publication is accompanied by a CD containing useful information on those who took ship for Amazonia, Rio de Janeiro, Vitória, or Santos. The editors microfilmed documents in the Arquivo Público Estadual do Ceará. Copies of the films are in the Centro de Estudos de Demografia Histórica da América Latina of the Universidade de São Paulo and in the Departamento de História of the Universidade Federal do Ceará. This booklet is a partial guide to the materials.

Study of the *Sertão* and the origins of the Canudos crisis have been substantially advanced by Monica Duarte Dantas' book *Fronteiras movediças* (item **2014**). She analyzes the 70 years before the formation of Antonio Conselheiro's town, recreating the daily life of the surrounding districts of the *Sertão* to find out where the people of Canudos came from. The economic and political changes that she unearthed collided with existing social practices and local customs that guaranteed various forms of access to land, including ability to negotiate usage, if not ownership, and maintenance of degrees of personal autonomy in a world over which *sertanejos* had little control. At the margins of Brazilian society, they benefited from mutual aid in order to survive. The society she studied was made up of poor whites, freed Africans, runaway slaves, and Indians. Canudos was not an overnight creation but the result of decades of social change.

The tragedy of Canudos continues to fascinate and to frustrate scholars interested in Brazil. That shameful affair and his book, *Os Sertões*, established the reputation of Euclides da Cunha and tied him permanently to any discussion of the Bahian backlands. The collection of essays produced in France (item **1983**) begins with him and is permeated by references to him. Katia de Queirós Mattoso shows how images of the *Sertão* and its people link the writings of Euclides and João Capistrano de Abreu. The role of collective mental suggestion and even illness suggests the influence of the work of Nina Rodrigues. Those interested in the effects of the past on popular culture will want to read the chapters on film portrayals of Canudos and the *Sertão*, as well as the final chapter on the impact of Mario Vargas Llosa's novel (1981). The fame of *Os sertões* overshadowed the many interesting and revealing books written by participants in the suppression of the community, and to some extent has discouraged deeper research. Frederico Pernambucano de Mello (item **2076**) makes ample use of this largely ignored bibliography and probed contemporary newspapers for eyewitness accounts. He also brings a depth of local, regional knowledge that helps him to understand the documentary record. Clearly, there is yet more to learn about the events in the Bahian *Sertão* of 1897.

Raúl Gouveia Fernandes (item **2031**) demonstrates this assertion in his *Luso-Brazilian Review* article. He observes that Euclides da Cunha wrote *Os Sertões* with future historians in mind, and so continues to captivate scholars. In the course of writing da Cunha changed his views of the *sertanejos* as lesser beings to the strong, defiant "bedrock" of the Brazilian nation. Those people massacred at Canudos, "in the greatest scandal of our history," were only "defending their invaded home, nothing more" (p. 58). Euclides' impassioned curiosity continues to attract readers. It is with reason that *Os Sertões* continues to be a key source for the history of Canudos and that it keeps alive in the Brazilian memory the painful drama of its destruction. One of the contemporary accounts was written by another journalist to witness the fighting at Favela hill. Manoel Benício sent biting reports to his paper and had to flee the likely vengeance of angry army officers. His writings are often compared and judged against those of Euclides. In his *O Rei dos jagunços de Manuel Benício* (item **1975**), Benício emphasized a truth that the affair had suppressed, namely that "the *Sertão* also is Brazil and the *jagunço* is a Brazilian marginalized by civilization, left to the mercy of the 'Law of Nature'" (p. 30). The introduction by Silvia Maria Azevedo is well done and very helpful in clarifying the literary criticisms of this and other books on Canudos.

There is now a subfield of Brazilian studies devoted to the life and work of Euclides [Rodrigues Pimenta] da Cunha. Roberto Ventura produced a fine biography (item **2134**) of Euclides, which tragically he could not complete due to his death in an auto accident returning home from a symposium on Euclides. Some parts of the biography are fuller and more finished than others. The periods of the coming of the republic, the *"encilhamento,"* the political repression during Deodoro's presidency, and the Fleet's revolt are complete, while the section on Euclides' turbulent family life is not. Regarding the Canudos affair, Ventura took the unusual tack of placing Euclides and Antonio Conselheiro in a parallel comparison. Both were orphans who had a traumatic experience involving adultery; both were builders, one of bridges, the other of churches; and each was marked by the republican cause. "The fanatic that was transformed into a historic personage is a literary construction of the writer" (p. 14).

The gaps in our knowledge of Euclides da Cunha's life have been filled by a new, complete biography by Frederic Amory (item **1966**). He provides an exhaustive reconstruction of the author's life and work. He delves into Euclides upbringing, his cadet years, when he came under the influence of Benjamin Constant and positivism, and his gradual disenchantment with the *Praia Vermelha* military school. Oddly most historians of the era have ignored Euclides' involvement in the extreme republican faction labeled *Florianistas* or Jacobins, which was solidified by his marriage to Ana Ribeiro, the daughter of the infamous officer Solon Ribeiro, who had delivered the expulsion order to Pedro II. There is evidence that Euclides was among the plotters against the empire. His brief army service set him on his civilian career as a civil engineer. Amory's discussion of his sometime work as a journalist and his path to and reports from Canudos make compelling reading. In all Euclides spent only 15 to 18 days at Canudos. Historians might wish that Amory had explored his subject's sources more deeply, but they will benefit from his comparison of the work of Euclides and that of Manoel Benício. The details of the writing, publishing, and subsequent history of Os Sertões is all included, as is the turmoil caused by his wife's infidelity that led to Euclides' brutal murder at the hands of her lover. This is an extremely welcome study.

Canudos did not end violence in the Sertão. The region was beset by armed, highly mobile gangs called cangaços through to the late 1930s. Aside from the work of Linda Lewin and Billy Chandler, much that has been written about that phenomenon has been more romantic than based on serious research. Hilário Lucetti and Magérbio Lucena reduced that deficiency with their biography (item 2064) of Virgulino Ferreira da Silva, known by the nickname Lampião, and his closest lieutenants. At the outset, the authors make the important comment that no matter how unfairly a person is treated, no one is forced into a life of crime, pillage, torture and murder; it is a choice. The book describes the band's organization, internal rules, and its principal attacks, such as the failed one on Mossoró, Rio Grande do Norte (1927). Lampião was not a modern Robin Hood, taking from the rich and giving to the poor, he was indiscriminate in robbing and murdering those who crossed his path. His cangaço had no ethics. The authors also discuss the "coiteiros," paid informers, local landowners, or political figures who protected the cangaceiros and profited from their thievery. This fascinating, well-written book brings to light the violent underbelly of the Old Republic.

Some of the most impressive research and analysis in the literature reviewed here dealt with labor history. Two excellent articles broke new ground with their incisive, even imaginative analyses of dock workers in Rio de Janeiro in the first decades of the 20th century. The Journal of Latin American Studies and the HAHR published within months of each other these connected but independent studies. Kit McPhee (item 2075) led off with a provocative, well-researched, and well-reasoned article that is founded on actual history, rather than on ideological or racially based interpretations. The Afro-Brazilian dock workers had traditions going back into the 19th century that governed their preference for mediation in resolving labor problems. Their attitudes clashed with the ideas of immigrants who tried to implant European models. Surprisingly their "Brazilianness" gave them common ground in dealing with government officials. In fact, McPhee concluded that it "was the single factor that distinguished the coffee workers from their competitors, and it allowed these men to lose their blackness by gaining an ethnicity" (p. 175). María Cecília Velasco e Cruz (item 2131) followed with an equally excellent piece of work. She asks: Who were the dock workers? What were their traditions? How were they related to the "slaves for hire" in the first decades of the 19th century? African origins, such as being from Mina, had importance. This revisionist interpretation of labor history gives an example of what is possible when conventional explanations are seriously questioned. The Resistência society that was at the center of both articles still exists and the authors' keen research explains why. Surplus labor supply seemingly did not always mean that the bosses would win. Velasco e Cruz also explains how blacks kept certain spaces in an increasingly whiter city. Both of these scholars deserve a wide readership. Work like this could revitalize labor history and give it a more Brazilian focus.

Discomfort with conventional analysis emphasizing European origins of Brazil's labor movement is evident in Antonio Luigi Negro and Flavio Gomes' article (item **2086**) wherein they point out that studies on slave and immigrant labor do not interact and thus have created a hiatus in the historiography. The article is a stimulating journey through the historical literature on labor. The authors object to the conventional boundaries of research on labor history in their efforts to comprehend the complexity and diversity in the ways in which historians have dealt with the history of Brazilian labor. Seemingly Marcelo Badaró Mattos (item **2073**) agrees that new approaches are necessary. He shows how slave and free labor eventually combined to form a labor movement in Rio de Janeiro. He emphasizes what is sometimes forgotten, namely that the slaves had experience with social organizations in their religious brotherhoods (*irmandades*), in negotiating work practices with owners and overseers, and in organizing and governing *quilombos*. The bulk of his pages deal with the 19th century as would be expected, but the important and formative years from 1890 to 1910 need to be fleshed out more to strengthen this useful analysis.

Another area of exciting research is that of health history. In the 19th century Brazil had a reputation as a dangerous, disease-ridden place. The items reviewed here are filling a serious lacuna in Brazilian historiography. Denise Bernuzzi de Sant'Anna's *Cidade das águas* (item **2106**) tells the history of São Paulo's water supply and use by examining the city's public policies, disasters, and degradation of its environment. The book runs from the construction of the first waterspouts and fountains to the electric power plants on the Rio Tietê. Rivers contributed to the selection of the city's site and guided its history. Today many of the smaller streams have been channeled underground and paved over, their presence revealed only by street and plaza names, while the larger rivers are bordered by expressways. Sant'Anna does a fine job linking water and electricity and describing the tremendous effects that combination had on São Paulo.

Henriquez Cukierman (item **2011**) wrote an excellent biography of Oswaldo Cruz and the story of how he led the struggle to eliminate yellow fever from Rio de Janeiro by applying the methods of mosquito control the American military used in Cuba. In the process Cruz earned the nickname General Mata-Mosquito. Along the way Cukierman examines public health as public policy, how Cruz developed his famous institute at *Manguinhos*, how he built the Moorish "castle" as its headquarters, and how he combated bubonic plague and small pox. There is a finely detailed chapter on the Vaccination riots of 1904. Equally fine is a long chapter on the 1912 scientific expedition of Arthur Neiva and Belisário Penna through the *Triângulo Mineiro*, Goiás, Piauí, Pernambuco, and Bahia. Those interested in the history of science and health in Latin America should not miss this book.

More attention is being paid to Brazil's experience with the pandemic Spanish flu of 1918. Christiane Maria Cruz de Souza (item **2120**) investigated the flu's impact on Salvador da Bahia in September to December 1918. She used local newspapers to analyze the politics of the city, its sanitary conditions, and the weaknesses of its public health policies and services. The harsh inequalities of the time were highlighted by the murderous epidemic. Adriana Costa da Goulart (item **2046**) plunges even more deeply into the disaster in Rio de Janeiro. The Spanish flu sent 600,000 Cariocas to their beds and created a crisis that could only be called social chaos. The dead were piled in the streets. Those who could walk debated whether the republican model created obstacles to good government; the newspapers blamed the director of public health, accusing him of trying to undo the work of Oswaldo Cruz. Director succeeded director until Carlos Chagas, head of the *Instituto Oswaldo Cruz*, took charge. President Wenceslau Braz, accused of incompetence, lost prestige while the scientific community won increased public confidence because scientists could protect the public from unseen biological threats. This is a well-researched and well-written article. It would be interesting to see if there are links between this crisis and the political-military unrest of the 1920s. [FDM]

MODERN PERIOD (SINCE 1919)

The moving wall of roughly one-and-a-half generations that relegates an era to the care of historians has by now reached 1970. Modern historiography is confronting new sets of sources: social statistics generated by the growth of public bureaucracies after 1930 and interviews with witnesses of events, made possible by the longer life spans of the 20th century. Certain topics have been reclaimed by other disciplines, so that sociologists study race relations across the 20th century, and economists not only analyze standardized national accounts series beginning in 1950, but also "data mine" digitized statistics from the 19th century. Perhaps this division of labor explains why 20th-century economic history was underrepresented in recent monographs by Brazilian historians; Queiroz (item **2097**) on the economic and political side effects of the Noroeste rail line from São Paulo to Bolivia and Paraguay was an exception.

Some of the best recent history meets this challenge by combining traditional archival research with oral history interviews and with reanalysis of the prodigious quantity of idiosyncratic data published in government reports. Two exemplary histories make the best of eclectic sources to study interactions between state and society: Fischer (item **2035**) on the pursuit of citizenship rights by poor people in Rio de Janeiro *favelas* since 1920 and Hentschke (item **2049**) on the relation between Vargas' educational policy and local-level school practice. The density of their research sets a benchmark for studies of social policy in the Vargas era.

Histories centering on rhetoric, symbols, myths, and imaginations have emerged as an autonomous field. While still subordinate to traditional periodizations of political economy, they seem to converge on the insight that some cultural transformation during the 1950s consolidated urban, consumerist mass culture. The most perspicacious of these cultural histories, Gonçalo Júnior (item **2054**) on comic book authors, audiences, publishers, and censors, is a work of semi-popular journalism. Oliveira (item **2087**) centers on myths about the plans for Brasília, and Wolfe (item **2135**) on "automobility" across the 20th century, rather than the automobile industry *per se*, both pivoting on the Kubitschek era. Franco Júnior (item **2037**) offers an exhaustive inventory of interpretations of soccer. Most cultural history research embroiders rather than challenges conventional historical wisdom. There is a touch of revisionism in the claim of Ferreira (item **2033**) that public rhetoric traces a developing mood and "imaginary" of Trabalhista party followers, 1945–64, that constituted a new political subculture. Cultural history tends to focus on leisure and consumer culture, while less commodified dimensions of cultural life, such as religion, receive little attention, with the exception of Romo (item **2104**) on the legitimization of Afro-Bahian religion and culture and a collection of documents about Protestants by Reily (item **2099**).

The transnational history of US-Brazilian relations around World War II include some cultural histories. In a rare piece of historiography with a sense of humor, Tota (item **2128**) reviews the exchange of stereotyped mutual perceptions. Pedreira (item **2091**) zeroes in on interactions around the Natal airbase. Campos (item **1987**) on ma-

372 / Handbook of Latin American Studies v. 66

laria control in strategic zones of the Amazon could be added to the list, though it leans more to institutional than cultural history. The most solid subfield of Brazilian historical research is the institutional history of public health, partly because it benefits from triangulating the good archives of Brazilian medical institutions with archives outside Brazil. Public health histories include Faria (item **2026**) on Rockefeller Foundation aid to São Paulo public health, and perhaps most interesting, Sanglard (item **2105**) on Guilherme Guinle's private patronage of hospitals and medical researchers.

This section includes Brazil's abundant and best-selling genre of popular biography, much of it subscholarly hagiography about figures of the Vargas era; Fausto's work (item **2028**) on Getúlio Vargas is good enough to merit special mention. On the 1930s and the Vargas era, perhaps the most novel contribution was the confrontation of the Salazar and Vargas regimes in the articles of *O corporativismo em português* (item **2114**). The good articles about Vargas in *Seminário Internacional Da Vida para a História* (item **2113**) are much more fragmentary. Perhaps the most insightful of the monographs on discrete topics in politics in the 1920s and 1930s is Soihet (item **2119**) on the feminist Bertha Lutz; also notable is Lustosa (item **2066**) on the Integralistas.

Studies on immigration and ethnic groups, another prolific genre, appeared in eclectic collections of articles, such as the outstanding *Cem anos* (item **1997**) on the Japanese and *Franceses* (item **2036**) on the French. Even the single-authored Falbel (item **1906**) on the Jews is a collection of pieces, not an integrated monograph, and Valduga (item **2129**) is microhistory, the "biography" of a Catholic Italian newspaper in Rio Grande do Sul. Opening the secret police archives of São Paulo has led to a number of small thesis books that target a nationality during the Vargas era: Perazzo (item **2093**) on Axis prisoners of war; Santos (item **2109**) on Italian antifascists; and Zen (item **2136**) on Lithuanians.

The expansion of Brazilian graduate programs in history has led to thesis research outpacing the capacity of university presses. Some Master's theses are still published as small monographs rather than articles, and regional university presses will publish even a cookie-cutter topic such as Campos (item **1988**) on representations of women in the small-town press. But now what is published as a small monograph may be a slimmed-down PhD dissertation rather than a MA thesis. And omnibus samplers of dissertation-based articles by doctoral students in one program, such as the USP Economic History department Congresso de Pós-Graduação (item **2005**), or one team, such as Universidade de Brasília students in *Histórias de violência* (item **2052**), are becoming common. The free online archive of academic journal articles at the SciELO (Scientific Electronic Library Online) Brazil website, with indexed, machine-translated English abstracts of articles, distributes much MA-level research (http://www.scielo.org). The Plataforma Lattes curriculum vitae system allows for limited searching of junior scholars' theses and article topics (http://www.plataformalattes.net), and various thesis depositories, such as the CAPES Banco de Teses (http://www.capes.gov.br/servicios/banco-de-teses) and the IBICT (Instituto Brasileiro de Informação em Ciência e Tecnologia) Biblioteca Digital Brasileira de Teses e Dissertações (http://bdtd.ibict.br), index or distribute theses. The publication of a MA thesis may say more about the sociology of patronage or vagaries of fortune than the importance of its research.

A perennial thesis topic is the history of leftists, particularly "the lives of communists." Studies range from *Velhos vermelhos* (item **2132**) on Paraná leadership, to Battibugli (item **1974**) on Spanish Civil War internationalists and Bernardes (item **1976**) on Laura Brandão, wife of a leader. A nostalgic tone pervades this field. Even an excellent collection of articles such as the three-volume *Esquerdas no Brasil* (item **2004**) suffers from partisan blind spots and a narrow definition of "the" lefts. And the literature shades into celebratory or highly partisan histories settling accounts, such as Giannotti (item **2043**) on labor, or *O Brasil de João Goulart* (item **1982**) on the Goulart legacy.

In recent years the historiography of the post-1964 dictatorships and resistance movements has become less one-sided, as apologists of the coup push back. *Simpósio "Quarenta Anos do Golpe de 1964"* (item **2117**) offers a good sampling of scholarly research, including some papers analyzing media debates justifying 1964. One example of pushing back is the publication of Frota (item **2039**), a posthumous memoir defending his authoritarian nationalist position against Geisel's political opening. The outstanding exemplar of truth-commission works, a quite common genre since 1985, is *Dossiê ditadura* (item **2020**), which documents a provisional list of persons killed by official repression. Research on political repression now confronts a mix of selectively declassified documents and participants' self-interested testimony. The contrast between *Operação Araguaia* (item **2080**) and Studart (item **2122**) is instructive: both chronicle the Araguaia guerilla, relying on unattributable sources, yet the former sweeps the problem under the carpet while the latter faces it head on.

Outside the history of resistance and repression, distance from events seems to have permitted good, mundane political history of the 1960s and 1970s like Cittadino (item **2002**) on the transition from populist to authoritarian politics in Paraíba, Dominguez Perez (item **2019**) on Carlos Lacerda's administrative style as governor, and Parucker (item **2090**) on the Sergeants' revolt of 1963. A lone memoir on contemporary politics, Rodrigues (item **2103**) on the rubber tappers' movement of the 1990s, testifies to the routinization of violence in a democratic system. [DB]

GENERAL

1904 Bem traçadas linhas: a história do Brasil em cartas pessoais. Organização de Renato Lemos. Rio de Janeiro Br. Bom Texto, 2004. 479 p.: bibl., ill.

Renato Lemos has gathered a large selection of the correspondence of notable Brazilians from the 1840s to the 1980s. The letters are arranged in chronological order grouped by five generations spanning those 14 decades. For each generational grouping, Lemos provides an introduction setting out the major themes of the era. Unhappily there is no index, nor listing of the names of the letter writers. [FDM]

Brandão, Paulo Roberto Baqueiro. Geografias da presença galega na cidade da Bahia. See *HLAS 65:1289.*

1905 Calavia Sáez, Oscar. La fábula de las tres ciencias: antropología, etnología e historia en el Brasil. (*Rev. Indias*, 65:234, mayo/agosto 2005, p. 337–354, bibl.)

Writing anything that proposes comparison requires more or less equal depth, detail, and temporal coverage of each subject. This article compares anthropology and ethnology with a very unequal nod in the direction of history. It is a shame because the two major sections are quite good, interesting, and provocative. The author's basic view is that Brazilian history was by and for whites, ethnology was focused on Indians, and anthropology was the study of African and Afro-Brazilian people. The three disciplines were committed, in his view, to building the Brazilian nation. [FDM]

1906 Falbel, Nachman. Judeus no Brasil: estudos e notas. São Paulo: Humanitas: EDUSP, 2008. 821 p.: bibl., ill., index.

São Paulo-focused collection of essays and research material on topics in Jewish history, including journalists of the Yiddish press; post-1891 settler colonies; associations, community formation, and community leaders; the Zionist movement; and prostitution. Useful starting point for researchers. [DB]

1907 Hausser, Christian. Auf dem Weg der Zivilisation: Geschichte und Konzepte gesellschaftlicher Entwicklung in Brasilien, 1808–1871 [On the way to civilization: history and concepts of social developments in Brazil, 1808–1871]. Stuttgart, Germany: Franz Steiner, 2009. 349 p.: bibl. (Geschichte) (Beiträge zur Europäischen Überseegeschichte, 96)

This work provides a close examination of historiographic concepts in 19th-century Brazil. After a discussion of the concept of "history" in Brazil from discovery to 1800, the author examines *Historia geral do Brasil* (1854) by Adolfo de Varnhagen and *Historia dos principaes successos políticos do Império do Brasil* (1826) by José da Silva Lisboa, among other works. He includes institutional aspects such as the foundation of the Instituto Histórico e Geográfico Brasileiro. [F. Obermeier]

Hemming, John. Tree of rivers: the story of the Amazon. See *HLAS 65:357.*

1908 Histórias do movimento negro no Brasil: depoimentos ao CPDOC. Organização de Verena Alberti e Amilcar Araujo Pereira. Rio de Janeiro: Fundação Getúlio Vargas, CPDOC: Pallas, 2007. 526 p.: bibl., ill. (some col.), index.

Based on four years of research and interviews, this work, produced by the oral history experts at the Centro de Pesquisa e Documentação de História Contemporânea do Brasil (CPDOC), contains personal narratives of leaders of the black movement in Brazil. Organized topically, the chapters also loosely follow the chronological development of the black movement by relating significant moments in the lives of key actors and describing events on the national stage: "Consciousness of Negritude" (i.e., Black Consciousness); "External Influences and Ideas," "Politics in Brazil," "Organization of the Black Movement," etc. Includes a discussion of university quotas and the passage of Lei 10.639, which mandates the teaching of Afro-Brazilian history and culture in all Brazilian schools. Appendices include a chronology of the black movement along with a brief bibliography and color re-

productions of posters from the movement. Also includes brief biographical sketches of women involved in the anti-slavery movement in Brazil. [K. McCann]

1909 Langfur, Hal. Moved by terror: frontier violence as cultural exchanges in late-colonial Brazil. (*Ethnohistory/Columbus,* 52:2, Spring 2005, p. 255–289, bibl., ill., map)

An article that rejects the contention that violent indigenous resistance to colonization had become all but ineffectual by the late colonial period on the frontiers of Portuguese America. Based on archival evidence, the author argues that successful raiding and military maneuvers by such groups as the Botocudo and the Puri to counter violence by Luso-Afro-Brazilian society was an essential part of cultural interaction that evolved into a shared language and praxis, at once symbolic and concrete. He writes, in sum, of "mutual brutality constituting cultural commerce, as warring parties found in terror an essential means of communication and exchange." [S. Ramírez]

Possamai, Zita Rosane. O circuito social da fotografia em Porto Alegre, 1922 e 1935. See item 170.

1910 Rodrigues, Jaime. De costa a costa: escravos, marinheiros e intermediários do tráfico negreiro de Angola ao Rio de Janeiro, 1780–1860. São Paulo: Companhia das Letras, 2005. 420 p.: bibl., ill. (some col.), index, maps.

Extensively researched in Portuguese and Brazilian archives, exploiting many new sources, this work elucidates activities of understudied intermediaries who facilitated slave trade between Angola and Rio de Janeiro, including ship captains, free and enslaved sailors, inland and coastal slave traders, smugglers, Portuguese and Brazilian authorities, and African chieftains, among others. Example of increasingly transatlantic perspective enhancing recent studies of Brazilian slavery. [HL]

1911 Os senhores dos rios. Organização de Mary Del Priore e Flávio Gomes. Rio de Janeiro: Elsevier: Campus, 2004. 315 p.: bibl., ill.

Collection of 10 essays that coheres admirably, focused on the Amazon basin as a place exoticized or forgotten by history. As an alternative, proposes a "de-centered" understanding of the region's past in which Brazil's geographic margins and their inhabitants, pushed aside by a nationalist historiography, acquire new significance. Most contributors consider the colonial period, but several cover the 19th and 20th centuries. [HL]

1912 The Yoruba diaspora in the Atlantic world. Edited by Toyin Falola and Matt D. Childs. Bloomington: Indiana Univ. Press, 2004. 455 p.: bibl., ill., index. (Blacks in the diaspora)

State-of-the-field collection of 19 essays, including several by leading Brazilian historians. Serves as a valuable corrective to the preponderance of Euro-American topics that characterize Atlantic world historical studies. Coverage includes Yoruba origins, diaspora in the Americas, cultural foundations, and return migration. [HL]

COLONIAL

1913 A abertura dos portos. Organização de Luís Valente de Oliveira e Rubens Ricupero. Textos de Ângela Domingues *et al.* São Paulo: Editora Senac São Paulo, 2007. 352 p.: bibl., ill. (some col.).

New interpretations of an old historiographical problem, the opening of Brazilian ports to friendly nations in the wake of the Portuguese Crown's forced transfer to the colony in 1808. More than a dozen Brazilian and Portuguese scholars evaluate the economic, political, geopolitical, and cultural aspects of this transformative event of the independence era. [HL]

1914 Algranti, Leila Mezan. Livros de devoção, atos de censura: ensaios de história do livro e da leitura na América portuguesa, 1750–1821. São Paulo: Editora Hucitec: FAPESP, 2004. 301 p.: bibl. (Estudos históricos; 54)

Seeks to understand which religious books colonists read, how they practiced the act of reading, and what impact reading had on their lives. Identifies marked consistency in books circulating in both Portugal and Brazil, despite the Atlantic crossing and distinct conditions of life in the colony. Regulated by Church and state censors, consumed by a relatively small literate sector of the population, these books and their influence reveal the often-coercive power

exercised by the Church, even at great distances, in its attempt to teach devotion while controlling the act of reading. Special emphasis on the reading practices of women in convents and the growing preference among a broader public for nonreligious texts during the independence era. [HL]

1915 Anastasia, Carla Maria Junho. A geografia do crime: violência nas Minas setecentistas. Belo Horizonte, Brazil: Editora UFMG, 2005. 159 p.: bibl., ill. (some col.), maps (some col.). (Humanitas; 100)

Important study of crime, contraband, and violence in the *sertões* (backlands) of Minas Gerais views pervasive illegality as a consequence of the absence of institutionalized state authority, which relinquished territorial control to local strongmen. See also item **1950**. [HL]

1916 Andrade, Francisco Eduardo de. A invenção das Minas Gerais: empresas, descobrimentos e entradas nos sertões do ouro da América portuguesa. Belo Horizonte, Brazil: Editora PUC Minas: Autêntica, 2008. 395 p.: bibl., ill., maps. (Col. Historiografia de Minas Gerais. Série Universidade; 1)

Highly original revisionist interpretation of the *bandeirantes* (backwoodsmen) from São Paulo who in the late 17th and early 18th century discovered and then struggled to retain control of great mineral wealth in the region that later would be named Minas Gerais. Examines their expeditions and discoveries not simply as dramatic events to be cataloged but as social constructs with specific historical origins and meanings to be understood in light of Portuguese traditions, legal regimes, symbolic power, and patronage networks. Adepts of Brazil's backlands, these men often proved unable to navigate the intricacies of metropolitan political culture. See also item **1945**. [HL]

1917 Apolinário, Juciene Ricarte. Os Akroá e outros povos indígenas nas fronteiras do Sertão: políticas indígena e indigenista no norte da capitania de Goiás, atual Estado do Tocantins, século XVIII. Goiânia, Brazil: Fundação Cultural do Estado do Tocantins: Editora Kelps, 2006. 276 p.: bibl., ill. (some col.), maps (some col.).

Meticulous study, uncovering many new sources, of the Akroá and other indigenous peoples who suffered an 18th-century extermination campaign in what was then northern Goiás (now the state of Tocantins) as well as in southern Piauí. The decline of mining and transformation to an agricultural and pastoral economy intensified pressure on native lands. Colonists attacked and enslaved Indians, despite Crown policies that declared their liberty. The Akroá responded with multiple strategies, including warfare and rebellion, peace negotiations, and alliances with other indigenous and non-native groups. [HL]

1918 Assunção, Paulo de. Ritmos da vida: momentos efusivos da família real portuguesa nos trópicos. Rio de Janeiro: Arquivo Nacional, 2008. 298 p.: bibl., ill.

Cultural history of public rituals and celebrations honoring the lives of the Portuguese royal family during its 13-year sojourn in Brazil, 1808–21. The Catholic calendar and rites of passage—including royal birthdays, marriages, and deaths—structured civic and religious commemorations that reinforced links between monarch and vassal in an emerging public sphere. Perpetuating a heroic image of Prince Regent João, later João VI, the accounts, poems, and sermons that accompanied such public spectacles helped consolidate the monarch's political power and maintain social hierarchy. [HL]

1919 Aymoré, Fernando Amado. Die Jesuiten im kolonialen Brasilien: Katechese als Kulturpolitik und Gesellschaftsphänomen, 1549–1760. Frankfurt, Germany; New York; Oxford; Wien: Lang 2007. 425 p. (Europäische Hochschulschriften/3, 1069)

This thesis about the Jesuits in colonial Brazil focuses on their contribution to the country's cultural development mainly in linguistics (indigenous languages such as Tupi were promoted as *lingua franca* for missionary purposes), literature (dramas written by José de Anchieta), and selected historical works (João Daniel, *Tesouro descoberto do Rio Amazonas*, written around 1776). [F. Obermeier]

1920 Barata, Alexandre Mansur. Maçonaria, sociabilidade ilustrada e independência do Brasil, 1790–1822. Juiz de Fora, Brazil: Editora UFJF; São Paulo: Annablume, 2006. 338 p.: bibl.

Incisive study of Freemasonry during Brazil's independence era, this revised doctoral thesis focused on Rio de Janeiro examines not only the role of the fraternal organization in advancing the cause of independence and the political differences that arose among its members, but also the broader context of new spaces of sociability emerging during the period and the transatlantic connections between freemasons in Brazil and Europe. [HL]

1921 Billé, Philippe. La faune brésilienne dans les écrits documentaires du XVIe siècle. Paris: Champion, 2009. 478 p.: bibl., indexes. (Les géographies du monde, 12)

Useful study about the Brazilian fauna as recorded in 16th-century documents about Brazil written by Vaz da Caminha, Antonio Pigafetta, Gaspar de Carvajal, the Jesuits Manuel da Nóbrega, José de Anchieta and Fernão Cardim, the German Hans Staden, the Portuguese Pero Magalhães de Gândavo, and the French travelers André Thevet and Jean de Léry. Given that many of the original names for animals in the indigenous Tupi language have been assumed as "loanwords" in European languages, the material is also of interest for linguists. [F. Obermeier]

Cabral, Diogo de Carvalho and **Susana Cesco.** Árvores do rio, floresta do povo: a instituição das "madeiras-de-lei" no Rio de Janeiro e na ilha de Santa Catarina (Brasil) no final do período colonial. See *HLAS 65:1295.*

1922 Calainho, Daniela Buono. Agentes da fé: familiares da Inquisição portuguesa no Brasil colonial. Bauru, Brazil: EDUSC, 2006. 202 p.: bibl., ill. (Col. História)

Early example, originally a MA thesis, of growing interest in the bureaucratic agents as opposed to the victims of the Inquisition, studies the so-called *familiares*, lay and clerical officials who comprised the institution's administrative staff in Portuguese America. Does not offer the depth of research made possible by a more focused regional study, but provides an informative overview of the colony as a whole. Demonstrates the use of the Inquisition by these appointees as a means of social ascension and power. See also *HLAS 64:1656.* [HL]

1923 Calazans Falcon, Francisco José.
O império luso-brasileiro e a questão da dependência inglesa: um estudo de caso; a política mercantilista durante a Época Pombalina, e a sombra do Tratado de Methuen. (*Nova Econ./Belo Horizonte,* 15:2, maio/agosto 2005, p. 11–34, bibl.)

Re-evaluation of Luso-Brazilian and British economic relations during the second half of the 18th century, highlighting the ambiguity of interactions that demonstrated Portugal's dependence on England but also its capacity to defend certain imperial prerogatives. [HL]

1924 Caldeira, Jorge. O banqueiro do sertão. Vol. 1, Mulheres no caminho da prata. Vol. 2, Padre Guilherme Pompeu de Almeida. São Paulo: Mameluco, 2006. 2 v.: bibl., ill., maps.

Definitive biography of the priest and backlands entrepreneur Guilherme Pompeu de Almeida (1656–1713) emphasizes early development of internal social networks and commercial activity beyond the reach of Spanish and Portuguese crowns. Vol. 1 establishes the importance of 16th-century inland silver and foodstuffs trade linking Potosí, Assunción, Buenos Aires, and the Captaincy of São Vicente (later São Paulo). Commercial networks depended on colonist alliances with Tupi-Guarani women and challenged the power of state and Church, the latter in the form of the Jesuit missionary endeavor. Vol. 2 follows Almeida as he abandoned Jesuit training to become a secular priest in the interior of São Paulo and built his fortune as a financier of ventures that profited from discoveries of gold in the region that would become Minas Gerais. Sees in such internal economic development the origins of a distinctive Brazilian society, culture, and economy. [HL]

1925 Cavalcanti, Nireu Oliveira. O Rio de Janeiro setecentista: a vida e a construção da cidade da invasão francesa até a chegada da Corte. Rio de Janeiro: J. Zahar, 2004. 443 p.: bibl., ill. (some col.), maps.

Author's training as both historian and architect underlies innovative approach of this valuable, painstakingly researched and illustrated contribution. First part surveys factors responsible for the city's spatial, political, and economic development during the century preceding (and including the

arrival of) the exiled Portuguese Court in 1808. Second part, focusing primarily on elites, explores professional, intellectual, artistic, and religious groups and institutions that contributed to an urban cultural dynamism exceeding that which historians have traditionally acknowledged. Third part highlights the importance of those who built the city and shaped its urban space, including property owners, real estate investors, architects, artisans, and tradesmen. See also *HLAS 64:1597.* [HL]

1926 Chambouleyron, Rafael. Escravos do Atlântico equatorial: tráfico negreiro para o estado do Maranhão e Pará (século XVII e início do século XVIII). (*Rev. Bras. Hist./São Paulo,* 26:52, julho/dez. 2006, p. 79–114, tables)

Well-researched analysis of the understudied African slave trade to the greater Amazon region, focusing primarily on the 17th century. Emphasizes three elements that made this trade distinctive: the presence of epidemic disease, the trade's emerging profitability for the royal treasury, and the pervasive use of indigenous laborers. [HL]

1927 Correspondência Luso-Brasileira.
Vol. 1, Das invasões francesas à corte no Rio de Janeiro, 1807–1821. Estudo, organização e notas de António Manuel Monteiro Cardoso e António d'Oliveira Pinto da França. Lisboa: Imprensa Nacional-Casa da Moeda, 2008. 1 v.: bibl., ill. (some col.).

Contains 68 annotated letters exchanged first in Portugal and then across the Atlantic by members of the elite Pinto da França and Garcez families, 1807–23. Topics include failed resistance to French invasion of Portugal, urban life in Salvador da Bahia, court culture and politics in Rio de Janeiro, the 1817 revolt in Pernambuco, and the 1820 Liberal Revolution in Porto, as well as the personal concerns and affairs of these transatlantic elites in a turbulent era. [HL]

1928 Ferreira, Alexandre Rodrigues.
Viagem filosófica ao Rio Negro. Organização, atualização, anotação e ampliação de Francisco Jorge dos Santos, Auxiliomar Silva Ugarte, e Mateus Coimbra de Oliveira. 2a. ed. Manaus, Brazil: EDUA: Editora INPA, 2007. 662 p.: bibl., col. ill., indexes.

Minimally revised edition of 1785 account of a scientific expedition along Rio Negro, part of Ferreira's broader exploration of the Amazon and Mato Grosso regions. Contains six new indexes organized according to individual and place names, plant and animal life, ethnic groups, and medical terms and diseases. [HL]

1929 Gonçalves, Regina Célia. Guerras e açúcares: política e economia na capitania da Parayba, 1585–1630. Bauru, Brazil: EDUSC, 2007. 329 p.: bibl. (História)

Construing the constant state of war against the native Potiguara Indians as the defining characteristic of the early history of this northeastern region, the author traces the initial Portuguese occupation, the resulting interethnic conflict, and the consolidation of a regional elite of sugar plantation owners tied to similar elites in neighboring captaincies, especially Pernambuco. [HL]

1930 A Inquisição em xeque: temas, controvérsias, estudos de caso. Organização de Ronaldo Vainfas, Bruno Feitler, e Lana Lage da Gama Lima. Rio de Janeiro: EdUERJ, 2006. 280 p.: bibl.

Collects essays by leading scholars of the Portuguese Inquisition, organized according to four themes: the institution's structure and activities; its social agents; its repression of New Christians and those accused of practicing Judaism; and its crackdown on heresy and homosexuality. [HL]

1931 Karasch, Mary. Free women of color in central Brazil, 1779–1832. (*in* Beyond bondage: free women of color in the Americas. Edited by David Barry Gaspar and Darlene Clark Hine. Chicago: Univ. of Illinois Press, 2004, p. 237–270, bibl., tables)

Uses census, lay confraternity, and other records to study free women of color in the frontier society of the captaincy (and later province) of Goiás. During a period when slavery was declining, these women came to comprise the largest sector of the region's population in sharp contrast to frontier regions in North America. See also item **1972**. [HL]

1932 Kraay, Hendrik. Arming slaves in Brazil from the seventeenth century to the nineteenth century. (*in* Arming

slaves from classical times to the modern age. Edited by Christopher Leslie Brown and Philip D. Morgan. New Haven, Conn.: Yale Univ. Press, 2006, p. 146–179)

Most important survey to date of the widespread practice of arming Brazilian slaves, by both masters and the state. Rather than conceiving this phenomenon as antithetical to slavery, Kraay argues that its generally careful management over three centuries demonstrates the strength of the slave regime. [HL]

1933 Langer, Protasio Paulo. Os guarani-missioneiros e o colonialismo luso no Brasil Meridional: projetos civilizatórios e faces da identidade étnica, 1750–1798. Porto Alegre, Brazil: Martins Livreiro Editor, 2005. 252 p.: bibl., ill., maps.

Although more comprehensive studies of the Guarani under colonial rule exist, this one is distinguished by its use of a particularly wide variety of Portuguese if not Spanish sources and its focus on the second half of the 18th century, when Jesuit missionaries were expelled from indigenous villages. Lay directors took over governance under Pombal's Indian Directory legislation, requiring the Guarani to refashion their ethnic identity, but the experience under Jesuit tutelage remained a touchstone. See also *HLAS 62:1461*. [HL]

1934 Lara, Silvia Hunold. Fragmentos setecentistas: escravidão, cultura e poder na América portuguesa. São Paulo: Companhia das Letras, 2007. 430 p.: bibl., ill. (some col.), index.

Indispensable study of urban social relations in Rio de Janeiro and Salvador da Bahia during the final decades of the 18th century posits the increasing racialization of the colonial social hierarchy as metropolitan and colonial elites responded with alarm to a fast-growing population of peoples of color, both free and enslaved. Seeking to reassert their position of dominance, elites devised new social and political means by which to exclude nonwhite populations from a full range of privileges, emphasizing the proximity to slavery of even free persons of mixed African and Portuguese ancestry. Inspired by A.J.R. Russell-Wood's classic work on free persons of color (see *HLAS 46:3508* and *HLAS 47:8403*). [HL]

1935 Leopoldina, Empress, consort of Pedro I, Emperor of Brazil. Cartas de uma imperatriz. Seleção e transcrição das cartas de Bettina Kann e Patrícia Souza Lima. Artigos de Andréa Slemian *et al.* Tradução de Guilherme João de Freitas Teixeira e Tereza Maria Souza de Castro. Coordenação editorial de Angel Bojadsen. São Paulo: Estação Liberdade, 2006. 494 p.: bibl., ill. (some col.), index.

Collects 315 letters, many never published, written by the Austrian archduchess and later Brazilian empress consort, who witnessed and actively participated in Brazil's transformation from colony to independent nation, endured an unhappy arranged marriage to Pedro I, gave birth to seven children (including Pedro II), and died at 29 after a miscarriage. Arranged chronologically, with helpful appendixes and fine illustrations, the volume includes letters written to the Austrian royal family, her husband and his parents, and other leading figures of the independence era. Five introductory essays contextualize her life. [HL]

1936 Libby, Douglas Cole and Zephyr Frank. Exploring parish registers in colonial Minas Gerais, Brazil: ethnicity in São José do Rio das Mortes, 1780–1810. (*CLAHR*, 14:3, Summer 2005, p. 213–244, tables)

Report on quantitative research in progress, demonstrates that baptismal, census, and marriage records provide invaluable sources for understanding the logic of the mining district's complex ethnic and social categories, marriage practices, motherhood, legitimacy, and miscegenation. [HL]

1937 Machado, Cacilda da Silva. A trama das vontades: negros, pardos e brancos na produção da hierarquia social do Brasil escravista. Rio de Janeiro: Apicuri, 2008. 218 p.: bibl., ill. (Distâncias)

Slightly revising the author's doctoral dissertation, this demographic history, interwoven with careful social analysis, examines race relations at the turn of the 19th century in the community of São José dos Pinhais (then in the captaincy of São Paulo, now in Paraná). Social hierarchy included proportionately fewer slaves in smaller holdings than in plantation zones, more *agregados* (free dependents), and many free persons of African ancestry. Finds a constant state of tension as slaves and their descendants sought to emerge and distance themselves from slavery, often by seeking free marriage partners, while landowners competed for *agregados* and struggled to maintain their slave holdings. [HL]

Machado, Lilia Maria Cheuiche. Sítio cemitério dos Pretos Novos: análise biocultural, interpretando os ossos e os dentes humanos. See *HLAS 65:364.*

1938 Martel, H.E. Hans Staden's captive soul: identity, imperialism, and rumors of cannibalism in sixteenth-century Brazil. (*J. World Hist.*, 17:1, March 2006, p. 51–69)

Reviewing dated debates on veracity of Tupinambá cannibalism through rereadings of Jean de Léry and especially Hans Staden, asserts that coastal indigenous peoples "played cannibal" in order to inspire fear in European antagonists. Does not address much recent scholarly output on Brazil's coastal peoples, primarily in Portuguese, which draws stronger conclusions from a far wider range of sources. [HL]

1939 Massimi, Marina. Palavras, almas e corpos no Brasil colonial. São Paulo: Edições Loyola, 2005. 329 p.: bibl.

Interdisciplinary study, as much psychology and philosophy as history, of the pervasive art and praxis of the colonial religious sermon. Argues that sermons served a critical cultural function, which the faithful prized, transmitting a full range of concepts, practices, beliefs, and notions of the self founded on classical, medieval, and renaissance traditions. [HL]

1940 Mattos, Hebe Maria. *Pretos* and *pardos* between the cross and the sword: racial categories in seventeenth century Brazil. (*Rev. Eur. Estud. Latinoam. Caribe*, 80, abril 2006, p. 43–55, bibl.)

Using two case studies, challenges scholars who see designations of racial mixture (e.g., "mulato" and "pardo") as indeterminate colonial inventions. Posits that specific demographic and legal elements of Portuguese expansion accounted for the historical utility of these and other racial categories in the Iberian Atlantic. [HL]

1941 Mello, Evaldo Cabral de. Nassau. Coordenação de Elio Gaspari e Lilia M. Schwarcz. São Paulo: Companhia Das Letras, 2006. 289 p.: bibl., ill., index, map. (Perfis brasileiros)

Much-needed biography of the governor of Dutch Brazil, debunking many myths, by a leading expert of the period. Like other works in this "profiles" series, this publication is designed for wide readership and is therefore frustrating as scholarship, lacking notes and full bibliography, although a concluding essay on supplementary readings is helpful. [HL]

Noelli, Francisco Silva and **Lúcio Menezes Ferreira.** A persistência da teoria da degenerção indígena e do colonialismo nos fundamentos da arqueologia brasileira. See *HLAS 65:378.*

1942 Oliveira, Maria Lêda. A historia do Brazil de Frei Vicente do Salvador: história e política no Império português do século XVII. Brazil: Odebrecht: Versal Editores, 2008. 2 v.: bibl., ill. (some col.), indexes, 1 CD-ROM.

Definitive edition, stunningly illustrated, of Salvador's early 17th-century history of Portuguese America. Vol. 1 includes Oliveira's essays on the Franciscan friar's life, on the Baroque milieu in which he wrote, and on the historical and historiographical legacy of his work. Vol. 2 opens with an introductory essay examining previous editions of the *Historia,* followed by a new critical, annotated edition, enhanced with glossary and indexes. [HL]

1943 Pedreira, Jorge Miguel Viana and **Fernando Dores Costa.** D. João VI: um príncipe entre dois continentes. São Paulo: Companhia das Letras, 2008. 491 p.: bibl., ill. (some col.), index.

Judicious, carefully researched biography of the Portuguese monarch who fled Napoleon's armies to reside 13 years in Brazil. Clarifies the complex relations among Portugal, Brazil, Spain, France, and England during his troubled reign. Devotes some attention to court life, and less to Brazil's interregional politics. Achieves a balance between Brazilian and Portuguese historiographies, the latter of which has tended to view this ruler unfavorably as an ineffectual king who "lost" Brazil. [HL]

Pesquisas Antropologia. See *HLAS 65:381.*

1944 Raminelli, Ronald. Viagens ultramarinas: monarcas, vassalos e governo à distância. São Paulo: Alameda, 2008. 312 p.: bibl., col. ill., index.

Valuable contribution to the history of Luso-Brazilian science and its important function as an arm of the state, attributes a critical role in maintaining imperial ties and strengthening long-distance governance to naturalist-voyagers. During the second half of the 18th century, increasing numbers of young, elite men, born in Brazil then educated in Enlightenment thought at the Univ. de Coimbra, left Portugal on overseas journeys as Crown agents. Their scientific surveys of distant reaches of the Empire earned royal patronage, rewards, and appointments, often making them central figures in colonial administration. These endeavors tended to lapse, hampering the development of Portuguese science as their bureaucratic commitments intensified. After the royal court's transfer to Rio de Janeiro in 1808, they continued to favor maintaining ties with Lisbon and to reinforce traditional social hierarchies, only hesitantly embracing the cause of independence. [HL]

1945 Romeiro, Adriana. Paulistas e emboabas no coração das Minas: idéias, práticas e imaginário político no século XVIII. Belo Horizonte, Brazil: Editora UFMG, 2008. 431 p.: bibl. (Humanitas)

Probing revisionist history of conflict pitting São Paulo-born discoverers of extravagant gold deposits against settlers from other regions of the colony and especially from Portugal who rushed to displace them, provoking armed conflict in 1708 in the region that would become Minas Gerais. Author posits a broad context for this violent episode, tracing it to 17th-century tensions and demonstrating its continued influence on Portuguese Crown policy for the rest of the century. Argues that conflict was not merely the product of competition for mineral wealth but also of disparate political cultures and historical experiences. See also item **1916.** [HL]

Rosas Moscoso, Fernando. Del Río de La Plata al Amazonas: el Perú y el Brasil, en la época de la dominación ibérica. See item **1449.**

1946 Santos, Beatriz Catão Cruz. O Corpo de Deus na América: a festa de Corpus Christi nas cidades da América portuguesa—século XVIII. São Paulo: Annablume, 2005. 194 p.: bibl., ill.

A slightly revised dissertation, this theoretically informed study of Corpus Christi feasts and processions in Brazil's principal colonial cities, as well as in Portugal itself, analyzes ecclesiastical, civil, and popular aspects. Author argues that, exercising its power through municipal councils, Portuguese monarchy appropriated this important Catholic festival, investing it with increasing solemnity, in order to extend its power and reinforce hierarchies in the colony, even as various social groups asserted distinctive popular religious traditions. [HL]

1947 Schiffner, Wolfgang. Unter Menschfresser-Leuthen Hans Stadens Brasilienbuch von 1557 = Entre as gentes antropófagas. Texte von Wolfgang Schiffner in Zusammenarbeit mit Eckhard E. Kupfer und Franz Obermeier. Herausgegeben von Sven-Hinrich Siemers für das Regionalmuseum Wolfhager Land. Wolfhagen, Germany: Regionalmuseum Wolfhager Land, 2007. 100 p.: ill. (Sonderausstellungen/Regionalmuseum Wolfhager Land, 5)

Exhibition catalog in German and Portuguese issued to mark the 450th anniversary of the 1557 publication of Hans Staden's *Warhaftige Historia* (Marburg, Germany). Staden's account of his journey to Brazil and capture by the Tupinamba peoples is thought to be the first 16th-century publication about Brazil. After his return from South America, Staden lived in the small town of Wolfhagen. Today the Wolfhagen Regional Museum maintains a small section dedicated to the explorer. The publication is from a special 2007 exhibition celebrating the writings and travels of Staden. The exhibition also traveled to various towns in Brazil. [F. Obermeier]

1948 Shellard Corrêa, Dora. Historiadores e cronistas e a paisagem da colônia Brasil. (*Rev. Bras. Hist./São Paulo*, 26:51, jan./junho 2006, p. 63–87)

Contrasts conventional modern scholarly portrayals of 16th-century Brazil as a virgin landscape with early colonial chronicles that depict territories densely inhabited and altered by indigenous peoples. [HL]

1949 Silva, Ana Rosa Cloclet da. Inventando a nação: intelectuais ilustrados e estadistas luso-brasileiros na crise do antigo regime português, 1750–1822. São Paulo: Editora Hucitec: FAPESP, 2006. 445 p.: bibl. (Estudos históricos; 63)

Important study of the dissolution of Portuguese imperial control over Brazil and the coeval implementation of various projects to build a modern transatlantic state and, ultimately, to envision a new nation. Traces the intellectual and political contributions of statesmen informed by Enlightenment ideals, emphasizing three key and connected reformists: the Marquis of Pombal, José I's autocratic prime minister; Rodrigo de Sousa Coutinho, Pombal's godson and João VI's Minister of War and Foreign Affairs; and especially José Bonifácio de Andrada e Silva, Coutinho's protégé and eventually the grey eminence of Brazilian independence. Silva's commitment to a model based on a constitutional monarchy—realized in 1820, two years before independence—is placed in historical context and viewed as an expression of a longstanding dialectic of tradition and modernity. [HL]

1950 Silva, Célia Nonata da. Territórios de mando: banditismo em Minas Gerais, século XVIII. Belo Horizonte, Brazil: Crisálida, 2007. 325 p.: bibl., map.

Study of rural banditry in Brazil's primary colonial mining district. Departing from traditional focus on region's towns and villages, author examines frontier zones, whose rural potentates urban inhabitants viewed as violent and rebellious rustics. Argues that these charismatic men were adept at accumulating private power that undermined the Crown's aspirations to exert control over remote lands. Far from being exotic and irrational, their political culture melded longstanding Portuguese practices to local traditions. See also item **1915**. [HL]

1951 Silva, Lina Gorenstein Ferreira da. A Inquisição contra as mulheres: Rio de Janeiro, séculos XVII e XVIII. São Paulo: Associação Editorial Humanitas: FAPESP: LEI-USP, 2005. 477 p.: bibl., ill. (Histórias da intolerância; 1)

First systematic study of women condemned by the Portuguese Inquisition in Brazil for practicing Judaism, based on cases of 167 women born or resident in Rio de Janeiro who suffered persecution and imprisonment, many of whom were from elite families. Describes these women as thoroughly assimilated into Iberian culture but nevertheless vulnerable because of their status as "New Christians," whether or not they were "crypto-Jews." Themes include anti-Semitism, family life, female education, marriage, and religious faith. [HL]

1952 Silva, Maria Beatriz Nizza da. D. João: Príncipe e Rei no Brasil. Lisbon: Livros Horizonte, 2008. 143 p.: bibl. (Col. Horizonte histórico)

Conceived as an attempt to address a perceived gap in the Portuguese (as opposed to Brazilian) historiography concerning the Crown's 13-year sojourn in Brazil, 1808–21. Readable and concise. More thorough treatments available in both classic (see *HLAS 11:2626*) and recent (see item **1943**) studies. [HL]

1953 Silva, Maria Beatriz Nizza da. A primeira gazeta da Bahia: *Idade d'Ouro do Brazil.* 2a ed. rev. e ampliada. Salvador, Brazil: EDUFBA: Academia de Letras da Bahia, 2005. 372 p.: bibl. (Col. Cipriano Barata)

New edition expands examination of Bahia's first newspaper, published 1811–23. Slim on analysis, best used as a reference work pointing to key subjects covered by the paper, including the urbanization of Salvador da Bahia, the development of the city's surrounding region, and the characteristics of its social groups, daily life, and cultural institutions. [HL]

1954 Silveira, Marco Antonio. Acumulando forças: luta pela alforria e demandas políticas na capitania de Minas Gerais, 1750–1808. (*Rev. Hist./São Paulo*, 158, primer semestre 2008, p. 131–156, bibl.)

Argues that peoples of African descent in Minas Gerais, emboldened by their demographic expansion in the second half of the 18th century, successfully pressed for greater political powers by sending collective petitions to the Crown's Overseas Council. Builds on insights originally articulated by A.J.R. Russell-Wood (see *HLAS 46:3508* and *HLAS 47:8403*). [HL]

1955 Slemian, Andréa. Vida política em tempo de crise: Rio de Janeiro, 1808–1824. São Paulo: Aderaldo & Rothschild Editores, 2006. 283 p.: bibl., maps. (Estudos históricos; 64)

A revised and expanded MA thesis examining the changing political culture and new modes of sociability in Rio de Janeiro after it became home to the exiled Portuguese Court. Among other developments, this research considers the installation of state institutions such as new police administration (Intendência Geral de Polícia); the persecution of persons and ideas deemed foreign and otherwise threatening to the empire's stability; the implications of Portugal's 1820 Liberal Revolution for competing political projects across the Atlantic; the emergence of a vibrant press after royal censorship was lifted the following year; the rise of anti-Portuguese sentiments and Freemasonry in the wake of independence. [HL]

1956 Sons, formas, cores e movimentos na modernidade Atlântica: Europa, Américas e África. Organização de Júnia Ferreira Furtado. São Paulo: Annablume; Belo Horizonte, Brazil: FAPEMIG: Pós Graduação História, UFMG, 2008. 506 p.: bibl., ill. (chiefly col.). (Col. Olhares)

Diverse collection of 25 essays by leading historians of Portuguese America and the south Atlantic world, 16th–19th centuries, grouped according to innovative themes: 1) sound, sonority, and language; 2) forms of power and the inversion of order; 3) images and narratives; 4) colors and the colored; and 5) empires in movement. [HL]

1957 Staden, Hans. Hans Staden's true history: an account of cannibal captivity in Brazil. Edited and translated by Neil L. Whitehead and Michael Harbsmeier. Durham, N.C.: Duke Univ. Press, 2008. 206 p.: bibl., ill., index, maps. (The cultures and practice of violence series)

First English translation since 1928 of German gunner's famed account of his nine-month captivity among the Tupinambá, with a probing critical introduction examining the nature of early modern travel writing, Christian testimonial, ethnographic experience and description, and their bearing on the ritual cannibalism recounted by Staden. Also notable for illustrations, which reproduce underappreciated woodcuts published in the first 1557 German edition. For translation specialist's comment, see item **3306**. [HL]

1958 Sweet, James H. Mistaken identities?: Olaudah Equiano, Domingos Álvares, and the methodological challenges of studying the African diaspora. (*Am. Hist. Rev.*, 114:2, April 2009, p. 279–306, bibl., map)

Subtle analysis of the construction of identities by slaves inhabiting a pluralistic Atlantic world, adding important insights to longstanding debates opposing African cultural retention to American creolization. Calls for a more fluid, situational understanding of individual identity whereby African cultural forms could be retained even as changing circumstances led slaves to assert, mute, or conceal such forms. [HL]

1959 Vainfas, Ronaldo. Traição: um jesuíta a serviço do Brasil holandês processado pela Inquisição. São Paulo: Companhia das Letras, 2008. 384 p.: bibl., ill., index.

Highly readable account of the life of Manoel de Moraes, an extraordinary Brazilian-born Jesuit missionary of mixed European and Indian ancestry active in Pernambuco when Dutch invaded in 1630. Moraes first fought for the Portuguese, then switched sides to help lead Dutch forces, migrated to the Netherlands, and converted to Calvinism; hence, his reputation as a traitor. Eventually he returned to Brazil as a merchant, again embraced Catholicism, but was imprisoned, tried, and condemned by the Inquisition. Author employs this anti-heroic tale, the fruit of impressive archival research, to elucidate the social, religious, and political tensions of the era. [HL]

1960 Viana, Larissa. O idioma da mestiçagem: as irmandades de pardos na América portuguesa. Campinas, Brazil: Editora Unicamp, 2007. 238 p.: bibl., ill. (Col. várias histórias; 26)

Contests the traditional view that racial lines dividing lay brotherhoods benefited only dominant whites. Focusing on but not limited to Rio de Janeiro's Catholic confraternities organized by free persons of color, especially between mid-17th and late 18th century, the author argues that brotherhood members, usually of mixed racial descent, pursued individual and collective religious, social, and cultural objectives by

participating in such organizations, forging a distinctive communal identity founded on being born in Brazil, distant from African origins, and no longer enslaved. [HL]

1961 Wadsworth, James E. Jurema and batuque: Indians, Africans, and the Inquisition in colonial northeastern Brazil. (*Hist. Relig./Chicago*, 46:2, Nov. 2006, p. 140–161)

Focusing on indigenous and Afro-Brazilian challenges to religious orthodoxy during the 18th century, gauges the reach and limitations of the Inquisition in the northeastern captaincies of Paraíba and Pernambuco. Explains the failure to repress these enduring expressions of ethnic identity, which were condemned as demonic, by emphasizing both internal and external constraints on inquisitional power. [HL]

NATIONAL

Acevedo Marin, Rosa Elizabeth. Julgados da terra: cadeia de apropriação e atores sociais em conflito na Ilha de Colares, Pará. See *HLAS 65:1275.*

1962 Alemão, Francisco Freire. Diário de viagem de Francisco Freire Alemão: Fortaleza-Crato, 1859. Fortaleza, Brazil: Museu do Ceará, Secretaria da Cultura do Estado do Ceará, 2006. 235 p.: bibl., ill., map. (Col. Comissão Científica de Exploração; 3)

Story of an expedition by the Comissão Científica de Exploração, organized by the Instituto Histórico e Geográfico Brasileiro (IHGB) to study the geography, natural resources, and populations spread along the fringes of Brazilian territory. Behind the effort was a deliberate public policy to develop a discourse of knowledge that would secure a prominent international position for Brazil as a producer of scientific knowledge. The leader of the expedition was Francisco Freire Alemão, a medical doctor and naturalist and long time member of IHGB. The life, place, and ambience of mid-19th century Ceará comes alive in these pages. Those interested in Brazil's self-discovery and identity formation will find much of interest here. [FDM]

1963 Alves, Paulo. Anarquismo e anarco-sindicalismo: teoria e prática no movimento operário brasileiro, 1906–1922. Curitiba, Brazil: Aos Quatro Ventos, 2002. 92 p.: bibl.

The labor movement in the 1920s was deeply marked by ideologies. The debates about their role in Brazilian society influenced the directions the labor movement took. The author examines the movement's formative ideas, analyzes the political and ideological debates, and describes state repression of the movement. [FDM]

1964 Alves de Oliva, Terezinha. Fausto Cardoso: herói de Sergipe. (*Rev. Inst. Hist. Geogr. Sergipe*, 35, 2006, p. 18–43, bibl., photo)

Local history of Sergipe. Examines how the assassinated Fausto Cardoso (1906) was transformed from a defeated politician into a symbol against arbitrary rule. [FDM]

1965 Amaral, Braz do. Recordações históricas. 2a ed., rev. Salvador, Brazil: Academia de Letras da Bahia: Assembléia Legislativa do Estado da Bahia, 2007. 414 p.: bibl., ill.

The book would interest those studying Bahia. The chapters are short essays that originally appeared in the *Jornal de Notícias* (Salvador). The collection was published in Porto, Portugal, in 1920. Unhappily not all the essays are dated and their placement in the book is accidental and disordered. While topically they deal with incidents in Bahian or Brazilian history, at least one essay is on the destruction of the Roman oligarchy, with no hint as to why it was included. Braz do Amaral taught history in the Ginásio da Bahia and was a figure in the intellectual scene of Salvador in the early 20th century. A few essays include reprints of archival documents. [FDM]

1966 Amory, Frederic. Euclides da Cunha: uma odisseia nos trópicos. Cotia, Brazil: Ateliê Editorial, 2009. 432 p.

This is a new, complete biography providing an exhaustive reconstruction of the author's life and work. The book is the winner of two major Brazilian book prizes: Prêmio Euclides da Cunha da Academia Brasileira de Letras 2009 and the Prêmio Jabuti de Biografia 2010. Highly recommended. [FDM]

1967 Andrade, Joaquim Marçal Ferreira de. História da fotorreportagem no Brasil: a fotografia na imprensa do Rio de Janeiro de 1839 a 1900. Coordenação editorial de Mary Del Priore. Rio de Janeiro: Elsevier: Edições Biblioteca Nacional, 2004. 281 p.: bibl., ill.

This study examines the development of Brazilian photojournalism as it advanced in the more technically developed countries of the north Atlantic. The author explains how the technical aspects of page design and the processes of printing images affected what the illustrated press could achieve. He treats the first instances when photos were used to heighten readers' understanding of events, such as the Paraguayan War and droughts in Ceará. [FDM]

1968 Andreatta, Verena. Cidades quadradas, paraísos circulares: os planos urbanísticos do Rio de Janeiro no século XIX. Apresentação e colaboração de Manuel Herce Vallejo. Rio de Janeiro: Maud X, 2006. 212, 29 p.: bibl., ill. (some col.), maps (some col.).

This is a beautiful book that will be enjoyed by those wondering how Rio got to be as it is today. It analyzes the three great reform plans of 1843, 1875–76, and 1903–06. The maps are excellent and the accompanying drawings, paintings, and photos are worth careful study. [FDM]

Andrews, George Reid. Workers, soldiers, activists: black mobilization in Brazil and Spanish America, 1800–2000. See item **393**.

1969 Araújo, Rita de Cássia Barbosa de. As praias e os dias: história social das praias do Recife e de Olinda. Recife, Brazil: Prefeitura do Recife, Secretaria de Cultura, Fundação de Cultura Cidade do Recife, 2007. 547 p.: bibl., ill. (some col.), index, map.

This book interprets the forms of occupation, use, and social meanings attributed to the beaches of Recife and Olinda. The author stresses the century between 1840 and 1940, during which sea bathing became the fashion and beaches became the place of cures, recreation, rest, and socializing. The author breaks from the usual middle and upper class focus of such books to pay attention to the incorporation of lower class people into the beach scene. The changing views of the seaside as a place of enjoyment and health were related to changes in attitudes toward cities, recreation, and health. To some extent sugarcane production polluted so many northeastern rivers that bathers had little choice but to turn to the beaches. The existence or not of street car lines connecting beaches to the cities opened or closed off access. The newspapers of Pernambuco were a key source as there were next to no appropriate studies. [FDM]

1970 Assis Brasil, Joaquim Francisco de. Assis Brasil um diplomata da República. v. 1, Buenos Aires, Lisboa & Washington. v. 2, Buenos Aires & Volta à diplomacia. Rio de Janeiro: CHDD/FUNAG, 2006. 2 v.

Assis Brasil was a leading figure in the Brazilian republic who contributed to the growth of republican sentiment in the 1880s and to governmental theory in the 1890s. A gaúcho, he stood against *castilhismo* in Rio Grande do Sul and was an ardent defender of his home state. He advocated modernization of agriculture. This book is focused on his diplomatic career. It is a collection of correspondence from the Arquivo Histórico do Itamaraty. Alvaro da Costa Franco introduces the volumes with intriguing essays. Those interested in Brazilian relations with Argentina, Portugal, and the US will want to examine these letters. [FDM]

1971 Backes, Ana Luiza. Fundamentos da ordem republicana: repensando o pacto de Campos Sales. Brasília: Plenarium, 2006. 308 p.: bibl. (Col. Parlamento em teses; 1)

The Campos Sales pact made the republican model functional a la brasileira. This was the author's doctoral dissertation at the Universidade Federal do Rio Grande do Sul. She reviews the tumultuous development of the republic in the 1890s, with a steady focus on how politics was reflected in the congress. [FDM]

1972 Barickman, B.J. and Martha Few. Ana Paulinha de Queirós, Joaquina da Costa, and their neighbors: free women of color as household heads in rural Bahia, Brazil, 1835. (*in* Beyond bondage: free women of color in the Americas. Edited by David Barry Gaspar and Darlene Clark Hine. Chicago: Univ. of Illinois Press, 2004, p. 170–201, graphs)

Uses census data to reveal the significant presence of household heads who were freeborn and freed women of color in one of the most important slaveholding regions of the Americas. Addresses lacuna in scholarship that conventionally focuses on race or gender rather than their intersection. Some of these women became slaveholders, while most suffered poverty and insecurity. See also item **1931.** [HL]

1973 Barreiro, José Carlos. Imaginário e viajantes no Brasil do século XIX: cultura e cotidiano, tradição e resistência. São Paulo: Editora UNESP, 2003. 243 p.: bibl., ill.

This book provides a lively portrait, from an unexpected point of view, of the beginnings of contemporary Brazilian society. This is truly a fascinating book that lends texture and depth to the often superficial images of 19th-century Brazil. What gives this work its special strength is its closeness to primary sources. [FDM]

1974 Battibugli, Thaís. A solidariedade antifascista: brasileiros na guerra civil espanhola, 1936–1939. São Paulo: EDUSP; Campinas, Brazil: Autores Associados, 2004. 236 p.: bibl., ill., maps.

Revised master's thesis, based partly in oral history archives, follows political careers of a cohort of 16 Brazilians, most of them communists who fought in International Brigades. [DB]

1975 Benício, Manoel. O rei dos jagunços de Manoel Benício: entre a ficção e a história. Introdução, atualização ortográfica, notas e glossário de Sílvia Maria Azevedo. Fotografias de Flávio de Barros. Rev. ed. São Paulo: EDUSP, Editora da Univ. de São Paulo, 2003. 350 p.: bibl., ill., map.

Manoel Benício and Euclides da Cunha were the principal journalists to witness some of the fighting at Canudos. The introduction by Azevedo is well done and very helpful in clarifying the literary criticisms of this and other books on Canudos. Manoel Benício deserves more attention from historians. This publication gives scholars a major source, complete with new notes and clarifications. Includes an excellent glossary of unusual terms. [FDM]

1976 Bernardes, Maria Elena. Laura Brandão, a invisibilidade feminina na política. Campinas, Brazil: CMU Publicações, Centro de Memória-Unicamp, 2007. 196 p.: bibl., ill.

Revised master's thesis, whose sources include interviews with family, poet's writings and correspondence, using career of Communist leader Octávio Brandão's wife to illuminate women's lives in literary and radical circles in Brazil and Soviet exile, 1915–1942. [DB]

1977 Bibiani, Regina Elísia de M.L.
Iconografia e iconologia das medalhas da Campanha do Paraguai concedidas ao Excército brasileiro. (*An. Mus. Hist. Nac.*, 2006, p. 190–206, photos, tables)
Author analyzes the symbolism of the medals awarded soldiers during the war. She proposes to interpret the iconological message aimed at maintaining the memory of the war. The article is illustrated with photos of the medals. Each one is described and discussed. [FDM]

1978 Bigio, Elias dos Santos. Linhas telegráficas e integração de povos indígenas: as estratégias políticas de Rondon, 1889–1930. Brasília: CGDOC FUNAI, 2003. 357 p.: bibl., ill., maps.
Cándido Mariano da Silva Rondon is often presented in historical studies as a "hero" of Brazilian integration. Realistically, Elias Bigio treats him as a remarkable man engaged in a heroic effort to lay telegraph lines through the Mato Grosso jungle. He based his study on little-used sources focusing on the alliances—local, state, nation—that were necessary to support this effort. This book offers a broad vision of the telegraph line construction by showing how it also dealt with gathering geographic, geologic, biologic, and ethnographic data. Fifteen new rivers were added to the map of Mato Grosso and many more were explored. Rondon's units "pacified" some 30,000 Indians. [FDM]

1979 Borges, Valdeci Rezende. A cidade do Rio de Janeiro imperial: construindo uma cultura de corte. (*Estud. Ibero-Am./ Porto Alegre*, 31:1, junho 2005, p. 121–143)
The article discusses some of the impressions of writer José de Alencar on the transformation of Rio de Janeiro from a colonial city into a Europeanized one in the years from 1850 to 1870. [FDM]

1980 Botelho, Tarcisio R. Censos e construção nacional no Brasil Imperial. (*Tempo Soc./São Paulo*, 17:1, 2005, p. 321–341, bibl.)

The author uses the censuses of 1852 and 1872 as factors in the process of building a national state. The census of 1872 provided the first real portrait of the Brazilian people. [FDM]

1981 Braga, Cláudio da Costa. O último baile do Império: o baile da Ilha Fiscal. Brazil: s.n., 2006. 113 p.: bibl., ill. (some col.).
The grand ball at the Ilha Fiscal on November 9, 1889, is emblematic of the end of the Brazilian empire. This well-illustrated book reviews the reasons for the event, the struggle for invitations, the elaborate preparations, the obvious absence of army officers, the ostentatious presence of elaborately uniformed National Guard officers, and the opulent menu and decorations. It was all a wonderful façade that hid the reality of the moment, the imminent collapse of the Bragança monarchy. [FDM]

1982 O Brasil de João Goulart: um projeto de nação. Organização de Oswaldo Munteal, Jacqueline Ventapane e Adriano de Freixo. Rio de Janeiro: Editora PUC Rio; Contraponto, 2006. 237 p., 12 p. of plates: bibl., ill., ports.
Anthology of speeches, economic plans, and political essays from Goulart's era, presenting or analyzing his project of nationalist development, combined with contemporary pieces claiming his legacy passed to Leonel Brizola in the 1990s. [DB]

1983 Le Brésil face à son passé, la guerre de Canudos: quand les Brésiliens découvrent le Brésil, Euclides da Cunha, l'écriture et la fabrique de l'histoire. Organiser d'Idelette Muzart-Fonseca dos Santos & Denis Rolland avec Albert Bensoussan *et al.* Paris: Harmattan, 2005. 215 p.: ill., maps. (Recherches Amériques latines)
The tragedy of Canudos (1897) has a deep grip on scholars interested in Brazil. This collection of essays is a French-Brazilian effort. The effects of the past on popular culture are discussed here. Those interested in the *Sertão* will find much of worth. [FDM]

1984 Brierly, Oswald Walters, Sir. Diários de viagens ao Rio de Janeiro: 1842–1867. Apresentação e organização de Pedro da Cunha e Menezes. Rio de Janeiro: Andrea

Jakobsson Estúdio, 2006. 148 p.: bibl., ill. (some col.), col. maps.

By the 1870s Rio de Janeiro was a busy watering and supply port-of-call for international shipping. Many vessels carried on board naturalists whose task was to acquire and study flora and fauna. Oswald W. Brierly visited Rio on British vessels passing between Australia and Great Britain. This book contains a detailed introduction, his diaries, and numerous reprints of his drawings and watercolors. [FDM]

1985 Bulhões, Antônio. Diário da cidade amada: Rio de Janeiro, 1922. v. 1, Janeiro, fevereiro, março, abril. v. 2, Maio, junho, julho, agosto. v. 3, Setembro, outubro, novembro, dezembro. Rio de Janeiro: Sextante Artes, 2003. 3 v.: bibl., ill., index.

This is a tour de force, even if a bit confusing at first glance to grasp its organization. Its fascinating 2000 pages embrace the city's history, culture, people, politics, and more. It is structured as a diary of 1922, marking the first centenary of Brazilian independence, but it reaches far into the past and future as well. Bulhões is descriptive, analytical, even lyrical as he weaves in considerable detail. His volumes are based on deep research. The hundreds of photos and illustrations are a researcher's delight. While Rio de Janeiro holds center stage, the national enters the mix constantly. Rio served as a mirror of Brazil. Happily, there is an index. [FDM]

1986 Cabeda, Coralio Bragança Pardo. Logística e fornecedores na guerra do Paraguai. *(Rev. Inst. Hist. Geogr. Rio Gd. Sul*, 141, 2006/2007, p. 9–17)

Logistics can determine the outcome of wars. The Brazilian system of civilian contractors never worked effectively in the Paraguayan war. The lessons of the conflict were not absorbed and so the army suffered another logistical breakdown at Canudos. [FDM]

1987 Campos, André Luiz Vieira de. Políticas internacionais de saúde na Era Vargas: o Serviço Especial de Saúde Pública, 1942–1960. Rio de Janeiro: Editora Fiocruz, 2006. 318 p.: bibl., ill., index, maps. (Col. História e saúde)

Traces the US-Brazilian cooperative health program SESP [Serviço Especial de Saúde Pública] from its wartime campaigns of anti-malaria spraying, to protecting military bases and strategic rubber and mineral zones, through its postwar reorientation toward public health training and planning in underdeveloped regions, especially the Amazon. Solidly researched in both US and Brazilian archives. [DB]

1988 Campos, Raquel Discini de. Mulheres e crianças na imprensa paulista, 1920–1940: educação e história. São Paulo: Editora UNESP, 2009. 223 p.: bibl., ill., maps.

Illustrated survey of representations of women and children in small-town newspapers of the São José de Rio Preto region of São Paulo demonstrates dissemination of metropolitan themes with a few local variants such as the theme of bandeirante pioneer origins. [DB]

1989 Campos, Raquel Discini de. A "princesa do sertão" na modernidade republicana: urbanidade e educação na Rio Preto dos anos 1920. São Paulo: Annablume; São José do Rio Preto, Brazil: Secretaria Municipal de Cultura, 2004. 185 p.: bibl., ill. (some col.).

The subject here is the city of São José do Rio Preto in the northwest of São Paulo state. The author used the city's newspapers to describe the "progress" from an entry point into the *sertão* and on to a modern town. Journalist, teachers and schools, lawyers, doctors and hospitals, and local commerce all get attention. For those wanting to escape from studying Brazil's big cities, this book provides a clear, useful examination of urbanization in the "interior." [FDM]

1990 Cancian, Elaine. A cidade e o rio: escravidão, arquitetura urbana e a invenção da beleza: o caso de Corumbá, MS. Passo Fundo, Brazil: Univ. Passo Fundo, UPF Editora, 2006. 296 p.: bibl., ill. (Col. Malungo; 11)

The author shows that slavery can be studied from the perspective of a city's architecture. She expends 78 pages reviewing statements by various historians relative to slavery, some even dealing with Mato Grosso, but while interesting they do not advance her case. She is on topic when she turns to the development of Cuiabá and Corumbá. There is rich detail on daily life in the houses of the two cities' slaveholders. There are some useful tables giving names of slaves, those of their owners (some of whom were black women), and some comments about their abilities and locations. [FDM]

1991 Cândido, Tyrone Apollo Pontes. Trem da seca: sertanejos, retirantes e operários, 1877–1880. Fortaleza, Brazil: Museu do Ceará, Secretaria da Cultura do Estado do Ceará, 2005. 127 p.: bibl., ill. (Col. Outras histórias; 32)

Part of a series of small books published by Fortelaza's Museu do Ceará, *Trem da seca* tells how Cearense sertanejos fleeing the great drought of 1877–79 became railroad workers. They were ill prepared for the long drought. They swarmed into Fortaleza frightening the urban elite. An estimated 2,147,000 were set adrift by the crisis. The Baturité railroad project allowed thousands of them to be put to work. Cândido's well-researched study examines government policies that combined the railroad's need for labor with the desire to keep the rural-urban migration in hand. Public works were to feed the starving. [FDM]

1992 Cánovas, Marília Klaumann. Hambre de tierra: imigrantes espanhóis na cafeicultura paulista, 1880–1930. São Paulo: Lazuli Editora, 2005. 351 p.: bibl., ill., maps.

This is immigration history at its best. The reader gets a clear idea about who the immigrants were, where they came from, and what they hoped to gain. The discussion of Brazil's immigrant policies and methods of attraction and reception are deeply informed and useful. [FDM]

1993 Carvalho, Marcus J.M. de. O outro lado da Independência: Quilombolas, negros e pardos em Pernambuco, Brasil, 1817–1823. (*Luso-Braz. Rev.*, 43:1, June 2006, p. 1–30)

Quilombos did not just have local effects. Carvalho's deeply researched study shows that they could have national impacts. Elite fears of the inhabitants of the quilombo near Recife led slave masters to arm their slaves and to decide against attempts at independence. They came to believe that they needed imperial military forces to suppress the quilombos or risk a Haitian-style slave revolt. So unity with Rio de Janeiro was solidified and we have yet another factor contributing to Brazilian national unity. [FDM]

1994 Cascardo, Francisco Carlos Pereira. O tenentismo na Marinha: os primeiros anos, 1922 a 1924. São Paulo: Paz e Terra, 2005. 825 p.: bibl., ill.

The navy had its tenentes too. Even before the raising of Fort Copacabana in July 1922 there was a repressed conspiracy among navy pilots to attack the president. Retired naval officer Cascardo has produced a massive, detailed study that will require some rewriting of the usual history of those crucial years of the 1920s. The research is impressive and warrants the attention of students of the era. [FDM]

1995 Castro, Adler Homero Fonseca de. Navios, museus e a resistência negra: o quilombo da Cabaça como estudo de caso. (*An. Mus. Hist. Nac.*, 2006, p. 46–69, ill., maps, photos)

This is a very elaborate study of some rock paintings near Diamantina, Minas Gerais. It shows that scenes of naval vessels were most likely done by African slave fugitives. [FDM]

1996 Castro, Maria Werneck de. No tempo dos barões: histórias do apogeu e decadência de uma família fluminense no ciclo do café. Organização, pesquisa e notas de Moacir Werneck de Castro. Rio de Janeiro: Bem-Te-Vi, 2004. 212 p.: bibl., ill. (some col.).

This is a family memoir that adds depth to Stanley J. Stein's famous portrayal of the Lacerda Werneck in his *Vassouras: A Brazilian Coffee County, 1850–1900* (see *HLAS 22:3889*). The book was organized and completed after the author's death by her brother Moacir. It is an inside look into the lives of the declining fazendas families of the Paraíba valley. The role of women on the decadent fazendas of the transition from slavery was fundamental in preserving such declining elite families. Many women administered the fazendas when faced with their husbands' inaptitude or absence. Castro adds depth to discussions of the interethnic relations of that time and place and the pains of adjustment. Those interested in the formation of landowning families will find much of value here. In discussing the barons of coffee she gives most attention to her great-grandfather Francisco Peixoto de Lacerda Werneck, Baron of Pati do Alferes, owner of seven fazendas and more than 1000 slaves. Includes 45 pages of excellent photos. [FDM]

Cavenaghi, Airton José. O território paulista na iconografia oitocentista: mapas, desenhos e fotografias, análise de uma herança cotidiana. See *HLAS 65:1301.*

1997 Cem anos da imigração japonesa: história, memória e arte. Organização de Francisco Hashimoto, Janete Leiko Tanno e Monica Setuyo Okamoto. São Paulo: UNESP: apoio Fapesp, 2008. 371 p.: bibl., ill. (some col.).

Good collection by leading scholars on various aspects of Japanese migration to Brazil, social life and literature of Japanese-Brazilians, and return migrations to Japan. [DB]

1998 César, Guilhermino. Origens da economia gaúcha: o boi e o poder. Porto Alegre, Brazil: Instituto Estadual do Livro: Corag, 2005. 220 p.: bibl. (Meridionais)

The discoveries of gold in Minas Gerais and the consequent need for food and animal transport turned the attention of the Portuguese Crown to great wild herds in what would become Rio Grande do Sul. The author develops the history of the resulting economy with style and energy. Tropeiros, estancias, Jesuits, Indians, struggles with the Spanish, and sponsored settlement are brought into his story. The author was a Mineiro who fell under the spell of Rio Grande. [FDM]

1999 Chazkel, Amy. Beyond law and order: the origins of the *Jogo do Bicho* in republican Rio de Janeiro. (*J. Lat. Am. Stud.*, 39:3, Aug. 2007, p. 535–565)

This is an imaginative, well-researched and clearly written article. The unsuccessful attempts to suppress the *Jogo do Bicho*, a gambling game, came from the authorities' desire to police Rio de Janeiro, which also created crimes out of *capoeira* and *macumba*. Chazkel did an excellent job explaining and analyzing these peculiar attempts at preserving order and progress. [FDM]

2000 Christoffoli, Angelo Ricardo. Uma história do lazer nas praias: Cabeçudas, SC, 1910–1930. Itajaí, Brazil: Univali Editora, 2003. 187 p.: bibl., ill.

This is a contribution to the history of leisure. The beaches of Itajaí, Santa Catarina, are among the most beautiful of southern Brazil. Christoffoli examines how and why German-Brazilians were drawn to Cabeçudas beach and what they did there. It was, he notes, the first Catarinense beach to develop the physical conditions to create an atmosphere appropriate to maintaining health and restoring energies. [FDM]

2001 Cidades negras: africanos, crioulos e espaços urbanos no Brasil escravista do século XIX. Textos de Juliana Barreto Farias *et al.* São Paulo: Alameda, 2006. 174 p.: bibl. (Passado presente)

In the popular imagination African slavery is often rural, especially on agricultural plantations, but there was also slavery in the cities. The authors focus here on port cities and how the captives reshaped their lives resurrecting African practices, ways, foods, music, dance, and language. It is well-written and based on solid research. Its final chapter "Recriando Áfricas" is absorbing and the essay on sources is very helpful. [FDM]

2002 Cittadino, Monique. O poder local e ditadura militar: o Governo João Agripino: Paraíba, 1965–1971. Bauru, Brazil: Editora da Univ. do Sagrado Coração, 2006. 423 p.: bibl., ill.

Well-researched political history of Paraíba focuses on the career of João Agripino Filho and his gubernatorial administration, 1966–71, to exemplify the tactical and ideological flexibility of "traditional" family-based politicians of the Northeast. Good narration of how creative political alliances with populists, such as Pedro Gondim, trumped affiliation with conservative parties, such as the UDN and ARENA, and prolonged survival of certain powerful families. Analysis of economic policy and economic transformation is less illuminating because of narrow focus on 1960s. [DB]

2003 Claudio, Affonso. História da propaganda republicana no estado do Espírito Santo. Organização de texto de Estilaque Ferreira dos Santos. Vitória, Brazil: Gráfica Espírito Santo, 2002. 163 p.: bibl.

This is a manuscript written in the 1920s by a republican from Espírito Santo that was held in the Instituto Histórico e

Geográfico Brasileiro until this publication. It sets the republican movement at the state level and thereby provides a local view of well-known national events. [FDM]

2004 Coleção As esquerdas no Brasil. v. 1, A formação das tradiçoes, 1889–1945. v. 2, Nacionalismo e reformismo radical, 1945–1964. v. 3, Revolução e democracia, 1964-. Organização de Jorge Ferreira e Daniel Aarão Reis. Rio de Janeiro: Civilização Brasileira, 2007. 3 v.: ill.

Good three-volume compilation of clearly written essays by leading scholars about aspects of the Brazilian left. The left is defined as movements "in favor of equality" from 1889 to the present, but in practice centers on the Communist Party and post-1945 nationalisms. Emphasizes both paradigmatic leaders and interesting marginal figures. Excellent starting point for research on select topics, but not a substitute for surveys of political history. Certain topics that might help to understand 20th-century radicalism are omitted (abolitionism of the 1880s, tenentismo, liberalism) and others are slighted (feminism). [DB]

2005 Congresso de Pós-Graduação em História Econômica da USP, 2nd, Universidade de São Paulo. Departamento de História, 2004. História econômica: agricultura, indústria e populações. Organização de Esmeralda Blanco Bolsonaro de Moura e Vera Lúcia Amaral Ferlini. São Paulo: Alameda, 2006. 485 p.: bibl., ill.

Graduate student and faculty papers from Universidade de São Paulo "Economic History" group present an interesting snapshot of past and current research interests. Topics are mostly women's history, institutional history of São Paulo, international relations, and demography, but also conventional market economy topics such as commerce. [DB]

2006 O Conselho de Estado e a política externa do Império: consultas da Seção dos Negócios Estrangeiros, 1858–1862. Organização do Centro de História e Documentação Diplomática. Organização do Rio de Janeiro: FUNAG, 2005. 450 p.: bibl., index.

The Council of State was the pinnacle of the imperial elite. Its foreign relations decisions can be studied in these volumes containing reports (consultas) submitted for discussion. These documents from the foreign ministry's archive include critical reviews, opinions, and reports by ministry staff. They are a necessary source for the study of Brazilian foreign relations during the empire. [FDM]

2007 O Conselho de Estado e a política externa do Império: consultas da Seção dos Negócios Estrangeiros, 1863–1867. Organização do Centro de História e Documentação Diplomática. Rio de Janeiro: FUNAG, Fundação Alexandre de Gusmão, 2007. 413 p.: bibl., index.

For annotation, see item **2006**. [FDM]

2008 Corrêa, Antonio Eutalio. A fragata Leopoldina e a missão Grenfell no Pará. Belém, Brazil: UNAMAZ, 2003. 306 p.: bibl., ill., maps.

This book analyzes and documents the intrigues that occurred during the transition of Pará from Portuguese colony to province of the new imperial Brazil. It describes the 1823 mission of English mercenary John Pascoe Grenfell to Belém to pressure the local ruling junta to accept the independence of Brazil. The work is based on unused documents from the Arquivo Público do Pará and consequently is rich in details. Grenfell's letters are full of sarcastic remarks about the Brazilians and clearly show that he used his authority to confiscate the wealth and property of opponents of the Rio de Janeiro regime, as well as to order executions of the most obstinate enemies. The book is a serious contribution to the complex history of Brazil's often misunderstood independence. [FDM]

2009 Corrêa, Valmir Batista. Fronteira oeste. 2a ed., rev. e ampliada. Campo Grande, Brazil: Editora UNIDERP, 2005. 190 p.: bibl.

The basic history of Mato Grosso do Sul centers on cattle ranching and the collection of erva matte. Its colonial history was shaped by the imperial struggles of Portugal and Spain. The important matte laranjeiras received due attention, but much is yet to be learned. Southern Mato Grosso relations with Bolivia and Paraguay will surprise those not familiar with the region. Highly recommended. [FDM]

2010 Couceiro, Luiz Alberto. A disparada do burro e a cartilha do feitor: lógicas morais na construção de redes de sociabilidade entre escravos e livres em fazendas do Sudeste, 1860–1888. (*Rev. Antropol./São Paulo*, 46:1, jan./junho 2003, p. 41–83, bibl.)

The article examines relations among slaves, free farmers, and administrators on fazendas in the last decades of slavery. Focuses on the tensions caused by the importation of slaves from the northeast and the readjustments that were necessary to keep the peace. [FDM]

2011 Cukierman, Henriquez. Yes, nós temos Pasteur: Manguinhos, Oswaldo Cruz e a história da ciência no Brasil. Rio de Janeiro: Relume Dumará: FAPESP, 2007. 439 p.: bibl., ill., maps.

An excellent biography of Oswaldo Cruz and the story of the elimination of yellow fever from Rio de Janeiro. The author examines the history of Cruz's institute at Manguinhos, and how and why he built the Moorish castle as its headquarters. He clarifies much about the vaccination riots of 1904, and much else that has escaped other historians. Those interested in the history of science and health in Latin America should not miss this book. [FDM]

Cunha, Euclides da. Backlands: the Canudos Campaign. See item **3304**.

2012 Cunha, Olivia Maria Gomes da. Learning to serve: intimacy, morality, and violence. (*HAHR*, 88:3, Aug. 2008, p. 455–491)

The author does several important things in this article. She examines the history of the domestic training school of Nossa Senhora do Amparo in Petrópolis, the ideology behind it, and how it was linked to ideas about domestic work. With slave emancipation of the horizon, there was rising concern for preparing free labor to work in family homes. She also analyzes attempts to legally interpret, regulate, and organize such work. Along the way she discusses little-known feminist publications that had roles in the debates about domestic servants and educating young women. [FDM]

2013 Daibert Junior, Robert. Isabel, a "redentora" dos escravos: uma história da princesa entre olhares negros e brancos, 1846–1988. Bauru, Brazil: FAPESP: EDUSC, Editora da Univ. do Sagrado Coração, 2004. 284 p.: bibl., ill. (some col.). (Col. História)

How was the public image of Princess Isabel constructed and resignified from her birth to her positioning among the civic heroes of Brazilian history? Daibert carries his examination from her birth to the centenary celebrations of her signing the act of abolition. Among its other strong points the text has an enlightening discussion of African views of royalty that were carried to Brazil. There are excellent illustrations and photos. [FDM]

2014 Dantas, Monica Duarte. Fronteiras movediças: a comarca de Itapicuru e a formação do arraial de Canudos (relações sociais na Bahia do século XIX). São Paulo: Editora Hucitec: Aderaldo & Rothschild Editores: FAPESP, 2007. 476 p.: bibl., ill. (some col.), maps. (Estudos históricos; 66)

The author is intrigued with the question "where did the people of Canudos come from?" She analyzes the daily life of the surrounding districts of the *sertão* in the 70 years before Conselheiro established his town. Canudos did not appear suddenly, but was the product of decades of social change. [FDM]

2015 D'Avila, Luiz Felipe Chaves. Os virtuosos: os estadistas que fundaram a República brasileira. São Paulo: A Girafa, 2006. 239 p.: bibl., ill., indexes.

This is a historical essay about the first two decades of the Brazilian republic. It is based on secondary literature and focused on Presidents Prudente de Morais, Rodrigues Alves, and Campos Sales, who D'Avila argues laid the foundation for democratic rule. The author tells a good story. Some of his tales could well enliven lectures on the period. [FDM]

2016 De sertões, desertos e espaços incivilizados. Organização de Angela Mendes de Almeida, Berthold Zilly e Eli Napoleão de Lima. Rio de Janeiro: MAUAD: FAPERJ, 2001. 301 p.: bibl., ill., maps.

The question here is what to do with the vast *sertões* and their uneducated populations. The 19 chapters confront the place of the inhabitants of the countryside in the formation of national identity. Three chapters examine the idea of the *sertão* and of the "interior" in the writings of Caio Prado Junior, Sérgio Buarque de Holanda, Gilberto Freyre, Paulo Prado, and Manoel Bomfim.

Five chapters are devoted to discussion of Canudos from the perspectives of Olavo Bilac, Machado de Assis, and Euclides da Cunha, and one provides a historiographic overview. [FDM]

2017 Dezem, Rogério. Matizes do "amarelo": a gênese dos discursos sobre os orientais no Brasil, 1878–1908. São Paulo: Associação Editorial Humanitas: FAPESP: LEI-USP, 2005. 306 p.: bibl., ill. (Histórias da intolerância; 4)

The end of African slavery and the search for replacement labor is the background against which Rogério Dezem sets his study of Japanese immigration. Excellent illustrations. [FDM]

2018 Dias, Antônio Gonçalves. Gonçalves Dias na Amazônia: relatórios e diário da viagem ao Rio Negro. Introdução de Josué Montello. Rio de Janeiro: Academia Brasileira de Letras, 2002. 203 p.: ill. (Col. Austregésilo de Athayde; 5)

In mid-19th century, Amazonia was the great unknown and Gonçalves Dias was one of those sent to report on the region. He had participated in the earlier expedition to Ceará, was a mulatto from São Luís, Maranhão, and a poet of note. His writings will stimulate those interested in Amazonian problems. [FDM]

2019 Dominguez Perez, Maurício. Lacerda na Guanabara: a reconstrução do Rio de Janeiro nos anos 1960. Rio de Janeiro: Odisséia Editorial, 2007. 319 p.: bibl., ill.

Study of Carlos Lacerda as governor administering the newly created state of Guanabara, 1960–65, overseeing major infrastructure projects and expanding public services. Concludes that fiscal windfalls to the city-state were not responsible for his accomplishments, and that Lacerda's moralistic, personalist style, often destructive in national politics, may have been constructive in hands-on supervision of municipal government. [DB]

2020 Dossiê ditadura: mortos e desaparecidos políticos no Brasil, 1964–1985. Organização do Comissão de Familiares de Mortos e Desaparecidos Políticos, IEVE—Instituto de Estudos sobre a Violência do Estado. 2a ed. rev., ampliada e atualizada. São Paulo: IEVE, Instituto de Estudos sobre

a Violência do Estado: Imprensa Oficial, 2009. 767 p.: bibl., ill., index.

New and greatly expanded compilation of short biographies of 436 persons either killed without acknowledgement by the state (159 "disappeared") or killed in acknowledged confrontations or when in acknowledged custody ("official deaths") during the military dictatorship. Each entry cites sources, mainly in recently declassified government documents. Includes some non-Brazilians and Brazilians killed abroad. Not a complete register of state repression, as it does not document nonlethal exiles, arrests, and tortures, and does not cover persons killed outside of "political" contexts during that period, such as 1,100 to 1,700 who have been listed as killed in rural land disputes. Complements and updates *HLAS 51:4037*. [DB]

2021 Duarte, Regina Horta. Pássaros e cientistas no Brasil: em busca de proteção, 1894–1938. (*LARR*, 41:1, 2006, p. 3–26, bibl.)

The worldwide popularity of feathers in women's hats created an enormous market. During the first republic hunters decimated bird populations to the point that naturalists raised alarms. These scientists charged the government with abandoning Brazil's natural resources. Because many of the species were insect eaters, the scientists argued that farmers needed to protect birds to keep the natural balance. Continued economic growth and even modernity were at stake. Under Vargas, the protection of birds was used to reinforce the values of the authoritarian regime. [FDM]

2022 Dutra, Eliana Regina de Freitas. Rebeldes literários da República: história e identidade nacional no *Almanaque Brasileiro Garnier*, 1903–1914. Belo Horizonte, Brazil: Editora UFMG, 2005. 253 p.: bibl., ill. (Humanitas; 123)

The *Almanaque Brasileiro Garnier* was published by the Livraria Garnier Frères (1844–1920s) of Rio de Janeiro beginning in 1901. The bookstore was a publishing house and meeting place of Rio's intellectuals. Almanacs had an educative and propagandistic mission of spreading information. Many of those renowned writers contributed to the *Almanaque*. Its contributors debated issues of national identity, such as language, literature, art, science, health, history, and folklore. This is a well-written and well-researched book. [FDM]

2023 Em família: a correspondência de Oliveira Lima e Gilberto Freyre. Organização, introdução e notas de Ângela de Castro Gomes. Campinas, Brazil: CECULT, Centro de Pesquisa em História Social da Cultura: Mercado de Letras, 2005. 295 p.: bibl., ill. (Col. Letras em série)

The correspondence of two of Brazil's greatest intellectuals is important and sheds light on their points of view and on their relationship. Oliveira Lima was an example of an intellectual combining historical research and/or literary work with a diplomatic career. The annex includes reprints of Freyre's articles in newspapers and scholarly journals and various commentaries on Oliveira Lima's writings. It contains material of interest to students of Brazilian-American relations. Oliveira Lima saw the US as a good ally and as "a model republican nation, modern and industrial, that could serve as inspiration for a "backward" Brazil . . ." (p. 17). The letters show the development of a paternal friendship and shed light on Freyre's student years at Columbia University. Highly recommended. [FDM]

2024 Encontro de Historiografia e História Política, Univ. Federal do Rio de Janeiro. Programa de Pós-Graduação em História Social, 2005. Anais: 10 e 11 de outubro de 2005. Organização do Programa de Pós-Graduação em História Social, Instituto de Filosofia e Ciências Sociais, Univ. Federal do Rio de Janeiro. Promoção e organização de Manoel Luiz Salgado Guimarães. Rio de Janeiro: 7Letras, 2006. 265 p.: bibl.

The essays in this collection were presented at a conference at the Universidade Federal do Rio de Janeiro. They are preoccupied with historiography and especially the work of Francisco Adolfo de Varnhagen, Euclides da Cunha, Capistrano de Abreu, and Gilberto Freyre. They tend to be philosophical and concerned with well-traveled paths and perspectives. [FDM]

2025 Ermakoff, George. Rio de Janeiro: uma crônica fotográfica, 1840–1900. Tradução de Carlos Luís Brown Scavarda. Rio de Janeiro: G. Ermakoff Casa

Editorial, 2006. 259 p.: bibl., ill. (some col.), index.

The photos in this book must be seen by those interested in the history of Rio de Janeiro. The street scenes reveal a Rio long gone, but intriguing. The book is enriched by photos of individuals and families. [FDM]

2026 Faria, Lina Rodrigues de. Saúde e política: a Fundação Rockefeller e seus parceiros em São Paulo. Rio de Janeiro: Editora Fiocruz, 2007. 206 p.: bibl., ill., index. (Col. História e saúde)

Archivally based study of Rockefeller Foundation programs in São Paulo brings out the role of physician Geraldo Horácio de Paula Souza as intermediary in the 1920s, founding the Institute of Hygiene and rural health centers. Ironically, in the 1930s opponents cemented the place of the Institute by folding it into the new Univ. de São Paulo public health school. Also studies Rockefeller promotion of nursing education. [DB]

2027 Farias, Juliana Barreto; Carlos Eugênio Líbano Soares; and Flávio dos Santos Gomes. No labirinto das nações: africanos e identidades no Rio de Janeiro. Rio de Janeiro: Presidência da República, Arquivo Nacional, 2005. 334 p.: bibl., ill. (Prêmio Arquivo Nacional de Pesquisa-2003)

This is a very interesting book whose three authors successfully merged their research and writing to produce a solid whole. It won the research prize of the Arquivo Nacional in 2003. It deals with the multi-ethnic African captives who were transformed into "Africans" and all but lost their earlier identities. But many managed to keep their old identities and used them in a variety of ways. This is an important book that adds richness and detail to the history of slavery. [FDM]

2028 Fausto, Boris. Getúlio Vargas. Coordenação de Elio Gaspari e Lilia M. Schwarcz. São Paulo: Companhia Das Letras, 2006. 233 p.: bibl., ill., index. (Perfis brasileiros)

Popularizing concise biography of Brazil's most formative 20th-century leader by a senior historian of the 1930s. Relatively sympathetic, attributing repression, alignment with Axis, and other misdeeds to "reasons of state" or "the times." Exerts itself to integrate private life and sense of personal development into political biography, and to explain Vargas' charisma. No footnotes, but indication of sources in short bibliographical essay. [DB]

2029 Fernandes, Ana Carla Sabino. A imprensa em pauta: jornais *Pedro II, Cearense* e *Constituição*. Fortaleza, Brazil: Museu do Ceará, Secretaria da Cultura do Estado do Ceará, 2006. 127 p.: bibl. (Col. Outras histórias; 47)

This is a study of three Cearense newspapers: the supposedly liberal (*Cearense,* 1846–91) and the conservative (*Pedro II,* 1840–89 and *Constituição,* 1863–89). The book was drawn from Fernandes' master's thesis at the Universidade Federal do Ceará. She delves briefly into the operation of the newspaper business in Fortaleza. Reporting on the droughts and the influx of refugees and the government's attempts at relief was heated and politically slanted. Researchers interested in urban development, politics, or social life will find some leads here. [FDM]

2030 Fernandes, Josué Corrêa. Saga da esperança: socialismo utópico à beira do Ivaí. 2a. ed., rev. e ampliada. Curitiba, Brazil: Sesquicentenário: Secretaria de Estado da Cultura, Imprensa Oficial do Paraná, 2006. 233 p.: bibl., ill.

This is a biography of Jean-Maurice Faivre, a French medical doctor who immigrated to Brazil during the first empire. He was one of the founders of what became the Academia Nacional de Medicina and created a center for the free health care for the poor. He later worked at a leper colony at the hot spring waters of Caldas Novas and Caldas Velhas in Goiás where he studied the disease. He founded a utopian agricultural community with French immigrants, which had a long history. Among its products was excellent cachaça. The history of utopian settlements is rare in Brazilian historiography. [FDM]

2031 Fernandes, Raúl C. Gouveia. Euclides e a literatura: comentários sobre a "moldura" de Os Sertões. (*Luso-Braz. Rev.,* 43:2, Dec. 2006, p. 45–62, bibl.)

Os Sertões continues to fascinate scholars. In the course of writing the book da Cunha changed his views of the *sertanejos* as lesser beings to the strong, defiant "bedrock" of the Brazilian nation. Canudos

was, da Cunha wrote, "the greatest scandal of our history." *Os Sertões* continues to be a key source for the history of Canudos and keeps alive in the Brazilian memory the painful drama of its destruction. [FDM]

2032 Ferreira, Gabriela Nunes. O Rio da Prata e a consolidação do Estado imperial. São Paulo: Editora Hucitec, 2006. 239 p.: bibl., ill. (some col.), maps. (Estudos históricos; 62)

Theoretically sophisticated study by historically inclined political scientist of Brazil's efforts in the first half of the 19th century to exert diplomatic and military power over the Río de la Plata region, which embroiled the young nation in conflicts with Argentina and Uruguay, testing its foreign policy, clarifying its ill-defined territorial limits, and ultimately strengthening the authority of a centralized state vis-à-vis regional potentates. [HL]

2033 Ferreira, Jorge Luiz. O imaginário trabalhista: Getulismo, PTB e cultura política popular, 1945–1964. Rio de Janeiro: Civilização Brasileira, 2005. 390 p.: bibl., ill.

Intelligent reconstruction of the texture of political moods, using memoirs and generous quotation from highly polarized newspapers and speeches. Also attempts to find principled coherence and development in the political "collective language" of Partido Trabalhista Brasileiro leaders and followers through analysis of key episodes such as the 1945 pro-Vargas "queremista" movement; the rise of João Goulart's popularity as labor minister; popular trauma and riots after Vargas' suicide in 1954; the 1955 and 1961 near-coups; and the language of rallies in 1963. [DB]

2034 Figueiredo, Osorio Santana. Plácido de Castro, o colosso do Acre. São Gabriel, Brazil: s.n., 2007. 184 p.: bibl., ill.

This is a popular rather than a scholarly biography of the Brazilian military leader of the acquisition of Acre. [FDM]

2035 Fischer, Brodwyn M. A poverty of rights: citizenship and inequality in twentieth-century Rio de Janeiro. Stanford, Calif.: Stanford Univ. Press, 2007. 464 p.: bibl., index.

Richly detailed study of how poor people living in Rio de Janeiro related to services and rights promised by the state, emphasizing the period from 1920 to 1960. Discusses the slow extension of basic urban services to new, poor neighborhoods, particularly to favela shantytowns; identifies paradoxes and gaps in recognition as "workers" by the new labor bureaucracy; and measures the role of social prejudice in inflecting outcomes in the criminal courts. Superb analysis of muddled land rights and of the struggles by informal neighborhoods to defend property against other private claimants and government urban renewal programs. Demonstrates political mobilization long before 1950s and catalytic role of Communist organizers in urban politics. Based in a wide range of documents including criminal and civil cases and early social surveys by government agencies. [DB]

2036 Franceses no Brasil: séculos XIX–XX. Organização de Laurent Vidal e Tania Regina de Luca. São Paulo: Editora UNESP, 2009. 486 p.: bibl., ill. (some col.), maps (some col.).

Good collection of studies by leading scholars discusses French labor and small-business migration to Brazil in the 19th century; transmission of ideologies and styles; French agricultural settlements; and the lives of some outstanding French migrants and visitors. [DB]

2037 Franco Júnior, Hilário. A dança dos deuses: futebol, cultura, sociedade. São Paulo: Companhia das Letras, 2007. 433 p.: ill. (some col.).

Treatise on the contemporary meanings of soccer worldwide is primarily a compendium of disciplinary perspectives indiscriminately arrayed as approaches to the "metaphors" in soccer. Two chapters smoothly intertwine the histories of politics and soccer in Brazil, but say little about the controversial recent restructuring of leagues. Lightly footnoted, based primarily in secondary literature and some newspaper articles. [DB]

2038 Frank, Zephyr. Wealth holding in southeastern Brazil, 1815–60. (HAHR, 85:2, May 2005, p. 223–257, graph, tables)

This is an important contribution to the study of a slave-holding society. Frank's research in 1,220 estate inventories in Rio de Janeiro, São João del-Rei and São José in Minas Gerais, and São Paulo provided interesting conclusions, such as that slaves were "much more important to middling and small wealth holders than their wealthy cousins" (p. 256). [FDM]

2039 Frota, Sylvio. Ideais traídos. Rio de Janeiro: Jorge Zahar Editor, 2006. 662 p.: bibl., ill., index.

Posthumously published memoir, drafted between 1978 and 1980, by ousted "hard-line" military minister who opposed President Ernesto Geisel's gradual political liberalization. Provides interesting counterpoint to Geisel- and Golbery-centered histories of the military dictatorships, such as Elio Gaspari's A ditadura encurralada (see HLAS 62:2213), and includes unpublished documents. [DB]

2040 Gadelha, Francisco Agileu de Lima. O Ceará na trilha da nova fé: o presbiterianismo no Ceará, 1883–1930. Fortaleza, Brazil: Ed. UECE, 2005. 125 p.: bibl.

This book analyzes the establishment and growth of the Presbyterian church in Ceará against the background of the spread of Protestantism in Brazil. It is arranged in three chapters: the first reviews the insertion of Protestant denominations in the empire and the political, social, and economic events involved in the process. The second chapter examines Protestantism in Ceará and the often hostile reactions of the people and the Catholic clergy. It also deals with sharp divisions among the Presbyterians. The final chapter traces the profile of Rev. Natanael Cortez, one of the most active pastors in Fortaleza. Though the author speaks of documentary sources all the notes refer to published secondary sources. [FDM]

2041 Garmes, Hélder. O romantismo paulista: os Ensaios Literários e o periodismo acadêmico de 1833 a 1860. São Paulo: Alameda, 2006. 286 p.: bibl., index.

This is a study of the monthly periodical Ensaios Literários published from 1847 to 1850 by students of the Academia de Ciências Sociais e Jurídicas de São Paulo. Among its contributors figured names that would later be famous writers, such as José de Alencar, Bernardo Guimarães, and Francisco Otaviano. It provides an analytical view into the student life of the era. [FDM]

2042 Gaudêncio, Francisco de Sales.
Joaquim da Silva: um empresário ilustrado do Império. Bauru, Brazil: EDUSC, 2007. 351 p.: bibl., ill. (História)

A biography of a self-made businessman and cultural figure of Areia, in the Brejo area of Parahyba do Norte during 1820–99. The author's description of Joaquim da Silva's education will be helpful to those interested in upward social mobility in the interior of the Northeast. His discussion of life, economy, society, and politics in the Brejo should be helpful to researchers of the era. [FDM]

2043 Giannotti, Vito. História das lutas dos trabalhadores do Brasil. Rio de Janeiro: Mauad X, 2007. 311 p.: bibl.

Sketchy history of 20th-century politics and labor organizations by labor leader and intellectual. Describes, but cannot explain, repeated failures of unification other than as betrayals. Ends with enigma of Lula's election in 2002. Interesting document for researchers. [DB]

2044 Golletti Wilkinson, Augusto. Guerra contra el Imperio del Brasil: a la luz de sus protagonistas. Buenos Aires: Editorial Dunken, 2003. 358 p.: bibl., ill., maps.

The long off-and-on struggle between Portugal and Spain over control of the eastern bank of the Rio de la Plata exploded into open war after Brazil took up the colonial-era claim. The República Oriental del Uruguay owes its existence to the contenders' inability to accept the other's claims. [FDM]

2045 Gomes, Flávio dos Santos. Histórias de quilombolas: mocambos e comunidades de senzalas no Rio de Janeiro, século XIX. Ed. rev. e ampliada. São Paulo: Companhia das Letras, 2006. 430 p.: bibl., ill., index.

An influential study of runaway slave communities in a revised and expanded edition. For review of 1st ed., see *HLAS 58:3275.* [HL]

2046 Goulart, Adriana Costa da. Revisitando a espanhola: a gripe pandêmica de 1918 no Rio de Janeiro. (*Hist. Ciênc. Saúde Manguinhos,* 12:1, jan./abril 2005, p. 101–142, bibl., ill.)

The Spanish flu created social chaos. The dead lined the streets. The government seemed incapable of adequate response until Carlos Chagas, head of the Instituto Oswaldo Cruz, took charge. The status of scientists increased as a result. This is a well-researched and well-written article [FDM]

2047 Gouvêa, Fernando da Cruz. Visão política de Machado de Assis e outros ensaios. Recife, Brazil: Companhia Editora de Pernambuco, 2005. 392 p.: bibl.

This is a collection of the author's essays on a variety of topics, most of which have some relationship to Pernambuco. In addition to the title essay on Machado de Assis, some of the other topics are Britishers in Pernambuco, rural landowners in Brazilian political life, the Partido Liberal after the Praieira revolt, the uprising of prisoners in the Fortaleza de Santa Cruz (Rio) in 1892, Bishop Dom Vital de Olinda, the emperor as seen by a young republican, diplomat Visconde de Cabo Frio, and Oliveira Lima. [FDM]

2048 Guimarães Neto, Regina Beatriz. Cidades da mineração: memória e práticas culturais: Mato Grosso na primeira metade do século XX. Cuiabá, Brazil: EdUFMT: Carlini & Caniato Editorial, 2006. 272 p.: bibl., ill., col. maps.

This is both family and regional history. The author rejects the "wild west" image of violence that characterizes much of the writing on Mato Grosso. She concentrates on the story of small towns as centers of civilization in the *sertão.* Her history mixes cattle and diamonds with internal migrations from Pará and Minas Gerais. The end of the Amazon rubber boom pushed migrants south into the diamond fields. Her oral histories of such migrants are valuable. [FDM]

2049 Hentschke, Jens R. Reconstructing the Brazilian nation: public schooling in the Vargas era. Baden-Baden, Germany: Nomos, 2007. 518 p.: bibl., ill., index, maps.

Densely researched history of Brazilian school policy and practice in the 20th century through the 1961 Lei de Diretrizes e Bases reform, based in case studies, not of capital cities but rather of secondary cities, in Rio de Janeiro and Rio Grande do

Sul. Rio Grande do Sul's positivist political culture influenced Getúlio Vargas' national educational policies, partly by legitimating a partnership delegating secondary schools to the Catholic Church, but Vargas' government easily absorbed other reform programs. Good analysis of reformers and policy issues such as suppression of foreign-language schools in 1938 and ideological conflict between Catholics and Escola Nova liberals, but most original in its attempt to combine educational statistics and local school records to explore the puzzling problem of the persistent low quality of primary education. [DB]

2050 História geral do Rio Grande do Sul. v. 2, Império. Coordenação geral de Nelson Boeira e Tau Golin. Direção de Helga Iracema Landgraf Piccolo e Maria Medianeira Padoin. Passo Fundo, Brazil: Méritos Editora, 2006–2007. 1 v.: bibl., ill., maps (some col.).

This volume is the second of five covering the history of the gaúcho state. This ambitious project, involving 22 contributors, represents an attempt to stimulate historical research on the state by opening new topical paths and raising broader or different questions regarding its development. The editors provide a listing of 15 general topics needing research (p. 10–11). The volume is handsomely illustrated with many maps, drawings, paintings, and photographs. [FDM]

2051 A história na política, a política na história. Organização de Cecília Helena de Salles Oliveira, Maria Ligia Coelho Prado e Maria de Lourdes Mônaco Janotti. São Paulo: Alameda, 2006. 290 p.: bibl. (Série Coletâneas/Programa de Pós-Graduação em História Social, Univ. de São Paulo, Faculdade de Filosofia, Letras e Ciências Humanas)

This is a collection of essays presented in a conference held at Universidade de Campinas (SP) in 2004. The essays examine the directions that politics were assuming in historical research and historiography. In the 1980s, the mobilization of labor as a political force introduced new forms of political practice in Brazil. The political vocabulary expanded to incorporate the developing political forces. The perplexity

that Brazilians felt while witnessing the labor politicians behaving similarly to the old ruling elites moved these historians to reconsider the conventional approaches to historical study. The fascination of some of the authors with the writings of Hannah Arendt is notable and worrisome. [FDM]

2052 Histórias de violência, crime e lei no Brasil. Organização de Elizabeth Cancelli. Brasília: Editora UnB, 2004. 259 p.: bibl., ill.

Uneven collection of papers, some by senior scholars, on topics concerning violence and the criminal justice system, from the colonial period to the present. [DB]

2053 Holloway, Thomas H. The defiant life and forgotten death of Apulco de Castro: race, power, and historical memory. (*Estud. Interdiscipl. Am. Lat. Carib.*, 19:1, enero/junio 2008, http://www.tau.ac.il/eial)

This is an article that every historian of Brazil should read and contemplate. Apulco de Castro tried to call a cheating junior army officer to task for not paying his debts and paid for his audacity with his life. This 1883 crime has been largely forgotten because it was so shameful. Holloway has done a true service by bringing it to the fore. [FDM]

2054 Júnior, Gonçalo. A guerra dos gibis: a formação do mercado editorial brasileiro e a censura aos quadrinhos, 1933–1964. São Paulo: Companhia das Letras, 2004. 433 p.: bibl., ill. (some col.), index.

Outstanding journalist's account of comic book business history and policy, organized around the David and Goliath rivalry between publishers Adolfo Aizen of Ebal and Ricardo Marinho of the Globo conglomerate. Weaves together issues of cultural nationalism, market protection, and the censorship of "immorality" that could corrupt children. No footnotes; based in interviews, printed material, and government documents. Fascinating appendix reprints proposed censorship laws and comics codes. [DB]

2055 Karepovs, Dainis. A classe operária vai ao Parlamento: o Bloco Operário e Camponês do Brasil, 1924–1930. São Paulo: Alameda, 2006. 178 p.: bibl. (Passado presente)

The title describes the contents very well. The Communist Party gets fulsome treatment. It provides a useful perspective on 1920s politics. [FDM]

2056 Karsburg, Alexandre de Oliveira. Sobre as ruínas da velha matriz: religião e política em tempos de ferrovia: Santa Maria, Rio Grande do Sul, 1880–1900. Santa Maria, Brazil: Editora UFSM, 2007. 325 p.: bibl., ill.

This book is a great help in understanding how the empire's loss of support by Ultramontane Catholicism played out at the local level. It is a good example of history written from the bottom up. Santa Maria da Boca do Monte is the stage on which the drama is set. The arrival of the railroad symbolized the progress that modernity was bringing, but the new Catholicism was part of the package. Those interested in religion in Brazil must read this book. [FDM]

2057 Kittleson, Roger Alan. Women and notions of womanhood in Brazilian abolitionism. (*in* Gender and slave emancipation in the Atlantic world. Edited by Pamela Scully and Diana Paton. Durham, N.C.: Duke Univ. Press, 2005, p. 99–120)

Women were not bystanders in Brazil's abolition movement, but rather active, vocal participants. Kittleson observed that women who tried to use their role to expand the discussion in the more radical direction of rights for women were marginalized and isolated. Even so he concluded that feminizing the movement was key to its spread and limited slave owners' defense of enslavement. [FDM]

2058 Klanovicz, Jó. O Brasil no mundo rural doente: a construção do agricultor na literatura em dois momentos da história brasileira, 1914 e 1970. (*Luso-Braz. Rev.*, 44:1, June 2007, p. 45–60, bibl.)

The author focuses on thematic and descriptive coincidences between Monteiro Lobato's *Jeca Tatu* (1914) and the *Cartilha do agricultor* (1970) prepared by the Rio Grande do Sul government. Both present the rural worker as backward and diseased. In Lobato's view medical specialists were necessary to modernize the countryside. Social progress required hygiene, cleanliness, and health. This attitude blamed small growers for their misery and sickness, yet society

needed clean and healthy foods. This paradoxical situation reflected the confusion of the Brazilian elite in addressing poverty, health, and education. [FDM]

2059 Klas, Alfredo Bertoldo. A verdade sobre Abetaia: drama de sangue e dor no 40 ataque da F.E.B. ao Monte Castello. Curitiba, Brazil: Secretaria de Estado da Cultura: Imprensa Oficial do Paraná, 2005. 285 p.: bibl., ill., map.

The author was a lieutenant in the 11th Infantry Regiment. His underlying attitude is that the government did not keep its promises to the soldiers. War was a hell, but the return was another hell: "the hell of the Pátria that forgot us" (p. 19). The value of this book is also its weakness. The author believed that the German submarine attack on Brazilian ships was provoked by the Vargas government, allowing American air and naval bases in Northeast Brazil. He equated the Vargas regime with "Nazism." Throughout there is an undertone that the US dragged Brazil into the war. In sending the FEB without sufficient training, including explanation of what the war was about, against "an alert and brave enemy . . . they committed a crime in the name of Brazil" (p. 237). He correctly asks why there are not studies of the significant numbers of deserters (p. 262). The book is not based on much research; he lists 21 books and 2 articles in the bibliography. However, it deserves to be read for the author's personal experiences, for unusual details, and as a check against the exaggerated enthusiasm of typical books on the FEB. [FDM]

2060 Kuschel, Karl-Josef; Frido Mann; and **Paulo Soethe.** Mutterland: die Familie Mann und Brasilien. Düsseldorf, Germany: Artemis & Winkler, 2009. 263 p., 8 p. of plates: ill.

The mother of the renowned German writers Thomas Mann and Heinrich Mann, Júlia da Silva Bruhns (1851–1923) was a Brazilian born in Angra dos Reis with a German father. Her personal memoirs about her childhood in Brazil were later published as *Aus Dodos Kindheit*. Her personality influenced the entire Mann family and their sons' literary works. The study focuses on the relationship that the Mann family had with Brazil. A chapter on Stefan Zweig, an Austrian writer who emigrated to Brazil during the WWII and wrote about the country, is included. [F. Obermeier]

2061 Loner, Beatriz Ana. La lenta construcción de identidades colectivas: trabajadores en el final del Imperio. (*Entrepasados/Buenos Aires*, 15:29, 2006, p. 27–41, ill.)

The author is in the History Department at Universidade Federal de Pelotas, whose city is the focus of her article. In it she studies the process of identity formation among the city's workers. She noted that discrimination was strong, but where it appeared blacks reacted by forming mutual aid groups. [FDM]

2062 Lopes, Ivone Goulart. Asilo Santa Rita: educação feminina católica, 1890–1930. Cuiabá, Brazil: EdUFM, 2006. 93 p.: bibl., ill. (Educação & memória; 1)

This is a study of female education in Mato Grosso. This school, under the control of the Diocese of Cuiabá, still exists, and offered not only primary education, but also art, music, and domestic skills. The study is based on archival records and oral histories. The author's intention was to emphasize the role of nuns in the education of women in Brazil. The peculiarities of educating women in Mato Grosso received ample attention. [FDM]

2063 Loureiro, Antonio José Souto. O Amazonas na época imperial. 2a. ed., rev. pelo autor. Manaus, Brazil: Valer Editora, 2007. 332 p.: bibl., ill. (Memórias da Amazônia)

This is less a history than a collection of data on a wide range of topics, such as listing the names of members of provincial government. In fact lists are a major feature of this book. Data on the "new market" of Manaus (1880), on street lighting (1882), and piped water (1880) are to be found here. [FDM]

2064 Lucetti, Hilário and Magérbio Lucena. Lampião e o estado maior do cangaço. 2a ed. rev. e ampliada. Fortaleza, Brazil: Banco do Nordeste, 2004. 374 p.: bibl., ill.

The *cangaço* was a northeastern phenomenon that merits careful study. Happily, this valuable contribution should stimulate more research and analysis. It is

a biography of Virgulino Ferreira da Silva, *Lampião*, and his closest lieutenants. This is a fascinating, well-written book that opens the violent underbelly of the Old Republic to view. [FDM]

2065 Lustosa, Isabel. D. Pedro I. Coordenação de Elio Gaspari e Lilia M. Schwarcz. São Paulo: Companhia Das Letras, 2006. 340 p.: bibl., ill., index. (Perfis brasileiros)

The latest in a long line of biographies of Brazil's first emperor describes him as the nation's most fascinating historical figure and a "hero without character." Like other works in this "profiles" series, designed for wide readership but frustrating as scholarship, lacks notes and bibliography. [HL]

2066 Lustosa, Rogério. O integralismo nas águas do Lete: história, memória e esquecimento. Goiânia, Brazil: ABEU, Associação Brasileira de Editoras Universitárias: Editora da UCG, 2005. 152, 11 p.: bibl.

Unsurprising master's thesis on "memories" of Integralista fascist movement finds that schoolbooks and mainstream press diminished it as a mass movement and reduced it to a form of Nazism, while 1990s nationalist fringe groups venerate and claim its legacy. [DB]

2067 Mac Cord, Marcelo. O rosário de D. Antônio: irmandades negras, alianças e conflitos na história social do Recife, 1848–1872. Recife, Brazil: Editora Universitária UFPE; São Paulo: FAPESP, 2005. 294 p.: bibl.

Religious practices and political and social life mixed in ways that many researchers have overlooked. This book on the social history of the *irmandade* of Nossa Senhora do Rosário dos Homens Pretos in the parish of Santo Antônio in Recife opens new perspectives. It shows clearly how Catholic practices, the daily lives of the members of the *irmandade*, and provincial political life were interrelated. Mixed into the story is the clash between Luso-Afro-Brazilian Catholicism and the Roman Ultramontane variety. The author gives life to the Reis do Congo and much else of 19th-century Recife. [FDM]

2068 Machado, Maria Helena Pereira Toledo. From slave rebels to strikebreakers: the quilombo of Jabaquara and the problem of citizenship in late-nineteenth-century Brazil. (*HAHR*, 86:2, May 2006, p. 247–274, bibl.)

Presents the story of a runaway slave encampment organized and supported by abolitionists within the city limits of Santos. It raises questions about agency and appropriate names. Residents of the *quilombo* of Jabaquara were drawn into the dock strike of 1891 as strike breakers. This is good social history with real life importance. [FDM]

2069 Maestri Filho, Mário José. Uma breve história do Rio Grande do Sul: da pré-história aos dias atuais. v. 2, O império: da consolidação à crise do escravismo, 1822–1889. Passo Fundo, Brazil: Univ. de Passo Fundo, UPF Editora, 2005. 1 v.: bibl.

Likely intended as review text for schools in Rio Grande do Sul. It is a quick and easily read summary based on secondary literature. [FDM]

2070 Maestri Filho, Mário José. Uma breve história do Rio Grande do Sul: da pré-história aos dias atuais. v. 3, A república velha: desenvolvimento, consolidação e crise do capitalismo regional, 1889–1930. Passo Fundo, Brazil: Univ. de Passo Fundo, UPF Editora, 2006. 1 v.: bibl.

Rio Grande's positivism is analyzed here. The positivists favored abolition of slavery without compensation for slave owners. They argued for property taxes and elimination of contraband, which clashed with the views of *latifúndarios*. The author explains the socioeconomic tensions of the era and how, with the coming of the republic, they multiplied into one of the most violent regional civil wars in Brazil's history. This well-written book is based on extensive secondary sources. Its clear language and skillful summary accounts will be useful for researchers seeking to understand the role of Rio Grande do Sul in the Old Republic. [FDM]

2071 Maretti, Maria Lídia Lichtscheidl. O Visconde de Taunay e os fios da memória. São Paulo: Editora Unesp, 2006. 351 p.: bibl., ill., map.

A study of the work of Alfredo d'Escragnolle Taunay, author of *A retirada da Laguna* (1871). The author seeks to broaden the space in Brazilian literary studies devoted to "minor" writers and to

deepen the links their works have to social organization, mentality, and culture. The book mixes biography and criticism. Readers seeking to add dimension to studies of the late 19th century will find it useful. [FDM]

2072 Martins, Antonio Marco Ventura. Um império a constituir, uma ordem a consolidar: elites políticas e Estado no sertão, Franca, SP, 1824–1852. Franca, Brazil: Ribeirão Gráfica e Editora, 2004. 219 p.: bibl., map.

The author sees the great themes of Brazilian historiography as set against a background of a constant struggle between liberty and authority. The work of Oliveira Vianna, Richard Graham, and Raymundo Faoro is analyzed, dissected, and compared. The author used the municipio of Franca (SP) as the scene in which to examine the roles of the municipal council and the local Guarda Nacional. There is an interesting discussion of the interaction between local and national elites in the formation and consolidation of the national Brazilian state. [FDM]

2073 Mattos, Marcelo Badaró. Esclavizados y libres en la formación de la clase trabajadora: en busca de la conciencia de clase, Río de Janeiro, 1850–1910. (*Entrepasados/Buenos Aires*, 15:29, 2006, p. 9–26, ill.)

Author seeks to show how slave and free labor eventually combined to form a labor movement. He noted what is sometimes forgotten, namely that the slaves had experience with social organizations, with negotiating work practices with owners and overseers, and with organizing and governing quilombos. The bulk of its pages deal with the 19th century. [FDM]

2074 Mazzoco, Maria Inês Dias and **Cecília Rodrigues dos Santos.** De Santos a Jundiaí: nos trilhos do café com a São Paulo Railway = From Santos to Jundiaí: on the coffee tracks with the São Paulo Railway. São Paulo: Magma Editora Cultural, 2005. 240 p.: bibl, ill. (some col.).

Discusses the railroad that opened the interior of São Paulo to the world. The short 139 km line overcame the escarpment that separates the Paulista plateau from the sea. Nicknamed the "Inglesa," this British-built railway began in 1867 and was reconstructed between 1996 and 2005. This book is full of wonderful photos of people, equipment, bridges, documents, maps, and many trains. Those interested in the history of coffee and the development of São Paulo will want to see this book. [FDM]

2075 McPhee, Kit. "A new 13th May": Afro-Brazilian port workers in Rio de Janeiro, Brazil, 1905–1918. (*J. Lat. Am. Stud.*, 38:1, Feb. 2006, p. 149–177, bibl., ill.)

This is a provocative, well-researched and well-reasoned article that is solidly founded on actual history, rather than on ideological or racially based interpretations. The attitudes of Afro-Brazilian dock workers clashed with the ideas of immigrants who tried to implant European models. Work like this could revitalize labor history. [FDM]

2076 Mello, Frederico Pernambucano de. A guerra total de Canudos. São Paulo: A Girafa, 2007. 367 p.: bibl., ill., index, maps.

Canudos continues to fascinate scholars. The author observed that the fame of Euclides da Cunha's *Os sertões* discouraged deeper research. The author made ample use of largely ignored bibliography by those involved in the disaster and probed contemporary newspapers for eyewitness accounts. His deep local knowledge enlivens his writing. There is more to be learned about Canudos. [FDM]

2077 Mello, Maria Tereza Chaves de. A República consentida: cultura democrática e científica do final do Império. Rio de Janeiro: ANPUH Rio de Janeiro: EDUR: FGV Editora, 2007. 244 p.: bibl., ill.

The collapse of the empire and the onset of the republic continue to fascinate. This book probes the empire's last decades for discussion and the strengthening of the republican idea. In that era, "Rio de Janeiro monopolized national life" (p. 55) so what happened there and on its principal streets had an outsized importance. This is an important book. [FDM]

2078 Mesquita Júnior, Geraldo. O Tratado de Petrópolis e o Congresso Nacional. Organização do Senado Federal, Gabinete do Senador Geraldo Mesquita Júnior. Brasília: Senado Federal, 2003. 327 p.: ill. (Documentos para a história do Acre)

This book is a re-edition of congressional documents relative to the 1903 treaty with Bolivia. The introduction reviews the history of the Acre crisis. The congressional debates add detail and substance. The correspondence between Rio Branco and Rui Barbosa is a plus, as is Carlos Henrique Cardim's essay on their differences. [FDM]

2079 Monsma, Karl. Symbolic conflicts, deadly consequences: fights between Italians and blacks in western São Paulo, 1888–1914. (*J. Soc. Hist.*, 39:4, Summer 2006, p. 1123–1152)

This impressive piece of research and analysis examines the everyday relations between Italian immigrants and Afro-Brazilians. Argues that racism did not develop into racial preference and segregation because once the fear of black revolt faded, it was replaced with fear of immigrant violence and strikes. [FDM]

2080 Morais, Taís. Operação Araguaia: os arquivos secretos da guerrilha. São Paulo: Geração Editorial, 2005. 656 p.: bibl., ill., index, maps.

Journalist's reconstruction of the 1972–74 Araguaia rural guerilla war in human interest episodes from all sides. Claims to be based on interviews with survivors and "three years" of research in declassified government documents, but frustrates critical understanding of controversial events by omitting footnotes and displaying facsimile fragments from "secret" documents as trophies, not as usable documents. See also item **2122**. [DB]

2081 Morettin, Eduardo Victorio. Dimensões históricas do documentário brasileiro no período silencioso. (*Rev. Bras. Hist./São Paulo*, 25:49, jan./junho 2005, p. 125–152, bibl.)

This article deals with documentaries made in Rio de Janeiro and São Paulo during the silent film era. Specifically the author discussed the 1913 film *Caça à raposa*. He concludes that the Paulista coffee-elite wanted images that supported their social status. The imagery of the bandeirante, then the rage in the writing of history, was used to make the elite appear as inheritors of the expansive roles of such figures. Immigrants did not fit into that framework and the themes of their film work were ambiguous. [FDM]

2082 Mott, Maria Lucia et al. As parteiras eram "tutte quante" italianas, São Paulo, 1870–1920. (*Hist. Quest. Debates,* 24:47, julho/dez. 2007, p. 65–94, graphs, photo, tables)

This article deals with midwives during the Italian immigration. The article challenges the view that midwives, trained in Europe, lacked proper credentials. Author used Health Service inspection records. [FDM]

2083 Moura, Denise Aparecida Soares de. Sociedade movediça: economia, cultura e relações sociais em São Paulo, 1808–1850. São Paulo: Editora Unesp, 2006. 325 p.: bibl., ill.

This is a provocative reinterpretation of São Paulo's history that challenges established scholars Silva Bruno and Richard Morse. This book should be required reading for those interested in Brazilian urbanization and economic development. [FDM]

2084 Nação e cidadania no Império: novos horizontes. Rio de Janeiro: Civilização Brasileira, 2007. 473 p.: bibl., ill.

The essays in this book are carefully researched and well written. Their reading will profit scholars regardless of interests and specialties. The essays reveal a dynamic debate about the nature of Brazilian political citizenship and about the ways to create a national identity. How does historiography affect such identity? This is an excellent collection. [FDM]

2085 Nascimento, Jorge Carvalho do. Notas para o estudo da imigração alemã em Sergipe. (*Rev. Inst. Hist. Geogr. Sergipe,* 35, 2006, p. 151–175, bibl.)

Discussion of efforts to bring European immigrants to Sergipe, centering on Germans who arrived in 1839. [FDM]

2086 Negro, Antonio Luigi and Flávio Gomes. Além de senzalas e fábricas: uma história social do trabalho. (*Tempo Soc./São Paulo,* 18:1, junho 2006, p. 217–239, bibl.)

The authors point out that studies on slave and immigrant labor do not interact and thus create a hiatus in the historiography. They object to the conventional boundaries of research on labor history in their search for ways to comprehend the complexity and diversity in how historians have dealt with the history of Brazilian labor. [FDM]

2087 Oliveira, Márcio de. Brasília: o mito na trajetória da nação. Brasília: Paralelo 15, 2005. 273 p.: bibl., ill., maps. (Biblioteca Brasília; 1)

Study of tactical myth-making, by both President Kubitschek and architects, about plans and construction of the new capital city. Based in printed materials. Includes a useful inventory of "facts" distorted or trimmed from most conventional accounts. Yet agrees that the Brasília project forged the ideology of "national-developmentalism." [DB]

2088 Ottoni, Teófilo Benedito. Notícia sobre os selvagens do Mucuri. Organização de Regina Horta Duarte. Belo Horizonte, Brazil: Editora UFMG, 2002. 184 p.: bibl., maps. (Inéditos & esparsos; 8)

This interesting book contains the 1850s reports of Teófilo Benedito Ottoni on his efforts to open the Mucuri river area of northeastern Minas Gerais to settlement. He provided a surprisingly sympathetic description of the natives and dismay at how the military forces treated them. This is an up-close tale of the destruction of the Mucuri section of the dense Atlantic forest to provide cleared land for cattle fazendas. The terrible results can still be seen today. The documents are given context by an excellent introductory essay. [FDM]

2089 Parente, Temis Gomes. O avesso do silêncio: vivências cotidianas das mulheres do século XIX. Goiânia, Brazil: Editora UFG, 2005. 164 p.: bibl., ill.

This book looks at women in northern Goiás, the present-day state of Tocantins. The creation of the state in 1988 has caused some reordering of scholarship on central Brazil. Tocantins needs a past and its resident historians are obliging. The author's objective was to break the silence with which history has regarded the women of the region. Daily life was not well documented, but the author carefully studied her base documents: wills, estate inventories, and parish records; and employed good imagination to reconstruct daily life. Parente attributes the silence regarding women of that time and place to the low esteem that men had for women. Yet the history she provides of what was a rustic, isolated frontier is an interesting and surprisingly clear one. [FDM]

2090 Parucker, Paulo Eduardo Castello. Praças em pé de guerra: o movimento político dos subalternos militares no Brasil (1961–1964) e a Revolta dos Sargentos de Brasília. São Paulo: Editora Expressão Popular, 2009. 288 p.: bibl.

This 1992 master's thesis based in trial records and interviews provides a useful, detailed account of noncommissioned officers' movement for representation of career grievances and ideals of political nationalism, with a detailed chronology of 1963 Sergeants' Revolt in Brasília. [DB]

2091 Pedreira, Flávia de Sá. Chiclete eu misturo com banana: carnaval e cotidiano de guerra em Natal, 1920–1945. Natal, Brazil: Editora da UFRN, 2005. 295 p.: bibl., ill.

Based primarily in newspapers and oral interviews, compares carnaval in Rio Grande do Norte and Rio de Janeiro, surveys local cultural exchanges and sexual tensions due to establishment of US airbase in Natal, and takes a close look at proposals to cancel frivolous (and potentially satirical) Carnival during wartime. [DB]

2092 Pedrosa, José Fernando Maya. A catástrofe dos erros: razões e emoções na guerra contra o Paraguai. Rio de Janeiro: Biblioteca do Exército Editora, 2004. 301 p.: bibl., ill., maps. (Publicação/Biblioteca do Exército Editora; 757. Col. General Benício; 412)

Retired army colonel, with years of experience in Paraguay, takes on the disastrous war of the 19th century. Pedrosa divides his book into five sections: historic Paraguay; Uruguay in crisis; Mitre and Pedro II; the disarmed pre-war empire; and the peace treaty. Richly annotated and calmly analytical, it should be read by military history and foreign relations specialists. [FDM]

2093 Perazzo, Priscila Ferreira. Prisioneiros da guerra: os "Súditos do eixo" nos campos de concentração brasileiros, 1942–1945. São Paulo: Humanitas: Imprensa Oficial, 2009. 378 p.: bibl., ill. (Histórias da repressão e da resistência; 5)

Study of internment camps and prisons for Axis subjects, which the author insists should be called "campos de concentração." Because Japanese subjects were often interned in their own agricultural settlements, and Italians were often not interned, this research tends to focus on German internees. Points out that, after joining Allies, Brazil's dictatorial government had to adopt humanitarian discourse regarding treatment of prisoners. [DB]

2094 Pereira, Cristiana Schettini. Que tenhas teu corpo: uma história social da prostituição no Rio de Janeiro das primeiras décadas republicanas. Rio de Janeiro: Presidência da República, Arquivo Nacional, 2006. 264 p.: bibl., ill. (Prêmio Arquivo Nacional de Pesquisa-2003)

This book won the Arquivo Nacional's prize for research in 2003. It fills a lacuna in Brazilian historiography. The author analyzes prostitution from the point of view of the practitioners and sets them and their struggles in the context of the early republic. Her deep research in public records is imaginative. This is excellent social history. [FDM]

2095 Pereira, Robson Mendonça. Washington Luís e a modernização de Batatais. São Paulo: Annablume, 2005. 223 p.: bibl., ill. (Selo universidade; 307. História)

Power in Brazil's "Old Republic" was concentrated in the "politics of the Governors" system, which gave taxing authority to the state governments. Local municipalities lost much of the autonomy that they had exercised in the colonial period. Their efforts to finance their activities and services weighed heavily on their small populations. The bulk of Brazilians lived in the countryside distant from tax collectors. The author examines Washington Luís' governorship of São Paulo, symbolized by his efforts to tax the great rural properties. Those interested in the interaction of municipal and state government will find much to ponder. [FDM]

Processos de territorialização: entre a história e a antropologia. See HLAS 65:1375.

2096 Quase-cidadão: histórias e antropologias da pós-emancipação no Brasil. Organização de Olivia Maria Gomes da Cunha e Flávio dos Santos Gomes. Rio de Janeiro: Editora FGV, 2007. 452 p.: ill.

The movement from a slave-based economy and society through emancipation to freedom and citizenship was rocky and full of detours. This worthwhile anthology brilliantly renews the discussion about slavery, color, citizenship, political rights, power, and freedom. [FDM]

2097 Queiroz, Paulo Roberto Cimó. Uma ferrovia entre dois mundos: a E.F. Noroeste do Brasil na primeira metade do século 20. Bauru, Brazil: EDUSC; Campo Grande, Brazil: Editora UFMS, 2004. 526 p.: bibl., maps. (Col. História)

Highly empirical analysis of the mature stages of a frontier railroad that connected southern Mato Grosso to Bolivia, Paraguay, and São Paulo, attempts cost-benefit analysis of regional economic and geopolitical impacts of money-losing state-owned railroad. [DB]

2098 Os refugiados da seca: emigrantes cearenses, 1888–1889. Organização de Nelson Nozoe, Maria Silvia C. Beozzo Bassanezi e Eni de Mesquita Samara. São Paulo: NEHD: CEDHAL; Campinas, Brazil: NEPO, 2003. 42 p.: bibl., maps.

This publication is accompanied by a CD containing the names and personal data of drought refugees who took ship for Amazonia or for Rio de Janeiro, Vitória, or Santos. This booklet is a partial guide to the materials. [FDM]

2099 Reily, Duncan Alexander. História documental do protestantismo no Brasil. 3a ed. rev. pelo autor. São Paulo: ASTE, 2003. 458 p.: bibl., indexes.

Third edition of a collection of short excerpts from documents, all translated into Portuguese, interwoven with running commentary on Protestant churches in Brazil through 1980. More than half of the book deals with pre-1920 period, emphasizing Church-state relations. Useful for researchers, especially by combining history of German immigrant churches with history of missionary churches. No substantive changes from second edition of 1983. [DB]

2100 Ribeiro, Luiz Cláudio M. A invenção como ofício: as máquinas de preparo e benefício do café no século XIX. (*An. Mus. Paul.*, 14:1, jan./junho 2006, p. 121–165, bibl., ill., photos)

The article examines the mechanization of coffee production between 1860 and 1882. The machinery developed by Brazilian inventors updated the agricultural equipment that modernized the finishing process on slave-labor coffee fazendas. [FDM]

2101 Rio Branco, José Maria da Silva Paranhos, Visconde do. Com a palavra, o Visconde do Rio Branco: a política exterior no Parlamento Imperial. Organização de Alvaro da Costa Franco. Rio de Janeiro: CHDD/FUNAG, 2005. 570 p.

These are the speeches on foreign relations of the Visconde do Rio Branco (father of the Baron) given in the Chamber and Senate of Brazil's Imperial Parliament. Their principal theme is policy toward the Rio de la Plata region. His leadership, particularly in the decades from 1850 to the 1870s, was "fundamental in the construction of the thought process of Brazilian foreign policy" (p. 17). [FDM]

2102 Rio Branco, a América do Sul e a modernização do Brasil. Organização de Carlos Henrique Cardim e João Almino. Prefácio de Fernando Henrique Cardoso. Brasília: Comissão Organizadora das Comemorações do Primeiro Centenário da Posse do Barão do Rio Branco como Ministro de Estado das Relações Exteriores, Fundação Alexandre de Gusmão, Instituto Rio Branco, Instituto de Pesquisa de Relações Internacionais: EMC Edições, 2002. 543 p.

For students of Brazilian foreign relations this is a book not to be missed. It is a collection of 27 essays presented at a seminar held at the Itamaraty in Brasília in August 2002 to commemorate the centenary of the ministry of José Maria da Silva Paranhos Júnior, the Baron of Rio Branco. The authors are a distinguished mix of diplomats and academic specialists. They study the development of the intellectual bases, the traditions and methods, and the functioning of the republic's foreign relations. They provide insights into the functioning of the foreign ministry under Rio Branco. [FDM]

Rio de Janeiro: formas, movimentos, representações: estudos de geografia histórica carioca. See *HLAS 65:1383.*

2103 Rodrigues, Gomercindo. Walking the forest with Chico Mendes: struggle for justice in the Amazon. Edited and translated by Linda Rabben. Introduction by Biorn Maybury-Lewis. Austin: Univ. of Texas Press, 2007. 187 p.: bibl., ill., index, map.

English translation, framed by academic essays, of anecdotal memoir by government agronomist who supported rubber tappers' cooperative movement. Chronicles their political mobilization, repression, and assassination of leader Chico Mendes. Briefly discusses establishment of "extractive reserves," which limit forest land use to relatively sustainable activities such as rubber tapping and Brazil nut gathering. [DB]

2104 Romo, Anadelia A. Brazil's living museum: race, reform, and tradition in Bahia. Chapel Hill: Univ. of North Carolina Press, 2010. 221 p.: bibl., index.

Intellectual history of the transformation in upper-class attitudes and public policy toward Bahia's African heritage in the early 20th century, emphasizing Bahians' imitative and competitive responses to Gilberto Freyre's Recife-centered initiatives in the 1930s and the contribution of anthropologists to defining Salvador as a center of authentic folklore. [DB]

2105 Sanglard, Gisele. Entre os salões e o laboratório: Guilherme Guinle, a saúde e a ciência no Rio de Janeiro, 1920–1940. Rio de Janeiro: Editora FIOCRUZ, 2008. 303 p.: bibl, ill. (Col. História e saúde)

Broad-ranging (half of it covering events before 1920), well-researched, yet somewhat inconclusive study of the multifaceted philanthropy and patronage of Guilherme Guinle and Candido Gafrée, particularly in its relations to the careers of the scientist Carlos Chagas and to the rise of government-funded public health programs after 1919. Guinle and Gafrée funded institutions such as hospitals, anti-syphilis campaigns, and cancer research at the Instituto Oswaldo Cruz, but Guinle also exercised personal patronage to advance the careers of talented friends. [DB]

2106 Sant'Anna, Denise Bernuzzi de. Cidade das águas: usos de rios, córregos, bicas e chafarizes em São Paulo, 1822–1901. São Paulo: Editora Senac São Paulo, 2007. 318 p.: bibl., col. ill.

This book tells the history of São Paulo's water supply, its public water policies, disasters, and degradation of its environment. Those interested in modern-day São Paulo will find this book highly useful. [FDM]

2107 Santos, Fabiane Vinente dos. "Brincos de ouro, sais de chita": mulher e civilizacão na Amazônia segundo Elizabeth Agassiz em Viagem ao Brazil, 1865–1866. (Hist. Ciênc. Saúde Manguinhos, 12:1, jan./ abril 2005, p. 11–32, bibl.)

Discusses the Amazonian woman as portrayed in Agassiz's Viagem ao Brasil. Author highlights the divergence between Agassiz's North American viewpoint and the local population's lifestyles. [FDM]

2108 Santos, Martha S. On the importance of being honorable: masculinity, survival, and conflict in the backlands of northeast Brazil, Ceará, 1840–1890. (Americas/Washington, 64:1, July 2007, p. 35–57, graph, table)

Well researched and cogently argued, this article sees assertions of honor by poor sertanejos as a mechanism used to defend their use of land, water, and livestock. The fragile land-owning structure of Ceará and the inability of the empire to guarantee property boundaries encouraged a constant assertion of honor as a marker of respectability and as a proprietor. Such declarations partly were aimed at fending off potential claims of large landowners on the sertanejo's labor. This research attacks the idea that Mediterranean notions of honor can be applied easily to Northeast Brazil. [FDM]

2109 Santos, Viviane Teresinha dos. Italianos sob a mira da polícia política: vigilância e repressão no estado de São Paulo, 1924–1945. São Paulo: Humanitas: FAPESP: PROIN, 2008. 340 p.: bibl., ill. (Histórias da repressão e da resistência; 8)

Revised master's thesis, based in secret police dossiers, provides generous empirical documentation, illustrated with photos, of surveillance of "undesirable" Italian nationals. After 1930 targets were primarily anti-fascists, whom the police lumped together as "Communists." Also covers surveillance of Italian fascists after 1938 nationalist crackdown on foreign organizations and 1942 affiliation with Allies, but says less about this shift in orientation. [DB]

Sattamini, Lina Penna. A mother's cry: a memoir of politics, prison, and torture under the Brazilian military dictatorship. See item **3305.**

2110 Schwarcz, Lilia Moritz. A mestizo and tropical country: the creation of the official image of independent Brazil. (*Rev. Eur. Estud. Latinoam. Caribe*, 80, April 2006, p. 25–42, bibl., ill., photos)

Schwarcz portrays Brazil as an "imagined community" creating a conscious self image "founded upon certain cultural roots that were . . . selected and delimited" (p. 26). In the process, it "conferred legitimacy" upon the new empire. The article is a shorter version of ideas she presented more extensively in her book, *As barbas do imperador: D. Pedro II, um monarca nos trópicos* and the English translation, *The Emperor's beard* (see *HLAS 60:3331*). [FDM]

2111 Sêga, Rafael Augustus. Tempos belicosos: a Revolução Federalista no Paraná e a rearticulação da vida político-administrativa do Estado, 1889–1907. Curitiba, Brazil: Aos Quatro Ventos: Editora CEFET-PR, 2005. 260 p.: bibl.

This book analyzes Paraná's politics during the reorganization after the overthrow of the monarchy. The violence that the state suffered further undermines the myth of pacific change. Sêga takes pains to show the historic links between the state and Rio Grande do Sul. The construction of a national oligarchic government based on an agrarian-export model marginalized Paraná and Santa Catarina. The work reflects its extensive bibliography, but unfortunately shows no archival research. [FDM]

2112 Seminário Internacional "170 Anos da Revolução Farroupilha," *Porto Alegre, Brazil, 2005.* Os caminhos de Garibaldi na América. Organização de Omar L. de Barros Filho *et al.* Porto Alegre, Brazil: Laser Press Comunicação, 2007. 191 p.: bibl., ill. (some col.). (Col. Sujeito & perspectiva; 3)

This "conference" book sheds light on the somewhat vague impressions historians have of Garibaldi's time in Brazil and Uruguay. [FDM]

2113 Seminário Internacional Da Vida para a História—o Legado de Getúlio Vargas, *Memorial do Ministério Público do Rio Grande do Sul, 2004.* Da vida para a história: reflexões sobre a Era Vargas. Organização de Gunter Axt. Porto Alegre, Brazil: Memorial do Ministério Público, 2005. 234 p.: bibl., ill. (some col.). (Col. Sujeito & perspectiva; 2)

Brief conference papers by eminent scholars have no consistent focus but offer good glimpses of aspects of Vargas' career from his youth, through his presidencies and political defeats, up to policies of his governments. [DB]

2114 Seminário "Salazarismo e Varguismo: Duas Ditaduras em Comparação," *Instituto de Ciências Sociais da Universidade de Lisboa, 2006.* O corporativismo em português: estado, política e sociedade no salazarismo e no varguismo. Organização de António Costa Pinto e Francisco Carlos Palomanes Martinho. 1a. ed. em Portugal. Lisboa: ICS, Impr. de Ciências Sociais, 2008. 365 p.: bibl., ill.

Papers of a symposium comparing aspects of Getúlio Vargas' Estado Novo (1937–45) and Antonio Salazar's Estado Novo, with emphasis on interwar years. Not strictly restricted to theme of corporativist institutions, but also ideas and parties. Suggests more differences than similarities, except in common definitions of enemies and in repressive institutions. Interesting paper by Jorge Ferreira highlights curious function of the Secretariat of the Presidency of the Republic, gatekeeper of correspondence with Vargas that built populist patronage relationship with workers. [DB]

Os senhores dos rios. See item **1911.**

2115 Silva, Alberto da Costa e. Comprando e vendendo Alcorões no Rio de Janeiro do século XIX. (*Estud. Av.*, 18:50, jan./abril 2004, p. 285–294, bibl., photos)

Korans were for sale in a Rio de Janeiro bookstore. There was a Muslim community partly made up of freed slaves in Rio de Janeiro that existed into the 20th century. A fascinating study. [FDM]

2116 Silveira, Eder. Sanear para integrar: a cruzada higienista de Monteiro Lobato. (*Estud. Ibero-Am./Porto Alegre*, 31:1, junho 2005, p. 181–200, ill.)

The well-known writer Monteiro Lobato is less known for his participation in campaigns for hygiene and eugenics in Brazil. Good education and medical care could raise the sickly rural population. Debates over immigration enter into the discussion. [FDM]

Silveira, Rogério Leandro Lima da. Cidade, corporação e periferia urbana: acumulação de capital e segregação espacial na (re)produção do espaço urbano. See *HLAS 65:1398.*

2117 Simpósio Internacional "Quarenta Anos do Golpe de 1964: Novos Diálogos, Novas Perspectivas," *Universidade Federal de São Carlos, 2004.* O golpe de 1964 e o regime militar: novas perspectivas. Organização de João Roberto Martins Filho. São Carlos, Brazil: EdUFSCar, 2006. 223 p.: bibl.

Papers by Brazilian and US scholars on 1964–78 authoritarian governments. Several review recent debates in the Brazilian press over explaining the 1964 military coup and interpreting its legacies. [DB]

2118 Siqueira, Jacy. Um contrato singular: e outros ensaios de história de Goiás. Goiânia, Brazil: Editora Kelps, 2006. 239 p.: bibl.

Local history at its narrowest, treats the town of Pires do Rio, which was known earlier as Brejo. Its founding is in dispute but relates to the extension of the railroad in Goiás. Comments on other parts of Goiás drift in here and there. [FDM]

2119 Soihet, Rachel. O feminismo tático de Bertha Lutz. Florianópolis, Brazil: Editora Mulheres; Santa Cruz do Sul, Brazil: EDUNISC, 2006. 302 p.: bibl., port. (Série Feministas)

Brief biographical essay on key feminist leader defends her moderate tactics in obtaining the vote and work rights against criticism by historians such as Susan Besse (*Restructuring Patriarchy*; see *HLAS 57:5219*) that these tactics merely modernized bourgeois patriarchy. Half of the volume is an anthology of excerpts from Lutz's writings. [DB]

2120 Souza, Christiane Maria Cruz de. A gripe espanhola em Salvador, 1918: cidade de becos e cortiços. (*Hist. Ciênc. Saúde Manguinhos*, 12:1, jan./abril 2005, p. 71–99, bibl., graph)

This is an investigation of the Spanish flu that spread in Salvador in 1918. Souza analyzes the politics of the era, sanitary conditions, and the weaknesses of public health policies and services. [FDM]

2121 Streit, Isléia Rossler. Entre ditos e não-ditos: o coronelismo e a imigração. Passo Fundo, Brazil: Univ. de Passo Fundo, UPF Editora, 2003. 147 p: bibl., ill., maps.

The subject here is the relationship between the politics of coronelismo in the north of Rio Grande do Sul and the immigrants who colonized the region centering on the municipio of Saldanha Marinho. Oral histories and personal letters in regional and private archives stand out among the archival sources. The question of how local colonels related to the immigrants is an important one. The author highlights the role of colonization companies. She studies the land conflicts and political disputes in the region to explain the functioning of public and private power in Rio Grande do Sul of the era. [FDM]

2122 Studart, Hugo. A lei da selva: estratégias, imaginário e discurso dos militares sobre a guerrilha do Araguaia. São Paulo: Geração Editorial, 2006. 383 p.: bibl., ill., map.

Master's thesis by senior journalist studies three phases in military tactics during Araguaia guerrilla war. After conventional military campaign tactics failed, final phase involved massive infiltration by military intelligence officers and escalation in torture and execution of prisoners. Excellent discussion of problems arising from author's collaboration with a group of military officers who for their own reasons compiled his major source: an archive of documents, memoirs, and sometimes pseudonymous interviews reconstructing the campaign. Thus he claims to be able to analyze only military strategies and "discourses." Compare to item **2080**, which is based largely on interviews with survivors. [DB]

2123 Summerhill, William Roderick. Big social savings in a small laggard economy: railroad-led growth in Brazil. (*J. Econ. Hist.*, 65:1, March 2005, p. 72–102, bibl., map, tables)

This article assesses the direct and indirect effects of railroads in Brazil. High transportation costs were a constant obstacle to economic growth. Subsidies became the rule and by 1914 61 percent of railroads were government-owned. Summerhill concludes that investment in rail was not the best choice for a country in need of education. [FDM]

2124 Tasca, Vilma Lourdes Bohm. A terra onde corre leite e mel: memórias da imigração sueca inserida na região colonial italiana da serra gaúcha. Porto Alegre, Brazil: Est Edições, 2005. 93 p.: bibl., ill., maps.

A family's story as part of Swedish migration to Brazil. The current queen of Sweden has Brazilian roots. [FDM]

2125 Tavares, Francisco da Silva. Diário da Revolução de 1893. Organização de Coralio Bragança Pardo Cabeda, Gunter Axt e Ricardo Vaz Seelig. Porto Alegre, Brazil: Ministério Público do Rio Grande do Sul, Memorial, 2004. 2 v.: bibl., ill. (Série Memória política e jurídica do Rio Grande do Sul; 3)

The diaries of the Tavares brothers were unknown for 110 years so their publication is important. During the so-called Revolução de 1893, Joca was the commanding general of the Libertador army and Francisco was one of the main civilian instigators of the revolt. The diaries constitute a small archive of the revolt and reproduce correspondence with leaders, such as Gaspar Silveira Martins, Admiral Saldanha da Gama, and General Aparicio Saraiva. The relations of the gaúcho forces and the rebellious navy get some clarification in these pages. The two volumes are a new source for the study of the tumultuous early years of the republic. [FDM]

2126 Teixeira, Rodrigo Corrêa. Ciganos em Minas Gerais: uma breve história. Belo Horizonte, Brazil: Crisálida, 2007. 174 p.: bibl.

The gypsies or Rom of Brazil have been little studied so this fine book is very welcome. It covers the 18th century to the early 20th century. No one knows how many gypsies are in the country. This excellent study provides a different angle from which to view Brazilian history. [FDM]

2127 Torres, Euclides. A patrulha de sete João. Porto Alegre, Brazil: Já Editores, 2005. 202 p.: bibl., ill.

This small book centers on the diary of the author's great grandfather who was one of 1,770 German mercenaries hired by Brazil in 1851 to fight against Juan Manuel de Rosas. He kept a record of his adventure in the Rio de La Plata campaign. He did not get the land he had been promised but made his life in the Caçapava area of Rio Grande do Sul marrying a local Indian girl and fathering 11 children. The story here runs to the bloody 1890s. The text is without notes and the bibliography is limited, but happily the book is well-written. [FDM]

2128 Tota, Antônio Pedro. The seduction of Brazil: the Americanization of Brazil during World War II. Translated by Lorena B. Ellis. Foreword and commentary by Daniel J. Greenberg. Austin: Univ. of Texas Press, Teresa Lozano Long Institute of Latin American Studies, 2009. 159 p., 25 p. of plates: bibl., ill., index. (LLILAS Translations from Latin America series)

Lively brief history of planned and unplanned cultural exchanges between Brazil and the US in the 1940s. Nelson Rockefeller's Office of the Coordinator of Inter-American Affairs commissioned propaganda but also brokered entertainment industry exchanges, in which Carmen Miranda became a touchstone. Each public happily, though with touches of irony and skepticism, absorbed anti-authoritarian stereotypes offered by the other: American post-Puritan democratic irreverence and Brazilian easygoing eroticism. [DB]

2129 Valduga, Gustavo. Paz, Itália, Jesus: uma identidade para imigrantes italianos e seus descendentes—o papel do jornal Correio Riograndense, 1930–1945. Porto Alegre, Brazil: EdiPUCRS, 2008. 291 p.: bibl., ill.

Master's thesis uses Italian-language Catholic newspapers, 1912–45, to suggest that priests ministering to Italian immigrants eased adaptation by emphasizing the "Catholic" solidarity of all Italians, and then, after the 1931 rapprochement of Brazilian Church and state, the "Catholic" nature of Brazil. The Staffeta/Correio Riograndense was above all obedient to authority; it dropped support of Integralismo after the government ban in

1938, and of Mussolini's fascism—and even the Italian language—after the government's anti-Axis crackdown in 1942. [DB]

2130 Vargas, João Tristan. O trabalho na ordem liberal: o movimento operário e a construção do Estado na Primeira República. Campinas, Brazil: CMU Publicações, Centro de Memória-Unicamp, 2004. 365 p.: bibl.

There are copious notes at the end of each chapter, but there is no essay on sources or bibliography. The author is focused on the "possibility of creating laws [governing] work, that is, fixing social rights in law" (p. 361). Freedom to strike and the establishment of legal protections for workers consumes much of this book. In the first or old republic, workers' rights were not expanded and the labor movement "was harshly repressed while workers were excluded from citizenship" (p. 364). [FDM]

2131 Velasco e Cruz, María Cecília. Puzzling out slave origins in Rio de Janeiro port unionism: the 1906 strike and the Sociedade de Resistência dos Trabalhadores em Trapiche e Café. (*HAHR*, 86:2, May 2006, p. 205–245, bibl.)

This is an excellent piece of work. The author seeks to answer the following questions: Who were the dock workers? What were their traditions? How were they related to the slaves for hire in the first decades of the 19th century? Surplus labor supply seemingly did not undermine the workers. Velasco e Cruz's work deserves a wide readership. [FDM]

2132 Velhos vermelhos: história e memória dos dirigentes comunistas do Paraná. Organização de Adriano Codato e Marcio Kieller. Curitiba, Brazil: Editora UFPR, 2008. 299 p.: bibl., ill. (Série Pesquisa; 135)

Two introductory essays, one on women in the party, and a collection of documents and 10 interviews with Communist Party leaders in Paraná, emphasizing 1945–64 period. Useful for researchers. [DB]

2133 Velloso, Mônica Pimenta. A cultura das ruas no Rio de Janeiro, 1900–1930: mediações, linguagens e espaço. Rio de Janeiro: Edições Casa de Rui Barbosa, 2004. 110 p.: bibl., ill. (Col. FCRB. Estudos; 1)

This study looks at the relationship between elite and popular cultures. It stresses the roles of the malandro and the bohemian intellectual, and the spread of elements of the marginalized Afro-Carioca culture. The author's knowledge of early 20th-century society is impressive. She successfully shows how the subculture was transformed into a key element of national identity. Her use of cartoons is intriguing and sets an example for other historians. [FDM]

2134 Ventura, Roberto. Retrato interrompido da vida de Euclides da Cunha. Esboço biográfico de Roberto Ventura. Organização de Mario Cesar Carvalho e José Carlos Barreto de Santana. São Paulo: Companhia das Letras, 2003. 349 p.: bibl., ill.

This biography of Euclides da Cunha made incomplete by the accidental death of its author. It is very readable and clearly was on the way to being a major study. [FDM]

2135 Wolfe, Joel. Autos and progress: the Brazilian search for modernity. Oxford; New York: Oxford Univ. Press, 2010. 269 p.: bibl., index.

Broad social and cultural history, light on business history, traces ideals and implementations of "automobility" across political periods. Dominant motif was Henry Ford's utopia of consumerist industrialization. Cars, trucks, and even buses symbolized aspirations to progress, national integration, and prosperity. As a technological option, they channeled private and public investments. By the 1990s, some version of dreams had been realized in the form of an automobile industry with organized workers. [DB]

2136 Zen, Erick Reis Godliauskas. O germe da revolução: a comunidade lituana sob vigilância do DEOPS, 1924–1950. São Paulo: Associação Editorial Humanitas: FAPESP: LEI-USP, 2005. 222 p.: ill., index. (Inventário DEOPS; 13. Módulo VI, Comunistas)

Summary overview of Lithuanian associations, newspapers, and Communist militants, introducing documents of interest to historians: transcription of 200 secret police records on Lithuanian suspects from secret police files that lumped them as a "language group." Political policing continued past 1945. [DB]

LITERATURE

SPANISH AMERICA
20th Century Prose Fiction
Mexico

ÉDGAR COTA TORRES, *Assistant Professor of Spanish, University of Colorado, Colorado Springs*

LA CREACIÓN DE MÉXICO como nación ha sido caracterizada por una complejidad histórico-social la cual se manifiesta como una constante en la evolución del país. El ámbito literario, especialmente la narrativa de los últimos años, ha reflejado estos movimientos sociales los cuales parten de distintas vertientes. La ola de violencia que se ha desatado en regiones del territorio mexicano combinada con el interés editorial de publicar lo que más se vende, ha dado pie a una temática que ya no es nueva en las letras de este país. Hasta hace unas décadas resultaba poco común, e incluso sorprendente, publicar novelas de corte atrevidamente violento. Hoy en día, desafortunadamente, se ha convertido en la norma: historias relacionadas al narcotráfico, las muertas de Juárez, los secuestros e incluso la corrupción política. Dentro de esta categoría resalta la obra de Víctor Ronquillo titulada *La Reina del Pacífico y otras mujeres del narco* (item **2216**), *Crónicas de sangre* de Ricardo Ravelo (item **2213**), *If I Die in Juárez* de Stella Pope Duarte (item **2163**), *La reina baila hasta morir* de Eve Gil (item **2178**) y *Dilemas* de Arturo Villaseñor (item **2234**).

En relación, hasta cierto punto, con la temática de la violencia, también se observa una producción que analiza la situación fronteriza entre Centroamérica, México y los EE.UU. Éste es el caso de *Lejanía* (item **2189**) de Gabriel Hernández García, *Al otro lado* (item **2235**) de Heriberto Yépez y *Tecateando el recuerdo: recuentos y recreaciones fronterizas* (item **2230**) de José Manuel Valenzuela Arce. No está por demás resaltar que la violencia no es la única temática que emana de las regiones fronterizas. En las anteriores obras también se observa un cuidadoso trato del peculiar lenguaje de estas áreas así como las situaciones alternas que se generan en aquellos espacios donde convergen países y tradiciones diversas.

Otra constante de la narrativa contemporánea mexicana es el coqueteo del pasado con el presente que se establece en la novela histórica. Estas obras son un esfuerzo por rescatar sucesos o personajes del pasado con el propósito de que sean esclarecidos, reescritos o cuestionados bajo la luz del pensamiento actual. Sin duda, los libros de Pedro Ángel Palou *Morelos: morir es nada* (item **2212**) y *Cuauhtémoc: la defensa del Quinto Sol* (item **2211**) son unos exitosos ejemplos de esta narrativa. Otras obras destacables de esta corriente son: *México acribillado* (item **2200**) de Francisco Martín Moreno y *Presidente legítimo* (item **2167**) de Francisco Estrada.

Aludiendo, hasta cierto punto, a la anterior producción literaria, no se puede soslayar el esfuerzo de un buen número de estados así como de instituciones como Conaculta (Consejo Nacional para la Cultura y las Artes) por promover la literatura. Por lo general, estos organizaciones funcionan como un escaparate para los nuevos y también para los no tan nuevos escritores regionales. Producto de esta iniciativa son Ramón Betancourt, autor de *Pájaros ciegos* (item **2150**) del Fondo Editorial de Baja California; Antonio Cordero, *Tornaviaje* (item **2160**) de la Secretaría de Cultura del Estado de Jalisco; Arturo Arredondo autor de *El camino a Bagdad está lleno de tentaciones* (item **2143**) del Consejo Estatal para las Culturas y las Artes de Chiapas, entre otros. Las temáticas dentro de esta categoría suelen ser variadas, se destaca una tendencia por contar historias personales y no necesariamente divulgar más las representaciones violentas del crimen organizado.

Dentro del grupo de los más reconocidos escritores mexicanos, sobresale, por un lado, el trabajo reciente de escritores como Carlos Fuentes, Elena Poniatowska y Carlos Monsiváis, y por otro, las antologías, intentos de justicia literaria, de escritores de la talla de Elena Garro, Margo Glantz y Nellie Campobello. A grandes rasgos y con una anticipada disculpa por la exclusión de importantes figuras literarias, los anteriores autores son sólo algunos de aquellos que han aportado obras recientes a la narrativa mexicana.

Como se ha podido observar, la narrativa contemporánea mexicana se inclina cada vez más a temas relacionados con los problemas socioeconómicos del país y con la violencia que se ha generado ya sea por hechos sociales como la pobreza, o por situaciones relacionadas con las drogas y las pandillas. Por lo tanto, las casas editoriales están hoy en día más interesadas en este tipo de temática, especialmente cuando se trata de publicar escritores no canónicos que se tienen que ceñir a estas premisas. Claro está que escritores consagrados como Fuentes o Poniatowska pueden darse el lujo de publicar cualquier temática y con el respaldo de las mejores editoriales a nivel mundial. Otro aspecto que cabe mencionar es que aun se publican textos que incursionan en temas más personales, de índole psicológico o feministas. Sin embargo, estos textos se presentan más esporádicamente y no son una parte central de este estudio.

PROSE FICTION

2137 Aboytia, José Juan. Ficción barata. Mexicali, Mexico: Consejo Nacional para la Cultura y las Artes: Instituto de Cultura de Baja California, 2009. 135 p.

La acción se desarrolla cuando el protagonista Hugo Piñero inicia la búsqueda de su amigo desaparecido en la frontera entre México y los Estados Unidos. Ese recorrido también se convierte en una búsqueda, un reflejo de una realidad fronteriza. Una frontera, que como todo sitio, cuenta con virtudes y desventajas.

2138 Adame Martínez, Homero. 14 voces por un real. San Luis Potosí, Mexico: Editorial Ponciano Arriaga, Gobierno del Estado de San Luis Potosí: Verdehalago,

2007. 155 p. (Literatura mexicana. Narrativa contemporánea)

Real de Catorce, un pueblo en la ciudad de San Luis Potosí, México, es el protagonista de los relatos presentados en este libro. Las historias son narradas por 14 personajes que nada tienen que ver entre sí y que por ende brindan variadas aproximaciones e interpretaciones sobre el sitio.

2139 Aguilar Camín, Héctor. La provincia perdida. México: Planeta, 2007. 320 p. (Autores españoles e iberoamericanos)

Novela madura y bien lograda que mantendrá el interés del lector a través de sus 320 páginas. Una de las temáticas principales se basa en la búsqueda del protagonista de un balance entre incorporarse al México "moderno" o mantener sus raíces.

Finalmente, se percatará que la modernidad no es tal y que sus raíces no son tan profundas como él lo pensaba.

2140 Aguilar Zéleny, Sylvia. Una no habla de esto. México: Consejo Nacional para la Cultura y las Artes, 2007. 96 p. (Fondo editorial tierra adentro; 344)

Para Sylvia, la protagonista de esta breve historia, el sumergirse en la escritura de un diario resulta el mejor de los remedios para no compartir en voz alta las intrínsecas historias de su vida. A través de géneros como poesía, cuento y ensayo se arriba a una escritura fresca y amena que invita a la reflexión y al autoanálisis existencial.

2141 Alcocer, Ernesto. Perversidad. Barcelona, Spain: Ediciones Destino, 2007. 266 p.

Partiendo de noticias trastocadas y de ciertas reglas que no todos respetan en la sociedad del México contemporáneo, el autor produce una selección de seis relatos bien elaborados; los últimos dos en colaboración con Santiago Bolaños. La perversidad, el hilo conductor del libro, muestra otra cara del sentir humano.

2142 Ariceaga, Alejandro. Obra alejandrina. Selección y prólogo de Eduardo Osorio. Toluca, Mexico: Instituto Mexiquense de Cultura, 2007. 338 p. (Raíz del hombre) (Biblioteca mexiquense del bicentenario)

Antología de la obra del escritor Alejandro Ariceaga la cual es muy recomendable por la frescura y amenidad que impregnan los relatos. Este libro se compone de las colecciones de cuentos tituladas "Cuentos alejandrinos", "La otra gente", "La identidad secreta del camaleón antiguo", "A corto plazo", "Ciudad tan bella como cualquiera", "Bustrófedon y otros bichos", y "Placeres3".

2143 Arredondo, Arturo. El camino a Bagdad está lleno de tentaciones. Ilustraciones de Óscar Mayorga. Tuxtla Gutiérrez, Mexico: Consejo Estatal para las Culturas y las Artes de Chiapas, 2007. 169 p.: ill. (Col. Hechos en palabras. Narrativa; 9)

Cuentos que oscilan entre el periodismo y la literatura y que gracias a ese coqueteo, resultan historias atractivas, interesantes, y en algunos casos, prácticas. El libro está dividido en tres partes: "Varia invención", "Agencia noticiosa" y "Tinta fresca".

2144 Arrioja Vizcaíno, Adolfo. Mamá Carlota: el fin de la fugaz emperatriz de México. México: Mr (Martínez Roca), 2008. 229 p. (Novela histórica)

La narración de esta novela histórica inicia en el Castillo de Chapultepec, Ciudad de México, en 1866. El valor de esta novela recae en la profunda investigación por medio de la cual se rescatan eventos que en ocasiones han sido olvidados en los textos de historia.

2145 Atrapadas en la madre. Compilación de Beatriz Espejo y Ethel Kolteniuk. México: Alfaguara, 2007. 255 p.

Antología que conjunta 19 cuentos, todos escritos por mujeres y de temáticas relacionadas a la maternidad en México. En esta selección se destacan obras de Elena Garro y Rosario Castellanos así como de Margarita Ponce y Beatriz Espejo, entre otras. En estas historias destaca un lenguaje directo, un poderío narrativo que abunda en la elocuencia y comunicación femenina.

2146 Basurto Flores, Oswaldo. El amor siempre mata. México: Sociedad Dokins para la Nueva Practica Artísticas, 2008. 205 p.

Interesante título para una novela en la que el eje central es el amor y sus múltiples manifestaciones. Todo parece indicar que en esta novela, el amor, más que matar, renueva, es decir, al encontrar un amor se muere una costumbre, una forma de ser pero nace una nueva. Por lo tanto, la terminación y la iniciación van de la mano en la trama de esta narración.

2147 Bátiz Zuk, Martha. Boca de lobo: novela corta a dos voces y un cuaderno. Toluca, Mexico: Instituto Mexiquense de Cultura, 2008. 132 p.

Novela corta, de precisa estructura, narrada por las hermanas Tamara y Damiana Guerra, la protagonista. Ellas cuentan lo problemático de su vida y de su hermano, al convivir en un hogar donde impera la violencia doméstica y donde cotidianamente deben de luchar por combatir los obstáculos que se les presentan.

2148 Bellinghausen, Hermann. Encuentros con mujeres demasiado guapas. México: Ítaca, 2008. 121 p.

En este libro se reúnen más de 30 relatos breves en los que el lector puede descubrir que todas las mujeres tienen algo muy peculiar; una belleza innata ante la cual el hombre generalmente sucumbe. Es a través de la figura femenina que Bellinghausen comparte historias que nos dan una pequeña lección de vida.

2149 Best of contemporary Mexican fiction. Edited by Álvaro Uribe. Translation edited by Olivia Sears. Champaign, Ill.: Dalkey Archive Press, 2009. 529 p. (Latin American literature series)

Antología bilingüe que incorpora 16 cuentos de excelentes escritores nacidos entre 1945–72 y que publican en México. La introducción de Álvaro Uribe además de contextualizar la obra presentada, también brinda un panorama esclarecedor de la historia literaria del cuento mexicano. Sin duda, los relatos cuentan con todos los méritos para ser parte de esta antología, además el hecho de que aparezcan en español y en inglés colabora a que éstas obtengan mayor difusión. Para el comentario del especialista de traducción, ver item **3242**.

2150 Betancourt, Ramón. Pájaros ciegos. Mexicali, Mexico: Fondo Editorial de Baja California, 2008. 113 p.

Colección de cuentos en la que predomina un humor negro y una búsqueda de justicia. Betancourt logra en estos relatos directos, sucintos y precisos, una aproximación a la angustiosa vida de los personajes que no sólo habitan las páginas de este libro sino también la sociedad en la que muchos de nosotros compartimos nuestra existencia.

2151 Blum, Liliana V. El libro perdido de Heinrich Böll. México: Editorial Jus, 2008. 86 p. (Contemporáneos)

El libro del autor alemán, Heinrich Böll, pasa de mano en mano, y así presenta la triste y compleja situación de las protagonistas que aparecen en los cinco relatos de Blum. Cada historia, cuidadosamente trabajada, parte de un conflicto entre la mujer y su entorno y destaca la perseverancia de éstas.

2152 Boullosa, Carmen. El fantasma y el poeta. México: Sexto Piso, 2007. 132 p.: ill. (Narrativa Sexto Piso)

De los 15 relatos de este texto, el mejor logrado es el que le otorga título al libro, "El fantasma y el poeta". En éste, el fantasma de Jan Rodrigues inicia narrando sus encuentros con el poeta Rubén Darío y posteriormente describe anécdotas, o bien podrían ser leyendas, del escritor Octavio Paz.

2153 Boullosa, Carmen. La virgen y el violín. Madrid: Ediciones Siruela, 2008. 248 p.: col. ports. (Nuevos tiempos; 126)

Novela por demás interesante y cautivadora ya que rescata un periodo de hace más de 500 años y a algunas artistas femeninas de la época. La acción gira en torno a la pintora Sofonisba Anguissola e involucra a figuras como Miguel Ángel y el nieto de Moctezuma.

2154 Campobello, Nellie. Obra reunida. México: Fondo de Cultura Económica, 2007. 378 p.: bibl. (Letras mexicanas)

Esta obra es un ambicioso intento por recuperar la obra de Campobello. Sin duda, su obra maestra es "Cartucho", en ésta ofrece una mirada fresca y de otra perspectiva de la Revolución Mexicana. No obstante no se limita a ésta y también aparecen obras de "Yo! Versos", "Las manos de mamá", "Apuntes sobre la vida militar de Francisco Villa", y "Tres poemas de Abra en la roca".

2155 Carrera, Mauricio. Travesía: crónicas marineras. México: Instituto Chihuahuense de la Cultura: Chihuahua Gobierno del Estado: Consejo Nacional para la Cultura y las Artes, 2008. 187 p. (Ficticia)

Dieciséis crónicas marineras narradas desde las entrañas del autor durante viajes de juventud por el Caribe. Aventuras en las que además de la satisfacción, se hace patente un temor ante el poderío de la naturaleza y lo minúsculo que resulta el humano ante ella. Lectura por demás placentera y llena de intriga.

2156 Carrillo Arciniega, Raúl. En la tierra de Op. México: Ediciones y Gráficos Eón; Charleston, S.C.: College of Charleston, 2009. 115 p. (Col. Narrativa)

Novela situada en el México de los años 80. A través de la historia el protagonista se desarrolla física y psicológicamente pasando por una serie de experiencias religiosas, escriturales e incluso pornográficas. Además de ese crecimiento también descubrirá la expresión literaria del lenguaje. Esta novela, debido a las constantes reflexiones, coquetea con el género del ensayo.

2157 Cerda, Martha. Cuentos y recuentos: antología personal. Guadalajara, Mexico: Ediciones Arlequín, 2007. 158 p. (Col. El gran padrote)

Selección de 42 relatos publicados entre 1988 y 2006. La autora en su presentación menciona que más que seguir un orden cronológico, los ha organizado por categorías: realista, fantástico, misterio, etc. Como se podrá comprobar la gama temática de esta selección es bastante abarcadora a pesar de la brevedad de los cuentos.

2158 Una cierta alegría en no saber a dónde vamos: cuento de Guanajuato, 1985–2008. Edición de Jorge Olmos Fuentes. León, Mexico: León H. Ayuntamiento, Instituto Cultural de León, 2009. 238 p.

Colección de cuentos de escritores que radican en Guanajuato y que han aparecido entre 1985 y 2008. Este conjunto narrativo destaca y rescata obras que, se espera, dice el compilador, sean atractivas y amenas para el lector que goza de este género narrativo.

2159 Clavel, Ana. Las violetas son flores del deseo. México: Alfaguara, 2007. 131 p.

La autora, brinda una realidad clandestina fundada en el incesto y lo que este tipo de obsesión puede crear en el ser humano. Julián Mercader, el protagonista, como alternativa al incesto, crea unas muñecas que llama las Violetas; éstas llaman tanto la atención que se hacen muy populares y, en poco tiempo, existe una demanda por obtener estas creaciones. Sin duda alguna, esta situación pone en evidencia el lado oscuro de la humanidad y en especial, el de los hombres.

2160 Cordero, Antonio. Tornaviaje. Guadalajara, Mexico: Secretaría de Cultura del Estado de Jalisco: CONACULTA, 2007. 242 p.

Novela que podría ubicarse entre las de aventuras de viajes, sin embargo también narra hechos verídicos con lo que se da un balance de realidad y ficción que resulta atractivo para todo lector. La empresa inicia en 1564 con la salida de cuatro navíos de Jalisco rumbo a las Filipinas en busca de una ruta de retorno a través del Pacífico.

2161 Cuentos mexicanos: de los orígenes a la Revolución. Compilación e introducción de Luis Leal. Miami, Fla.: Stockcero, 2007. 182 p.

Colección de cuentos muy completa, 31 relatos, que hace un recorrido desde los mitos mayas y la época colonial hasta el periodo de la Revolución Mexicana. Además cuenta con una breve introducción de Luis Leal. En esta colección se encontrarán obras de Fray Bernardino de Sahagún, Amado Nervo, Gregorio López y Fuentes y Nellie Campobello, entre otros.

2162 Deblock, Lucía. Algo me dice tu silencio. Veracruz, Mexico: Instituto Veracruzano de la Cultura, 2007. 78 p. (Cuadernos del baluarte)

En seis de los ocho cuentos que componen este libro, la mujer aparece como protagonista. Sin embargo esto no implica que sean relatos feministas ya que en cada historia se presentan, de manera muy peculiar y bien trabajada, situaciones que tanto hombres como mujeres podrían compartir.

2163 Duarte, Stella Pope. If I die in Juárez. Tucson: Univ. of Arizona Press, 2008. 328 p. (Camino del sol)

Una novela en inglés basada en las atrocidades que durante años han teñido de sangre la ciudad fronteriza de Ciudad Juárez. La autora comparte, por medio de las tres jóvenes protagonistas, el secreto de los crímenes y el dolor que estos implican en las familias de las víctimas.

2164 Esmerio, Juan. Meteoro y otras historias de sol. Culiacán, Mexico: Umbral Ediciones, 2008. 175 p. (Col. De cuento; 1)

El libro incorpora doce relatos entre los que destacan "Estofado", "Licores", "Vuelo", "Sol" y el que da nombre al libro, "Meteoro". El autor comparte historias locales de su estado natal, Sinaloa. Al parecer, se busca una reivindicación, en caso de ser necesaria, de su estado el cual es frecuentemente asociado al mundo de las drogas y la violencia.

2165 El espejo de Beatriz: antología. México: Instituto de Cultura de Yucatán: Ficticia, 2008. 186 p.

Este libro recoge los primeros lugares y las menciones honoríficas del Premio Nacional de Cuento Beatriz Espejo de 2001 a 2007. Por esta razón tanto en cuestiones temáticas, como estilísticas, los 15 relatos tienen personalidad propia y no se asemejan al resto de los seleccionados. En lo que sí se relacionan es en la narración de historias humanas que sin duda dejarán una grata impresión en sus lectores.

2166 Esquinca, Bernardo. Los niños de paja. Oaxaca de Juárez, Mexico: Editorial Almadía, 2008. 123 p. (Mar abierto)

Este libro consiste de ocho cuentos breves y concluye con uno más extenso que le da el título a la obra. La virtud del texto recae en una excelente conducción narrativa que atrae rápidamente al lector. No obstante, algunos finales aparentan una falta de persuasión, o bien si se quiere, podrían ser una invitación al lector para que colaborare, si así lo desea, en las conclusiones de los casos detectivescos.

2167 Estrada Correa, Francisco. Presidente legítimo: memorias de Miguel Henríquez Guzmán: ¿novela histórica? México: s.n., 2009. 255 p.: ill.

Novela que parte, como toda novela histórica, de una minuciosa labor investigativa. El autor intenta esclarecer sucesos del pasado que involucraron al presidente Miguel Henríquez Guzmán en su lucha por alcanzar una democracia. Esta novela bien podría reflejar, hasta cierto punto, el proceso de democratización por el que pasa el México de hoy.

2168 Eudave, Cecilia. Bestiaria vida. México: Instituto de Cultura de Yucatán: Gobierno del Estado de Yucatán: Ficticia Editorial, 2008. 98 p.

Breve historia en la cual la protagonista da vida a un universo ficticio, una práctica onírica en la que transporta al lector a un mundo fascinante y fantástico. Obra que tiene la capacidad de cautivar ya que en ésta aparentemente se describe y refleja la realidad desde otra dimensión de la misma.

2169 Fernández, Bernardo. Gel azul. México: Suma de Letras, 2009. 288 p.

Este volumen reúne dos novelas: "Gel azul" y "El estruendo del silencio". Ambas son representativas de la ciencia ficción, un género que Fernández maneja exitosamente. La primera podría ubicarse en el violento presente donde el tráfico de órganos se ha convertido en una lucrativa opción. La se-

gunda, de carácter futurista, trata de naves espaciales y robots.

2170 Fernández, Bernardo. Ojos de lagarto. México: Editorial Planeta Mexicana, 2009. 260 p.

Novela juvenil de historia muy original donde se mezcla la ficción con la realidad y que cuenta con la dosis exacta de misterio. La trama se basa en el mundo de cazadores de animales exóticos entre 1829 en el Congo y 1923 en la verdadera ciudad subterránea de la Chinesca en Mexicali, México.

2171 Figueroa Neri, Fabiola. Leve cotidiano. Guadalajara, Mexico: Ediciones El Viaje, 2009. 75 p. (Col. Sin Límite)

Conjunto de breves relatos unidos por el transcurrir cotidiano de la vida. Algunas historias tienen un tono un tanto poético mientras que otras se apegan estrictamente a una prosa directa y bien pulida.

2172 Fuentes, Carlos. "Cien años de soledad" y un homenaje: discursos. México: Fondo de Cultura Economica, 2007. 40 p. (Centzontle)

Esta edición surge como parte de la celebración de los 80 años del Premio Nobel colombiano y los 40 años de la novela *Cien años de soledad*. En ella se reúne un texto de Carlos Fuentes en homenaje a Gabriel García Márquez y un vibrante discurso en el cual el autor comparte las condiciones en que escribió esta obra cumbre.

2173 Fuentes, Carlos. Todas las familias felices. Madrid: Alfaguara, 2006. 411 p.

Obra de 16 cuentos en los que el común denominador es la infelicidad y fatalidad familiar. Además a cada relato le acompaña un "coro" en los que la violencia cruda y abrupta se hace patente. La infelicidad y la violencia llegan a todos los estratos sociales desde la familia presidencial hasta la familia tradicional, desde una pareja gay hasta un matrimonio en el que el machismo es la norma. Este libro es una radiografía parcial del México violento y por ende, de Latinoamérica. No se trata de una casualidad que la palabra final del libro sea "violencia". Para el comentario de la traducción al inglés del especialista en traducción, ver item **3244.**

2174 Ganadores del cuarto certámen literario Pedro F. Pérez y Ramírez, Peritus. Coordinación editorial de Ana María

Pérz Román de Cortez. Mexicali, Mexico: Fundación Pedro F. Pérez y Ramírez "Peritus" A.C., 2009. 213 p.: bibl., ill.

Este libro recopila a los ganadores del cuarto certamen literario Pedro F. Pérez y Ramírez que se lleva a cabo en la ciudad fronteriza de Mexicali, Baja California. Entre sus páginas se pueden encontrar las obras de las promesas literarias de esta región tanto en poesía como en narrativa histórica. Si bien, se trata, en su mayoría, de un ejercicio iniciador, también se destacan destellos de una verdadera vocación y seria producción literaria.

2175 García Bergua, Ana. Isla de bobos. México: Planeta Editorial, 2007. 251 p. (Biblioteca breve)

Novela situada a principios del siglo XX durante la época de la Revolución Mexicana y basada en un suceso verídico que aconteció en la isla de Clipperton, al sudoeste de Michoacán. La trama se concentra en los escasos habitantes de la isla que fueron abandonados a su suerte. Además de la narración de tan precaria situación, el autor se concentra en los fuertes lazos humanos que se desarrollan durante las pericias insulares.

2176 García Bergua, Ana. Pie de página. México: Ediciones Sin Nombre: Consejo Nacional para la Cultura y las Artes, 2007. 141 p. (Los libros del arquero)

Las crónicas de este texto confirman la multiplicidad de historias de las que tanto humanos como objetos son testigos en el transcurso del tiempo. La nostalgia y el añorado porvenir se mezclan para brindar un sentimiento que de una manera u otra nos permite seguir adelante en nuestra existencia.

2177 Garro, Elena. Obras reunidas. Introducción de Lucía Melgar. México: Fondo de Cultura Económica, 2006. 1. v. : bibl.

La narrativa de esta escritora es de suma importancia para tener un buen conocimiento de la literatura mexicana del siglo XX. Su temática dentro del cuento es variada, sin embargo se destacan temas como la rebeldía de la mujer ante la sociedad patriarcal y el abuso de las clases privilegiadas hacia los desfavorecidos. Los cuentos reunidos forman parte de los libros La semana de colores, Andamos huyendo Lola y por último un relato inédito.

2178 Gil, Eve. La reina baila hasta morir. México: Ediciones Fósforo, 2008. 113 p. (Col. Narrativa)

Relatos que atañen sobre los temas de las relaciones humanas poco usuales. Ya sea a través del Internet como en el caso de "Cenicienta Hardcore" o desde la recuperación de un secuestro en "Alicia o el diablo", los personajes de Gil muestran la genialidad de su creadora. Historias intensas, irreverentes y a la vez totalmente deleitosas.

2179 Gil, Eve. Virtus. México: Editorial Jus, 2008. 123 p.

Virtus, novela un tanto futurista, o bien, si se quiere, apocalíptica, en la que se desarrolla una realidad novelística bastante oscura del México venidero. La tecnología está al servicio de un grupo de humanos que buscan saciar su avaricia y su sed de poder sin tomar en cuenta al resto de sociedad.

2180 Glantz, Margo. Obras reunidas. México: Fondo de Cultura Económica, 2008. 1 v.

Afortunadamente, este libro es parte del paulatino rescate de la obra de esta prolífica escritora. En esta selección, muy completa de la obra narrativa, se abordan géneros como: novela, autobiografía, ensayo, reportaje, crónica y memorias. Los seis tomos que se reúnen en esta obra son: "Las genealogías", "El día de tu boda", "Doscientas ballenas azules", "Síndrome de naufragios", "De la amorosa inclinación a enredarse en cabellos" y "Apariciones".

2181 Glantz, Margo. Saña. México: Ediciones Era, 2007. 233 p. (Biblioteca Era)

Narraciones ensayísticas y fragmentadas que versan en una multiplicidad impresionante de temas. Las meditaciones del texto podrían resultar en una placentera y analítica visión de la cotidianidad y de aquello que todavía se desea lograr para dejar detrás las nostalgias.

2182 Gollnick, Brian. Reinventing the Lacandón: subaltern representations in the rain forest of Chiapas. Tucson: Univ. of Arizona Press, 2008. 225 p.: bibl., index.

Un estudio ambicioso y completo de la gente indígena del estado de Chiapas, México y de la selva lacandona. El contenido incluye aproximaciones históricas, literarias, ecológicas y sociales contemporáneas.

Este es un estudio que todo investigador serio debe de consultar para partir de una base sólida y actualizada sobre el tema presentado.

2183 Guedea, Rogelio. Para, caídas. Colima, Mexico: Gobierno del Estado de Colima, Secretaría de Cultura; México: Ficticia, 2007. 129 p. (Biblioteca de cuento contemporáneo; 3)

Una refinada estructura y una narrativa más que sucinta, es el ingrediente principal de este libro compuesto por 96 minificciones. Estas brevísimas historias exploran las situaciones cotidianas de la vida mediante las cuales se muestran diversas alternativas en el peregrinar de la vida.

2184 Guerrero Martínez, Maurizio. Los cojos. Guanajuato, Mexico: Ediciones La Rana, 2009. 93 p.

Los personajes de los tres cuentos que componen este libro se ven atrapados en situaciones desfavorables de las cuales no pueden salir. De allí que su cojera, más que física, sea espiritual. A pesar de la tristeza que envuelve a los personajes, los cuentos tienen la capacidad de producir un humor áspero con el que el lector puede identificarse.

2185 Guevara del Angel, Itzel. Santas madrecitas. México: Consejo Nacional para la Cultura y las Artes, 2008. 90 p. (Fondo editorial tierra adentro; 379)

Catorce cuentos breves en los que la incógnita y la presencia femenina es la constante. Guevara del Ángel presenta el mundo cotidiano en el que sus lectores podrán relacionarse fácilmente con los hechos que marcan la vida de sus protagonistas: madres abnegadas, madres libres, madres profesionales, al fin y al cabo, madres.

2186 Haghenbeck, Francisco G. Solamente una vez. México: Planeta, 2007. 284 p.

Novela basada en la figura de uno de los mejores compositores mexicanos, Agustín Lara. Obra, basada en datos históricos y de buena hechura por medio de los cuales un entrevistador conoce de cerca una etapa de la vida de esta leyenda.

2187 Hecho en México. Edición de Lolita Bosch. Barcelona, Spain: Mondadori, 2007. 407 p., 16 p. of plates: bibl., ill. (chiefly col.), map. (Literatura Mondadori; 340)

Este libro es una recopilación panorámica autónomamente seleccionada por Bosch. En esta apasionada colección se incluyen: ensayos, poesías, canciones, historias, fotografías de expresiones artísticas, una cronología e incluso un mapa. Sin duda alguna, el lector encontrará en estas páginas un auténtico producto hecho en México.

2188 Hernández, Luisa Josefina. Roch: novela hagiográfica. Xalapa, Mexico: Univ. Veracruzana, 2008. 251 p. (Ficción)

Esta novela hagiográfica y con matices históricos guía al lector por la vida del santo Roch. Esto no significa que sea una obra religiosa sino más bien una narrativa que se adentra en la vida de los personajes que rodean al protagonista.

2189 Hernández García, Gabriel. Lejanía. Tuxtla Gutiérrez, Mexico: UNICACH, Univ. de Ciencias y Artes de Chiapas, 2008. 202 p. (Col. Selva Negra) (Col. Boca del cielo)

Novela por demás interesante e impactante. Los protagonistas, José y Alcira, han decidido emigrar de Centroamérica a los Estados Unidos. Sin embargo, ese es sólo el primer pasó, ya que para lograr su objetivo se verán involucrados en una extensa serie de conflictos e injusticias.

2190 Jandra, Leonardo da. La almadraba. México: Planeta Editorial Mexicana, 2008. 323 p. (Autores españoles e iberoamericanos)

Esta novela concluye la trilogía compuesta por las obras tituladas "Huatulqueños" y "Samahua." Una historia de aventura y respeto al mar y a la naturaleza en la cual la almadraba, una especie de red para pescar, se convierte en una metáfora de la vida. El tono humanista de esta novela crea conciencia en sus lectores y un sincero interés por la vida del mar.

2191 Krauze, Daniel. Cuervos. México: Planeta, 2007. 179 p.

Esta novela podría ser una radiografía, no tan parcial, de la juventud de la clase alta mexicana. Un mundo donde abunda el sexo, las drogas, el alcohol y una vida llena de irresponsabilidad y frivolidad. Todo esto se maneja por medio del dinero y las influencias pero, como en toda etapa, se llega a un límite y se afrontan y sufren las consecuencias de ciertas actitudes y excesos.

2192 Lavín, Mónica. Hotel Limbo. México: Alfaguara, 2008. 226 p.

Darío, pintor de desnudos, y Sara, su modelo, son los protagonistas de esta intensa y apasionada novela. Ambos desarrollan una relación erótica en la habitación 301, lugar de sus citas. La autora, a través de su estilo narrativo, intenta recrear ese espacio erótico, donde la sexualidad no sólo se apodera de los personajes sino también de los lectores que contemplan las pinturas de Darío.

2193 Lavín, Mónica. Retazos. México: Editorial Praxis, 2007. 84 p.: ill. (El Puro cuento)

Prosas breves, dice su autora, retazos como título, fragmentos breves de un razonamiento como definición. Esta colección de más de 40 breves narraciones acompañadas de dibujos, plasma historias que aparentemente se habían quedado en el tintero, pero que ahora son atrapadas en las páginas de este apacible libro.

2194 Leeworio Gallardo, Melquiades. La pesadilla. Toluca, Mexico: Instituto Mexiquense de Cultura, 2008. 173 p. (Biblioteca Mexiquense del Bicentenario) (Piedra de fundación)

Tal y como el título lo sugiere, la trama de la novela gira en torno al mundo onírico. Un mundo que se confunde con la realidad y viceversa. Es así como el estilo del autor crea un ambiente propicio para el erotismo, el misterio e incluso el miedo.

2195 León, Lorenzo. La realidad envenenada o de la arquitectura del horror. Oaxaca de Juárez, Mexico: Editorial Almadía: Ciclo Literario Editorial, 2007. 166 p.

En esta serie de relatos, frescos y rigurosos, el común denominador es el horror y una trepidante narración. De hecho, desde un inicio, los cuentos acaparan la atención e interés del lector para que éste continúe por las páginas impregnadas de terror que despliega el libro.

2196 La literatura mexicana del siglo XX. Coordinación de Manuel Fernández Perera. México: Fondo de Cultura Económica: Consejo Nacional para la Cultura y las Artes: Univ. Veracruzana, 2008. 498 p.: bibl. (Biblioteca Mexicana: Serie Historia y Antropología)

Esta obra, dividida en 10 capítulos correspondientes a las décadas del siglo anterior, es una serie de estudios literarios. La organización del texto y el excelente conocimiento de los autores, quienes hacen una excelente labor en cada apartado, colaboran para que esta colección sea codiciada por los estudiosos de la literatura mexicana.

2197 Lobo, Fernando. Relato del suicida. Oaxaca de Juárez, Mexico: Editorial Almadía, 2007. 62 p. (Mar abierto)

El protagonista Tadeus Giménez, profesor de metafísica, se ve involucrado en una crisis filosófica que lo motiva a dedicarse, de tiempo completo, a quitarse la vida. Conforme se avanza en la lectura de esta novela de suspenso, el lector se percata que la tarea de suicidarse podría ser más compleja de lo esperado.

2198 Macluf, Lourdes. Si hubiera mar—. México: Alfaguara, 2007. 199 p.

Esta virtuosa novela desvela el complejo proceso escritural en el cual se enmaraña la autora y del cual, sin duda, sale avante. Además cuenta con un matiz nostálgico en el que se retorna al México de los años 40.

2199 Martín del Campo, David. Perro dog: doce cuentos. México: Alfaguara: Santillana Ediciones Generales, 2007. 126 p. (Serie roja)

Doce cuentos, frescos y de aparente sencilla estructura, son los que dan cuerpo a este libro. Cada historia podría ser una breve y estremecedora, lección de vida. Por lo tanto, resulta bastante factible el hecho de que el lector se vea reflejado en las situaciones que del Campo ha creado.

2200 Martín Moreno, Francisco. México acribillado: una novela histórica en cuatro actos. 2. ed. México: Alfaguara, 2008. 585 p.

Novela histórica que cuestiona un capítulo de la historia oficial de México, el del asesinato de Álvaro Obregón a principios del siglo XX. Partiendo de sucesos verídicos, el autor añade una dosis de imaginación enmarcada por un estilo directo y ante todo, de una serie de personajes que poco han sido estudiados en la historia mexicana pero que sin lugar a dudas, son de suma importancia para comprender los acontecimientos de la época.

2201 Martínez-Belli, Laura. Por si no te vuelvo a ver. México: Planeta, 2007. 244 p. (Autores españoles e iberoamericanos)

Al inicio de esta emotiva novela, Mercedes es arrancada de su niñez al ser vendida a un prostíbulo. Posteriormente, da a luz, a pesar de los múltiples intentos de aborto, a Gilberto. El niño crece en el burdel rodeado de prostitutas en un ambiente no apto para él. Finalmente, Mercedes entrega a su hijo en adopción a un hombre adinerado quien lo educa. Gilberto se convierte en pintor y en ayudante de Diego Rivera durante la época de la Revolución Mexicana.

2202 Ménez Espinosa, Omar. Las flechas de apolo. Toluca, Mexico: UNAM, 2008. 211 p. (Arte Novela)

Novela situada en la pequeña ciudad de San Joseph Tolotzinco en 1829. La comunidad se ve afectada por una fuerte epidemia de viruela. Durante esa época no existían los medicamentos o vacunas actuales, de manera que el combate de esta enfermedad es el hilo que une la trama de la historia.

2203 Moch, Jorge. Dónde estás, Alacrán? México: Planeta Editorial, 2008. 279 p.

Literatura negra en la que se plasman, bajo el riesgo de llegar a ofender a personajes actuales, temas dentro de la sociedad y política mexicana. Sin duda, la búsqueda detectivesca le da un ritmo vertiginoso a la trama de esta bien lograda novela.

2204 Monsiváis, Carlos. Pedro Infante, las leyes del querer. México: Aguilar, 2008. 278 p.: ill. (some col.)

Una crónica-ensayo que con dejos de nostalgia, pérdida y orgullo repasan la vida del máximo ídolo mexicano, Pedro Infante. Una obra indispensable para aquellos que deseen adentrarse no sólo en la vida de este personaje sino en la época de ese México que muchos continúan añorando; la época de oro del cine mexicano.

2205 Montemayor, Carlos. La fuga. México: Fondo de Cultura Económica, 2007. 162 p. (Letras Mexicanas; 142)

Novela que narra, durante la década de los 70, la fuga del guerrillero Ramón Mendoza de las Islas Marías. Ramón en su búsqueda de libertad está dispuesto a todo para no permanecer prisionero bajo un sistema carcelario que en lo particular considera injusto. La narración de la novela es

eficaz y efectiva, mientras que el trasfondo político le otorga una seriedad que bien podría ubicar la trama en diversos periodos turbulentos de México.

2206 Naró, Rodolfo. El orden infinito. México: Planeta, 2007. 309 p.

Novela que va más allá de lo histórico ya que en ésta se conjugan diversos géneros y estilos como realismo mágico, varias voces narrativas y un número copioso de personajes. Además es un proyecto bastante ambicioso porque, a través de la protagonista Nina Ramos, se hace un recorrido de cien años de la historia de México. Novela bien estructurada e interesante que podría resultar un reto para lectores principiantes.

2207 Orea Marín, Augusto. La muerte del judío. Guadalajara, Mexico: Secretaría de Cultura del Gobierno del Estado de Jalisco, 2007. 440 p. (Col. Clásicos jaliscienses)

En esta novela destaca un estilo definido del autor ya que ha publicado más de dos decenas de libros por lo que cuenta con un sitio prodigioso en las letras jaliscienses. En este caso comparte la vida del judío, en un pueblo del sur de México, y todas las aventuras que lo rodean por su peculiar apariencia.

2208 Ortega Ojeda, Alfredo T. La inapetencia de Pedro. Autlán de la Grana, Mexico: Centro Universitario de la Costa del Sur: Univ. de Guadalajara, 2008. 162 p.

Colección de relatos de temática variada y en los que depuradamente se narran situaciones que involucran a diversos personajes. Los temas trabajados en este colección son enmarcados por la vida urbana y por un ritmo estrepitoso que, en ocasiones, genera confusión y alteración.

2209 Ortuño, Antonio. El jardín japonés. Madrid: Páginas de Espuma, 2007. 102 p. (Col. Voces literatura; 79)

Colección de cuentos agresivos que se alejan de los patrones narrativos tradicionales latinoamericanos. Aparentemente, el objetivo es encontrar, partiendo de la nostalgia, la ironía e incluso la violencia, narraciones que capten, en todo momento, la atención del lector.

2210 Osorio, Eduardo. El enigma Carmen: diálogos para su réquiem. Toluca, Mexico: Instituto Mexiquense de Cultura,

2008. 148 p. (Cruce de milenios) (Biblioteca mexiquense del bicentenario)

Carmen, la protagonista de esta intrigante novela, es asesinada misteriosamente. La investigación de este crimen se complica ya que además de haber contado con un ex-esposo diplomático, sostuvo varias aventuras con personajes importantes de su entorno. Conforme se va esclareciendo el caso, el lector se va percatando de la influencia de esta mujer en la vida de sus amantes y simultáneamente, de los puestos que ella desempeñó.

2211 Palou, Pedro Ángel. Cuauhtémoc: la defensa del Quinto Sol. México: Editorial Planeta Mexicana, 2008. 210 p.: bibl., maps. (Autores españoles e iberoamericanos)

Palou revisa la "historia oficial" del personaje histórico Cuauhtémoc. El narrador, el sirviente llamado Ocuilin, hace un recorrido detallado de la vida del último emperador azteca. Si bien, se llega a la conclusión que su final fue trágico, el autor pone en tela de juicio algunos acontecimientos que marcaron la decadencia de la civilización azteca.

2212 Palou, Pedro Ángel. Morelos: morir es nada. México: Editorial Planeta Mexicana, 2007. 269 p.: bibl., maps. (Autores españoles e iberoamericanos)

Obra en la que se pone al descubierto, a través de Jerónima Aguilar, el lado humano del héroe de Independencia, José María Morelos y Pavón. Esta es una novela biográfica en la que Palou, como creador, se toma cierto albedrío estilístico y narrativo con el que enriquece esta fascinante historia.

2213 Ravelo, Ricardo. Crónicas de sangre: cinco historias de los Zetas. México: Random House Mondadori, 2007. 127 p. (Col. De bolsillo)

Cinco crónicas que narran, sin tapujos, el funcionamiento de los Zetas, una de las bandas criminales más temidas en el territorio mexicano. La crueldad de estas historias es tan gráfica, que bien se podría deducir que son parte de una ficción, desafortunadamente, forman parte de la cotidianidad del México actual.

2214 Robleda, Eugenia. Bosque dorado teñido de sangre. México: Fondo Editorial Tierra Adentro: Consejo Nacional para la Cultura y las Artes, 2007. 173 p. (Fondo editorial tierra adentro; 338)

Los protagonistas de los cuentos de este texto son entes fabulosos, tales como vampiros, hadas e incluso insectos. Estos seres y sus misterios deambulan por la noche e interactúan con las personas, más allá de sus pesadillas. La autora, por medio del misterio, recrea los temores que sin duda acecharán a sus lectores.

2215 El rock es puro cuento. Prólogo de Guillermo Fadanelli. Presentación de Xardiel Padilla. Selección de José de la Paz. Monterrey, Mexico: La Rocka: Univ. Autónoma de Nuevo León, 2007. 130 p.

Esta antología de 17 historias es producto de un certamen de cuentos enfocados al rock. Los autores, en su mayoría jóvenes, además de compartir un gusto por ese género musical, también plasmaron, en muchos casos, sus inquietudes iniciales dentro del ámbito literario. Por lo tanto, el mérito de estos relatos recae en la frescura y experimentación literaria que, como el rock, suelen ser compartidos por los jóvenes y también por los no tan jóvenes.

2216 Ronquillo, Víctor. La Reina del Pacífico y otras mujeres del narco. México: Planeta Editorial, 2008. 205 p. (Temas de Hoy)

El autor, formado como periodista por muchos años, presenta nueve historias que tienen en común, como lo delata su título, que las protagonistas son mujeres relacionadas al mundo del narcotráfico. Estas historias constatan que el inframundo de esta redituable actividad no es sólo para los hombres. Hoy en día existen mujeres que operan en los cárteles más poderosos de México y Latinoamérica.

2217 Ruisánchez, José Ramón. Nada cruel. México: Ediciones Era: Consejo Nacional para la Cultura y las Artes, 2008. 196 p.

Novela de ritmo trepidante, cuenta una historia sobre hermandad y las diversas dicotomías en las que Raúl y Santi se ven involucrados: lealtad-traición, amigos-enemigos, amor-odio. La novela experimenta con diálogos bastante ágiles e intensos y provocan una lectura de un ritmo similar.

2218 Ruy Sánchez, Alberto. La mano del fuego: un Kama Sutra involuntario. México: Alfaguara, 2007. 364 p.

Obra cuya trama gira en torno al erotismo, al deseo, a esa mano de fuego que acaricia al palpar otro cuerpo y descubrir los puntos sensibles de éste. Ruy Sánchez ya ha tratado este tema de magistral manera y ésta no es la excepción, ya que conforme se avanza en la lectura, el deseo de continuar devorando las páginas de la novela incrementa.

2219 Sandoval Medina, Albaro. Lodo en tierra santa. México: Consejo Nacional para la Cultura y las Artes: Centro Cultural Tijuana, 2007. 181 p. (Col. Tierra adentro; 333)

El autor presenta una sociedad mexicana donde la esperanza ha dejado de existir, es decir, un país en ruinas que ha sucumbido, en su totalidad, ante las fuerzas de la violencia y la injusticia. Si bien, estamos ante una novela de ficción, podría parecer, desafortunadamente, que no está muy lejos de lo que, para algunos, se está convirtiendo en una dolorosa realidad.

2220 Santos Guevara, Criseida. Rhyme & reason. México: Consejo Nacional para la Cultura y las Artes, Dirección General de Publicaciones, 2008. 165 p. (Fondo editorial tierra adentro; 375)

Historia en la que el ritmo (rhyme) como se estipula en el título, es parte fundamental de la estructura de la novela. Además cuenta con una fuerte influencia del hip-hop, expresión con la que sus personajes marginados logran expresar sus más profundos sentimientos. Por último, el uso de términos e incluso frases en inglés enmarcan y otorgan mayor autoridad al mundo de rhyme & reason por el que deambula la protagonista Claudia Cisneros.

2221 Sarabia, Antonio. Troya al atardecer. Barcelona, Spain: Otra Orilla, 2007. 263 p.

Esta historia que se podría catalogar como novela histórica, reúne los componentes necesarios para mantener la atención del lector de principio a fin. Sin bien, no cabe duda que la historia de Troya ha sido estudiada en múltiples ocasiones, el toque peculiar de la presente es que se concentra en la vida de personas y en la búsqueda de su propia identidad.

2222 Schmidhuber de la Mora, Guillermo. Mujeres del volcán de Tequila: Teuchitlán. Guadalajara, Mexico: Univ. de Guadalajara, 2007. 212 p.

Excelente novela en la que se hace hincapié en la fuerza y persistencia de siete mujeres del Valle del Volcán en Teuchitlán, Jalisco. A pesar de mantener un arraigado sentido de maternidad y de la familia, esto no implica que permitan ser atropelladas por el imperante machismo de su entorno.

2223 Segura, Gerardo. ¿Quién te crees que eres? Mexico: Gobierno del Estado de Coahuila de Zaragoza, 2007. 124 p.

Obra narrativa cargada de suspenso y de sucesos inesperados. El protagonista inicia una pesquisa en la que surgen más preguntas que respuestas y en la que más de una ocasión se encuentra al borde del rotundo fracaso. El autor jamás se verá involucrado en ese tipo de desenlace gracias a una narrativa sucinta y a la cantidad exacta de detalles.

2224 Servín, Juan Manuel. Al final del vacío. México: Mondadori, 2007. 290 p. (Literatura Mondadori)

Novela cruda en la que el protagonista inicia la búsqueda de su mujer en la Ciudad de México. Por medio de su pesquisa descubrimos una ciudad en la que reina el caos, y la violencia forma parte del día a día. El México que presenta Servín es un tanto apocalíptico o dantesco, escenario que en ocasiones aparente convertirse en el protagonista de la historia.

2225 Sicilia, Javier. La confesión: el diario de Esteban Martorus. México: Editorial Jus, 2009. 277 p. (Tradición y ruptura)

Novela fuerte y valiente en la que se denuncian algunas de las situaciones conflictivas en las que se ha visto involucrada la Iglesia católica. La narración parte una confesión, del diario del padre Esteban Martorus y de la estrecha relación de éste con la población de Ahuetepec, México.

2226 Soler Frost, Pablo. Yerba americana. México: Ediciones Era: Consejo Nacional para la Cultura y las Artes, 2008. 187 p. (Biblioteca Era)

Novela que inicialmente fue un guión de cine, razón por la que relucen las técnicas fílmicas en esta obra. Desafortunadamente, a causa de lo anteriormente mencionado, en ocasiones no se desarrolla de manera convincente la trama central de la obra. Los protagonistas, Pato, Andrés y Ecuador, recorren México y Estados Unidos en un viaje que cambiará su vida.

2227 Toriz, Rafael. Animalia. Ilustraciones de Edgar Cano. Guanajuato, Mexico: Univ. de Guanajuato, Biblioteca Universitaria, Programa Editorial, 2008. 87 p.: ill. (Anaquel; 18)

El reino de animalia que presenta el autor está enmarcado por un humor burlón, casi una sátira contra lo preestablecido. En cuestiones de género, es un texto que se rehúsa a ser catalogado ya que hay ensayo, cuento, ficción e incluso dibujo, eso sí todo dentro del reino de animalia, y de un entorno bucólico.

2228 Trueba, Eugenio. Los pasos finale. Guanajuato, Mexico: Azafrán y Cinabrio Ediciones, 2007. 161 p. (Autores contemporáneos)

Novela nostálgica en la que se hace un recuento de las memorias de toda una vida: alegrías, tristezas, aventuras, añoranzas, amoríos y más. Un balance de vida que a la vez es una invitación para que, los que así lo dispongan, continúen llenando su existencia de recuerdos y hechos memorables, esos que suelen acompañarnos hasta nuestros últimos días.

2229 Uribe, Eduardo. Infiernos particulares. México: UNAM, Coordinación de Difusión Cultural, Dirección de Literatura, 2008. 105 p. (Textos de difusión cultural. Ediciones de punto de partida; 4)

Los personajes de los relatos viven en un infierno interno, llevan un yugo del cual no se pueden liberar. Los cuentos tambien muestran una ironía y en ocasiones una crudeza que expone las diferentes manifestaciones del sufrimiento humano. La crueldad de las historias invita a la reflexión y a la aproximación a los sucesos de la vida desde diversas perspectivas.

2230 Valenzuela Arce, José Manuel. Tecateando el recuerdo: recuentos y recreaciones fronterizas. Tijuana, Mexico: Consejo Nacional para la Cultura y las Artes: Fondo Regional para la Cultura y las Artes del Noroeste, 2007. 163 p. (Col. literatura)

Quince relatos fronterizos, bajacalifornianos, dan cuerpo a este libro. Como un intento de capturar la vida ágil de la frontera, el autor recurre a una escritura elaborada y al lenguaje coloquial de esa entidad. No obstante, se hace patente una nostalgia que emana de las historias del pasado que posiblemente no retornarán.

2231 Vega-Gil Rueda, Armando. Cuenta regresiva. México: Ediciones B México, 2007. 355 p. (Ficcionario)

Colección extensa de 31 cuentos breves dividida en ocho secciones que fue galardonada con el Premio Nacional de Cuento San Luis Potosí 2006. La narración de las historias es ágil y cuenta con variadas temáticas desde las mitológicas hasta las fantásticas. La estructura ha sido cuidadosamente trabajada y los desenlaces han sido pulcramente elaborados para mantener al lector al filo de la página.

2232 Velasco, Xavier. Éste que ves. México: Alfaguara, 2007. 241 p.

Obra en la que la narradora y protagonista adulta, Violetta, cuenta lo que fue la niñez del niño del cual no se rebela el nombre. El autor rescata a ese niño que fue, ese que permanecerá en su memoria hasta la muerte. Ahora se le proporciona al niño, al autor, la oportunidad de alzar la voz y ser escuchado, situación opuesta a la que vivió en su niñez.

2233 Venegas, Socorro. La noche será negra y blanca. México: Ediciones Era: Dirección de Literatura, UNAM, 2009. 133 p.

A pesar del delicado tema, la búsqueda del padre por su hija Andrea, esta novela por demás agradable, cuenta con una narrativa ágil y sencilla. Por lo tanto, es de muy amena lectura y bastante cautivadora para todo tipo de lector.

2234 Villaseñor, Arturo. Dilemas. Guadalajara, Mexico: Editorial Paraíso Perdido, 2008. 71 p. (Col. El Taller del Amanuense)

Siete relatos cuidadosamente elaborados y perspicaces que abarcan desde temas amorosos y de soledad hasta tópicos de amistad y secuestro. Lo que sí es una constante es que en estas historias se observa un reflejo de las situaciones que se llevan a cabo en algunas de las sociedades latinoamericanas.

2235 Yépez, Heriberto. Al otro lado. México: Planeta, 2008. 322 p.

Novela en la que se hace un ambicioso recorrido por las avenidas de Tijuana. Por medio del protagonista, Tiburón, el autor comparte intensas aventuras en su ciudad natal para así involucrar a sus lectores por ese deambular en el que frecuentemente saltan obstáculos y se crean nuevos límites.

Central America

JANET N. GOLD, *Professor of Spanish, University of New Hampshire*

THE SHORT STORY continues to be the preferred genre for many Central American fiction writers. Recognized masters of the short story such as Rodrigo Soto, Jacinta Escudos, and Dante Liano have added to their already impressive *oeuvre*, and a number of new voices were published in anthologies and single author works. There is tremendous thematic and stylistic variety among short fiction writers, but it is noteworthy that urban settings and characters, often marginalized, quirky, or disenfranchised, have definitely assumed prominence over rural locales and indigenous or traditional characters.

Some of the new anthologies follow the scholarly tradition of including works and authors that represent the stylistic and thematic trends of a particular country. A notable exception is Méndez's *Tiempo de narrar: cuentos centroamericanos* (item **2259**), whose selection includes writers from all seven countries of the isthmus (the inclusion of a Belizean writer is rare in Central American anthologies), men and women, internationally known writers, as well as others of local readership. With the publication of *Narradoras costarricenses: antología de cuentos* (item **2254**), Muñoz has now published anthologies of short stories by women writers of Guatemala (see *HLAS 62:2376*), Honduras (2003), El Salvador (2004), and Costa Rica (2006), invaluable contributions that make a wide range of previously difficult to access Central American short fiction available internationally. In addition to carefully researched selections of stories from the 19th century to the present, Muñoz introduces his anthologies with informative and thoughtful essays that contextualize and analyze the writers and their stories.

In a less academic vein, recent collections of stories in the series *Nuevas especies* showcase writing from Costa Rican Delia Barahona's workshop "Taller de la Palabra," whose participants, sociologists, agronomists, doctors, lawyers, and so forth, come together to share their work (see items **2244** and **2261**). A stated extra-textual concern of the series is the homogenization of culture in a rapidly globalizing Costa Rica and the stories are attempts to reclaim the centrality of the local.

The incursion into fiction by practitioners of other genres and by professionals in other fields has resulted in some original hybrid works, such as *Noticias de Villaflor* by Nicaraguan sociologist Jorge Canda (items **2238**), who creates a fictional utopian community to dramatize social problems and their potential solutions. It is apparent that the harsh realities of contemporary Central America and the desire to use fictional texts to send a message of urgency to readers are the driving forces behind these hybrid texts with themes of social concerns (for example, street children, domestic violence, environmental destruction). But of course anger, urgency, and frustration have long been present in Central American fiction and writers continue to grapple with how to channel these passions. Costa Rican writer and environmental activist Rossi takes on the challenge in her monumental historical novel *Limón reggae* (item **2257**), creating sometimes larger than life characters whose thoughts and conversations convey the sweep of political corruption, idealism, and despair in the last decades of the 20th century, while Castellanos Moya's intense psychological tour de force, *Insensatez* (item **2242**), probes the complexities of the individual's response to violence.

A disheartening setback in Central American letters has been the response by the Ortega administration of Nicaragua to writing that it perceives as critical of its policies or prominent figures. Official criticism of Ernesto Cardenal's memoir, *La revolución perdida* (item **2240**) and subsequent threats to incarcerate the venerable priest, poet, and long-time activist were met with immediate disbelief and public protest both in Nicaragua and throughout the international community, which was apprised of these developments through the web. A similar attempt to censure Sergio Ramírez, who has been eloquent and outspoken in his criticism not only of the Ortega regime, but of the Nicaraguan revolutionary process in general, was met with outrage in blogs and web pages. The tense political situation in neighboring Honduras has inspired a national outpouring of resistance via creative expression in all genres and media, from video to music to the written and spoken word. Both of these situations have dramatized the increasingly prominent role that the Internet plays in Central American cultural expression. Online reviews and blogs publish short fiction, book reviews, news about literary conferences, critical essays, and the personal musings of writers.

Readers of Central American fiction mourned the loss in 2007 of two preeminent cultural figures: Franz Galich, whose proposed Cuarteto de Centroamérica remains unfinished, and Roberto Castillo, philosopher and author of short fiction and novels, the most recent being *La guerra mortal de los sentidos*.

PROSE FICTION

2236 Ak'abal, Humberto. De este lado del puente: relatocuento. Totonicapán, Guatemala: Ediciones Tz'ukulik, 2006. 142 p.

A collection of "cuentorelatos" by celebrated Guatemalan poet Humberto Ak'abal. Some of the pieces were also included in his first prose publication, *Grito en la sombra* (2001). Like his poetry, these short narratives reflect elements of his K'iché Maya worldview and experiences, such as a closeness with nature imbued with awe and respect and the suffering wrought by poverty and alcohol. They are quirky, intimate, and deceptively simple.

2237 Belli, Gioconda. El infinito en la palma de la mano. Barcelona: Seix Barral, 2008. 237 p.: bibl.

An imaginative recreation of the story of Adam and Eve, told from the perspective of an inquisitive, questioning and gently feminist Eve, in what we have come to recognize as Belli's lush, lyrical prose. The novel was awarded the Premio Biblioteca Breve (Spain) as well as the Premio Sor Juana Inés de la Cruz (Mexico), perhaps more as a well-deserved homage to the author's lifetime accomplishments than due to the merits of the novel, which is beautifully written but predictable.

2238 Canda, Jorge. Noticias de Villaflor. Managua: Amerrisque, 2006. 281 p.

A hybrid of novel, didactic essay, and ethical reflection, this text exemplifies the phenomenon of individuals successfully established in nonliterary careers who are bringing their particular knowledge and expertise to the writing of fiction. In this case, sociologist Jorge Canda creates a fictional utopian community concerned with neoliberal economics, environmental destruction, and other contemporary social ills. The informational and didactic elements of his text are skillfully woven into the narrative but are sometimes heavy-handed and tedious.

2239 Cardenal, Ernesto. Las ínsulas extrañas. Managua: Anamá Ediciones Centroamericanas, 2002. 559 p.: index. (Memorias; 2)

In this second volume of his memoirs (vol. 1 was published as *Vida perdida* along with *Los años de Granada* under separate cover), Cardenal recounts his years in a seminary in Colombia and the founding of the now legendary community on the island of Solentiname in Lake Nicaragua. His narrative is peopled by a fascinating cast of characters and enriched by his honest and intimate musings on his personal evolution as a poet, mystic, priest, and revolutionary. The onomastic index assists the reader interested in locating references and anecdotes about personages as varied as Camilo Torres, Alan Ginsberg, and former California Gov. Jerry Brown.

2240 Cardenal, Ernesto. La revolución perdida. Managua: Anamá Ediciones Centroamericanas, 2003. 666 p.: ill., index. (Memorias; 3)

The author's first-hand account of Nicaragua's Sandinista Revolution, replete with anecdotes that communicate with the immediacy of orality, is the weaving together of an extraordinary life and a monumental piece of history. He tells a story rich with portraits that range from elementary school children to campesino poets to world leaders. With candor and directness and an impressive humility for such a major player, he recalls a seemingly endless flow of encounters, strategies, and dreams that made up the idealistic Sandinista Revolution. In the second half, he narrates the adventure of envisioning, organizing, and maintaining the revolutionary government, of which he was the Minister of Culture. The volume ends with a deep sadness and a nostalgia for the loss of those hopes and ideals and an indictment of certain Sandinista leaders who abandoned the ethics that initially characterized the Revolution.

2241 Castellanos Moya, Horacio. Desmoronamiento. Barcelona: Tusquets Editores, 2006. 210 p. (Col. Andanzas; 616)

In this narrative triptych, that begins with an extended dialogue, continues in the form of letters and ends with a monologue, Castellanos Moya dramatizes the falling apart of a politically connected Honduran family. Their estrangement begins in 1963 when the daughter leaves Honduras to live in El Salvador with her leftist Salvadoran husband, is aggravated by the 1969 war between the two countries, and finally collapses with the death of the matriarch 30 years later. A poignant portrait of the negative consequences of passionate nationalism.

2242 Castellanos Moya, Horacio. Insensatez. Barcelona: Tusquets Editores, 2005. 155 p. (Col. Andanzas; 582)

This first-person novel in 12 chapters explores the complex emotions and psychology of the narrator, who has accepted the job of copyediting a 1,100 page document that describes, in the words of the victims and witnesses, the torture and killing of the indigenous people of an unnamed Central American country. An important if excruciating portrait of the toll violence takes on human sensibility.

2243 Castillo, Roberto. La tinta del olvido. San José: Editorial Costa Rica, 2007. 98 p.

An intriguing blend of science fiction and magical realism characterizes this last collection of stories by Honduran writer Roberto Castillo, published shortly before his untimely death in January 2008. Castillo's fascination with time, history, and memory informs these 12 stories, all of them rich in intertextualities and flights of the imagination, yet still rooted in the people and places of his country.

2244 Cuentos: espíritus locales. San José: Editorial Lumbre, 2006. 224 p. (Col. Nuevas especies; 2)

Volume 2 of the collection *Nuevas especies* brings together stories by the eight writers who contributed to vol. 1, *21 cuentos primitivos* (see item **2261**), as well as five additional voices. The inclusion of established writers such as Rodrigo Soto testifies to the positive reception of the first volume. The collection attempts to draw attention to the cultural specificities of Costa Rica and to be an antidote to the homogenizing effects of globalization.

2245 Darío, Rubén. Cuentos completos. Managua: Anamá Ediciones Centroamericanas, 2005. 329 p.: bibl.

This 2005 compilation of Darío's short fiction includes 96 texts and reproduces the opening remarks by Ernesto Mejía Sánchez as well as the classic study of Darío's work by Raimundo Lida that appeared in the first "complete" edition of Darío's short fiction, edited by Ernesto Mejía Sánchez and published in 1950 by Fondo de Cultura Económica with a total of 77 texts. According to Nicaraguan scholar and bibliophile Jorge Eduardo Arellano, 96 represents 10 more than the 86 in the next "complete" compilation, a second edition of Ernesto Mejía Sánchez's 1950 work by Julio Valle Castillo. The 10 additions to the master's oeuvre are found in an appendix, meticulously annotated, allowing future scholars to judge their authenticity.

2246 Darío, Rubén. Cuentos completos. Edición y compilación de Ernesto Mejía Sánchez; prólogo de Edgardo Buitrago; adiciones y nota de Julio Valle Castillo. Managua: Editorial Hispamer, 2007. 421 p.

This 2007 compilation of Darío's short fiction includes 89 texts: the 86 from Julio Valle Castillo's 1990 edition plus three additional texts placed in an appendix: "La pluma azul," "Verónica," and "Curiosidades literarias." In the prologue, a concise and very readable summary of Darío's entire oeuvre, Edgardo Buitrago acknowledges the 10 texts added to Valle Castillo's list by Jorge Eduardo Arellano in Editorial Anamá's 2005 edition (item **2245**), but gives no reason for including only three of them in this 2007 edition. It appears that the scholarly debate continues regarding which edition is the most accurate and complete.

2247 Escoto, Julio. El génesis en Santa Cariba. San Pedro Sula, Honduras: Centro Editorial, 2006. 400 p.

This magnum opus by Honduras' arguably most distinguished literary personage writing today recreates Afro-Caribbean history through an assemblage of characters of mythical proportions who live through colonization, evangelization, dictatorships, and revolutions. In the vein of so-called totalizing or master narratives that attempt to incorporate multiple and diverse facets of reality in a single text, Escoto employs parody, myth, and humor in this linguistically and stylistically Baroque text.

2248 Escudos, Jacinta. El diablo sabe mi nombre. San José: Uruk Editores, 2008. 102 p. (Col. Sulayom; 11)

A woman becomes a man; a young girl morphs into a crocodile; while her cat watches, a woman sinks her teeth into the flesh of a live bird. With these and 11 other stories of transgression, metamorphosis, and role reversals, Jacinta Escudos, one of Central America's most admired and anthologized fiction writers, creates charac-

ters, contexts, and exchanges at first glance surreal, but told with such directness, clarity, and understated conviction that the implausible becomes poetry.

2249 Flores, Ronald. El informante nativo. Colonia Centro América, Guatemala: F&G Editores, 2007. 211 p.

This provocative novel by one of Guatemala's most original, serious, and prolific young writers traces an indigenous family's responses to the challenges and opportunities of contemporary urban life. A sometimes awkward and often angry mix of cynicism and sincerity, sarcasm, and social critique, the text presents a complex range of sensibilities, social theories, and astute if acerbic commentary on Guatemalan identity.

2250 González, Arquímedes. Qué sola estás Maité. Managua: Anamá Ediciones, 2007. 163 p.

This second novel by González takes place in Nicaragua and Costa Rica, where the protagonists migrate after Hurricane Mitch. Numbing daily routines in the context of overwhelming natural disasters and the emotional displacement accompanying social migrations make the individual's desires for liberty and prosperity seem unreachable utopias. The novel's stylistic experimentation and sophisticated interplay of voices have been praised by such luminaries of Nicaragua's literary critical establishment as Sergio Ramírez and Erick Aguirre.

2251 González Huguet, Carmen. El rostro en el espejo. San Salvador: Editorial Rubén H. Dimas, 2005. 78 p.

A lyrical journey into the violent history of her inherited country and into the mysteries of her own family's past brings the protagonist unexpected experiences and discoveries and involves her in the healing of generations of victims and victimizers. This novella by a much admired Salvadoran poet carries a message of peace and hope, won by facing the sins of the past and enacting a ritual of forgiveness.

2252 Liano, Dante. Cuentos completos. Guatemala: Tipografía Nacional, 2008. 344 p. (Col. Clásicos de la Literatura Guatemalteca; 4)

This collection of short fiction includes both of the author's published volumes of short stories as well as the previously unpublished *El viaje de los mártires*. This valuable addition to Guatemalan letters allows the reader to trace Liano's stylistic and thematic changes over time and appreciate his often dry humor and his characteristically ironic amorality. Like his predecessor, Augusto Monterroso, the consummate master of the very short story, Liano's best narratives are brief, startling, and satisfying. Includes an incisive introduction by Luis Eduardo Rivera.

2253 Méndez Vides. El tercer patio. Guatemala: Alfaguara, 2007. 99 p. (Serie Roja. Contemporáneos)

Six short stories by the author of the award-winning novel *Las murallas* (1997), these expertly crafted narratives, all with youthful protagonists, take place in the time of President Arbenz and the 1954 coup. The title refers to the interiormost patio of colonial-style dwellings in Antigua, an allusion also to the need felt by many Guatemalans of the author's generation to live surreptitiously, hiding their true thoughts and feelings in the face of censorship and repression.

2254 Muñoz, Willy Oscar. Narradoras costarricenses: antología de cuentos. San José: Editorial Univ. Estatal a Distancia, 2006. 328 p.

A panoramic selection of 24 short stories by Costa Rican women from Rafaela Contreras de Darío (1868–93) to the present, and including consecrated writers from the past such as Yolanda Oreamuno and Carmen Lyra as well as writers currently active, among them Magda Zavala, Linda Berrón, and Anacristina Rossi. The youngest writer included, Ailyn Morera, was born in 1965. The introduction outlines the thematic evolution of Costa Rican women's stories and concludes that women's voices are a significant and integral contribution to Costa Rican fiction, often leading the way in an exploration of themes of national importance. A bibliography of Costa Rican women's narrative completes the volume.

2255 Ochoa López, Moravia. Las esferas del viaje: cuentos escogidos, 1962–2004. Selección y prólogo de Enrique Jaramillo Levi. Panama: Univ. Tecnológica de Panamá, 2005. 253 p. (Col. Testimonios Nacionales; 9)

Because this selection of short fiction draws from the author's published work over a span of approximately 40 years and also includes 11 previously unpublished pieces, the reader can observe Ochoa López's stylistic evolution and experimentation and appreciate her deepening lyricism. She works primarily with female protagonists to create stories that artfully integrate the characters' inner voices with their outer realities and social contexts. Distinguished Panamanian writer and critic Enrique Jaramillo Levi chose the stories and wrote the thoughtful prologue, which praises Ochoa López for her unique voice.

2256 Peña, Alfonso. Labios pintados de azul. San José: Ediciones Andrómeda, 2006. 133 p.: ill.

These six stories by the author of *Noches de celofán* and *La novena generación* are urban tales of surreal juxtaposition, dark humor, and open-ended ironies. The characters are a diverse collection of divas, mannequins, and everyday San José eccentrics. Includes a brief lyrical and appreciative introductory essay by Carlos Barbarita.

2257 Rossi, Anacristina. Limón reggae. Alcalá La Real (Jaén), Costa Rica: Alcalá Grupo Editorial, 2008. 302 p. (Col. Libros gran reserva; 12)

Like its precursor, *Limón Blues*, which portrayed the history of the Afro-Caribbean community of Costa Rica in the first decades of the 20th century, this novel by celebrated Costa Rican writer and environmental activist Anacristina Rossi offers a panoramic, richly detailed, and passionately narrated history lesson. The female protagonist, through her engagement with all of the significant political battles of Central America from the 1960s to the present, is a leftist Everywoman, a larger-than-life player whose utopian ideals and activist commitments draw her into community organizing, guerrilla combat, adopting a war orphan, and even participating in a tattooing ritual with a gang. Believability aside, Rossi's obvious familiarity with the recent history, politics, and social issues of the isthmus make this a valuable text for present and future generations of Central Americans.

2258 Soto, Rodrigo. Floraciones y desfloraciones: cuentos. San José: Editorial Univ. Estatal a Distancia, 2006. 175 p. (Col. Vieja y Nueva Narrativa Costarricense; 91)

The 20 stories in this collection confirm Rodrigo Soto, one of Costa Rica's most anthologized short story writers, as a confident and accomplished practitioner of the genre. Like a talented actor capable of playing a wide range of characters, Soto creates narrative voices that ring true. His often understated and colloquial style belies a sly perceptivity that piques and surprises.

2259 Tiempo de narrar: cuentos centroamericanos. Antología de Francisco Alejandro Méndez. Guatemala: Editorial Piedra Santa, 2007. 310 p.: ill. (Col. Mar de tinta. Letras centroamericanas; 6)

The 35 authors gathered together in this excellent anthology hail from all seven Central American countries and 11 of the short stories were written by women. Internationally recognized authors such as Sergio Ramírez and Rodrigo Rey Rosa share the limelight with writers of more limited or local fame. This refreshing inclusivity, coupled with a fine selection of stories, make this anthology highly recommended for readers desirous of a panoramic view of contemporay Central American short fiction.

2260 Valdés, Elías. Vainita de ishcanal: fábulas. Chiquimula, Guatemala: Impresión Impr. Club, 2005. 138 p.

These 32 fables employ the traditional form of a dialogue between animals and/or plants to dramatize an obvious moral lesson. By the celebrated author of the novel *Tizubin*, these simple, modest, and direct tales make talking animals seem entirely natural. The large print format and abundant use of regional words and expressions suggest that this book would be appropriate for use in a multicultural classroom.

2261 21 cuentos primitivos. San José: Editorial Lumbre, 2005. 203 p. (Nuevas especies)

Eight Costa Rican writers, all members of Delia Barahona's "Taller de la Palabra" writers' workshop, have joined their voices in this refreshing collection of stories that offer glimpses into the idiosyncracies, characters, and locales of Costa Rica's past and present. The authors represent a range of professions—agronomist, lawyer, sociologist, journalist—but share a love of the written word and the well-told story.

2262 La vida breve: antología del microrrelato en Honduras. Edición de Helen Umaña. Guatemala: Letra Negra Editores, 2006. 176 p.: ill.

An excellent introduction to the *microrelato* or very short story by Helen Umaña, Honduras' preeminent literary critic, historian, and anthologizer. A clear and concise description of the genre is followed by a varied sampling of brief fiction from Honduras beginning with examples from the indigenous and Garífuna oral tradition and continuing through the 20th century.

LITERARY CRITICISM AND HISTORY

2263 Caratula: revista electrónica. Managua: Fundación Luisa Mercado, Hivos. <http://www.caratula.net/>

A bimonthly electronic cultural review established in August 2004. Provides a forum for Nicaraguan culture that includes generous attention to contemporary regional and international writers, artists, and filmmakers. Full-text articles are archived and available online.

2264 Erick Aguirre: crítica, literatura y cultura en general por el escritor nicaraguense Erick Aguirre Aragón. Nicaragua. <http://erickaguirre.blogspot.com/>

Lengthy and thoughtful reviews of contemporary Central American fiction by this Nicaraguan writer and critic.

2265 Espacio fílmica: Jacintario. Cadiz, Spain: Delgado & Barrera. <http://www.filmica.com/jacintaescudos/>

Salvadoran writer currently living in Costa Rica, Jacinta Escudos maintains a lively and eclectic blog with interviews, opinions, and links to items of interest related to Central American culture.

2266 Istmo: revista virtual de estudios literarios y culturales centroamericanos. Wooster, Ohio: College of Wooster, Dept. of Spanish. <http://collaborations.denison.edu/istmo/>

Published online semi-annually since 2001, *Istmo* provides a scholarly forum for academic essays and reviews of Central American literature. Sponsored by the Instituto de Historia de Nicaragua y Centroamérica (IHNCA-UCA), the Centro de Investigación en Identidad y Culturas Latinoamericanas (CIICLA) and The College of Wooster and Denison University. Issues center on themes such as historiography, testimonial narratives, and autobiography. In Spanish. Full-text articles archived and available online.

2267 Maga: revista panameña de cultura. Panama: Univ. Tecnológica de Panamá. <http://www.utp.ac.pa/secciones/maga/maga.htm>

Maga, now archived with full text available online, is a semi-annual review sponsored by the Universidad Tecnológica de Panamá that has been publishing Central American poetry, fiction, essays, and news of cultural events since 1984. The editor, Enrique Jaramillo Levi, is a distinguished Panamanian writer and literary critic. The editorial board boasts such luminaries as Magda Zavala (Costa Rica), Vidaluz Meneses (Nicaragua), and Julio Escoto (Honduras).

2268 El ojo de Adrián: arte, literatura, Centroamérica. El Salvador. <http://www.elojodeadrian.com/>

Since its beginnings as a blog in June 2005, this eclectic and continuously evolving cultural space has published contemporary cutting edge art, music, poetry, short fiction, and cultural commentary from Central America in English and Spanish.

2269 Ronald Flores. [s.l.]: [s.n.]. <http://www.ronaldflores.com/>

This Guatemalan writer's blog is frequently updated with reviews and commentary on Central American fiction.

2270 Talpacojote: textos e imagenes. El Salvador. <http://talpajocote.blogspot.com/>

Salvadoran writer and cultural critic Miguel Huezo Mixco and artist María Tenorio contribute insightful reviews, photographs, and cultural commentary to their shared blog.

2271 Vargas Méndez, Jorge. Literatura salvadoreña 1960–2000: homenaje. San Salvador: Ediciones Venado del Bosque, 2008. 429 p.: bibl.

This ambitious attempt to document late-20th-century Salvadoran letters begins with a description of the country's sociopolitical context and continues with an exhaustive list of what appears to be most, if not all, writers of those four decades. Some are still alive, others have passed on, some have published their work, some have stopped writing. The author pays close and careful attention to all, mentioning biographical details of interest, participation in literary groups and workshops, and critical appraisals of their work. The number and variety of writers included make this a truly democratic contribution to the study of Salvadoran culture and reminds us that a national literature is the result of the works and interactions of many individuals and groups.

Hispanic Caribbean

DIANA ALVAREZ-AMELL, *Associate Professor of Spanish, Seton Hall University*
MYRNA GARCÍA-CALDERÓN, *Assistant Professor of Spanish, Syracuse University*

CUBA

LOS MAESTROS MODERNISTAS de la prosa cubana parecen dominar todavía el panorama de las letras del país, mientras los escritores más jóvenes inciden en narrativas que de un modo casi siempre oblicuo aluden a la convulsiva situación social del país. Los logros estéticos de Guillermo Cabrera Infante, Virgilio Piñera y Reinaldo Arenas, para mencionar los más notables, se imponen. Ante esa generación, en la ficción de los escritores contemporáneos la emigración, el exilio, la desconexión y la locura son temas privilegiados. Se publicó de manera póstuma el legendario título *La ninfa inconstante* de Guillermo Cabrera Infante (item **2285**), quien en vida solía contestar que ésta era la novela que escribía. Su viuda reunió sus capítulos descifrando las instrucciones dejadas en la impenetrable caligrafía del difunto escritor. Es un breve relato sobre las obsesiones y las traiciones del amor con el infalible trasfondo de La Habana de los años 50. Presentes están los juegos lingüísticos y conceptuales junto con las abigarradas alusiones culturales que caracterizaron el estilo de este escritor quien, no obstante, escribió prosa en un lenguaje diáfano, lejos del Neobarroquismo con el que a veces se identifica la literatura cubana.

La prosa esmerada en su claridad es también el mismo rasgo estilístico que caracteriza la prosa de Virgilio Piñera, aunque ambos escritores son en temática y otros aspectos estilísticos, dramáticamente diferentes. La importante colección de cuentos *Cuentos fríos; El que vino a salvarme* (item **2329**) se publica la emblemática editorial española Cátedra que con justicia divulga así la obra de uno de los que en vida fue de los grandes olvidados. Rescatado de manera póstuma en Cuba, en donde fue perseguido en vida, esta edición se suma a otras anteriores, aparecidas sobre todo en España, que ayudarán a divulgar la obra de uno de los grandes artífices de la prosa en español del siglo XX. Piñera empleó la lacónica ironía fría para presentar los aspectos absurdos de la existencia humana y la vida social, junto con cuentos de enorme sátira política que trascienden la temática incidental. Son cuentos que se leen hoy día y reflejan, como lo puede hacer una obra de arte, situaciones que se dan en la actualidad. La mecanización, la deshumanización, la corrupción y el sin sentido existencial son temas recurrentes en sus cuentos que nunca se desbordan en el sentimentalismo y se ajustan a las coordenadas que fija su "fría" ironía.

La editorial española Cátedra publica también la obra maestra de Reinaldo Arenas, *El mundo alucinante* (item **2278**), novela clave en su escritura y que marca un claro giro hacia el postmodernismo en las letras cubanas y latinoamericanas. Rescritura de las memorias del sacerdote mexicano decimonónico Fray Servando Teresa de Mier, su publicación cuando Arenas no había cumplido 30 años, significó que se estableciera un paralelismo entre escritor y sujeto novelado. En un curioso paralelismo entre su propia vida y la del fraile cuya vida noveló, Arenas fue perseguido y encarcelado por las autoridades de su país hasta que pudo huir en la confusión del éxodo del Mariel en los años 80. En la parodia postmoderna de Arenas, sin embargo, se esbozan los temas que desarrollará posteriormente, la rebeldía, la búsqueda por ampliar siempre los márgenes de la libertad y su aserto de la importancia de la expresión vital, artística e intelectual del individuo.

Antón Arrufat, el dramaturgo mejor conocido por su obra de teatro emblemática y censurada en los años 70 *Los siete contra Tebas* (ver *HLAS 56:4266*), prosigue ahora su carrera literaria restituido por las autoridades del país. Publica una breve colección de cuentos, la mayoría de corte fantástico, en que se privilegia el humor irónico y la atención a una prosa cuidada y despojada de artificios retóricos. *Los privilegios del deseo* incluye el cuento premiado "El envés de la trama", el más largo de la colección, sobre la obsesión literaria (item **2280**).

Otro escritor de la generación anterior, en este caso Orígenes, Lorenza García Vega sigue publicando con prosa experimental y elabora ejercicios estilísticos que recuerdan los de las vanguardias europeas en su "no-novela" en la que rompe con las expectativas de desarrollo de trama en su novela con un estupendo título

Devastación del Hotel San Luis (item **2304**). También cabe destacar que en Cuba se edita otra vez la historia sobre el contrabando de Enrique Serpa (item **2338**), un libro ambientado en la época antes de los 50 y es la novela más conocida de quien se dedicó principalmente al periodismo. De igual modo, reaparece la novela de Miguel Correa *Al norte del infierno* (item **2291**), novela emblemática del escritor que pertenece a la generación del Mariel. Tanto García Vega como Correa viven en Estados Unidos.

Llama la atención la cantidad de colecciones de cuentos sobre todo escrita por mujeres que aparecen en Cuba, ya sea de figuras establecidas en el ámbito nacional como Mirta Yáñez (item **2345**) o autoras más recientes como Aida Bähr (item **2281**). También es un género que aparece en la obra de escritores jóvenes como Ernesto Pérez Chang (item **2326**).

De los escritores que viven en Cuba pero son publicados fuera del país, preferiblemente en España y son, por tanto, conocidos en el exterior, cabe señalar Wendy Guerra, que publica novelas que de igual modo trata la temática femenina (item **2305**). No así Ena Lucía Portela cuyo locus literario en *Djuna y Daniel* (item **2330**) es París y escribe la historia novelada de la escritora británica de culto, Djuna Branes. Leonardo Padura, mejor conocido por su serie de novelas negras sobre el detective ficticio Mario Conde, en su novela más reciente *El hombre que amaba los perros* (item **2324**), se basa en la historia real aunque poco conocida de la vida habanera de Ramón Mercader, el asesino de Troski. Pedro Juan Gutiérrez publica una crónica de viajes dentro de la isla en la que aparecen imágenes duras que caracterizan al conocido escritor del llamado realismo sucio. La profesora Margarita Mateo Palmar hace su primera incursión en la novela con una historia que tiene como escenario el manicomio y como protagonista una mujer que ha perdido la cordura. La novela fue premiada en Cuba.

También aparecen las obras de varios escritores que viven fuera de Cuba. En primer lugar, cabe mencionar la novela histórica premiada por Alfaguara basada en la vida de un personaje histórico del circo internacional del siglo XIX, la cubana *Chiquita* de Antonio Orlando Rodríguez (item **2334**). Abilio Estévez radicado en Barcelona publica dos novelas sobre el desarraigo, *El navegante dormido* en 2008 (item **2297**) y *El bailarín ruso de Montecarlo* en 2010 (item **2296**). Daina Chaviano presenta tres cuentos largos en donde la imaginación y lo improbable deciden las tramas en *Historias de hadas para adultos* (item **2290**), prosiguiendo así una prolífica producción desde Cuba, como el caso de Estévez y de la popular escritora radicada en Francia, Zoé Valdés, quien publicó una historia con elementos de ficción en su crítica hacia el fenómeno político en Cuba (item **2340**). [DAA]

REPÚBLICA DOMINICANA

Mientras hay escritores como Amado Alexis Chala, Emilia Pereyra y Ligia Minaya Belliard que se han dedicado a escribir novelas, cabe recordar que los dos novelistas de origen dominicano más conocidos, Julia Álvarez y Junot Díaz, escriben en inglés. Lo que parece destacarse más en la República Dominicana es la amplia selección de cuentos y además la conservación del patrimonio literario con la publicación de textos importantes para la literatura dominicana. Sin duda, la publicación de una amplia selección de cuentos que incluyen a escritores importantes como Juan Bosch con el título *Colección pensamiento dominicano, volumen II, Cuentos* implica una conservación del acervo literario dominicano (item **2348**). De igual modo, ése parece ser el motivo de la recopilación de cuentistas femeninas que presenta la estudiosa Emelda Ramos. Ella ha reunido escritoras desde el principio del siglo XX hasta algunas muy recientes en una colección titulada *Antología de cuentistas dominicanas* (item **2276**). También se ve ese deseo de conservar el legado literario nacional en la publicación de la breve novela, *El terrateniente* (item **2275**), que había circulado sólo dentro de un círculo cerrado de amistades del autor y ahora reaparece para el público en general. El otro factor importante en esta literatura es el tema del éxodo dominicano que se destaca en la obra de escritores como Ligia Minaya Belliard (item **2318**) y Eduardo Lantigua (item **2308**). [DAA]

PUERTO RICO

In recent decades, Puerto Rican literature has shown an unrelenting march towards heterogeneity. If in previous decades it was relatively easy to pinpoint a few central literary figures and established publishing houses such as Ediciones Huracán or Editorial de la Universidad de Puerto Rico that led the way in creating, for better or worse, a sense of canonical literature, this no longer seems to be the case. Even the core circuits of critical evaluation of published works such as "En Rojo," "Diálogo," the literary supplements of newspapers such as *El Nuevo Día*, and recognized, well-established academic journals have been slowly substituted by more immediate, electronic means of dissemination such as online journals and blogs. The literary journals that still remain struggle for survival.

The works annotated for *HLAS 66* speak about a series of interesting trends and developments in the new millennium. Three, in particular, stand out. The craft of writing, its professional development, and the critical spaces that nurture their creation and growth are highlighted in several anthologies. Two of the works reviewed, *Vivir del cuento* (item **2344**) and *Cuentos de oficio. Antología de cuentistas emergentes en Puerto Rico* (item **2292**), originate from writers who have participated in writing workshops and graduate writing programs. In the past, writing workshops, such as the one established at the Universidad de Puerto Rico by Enrique Laguerre in the 1950s, later led by Emilio Díaz Valcárcel during the 1970s, masterfully guided by Edgardo Rodríguez Juliá at the end of the 20th century, and more recently directed by Mayra Santos-Febres, have multiplied. Some, like the one related to the Masters Program in Writing at the Universidad del Sagrado Corazón, have tried to develop professional writers; yet others, like the ones Mayra Santos-Febres has been involved with, have consistently insisted on the dissemination of the work through anthologies and individual volumes, more recently even exploring electronic technologies of distribution such as the blogosphere. Other short fiction anthologies, such as *Relatos en espiga. Cuentos del Grupo Guajana* (item **2333**), speak of a long-standing collaboration amongst writers who have been associated for half a century, and seem to have become their own interpretive community. *Hecho a mano* (item **2317**), also nurtured by a workshop model, goes even further by including texts written by two authors in a show of the ultimate type of teamwork. An interesting insight into the process of writing is offered by *El libro de las imaginadas* (item **2287**), a text that deliberately draws the reader's attention to the creative process and the idea of others consuming the text.

A second trend of great importance is the varied and nuanced representations of gender, sexualities, and the body that have appeared in some of the most exciting and innovative works in the last two decades in the island and its diasporas. *Los otros cuerpos* (item **2323**), for example, is a comprehensive anthology of gay, lesbian, and queer texts from Puerto Rico that clearly establishes the serious production of primary texts and first-rate criticism of queer literature in the island.

Other texts, such as *Nocturno y otros desamparos* (item **2273**), use the image of the body ravaged by both pleasure and pain in a contemporary world at odds with the celebration and/or stigmatization of the body as a space to reflect upon and tease out issues of power and difference. The novellas *Sexo y cura* and *Carnada de cangrejo en Manhattan* (item **2272**) brilliantly explore everyday desires where both the physical body as well as the abstracted views of it are put into play. Probably the most disturbing reflection of the body is the one provided by Pedro Cabiya in his haunting text *La cabeza* (item **2284**). It is important to note that several of the texts reviewed reflect either directly or indirectly on gender and writing.

Several of the works reviewed are part of an interesting trend to make the past present and provide critical and historical foundations for poetry, fiction, and thought. The Puerto Rican Collection of the Editorial de la Universidad de Puerto Rico has been working on a series titled *Clásicos no tan clásicos*. It has embarked on a project to reedit and make available to a contemporary reading public iconic Puerto Rican novels published between 1880 and 1930, but virtually unknown today. Three of the books reviewed are by José Elías Levis (items **2309**, **2310**, and **2311**) and are part of that revival. An ongoing project to bring together in a carefully researched critical edition the works of Ramón Emeterio Betances is represented by two entries (items **2282** and **2283**). A similar attempt is shown in the publication of the first two volumes of the poetry and complete works of Francisco Matos Paoli (items **2314** and **2315**).

Beyond the three developments just underscored, in the annotated texts newer voices make an impressive appearance, particularly the above-mentioned Pedro Cabiya and the refreshing, mature voice of Francisco Font Acevedo (item **2301**). Established writers such as Emilio Díaz Valcárcel (item **2294**), Luis Rafael Sánchez (item **2336**), Ana Lydia Vega (item **2341**), Marta Aponte Alsina (item **2277**), and Mayra Santos-Febres (item **2357**) offer evidence of their continued trajectory. Of particular note are Vega's and Santos-Febres' keen observations on everyday life, urban culture, race, gender, and sexuality, as well as the specter of violence. The latter appears as a theme and concern in a number of the books reviewed. Finally, poetry is alive and thriving as a number of books clearly demonstrate. Of particular note is *Contraocaso*, by Hjalmar Flax (item **2732**), which forces readers to think about the evanescence of time and the power of words. [MGC]

PROSE FICTION

2272 Acevedo, Rafael. Carnada de cangrejo en Manhattan. San Juan: Santo Domingo: Isla Negra Editores, 2008. 46 p.: bibl. (Col. la montaña de papel; 69)

This double volume contains two novellas where writing, semantics, everyday desires and passions are intertwined with mystery and deception. The title *Sexo y cura* is a clever play on words where characters and situations are eventually parodied by the narrator and the writer for their Freudian interpretation of dreams and castration complex. *Carnada* is the story of an aspiring writer who attempts to explain the man as

subject, whose everyday life is altered by his inability to capture the essence of language and meaning. Original ideas and witty, well-crafted writing. [MGC]

2273 Agosto Rosario, Moisés. Nocturno y otros desamparos. San Juan: Terranova Editores, 2007. 125 p.

Twelve short stories dealing with love in the times of AIDS. Devoid of the urge to moralize, and lacking melodrama, these stories tell the lives of the survivors, their erotic exploits, and the relationships that have impacted their lives. The stories dialogue with the best tradition of urban gay literature.

2274 Agramonte, Carlos. El monseñor de las historias. Santo Domingo: Editora Búho: Ediciones FECSD, 2007. 347 p.

El escritor que es académico en su país, es conocido por narrativas de tema histórico. Esta novela toma lugar en gran parte en un seminario y trata sobre la fe religiosa de los distintos personajes. [DAA]

2275 Amiama, Manuel Antonio. El terrateniente: novela. Santo Domingo: Sociedad Dominicana de Bibliófilos, 2007. 202 p. (Col. Bibliófilos 2000)

Curiosa publicación de una novela que escribió originalmente en 1960 un periodista que al principio fue colaborador y luego opositor de Rafael Trujillo. La novela circuló entre las amistades de una tertulia literaria y ahora se publica para el público lector en general. Se basa en un personaje de la historia dominicana del siglo XIX, ya que su protagonista es uno de los hijos de quien fue presidente de la República Dominicana, Cesáreo Guillermo. [DAA]

2276 Antología de cuentistas dominicanas. Antóloga de Emelda Ramos. Guatemala: Letra Negra Editores; Santo Domingo: Ediciones Ferilibro, 2007. 119 p. (Col. Iberoamericanos; 8)

Colección de cuentos escritos por escritoras dominicanas que abarca ejemplos de la producción femenina de este género en el siglo XX. Su editora Ramos señala su carácter representativo ya que incluye cuentos muy heterogéneos en tema y estilo literario. [DAA]

2277 Aponte Alsina, Marta. Sexto sueño. Madrid: Veintisiete Letras, 2007. 241 p. (Col. Las eras imaginarias)

The author's most ambitious project to date in which she clearly supports the notion that dreaming is tantamount to knowing. The novel's protagonist, an anatomist, reconstructs the life of a man while dissecting his body. The novel blends life and death in the process of recreating broken lives and marginal subjects. Dreams become revelations. Beautifully written. [MGC]

2278 Arenas, Reinaldo. El mundo alucinante: una novela de aventuras. Edición de Enrico Mario Santí. Madrid: Cátedra, 2008. 319 p.: bibl. (Letras hispánicas; 616)

Se edita la importantísima novela de Arenas, uno de los escritores cubanos y latinoamericanos más destacados del siglo XX. La novela censurada en Cuba es, como señala el académico Santí en su introducción, de gran audacia formal. Es una versión libre y paródica de las Memorias de Fray Servando Teresa de Mier. [DAA]

2279 Arroyo Pizarro, Yolanda. Los documentados: novela. San Juan: Ediciones Situm, 2005. 172 p. (Novela)

This novel takes place on the west coast of Puerto Rico and deals with a difficult issue: the undocumented migration of Dominicans. A first novel by a published poet, it vividly details the drama of displacement, including disillusion and prejudice. Behind the fluid narrative is serious research; the author conducted extensive interviews with affected subjects. [MGC]

2280 Arrufat, Antón. Los privilegios del deseo. La Habana: Editorial Letras Cubanas, 2007. 153 p.

Colección de nueve cuentos de corte ecléctico que incluye cuentos fantásticos. El autor conocido por la obra teatral Los siete contra Tebas, dramaturgia que recibió el premio de la Unión Nacional de escritores cubanos en 1968 y le creó graves dificultades en Cuba y significó el ostracismo por varias décadas. La obra llegó a ser estrenada en Cuba en el 2007. Arrufat está ahora rehabilitado políticamente al punto que en el año 2000 recibió el Premio Nacional de Literatura. [DAA]

2281 Bähr, Aida. Ofelias. La Habana: Letras Cubanas, 2007. 86 p.

Esta brevísima colección de siete cuentos recibió el Premio Alejo Carpentier en el año de su publicación. Como señala el título son historias sobre la situación de la mujer, aunque la autora rechaza la rúbrica de feminista. [DAA]

2282 Betances, Ramón Emeterio. Obras completas. Vol. 1. Edición de Félix Ojeda Reyes y Paul Estrade. San Juan: Ediciones Puerto, 2008. 1 v.

First volume of the complete works of Puerto Rican founding father Ramón Emeterio Betances, 1827–98. A 30 year collaborative project by Félix Ojeda Reyes (UPR) and Paul Estrade (Paris VIII), this volume contains intimate correspondence found in libraries and archives in France, Italy, US, Puerto Rico, Venezuela, Dominican Republic, Spain, Cuba, and Denmark. See also item **2283**. [MGC]

2283 Betances, Ramón Emeterio. Obras completas. Vol. 2. Edición de Félix Ojeda Reyes y Paul Estrade. San Juan: Ediciones Puerto, 2008. 1 v.

Second volume of the complete works of Puerto Rican founding father Ramón Emeterio Betances, 1827–1898. A 30 year collaborative project by Félix Ojeda Reyes (UPR) and Paul Estrade (Paris VIII), this volume contains Betances' medical and scientific writings. Topics include hygiene, eye care, public health, and a piece on abortion. See also item **2282**. [MGC]

2284 Cabiya, Pedro. La cabeza. 2. ed. San Juan: Isla Negra, 2008. 60 p. (Col. La montaña de papel)

Cabiya is one of the most innovative and fearless young contemporary Puerto Rican writers. After the resounding success of his two previous collections, in this text he brings together an interesting blend of erotic tales and science fiction. At times cruel and grotesque, this utterly original and disturbing book is well written and not easily forgotten. [MGC]

2285 Cabrera Infante, Guillermo. La ninfa inconstante. Barcelona: Galaxia Gutenberg: Círculo de Lectores, 2008. 283 p.

Por muchos años, Cabrera Infante respondía infaliblemente el título de esta novela a la pregunta de qué estaba escribiendo. Aparece de manera póstuma al cuidado de su viuda Miriam Gómez, la historia de amor entre una adolescente errática y un hombre inconstante. El relato lleva la impronta reconocible de Cabrera Infante con sus juegos verbales, su intertextualidad con la literatura y el cine y con el trasfondo de La Habana, su inolvidable ciudad, alegre y violenta, de los años 50. [DAA]

2286 Carballo, Antonio. Adiós, camaradas. Madrid: Editorial Funambulista, 2007. 248 p. (Col. Literadura)

Novela ganadora del Premio de Primera Novela Mario Lacruz en 2006 en Barcelona, el escritor cubano elabora en la historia de un cosmonauta ruso una sátira del totalitarismo. [DAA]

2287 Cardona, Sofía Irene. El libro de las imaginadas. San Juan: La Editorial Univ. de Puerto Rico, 2008. 229 p.

A fascinating and original look at the process of writing. These narrative pieces delve critically into everyday occurrences to create works of rich fiction. Three characters: the narrator, *n*, and Eva share their joys and difficulties in molding and creating their work, allowing the reader a glimpse into how to observe, organize, and ultimately shape these memorable characters. [MGC]

2288 Casanova, Tina. En busca del cemí dorado. Hato Rey, Puerto Rico: Publicaciones Puertorriqueñas, 2007. 393 p.

This book is a follow up to *El último sonido del caracol* (2005). It traces a Puerto Rican family 20 generations back to their Taíno roots in the context of a modern mystery. The text is a pretext to reflect on the Caribbean's indigenous past and its contributions to the history of the region. [MGC]

2289 Chalas, Amado Alexis. Ciudad de lodo: una historia de ayer. Santo Domingo: Dirección General de la Feria del Libro, 2007. 190 p.: bibl. (Ediciones Ferilibro; 109)

Novela de perfiles psicológicos de un escritor que fue uno de los fundadores del Círculo Literario Yélida. [DAA]

2290 Chaviano, Daína. Historias de hadas para adultos. Barcelona: Minotauro, 2007. 172 p. (Pegásus)

Libro compuesto de tres narraciones largas: "La granja"; "La dama del ciervo" y "Un hada en el umbral de la tierra". Las tramas están configuradas por la fantasía, el misterio y la mitología. [DAA]

2291 Correa Mujica, Miguel. Al norte del infierno. Introducción de Reinaldo Arenas. 3. ed. Brooklyn, N.Y.: Artimana Libros, 2007. 150 p.

El libro del autor que perteneció a la Generación del Mariel, con la que se conoció a un grupo de escritores y artistas plásticos, se inicia con un breve y brillante ensayo de Reinaldo Arenas, quien encabezó ese grupo que se reunió en una revista cultural titulada precisamente *Mariel*. Arenas señala que en este texto de Correa, la palabra: es la "única salvación, la única arma, la suprema rebeldía" y concluye que este es un libro "imprescindible tanto para los que quieran conocer la actual realidad cubana . . . como para los que deseen disfrutar del talento de un autor". La portada lleva la imagen de Clara Morera, una importante artista cubana. [DAA]

2292 Cuentos de oficio: antología de cuentistas emergentes en Puerto Rico. Edición de Mayra Santos-Febres. Carolina, Puerto Rico: Terranova Editores, 2005. 125 p.

Edited by Mayra Santos-Febres, this anthology of emerging short story writers in Puerto Rico contains stories by 18 writers, of which the majority were born in the late 1970s and early 1980s. Most of the writers participated in creative writing workshops organized by Santos-Febres. A diversity of styles and topics are included. [MGC]

2293 De La Habana ha llegado—: cuentos cubanos contemporáneos. Madrid: Editorial Popular, 2007. 145 p. (Letra grande. Serie maior; 9)

Colección en la que aparecen relatos de distintos escritores contemporáneos como Marilyn Bobes, Daniel Chavarría y Rogelio Riverón. Los cuentos son de distintas tendencias literarias, tales como el realismo mágico, el absurdo y además hay una exploración de la sexualidad. [DAA]

2294 Díaz Valcárcel, Emilio. El dulce fruto. Guaynabo, Puerto Rico: Alfaguara, 2007. 285 p.

This novel takes place in the 1940s in a fictional Puerto Rican mountain village called Ochocalles. A confusing time in the island's history and its adolescent protagonist's life, the narration details the uncertainties, chaos, and search for direction of both country and character. Contains historical elements, sociological depictions, and adolescent angst. [MGC]

2295 Duchesne Winter, Juan. Gotcha. San Juan: Editorial Tal Cual, 2008. 169 p.: ill. (OM)

Seventeen short stories, all from the perspective of the same narrator who doesn't hesitate to get involved in the action he is conveying or become unreliable to the reader. The stories explore contradictory messages, a rare collection

of characters portrayed from an ironic, enigmatic, and fascinating point of view. [MGC]

2296 Estévez, Abilio. El bailarín ruso de Montecarlo. Barcelona: Tusquets Editores, 2010. 194 p. (Col. Andanzas; 726)

Historia de un estudioso cubano que en lugar de asistir a la conferencia en España, se dirige por su cuenta a Barcelona. Un saldo de cuenta, que busca lo perdido y se enfrenta a las consecuencias del desarraigo. [DAA]

2297 Estévez, Abilio. El navegante dormido. Barcelona: Tusquets Editores, 2008. 377 p. (Col. Andanzas; 659)

El novelista radicado en Barcelona, regresa al tema de La Habana. La trama incluye a varias generaciones de mujeres que se encierran en una casona de playa en espera de un ciclón. En esta novela, la emigración, la huída y el destierro son elementos importantes en el desarrollo de la trama. [DAA]

2298 Fernández de Juan, Adelaida (Laidi). La vida tomada de María E. Laidi Fernández de Juan. Ciudad de La Habana: Ediciones Unión, 2008. 86 p.

La autora, doctora de medicina de profesión, es conocida en Cuba por los temas que se centran en torno a la mujer. Presenta aquí una breve colección de cuentos sobre la cotidianidad habanera. [DAA]

2299 Fernández Pequeño, José Manuel. Tres, eran tres: relatos. Bogotá; Santo Domingo: Grupo Editorial Norma, 2007. 155 p. (La otra orilla)

Narraciones que giran en torno al tema del viaje por parte de este escritor de origen cubano radicado en la República Dominicana. Como se señala en la entrevista que antecede estos relatos, el autor dedica estas narraciones al tema de la diáspora, tan presente en la vida y en las manifestaciones culturales cubanas, pero, aclara este autor, desde el punto de vista del individuo. No aspira a ver el viaje desde un punto de vista ni sociológico ni político de denuncia, sino explorar lo que significa en la trayectoria de sus personajes. [DAA]

2300 Figueroa, Sylvia. Para mirar de cerca. San Juan: Fragmento Imán Editores, 2007. 61 p.: ill.

A collection of poems that forces the reader to consider the limits and possibilities of the visual image and written word as potential ways of seeing and thinking. Contains poems and photos that establish a productive dialogue. Beautifully written, poses interesting questions about the need for caution and suspicion. [MGC]

2301 Font Acevedo, Francisco. La belleza bruta. San Juan: Editorial Tal Cual, 2008. 317 p.

A tour-de-force by a writer who doesn't hesitate to take readers through an intense voyage of contemporary Puerto Rico's most memorable characters and social ills. A decidedly human collection of short stories, the writer combines exquisite original writing with a deep sense of compassion creating a most memorable reading experience. [MGC]

2302 Franco, Rafael. Alaska. San Juan: Instituto de Cultura Puertorriqueña, 2007. 167 p. (Col. Premios de literatura 2006. Cuento)

Rafael Franco Steeves is one of the new generation of Puerto Rican writers to emerge in the 1990s. *Alaska* is a collection of stories and winner of the 2007 First National Short Story Prize from the Institute of Puerto Rican Culture. The 10 short stories deal with characters facing limit situations. [MGC]

2303 García, C.J. Terror, Inc. Guaynabo, Puerto Rico: Alfaguara: Ediciones Santillana, 2006. 199 p.

A first novel, its title comes from the American comic book horror series from Marvel Comics starring the antihero Terror. It takes place in Puerto Rico at the end of the 21st century. This psychological detective novel engages a central concern in the world in general, and Puerto Rico in particular: violence. [MGC]

2304 García Vega, Lorenzo. Devastación del Hotel San Luis. Buenos Aires: Mansalva, 2007. 220 p. (Col. Poesía y ficción latinoamericana; 14)

Integrante del legendario grupo cultural Orígenes, se desmarcó al escribir una crítica del mismo. Ésta es una novela que el autor cataloga de "mala". García Vega escribe en un estilo reminiscente de las vanguardias del siglo XX. Su relato rompe con

las expectativas de un desarrollo narrativo y con personajes con los cuales el lector pueda sentir afinidad. Es una novela de corte experimental. [DAA]

2305 Guerra, Wendy. Nunca fui Primera Dama. Barcelona: Bruguera, 2008. 290 p. (Bruguera narrativa)

Las historia de tres cubanas en la época posrevolucionaria que ejemplifican las distintas actitudes vitales. Aparece la figura de Celia Sánchez, una mujer conocida en el ámbito político cubano. [DAA]

2306 Gutiérrez, Pedro Juan. Corazón mestizo: el delirio de Cuba. Barcelona: Editorial Planeta, 2007. 284 p.

Crónica de viajes a lo largo de la Isla, en que apunta sus experiencias, siempre en el estilo del llamado realismo sucio que ha caracterizado su narrativa. [DAA]

2307 Lalo, Eduardo. Los países invisibles. San Juan: Editorial Tal Cual, 2008. 183 p. (Temporalidades)

This hybrid text is a philosophical reflection of the author's observations on space, place, geography, and change. Suspicious as he is of all literary projects that voluntarily submit themselves to the whims of the canon, Lalo's writing positions itself at the margins of such an exercise, becoming a unique performatory act. [MGC]

2308 Lantigua, Eduardo. Un pez atrapado en el desierto: narrativa. Dominican Republic: Ediciones Caliope, 2007. 133 p.

Conjunto de cuentos en algunos casos brevísimos que tratan de personajes en su mayoría de procedencia hispanoamericana afincado en Nueva York. Estos cuentos dan un registro del fenómeno de la emigración en la literatura dominicana. [DAA]

2309 Levis Bernard, José Elías. Estercolero. Edición de Carmen Centeno Añeses. San Juan: La Editorial Universidad de Puerto Rico, 2008. 190 p.: bibl., ill. (Col. puertorriqueña) (Clásicos no tan clásicos)

The novel explores the impact of hurricane San Ciriaco (Aug. 8, 1899) on Puerto Rico economically, demographically, and on the day-to-day lives of the common people. This critical edition by Carmen Centeno Añeses includes an updated bibliography, a chronology, and photos of the period. An example of trade union literature. [MGC]

2310 Levis Bernard, José Elías. Las novelas *El estercolero* (1899), *Estercolero* (1901). Estudio crítico de Estelle Irizarry. 3. ed. San Juan: Ediciones Puerto, 2008. 372 p.: bibl., ill., map.

Includes the original edition of *El estercolero*, published in Ponce, P.R., Imprenta de Manuel López, 1899; the 2nd corr. and rev. ed., published in Mayagüez, P.R., Imprenta de "El Progreso," 1901, and a critical study by Estelle Irizarry. [MGC]

2311 Levis Bernard, José Elías. Vida nueva. Introducción, edición y notas de Estelle Irizarry. San Juan: Ediciones Puerto, 2007. 422 p.: bibl.

This critical edition by Estelle Irizarry of Levis' 1910 novel includes an updated bibliography, a chronology, and photos of the period. The novel looks at Puerto Rican society after 1898. The text occasionally assumes a moralizing tone, at others it seems prophetic; its 1935 edition revealed the intricacies of Puerto Rico's shift from Spanish to US colony. [MGC]

2312 Martes Pedraza, Daniel. Acá abajo vive gente: novela. San Juan: Santo Domingo: Isla Negra Editores, 2008. 323 p. (Col. la montaña de papel)

A first novel that brings together a varied and, at times, disparate series of characters who all converge in a working class neighborhood of Santurce, Puerto Rico called Villa Palmeras in the 1960s. The author, a longtime union leader, uses a fluid and visually descriptive language to create characters dealing with familiar, unresolved social problems. [MGC]

2313 Mateo Palmer, Margarita. Desde los blancos manicomios. La Habana: Editorial Letras Cubanas, 2008. 234 p.

Esta primera novela de una conocida ensayista académica obtuvo el Premio Alejo Carpentier para la novela en el año de su publicación. Concierto de voces que tiene como eje el ingreso al manicomio de una mujer. Los personajes acongojados y desdichados en donde el mar en lugar de expansión es un infinito muro de contención. Los personajes aparecen enloquecidos y desorientados por la cotidianidad del país, la escasez siempre peor, la división de la familia por el éxodo de algunos. El manicomio, más que el simple locus, es la gran metáfora que resume la vida de los personajes en esta novela. [DAA]

2314 Matos Paoli, Francisco. Raíz y ala: antología poética. Vol. 1. Selección, introducción y notas de Luis de Arrigoitia. San Juan: Univ. de Puerto Rico, 2006. 1 v., 973 p.: ill.

Wide selection of poetic works by Puerto Rican poet Francisco Matos Paoli published between 1930 and 1979. Selection, introduction, and notes by Luis de Arrigoitia. Includes a revealing "Spiritual Autobiography" that speaks to his nationalist fervor and poetic connections. The anthology establishes eight creative periods. Volume I contains works from the first two. [MGC]

2315 Matos Paoli, Francisco. Raíz y ala: antología poética. Vol. 2. Selección, introducción y notas de Luis de Arrigoitia. San Juan: Univ. de Puerto Rico, 2006. 1 v., 973 p.: ill.

Second volume of a major anthology of the poetry of Puerto Rican poet Francisco Matos Paoli. Selection, introduction and notes by Luis de Arrigoitia. Contains "Cancioneros" published between 1969–80 as well as poems written through the end of his life (2000). A few pieces published posthumously are also included. [MGC]

2316 Medina Carrero, Alberto. Primer viernes: recuerdos de un joven escolar. Puerto Rico: Letra 2 Editores, 2007. 129 p. (Col. Álbum)

A personal memoir of self discovery told through the eyes of an adolescent who used the atonement evoked by the first Friday of the month in the religious Catholic calendar to learn about himself and his environment. The action takes place during the years of 1955–68. [MGC]

2317 Méndez, Helena and Andrés Candelario. Hecho a mano. San Juan: Isla Negra Editores, 2005. 83 p. (Col. El rostro y la máscara)

An interesting and innovative collaborative project. Two authors share the slim volume with several individual stories as well as a number of stories written together. The importance of writing workshops comes to bear (one of the authors, Andrés Candelario, was the driving force of one of them). Interesting attempt to erase the specificity of gender writing. [MGC]

2318 Minaya Belliard, Ligia. Mi corazón tiembla en la sombra: novela. Santo Domingo: Ediciones Librería La Trinitaria, 2007. 114 p.

Novela de corte detectivesco que aborda el problema de la frontera y la emigración. Es la segunda novela de esta escritora y periodista radicada en los Estados Unidos. [DAA]

2319 Monclova Vázquez, Héctor Iván. El dragón de la playa. San Juan: Santo Domingo: Isla Negra Editores, 2008. 131 p. (Col. el rostro y la máscara)

A collection of short stories that effortlessly weaves together contemporary urban short stories where magical realism meets the classical world, warriors from the ancient orient share narrative space with heroes of contemporary popular music such as Ismael Rivera, and where the craft of writing is assumed at the margins of canonical expectations. [MGC]

2320 Montañez, Carmen L. Pelo bueno, pelo malo. Carolina, Puerto Rico: Terranova Editores, 2006. 142 p.

This novel is a first novel by the author, narrated through fragmented monologues that reflect archetypal female voices. It tells the story of a woman who, in spite of her fears, is successful in assuming control of her life. Shows many elements of ambiguity, Caribbean hybridity and multiplicity of voices. [MGC]

2321 Morrison, Mateo. Un silencio que camina: novela. Santo Domingo: Editora Búho, 2007. 102 p.

Breve novela de un autor más conocido en la República Dominicana como poeta. La trama gira sobre un triángulo sentimental entre jóvenes que pone a prueba la amistad entre dos muchachos. [DAA]

2322 Ocasio, Carlos. Tríada de abril, cuentos. Guaynabo, Puerto Rico: OCA Books, 2006. 66 p.

The three texts in this first collection of short stories, set in San Juan, follow the downtrodden protagonists as they search for hope and a way out of their predicament. All three face limit situations: life, death, chaos, violence; all seek a second chance. Clear prose, lively dialogue. April is the cruelest month. [MGC]

2323 Los otros cuerpos: antología de temática gay, lésbica y queer desde Puerto Rico y su diáspora. Compilación de David Caleb Acevedo, Moisés Agosto Rosario y Luis Negrón. Introducción por Moisés Agosto Rosario. San Juan: Editorial Tiempo Nuevo, 2007. 403 p.

A comprehensive anthology of gay, lesbian, and queer texts from Puerto Rico. The collection includes poems, short stories, and excerpts from novels, alongside groundbreaking, critical essays. Combines works by classic authors such as Manuel Ramos Otero together with works by a younger generation of writers. All texts are in Spanish. [MGC]

2324 Padura, Leonardo. El hombre que amaba a los perros. Barcelona: Tusquets Editores, 2009. 573 p. (Andanzas; 700)

Historia que se basa en la vida de Ramón Mercader, el asesino de León Troski, que vivió y murió en Cuba. En un encuentro fortuito en la playa, un veterinario se encuentra con un misterioso hombre que dice llamarse "López" y tiene espléndidos perros. Es la última novela de este escritor que cultiva el género negro. [DAA]

2325 Pereyra, Emilia. Cenizas del querer. Santo Domingo: Editorial Letra Gráfica, 2007. 206 p. (Breve Letra Gráfica)

Segunda novela de la autora que recrea el ámbito de un pueblo del sur de la República Dominicana, en donde se escenifican los encuentros y desencuentros en un ambiente de traiciones sentimentales y prejuicios. [DAA]

2326 Pérez Chang, Ernesto. Variaciones para ágrafos: cuento. Ciudad de La Habana: Ediciones Unión, 2007. 137 p. (La Rueda dentada)

Breve colección de cinco cuentos previamente publicados en distintos periódicos y revistas. Se inicia con "Victoria Hugo", uno de los cuentos más conocidos de este escritor que ha recibido distintos premios literarios en Cuba. En estos relatos los personajes se desenvuelven en situaciones improbables e inusuales lo que dota a la trama un ambiente onírico en muchos casos. [DAA]

2327 Pérez Jiménez, Efraín. El piadoso. San Juan: Ediciones Puerto, 2005. 223 p.

A novel that attempts a familiar gesture: a reflection of Puerto Rican society in the first part of the 20th century. The impact of the presence of the US, the world wars, and the rural environment of the island are explored. [MGC]

2328 Pietri, Georgiana. Barabradya. San Juan: Editorial Instituto de Cultura Puertorriqueña, 2005. 215 p.

An experimental novel in which the author tells the story of several generations of a Puerto Rican family through highly sensitive characters, at times from the domain of the fantastic, others historically grounded. A train ride evokes a voyage that the story develops through the realms of psychology, semiotics, and play. [MGC]

2329 Piñera, Virgilio. Cuentos fríos; El que vino a salvarme. Edición de Vicente Cervera y Mercedes Serras. Madrid: Cátedra, 2008. 420 p.: bibl. (Letras hispánicas; 626)

Con esta nueva edición de la editorial Cátedra, se empieza a incorporar al importantísimo escritor cubano al legado general de la literatura en español. Piñera, escritor fundamental del siglo XX cubano, autor de cuentos imprescindibles y de la mejor obra teatral cubana de ese siglo, *Electra Garrigó*, no ha recibido aún su justo lugar, en parte debido al ostracismo político que se le impuso en Cuba hasta el final de su vida en 1979. Esta edición española recoge dos colecciones de cuentos, *Cuentos fríos* publicados originalmente en 1956 y *El que vino a salvarme* de 1970. Perteneciente al grupo Orígenes, se separa por diferencias estéticas con este grupo de escritores que dirigía el otro gran escritor cubano, José Lezama Lima, con quien estaba ligado Piñera en una relación complicada de amistad y distanciamiento. En estos cuentos, predomina el absurdo y la ironía. [DAA]

2330 Portela, Ena Lucía. Djuna y Daniel. Barcelona: Mondadori, 2008. 366 p. (Literatura Mondadori; 351)

Esta novela es la historia novelada, mitad hechos reales, mitad ficción, de la relación que unió a la escritora inglesa Djuna Barnes con el norteamericano Daniel Mahoney. El legendario locus de la bohemia del Barrio Latino de París es el escenario para la narración de esa amistad crispada por el amor, el alcoholismo y la literatura. [DAA]

2331 Ramos, Josean. Antes de la guerra. San Juan: Editorial Cultural, 2005. 255 p.

A war novel, Ramos traces the military experience of two expelled university students from recruitment and boot camp to their realization of the violence and horrors of war. Detailed attention paid to the depiction of the physical and psychological impact of learning how to kill. Includes moving stories of the 65th Infantry Regiment. [MGC]

2332 Ramos, Juan Antonio. La última aventura de la Pantera Rosa. Cataño, Puerto Rico: Ediciones SM, 2008. 150 p. (Gran angular. Alerta roja)

Ramos tackles in this novel a series of well-known social problems: family violence, social prejudice, drugs, and despair. Written as an homage to those who survive these ills, and based on a real story, the text also shows the redeeming power of love, solidarity, and, above all, imagination. Impeccably written. [MGC]

2333 Relatos en espiga: cuentos del Grupo Guajana. Selección, investigación, notas y bibliografía de Reynaldo Marcos Padua. San Juan: Ediciones Huracán, 2007. 232 p.: bibl.

During the tumultuous 1960s a group of Puerto Rican poets created a journal called *Revista Guajana*. Their political and esthetically revolutionary poetry reflected the heightened sensibilities of the time. This anthology includes 14 *Guajana* writers in their capacity as writers of fiction. Their work remains varied, diverse, and reflective of their time. [MGC]

2334 Rodríguez, Antonio Orlando. Chiquita. Bogotá: Alfaguara, 2008. 550 p.: ill.

Novela histórica basada en la vida de una cubana del siglo XIX que se hizo famosa en el circo en donde se mostraba como rareza precisamente por medir 26 pulgadas. Es la memoria imaginaria que se basa en los pocos documentos y fotografías de quien en vida viajó por el mundo como artista de vaudeville. La novela recibió el prestigioso premio Alfaguara en el año de su publicación. [DAA]

2335 Rodríguez Soriano, René. Betún melancolía. Santo Domingo: Dirección General de la Feria del Libro, 2008. 221 p. (Ediciones Ferilibro; 116)

Colección de cuentos escritos por este autor dominicano que se inició en las letras como poeta para luego transformarse en prosista. Esta colección fue presentada en la Feria del Libro de Santo Domingo y recoge relatos de distintas épocas. Según José Rafael Lantigua, su prologuista, en los cuentos de Rodríguez Soriano se nota el influjo de Cortázar y es uno de los narradores más importantes de finales del siglo XX en la literatura dominicana. [DAA]

2336 Sánchez, Luis Rafael. Indiscreciones de un perro gringo. Guaynabo, Puerto Rico: Alfaguara, 2007. 199 p.

Sánchez's novel recounts the story of the "First Dog" of the US during Bill Clinton's presidential term (1993–97). Thanks to Buddy, we are privy to the ins and outs of life in the White House including the juicy details of the Monica Lewinsky ordeal. Humor, parody, and witty double-entendre make for a memorable reading experience. [MGC]

2337 Sánchez-Boudy, José. Cuentos de una vida vivida. Miami, Fla.: Ediciones Universal, 2007. 105 p. (Col. Caniquí)

Colección de cuentos del prolífero escritor que en su obra se dedica a breves relatos de la vida diaria y las costumbres cotidianas de la Cuba republicana. [DAA]

2338 Serpa, Enrique. Contrabando. La Habana: Editorial Letras Cubanas, 2007. 190 p. (Biblioteca literatura cubana)

Se edita este libro del narrador vanguardista. La novela escrita originalmente en los años 30 capta el ambiente, el lenguaje de hombres de mar dedicados al contrabando. La novela es conocida por reflejar de manera certera mediante sus personajes, en donde se usa el monólogo interior, un momento particular en la historia nacional. [DAA]

2339 Ureña Rib, Fernando. Las cuatro patas del diablo: cuentos. Santo Domingo: Latin Art Museum, Fundación Ureña Rib, 2007. 277 p.: ill.

Estos textos del pintor dominicano van acompañados por sus propios dibujos. [DAA]

2340 Valdés, Zoé. La ficción Fidel. Barcelona: Planeta, 2008. 375 p. (Autores españoles e iberoamericanos)

¿Historia novelada o novela ahistórica? La novelista no reclama fidelidad histórica en su recuento de su historia-ficción con la que pretende desmontar los supuestos del fidelismo. [DAA]

2341 Vega, Ana Lydia. Mirada de doble filo. San Juan: Editorial Univ. de Puerto Rico, 2008. 357 p.: index.

A volume of contemporary chronicles, many of which had previously appeared in local Puerto Rican newspapers. Topics include space, place, urban life, popular culture, memory, public festivities, death, war, politics, and literature. Written as tales, testimonials, dialogues, obituaries, and critical articles, the essays are keen observations, many filled with satire and parody. [MGC]

2342 Vega Serova, Anna Lidia. Ánima fatua. La Habana, Cuba: Letras Cubanas, 2007. 279 p. (La novela)

Novela que narra la historia de una juventud escindida por la doble identidad cubana y rusa tal como es vivida por la joven protagonista. La novela es de corte autobiográfico ya que relata la vida de una adolescente de madre rusa y padre cubano. Narración femenina que narra las tensiones entre madre e hija. [DAA]

2343 Viajeros del rocío: 25 narradores dominicanos de la diáspora. Compilación de Rubén Sánchez Féliz. Santo Domingo: Secretaría de Estado de Cultura, Editora Nacional, 2008. 225 p. (Col. Ultramar)

Esta colección incluye a varios escritores que viven fuera de la República Dominicana y así se deja testimonio literario del fenómeno de emigración en este país. Se incluye un cuento de Junot Díaz, escritor de procedencia dominicana muy conocido en los Estados Unidos. [DAA]

2344 Vivir del cuento: antología. Textos de Algrín Carmona, Juan Félix et al. Viejo San Juan: Terranova Editores, 2009. 141 p.

This anthology of contemporary short stories is a product of the Sagrado Corazón University's writer's workshop, directed by Luis López Nieves. Eight writers, Juan Félix Algarín Carmona, Isamari Castrodad, Shara Lávender, Blancairis Miranda-Merced, Héctor Morales Rosado, Luccia Reverón, Sandra Santana Segarra and Andrés O'Neill, contribute three stories each to this varied collection. [MGC]

2345 Yáñez, Mirta. El búfalo ciego y otros cuentos. Ciudad de La Habana: Ediciones UNIÓN, 2008. 181 p.

Colección de cuentos de una escritora conocida en Cuba. Tratan sobre la vida de todos los días. [DAA]

LITERARY CRITICISM AND HISTORY

2346 Cancio Isla, Wilfredo. Crónicas de la impaciencia: el periodismo de Alejo Carpentier. Madrid: Editorial Colibrí, 2010. 381 p.: bibl., index.

Cuban-American journalist Wilfredo Cancio assembled here a large number of contributions by Alejo Carpentier to newspapers in Spain and Latin America starting in the 1920s. The renowned literary critic Roberto González Echevarría has noted that the breadth of coverage in this work provides an important insight into Carpentier. [G.M. Dorn]

2347 Carpentier, Alejo. Cartas de Carpentier. Edited by Roberto González Echevarría. Madrid: Editorial Verbum, 2008. 182 p.: bibl., ill. (Verbum ensayo)

Important compilation of correspondence between Cuban master Alejo Carpentier and literary critic Roberto González Echevarría, who is the the world renowned expert on the iconic Cuban literary figure. In addition to the 26 letters and a telegram, the work features an introduction, insightful critical essays, and a hitherto unpublished interview with Carpentier in 1973. Of interest to all those studying Cuban literature. [G.M. Dorn]

2348 Colección pensamiento dominicano. v. 2, Cuentos. Santo Domingo: Banreservas: Sociedad Dominicana de Bibliófilos, 2008. 1 v.: bibl.

Como indica el título, es una colección de ensayos que analizan el cuento dentro de la literatura dominicana, además de los cuentos mismos. Incluye varios ejem-

plos de diversos autores entre los cuales se destacan uno de los escritores más conocidos de la República Dominicana, Juan Bosch además del conocido Virgilio Díaz Grullón. [DAA]

2349 Díaz Infante, Duanel. Palabras del trasfondo: intelectuales, literatura e ideología en la Revolución Cubana. Madrid: Editorial Colibrí, 2009. 213 p.: bibl.

Análisis de las distintas posturas ideológicas adoptadas por los escritores cubanos. Es un repaso apasionado no académico de los distintos momentos en que la literatura y la política se han encontrado y han chocado, desde los sesenta con las polémicas culturales y la represión de manifestaciones culturales, para pasar a los setenta cuando según Díaz se impone la doxa para llegar al "deshielo" a partir de la caída del muro de Berlín y la desaparición de la Unión Soviética. [DAA]

2350 Ette, Ottmar. Una literatura sin residencia fija: insularidad, historia y dinámica sociocultural en la Cuba del siglo XX. (*Lect. Econ.*, 62, enero/junio 2005, p. 729–754, bibl.)

Estudio que señala la tensión territorial en la literatura cubana en la que escritores fundamentales a ella han escrito y publicado fuera de Cuba. Este fenómeno se registra desde el siglo XIX con escritores tales como José María Heredia, Cirilo Villaverde y Gertrudis Gómez de Avellaneda, para mencionar algunos de los más destacados. También la extraterritorialidad es característica de José Martí. El profesor Ette elige precisamente el diario de campaña escrito por Martí justo antes de su muerte como metáfora para señalar el elemento de lo huidizo y la inestabilidad que caracteriza a la literatura cubana. [DAA]

2351 Fernández Fe, Gerardo. Cuerpo a diario. Argentina: Tsé Tsé, 2007. 145 p. (Paradoxa. Ensayos)

Ensayo compuesto de observaciones fragmentarias sobre escritores en muchos casos sometidos a los avatares de las tragedias históricas. [DAA]

2352 Irizarry, Guillermo B. José Luis González: el intelectual nómada. San Juan: Callejón, 2006. 296 p.: bibl. (Col. en fuga. Ensayos)

One of the most comprehensive studies to date of the body of work of Puerto Rican writer and critic José Luis González. Divided into 10 chapters, the author organizes his reflection around the concepts of nomadism, faciality, territoriality, reterritoriality. Highly theoretical approach, innovative reading, and up-to-date bibliography.

2353 Kumaraswami, Par. Cultural policy, literature and readership in revolutionary Cuba: the view from the 21st century. (*Bull. Lat. Am. Res.*, 26:1, Jan. 2007, p. 69–87)

Presenta el desarrollo histórico desde los años 60 hasta los 90, el llamado "Periodo especial" en Cuba, de las ideas sobre la función de la literatura, el autor y la relación de éste con la política y el lector desde las directrices que impusieron los sectores revolucionarios del gobierno. La autora entiende que hubo un impulso democratizante en los años 60 y hasta llegar a los años actuales en donde el escritor según ella se enfrenta no sólo al capitalismo enemigo de los EE.UU. sino además a los retos del incipiente capitalismo interno. [DAA]

2354 Mateo Palmer, Margarita. El palacio del pavo real: el viaje mítico. Ciudad de La Habana: Ediciones Unión, 2007. 158 p.: bibl.

Estudio académico de la novela escrita por el guyanés Wilson Harris. Ganador del premio de la UNEAC, se basa el análisis en las estructuras míticas del relato según las ideas sobre el mito de Joseph Campbell. [DAA]

2355 Méndez, Roberto. Otra mirada a La Peregrina. La Habana: Letras Cubanas, 2007. 339 p.: bibl.

Estudio sobre Gertrudis Gómez de Avellaneda que ganó el Premio Alejo Carpentier de ensayo en el año de su publicación. El ensayo crítico pretende una revalorización de la obra de la poeta y dramaturga cubana del siglo XIX que vivió gran parte de su vida en España. Este estudio reclama una redefinición de su lugar en el canon de la poesía cubana. [DAA]

2356 Rojas, Rafael. Motivos de Anteo: patria y nación en la historia intelectual de Cuba. Madrid: Editorial Colibrí, 2008. 402 p.: bibl.

Repaso de las distintas corrientes intelectuales presente en los escritores tales como José Martí, Fernando Ortiz, Jorge Mañach, José Lezama Lima y como se desarrollo el concepto de patria en sus escritos. Rojas se remonta a escritores desde fines del siglo XVIII cubano en su análisis. [DAA]

2357 Santos-Febres, Mayra. Sobre piel y papel. San Juan: Ediciones Callejon, 2005. 233 p.

This collection of brief essays includes newspaper columns, lectures, and essays previously published or delivered by the author in different countries during a 10-year span. Divided into three sections, the majority of essays deal with the author's recurring interests: gender, race, literature, sexuality, and Puerto Rican and Caribbean culture. [MGC]

2358 Serra, Ana. The "new man" in Cuba: culture and identity in the Revolution. Gainesville: Univ. Press of Florida, 2007. 210 p.: bibl., ill., index. (Contemporary Cuba)

En este estudio, la profesora Serra analiza cómo han interactuado la literatura de escritores adscritos a los postulados del gobierno de la Revolución Cubana. A partir del postulado guevariano del "hombre nuevo", la propuesta oficial fue recibida por escritores afines al gobierno, que sin embargo, según este estudio, aún en los escritores más comprometidos con el régimen, surgen divergencias y cuestionan al final esos mismos supuestos. Es un análisis de la literatura oficial que según la autora no ha sido estudiada todavía a fondo. Para el comentario del historiador, ver item **1347**. [DAA]

2359 Sklodowska, Elzbieta. Espectros y espejismos: Haití en el imaginario cubano. Madrid: Iberoamericana; Frankfurt am Main: Vervuert, 2009. 341 p.: bibl., index. (Nexos y diferencias; 25)

Estudio de un interesante fenómeno en la historia cubana y haitiana, la relación histórica y literaria entre ambos países. La autora, profesora en Washington University, se remonta a la Revolución haitiana que tantas repercusiones tuvo en la historia y en la cultura, sobre todo la parte oriental, de Cuba hasta llegar a la fabulación de Haití en el conocido libro La isla que se repite de Antonio Benítez Rojo. [DAA]

Andean Countries

CÉSAR FERREIRA, *Professor of Spanish, University of Wisconsin-Milwaukee*
JOSÉ CARDONA-LÓPEZ, *Associate Professor of Spanish, Texas A&M International University*

COLOMBIA AND VENEZUELA

LAS REALIDADES POLÍTICAS Y SOCIALES de la Colombia de las últimas décadas del siglo XX son objeto de recreación en su narrativa del bienio pasado. La de los años ochenta aparece en la novela de Piedad Bonnett (item **2397**); sus personajes están relacionados con un grupo armado urbano que enfrenta un gobierno caracterizado por su feroz represión, la que incluye tortura y desapariciones. Bogotá es el escenario principal del desarrollo narrativo, como también lo es en *La mujer que sabía demasiado*, novela de Silvia Galvis (item **2400**), la mejor entre las publicadas en los últimos años. Con una excelente narración, de factura propia de la gran novela negra, se recrean los años de un gobierno altamente comprometido con el narcotráfico. Corrupción desmedida desde la primera casa de gobierno y ajuste de cuentas a plomo limpio y callejero circula en páginas que se leen con mucha tensión. Medellín es el espacio urbano para la obra de Héctor Abad Faciolince (item **2393**). Bella novela autobiográfica, construida desde la memoria del amor intenso que un hijo le profesa a su padre, hombre honesto y luchador social incansable. En la novela colectiva *La sucursal del cielo* (item **2409**) aparece Cali, ciudad arrinconada por la violencia y despropósitos del narcotráfico en los años noventa.

En la novela de José Luis Díaz-Granados (item **2398**), el personaje narrador crece en sus aspiraciones de escritor en medio de las calles y esquinas de los 1960s y 1970s de la Bogotá del emblemático barrio Palermo. Esa misma ciudad, con todas sus trasformaciones de un siglo, circula en *Necesitaba una historia de amor y otros cuentos de Bogotá* de Roberto Rubiano Vargas (item **2407**), excelentes relatos que hablan de una ciudad que no se inmuta ante sus tantas angustias y llagas.

En los cuentos de Emma Lucía Ardila Jaramillo (item **2395**), una delicada voz femenina da cuenta de la situación violenta del país mientras narra historias de mujeres y parejas. La violencia en el campo se aborda en la novela de Adolfo Ariza Navarro (item **2396**), narración de estructura experimental muy bien lograda. A tono con los tiempos que corren está la novela de Albeiro Patiño Builes (item **2405**), narración de suspenso en la que delincuentes del mundo de la infomática quieren ser famosos y juegan con la ley al gato y al ratón.

La Venezuela de la segunda mitad del siglo pasado y lo que va del actual aparece en su narrativa, la que de manera general se caracteriza también por la ironía y el buen humor. *Beso de lengua*, novela de Orlando Chirinos (item **2496**), vierte en sus páginas la lucha estudiantil y guerrillera de los 1960s y 1970s, con mucha presencia de la cultura popular. En cambio la Venezuela del siglo XXI, con sus nuevos libretos sociales y políticos destaca en las obras de Héctor Bujanda (item **2495**) y Adriana Villanueva (item **2509**). En todas estas novelas el lugar de las acciones es Caracas, escenario de profundas inclemencias sociales. La misma ciudad y sus registros lingüísticos de las clases bajas y sectores marginales comparecen en *Caracas cruzada* de Vicente Ulive-Schnell (item **2508**), texto de gran audacia narrativa.

Cabe mencionar que la narrativa policíaca, tanto en novela como en cuento, muestra excelentes desarrollos en la literatura venezolana. En este sentido destacan la novela de Roberto Echeto (item **2497**) y los libros de cuentos de Fedosy Santaella (item **2505**) y Omar Mesones (item **2501**). En todos ellos los personajes hablan con un lenguaje muy crudo y predomina el punto de vista narrativo del delincuente. En *La muerte en la víspera*, novela de suspenso de Pedro Rangel Mora (item **2504**), aparece una sociedad corrupta desde los organismos de control policial.

Como lo ha sido en el pasado, en la producción literaria venezolana del bienio destaca también la narrativa breve. Una voz femenina de lenguaje procaz narra historias de amor violentas en *Cállate poco a poco*, cuentos de Enza García Arreaza (item **2498**), libro ganador del V Concurso de Monte Avila 2007 para autores inéditos. Nuni Sarmiento (item **2506**) y Stefanía Mosca (item **2502**) continúan con la excelente tradición venezolana del cuento muy breve. Estos libros refieren una visión muy irónica del mundo y la sociedad. Igual sucede en *Viviana y otras historias del cuerpo*, cuentos de Miguel Gomes (item **2499**) escritos en una prosa elegante que recrea asuntos de la erótica en ambientes intelectuales. [J.C.L.]

BOLIVIA, ECUADOR, PERU

ENTRE LOS LIBROS BOLIVIANOS publicados en este milenio, vale la pena destacar la gran variedad de registros discursivos de la que goza su producción novelística. A las nuevas contribuciones de escritores como Edmundo Paz Soldán, Edgar Avila Echazú, Wolfango Montes y Enrique Mocha Monroy, Verónica Ormachea Gutiérrez y Giovanna Rivero Santa Cruz, se suma una importante producción en el cuento, gracias a los aportes de Rodrigo Hasbún, Gonzalo Lema, Alfonso Murillo y María Soledad Quiroga, entre otros. Asimismo, destaquemos las diversas antologías de cuentos que recopilan importantes textos y autores de la literatura boliviana. En términos temáticos, subrayemos el buen cultivo de la novela histórica en las letras bolivianas, así como la abundancia de relatos que retratan los dilemas humanos que tienen como telón de fondo a la ciudad de La Paz.

Como en Bolivia, la novela ecuatoriana también indaga sobre los vaivenes históricos y políticos del país en los relatos de Marcelo Cevallos Rosales, Marcela Costales, Diego Cornejo Menacho, Alfonso Reece Dousdebes y Byron Rodríguez Vásconez. Al mismo tiempo, es prolífica la producción cuentística a través de nombres como Gabriela Alemán, Aminta Buenaño, Alex Ron y Jorge Velasco Mackenzie, entre otros. Destaquemos, asimismo, las importantes antologías sobre el cuento ecuatoriano que se han publicado a partir de la revista *Letras del Ecuador*. Otro grupo de textos como los pertenecientes a Rocío Barba Durán, Leonardo Valencia o Giulia Zunino buscan contrastar las experiencias de personajes ecuatorianos fuera de un contexto estrictamente nacional.

En el Perú, Mario Vargas Llosa, laureado con el Premio Nobel de Literatura en 2010, vuelve a mostrar sus grandes dotes de novelista con la publicación de una novela mayor: *El sueño del celta* (item **2488**). También entregó un notable estudio sobre la obra de Juan Carlos Onetti. Otros nombres importantes de la literatura peruana contemporánea como Jorge Eduardo Benavides, Alfredo Bryce Echenique, Alonso Cueto, Eduardo González Viaña, Augusto Higa, Edgardo Rivera Martínez, Iván Thays, Siu Kam Wen y Carlos Eduardo Zavaleta también publicaron importantes títulos en la novela y el cuento que los reafirmaron como protagonistas de las letras de su país. También vale la pena destacar la buena producción, tanto en calidad como en cantidad, de escritoras como Leyla Bartet, Alicia Bisso, Pilar Dughi y Bertha Martínez Castilla, entre otras. Asimismo, conviene subrayar la consolidación de una serie de escritores aparecidos en años recientes como Sergio Galarza, José Guich Rodríguez, Lorenzo Helguero, José de Piérola y Carlos Yushimoto, entre otros nombres, cuyo talento para narrar es indudable y garantiza un buen relevo generacional en las letras peruanas en años venideros. [C.F.]

LITERARY CRITICISM AND HISTORY

Ecuador

2360 Pérez, Galo René. Agua que se va por el río: vida autocontemplada. Quito: Casa de la Cultura Ecuatoriana Benjamín Carrión, 2007. 284 p.

Libro de memorias donde Pérez relata su experiencia vital y sus experiencias literarias que abarcan más de medio siglo. Lo colectivo y lo histórico se despliega alrededor de circunstancias y anécdotas individuales del autor. Este libro forma una suerte de tríptico con las dos biografías anteriores de Pérez sobre Juan Montalvo y Manuelita Sáenz. [C.F.]

Peru

2361 Cueto, Alonso. Sueños reales. Lima: Seix Barral, 2008. 208 p.: bibl. (Tres Mundos. Ensayo)

Libro que recopila una serie de ensayos escritos de este novelista y periodista que exploran las biografías y peculiaridades literarias de nombres notables de las letras como Nabokov, Nerval, Carroll, Faulkner, Víctor Hugo, Carver, Henry James y, del lado peruano, Bryce, Arguedas, Martín Adán, Fernando de Szyszlo y Julio Ramón Ribeyro, entre otros. La naturaleza de su inspiración y su actitud con respecto a la creación son algunos de los detalles comunes en los que el autor hace hincapié. [C.F.]

2362 Cumbre Iberoamericana, 9th, Lima, 2001. Las guerras de este mundo: sociedad, poder y ficción en la obra de Mario Vargas Llosa. Lima: Planeta, 2008. 251 p.

Conjunto de ponencias que se presentaron en un congreso sobre la obra de Vargas Llosa. El eje central del mismo son las relaciones de Vargas Llosa con el poder y cómo las relaciones de sus personajes se estructuran en función de las tentaciones del poder. Narradores como Jorge Edwards, Nélida Piñón y Antonio Tabucchi, ensayistas como Enrique Krauze, C.A. Montaner, científicos sociales como Juan Ossio y Gonzalo Portocarrero, historiadores como J.L. Orrego y Manuel Burga, hombres de teatro y cine como Luis Peirano, Alonso Alegría y Francisco Lombardi comentan la obra del novelista y su condición de ciudadano del mundo, comprometido siempre con los grandes ideales de la modernidad. [C.F.]

2363 Galdo Marín, Juan Carlos. Alegoría y nación en la novela peruana del siglo XX: Vallejo, Alegría, Arguedas, Vargas Llosa, Scorza, Gutiérrez. Lima: Instituto de Estudios Peruanos, 2008. 280 p.: bibl. (Serie Lengua y sociedad; 29)

Analizando las novelas *El tungsteno*, de Vallejo; *El mundo es ancho y ajeno*, de Alegría; *El sexto*, de Arguedas; *Conversación en La Catedral*, de Vargas Llosa; *Redoble por Rancas*, de Scorza; y *La violencia del tiempo*, de Gutiérrez, Galdo devela cómo esos seis autores imaginan la nación peruana en el siglo XX. El autor traza conexiones y diferencias entre las alegorías del Perú que proponen, relacionándolas con las experiencias sociohistóricas ficcionalizadas en sus tramas. [C.F.]

2364 González Vigil, Ricardo. Años decisivos de la narrativa peruana. Lima: Editorial San Marcos, 2008. 431 p. (Col. Súmmum)

Libro que reúne más de 130 textos de este importante crítico peruano, desde breves artículos periodísticos hasta extensos ensayos. Gran parte de ellos analiza obras de los narradores de la "generación del 50", especialmente las de Julio Ramón Ribeyro y Carlos Eduardo Zavaleta. Otro grupo de narradores cuyas obras son objeto de estudio es el que apareció a finales de los años 60 y que se congregó en torno a la revista *Narración*: Miguel Gutiérrez, Oswaldo Reynoso, Gregorio Martínez, Antonio Gálvez Ronceros, Juan Morillo y otros. Ellos, junto con Rivera Martínez y Bryce Echenique, constituyen para González Vigil la trascendental "generación del 68". [C.F.]

2365 Mario Vargas Llosa: la libertad y la vida. Textos de Fernando de Szyszlo *et al.* 1a reimpresión. Lima: Editorial Planeta Perú: Pontificia Univ. Católica del Perú, 2008. 251 p.: facsims., ill., ports. (some col.).

Libro que repasa la vida y la obra del importante escritor peruano, en el que la principal protagonista es la imagen. Decenas de fotografías—muchas de ellas inéditas y pertenecientes al álbum familiar de los Vargas Llosa—pueblan estas páginas y nos llevan por un viaje imaginario por distintas ciudades y lugares (Arequipa, Piura, Lima, París, Londres, Madrid, etc.), tiempos y personajes, todos ellos íntimamente relacionados con la trayectoria vital, intelectual y creativa del autor. Y entre las imágenes y documentos aparecen las palabras, textos de amigos, escritores, artistas y académicos que han jugado un papel especial en la vida del novelista. La política, el cine, el teatro y el periodismo son actividades que nos muestran a un hombre comprometido con su tiempo. [C.F.]

2366 Para leer a Luis Loayza. Recopilación de César Ferreira y Américo Mudarra. Textos de Gerardo Castillo *et al.* Lima: Ediciones del Vicerrectorado Académico, Univ. Nacional Mayor de San Marcos, 2009. 293 p.: bibl.

Conjunto de artículos sobre este importante escritor perteneciente a la generación del 50. Destaca la sección dedicada al libro *El avaro* de Loayza, así como los que se dedican a su obra cuentística y novelística. Se incluye, además, una vasta bibliografía de y sobre Loayza. [C.F.]

2367 Tauzin Castellanos, Isabelle. El otro curso del tiempo: una interpretación de *Los ríos profundos.* Lima: IFEA, Instituto Francés de Estudios Andinos: Lluvia Editores, 2008. 228 p.: bibl. (Col. Biblioteca andina de bolsillo; 29) (Col. Alasitas)

Este estudio invita al lector a descubrir la compleja temporalidad que estructura la obra maestra de José María Arguedas, *Los ríos profundos.* La novela no predica en absoluto una vuelta atrás ni menos aún una utopía arcaica. Al contrario, cuando se alude al pasado es para explicar la fuerza y la resistencia de los hombres del presente, que son capaces de movilizarse contra la peste, alegoría del mal que se cierne y aplasta a los desvalidos. [C.F.]

2368 Varona, Dora. Ciro Alegría y su sombra: biografía ilustrada. Lima: Planeta, 2008. 335 p.: ill., ports. (Biblioteca Ciro Alegría)

La viuda del autor de *El mundo es ancho y ajeno* acomete aquí una biografía de Ciro Alegría con ribetes indudablemente novelescos. Varona entrega una versión íntima y humana del escritor con quien vivió desde 1957, año en el que contrajeron matrimonio. Sin lugar a dudas, se trata de un documento

de primera mano para conocer más sobre el mundo que rodeó al escritor. El volumen viene acompañado de fotografías del archivo familiar. [C.F.]

PROSE FICTION

Bolivia

2369 Avila Echazú, Edgar. Juana Manuela recuerda—: y otros relatos. La Paz: Plural Editores, 2006. 165 p. (Col. "La nao")

Novela sobre la escritora Juana Manuela Gorriti escrita a la manera de un monólogo durante los últimos cinco días de su existencia y ya refugiada en casa de unos parientes en Buenos Aires. La protagonista recrea su vida en su ciudad natal de Salta y los reveses sufridos por su padre ante uno de los caudillos federalistas de la Argentina post-independentista; en Tarija, donde se casó con el futuro presidente boliviano Manuel Isidoro Belzú; en La Paz y Oruro, escenarios de sus amores con el Vencedor de Ingavia, José Ballivián; y en Lima, ya vieja y dedicada a la enseñanza. [C.F.]

2370 Barrientos, Maximiliano. Los daños. Santa Cruz de la Sierra, Bolivia: La Mancha Editorial: Editorial La Hoguera, 2006. 167 p. (Serie La mancha) (Cuentos)

Los cuentos de *Los daños* constatan esa desesperada contemporaneidad del tercer milenio, el desapego, y casi la amoralidad. Con una clara influencia de la generación Beat norteamericana, Barrientos apuesta por una prosa minimalista y la creación de una serie de personajes que destacan por una existencia mediocre en su obligado ingreso a la adultez. [C.F.]

2371 Cabrera Maraz, Hernán. Desaparecidos. Santa Cruz de la Sierra, Bolivia: Sello Mancha, Fondo Editorial de Hoguera, 2006. 94 p. (Novela)

El periodismo y la ficción se fusionan para crear una novela que oscila entre el testimonio y la ficción, donde el protagonista es el general Hugo Banzer. Del 19 al 21 de agosto de 1971, el país vivió jornadas de violencia y muerte hasta que se consolidó la dictadura banzerista. El ambiente de esos días, los protagonistas, los lugares, las víctimas y las desapariciones están narradas a través de fragmentos de noticias de periódicos de la época, que sirven como enlace con los hechos sucedidos. El uso de las entrevistas como fuentes de la información de la que se alimenta el relato es una muestra del buen oficio del escritor. [C.F.]

2372 Camacho, Georgette de. Tan solo en su agonía: novela. La Paz: Plural Editores: Summa Artis, 2007. 194 p.

Novela que relata algunos acontecimientos ubicados en la época de la dictadura en Bolivia, fusionando la ironía, el humor y el realismo. Aunque la historia como tal transcurre en un tiempo indeterminado, se rescata del olvido ciertas situaciones que ilustran la memoria colectiva de un pueblo. [C.F.]

2373 Los diez mejores cuentos de la literatura boliviana. Contribuciones de Augusto Céspedes *et al.* Investigación de César Verduguéz Gómez. La Paz: Plural Editores, 2007. 235 p.: bibl.

Excelente antología del cuento boliviano. Se incluye una breve semblanza de cada uno de los autores escogidos y un pequeño comentario crítico sobre su obra. Entre los autores incluidos figuran Augusto Céspedes, Porfirio Díaz Machicao, Néstor Taboada Terán, Alcides Arguedas y René Bascopé Aspiazu. [C.F.]

2374 Hasbún, Rodrigo. Cinco. Bolivia: Editorial Gente Común, 2006. 118 p. (Narrativa)

Conjunto de cuentos en los que nos adentramos en travesías por la intimidad de los personajes, la mayoría de ellos jóvenes que empiezan a dejar de serlo. Son fotografías de lugares y de la desaparición de esos lugares. Estamos ante crónicas detalladas y precisas de batallas que suceden en el interior de las habitaciones o en autos que atraviesan la ciudad en un atardecer de domingo, batallas silenciosas en camas de moteles o en baños de departamentos. La crónica de lo que hubo antes de esas batallas y paraísos solitarios, paraísos que se alejan ante el paso del tiempo. [C.F.]

2375 Lema Vargas, Gonzalo. Contra nadie en la batalla. Santa Cruz de la Sierra, Bolivia: Grupo Editorial Hoguera, 2007. 351 p. (Mancha. Literatura adultos)

Novela cargada de alta afectividad, donde los dramas personales y los encuentros y desencuentros de una familia se desarrollan en medio de un contexto altamente político. El relato se inicia en la época del golpe de Barrientos en 1964 y termina en la guerra del agua en Cochabamba en 2000. El relato gira en torno a la vida de sujetos que poseen lazos estrechos, cuya unidad se ve en peligro en medio de una revolución fallida. El personaje de Benjamín es el principal testigo de todo este periodo. [C.F.]

2376 Lema Vargas, Gonzalo. Después de ti no hay nada. Cochabamba, Bolivia: Editorial Los Amigos del Libro, 2006. 162 p.

Conjunto de 13 relatos que cuentan diversas historias sobre personajes que no saben por qué tienen que vivir esas situaciones existenciales. El primer cuento, "Cartas desde la soledad", evoca el tema de la migración permanente de los bolivianos, pero esta vez motivado por un problema de amor. Otro de los relatos refleja algunas anécdotas que le tocó vivir al autor en su condición de vocal de la Corte Nacional Electoral. Destaca el buen oficio para el género breve de este novelista. [C.F.]

2377 Lema Vargas, Gonzalo. Si tú encuentras a Mari Jo. Bolivia: Editorial Gente Común, 2007. 192 p. (Novela)

Novela ambientada en los años 70 en Bolivia sobre el mundo del fútbol boliviano. La historia es protagonizada por un jugador del equipo Wilsterman llamado "Granuja", un personaje ficticio inventado para la novela. La novela recupera tres grandes partidos del popular equipo boliviano para contar una historia de amor y de triunfos frustrados. [C.F.]

2378 Mendieta Paz, Pablo. La noche oscura y otros relatos. La Paz: Plural Editores, 2005. 175 p.

Primer libro de relatos de este escritor, abogado y músico compuesto por 22 textos. En ellos se exploran temas como el asombro ante la realidad, la fantasía y la sorpresa en la vida cotidiana. Destaca un tono coloquial y un lenguaje claro y directo para narrar la experiencia vital de los personajes. [C.F.]

2379 Montaño Balderrama, Celso. Corazón de Bolivia: novela. 2. ed. Cochabamba, Bolivia: Grupo Editorial Kipus, 2007. 310 p.

Novela que funde una serie de géneros (poesía, novela psicológica, ensayo político) y cuya trama tiene como fondo el despido de 50 mil mineros y su relocalización en 1985, luego de la aplicación de la ley 21060, cuando el futuro presidente boliviano,

Gonzalo Sánchez de Lozada, era ministro de planificación de Bolivia y se benefició personalmente con la medida. [C.F.]

2380 Montes, José Wolfango. Bolivia, adiós! Recopilación de Mauricio Méndez J. Santa Cruz de la Sierra, Bolivia: Editorial La Hoguera, 2006. 305 p. (Novela. Serie la mancha)

Novela donde se cuenta las desventuras de una Bolivia habitada por politicos aparentemente intocables y que desnuda el turbio mundo del poder en el país. Se cuenta la historia de una secta religiosa llamada los nazarenos que está provocando el final de la civilización occidental. Montes sorprende con una historia bastante original sobre un posible futuro predecible de la nación boliviana, una distopia donde se puede apreciar el fin de una vida de lucha republicana y democrática. [C.F.]

2381 Murillo, Alfonso. El hombre que estudiaba los atlas. La Paz: Plural Editores, 2006. 78 p.

De los siete relatos de este volumen, cinco se desarrollan en un ambiente que es crepuscular y citadino. Nada de claridades campesinas, sino la luz de la luna urbana o el pálido reflejo de los atardeceres en el señorío de Sopocachi de La Paz a mediados del siglo XX. Dos textos, "Final de un oficio" y "Leyenda al pie", tienen características fantásticas y, mirados en conjunto, muchos textos exploran el género policial. [C.F.]

2382 Ormachea Gutiérrez, Verónica. Los ingenuos. La Paz: Alfaguara, 2007. 472 p. (Alfaguara)

Novela histórica que cuenta la historia de amor entre Juliana, una mujer de la oligarquía, y Sebastián, un sindicalista mestizo. Su telón de fondo es la Revolución Boliviana de 1952. El relato destaca las divisiones sociales imperantes en la sociedad de la época, destacando la miopía de las oligarquías latinoamericanas ante fenómenos revolucionarios como los aquí narrados. Destaca la prosa fluida y bien lograda de esta escritora boliviana. [C.F.]

2383 Paz Soldán, Edmundo. Los vivos y los muertos. Madrid: Alfaguara, 2009. 206 p.

Primera novela ambientada fuera de Bolivia de este importante narrador. La trama ocurre en una pequeña población norteamericana del estado de Nueva York donde sus jóvenes habitantes van construyendo un mundo de aspiraciones truncadas, secretos inconfesables y pasiones desatadas. Poco a poco se suceden en un breve espacio de tiempo una serie de muertes que expresan la frustración de los personajes. Destaca el estilo crudo y directo del relato que nos va conduciendo de la mano de sus protagonistas por un camino sin retorno al lado más oscuro de las relaciones humanas. [C.F.]

2384 Quiroga, María Soledad. Islas reunión. La Paz: Plural Editores, 2006. 126 p.

Conjunto de cuentos donde la palabra es una realidad en sí misma. Se trata de textos donde Quiroga explora esa zona simbólica que parece ambigua y que participa de lo real y también de lo fantástico. En realidad, ella es la puerta que permite transitar de un ámbito a otro. Ambos espacios son reales y al mismo tiempo fantásticos, pero los identificamos de manera distinta y nos situamos en uno de ellos porque la ambivalencia no resulta cómoda. [C.F.]

2385 Reck López, Centa. Zona rosa: novela. La Paz: Editorial Gente Común, 2006. 182 p.

Novela que está estructurada sobre una historia de amor entre más de dos personas, un hecho que socava el interior de cada uno de los individuos. Las miradas y las voces del relato pertenecen a las protagonistas pues el hombre acá es un mero objeto. Destaca el mundo interior femenino que la escritora recrea con buen oficio. [C.F.]

2386 Rivero Santa Cruz, Giovanna. Contraluna. Santa Cruz de la Sierra, Bolivia: Fondo Editorial de la Hoguera: La Mancha Editorial, 2005. 150 p.: ill.

Nuevo libro de cuentos de esta periodista y novelista. En sus relatos no hay emociones sutiles, tampoco quietas epifanías. Los personajes están siempre poseídos por pasiones extremas y deambulan por el mundo expresándose con fuerza. En sus relatos destaca la presencia de la ironía y abunda el sarcasmo y humor negro. La mujer aparece en estos textos como un ser que no sólo ama sino que es también capaz de desear con más fuerza que los hombres. En esta constante lucha entre los sexos, la tibieza masculina poco puede ante el exceso femenino. Así, los hombres y las mujeres están destinados a desencontrarse.

2387 Rocha Monroy, Enrique. Casa de la vida umbral de la muerte: homenaje a los 50 años de escritor. La Paz: Producciones "CIMA", 2007. 215 p.

Novela que cuenta con sutileza y agilidad narrativa la historia de un boliviano que gana la lotería, pero es escamoteado. Destaca la habilidad del escritor para retratar la euforia y la miseria del protagonista. La novela llegó a ser finalista en el premio "Rómulo Gallegos" de Venezuela. [C.F.]

2388 Rocha Monroy, Ramón. Que solos se quedan los muertos!: vida (más allá de la vida) de Antonio José de Sucre: novela. Santa Cruz de la Sierra, Bolivia: Editorial El País, 2006. 541 p.

Ambiciosa novela histórica sobre Antonio José de Sucre que está contada en varios planos y tiempos. El relato se abre en el año 1900 con un homenaje de aquel Ecuador del revolucionario Eloy Alfaro y luego se adentra en el tiempo heroico de las batallas emancipadoras en América. La narración eje explota la peripecia dramática del asesinato de Sucre, para luego entrar de lleno en la investigación y búsqueda de la verdad que inicia el recuento de su vida; esto es, los avatares de la lucha política de Sucre y de los hombres y mujeres que rodean al Gran Mariscal en su periplo vital. [C.F.]

2389 Rodríguez, Antoine. La hoyada y los perros. La Paz: Plural Editores; Madrid: SEPHA, 2005. 154 p.

Relatos caracterizados por los tránsitos y desplazamientos múltiples de sus personajes. Pero a diferencia de aquellos relatos de itinerario que narran peripecias en continuo movimiento, estos logran, además, detenerse y residir en el mundo de manera cotidiana silenciosa y significativa. [C.F.]

2390 Scott Moreno, Eduardo. La doncella del bárón Cementerio. La Paz: Alfaguara, 2005. 374 p.

Novela narrada desde un lenguaje denso que rezuma un agotador enciclopedismo, a ratos injustificado y decorativo. El protagonista es un francés psicoanalista que, en búsqueda de nuevos rumbos en un sitio exótico, mantiene una relación con la coprotagonista, su novia haitiana. La obra sigue el derrotero pseudointelectual del protagonista, mezclando recuerdos y postales de infancia. [C.F.]

2391 Vargas, Manuel. Nocturno paceño. La Paz: Correveidile, 2006. 146 p.

Libro que consta de 16 relatos que pueden ser leídos de forma independiente y en un orden cualquiera pero que, en su conjunto, conforman una novela. La acción transcurre en La Paz, con escapadas al Altiplano y los yungas, y a las minas de Potosí y Oruro. El trasfondo es la noche, el frío y los siete años de la dictadura de los años 70 en Bolivia. Los personajes son jóvenes universitarios y muchachas que los acompañan en sus venturas y desventuras políticas o amorosas. [C.F.]

2392 Viscarra, Víctor Hugo. Ch'aqui fulero: los cuadernos perdidos de Víctor Hugo. La Paz: Correveidile, 2007. 150 p.

Libro póstumo de relatos breves de este escritor boliviano que, en la vena de Charles Bukowski, relata las vivencias de alcohólicos, artilleros, prostitutas y homosexuales en el submundo nocturno de la ciudad de La Paz. [C.F.]

Colombia

2393 Abad Faciolince, Héctor Joaquín. El olvido que seremos. Bogotá: Planeta, 2006. 274 p. (Autores españoles e iberoamericanos)

La relación de mucho amor entre un padre y un hijo. El padre, un socialista frente al ambiente muy católico en su familia y la sociedad, morirá asesinado por unos sicarios. La primera parte de la novela está dedicada a exponer ese amor entre padre e hijo. Ya en la segunda la narración adquiere un ritmo vibrante, hasta culminar con el asesinato del padre del narrador y el intenso dolor de éste. [J.C.L.]

2394 Alape, Arturo. Conversación con la ausencia y otros relatos. Edición de Carlos Vásquez-Zawadzki y Manuel Ruiz Montealegre. Bogotá: Editorial Planeta Colombiana, 2007. 131 p. (Seix Barral Biblioteca breve)

Relatos de viaje por aire, mar y tierra. El viajero recuerda pasajes y personajes de su vida, acontecimientos suyos o del país. Hay relatos de una Bogotá que se trasforma mientras los personajes insisten en quedarse en el pasado. Una prosa que fluye lenta, hermosa en imágenes y reflexiones, con lo que el libro logra ser también un viaje al interior del ser.

2395 Ardila Jaramillo, Emma Lucía. Nos queremos así: cuentos. Medellín, Colombia: Fondo Editorial, Univ. EAFIT, 2007. 81 p. (Letra por letra)

Cuentos sobre parejas. Mujeres que poco a poco llegan a envolverse en situaciones terminales, muchas de ellas con la presencia de la violencia colombiana. Quince cuentos narrados por una voz femenina a medio tono. Destaca "Fetiche", gran cuento en que se narran las paranoias de una madre luego de permitir que su hijo apareciera en una valla publicitaria. [J.C.L.]

2396 Ariza Navarro, Adolfo. Afuera estaba la noche. Neiva, Colombia: Fundación Tierra de Promisión, 2006. 113 p.

A un pueblo arrasado por la violencia entre grupos armados, una mujer va en busca de quienes vivieron con su padre. Ahora en el pueblo todos son cadáveres y la mujer habla con otra que conoció a su padre. Cada uno de los capítulos es nombrado con el orden de los tragos bebidos desde una botella de licor durante la conversación que sostienen las dos mujeres. [J.C.L.]

2397 Bonnett, Piedad. Siempre fue invierno. Bogotá: Alfaguara, 2007. 329 p.

Un médico se enamora de una intelectual de familia adinerada. Al médico le matan su hermano revolucionario y su novia lo abandona para irse con otro hombre. Trascurren los años de un gobierno colombiano caracterizado por sus políticas altamente represivas. Al final se sugiere que el médico acaba siendo un desaparecido más por las fuerzas militares. [J.C.L.]

2398 Díaz Granados, José Luis. Los años extraviados. Bogotá: Planeta, 2006. 143 p.

Un escritor de cuentos admira fervorosamente a Gabriel García Márquez, de quien es primo. Tiene grandes anhelos en su vida, como el publicar su primera novela, de la que apenas ha escrito 100 páginas. Texto en fragmentos, algunos narrados en primera persona, otros en tercera. Es una novela de aprendizaje, narrada en forma ágil y con humor. [J.C.L.]

2399 Francisco, Miguel de. El enano y el trébol y otras narraciones. Bogotá: Mondadori, 2008. 199 p. (Literatura Mondadori)

Tres textos. Un relato barroco en la Madrid del siglo XVII; una novela corta ambientada en la Bogotá de los años 70 del siglo XX y por último una narración sobre una casa bogotana habitada por muchas personas. Destaca la prosa elegante de un autor desarraigado del mundo y pesimista, pero fiel con el espacio para la alegría y la libertad que para él siempre fue la literatura. [J.C.L.]

2400 Galvis, Silvia. La mujer que sabía demasiado. Bogotá: Planeta, 2006. 229 p.

Un detective y su ayudante investigan el asesinato de una mujer y descubren que el alto gobierno, desde el presidente, está comprometido en el crimen. Tras todo lo narrado el referente inmediato es la Colombia de la segunda mitad de los 1990s. El detective y su novia terminan asesinados. Se narran muchos eventos, al tiempo que aparece la erudición respecto de autores clásicos de lo policíaco. [J.C.L.]

2401 García Saucedo, Jaime. El jardín de los dóberman. Colombia: J. García Saucedo, 2006. 95 p.

La historia trascurre en Barranquilla, Bogotá y otras ciudades del continente americano. Trata de la nostalgia por un amor de un profesor de literatura en medio de la situación de Panamá durante el gobierno de Noriega. Casi toda la narración corre a cuenta del profesor, quien regresa a suicidarse en Bogotá. Al final ya la voz narrativa es de otro personaje, y es cuando la prosa se vuelve ampulosa. [J.C.L.]

2402 Iriarte, Helena. Llegar hasta tu olvido. Bogotá: I/M Editores, 2006. 158 p.

Una mujer viaja a visitar los lugares donde creció, a la gente con quien creció, y se encuentra con su mamá casi a punto de morir. La hija le agradece a la madre por haberla traído al mundo. Es un viaje a la memoria y al mundo de los sueños. Prosa hermosa, de la nostalgia y el recuerdo, con notables hallazgos poéticos para hablar del paisaje y de la vida. [J.C.L.]

2403 Jaramillo Valdés, René. Los cadáveres por el río bajan sin sombra y otros cuentos. Medellín, Colombia: Ediciones Mascaluna, 2006. 108 p.

Cuentos cuyo tema general es la violencia actual del campo y la ciudad colombianos. Medellín es la ciudad más presente, con sus llagas sociales tan fatales. Algunos cuentos, los mejor logrados, son metáforas del conflicto colombiano y de la creación literaria. En este sentido destacan el que da título a la colección y "Cartas letales". Las tramas de los cuentos tienen excelente elaboración. [J.C.L.]

2404 Pardo, Jorge Eliécer. Transeúntes del siglo XX. Bogotá: Pijao Editores, 2007. 382 p.

Narraciones en cuyas páginas trascurren historias que refieren la violencia del campo colombiano de medio siglo, como también la vida de los años recientes, tan nutrida con los efectos de los espacios virtuales del mundo digital. Son cuatro libros de cuentos en uno solo, que dan cuenta de 30 años de trayectoria del autor. Textos que en forma sencilla narran eventos, muchos de ellos son microficciones. [J.C.L.]

2405 Patiño Builes, Albeiro. Bandidos y hackers. Medellín, Colombia: Univ. de Antioquia, División de Extensión Cultural: Editorial Univ. de Antioquia, 2007. 176 p. (Col. Premios nacionales de cultura de Universidad de Antioquia)

Novela de suspenso sobre el robo de información a grandes corporaciones en el mundo de la informática. Delincuentes solitarios frente a una computadora haciendo sus fechorías de manera silenciosa. Uno de los narradores termina por robar unos diamantes, y el mismo día en que la policía va por él a su casa acaba de escribir la novela que el lector tiene en sus manos. [J.C.L.]

2406 Rodríguez, Juan Carlos. El viento agitando las cortinas. Caracas: Mondadori, 2008. 159 p. (Literatura Mondadori)

Tres relatos en los que en cada uno el narrador y protagonista es un hombre de edad madura, intelectual, que recrea su presente y su pasado en una Bogotá que poco a poco se transforma y moderniza. En el primer relato el narrador habla de sus fetiches eróticos, en otro regresa de Quito a Bogotá a reencontrarse con sus amigos, y en el tercero es un asiduo usuario del correo electrónico con una amiga. La narración corre muy lenta. [J.C.L.]

2407 Rubiano Vargas, Roberto. Necesitaba una historia de amor: y otros cuentos de Bogotá. Bogotá: Villegas Editores, 2006. 348 p. (Col. Turquesa. Narrativa)

Cuentos que narran historias en una Bogotá que se trasforma desde la provincial de comienzos del siglo XX hasta la de los primeros años del XXI. Destaca una ciudad impasible ante la vida dura y el ambiente de robos y asesinatos en que viven los personajes. Las narraciones poseen un amable tono coloquial, con tramas en las que no falta el enigma de orden policíaco. [J.C.L.]

2408 Serrano, Enrique. Donde no te conozcan. Bogotá: Editorial Planeta Colombiana, 2007. 300 p.: map. (Seix Barral Biblioteca breve)

Desde los años de la peste negra del siglo XIV se cuenta de una saga de judíos de España, de su gran conocimiento de la medicina, su persecución y conversión. Representantes de aquella saga llegan a América, como si por fin hubiesen encontrado una tierra para vivir sin incomodidades. Con una prosa muy sencilla se hace gran erudición sobre los judíos en la edad media española. [J.C.L.]

2409 La sucursal del cielo. Santiago de Cali, Colombia: Calíope taller literario, 2002. 153 p.

Vidas y episodios de una Cali de los años 90s, plagada por los estragos y personajes del narcotráfico. El lector acude a páginas en que la ciudad va desmoronándose. Novela en seis capítulos, cada uno escrito por una persona diferente. Entre los personajes y las situaciones hay mucho estereotipo. Destaca la ironía del nombre de la novela, pues de lo que se habla es más bien de una sucursal del infierno. [J.C.L.]

2410 Toro, Hernán. Ceremonias privadas. Cali, Colombia: Programa Editorial Univ. del Valle, 2007. 102 p. (Col. Artes y humanidades. Cuentos)

Ocho cuentos en los que prima lo fantástico. Seres de otro tiempo y cultura que todavía están presentes, sucesos que ocurren en tiempos y espacios paralelos a los de la realidad objetiva. Cuentos bien diseñados, construidos como juegos intelectuales. En la mayoría de ellos se nota la cultura del libro. "La cantante a capella" es uno de los mejores; trata sobre el tiempo de la ensoñación y el de la realidad objetiva. [J.C.L.]

Ecuador

2411 Alemán Salvador, María Gabriela.
Album de familia. Lima: Estruendo-
mudo, 2010. 89 p.

En los ocho cuentos de este libro,
Ecuador encarna tanto el límite como el
marco de lo que se cuenta. Es un país en
trámite de cambio, donde nada es lo que
aparenta: el esposo de Lorena Bobbit, la Emperatriz de las Islas Encantadas y Robinson
Crusoe son algunos de los personajes que
aparecen. Estos constituyen la entrada a una
ficción sin moralejas que incita al lector a
confiar en su imaginación. Alemán presenta
anécdotas y reflexiones vinculadas al acto
de narrar y, a su vez, misterios que afrontan
la complejidad de la memoria más entrañable: la memoria de familia. [J.C.L.]

2412 Becerra C., Jorge W. Camas calientes.
Quito: Triana Editorial, 2005. 339 p.
(Col. Narrativa)

Novela en que los personajes ecuatorianos descubren la tragedia cotidiana de
los emigrantes tras viajar a España en busca
del sueño español. Algunos de los que viven
en Pueblo Nuevo se han conocido en el Bar
de Rossi, especie de punto de encuentro
en el que se confunden y entrecruzan sus
vidas. A la difícil relación entre Danielle y
su madre, que constituye el eje de la obra, se
unen otras historias que nos invitan a conocer una vasta galería de personajes como
Giselle, la femme fatale de las diminutas
minifaldas, que se fue a España en busca de
aventuras; la de Vanesa, la prostituta de al-
tísimos tacones de cristal, confundida entre
el bien y el mal; la del mesero, convertido en
cabeza de una naciente red de delincuentes,
entre otros. [J.C.L.]

2413 Buenaño Rugel, Aminta. Mujeres
divinas. Guayaquil, Ecuador: baez.
editore.es, 2006. 188 p.

Conjunto de cuentos en los que
aparecen personajes femeninos en situaciones aparentemente comunes como el
primer amor, la maternidad, la menopausia,
mostrando—en tonos íntimos y poéticos—
la divinidad rescatada de las mujeres y de su
lucha contra las intrigas sociales, la marginación y sus propias limitaciones. [J.C.L.]

2414 Carrión, Pepé. El cuento de nunca
acabar. Quito: Casa de la Cultura
Ecuatoriana Benjamín Carrión, 2005. 269 p.

Cuentos que destacan por su estilo
diáfano en los que el escritor va dibujando
un retrato reivindicador sobre Manuela
Sáenz. Al mismo tiempo, aparecen una serie
de perfiles sobre la historia ecuatoriana
hasta arribar al momento actual. [J.C.L].

2415 Cevallos R., Marcelo. Los fantasmas
de Carondelet. Quito: b-line Cinearte,
Sección Editorial, 2006. 385 p.

El ex-secretario de comunicación de
la Presidencia del Ecuador usa su experiencia en el Palacio de Gobierno para inspirar
una trama histórica y romántica ambientada en los pasadizos de la emblemática
construcción donde vive el Presidente de la
República. La novela reflexiona en su trama
sobre la historia y la política en el Ecuador,
pero sobre todo se interna en el mundo de lo
humano y del amor en medio de los conflictos del poder y la corrupción. [J.C.L].

2416 Cornejo Menacho, Diego. Miércoles
y estiércoles. Quito: Alfaguara: Santillana, 2008. 133 p.

Segunda novela de este importante
narrador ecuatoriano con dos fuentes: la
primera es un hecho de la vida real, el asesinato de los hermanos Santiago y Andrés
Restrepo durante el gobierno de León Fe-
bres Cordero entre 1984 y 1988; la segunda
es Raymond Chandler, cultivador de la
novela negra en los Estados Unidos y que la
definió alguna vez como "el simple arte de
matar". El relato es un agudo comentario
sobre los derechos individuales en la sociedad ecuatoriana. [J.C.L].

2417 Costales, Marcela. Memorial de la
ciudad de los espejos. Quito: Ediciones Abya-Yala, 2006. 162 p.

Novela histórica que trata de reflejar
el especial poder del alma de la libertadora
Manuela Sáenz y la esencia de relación de su
amor y comunión de objetivos con el Libertador Simón Bolívar y la gesta de la emancipación americana. [J.C.L]

2418 Durán Barba, Rocío. Ecuador, el velo
se levanta. Quito: Editorial Conejo,
2007. 375 p.

Libro que trata de un reencuentro con
el escritor francés Henri Michaux, autor de
Ecuador, un libro que le valió renombre y
con el cual difundió una imagen peyorativa
del país en el mundo. En esta novela, Michaux vuelve a la vida para convertirse en

actor. El relato sirve a la autora no sólo para rebatir el diario de viaje de Michaux, sino para descubrir el Ecuador de ayer y del presente. A lo largo de la novela desfila el país con sus paisajes andinos y marinos, ciudades, pueblos, comunidades indígenas, la selva, puntos históricos y leyendas. [J.C.L.]

2419 Espinosa, Roque. Me descambias la vida. Quito: Editorial Conejo, 2006. 185 p.

Espinosa busca en estos cuentos escenarios lejanos (por ejemplo, un castillo en Portugal), para que su viaje interior alcance matices mayores. Se trata de cuentos escritos a renglón seguido, como si se tratase de narrar una sola y múltiple vida. Aparecen, así, planos simultáneos que se encuentran, se desencuentran, se sobreponen y componen la complejidad de lo cotidiano. A ratos los relatos se postulan como una suerte de fuga; en otros, como una confesión vehemente. [J.C.L.]

2420 Gudiño, Renato. Destino de papel: novel. Quito: Editorial El Conejo, 2007. 187 p.

Novela que utiliza los inexplorados potenciales de la mente humana para crear un universo paralelo que toma como base la posibilidad de la transmutación. El relato plantea la eterna lucha entre el bien y el mal a través del personaje de Donna, transformada en Maya, quien se enfrenta a un personaje oscuro llamado Lucard. [J.C.L.]

2421 Letras del Ecuador 100: cuento. Tomo 1, Selección de cuento de la revista *Letras del Ecuador*, 1945–1949. Textos de Ángel Felicísimo Rojas et al. Quito: Casa de la Cultura Ecuatoriana Benjamín Carrión, Dirección de Publicaciones, 2007. 241 p.

Volumen que reúne una selección de relatos de escritores ecuatorianos publicados en los primeros números de la revista *Letras del Ecuador* entre 1945 y 1949. Destaca en esta selección la presencia de nombres fundamentales de la literatura ecuatoriana como César Dávila Andrade, Jorge Icaza, Pedro Jorge Vera y Joaquín Gallegos Lara, entre otros. [J.C.L.]

2422 Letras del Ecuador 100: cuento. Tomo 2, Selección de cuento de la revista *Letras del Ecuador*, 1950–1954. Textos de Ángel Felicísimo Rojas et al. Quito: Casa de la Cultura Ecuatoriana Benjamín Carrión, Dirección de Publicaciones, 2007. 352 p.

Segundo volumen que reúne una selección de relatos de escritores ecuatorianos publicados en los primeros números de la revista *Letras del Ecuador* entre 1950 y 1954. Sobresale en esta selección la presencia de nombres fundamentales de la literatura ecuatoriana como César Dávila Andrade, Jorge Icaza, Sergio Núñez, Adalberto Ortiz y Eugenia Viteri, entre otros. [J.C.L.] Para el comentario sobre Tomo 1, ver item **2421**.

2423 Madriñán, Rocío. El cadáver prometido. Quito: RM Editores, 2006. 125 p.

Novela detectivesca en la que el protagonista, el inspector Sánchez Montalvo, debe resolver un crimen. Así, la trama del mismo, acaba siendo parte de ella. Madriñán ubica la historia en un contexto muy ecuatoriano, lo que se convierte más en un mérito que en una limitación, pues le permite construir los personajes en íntima relación con los procesos de una sociedad en concreto, con sus mentiras, sus crueles imaginarios, sus ámbitos sórdidos y las soledades que la pobreza anida. [J.C.L.]

2424 Maldonado, Lucrecia. Salvo el calvario. Quito: Editorial Planeta del Ecuador, 2005. 237 p.

Novela que tiene dos historias centrales de dos hombres jóvenes, narradas desde diversas ópticas que se complementan en el relato. Al más joven de los personajes, aprendiz de poeta y bohemio, le descubren leucemia. Luego de un largo y penoso tratamiento, regresa para encontrarse con sus amigos y su familia. La leucemia retorna y no le queda más que enfrentar la muerte, pero lo hace en compañía del otro joven personaje, un médico. Este último, de nombre Fernando, acicateado por los sentimientos que le provocan la enfermedad de su amigo, se enfrenta al reconocimiento de su homosexualidad. Los dos jóvenes se marchan a la Amazonía para pasar juntos el tiempo que al enfermo le queda de vida. Cuando Fernando retorna, se encuentra con el rechazo de su familia y se marcha a España donde puede vivir su homosexualidad y su verdadera vocación, la música. Aquí se establece un juego de historias: la leucemia, la enfermedad del cuerpo que conduce a la muerte, es simultánea al descubrimiento de la homosexualidad, un tema que en una sociedad homofóbica conduce a la muerte social. [J.C.L.]

2425 Mejía, Manuel Esteban. Trinitarias. Quito: Editorial El Conejo, 2007. 206 p.

Novela en la que se narra la cotidianidad en la ciudad de Guayaquil. La historia se centra en la vida de un abuelo y un niño que cohabitan en la Isla Trinitaria. El autor evidencia el pasado, el presente y el futuro de un lugar que cada vez más se ve invadido por la ciudad. Asimismo, el relato toma en cuenta la creación de nuevos suburbios debido a la modernidad que se expresa en la expansión de los linderos del principal puerto del Ecuador. [J.C.L.]

2426 Menoscal, Renato. Balada para terroristas. Ecuador: Quimera Ediciones, 2006. 187 p. (Col. Litera)

Novela que combina multiplicidad de discursos eróticos, cómicos y cinematográficos y plantea el tema del terrorismo. Se trata de un libro que consta de tres historias de humor estrechamente conexas: la carrera musical en el ámbito local e internacional del hiphopero ecuatoriano Marc Toine rodeada de jocosas aventuras; una familia real europea seriamente cuestionada y envuelta en escándalos; y una guerra de fanáticos religiosos africanos que despide olores escatológicos hacia el resto del mundo. [J.C.L.]

2427 Páez, Santiago. Crónicas del breve reino: tetralogía. Quito: Paradiso Editores, 2006. 475 p.: bibl. (Cantidad hechizada; 18. Narrativa)

Novela que forma parte de una tetralogía de este prolífico escritor. La acción comienza en el París de 1911 y recorre, además de la geografía ecuatoriana, ciudades como el Hamburgo posterior a la Segunda Guerra Mundial, el Cuzco y la Estación Espacial Internacional en pleno siglo XXI. Concebida como una novela total, es una reflexión sobre el rol de la literatura y el destino de las sociedades. [J.C.L.]

2428 Reece Dousdebés, Alfonso. Morga. Quito: Alfaguara, 2007. 263 p.

Novela histórica que recrea la vida del doctor Antonio de Morga, presidente de la Real Audiencia de Quito de 1615 a 1636. Fino observador de las naciones conquistadas por España, el libro narra los placeres y emociones que Morga encontró en el Nuevo Mundo, desde su amor por una mestiza, pasando por su relación con grandes artistas quiteños y teólogos de la época. [J.C.L.]

2429 Reinoso Barzallo, Yolanda. Días de arena y dátiles. Quito: Editorial El Conejo, 2006. 186 p.

El novela que nos introduce en el misterioso mundo de la cultura del Medio Oriente, acechada por la creciente invasión de valores de la sociedad de consumo. Cornelia, la protagonista, es una joven profesional que viaja a los Emiratos Árabes, para dirigir la primera biblioteca de una universidad. El relato registra en cada una de sus páginas y con un lenguaje directo las contradicciones que conviven en una misma cultura desde la sensibilidad de una mujer que ha experimentado en su país de origen las profundas huellas de una sociedad marcada por un mundo excluyente. En su nuevo destino, Cornelia se enfrenta a un sinnúmero de restricciones que fortalecen un poder anónimo y absolutista, y anula, para una mujer hecha en Occidente, parte de su ser femenino. [J.C.L.]

2430 Ribadeneira, Alejandro. Las traigo muertas: cuentos. Quito: Eskeletra Editorial, 2005. 193 p.: ill.

Libro de cuentos que rezuma un intenso perfume de descontento y rabia contenida con la realidad. El autor recurre a la palabra y a una particular sintaxis para emprender contra la política y los políticos, el modo de ser nacional, el lenguaje de los jóvenes, los divos de los medios de comunicación, la cultura del alcohol, los símbolos de la jerarquía social en un país excluyente como el Ecuador, el machismo y la telebasura. El libro ofrece una literatura que maneja con habilidad el lenguaje coloquial y los giros idiomáticos nacionales, mientras los nombres de sus personajes remiten al lector a protagonistas de la vida pública ecuatoriana. [J.C.L.]

2431 Rodríguez Vásconez, Byron. La guerra de la funeraria. Quito: Planeta, 2007. 353 p.: bibl.

Novela que cuenta el frustrado golpe de estado en contra del gobierno del Gen. Guillermo Rodríguez Lara el 1 de septiembre de 1975. En esa ocasión, el Gen. González Alvear atacó el palacio de Carondelet para derrocar al dictador. Escrita a caballo entre el periodismo y la ficción, en el relato abundan datos históricos e información curiosa que hace por momentos que el texto sea leído como si fuera un reportaje veraz e incuestionable. [J.C.L.]

2432 Ron, Alex. Historias de aerosol: cuentos. Quito: Eskeletra Editorial: Guayas: Casa de la Cultura Ecuatoriana, Núcleo de Guayas, 2005. 120 p.: ill.

Volumen de cuentos que reivindica la transformación que ejerce la metáfora pública del graffiti sobre las existencias solitarias de mujeres y hombres que habitan el vacío de la modernidad. Destacan los personajes rebeldes y aventureros que viven enfrentados a una vida siempre al borde del abismo. [J.C.L.]

2433 Serrano Sánchez, Raúl. Catálogo de ilusiones: cuentos. Quito: Eskeletra Editorial, 2006. 152 p.

Conjunto de cuentos que se postula como un muestrario de personajes esperpénticos, de pasiones torcidas. Se trata de una galería de hombres y mujeres llenos de sueños rotos. La historia y la vida cotidiana son elementos en descomposición y sirven como un escenario natural para contar la vida ecuatoriana. [J.C.L.]

2434 Valencia Assogna, Leonardo. Kazbek. Madrid: Editorial Funambulista, 2008. 117 p.: ill. (Col. Literadura)

Kazbek, trasterrado a Barcelona desde su Guayaquil natal, recibe de un amigo artista el encargo de poner palabras a una colección de grabados formada por 16 "bichos". Pese a que tiene pendiente escribir su Gran Novela, el escritor aceptará el encargo y se pondrá a ello. La sencillez de esta trama, sin embargo, esconde una notable sofisticación. Y es que Kazbek, al mismo tiempo que narra la elaboración del encargo, lo contiene con delicadeza. Aquí están los "bichos" del amigo artista y los pequeños poemas en prosa que el escritor dedica a cada uno, además de una teoría y práctica del arte. [J.C.L.]

2435 Vásconez, Carlos. El violín de Ingres. Ecuador: Editorial Ziete, 2005. 179 p.

Novela que narra la historia de Oscurimbad, un pobre iletrado y degradado sujeto parisino que, por trabajos del destino, se ve abordado por una melodía que lo poseerá sin tregua hasta consumirlo. Se trata de una novela de contrastes y de laberintos mentales, de alegres y meticulosas fantasías que conllevan más de una sorpresa. [J.C.L.]

2436 Velasco Mackenzie, Jorge. La mejor edad para morir: cuentos. Quito: Eskeletra Editorial, 2006. 151 p.

Conjunto de cuentos de este importante novelista cuyo eje en las nueve narraciones que contiene el volumen es la marginalidad. Los personajes se mantienen excluidos de un mundo que los expulsa y los recluye en espacios asfixiantes de los que les resulta imposible huir. Velasco reconstruye en sus narraciones una geografía en medio de la cual se puede intuir referentes reales— Guayaquil, Babahoyo, Nueva York, la China imperial—, pero que siempre mantiene su naturaleza opresiva, que genera una atmósfera que solamente existe en el interior la literatura del autor guayaquileño, sin que importe demasiado donde se sitúe la acción de los cuentos. Es recurrente el motivo de la búsqueda en los protagonistas de los cuentos. Ya sean marineros, artistas, periodistas o guerreros, todos están obsesionados con encontrar algo—una mujer, un símbolo, la solución de un crimen—aunque en realidad cada personaje pretende hallarse a sí mismo. [J.C.L.]

2437 Zunino, Giulia. ¿Dónde está Monse? Quito: Editorial el Conejo, 2007. 163 p.

Novela que narra fragmentos de la historia de la familia Montserrat a través de una mujer de 80 años de ascendencia ítalo-ecuatoriana que pasa sus días rememorando el pasado en compañía de su amiga Ceci. Sus relatos se ambientan en el Ecuador y en Italia, desde finales del siglo XIX, hasta el 2005. Zunino recrea la vida, costumbres y tradiciones ecuatorianas que surgen de la migración y la mezcla de culturas. [J.C.L.]

Peru

2438 Adaui Sicheri, Katya. Un accidente llamado familia. Lima: Grupo Editorial Matalamanga, 2007. 106 p. (Cuento; 9)

Primer libro de relatos de esta periodista donde la se examina las marcas que la vida deja en los diversos componentes de una familia. Estos 17 relatos no temen mostrar las heridas que a veces se abren a vista y paciencia de los seres más cercanos en medio de una cotidianidad a menudo misteriosa y conflictiva. [C.F.]

2439 Aguila, Irma del. Moby Dick en Cabo Blanco. Lima: Estruendo Mudo, 2009. 150 p. (Cuadernos esenciales; 28)

Ernest Hemingway se convirtió en un modelo de escritor para muchos narradores en ciernes, sobre todo por su vida aventurera, llena de hazañas bélicas, de caza y de pesca. Esta novela recrea la visita de Hemingway, en 1956, a Cabo Blanco, en el norte del Perú. Quien investiga sobre ese episodio es Cristina, una periodista limeña de nuestro tiempo. Después de leer lo escrito sobre Hemingway en periódicos, revistas y libros, ella viaja a Cabo Blanco, a entrevistar a los pocos testigos que aún sobreviven. Así, va descubriendo que, como toda leyenda, la de Hemingway está hecha de muchas exageraciones y mentiras y que el escritor no fue protagonista de todas las proezas que se le atribuyen. [C.F.]

2440 Alfredo Bryce Echenique, una vida de novela. Lima: Aguilar, 2010. 221 p.: facsim., ill.

Una vida de novela es un trabajo recopilatorio sobre el autor de *Un mundo para Julius* (see *HLAS 34:3605*). Este consiste en una colección de cartas dirigidas al autor por parte de otros escritores, de admiradores o de amigos, además de viejas fotografías, en muchos casos inéditas, una entrevista con Bryce y textos escritos sobre su obra. [C.F.]

2441 Ampuero, Fernando. Hasta que me orinen los perros. Lima: Planeta, 2008. 159 p. (Autores españoles e iberoamericanos)

Novela en que este escritor y periodista intenta retratar de modo realista el rostro callejero de la ciudad de Lima. El libro cuenta la vida de un grupo de taxistas limeños dedicados a la delincuencia. Destaca una prosa limpia y funcional, a medio camino entre la ficción y la crónica urbana, como en muchos de los relatos de Ampuero. [C.F.]

2442 Antología del relato brichero: Pachamama club. Selección de Fernando Pomareda. Lima: Estruendo Mudo, 2007. 172 p. (Col. Cajas; 3)

Este libro reúne una serie de cuentos que tienen como protagonistas a esos jóvenes—hombres y mujeres—cuyo oficio consiste en "levantarse" gringos(as) con la finalidad principal de vivir a sus expensas e irse a vivir a sus países de origen, o sencillamente robarles. Los relatos muestran situaciones insólitas e incluso ridículas, al tiempo que divertidas por las delirantes

estrategias seductoras utilizadas por los bricheros y la candidez de sus víctimas. Si hay dos relatos que sobresalen claramente en el libro son "Buscando un Inca" de Luis Nieto Degregori, y "Los cuatrocientos golpes" de Oswaldo Chanove. Destaquemos también los relatos "Cazador de gringas" de Mario Guevara, y "Visa woman" de Carlos Rengifo. [C.F.]

2443 Bartet, Leyla. A puerta cerrada. Lima: PEISA, 2007. 140 p. (Serie del río hablador)

Nueva colección de relatos de esta cuentista. Misterio y erotismo recorren las páginas de este libro en el que, con gran manejo del suspenso y notable capacidad narrativa, Bartet nos invita a explorar las pulsiones básicas que determinan el rumbo de nuestras vidas. Devotos del silencio, sus personajes se entregan a la pasión y al desenfreno, y se despojan de toda atadura cuando acuden al encuentro de situaciones definitivas, como asesinatos, traiciones, venganzas y locura. [C.F.]

2444 Belevan, Harry. Cuentos de bolsillo. Lima: Univ. Ricardo Palma, Editorial Universitaria, 2007. 115 p. (Serie Ficciones)

Libro que reúne 67 relatos breves, algunos en forma de apostillas, sobre el amor, la amistad y la muerte. Destaquemos la originalidad del autor para tratar temas universales, así como su agudeza con el lenguaje narrativo. [C.F.]

2445 Benavides, Jorge Eduardo. La paz de los vencidos. Lima: Alfaguara, 2009. 187 p.

Novela escrita a manera de diario íntimo en el que el protagonista, un aspirante a escritor radicado en la isla de Tenerife, cuenta sus pequeños encuentros y desencuentros con sus vecinos, colegas y amigos. Estos últimos son tan solitarios y desarraigados como él. A pesar de la naturaleza solitaria de los personajes, Benavides le da al relato un tono optimista y desenfadado, gracias a una prosa ingeniosa y el peculiar sentido del humor del narrador. [C.F.]

2446 Bisso, Alicia. Algunas fotos tuyas. Lima: Solar, 2008. 88 p. (Col. Pandemonio. Narrativa)

Los cuentos de este volumen están llenos de claroscuros, de vuelcos emocionales que logran una especie de reconciliación hacia el final del libro. Las imágenes y los escenarios finamente construidos expresan sentimientos muy variados: por un lado, el dolor de la soledad, de las rupturas, de los vacíos que se generan en los vínculos por aquellas frases no dichas, aunque muy sentidas. Pero también una sonrisa querida, el olor de la persona amada, la canción a través de la cual ella nos pertenece. [C.F.]

2447 Bisso, Alicia et al. Matadoras: nuevas narradoras peruanas. Lima: Estruendo Mudo, 2008. 205 p.: ill. (Cuadernos esenciales; 21)

Antología de cuentos que reúne a 13 nuevas narradoras del Perú. Estas escritoras se distancian de la generación anterior en su manera de ejercer eso que se suele llamar literatura femenina. En verdad, ninguna de ellas considera su trabajo marcado por una perspectiva de género. Destaca un grupo de cuentos más vivenciales de Bisso, Díaz, Ulloa, Pacheco, Del Río y Villena, y otro poblado por las que ejercen opciones más literarias de Klatic, Noltenius, Adaui, Gadea, Cáceres y Belevan. [C.F.]

2448 Bossio Suárez, Sandro. Crónica de amores furtivos. Lima: Editorial San Marcos, 2008. 184 p. (Col. Súmmum)

Segundo libro de este escritor que es una recopilación de 16 cuentos de variado registro: policiales, históricos, fantásticos, realistas. A la eficacia de su lenguaje en los relatos hay que sumar un destacable manejo de las técnicas narrativas y el acertado desarrollo de algunas tramas. Varios relatos tienen incluso un final sorpresivo que parece dar vuelta a lo narrado hasta entonces. "Retornos", "El juego de las equivalencias" y "En busca del Paititi" están entre los más logrados cuentos del libro y combinan atmósferas realistas con finales fantásticos. [C.F.]

2449 Bryce Echenique, Alfredo. La esposa del Rey de las Curvas: cuentos. Lima: PEISA, 2008. 145 p. (Serie del río hablador. Peisa)

Libro de cuentos en el que Bryce es fiel a su estilo oral, con largos monólogos llenos de digresiones y retorcimientos, en los que un antihéroe cuenta sus peripecias y desventuras. Destacan relatos como "La funcionaria linguista", "La esposa del Rey de las Curvas" o "La chica Pazos". [C.F.]

2450 Calderón Fajardo, Carlos. El huevo de la iguana. Lima: Editorial San Marcos, 2007. 425 p. (Col. Diamantes y pedernales; 11)

Versión definitiva de la novela La conquista de la maravilla que ganó el premio Gaviota Roja en 1982 y cuya primera parte fuera publicada en 1983 bajo el título Así es la pena en el paraíso. El libro narra la historia de amor de Toño Farías y Encarnación Zapata en el contexto de una ciudad-capamento petrolero en Talara, en el norte del Perú, en la década de los años cincuenta, por cuyos intersticios se colaba un mundo de mitos, de espíritus, de almas en pena en el cual solo podían intervenir brujos y curanderos. En más de un sentido, esta novela es un viaje al pasado de un hombre que, a través de sus sueños, recuerda su infancia, adolescencia y juventud en Talara. Destaca el lenguaje onírico del relato cercano al realismo mágico. [C.F.]

2451 Calderón Fajardo, Carlos. La noche humana. Lima: PETROPERÚ, Ediciones COPÉ, 2008. 245 p.

Novela que rinde homenaje a Milú, amiga del poeta César Vallejo, esposa de Gonzalo More y competencia amorosa de Anais Nin. En ella el autor hace referencias sobre las vidas azarosas de los artistas e intelectuales peruanos que viajaron a París entre las décadas de 1920 y 1970. [C.F]

2452 Colchado Lucio, Oscar. Noticias del gran bandido. Lima: Bruño, 2010. 140 p.

Novela que narra la historia de Luis Pardo, llamado el Gran Bandido. Temido y amado, Pardo robaba a comerciantes y ricos hacendados para socorrer a los pobres y explotados campesinos. La policía y el ejército lo perseguían sin tregua, achacándole crímenes y latrocinios que mayormente no había cometido. Luis Pardo con ayuda de los mismos campesinos, logró evadir muchas veces a sus perseguidores, hasta que sucumbió trágicamente en 1909. [C.F.]

2453 Congrains Martín, Enrique. 999 palabras para el planeta tierra. Lima: Ediciones HuaitaPuquio, 2008. 445 p.: ill.

Cultivador de una novelística urbana de corte realista en la década de los años 50, Congrains muestra aquí una nueva faceta de su trabajo creativo: novelas imaginativas del futuro, pero ajenas a las convenciones de la ciencia ficción. En febrero del 2015, cerca de las líneas de Nazca, una nave espacial le pide a Toribio Huaita que el presidente peruano acuda el 16 de marzo y reciba oficialmente el encargo de redactar un artículo de 999 palabras sobre el planeta Tierra para la "Gran Enciclopedia Intergaláctica". Se trata de una obra que se ubica entre la sátira y la alegoría grotesca y agridulce para representar el porvenir al que puede conducirnos el estado actual de la humanidad con sus prejuicios y dilemas políticos y económicos. [C.F.]

2454 Cueto, Alonso. La venganza del silencio. Lima: Planeta, 2010. 319 p. (Autores Españoles e Iberoamericanos)

Novela que es un relato policial de trasfondo moral que explora los cimientos sentimentales, sociales y económicos sobre los que se levantan las relaciones en las clases altas latinoamericanas. Luego de la muerte de sus padres en un accidente automovilístico, Antonio se muda a casa de sus tíos, Adolfo y Adriana, quienes se encargarán de cuidar de él como si se tratara de su propio hijo. Desde entonces, los años de Antonio pasan bajo la mirada amable de su tío y el severo carácter de su tía hasta que el joven decide irse a estudiar a Europa. A su regreso a Lima, Antonio percibe los cambios que han ocurrido durante su ausencia; la rigurosidad de los hábitos que estructuraban la casa de sus tíos se han visto alterados por fuerzas invisibles que despiertan su curiosidad. Al cabo de unos días, durante una salida nocturna, Antonio descubrirá una verdad que pondrá en vilo sus creencias familiares, una verdad en la que el sexo, la mentira y la distancia insalvable que existe entre las clases sociales se confundirán en una espiral de confusión que deja a la familia sin sentido. El asombro de Antonio se intensificará con el asesinato de su tío, que aparece muerto de un balazo en una calle alejada de la casa familiar. [C.F.]

2455 Díaz Herrera, Jorge. Pata de perro: novela. Lima: Editorial San Marcos, 2007. 327 p. (Col. Súmmum)

Novela cuyo protagonista, Pol, verdadero "pata de perro", es un combatiente de la sobrevivencia cotidiana. Drama, reflexión y no poca vitalidad hay en este personaje que revela, en muchas maneras, la vida peruana y dialoga con la tradición de la novela picaresca. [C.F.]

2456 Díaz Herrera, Jorge. Las tentaciones de don Antonio. Lima: San Marcos, 2008. 186 p.: index. (Col. Súmmum)

Quince cuentos de este prolífico autor peruano poblados por personajes que luchan por construir su propia felicidad, pero que en el fondo terminan por naufragar en la desventura. Destaca la lograda dualidad entre tragedia y comedia de los textos. [C.F.]

2457 17 fantásticos cuentos peruanos. Recopilación de Gabriel Rimachi Sialer y Carlos M. Sotomayor. Lima: Casatomada, 2008. 224 p.: ports. (Casatomada narrativa)

Libro que explora, a partir de sus propias coordenadas, la producción narrativa de autores peruanos en los delirantes rumbos de la dimensión desconocida. El corpus cubre voces nacidas entre 1933 y 1979; por lo tanto, debe afirmarse que los cuentos seleccionados pertenecen al período de la maduración luego de que los pioneros modernistas y la explosiva Vanguardia tendieran los rieles para el género. [C.F.]

2458 Dughi Martínez, Pilar. La horda primitiva. Lima: PEISA, 2008. 168 p.: index. (Serie del río hablador)

Volumen que reúne textos inéditos y otros cuentos que pertenecen a los libros *La premeditación y el azar* y *Ave de la noche* seleccionados por Dughi antes de morir en 2006. Conocedora de las técnicas de la narrativa moderna y seguidora de Chéjov en estos relatos póstumos, Dughi se interesa más por lo que sucede en el fuero interno de sus protagonistas que por narrar una historia al estilo clásico. Por ello, destacan aquí una serie de personajes atormentados como el adolescente de "A mí no me importa"; la muchacha que cuida a su anciano padre a costa de su felicidad en "Hay que lavar", o la solitaria profesora, que escribe sobre Schopenhauer en "Los guiños del destino". Cada uno de ellos debe tomar en algún momento de su vida una decisión importante y dar un paso adelante; es en ese momento que la conciencia de los protagonistas va hacia lo definitivo que el relato acaba y que el lector deberá completar. [C.F.]

2459 Effio Ordóñez, Augusto. Lecciones de origami. Lima: Grupo Editorial Matalamanga, 2006. 126 p. (Matalamanga. Cuento; 6)

Primer volumen de cuentos de este escritor donde destaca su gran cuidado del lenguaje narrativo. Uno de sus temas recurrentes es la figura del burócrata público. Reminiscentes de Kafka, los cuentos de Effio transmiten la burocrática mirada de ese emblemático sujeto y el infernal procesar de expedientes. Todo ello lleva a los personajes a explorar círculos concéntricos hacia la esfera de la corrupción como un modo de vida; vale decir, el engaño, tolerado por las partes, la funcional mentira burocrática y la convivencia con lo ilegal en la vida peruana. [C.F.]

2460 Ferrini, Ernesto. Los crímenes del caso Mariposa. Lima: Planeta, 2008. 240 p. (Autores españoles e iberoamericanos)

Segunda novela de este escritor. Escrita bajo el formato policial también despliega un buen uso de un humor inteligente como arma reveladora de la realidad. El periodista y ensayista peruano Eric Frattini publica su primera novela, *El Quinto Mandamiento,* un relato de intriga sobre "lo que los poderosos son capaces de hacer para mantener su poder", inspirado por sus investigaciones sobre los servicios de inteligencia del Vaticano. Para Frattini, aquellos son "los mejores del mundo, por delante incluso de la CIA, ya que se componen de una red con fuentes repartidas por todo el mundo". A partir de su propia documentación, y de sus visitas a lugares reales en los que se ambienta la historia—como el Monasterio de Vila Mondragone, en la ciudad italiana de Frascati—, Frattini recrea el funcionamiento interno del Vaticano, desde donde el cardenal Lienart, personaje principal de la obra, despliega sus oscuros propósitos. [C.F.]

2461 Freire Sarria, Luis. La tradición secreta de Ricardo Palma. Ilustraciones de Mario Molina. Lima: PEISA, 2008. 110 p.: ill., index. (Contraseña)

En esta novela, Freire parte de una imaginario a carta firmada por Palma que revela la existencia de una versión modificada de la tradición "El carbunco del diablo". Esta señala las pistas para encontrar el tesoro robado del siglo XVI al pirata holandés Jacques Clerk l'Hermite. La carta cae en manos de un joven narrador, Jorge Buendía, quien decide lanzarse en búsqueda del tesoro Para suerte de Buendía, el mismo Palma vuelve a la vida y decide ponerse de su parte. Freire construye un relato hila-

rante que conduce al lector por lugares emblemáticos de la vieja ciudad de Lima. [C.F.]

2462 Galarza, Sergio. Paseador de perros. Lima: Alfaguara, 2008. 110 p. (Alfaguara)

Primera novela de este reputado cuentista que tiene lugar en Madrid. Allí un joven migrante busca adaptarse a España desde su oficio de paseador de perros, gatos y hasta de un mapache. Galarza relata su historia a través de estampas de gentes y lugares que poco a poco van plegándose a su vida, auscultados con sinceridad y pertinencia. [C.F.]

2463 Gallardo, Carlos. Espuma! Lima: Estruendo Mudo, 2008. 337 p. (Cuadernos esenciales; 25)

Primera novela de este joven escritor. Se trata de un retrato hiperrealista de su propia generación, elaborado a partir de la historia de un grupo de estudiantes del colegio Claretiano y escrito en el peculiar lenguaje de los adolescentes limeños de fines del siglo pasado. El protagonista de este relato es Carlos Mantilla, un joven aspirante a escritor. Alrededor de él están sus compañeros de promoción: Javier, Eduardo, Marx, entre otros. Todos ellos narran sus primeras incursiones en el mundo adulto, la tensión de los exámenes de ingreso a la universidad y el descubrimiento del amor y del sexo. [C.F.]

2464 Garayar, Carlos. El cielo sobre nosotros. Lima: Alfaguara, 2007. 332 p.

Novela que tiene como temas principales el amor y la enfermedad. Un jóven alférez, Juan Siélac, es destacado a un pueblo en la selva. Deshauciado, allí vive una historia de amor con la enfermera Soria en un hospital que es un espacio de exilio y reclusión. Con ecos de *La montaña mágica* de Thomas Mann, la novela de Garayar presenta la enfermedad no sólo como un mal concreto, sino como una poderosa metáfora de la condición humana. [C.F.]

2465 González Viaña, Eduardo. El corrido de Dante. Houston, Tex.: Arte Público Press, 2006. 312 p.

Novela sobre la inmigración latinoamericana en los Estados Unidos. Los personajes Dante, su esposa fallecida Beatriz y el burro Virgilio reeditan los caminos a veces bellos y a veces atroces de Dante Alighieri, entre el cielo y el infierno, y de los latinoamericanos en el mismo territorio norteamericano. [C.F.]

2466 Güich Rodríguez, José. Los espectros nacionales. Lima: Editorial San Marcos, 2008. 153 p. (Col. Súmmum)

Libro de cuentos compuesto por ocho relatos de variada índole realista y fantástica con un amplio juego de referencias intertextuales. Desde el cuento que da título al libro, queda claramente establecida la dinámica de los relatos: Joao Pereira, "ciudadano octogenario de Río de Janeiro", vuelve al estadio Maracaná 50 años después de presenciar la recordada derrota de su selección ante la de Uruguay. Y aunque sólo desea ver el debut de su nieto como futbolista, vuelve a vivir la humillante final del Mundial de 1950. Otro salto cronológico, aunque hacia el futuro, es el realizado por el protagonista de "Intersecciones"; y en "Los pasajes errantes" un científico de mediados del siglo XXI vuelve a la Lima de 1950 para averiguar sobre el escritor Julio Ramón Ribeyro. En otros cuentos los saltos se producen también entre la realidad y la ficción—en "La penumbra" los protagonistas son Miguel de Cervantes y Don Quijote—, entre identidades personales ("Vórtice en Prescott") y hasta universos paralelos, como en "El otro monitor", que plantea la existencia de un monitor Huáscar fantasma que colabora con el real en la Guerra del Pacífico entre Perú y Chile. [C.F.]

2467 Helguero, Lorenzo. El amor en los tiempos del cole; Fiesta de promoción. Lima: Estruendo Mudo, 2008. 45, 106 p. (Cuadernos esenciales; 22)

Volumen dividido en dos partes. La primera, *El amor en los tiempos del cole*, apareció publicado por vez primera en el 2000. Desde el título, este texto mostraba una travesura literaria: la aplicación de un corte que mutilaba la sílaba final de la ilustre novela de García Márquez para instalarnos en el ámbito escolar; allí donde bullen los amores furtivos, las promesas incumplidas, las ternuras odiosas. A medio camino entre la poesía y las estampas en prosa, es claro que se trata de un libro de culto en las letras peruanas, que retrata la imagen de un adolescente trémulo, tristísimo y trastornado al contemplar su rostro en la pantalla de su memoria, como un vivaz y maltrecho

dibujo animado. En la segunda parte, encontramos *Fiesta de promoción*, una treintena de cuentos brevísimos, que recrean las tribulaciones que pasan unos muchachos los días previos a la fiesta que culmina su educación secundaria. Todos los relatos ilustran esa hoguera de vanidades por la que deben pasar los estudiantes de un colegio de clase alta para esa ocasión. [C.F.]

2468 Helguero, Lorenzo. Entre el cielo y el suelo. Lima: Alfaguara, 2008. 141 p.

Primera novela de este importante poeta de la generación del noventa. El relato está dividido en cinco secciones, narrada cada una por un personaje distinto, con monólogos que brotan diferenciados por sus propios registros. Todos ellos sirven para evocar el romance entre Carlos y Clara, los amantes que ahora se encuentran separados por el viaje del protagonista. Destaca el estilo humorístico y lúdico del libro. [C.F.]

2469 Higa Oshiro, Augusto. La iluminación de Katzuo Nakamatsu. Lima: Editorial San Marcos, 2008. 127 p. (Col. Súmmum)

La novela—que es un informe de Benito Gutti—cuenta la historia de Katzuo Nakamatsu, un descendiente de un migrante japonés en el Perú. Nakamatsu trabaja como profesor de literatura en una universidad, pero de pronto, sin mayores explicaciones, es despedido. Desempleado, con síntomas de males psiquiátricos, empieza a errar por barrios pobres de la ciudad, centros nocturnos de mala muerte, pero siempre escuchando voces. Cuando Nakamatsu pierde finalmente la razón y es hospitalizado, recibe la asistencia, además de médica, de una médium, la yuta Miyagui, quien le establece un puente con el pasado de su padre y la vida humillada y perseguida de los migrantes japoneses durante el gobierno de Manuel Prado en la primera mitad del siglo XX. Con gran destreza, la novela entrelaza un presente y un pasado de historias ominosas. [C.F.]

2470 Lauer, Mirko. Orbitas, tertulias. Lima: Hueso Húmero Ediciones: Ediciones El Virrey, 2006. 168 p.

En esta novela se prolonga la preocupación del autor por acontecimientos misteriosos en el puerto de Cerro Azul, en el valle de Cañete al sur de Lima. El misterioso personaje que en 1988 voló a San Francisco,

California, en busca de un antiguo habitante de Cerro Azul de los años 30 en *Secretos inútiles*, la primera parte de esta trilogía, esta vez da vueltas en mototaxi por el valle cumpliendo un periplo de 24 horas que incluye citas y encuentros inesperados. Un día que gira en torno a un objeto imposible, que hasta hace unas horas dormía enterrado, girando al fondo de un laberinto sin salida. [C.F.]

2471 Lauer, Mirko. Tapen la tumba: una novela. Lima: Ediciones El Virrey: Hueso Húmero Ediciones, 2009. 165 p.

Novela de este poeta y periodista que cierra su "tríptico de Cerro Azul" que iniciaron las novelas *Secretos inútiles* y *Órbitas, tertulias* (ganadora del premio Juan Rulfo; ver item **2470**). En ella se superponen las voces de críticos literarios como Abelardo Oquendo, políticos como Luis Alberto Sánchez y hasta la del propio Lauer, para así desarrollar una singular narración no exenta de guiños a la historia contemporánea del Perú. Se trata de una novela experimental que se despliega con frases descriptivas de aliento cotidiano, vanguardista en estructura y modernista en contenido. [C.F.]

2472 Martínez Castilla, Bertha D. El despertar de las sombras: novela. Lima: Editorial San Marcos, 2007. 241 p. (Biblioteca de narrativa peruana contemporánea; 78)

Novela que transcurre en Santa Rosa de Ocopa, en la sierra central del Perú, en los años 60. La trama desenvuelve una inusitada historia de amor entre el padre Iluminato, un monje franciscano de origen español, y una muchacha del lugar, que lleva el nombre de María de los Angeles pero a quien se conoce como "La Angel". La novela enfrenta un contrapunto entre la pasión del sacerdote y la de su ángel carnal, evocada con un gran tono lírico. El telón de fondo de esta suerte de novela costumbrista es la preparación de una rebelión guerrillera en el pueblo contado desde la imaginaría popular. [C.F.]

2473 Miró Quesada, Patricia. Herencia de familia. Lima: Editora Mesa Redonda, 2008. 135 p.: index. (Serie Narrativa)

Debut literario de esta escritora con un conjunto de diez cuentos que interrogan de distinta manera sobre lo que realmente se transmite de generación en generación: asuntos como el amor, el desamor, los silen-cios, la esperanza. Tomando como eje de sus historias a mujeres que han logrado obtener un grado de madurez en su vida, la autora se sumerge en las heridas, nostalgias y sueños de sus personajes para ver hasta qué punto todo ello es reflejo de su vida familiar. De esta manera, el pasado se convierte en el vector temporal privilegiado desde el cual los diferentes actores de estas historias van tejiendo y destejiendo su presente. [C.F.]

2474 Niño de Guzmán, Guillermo. Algo que nunca serás. Lima: Planeta, 2007. 121 p. (Autores españoles e iberoamericanos)

Tercer libro de relatos de este importante cuentista perteneciente a la generación del 80. La mitad de estos cuentos pueden clasificarse como relatos fantásticos. Otros textos como "Sombras nada más" y "Viejo ángel de medianoche" se centran en temas que ya estaban presentes en sus libros anteriores como el desamor, la derrota, la vida nocturna y el escepticismo. Destaca, asimismo, el cuento "La vida sexual de Borges", una magnífica parodia del escritor argentino. [C.F.]

2475 Noltenius, Susanne. Crisis respiratoria. Lima: Estruendo Mudo, 2006. 143 p. (Cuadernos esenciales; 9)

Ante el fracaso de la comunicación, y con la conclusión inevitable de que los individuos están solos, "actuando" para cumplir con sus funciones y expectativas en una ciudad codificada por las apariencias. Este es un libro de relatos que expone con precisión los síntomas de la infelicidad en medio de relaciones amorosas y filiales aparentemente estables, y presenta los vacíos invisibles de lo cotidiano: el efecto del tiempo, el hastío, el desengaño y la necesidad salvadora, en la quietud del hogar, en la ciudad o en los viajes, de escapar y de decir. [C.F.]

2476 Ollé, Carmen. Una muchacha bajo su paraguas y otros relatos. 2. ed. Lima: Editorial San Marcos, 2008. 189 p.: ill. (Col. Súmmum)

Segunda edición de una novela corta que esta importante poeta publicó originalmente en el 2002 (ver *HLAS 62:2521*). Se trata de un recorrido por un París que está en el otro lado del París turístico o de postal: un París áspero, triste, en el que los inmigrantes latinoamericanos de fines de los años setenta sobreviven y buscan los restos

de la Ciudad Luz y sus mitos. La edición
viene acompañada por un conjunto de relatos que son viñetas que expresan confusión
y azar. [C.F.]

2477 Piérola, José de. El camino de regreso. Bogotá; Lima: Grupo Editorial
Norma, 2007. 420 p. (La otra orilla)

Novela que viene a cerrar una trilogía
del autor sobre la violencia y el terror que
envolvió al Perú a partir de la lucha armada
de Sendero Luminoso. El protagonista de
esta novela es Fernando, un joven ingeniero
cuyo padre ha muerto víctima de un aten-
tado terrorista y cuyo hilo conductor es
precisamente la constante amenaza de la
muerte. Encontrar el "camino de regreso"
(entendido como una recuperación del orden
y de una racionalidad que permitan la convivencia en la sociedad peruana) es una tarea
en que el protagonista y otros personajes se
juegan nada menos que la vida. [C.F.]

2478 Piérola, José de. Sur y norte. Lima:
Grupo Editorial Norma S.A.C., 2008.
222 p. (La otra orilla)

Libro que reúne los mejores cuentos
de este premiado escritor como "La viuda
de Cayara", "El futuro en la mirada", "Mañana lo buscamos" y "Hallazgo en la calle
42". Se trata de una serie de historias de
inmigrantes perdidos en un mundo que
recorren con asombro y que nunca alcanzan
a comprender. [C.F.]

2479 Ponce, Víctor Andrés. Las muertes
de Emilio. Lima: Grupo Editorial
Norma, 2008. 290 p. (La Otra orilla)

Novela escrita por este escritor y
periodista donde el dogmatismo ideológico,
la ética periodística y la creatividad literaria
dan forma a una historia donde cada personaje busca encontrarse consigo mismo y así
poder redimirse. [C.F.]

2480 Reátegui, Roberto. A fin de cuentas.
Lima: Planeta, 2008. 206 p. (Autores
españoles e iberoamericanos)

Nueva novela de este periodista y
escritor. Un hombre que apenas pasa la
cincuentena se interna en un hospital para
ser tratado de un cáncer maligno. Con la
certeza que el fin se acerca, comienza a
anotar en un cuaderno todos sus recuerdos,
evocando el tiempo cuando estaba sano y
más o menos feliz. La confrontación con su
estado actual da pie a una larga reflexión

sobre el bienestar; las mieles de la salud y
los sinsabores ácidos de la enfermedad, a la
que execra y apostrofa con una rudeza conmovedora. [C.F.]

2481 Rivera Martínez, Edgardo. Cuentos
del Ande y la neblina, 1964–2008.
Lima: Punto de Lectura, 2008. 495 p. (Punto
de lectura. Narrativa)

Los cuentos escritos hasta 1999 han
sido reunidos aquí de acuerdo al criterio que
sirvió para la primera edición de los cuentos completos de este importante escritor
peruano en 1999; es decir, una edición que
tomó en cuenta los temas, los escenarios,
las afinidades, los contrastes, el conjunto de
que formaban parte y el año de su aparición.
A ellos se agregan los que aparecieron bajo el
título de *Danzantes de la noche y la muerte*
en 2006 y, finalmente, dos inéditos, "Ileana
Espíritu" y "El Tucumano" fechados en
el 2008. El título alude al escenario de los
relatos, esto es, al mundo andino, que es el
prevaleciente, y al de una Lima signada por
la neblina de sus largos inviernos. [C.F.]

2482 Rivera Martínez, Edgardo. Diario de
Santa María. Lima: Alfaguara, 2008.
197 p. (Alfaguara)

Nueva novela de este importante escritor peruano que confirma diversas constantes en su universo literario, que establece
como siempre un fructífero diálogo entre
el mundo andino y el mundo occidental.
Ambientada en Ocopa, en la sierra central
del Perú, en el imaginario Colegio de Edu-
candas de Nuestra Señora de Santa María,
esta novela narra un año decisivo en la educación sentimental de Felicia de los Ríos:
1935, cuando estudió interna el último año
de secundaria, pasando de los 17 años a los
18 de edad. En ese entonces sintió el ardor
sexual, no solo despertado por un novicio de
Ocopa, sino sobre todo por una compañera
de cuarto, la francesa Solange, desinhibida y
más madura que ella. En ese tiempo, Felicia
escribió el diario que contiene esta novela
y, compartiendo lecturas con Solange, des-
cubrió su vocación por la creación literaria.
Destaca, como siempre, el gran lirismo de la
prosa de Rivera Martínez. [C.F.]

2483 Ruiz Rosas, Teresa. La falaz posteri-
dad. Lima: Editorial San Marcos, 2007.
363 p. (Col. Diamantes y pedernales; 12)

Novela que se inicia con la aparición
de Dora Bakarel en busca de reconocimiento

a la autoría del guión Kuhle Wampe o ¿De quién es el mundo?, primera película del 'cine proletario' en Alemania, en las postrimerías de la Republica de Weimar, obra de Slatan Dudow más que de Bertolt Brecht, como figura en la mayoría de los registros. Es a través de este hecho y sus connotaciones jurídicas, que Dora Bakarel, única hija del realizador, y Silvia Olazábal, periodista y cinéfila, se acercan hasta la inevitable complicidad. Ruiz Rosas es narradora y traductora literaria con varios premios literarios importantes en su haber. [C.F.]

2484 Siu, Kam Wen. La vida no es una tómbola. Lima: Univ. Nacional, Mayor de San Marcos, Ediciones del Vicerrectorado Académico, 2008. 295 p.

Novela de este importante narrador de origen chino. En ella, Héctor, nombre impuesto a un niño chino que emigra al Perú a los nueve años de edad, es el hijo de un tendero que quiere transmitirle su visión práctica de la vida. Héctor terminará despreciándola en aras de su vocación literaria. Con mil sinsabores, el protagonista termina sus estudios en una carrera que no le interesa. Paralelamente, asistimos a sus frustraciones en el terreno amoroso. También se cuenta la existencia fracasada del tío de Héctor y de una bella mujer sin premios en la tómbola del mundo. Sin lograr urdir un gran fresco de la colonia china en el Perú, muestra una faceta importante de una sociedad pluricultural y multiétnica. [C.F.]

2485 Sumalavia, Ricardo. Que la tierra te sea leve. Barcelona: Bruguera, 2008. 156 p. (Bruguera narrativa)

Se puede decir que el tema central de esta primera novela de Sumalavia es, de alguna manera, la búsqueda: la búsqueda del hermano perdido, por un lado, y la del hermano literario, por otro. Y en ambas búsquedas el relato trata de establecer correspondencias, crear un tramado que articule toda la novela. Por un lado, con la historia de César y la búsqueda de su hermano, el enano Féfer, en pleno centro de una Lima noctámbula: y, por otro, la de un joven aspirante a escritor que trata de hallarse a sí mismo a través de libros, viajes y, especialmente, las búsquedas emprendidas por otros escritores. El relato propone un proceso en el que se construye una identidad que va mutando en su propia construcción. [C.F.]

2486 Thays, Iván. Un lugar llamado Oreja de Perro. Barcelona: Editorial Anagrama, 2008. 212 p. (Narrativas hispánicas; 445)

Novela finalista del premio Anagrama de novela de este importante narrador peruano. En ella, un joven periodista limeño que sufre la temprana muerte de su hijo y la ruptura de su matrimonio, ha llegado a un remoto pueblo en Ayacucho, en la sierra sur del Perú, para cubrir el lanzamiento oficial de un programa de asistencia social. El personaje será testigo involuntario de trágicos sucesos que le permitirán conocerse a sí mismo. [C.F.]

2487 Tola, Raúl. Toque de queda. Lima: Planeta, 2008. 126 p. (Autores españoles e iberoamericanos)

Libro de cuentos que alterna historias llenas de ternura y brutalidad que transcurren en la década los ochenta en el Perú: un período de violencia y orfandad donde las calles se convirtieron en un territorio de guerra sin vencedores y en el que la muerte aguardaba a la vuelta de la esquina. En ese contexto, una generación como la del autor aprendió a descubrir la belleza cuando todo parecía perdido. [C.F.]

2488 Vargas Llosa, Mario. El sueño del celta. 2a ed. Madrid: Alfaguara, 2010. 454 p.

La aventura que narra esta novela empieza en el Congo en 1903 y termina en una cárcel de Londres en 1916. Se cuenta la peripecia vital del irlandés Roger Casement. Héroe y villano, traidor y libertario, Casement fue uno de los primeros europeos en denunciar los horrores del colonialismo. De sus viajes al Congo Belga y a la amazonía peruana quedaron dos informes memorables que conmocionaron a la sociedad de su tiempo, pues tras ellos se revelaba una verdad dolorosa: no era la barbarie africana ni amazónica la que volvía bárbaros a los civilizados europeos, en nombre del comercio, la civilización y el cristianismo. Estos dos viajes y lo que allí vio, cambiarían a Casement para siempre, haciéndole emprender otra travesía, en este caso intelectual, tanto o más devastadora, que lo llevó a enfrentarse a una Inglaterra que admiraba y a militar activamente en la causa del nacionalismo irlandés. [C.F.]

2489 Yushimito, Carlos. Las islas. Lima: [SIC] Libros, 2006. 159 p. (Col. Breve)

Conjunto de ocho cuentos ambientados en la ciudad de Río de Janeiro, en Brasil donde los personajes habitan las favelas situadas en los alrededores de la ciudad. Los seres que recorren estos relatos son marginales, sin embargo, más allá de sobrevivir en un ambiente colmado de carencias, ellos no son absorbidos por la condición de su entorno, sino que escapan a sus angustias y encuentran que el vivir está más allá de la simple existencia. [C.F.]

2490 Zavaleta, Carlos Eduardo. Huérfano de mujer. Lima: Alfaguara, 2008. 109 p.

Nueva novela de este importante escritor de la Generación del 50. Su trama principal es el enamoramiento y matrimonio de Claudio Rojas, un joven provinciano andino, y Rosa, una muchacha limeña parecida a Susan Hayward, educada con las pautas tradicionales de una Lima tradicional. Luego, la penosa enfermedad y prematura muerte de Rosa, quien deja a Claudio en un vacío que lo hace sentirse sumido en una gran soledad. El hilo secundario es la formación de Claudio como historiador y la evolución de Lima hasta el "desborde popular" de décadas recientes. [C.F.]

2491 Zeballos Rebaza, Roberto. Tigre hircana. Lima: Banco Central de Reserva del Perú, 2007. 171 p.

Con el trasfondo de una antigua ciudad de provincia, esta novela constituye un relato sobre la inevitable pérdida del mundo de la infancia y la necesidad de lidiar con circunstancias desagradables, desencantos y sentimientos inesperados. Haciendo uso de un lenguaje intimista y reflexivo, el protagonista y narrador de esta historia evoca su resistencia para aceptar los cambios y las consecuencias del ineludible paso del tiempo. [C.F.]

Venezuela

2492 Belmonte, Luis Enrique. Salvar a los elefantes. Caracas: Editorial Equinoccio, 2006. 122 p. (Col. Papiros. Serie Narrativa)

En la novela corta que le da título al libro, un emigrante venezolano se ha quedado solo en Barcelona y su refrigerador va dañándose poco a poco a medida que pasa el verano. Hay ocho otros textos, todos relacionados entre sí y con la novela. Una prosa sencilla que registra cosas pequeñas de la vida, de los objetos, para exprimir de ellos sus posibilidades de humor. [J.C.L.]

2493 Blanco Calderón, Rodrigo. Una larga fila de hombres. Caracas: Monte Avila Editores, 2005. 139 p. (Col. Las formas del fuego. Narrativa)

Cuatro cuentos y una novela corta. "Uñas asesinas" es la novela corta escrita en forma de diario. En ella un estudiante de literatura quiere desentrañar unos asesinatos en serie y, mientras lo hace, halla razones esenciales de su propia vida y de Caracas. En todas las narraciones aparecen alusiones a la escritura misma del texto que se lee, con lo que hay autorreflexión narrativa. [J.C.L.]

2494 Britto García, Luis. Arca. Caracas: Editorial Planeta Venezolana, 2007. 228 p. (Biblioteca breve)

Es un libro misceláneo de cuentos breves, reflexiones y textos en verso. Como es costumbre en este autor, su lenguaje frecuenta la paradoja y la ironía, con lo que las narraciones logran cargarse de sorpresa y humor. Lo mejor de este libro se encuentra en "Invenciones atroces", sección de 28 reflexiones, muchas a la manera de aforismo. [J.C.L.]

2495 Bujanda, Héctor. La última vez. Bogotá: Grupo Editorial Norma, 2007. 150 p. (La otra orilla)

Un hombre muere de SIDA y el día de su entierro, en el mismo cementerio, su padre desaparece de la vista de todos para unirse a la guerrilla de un movimiento bolivariano. Esta circunstancia que da entrada a la novela congrega tres momentos de la historia de Venezuela que luego aparecerán en la narración: el caracazo de 1989, el golpe militar de 1992, los gobiernos que siguieron y la época actual del chavizmo. [J.C.L.]

2496 Chirinos, Orlando. Beso de lengua. Caracas: Planeta, 2007. 257 p.: index. (Autores españoles e iberoamericanos)

Novela en fragmentos que narran luchas estudiantiles de hace décadas y los avatares de un grupo de izquierda. Es la visita a un pasado para dar cuenta de la corrosión del tiempo en las cosas y lo seres. Hay presencia de obras y autores de la literatura universal, como también elementos de la cultura popular, sobre todo en sus expresiones musicales del Caribe y de Argentina. [J.C.L.]

2497 Echeto, Roberto. No habrá final. Caracas: Alfa Grupo Editorial, 2006. 223 p. (Alfa 7 Thriller)

Siete maleantes cuentan alternadamente sus fechorías. Con un lenguaje muy crudo se relatan historias, todas disparatadas, a veces definitivamente absurdas. Mientras ocurren las narraciones, hay música de fondo, sobre todo clásica, interpretada por Ismael con su violín. Novela policíaca en la que predomina el punto de vista del facineroso. [J.C.L.]

2498 García Arreaza, Enza. Cállate poco a poco. Caracas: Monte Ávila Editores Latinoamericana, 2007. 72 p. (Col. Las formas de fuego. Narrativa)

Doce cuentos en los que predominan las relaciones difíciles y brutales entre parejas. El lenguaje es descarnado y sucio, con logros de inolvidables imágenes como en "Disidencias" y aún de bellas metáforas como en "Cállate poco a poco". En varios de los cuentos aparecen niñas enamoradas locamente de hombres violentos. [J.C.L.]

2499 Gomes, Miguel. Viviana y otras historias del cuerpo. Caracas: Mondadori, 2006. 229 p. (Col. Literatura Mondadori)

Trece cuentos en que los personajes son seres de clase media, de origen hispano y que viven en ámbitos de Nueva Inglaterra. Se narran anécdotas que dan cuenta de las diversas maneras que ellos tienen para asumir su vida íntima, su erotismo. En muchos de los cuentos destaca el ambiente de campus, con un humor e ironía de gran sutileza. [J.C.L.]

2500 Guerra, Rubi. La tarea del testigo. Caracas: Fundación Editorial el Perro y la Rana, 2007. 92 p.: ill.

Trata sobre los años del poeta José Antonio Ramos Sucre como cónsul de Venezuela en Ginebra, y su implacable insomnio que por tanto tiempo lo acompañó. Transcurre la década del 30 del siglo XX, y en la novela el insomnio llega a ser una metáfora de la época difícil que Europa está viviendo. Aparecen fragmentos de textos de Ramos Sucre reescritos por el autor. Hay metaficción. [J.C.L.]

2501 Mesones, Omar. Inventario y otros relatos. Caracas: Casa Nacional de las Letras Andrés Bello, 2007. 208 p.

Cuentos de mucha crudeza y violencia en el mundo de la delincuencia, escritos en una prosa vertiginosa. Caracas aparece como una ciudad sucia y cargada de maleantes. En "300 gramos de sexo de baja pureza", entre música y sexo dos hombres quieren comprar marihuana pero deberán presenciar el asesinato de dos mujeres por parte del expendedor. [J.C.L.]

2502 Mosca, Stefania. Mediáticos. Caracas: Monte Ávila Editores Latinoamericana, 2007. 163 p. (Continentes)

Colección de textos breves en los que predomina la mirada femenina del mundo. En "Patz", una mujer con su vivir y actuar perfecciona la vida; en "Historia del payaso Harry", un payaso hace una acrobacia increíble a la edad de 60 años y el público, envidioso de su hazaña, no lo aplaude. La autora confecciona en este libro, con fina ironía, una sutil burla del mundo. [J.C.L.]

2503 Policastro, Cristina. La dama del segundo piso. Caracas: Alfaguara, 2005. 205 p.

María Adelaida, una mujer que ha sido rebelde y antimachista, cumple 85 años, y con ese motivo hace un recuento de su vida. Su abuelo fue miembro del gabinete del dictador Juan Vicente Gómez, por lo que ella llega a ser un testigo de excepción de la historia del poder en Venezuela, frente a todo el machismo y los tabúes de esta sociedad. [J.C.L.]

2504 Rangel Mora, Pedro. Muerte en la víspera. Caracas: Mondadori, 2008. 165 p.: index. (Literatura mondadori)

Novela escrita a fragmentos para registrar la corrupción de la sociedad, sobre todo la de los cuerpos policiales. En el fragmento que da título a la novela, un abogado inescrupuloso se alía con un comisario enemigo suyo para investigar el asesinato de una detective, en el que está comprometido otro comisario. Novela experimental, bien escrita y de mucho suspenso. [J.C.L.]

2505 Santaella Kruk, Fedosy. Piedras lunares. Barcelona: Ediciones B, 2008. 150 p. (Ficcionario)

Cuentos policíacos en los que se refieren historias muy violentas de maleantes. Hay mucho suspenso en los textos, el que a veces asciende hasta el horror. Narraciones con buen humor e ironía. Destaca "Un tal William", sobre un bestial asesino a sueldo de imagen impecable e incapaz de matar una mosca. El lenguaje es sencillo, coloquial y con muchos giros propios del habla juvenil. [J.C.L.]

2506 Sarmiento, Nuni. Revés. Mérida, Venezuela: Siembraviva Ediciones, 2003. 96 p.: col. ill.

Narraciones entretenidas en que se refieren historias extrañas y absurdas. En "Un . . .", un animal decide borrar su nombre para que nadie pueda hacer nada con él; en "El castillo", una mamá le lee a su hija moribunda "El castillo" de Kafka, y la mamá se pierde en esta novela y conversa con Miguel de Unamuno. En los textos hay mucha ironía y sátira. [J.C.L.]

2507 Socorro, Milagros. El abrazo del tamarindo. Caracas: Alfaguara, 2008. 110 p. (Alfaguara)

Para vincularse a un grupo de mujeres, una adolescente debe dar su virginidad a un hombre. El grupo de mujeres se integra alrededor de la organización de un grupo de música vallenata que habita un pueblo de la frontera colombo-venezolana. En las páginas de esta novela hay crudeza y poesía que habla del cuerpo femenino desde lo más interior de ese mismo cuerpo. [J.C.L.]

2508 Ulive-Schnell, Vicente. Caracas cruzada: el solfeo de Caracas. Caracas: Fundación Editorial Perro y Rana, 2006. 183 p. (Col. Páginas venezolanas. Serie Contemporáneos; 30)

Novela escrita en fragmentos, cada uno titulado con el nombre de un personaje. Individuos de diferentes clases sociales van hacia el centro de Caracas y en la narración se exhiben pedazos de sus vidas. Al final, cinco de ellos acaban implicados en un aparatoso accidente de autos. La ciudad se presenta como un ser infernal que engulle y tritura vidas. La prosa da cabida a diversos registros del habla urbana. [J.C.L.]

2509 Villanueva, Adriana. El móvil del delito. Caracas: Ediciones B, Grupo Zeta, 2006. 197 p. (Ficcionario)

En 24 capítulos y un epílogo se narra sobre el robo de un móvil de Cálder, la investigación del hecho y el regreso del móvil a su sitio. En las páginas circula la Venezuela del siglo XXI, el caos de Caracas y la pobreza, mientras los personajes viajan a un pasado de años universitarios sin preocupaciones. Es una novela policiaca, de prosa alegre y lenguaje coloquial, con humor e ironía. [J.C.L.]

Chile

JOSÉ PROMIS, *Professor of Latin American Literature and Literary Criticism, University of Arizona*

LA PRODUCCIÓN NOVELESCA chilena que va del año 2007 al 2009 confirma un fenómeno que se viene manifestando históricamente desde hace más de un decenio: el considerable aumento de la producción narrativa nacional tanto en términos cuantitativos como cualitativos. Gran cantidad de novelas son publicadas bajo el sello de editoriales transnacionales, pero también aparecen muchas editadas por pequeñas editoriales surgidas después de 1980. También durante este trienio fallecen dos grandes narradores chilenos: Hugo Correa (1926–2008) y Volodia Teitelboim (1916–2008).

Puede decirse que la novela chilena del trienio se inserta en las tendencias temáticas y discursivas que el género exhibe a nivel continental, pero a la vez manifiesta interés hacia asuntos característicos que son consecuencia de la dictadura militar de las décadas de los 70 y 80. Se advierte, eso sí, que tales asuntos son tratados ahora con diferentes perspectivas y puntos de vista que arrojan interpretaciones novedosas sobre ellos. Novelas como *El libro de Carmen* y *Carne de perra* (items **2531** y **2544**) desarrollan el tema de la tortura, ampliamente trabajado en la narrativa nacional desde hace más de dos décadas, pero en la primera se intenta contemplar el otro lado de la maldad y en la segunda se escudriña la interioridad de un agente de la dictadura forzado a desempeñar dicho papel. Por su parte, *Yo tenía un compañero* (item **2548**) enfoca a quienes participaron en el golpe de 1973, no por razones ideológicas, sino obligados por la obediencia y la lealtad juradas a la institución militar.

La búsqueda de raíces es otro tema reiterado desde hace años en la novela chilena contemporánea. Muchos críticos afirman que también es una reacción contra los intentos de la dictadura militar para borrar radicalmente el pasado inmediato nacional. En este trienio se nota un interés hacia el rescate de la historia cultural chilena de los decenios inmediatamente anteriores a 1970. *El zapato perdido de la Marilyn* (item **2524**) enfoca este ambiente en la década de los años 50 y *Todas íbamos a ser reinas* (item **2517**) es la ficción con base biográfica de un grupo de travestís que revolucionaron el medio artístico nacional en los años 70. La novela más importante dentro de esta tendencia es *La casa de Dostoievski* (item **2521**), recreación de la atmósfera, las preferencias y las inquietudes de donde surgieron los miembros de la llamada *generación de 1950*, sin duda el más importante grupo de narradores contemporáneos chilenos.

También dentro de esta tendencia hay que destacar la significativa labor de rescate de textos clásicos chilenos. *La secretísima: los cuentos de Román Calvo, el Sherlock Holmes chileno* (item **2520**) es una antología de lectura indispensable para quienes se interesen por estudiar el desarrollo de la novela policial en Chile; y *En Tontilandia* se reúnen artículos de crítica social que definen la ideología de uno de los ensayistas más interesantes de la primera mitad del siglo XX (item **2536**).

La segunda gran línea temática que exhibe la novela chilena durante el trienio en cuestión tiene que ver con la representación de problemas sociales específicos y la relación del individuo con sus circunstancias, que son dominantemente caracterizadas como propias de una sociedad de economía neoliberal que reemplaza los valores del espíritu con los del consumismo y la adquisición de objetos, a los que considera síntomas de bienestar y progreso. En textos como *Puro hueso* (item **2522**) se denuncian problemas de marginalidad, desequilibrio y olvido sociales; *Ciudadanos de baja intensidad* (item **2534**) representa las formas de comunicación de las llamadas tribus urbanas; *Cuentos de barrios* (item **2540**) pretende rescatar el alma popular chilena a punto de desaparecer en la modernidad. En el otro extremo de las variantes temáticas, *Vendo casa en el Barrio Alto* (item **2546**) es una sátira inclemente de lo que su autora considera el triunfo de la inmovilidad social chilena sobre los programas de reforma social. Otras novelas se orientan hacia problemas individuales de carácter más íntimo. *Dile que no estoy* (item **2519**) ejemplifica el interés de muchos novelistas jóvenes hacia el deterioro de las relaciones familiares y *El resto es silencio* (item **2525**) resume la línea temática de la soledad y la incomunicación contemporáneas. El motivo de la fragilidad familiar sigue presente en la novela chilena, como lo ejemplifican bien *El amante sin rostro* (item **2532**) y *La barrera del pudor* (item **2545**).

Finalmente, debe destacarse también la proposición de nuevas formas de discurso que ofrecen muchas novelas del trienio, o la aparición de novelas que además de relatar una historia constituyen una reflexión sobre las características del género literario en las actuales circunstancias históricas: *Locuela* (item **2529**) o *Los gritos de las sombras* (item **2514**) ejemplifican bien esta última inquietud, mientras que *El resto es silencio* exhibe el estilo que se ha llamado "esencialista", sencillo, directo, desnudo de retórica, que practican muchos narradores chilenos jóvenes.

PROSE FICTION

2510 Ampuero, Roberto. El caso Neruda.
Bogotá: Editorial Norma, 2008. 330 p.
(La otra orilla)
Novela que sin duda satisface la
curiosidad de todos los admiradores del
detective Cayetano Brulé. Relato de las
circunstancias que transformaron a este
personaje en el investigador privado de la
serie de novelas policiales publicadas por
Ampuero a partir de ¿Quién mató a Cristián
Kustermann? en 1993.

2511 Banderas Grandela, Felipe. El éxodo
de Mariana. Santiago: Editorial
Cuarto Propio, 2008. 218 p. (Serie Narrativa)
Primera novela del autor donde se
relata una historia de amor desarrollada en
una atmósfera cuyo sentido más profundo
escapa incluso a quienes viven en su interior. Relato que ejemplifica bien las preferencias de los narradores más jóvenes del país.

2512 Barahona Saldías, Mario Eugenio. De
casa en casa. Santiago: Editorial Forja,
2008. 194 p.
Evocaciones de la infancia campesina
que usa la ficción para rellenar los espacios
vacíos que la memoria ha olvidado. Pero la
fuga hacia el pasado es engañosa porque el
verdadero propósito de la evocación es comprender las heridas de la actualidad.

2513 Blanco, Guillermo. Una loica en la
ventana. Santiago: LOM Ediciones,
2008. 209 p. (Narrativa)
Un adolescente viaja al sur de Chile
para visitar a su familia paterna, con quien
no ha tenido contacto durante muchos años.
Comienza una historia de amor con una
prima e inicia un viaje hacia el pasado familiar y nacional donde descubre misterios que
nadie menciona.

2514 Burotto, Susana. Los gritos de las
sombras. Santiago: Mosquito Comu-
nicaciones, 2009. 219 p.
Premio Oscar Castro de Novela 2007.
Un estudiante de literatura escribe una tesis
sobre un oscuro escritor chileno exiliado después del golpe militar y fallecido en París para
comprobar la importancia de lo biográfico en
la creación artística. La novela se ofrece así
como una reflexión sobre los contactos de la
verdad de la literatura y de la vida.

2515 Bustamante, Oscar. El jugador de
rugby. Santiago: Aguilar Chilena de
Ediciones, 2008. 310 p. (Alfaguara)

La novela gira en torno a uno de los
motivos más recurrentes en la narrativa chilena contemporánea: el tránsito de la adolescencia a la madurez, que en este caso tiene
lugar en una escuela de Inglaterra, donde
estudia un adolescente chileno proveniente
de una familia a punto de quebrarse.

2516 Cáceres Marchesi, Claudio Armando.
Praemeditatio malorum. Xalapa, Mexico: Univ. Veracruzana, 2008. 168 p. (Ficción)
Notable relato donde una disposición
lingüística aparentemente caótica o laberín-
tica es congruente con una atmósfera de pérdida donde las verdades han sido reemplaza-
das por la incertidumbre y la desconfianza.

2517 Cardoch Zedán, Branny. Todas íbamos a ser reinas. Santiago: Forja,
2009. 235 p.
El verso de Gabriela Mistral sirve como
título para la historia novelada del llamado
Blue Ballet, un grupo de travestis que revolucionaron el medio artístico chileno durante
los años 70. Relato convincente, lleno de ca-
lidez y comprensión humana hacia el mundo
de los "otros", de individuos hasta ahora excluidos de la llamada normalidad social.

2518 Colodro, Max. Letras de una traición.
Santiago, Chile: Editorial Universitaria, 2008. 174 p. (Col. El Mundo de las Letras)
Relato que gira en torno al descifra-
miento del famoso y enigmático manuscrito
Voynich que existe en la Biblioteca Beinecke
de la Univ. de Yale. Un estudiante chileno
logra descodificar el manuscrito pero su
triunfo constituye también su perdición.
Excelente relato de aventuras e intrigas,
inusual en el medio literario chileno.

2519 Costamagna, Alejandra. Dile que no
estoy. Santiago: Planeta, 2007. 260 p.
(Autores españoles e iberoamericanos)
Excelente novela donde la autora
manifiesta una vez más la atracción que
ha demostrado desde sus primeros relatos
para escudriñar relaciones familiares que se
deterioran irremisiblemente. En este caso se
disuelve una típica familia de clase media,
proveniente del sur de Chile. Su historia
sirve para contraponer la vida urbana frente
a la provinciana y, en último término, al
arte con la realidad.

2520 Edwards, Alberto. La secretísima: los
cuentos de Román Calvo, el Sherlock
Holmes chileno. Santiago: Ediciones B, 2007.
342 p. (Dulce patria)

Selección de los cuentos de intriga y misterio que Alberto Edwards publicó en la revista *Pacífico Magazine* entre 1913 y 1921, y en donde aparece la figura del investigador Román Calvo, versión nacional del analítico detective inglés. Pero además estos cuentos ofrecen la imagen de una desaparecida sociedad aristocrática criolla, contemplada desde una mirada asimismo conservadora.

2521 Edwards, Jorge. La casa de Dostoievsky. Santiago: Planeta, 2008. 329 p. (Autores españoles e iberoamericanos)

Novela ganadora del Premio Iberoamericano Planeta-Casa de América y una de las más importantes publicadas en estos años. Con toda razón ha sido llamada novela generacional: aunque es una ficción que posee muchos elementos autobiográficos y retrata los ambientes, preferencias e inquietudes de donde surgieron los miembros de la generación del 50.

2522 Fuentes, Roberto. Puro hueso. Santiago: Editorial Cuarto Proprio, 2007. 274 p. (Serie Narrativa)

Relato que se ubica en la línea de escritores sociales del pasado, como Nicomedes Guzmán, pero que indaga nuevos modos para representar los problemas de marginalidad, injusticia y desequilibrio social denunciados por aquellos.

2523 Gil, Antonio. Cielo de serpientes. Santiago: Seix Barral Biblioteca Breve, 2008. 163 p. (Seix Barral biblioteca breve)

Inspirada en el hallazgo de la momia de un niño inca en el cerro El Plomo, la novela desarrolla a través de diferentes voces, entre las que destaca la del niño Cauri Pacssa, el conflicto entre el carácter sagrado de la naturaleza y las costumbres ancestrales y los intereses de las mafias que trafican con los restos arqueológicos de las antiguas culturas andinas.

2524 Goles, Eric. El zapato perdido de la Marilyn. Santiago: LOM, 2008. 132 p. (Col. Narrativa)

Mediante dos secuencias narrativas con fuertes referentes biográficos y una tercera de contenido absolutamente imaginario, la novela recrea la adolescencia del autor en la ciudad de Antofagasta y a través de ella el ambiente de la cultura popular chilena durante los años de 1950.

2525 Guelfenbein, Carla. El resto es silencio. Santiago: Planeta, 2008. 304 p. (Autores españoles e iberoamericanos)

La autora ha impuesto un nuevo modo de contar, sencillo, directo, desnudo de retórica, en la prosa chilena contemporánea. En esta novela presenta a tres personajes involucrados en una historia de amor y redención: un cirujano, su segunda esposa y su hijo representan una familia de la actualidad enfrentada a los problemas de la soledad y la incomunicación.

2526 Guzmán, Jorge. Con ojos de niño. Santiago: LOM Ediciones, 2008. 152 p. (Narrativa)

Novela ganadora del Premio de la Crítica 2009 otorgado por la Universidad Diego Portales. Excelente narración donde los temas del mundo de los adultos se contextualizan en un primer plano inaugurado por la mirada de los niños. La historia tiene lugar en Santiago y Valparaíso a fines de los años 30.

2527 Jauregui Castro, Elías. Trece. Santiago: RIL Editores, 2009. 156 p.

Primera publicación del autor. Como lo indica el título, se reúnen 13 relatos de variadas formas y tendencias, desde la ficción científica hasta la parodia del costumbrismo y regionalismo, para romper con las formas del realismo tradicional, pero no con su propósito de denunciar los desequilibrios sociales que el autor percibe en la realidad circundante.

2528 Jerez, Fernando. Nostalgias y desdenes. Santiago: Simplemente Editores, 2009. 193 p.

El motivo del inesperado abandono de un amante sirve para contemplar distintas formas de soledad y de supervivencia en una sociedad como la actual donde los roles han sido definidos con precisión y la verdad depende del punto de vista de quien la enuncia.

2529 Labbé, Carlos. Locuela. Cáceres, Spain: Periférica, 2009. 249 p. (Biblioteca portátil; 33)

Novela que se destaca debido a su inteligente uso de las convenciones del género policial para proponerse como un texto que socava sus propios estatutos literarios para fundar otro tipo de lectura donde los límites tradicionales de lo real y lo ficticio son cuestionados o sencillamente no tienen validez.

2530 Lillo, Marcelo. El fumador y otros relatos. Santiago: Mondadori, 2008. 130 p.

Los críticos chilenos han afirmado que los 10 cuentos reunidos en este volumen muestran al autor como uno de los más interesantes narradores chilenos contemporáneos. En todos ellos destaca una nueva manera de representar actitudes y comportamientos banales o insignificantes, pero profundamente humanos.

2531 London, María. El libro de Carmen. Santiago: Editorial Forja, 2008. 101 p.

Novela que retoma el tema de la destrucción física, psicológica y afectiva de la mujer en manos de torturadores amparados por regímenes militares, pero contemplado desde una perspectiva novedosa que trata de iluminar el otro lado del mal.

2532 Marchant Lazcano, Jorge. El amante sin rostro. Santiago: Tajamar Editores, 2008. 297 p. (Col. narrativa/Tajamar Editores)

Historia de una familia que abarca tres generaciones y que tiene como núcleo del relato la inevitable desintegración de sus miembros debido a factores que van más allá de la pura consanguinidad. Continúa las preocupaciones narrativas que el autor ha materializado magistralmente en sus novelas anteriores.

2533 Maturana, Andrea. No decir. Santiago: Alfaguara: Aguilar Chilena de Ediciones, 2006. 200 p.

Incluye 12 interesantes relatos breves que giran en torno a un motivo central común: el silencio impuesto por distintas razones sobre los individuos y la imposibilidad del esfuerzo que estos hacen para mantener ocultos determinados secretos.

2534 Mellado, Marcelo. Ciudadanos de baja intensidad. Santiago: Caligrafía Azul, 2007. 157 p. (Libros La calabaza del diablo)

Premio de la Crítica 2008. Cuentos que constituyen una especie de antropología poética de las nuevas formas de chilenidad que revela el comportamiento de las tribus urbanas y que se manifiesta a través del lenguaje del vituperio, la protesta y el insulto.

2535 Mihovilovich Hernández, Juan. Desencierro. Santiago: LOM Ediciones, 2008. 233 p. (Col. Narrativa)

Novela donde se asiste a un lento viaje de desvarío hacia el fondo de una conciencia marcada por un profundo sentimiento de culpa moral. Excelente relato donde se recogen los temas más característicos de la totalidad de la obra del autor.

2536 Prieto, Jenaro. En Tontilandia. Santiago: Ediciones B Chile, 2006. 366 p. (Dulce patria)

Atractiva selección de artículos periodísticos que definen la personalidad y la ideología de uno de los narradores y ensayistas más interesantes de la primera mitad del siglo XX, presentada por Alejandra Costamagna. Tontilandia fue el país inventado por Prieto para parodiar los hábitos y costumbres de los chilenos que más le incomodaban.

2537 Rimsky, Cynthia. Los perplejos. Santiago: Sangría, 2009. 385 p.

La estructura de la novela se sostiene sobre dos secuencias argumentales: una presenta la biografía del sabio judío Maimónides; en la otra se relatan las vicisitudes que vivió su autora para escribirla. La novela cuestiona así conceptos como el de la autonomía de la obra literaria, o del carácter binario de la verdad.

2538 Rivas Rudisky, Ramiro. En malos pasos. Santiago: Bravo y Allende Editores, 2009. 121 p.

Interesante conjunto de cuentos que ilustran el temple de desilusión y escepticismo histórico que se manifiesta en numerosos relatos chilenos contemporáneos.

2539 Rivera Letelier, Hernán. Mi nombre es Malarrosa. Santiago: Alfaguara, 2008. 254 p.

El desierto salitrero del norte de Chile es nuevamente el escenario y el protagonista de esta novela. En todos sus relatos anteriores Rivera Letelier ha sido capaz de otorgar a la existencia pampina una fisonomía radicalmente novedosa, colorida y melodramática, que en esta novela se acentúa aún más. Rivera Letelier es sin duda uno de los narradores preferidos por el público chileno.

2540 Rojo Redolés, Rolando. Cuentos de barrios. Santiago: Bravo y Allende Editores, 2008. 119 p.

Conjunto de cuentos que pretenden rescatar lo que el autor entiende como el alma popular de los viejos barrios de Santiago que van desapareciendo reemplazados por los nuevos edificios de la modernidad.

2541 Sepúlveda, Luis. La sombra de lo que fuimos. Madrid: Espasa, 2009. 174 p. (Espasa narrativa)

Tres antiguos extremistas de la Unidad Popular se juntan para rescatar un tesoro escondido durante la época de la dictadura militar. Novela que se inscribe en la tendencia de representar el estropicio causado por la destrucción de los antiguos ideales reformistas.

2542 Sepúlveda Caraball, Paz. Instantáneas y retratos. Santiago: Cadaqués, 2008. 203 p.: bibl.

El volumen reúne cuentos de distinta extensión y estilo narrativo que comparten un propósito común: desechar las engañosas imágenes construidas por los sentidos para descubrir las verdades ocultas por el racionalismo, los temores o los intereses particulares.

2543 Serrano, Marcela. La llorona. Barcelona, Spain: Planeta, 2008. 167 p. (Autores españoles e iberoamericanos)

La autora crea la voz de una narradora campesina, cuya hija ha fallecido a los pocos días de nacer, quien denuncia el tráfico clandestino de recién nacidos que ocurre en países hispanoamericanos, y que no es sino otra manifestación de la lucha de los débiles contra poderes ilimitados y al parecer invencibles.

2544 Sime, Fátima. Carne de perra. Santiago: LOM Ediciones, 2009. 122 p. (Narrativa)

La historia de una muchacha torturada física y psicológicamente en los años del régimen militar chileno es el engranaje de un plan diseñado para asesinar a una conocida figura política opositora. Esta situación sirve además para comprobar la efectividad del llamado síndrome de Estocolmo.

2545 Simonetti, Pablo. La barrera del pudor. Bogotá: Grupo Editorial Norma, 2009. 238 p. (La otra orilla)

Al igual que en sus dos novelas anteriores, el autor indaga las profundas complejidades de las relaciones humanas. En este caso, una mujer asume la responsabilidad narrativa para auscultar las razones de su fracaso matrimonial y de sus inútiles esfuerzos para recuperarlo.

2546 Subercaseaux, Elizabeth. Vendo casa en el barrio alto: Alberto Larraín Errázuriz Propiedades. Santiago: Catalonia, 2009. 239 p.

La historia satírica de un vendedor de propiedades que vende casas según la "casta" social en que cataloga a sus clientes sirve para llevar a cabo uno de los mejores y más demoledores retratos de la rígida estratificación social del Chile actual.

2547 Torres, Siret. No llevados ni traídos. Santiago: AGUILAR: El Mercurio, 2008. 243 p.

La voz de un adolescente desarrolla la historia de su familia a lo largo de tres generaciones, en un movimiento narrativo que enlaza los acontecimientos privados con el contexto histórico en que tienen lugar. Recibió el Premio Revista de Libros 2008.

2548 Villegas Morales, Juan. Yo tenía un compañero. Santiago: RiL Editores, 2009. 298 p. (Narrativa)

Novela de sólida e impecable composición. Un profesor chileno de literatura en una universidad de los Estados Unidos rememora la figura de su padre, suboficial de ejército y por lo mismo obligado participante en los acontecimientos del golpe militar de 1973.

Argentina

CLAIRE EMILIE MARTIN, *Professor of Spanish, California State University, Long Beach*
LAURA R. LOUSTAU, *Associate Professor of Spanish, Chapman University*
with **MARIA NELLY GOSWITZ,** *Lecturer, California State University, Long Beach, Instructor, Rio Hondo Community College*

ES POSIBLE IDENTIFICAR algunas tendencias temáticas y estilísticas en las novelas publicadas en la Argentina entre el 2005 y el 2008. Se debe subrayar la recurrencia temática de la representación de la violencia de estado durante la última dictadura militar. Algunos de los textos reconstruyen pasados personales e históricos de aquellos años: Saccomanno (item **2601**), Negroni (item **2593**), Fainsten (item **2565**), Yudicello (item **2609**), Gorodischer (item **2577**), Muchnick (item **2591**), Prenz (item **2598**) y Rivera (item **2596**).

La representación de la violencia de estado se observa en la novela de Cristian Rodríguez, *Madruga negra* (item **2599**), la cual se ocupa del mundo sórdido del victimario. Norma Huidobro, cuya novela, *El lugar perdido* (item **2581**), ganadora del Premio Planeta 2007, indaga en el mundo del poder y de la persecución política durante la década de los 70 en un pueblo del interior de la Argentina. La novela de Susana Cella (item **2559**), por su parte, presenta oblicuamente el tema de los hijos apropiados y de los mundos inciertos en los que sobreviven algunos de los hijos de desaparecidos. Cristina Feijóo (item **2567**) trata el tema de la violencia de estado desde la mirada infantil. Es notable la presencia y la vigencia de las representaciones de la violencia de última dictadura militar en la narrativa, relatadas desde diferentes perspectivas y con estilos muy diversos y renovadores.

Continuando con la vena histórica de las últimas décadas, las novelas de Colombo, *Aventuras de un porteño en tiempos de la colonia* (item **2560**), Mairal, *El año del desierto* (item **2588**) y Forn, *María Domecq* (item **2570**), recrean el pasado atentos a las resonancias con el presente.

La ciudad de Buenos Aires aparece como testigo de sucesos de gran amplitud: de la devastadora enfermedad del SIDA en la década de los 80 (item **2610**); de la pobreza y las consecuencias sociales de las políticas neoliberales en los años 90 (item **2583**); de la crisis económica del 2001 (item **2592**); así como del mundo corrupto e inmoral de los políticos (item **2555**) y del consumismo y deterioro de ciertos valores humanos visto en los libros de Beltrán (item **2554**), Brindisi (item **2556**), García Lao (item **2572**) y García Mansilla (item **2571**).

Abundan los relatos sobre las relaciones familiares en la literatura argentina de estos años, especialmente entre padres e hijos y entre parejas, tal como lo exploran Ramos en *La ley de la ferocidad* (item **2597**), Guebel en *Derrumbe* (item **2579**), González en *Arte menor* (item **2575**), Fernández Díaz en *Fernández* (item **2568**) y Fernández Moreno en *La profesora de español* (item **2569**).

Se destacan miradas de narradoras mujeres que desafían los modelos familiares tradicionales y se adentran en búsquedas personales en donde coexisten la verdad y la falsedad de lo cotidiano: *El espejo de Rosaura Acebedo* de Alicia Cámpora (item **2557**), *Las primas* de Aurora Venturini (item **2606**), *Historia de mujeres oscuras* de Alejandra Laurencich (item **2586**) y *Siesta nómade* de Débora Vázquez (item **2605**).

En cuanto a las colecciones de cuentos, se distinguen dos vertientes importantes de narradores jóvenes, nacidos en la década de los años 70: los que escriben relatos audaces sobre sexo (item **2564**), abarcando temas desde el sadomasoquismo al sexo cibernético, y aquellos que incursionan en los relatos policiales (item **2582**). La particularidad de estos últimos es que se basan en hechos de la realidad argentina para luego ficcionalizarlos y reescribirlos. La edición y el prólogo de ambas antologías están a cargo de Diego Grillo Trubba. Florencia Abatte ha editado *Una terraza propia: nuevas narradoras argentinas* (item **2549**), colección de cuentos de narradoras nacidas entre 1963–83.

Es de notar la publicación de las obras completas de la cuentística de varios autores consagrados: Héctor Tizón (item **2604**), Antonio Di Benedetto (item **2563**) y Ricardo Piglia (item **2595**). [LRL and CEM]

PROSE FICTION

2549 Abatte, Florencia. Una terraza propia: nuevas narradoras argentinas. Buenos Aires: Grupo Editorial Norma, 2006. 284 p. (El dorado)

La colección de cuentos de 23 jóvenes autoras nacidas entre 1963–83 reúne relatos de gran variedad temática y de estilo y perspectivas dispares. Las narrativas se hallan acopladas en grupos muy generales y hasta algo caprichosos, de acuerdo al diseño de la prologuista, que obedecen a corrientes temáticas como la locura, la imaginación, los sueños, las tierras lejanas, el sexo, la pornografía, la ciudad y sus personajes. [CEM]

2550 Aira, César. La vida nueva. Buenos Aires: Mansalva, 2007. 77 p. (Poesía y ficción latinoamericana; 15)

La relación íntima entre un editor y el joven escritor novato es narrada en primera persona desde la memoria de este último quien recuerda las vicisitudes de la publicación de su libro y las conversaciones telefónicas con su amigo y editor Horacio Achával. La fluidez de las charlas telefónicas que se suceden a través de las décadas dejan al descubierto el humor, la ironía, la erudición y el poder magistral de la palabra que ejerce el autor en esta breve y deslumbradora obra. [CEM]

2551 Almada, Selva. Una chica de provincia. Buenos Aires: Gárgola, 2007. 173 p. (Col. Laura Palmer no ha muerto)

Tres cuentos se incluyen en esta colección: "Niños", "Chicas lindas" y "En familia", los cuales están atravesados por las vivencias de niños y adolescentes en un pueblo de Entre Ríos, provincia de donde procede la autora. En los dos primeros cuentos se narran historias iniciáticas especialmente las primeras experiencias de los niños con la muerte de los seres humanos y de los animales. "En familia", por su parte, relata un suicidio y las tensiones familiares que causan la ausencia y el abandono de seres queridos. Con un lenguaje íntimo—sin ser nostálgico—y cargado de imágenes sensoriales, Almada exalta mundos sencillos y profundos que atrapan y cautivan al lector. [LRL]

2552 Andahazi, Federico. La ciudad de los herejes. Buenos Aires: Planeta, 2005. 299 p.

Novela que narra la falsificación del Sudario de Turín o el Santo Sudario. Andahazi intercala hechos históricos y una ficticia trama amorosa entre Christine, la hija del codicioso y perverso duque Geoffroy de Charny, y el joven monje Aurelio. A pesar que los amantes logran desafiar los deseos perversos del duque durante un tiempo finalmente son víctimas del horror y ambos padecen un fatídico final. En esta apasionante novela se entrelazan el poder y la hipocresía de la iglesia y el estado, las bajezas humanas y la fuerza del amor. [LRL]

2553 Bajo, Cristina. El jardín de los venenos. Buenos Aires: Editorial Sudamericana, 2005. 479 p. (Narrativas)

Novela histórica antes publicada como *Sierva de Dios: ama de la muerte* recopila y cuestiona a través de los 48 relatos la vida de Sebastiana, una joven que vive en Córdoba en el siglo XVIII. La inclusión de los acápites "las confesiones" otorgan a la novela un carácter personal que le sirven a la protagonista para exponer las causas de su embarazo, su condena matrimonial, su experiencia en el convento, y su plan de venganza ante las personas que la empujan a tomar justicia por sus propias manos. *El jardín de los venenos* destaca el quehacer de su protagonista por subsistir usando armas naturales que la ayudan en su plan de venganza. [MNG]

2554 Beltrán, Jorge. Golpe de suerte. Buenos Aires: Corregidor, 2006. 255 p.

La amistad con un hombre mayor, sofisticado y rico le depara al joven protagonista un inesperado reverso de fortuna que lo llevará a Nueva York para cumplir con la voluntad de su amigo. La trama cerrada, cuidadosamente desarrollada que se aproxima a la novela detectivesca o al "thriller" acopla las voces de personajes de alto valor sicológico. El suspenso narrativo, la indagación en los sentimientos de soledad, de solidaridad y de ambición son tratados con mesura e inteligencia por un autor que controla magistralmente su oficio. [CEM]

2555 Bredam, Orlando van. Teoría del desamparo. Buenos Aires: Emecé, 2007. 211 p. (Emecé cruz del sur)

Premio Emecé 2007. Novela que mezcla el género policial con la comedia negra. Se inicia con un hallazgo inesperado.

Catulo Rodríguez, un hombre de clase media, descubre una mañana, en el baúl de su auto, el cadáver de un diputado nacional. La investigación que inicia Catulo junto a un detective intuitivo pero inexperto los lleva a entremezclarse con el mundo corrupto e inmoral de los políticos y sus secuaces. [LRL]

2556 Brindisi, José María. Frenesí. Buenos Aires: Emecé, 2006. 123 p. (Emecé cruz del sur)

Premiada por la Secretaría de Cultura del GCABA, con el premio novela corta Casa del Escritor 2005, Frenesí retrata a través de sus cinco protagonistas a una generación que es víctima de la coyuntura política y social de principios de los noventa. La promesa de vivir con frenesí y sin miedo a que el tiempo los doblegue es el pacto que se hacen cuando bordean los 29 años. Sin embargo, este pacto resulta al final la paradoja de la historia. El fracaso como generación revela su impotencia ante la historia y silenciamiento paulatino de sus voces. [MNG]

2557 Cámpora, Alicia. El espejo de Rosaura Acevedo. Buenos Aires: Corregidor, 2006. 141 p.

Novela que intercala la historia personal de una mujer de unos 50 años con la historia política de su país. En ese entretejido sobresale la relación de la narradora, Rosaura Acevedo y su abuela homónima quien la insta permanentemente a romper los modelos familiares para cumplir con las anheladas expectativas de la diferencia. [LRL]

2558 Castillo, Abelardo. Los mundos reales V: el espejo que tiembla. Buenos Aires: Seix Barral, 2005. 125 p. (Seix Barral Biblioteca breve)

Con dominio absoluto sobre la forma y el contenido del material cuentístico, Castillo continúa recreando nuevos mundos reales y fantásticos por los que transitan sus personajes. Entre ellos deambulan fantasmas amenazadores, la foto risueña de una amante muerta compartida entre dos hombres que la lloran cada cual a su manera, una joven hippie que nunca envejece ante la desesperación del amante, una niñita que escribe a los Reyes Magos. El humor, la pasión, la risa, la ironía y el compendio de emociones humanas impregnan a los

personajes de Castillo quien los vuelve de carne con su prosa prolija, nítida, reveladora. [CEM]

2559 Cella, Susana. Presagio. Buenos Aires: Santiago Arcos Editor, 2006. 233 p. (Parabellum. Ficciones; 17)

Una maestra, Marisa, sale una mañana temprano rumbo a la escuela y encuentra un bebé abandonado con una medallita sostenida por una cinta oscura de cuero trenzado. La joven lo recoge y lo lleva a casa de sus padres quienes amparan al bebé y lo crían como propio. La novela se desarrolla en una maraña de engaños y mentiras que atañen no sólo a la historia del Cocoliso (así apodado por Marisa) sino también a la de los familiares y amigos que de alguna manera se conectan con Marisa y sus padres. A lo largo de la novela aparecen oscuros presagios que van anticipando posibles peligros. Los personajes viven mundos inciertos y de profundo desasosiego. [LRL]

2560 Colombo, Jorge A. Aventuras de un porteño en tiempos de la Colonia. Buenos Aires: Editorial Distal, 2006. 160 p.

Novela de ágil estructura narrativa, tiene como telón de fondo personajes de la historia colonial en Hispanoamérica. Los relatos que forman esta colección revelan el universo ficcional del que Colombo se vale para ofrecer a sus lectores una mirada diferente del pasado. La voz narrativa no evade el ojo acusador y crítico hacia los colonizadores españoles en tierras americanas. [MNG]

2561 Corbacho, Luis. Mi amado Míster B. Barcelona: Egales Editorial, 2006. 308 p. (Salir del armario; 101)

Novela que narra una intensa relación amorosa entre Martín Alcorta, un joven editor de una revista porteña, Soho BA, y un reconocido escritor y conductor de T.V. peruano, Felipe Brown. La pareja se conoce en el bar del Hotel Plaza en Buenos Aires, donde Martín y su compañero Fernando improvisan una entrevista a Brown. La conexión entre Martín y Felipe es instantánea. Los encuentros tienen lugar en Santiago, Lima, Miami, Buenos Aires, donde los protagonistas viven intensas experiencias sexuales. Con una entretenida prosa, Corbacho trata una amplia variedad de temas, tales como las relaciones a larga distancia, la homosexualidad y el compromiso. [LRL]

2562 Correa Luna, Hugo R. La pura realidad. Buenos Aires: Losada, 2007. 169 p. (Narrativa)

Novela que mezcla lo cotidiano con lo metafísico. Una pareja de clase media, Nelly y Guille se preparan para un viaje al sur de la Argentina cuando reciben una carta desde Australia, lugar en el que nunca han estado. El desconcierto es mayor cuando al leer la carta, se dan cuenta que un tal George se dirige a ellos con suma familiaridad. El desconocido incluye también fotos de los tres en Australia. A pesar de que Guille y Nelly tratan de olvidar el hecho, adelantando las vacaciones; al regreso encuentran una nota de George diciendo que ha estado en Buenos Aires y que pronto regresará. La novela indaga en el desconcierto y lo inexplicable sin ofrecer ninguna solución ni respuesta al enigma. [LRL]

2563 Di Benedetto, Antonio. Cuentos completos. Edición de Jimena Néspolo y Julio Premat. Introducción de Julio Premat. Buenos Aires: Adriana Hidalgo Editora, 2006. 705 p. (La lengua/Cuento)

Esta cuidadosa colección de toda la obra cuentística de Di Benedetto incluye *Mundo animal* (1953), *Cuentos claros* (1957), *Declinación y angel* (1958), *El cariño de los tontos* (1961), *Absurdos* (1978), *Cuentos del exilio* (1983), cuatro cuentos inéditos y una docena de cuentos reescritos por Di Benedetto. [CEM]

2564 En celo: cuentos: los mejores narradores de la nueva generación escriben sobre sexo. Selección de Diego Grillo Trubba. Buenos Aires: Editorial Sudamericana, 2007. 211 p. (Reservoir books. Nuevos escritores; 1)

Colección de cuentos escrita por 19 autores los que en su gran mayoría nacieron en la década de los 70. Valiéndose de diferentes estilos, multiplicidad de tonos y estrategias narrativas presentan audaces y originales relatos sobre el sexo. Los temas escogidos abarcan, entre otros, el sadomasoquismo, el travestismo y el sexo cibernético. [LRL]

2565 Fainstein, Graciela. Detrás de los ojos. Buenos Aires: Icaria Editorial, 2006. 199 p.

Novela autobiográfica que reconstruye la noche de 1976 en que Graciela, su novio Dani y su amiga Pupi son secuestrados por las fuerzas de seguridad del estado argentino. Graciela es brutalmente torturada y liberada al tercer día. La novela aboga por la trascendencia de la memoria no sólo la de Graciela sino la de una generación que confió demasiado en sus dirigentes y que se sintió abandonada e incomprendida después del infierno que les tocó vivir. En su relato la autora se vale de citas de Jorge Semprún, Simone Weil, Elie Wiesel y Theodor Adorno, entre otros, para tejer su propio relato y el de su familia. [LRL]

2566 Fasce, María. La naturaleza del amor. Buenos Aires: Emecé Editores, 2008. 316 p. (Emecé cruz del sur)

Ana es una editora argentina que en el año 2001 se traslada a Barcelona motivada por la crisis económica y una desilusión amorosa con Claudio, un hombre separado con tres hijas. En Barcelona, Ana entabla una amistad enriquecedora con Isabel, otra mujer argentina que está en busca de su genealogía familiar y con Nicolás, un artista cuyo interés por la alquimia fascina a la protagonista y de quien Ana se enamora y tiene un hijo. En esta novela Fasce indaga en los misterios del amor y de las relaciones humanas. [LRL]

2567 Feijóo, Cristina. La casa operativa. Buenos Aires: Planeta, 2007. 284 p.

Manuel, un hijo de una mujer desaparecida durante la última dictadura militar reconstruye en el presente y con la colaboración de Dardo, un militante sobreviviente, la semana que el entonces niño vivió a los cuatro años en una casa operativa de Rosario, donde se alojó con su madre y otros tres integrantes de las Fuerzas Armadas Revolucionarias para vigilar a un militar que eventualmente resulta asesinado a manos de otra organización guerrillera. El narrador escribe desde un espacio personal, de búsqueda ("aunque nunca dejaré de buscarla, algo de mi madre queda en estas páginas"). El relato ahonda más que nada en lo cotidiano de la experiencia y las emociones humanas.

Novela Finalista del Premio Planeta 2006 Argentina. [LRL]

2568 Fernández Díaz, Jorge. Fernández. Buenos Aires: Editorial Sudamericana, 2006. 250 p.

Un hombre como tantos, un cuarentón que ha vivido y fracasado, se reencuentra fortuitamente con su amor de adolescente en la oficina del dentista. Este encuentro produce un vaivén de recuerdos episódicos que presenta personajes apasionantes por su humanidad que han formado parte del universo de Fernández y por extensión del argentino común. Hijo de inmigrantes, vive junto con su generación las vicisitudes y violencias, las esperanzas postergadas y el cinismo de las últimas tres décadas del siglo XX. El narrador hace alarde de una prosa ágil, vigorosa, humorística articulada desde el lenguaje de su generación. [CEM]

2569 Fernández Moreno, Inés. La profesora de español. Buenos Aires: Alfaguara, 2005. 246 p.

Las experiencias que vive Isabel como exiliada en España debido a la debacle económica argentina del año 2001, recrean a través de la ficción, un momento específico de la vida de su propia autora. La voz narrativa entreteje la vida de Isabel, mujer de 56 años dentro de un contexto lingüístico y social que la confunde y la reta sobre su propio lenguaje, sus costumbres y sus tradiciones. Sin embargo, la desolación que enfrenta su protagonista se esfuma cuando se transporta a través de los sueños a su hogar en Buenos Aires, a sus recuerdos y a su historia. [MNG]

2570 Forn, Juan. María Domecq. Buenos Aires: Emecé, 2007. 236 p. (Emecé cruz del sur)

La narrativa de Forn entrelaza la historia íntima, "la pequeña historia", con la de la Argentina, el Japón y el delirante mundo de la ópera "Madama Butterfly". El protagonista narrador, luego de sufrir un coma pancreático, nos guía a tientas por una ficción deliciosa que le confiere la prodigiosa virtud de allegarse a un bisabuelo Almirante benefactor del pueblo japonés, una mujer que debería estar muerta pero que le enseña a vivir, un japonés radicado en Brasil quien quizás revele secretos impensables. La

literatura, la música, la historia cobran vida en las páginas eruditas y magistrales de esta novela. [CEM]

2571 García Lao, Fernanda. Muerta de hambre. Buenos Aires: El Cuenco de Plata, 2005. 217 p. (Nueva narrativa)

Primer Premio de Novela Fondo Nacional de Las Artes 2004. A través de la primera persona de una jovencita obesa, inteligente y en batalla contra sí misma y contra el mundo incapacitado para entenderla, la voz narrativa nos fuerza a mirarnos y mirar a una sociedad enferma de inmundicia. El cuerpo femenino como cárcel decide no ya borrarse en una purgación anoréxica, sino rebelarse en el exceso y literalmente reventar, estallar ante la indiferencia y la mediocridad. Si bien el humor y la ironía permean el discurso de la joven, la herida aflora a cada instante, furibunda, maloliente, pero verdadera. La novela choca, lastima, hiede y nos acerca a esa sensibilidad encarnada en la boca de una adolescente quien mira al mundo con una mirada lúcida y despiadada. [CEM]

2572 García Mansilla, Julia. Country club. Argentina: Ediciones Deldragón, 2005. 205 p.: bibl. (Novela Deldragón)

Con humor, ironía y compasión, la narradora ofrece una visión inquietante de los estratos sociales de la sociedad argentina de la última década. Siguiendo los pasos de una familia tipo clase media alta que rechaza la vida en la capital para instalarse en un "country club" de gran renombre y alta seguridad, la narración muestra un desfile de personajes que luchan a su manera por lograr sus propias quimeras. Las empleadas domésticas extranjeras y algunos personajes marginalizados por su conducta actúan como contrapunto a la demencia esnobista de los habitantes de este mundo vacuo y artificial. [CEM]

2573 Giardinelli, Mempo. Luminoso amarillo y otros cuentos. Caracas: Monte Ávila Editores Latinoamericana, 2007. 124 p. (Continentes)

Colección que reúne 19 cuentos que toman lugar en diferentes espacios y tiempos: un viaje aéreo junto a Jorge Luis Borges, una noche de Navidad en un tren averiado en el monte chaqueño y un hombre subido a un árbol que observa y goza al espiar una mujer desnuda en la casa vecina, entre otros. El cuento "Luminoso amarillo", que le da nombre a la colección, trata el tema de la extrema pobreza en un caserío toba y la necesidad de vender el cuerpo de una joven india. En todos los cuentos, sobresale la estupenda descripción de los ambientes naturales así como las desenfrenadas pasiones humanas. [LRL]

2574 Gómez, Carlos María. Highsmith: novela. Buenos Aires: Ediciones Simurg, 2005. 254 p.

Dos historias que comparten el mismo eje temático, a pesar que son presentadas de manera independiente sirven de base a la novela de Gómez. Por un lado, Tom Ripley es el protagonista de la obra ficcional de Patricia Highsmith, quien goza de una vida holgada en París pero sobre el que gira un pasado turbio y dudoso. Por otro lado, Marcos Dellepiane escritor y protagonista de la segunda historia, reside en Buenos Aires y busca a través de su ficción esclarecer y completar lo que quedó pendiente en la vida de Ripley. Tres voces que sincronizan en una sola (la de Gómez) para mostrar una obra que magnetiza por su complejidad narrativa y que entrelaza lenguajes ajenos pero al mismo tiempo conserva la autenticidad en cada relato. [MNG]

2575 González, Betina. Arte menor. Buenos Aires: Clarín: Alfaguara, 2006. 181 p.

La narrativa se encauza a partir de la voz de una hija ya adulta quien busca desentrañar el misterio de su padre, escultor, poco presente durante su infancia y mujeriego empedernido. Luego de su muerte accidental, la joven intenta recuperar la figura paterna mediante pesquisas llevadas a cabo en entrevistas con las amantes del padre y mediante los recuerdos que ella evoca. Por medio de su trama detectivesca, su humor, sus vuelos imaginativos y su lenguaje, esta primera novela logra recrear a un hombre en toda su complejidad a través de la ausencia y del silencio. [CEM]

2576 Gorodischer, Angélica. Querido amigo. Buenos Aires: Edhasa, 2006. 262 p. (Novela Edhasa)

Un enviado de su majestad británica a principios del siglo XIX le escribe a un amigo sus extrañas experiencias desde una fantástica tierra, toda ella tapizada de seda blanca, donde los hombres se complacen en compartir sus mujeres con sus allegados. La novela expresa la inmersión casi involuntaria del personaje en este mundo de valores antitéticos a la Inglaterra victoriana, pero a la vez enormemente seductores y razonables para la sociedad de los "abdassiris". Gorodischer ha creado un mundo con sus reglas y sus códigos los cuales revelan la hipocresía y quizás lo erróneo de los valores europeos en cuanto a la sexualidad, pero que al mismo tiempo revelan los males eternos de la esclavitud y el comercio del cuerpo femenino. [CEM]

2577 Gorodischer, Angélica. Tumba de jaguares. Buenos Aires: Emecé Editores, 2005. 218 p. (Emecé cruz del sur)

El acto de la escritura permite sobrevivir precariamente el horror de la realidad del padre de una "desaparecida", y al inventar mundos donde dejar parte de ese dolor, el autor de la novela y los personajes, quienes a su vez escriben sus propias ficciones, reflejan y canalizan el miedo, la locura, el amor y la muerte. Novela política cargada de poesía, Tumba de jaguares absorbe y magnetiza por su complejidad y seguridad narrativas, la intimidad de sus voces, la emoción de su lenguaje. [CEM]

2578 Gruss, Irene. Una letra familiar. Buenos Aires: Bajo la Luna, 2007. 74 p. (Col. Buenos y breves; 4)

Una letra familiar es la primera publicación en prosa de la consagrada poeta Irene Gruss. La niña protagonista no sólo registra en su diario lo que experimenta en su núcleo familiar en sus años de infancia y pubertad, sino que también anota los acontecimientos políticos y sociales de la Argentina en los años 70. Con una trama sencilla, ágil y narrada a través de la cándida voz de la niña a modo de diario personal, Gruss revaloriza "el querido diario" como género discursivo y le otorga a éste agencia sobre la historia y la política de su país. [MNG]

2579 Guebel, Daniel. Derrumbe. Buenos Aires: Mondadori, 2007. 188 p. (Literatura Mondadori)

El protagonista de esta novela se hunde ante la separación conyugal y la posibilidad de perder el amor de su pequeña hija Ana. La novela se inicia el último día del año cuando Paula decide abandonar al narrador. El protagonista narra el derrumbe presente y pasado en su vida pero también su responsabilidad por cuidarse y sobrellevar la infelicidad que entendía como circunstancial. Criado por una familia adoptiva de carácter depresivo, el protagonista y su hermana fueron testigos y partícipes de abusos físicos y verbales. La novela narra el descenso del personaje a un mundo indigente y desolador. [LRL]

2580 Gusmán, Luis. El peletero. Buenos Aires: Edhasa, 2007. 246 p. (Novela)
Dos vidas de seres drásticamente diferentes pero ambos signados por las derrotas de su sendos pasados se cruzan inesperadamente. Landa, el peletero que heredó de sus padres inmigrantes el negocio y Hueso, habitante del maloliente riachuelo colaboran para dar sentido a sus vidas en busca de una venganza. Esta novela de personajes ambiguos, antiheroicos y descarnadamente humanos, escarba con sensibilidad e inteligencia la responsabilidad del individuo frente a los males que aquejan a la humanidad y al planeta. [CEM]

2581 Huidobro, Norma. El lugar perdido. Buenos Aires: Clarín: Alfaguara, 2007. 221 p.
Ganadora del Premio Clarín de Novela, 2007, *El lugar perdido* tiene lugar en Villa del Carmen, un pequeño pueblo ubicado en la provincia de Jujuy. Es el año 1977. Un oficial de policía porteño llega al pueblo en busca de Matilde Trigo, quien ahora vive en Buenos Aires y que es pareja de un militante ferroviario, supuesto subversivo. La novela se centra en la búsqueda de unas cartas que Matilde le ha enviado a su mejor amiga, Marita, quien protege fielmente a su amiga. Con un lenguaje simple, lírico y profundo al mismo tiempo, la novela ahonda en el poder de las relaciones humanas y el drama de la persecución política. [LRL]

2582 In fraganti: los mejores narradores de la nueva generación escriben sobre casos policiales. Selección de Diego Grillo Trubba. Buenos Aires: Reservior Books, 2007. 303 p. (Cuentos; 2) (Nuevos escritores; 2)
Veintiún cuentos conforman esta colección. La particularidad es que fueron escritos por jóvenes que pertenecen a las nuevas generaciones de escritores argentinos. Lo que caracteriza al grupo es precisamente el abanico de temas y enfoques a la hora de abordar los hechos policiales. Los casos policiales que narran tratan sobre violaciones, abusos, tráfico de personas, robos y asesinatos, entre otros, y están motivados por venganza, codicia e incomprensión. En la mayoría de los cuentos se reconocen hechos reales que acontecieron en algún momento de la realidad argentina y que los autores ficcionalizan y reescriben sin tapujos y sin límites. [LRL]

2583 Iparraguirre, Sylvia. El muchacho de los senos de goma. Buenos Aires: Alfaguara, 2007. 345 p.
Cris, un adolescente que se va de su casa, Mentasti, un profesor de filosofía que acaba de regresar de un infructuoso viaje a Bolivia, y la señora Vidot, cuyo marido acaba de fallecer en un accidente, entrecruzan sus destinos en la Buenos Aires de los años 90 donde se evidencian la pobreza y la proliferación de los vendedores ambulantes. A lo largo de la novela, los tres personajes buscan respuestas a sus cuestionamientos personales tanto a través de otras relaciones humanas como de las ideas de Wittgenstein que se intercalan a lo largo de la narración. [LRL]

2584 Kaufmann, Paola. El campo de golf del diablo: cuentos. Buenos Aires: Suma de Letras Argentina, 2006. 204 p. (Punto de lectura)
Primer Premio del Fondo Nacional de las Artes, año 2000. Diez cuentos narrados con precisión lingüística y una mirada aguda sobre los comportamientos y las relaciones humanas. La movilidad física y mental atraviesa los relatos que se resisten a ubicarse en espacios y tiempos estables. Las relaciones entre hermanos, de parejas, de amigos, entre profesor y alumna, entre doctor y paciente, son algunos de los escenarios humanos donde se desarrollan estos cuentos que abogan por lo imperfecto y lo inesperado. [LRL]

2585 Kociancich, Vlady. La ronda de los jinetes muertos. Buenos Aires: Seix Barral, 2007. 183 p. (Biblioteca breve)
Siete cuentos que narran historias familiares en las cuales la realidad y la

imaginación se entrelazan para ahondar en temas como el amor, la amistad y la soledad. Los espacios y tiempos de los cuentos son muy diversos: un bazar en el Cairo, un barrio en Buenos Aires, una finca en Bali, un persistente recuerdo de una casa en Polonia. Caracteriza algunos de los cuentos una intertextualidad representada, entre otros, por los escritos de Heródoto del siglo V y la obra de William Shakespeare, *El Mercader de Venecia*. [LRL]

2586 Laurencich, Alejandra. Historias de mujeres oscuras. Buenos Aires: Grupo Editorial Norma, 2007. 230 p. (Col. El Dorado)

Diecisiete relatos conmovedores y variados sobre mujeres que experimentan culpas y miedos pero que las caracterizan la entereza y la constancia. Con una prosa ágil y contundente los cuentos narrados en primera y tercera persona retratan vivencias emocionales, físicas y mentales de mujeres que engañan, sufren, trabajan, discuten, viajan y sobre todo existen en espacios y tiempos distintos, aunque las aúna la búsqueda de una cierta felicidad propia. [LRL]

2587 Lojo de Beuter, María Rosa. Cuerpos resplandecientes: santos populares argentinos. Buenos Aires: Editorial Sudamericana, 2007. 209 p.: ill.

Texto que cuenta con 10 relatos ficcionalizados sobre santos populares argentinos, entre los que se encuentran la Difunta Correa, el Gauchito Gil, la Telesita, Ceferino Namuncurá y Gilda, entre otros. El texto consta de una bibliografía que incluye textos históricos, antropológicos, filosóficos, testimoniales y biográficos sobre los santos populares. Una introducción a los relatos indaga en las condiciones de santificación popular, la dimensión política y simbólica del culto popular así como en la poética corporal de los santos populares. [LRL]

2588 Mairal, Pedro. El año del desierto. Buenos Aires: Interzona, 2005. 273 p.

Novela que recrea la historia argentina valiéndose de la propia historia política, social, económica y literaria de ese país. Mairal recrea a través de María, su protagonista, un viaje histórico que transporta al lector de la civilización a la barbarie retratada por Sarmiento en *Facundo* o plas-

mada en el poema "La cautiva" de Esteban Echeverría. Los malones, los baqueanos, el matadero y la naturaleza son elementos que evocan la barbarie y que el autor utiliza para cuestionar con un sentido dramático y conmovedor la crisis por la que atraviesa su país 200 años más tarde. [MNG]

2589 Masetto, Antonio dal. Señores más señoras. Buenos Aires: Editorial Sudamericana, 2006. 190 p. (Relatos)

Señores más señoras es una colección de 40 relatos incluidos en cinco capítulos. Con la espontaneidad y la naturalidad que exige una situación particular de la vida cotidiana, los relatos de esta colección retratan ese mundo real para mostrar un variado universo donde confluyen las anécdotas, las experiencias vitales. Relatos, como "Almendros" y "Bolero", desmenuzan con brevedad y astucia las etapas vivenciales de todo ser humano. [MNG]

2590 Modern, Rodolfo E. La salsera de Meissen. Buenos Aires: Editorial Sudamericana, 2005. 188 p. (Narrativas)

Esta colección de 40 relatos de extensión variada contiene narraciones donde la imaginación desbordante de Modern atrapa al lector mediante su acertada capacidad lúdica. El cuento infantil, la recreación biográfica, la reescritura mitológica o novelística, la evocación de un paisaje, un hecho histórico, de un personaje o de un objeto, se transforman en manos del cuentista en material lírico, en un juego literario perfecto que une la realidad a la imaginación. [CEM]

2591 Muchnik, José. Chupadero. Buenos Aires: El Farol, 2005. 237 p.

Novela filosófica y política, *Chupadero* deja al descubierto las atrocidades perpetradas durante la represión de los años 70 en Argentina. Los 27 capítulos que la constituyen entrelazan una serie de relatos que mantienen en vilo a su lectoría. Las historias cruzadas y los cambios abruptos de narradores sirven para revelar el caos, el dolor, la impotencia y la injusticia de las que miles de familias argentinas fueron víctimas. Es una loa a la memoria de miles de desaparecidos y un intento por mostrar lo indescifrable a través de la ficción. [MNG]

2592 Muleiro, Vicente. La balada del asador. Buenos Aires: Planeta, 2007. 205 p. (Autores españoles e iberoamericanos)

Es el año 2001 en Buenos Aires. Leo, un asador "amateur", relata su historia personal intercalada con los acontecimientos sociopolíticos y económicos de la época. La relación con Cynthia, su segunda pareja, se resquebraja mientras su hijo Facundo (Fackyou, Fac o Facu) transita por la adolescencia de una ciudad sin leyes ni orden. La narración es ágil y fluida con un ritmo que acompasa las vertiginosas caídas de los personajes y del ambiente que los rodea. [LRL]

2593 Negroni, María. La anunciación. Buenos Aires: Seix Barral, 2007. 229 p. (Biblioteca breve)

Novela que trata de reconstruir desde lo íntimo y lo personal hechos y memorias de los violentos años 70 en la Argentina. Caracterizan la narrativa la fragmentación, lo onírico y el vaivén entre múltiples espacios y tiempos. En Roma, la narradora dialoga con un interlocutor, Humboldt, quien ha sido testigo y partícipe de algunas experiencias compartidas que ella intenta recordar. [LRL]

2594 Ortiz, Marta. El vuelo de la noche: cuentos. San Juan: La Editorial, Univ. de Puerto Rico, 2006. 221 p.

Primer Premio Emilio Díaz Varcárcel de la Bienal Internacional de Literatura Puerto Rico 2000. Los cuentos que constituyen esta colección despliegan una gran amplitud de registros protagónicos que llevan en común la angustia y la esperanza de una humanidad doliente pero aún llena de plenitudes. La narradora sigue con firmeza los vaivenes de sus personajes, y con un lenguaje que oscila entre lo lírico y lo cotidiano, desmenuza lo más íntimo del ser y su circunstancia. [CEM]

2595 Piglia, Ricardo. La invasión. Barcelona: Editorial Anagrama, 2006. 194 p. (Narrativas hispánicas; 404)

Segunda edición corregida y aumentada de la edición original de 1967 premiado por Casa de las Américas en ese año. Además de los 10 relatos originales, Piglia ha añadido cinco cuentos ya publicados en revistas literarias en la misma época y dos inéditos que inician y cierran la colección. Ambos relatos, "El joyero" y "Un pez en el hielo", demuestran el dominio y la madurez del autor desde esa tempana narrativa. La temática que surgirá más adelante en la obra de Piglia se encuentra ya no sólo latente sino desarrollada en los relatos que abordan la historia, las relaciones humanas, la soledad, la niñez, el arte. [CEM]

2596 Prenz, Juan Octavio. El señor Kreck. Madrid: Losada, 2006. 309 p.

La vida de un apacible e irrefutablemente correcto agente de seguros dará un vuelco hacia el horror a partir de un pequeño gesto de rebeldía personal. Ubicada durante la dictadura en los años 70, la novela revela los efectos kafkianos que ésta ejerce sobre la sociedad y sobre los individuos. El inocente y algo excéntrico personaje mantiene su dignidad y defiende su verdad a través de todo su calvario ante la iniquidad de sus torturadores y la cobardía y hostilidad de los vecinos y colegas que se apartan de él y de su esposa. El mundo del "extranjero" Kreck se vuelve metáfora de la Argentina bajo la dictadura de los 70. [CEM]

2597 Ramos, Pablo. La ley de la ferocidad. Buenos Aires: Alfaguara, 2007. 364 p. (Alfaguara)

La noticia de la muerte del padre de Gabriel en una fría mañana porteña genera una novela sobre las relaciones familiares, el alcohol, las drogas y el sexo, entre otros temas. El protagonista avanza por los que parecen ser túneles oscuros e interminables (como cuando compra harina y veneno para ratas y hace panes que luego da a las palomas), pero por momentos, encuentra espacios renovadores gracias a su propia escritura y a la catarsis de emociones que le brinda el relato sobre las relaciones entre él y su padre. [LRL]

2598 Rivera, Andrés. Traslasierra. Buenos Aires: Seix Barral, 2007. 84 p. (Biblioteca breve)

La brevedad del relato agudiza el impacto de esta novela escrita en forma de contrapunteo narrativo de padre e hija. Los personajes se hallan unidos profundamente por una mujer, Rebeca, madre y amante judía de Gerhard Schrader, oficial alemán fiel a Hitler que llega al sur argentino con su pequeña hija. La pasión, la crueldad, el erotismo y el crimen que se entretejen en las vidas de los dos personajes y sobre aquellos seres que los rodean, tienen como telón de fondo la represión de los años 70. [CEM]

2599 Rodríguez, Cristian. Madrugada negra. Buenos Aires: A. Hidalgo Editora, 2007. 191 p. (La lengua. Novela)

Novela, ganadora del Premio Biblioteca Nacional de Novela 2007, que se ocupa del mundo sórdido de un torturador de la última dictadura militar. El protagonista, Miguel Arribeño, es un ser detestable que deambula por las calles como un espectro perseguido por las memorias de los tormentos que infligió a hombres y mujeres. La novela, narrada en tercera persona, se vale de un lenguaje novedoso, según explica el autor, muy barroco, donde se emplean los verbos sin sujeto—siguiendo la modalidad castrense—así como la perífrasis, las aliteraciones, la deconstrucción de la conjugación verbal y el uso del infinitivo, "Los custodios que no abandonan el emblema de los anteojos negros. Retomar oficios afuera. Fusilamientos en masa, el pozo" (p. 118). [LRL]

2600 Sábato, Mario. India Pravile. Buenos Aires: Emecé, 2005. 328 p.

Un director de cine deprimido y amargado en lucha enconada con un mundo hostil que no lo comprende ni él entiende se aferra a un pasado que ya nadie parece recordar. La soledad y la rabia lo aíslan de todo y de todos hasta que su nieto de 14 años comienza a talar su dura caparazón. El humor, el sarcasmo, y el lenguaje mordaz, rápido y cinemático de esta obra, llevada al cine antes de ser publicada, dejan abierta la llaga de la incomprensión e incomunicación entre los seres, entre las generaciones, pero a su vez prometen la posibilidad de redención. [CEM]

2601 Saccomanno, Guillermo. 77. Buenos Aires: Planeta, 2008. 273 p. (Autores españoles e iberoamericanos)

El profesor Gómez es un hombre de más de 80 años que recuerda el frío invierno del año 1977 en una ciudad hundida por la pobreza y el terror. Su experiencia personal como homosexual y simpatizante del peronismo se entrelaza con historias de sus propios estudiantes desaparecidos así como la de sus padres. Al no encontrar respuestas en Dios y la iglesia, estos se refugian en charlatanas y clarividentes para saber el paradero de sus hijos. [LRL]

2602 Sagasti, Luis. Los mares de la luna. Buenos Aires: Editorial Sudamericana, 2006. 254 p. (Narrativas)

La invitación que recibe Julián en su oficina para asistir a una fiesta lujosa y en una estancia exclusiva, propicia que éste y su esposa Emilia se sumerjan en ese mundo farandulero y banal del que gozan los privilegiados de la alta sociedad. La novela va más allá del relato de las frivolidades y derroches propios de una fiesta de una clase social pudiente. Sagasti, a través de las expresiones inconclusas de sus personajes y de las misteriosas apariciones y desapariciones de los mismos, reflexiona sobre las realidades individuales y colectivas inacabadas que siguen buscando a través de la memoria para responder a profundos interrogantes. [MNG]

2603 Semán, Ernesto. Todo lo sólido. Buenos Aires: Aurelia Rivera, 2007. 244 p. (Narrativa)

Novela finalista del Concurso EMECÉ de Novela 2007. Tres argentinos Gabriel, Laura y Bernardo viven en Brooklyn. Un incendio en el departamento que comparten Gabriel y Laura en septiembre de 2001 le da impulso a la novela. La pareja se refugia con Bernardo, un abogado razonable y centrado cuyo personaje contrasta con el mundo de la drogadicción y la violencia en el que habita Gabriel. El regreso de los tres personajes a Buenos Aires complejiza la novela y ahonda en el suspenso que se crea a lo largo de la narración. [LRL]

2604 Tizón, Héctor. Cuentos completos. Prólogo de Leonor Fleming. Buenos Aires: Alfaguara, 2006. 484 p. (Alfaguara)

Esta edición contiene 52 relatos de Tizón antes publicados en cinco volúmenes. Se conserva el orden cronológico aunque no la organización de las obras en que primero aparecieron publicados. Cuenta el volumen con un prólogo de Leonor Fleming y un apéndice con tres textos de Tizón. El mundo de la puna jujeña y sus personajes recreados a través del lenguaje colorido del paraje austeramente bello del norte fronterizo pueblan muchas de las narrativas. El exilio y el ser desarraigado forman parte de su otra vertiente temática de alto valor artístico. [CEM]

2605 Vázquez, Débora. Siesta nómade. Rosario, Argentina: Beatriz Viterbo Editora, 2006. 88 p. (Ficciones)

Colección de 24 relatos breves que incursionan en una variedad de temas y de personajes; una coleccionista falsa, la espera de un profesor que no llega, un violinista suplente y una mujer en una playa desconocida y fría, entre otros. Los relatos son retazos de vida, descripciones de lo esperado e inesperado, existencias que transcurren entre la verdad y la falsedad de lo cotidiano. [LRL]

2606 Venturini, Aurora. Las primas. Buenos Aires: Página 12, 2007. 166 p.

Novela galardonada con el Premio Nueva Novela Página/12-Banco Provincia. Yuna, la protagonista y narradora es una niña aparentemente subnormal cuya capacidad para pintar y contar historias es innegable. Conmovedora y por momentos cruel, la novela narra las desdichas de una familia disfuncional, de clase media que reside en la ciudad de La Plata en los años 40. [LRL]

2607 Vidal, Raúl. Pagué y salí. Córdoba, Argentina: Alción Editora, 2006. 89 p.

Primer volumen de relatos de Vidal, incluye seis cuentos que impactan por la complejidad de su estilo narrativo. Los personajes de cada historia y los espacios en que éstos se mueven dejan al descubierto cuestionamientos sobre un dolor latente y un universo sombrío que todavía rodea la vida y la historia del pueblo argentino. A través de un lenguaje íntimo y analítico esta novela política y psicológica intenta recuperar del olvido esos recuerdos que puedan aliviar el dolor de una nación. [MNG]

2608 Waisbrot, Daniel. Y al volver la vista atrás. Buenos Aires: Ediciones Deldragón, 2006. 183 p. (Novela deldragón)

Tres compañeros de estudios universitarios se encuentran en una cena 20 años más tarde. En el transcurso de las horas, los tres sicoanalistas recuperan de alguna manera los recuerdos, algunos a medias olvidados, otros violentamente presentes. La narrativa en primera persona se mueve ágilmente del presente que los reúne hacia el pasado y la juventud durante los años 70, escarbando entre los despojos de la memoria el destino que ignoraban y el presente que no logran comprender. [CEM]

2609 Yudicello, Lucio. El sangrador. Córdoba, Argentina: El Emporio Ediciones, 2006. 140 p.

Novela finalista por dos años consecutivos del Premio Clarín en los años 2004 y 2005, impacta por lo que deja entrever entre líneas. Narrada en primera persona, el autor se vale de la enfermedad de su protagonista Abelardo Pinto y de su cargo como miembro del comité vecinal del barrio Los Ligustros para conectar el pasado y el presente de la historia de un pueblo donde las interrogantes siguen aún sin respuesta y donde los desaparecidos y olvidados parecen ser por primera vez escuchados. [MNG]

2610 Zeiger, Claudio. Adiós a la calle. Buenos Aires: Emecé, 2006. 253 p. (Emecé cruz del sur)

Las calles de la ciudad de Buenos Aires durante la década de los 80 son testigo de encuentros amorosos y de la aparición de la enfermedad más devastadora y menos entendida del siglo XX, el SIDA. Horacio Calvo, el protagonista, y sus amigos homosexuales se mueven en un círculo que no queda fuera del gran impacto de este mal. [LRL]

LITERARY CRITICISM AND HISTORY

2611 Gorodischer, Angélica. A la tarde, cuando llueve. Buenos Aires: Emecé, 2007. 225 p. (Cruz del sur)

Esta colección de ensayos es una recopilación de presentaciones efectuadas por Gorodischer en diferentes conferencias en las dos últimas décadas. Lo valioso de la colección radica en la relación que se establece entre el lector y la escritora. La autora cuenta sus vivencias—como si estuviera charlando con su lectoría—, comparte sus emociones y, como escritora, estimula a otras mujeres a seguir escribiendo. Este texto le permite a ese lector de cafés y de bibliotecas, reflejo de ella misma, ingresar de forma íntima al mundo de la escritora y aprender de sus experiencias literarias sobre los libros que la conmovieron, los temas universales, el amor, el sexo, el sueño, la locura, la imaginación, la escritura y el compromiso. [MNG]

Poetry

LESLIE BAYERS, Assistant Professor of Spanish, St. Mary's College of Maryland
FRANCISCO CABANILLAS, Associate Professor of Spanish, Bowling Green State University
JUAN DUCHESNE-WINTER, Professor of Latin American Literature, University of Pittsburgh
HÉCTOR JAIMES, Associate Professor of Spanish, North Carolina State University
JILL S. KUHNHEIM, Professor of Spanish, University of Kansas
ELIZABETH MONASTERIOS, Associate Professor of Spanish, State University of New York, Stony Brook
OSCAR SARMIENTO, Professor of Spanish, State University of New York, Potsdam
JACOBO SEFAMÍ, Professor of Spanish, University of California, Irvine

MÉXICO

EN EL PERIODO que va de 2007 a 2010 continúa la tendencia a publicar antologías de poesía mexicana actual. Llama la atención, en particular, la reaparición de los anuarios de poesía mexicana, editados desde 2005 por el Fondo de Cultura Económica.

De los libros individuales reseñados en este periodo, es importante la aparición de la poesía y la poética de López Velarde (item **2770**) en las ediciones de Ayacucho, y la poesía completa de Ramón Xirau (item **2851**), un escritor que, a pesar de haber vivido en México la mayor parte de su vida, escribe en su lengua materna, el catalán. La gran mayoría de los escritores reseñados en este periodo han nacido en las décadas de los 50, 60 y 70. Algunos de ellos (Esquinca, Bravo Varela, Fabre) han sido publicados por la Editorial Pre-Textos de Valencia (España). El proyecto en poesía de la Editorial Bonobos es fascinante; otras editoriales distinguidas, como Era, Fondo de Cultura Económica y Conaculta, siguen comprometidas con la publicación de libros de poetas mexicanos.

En cuanto a los libros de crítica, apareció una nueva recopilación de Enrico Mario Santí sobre Octavio Paz (item **2861**); un libro sobre la generación de medio siglo en México (Sabines, Castellanos, Segovia, entre otros) (item **2859**) y otro sobre poetas mujeres a lo largo del siglo XX. En 2010 lamentamos el fallecimiento de los escritores Alí Chumacero (1918–2010), Carlos Montemayor (1947–2010) y Esther Seligson (1941–2010). [JS]

CENTROAMÉRICA

En el período que nos concierne, destacan las antologías colectivas de poetas contemporáneos y actuales, y las antologías individuales de poetas recientes y no tan recientes ya consignados a una tradición, no siempre muy conocidos. La contribución más notable de estos últimos tres años al legado de la poesía centroamericana quizás sea la antología de Mario Campaña, *Pájaro relojero* (item **2650**), que incluye, a veces completos o casi completos, los poemarios más importantes de 13 de los grandes poetas de la región en el siglo XX. No se incluye a Darío, podemos presumir que se arranca desde la poesía posmodernista. Pero se incluye en su totalidad *El soldado desconocido*, de Salomón de la Selva, y una cantidad considerable de poemas de Pablo Antonio Cuadra. La selección de Dalton es amplia y balanceada. Las de Cardenal y Coronel son depuradas. Se nos regala, además la poesía de dos figuras menos conocidas fuera de sus países que seguro llamarán la atención en el futuro por la fuerza renovadora de su lenguaje lírico: el salvadoreño Alonso

Quijadurías (1940) y la guatemalteca Isabel de los Ángeles Ruano (1945). Ellos se separan de las corrientes predominantes en sus respectivos ámbitos nacionales, el primero con un verso alegórico-reflexivo, la segunda con una voz intimista.

Entre las antologías individuales de poetas ya consignados en la tradición, que requieren sin embargo mayor difusión y atención, sobresale la dedicada al guatemalteco Carlos Illescas, *La rosa bien temperada* (item **2753**), quien perteneció al grupo literario Acentos creado en 1940 y forjó poemas de gran rigor expresivo dignos de figurar en las mayores antologías de la lengua pese la desigual calidad de parte de su considerable producción.

Convocan la lectura atenta dos poemarios individuales de André Cruchaga, salvadoreño, y Gerardo Guinea Diez, guatemalteco. El primero nos ofrece en *Oscuridad sin fecha* (item **2713**) un excepcional despliegue de poesía meditativa con foco existencial, que abreva en las fuentes de la tradición lírica coronada en el siglo XX por autores como Vallejo, Celan y Espriu, y además logra articular una voz original, singularmente conmovedora en torno a las experiencias esenciales de la soledad, la muerte y la enfermedad, según se modifican en el mundo contemporáneo. El segundo hilvana en *Casa de nosotros* (item **2748**) una secuencia amorosa compuesta de fragmentos musicalmente encadenados por un fraseo cercano a los blues. Tanto este tipo de poemario como las antologías panorámicas de la producción actual (anotadas a continuación) sugieren que lo mejor del taller poético centroamericano se aleja crecientemente de los temas cívicos, en parte forjados al calor de los intensos conflictos bélicos que asolaron la región, y de las formas conversacionales inauguradas tempranamente por un Salomón de la Selva, que luego protagonizaron la segunda mitad del siglo XX, para incursionar ahora en registros reflexivos, intimistas, articulados a formas más cancioneriles que conversacionales o discursivas. [JDW]

EL CARIBE

Entre la antología que se aboca a compilar una tradición poética hecha, terminada, como en el primer volumen dedicado a la poesía de Cintio Vitier (item **2865**), y la que, como en el caso de la poesía de Luis Palés Matos, reorganiza temáticamente la obra (item **2651**), están el homenaje crítico a poetas medulares como Nicolás Guillén (item **2860**) y la antología de la nueva, *"post-edípica"* poesía puertorriqueña del siglo XXI (item **2659**). En el caso de la poesía dominicana, cinco antologías se entrecruzan: 1) la que recoge la producción poética del sur de la isla, no como marcador regional sino antropológico (item **2620**); 2) las dos que, desde la diáspora, conectan lo dominicano con el universo poético hispanoparlante (items **2630** y **2665**); 3) la que parte de lo citadino (item **2633**); 4) la que, enfocada en la mística del interiorismo, incluye la producción dominicana junto a la española. Cabe destacar la colección de ensayos sobre el pensamiento poético de Jorge Luis Arcos (item **2858**) y el estudio de la música de Silvio Rodríguez como poesía de Suyín Morales Alemañy (item **2863**).

En el caso de la poesía puertorriqueña, tanto la editorial Isla Negra como Terranova marcan el ritmo de publicaciones. Entre los poetas establecidos, la voz de Rosario Ferré se plantea una reflexión afirmativa, gozosa y elocuente sobre la lengua, lo lingüístico, el español y el inglés, que abre nuevos espacios (*fisuras*) en su obra (item **2731**). Por otro lado, abundan las buenas voces de la nueva poesía puertorriqueña, una producción que, en general, parecería mantener una proximidad solidaria con la academia, como en el caso de Juanmanuel González Ríos (item **2744**). Viejos entre los nuevos, el erotismo soberano de Mairyn Cruz-Bernal reaparece en el contexto de un viaje a Colombia, donde "todos los hombres que vi / besaron mis labios" (item **2714**); la poesía desde la tradición literaria de Javier Ávila se reinventa a partir de "lo que no quedó nunca en el recuerdo" (item **2676**); Elidio La Torres Lagares se entrega al vicio literario del doble sentido (item **2760**); el apalabramiento encarna el poemario de Mara Pastor (item **2796**). El cruce con lo dominicano, en la poesía de Carlos Roberto Gómez Beras, se da desde lo amoroso (item **2742**).

En cuanto a la poesía dominicana, el homenaje a Pedro Mir reafirma la presencia del poeta que puso a la isla en el mapa de la poesía del siglo XX (item **2777**). Desde la diáspora, sobresale la producción de Rei Berroa; como poeta, "triste el que se fuera/con el sexo sin usar" (item **2688**), y como antólogo (items **2665** y **2630**). El cruce con lo puertorriqueño se da, por un lado, en el poemario enamorado del amor de Alexis Gómez, una experiencia vivida entre el puerto de Mayagüez y el de Santo Domingo "Hacia Mayagüez me voy/en el temblor de tu cuerpo" (item **2743**); y por el otro, en la publicación de Pastor Moya, el poeta dominicano más atrevido, creador de una *poética de la locura,* en la editorial puertorriqueña y dominicana de Isla Negra, "viene LEZAMA montando/un caballo hirviente y blanco/que huye de lo blanco" (item **2787**). Menos esperado, el cruce con lo argentino se da en la propuesta épica y trágica de Mónica Volonteri, una escritora argentina-dominicanizada, "releyendo a Rimbau/y/escupiendo a Junot Díaz" (item **2849**). Desde la diáspora, se apuesta al sueño de reconciliación con todo lo que simboliza Haití (item **2846**).

En cuanto a la poesía cubana, Miguel Barnet plantea un itinerario de su obra poética que asegura, por todo lo que le falta por vivir y escribir, incompleto (item **2679**); un itinerario que, en otro poemario (item **2680**), marcado también por la "poética de la travesía", acopla las rutas internas con las externas, "Amo estas calles [de Francia] que no se parecen a las mías". La persistencia de Gustavo Guerrero recopila la producción poética de Severo Sarduy, seguro de que lo mejor de éste se encuentra en el barroquismo de la poesía sarduyana (item **2829**). Desde los oleajes de la poesía alternativa, el poemario de Ricardo Alberto Pérez estalla frente a la solemnidad demasiado establecida de lo literario domesticado, "Natalia cepillaba/y cantaba y cuando el semen/también se había/acumulado/Oral-B, lo descubría" (item **2798**); un estallido, más o menos paralelo al de Reina María Rodríguez, desconfiado de las apariencias capturadas, "Coger y dejar sin que el anzuelo penetre" (item **2813**). Desde la otra orilla del exilio, la contundencia prolífica de José Kozer vuelve a insistir en la intuición poética, "el agua que me llega a la cintura/me recubre de yedra (lianas) somos (en última instancia) sombras" (item **2759**). [FC]

COLOMBIA Y VENEZUELA

En este período, el empuje de las políticas culturales del gobierno venezolano, orientadas a fomentar la cultura en todos sus ámbitos, así como la lectura y la creación literaria, quedan reflejadas en una amplia lista de publicaciones por dos de las casas editoriales estatales más importantes: Monte Ávila Editores Latinoamericana y El Perro y la Rana. Asimismo, los festivales internacionales de poesía en Venezuela, y en la ciudad de Medellín (Colombia), que toman lugar anualmente, han contribuido a que la poesía se constituya también en una forma de socialización y difusión cultural. En cuanto a la producción literaria misma, aparecen una serie de antologías que, por un lado, recogen la obra de poetas con una trayectoria reconocida en Venezuela, pero por otro lado, también aparecen antologías de poetas menos conocidos. Entre el primer grupo de antologías, aparecen: *Lugar de pasaje: antología poética* de María Auxiliadora Álvarez, una poetisa que experimenta con el lenguaje y las imágenes (item **2612**); *En lugar del resplandor: antología poética* de Luis Alberto Crespo, un poeta reflexivo y en constante renovación (item **2637**); *La sagrada familia (antología 1968/2000)* de Enrique Hernández-D'Jesús, poeta culto que desafía al lector con sus temas y humor (item **2644**); *Amarrando la paciencia a un árbol: antología poética 1979–2007* de Mharía Vázquez Benarroch, una poetisa que se dio a conocer en los 80s tras haber obtenido premios literarios importantes, y cuya poesía reflexiva perdura en el tiempo (item **2662**). Entre las antologías de poetas menos conocidos están: *Pasadizo: poesía reunida 1994–2006* de Luis Enrique Belmonte (item **2625**); *Sólo el mar: antología personal* de Celso Medina (item **2647**) y *Lámpara y silencio: antología poética* de César Seco (item **2660**). Otra antología importante, esta vez de poetas colombianos, pero publicada en Venezuela, es: *Antología de la poesía colombiana (1958–2008)* preparada por Iván Beltrán Castillo (item **2617**). Se trata de una antología muy bien cuidada, y con una selección de poetas reconocidos, así como de nuevas voces, como Enrique Rodríguez Pérez, Juan Felipe Robledo, Winston Morales Chavarro, John J. Junieles, Federico Díaz-Granados, Juan Sebastián Gaviria y Robert Max Steenskist. Finalmente, encontramos nuevas voces en Venezuela: Mariela Casal (*Hotel*) (item **2704**), Mirih Berbin (*Mareas*) (item **2686**), Alexis Romero (*La respuesta de los techos)* (item **2818**), María Clara Salas (*1606 y otros poemas)* (item **2824**), José Javier Sánchez (*Código postal 1010* y *Fragmentos para una memoria)* (items **2826** y **2827**) y Rafael Castillo Zapata (*Estancias)* (item **2708**). Entre este grupo, la poética de Casal, por ser radical e integral a la vez, y la poética de Sánchez, por ser renovadora en su tono conversacional y anecdótico, pueden considerarse poéticas revolucionarias. [HJ]

PERU

An impressive assortment of poetry reviewed for this essay confirms a thriving tradition in Peru. Among welcome reprints of work by internationally celebrated voices is a new edition of César Vallejo's seminal *Los heraldos negros* (item **2845**), which includes an informative essay and notes by critic Ricardo González Vigil. A transcription (and accompanying audio DVD) of a reading Blanca Varela gave in Spain a decade ago (item **2847**), including poems and framing anecdotes personally selected by the poet, offers an appealingly personalized view of her renowned work. Carlos Germán Belli's new compilation of previously published verse (item **2684**) spotlights a modern voice brilliantly rendered in classical forms. Publications of the complete poetry of Xavier Abril (item **2666**) and Rodolfo Hinostroza (item **2751**) assemble their celebrated works, while other established poets, including Santiago Aguilar (items **2667** and **2668**), Raúl Brozovich (item **2693**), Isaac Goldemberg (item **2741**), Pablo Guevara (item **2746**), Cronwell Jara (item **2757**), and Roger Santiváñez (item **2828**) offer notable new collections. Hildebrando Pérez's sampling of recent writing by Antonio Cisneros, Washington Delgado, José Wantanbe, Marco Martos and several others (item **2862**) similarly displays fresh work by well-known poets.

At the same time, an explosion of independent publishing houses in Peru has created new spaces for the dissemination of emerging voices. Two notable books circulated thanks to this trend are Paul Guillén's *La transformación de los metales* (item **2747**) and Manuel Fernández's *Octubre* (item **2729**). The motif of alchemy announced in Guillén's title suits this accomplished text, which layers contemplations of art and cosmology—striking chords both contemporary and timeless—upon an erudite base informed by a wide range of texts and traditions. His dense free verse is hermetic, but not alienating; like the liquid metaphors that saturate his work, cycling through images of life and death, Guillén's graceful verse flows pleasantly. Fernández's text, for its part, is firmly rooted in Peruvian history, framed by the years in which Juan Velasco Alvarado and Alberto Fujimori commenced their respective dictatorships (1968–1992). Yet public and private histories mingle in this book, which sets non-sequential fragments of a couple's intimate life against that backdrop. Fernández moves between poetic prose, minimalist verse, cadenced lines, journalistic language, and cinematic perspectives in his ambitious book, evoking an array of intertexts. These are only two of several praiseworthy younger voices; engaging collections by Andrea Cabel (item **2697**), Rafael Espinosa (item **2725**), and Claudia Ulloa Donoso (item **2843**) similarly invigorate the contemporary scene.

The biennial Copé poetry prize continues to promote commendable work, as a compilation of poems by finalists in the XII competition (item **2618**) demonstrates. The gold and silver award-winning collections, respectively Chrystian Zegarra Benites' *Escena primordial y otros poemas* (item **2854**) and Rocío Silva Santisteban's *Las hijas del terror* (item **2835**), are distinct in approach yet commensurate in impact. In his title poem, Zegarra's long, dense, introspective lines of free verse—rich with allusions to diverse artistic and intellectual works—fight to create sanctuary amid the speaker's sense of powerlessness and disillusionment. At times Zegarra renders cinematic angles, framing his lines as cloudy, black-and-white reconstructions of history on a screen-like page. Visions of guilt-ridden exile in a hectic foreign city, blurred images of death, and an ironic awareness of the limitations of poetry linger in the reader's mind. A perceptible undercurrent in Zegarra's work, political violence is the main concern in Silva Santisteban's. Well-known for both literary and journalistic writing, the poet combines those two veins powerfully in a collection that centers on the brutality suffered by women at the hands of government and insurgent forces alike during the civil war of the 1980s and 90s. As her prologue clarifies, Silva Santisteban's verse draws from the statements of women who courageously bore witness to violence during the hearings of the Truth and Reconciliation Commission (which culminated in the eye-opening Final Report of 2003). Photographs interspersed throughout the book complement its testimonial nature. Varying in style and perspective, the book is at once lyric and denunciatory.

Though perhaps less patently than in Silva Santisteban's collection, reflections on the internal conflict make their way into other texts reviewed for this essay. Violeta Barretos' remarkable *El jardín de las delicias* (item **2681**) provides just one case in point: while her book's innovative explorations of artistic, natural, and human creation are broad in scope, the poem at the core of the book, "El infierno musical (Perú: 1980–2000)," poignantly explores the legacy of the war.

Finally, a number of recent works by émigrés, including the aforementioned texts by Santiváñez, Goldemberg, Ulloa, and Zegarra, continue to expand the base and reach of contemporary Peruvian poetry. A proliferation of blogs interfacing with Peruvian letters links dispersed writers and readers virtually; among them, Paul Guillen's *Sol negro* (http://sol-negro.blogspot.com) remains indispensable for news and notes relating to Peruvian poetry. [LB]

CHILE

La poesía chilena mantiene su curso abierto y multifacético reconociendo en los trabajos de generaciones anteriores el origen de posibilidades inéditas de expresión que no pasan simplemente por un solo puente conductor—por ejemplo, el de la antipoesía—sino que encuentran su fortaleza y fortuna en todo un abanico de propuestas. En esta diversidad de opciones sin rumbo prefijado cada vez sobresalen más en la actualidad las voces diversas de las poetas mujeres y se advierte la riqueza de los poetas indígenas que introducen el bilingüismo como una realidad base de su producción. En este sentido, la poesía chilena insiste en aseverar textualmente que el poeta no tiene un solo rostro ni una identidad conocida de antemano; muy por el contrario, se trata de desbordar lo ya consumido y consumado, ejerciendo el poder de imaginarse o saberse otros, paradójicos, desconcertantes y desconcertados, dentro de un escenario cultural democrático que participa de un universo latinoamericano globalizado intensamente consciente de sus particularidades y diferencias.

Las fundaciones Neruda, Huidobro, Pablo De Rokha continúan promoviendo el patrimonio cultural representado por los poetas que les dan nombre. Llama la atención también el rol que viene cumpliendo la Universidad Diego Portales, tanto por la evidente importancia que le ha asignado a publicar de manera rigurosa y con una calidad evidente a poetas cuyas propuestas poéticas han adquirido un perfil substancial, como por el "Premio de la crítica" que busca darle relevancia a la escritura emergente de nuevos poetas chilenos. Editoriales como LOM, Cuarto Propio y otras continúan ampliando la importante gama de poetas publicados. Es también evidente que el Internet ha hecho posible una expansión de las posibilidades de publicación y el acceso mediante el formato video a lecturas de poetas mayores y jóvenes que están muy activos. Un ejemplo de esto último es el encuentro latinoamericano de poetas del 2008 titulado "Poquita Fe" que se encuentra accesible en YouTube. Otra posibilidad innovadora la ha introducido la colección "Libros de mentira", no sólo porque hace posible un acceso internacional instantáneo del libro sino por las evidentes posibilidades gráficas de producir un objeto visualmente sofisticado como lo deseara Juan Luis Martínez.

Para buena fortuna de la poesía chilena la obra injustamente olvidada de Winétt de Rokha ha sido editada cuidadosamente por Javier Bello en *El valle pierde su atmósfera* (item **2817**). Como señala Adriana Valdés en uno de los ensayos del libro, hay todavía que determinar lo más valioso de su escritura, pero, sin duda, esta edición es un paso crucial para apreciar la intensidad vanguardista de su propuesta poética. Por otro lado, una alternativa diferente, que se distancia del deslumbramiento vanguardista y se mantiene en una suerte de transparencia afectiva, se encuentra en la publicación de *Ángelus del mediodía* (item **2789**) de Eliana Navarro. ¿De qué manera el discurso de las poetas contribuyó a poblar de otras voces el monumental escenario cultural chileno de los años 50? Las obras disímiles de ambas escritoras ofrecen una respuesta compleja a la pregunta.

El tomo cuarto de la *Antología crítica de la poesía chilena* (item **2614**) editado por Naín Nómez ofrece un excelente panorama de la producción poética de los años 50 y 60. La virtud mayor del libro reside en su amplitud acuciosa respecto de los autores seleccionados como una estrategia de comprensión plural de las posibles tendencias emergentes y divergentes en una década de producción poética determinada.

Oscar Hahn y Omar Lara reciben el prestigioso Premio Iberoamericano Casa de América de Madrid por sus libros *En un abrir y cerrar de ojos* (item **2749**) y *Papeles de Harek Ayun* (item **2765**), respectivamente. La obra de Hahn remite a fuentes clásicas del Siglo de Oro renovadas desde la perturbadora experiencia de lo contemporáneo y la de Lara adquiere su peculiar intensidad mezclada a una nostalgia escueta, que sin volverse reconcentrada no pierde de vista su crítica capacidad de asombro.

El fallecido Gonzalo Millán realiza una asombrosa labor de contención emocional que sitúa su escritura en una suerte de hiperrealismo en *Autorretrato de memoria* (item **2776**). Es singular encontrar una escritura tan autobiográfica que, al mismo tiempo, toma distancia y deja que los hechos, las situaciones hablen por sí mismos expresándolo todo tan certeramente.

La preocupación ecológica adquiere tonalidades religiosas y un espesor específico en relación a la fauna chilena en extinción en los vibrantes poemas de *Día quinto* (item **2834**) de Manuel Silva Acevedo. En poemas de relativa extensión el poeta celebra la diversidad animal como parte de la maravilla de la creación del mundo y deplora su desaparición irremediable.

La publicación de *Canciones oficiales* (item **2715**) de José Ángel Cuevas solidifica la voz de este poeta que ha venido perfilándose como la voz desencantada de aquellos que militaron en un proyecto histórico devastado y que se resisten a confiar en un proyecto democrático falto de utopía. La voz del poeta habla desde el persistente fracaso de una manera mordaz y amarga.

Por otro lado, la publicación de la poesía completa de Roberto Bolaño en *La universidad desconocida* (item **2690**) establece el fervor poético de este autor cuya escritura se resiste a quedar fijada en un solo territorio y se abre, de manera díscola, a los desplazamientos vagabundos de un sujeto al margen. La extraterritorialidad de Bolaño, su desplazamiento entre fronteras culturales, lingüísticas y literarias, se vuelve una pasión de escritura permanente.

La poesía de Carmen Berenguer encuentra pleno reconocimiento en el prestigioso Premio Iberoamericano de Poesía Pablo Neruda. La obra de esta poeta que comienza a publicar en los años 80 se sitúa en la discordia de los márgenes culturales con un discurso neobarroco intensamente figurativo y provocador. No hay palabra certera a menos, parece decir Berenguer, que se cumpla como acertijo y laberinto liberador de ecos inusitados. Por su parte, la poesía epigramática de Jorge Montealegre en *No se puede evitar la caída del cabello* (item **2781**)—su humor incisivo enfocado en lo erótico y la vejez—es reconocida con el Premio Altazor. Este es un premio dado por sus pares artistas.

La diestra utilización del libro electrónico que puede incluir un énfasis creativo en lo audiovisual se articula con acierto en la iniciativa "Libros de mentira". Poetas ampliamente reconocidos como Oscar Hahn, Armando Uribe, Delia Domínguez, Claudio Bertoni y Raúl Zurita han sido publicados, así como poetas cuyas voces ya presentan un perfil propio: Carmen Berenguer, Elvira Hernández, Eric Polhamer, Jorge Montealegre y Elicura Chihuailaf. Importa señalar aquí la diversidad de propuestas representadas: por ejemplo, la ruptura inteligente con el intimismo de Hernández, la exploración de una poética budista en Polhamer, la dignificación de lo mapuche en Chihuailaf, y la incursión en el cine mudo plasmada de manera visualmente brillante en el libro de Montealegre. La voz de Zurita continúa, por su parte, su recorrido alucinado ahora explorando las consecuencias de un holocausto nuclear.

El Premio Pablo Neruda, otorgado por la Fundación Pablo Neruda, ha venido reconociendo el trabajo de los poetas más jóvenes: Héctor Hernández Montecinos (2009), Rafael Rubio (2008), Javier Bello (2007) y Malú Urriola (2006). También el

Premio de la Crítica, otorgado por la Universidad Diego Portales, ha reconocido a nuevas voces: Juan Cristóbal Romero (2009), Yanko González (2008) y Andrés Anwandter (2007).

Los más jóvenes insisten en su derecho a definir un lenguaje que los represente sin atavismos. Por ejemplo, Germán Carrasco en *Multicancha* (item **2702**) utiliza un lenguaje aparentemente distanciado y abstracto que, sin embargo, incorpora lo social, lo latinoamericano, lo díscolo como problemáticas vitales. Javier Bello en *Letrero de albergue* (item **2685**) despliega su voz en lo onírico, prefiriendo entrever visiones que dan cuenta fragmentariamente de experiencias oscuramente revelables. Antonia Torres en *Inventario de equipaje* (item **2841**) indaga de manera lúcida en el luto, o la relación de pareja, o el espacio del sur como instancias poéticas cruciales y definidoras. Oscar Saavedra Villarroel en *Tecnopacha* (item **2822**) construye una alegoría postmoderna sobre un universo sudamericano globalizado y tecnológico que se funda en el extravío y en el desconcierto. Antonio Silva en *Matria* (item **2832**) celebra la diferencia del sujeto homosexual popular con una palabra lúdica, sensual e irreverente. Christian Formoso en *El cementerio más hermoso de Chile* (item **2733**) reescribe la diversidad multiétnica de Magallanes a través del símbolo del cementerio como quien da testimonio, a través de la crónica poética, de un luto nutricio del cual renacer históricamente. [OS]

ARGENTINA, URUGUAY Y PARAGUAY

A pesar del tumulto económico en la región rioplatense, había una gran cantidad de libros de poesía publicados entre 2006–08. Muchos de ellos son volúmenes delgados con estilo lírico y temas bastante tradicionales—poesía del amor, desahogo personal—los que no se comentan en detalle aquí, pero su publicación indica la fuerza perpetua de este modo de poetizar. En este grupo de libros también aparecen varios nombres conocidos con nuevas colecciones: Juan Gelman (item **2738**), Juan L. Ortiz (item **2792**), Mirta Rosenberg (item **2819**), y cuarto títulos que muestran el gran interés en la obra del argentino Leonides Lamborghini (ítems **2761**, **2762**, **2763** y **2764**). Fallecido en 2009, este poeta admirado quería ver "lo cómico en el horror", afirmando en su propia poesía que "lo que no es loco no es verdad". Tomó tiempo para que la crítica afirmara la importancia de la experimentación de este gran poeta, pero al fin del siglo XX, su escritura, que combina elementos de la cultura popular con la elite, recibió más y más atención y la re-edición de sus libros lo evidencia.

El interés en esta combinación de lo alto y lo bajo se observa de otra manera en la obra del pampeano Juan Carlos Bustriazo Ortiz (item **2696**). A diferencia de Lamborghini, que escribe desde la ciudad (o el exilio) y muestra un compromiso político desafiante a través del humor y la parodia, Bustriazo Ortiz viene de las provincias y vivía una vida verdaderamente ambulante dentro de la Argentina. Deambula por las formas poéticas desde lo verdaderamente popular hasta estilos más innovadores; además de su colección notada aquí publicó un disco compacto, *Hereje bebedor de la noche* (Ediciones Espacio Hudson, 2007), que refuerza el componente oral de su producción.

Las transformaciones sociales del principio de esta década continúan y con ellas ha surgido una nueva poesía urbana que comunica la experiencia de manera directa que unos críticos han llamado "hiperrealista". Así muchos poetas jóvenes luchan en contra de la enajenación y dan voz a su desilusión por la ironía y referencias a los nuevos márgenes sociales, ampliando la definición y los estilos de la poesía social (se ve esta trayectoria en la poesía de Appratto, Daneri, Falcone,

Mileo, Peyseré, Zito Lema). Hay poesía en estos años que también incorpora el cine, los medios masivos y la cultura popular, tanto en forma como contenido (por ejemplo, las obras de Moisés, De Jager). Los poetas también encuentran nuevas maneras de descubrir lectores más allá del texto: por el *performance*, la poesía en la red, las formas hipertextuales, y blogs, como el de Bárbara Belloc (see http://www .evolucionariarevolucionaria.blogspot.com/). Hay otros sitios en la red que dialogan sobre la poesía rioplatense desde ángulos distintos como: http://Zapatosrojos .com.ar, http://revistavox.org.ar o http://poesiaeljabali.com. En Uruguay, poetas/ intérpretes como Clemente Padín y Luis Bravo continúan haciendo sus poemas/ performances multi-genéricos que son accesibles en la red, en CD y DVD, pero sus obras recientes todavía no aparecen en la Biblioteca del Congreso.

En contra de o complementario a la exploración de otros medios para la circulación de la poesía, en un viaje reciente a Montevideo encontré una serie de libros que llaman la atención a las calidades físicas del texto, al libro como objeto bello, publicados por el editorial Yuagurú de Gustavo Wojciechowski (conocido como Maca). Maca mismo publicó su propio libro/caja de poemas/postales (en un estilo que recuerda los *Artefactos* de Nicanor Parra), *Aquí debería ir el título* (Montevideo: Yuagurú, 2008), desafiando el libro convencional de manera que recuerda las vanguardias y la poesía concreta. Su editorial también presenta las obras de varios otros autores que siempre tiene un aspecto físico, visual, como *Toda la noche/O varios* de Ana Cheveski (Montevideo: Yuagurú, 2007), un libro que incorpora dos poemarios con largos poemas posmodernos y experimentales que se leen en dos distintas rutas: una hacia el centro del texto donde se tiene que dar la vuelta al libro para entrar en el otro.

Unas poetas argentinas cuya obra no conocía antes emplean un acercamiento íntimo para crear un diálogo sobre temas más universales: la relación madre-hija en el libro de Roxana Páez (item **2795**) y algunos de sus antecedentes artísticos y po- líticos en la obra de Edna Pozzi. La antología de Anna Becciu (item **2683**) también pone de relieve sus influencias tanto antiguas como contemporáneas de manera algo dialógica, y María Casiraghi (item **2706**), entre otros autores, dialoga con la ciudad. Silvia Montenegro emplea un diálogo entre personajes marcados por sus papeles genéricos (masculinos/femeninos) para hacernos ver estas relaciones desde ángulos nuevos (item **2782**). Así que la poesía de todas estas autoras emplea formas distintas para manifestar rasgos intertextuales y/o dramáticas en la lírica. [JK]

ANTHOLOGIES

2612 Alvarez, María Auxiliadora. Lugar de pasaje: antología poética. Prólogo de Julio Ortega. Selección de Linde M. Brocato. Caracas: Monte Ávila Editores Latinoameri- cana, 2009. 356 p. (Altazor)

La antología reúne el cuerpo poético de una de las voces femeninas más emble- máticas de la poesía venezolana. La poesía de Álvarez es lingüísticamente desafiante e innovadora; también se podría caracterizar como una poesía que juega con los espacios internos del poema. Los multiples ángulos poéticos que se contienen en esta antolo- gía, demuestran que se trata de una obra viva, dinámica, y en constante evolución. [HJ]

2613 Anillo de silencio: Centroamérica en la poesía. Selección y prólogo de Jorge Boccanera. Buenos Aires: Ediciones del IMFC, 2009. 124 p. (Desde la gente)

Reúne una muestra de poesía centro- americana contemporánea. Incluye de 6 a 16 poetas por país. La selección es balanceada en cuanto a los autores inclui- dos, pero no en la calidad de los poemas de cada autor. Datos bibliográficos mínimos. [JDW]

2614 Antología crítica de la poesía chilena. t. 4, Modernidad, marginalidad y fragmentación urbana, 1953–1973. Selección, introducción, notas y bibliografía de Naín Nómez. Santiago: LOM Ediciones, 2006. 655 p.: bibl., index. (Col. Entre mares. Poesía)

En la introducción Nómez establece los parámetros teóricos básicos de su selección que se basa en una lectura inclusiva de diversas propuestas poéticas que dialogan y difieren entre sí en los años 50 y 60. Nómez presta especial atención al contexto histórico global y latinoamericano de ambas décadas. Tomando como eje central la antipoesía de Nicanor Parra encuentra tres líneas de desarrollo que ve articuladas en los poetas de los 50 y luego desplegadas más allá de la complejidad nostálgica de la poesía lárica y de la crítica (auto)irónica del ciudadano de la urbe moderna latinoamericana. La antología divide en dos partes los poemas seleccionados: la primera secuencia va desde 1953 a 1963 y la segunda desde 1964 a 1973. Los poemas de cada autor seleccionado corresponden, por lo general, a distintos momentos de su obra y vienen precedidos por un breve ensayo introductorio que cuidadosamente ofrece una reflexión sobre la biografía, la obra de cada poeta y su recepción crítica. La antología incluye una bibliografía general de otras antologías, textos teóricos y críticos. Libro esencial para entender de manera más detallada la producción poéticas de las décadas que preceden al corte histórico del golpe de estado de 1973. [OS]

2615 Antología de la decima tanática cubana. Compilación de Odalys Leyva Rosabal. Controversia de Francisco Henríquez y José Luis Mejía. México: Frente de Afirmación Hispanista, 2007. 2 v.: bibl.

Tras una introducción que rastrea el tópico de la muerte a través de las culturas y religiones del mundo, "Los pitagóricos creían en la inmortalidad y en la transmigración del alma", la compiladora se pregunta cuánto de cubana tiene la décima: "Sin concederle nacionalidad a la décima, me atrevo a decir que en Cuba se habla en octosílabos". La selección de poemas incluye los siglos XIX y XX. [FC]

2616 Antología de la poesía arequipeña, 1950–2000. Edición de Tito Cáceres Cuadros. Arequipa, Peru: Editorial UNSA, 2007. 373 p.

Complementing a previous anthology, this one compiles poetry written in the second half of the 20th century. Though all hailing from Arequipa, many of the more than 50 poets included have relocated to Lima or abroad. The anthology predictably offers a broad diversity of voice, though Cáceres (who presents succinct characterizations of each poet's approach in his introduction) notes that they tend to avoid traditionalism in favor of universalism. [LB]

2617 Antología de la poesía colombiana: 1958–2008. Selección y prólogo de Iván Beltrán Castillo. Caracas: Fundación Editorial el Perro y la Rana: Ministerio del Poder Popular para la Cultura, 2008. 733 p.: index. (Col. Poesía del mundo. Serie Antologías)

La antología recoge la producción reciente de la poesía colombiana, donde figuran voces clásicas, pero también, voces nuevas. Asimismo, cada poeta cuenta con una breve presentación de su obra. La antología está compuesta por los siguientes poetas: Gonzalo Arango, Jaime Jaramillo Escobar, Eduardo Gómez, Mario Rivero, José Arango, Nicolás Suescún, Giovanni Quessep, Jotamario Arbeláez, Miguel Méndez Camacho, Armando Romero, Raúl Henao, Raúl Gómez Jattin, María Mercedes Carranza, Juan Manuel Roca, Juan Gustavo Cobo Borda, Antonio Correa Losada, Luz Mary Giraldo, Fernando Rendón, Piedad Bonnet, Santiago Mutis Durán, Julio César Arciniegas, Amparo Osorio, Guillermo Martínez González, Eduardo García Aguilar, William Ospina, Javier González Luna, Hernando Guerra Tovar, Jorge Torres Medina, Armando Rodríguez Ballesteros, Gabriel Jaime Franco, Mery Yolanda Sánchez, Orietta Lozano, Fernando Linero, Gustavo Adolfo Garcés, Álvaro Marín, Flóbert Zapata, Fernando Herrera Gómez, Nicanor Vélez, José Zuleta Ortiz, Mauricio Contreras Hernández, Miguel Torres Pereira, Luz Helena Cordero Villamizar, Gabriel Arturo Castro, Ramón Cote Baraibar, Myriam Montoya, Gonzalo Márquez Cristo, Enrique Rodríguez Pérez, Juan Felipe Robledo, Winston Morales Chavarro, John J. Junieles, Federico Díaz-Granados, Juan Sebastián Gaviria y Robert Max Steenskist. [HJ]

2618 Antología de los ganadores y finalistas de la XII Bienal de Poesía "Premio Copé 2005". Lima: PETROPERÚ

Ediciones COPÉ, Departamento de Relaciones Corporativas de Petróleos del Perú, 2007. 104 p.

This compilation of poems by finalists for the Copé poetry prize highlights an array of emerging and mature talent. A departure from rigid versification characterizes an otherwise diverse anthology that includes economic verse, dense poetic prose and complex semantic contortions; personal, social, regional, and distinctly globalized perspectives mingle here. [LB]

2619 Antología mayor: movimiento Interiorista. Selección de Fausto Leonardo Henríquez. Guatemala: Letra Negra, 2007. 189 p.: port. (Iberoamericanos; 9)

Selección de poesía del Movimiento Interiorista (República Dominicana, 1990) el cual tuvo también ramificaciones en Centroamérica. Los 16 autores representados articulan visiones interiores en un lenguaje depurado que desarrolla las "3 M" de la disciplina interiorista: mito, mística y metafísica. Destaca el lirismo de Sally Rodríguez. [JDW]

2620 Antología poética del sur. Compilación de Juan B. Nina. Santo Domingo: Dirección General de la Feria del Libro, 2007. 260 p. (Ediciones Ferilibro; 107)

Compilación preparada por un poeta, Nina; muestra de la poesía sureña dominicana (San Cristóbal, Peravia, San José de Ochoa, Azua, Barahona, San Juan, Bahoruco, Elías Piña, Independencia y Pedernales) no sólo como singularidad geográfica sino sobre todo, según Odalís G. Pérez en el prólogo, como diferencia antropológica: "El poeta del Sur, al igual que el hombre del Sur, reproduce una línea de ser en el texto-cultura . . . donde raíz y muerte conducen a una finalidad que no es simplemente regional, sino más bien poética y ontológica". [FC]

2621 Antología poética: Premio Pablo Neruda, 1987–2005. Textos de Gonzalo Millán et al. Santiago: Fundación Pablo Neruda, 2006. 321 p.

El premio Pablo Neruda, que se otorga anualmente a poetas menores de 40 años, está representado aquí por 14 hombres y cuatro mujeres. El poeta inicial es Gonzalo Millán (1947–2006) y el más reciente Germán Carrasco (1971). A pesar de que esta antología no pretende abarcar toda la diversidad de la producción chilena que va de finales de los años 60 a la fecha, incluye una gama de propuestas poéticas claramente significativas que pasan por el poema breve, fragmentario, hasta el poema extenso y de corte narrativo; la poesía que se entiende a sí misma como un encuentro sacrificial o ácido y sarcástico con el horror del trauma en dictadura, y la que propone un lenguaje distanciado, más reconcentrado, intencionalmente opaco aunque centrado en momentos críticos experimentados en los avatares de la democracia. [OS]

2622 Anuario de poesía mexicana, 2006. Selección y prólogo de Pura López Colomé. México: Fondo De Cultura Económica, 2007. 329 p.: bibl. (Tezontle)

A partir del 2004, se reinician los anuarios de poesía mexicana. Se trata de selecciones de textos aparecidos en publicaciones periódicas a lo largo del año en cuestión. Así, esta recopilación mide el pulso de la poesía actual, en un corte sincrónico que reúne escritores tan diversos de varias generaciones. López Colomé decidió a la vez organizar el material a través de ocho ejes temáticos: "voz cantante", "Dios", "los reinos vegetal y animal", "el ser humano", "luz y agua", "viaje", "tiempo" y "voz callante". [JS]

2623 Anuario de poesía mexicana, 2007. Selección y prólogo de Julián Herbert. México: Fondo de Cultura Económica, 2008. 226 p. (Tezontle)

Al igual que las ediciones anteriores, este anuario recopila poemas publicados en revistas y suplementos durante 2007. El volumen se organiza por orden alfabético del apellido de los autores. Herbert apunta muy bien que la antología obedece al azar del tiempo (el año 2007). También señala su criterio de selección: "nada de cuotas o representaciones; únicamente poemas", intentando también trascender sus propios gustos, pero siempre atañéndose a dos elementos que considera relevantes en la composición poética: tensión y levedad. [JS]

2624 Arellano, Luis Alberto and **Román Luján.** Le pays sonore: 9 poètes mexicains = El país del ruido. 9 poetas mexicanos. Traduit de l'espagnol par Françoise Roy. Trois-Rivières, Canada: Écrits des Forges, 2008. 260 p.

Selección bilingüe de nueve poetas mexicanos nacidos en la década de 1960: Luis Armando Malpica, Laura Solórzano, Juan Carlos Bautista, Anne-Marie Bianco (pseudónimo de Cristina Rivera Garza), Jorge Fernández Granados, José Eugenio Sánchez, Luis Enrique Gutiérrez O.M., Ángel Ortuño y Mónica de la Torre. Se trata de poéticas emergentes, variadas, que a pesar del esfuerzo de los editores por formular ciertas pautas en común (por ejemplo, el humor que parece ser una constante en la mayoría de ellos) muestran una diversidad de propuestas poéticas que van desde la elaboración barroca en Solórzano al lenguaje coloquial, corrosivo de José Eugenio Sánchez. [JS]

2625 Belmonte, Luis Enrique. Pasadizo: poesía reunida 1994–2006. Prólogo de Daniel Molina. Caracas: Monte Ávila Editores Latinoamericana, 2009. 313 p. (Altazor)

Esta antología recoge la obra de uno de los poetas más activos y prolíficos en Venezuela. Su obra busca constantemente desafíos temáticos, y se sirve de la narración para describirle al lector escenas imaginarias que transitan a través de un laberinto desesperanzador. Médico de profesión, Belmonte no oculta la crudeza de un lenguaje que se desborda en lo profiláctico. [HJ]

Benegas, Noni. Burning cartography. See item **3209**.

2626 Berenguer, Carmen. Chiiit, son las ventajas de la escritura: antología poética. Selección y prólogo de Raquel Olea. Santiago: LOM Ediciones: Editores Independientes, 2008. 261 p. (Col. Bolsillo)

Esta antología, que incluye poemas de todos los libros publicados por Berenguer— el primero de 1983 y el último hasta la fecha de 2006—es una excelente muestra de la rica producción de la poeta. En el prólogo, la editora Raquel Olea señala que: "Lo particular de una escritura siempre se juega en la novedad de la forma más que en lo dicho parece señalar esta poesía con sus provocaciones al oído y a los sentidos comunes reglamentados por la obediencia al mandato formal. Berenguer elige las verdades del incumplimiento". Incluye el discurso de Berenguer al recibir el premio Iberoamericano de Poesía Pablo Neruda 2008. [OS]

2627 Boti y Barreiro, Regino Eladio. La visita de los dioses: antología poética. La Habana: Letras Cubanas, 2004. 204 p.: ill. (Biblioteca Literatura Cubana)

Antología cuidadosamente anotada del modernista tardío cubano que en la década de 1920 anticipa la antipoesía de Nicanor Parra, la ciencia-ficción, el erotismo franco y aspectos de la vanguardia posterior. El poemario Kodak-Ensueño (1929) articula la palabra lírica a las formas fotográficas y cinematográficas. Versos extraordinariamente precisos y sugerentes. [JDW]

2628 Bracho, Coral. Firefly under the tongue: selected poems of Coral Bracho. Translated by Forrest Gander. New York: New Directions Book, 2008. 133 p.

Primera antología de la poesía de Bracho (Mexico, 1951) traducida al inglés. Bracho es una de las poetas que mayor influencia han ejercido en las nuevas generaciones y sus libros iniciales son venerados por su ritmo cadencioso y por su sintaxis tan abierta y ambigua. Gander logra capturar esa sensualidad y voluptuosidad en un inglés que fluye tan bien como en el español. Para esta edición se traducen textos de todos sus libros hasta la fecha, incluidos tres poemas no recogidos en libro. Para el comentario del especialista en traducción, ver item **3212**. [JS]

2629 Cardenal, Ernesto. Poesía completa. Buenos Aires: Editorial Patria Grande, 2007. 560 p. (Identidades; 21, 24)

Con brevísimo y certero prólogo de Luis Alberto Angulo a una compilación del gran poeta nicaragüense manejable por el público general. [JDW]

2630 Cauteloso engaño del sentido: antología poética. Prólogo, selección y notas de Rei Berroa. Santo Domingo: Teatro de la Luna, 2007. 254 p. (Col. Libros de la luna; 2)

Se reúnen en esta antología a los poetas hispanoparlantes de Latinoamérica, España y Estados Unidos (Ecuador, Paraguay, España, Nicaragua, Puerto Rico, Argentina, México, Colombia, República Dominicana, Estados Unidos) que en 2006 y 2007 participaron en el XIV y XV Maratón de Poesía "La pluma y la palabra," celebrado en la zona metropolitana de Washington D.C. como parte de las actividades culturales para la comunidad latina. [FC]

2631 Chuchón Huamaní, Serafina. Sentimiento ayacuchano: recopilación de waynos, pasacalles, carnavales, yaravíes, pumpines y obligados. San Borja, Peru: Ediciones Altazor, 2007. 439 p.

This book offers transcriptions of hundreds of enduring popular songs from Ayacucho in Quechua and Spanish. Spanning themes including love, loss, migration and displacement, Andean flora and fauna, religion, and music, the collection offers a rich tapestry of expression. [LB]

2632 Un ciervo besa las manos de los niños. Memoria Poética: Tercer Encuentro Internacional de Poetas: "El turno del ofendido": El Salvador, mayo 2006. Recopilación de Vladimir Baiza et al. Coordinación general de El turno del ofendido de Otoniel Guervara. San Salvador: Fundación Metáfora, 2006. 224 p.: ports.

Antología de poetas tipo ómnibus que junta poetas sigloveintistas de rango casi clásico con novísimos procedentes de Centroamérica y otros países. Entre los menos conocidos sobresalen los poemas de Edgardo Nieves Mieles (Puerto Rico, 1962) y Consuelo Hernández (Colombia, 1952). [JDW]

2633 La ciudad en nosotros: la ciudad en la poesía dominicana: antología. Selección, notas y prólogo de Soledad Alvarez. Santo Domingo: Ediciones de la Secretaría de Estado de Cultura, 2008. 258 p.: bibl.

Entre la "Presentación" de Basilio Belliard (poeta antologado), que pone en contexto general el tópico de la ciudad en la literatura occidental y latinoamericana, y el prólogo de la investigadora (y poeta antologada) Soledad Álvarez, se establece el punto de partida a partir del cual surge "la ciudad textual" que la antología evidencia: cuando, a partir del último tercio del siglo XIX, con José Joaquín Pérez, Salomé Ureña de Henríquez y Gastón Fernando Deligne, aflora a la literatura la "tensión entre la concepción rural y la emergente realidad urbana, entre el presente y el pasado". [FC]

2634 Colección pensamiento dominicano. v. 1, Poesía y teatro. Santo Domingo: Banreservas: Sociedad Dominicana de Bibliofilos, 2008. 1 v.: bibl.

En lo que toca a la poesía, el presente volumen se centra en una muestra antológica de cuatro poetas dominicanos—Domingo Moreno Jimenes, Franklin Mieses Burgos, Julio Antonio Alix y Salomé de Henríquez—seguida de un muestreo de la poesía dominicana en general. En la antología de autores una visión crítica ubica el universo de los poetas; en la última parte, un mapa de la poesía dominicana la contextualiza. [FC]

2635 El corazón de Venezuela: patria y poesía. Recopilación de Luis Alberto Angulo y Luis Ernesto Gómez. Caracas: Ediciones de la Presidencia de la República, 2009. 408 p. (Col. Oromae)

Se trata de una gruesa antología reunida bajo el tema de la "patria". El compendio agrupa cronológicamente los poemas que, desde el siglo XIX hasta el presente, evocan el tema nacionalista. En este sentido, el libro es una antología, pero también, una historia de la literatura venezolana. [HJ]

2636 Cruce de poesía: Nicaragua-El Salvador. Selección y notas de Marta Leanor González, Juan Sobalvarro y Luis Alvarenga. Managua: Ediciones 400 Elefantes, 2006. 200 p.

Antología de poetas jóvenes de los últimos 25 años en Nicaragua y El Salvador. Recoge varios poemas perdurables de Carlos Castro Jo (Bluefields, 1960), Nick Aguirre (Managua, 1961) y otros. [JDW]

2637 En lugar del resplandor: antología poética. Textos de Luis Alberto Crespo. Caracas: Monte Avila Ed. Latinoamericana, 2007. 234 p. (Biblioteca básica de autores venezolanos; 46)

Esta antología refleja la variada y nutrida obra de Luis Alberto Crespo, uno de los principales poetas venezolanos del siglo XX. Parte de su obra gira en torno a la memoria personal; esto es, la edificación del "yo". Al mismo tiempo, encontramos poemas intimistas y reflexivos. Pero el grueso de su obra lo constituyen poemas breves, no obstante, cargados de escenas y pensamientos. El prologuista, Gonzalo Ramírez Quintero, escribe: "el poema se le da como una iluminación fragmentaria. Al elegir fragmentos como procedimiento compositivo testimonia, a la par que su inmensa devoción por el silencio, una raigal necesidad de que las palabras digan más de lo que dicen". [HJ]

2638 Estrella, Ulises. Antología poética esencial, 1960–2006. Quito: Casa de la Cultura Ecuatoriana Benjamín Carrión, 2007. 219 p.: bibl. (Palabra viva)

El volumen reúne la extensa producción poética de Ulises Estrella (Quito, 1939), seleccionada y antologada por el mismo autor. Además de la obra publicada, quedan incluidas composiciones inéditas y una breve nota introductoria de Estrella, que explica los criterios que han guiado la organización del volumen. Se entera el lector que la dinámica de esta antología no está dada por el orden cronológico, sino más bien por el seguimiento y articulación de las mayores preocupaciones éticas y estéticas que han guiado la obra de Estrella: el tzantzismo de los 70, la poética urbana, la historia ecuatoriana, su enfrentamiento con la modernidad, y el diálogo del poeta con la poesía universal. [EM]

2639 Galarza Zavala, Jaime. Antología poética. Quito: Casa de la Cultura Ecuatoriana Benjamín Carrión, 2007. 344 p. (Palabra viva)

El volumen que se reseña reúne la producción poética de Jaime Galarza (Cuenca, 1930), posiblemente uno de los escritores ecuatorianos que más tozudamente ha desafiado el imperio de la violencia en su país a través del lenguaje poético. La antología, autorizada y organizada por el mismo autor, incluye composiciones tomadas de *El aire del hombre* (1968), *Poemas sin permiso* (1973), *Palabra marginada* (2006), *Línea imaginaria* (1989) y *la flor y el fusil* (1967). El toque de originalidad lo da el conjunto de poesía carcelaria que aparece al final del volumen, titulada "Versos libres en la prisión" y escrita en cuatro diferentes centros ecuatorianos de reclusión entre agosto 1965 y marzo 1966. Un prefacio o estudio introductorio habría sido el complemento ideal para esta antología. [EM]

2640 Galarza Zavala, Jaime. Palabra marginada: selección poética. Quito: Casa de la Cultura Ecuatoriana Benjamín Carrión, 2006. 192 p. (Oroletras)

Con esta antología el Núcleo Provincial de El Oro de la Casa de la Cultura Ecuatoriana Benjamín Carrión inaugura su propia línea editorial: Oroletras. El propósito de esta iniciativa cultural es la difusión, a escala nacional, de escritores, científicos e investigadores orenses. La antología que se reseña constituye el primer número de Oroletras, y recoge la excelente obra poética de Jaime Galarza Zavala (Cuenca, 1930). Dueño de una poética sobria, crítica frente al poder en cualquiera de sus manifestaciones, y sobre todo ágil en el uso del lenguaje y del humor, Galarza Zavala nos ofrece una hermosa muestra de su poesía. Enriquece el volumen un escrito personal, titulado Palabra Marginada, que constituye la mejor introducción a la obra de este poeta ecuatoriano. Hay que lamentar, sin embargo, el descuido de la edición, que por lo menos en el volumen reseñado, confunde la paginación y elimina las páginas 13 y 14. [EM]

2641 Golpes de agua: antología de poesía cubana de tema religioso. Selección y prólogo de Leonardo Sarría. La Habana: Editorial Letras Cubanas, 2008. 2 v.: bibl. (Biblioteca literaria cubana)

Partiendo de la proximidad histórica entre religión y poesía, una que, según Sarría, George Santayana planteó mejor que nadie, "Nuestra religión es la poesía en la que creemos", se rastrea el arco de la poesía cubana que va de José Surí (1696–1762) hasta Ángel Augier (1910–2009) en busca del "sentimiento de lo trascendente", esté en lo religioso, en lo político o como en el caso de José Martí, mezclado lo primero con lo segundo: "Llama la atención que ["Virgen Martía" de Martí] el ansia independentista y los sufrimientos del coloniaje se acompañen o nazcan del sentimiento religioso". [FC]

2642 El güegüense al pie de Bobadilla: poemas escogidos de la poesía nicaragüense actual. Managua: PAVSA, 2008. 553 p.: bibl.

Esta antología incluye una amplísima selección y una introducción extraordinariamente informativa sobre la escena poética en la Nicaragua contemporánea. Anotaciones útiles sobre cada poeta. [JDW]

2643 Hahn, Óscar. Hotel de las nostalgias. Peru: Lustra Editores, 2007. 78 p.

Esta breve antología reúne poemas publicados desde el año 1961 al 2006 en siete libros del poeta. El título proviene de un poema que hace explícita la mirada cáustica del autor respecto de su propia generación: la de la década del 50. [OS]

2644 Hernández d'Jesús, Enrique. La sagrada familia: antología, 1968–2000. Caracas: Fundación Editorial Perro y Rana: República Bolivariana de Venezuela, Gobierno Bolivariano, 2007. 334 p. (Col. Poesía venezolana. Contemporáneos)

Ésta era una antología necesaria, pues reúne la obra principal de un clásico de la poesía venezolana contemporánea. Hernández-d'Jesús juega con la cotidianidad y la memoria; su poesía no es profética ni lírica, más bien tiene la capacidad de desdibujar las realidades imaginarias que presenta. Asimismo, es un poeta que juega con el humor y le deja al lector un halo de incertidumbre. [HJ]

2645 Historia y antología de la poesía gauchesca. Buenos Aires: Ediciones Margus, 2004. 727 p.: bibl. (Col. Cofre)

Colección bien realizada de poesía gauchesca con una introducción informativa de Fermín Chávez. Incluye estudios por Guillermo Ara, José Gabriel, Ángel Nuñez, Aurora Venturini y una visión panorámica de la poesía gauchesca. Hay introducciones breves a cada poeta y se incluyen las obras de Bartolomé Hidalgo, Juan Gualberto Godoy, Hilario Ascasubi, Estanislao Del Campo, José Hernández, Antonio D. Lussich, Leopoldo Lugones y Miguel D. Etchebarne, entre otros. [JSK]

2646 La Hoz, Luis. 10 aves raras de la poésia peruana. Lima: Fondo Editorial Cultura Peruana, 2007. 106 p.

La Hoz aims to expose 10 commendable poets absent from the Peruvian canon due to one "rarity" or another. Brief biographical and critical notes accompany each sampling of poems, many representative of the 70s generation. This range of engaging voices hints at countless other buried talents. [LB]

2647 Medina, Celso. Sólo el mar: antología personal. Prólogos de Carmen Ruiz Barrionuevo y Lubio Cardozo. Caracas: República Bolivariana de Venezuela, Monte Ávila Editores Latinoamericana, 2008. 157 p.: index. (Altazor)

La antología de Medina tiene la virtud de contener un amasijo de voces y pasajes poéticos que muestran no solamente las distintas etapas del poeta, sino su capacidad de hacer del lenguaje un verdadero universo de lo posible. En la antología aparecen poemas epigramáticos, autorreferenciales, y reflexivos que al final llegan a conformar las figuras del "yo" a través de una lógica que permea todos los poemas. [HJ]

2648 Noble Katerba: persistencia vital. Agrupación poética de Noble Katerba. Lima: Casa Barbieri Editores, 2007. 104 p.

This anthology unites works from nine members the poetic group Noble Katerba (formed by the confluence of Neo-Babel, Estigma, and Mural in the early 90s) and attests to ardent creativity, fueled by workshops and recitals, during a period of social disquiet and political violence. A wide range of style and themes reveals a fostering of originality in place of any prescribed approach. [LB]

2649 Nueva poesía hispanoamericana. Compilación de Leo Zelada. 15. ed. Lima: Ediciones Lord Byron, 2006. 124 p.

This is the fifteenth in a series of compilations regularly edited by Zelada, in which emerging and established poets offer current work addressing a unifying theme. Here, more than 50 poets representing various countries ruminate on the city. Commendable for its endeavor to create a pan-Hispanic dialogue, this volume allows readers to become acquainted with a diversity of contemporary poetic expression in Spanish. [LB]

2650 Pájaro relojero: poetas centroamericanos. Barcelona: Galaxia Gutenberg: Círculo de Lectores, 2009. 877 p.: bibl.

Mario Campaña proporciona un ameno contexto histórico-literario a su antología de 13 poetas clásicos sigloveintistas de la región. Junto a nombres predecibles que van de Cardoza y Aragón, a Dalton, sorprende agradablemente la inclusión de dos significativos autores menos conocidos: Alfonso Quijadurías (El Salvador, 1940) e Isabel de los Ángeles Ruano (Guatemala, 1945). [JDW]

2651 Palés Matos, Luis. Fiel fugada: antología poética de Luis Palés Matos. Edición de Noel Luna. San Juan: La Editorial, Univ. de Puerto Rico, 2008. 320 p.: bibl., ill., index.

Novedosa edición de la poesía palesiana organizada por temas recurrentes en su obra (ocho en total): "el deseo y la muerte", la imantación por las "formas

elementales de la vida", el "imaginario acuático", las "estéticas de vanguardia", el poeta
"esencialmente romántico", la primacía
de la "imaginación", lo femenino y lo afro-
antillano. Además de una cronología y una
bibliografía selecta, esta edición contiene
un "Abecé de Palés", en el que ordena "alfabética y temáticamente citas provenientes
de la prosa de Luis Palés Matos, así como de
parte de la crítica palesiana". [FC]

**2652 Poemas de amor y rebeldía social:
poetas del mundo, antiguos y contemporáneos.** Selección, prólogo y notas
de Balmes Lozano Morillo. Lima: Arteidea
Editores, 2006. 2 v.: indexes.

This ambitious anthology congregates
hundreds of international poems written
between 4,000 B.C. and the mid-20th century around the central themes of popular
struggle and conciliatory love, principles
enhanced by the egalitarian and dialectical
gesture of situating world-renowned poets
alongside lesser-known voices from diverse
nations. [LB]

**2653 Poesía ecuatoriana: antología esen-
cial.** Edición de Edwin Madrid. Madrid: Visor Libros, 2007. 421 p. (La Estafeta
del viento; 4) (Col. Visor de poesía)

Publicada por una casa editorial
española y compilada por Edwin Madrid
(Quito, 1961), uno de los poetas más representativos de la poesía ecuatoriana actual,
esta antología ofrece una muestra exqui-
sita de la contribución poética de este país
a la literatura latinoamericana del siglo
XX. Acompaña al volumen un prólogo del
antologador que invita a reflexionar en
torno a la particularidad de la poesía (y por
extensión de la literatura) ecuatoriana,
planteando acuciantes preguntas: ¿Existe
una literatura específicamente ecuatoriana?
¿Cuánto importa la existencia de una poe-
sía ecuatoriana? Los poetas antologados
son: Medardo Ángel Silva, Hugo Mayo,
Jorge Carrera Andrade, Gonzalo Escudero,
Gangotena, Lydia Dávila, César Dávila
Andrade, Efraín Jara Idrovo, Jorge Enrique
Adoum, Francisco Granizo Ribadeneira,
Carlos Eduardo Jaramillo, David Ledesma
Vásquez, Euler Granda, Fernando Cazón
Vera, Antonio Preciado, Humberto Vinueza,
Julio Pazos, Iván Carvajal, Iván Oñate, Jorge
Martillo Monserrate, Roy Sigüenza, y Paco
Benavides. [EM]

**2654 Poesía mística del interiorismo:
antología de la lírica teopoética y
protomística.** Textos de Bruno Rosario
Candelier. Santo Domingo: Ateneo Insular
Internacional, 2007. 341 p.: bibl. (Col. "En la
interior bodega"; 6)

Dividido en tres partes, la primera,
dedicada a la "Orientación espiritual y estética", aborda en 9 ensayos la relación entre
la conciencia mística, el lenguaje poético
y la trascendencia: "La Poética Interior
presta su atención a la íntima urdimbre
humana como prototipo ideal con vocación
trascendente". Las dos restantes, agrupan la
producción de poemas interioristas en términos internacionales (mayormente poetas
españoles) y dominicanos, como Juyan
Francisco Barranco: "Todo se vincula con el
Todo". [FC]

2655 Poetas argentinas, 1961–1980. Buenos Aires: Ediciones del Dock, 2007.
310 p. (Pez náufrago. Poesía)

Incluye 53 poetas. La colección refleja
la profusión de poéticas y de producción en
el país en estos años. Incluye sólo la fecha de
nacimiento de los autores como información
biobibliográfica, pero identifica de cuáles
libros vienen las selecciones. [JSK]

**2656 Los poetas interiores: una muestra
de la nueva poesía argentina.** Madrid:
Amargord, 2005. 320 p.: bibl. (Col. Los orfe-
bres; 7)

Una colección que incluye poetas
de Buenos Aires y otras regiones del país
nacidos desde 1965 y expone una visión
"interior" (no objetivista) compartida por los
autores. [JSK]

**Praises and offenses: three women poets
from the Dominican Republic.** See item
3200.

2657 Preciado, Antonio. Antología personal. Antonio Preciado. Quito: CCE
Benjamín Carrión, 2006. 316 p.: ill. (Palabra
viva)

Valiosa y cuidadosamente preparada,
esta colección reúne el trabajo del poeta
afroecuatoriano Antonio Preciado (Esmeralda, 1941) desde el primer poemario, *Jolgo-
rio* (1961), hasta *De boca en boca* (2005). Al
margen de la ausencia de un ensayo o nota
introductoria que le habría hecho justicia a
esta magnífica colección de poesía, el volumen ofrece una excelente ocasión para apre-

ciar una obra poética dueña de voz propia y con capacidad de articular en el Ecuador un proyecto poético de alcance nacional. [EM]

2658 Rodríguez Ballesteros, Armando. Lunada poética: poesía costarricense actual. San José: Ediciones Andrómeda, 2005. 237 p.: bibl.

Inclusiva, muy actualizada; datos bibliográficos sobre los autores. Útil mapa del escenario poético costarricense. [JDW]

2659 Los rostros de la Hidra: antología de revistas y poetas del siglo XXI. Edición de Julio César Pol. San Juan: Isla Negra; Río Piedras, Puerto Rico: Publicaciones Gaviota, 2008. 283 p.: bibl.

Texto clave en la nueva (de 1995 a 2005) poesía puertorriqueña (de la isla); una propuesta que, además de abrir un abanico (70 poetas incluidos, a dos poemas por cada poeta) de estilos y temáticas, busca constituirse en la casa literaria—en "la revista"— de esa "generación (post)-edípica". Entre la poesía "escrita o textual", "introspectiva" o "artesanal", escrita en español, y la "poesía oral", "performativa", influida por la poesía nuyorican, escrita en una mezcla de español e inglés, "ingleñol", se silencia o se manifiesta, respectivamente, el espacio "político-nacional inmediato". Incluye una historia breve de las 4 revistas literarias que le dieron vida a los poetas en ciernes. [FC]

2660 Seco, César. Lámpara y silencio: antología poética (1987–2004). Caracas: Monte Avila Editores Latinoamericana, 2007. 246 p. (Col. Altazor)

El rasgo característico de esta antología es el cuidadoso manejo del lenguaje que observamos a través de poemas que no se desbordan más allá de sí mismos, sino que se contienen para celebrar la "poesía" y los poetas. Una poesía madura que se esmera por expresar, a la vez, sabiduría de vida y de literatura. No son poemas programáticos, pues le dan al lector una sensación abierta de la experiencia poética. [HJ]

2661 Selva, Salomón de la. Antología mayor. Managua: Fundación UNO, 2007. 1003 p. (Col. Cultural de Centro América; 16–17. Serie literaria)

Reúne la poesía del brillante nicaragüense-estadounidense, secretario de Samuel Gompers, pareja romántica de Edna St. Vincent Millay y asesor del presidente mexicano Miguel Alemán. Se destacan "Tropical Town and Other Poems" y "El soldado desconocido". [JDW]

2662 Vázquez Benarroch, Mharía. Amarrando la paciencia a un árbol: Antología poética 1979–2007. Caracas: Monte Avila Editores Latinoamericana, 2009. 1 v.

La antología recoge la obra poética de una de las voces femeninas más sólidas en la poesía venezolana. La base de esta solidez la encontramos en la precisión del lenguaje, la sabiduría cómo se intercalan las pausas internas, y la manera de mostrar el sentimiento de desasosiego y asombro que inunda toda la antología. Aunque el tema del amor es recurrente, los poemas no son necesariamente románticos, ya que intentan esclarecer los misterios de la vida y los enigmas mismos del lenguaje. La última parte ofrece una reflexión sobre la creación poética. [HJ]

2663 25 poetas argentinos contemporáneos. Compilación de Osvaldo Svanascini. Buenos Aires: Ediciones Papiro, 2005. 218 p.

Selección de poetas renovadores que, según el editor, se destacan por su rigor estilístico. La colección funciona como una visión amplia de la poesía en estos años. [JSK]

2664 Vinueza, Humberto. Constelación del instinto. Quito: Casa de la Cultura Ecuatoriana Benjamín Carrión, 2006. 196 p.

En este nuevo poemario Humberto Vinueza (Guayaquil, 1942) ofrece una poesía que sin desentenderse de su característico rechazo por el progresismo y las promesas incumplidas de la modernidad, transita hacia espacios "donde todavía se espera enjambres de algún jardín" y donde el sujeto puede "abandonar su vigilancia" y comenzar a "vigilar su abandono" (notable en el caso de Vinueza, que se inició como Tzántzico), queda plenamente expresado en la abstración del título del libro: *Constelación del instinto.* Habrá que espera las próximas composiciones de Vinueza para apreciar el impacto que este giro ha de tener en su poética. [EM]

2665 Voces y memorias de la Luna: antología poética. Prólogo, selección y notas de Rei Berroa. Santo Domingo: Teatro de la Luna, 2006. 173 p.: bibl., ill. (Col. Libros de la luna; 1)

Se reúnen en esta antología 10 poetas hispanoparlantes de República Dominicana, Argentina, México, Colombia, Venezuela, España y Chile (Luis Alberto Ambroggio, Indran Amirthanayagam, Rei Berroa, Mario Bojórquez, Juan Carlos Galeano, Arturo Gutiérrez Plaza, Consuelo Hernández, Gladys Ilarregui, José Mármol, María Ángeles Pérez y Marcelo Rioseco), para tratar temas como el amor que vence por encima de la guerra; los desastres naturales y su relación con los humanos; la reivindicación de la memoria de los seres queridos; el odio que nos invade a todos por encima del amor; la relación lúdica entre los humanos y las cosas; el itinerario de una mujer que emigra; la humanización de lo divino; la paradoja entre la vida y la muerte; la perfección y el fulgor de la palabra; la costumbre de la soledad. [FC]

BOOKS OF VERSE

2666 Abril, Xavier. Poesía soñada. Prefacio de Clara Abril de Vivero. Edición y estudio introductorio de Marco Martos Carrera. Lima: Fondo Editorial UNMSM: Academia Peruana de la Lengua: Univ. de San Martín de Porres, Facultad de Ciencias de la Comunicación, Turismo y Psicología, 2006. 353 p. (Serie Clásicos sanmarquinos)

This welcome anthology unites the complete poetry of a prominent Peruvian figure in the international avant-garde movement who deserves more recognition. In his introduction, Martos describes Abril's poetry as an artistic intermediary between Eguren and Vallejo, fusing a surrealist base with vestiges of symbolism, reconciling vanguardism and tradition. [LB]

2667 Aguilar, Santiago. La celebración continúa. Trujillo, Peru: Ediciones Algo te Identifica, 2006. 102 p.

Aguilar celebrates the human link in a chain of cosmic forces—from divinity to grass (framed as the poetry of the landscape), stones, family, and love—and calls for greater solidarity. Aguilar's merging of Christian and Andean imagery complements the motif of continuation, also accentuated by long lines of free verse and echoes of Whitman, Vallejo, Neruda, and others. [LB]

2668 Aguilar, Santiago. Celebración del memorial oculto. Trujillo, Peru: Ediciones Algo te Identifica, 2007. 118 p.

This book closes the cycle that includes Aguilar's two preceding works (see item **2667** and the similarly named *Celebración Continua* (2000)). Long lines of freeverse alternate with stanzas whose blocking evokes stonework, weaving, dialogue, and other images, visually complementing poetic reconstructions of Andean suppression and revindication, faith, love, and the struggle for global human rights. [LB]

2669 Alliende Luco, Joaquín. Sámara: semilla alada. Selección y prólogo de Delia Domínguez. Santiago: Grijalbo, 2005. 199 p.: ill.

Colección de haikus que no siguen el formato clásico y que expresan a través de una intensa y certera imaginación asociativa una visión religiosa marcada por el cristianismo. [OS]

2670 Andrade, Martín. Clepsidra. Córdoba, Argentina: Editorial de la Univ. Católica de Córdoba, 2005. 57 p. (De puño y letra, Calíope; 14)

Poemas breves de lenguaje preciso que se concentran en situaciones humanas límites para darles una magnitud esencial. [OS]

2671 Anselmi Samanez, Rafael. Sueltos de bar. Lima: Tranvías Editores, 2006. 83 p. (Col. Olivetti. Narrativa)

Anselmi's 71 "annotations," crafted while waiting in bars, cafés, and homes, are minimalist works rendered in poetic prose and surrounded by contemplative white space. Lyric technique deepens these fleeting meditations laden with existential questioning, yearning, and nostalgia. [LB]

2672 Appratto, Roberto. Levemente ondulado: poemas, 1990–2003. Montevideo: Librería Linardi y Risso, 2005. 87 p. (Col. La hoja que piensa: 7)

Una mezcla de poemas en prosa y líricas de 1990 a 2003. Appratto juega con la presentación visual de su poesía, omitiendo, a veces, puntuación y el uso de mayúsculas para representar la voz interna y su conciencia. Hay atención a lo visual por medio de la anáfora y el uso del ojo para leer y para observar una mujer particular. Se identifica la voz poética como uruguaya cuando trata la situación cambiante del país mientras explora la escritura misma como un modo de escapar del sufrimiento individual. [JSK]

2673 Aráoz, Inés. Echazón: y otros poemas. Buenos Aires: Grupo Editor Latinoamericano, 2008. 95 p. (Nuevohacer)

El título, el cual viene de un término náutico que refiere a lo que se tira de un barco para mantenerlo a flote, anuncia las circunstancias del viaje de este poemario. Esta poeta tucumana nos traslada por las palabras, examinando su medio de transporte en camino, en un itinerario tanto emocional como simbólico. [JSK]

2674 Arce, Manuel José. Anclado en esta tierra: antología. Guatemala: Dirección General de Cultura y Artes, 2007. 118 p.

Selección de la poesía del dramaturgo guatemalteco. Se destacan por su fuerza los poemas escritos en el exilio en Francia poco antes de su muerte en 1985, los cuales denuncian con verbo depurado y directo las atrocidades del régimen militar. [JDW]

2675 Auris Villegas, W. David. Mañana cuando me vaya, piensa en mí: poemario. Lima: Editorial San Marcos, 2006. 104 p.

Images of displacement, disappearance, solitude, war, ruins, and bittersweet return predominate in this collection. Winding through a labyrinth of disparate epochs and global spaces, the poems are linked by contemplations of a universal cycle of violence and sprinkled with restrained moments of optimism. [LB]

2676 Ávila, Javier. Criatura del olvido. San Juan: Terranova Editores, 2007. 95 p.: ill.

Poemario estructurado en dos partes principales—"La memoria del tiempo", basada en una cita de Jorge Luis Borges sobre la voluntad de recordar, y "Repertorio del terror", con una cita de Nicanor Parra sobre el olvido de la amada—y una unidad más pequeña, "Serie del catedrático", sin cita, de ocho páginas, sobre el desgaste y el deterioro. Empapada de tradición literaria, y marcada por la mejor economía verbal— "morir así/degradado/por la cruel debilidad/ de un cuerpo que ya no me reconoce", aquí la poesía se levanta, según Echevarría, con lo que, paradójicamente, no quedó nunca en el recuerdo: "La fuga es así". [FC]

2677 Azarru, Juan Eduardo de. Adagios, requiems, allegros. Asunción: Arandura Editorial, 2006. 74 p.: ill.

Se ve la musicalidad de la poesía de Azarru en este poemario que muestra la poesía como un género móvil, inseguro de su destino final y su relación a la memoria y el olvido. Azarru no emplea lenguaje erudito ni se queda dentro de la métrica tradicional, sino afirma por sus recursos estilísticos que su meta es comunicarse con sus lectores. [JSK]

2678 Barco, Oscar del. Poco [y] pobre [y] nada. Córdoba, Argentina: Alción Editora, 2005. 192 p.

El título hace referencia a las subdivisiones de la colección y por todo el texto la voz poética refiere a palabras, letras, el balbuceo, y el sonido en su búsqueda de lo poético. La expresión lírica también se asocia con el vuelo de las aves y el mar, y el autor juega con la presentación visual de sus versos, un proceso que aumenta más hacia el fin del libro. [JSK]

2679 Barnet, Miguel. Itinerario inconcluso. La Habana: Ediciones Unión, 2007. 252 p. (Bolsilibros Unión)

Reunión de varios poemarios anteriormente publicados, como, entre otros, *Poemas berlineses, Poemas chinos, Cuaderno de París*, en los que el escritor cubano demuestra "sus diversos rostros, los diversos timbres de su poética", según el prólogo de Gaetano Longo, para quien la poesía de Barnet no es nunca "un puro ejercicio de estilo", ni un "acto estilista" ni un arte "para unos pocos íntimos", sino "una poesía indispensable, viva, poesía que respira y se mueve entre la gente". [FC]

2680 Barnet, Miguel. Vestido de fantasma y otros poemas. La Habana: Editorial Letras Cubanas, 2006. 115 p.: ill. (Letras Cubanas Poesía)

Dividido en dos partes, como señala Bailia Papastamatíu en la introducción, "Tatuado en la máscara del tiempo", el poemario está unido por la "poética de la travesía". Por un lado, el viaje hacia la interioridad del sujeto en la primera parte, "estamos solos ella y yo/en la imposible ventura de la vida"; por el otro, el "Cuaderno de París" en la segunda, "Amo estas calles que no se parecen a las mías". Ante la vacuidad final de todo, Barnet apuesta a la perdurabilidad de la escritura: "el medio más privilegiado para perpetuarse, más cierto que . . . la ilusión de permanecer fantasmalmente en la casa o a través del ser amado". [FC]

2681 Barrientos, Violeta. El jardín de las delicias. 2. ed. Lima: Hipocampo Editores, 2006. 60 p. (Poesía)

The book's title, triptych structure, and ekfrastic nature reveal a dialogue with Bosch's *The Garden of Earthly Delights*, yet the work calls for a transcendence of socially constructed judgments. In semantically rich yet penetrable free verse, minimalist and more extended poems probe the essence of creation and being. The longest poem, at the heart of the book, is distinctly national in focus, portraying the violence of the civil war. [LB]

2682 Bastías, Waldo. Estación de tránsito: (poesía reunida). Caracas: República Bolivariana de Venezuela, Gobierno Bolivariano: Fundación Editorial el Perro y la Rana, 2007. 227 p. (Colección Poesíavenezolana. Contemporáneos)

Poemas que de manera escueta representan las contradicciones y los conflictos a veces virulentos que experimenta el sujeto sin dejar de lado la fuerza erótica del deseo que lo sobresalta. Reúne todos los poemas publicados hasta la fecha por el autor. [OS]

2683 Becciú, Ana. La visita y otros libros. Barcelona: Bruguera, 2007. 194 p.

Este libro reune cuarto poemarios de la autora (1972–2002), los cuales tratan el tema de la identidad en relaciones tanto familiares y amorosas como nacionales. Los poemas varían entre los líricos, condensados, hasta los poemas en prosa, y dialogan con autores como San Juan de la Cruz, cantigas de amigo medievales y con autores más contemporáneos como Clarice Lispector. [JSK]

2684 Belli, Carlos Germán. Sextinas, villanelas y baladas. Madrid: Visor Libros, 2007. 53 p. (Col. Visor de poesía; 634)

One of Peru's most distinguished poets, Belli is a master at crafting a contemporary voice within classical form, as evidenced by this sampling of sestinas, ballads, and villanelles. In brief prose pieces framing the book, the poet explains that orderly, closed verse provides refuge from the limitations of language and the fragmentation and emptiness of modern life, themes that run through these complex, exquisitely rendered poems. [LB]

2685 Bello, Javier. Letrero de albergue. Huelva, Spain: Diputación Provincial de Huelva, 2006. 73 p. (Col. de poesía Juan Ramón Jiménez; 47)

La fluidez de las imágenes yuxtapuestas da cuenta del esplendor de lo inusitado en un lenguaje que no cesa de entregar aristas de una realidad entrecortada, siempre más sorprendente cuanto más incomprensible. Este libro recibió el XXVI premio Hispano-americano de poesía "Juan Ramón Jiménez" concedido por la diputación de Huelva, España. [OS]

2686 Berbin, Mirih. Mareas. Caracas: El Perro y la Rana, 2008. 56 p.

Una voz nueva cuya poesía es esencialista: gira en torno a las esencias. El lenguaje no se presenta como experimentación o como desafío, sino como pura transparencia para darle significado a la forma, y forma al significado. En este sentido, los poemas que componen *Mareas* son vestigios que van armando un universo íntimo que involucra la naturaleza, pero también los espacios interiores y exteriores. [HJ]

2687 Bergaño y Villegas, Simón. Poemas. 3a ed. Guatemala: Tipografía Nacional, 2008. 120 p. (Clásicos de la Literatura Guatemalteca; 2)

Tercera edición del significativo díptico La Vacuna y "Silva de economía política", el cual fue publicado en 1808 en Nueva Guatemala por un precursor de la independencia centroamericana. Valioso documento de la Ilustración hispánica en América. Esta edición no anotada cuenta con el prólogo a la edición de 1959 de César Brañas. [JDW]

2688 Berroa, Rei. Libro de los fragmentos y otros poemas. Caracas: Ministerio de la Cultura, Fundación Editorial el Perro y la Rana, 2006. 166 p.: bibl. (Col. Poesía del mundo. Serie contemporáneos)

Poeta establecido de la diáspora dominicana. Este poemario se divide en dos partes. En la primera, un "Pórtico para el lector", tan ficticio como Don Quijote, se simula el hallazgo de un manuscrito antiguo sobre poesía y erotismo, escrito por el poeta andaluz Abu Abad Allah Muhammad Ibn Abbad. En la segunda, la muestra de poemas incluye títulos como "Acid Rain" y el poema "VII": "Triste el que se fuera/con el sexo sin usar,/dijéramos, tal vez,/a medio hacer o sin abrir". El poemario termina con un ensayo titulado "Filiación: la poesía, el hombre". [FC]

2689 Bertoni, Claudio. Para una joven amiga que intentó quitarse la vida. Santiago: Libros de Mentira: Consejo Nacional de la Lectura y las Artes, 2009. 33 p.
Secuencia de poemas de lenguaje desenfadado y directo sobre situaciones eróticas. Incluye fotos tomadas por el poeta-fotógrafo. [OS]

2690 Bolaño, Roberto. La universidad desconocida. Barcelona: Editorial Anagrama, 2007. 459 p. (Narrativas Hispánicas; 406)
Fundamental recopilación de poemas escritos entre 1978 y 1994 que también incluye textos en prosa. Hay interesantes notas explicativas de algunos textos, una bibliografía detallada de los textos publicados, y una historia del origen del libro. El título celebra la formación literaria personal del escritor como alternativa radicalmente creativa. El carácter díscolo, desconcertante, geográficamente dislocado, visionario y pesadillesco de Bolaño se encuentra poéticamente comprimido en estas páginas. [OS]

2691 Bravo Varela, Hernán. Sobrenaturaleza. Valencia, Spain: Pre-Textos, 2010. 80 p. (Poesía)
Bravo Varela (México, 1979) ya figura como uno de los poetas (y ensayistas) importantes de su generación. El título de este libro remite sin duda a la poética del cubano Lezama Lima. En la primera sección se establecen diálogos con poetas marginales como Marosa di Giorgio o Luis Hernández (sobre quienes escribe en Los orillados), y tantos otros interlocutores (hay allí un poema en diálogo sobre la vaca con Enrique Fierro). En la segunda parte se dedican sendos textos en prosa a todas las letras del alfabeto griego, como si a partir de allí se pudiera instaurar una poética que emana del abecedario como gestión del mundo. [JS]

2692 Brodsky B., Camilo. Las puntas de las cosas. Santiago: Editorial Cuarto Propio, 2006. 75 p. (Botella al Sur, Poesía)
La mirada descarnada, suelta, sobre la existencia cotidiana y sus avatares trágicos también descubre en la relación con la mujer

y con el sufrimiento posibilidades para el asombro y la empatía. [OS]

2693 Brozovich, Raúl. El duro oficio de vivir. Peru: Rectorado de la Univ. Nacional de San Antonio Abad del Cusco, 2006. 289 p.
This book gathers works sporadically published by the respected cuzqueño poet (who died in 2006) and includes an informative interview by Mario Guevara Paredes. Fed by an eclectic range of influences, these works explore indigenismo, revolution, bohemian life, love, pop culture, and art. Brozovich's social commitment stands out without overshadowing his lyric sensibility. [LB]

2694 Bustos, David. Peces de colores. Santiago: LOM Ediciones, 2005. 79 p. (Col. Entre mares. Poesía)
El desaliento crítico frente a las experiencias vitales se mezcla a la perplejidad y aunque los "peces de colores" o espejismos del deseo no atrapan al poeta lo mantienen íntimamente ligado a la fascinación y a la sospecha. [OS]

2695 Bustos, Miguel Angel. Visión de los hijos del mal: poesía completa. Buenos Aires: Editorial Argonauta, 2008. 457 p.: ill., index. (Biblioteca de poesía; 13)
Incluye un prólogo y notas por Emiliano Bustos y un apéndice con poesía de Juan Gelman. Reune siete colecciones en textos que mezclan la lírica con la poesía en prosa. Según Bustos, la crítica ha enfatizado lo amoroso, lo sereno, y las transparencia armónica de los poemas tempranos mientras los finales dialogan con hechos históricos como el masacre Trelew, y los asesinatos de Victor Jara y Pablo Gustavo Laguzzi. [JSK]

2696 Bustriazo Ortiz, Juan Carlos. Herejía bermeja: obra poética. Buenos Aires: Ediciones en danza, 2008. 206 p.: bibl., ill., index.
Este poeta de La Pampa se ha caracterizado como un "trovador errante" y "una de las mayores voces poéticas de la provincia". Este emplea un vocabulario idiomático, regional, y formas como la milonga. Su obra se desconoce en gran parte porque ha quedado inédita hasta ahora. Esta edición, coordinada por Javier Cófreces, reune la voz popular de su poesía más temprana, así como su poesía más reciente, la cual tiene

lazos con las vanguardias. Incluye un estudio introductorio, cronología, testimonios del autor, y un índice de artículos sobre el poeta. [JSK]

2697 Cabel García, Andrea. Las falsas actitudes del agua. 2. ed. Lima: Editora Mesa Redonda, 2007. 62 p.: ill. (Taquicardia)

In his prologue, Raúl Zurita commends the originality and maturity of this young poet. As its title intimates, the collection evades precise description: vivid metaphors lead to vague referents, yet scenes and feelings (often of longing) are familiar, and love and family are discernible concerns. The verse is free and varied, but in the central portion of the book, minimalist, fragmented lines become dense through their separation by slashes rather than space, creating a formally consistent core in a book full of texture and movement. [LB]

2698 Cámeron, Juan. Ciudadano discontinuado. Santiago: Libros de Mentira: Consejo Nacional de la Lectura y las Artes, 2009. 39 p.

Experiencias con otros lenguajes y otros territorios y testimonios de relaciones personales y amistades de una manera directa, casi conversacional. [OS]

2699 Camerotto, Silvia. 420 minutos de abstinencia. Buenos Aires: Ediciones del Dock, 2008. 56 p. (Pez náufrago. Poesía; 28)

Es el primer poemario de Camerotto. El primer verso, "que querías de mí", nos da una pista acerca de su filosofía poética. La autora establece una voz poética interesante: fuerte, combativa, inquisitiva. Mantiene una voz femenina, pero también rompe con las expectativas de su género y mezcla los dos géneros en su auto-descripción: "Soy el hijo que no fui/la otra que fui/la otra que soy". [JSK]

2700 Canal Feijóo, Bernardo. Penúltimo poema del fútbol. Buenos Aires: El Suri Porfiado, 2007. 44 p.: ill., index. (Poesía)

Re-publicación 80 años después de la primera edición de esta poesía que se lee como anotaciones de un partido de fútbol, sin embargo, sigue siendo vigente. Títulos como "Patada", "Penal", "Réferi", "Gol" enfatizan los aspectos futbolísticos, pero la voz poética hace paralelos fuertes entre lo deportivo y lo político, por ejemplo, cuando escribe que "la patada es la hija de la demo-

cracia". Incluye los dibujos originales del autor que se mezclan con la palabra escrita. Los poemas son de extensión muy variada: algunos son escritos en formato de prosa, con párrafos descriptivos muy largos, y otros son de unos dos o tres versos. [JSK]

2701 Carr M., José Antonio. Reino adentro: más allá de la rosa. Panamá: Instituto Nacional de Cultura, Direccion Nacional de Las Artes, Departamento de Letras, 2007. 59 p. (Col. Ricardo Miró. Premio poesía; 2006)

Poemario breve premiado en Panamá cuyos versos fluyen con una ductilidad rítmica y temática afín a la tradición oral. Destaca "Los muertos y la hora" por su intensidad lírica y dramática. [JDW]

2702 Carrasco, German. Multicancha. Mexico: EBL, 2006. 89 p. (Poesia latinoamericana; 2)

Una poesía que busca distanciarse de la figura del poeta como un sujeto sacrificial y que se concentra, mediante un lenguaje tanto deliberadamente inconexo como figurativo, en la circunstancia latinoamericana, lo natural representado, por ejemplo, en un Ombú de Buenos Aires y lo social a través de personajes marginales. [OS]

2703 Carvalho, Homero. Los reinos dorados. Bolivia: Grupo Editorial La Hoguera, 2007. 85 p.: ill. (La mancha. Literatura adultos)

El referente poético de este poemario es la selva boliviana, sus ríos, sus árboles y animales misteriosos que, reunidos bajo el rigor de la palabra poética, conforman los *Reinos Dorados* de Homero Carvalho. Hay ciertamente mucha belleza en estos poemas, y por supuesto un gran esfuerzo por hacer del verso un pincel histórico que con agilidad nos va mostrando el esplendor de un mundo *feliz* no tocado por la máquina moderna, pero que finalmente cede ante el impacto cultural de la conquista. A estos *Reinos dorados* llegaron los conquistadores fundando barbarie, pero *algunos*, "iluminados por el verbo", llegaron para "encontrar un hogar", y en el proceso "nos legaron la lengua castellana" e instalaron un "nuevo tiempo". A esa lengua (castellano) y a ese Tiempo (moderno-mestizo) le apuesta el poeta. El precio, claro, es el difícil acomodo de los *Reinos dorados* a ese *nuevo tiempo*. [EM]

2704 Casal, Mariela. Hotel. Caracas: Editorial Diosa Blanca, 2008 1 v.

Casal busca ser una artista integral en este poemario. Por un lado, aparece el aspecto visual, el cual queda expuesto doblemente: a través de los poemas escritos a mano que aparecen en la primera parte del poemario (en la segunda parte encontramos la versión mecanografiada de estos poemas), y en el video que acompaña el libro, donde la autora recorre las instalaciones del abandonado Hotel Humboldt de la ciudad de Caracas, con su misma voz que—más que recitar—, pronuncia algunos de los poemas. Por otro lado, encontramos también el apecto sonoro, igualmente reflejado doblemente: a través de la voz del video, pero también, a través de la palabra "hotel" que se repite constantemente, y que crea un eco en el poemario. Pero, más allá de estos aspectos, la poética de Casal intenta presentar una "estética radical", pues no podríamos decir que los poemas se limitan a dibujar el desamor o el desencuentro, como en efecto lo hacen, de manera minimalista y profética, sino que buscan renovar el lenguaje, el efecto visual, y la posición del lector que necesaria y dinámicamente se reubica en poemas que los podríamos definir como espaciales: tránsito, recorrido, viaje. [HJ]

2705 Casas Silva, Francisco. Romance de la inmaculada llanura. Providencia, Santiago: Editorial Cuarto Propio, 2008. 60 p. index. (Poesía)

La densa descripción de una relación amorosa homoerótica se intersecta con el trazado de una pintura en la voz de un hablante que fluctúa de género. [OS]

2706 Casiraghi, María. Turbanidad. Córdoba, Argentina: Alción Editora, 2008. 91 p.

Desde la primera página de este poemario, marcada por un epígrafe de Charles Bukowsky ("lo que cuenta es observar las paredes/yo nací para hacer esto"), se encuentran observaciones íntimas de una ciudad personificada. La voz poética se enfoca mucho en la experiencia, muchas veces contradictoria, de vivir en un ambiente urbano: "Todos llevamos adentro una ciudad". Además de lo interno-externo, otros binarios cuestionados aquí incluyen: vida-muerte, lo artificial-lo natural, ruido-silencio. [JSK]

2707 Cassaus, Víctor. Perfume (y secuencia) de mujer. La Habana: Letras Cubanas, 2007. 122 p. (Poesía)

Entre sus 11 libros de poesía, el poeta cubano hace una selección de poemas en torno al amor, "sobre todo/cuando me ensimismo/en ti misma"; la amante, "El universo será (o no) infinito/Pero hoy/específicamente hoy/comienza y termina/en tus piernas"; o la desamada, "Después del amor y un poco antes del olvido/rompiste y quemaste todos los poemas . . . que una vez te entregué". Pero también la poesía juega con el amor, "Esta mujer no conoce a Goethe ni a Coleridge", y con algunas variantes de un chiste porteño, "Vos sos/esa pequeña argentina/que todos debieran/llevar dentro". [FC]

2708 Castillo Zapata, Rafael. Estancias. Caracas: Editorial Equinoccio: Univ. Simón Bolívar, Dirección de Cultura, 2009. 93 p. (Col. Papiros. Serie Poesía)

Los breves poemas en prosa de Castillo Zapata dan señal de restos o vestigios, pero que apuntan hacia un universo más rico y enigmático. El prevaleciente signo interrogatorio muestra una actitud filosófica ante una realidad que los poemas desdibujan. El depurado lenguaje del libro, al mismo tiempo, da signos de una poesía cerrada en sí misma, a manera de claustro. [HJ]

2709 Cerón, Rocío. Tiento. Fotografías de Valentina Siniego. Música de Enrico Chapela. Monterrey, Mexico: Univ. Autónoma de Nuevo León, 2010. 75 p.: ill. (Palabra en poesía)

Promotora de proyectos artísticos en colaboración (reuniendo música, arte y poesía), Cerón (México, 1972) propone en este libro un acompañamiento con la música para violoncello de Enrico Chapela (accesible en el blog de la autora), y las fotografías de Valentina Siniego. El poema mismo traza la voz de tres mujeres: la abuela, la madre y Eleonora, en tanto se trazan rutas en diferentes espacios, como si fuera una mudanza, una migración, que significa pérdidas y vislumbres de tierras ignotas. [JS]

2710 Chávez Camacho, Benjamín. Pequeña librería de viejo. La Paz: Plural Editores, 2007. 89 p.: ill.

Con este poemario Benjamín Chávez (1971) obtuvo el Premio Nacional de Poesía Yolanda Bedregal 2006. Uno a uno, los poemas que componen el volumen testimonian momentos, experiencias, imágenes, pensamientos y hasta la presencia de objetos que en circunstancias determinadas participan en la construcción de un universo personal. Lo enormemente creativo es que en la lógica de estos poemas, semejantes "testimonios" son percibidos como "pedradas" dirigidas al hablante, pues aquí el universo del poeta está forjado con estas "piedras" que le avienta la vida. Magistral manera de significar la condición de "apedrado" que vive el poeta. [EM]

2711 Chihuailaf, Elicura. Soñar en el azul. Santiago: Libros de Mentira: Consejo Nacional de la Lectura y las Artes, 2009. 53 p.

El poeta valora la cultura indígena y lo demuestra con sutileza en poemas que rememoran experiencias vitales y que también celebran una cosmovisión personal y comunitaria de la existencia. Incluye textos en lengua mapuche. [OS]

2712 Cruchaga, André. Caminos cerrados. México: Editorial Praxis, 2009. 102 p.

En este volumen el poeta nacido en Chalatenango (El Salvador, 1957) despliega un estro profético de escarnio de los poderes mundanos a los cuales adjudica la guerra y la destrucción generalizada de la vida. El lenguaje es elevado y figurado, si bien abundan los versos sentenciosos y declarativos. [JDW]

2713 Cruchaga, André. Oscuridad sin fecha = Data gabeko iluntasuna. San Salvador: s.n., 2006. 97 p.

47 poemas se ajustan a la medida estricta de la página en una meditación que asume el más elevado lenguaje lírico occidental. El tono melancólico y la concisión sugerente recuerdan a poetas peninsulares como Salvador Espriu y Jaime Gil de Biedma. Edición bilingüe castellano-vasco: traduce la poeta María Eugenia Lizeaga. [JDW]

2714 Cruz-Bernall, Mairym. Ensayo sobre las cosas simples. Bogotá: Común Presencia Editores, 2006. 79 p.: ill. (Col. Los conjurados; 23)

Puente ocasional entre lo puertorriqueño que marca a la voz poética y la cercanía pasajera colombiana que la deleita, "En Bogotá todos los hombres que vi/besaron mis labios". Dueña de una sexualidad, como

poco, epistemológica, desde la que fluye lo poético sin salirse de las palabras. Poesía de versos cortos que nombran con pasión inagotable la geografía del amor provocado: "tengo todavía un poema más/un hombre por el instante del beso". De esa feminidad soberana surge la reflexión metapoética que rellena las lagunas entre el deseo y "lo que no se puede capturar": "aquello inasible/indefendible/que sabemos ausente/la causa por la cual escribo este poema/la razón por la cual no quiero que pienses/que ya no te espero". [FC]

2715 Cuevas, José Angel. Canciones Oficiales. Santiago: Ediciones Univ. Diego Portales, 2009. 197 p.

La ácida radiografía del fracaso de un proyecto generacional por establecer cambios políticos y culturales que se vieron cortados por el golpe militar de 1973 y el terror consiguiente se presenta como una forma de resistencia al triunfalismo y el individualismo que el poeta observa y deplora en democracia. Incluye poemas de cuatro libros publicados entre 1992 y el 2000 y 33 nuevos poemas bajo el título "Estación delirio". [OS]

2716 Cuevas, José Angel. Lírica del edificio 201. Buenos Aires: Black & Vermelho, 2007. 63 p.

Con sarcasmo, el poeta se presenta como un ciudadano al margen, marcado por un visceral descreimiento del presente y anclado en lo que valora como su cruda honestidad a toda prueba. [OS]

2717 Curbelo Rodríguez, Jesús David. Sonetos imperdonables. Camagüey, Cuba: Editorial Ácana, 2006. 141 p. (Col. Premio)

Poeta muchas veces premiado en Cuba—2001 y 2004, fechas más recientes. En este poemario se trata de una selección personal que capture el proceso de escribir sonetos durante más de 20 años, de modo que el lector vea "el movimiento de mi espíritu y mis tropiezos con el dominio de la forma". Dividido en cuatro partes: 1) los sonetos iniciales; 2) el despegue; 3) el abandono de la forma; 4) los sonetos que le hubiera gustado escribir. El libro termina con una traducción al español de sonetos escritos por grandes poetas en italiano, inglés, francés y portugués. [FC]

2718 Daneri, Alberto. Fuego de palabras. Argentina: Libros de Tierra Firme, 2007. 79 p. (Col. de poesía Todos bailan; 349)

Esta colección incorpora la poesía de Daneri entre 2001–2003, en la cual se combina poesía social y testimonial, dirigiéndose a los temas de la dictadura y el exilio. En estos términos se discute la memoria y la relación entre pasado, presente y futuro. Hay cierta negación del presente que se comunica por las palabras y por los espacios o el espacio en blanco entre palabras y versos en la página. [JSK]

2719 Delgado, Wáshington. La palabra en el tiempo. Lima: Lustra Editores, 2007. 141 p.

This chronologically organized selection of 80 poems, drawn from Delgado's nine published collections, offers an introduction to the renowned poet's work. Compiler Ruiz Velazco explains that he aims to represent not only his personal favorite and Delgado's most emblematic works, but also the diversity of an oeuvre that exceeds any limitations mistakenly implied by Delgado's categorization within the 50s generation. [LB]

2720 Delmar, Patricia. Rouge: poemas rojos. Córdoba, Argentina: Alción Editora, 2008. 89 p.

Este libro sigue la evocación de emoción a través del color que se empezó en sus poemarios anteriores, Azul y Amarillo. Aquí tenemos la pasión y la lucha en poemas a menudo breves como un haiku. Nos proporciona pequeñas impresiones de la vida porque Delmar tiene un enardecimiento por la minucia de la vida diaria. [JSK]

2721 Díaz, Martín. Cuaderno de un clochard. Córdoba, Argentina: Alción Editora, 2008. 75 p.

El poeta emplea la perspectiva de un clochard, o vagabundo, para crear un tono ambulante, pero no sólo describe el acto físico de ambular sino que también viaja por el tiempo, por los recuerdos, por la historia. Se escribe en una mezcla de primera persona (los pensamientos escritos del clochard) y tercera persona (las observaciones del poeta que encuentra el cuaderno y añade sus propias observaciones), algo que contribuye a la sensación fuerte de un diálogo, lo cual es algo que se revela explícitamente al final del poemario. [JSK]

2722 Dlugosz Salas, Alain. Tawa. Peru: Instituto Nacional de Cultura Cusco, 2005. 87 p.: ill. (Poesía)

The poet's compact, conceptual works, infused with natural imagery, express the circularity of time and space through content and form. Reciprocity and duality, tenets fundamental to indigenous worldviews, are captured through the driving theme of tawa ("four" in Quechua) and enhanced by quadripartite visual icons from Andean and other Native American groups on every fourth page. [LB]

2723 Durán, Claudio. La infancia y los exilios. Santiago: Editorial Cuarto Propio, 2006. 62 p. (Col. Uvas de la ira. Poesía)

Las ciudades son lugares en los que el sujeto ha dejado huellas fuertemente personales que reencuentra y en las que se detiene cuidadosamente al recorrerlas luego de años de exilio. [OS]

2724 Espaillat, Rhina P. Agua de dos ríos: poemas, prosa y traducciones: una colección bilingüe. Santo Domingo: Secretaría de Estado de Cultura, Editora Nacional, 2006. 201 p.: bibl. (Col. Ultramar)

Escritora dominicana de la diáspora, varias veces galardonada en los Estados Unidos por su poesía en inglés—en el año 2003 obtuvo el Premio Nacional de Poesía con Playing at Stillness (Jugando a la quietud). Importante muestra bilingüe del trabajo de Espaillat, a quien, como dice Silvio Torres-Saillant en la introducción, "Su origen de inmigrante caribeña no la acongoja". En vez, "reconociéndose hija de la historia, mira a la historia para entender la naturaleza de su desarraigo". Texto importante que se suma a la también importante tarea de unir las orilla caribeñas en toda su variedad de idiomas. [FC]

2725 Espinosa, Rafael. El anticiclón del Pacífico Sur. Lima: Ritual de lo Habitual Ediciones, 2007. 60 p.

Espinosa's title—tellingly presented backwards and forwards on the book's cover and spine—captures the destabilizing sense of oppositional movement running through his poems. Locality and universality, interiority and outer geographies, detachment and social engagement, and modernity and timelessness merge through rich, sometimes formally experimental language, whose meaning is pleasingly indistinct yet perceptible. [LB]

2726 Esquinca, Jorge. Descripción de un brillo azul cobalto. Valencia, Spain: Pre-Textos, 2008. 59 p. (Col. La cruz del sur; 956)

Esquinca (México, 1957) hace confluir en este poemario circunstancias personales con evocaciones literarias y culturales: la agonía de su padre en un hospital coincide en el mismo plano discursivo del poema con el último día en la vida de Gérard de Nerval; el paisaje francés desemboca en una rememoración de la infancia en México. Todo es una confluencia que hace latir en los versos una persistente melancolía en uno de los libros más sugerentes y logrados del autor. [JS]

2727 Fabre, Luis Felipe. La sodomía en la Nueva España. Valencia, Spain: Pre-Textos, 2010. 92 p. (Poesía)

Libro basado en la lectura (confesiones, cartas, edictos, testimonios) que realizó Fabre (México, 1974) acerca de la persecución de homosexuales en la Nueva España durante 1657 y 1658. Compuesto por tres poemas largos, uno en forma de auto sacramental ("Retablo de sodomitas novohispanos") donde se representa la persecución, de modo semejante a los juicios que se realizaron contra los conversos por prácticas "judaizantes"; y los otros dos en forma de "anexos". El último es un brillante poema que relata la condena a la hoguera para Gerónimo Calbo, quien había ignorado diferencias de edad, raza o posición social, en sus deseos carnales. [JS]

2728 Falcone, Jorge. Canto hereje: textos poéticos. Buenos Aires: Ediciones Baobab, 2005. 144 p.: ill. (Col. Palabra militante)

El autor dedica su libro a una serie de nombres que representan "los intelectuales más subversivos" que conoce, así señalando su inspiración hacia la poesía rebelde que nace de la crisis y la miseria. Su estilo es a veces panfletaria, a veces íntima, pero siempre se basa en la poesía hablada, en un estilo oral, directo, que dialoga con el arte visual por los collages de Gabriela Podestá. Su estilo aquí textualizado crece de su antología oral, "Falcompact", producida en 1999. [JSK]

2729 Fernández, Manuel. Octubre. Lima: Estruendo Mudo, 2006. 87 p.

Public and private discourses dialogue in this accomplished work; the daily life of a couple from La Breña is set against three decades of history, framed by Velasco and Fujimori's respective coup-d'états. Grouped in nonconsecutive chronological moments, the poems present distinct registers, intertexts, and perspectives, offsetting the spectacle of official history with a bittersweet intimate one. [LB]

2730 Fernández Granados, Jorge. Principio de incertidumbre. México: Ediciones Era: Univ. de las Américas; San Luis Potosí: Secretaría de Cultura de San Luis Potosí, 2007. 98 p. (Biblioteca Era)

Fernández Granados (México, 1965) es un poeta versátil, con diferentes recursos en su estrategia discursiva. Lo mismo usa el verso largo, a veces en forma de prosa; las repeticiones sonoras, el uso de la anáfora, la incisiva ironía, o la incorporación de frases o versos de múltiples fuentes. Este libro gira en torno a un tema peculiar de nuestro tiempo: la incertidumbre, que lo mismo se da en el seno mismo del poema, como un cuestionamiento de la forma, que a través de sus tres secciones: identidades (movimiento), dimensiones (espacio) y eventos (tiempo). [JS]

2731 Ferré, Rosario. Fisuras. Prólogo de Julio Ortega. San Juan: Ediciones Callejón, 2006. 123 p. (Col. de poesía) (El farolito azul)

Desde lo lingüístico, "esa lengua que sostiene mi alma/como el esqueleto sostiene mi cuerpo", al órgano de la lengua, uno "poderoso [que]:/tiene muchas notas/y varios teclados". De la palabra que "nace/detrás de un fanal de hueso", al poema "fuerte como un ángel/y demasiado soberbio para reconocerlo". Desde el Bill Gates que "anunció que la letra ñ/no se eliminaría de sus programas", hasta la lucha entre el inglés y el español, "Dos reyes machos no caben/dentro de un misma cueva". Según Ortega, éste es "el libro más afirmativo, gozoso y elocuente" de Ferré, una "poesía inmediata, descarnada, urgida, a la vez severa y sensual", donde, por supuesto, hay espacio para el humor, una "Oda al tembleque", otras al teléfono y al lechón a la varita; donde no falta el saludo al padre muerto,

"Vivió muchos años/y todos creían que era inmortal". [FC]

2732 Flax, Hjalmar. Contraocaso. San Juan: Instituto de Cultura Puertorriqueña, 2007. 96 p.

This collection reminds us that poetry is a battle against time. The decline of time is cleverly expressed by the irony that penetrates everyday life in an attempt to disguise the future. The five main sections: "Interrogations," "Intuitions," "Cities," "Considerations," and "Divertimentos" follow the collections' philosophical considerations. A variety of poetic forms are used. [M. García Calderón]

2733 Formoso Babic, Christian. El cementerio más hermoso de Chile. Providencia, Santiago: Editorial Cuarto Propio, 2008. 357 p. (Col. Uvas de la ira. Poesía)

El espacio del cementerio magallánico en Punta Arenas le permite al poeta crear un macrocosmos histórico donde se manifiestan las experiencias trágicas de un colectivo de voces, a las que revive como si fuera un médium, un testigo en tránsito desde el luto hacia otra vida posible. [OS]

2734 Fressia, Alfredo. Senryu, o, El árbol de las sílabas. Montevideo: Linardi y Risso, 2007. 107 p. (La hoja que piensa; 13)

En su ensayo introductorio, Fressia explica que el género de su poesía es el senryu (y no el haiku), y que este enfoque le permite más libertad temática. El autor describe su "árbol de símbolos" en términos del mestizaje y mientras todos los poemas incorporan imágenes naturales, también incluyen imágenes del contexto histórico: bombas, el exilio, la verdad/mentira, la patria, y los gauchos. Por medio de citas y referencias abre un diálogo con otros poetas como Baudelaire, Enrique Fierro, y Gustavo Wojciechowski. [JSK]

2735 Galarza, Rodrigo. Parque de destrucciones. Buenos Aires: El Suri Porfiado, 2007. 45 p.: index. (Poesía)

El primer verso de este poemario dirige la atención a una voz poética con rasgos nerudianos, sobre todo de "Las alturas de Macchu Picchu": "Soy él que hundió su pulso en la niebla". Tiene un tono épico y sigue el hilo conductor de "caminar entre ruinas", aunque está ubicada la voz en Madrid, y no en Macchu Picchu. Se lee como

un mapa deconstruido de la ciudad, hecho por una voz que es, a la vez, presente y ausente, desorientada y reflexiva. [JSK]

2736 Gamarra Rivero, Matilde. Trabajo de campo. Lima: Editorial el Río, 2008. 176 p.

Organized in four "recorridos" (journeys) evoking distinct dispositions (the bookends are "melancholy-schizoidal" and "jocus x ludus"), Gamarra's reflective poems—some in free verse, some more formally rigid, many laconic—move between child and adulthood, light and shadow, and life and death, contemplating fear, sensuality, the passage of time, and other impressions gathered along an existential pilgrimage. [LB]

2737 Gandolfo, Francisco. Versos para despejar la mente. Rosario, Argentina: Editorial Municipal de Rosario, 2006. 324 p.

Una colección de tres de sus obras publicadas entre 1968–1977. Gandolfo emplea un lenguaje coloquial, anti-poético, y a veces narrativo, incorporando ironía y humor. [JSK]

2738 Gelman, Juan. País que fue será: México, 2001–2002. Buenos Aires: Seix Barral, 2004. 94 p. (Biblioteca Breve)

Una colección de poemas del poeta argentino tal vez más conocido hoy en día. Gelman emplea su estilo típico con trastornos de tiempos verbales para tratar temas como el amor, la nostalgia, la poesía, Argentina y aun Iraq en 2003. [JSK]

2739 Giannuzzi, Joaquín O. Un arte callado. Buenos Aires: Ediciones del Dock, 2008. 83 p. (Pez náufrago)

Una edición posterior, dado que el poeta falleció en 2004, con poemas que llaman la atención por su brevedad. Aunque son breves, tienen una temática variada: lo cotidiano se mezcla con lo político y lo metafísico. [JSK]

2740 Godino, Rodolfo. Viaje favorable, 1954–2004. Córdoba, Argentina: Ediciones del Copista, 2004. 401 p.: bibl. (Col. Fénix; 21)

Godino intenta mantener la vida del lenguaje y la memoria a través de la poesía. La suya es una poesía formal ("posclásica" según Ricardo Herrera), la cual incluye elegías, arte poéticas, canciones, en un estilo a veces simbolista, a veces hermética. El volumen incluye una extensa bibliografía, estudios, artículos, reseñas y una entrevista, y un camino muy completo para empezar a explorar el trabajo de este poeta. [JSK]

2741 Goldemberg, Isaac. Libro de las transformaciones. Prólogo de Eduardo Espina y Róger Santiváñez. Lima: Univ. Nacional Mayor de San Marcos, 2007. 99 p.

As Róger Santiváñez observes in his prologue, this collection by celebrated writer Goldemberg interrogates God, identity, history and the written word itself. The latter becomes both the subject of self-reflexive irony and a potential conduit between humanity and divinity. Simultaneously expressing skepticism and faith—thus both grounded and transcendent—the poems weave Jewish, Christian, and Andean symbolism into trans-galactic explorations reaching from Peru to the Hudson River and far beyond. [LB]

2742 Gómez Beras, Carlos Roberto. Aún, 1992–1989. San Juan: Isla Negra Editores, 2007. 182 p. (Col. El Canon secuestrado)

Poeta dominicano-boricua, cuya poesía reelabora desde la tradición literaria tópicos establecidos por la poesía de siempre, sobre todo el amor: "La lluvia oxidante de su cabellera/que cae en mi como la noche sobre un arado". Premio Nacional de Poesía del Pen Club de Puerto Rico con el poemario *Viaje a la noche* (1989)—"de noche/cuando la virginidad/es un charco de promesas"—, incluido en *Aún*, junto a tres poemarios anteriores (*Animal de sombras*, 1992; *Poesía sin palabras*, 1991; *La paloma de la plusvalía*, 1990). Poeta de lo amoroso, de la palabra tersa y de la memoria (erótica y literaria): "Sin poder evitar las palabras/ regreso a su imperio de gemidos/a su casa de sílabas manoseadas/(míralas como chillan Octavio)". [FC]

2743 Gómez Rosa, Alexis. Ferryboat de una noche invertebrada. Santo Domingo: Secretaría de Estado de Cultura, Editora Nacional, 2006. 92 p.

Poeta varias veces ganador del premio dominicano de poesía "Casa de Teatro". Por este poemario enamorado del amor, "Las sábanas que guardan las miserias/babosas del último inquilino", obtuvo el Premio Nacional de Poesía Salomé Ureña de Henríquez

en 2006: "Escrito el amor, es confidencia. Inter (venido) el amor,/es una fiesta". Dividido en dos partes y en dos islas, "Puertos y singladura I" (escrita en Santo Domingo, R.D.) y "Puertos y singladura II" (escrita en Mayagüez, Puerto Rico: "Hacia Mayagüez me voy/en el temblor de tu cuerpo"), el poeta transforma el viaje nocturno de un puerto al otro, "El ferryboat gime/como león de mar,/es una vaca marina,/trepando la oscuridad/boca de lobo", en una aventura de amor que termina, como tantas, en el recuerdo: "En este instante/aquí todo es memoria". [FC]

2744 González Ríos, Juanmanuel. Sobre todo tus silencios. San Juan: Isla Negra Editores, 2006. 62 p. (Col. Josemilio González)

Poemario—ha publicado otros en 2008 y 2009—de un poeta joven, formado, como plantea Mercedes López-Baralt en el prólogo, en la "patria chica" de la Universidad de Puerto Rico, que se destaca por su elocuente intertextualidad; un diálogo fértil con poetas y músicos del que se desata "una polifonía de voces en sus versos: la frivolidad erótica se opone a la pasión más tierna, el escepticismo al compromiso político, el amor filial al abismo de la violencia". [FC]

2745 Granizo, Francisco. Francisco Granizo. Quito: Casa de la Cultura Ecuatoriana Benjamín Carrión, 2005. 220 p. (Poesía junta; 1)

A partir del año 2005, la Casa de la Cultura Ecuatoriana Benjamín Carrión viene publicando la obra de los poetas vivos más representativos de la literatura ecuatoriana en una colección titulada Poesía Junta. Se trata de un proyecto de alcance nacional que además de dar a conocer la producción poética de este país, apunta a una reforma cultural educativa que podría tener importantes consecuencias a corto y largo plazo, sobre todo por su potencial de impactar la currícula escolar y universitaria. Los volúmenes aparecen en formato grande, elegante y cuidadosamente diagramados y en muchos casos acompañados de prólogos y/o separatas que ofrecen una introducción general a la obra antologada. A esto, se suman las notas de Marco Antonio Rodríguez (Presidente de la Casa de la Cultura Benjamín Carrión) que aparecen en la contratapa de los volúmenes y que contribuyen al entendimiento del proyecto Poesía Junta. Los números que aquí se reseñan corresponden a la obra de Francisco Granizo (Quito, 1925–2009), con lo qual se inicia la colección Poesía Junta, Filoteo Samaniego Salazar (Quito, 1928) (ver item **2825**), Manuel Zabala Ruiz (Riobamba, 1928) (ver item **2853**), Carlos Eduardo Jaramillo (Loja, 1932) (ver item **2758**), Violeta Luna (Guayaquil, 1943) (ver item **2772**), y Julio Pazos (Baños de Agua Santa, 1944) (ver item **2797**). La obra de Granizo (ya considerada esencial para el entendimiento de la poesía ecuatoriana del siglo XX) se presenta con un Prólogo de María Gabriela Borja seguido por cuatro poemarios de este poeta: "Nada más el verbo" (1969), "Muerte y caza de la madre" (1978), "El sonido de tus pasos" y "Fedro: Drama en seis escenas de un acto", que se publican por primera vez. [EM]

2746 Guevara, Pablo. Hospital. Lima: Editorial San Marcos, 2006. 53 p.

Guevara probes his own transience in these moving poetic-prose pieces, begun in a hospital bed in early September 2006 and finished at home later that month. Published one month after the respected poet's death, Guevara's final poems poignantly contemplate sickness, life, and death. [LB]

2747 Guillén, Paul. La transformación de los metales. Lima: Trpode Editores, 2005. 84 p.

Guillén's hermetic free verse contemplates an eternal cycle in which humanity, struggling to make sense of the world, vertiginously heads toward death, the only certainty. The title image of alchemy fits a poetic quest that fuses ontological, spiritual, scientific, and artistic questions. Conspicuous, diverse epigraphs attest to the rich array of traditions feeding Guillen's sophisticated voice. [LB]

2748 Guinea Diez, Gerardo. Casa de nosotros. Ciudad de Guatemala: Letra Negra, 2009. 63 p.: ill. (Poesía centroamericana; 38)

Composición lírico-narrativa que desarrolla una historia de amor con profundidad sicológica, expresividad y musicalidad moderna afín al jazz (blues). Sugiere nuevos caminos para la lírica centroamericana. [JDW]

2749 Hahn, Óscar. En un abrir y cerrar de ojos. Madrid: Visor Libros, 2006. 48 p. (Col. Visor de poesía; 619)

Libro ganador del sexto premio Casa América de poesía americana. Con un lenguaje preciso, el poeta regresa a sus continuas obsesiones—amor, muerte, presencias fantasmales, fusión de épocas, religión—y elabora su rechazo del poder abusivo, la explotación y la esclavitud. [OS]

2750 Hernández, Elvira. Síndrome de Osiris. Santiago: Libros de Mentira: Consejo Nacional de la Lectura y las Artes, 2009. 24 p.

Poemas de lenguaje reconcentrado que reflexionan sobre partes del cuerpo de una manera reflexiva y sutil, sin fáciles concesiones emocionales, y en que el sujeto genérico no es evidente. [OS]

2751 Hinostroza, Rodolfo. Poesía completa. Edición de Fernando de Diego Pérez. Madrid: Visor Libros, 2007. 263 p. (Col. Visor de poesía; 658)

This gathering of Hinostroza's complete poetry, succinctly contextualized in the editor's introduction, accentuates the diversity of structure and content—a challenge to literary and social categories—within and between this exceptional writer's three collections. Case in point: though situating him within the "generación del 60," the innovative works of *Contra natura* (1971) resist repressive taxonomies, while the introspective genealogy of *Memorial de Casa Grande* (2005) personalizes Peruvian history. [LB]

2752 Ibargoyen Islas, Saúl. Poemar. México: Biblioteca Universitaria, Programa Editorial, Univ. de Guanajuato, 2007. 84 p. (Ex libris; 9. Poesía)

El poeta, quien es de Montevideo, ha escrito un poemario activo y vital, en el cual el verbo tiene un papel central (como se ve en el título del poemario). Cada poema también se intitula con un verbo, y se organiza de manera alfabética. Los poemas se escriben de una estrofa, o de muchos versos o de unos pocos, mientras la temática es una mezcla de temas cotidianos y existencialistas. [JSK]

2753 Illescas, Carlos. La rosa bien temperada: póesia escogida (1958–1999). Guatemala: Magna Terra editores, 2006. 126 p.: bibl.

Los compiladores entresacan poemas de 11 libros de este miembro del grupo literario guatemalteco Acento (1940), quien cultivó en su exilio mexicano una obra de especial rigor estético, vinculable a la tradición hispánica clásica. Algunos poemas, como "Memoria del espejo", se parangonan con los más excelsos del corpus hispanoamericano. [JDW]

2754 Izaguirre, Ester de. Morir lo imprescindible: obra poética. Buenos Aires: Vinciguerra, 2006. 273 p.: ill. (Col. Metáfora)

El título de esta colección viene de un poemario de la polaca Wislawa Szymborska cuyo título se traduce como Podría haber. Este crea una atmósfera nostálgica para esta selección de poesía de 1960 a 1992. Sus poemas se centran en la oposición entre la vida y la muerte, porque vivir implica tener voz, hablar, escribir, mientras morir es silenciarse, porque después de morir uno no puede leer ni escribir la poesía. [JSK]

2755 Jager, Jan de. Casa de cambio: traducciones y afines. Buenos Aires: Nuevohacer, Grupo Editor Latinoamericano, 2004–2007. 3 v. (Col. Escritura de hoy)

"Cambio" es la palabra clave para esta poesía multilingüe, visual, y sonora. Además de sus propias experimentaciones con las lenguas, De Jager nos ofrece "trancelations" de Néstor Perlongher, John Donne y Cole Porter—una gama de escritores que nos hacen escuchar/ver las diferencias y coincidencias linguísticas. [JSK]

2756 Jaimes, Héctor. (Dis)pensares. Caracas: El Perro y la Rana, 2009. 1 v.

En 13 poemas, Jaimes presenta una nueva poética que gira en torno a sensaciones y sentimientos profundos, desde el amor y la memoria, donde el lenguaje sirve resueltamente como un instrumento de experimentación. La escritora Rosa Elena Pérez Mendoza ha señalado que el libro "se nos representa como un canto liberado de viejas ataduras, áridos formalismos o axiomas y, por tanto, más próximo al sentir, a la sensación, siempre flanqueada por lo meditativo, pero jamás arrollada por la meditación, ya que podríamos decir que en este caso la reflexión propicia y potencia un mundo sensitivo que termina imponiéndose". [HJ]

2757 Jara Jiménez, Cronwell. Manifiesto del ocio. Lima: Editorial San Marcos, 2006. 220 p.: ill.

The title of this sizeable collection encapsulates its celebration of the creative and spiritual fruits that leisure—characterized in Ricardo González Vigil's prologue as freedom from mundane social contracts—affords. Combining strokes of Andean cosmology, Eastern and Western mysticism and philosophy, and a wide array of literary influences (conceptismo stands out), Jara promotes anti-dogmatism through his verse. [LB]

2758 Jaramillo, Carlos Eduardo. Carlos Eduardo Jaramillo. Quito: Casa de la Cultura Ecuatoriana Benjamín Carrión, 2006. 426 p. (Poesía junta; 6)

El volumen se abre con un Prólogo de Rafael Díaz Ycaza y antologa prácticamente toda la extensa obra de Jaramillo: Maneras de vivir y de morir (1965), La trampa (1964), La noche y los vencidos (1967), El hombre que quemó sus brújulas (1966), Las desvelaciones del Jacob (1970), Una vez la felicidad (1972), Crónica de la casa, los árboles y el río (1973), Viaje al planeta Eurídice (1973), Perseo ante el espejo (1974), La edad de fuego (1977), Tralfamadore (1977), Nefertiti la bella ha venido (1980), Blues de la calle Loja (1991), Canciones levemente sadomasoquistas (2000) y una breve selección de poemas sueltos. [EM]

2759 Kozer, José. En feldafing las cornejas. México: Editorial Aldus: Univ. del Claustro de Sor Juana, 2007. 140 p. (Poesía. Col. El Caracol de Poesía)

Escritos tras una breve estancia en el sur de Münhen, "EN LOS BOSQUES DE FELDAFING UNA NINFA RECIÉN SALIDA DEL LAGO STARNBERG." En los más de 50 frondosos poemas del libro—ninguno más corto que "Silogismo": "EL AGUA ES ARROGANTE./El pez aligera sus heces en el agua./Agua donde el pez ensucia se va de bruces a los pantanos."—, la intuición deviene en contemplación minuciosa y poética del mundo: "el agua que me llega a la cintura/me recubre de yedra (lianas) somos (en última instancia) sombras; me asperjan: primeras raíces adventicias (aéreas) habré afincado/demasiado las pezuñas". En ocasiones, más allá de "la acostumbrada oscuridad" de este poeta cubano del exilio, la escritura se hace clara, rasgos de una "objetividad emocional" que agiliza la lectura. [FC]

2760 La Torre Lagares, Elidio. Vicios de construcción. San Juan: Terranova Editores, 2008. 78 p.: ill.

Poemario dividido en tres partes, en las que, como malos hábitos—sí, la muerte protagónica con la que empieza y termina el libro—, se agrupan los poemas: "Vicios estructurales," "Vicios funcionales" y "Vicios de terminación". Propuesta del poeta puertorriqueño, también novelista, de abordar con dignidad literaria—una cita de Paul Auster al principio y una de Whitman al final—el doble sentido. Por un lado, el vicio de fabricación edilicia y por el otro el lingüístico-literario, como en el poema homónimo, en el que se trenza la mala arquitectura, el recuerdo de la familia rota (o con goteras)—el abandono del padre, la muerte de la abuela, el recuerdo doloroso del pasado—y la necesidad edificante, a pesar de las errancias, de la palabra. [FC]

2761 Lamborghini, Leónidas C. Antología poética. Buenos Aires: Fondo Nacional de las Artes: Cultura Nación, Secretaría de Cultura, Presidencia de la Nación, 2006. 144 p. (Poetas argentinos contemporáneos; 36)

Incluye obras desde "El solicitante descolocado" hasta "La risa canalla" (1955–71), con una introducción por Noe Jitrik que comenta el fraccionamiento de las frases y la desarticulación de palabras como representativos de la áspera vida social en la poesía de Lamborghini. [JSK]

2762 Lamborghini, Leónidas C. Encontrados en la basura: poemas. Buenos Aires: Paradiso, 2006. 88 p. (Paradiso poesía)

En este poemario Lamborghini dialoga con la literatura en varios niveles; personajes y autores como Francesca y Paolo, Dante, Quevedo y Lewis Carroll aparecen. Se encuentran también secciones tan diversas como el "Cancionero del pillo" hasta "Quarks". [JSK]

2763 Lamborghini, Leónidas C. El jugador, el juego. Buenos Aires: Adriana Hidalgo Editora, 2007. 109 p. (La lengua. Poesía)

Serie de poemas basada en el ajedrez con 12 partes poetizando el juego. Se presencia un salto a una sección barroca, con

referencias a o reescrituras de Quevedo, Fray Luis, San Juan, Góngora que pueden parecer desconectadas, pero al final se descubre de que todo nos remite al juego, la invención y reiteración de la poesía. [JSK]

2764 Lamborghini, Leónidas C. El solicitante descolocado. Buenos Aires: Paradiso, 2008. 159 p. (Paradiso poesía)

Publicado por primera vez en 1955, este libro elabora una parodia de Martín Fierro por medio de un género que Lamborghini nombra el "gauchesco urbano". Ciertos poemas desarrollan una payada entre el solicitante descolocado y el saboteador arrepentido para provocar la risa crítica, mientras otros poemas dialogan con la situación política y la historia argentina. [JSK]

2765 Lara, Omar. Papeles de Harek Ayun. Madrid: Visor Libros, 2007. 56 p. (Col. Visor de poesía; 661)

En este libro, que recibió el Séptimo premio Casa América de Poesía Americana, Lara hace memoria de relaciones amorosas que lo obsesionan aún en su exilio y también critica el país en democracia por lo que el poeta entiende como un olvido aberrante de las aspiraciones de justicia de los perseguidos políticos bajo dictadura. [OS]

2766 Lavín Cerda, Hernán. La sublime comedia. México: Editorial Praxis, 2006. 198 p.

El libro oscila entre la prosa poética y el verso libre y se despliega como una meditación fervorosa sobre lo erótico, las voces de otros poetas, las encrucijadas de la existencia. Dos espacios cruciales: Chile y México. "Escribimos en una lengua moribunda/pero resucitamos a cada instante". [OS]

2767 Letras del Ecuador 100: poesía: selección de poesía de la revista Letras del Ecuador, 1945–1954. Quito: Casa de la Cultura Ecuatoriana Benjamín Carrión, 2007. 597 p.

Este volumen reúne la poesía de poetas ecuatorianos que publicaron en los primeros 100 números de la revista Letras del Ecuador, órgano de la Casa de la Cultura Ecuatoriana que Benjamín Carrión fundó en 1944. Entre los poetas publicados figuran Pedro Jorge Vera, César Dávila Andrade, Luis Yépez Calisto, Adalberto Ortiz, Jorge Guerrero, Gonzalo Escudero, Alejandro Carrión y Mirtha Gandolfo—la única figura femenina. Cronológicamente, las publicaciones van de 1945–1954. [EM]

2768 Llinás, Julio. De las aves que vuelan: antología personal. Buenos Aires: Editorial Argonauta, 2008. 150 p.: ill., index. (Biblioteca de poesía; 12)

Con un lenguaje poético preciso y algunos rastros del surrealismo, Llinás considera la vida y la memoria a través de experiencias personales y comunes a muchos de sus lectores. [JSK]

2769 López-Coño, Dagoberto. Cantos de ámbar = Songs of amber. Santo Domingo: Secretaría de Estado de Cultura, Editora Nacional, 2007. 131 p.: ill. (Col. Ultramar)

Dividido en cuatro partes porosas que tejen una historia poética (y bilingüe) del ámbar, "Fosilizado el ámbar ya no muere/ni en la luz ni en la calma de los tiempos", surgen los personajes, como el trabajador, "Cómo duele el dolor que se eterniza/gravitando en la sangre del minero", y la pitonisa, María Piringo ("espíritu del ámbar y la lluvia"), "la risa y el afán del ámbar", cuyos presagios, si no los escuchamos, "moriremos fosilizados bajo la piel del ámbar", según Diógenes Abreu en la presentación, "Fósiles de la memoria". [FC]

2770 López Velarde, Ramón. Poesía y poética. Selección, prólogo, bibliografía y cronología de Guillermo Sheridan. Caracas: Fundación Biblioteca Ayacucho, 2006. 342 p. (Biblioteca Ayacucho; 235)

López Velarde (1888–1921) es uno de los poetas más venerados en México y sin embargo no ha alcanzado la misma distinción en el extranjero. Este volumen recoge su poesía completa y una selección de sus ensayos sobre poesía y arte. Cuenta con un prólogo extenso de Sheridan y con una cronología. Seguramente esta edición ayudará a difundir a uno de los mejores poetas mexicanos del siglo XX. [JS]

2771 Lorenzano, Sandra. Vestigios. Valencia, Spain: Pre-Textos, 2010. 53 p. (Pre-textos. Poesía; 1056)

En este primer libro de poemas de Lorenzano (Buenos Aires, 1960, residente en México; argen-mex, como a ella le gusta autodefinirse), los versos aluden a historias incompletas, inconexas, dichas al sesgo; dejan a los lectores atónitos, con muchas incógnitas (sin duda vinculados a la época de la dictadura en Argentina). Pero los silencios son también respuestas; no se necesita decir más para comprender el dolor, el trauma, las posibles torturas por las que pasaron los seres: "La piel que cubre las clavículas, lastimada, dolorida, sangrante . . ." (6). *Vestigios* es también el punto de encuentro en que el amor aparece en medio del naufragio. [JS]

2772 Luna, Violeta. Violeta Luna. Quito: Casa de la Cultura Ecuatoriana Benjamín Carrión, 2005. 451 p. (Poesía junta; 7)

Un prólogo/estudio de Xavier Oquendo Troncoso abre este volumen que antóloga *in extenso* gran parte de la obra poética de Luna: *Con el sol me cubro* (1967), *Posiblemente el aire* (1970), *Ayer me llamaba primavera* (1973), *La sortija de la lluvia* (1980), *Corazón acróbata* (1984), *Memoria del humo* (1987), *Las puertas de la hierba* (1994), *Una sola vez la vida* (2000) y *La oculta candela*, que se publica por primera vez. [EM]

2773 Martí Brenes, Carlos. Rara Avis. San Juan: Isla Negra Editores, 2006. 106 p. (Col. Filo de juego)

Poeta cubano cuya poesía, en 1975 con *El hombre que somos*, y en 1996, con *Te llamaré Logor*, ha sido galardonada en Cuba. Poemario dividido en tres partes, "La ronda" ("Soy/La presa que el ser de barro/Espera en sus lamentaciones"), "El golpe" ("Me resisto a ser el cuerpo efímero y delirante/de la aves más bien solemnes que rondan/los páramos") y "La fuga" ("el poeta gira su cuello sobre el universo y escucha/nuevamente . . . como si la ceniza de su estirpe se fugara en la manos frágiles del tiempo.") Poemario cuyo "estudio insondable del alma y el cuerpo . . . convoca a todas las aves raras que conforman la literatura, o sea, el estudio de la vida", según Alinaluz Santiago Torres. [FC]

2774 Mattoni, Silvio. La división del día. Buenos Aires: Mansalva, 2008. 139 p. (Poesía y ficción latinoamericana; 20)

Este poeta de Córdoba muestra su trayectoria con esta colección que incluye temas históricos, clásicos, e historia familiar en poemas a veces dramáticas, narrativos y líricos. Su estilo es conversacional y crea personajes y voces distintas en su obra. [JSK]

2775 Mileo, Eduardo. Poemas del sin trabajo. Buenos Aires: Ediciones en Danza, 2007. 102 p. (Ediciones en Danza)

Claramente poesía social, Mileo escribe poemas situacionales, éticos, que salen de las circunstancias económicas del trabajador argentino en los últimos años. Hay, por ejemplo, una sección en la que sueña el hablante con un plomero, electricista, pintor, músico, poeta, entre otros oficios. [JSK]

2776 Millán, Gonzalo. Autorretrato de memoria. Santiago, Chile: Ediciones Univ. Diego Portales, 2005. 44 p. (Col. Poesia)

Una pormenorizada acumulación de detalles le permite al poeta escribir un recuento autobiográfico donde su aguda perspectiva, desdramatizada, surge siempre entrelazada a cada circunstancia, espacio y dilema vivido. [OS]

2777 Mir, Pedro. Hay un país en el mundo: si alguien quiere saber cuál es mi patria: poemas. Presentación de Julio César Valentín. Ilustraciones de Guillo Pérez. Santo Domingo: s.n., 2007. 116 p.: ill.

Como homenaje al poeta nacional dominicano, muerto en el año 2000 a los 87 años, surge esta edición ilustrada por Guillo Pérez, agenciada por la Cámara de Diputados de la República Dominicana, como reconocimiento "para toda la vida" a la palabra encarnada de un hombre que en su memorable poema "Hay un país en el mundo", publicado por primera vez en el año 1954, "refundaba la Patria con el corazón de sus versos", como explica Julio Valentín. [FC]

2778 Mitre, Eduardo. Vitrales de la memoria. Valencia, Spain: Editorial Pre-Textos, 2007. 84 p. (Col. La Cruz del Sur; 859)

Eduardo Mitre (Oruro, 1943) es sin duda uno de los poetas más destacados de la literatura boliviana actual y un crítico literario que ha contribuido notablemente al estudio de la producción poética de su país. Con este nuevo poemario Mitre se interna en los laberintos de la memoria, permitiendo que el recuerdo poetizado del pasado (re)constituya el presente del hablante. A manera de vitrales que permiten *ver* y *re-visar* el pasado desde las ansiedades y experiencias del presente, los poemas de este libro desatan la memoria en todas las

direcciones: el Altiplano boliviano, Cochabamba, Tarija, Manhattan, la infancia, Bruselas, personajes públicos y privados, son convocados con la secreta esperanza de hacerles saber que "nunca se quedaron atrás", que sin ellos sería imposible "trazar la travesía de uno hacia sí mismo". En este sentido *Vitrales de la memoria* es probablemente el libro más personal de Mitre y uno que el lector encontrará simplemente irresistible. [EM]

2779 Moisés, Juan Carlos. Museo de varias artes. Viedma, Río Negro, Argentina: El Camarote Ediciones, 2006. 69 p. (Biblioteca patagónica. Poesía)

Moisés abre su colección con una guía para "visitantes" a su museo, avisándonos al final que podemos llevar un papel entre los objetos que observamos. El texto que sigue consta de tres poemas que son "árboles": un albaricoquero, un manzano, y un circuelo. El hablante enfatiza los cambios constantes en la naturaleza para crear un lazo entre la manera en que el lector se acerca a los textos, u objetos en el museo. Hay una serie de ensayos al final por tres otros autores que comentan el cambio constante de estos árboles. [JSK]

2780 Montealegre, Jorge. Ecran: Los ojos de Buster Keaton. Santiago: Libros de Mentira: Consejo Nacional de la Lectura y las Artes, 2009. 44 p.

La figura de Buster Keaton le sirve a Montealegre para jugar con la idea del poeta como mimo y acróbata que se desliza por la cuerda floja de la pantalla en blanco y negro siempre al tanto de los riesgos que toma, de la muerte que lo divisa y lo espera. Incluye diversas fotografías de Keaton. [OS]

2781 Montealegre, Jorge. No se puede evitar la caída del cabello. Santiago: Ediciones Asterión, 2007. 75 p. (Col. Geomundos)

Textos epigramáticos que con agudo humor vislumbran el proceso de envejecimiento del sujeto, la permanencia del juego erótico en la relación de pareja y la presencia persistente de la muerte. Este libro recibió el premio Altazor 2008. [OS]

2782 Montenegro, Silvia. Los príncipes oscuros. Buenos Aires: Ediciones Último Reino, 2008. 67 p.

Otro diálogo poético entre la figura clásica del príncipe azul y una voz poética femenina y contemporánea. Se trata abiertamente el desencanto que llega a la hora de entender que los cuentos de hadas no son realistas; pero de una manera novedosa—al dar voz al príncipe, el poemario explora cómo la presencia masculina (y no solamente la femenina) se ve afectada por las fábulas y por las expectativas infantiles utópicas. [JSK]

2783 Morales, Gary. La jornada poética del Haijin. San Juan: Terranova Editores, 2007. 94 p.

Tributo a la tradición japonesa, desde una caribeñidad puertorriqueñizada: "en el caribe/se considera perla/la borinquen". Por ello, "el coquí canta/sobre la gran montaña/despertó eco." La mayoría de los temas abordados—20 en total—persiguen la universalidad propia del haiku, que con poco apalabra el mundo: "¿cómo es la vida?/con onza de placer/libra el dolor". [FC]

2784 Moreno Heredia, Eugenio. Eugenio Moreno Heredia. Quito: CCE Benjamín Carrión, 2005. 306 p.: ill. (Memoria de vida; 4)

Este volumen cuenta con un breve Prólogo de Susana Cordero de Espinosa, un extenso estudio lingüístico literario de Sonia Moreno O. y una serie de ilustraciones de Oswaldo Moreno Heredia. Los poemarios antologados son: *Caravana de la noche* (1948), *Clamor del polvo herido* (1949), *La voz del hombre* (1950), *Poemas de la paz* (1953), *Baltra* (1960), *Poemas para niños* (1964), *Ecuador, padre nuestro* (1968), *Sólo el hombre* (1972), *Antología* (1974), *Trilogía de la patria* (1978), *A tiempo de salvarnos* (1981), *Poesía* (s/f), *Gallito de Barro* (1981), *Presente vivo* (s/f) y un conjunto de poemas inéditos. También se reseñan el volumen Paco Tobar García (1926–97) (ver item **2840**). [EM]

2785 Morrison, Mateo. Espasmos en la noche. Santo Domingo: Publicaciones de la Univ. Autónoma de Santo Domingo, 2007. 92 p. (Col. Literatura y sociedad; 83)

Ganador del Premio Nacional de Literatura de la República Dominicana, 2010; poeta, ensayista y gestor cultural desde la década de 1960, para quien la poesía, en vez de transformar el mundo, sólo puede aspirar a mejorarlo: "Un imán en la sombra/me hace perder el equilibrio." En este poemario breve, de versos cortos, de reflexión filosófica matizada por la cercanía de la cotidianidad, de hondo agradecimiento maternal, la voz poética, "un combatiente/del recuerdo", reincide en uno de sus temas emblemáticos (el amor): "Por ejemplo acariciar/las formas vegetales de mi mujer,/ múltiples verduras su cuerpo,/signos eróticos por toda la cocina". [FC]

2786 Moscona, Myriam. De par en par. México: Instituto Mexiquense de Cultura; Metepec, Mexico: Bonobos, 2009. 1 v. (unpaged): ill. (Bonobos poesía) (Col. Reino de nadie)

En "Negro marfil", Moscona (México, 1955) hacía acompañar sus textos por imágenes de lo que parecen graffitis en paredes carcomidas. También incursionó propiamente en la poesía visual, con un librito donde coloca los nombres de poetas mexicanos conformando con ellos el mapa de México; o escribiendo (literalmente tejiendo) en una tela el poema "ver verde". En este bello libro Moscona recurre a la poesía que se refleja: simetrías y asimetrías de los contrastes. El libro está hecho para que se abra como una ventana o una puerta, volteando las páginas hacia la izquierda y la derecha, haciendo de la línea de en medio el filo del espejo que remite a un lado y al otro sus encuentros y desencuentros. [JS]

2787 Moya, Pastor de. Jardines de la lengua. San Juan: Isla Negra Editores, 2009. 93 p. (Col. El canon secuestrado)

Considerado como "la voz poética más atrevida de la reciente poesía dominicana" (Eugenio García Cuevas), "columnas luminosas escritas de pájaros", fundador de una "poética de la locura" (Fernando Valerio-Holguín), los poemas de este breve poemario tripartita (*El humo de los espejos*, 1985; *El alfabeto de la noche*, 1995; *Jardines de la lengua*, 2002) se mueven en su propia gravedad: "abre los tentáculos del vientre/ muérdeme duro hasta abrirme/recuerda al hombre que es porcelana solamente." Toda una segunda naturaleza, "aquí están las bocas/verticales y ceñidas hacia el árbol/dos lagartos muertos sobre los pezones/de la niña dormida", reclamando la autonomía de la página, "viene LEZAMA montando/un caballo hirviente y blanco/que huye de lo blanco", sin jamás saturar el vacío: "aquí es donde se derrama el párpado/para que los fetiches inventen la noche". [FC]

2788 Mujica, Wilfredo. Antología. Madrid: Ediciones Lord Byron, 2007. 100 p. (Col. Prometeo desencadenado)

Leo Zelada's prologue locates Mujica's poetry within the tradition of socially engaged (but undogmatic) poetry. Melancholic undertones are balanced by optimism in varyingly personal, testimonial, minimalist, and complex free verse exploring childhood, exile, desire, poetry, and human rights. [LB]

2789 Navarro, Eliana. Angelus de mediodía. Santiago: Editorial Universitaria, 2007. 398 p.: bibl., ill. (Col. El poliedro y el mar)

Se incluye los poemas publicados desde 1951 a 1995 por la poeta, además de dos cuentos y ensayos, una sección iconográfica con fotos de distintos momentos de la vida de la escritora, cronografía, bibliografía, y tres estudios sobre su poesía. En uno de ellos Pedro Lastra señala: "Me atrae la singular tonalidad de esta poesía, sustentada en una visión serena del mundo y del tiempo, y cuyas expresiones más intensas se dan en la confrontación, igualmente serena, de la vida y la muerte". [OS]

2790 Nogueras, Luis Rogelio. Hay muchos modos de jugar: antología poética. Edición de Jesús García Sánchez. Madrid: Visor Libros, 2007. 183 p. (Visor de poesía; 652)

Nogueras fue uno de los poetas importantes que surgieron con la Cuba revolucionaria, ganador de varios premios nacionales, como el de Casa de las Américas en 1981. La antología incluye una muestra de los siete poemarios importantes del poeta, en cuya poesía, según García Sánchez, "sobresale la defensa de la imaginación con humor y con sarcasmo, la acertada fusión de lo culto con lo popular, el empleo de la ironía contra la vulgaridad y el desprecio a los dogmatismos." El libro termina con una entrevista que le hiciera Wilfredo Catá, "Zen: la verdad es concreta". [FC]

2791 Olcese, Angélica. La mano que escribe: poesía, 1996–2006. Córdoba, Argentina: Ediciones del Copista, 2007. 150 p. (Col. Fénix; 42)

La preocupación por el reflejo de sí misma lleva a la poeta a escrutarse no como un sujeto simplemente narcisista sino como un ojo que da cuenta de su propia irrealidad, así como la irrealidad de los otros a los que observa a partir de la lucidez del luto. [OS]

2792 Ortiz, Juan L. El Gualeguay. Rosario, Argentina: B. Viterbo Editora, 2004. 287 p.: bibl. (Ficciones; 55)

Con estudio y notas de Sergio Delgado, este es el poema más extenso y mayor concebido de la obra de Ortiz. Es un poema autobiográfico en el sentido personal y nacional, el cual emplea el río como tema contando la historia vista desde la perspectiva fluvial. El río también es una fuerza latente en la poesía. Es la primera vez que aparece el poema como libro aparte. El estudio y notas al final son muy útiles. [JSK]

2793 Ortiz Sánchez, Jorge. Autorretrato acodado. La Paz: Plural, 2006. 197 p.

Desde su mismo título, este libro es un reto a la lectura y a la paciencia. Premeditadamente extraño, alejado de toda convención, autónomo hasta la desesperación, el libro de Ortiz Sánchez (Tarija, 1956) quiere y no quiere ser leído. Si bien sus geniales provocaciones (por ejemplo estar dedicado "a la ciudad de La Paz del Alma" o sostener que "el ascenso de los letrados no carga con el espíritu en expansión") invitan a la lectura, la densidad de su escritura (197 páginas, 90 poemas super-compactos e irreverentes, enumerados a la manera de Trilce, con números latinos) y una general acidez del lenguaje, agobian al más entusiasta. ¿Así se habrán sentido los lectores de textos vanguardistas a principios del siglo XX? La sola sospecha inclina a favor del poeta, y para aquéllos(as) que se animen a tomar el libro, vaya un guiño de complicidad: empiecen por el poema LXXII. [EM]

2794 Pacheco, José Emilio. Como la lluvia: poemas, 2001–2008. México: El Colegio Nacional: Ediciones Era, 2009. 205 p.

Consistentemente, Pacheco (Ciudad de México, 1939) hace entrega de sus poemas cada cuantos años. Este nuevo volumen se mantiene fiel a una voz que se consolidó desde 1969. Pacheco es el poeta de la cotidianeidad que observa con agudeza y pesimismo la transitoriedad y las novedades del momento. Pacheco vuelve, asimismo, en este volumen a los diferentes registros que se asocian con su estilo: poemas epigramáticos, breves, que en pocos versos emiten juicios críticos sobre innumerables asuntos;

homenajes a poetas de la tradición, en particular a los poetas del Siglo de Oro español y a los modernistas; o los textos reflexivos acerca de la enfermedad, la transitoriedad del tiempo y la muerte. [JS]

2795 Páez, Roxana. Madre ciruelo. Córdoba, Argentina: Alción Editora, 2007. 122 p.

Las transiciones de la vida—la maternidad, al nacimiento, la muerte—une esta colección que se basa en los diálogos entre una hija y una madre. Mientras el tema en sí no es novedoso, lo original de esta poeta joven es su creación de una atmósfera transicional y cambiante en cada poema. [JSK]

2796 Pastor, Mara. Alabalacera. Carolina, Puerto Rico: Terranova, 2006. 59 p.: ill.

Apalabrado de principio a fin, "Deambulando te quedas,/verso,/Aleatoria/caída de páginas funámbulas", el poemario de esta joven poeta no podía sino estructurarse en su propia plasticidad verbal. La primera parte se titula "Ala", la segunda, "Bala" y la tercera, "Cera". Metapoesía marcada con olor a mujer, "En esos momentos, sé que sobreviviré acribillada". Tráfico centrífugo y centrípeto en varias direcciones: "La bala puede ir en esta dirección/o da lo mismo si va en la otra". Fragmentos todavía calientes de deseo: "La mujer de cera se derrite en sí misma, en sus placeres". [FC]

2797 Pazos, Julio. Julio Pazos. Quito: Casa de la Cultura Ecuatoriana Benjamín Carrión, 2006. 530 p. (Poesía junta; 8)

Un extenso prólogo de Carlos Aulestia inaugura este volumen, estableciendo de entrada las coordenadas estéticas con que trabaja la poesía de Pazos. La antología que sigue reproduce, en 515 páginas, los textos completos de *La ciudad de las visiones* (1980, Premio Nacional de Literatura "Aurelio Espinosa Pólit"), *Levantamiento del país con textos libres* (1984, Premio "Casa de las Américas"), *Oficios* (1988), *Contienda entre la vida y la muerte o personajes volando en un lienzo* (1985) y *Mujeres* (1993, Premio Nacional de Poesía "Jorge Carrera Andrade"). Además, se antologan composiciones tomadas de otros libros. [EM]

2798 Pérez, Ricardo Alberto. Oral-B. La Habana: Letras Cubanas, 2007. 93 p.

Premio Poesía Nicolás Guillén, 2006. Tributo (de muchas maneras) a la boca. Un poemario minimalista, "Pasmar el instante sagrado/dejarlo tieso. Que entre/la piña/laqueada/hasta la médula", preñado de sorpresas poéticas, "José ha puesto su familia/en el poema . . . Kozer sabe, como Velásquez, de esas cosas"; metapoéticas, "El poema es un círculo/Una fuerza centrípeta"; absurdas, "termino pensando/que la única ficción/que poseo/es mi vejiga"; humorísticas, "Natalia cepillaba/y cantaba . . . y cuando el semen/también se había/acumulado/Oral-B, lo descubría". [FC]

2799 Pérez Martín, Norma. Poesía: selección, 1963–2003. Buenos Aires: Vinciguerra, 2004. 199 p.: ill. (Col. Metáfora)

Ya que no se pueden encontrar muchos de sus libros, este volumen nos da acceso a la poesía de Pérez Martín cuyos temas incluyen el vacío, el silencio, la melancolía, la memoria, y la muerte. El hablante poético incorpora imágenes de la vida diaria, de destinaciones turísticas, y de textos autóctonos. Mientras que la autora afirma que muchos de los textos se crearon "en tiempos de cenizas, martirios y crucifixiones individuales y sociales" todavía mantiene esperanza para el futuro. [JSK]

2800 Peyseré, Paula. Las afueras. Buenos Aires: Siesta, 2007. 61 p.: ill., maps.

Libro intrigante de una joven poeta argentina en el cual se combinan imágenes visuales con entradas y fechas de diario, para así, poetizar la vida y los objetos comunes y corrientes de la vida urbana. Abre con mapas y tarjetas postales y termina con poemas que notan el día y la hora de su composición para crear una crónica poética desde una perspectiva "más moderna que habita la pobreza". [JSK]

2801 Plascencia Ñol, León. Satori. México: Consejo Nacional para la Cultura y las Artes, 2009. 83 p. (Práctica mortal)

Este libro de Plascencia Ñol (Ameca, Jalisco, México, 1968) reúne tres poemas, escritos en circunstancias diferentes: "Pentimento" es un texto basado en las imágenes evocadas por una montaña roja en Seúl, Corea. "La cordillera" evoca los ojos de una adolescente en un atardecer en Bogotá, Colombia. Y "Satori" remite a la plenitud en una playa de la Costa Alegre de Jalisco. En los tres casos, se trata de epifanías, una poesía iluminada que hace de la fulguración su motivo principal. El autor además inserta versos de varias épocas y tradiciones, dándole un entramado intertextual a sus poemas, enriqueciendo así su dicción poética. [JS]

2802 Plaza, Ramón. Apuntes para un resumen de vida: obra poética inédita. Córdoba, Argentina: Alción Editora, 2005. 409 p.: bibl., ill.

En esta obra completa (1956–91) organizada por Plaza mismo antes de su muerte, vemos el compromiso social de su poesía, la cual incorpora imágenes de la vida diaria y yuxtapone lo colectivo y lo individual. [JSK]

2803 Polhamer, Eric. La hamaca interior. Santiago: Libros de Mentira: Consejo Nacional de la Lectura y las Artes, 2009. 1 v.

Con humor y soltura, el poeta da cuenta de un universo budista desde el cual es posible celebrar el instante y hacerlo desprender una mirada lúcida y lúdica de niño o adulto travieso. [OS]

2804 Pozzi, Edna. El libro de Juan: textos elegidos. Buenos Aires: Vinciguerra, 2004. 225 p. (Páginas universales)

Dice la poeta que el Juan del libro es quien desenterró el cuerpo de Teresa de Avila. También es Juan de la Cruz, Juan el discípulo y Juan Gris, "el Juan de mis primeros poemas". Incluye poesía, cuento, ensayo, fragmentos de novela, diario. Emplea un tono íntimo para desarrollar ciertos temas (como la madre en su "Serie de la madre militante") de manera clara, razonada, y no muy experimental, en términos de estilo. [JSK]

2805 Pulgar Vidal, Javier. Algo sobre el indio, o, El indio que yo conocí. Lima: Univ. Alas Peruanas, 2007. 300 p.: bibl., facsims, ill.

In this recently unearthed text, originally written for a college course in 1931, a young Pulgar Vidal (later a well-known geographer) voiced reflections on the oppression of indigenous Peruvians through verse. Interspersed with photos by Martín Chambi and others, the book's long, free-verse poems combine history, ethnography, and subjective analysis, offering a testament to indigenismo. [LB]

2806 Ramírez Mella, Edgar. Estación de lirio: máquina emotiva, 1974–1980, estación de lirio, 1997–2000. San Juan: Isla Negra Editores, 2006. 117 p. (Col. Josemilio González)

Dos poemarios (dos tiempos) en uno. El primero, de los años 70, empieza con una cotidianización de la muerte, "La muerte huele a costra vieja,/a ropa sucia y manzanas descompuestas". El segundo poemario, de los años 90, empieza con una soledad fría, "Las olas ladran a lo lejos,/ . . . un fluido frío, con la brisa y el agua,/ . . . Estoy solo, mirando los recuerdos de ciudades gigantes, . . . ahora, que el silencio me hace pensar . . ." Treinta años de poesía alineados en un libro que se deja tocar y leer en su nostalgia compartida: "Adentro, más adentro. Subir, subir con vértigo: caer,/caer al fondo del abismo de uno mismo . . ." De lo político en el primer poemario (aquellas muertes que cobró la emboscada en el Cerro Maravillas), "Ave mal, oscura e incierta,/pájaro fétido de Hades", al vidente del segundo poemario "que observa en cinemascope el thriller de aquéllas [ciudades], y su yo cosmogónico", según Letica Ruiz Rosado. [FC]

2807 Ramírez Santacruz, Gilberto. Obra poética. Asunción: Arandura editorial, 2006. 687 p.

Obra completa de este poeta paraguayo que escribe su poesía comprometida con una mezcla de rima consonante y verso libre. Un luchador por los derechos humanos, el poeta incorpora palabras en guaraní en su obra y su último poemario se escribió completamente en la lengua indígena. Además de temas como la justicia social, Ramírez Santacruz también trata temas universales, como el amor. [JSK]

2808 Rauskin, J.A. La rebelión demorada. Asunción: Arandura editorial, 2005. 109 p.

Último poemario del poeta paraguayo quien empezó a publicar en los años 70. En este libro se trata la poesía como un género enlazado a la naturaleza y los versos son "caminos" que nos llevan a "un arroyito, un puente, un aire fresco". El hablante también enfatiza los elementos orales de la poesía, empleando el verbo "cantar", imágenes de los pájaros cantando, la mano y la mejilla como productores de la lírica. [JSK]

2809 Rebollo-Gil, Guillermo. La carencia. Edición de Yara Liceaga. San Juan: Terranova Editores, 2008. 62 p.: ill.

En vez de la nada, 22 poemas hete-
róclitos que, "bienvenidos/a la carencia",
necesitan llenar el vacío de "artefactos/
que podrían atestiguar que hubo algo
vivo/coleando/aquí". Jugando en serio a una
escritura poética, "la ropa amontonada en el
piso/del baño/tiene más carácter que yo", sin
tener que inventarse un nombre propio, "el
erotismo depende del contacto íntimo/con
la muerte (Bataille)". La carencia, "acaricio
tu abdomen con el mismo gusto que me
provocaría/tocar la copia de una pintura
famosa", es lo que produce, "como en una
mala película" (cita de Frank O'Hara), la distancia apaciblemente—a veces surrealista—
metapoética: "es ficción, querida,/y mi
personaje es muy superficial". [FC]

2810 Rebollo-Gil, Guillermo. Teoría de
conspiración. San Juan: Isla Negra
Editores, 2005. 59 p. (Col. Filo de juego)

A fresh, self-reflexive collection of
poems where the poet consolidates his position as social, political, cultural, and poetic
commentator of contemporary society. His
provocative and performative style insists
on the need to take a closer look at the ways
of the contemporary world. These poems
show a mature poetic voice. [M. García
Calderón]

2811 Ríos-Cordero, Hugo. Al otro lado de
tus párpados. San Juan: Isla Negra Editores, 2006. 75 p. (Col. Josemilio González)

Aunque el presente, según este poeta
puertorriqueño, "podría aspirar a ser un
poemario o un libro de poemas . . . prefiere
que se le conozca como un catálogo . . ."
Una "enumeración" organizada en cuatro
partes. La primera, subterránea, sonámbula,
oscura, "me pregunto/desde lo más profundo
del sueño/(al que otros llaman vida)/¿qué
habrá/al otro lado de tus párpados?" La
segunda, evanescente, "siempre puede más
el silencio/que la palabra escrita". La tercera, religiosa, filosófica, "Revélame Señor,
tu inexistencia/o confunde mi sueño con la
espera". La cuarta, entrópica, "Entonces, me
di cuenta/que era yo el espejismo", titulada
"Casi poemas", regresa a la oscuridad origi-
naria, "Y si la poesía es himno/entonces,/no
es necesario aplaudir". [FC]

2812 Rodríguez, Augusto. Matar a la bestia, 2004–2007. Guadalajara, Mexico:
Gobierno de Jalisco, Secretaría de Cultura;

Tlaquepaque, Mexico: Mantis Editores,
2007. 85 p. (Col. Terredades)

En este poemario Augusto Rodríguez
(Guayaquil, 1979) reúne una selección de sus
anteriores libros (Mientras ella mata mosquitos, 2004; Animales salvajes, 2005; La
bestia que me habita, 2005, y Cantos contra
un dinosaurio ebrio, 2007) además de una
muestra de prosa poética perteneciente a un
manuscrito todavía no publicado: El beso de
los dementes. Definitivamente marcada por
la experiencia baudelairiana de la modernidad y por una poética del despojo que remite
a Vallejo, la poesía de Rodríguez interpela
sin piedad a su tiempo y al logos que lo construye. Denuncia que toda infancia ocurre en
medio de ciudades ultrajadas y dioses que
duermen, y que al sujeto, en medio de semejante desierto, sólo le queda seguir viviendo,
como vagabundo, "su quinta guerra mundial". Con acierto, alguna crítica ha perci-
bido en los poemas de Rodríguez "violencia
pura y hermosa", "poesía salvaje". [EM]

2813 Rodríguez, Reina María. Catch and
release. La Habana: Editorial Letras
Cubanas, 2006. 99 p. (Poesía)

Poeta más establecida en la literatura
cubana de la Revolución. Su poesía ha sido
ganadora de varios premios nacionales e
internacionales, como por ejemplo el de la
Revista Plural de México en 1991. En este
poemario, que, desde el título en inglés, nos
invita a su universo de dualidades, "En el
vientre de la ballena, en el mío,/una sensación de inmensidad vacía", el juego entre la
proximidad y la distancia, "Coger y dejar sin
que el anzuelo penetre", entre el pasado y el
presente, "Si hubiera tenido una nana/que
se llamara Ana", desconfía en la eventual
estabilización literaria: "Cómo creció hasta
esconderse/detrás de un oso rojo de peluche,
la vida". [FC]

2814 Rodríguez Castillo, Luis. El monstruo
de los cerros. Lima: Petroperú, Ediciones Copé: Departamento de Relaciones
Corporativas de Petroperú, 2007. 59 p.

In this third-place winner of the 2005
Copé poetry competition, the humanized
voice of a mythical serial killer (ironically
framed as a poet) alternates with those of
his victims, expressing—in deceptively
informal language—that which becomes
monstrous through marginalization and
legendary through writing. Much blank

space pointedly surrounds simultaneously lyric and unsettling portraits of alienation, desire, creation, and death. [LB]

2815 Rodríguez Francia, Ana María. Contemplación de la utopía. Buenos Aires: Corregidor, 2008. 93 p.: index.

Poemario dividido en tres secciones. Los poemas individuales no tienen títulos sino números, y en cada seis páginas del poemario se encuentra una hoja en blanco con el mismo fragmento escrito en letra cursiva: "descalza y por las calles continuo la incomprensible búsqueda". En la tercera y última parte la forma poética se convierte en algo mucho más estructurado, trabaja el soneto ("Sonetos de peregrinos") y adopta un tono más místico y religioso, con alusiones abiertas a San Juan de la Cruz. [JSK]

2816 Rojas Díaz, Wilder. Avenida amarilla. Lima: Media Communications, 2007. 212 p.: ill.

The poet describes his collection as six books in one, composed between 1986 and 2001. Among a variety of existential observations, these often succinct poems contrast the melancholy of displacement and alienation in the city with nostalgia-laden natural imagery. In the final segment, decidedly 21st century, urban references disrupt modernista imagery, yet nature retains hope. [LB]

2817 Rokha, Winétt de. Winétt De Rokha: el valle pierde su atmósfera: edición crítica de la obra poética. Prólogo, recopilación y notas de Javier Bello. Providencia, Santiago, Chile: Cuarto Propio, 2008. 626 p.: ill. (Serie Historia cultural)

Esencial contribución al rescate de la escritura de esta importantísima escritora. El libro reúne libros publicados desde 1915 a 1949 y algunos poemas publicados póstumamente en 1951. En su prólogo, Bello no sólo da cuenta del contexto cultural, poético e histórico de la producción de Winétt de Rokha: elabora una lectura obra por obra realizando sus logros y la complejidad de su situación como poeta mujer. Además de los poemas de Winétt de Rokha se incluye una selección de poemas que Pablo de Rokha escribió para ella, una serie de ensayos y testimonios de escritores coetáneos de la poeta, ensayos críticos de estudiosos recientes de su escritura, cartas inéditas, y una espléndido registro iconográfico. [OS]

2818 Romero, Alexis. La respuesta de los techos. Coordinación editorial de Carlos Pacheco. Prólogo de Arturo Gutiérrez Plaza. Caracas: Editorial Equinoccio: Univ. Simón Bolívar, 2008. 128 p. (Col. Papiros. Serie Poesía)

Los poemas están escritos con sabiduría literaria, pero también, con sabiduría de vida. Hay un tono filosófico y reflexivo a través del cual el poeta interroga imágenes, vivencias, y cotidianidades. No obstante, en los poemas no encontramos resoluciones, sino un permanente enigma desbordado de humanidad. [HJ]

2819 Rosenberg, Mirta. El árbol de palabras: obra reunida, 1984–2006. Buenos Aires: Bajo la Luna, 2006. 250 p. (Bajo La Luna Poesía)

Este libro une cuatro colecciones de Rosenberg y también incluye poemas sueltos, algunas traducciones y un apéndice desarrollado por Olvido García Valdés sobre su poesía. El ojo atento de la poeta examina objetos, emociones, temas íntimos con un ritmo regular que refleja unos de los poetas que traduce aquí (Sharon Olds, Stevie Smith, Elizabeth Bishop). [JSK]

2820 Rosenmann Taub, David. Auge. Ed. 2007. Santiago: LOM Ediciones, 2007. 264 p. (Entre mares poesia)

El lenguaje críptico de un oráculo que observa su propia vida le sirve al poeta para descubrir en lo religioso y en lo familiar una manera de celebrar lo inesperado, lo sorprendente, lo singular. [OS]

2821 Rosenmann Taub, David. Los despojos del sol: anandas primera y segunda. Santiago: LOM Ediciones, 2006. 127 p. (Col. Entre mares. Poesía)

Como un oráculo obsesionado con las maravillas de lo cotidiano, el poeta se concentra en una serie de revelaciones intensamente religiosas que sólo un lenguaje críptico, en juego, permite vislumbrar. [OS]

2822 Saavedra Villarroel, Oscar. Tecnopacha. Jesús María, Lima, Peru: Editorial Zignos, 2008. 106 p. (Poesía)

La realidad sudamericana escindida en múltiples versiones contradictorias promueve ampulosamente su excentricidad étnica, territorial, generacional, tecnológica y globalizada. [OS]

2823 Sáenz Andrade, Bruno. Máscara desnuda los trazos de mi cara. México: Colibrí, 2007. 170 p. (As de oros)

En este nuevo poemario Bruno Sáenz (Quito, 1944) ofrece un extenso conjunto de poemas en verso y en prosa agrupados en cinco unidades mayores cuyos títulos ("De vestigios y veladas voces", "La voz y su sombra", "Una línea de sombra en la punta del lápiz", "Vanidad de la escritura, vanidad del silencio", y "El espíritu desciende como ala, como lengua") son indicativos del tipo de poética que se propone, definitivamente centrada en torno a una búsqueda de *voz* para *escribir* y, así, para pasar activo por la vida. [EM]

2824 Salas, María Clara. 1606 y otros poemas. Caracas: ExLibris, 2008. 121 p.

El tono reflexivo y pausado predomina a lo largo del poemario compuesto de 121 breves poemas. Por un lado, encontramos una voz poética que devela presagios, y repetidas escenas naturales; muchas de ellas, en el medio oriente. Por otro lado, encontramos una memoria desdibujada y ahistórica, pues no se le da al lector ningún contexto preciso. En el poemario, no obstante, el lenguaje está muy bien trabajado. [HJ]

2825 Samaniego Salazar, Filoteo. Filoteo Samaniego Salazar. Quito: Casa de la Cultura Ecuatoriana Benjamín Carrión, 2006. 220 p. (Poesía junta; 4)

Este volumen se inicia con las palabras de Agradecimento del autor, seguidas por un Prólogo de Edmundo Ribadeneira. El volumen antologa poemas tomados de *Agraz* (1952–54), *Relente* (1955–57), *Umiña* (1961), *Signos* (1963), *Signos II* (1967), *La uña de Dios* (1996), *El cuerpo desnudo de la tierra* (1973), *Los niños sordos* (1973–76), *Oficios del río* (1983), *Ciudad en vilo* (2000), *Voces, ecos y silencios* (1993–2001) y *Los testimonios* (1992 y 2004). [EM]

2826 Sánchez, José Javier. Código postal 1010. Caracas: Monte Avila Editores Latinoamericana: Fundación Red Nacional de Escritores de Venezuela, 2010. 124 p. (Col. Altazor)

El título del poemario nos da una señal: el número de un código postal en la ciudad de Caracas. La poesía de Sánchez es esencialmente una poesía urbana; en este sentido, la ciudad nutre las metáforas, las imágenes, y las voces. De la misma manera, se trata de una poesía personal, pero no intimista, que colinda con lo social y el acto conciente de la memoria. Sánchez es un poeta contemporáneo que, con este libro, se establece en la vanguardia de la poesía venezolana. [HJ]

2827 Sánchez, José Javier. Fragmentos para una memoria. Caracas: Fundación El Perro y la Rana, 2007. 63 p. (Col. Poesía venezolana. Contemporáneos)

El libro está compuesto por poemas de temas autobiográficos, políticos, amorosos, y reconstructivos, a través de la memoria. En un tono conversacional, la voz poética logra establecerse entre un grueso cúmulo de imágenes y situaciones que se van describiendo críticamente; además, se logra crear un universo poético con vida propia. [HJ]

2828 Santiváñez, Roger. Labranda. Lima: Hipocampo Editores: Asalto al Cielo, 2008. 76 p.

A sense of movement and liminality flows through Santiváñez's Baroque lines, filled with water imagery (and sometimes correspondingly saturated with alliteration). Grouped into distinct yet mutually transitional spaces ("Hall"—subdivided into "Winter," "Spring," "Summer," and "Fall"—, "Once again," and "Homenaje a Ezra Pound," an ars poética that circles back to the speaker's native Piura), Santiváñez's lush poems weave memories of Peru and the Mid-Atlantic into an interior lyricism. [LB]

2829 Sarduy, Severo. Obras. Prólogo de Gustavo Guerrero. México: Fondo de Cultura Económica, 2007. (Tierra firme)

Invitación a (re)descubrir—con poemas que anteceden a los del primer poemario oficial, *Big Bang* (1974), hasta los que escribió en estado moribundo, posteriores a *Un testigo perenne y delatado* (1993)—la obra poética del cubano escritor de novelas, ensayos y obras de teatro, pues, según Guerrero, es casi seguro que lo mejor de Sarduy (1937–93) se encuentre en su poesía, "el género más característicamente neobarroco de su obra, aquel donde la mezcla de tiempos, temas y estilos encarnó en una forma única de leer el pasado y decir el presente . . ." [FC]

2830 Sicilia, Javier. Tríptico del desierto. México: Ediciones Biblioteca Era: Instituto Cultural de Aguascalientes: Instituto Nacional de Bellas Artes, Consejo Nacional para la Cultura y las Artes, 2009. 87 p. (Biblioteca Era)

Ganador del Premio Nacional de Poesía Aguascalientes 2009, este libro de Sicilia (México, 1956) se remite a un espacio espiritual, incluso se podría decir religioso (católico), en donde se exploran diálogos con escritores tocados por lo divino, desde la Biblia a Dante, a los místicos españoles, a autores contemporáneos como Gorostiza o T.S. Eliot. Se trata de una poesía que aspira a una unidad, la de Dios, trascendiendo el espacio terrenal y mundano de la carne. [JS]

2831 Sigüenza, Roy. Abrazadero y otros lugares: poesía reunida, 1990–2005. Edición y estudio introductorio de Cristóbal Zapata. Azuay, Ecuador: Último Round, 2006. 242 p.

Con este volumen, que reúne gran parte de la producción poética de Roy Sigüenza (Portovelo, 1958), la Casa de la Cultura del Azuay y la Universidad de Cuenca dan a conocer una poesía que de muchas maneras enriquece la tradición poética ecuatoriana posterior a las vanguardias. Destacan los poemas breves, intensos, de *Ocúpate de la noche*, poemario publicado el año 2000, en el que Sigüenza forja una de las propuestas mejor logradas de poesía homoerótica ecuatoriana. Acompaña al volumen un extenso estudio introductorio de Cristóbal Zapata. [EM]

2832 Silva, Antonio. Matria. Providencia, Santiago: Editorial Cuarto Propio, 2007. 92 p. (Col. Uvas de la ira. Poesía)

El deseo homosexual se presenta desde lugares marginados al silencio, a lo constreñido, a los espacios circunscritos de lo popular citadino. La palabra funciona como un encantamiento y como un quiebre del discurso homogéneo, como una celebración de la vitalidad y la diferencia. [OS]

2833 Silva Acevedo, Manuel. Campo de amarte. Santiago: Editorial Cuarto Propio, 2006. 68 p. (Col. Uvas de la ira. Poesía)

Del carácter contradictorio del deseo amoroso y la energía visionaria producto de la confrontación de los amantes anta-

gónicos, surge, al modo de un panegírico surrealista sutilmente calibrado, una figura visionaria de la mujer. [OS]

2834 Silva Acevedo, Manuel. Día quinto. Santiago: Universitaria, 2002. 54 p.

Adoptando una voz profética de dimensiones ecológicas, el poeta condena la extinción de parte de la fauna del territorio chileno como resultado de la intervención de intereses económicos de corto plazo y también celebra la existencia singular de ciertas especies animales. [OS]

2835 Silva Santisteban, Rocío. Las hijas del terror. Lima: Petroperú, 2007. 80 p.: ill.

In this second-place winner of the 2005 Copé poetry competition, the poet denounces the violence endured by female bodies during the recent civil war. Interspersed with photographs and drawing on testimonies exposed during the Peruvian Truth and Reconciliation Commission's hearings, these intense poems—most rendered in accessible yet metaphorically complex free verse—protest rape, torture, poverty, death, and indifference. [LB]

2836 Suárez, Ignacio. Casi tango: poemas rotos. Montevideo: Rumbo Editorial, 2007. 220 p.

Incluye poemas que fueron musicalizados y, como lo implica el título, expone un diálogo entre la música y la palabra. [JSK]

2837 Tapia Anaya, Vilma. La fiesta de mi boda. La Paz: Plural Editores, 2006. 65 p.

Este es el quinto poemario de Vilma Tapia Anaya (La Paz, 1960), y sin duda el que consolida su presencia en la poesía boliviana contemporánea. Breve, conciso y concluyentemente certero en su alcance, el verso de Vilma Tapia atrapa inmediatamente al lector(a). El poemario entero es el discurrir de una trapecista del destino que celebra, en un día de bodas, el hecho de que "todo está en su lugar/también el desconcierto/las omisiones/los desencuentros". Y sin embargo, en sus encuentros con sus semejantes (otras como ella), la trapecista reúne, en una misma entidad, lo que en ella hay de humano, de animal, y de naturaleza. Reunidos los reinos, constituida la comunidad, voraces, esperan "algunas visitaciones". Un comentario de Alba María Paz en la contratapa del libro ayuda (e invita) al lector a recorrer estos hermosos poemas. [EM]

2838 Tavárez Vales, Amarilis. Realid(h)ades. San Juan: Isla Negra Editores, 2006. 60 p. (Col. Josemilio González)

Cofundadora de la revista literaria *El sótano 00931*, "loca, única, imitadora, multirítmica", según Mairym Cruz-Bernall; joven poeta puertorriqueña de una frontalidad asombrosa: "Me presento desnuda de idealismo/de pesares, prejuicios y reglas;/me presento bañada de esperanza/anhelos, deseos de vivir". En la "Invitación al libro", Sonia Gaia la muestra sin ropa, al decir que la poeta "transmite en sus versos las mismas preocupaciones de la mujer puertorriqueña de varias décadas atrás" (vinculación a la tierra, conversación sobre lo erótico y diverso, autocrítica en lo social y en lo íntimo): "Estoy descubriéndome./Soplo los dados en esta apuesta/y los lanzo sobre la cama". [FC]

2839 Teillier, Jorge. El cielo cae con las hojas: El árbol de la memoria; Los trenes de la noche y otros poemas. Santiago: Tajamar Editores, 2004. 107 p.: bibl. (Col. Edición limitada)

Reimpresión de tres libros iniciales publicados en 1958, 1961, y 1964 respectivamente, con los cuales Tellier estableció una poética del lar como espacio en disolución y del poeta como personaje errante. El prólogo de Federico Schopf indaga en esta poética subrayando el descreimiento vital del poeta en sus etapas finales. [OS]

2840 Tobar García, Francisco. Paco Tobar García. Quito: Casa de la Cultura Ecuatoriana Benjamín Carrión, 2005. 343 p.: ill. (Memoria de vida; 2)

Paralela a la colección Poesía Junta, la Casa de la Cultura Ecuatoriana Benjamín Carrión inició, en el año 2005, la colección Memoria de Vida, dedicada a difundir la obra de poetas olvidados por el canon literario (pero no necesariamente marginales). También en formato grande y cuidadosamente presentados, los volúmenes de esta colección ofrecen prólogos introductorios y una antología de sus obras. Un Prólogo de Luis Carlos Mussó abre este volumen, en el que se antologa la obra poética de Tobar García escrita a partir de 1969. Tres son los poemarios

antologados: *Canon perpetuo* (1969), *Ebrio de eternidad* (Quito, 1991) y *La luz labrada* (Guayaquil, 1996). El volumen incluye también una breve selección de poesía inédita, reunida en la sección titulada Voces. También se reseñan el volumen Eugenio Moreno Heredia (1926–97) (ver item **2784**). [EM]

2841 Torres, Antonia. Inventario de equipaje. Santiago: Editorial Cuarto Propio, 2006. 85 p. (Col. Uvas de la ira. Poesía)

El mundo familiar, el del espacio habitado, el de la pareja y de la casa, el de la ciudad al sur, se ven traspasados por el asombro, la fuerte presencia de la muerte, la fragilidad de la palabra como sustento nutricio. La tercera sección da título al libro; las dos primeras corresponden a libros previos: "Las estaciones aéreas" es de 1999 y "Orillas de tránsito" de 2003. Este último libro recibió el primer premio del segundo concurso regional ministerial de literatura Luis Oyarzún. [OS]

2842 Uk'u'x kaj, uk'u'x ulew: antología de poesía maya quatemalteca contemporánea. Selección e introducción de Emilio del Valle Escalante. Pittsburgh, Pa.: Univ. de Pittsburgh, Instituto Internacional de Literatura Iberoamericana, 2010. 423 p.: bibl. (Série clásicos de América)

Valle Escalante, who is a young scholar specializing in Maya literature, published this work as part of the Clásicos de América series of the University of Pittsburgh Institute of Ibero-American International Literature. It includes poems by 15 poems by Guatemalan poets in both Maya and Spanish, featuring several linguistic Maya language groups or communities. An important contribution. [G.M. Dorn]

2843 Ulloa Donoso, Claudia. Séptima madrugada. Lima: Estruendo Mudo, 2007. 158 p. (Cuadernos esenciales; 18)

Culled from the author's blog and arranged here in nonsequential entries, the poems and poetic prose pieces of this hybrid text—much of it written during bouts of insomnia exacerbated by the author's residence in Norway—chronicle restlessness, loneliness, nostalgia (for Peru and beyond), love, and the search for identity. The charismatic, often intimate voice of "Madru" (Ulloa's alter ego) will likely resonate with a plugged-in generation of readers. [LB]

2844 Uribe, Armando. Idem. Talca, Chile: Ediciones Derrame: Editorial Univ. de Talca, 2008. 216 p. (Col. Corporativa. Serie de textos institucionales)

Con un lenguaje profano, medido y epigramático, Uribe desenmascara todo falso idealismo y despliega su estado anímico, a veces amargo, a veces sarcástico, como un modo legítimo de mantenerse alerta frente al transcurso rutinario de la existencia ciudadana. [OS]

2845 Vallejo, César. Los heraldos negros. Prólogo de Luis Jaime Cisneros V. Edición, estudio y notas de Ricardo González Vigil. Lima: Alfaguara, 2006. 166 p. (Serie roja)

Originally published in 1919, this seminal work bridged modernismo and the avant garde and announced one of the most innovative voices in modern poetry. González Vigil's essay and notes are illuminating and encouraging, making this new critical edition especially attractive for students. [LB]

2846 Vallejo, Osiris. Saint Domingue, 2044. Santo Domingo: Secretaría de Estado de Cultura, Editora Nacional, 2006. 85 p. (Col. Ultramar)

Poemario ganador del Premio Letras de Ultramar, 2005, convocado por el Comisionado Dominicano de Cultura en los Estados Unidos. Poesía de la diáspora—"Ya no naufragas en el mar como solías,/sino en pleno centro de tierra enemiga"—que, desde la distancia y el olvido—"¿Es que acaso también emigró tu fantasma . . ."—, asume, desdoblada la voz poética, los vacíos de "la memoria rota", cuya recuperación sólo es posible mediante la incorporación del "otro yo" expulsado de la identidad oficial dominicana: la presencia africana que, al incorporarla, requiere un arreglo de cuentas con lo haitiano, "¿Hallará nuestro ser su espejo enamorado?" El título del poemario, un retorno al antiguo nombre de Haití, apunta hacia un futuro de integración (2044). [FC]

2847 Varela, Blanca. La voz de Blanca Varela. Edición de Marín Rodríguez-Gaona. Madrid: Publicaciones de la Residencia de Estudiantes, 2006. 55 p.: bibl., ill. (Poesía en la Residencia; 10)

This book offers a transcription of a reading given by Varela at the Student Residence in Madrid in 1997. Including the poet's introductory comments to her selection of career-spanning works, editorial notes, a brief biography, and an audio CD, this book is rich in its inclusion of framing anecdotes and spoken versions of the texts. [LB]

2848 25 años Premio Nacional de Literatura Efraín Huerta: Tampico, 1982–2006. Compilación de Sara Uribe. Mexico: Gobierno Municipal de Tampico, Dirección de Educación y Cultura: Centro Historico Tampico: M.A. Porrúa, 2007. 539 p.: ill.

Recopilación de los libros ganadores del Premio Efraín Huerta en poesía y cuento que ha otorgado el gobierno de Tampico desde 1982. Este volumen está dedicado exclusivamente a los poetas. Salvo un par de escritores no incluidos, se recogen todos los libros premiados. Algunos de los poetas incluidos: Tedi López Mills, María Baranda, Claudia Hernández de Valle-Arizpe, Mónica Nepote y Jair Cortés. Incluye una introducción de Raquel Huerta-Nava, en que se explica la relación de Efraín Huerta con el estado de Tampico. [JS]

2849 Volonteri, Mónica. Máximo Gómez bajando: épica casi tragedia. San Juan: Isla Negra Editores, 2006. 59 p. (Col. Filo de juego)

Poesía—látigo de una narratividad poética: "un amor directamente proporcional/al dosage de hormonas/que me inflan las tetas"—de una argentina inscrita—y no sólo porque reside allá—en el tejido social, literario y lingüístico de una dominicanidad translocal: "releyendo a Rimbau/y/escupiendo a Junot Díaz". Cínicamente épica, "Quiero escribir un poema épico/porque me da la gana", y trágica (la tragedia de la madre, de la Patagonia, del sexo, del amor y del Caribe, con las que termina el poemario), "dos géneros—la épica y la tragedia—en decadencia rescatados entre la metáfora y la acción de una poeta que, a veces, preferiría no serlo", según Alinaluz Santiago, "Yo no soy poeta/ni lo quiero ser". [FC]

2850 Welden, Oliver. Oscura palabra: Poesía 1970–2006. Málaga, Spain: Taller Artesanal de Impresión y Encuadernación de María Eugenia Concha Sirandoni, 2009. 97 p.

Un testimonio escrito del itinerario histórico del socialismo, la dictadura, y el exilio chilenos encarnado en la vida del poeta y de su generación. [OS]

2851 Xirau, Ramón. Poesía completa. Traducción de Andrés Sánchez Robayna. Ed. bilingüe. México: Fondo de Cultura Económica, UNAM, 2007. 614 p. (Tierra firme)

Aunque nació en Barcelona (1924), Ramón Xirau ha residido en México desde 1939. Conocido sobre todo como ensayista, crítico literario y filósofo, también tiene una obra poética bastante amplia, como lo comprueba esta recopilación. A pesar de tantos años en México, Xirau escribe en su lengua materna, el catalán. Con cierta influencia de Octavio Paz, se trata de una poesía ceñida, crítica, que busca el conocimiento y la luminosidad. [JS]

2852 Y—, en las tardes la imaginación. Contribuciones de Beba Rodríguez Estenssoro *et al.* Cochabamba, Bolivia: s.n., 2006. 178 p.

Esta colección reúne trabajos poéticos y narrativos de cuatro escritoras bolivianas nacidas en Cochabamba y establecidas en la escena cultural de esa ciudad. Acompaña al volumen una breve presentación de Vilma Tapia Anaya. El volumen convoca voces y escrituras que sin necesariamente proponer un proyecto literario, exploran, desde ángulos más bien convencionales, la interioridad del sujeto femenino. [EM]

2853 Zabala Ruiz, Manuel. Manuel Ruiz Zabala. Quito: Casa de la Cultura Ecuatoriana Benjamín Carrión, 2006. 220 p. (Poesía junta; 5)

Sin prólogo pero acompañado de una separata escrita por Marco Antonio Rodríguez, este volumen recoge la totalidad de la (breve) obra poética de Zabala Ruiz. [EM]

2854 Zegarra Benites, Chrystian Iván. Escena primordial y otros poemas. Lima: Ediciones COPÉ, 2007. 47 p.

While the speaker laments the limits of poetry in this first-place winner of the 2005 Copé poetry competition, long lines of dense, dynamic language protest otherwise. Poetry offers a bittersweet refuge from a chaotic world and a reconstructed link to a past fragmented by migration. Varied intertexts feed the poet's voice, while prominent cinematic references create a parallel between the page and the screen. [LB]

2855 Zeller, Ludwig. Amoroso y caníbal. Tlaquepaque, Mexico: Consejo para la Cultura y las Artes de Nuevo León: Mantis Editores, 2008. 53 p.: ill. (Col. Liminar)

El brillante lenguaje onírico de Zeller indaga en las obsesiones de un sujeto visionario cuya incesante búsqueda existencial en el abismo sólo encuentra asidero poético en la mujer como origen de todo conjuro, como materialidad sorprendente y salvación terrestre. [OS]

2856 Zito Lema, Vicente. Belleza en la barricada. Buenos Aires: Ediciones ryr, 2007. 220 p.

Colección que reúne la poesía social y testimonial de Zito Lema desarrollada entre los años 1971 y 2007. En el prólogo Julio Cortázar afirma que los poemas del autor representan la opresión de la dictadura, los desaparecidos, la memoria, el olvido y el exilio. Se actualizan los temas en términos de la opresión que continúa (en Afganistán, por ejemplo), ya que según Zito Lema el silencio sin justicia continúa hoy en día. [JSK]

2857 Zurita, Raúl. Little Boy. Santiago: Libros de Mentira: 2009. 52 p.

A la secuencia de sueños que hacen posible un hablante visionario que divisa el regreso de rostros y situaciones familiares desoladoras la continúa una serie de textos en los que el lenguaje de la canción indígena de los Andes se entremezcla con el entrecortado discurso de quien canta la desaparición de la paloma o símbolo del núcleo de la vida latinoamericana enraizada en una existencia pacífica. Este símbolo resulta necesario por cuanto su contrapunto esencial en el libro es la violencia nuclear. [OS]

GENERAL STUDIES

2858 Arcos, Jorge Luis. Desde el légamo: ensayos sobre pensamiento poético. Madrid: Editorial Colibrí, 2007. 236 p.: bibl. (Col. Literatura)

Afamado ensayista y poeta cubano, ganador de varios premios nacionales e internacionales como poeta y como crítico, en este libro de ensayos vuelca su mirada ensayística sobre la literatura cubana, en particular pero no exclusivamente la poesía. Junto a los tópicos que acostumbra a estudiar—el grupo Orígenes, María

Zambrano, el pensamiento poético, la poesía y los poetas cubanos—aborda temas como el de la censura, el canon cubano, lo sagrado, la utopía, la mentira, la juventud. [FC]

SPECIAL STUDIES

2859 Guedea, Rogelio. Poetas del medio siglo: mapa de una generación. México: UNAM, 2007. 151 p.: bibl. (Poemas y ensayos)

Guedea (México, 1974) destaca no sólo por su prolífica obra poética, sino por haber incursionado en la crítica literaria elaborando antologías y libros de ensayos. Aquí reúne crítica sobre seis poetas mexicanos nacidos en la década de 1920 y que figuraron hacia mediados del siglo: Jaime Sabines, Tomás Segovia, Rubén Bonifaz Nuño, Eduardo Lizalde, Rosario Castellanos y Jaime García Terrés. Salvo quizá Segovia, se trata de una generación que se distingue por su preocupación por lo cotidiano, el lenguaje coloquial y directo, las referencias entresacadas de motivos personales (en cierto modo, el exteriorismo que pregonaba Ernesto Cardenal). [JS]

2860 Homenaje a Nicolás Guillén. Xalapa, Veracruz, Mexico: Univ. Veracruzana, Instituto de Investigaciones Lingüístico-Literarias, 2006. 412 p.: bibl. (Col. Cuadernos; 49)

Memoria que recoge una selección de los trabajos críticos presentados en el congreso internacional que convocó la Universidad Veracruzana en 2002, en homenaje al centenario del nacimiento del poeta cubano. Desde los trabajos que abordan los nudos importantes de la poesía de Guillén—por ejemplo, "el vuelo estilístico", el compromiso político, el vanguardismo afrocubano, la musicalidad, la identidad nacional, la alteridad—hasta los que se enfrentan a facetas menos estudiadas—por ejemplo, Guillén y la guerra civil española, su relación con la pintura de Wilfredo Lam, su influencia en la música de Juan Luis Guerra—el aporte de este libro reconecta el legado de Guillén. [FC]

2861 Luz espejeante: Octavio Paz ante la crítica. Selección y prólogo de Enrico Mario Santí. México: UNAM, Era, 2009. 703 p.: bibl.

Nueva recopilación de ensayos sobre Paz. En la bibliografía de Verani (1997) ya figuraban 75 publicaciones de este tipo, siendo seguramente el autor más estudiado de México. En esta edición (en la que intervino el mismo Paz antes de morir) aparecen ensayos muy conocidos, como Cortázar, Cabrera Infante, Zambrano, Pizarnik, Pacheco, etc., junto a los de críticos que han dedicado libros a Paz. Cuatro secciones la conforman: el hombre y su obra; su poesía; su crítica de arte; y sus visiones políticas. [JS]

2862 Peréz Grande, Hildebrando. ¡A Galopar por las sábanas! poesía peruana del siglo XX (de paso al XXI). (*Actual/Mérida*, 62/63, mayo/dic. 2006, p. 109–150, bibl.)

Pérez compiles recent works by some of Peru's most influential poets, observing a creative shift in the writing of Antonio Cisneros, Washington Delgado, José Wantanabe, and Mariela Dreyfus, and a refinement of approach in works by Marco Martos, Elqui Burgos, Mario Montalbetti and Juan Cristóbal. Poems by Sandro Chiri and Eduardo Urdanivia Bertarelli round out this sampling. [LB]

2863 Rodríguez, Silvio. Silvio poeta. Compilación de Suyín Morales Alemañy. La Habana: Centro Cultural Pablo de la Torriente Brau, 2008. 187 p.: bibl. (Col. A guitarra limpia)

Libro ganador del Premio Ensayo Noel Nicola 2008 cuyo objetivo consiste en un estudio de las canciones de Silvio Rodríguez en tanto textos poéticos y en ofrecer una transcripción selectiva de las mismas. En cuanto a lo poético de las canciones, el estudio plantea que el cantautor cubano "extrae de cada asunto tratado" en las mismas "su esencia, su real significado", el cual, más allá de los "acontecimientos", de lo que "el poeta comunica" y lo que aprehende, consiste en su "transcendencia histórica y humana". [FC]

2864 Vergara, Gloria. Identidad y memoria en las poetas mexicanas del siglo XX. México: Univ. Iberoamericana, 2007. 221 p.: bibl.

Libro que estudia a 11 poetas mexicanas del siglo XX: Concha Urquiza, Dolores Castro, Rosario Castellanos, Enriqueta Ochoa, Ulalume González de León, Gloria Gervitz, Elva Macías, Elsa Cross, Verónica Volkow, Pura López Colomé y María

Baranda. El libro intenta hacer un recorrido por todo el siglo XX, poniendo atención a los cambios que se desarrollan en la percepción de estas escritoras, a través de una multiplicidad de temas que recorren sus obras. Hay obvias ausencias, pero la crítica deja muy en claro que no intentaba hacer una obra abarcadora de toda la poesía de mujeres del siglo XX. [JS]

2865 Vitier, Cintio. Poesía I. Compilación, prólogo y notas de Enrique Saínz. La Habana: Editorial Letras Cubanas, 2007. 360 p.: bibl., ill. (Obras; 8)

Primera compilación de la obra de Vitier, un poeta clave del siglo XX cubano, para quien, según Saínz en el prólogo, "no era posible el conocimiento sin el diálogo entrañable con la realidad en busca de la unidad de lo diverso". De la "angustia de raíz historicista" a la "revolución interior", Saínz delinea las dos partes en que se amontonan los poemas, formando dos geografías que desde temprano en su devenir poético Vitier sabía entrelazadas: "La publicación [de poesía] adquiere así el sentido de un acto simbólico: el adentro se vuelve un afuera, la intimidad un objeto . . ." [FC]

MISCELLANEOUS

2866 Henestrosa, Andrés. Andanzas, sandungas y amoríos. Edición de Mariliana Montaner. Grabados de Juan Alcáraz. México: Plaza y Valdés: UNAM, Dirección General de Publicaciones y Fomento Editorial, 2006. 68 p.: ill. (some col.).

This publication, put together by Mariliana Montaner to celebrate the 100th birthday (2006) of Andrés Henestrosa, contains several texts by the Mexican essayist, composer, and poet. With the collaboration of Henestrosa's daughter, Cibeles, the booklet is introduced by Jacob Zabludodovsky, illustrated with engravings by Juan Alcázar, and concludes with a biographical essay by Adán Cruz Bencomo which, in abbreviated fashion, gives a profile of the colorful Zapotec writer. [F. Ángel]

Drama

SANDRA M. CYPESS, *Professor of Spanish, University of Maryland*
PAOLA HERNÁNDEZ, *Assistant Professor of Spanish, University of Wisconsin, Madison*

MEXICO AND THE CARIBBEAN

THE VITALITY OF THEATRICAL EXPRESSION in Latin America is evident from both the diversity of materials and the varied geographical areas where plays are being published. Scholars will be pleased to find Howard Quackenbush's *Antología del teatro dominicano contemporáneo* (item **2868**) and *La mujer frente al espejo: antología anotada de dramaturgas dominicanas contemporáneas* (item **2917**). The first volume contains seven plays by recognized male playwrights, such as Reynaldo Disla, Haffe Serulle, and Iván García, while his second anthology offers 12 plays by Dominican women, making this more unfamiliar facet of Dominican theater more accessible. Disla, who received the Premio Casa de las Américas in 1985 for his politically acerbic *Bolo Francisco*, shows his mastery of puppet theater as well, in his anthology of 11 plays, *Piezas para títeres* (item **2890**). His fine ear for the Dominican accent is once again displayed in the dialogue of these works. Frank Disla shows the family interest in critical social commentary in *Un búfalo de El Paso, Texas* (item **2889**). The innovative structure and impressionistic techniques do not hide the criticism of the role of the US in Dominican life. Another anthology, which includes the winners of the Premio Internacional de Literatura Casa de Teatro for 2005, demonstrates a refreshing strength to the formerly weak national theater movement in the Dominican Republic. The winning playwrights include four Dominicans: Carlos Esteban Deive, Giovanny Cruz, Julissa Rivera Céspedes, and Amaurys Pérez, as well as two Cubans—José Luis García and Jesús del Castillo Rodríguez.

Cuban theater continues to develop in directions that were seen before, as shown by the works of Héctor Quintero and Abel González Melo, whose *Chamaco* (item **2901**), winner of awards in Spain and Cuba, deals with issues of homosexuality and urban violence. In Puerto Rico, Ramos-Perea remains active in publishing his many plays, with *Teatro escogido* (item **2922**) offering five plays in a projected seven-volume series.

In Central America, publications by Costa Ricans lead in number. One active group, Teatro Abya Yala, a well-established independent theater company in Costa Rica, is directed by Roxana Avila and David Korish, who have brought out *Dramaturgia invisible: quince años del Teatro Abya Yala en Costa Rica* (item **2874**); in addition to critical commentary, four playtexts are included. Critics also have an opportunity to study plays by a younger generation, such as those included in *Emergencias: dramaturgia costarricense contemporanea emergente* (item **2895**). Along with a helpful prologue by Adolfo Alborno Farías, works by three young playwrights highlight the problems of young people. Also significant is the first-time publication of a play by the Guatemalan Vicenta Laparra de la Cerda, *Tempestades del alma* (item **2908**). Written in the 19th century by the feminist who founded the women's journal, *La voz de la mujer*, the play shows De la Cerda's treatment of gender issues which contemporary audiences will appreciate. Another major piece of research is found in the Cátedra edition of *Las Casas, El Obispo De Dios: la audiencia de los confines* by Miguel Angel Asturias (item **2873**). Las Casas is a figure found in a number of plays, but here Asturias not only shows Las Casas as an indigenist sympathizer, but also provides many opportunities for indigenous voices to enter into the play.

Based on the numbers of publications, it appears that Mexican playwrights are by far the most prolific in the region, and no longer publish and perform only in the Distrito Federal. In addition, the thematics of the plays also reflect continued development of regional concerns. Plays are being published from Mexicali and Chihuahua to Veracruz. Playwrights with established reputations—Victor Hugo Rascón Banda, Hugo Salcedo, Oscar Liera, Enrique Mijares, Estela Leñero, and Barbara Colio—as well as members of younger generations who are not connected to any particular older playwright-mentor—Edgar Chías, Luis Enrique Gutierrez Ortiz Monasterio, Mariana Hartasánchez—are represented in this selection of plays.

In general, the plays being produced today are notable for a focus on dialogue and a decided decrease in the use of stage directions, as can be seen in a number of plays by Mexicans Hugo Salcedo, Luis Enrique Gutierrez Ortiz Monasterio, and Edgar Chías. Another trend that seems to be more widespread is the attention to the violence of daily life, which also affects the language used. Border issues, as in *Aduana fronteriza* (item **2892**) and Salcedo's plays, are also important. Most noteworthy, however, throughout Mexico, Central America, and the Caribbean, are the many plays that obviously refer to previous literary texts. Often the homage is burlesque, but without the disdain. The Dominican Pedro Antonio Valdez's *Reciclaje* (item **2939**) brings his technique to the fore with his title, but the literary recycling is also notable in Lavandero Pascual's *Esperando al gordo* (item **2942**), Salcedo's *El perseguidor de Tlaxcala* (item **2931**), Mariana Hartasánchez's *Canción de Gershwin* (item **2884**), and in the biblical rewritings of Adam and Eve by Carmen Quidiello de Bosch *(La eterna Eva y el insoportable Adán*, item **2917**) and Valdez *(Paradise,* item **2939**). Prostitution, stereotyping of homosexuals, and abortion are also given theatrical space by characters who often speak in direct, regional registers. Wide-ranging themes about contemporary life, avant-garde techniques, prolific intertextuality, and regional vocabularies reveal that theater in Latin America is responsive to a diverse audience. [SC]

SOUTH AMERICA

The vast range and number of plays and critical works annotated in this volume signals the continuing vitality and importance of Spanish American theater as a field of literature. Many of these publications usher in the arrival of a new generation of playwrights. This is the case with Argentine authors, such as Federico León and Rafael Spregelburd. Federico León in *Registros: teatro reunido* (item **2910**) expresses a need for plays that emphasize the role of acting and body movement on stage and deemphasize dramatic dialogues. This can be seen in plays, such as *Cachetazo de campo*, in which the actresses are nude and in tears for most of the play or in *Mil quinientos metros sobre el nivel de Jack*, in which actors are submerged in a bathtub and try to get out constantly. Rafael Spregelburd is considered to be one of the most prolific and successful playwrights of the new generation. His collection of plays, *Remanente de invierno* (item **2933**), is an excellent example of his extraordinary thematic and stylistic diversity. A fundamental issue in these texts is the constant non-realistic, absurdist, and fragmented dialogues with a variety of topics that separate themselves from direct political theater. For the most part, these plays, *Remanente de invierno, Cuadro de asfixia,* and *Raspando la cruz*, highlight the exasperated state of the human condition in our highly mediated, contemporary reality with dark humor, sarcasm, and irony (see item **2933**). In Argentine theater studies, Osvaldo Pellettieri coins the term "theater of disintegration" (see *Criminal* (item **2887**)). This type of theater, also seen in authors such as Rafael Spregelburd, Daniel Veronese, Federico León, and Alejandro Tantanián, breaks with realism, reintroduces absurdist techniques, and favors deconstruction of language through texts that are often fragmented, inconclusive, and complex.

In Peru, younger playwrights are also well represented in publications, sometimes sponsored by cultural organizations whose commitment to theater is strong. A case in point is *Ponemos tu obra en escena* (item **2920**), a collection featuring the works of three young playwrights: Gino Luque, Mariana de Althaus, and Lucero Medina. Their plays deal with the role of media in a postmodern world, the disorienting and disappointing search for meaning in life, and human suffering.

A new trend in theater publications is to emphasize the strong caliber of plays written by authors who are not just playwrights, but also directors, actors, and even translators. Jorge Dubatti has described Federico León and Rafael Spregelburd as "multiple" authors who pay close attention to all of theater's components. Other collections follow this trend. For instance, actor Carlos Gassols from Peru (see *Teatro completo* (item **2899**)) is an avid theater practitioner, writing for and from the stage. A similar case is the late Peruvian José Enrique Mavila, who as a director, playwright, and entrepreneur constantly worked to make Peruvian theater a stronger competitor in international circles. His plays published in *Teatro: José Enrique Mavila* depict his constant commitment to metatheatrical techniques (item **2912**). Equally valuable are Gustavo Geirola's interviews with theater directors from Argentina, Chile, Paraguay, and Uruguay (item **2955**). This book contributes to the growing demand for scholarly work beyond dramatic texts, emphasizing instead the importance of stage productions.

There are a growing number of anthologies with multiple objectives and rationales for their organization. Some are grouped by gender, or recognized female authors, such as *Siete obras de teatro peruano*, by the Peruvian playwright Sara Joffré (item **2905**). This book provides a useful assembly of her works that deal with topics such as political corruption, social injustice, and human miscommunication. Another anthology, *Dramaturgias*, seeks to draw attention to the work of a variety of Argentine women dramatists including Lola Arias, Laura Fernández, Agustina Muños, and Mariana Chaud (item **2893**). There are also those works that provide a strong historical, critical, and even analytical background to theater studies. For instance there are anthologies that group their works by less represented countries or regions, like *Antología del teatro ecuatoriano contemporáneo* (item **2869**), *Antología selecta del teatro boliviano* (item **2871**), and *Dramaturgia de la Patagonia argentina* (item **2894**). The first two provide succinct introductions with excellent historical information on theater group formation, productions, and audience reception. There are two collected works on rare anarchist plays from the early 20th-century: *Antología crítica de la dramaturgia anarquista de Chile* (item **2957**) and *Las descentradas y otras piezas teatrales* (item **2914**) from Argentina. Both works explore political and social issues in highly volatile times. Because the publication of some of these texts has been limited to "folletines" or newspapers in the past, they are excellent sources of information. It is worth noting that Salvadora Medina Onrubia's work is an exquisite example of early Argentine feminist plays (item **2914**).

The works of Susana Torres Molina and Patricia Suárez, both from Argentina, and Inés Stranger from Chile are also worth mentioning. Torres Molina has become one of the most recognized Argentine contemporary playwrights. Her plays tend to deal with the constant struggle between men's and women's worlds (see item **2938**). Patricia Suárez explores the world of Evita's mythical and iconic status in humorous and historically accurate plays (item **2935**). Inés Stranger's works seek to fuse history, culture, and politics of Latin America from a female perspective. Her plays question the patriarchal society, female roles in history, and their strong solidarity to each other (see item **2934**). Several useful histories of Latin American theater provide solid and well-researched information. Some, as in the case of Luis Chesney Lawrence (*Relectura del teatro venezolano* (item **2948**)) and Juan Andrés Piña (*Historia del teatro en Chile* (item **2958**)), introduce extremely valuable scholarship on the birth of national theater for Venezuela and Chile respectively. They both highlight the beginning of the 20th-century theater, paying close attention to European influences, "género chico," and the reaction of national theater groups. Others, such as Diana Taylor and Sarah Townsend, employ a broader scope that expands our understanding of theaters and ephemeral art and brings attention to performance practices. Their excellent volume of translations, *Stages of Conflict* (item **2961**), provides a wealth of historical and socio-cultural information and introduces a wide variety of texts to an English speaking audience. [PH]

PLAYS

2867 Aguirre, Coral. Sofía al borde de la luz: obra en dos actos. Monterrey, Mexico: Univ. Autónoma de Nuevo León, Secretaría de Extensión y Cultura, Facultad de Artes Escénicas, 2007. 57 p. (Drama; 12)

Inspired by Alejo Carpentier's novel *El siglo de las luces*, Aguirre focuses on Sofía as her main interest, and explores her relationships with Victor Hugues, Carlos, her brother, and her cousin Esteban. She struggles to be part of the masculine enterprise of revolution and appears as eager and fearless as the men in trying to assert her rights. [SC]

2868 Antología del teatro dominicano contemporáneo. Compilación de L. Howard Quackenbush. Santo Domingo: Ediciones Librería La Trinitaria; Provo, Utah: Brigham Young Univ., 2004. 2 v.: bibl.

Howard Quackenbush selected seven plays for this volume and wrote an Introduction to contemporary Dominican theater. He also provided a commentary after each play. Included are playwrights whose works are not easy to find elsewhere: *Hágase la mujer!* by Juan Carlos Campos; *Los lectores del ático* by Efraín A. Castillo Arredondo; *Un comercial para Máximo Gómez* by Reynaldo Disla; *Bianto y su señor* and *La danza de Mingó* by Haffe Serulle; and *Fábula de los cinco caminates* and *Andrómaca* by Iván García Guerra. [SC]

2869 Antología del teatro ecuatoriano contemporáneo. Edición de Genoveva Mora. Cuenca, Ecuador: Casa de la Cultura Ecuatoriana "Benjamin Carrión", 2002. 484 p.

This collection publishes 15 contemporary plays from Ecuador that are otherwise difficult to locate. The introduction provides background information on the creation of theater groups that helped expand theater practices in the country. Topics vary, but death seems to be the connecting thread for these nonrealistic, sometimes humorous plays that bring colloquial speech alive. The authors are: Jorge Dávila Vázques, Hugo Avilés Espinosa, Isidro Luna, Juan Carlos Terán Guerra, Arístides Vargas, Ximena Ferrín, Raymundo Zambrano, Viviana Cordero, Peki Andino, Patricio Vallejo Aristizábal, Guido Navarro, Cristian Cortez, and Patricio Estrella. [PH]

2870 Antología didáctica del teatro mexicano, 1964–2005. Coordinación y edición de Oscar Armando García. Compilación y selección de Ricardo García Arteaga, Alejandro Ortiz Bullé-Goyri y Armando Partida Tayzan. México: UNAM, Dirección General de Asuntos del Personal Académico, Facultad de Filosofía y Letras: Univ. Autónoma Metropolitana, Unidad Azcapotzalco: Ediciones y Gráficos Eón, 2008. 1 v.: bibl.

Volume 2 (1990–2005) contains, in addition to an introductory essay by Óscar Armando García and an interesting essay on theatrical anthologies ("Antologias de teatro mexicano de fines y principios de milenio") by Armando Partida Tayzán, 10 plays by dramatists who range from the renowned (Olmos, Salcedo, Héctor Mendoza) to the new (León Mora). Arranged in chronological order, they are *El eclipse* by Carlos Olmos; *El viaje de los cantores* by Hugo Salcedo; *Secretos de familia* by Héctor Mendoza; *Las perlas de la virgen* by Jesús González Dávila; *El ajedrecista* by Jaime Chabaud; *Superhéroes de la aldea global* by Luis Mario Moncada; *Las tremendas aventuras de la capitana Gazpacho (o de cómo los elefantes aprendieron a jugar a las canicas)* by Gerardo Mancebo del Castillo Trejo; *Belice* by David Olguín; *El cielo en la piel* by Edgar Chías; and *Mestiza Power* by Concepción León Mora. [SC]

2871 Antología selecta del teatro boliviano contemporáneo. Edited and with an introduction by Willy O. Muñoz. Santa Cruz, Bolivia: Fondo Editorial, Gobierno Municipal Autónomo de Santa Cruz de la Sierra, 2005. 405 p.: bibl.

This is a useful collection that provides theatrical and historical information on Bolivian theater of the 20th century. Muñoz's selection offers a variety of plays that show a diverse group of authors and techniques from the 60s to the 90s. These include: *El Monje de Potosí* by Guillermo Francovich; *La lanza capitana* by Raúl Botelho Gosálvez; *La peste negra* by Sergio Suárez Fiegueroa; *Guano maldito* by Joaquín Aguirre Lavayén; *La última fiesta* by Oscar Zambrano; and *El cofre de Selenio* by Luis Ramiro Beltrán. [PH]

2872 Aristóteles, César. La comedia más espantosa y otras obras. Monterrey, Mexico: Fondo Estatal Para la Cultura y las Artes, 2007. 227 p. (Teatro)

Includes four plays: *La comedia más espantosa, Casa y jardín, Homicidio en el proscenio,* and *Vaqueros en calzones.* Written between 1994 and 2004, they purposely flout theatrical traditions. All ignore the conventional division between stage and the audience and provide good examples of metatheatrical experimentation and the use of simultaneous scenes, as in *Casa y jardín,* when two different actions occur: one in the house and one in the garden. The members of the audience have to decide which action to follow. In *Homicidio en el proscenio,* actors mingle with the spectators and act from the space of the audience, confusing the public further because of the play within a play, each with no ending. [SC]

2873 Asturias, Miguel Angel. Las Casas, el obispo de dios: La audiencia de los confines: Crónica en tres andanzas. Edición de José María Vallejo García-Hevia. Madrid: Cátedra, 2007. 560 p.: bibl. (Letras hispánicas; 605)

Although Asturias is not as well known as a dramatist, this text tries to fill in the gaps by providing the complete playscript and notes to his representation of Bartolomé de las Casas as a man with an "indigenous heart." José María Vallejo García-Hevia prepared the edition, and includes a number of essays that contextualize the play. He also provides copious notes that explain vocabulary, historical references, or other expressions not common today. [SC]

2874 Avila, Roxana. Dramaturgia invisible: quince años del Teatro Abya Yala en Costa Rica. Heredia: Editorial Univ. Nacional, 2008. 242 p.: ill.

Teatro Abya Yala is a well-established independent theater group in Costa Rica, known for creating its own plays, which are either authored collectively or by its directors David Korish and Roxana Ávila. This volume includes a preface by Eugenio Barba, an essay about the group by Marco Guillén, and other essays by Roxana Ávila and David Korish, along with the texts of 4 plays: *El Caso Otelo, Romeo and Julieta, in Concert, Sade,* and *Nos esperamos.* [SC]

2875 Ayub, Georgina. Vestidos de ocasión. Chihuahua, Mexico: Univ. Autónoma de Chihuahua, 2008. 113 p. (Col. Flor de arena; 68)

This is the third anthology by Ayub, and consists of the one-act plays *Anoche soñé que soñaba, Vírgenes de papel, Buscando a la soledad, Cuando las cosas pasan,* and *Personal de compañía.* All the plays include two characters and explore their personal relationships, with *Personal de compañía* being especially witty. [SC]

2876 Berenschot, Denis Jorge. Performing Cuba: (Re)writing gender identity and exile across genres. New York: P. Lang, 2005. 165 p.: bibl. (Caribbean studies; 15)

This book focuses on three prototexts: *Memorias del subdesarrollo* by Edmundo Desnoes; *El lobo, el bosque y el hombre nuevo* by Senel Paz; and *The Greatest Performance* by Elías Miguel Muñoz. Berenschot analyzes the alterations in their works as they are transformed from prose to film and theater, and shows how these multiple rewritings affect gender performances. The theoretical frame for issues of gender and performance is derived primarily from Judith Butler. [SC]

2877 Blanco, Sergio. Diptiko: vol. 1 y 2. Paris, Skené, 2006. 234 p.

In this play of unrequited adolescent love, the seven characters make their way through an unknown city, full of longing and desire for someone who feels an equal amount of passion—for someone else. Frustrated love turns to aggression, and even violence, as the playwright explores the volatility of human emotions. *Diptiko* is one of many plays made freely available online by the Uruguayan government. The site, a cooperative effort by playwrights and the government, hosts a large database of plays (see http://www.dramaturgiauruguaya.gub.uy). [K. McCann]

2878 Blanco, Sergio. Opus sextum. Paris: Skené, 2005. 253 p.

Sergio Blanco is an important playwright who has revitalized the Uruguayan stage with his realistic, political, and social plays at national and international outlets. With crude and visually effective techniques, *Opus Sextum* mixes the world of a slaughterhouse and the multinational corporation that owns it with the struggles of a father and his sons to come together as a family. [PH]

2879 Blanco López, Gerardo. Dramaturgia. Caracas: Bagazos, 2003. 161 p. (Col. Dramaturgos)

As a way to promote Venezuelan playwrights, this collection publishes four of Blanco's most contemporary plays. *El pequeño reino del Anacardo* is a morbid look at women's lives under a man's overpowering control. *La cuadrilla* is a humorous play in which four old men decide to take control of their own lives, leave their urban life in order to live together, and share their life secrets as they wait for death on their own terms. In *La dama y el carnicero*, a butcher's refrigerator becomes the entrapped space where an unforeseen couple humorously plays with seduction, only to end tragically. *Los náufragos* takes place on a deserted island where two friends literally sail through their life stories only to find out how empty and unproductive they have been. [PH]

2880 Briceño, Neher Jacqueline; Claudia Barrionuevo; and Araceli Mariel Arreche. La casa de todos. Presentación de Carmen Márquez Montes. Madrid: Asociación de Directores de Escena de España, 2006. 232 p. (Serie Literatura dramática iberoamericana; 46)

With an introductory essay by Carmen Márquez Montes, this anthology presents the winner and runners up of the Premio "Maria Teresa León 2005." First prize went to *La casa de todos* by the Venezuelan Neher Jacqueline Briceño. With its circular structure and enclosed space in which seven characters try to avoid the dictatorship of Alfonso Estrada, Briceño combines elements of social reality and magical realism to comment on the harsh reality of life in a dictatorship. *No matarás Rompecabezas temático (policial) en 52 piezas y una coda*, by the Costa Rican Claudia Barrionevo, was awarded second place. It is an unconventional murder mystery with many scenes taking place simultaneously and not always in chronological order. In third place was *Notas que saben a olvido* by the Argentine Araceli Mariel Arreche, which deals with Alzheimer patients and the effect of the disease on the family. [SC]

2881 Chaud, Mariana. Budín inglés: sobre la vida de cuatro lectores porteños. Buenos Aires: Teatro Vivo, 2007. 92 p. (Col. Teatro vivo; 27)

This humorous play is part of the Biodrama project directed by Vivi Tellas. The main goal of Biodramas is to have playwrights write something authentic about real people who live in Argentina. *Budín ingles, sobre la vida de cuatro lectores porteños* tells the story of four readers whose lives are intertwined with world literature. While set in a realistic, middle-class family home, amongst mate, tea and coffee, the intertextual flavors invite the audience to travel around the world of books and to consider how books impact our lives. [PH]

2882 Cinco dramaturgos chihuahuenses. Compilación de Guadalupe de la Mora Covarrubias. Ciudad Juárez, Mexico: Gobierno Municipal, 2005. 329 p.: bibl. (Col. Contemporaneos; 1)

The five plays in this anthology represent "teatro fronterizo," with each play dealing with different aspects of life on the "border"—especially issues affecting Mexico and the US. *El deseo* by Victor Hugo Rascón Banda explores the unequal power relationship between a rich American woman and a young Colombian whom she marries despite the huge differences in their social class, age, and ideology. It serves as an allegory for the relations between the first and third worlds. *Coctel margarita* by Antonio Zúñiga combines violence, colloquial language, and humor to portray the life of those involved in drug trafficking. *Lomas de poleo* by Edeberto Galindo Noriega and *Antígona, las voces que incendian el desierto* by Perla de la Rosa explore the violence associated with the assassinations of young women in Ciudad Juárez. As the title indicates, de la Rosa makes use of the Antigone myth to add a universal resonance to what is a tragic loss of life in a border community. In *Almas de arena*, Guadalupe de la Mora Covarrubias focuses on the plight of those Mexicans who emigrate across the desert in search of work and a better life, only to find hardship and death. Guadalupe de la Mora and José Manuel García-García offer bio-bibliographic information as well as brief analyses of each play. [SC]

2883 Colio, Bárbara. Pequeñas certezas. Presentación de Ignacio García May. Madrid: Publicaciones de la Asociación de Directores de Escena de España, 2005. 231 p.

(Publicaciones de la Asociación de Directores de Escena de Espana. Serie Literatura dramática iberoamericana; 43)

Winner in 2004 of Spain's Premio María Teresa León, this play takes place in Mexico City and Tijuana, and deals with dysfunctional families and a new way of looking at the Mother figure. It also explores the idea of how different people see the same event from different perspectives. [SC]

2884 Concurso Nacional de Dramaturgia Manuel Herrera Castañeda, 7th, 2005. Obras finalistas del Séptimo Concurso Nacional de Dramaturgia Manuel Herrera Castañeda. Santiago de Querétaro, Mexico: Q Fondo Editorial, 2006. 177 p. (Dramaturgia)

Three plays were finalists in the Concurso: *En las montañas azules* by Edgar Chías; *Edi & Rudy* by Luis Enrique Gutierrez; and *Canción de Gershwin* by Mariana Hartasánchez. The plays share a common interest in avoiding stage directions and presenting dialogue-based theater in which the story is not as important as the expression of angst in view of the dehumanizing forces in contemporary society. *En las montañas azules* even eschews names for the various characters who express their worries and fears, as if personal identities no longer have meaning in the face of the chaos of life. *Edi & Rudy* are two friends whose conversation shows that they also have trouble with their families and with women. *Canción de Gershwin* is a farce that explores the effect of family power relations on gender roles. [SC]

2885 Córdoba, Gonzalo de. Teatro. Edición de Mauricio Méndez J. Santa Cruz de la Sierra, Bolivia: Editorial La Hoguera, 2006. 170 p. (Teatro. Serie Puraletra)

As an actor, director, and playwright, Gonzalo de Córdoba is a major figure in Bolivian theater. His three plays: *Las vísperas de un extraño funeral; Un grito en la plaza;* and *Huelga de amor de un hombre desesperado* bring humor, sarcasm, irony, and even magical realism to the forefront. He is also concerned with social justice and is a strong critic of society's customs and vices. [PH]

2886 Cruz Durán, Giovanny. Sobre ángeles y demonios: tragedia en dos actos. Santo Domingo: Secretaría de Estado de Nación, Editora Nacional, 2006. 74 p. (Col. Premios nacionales)

This award-winning play explores religious beliefs and their use for political purposes. Subtitled a "tragedy in two acts," the action takes place in 1958, during the Carnival period and ends with the crucifixion of one of the characters. [SC]

2887 Daulte, Javier. Criminal. Estudio preliminar de Osvaldo Pelletieri. Buenos Aires: Corregidor, 2006. 61 p. (Los fundamentales del teatro argentino; 4)

Staged in 1996 and awarded the prestigious ACE award for best director (Jaime Kogan) and best author (Javier Daulte), this play humorously portrays Daulte's excellent exploration of the world of psychology, marital relations, and the role of therapy for contemporary couples in Buenos Aires. Osvaldo Pelletieri's preliminary study gives a well-founded explanation of what he coined the "theater of disintegration" and of how this play fits this description. [PH]

2888 Deive, Carlos Esteban. Quien se atreve con un entremés de Cristóbal de Llerena?: comedia en tres actos. Santo Domingo: Casa de Teatro, 2005. 315 p.

This anthology contains the winners of the Premio Internacional de Literatura Casa de Teatro 2005. The winning playwrights include the Dominican Carlos Esteban Deive, for his historical play, *¡Quién se atreve con un entremés de Cristóbal Llerena!* The Cuban José Luis García, for *Historia de una foto*, a realistic play about how to survive in Cuba despite the poverty. Third place was given to the Dominican Giovanny Cruz, for *La conferencia*, a tour de force that breaks down the fourth wall and explores politics and art with irony and humor. Honorable Mention was given to the Dominican Julissa Rivera Céspedes for *Miches*, followed by plays by the Dominican Amaurys Pérez (*Dos mendigos, un muñeco y toda una ciudad*), and the Cuban Jesús del Castillo Rodríguez for *Volando con el fakir*. [SC]

2889 Disla, Frank. Un búfalo de El Paso, Texas: teatro. Santo Domingo: Editora Nacional, 2005. 73 p. (Col. Premios nacionales)

A two-person play with 10 scenes and an innovative structure, the themes are political and timely, despite the impressionistic techniques. Topics include the effects of US foreign policy in the Caribbean and globally, Vietnam, the military recruitment of Caribbeans into the US army, and the life of immigrants. [SC]

2890 Disla, Reynaldo. Piezas para títeres. Santo Domingo: Secretaría de Estado de Cultura, Editora Nacional, 2006. 191 p.: ill. (Col. Infantil y juvenil)

The first Dominican anthology of works for puppet theater, Disla's 11 plays are based on figures from Dominican folklore who express themselves in language that reflects a lively Dominican vocabulary and phrasing in the dialogue. One of the plays, *¡Ay, papa, no me des!* shows in its subtitle—*Pieza para actors y muñecos sobre la prevención del abuso infantil*—that Disla is very much concerned with contemporary social issues. [SC]

2891 Dramaturgia de la historia del Perú. Edición de Roberto Angeles. Asistencia de edición de Carlos Galiano. Lima: s.n., 2006. 356 p.: ill.

This collection brings together a variety of plays that deal with Peru's history, atrocities, trauma, indigenous rights, and the attempts of the younger generations to deal with historical amnesia and memory gaps. *Espinas* by Eduardo Adrianzén Herrán takes a retrospective look at the conquest and colonial times in Peru's society. *Ayacucho* by Guillermo Nieto is a realistic play where a father and son confront each other due to antagonistic political views. C. Fernando Casaretto Alvarado offers *Los peruanos de angamos* to portray a romantic idea of the Peruvian military while simultaneously showing how an everyday man can be the true heroic figure. Delfina Paredes is one of the two women represented in this anthology with her play, *Evangelina, retorna de la breña.* In it, she emphasizes the role of Peruvian women in history, as well as calling attention to the lack of representation of women's roles in the official history books. *Contacto* by Ricardo Velásquez and Roberto Angeles tells the story of two young men whose lives change dramatically due to political and social changes in Peru. *Pequeños heroes* by Alfonso Santistevan is an introspective play in which the main protagonist is a woman who questions her role as a teacher in a country where civil wars have made people lose their own faith.

In a similar vein, Aldo Miyashiro writes *Un misterio, una pasión,* a play in which historical events of the 1980s-90s are intertwined with sports events to bring attention to the many painful and devastating effects of the war. Marina de Althaus offers *Ruido,* a play that emphasizes the inner struggles of younger Peruvian generations whose childhood memories of the war are full of anguish and fear. [PH]

2892 Dramaturgia joven de Nuevo Laredo. Compilación de Enrique Mijares. Ciudad Victoria, Mexico: Gobierno de Tamaulipas, 2007. 187 p. (Col. Nuevo siglo; 13)

This anthology includes the results of an effort to encourage playwriting in all parts of Mexico, which Enrique Mijares has been effective in bringing to the public's attention. In addition to his prologue, the 10 plays included are *Aduana fronteriza* by Rogelio Córdova; *House* by César Gutiérrez García; *Un sueño americano* by Luis Gutiérrez García; *Aborto* by Cynthia Guzmán Flores; *Proyecto ciudadano* by Maria Inés López López; *Amiguita* by Osvaldo Rodríguez; *El elegido* by Abraham Sanchez; *Prueba de amor* by Cynthia Isabel Sánchez López; *Circo color nostalgia* by Luis Edoardo Torres; and *Cuidados intensivos* by Maria de Jesús de Valle. The themes of the plays explore contemporary problems, from border issues (*Aduana fronteriza; Un sueño americano*) to gender relations (*Aborto; Amiguita; Cuidados intensivos*) and questions of identity (*House; Circo color nostalgia*). [SC]

2893 Dramaturgias. Compilación de Juan Manuel Nadalini. Prólogo de Mariana Obersztern. Buenos Aires: Editorial Entropía, 2008. 253 p. (Antología)

With the aim to give women playwrights more recognition, this volume presents seven young female authors. In *Poses para dormir,* Lola Arias shows the strong friction between the world of illusions and the real life in a raw and apocalyptic way. *Cien pedacitos de mi arenero* by Laura Fernández is a dark and somber ceremony where five men try to put an end to female seduction. Agustina Muñoz in *El calor del cuerpo* explores the life of four characters that are stuck desiring something they can never attain. *Ifigenia en* by Agustina Gatto is a retrospective look at family genealogy that questions the role of family memory and its effect on a person's development as an adult. Julieta de Simone writes *Cebo*, a play where the invasion of rats brings a repulsive yet corrupted way to proliferate for the characters. *Sigo mintiendo* is a humorous play about love and seduction that Mariana Chaud retells in a retrospective fashion. With *Algo de ruido*, Romina Paula postulates the life of two men who live as one and are expecting a woman's visit so that they can feel alive. [PH]

2894 Dramaturgos de la Patagonia argentina. Edición de Ana Ferrer y Lucía Laragione. Buenos Aires: Argentores, Sociedad General de Autores de la Argentina, 2007. 358 p. (Teatro. Serie Regionales)

This collection of 19 plays is an original publication that asserts the strong artistic contributions of well-established young playwrights in Argentina's southern provinces of Tierra del Fuego, Santa Cruz, Chubut, Neuquén, Río Negro, and La Pampa. There is a wide range of topics that relate to life in Patagonia. Some texts are more existential and deal with humanistic concerns of corruption, abandonment, and solitude, such as *¡Ay, Riquelme! (El Primer Mundo te pasó por encima)* by Oscar Benito; *El Titi ¡La victrola no!* by Edgardo Enrique Plaza and José Luis Blanco; *Luciérnagas curiosas* by Eduardo Bonafede; *El banquito* by Juan Aldo Umazano; and *El tragaluz* by Juan Carlos Moisés. Other plays like *Fortín Tebas* by Walter Cazenave; *Ya camina: La niebla de Malvinas* by Ademar Elichiry and *Malahuella* by Carol Yordanoff have a documentary and historical preoccupation with different social, political, and environmental issues in the Patagonia. Another common thread that connects some of these plays is the use of mythical or iconic figures of this area. Plays like *Barioletto y Germinal* by Alejandro Finzi, *La campana: parábola teatral en cuatro cuadros y un breve epílogo milagroso* by Guillermo Julio Gazia, and *San Juancito de Realicó: pieza satírica en tres cuadros* by Pedro Eugenio Pico illustrate the ongoing mythical beliefs that connect the environment to its people. Finally, *Es bueno mirarse en la propia sombra* by Luisa Calcumil brings to the foreground the life and struggles of the Mapuche lifestyle, their culture and marginal place within the

hegemonic society of Patagonia. Each play is introduced by a short and useful synopsis and detailed information on staging. [PH]

2895 Emergencias: dramaturgia costarricense contemporanea emergente. San José: Ediciones Perro Azul, 2008. 164 p. (Teatro)

In addition to a prologue by Adolfo Alborno Farías, works by three young playwrights are included: *El dolor de la carne* by Mabel Marín, *El largo adios* by Kyle Boza, and *El pudridero (Fotografias de quien sabe donde)* by Alvaro Martínez. They all deal with the problems of young people, expressed in a colloquial language; violence and the impact of visual culture on today's youth are some of their thematic preoccupations. [SC]

2896 En la Frontera Norte, Ciudad Juárez y el teatro. Coordinación, compilación y prólogo de Enrique Mijares y Cecilia Bueno. Chihuahua, Mexico: Instituto Chihuahuense de la Cultura: Univ. Autónoma de Ciudad Juárez, 2008. 253 p. (Col. Coediciones)

Enrique Mijares has selected six plays which were produced during a workshop held in the US-Mexican border region. In his prologue he describes the works and the background of these relative newcomers, who depict the often brutal experiences of life on the border. The violence and racism of the border, as well as the economic hardships and drug trafficking, are themes of these plays: *No te entiendo, no me entiendes* by Cecilia Bueno; *Expedientes del odio* and *Richard Ramírez, mi hermano siamés* by Selfa Chew; *Petrus* by Santos Galvadón; *Cruce alterno* by Carlos Alberto Hernández; *Amor impune* by Guadalupe de la Mora; and *Laceraciones* by Virginia Ordóñez. [SC]

2897 Festival Internacional de Buenos Aires, *5th*, 2004-2005. Premio Germán Rozenmacher de nueva dramaturgia. Ed. trilingüe. Buenos Aires: Libros del Rojas, Univ. de Buenos Aires: Festival Internacional de Buenos Aires, 2005. 179 p.

The Germán Rozenmacher prize aims to promote younger playwrights and help them gain international recognition by publishing the best plays in a trilingual edition (Spanish, English, and French). The plays awarded the prize in 2004-2005 were

Princesa peronista by Marcelo Pitrola and *El baile del pollito* by Pablo Iglesias. *Princesa peronista* is a nostalgic view of "better" times under General Juan Domingo Perón's presidency. The "princesa" is left all alone with her memories of this government while the current time shows the highly corrupted version of the Peronists. *El baile del pollito* is a somber, existential, and violent play that intermingles music, guns, and war stories while two criminals are hiding from the police. [PH]

2898 Galindo Noriega, Edeberto. Amores que matan y otras obras. Ciudad Juárez, Mexico: Gobierno Municipal, 2005. 287 p. (Col. contemporáneos; 3)

From Chihuahua, Galindo was awarded the Premio Nacional de Dramaturgia 2007 "Víctor Hugo Rascón Banda" for *La furia de los mansos.* The title play, based on a real event, the death of a woman whose body was found dismembered, reveals his continued interest in social issues that deal with women's roles in a machista culture. The following plays are also included: *Arizona en llamas, Ruega por nosotros, Puente negro, Mírame alos ojos, y dime que me quieres.* Galindo explores issues relating to the border, immigration, and the violence that marks Mexican society today. [SC]

2899 Gassols Eizaguirre, Carlos. Teatro completo. Prólogo de Manuel Pantigoso. Lima: Univ. Ricardo Palma, Editorial Universitaria, 2005. 499 p.

The eight plays included in this collection by Carlos Gassols, an actor, director, and playwright, show his close relationship to the stage. There are three one-act plays. *Un hombre, unas palabras* is a metatheatrical monologue that brings attention to the art of acting while expressing the difficulties of losing a job. *Un día cualquiera* exposes a family's constant economic struggles to survive. *El chequecito* is a humorous cinematographic farce influenced by the theater of the absurd that denounces social injustices. *Segundo debut* is a two-act comedy based on Chekhov's play, *The Proposal,* in which a man asks for his neighbor's hand in marriage. Gassols creates a metatheatrical drama where characters are rehearsing Chekhov's play while humorously adding his own twists to the "proposal." *Amor a poquitos* resembles a "vaudeville" that

satirizes society's look at love and eroticism. The last three plays, *Lima y Gardel, una vez; Los inquilinos del buque;* and *Fantasmas de Lima vieja* deal with legendary icons, music, history, tradition, fiction, humor, and nationalism with a strong social focus on Peruvian history and culture. [PH]

2900 Goldenberg, Jorge. Teatro completo. Estudio crítico de Jorge Dubatti. Buenos Aires: Colihue, 2005. 224 p.: bibl., ill. (Colihue teatro. Dramaturgias argentinas)

Five plays form this collection. *Krinsky* retells the many stories created around Krinsky, a Russian immigrant who worked as a librarian in a Jewish center. *Cartas a Moreno* is a metatheatrical play that humorously tries to understand the role of the prominent figure Mariano Moreno in Argentine history. *Sería más sencillo* is a short monologue about mother and daughter relationships. *La lista completa* goes back to Krinsky as a main character who tries to survive in a changed world. *Fotos de infancias* is a witty and humorous play that confronts the ephemeral moment in which different childhood pictures are taken and what the actual pictures depict. [PH]

2901 González Melo, Abel. Chamaco: informe en diez capítulos para representar. Compilación y prólogo de Carlos Fundora. La Habana: Ediciones Alarcos, 2006. 76 p. (Col. Aire frío)

Winner of awards in Spain and Cuba, *Chamaco* takes place in Havana's Central Park during Christmas Eve, and offers a disturbing picture of male prostitution, urban violence, and police corruption in Havana, but the problems depicted could occur anywhere in contemporary society. [SC]

2902 Griffero Sánchez, Ramón. Tus deseos en fragmentos: fin del eclipse. Providencia, Santiago: Editorial Cuarto Propio, 2007. 97 p.: index. (Dramaturgia. Serie de libros del estudiante)

Ramón Griffero, well-known Chilean playwright, publishes two of his most recent plays. *Tus deseos en fragmentos* is a fragmented, funny, media-heavy play that depicts the desolate and lonely world of young adults: their friendships, their search for identity, their ways of communicating in a highly connected world (such as chat rooms), and their experiences with gay and straight sex. In *Fin del eclipse*, Griffero utilizes "mise en abyme" to create a play where theater is the only constant referent through the scenes, while still calling attention to the role of the author, the muse, and fiction as the main component of the stage. [PH]

2903 Guerra, Ibrahim. V.I.P. Caracas: Ediciones del Ministerio de la Cultura, 2006. 89 p. (Cada día un libro, Teatro)

V.I.P. is a realistic play that takes place in the successful and professional world of men, who act as if they own the world. Guerra offers an intense study of masculinity and men's castrating attitude towards others. [PH]

2904 Hernández, Luisa Josefina. Los grandes muertos. Presentación de Emilio Carbadillo. Prólogo de Fernando Martínez Monroy. México: Fondo de Cultura Económica, 2007. 542 p. (Letras Mexicanas)

Twelve plays are included along with an introductory note by Emilio Carbadillo and a prologue by Fernando Martínez Monroy. The plays are not the most well known of Hernández's production, and include *El galán de ultramar*, *La amante*, *Tres perros y un gato*, ending with *De lealtades y traiciones*, from 2002. The plays show her mastery of dialogue as well as her thematic focus on the middle class and the problems that arise from the changing role of women in society. [SC]

2905 Joffré, Sara. Siete obras de teatro. Lince, Peru: Univ. Inca Garcilaso de la Vega, Fondo Editorial, 2006. 226 p. (Serie Obras escogidas. Teatro peruano)

This is a very useful edition that assembles a variety of Sara Joffré's texts (five plays, one radio script and one monologue) written during different decades. *Se administra justicia* is a realistic play that tells the story of authoritative governments and corrupted judicial systems. *Se consigue madera* is an ethical journey that juxtaposes the world of the living and the dead when a man steals wood from coffins to build his own house. *Pre-texto* is a short, absurdist play that emphasizes human miscommunication through humorous and empty language. The radio script, *Pañuelos, bandera, nubes* uses suspense to unite a couple who

unbeknownst to them, share a complicated and similar past. *Monólogo N° 1* relates the story of an orphan who cannot get close to other people for fear of being rejected. [PH]

2906 Kartun, Mauricio. Chau Misterix: El partener; La Madonnita; La suerte de la fea. Buenos Aires: Losada, 2006. 191 p. (Col. Gran teatro)

Together with a critical and historical prologue, this book showcases four of Kartun's better known and critically acclaimed plays. Starting with *Chau Misterix*, followed by *El partener; La madonnita* and ending with *La suerte de la fea*. For review of *Chau Misterix* (1989), see *HLAS 52:4350*. [PH]

2907 Kartun, Mauricio. El niño argentino. Edición de Jorge Dubatti. Buenos Aires: Atuel, 2006. 184 p. (Biblioteca del espectador)

El niño argentino takes place at the beginning of the 20th century, when a young Argentine aristocrat travels to Europe taking along a cow and a caretaker so that he, "el niño," could have fresh milk during the trip. With this play, Kartun literally recycles archaic language, history as well as anecdotes, and recreates a time and space where issues of social class, political parties, and economic power are at stake. This edition includes interviews with the author, critical and analytical papers, together with information on staging and production. [PH]

2908 Laparra de la Cerda, Vicenta. Tempestades del alma: drama en tres actos y en verso. Guatemala: Ministerio de Cultura y Deportes, 2008. 99 p. (Col. Teatro. Serie Manuel Galich; 8)

This play by the 19th-century Guatemalan woman who founded *La voz de la mujer* has not been available before. Considered a pioneering feminist, her play deals with gender issues, especially the double standard that permits adultery for men and strict codes of behavior for women. She also focuses on the destructive effects of gossip in a closed society. [SC]

2909 Leñero Franco, Estela. Casa llena: Habitación en blanco. Monterrey, Mexico: Univ. Autónoma de Nuevo León, Secretaría de Extensión y Cultura, Facultad de Artes Escénicas, 2008. 74 p. (Drama; 13)

Casa llena is a realistic play that deals with the abuse of women by their mates and how Sara, the protagonist, no longer is willing to accept physical and mental abuse of her former partner Martin who wants to go back to their old way of life. Sara shows that she has fulfilled her dream of being complete unto herself by resisting Martin's bullying attempts to regain a foothold in her home and heart. *Habitación en blanco*, her first play, shows her early interest in the use of space as a dramatic object. Two men fight over their right to an apartment, but in the end they realize their own lack of power in the contemporary Mexican social hierarchy, in which drug cartels play a part. [SC]

2910 León, Federico. Registros: teatro reunido y otros textos. Compilación y nota epilogal a cargo de Jorge Dubatti. Buenos Aires: A. Hidalgo, 2005. 318 p.: ill. (Lengua. Teatro)

This collection brings together a variety of León's works. His play *Cachetazo de campo* portrays a symbolic use of the binary "civilization or barbarism" by having the main actor play the role of authoritative "campo" who abuses his own daughter. *Ex-Antuán* presents the difficult world of mentally handicapped people, *Mil quinientos metros sobre el nivel de Jack* takes place in a bathtub full of water, where family members literally have to avoid drowning in their daily routines. *El adolescente* deals with how teenagers perceive the violent world they live in. *Todos juntos* is a movie script about a couple's anguish of being together just because they cannot live apart. There is also one documentary performance or installation piece, *Museo Miguel Angel Boezzio* (investigación sobre el Museo Aeronáutico) that explores the scars of the Malvinas war veterans. León adds introductory commentaries to some texts together with excellent photographs and Jorge Dubatti writes the conclusion showing the "multiplicity" of León's creative endeavor. [PH]

2911 Liera, Oscar. Teatro escogido. Prólogo de Armando Partida Tayzan. México: Fondo de Cultura Económica, Fondo Regional para la Cultura y las Artes del Noroeste; Culiacán, Mexico: Dirección de Investigación y Fomento de Cultura Regional del Gobierno del Estado de Sinaloa, 2008. 501 p. (Letras mexicanas)

In addition to the prologue by Armando Partida Tayzan, 18 plays are included along with data about productions. This is a good introduction to the many facets of Liera's work—from the farsical *Las Ubárry* (1975) and *La piña y la manzana* (1979) to the hyperrealism and brutality presented in *Repaso de indulgencias* (1984). We see the Sinaloan influence in such plays as *El oro de la Revolución mexicana* (1984), *El jinete de la divina providencia* (1985) and *Los caminos solos* (1987). In *El camino rojo a Sabaiba* (1988) the regionalism continues, but the work is best at showing off Liera's ability to combine reality, myth, and history. [SC]

2912 Mavila, José Enrique. Teatro. Lima: Asociación Cultural Plan 9, 2006. 137 p.

The late José Enrique Mavila was a true theater practitioner who constantly worked to make Peruvian theater better known in international circles. This compilation is a sample of some of his work as a playwright. *Camino de Rosas* is a play with simple language about the everyday life and struggles of a middle-class couple. *Tres hermanos* is an introspective play that portrays the controversial relationship between three brothers in an intense psychological exploration. *El sol bajo el mar* is an intertextual play about life in the sea and their fisherman's poetic creativity. *Un director* is a metatheatrical play where actors are rehearsing *La vida es sueño*, and in their acting they find the immense creativity of theater, the understanding of truth, and the polyphony of the stage. A monologue, *Los sacrificios de una madre* is a short, funny story about a mother's retrospective look at motherhood. [PH]

2913 Medina, Dante. Mundus novus: Américo: obra en tres actos. Guadazapopaque, Mexico: Univ. de Guadalajara: Editorial Emprendedpres Universitarios, 2006. 64 p.

First presented in 2006, this historical play is about the life of Américo Vespucio and his belief that Columbus and other sailors had come to a New World and not India. His dialogues with the Catholic kings focus on political issues while his interactions with Columbus favor the sophistication of Vespucio. [SC]

2914 Medina Onrubia, Salvadora. Las descentradas y otras piezas teatrales. Estudio preliminar de Josefina Delgado. Buenos Aires: Biblioteca Nacional: Ediciones Colihue, 2007. 247 p.: bibl. (Col. Los raros; 14)

This collection of Medina Onrubia's plays showcases some of her feminist, eccentric, and anarchist plays of the early 20th century. The preceding study gives solid historical background on the author's life, work, and theater production, while the edition provides a great collection of plays that are rare and exquisite early feminist texts, such as *La solución; Las descentradas;* and *Un hombre y su vida.* [PH]

2915 Mijares, Enrique. Un aire de familia: cuarteto. Durango, Mexico: iMAC, 2006. 93 p.: ill.

Mijares recreates part of the history of his state of Durango in this play about the four Revueltas siblings who participated in different ways in the arts of Mexico during the first half of the 20th century—Fermín, Silvestre, José, and Rosaura. Each short play focuses on one of the Revueltas, but refers to all their lives as well. *Andamios interiores* is about Fermín, the painter; *Amiga que te vas* shows the life of Silvestre the musician; *Las condiciones requeridas* focuses on the political life of the novelist José and his incarceration; *El círculo de gis* introduces the least known of the family, Rosaura, who was an actress as well as an activist. [SC]

2916 Montes Huidobro, Matías. Cuba detrás del telón. Miami, Fla.: Ediciones Universal, 2008. 3 v.: bibl. (Col. Polymita)

Montes Huidobro turns his critical attention to the established playwrights Carlos Felipe (*Réquiem por Yarini*), Virgilio Piñera (*El gordo y el flaco, Aire frío, El filántropo*), Fermín Borges, Abelardo Estorino, Gloria Parrado, Manuel Reguera Saumell, Leopoldo Hernández; as well as José Triana, Antón Arrufat, Ezequiel Vieta and his own work as a playwright. He also refers to writers of what he calls the vanguardia and "nuevas promociones": Nicolás Dorr, Raúl de Cárdenas, Ignacio Gutiérrez, David Camps, Fulleda León, Eugenio Hernández Espinosa, José Milián, and René Ariza. [SC]

2917 La mujer frente al espejo: antología anotada de dramaturgas dominicanas contemporáneas. Recopilación de L. Howard Quackenbush. Santo Domingo: Ediciones Librería La Trinitaria; Provo, Utah: Brigham Young Univ. 2007. 383 p.: bibl.

An important contribution to a little studied area, Howard Quackenbush has selected 12 plays by Dominican women and included a critical essay about each one, along with a biobibliographic note. The plays vary in style and technique, but most critique the patriarchal system in which these women live. Included are *La eterna Eva y el insoportable Adán* by Carmen Quidiello de Bosch; *Whish-key Sour (Trago amargo)* by Sherezada (Chiqui) Vicioso; *¡Yo soy Minerva! (Confesionses más allá de la vida y la muerte)* by Mu-Kin Adriana Sang-Ben; *La querida de don José* by Germana Quintana; *Minerva y Manolo, amor y lucha* by Carmen Dinorah Coronado; *Por hora* and a piece work by Elizabeth Ocvalle; *Estrategias del otro yo: el mundo de Claudia* and *La tierra es de nosotros* by Carlota Carretero; *Espejismo* by Margaret Sosa; *Hermanas* by Josefina Muñoz; and *¿Estamos listos . . . ?* by Ana Mercedes Soto. [SC]

2918 Nery Alvarado, Sergio Manuel. Apóstol de la democracia. Monterrey, Mexico: Univ. Autónoma de Nuevo León, 2008. 105 p. (Teatro)

Capitalizing on the programs surrounding the 100th anniversary of the Mexican Revolution, Nery Alvarado offers a play focusing on Francisco Madero, and including as characters Porifirio Díaz, Pancho Villa, Emiliano Zapata, Felipe Angeles, and a host of other historical figures. [SC]

2919 Ostoa, Alejandro. Oficiantes de catedral y dos más de teatro. Toluca, Mexico: Instituto Mexiquense de Cultura, 2007. 196 p. (El espejo de amarilis)

In addition to *Oficiantes de catedral,* this anthology includes *El árbol de las aves con las alas rotas* and *El ombligo de Maribel. Oficiantes* refers to the various workers who come to the Plaza in front of the Cathedral in Mexico City to look for work. The play incorporates references to historical figures from the Aztec and colonial periods, in particular, Josefa Ortiz de Dominguez. Idiomatic language and sexually explicit dialogue and actions contrast with the location. *El árbol de las aves con las alas rotas* is a two-act tragicomedy that also uses Mexican regionalisms and has a diverse cast of characters wounded by life's problems. *El ombligo de Maribel* also has sexually explicit scenes. [SC]

2920 Ponemos tu obra en escena: Los número seis; El arca de Noé; Efímero. Lima: Asociación Cultural Peruano Británica, 2008. 169 p.

This collection publishes three plays by young up-and-coming Peruvian playwrights. Gino Luque writes *Los número seis* where the absurd role of mass media in a postmodern world seems to showcase how people cannot communicate face to face. *Efímero* by Mariana de Althaus is an enigmatic and symbolic play where a woman searches for meaning in her life. Lucero Medina with *El arca de Noé* comments on human suffering through the eyes of a boy who faces difficult life choices. [PH]

2921 Quintero, Héctor. Teatro escogido y otros textos. Prólogo de Jorge Rivas Rodríguez. La Habana: Letras Cubanas, 2006. 2 v.: bibl. (Repertorio teatral cubano)

The two volumes contain a prologue by Jorge Rivas Rodríguez and nine plays of Quintero, who was awarded the Cuban Premio Nacional de Teatro in 2004: *Contigo pan y cebolla*, *El premio flaco*, *Te sigo esperando*, *El lugar ideal*, *Sábado corto*, *El abrigo* and *La obra de arte*, and the monologues *Aquello está buenísimo* and *Antes de mí El Sahara*, a play that has not been published before. His humor and dialogue are notable and substantiate his popularity as a playwright in Cuba. [SC]

2922 Ramos-Perea, Roberto. Teatro escogido. San Juan: Publicaciones Gaviota, 2006. 342 p.

Included in this first volume of the seven that present all the plays of this Puerto Rican dramatist are *Melodía salvaje*; *Tuya siempre, Julita*; *Mistiblú*; *Morir de noche*; and *Besos de fuego*. The addendum, "El autor y su obra," provides a bio-bibliography that records the chronology of Ramos-Perea's premières. Ramos-Perea is known for imaginatively mining Puerto Rican history for his thematics, as exemplified in this anthology by *Tuya siempre* and *Julita*, which deals with a relationship between the

poets Julia de Burgos and Luis Llorens Torres. In *Mistiblú*, he includes the historical figures Casanova, the Count of Saint Germain, and the rock star Madonna. [SC]

2923 Rascón Banda, Víctor Hugo. Mujeres desde el umbral. México: Libros de Godot, 2007. 141 p. (Espejo de Godot)

This anthology provides access to three plays that focus on women: *Voces en el umbral*, one of the well-known plays of Rascón Banda; *Sazón de mujer*, and *Sabor de engaño*. *Sazón de mujer* takes place at a county fair in which three women are preparing to show off their special dishes. As they work, they talk about their personal stories. According to Rascón Banda's note, the three characters were inspired by women he met in Chihuahua. *Voces en el umbral* presents the story of a foreigner who comes to Northern Mexico to explore a gold mine and in his work, he exploits the native peoples who do the labor. His daughter recounts the story in flashbacks since the play opens when she is an old woman accompanied by her Tarahumara servant. The story examines the prejudices of the foreigners and their ill treatment of the indigenous and mestizo populations. In *Sabor de engaño*, two men and two women arrive in the capital of Mexico with great plans for their artistic endeavors, but fail to achieve their dreams. [SC]

2924 Rea, Juan Carlos. El predicador y la mujer pública: texto dramático en un acto. Mexicali, Mexico: Instituto de Cultura de Baja California, 2008. 63 p.

Based upon the dramatist's real-life encounter in a park, the one-act play centers on the dialogues between a priest, Malaquías, and a prostitute named Geraldina, but many other characters also bring their problems to the park. [SC]

2925 Renato Aguilar, Eric. Eric Renato Aguilar: hombre de teatro. Compilación de José Antonio López-Lavalle. Mérida, Mexico: Instituto de Cultura de Yucatán, 2008. 402 p. (Teatro)

This book provides a detailed perspective on Eric Renato Aguilar, the playwright, director, and actor whose untimely death in 1992 ended his many contributions to Yucatecan culture life. In Part One, aspects of his work with the Grupo Teatro de

Repertorio and an inventory of the plays Aguilar directed are included along with selections from critics offering brief analyses of his work. Part Two includes eight original plays: *Gastos superfluous*, a one-act monologue set in a train station; *Las 3 gracias . . . A dieta*, a three-act play inspired by a story by W. Somerset Maugham; *Para engañar al tiempo*, another one-act play that explores gender stereotypes; *Adagio para un recuerdo*, a study of the frustrations of not being able to attain one's dreams; *Gracias, Agatha Christie*, a three-act mystery in which Christie's Poirot is a character; *Secreto a voces*, a tour de force in which two sets of characters enact a funeral scene, first as two sisters, then as two brothers; *Todo lo que brilla no es oro* and deals with homosexuality the effects of AIDS, on a typical Yucatecan family; *Los peligros de Violeta*, a one-act farce with marionettes. [SC]

2926 Rivano, Luis. Antología de obras teatrales. Santiago: RiL Editores, 2008. 433 p.

Rivano has become an important playwright in contemporary Chilean theater. This anthology publishes nine of his plays that deal with a variety of topics, such as nostalgia, the imminent role of the past in the present, as well as the role of memory in personal events. *Los matarifes; El rucio de los cuchillos; Por sospecha; ¿Dónde estará la Jeannette?; Te llamabas Rosicler;* and *Escucho discos de Al Jolson, mamá* deal directly with these topics, while *Un gásfiter en sociedad* and *El hombre que compraba y vendía cosas* have a greater social and political component where the author brings up issues of marginalized classes. [PH]

2927 Rodríguez Febles, Ulises. El concierto y otras obras. Prólogo de Amado del Pino. La Habana: Letras Cubanas, 2007. 285 p. (Repertorio teatral cubano)

Five plays are in this edition: *El concierto*, which was awarded the Premio Virgilio Piñera and is his most well known play; *Carnicería, Huevos, Sputnik*, and *Oráculo*, which is a monologue. Always eager to experiment, the author "ahonda en el lenguaje, tanto en el vigoroso sistema de diálogos como en las auténticas imágenes que aporta al latente espectáculo", which, as Amado del Pino accurately notes, allows the reader to enter "un mundo de personajes, conflictos y situaciones, tan personal, desgarrador y auténtico". [SC]

2928 Roemer, Andrés. El otro Einstein. México: Miguel Angel Porrúa, 2008. 89 p.

In six scenes, Roemer presents the conflictive portrait of the great Nobel scientist as seen by the women who knew him as a multifaceted human being: Mileva Maric, Einstein's first wife, Elsa Löwenthal, his second wife, and Helen Dukas, his secretary from 1928 until his death in 1955. The three women wait to be interviewed by a *Time* reporter and as they wait they talk about the great man as they knew him—as a lover, father, son, and man of the world. As Einstein is unmasked from his iconic position, the audience members are also expected to review the personas they create in their own lives. [SC]

2929 Rojas Jiménez, Miguel. Tres historias de amor a flor de piel. San José: Editorial Costa Rica, 2008. 126 p.

Donde canta el mar has been published previously and presents the Costa Rican legend of La Llorona. The common thread running through the three plays is that none of the couples are able to have fulfilling relationships. The female characters are strong, yet trapped in unhappy circumstances. In general, Rojas always touches upon the deterioration of genuine human relationships and values in Costa Rican society in his plays. [SC]

2930 Sáenz, Jaime. Obra dramática. Edición de Leonardo García Pabón. La Paz: Plural Editores, 2005. 161 p.: ill.

This is an interesting collection that brings together three plays, *La máscara; Perdido viajero;* and *La noche del viernes*, which includes a CD of the production. Topics range from "mestizo" social problems, the "Altiplano" as a symbol of nationalism, to capitalism that forces Bolivian economy into subordination. [PH]

2931 Salcedo, Hugo. El perseguidor de Tlaxcala y otras obras de teatro. Mexicali, Mexico: Univ. Autónoma de Baja California, Departamento de Editorial Universitaria, 2008. 133 p.

Three plays are included: *El perseguidor de Tlaxcala, Los choros*, and *Rasgar la noche*. The first play was inspired by the precolumbian ball games, the Flowery Wars, as well as the short stories of Cortázar, Elena Garro, and Carlos Fuentes. The innovative use of a theatrical space that reconstructs a jai-alai court reflects Salcedo's point of view. *Los choros* offers a more realistic exploration of the conflicts among the members of a family in Baja California who refuse to face their straitened economic situation or their dislike for each other. Like the mussels of the title, they hide their own special gifts in a hard exterior until they are forced to expose their inner thoughts. *Rasgar la noche* presents a young man and woman who wind up in bed but have no great interest in each other until the last scene when the secret of their meeting is finally revealed. [SC]

2932 Schmidhuber de la Mora, Guillermo. Dramaturgia mexicana: fundación y herencia. Guadalajara, Mexico: Univ. de Guadalajara, Coordinación General Académica, Unidad para el Desarrollo de la Investigación y el Posgrado, 2006. 214 p.: bibl., ill., index.

Schmidhuber presents an historical record of the rich theatrical tradition in Mexico, with brief reviews of the colonial period, the 19th century, and then offering more in-depth analyses of the 20th-century experimental movements represented by Teatro Ulises, Teatro Orientación, and the contributions of Rodolfo Usigli. He provides brief overviews of the work of Elena Garro, Héctor Azar, Hugo Arguelles, and Vicente Leñero, and includes a final chapter on the "nueva dramaturgia mexicana." [SC]

2933 Spregelburd, Rafael. Remanente de invierno: Canciones alegres de niños de la patria; Cuadro de asfixia; Raspando la cruz; Satánica; Un momento argentino. Buenos Aires: Losada, 2005. 283 p. (Nuevo teatro)

This collection brings together a variety of Spregelburd's plays that encompass 20 years of his works and is accompanied by Jorge Dubatti's prologue, which contextualizes the plays and productions. Spregelburd's own recollections of his writing and productions are also present in this edition. In *Remanente de invierno*, television characters invade the "real" theater characters similar to that of the theater of the absurd, bringing a deconstructive and dehumanized effect

to the stage. *Canciones alegres de niños de la patria* is a short one-act play that deals with the end of a war and the beginning of peace and a new order, but the characters seem elusive and unable to adapt. *Caudro de asfixia* is loosely based on Ray Bradbury's *Fahrenheit 451* with a "criollo" touch, where characters suffer from amnesia and are constantly trying to remember their lines. *Raspando la cruz* is an intertextual play that brings together a variety of texts from Umberto Eco and Nietzsche to Nazi history in order to recreate ideas about WWII in a detective genre. *Satánica* explores the confines of satanic devotion and life. *Un momento argentino* is perhaps one of his most social and political plays that reveals the anguish of the economic crisis of 2001. [PH]

2934 Stranger Rodríguez, Inés Margarita. Cariño malo; Malinche; Tálamo. Providencia, Santiago: Editorial Cuarto Propio, 2007. 131 p.: index. (Dramaturgia. Serie libros del estudiante)

This collection offers three plays about women's roles in sociopolitical history as well as intimate events through different times in Latin American history. *Cariño malo* relates the loss of female identity in a patriarchal society. Three heroines, Victoria, Eva, and Amapola, try to find themselves through memory, mourning, and solidarity. Stranger uses five female characters to stage the ambiguous Latin American heroine and anti-heroine figure of "La Malinche" in order to portray her many conflicting sides: intelligent, bilingual, and politically involved character, while also showing her more vulnerable interpretation as a prostitute, traitor, and "la chingada." *Tálamo* brings attention to the private and close intimacy of two couples' wedding night in the past and in the present. [PH]

2935 Suárez, Patricia and **Leonel Giacometto.** Trilogía peronista: Las 20 y 25; Puerta de hierro; La eterna. Buenos Aires: Teatro Vivo, 2005. 110 p. (Teatro vivo; 23)

This trilogy explores historical and mythical aspects of Juan Domingo Perón and Evita. *Las 20 y 25* is a humorous play that provides an interesting perspective of Evita's life retold by her maids. *Puerta de hierro* brings together the actress Ava Gardner and Perón in a melancholic and nostalgic manner. *La eterna* is a humorous monologue where Evita comes to life to confront her own emaciated body after 17 years of exile. [PH]

2936 Teatro de Quimeras. Compilación de Jorge Prada Prada y Fernando Ospina Sánchez. Bogotá: Ediciones Teatro Quimera, 2006. 272 p.: ill.

This book provides a critical and historical perspective of the Colombian Experimental Grupo de Teatro Quimera since its inception in 1985. This important contribution is followed by a selection of plays: *El mundo perfecto; El conuco del tío conejo; Outside ¡Okey!; El pan de cada día;* and *En el umbral.* [PH]

2937 Teatro mexicano decimonónico. Selección y prologo de Eduardo Contreras Soto. México: Ediciones Cal y Arena, 2006. 833 p. (Los Impresindibles)

This important anthology for those interested in Mexican theatrical history contains 15 plays written between 1817 and 1905, representing the work of 12 dramatists. Eduardo Contreras Soto provides an introduction. Lizardi's *Pastorela en dos actos,* Gorostiza's *Contigo pan y cebolla,* and Fernando Calderón's *A ninguna de las tres* are among the more well-known plays included, while Alfredo Chavero's *Quetzalcoatl* and Constancio Suárez's *El fandango de los muertos* are worthy of further study. [SC]

2938 Torres Molina, Susana. Extraño juguete; Y a otra cosa mariposa. Buenos Aires: Teatro Vivo, 2008. 123 p. (Col. Teatro Vivo; 30)

This book compiles two of Torres Molina's better-known plays. *Extraño juguete* (1977) deals with the life of two women and a door-to-door salesman who learn from each other's life experiences. In *Y a otra cosa mariposa* (1981), Torres Molina explores the masculine world with a twist: all actors are women dressed as men. While they act like men, there is constant tension between their true masculine identities and how they are supposed to act according to society's standards. [PH]

2939 Valdez, Pedro Antonio. Reciclaje: flor de textos teatrales. San Juan: Santo Domingo: Isla Negra Editores, 2006. 98 p.: ill. (Col. Los pies de Edipo)

The five dramatic pieces included here are based on previous texts: *Paradise* offers a retelling of biblical Adam and Eve; *Máscaras crueles* is inspired by the etchings of Goya; *Parasitum* is a retelling of Red Riding Hood; *Operación Don Quijote* is a riff on the work of Cervantes; and *Retrato de familia* explores memories and family myths and their effect on individuals. [SC]

2940 Vargas Llosa, Mario. Al pie del Támesis. Fotografías de Morgana Vargas Llosa. Lima: Alfaguara, 2008. 82 p.: ill.

The background for this play is closely related to Vargas Llosa's own novel, *Los cachorros* (1967), where the two protagonists suffer a devastating sexual experience as children that marks their lives later. With a symbolic approach, the play retells the story of two adult men meeting in England half a century later, where one comes disguised as his "sister" when in reality it is the man himself—with a sex change. Their struggles with the past, their sexual orientation, and their own identities are central topics. The book offers a prologue and pictures from rehearsals. [PH]

2941 Vargas Llosa, Mario. Teatro: obra reunida. Madrid: Alfaguara, 2006. 555 p. (Biblioteca Mario Vargas Llosa)

This collection brings together five plays: *La señorita de Tacna; Kathie y el hipopótamo; La Chunga; El loco de los balcones;* and *Ojos bonitos, cuadros feos.* Topics vary from family, age, pride, destiny, to love, desire, hope, and "machismo." [PH]

2942 Veracruz: dramaturgia del puerto. Selección y prólogo de Enrique Mijares. Durango, Mexico: Univ. Juárez del Estado de Durango, 2007. 207 p. (Teatro de frontera; 19)

With a prologue by dramatist and critic Enrique Mijares, this volume includes *Perseos* and *Canción de Amor* by Daniel Domínguez; *Homo Zapping y Ragnarok a.k.A.: El ocaso de los dioses* by Gabriel Fuster; *Levanten las manos* by Humberto Hernández; *La otra vida* and *Esperando al gordo* by Ezequiel Lavandero Pascual; *Levantamiento de sepulcros* by Andrés Mata; *Fobia* by Luis Armando Torres Camacho; *El romance* by Arminda Vázquez Moreno; *Intrafamiliar* by Jorge Alejandro Vega; and

Die go by Carlos Vigil. A number of the plays weave motifs from previous texts into these very modern theatrical expressions. *Perseos* not only refers to the Greek myth, but also uses poetry by Gilberto Owen; another example is the obvious reference to Beckett's play in *Esperando al gordo*, but Lavandero Pascual explores the same philosophical questions in an audaciously humorous style. *Die go* incorporates folkloric references and a critique of multimedia's influence on Mexican culture. [SC]

2943 Viñas, David. Rodolfo Walsh y Gardel: monólogo final. Buenos Aires: Peón Negro, 2008. 58 p.

This monologue brings together two real Argentine figures: Rodolfo Walsh, who was disappeared during the last military dictatorship due to his political activism, and an interlocutor, Carlos Gardel, the legendary tango singer. The play pays homage to those people who fought for a better life during hard and authoritative times, while emphasizing the immortal state of both Gardel and Walsh in Argentine consciousness. [PH]

2944 Winer, Víctor. Postal de vuelo y otras piezas teatrales: Freno de mano; Luna de miel en Hiroshima; Un toque de inspiración; Examen de Carnaval. Estudio crítico de Pablo Mascareño. Buenos Aires: Ediciones Colihue, 2005. 149 p. (Colihue teatro. Dramaturgias argentinas)

Five of Víctor Winer's best plays are compiled in this edition together with contextual information about the author's life and work. *Postal de vuelo* is a sordid play with grotesque overtones about poverty and desperation, where four characters are unable to find a way out of this somber and dark world. *Freno de mano* is an allegorical play that foreshadows many of the events that took place during the 2001 Argentine economic crisis through a couple's struggles, repossessions, and forced exile. *Luna de miel en Hiroshima* takes a closer look at moral values, corruption, the symbolic use of "ghost trains" and their affect on post-dictatorial society, and illegal use of power when a teacher marries a handicapped woman for money. *Un toque de inspiración* is about a writer who needs to be inspired to write about the desert. *Examen de Carnaval* is a short, humorous play that takes place in

a train station where ghosts return to question why the protagonist left town. [PH]

2945 Yeras, Roberto D. M. Noria. La Habana: Ediciones Alarcos, 2006. 63 p. (Col. Aire frío)

Set in a bar in Havana during the 1990s, the characters—five men and two women—all speaking in a regional Cuban accent that the text faithfully transcribes, suffer from the depression of having little money, no work, and no hope for a better future. [SC]

THEATER CRITICISM AND HISTORY

2946 Belgrave, Claire. Theatre in the Bahamas: from Ol' story to Rep Theatre. Nassau, Bahamas: Guanima Press, 2007. 264 p.: bibl.

This book fills a void by presenting the evolution of theater in the Bahamas. It traces the movement from forms of drama in the oral tradition and amateur theater to contemporary theatrical expressions like the Dundas Repertory Company. Nine chapters cover, in chronological order, theatrical activities, the contributions of theater groups, and actors from the early years of the 20th century until 1992. Belgrave includes descriptions of play performances, play synopses, many photos, and descriptions of the political context to put the work of the playwrights into an historical perspective. [SC]

2947 Bermúdez, Sari. Voces que cuentan. México: Plaza y Janés, 2002. 320 p.

This book includes 29 interviews conducted by Sari Bermúdez with some of the most important and influential writers, critics, and cultural icons in the 90s. She includes Elena Garro, Carlos Monsivais, Elena Poniatowska, Octavio Paz, José Agustín, as well as Enrique Krauze, Raquel Tibol, Oliver Stone, and Edward James Olmos. [SC]

2948 Chesney Lawrence, Luis. Relectura del teatro venezolano, 1900–1950: los orígenes de la dramaturgia moderna. Caracas: Fondo Editorial de la Facultad de Humanidades y Educación, Univ. Central de Venezuela, 2008. 349 p.: bibl., chart.

With exquisite historical background, Chesney Lawrence presents an excellent and important study of Venezuelan theater during the first half of the 20th century. His attention to social and cultural events is fused with the publication and production of plays, and thus, he presents the inception of the "sainete," its significance and relevance on a new and modern national theater, as well as the avant-garde playwrights and their roles in nationalizing the Venezuelan stage. He gives succinct information and analysis of the later decades from the 1920s, 30s, 40s, and concludes with the 50s and the new tendencies of the modern stage of the time. [PH]

2949 Davini, Silvia Adriana. Cartografías de la voz en el teatro contemporáneo: el caso de Buenos Aires a fines del siglo XX. Bernal, Argentina: Univ. Nacional de Quilmes Editorial, 2007. 259 p.: bibl. (Col. Textos y lecturas en ciencias sociales)

This book approaches the study of voice, gestures, and acting in the theater as its core artistic manifestation through history. With a critical study on rhetoric, Davini explores the link between the oral tradition of theater vis-à-vis the written text, while she emphasizes her studies on the interconnections between acting, text, and voice in the theater of Buenos Aires in the 1990s. Her study also focuses on the role of professional actors, voice schools, sound design, and some of the most pertinent playwrights, such as Ricardo Bartís and Rafael Spregelburd, who write for the theater, paying close attention to the actors' voice and presence on stage. [PH]

2950 De Shakespeare a Veronese: tensiones, espacios y estrategias del teatro comparado en el contexto latinoamericano. Edición de Graciela González de Díaz Araujo. Compilación de M. Micaela Amorós. Buenos Aires: Editorial Nueva Generación, 2007. 559 p.

This collection compiles 39 conference papers from the II Congreso Argentino Internacional de Teatro Comparado. It opens with an introduction on comparative theater by Graciela González de Díaz Araujo followed by Jorge Dubatti's keynote paper on "El concepto de micropoética en los estudios de teatro comparado." With varying degrees, all contributions touch on the key issues related to the studies of comparative theater in Argentina. For instance, José Francisco Navarrete considers "Circulación y recepción del teatro italiano en Mendoza," an historical approach to understanding the interconnections between 19th- and 20th-century theaters. In a more comparative line, Susana Tarantuviez offers a succinct study with "Macbeth es mujer: la construcción del sujeto femenino de Shakespeare a Gambaro." In a similar vein, both Marcela Montero's "Bernarda Alba: portavos de la obsesión," and Verónica Sentis Herrmann's "Las pelotas, ¿Civilización o Barbarie? Anotaciones sobre la resignificación de una obra europea en el contexto latinoamericano" trace the connections between European and Latin American theater. [PH]

2951 Dosio, Celia. El Payró: cincuenta años de teatro independiente. Buenos Aires: Emecé Editores, 2003. 235 p.: bibl., ill. (Emecé Argentina. Historia)

In celebration of the 50th anniversary of the Independent Theatre Payró, Celia Dosio has compiled an excellent historical and archival work on the production, set designs, directors, and playwrights who at one point were part of this theater. The work provides detailed stage information, behind-the-scenes photographs, and interviews of key members of the Payró in different decades, such as Diego Kogan, Onofre Lovero, Fabiana Lusardi, Luis Ordaz, and Jorge Goldenberg. This study also expands on the historical weight of "teatro independiente" in Argentina, and traces El Payro's birth, previously known as "Los Independientes," as the first theater built by a collective or co-op. The final chronology of Payro's premieres from 1953 to 2002 shows the variety of the productions ranging from international playwrights, such as Eugene O'Neill, Molière, Orson Welles, and Franz Kafka to national names, such as Agustín Cuzzani, Carlos Somigliana, Eduardo Pavlovsky, Roberto Cossa, and Eduardo Rovner, among others. [PH]

2952 Dubatti, Jorge. Concepciones de teatro: poéticas teatrales y bases epistemológicas. Buenos Aires: Colihue, 2009. 211 p.: bibl. (Colihue Universidad. Teatro)

This book offers new perspectives on theater studies in Argentina. Combining theater philosophy, comparative theater, comparative poetics, and theater cartography, Dubatti delves into the basic epistemology of theater history through 19th and 20th century European drama. [PH]

2953 Extraños en dos patrias: teatro latinoamericano del exilio. Edición de Heidrun Adler y Adrián Herr con la colaboración de Almuth Fricke. Frankfurt, Germany: Vervuert; Madrid: Iberoamericana, 2003. 213 p.: bibl. (Teatro en Latinoamérica; 12)

Exile has been a topic of much reverence in Latin America and this book aims to find critical voices that study how theater has shown and reacted to political exile in the 20th century. Osvaldo Dragún speaks from the diaspora and offers invaluable information about theater companies who were exiled in France. Both Guillermo Heras and Nora Eidelberg describe the difficulties of staging Latin American plays in Spain due to cultural and linguistic differences. Osvaldo Pellettieri emphasizes the theater influences brought by Italian immigrants such as the "grotesco criollo." George Woodyard also traces the immigration effect on Roberto Cossa, Jorge Díaz, and Arístides Vargas' plays. Jorge Febles, Frauke Gewecke, Heidrun Adler, and Christilla Vasserot discuss Cuban and Cuban American theater and the role of exile in many of their plays. Iani Moreno and Uta Atzpodien focus on borderland issues in the Mexican border with the US, as well as the inner borders of Mexican indigenous cultures. [PH]

2954 Fuentes Ibarra, Guillermina. Cuatro propuestas escénicas en la Ciudad de México: Teatro Panamericano, de las Artes, Teatro de Medianoche y la Linterna Mágica, 1939–1948. México: UNAM, Dirección General de Publicaciones y Fomento Editorial: Instituto Nacional de Bellas Artes, 2007. 300 p.: bibl., ill.

A very useful text that contains documentation, photos, programs, and biographical sketches. Describes the work of four theatrical groups that produced plays in the 1940s in Mexico City: Fernando Wagner's Teatro Panamericano; Seki Sano's Teatro de Las Artes, Rodolfo Usigli's Teatro De Medianoche and Ignaio Retes' La Linterna Mágica. This is an important aid for researchers trying to understand the historiography of Mexican theater. [SC]

2955 Geirola, Gustavo. Arte y oficio del director teatral en América Latina: Argentina, Chile, Paraguay y Uruguay. Buenos Aires: Editorial Nueva Generación, 2007. 500 p.

Geirola embarks on his second volume of interviews with theater directors conducted between 2004 and 2006. This time his focus is a rich and heterogeneous mix of highly acclaimed theater directors. The book begins with interviews of some of the most renowned directors from Argentina, from the late Alejandra Boero, Adhemar Bianchi, and Agustín Alezzo to Hector Rodríguez Brussa, Laura Yusem, Ricardo Bartís, and Claudio Gallardou. This extraordinary and diverse group of directors offers great insights into the world of stage production, the behind-the-scenes life of theater, and the interesting world of "teatro off" in Argentina. Chile also offers its dynamic group of directors, ranging from well-known artists like Ramón Griffero and Rodrigo Pérez to the sometimes-controversial Alberto Kurapel and the lesser-known directors, such as Ana Harcha and Angel Lattus. From Uruguay, Geirola contributes more interviews by well-known directors Rubén Yáñez, Jorge Denevi, Jorge Esmoris, and, from the younger generation of women directors, Nelly Goitino and Mariana Percovich. There are also interviews with directors Julio Saldaña and Tana Schembori from Paraguay. [PH]

2956 Martínez, Clara and **Julieta Orduña.** Una aventura llamada teatro: Aguascalientes en el siglo XIX. México: Escenología, 2005. 215 p.: bibl., ill. (Col. Escenología; 7)

A useful text filled with documents, photos, and information about the theater scene of 19th-century Aguascalientes. [SC]

2957 Pereira Poza, Sergio. Antología crítica de la dramaturgia anarquista en Chile. Santiago: Editorial Univ. de Santiago, 2005. 358 p.: bibl.

Pereira Poza assembles a well-founded historical and critical study together with the publication of seven "forgotten" anarchist plays with high political and social overtones. These plays are *Los Grilletes* by Alfred Aaron; *Suprema Lex* by Rufino Rosas; *Los cuervos* by Amrando Treviño; *Flores rojas* by Nicolás Aguirre

Bretón; *Un hombre* and *El sábado* by Adolfo Urzúa Roxas; and *Los vampiros* by Nicolás Aguirre Bretón. [PH]

2958 Piña, Juan Andrés. Historia del teatro en Chile, 1890–1940. Santiago: RiL, 2009. 413 p.: bibl., ill., ports. (Bibliodiversidad)

This book is a solid, well-researched study of Chilean theater that bridges the end of the 19th century and the beginning of the 20th. The author pays close attention to the European influences that transformed Chilean theater, and thus offers great historical information and analysis on "género chico" from Spain and Chile, Spanish and Chilean zarzuelas, the role of Chilean actors, theater groups, and production companies, as well as providing vast information on audience response, journalistic accounts, and the role of media during this time. The book is divided into three parts: "Los espectáculos del Chile finisecular (1890–1917)"; "Nacimiento y apogeo del teatro chileno (1918–1930);" and "De la consolidación a la crisis (1931–1940)." [PH]

2959 Pino, Amado del. Acotaciones: crítica teatral (1985–2000). La Habana: Ediciones UNIÓN, 2005. 253 p.: bibl., index.

This is a useful and invaluable compilation by journalist Amado del Pino, who has collected many of his performance reviews of Cuban theater written between 1985 and 2000. Some of the recurring themes are Brecht and Lorca's influence on the Cuban stage, the production of plays by Vicente Revuelta, Roberto Blanco, and Berta Martínez, the new generation of Cuban playwrights in the 1990s, the role of theater festivals, and the resistance and resilience of theater groups that work outside of La Habana. [PH]

2960 Reyes de la Maza, Luis. El teatro en México durante la Revolución, 1911–1913. México: Escenología, A.C., 2005. 431 p. (Col Escenología. Consulta; 6)

Reyes de la Maza begins with a preliminary study of the major trends and figures and then includes chapters on each year from 1911–13, describing the many plays that were produced in those years, offering material from playbills or newspapers. The book is useful for students of theater and historians who wish to get a

sense of the cultural scene of these crucial years of the Revolution. [SC]

2961 Stages of conflict: a critical anthology of Latin American theater and performance. Edited by Diana Taylor and Sarah J. Townsend. Translation coordination by Margaret Carson. Ann Arbor: Univ. of Michigan Press, 2008. 325 p.: bibl., ill.

This is the first English-language collection that provides a selection of theater and performance practices in Latin America of indigenous theater, European style plays, and popular performances dating back to the conquest and covering over 500 years. The introduction gives succinct and solid historical, political, and cultural perspectives of Latin America, while situating theater and performance as cultural practices that constitute society's own perception of history. The plays are: *Rabinal Achi* (Guatemala); *Final Judgment* (Andrés de Olmos); *The End of Atau Wallpa, a Tragedy* (Jesús Lara); *The Loa for the Auto Sacramental of the Divine Narcissus* (Sor Juana Inés de la Cruz); *Los Comanches* (US/Mexico Border); *The Jealous Officer, or the Fearsome Slave Catcher* (Luís Carlos Martins Pena); *Juan Moreira* (Gutiérrez/Podestá); *After Death* (Luisa Capetillo); *The Candle King* (Oswald de Andrade); *Electra Garrigó* (Virgilio Piñera); *Night of the Assassins* (José Triana); *The Camp* (Griselda Gambaro); *Documents from Hell* (Enrique Buenaventura); *Personal Belongings* (Diana Raznovich); *Isabel Banished in Isabel* (Juan Radrigán); *Denise Stoklos in Mary Stuart* (Denise Stoklos); *Adiós Ayacucho* (Julio Ortega/Miguel Rubio); *Manteca* (Alberto Pedro Torriente); and *The Demon's Nun* (Cruz Cruz/Juárez Espinosa). For comment by translation specialist, see item **3288**. [PH]

2962 Teatro argentino y crisis, 2001–2003. Edición, estudio preliminar y dirección de Osvaldo Pellettieri. Buenos Aires: Eudeba, 2004. 279 p.: bibl. (Teatro en Eudeba)

This collection of 11 essays expresses different views of how the economic crisis of 2001 affected the theater scene. Osvaldo Pellettieri opens the edition with his preliminary study tracing a historical link between different crises in Argentina during the 20th century (economic or political) and how they influenced the theater in creative forms such as political theater, *Teatro abierto*, and Theater of Disentegration. Laura Cilento in "El discurso de la crítica: más cerca de la epopeya que del Apocalipsis" discusses the role of theater journalists during the crisis. Javier Daulte contributes "Producción artística y crisis" and offers his own experience as a playwright writing and directing during this time. In a different vein, Cristina Piña writes "El teatro extranjero en Buenos Aires durante la crisis: entre la sordera y la atención vigilante," where she makes a connection between the plays performed, such as *Un enemigo del pueblo* by Henrik Ibsen or *Decadencia* by Stefen Berkoff, and the way the audience closely relates to them due to the economic struggles. Martín Rodríguez contributes "El teatro dominante y la crisis: de los 'pactos de interés' a los 'pactos de deseo,'" as an anlysis of the reaction of Argentine society to the post-crisis. In a positive light, Beatriz Trastoy observes in "El teatro argentino en tiempos de crisis: nuevas reflexiones, nuevos temas, nuevos personajes, nuevas propuestas escénicas" that there was more production and more audience who went to see theater as a way to cope with the crisis. The other essays focus on different venues of theater such as children's theater, varieté, and interviews with theater practitioners and their views about theater and the economic crisis. [PH]

BRAZIL
Novels

REGINA IGEL, *Professor of Spanish and Portuguese, University of Maryland, College Park*

INTO THE SECOND DECADE OF THIS CENTURY, Brazilian literature shows significant signs of a tendency towards globalization of its themes and characters. Many novels are created within a setting that leaves behind the limitations of "regionalism" and similar nationalistic labels. Some narratives are internationalized by authors who place plots in several parts of the world, while characters demonstrate fears, hopes, and other universal feelings, not restricted to local Brazilian circumstances. Nevertheless, the characters of most of these novels remain associated with their natural Brazilian cultural roots.

This trend is illustrated in *Um livro em fuga* by Edgard T. Ribeiro (item **2986**), whose title reflects an ambiguity that can be interpreted as "a flight" and "a vanishing line," both connected to a narrative placed beyond national boundaries, in a faraway land where the author, a Brazilian diplomat, was serving his country. Similarly, in *O movimento pendular* by Alberto Mussa (item **2982**), a love triangle travels across regions and time outside Brazil. Also involved with love in several landscapes within and beyond its frontiers is *Heranças* by Silviano Santiago (item **2987**). An international dimension is equally found in *O mundo como obra de arte criada no Brasil* by Renato Pompeu (item **2985**), a story where an amalgamation of all cultures in the world is sought. A "character" of universal recognition is Albert Einstein in the historical novel *O plágio de Einstein* by Carlos Alberto dos Santos (item **2988**). Santos deals with a supposed plagiarism by the scientist, which was an international scandal at the time of the revolutionary equation, and still is. In *Goethe e Barrabás* by Deonísio da Silva (item **2989**), the narrative portrays characters intending to change Brazil, and includes universal symbols and biblical meanings. Also dealing with foreigners as characters, *Pássaros de vôo curto* by Alcione Araújo (item **2966**) brings them to Brazil, where a British engineer and an American pianist travel deep into the backlands. In another story of an outsider trapped within the Brazilian landscape, *Black Music* by Arthur Dapieve (item **2971**) tells of a black American boy kidnapped and held prisoner in a Rio de Janeiro slum.

Besides these globalizing novels, traditional narratives with Brazilian characters and activities continue to be published, some written in a non-traditional manner. An example of the latter is *Acenos e afagos* by João Gilberto Noll (item **2983**), comprising one unique paragraph. Another example of an experimental novel is *O livro dos nomes* by Maria Esther Maciel (item **2976**), which introduces characters in alphabetical order, their stories overlapping as they meet in various locales. Bizarre topics are also part of the creative literary process, as in *Jonas, o copromanta* by Patrícia Melo (item **2978**), where the protagonist, a librarian in Rio de Janeiro, is actually a "reader of feces," declaring himself the inspiration for "Copromancia," a short story by Rubem Fonseca, an author idolized by Melo's main character. Further in the realm of writerly innovations is *Depois do sexo* by Marcelo Carneiro da Cunha (item **2970**), a combination of a puzzle and a novel, making the readers part of the narrative composition. Less uncommon, but still innovative, *A parede no escuro* by Altair Martins and awarded the São Paulo Literature Prize for First Novel in 2009 (item **2977**) deals with 14 narratives told by several characters about the loss of a father in a mysterious car accident. Atypical language is part of *Animais em extinção* by Marcelo Mirisola (item **2980**), whose narrator-protagonist uncovers the social ills of the underground of some Brazilian cities.

Urban environment is also the backdrop for *Tragédia da Rua da Praia: uma história de sangue, jornal e cinema* by Rafael Guimarães (item **2974**), awarded the Prize for Best Book in 2005, involving a brutal assault to a money exchange store in Porto Alegre, Rio Grande do Sul, in 1911. Though urban environment is prevalent in traditional and nontraditional Brazilian narratives, indigenous and backlands stories are also part of literary creativity as we enter the second decade of the 21st century. The city of Manaus is both the background and foreground of *Órfãos do Eldorado* by Milton Hatoum (item **2975**), a novel filled with allegories and indigenous legends whose scholarly sources are acknowledged by the author. While the latter emphasizes the abandonment of the forest community, another work located in the same Amazonian region, *Todas as coisas são pequenas* by indigenous author Daniel Munduruku (item **2981**), demonstrates the redeeming qualities of the jungle for a young man disillusioned by urban life.

Some of the literary essays emerging in recent years are both informative and based on sound scholarship. *Uma história do romance de 30* by Luís Bueno (item **2968**) is, as the title indicates, a study of the socio-political-literary atmosphere prevailing in Brazil shortly before and after 1930. The study focuses on novels by four authors who contributed the most to the establishment of the "social novel" (*romance social*): Cornélio Penna, Dyonélio Machado, Cyro dos Anjos, and Graciliano Ramos. Another study worthy of consultation is *O livro dos fragmentos* by Antonio Carlos Villaça (item **2994**), which includes excerpts of dialogues with some members of the Brazilian intellectual community during the 20th century, such as Gilberto Amado, Tristão de Athayde, Geraldo França Lima, and Guimarães Rosa, among others of equal renown. Quoting from many authors, sources, and theories, *Heróis de papel* by Jerri Roberto Almeida (item **2963**) explains literature as a cultural expression, beyond its esthetic dimension. Similarly, the study *Contando histórias, fazendo história: experiência com os poetas cordelistas do*

Cariri by João Bosco Alves de Sousa (item **2991**) analyzes popular culture by examining "literatura de cordel" (*string literature*) in Ceará.

A new generation is emerging and new topics are being explored in the history of Brazilian literature at the beginning of the second decade of this century. An attempt to globalize themes and characters is not only intriguing, but also of interest to all who approach Brazilian novels, whether as readers, scholars, or students. Nevertheless, traditional topics and narration styles still hold the focus of talented old and new writers.

2963 Almeida, Jerri Roberto. Heróis de papel: as representações sobre a Revolução Farroupilha na literatura. Porto Alegre, Brazil: Editora Alcance, 2007. 95 p.: bibl., ill.

In this study, the author views literature beyond its esthetic appeal, interpreting it as a cultural manifestation of some specific human experiences. In his attempt at combining literature and history, he looks for support on a series of theoretic frames, exemplified by concepts of "historic novel" and "historic fiction," cultural studies, and the relativity of national and regional identities. The text is rich in quotations by many authors, both Brazilians (Roberto da Matta, Ruben George Oliven, among others) and foreigners (Eric Hobsbawn, Adam Schaff, etc.).

2964 Almeida, Júlia Lopes de. Memórias de Marta: romance. Atualização dos textos, introdução, cronologia e notas de Rosane Saint-Denis Salomoni. Florianópolis, Brazil: Editora Mulheres; Santa Cruz do Sul, Brazil: Edunisc, 2007. 166 p. (Série Ensaios)

Re-edition of a book first published in 1888, when the author was 26 years old. She also wrote many other novels, short stories, plays, and children booklets, in total 40 books, in addition to having penned chronicles and educational articles for journals and magazines. In this novel, the trail-blazer in feminist literature in Brazil advocates for the education of women, as exemplified by the protagonist-narrator Marta, who is raised from extreme poverty to become a teacher and educator. The author, after more than 50 years of having her books kept as inconspicuous, is now the focus of studies by scholars, especially since the late 70s after her works began to be republished.

2965 Aragão, Adrino. A cabeça do peregrino cortada em triunfo pelos filhos do cão. Manaus, Brazil: Valer Editora: Edições Governo do Estado, 2005. 90 p.

This short narrative (less than 100 p.) is, nevertheless, a novel populated with strong characters who are ready to defend their freedom against the predatory activities of landowners. The time frame was a Brazil recently converted from a monarchy to a republic. The landscape is the vastness of the *sertão*. In addition to the skirmishes between those in favor of and against the new regime, there were popular rebellions against the land barons, with their manipulations to keep the population under a slavery disguised as something else. For its religious messages, its processions, fanaticism, the story seems to mingle the main topic of *Os Sertões*, by Euclides da Cunha, to some cinematographic scenes of the movie *Black God, White Devil* (*Deus e o Diabo na Terra do Sol*), directed by the iconic Glauber Rocha.

2966 Araújo, Alcione. Pássaros de vôo curto. Rio de Janeiro: Editora Record, 2008. 461 p.

This dense novel instigates the reader to reorganize the text, distributed as short descriptions of characters' activities. Two women, a lyric singer and her female friend, along with a driver, are involved with investigating the depth of the Brazilian backlands. A British engineer and an American pianist, both male adventurers, join the group. Though intended to keep a postmodern profile, the novel still follows traditional patterns of narrative.

2967 Azevedo, Fal. Minúsculos assassinatos e alguns copos de leite. Rio de Janeiro: Rocco, 2008. 203 p.

This narrative comprises two periods, past and present, which alternate short descriptive texts of an intimate nature. Graphic resources help in the separation of these periods, which were experienced by the female narrator. The two eventually become one story, mingling time and space. Feelings of impotence, anger, and attempts at reconciliation with the past and the people that populated it are strong elements in this long and original monologue.

2968 Bueno, Luís. Uma história do romance de 30. São Paulo: EdUSP; Campinas, Brazil: Editora Unicamp, 2006. 707 p.: bibl., indexes.

The often misunderstood literary movement initiated in the decade of the 30s in Brazil is examined in its convoluted and complex richness in political, social, and esthetic directions. The panoramic examination of the years that witnessed the 1930 Revolution and the 1937 installation of the Estado Novo, and the analyses of the so-called social novel (*romance social*) are funneled into the examination of four authors and their fictional works: Cornélio Penna, Dyonélio Machado, Cyro dos Anjos, and Graciliano Ramos. Other than following the established pattern of "right" and "wrong," of "left" and "right," the author indicates how the authors established their own style, vision, landscape, and frictions in their novels. Without ignoring, though, the premises of the social novel, they created their fictional worlds away from the narrowness of sending "social messages" in novels that, once political changes would take place, would become obsolete. The critic emphasizes how their novels, nevertheless, retain the spirit of the times or the restlessness of the people, keeping pace with their inner conflicts, and their intimate thoughts and reflections on their lives, their social environment, and on their conditions as participants of the neglected layer of Brazilian society.

2969 Caldeira, Almiro. O lume da madrugada: romance. Florianópolis, Brazil: Editora da UFSC, 2008. 256 p.

The author of *Rocamaranha* (see *HLAS 26:1962*) and *Arca açoriana* (see *HLAS 48:6126*), among other narratives related to the history of immigrants from the Azorean Islands to the south of Brazil, included this novel as part of his description, imaginary and real, of the state of Santa Catarina in the 19th century. As with most historical novels, this one remains close, within the possibilities of a fictional story, to dates and places. Thus, it is divided

in three parts, each headed by a date, from 1845–48. Emperor Pedro II and his wife spent one month in the area, in 1845, which stirred up the population of Desterro. The numerous characters move around flirtations, commitments, intrigues, envy, and other feelings pervading the town and the country in the region, before and after the Emperor's visit. The author utilized 19th-century terms in a successful attempt to create a realistic atmosphere of the times. A touch of the supernatural echoes through the novel, mainly with a mysterious "light" (lume), which is in the title, emerging from the ocean.

2970 Cunha, Marcelo Carneiro da. Depois do sexo. Rio de Janeiro: Editora Record, 2008. 314 p.

A sort of an interactive novel, the three stories related by three characters are constructed like a puzzle, which is put together as one reads. A doctor formerly addicted to cocaine meets a suicidal girl and they have an affair; then the same doctor and a female judge start a love story. Sex is part of the lives of all of the characters, but more important is what happens to them beyond their carnal agreement or discord. Exposed mostly through an extended dialogue, the writing tends towards a movie script inserted in the novel.

2971 Dapieve, Arthur. Black music. Rio de Janeiro: Objetiva, 2008. 116 p.

A slum area in Rio de Janeiro is the set for this narrative about the kidnapping of a black American boy, who was then a resident in the city. He remains a prisoner in a hut, surrounded by men wearing masks portraying Bin Laden. While his father does not pay the demanded ransom, he is in the hands of his captors, with whom he develops an ambiguous relationship. The story is narrated by the boy and by two of his captors, a woman and a man. Distinctive graphic patterns separate each version of the episode involving the hostage, drug dealers, and slum dwellers, who talk about their problems, frustrations, and dreams.

2972 Earp, Jorge de Sá. O novelo. Rio de Janeiro: 7 Letras, 2008. 203 p.

This novel completes the trilogy initiated by *O Olmo e a Palmeira* (2006) and *O Legado* (2007). The three tell stories related to social and geographical displacements of families hurt by political and economic circumstances. *O novelo* focuses, through personal narratives voiced by several characters, on changes that occurred in Brazil from the first quarter of the 20th century to the military rule of the 60s. The individual episodes are stylistically independent, though they complement each other, composing a large panoramic view of a certain Brazilian way of life for a period of 60 years.

2973 Garcia-Roza, Luiz Alfredo. Espinosa sem saída. São Paulo: Companhia das Letras, 2006. 210 p.

Detective Espinosa dives into one or two more complex crimes in Rio de Janeiro. This story is filled with crimes and mysteries as fits a detective novel. The narrative is rich in detailed description of interior spaces and nature. Intense dialogue is developed within the stories. For comment on translation of this novel, *Blackout: an Inspector Espinosa mystery*, see item **3294**.

2974 Guimaraens, Rafael. Tragédia da Rua da Praia: uma história de sangue, jornal e cinema. Porto Alegre, Brazil: Libretos, 2005. 304 p.: bibl., ill., maps.

Detailed account, mixed with fictionalized events, of a crime that shook up Brazil in 1911. Four immigrants invaded a money exchange post in downtown Porto Alegre, Rio Grande do Sul, executing its employee on the spot. The author, a journalist by training, combed archives, newspapers, and other documents in order to assemble the atmosphere of the times. The repercussion of the crime involved economic, social, and political dimensions. Pictures and a rich bibliography are included in the novel, which was awarded the Prize for Best Book in 2005.

2975 Hatoum, Milton. Órfãos do Eldorado. São Paulo: Companhia das Letras, 2008. 107 p. (Col. Mitos)

The same city of Manaus that appeared in the author's former novels returns as background and foreground in this narrative. Nevertheless, its profile is drawn entangled in reality, myth, legends, and folklore, engraved in the very lively routine of that urban site inlaid in the midst of a powerful forest. Orphans comprise a metaphor to the state of forlornness that Brazilians feel—either abandoned by parents, institutions, or government and, ultimately, by hopes nurtured during a lifetime. *Eldorado* is all of these things: a ship that sinks, a nonexistent city, a mirage. The people, Manaus' characters, reviving these *eldorados*, are also submersed in their hopeless way and paths of life. The author indicates, in the Acknowledgment, his scholarly sources for the narratives on the indigenous myths and legends. For comment on English-language translation, see item **3296**.

2976 Maciel, Maria Esther. O livro dos nomes. São Paulo: Companhia das Letras, 2008. 170 p.

Entertaining for its ability to stimulate a reader's curiosity, the narrative of the novel is driven by an innovative (though orderly) type of word play. The characters make their appearance in alphabetical order. The linguistic roots of each name are explained and a variety of philosophical interpretations are introduced. The characters meet in places where people and words interact. The author shows her ability to uncover hidden resources in the Portuguese language as used in Brazil by inserting new meanings within traditional concepts of love, hatred, harmony, and betrayal.

2977 Martins, Altair. A parede no escuro. Rio de Janeiro: Editora Record, 2008. 253 p.

Awarded the São Paulo Prize of Literature for First Novel (2009), multiple voiced narratives (14) focus on the loss of a father in a small family. He was a baker who died in a car accident; the driver's father was a witness to the crash that took away their neighbor's life. The novel turns around this topic, involving the daughter of the deceased, who takes over the direction of the bakery in spite of her plan to become a veterinary doctor. The young man who killed her father tries to reach a police district to confess, but the bureaucratic system hardly gives attention to him. An allegorical representation of a society filled with brutality, cruelty, and coldness, the novel presents some qualities of a telenovela, though in print.

2978 Melo, Patrícia. Jonas, o copromanta. São Paulo: Companhia das Letras, 2008. 173 p.

Jonas, an employee at the National Library in Rio de Janeiro, has the habit of guessing his future on his feces, as if he were performing the traditional "reading" of tea leaves. "Roman à clef," the narrative includes the cameo presence of Brazilian author Rubem Fonseca, author of "Copromancia," a short story that is perceived by the hero (or anti-hero) as a copy of his life as "copromanta" (a neologism meaning "excrement reader or interpreter"). Affected by what he considered to be plagiarism on the part of Fonseca, he expands his obsession to find the author with the help of three women, one of whom is also inclined to some esoteric habits. Melo's intention is to honor Fonseca, featuring Jonas as one of his obsessed followers.

2979 Miguel, Salim. Mare nostrum: romance desmontável. Rio de Janeiro: Editora Record, 2004. 174 p.

The 19 chapters comprising this novel are, in the author's words, "detachable," meaning that one does not need to read them in the traditional sequence from beginning to end. Being independent, their common trait is the sea. Like the regions conquered by the Romans around what today is the Mediterranean Sea, this "Mare nostrum" is the gathering of several stories, all bordered and infused by the sea as its main landscape. Mirroring its versatility, characters and stories are different, reverberating, in land, its nurturing calmness and its fatal perils.

2980 Mirisola, Marcelo. Animais em extinção. Rio de Janeiro: Editora Record, 2008. 174 p.

Irreverent language matches the development of some topics usually kept under wraps in Western society: pedophilia, transvestites, and prostitution. From São Paulo to Paraíba, the narrator-protagonist dives into the underground, tacitly not acknowledged by the law-abiding and conservative citizens, until some become the victims of thieves, assailants, and murderers. Sarcastic and sharp comments pervade the narrative, whose targets range from pretentious writers to arrogant editors to losers of all kinds. The author is a sort of an "enfant terrible" of contemporary Brazilian literature.

2981 Munduruku, Daniel. Todas as coisas são pequenas. São Paulo: ARX, 2008. 159 p.

Of indigenous origin from the state of Pará, the author is known for writing books for children in which he explains the indigenous Amazon culture for young readers. A graduate in philosophy and education, this is his first book for adults. Though it keeps, to a certain extent, a didactic tonality, the narrative refers to an urbanized and disenchanted young man who goes back to the forest community where he was born and finds the key to personal and universal happiness.

2982 Mussa, Alberto. O movimento pendular. Rio de Janeiro: Editora Record, 2006. 237 p.: ill.

Though a topic such as adultery might be thought to be exhausted, it emerges in this novel in a science-fiction mode that scrutinizes several love triangles across time and world regions. The author creates theorems, axioms, and other theoretic frameworks to prove, through equations and premises, that adultery or love among three people is as old as Adam, Eve, and God. More of a science-fiction narrative than a novel in the conventional sense of plot development, the work comprises several narrative avenues, thus resulting in a possible dispersion of readers' attention.

2983 Noll, João Gilberto. Acenos e afagos. Rio de Janeiro: Editora Record, 2008. 206 p.

Graphically, the novel comprises one and only one paragraph, though monologues, dialogues and puncutation are included. The basic story develops between two men who met in childhood, when one becomes obsessed with finding the other later in life. Homoeroticism, fixation for a love object, and passion are the themes of this search by the "engineer," who would bring spiritual comfort, physical plenitude, and love to the one who was married and had a son, yet was unable to forget the man of his life. Neither of them is named in the narrative, and their identities are equally blurred between male and female.

2984 Piroli, Wander. Eles estão aí fora: romance. Belo Horizonte, Brazil: Editora Leitura, 2006. 123 p.

Posthumous publication by an author who was a best-seller in Brazil, mainly because of his short stories. His texts, like those in this novel, are characterized by informal language, the characters' colloquialisms, and dialogues among members of a family, friends, and colleagues. The author is successful in addressing topics generated by intimate problems, generational frictions, and individual anguishes. Most probably, his background in journalism has contributed to his terse mechanism of writing and his preference for a direct approach to the plots, thus his inclination towards dialogues and monologues.

2985 Pompeu, Renato. O mundo como obra de arte criada pelo Brasil: romance-ensaio. São Paulo: Editora Casa Amarela, 2006. 211 p.

This essay-novel presents "Tatinha," a Brazilian *mestiza* who gathers in herself all the best and most attractive traits of humankind: high cheeks like a Chinese girl, light movements of an Indian dancer, etc. Characters from all over the world contribute to the composition of a song (samba, for good measure) that should be an *objet d'art*, which will become the symbol of an amalgamation of all cultures around the globe. Tatinha is in charge of gathering all the contributions, for which she travels in all directions of the planet. This huge mission will last from the 21st to the 50th century, though paradoxically the main character will never get older. The book comprises 30 parts, divided into more than 200 short chapters. Each chapter has a universal title: Toys, Woman, Work, etc. Light reading, but infused with reflections of philosophical, esthetical, and ethical dimensions. Author apparently intends to show the way for a social globalization, rather than the economic model that is the current trend.

2986 Ribeiro, Edgard Telles. Um livro em fuga. Rio de Janeiro: Editora Record, 2008. 238 p.

Following the example of some of his predecessors in the Brazilian diplomatic world (Guimarães Rosa, João Cabral de Mello Neto, Vinícius de Moraes, among many others), Telles is the protagonist-narrator of his experiences as diplomat in a region that is very far from his home country. In this novel, a sort of diary, he reflects on aging, caring for dying parents, commiseration for collective losses (like the ones due to tsunamis and earthquakes), nostalgic feelings for his family and home town. Amid his mulling incredulity over a rupture with a former girlfriend, he has bursts of hope and reconciliation with life's ups and downs, while learning about other people's feelings of despair, remorse, and frustration. Through a fine ironic filter, sometimes self-deprecating, the protagonist writes about his experience as an attentive listener and observer during a specific period of his career.

2987 Santiago, Silviano. Heranças. Rio de Janeiro: Rocco, 2008. 397 p.

Dynamic narrative about a member of Brazilian high society, who spends money and time with women in Brazil, Europe, and elsewhere. Told in the first person, the story uncovers the complex system of thoughts and decision-making of a cynical industrialist turned into a late-blooming philosopher.

2988 Santos, Carlos Alberto dos. O plágio de Einstein. Porto Alegre, Brazil: WS Editor, 2003. 101 p.: bibl., ill., map. (Série Narrativas)

Historical novel focusing on late scientist Albert Einstein as the target of accusations of plagiarism. According to the accusers, he might have copied the famous equation on relativity from an Italian amateur physicist, who exposed his discovery in an obscure scientific journal a few years before Einstein's extraordinary discovery. The author suggests that Einstein went much beyond the Italian's study. This may be the first Brazilian novel having as its main theme an international issue that, though fictionalized, is based on published biographies and other scholarly examinations of Einstein's life as a physicist.

2989 Silva, Deonísio da. Goethe e Barrabás. São Paulo: Novo Século, 2008. 190 p.

Including characters with names of canonical literary figures and biblical entities in the narrative, the author creates a sarcastic atmosphere while describing an affair, commenting on clergy celibacy, homosexuality, and on the frustrated plans for change in Brazil. A philosophical approach focuses on the nature of true love. This love is tentatively developed between a young woman, Salome, and a middle-aged man, Barrabás, who is married and an admirer of Goethe's *Faust*. Dialogues and other conversations stimulate characters into an attempt to neutralize their own demons and exorcize pessimism in relation to humankind.

2990 Sousa, Herculano Inglez de. O cacaulista: cenas da vida do Amazonas. 2a. ed. Belém, Brazil: Editora Universitária UFPA, 2004. 190 p.: ill. (Col. Amazônia)

Republication of a book that did not have an impact on the course of Brazilian literature when it was first published (1876). The author was 23 years old and this was his first novel. A second edition was published almost 100 years later; this is the third edition. Since the Amazon region is in the eye of the world nowadays, it is understandable that scholars, literary critics, and others became attracted to this narrative. In a pristine Portuguese, it describes a "primitive" Amazonian area along with the very first struggles for the possession of land and cocoa plantations, the beginning of a system of exploration of soil and people, and the habits of a population cultivating local traditions brought in by Portuguese settlers in the 17th century and also influenced by the Indians, all concentrated in the city of Obidos in the state of Pará. Referred to as a social-anthropological-historical novel, the story stimulates knowledge of important passages of the history of that region, involving characters that symbolize greed, perversion, betrayal, love, courage, and cowardice, all surrounded by the Trombetas river, a tributary of the Amazon, and inside and around the fringes of the forest.

2991 Sousa, João Bosco A. Contando histórias, fazendo história: experiência com os poetas cordelistas do Cariri. São Paulo: Editora PUCSP EDUC, 2007. 212 p.: bibl., ill. (Hipótese)

Focusing on the *literatura de cordel* (string literature) in the state of Ceará, the author examines in-depth texts by the *cordelistas* (narrators and poets). In his

study, the scholar enhances the areas of folklore, regional identity, national culture and traditions, and language.

2992 Tamm, Carlos. Esse rio sem ponte. Rio de Janeiro: 7 Letras, 2007. 103 p.

Complex and allegorical configurations of a string of disastrous events in a Brazilian rural landscape. In an obvious Shakespearian tragic atmosphere, mystery and philosophy embrace circumstances of crimes, death, and the pursuit of personal freedom involving members of a dysfunctional family. Good reading for lovers of cryptic language.

2993 Terron, Joca Reiners. Sonho interrompido por guilhotina. Rio de Janeiro: Casa da Palavra, 2006. 183 p.: ill.

This work can be read as a novel or a collection of short stories. The independent narratives include characters that are fictionalized authors (like the Brazilian Raduan Nassar and the American Wallace Stevens, among many others), and humble people in general (like the hopeful peasant migrant who finds soot and corpses in the big city). There is no specific continuity among the stories, other than the almost visible literary wire that gathers them all as a search, from the part of a writer, for the uncommon, the bizarre, and ultimately, the mission that an author may possibly have in life.

2994 Villaça, Antonio Carlos. O livro dos fragmentos. Rio de Janeiro: Civilização Brasileira, 2005. 157 p.

Renowned writer of memories (1928–2006) exposes, as the title indicates, slivers of the lives and thoughts of people who had an indelible influence in Brazilian arts, literature, and politics, among other areas. The author includes excerpts of conversations with recognized members of the intellectual elite of Brazil throughout the 20th century. Among them: Gilberto Amado, Tristão de Athayde, Geraldo França Lima, Guimarães Rosa, José Honório Rodrigues, Getúlio Vargas. Furthermore, the "fragments"— interviews and author's comments— describe a way of life, in the author's perspective, that was much more peaceful and less complex than the one being developed in 21st-century Brazilian society.

Short Stories

M. ANGÉLICA GUIMARÃES LOPES, *Professor Emerita of Literature, University of South Carolina, Columbia*

IN LITERARY TERMS, 2008 WAS DOUBLY IMPORTANT for Brazil as the year marked the centennials of two admirable short-story writers: Joaquim Maria Machado de Assis' death and João Guimarães Rosa's birth. Machado de Assis was the first major Brazilian short story writer, and the genre continues to be an integral part of the country's literature with stories published in books, newspapers, and magazines. Prestigious literary prizes, the Prêmio Jabuti chief among them, reward the best short writings. As W.D. Foster remarked, "The quantity of short stories produced in Brazil since the end of the 19th century is staggering. . . . The number of major names [suggests] the wealth of material and the intense sophistication of the genre in Brazil" (Margaret Sayers Peden, Ed., *The Latin American Short Story*. Boston, Mass.: Twayne, 1983, p. 1).

Among the works examined in this decade, some notable examples are written by veteran authors: Carone's collected short stories (item **3001**), for example, and two anthologies that unite several prominent writers, *Terriblemente felices* (item **3022**) and *Contos cruéis* (item **3006**). In addition, Engracio's classic, *Histo-rias de submundo*, has been deservedly reprinted (item **3009**).

New authors such as Almeida, Amaral, Fuks, Nami, Paiva, Nascimento Silva, N.A. da Silva, and Souza have produced accomplished stories. Some of these writers are obviously helped by their experience in other genres such as essays, journalism, and playwrighting. And Amaral is a cinematographer. Cavalcanti represents a different kind of beginner as he has published his first short stories in his early 70s.

Two important categories in the first millennium decade are "theme" collections and Spanish American/Brazilian anthologies. Among the former are Resende's scholarly *Cocaína*, which is also an historico-sociological opus as it examines the effects of narcotics in early-20th-century Brazilian society (item **3003**). The book reunites stories, essays, and a few poems. Another anthology, Fernandes' *Contos cruéis* (item **3006**), offers, in its organizer's words, "the most violent narratives in contemporary Brazilian literature." Fifteen of its authors are represented in Moriconi's *Os cem melhores contos brasileiros do século* (see *HLAS 60:4119*).

Moreira da Costa's subject is much more pleasant: popular music. The title *Aquarelas do Brasil* (Brazilian watercolors) is a reference to the famous samba by Ari Barroso, "Aquarela do Brasil" (1939), known in the US as "Brazil" (and recently used in television ads for Viagra and gambling). Many authors of different generations have been attracted to popular music as a subject. This anthology represents them well (item **2999**).

Another collection on a specific topic is Conte's competent and moving *A Livraria da esquina*, the subtitle of which, "Women's tales," stands for "Lesbian tales" (item **3005**). Also in the theme category is Moutinho's handsome *Contos sobre tela* bringing together 16 authors' stories on a particular painting or sculpture printed in the book (item **3007**). Yet another such volume is Franklin's *Dupla face de pedra* with *cordel* (stories on a string), which the author says are "the true . . . expression of Brazilian culture," accompanied by linocuts, cordel's classic illustrations (item **3010**).

The recent commendable effort at strengthening cultural and political ties among Latin American countries is evident in three splendid bilingual collections. From a seminar at the Banco do Brasil Cultural Center in Rio de Janeiro, Resende (*Cocaína*'s organizer) put together *A literatura latino-americana do século XX* (item **3018**). Eight stories by eminent contemporary authors accompanied by scholarly criticism are offered in Portuguese or Spanish.

Another such volume is the *15 cuentos brasileros/15 contos brasileiros* (item **3017**) organized by Oliveira, a Brazilian fiction writer, and Lavezzo, an Argentinian translator. Authors in the anthology are contemporary, born in the 1960s and 1970s. The third effort at bringing Brazilian short fiction to Spanish-speaking neighbors is *Terriblemente felices* (item **3022**). The Argentinian Cristian de Napoli is both translator and organizer of this fine and ambitious multi-generational book.

2995 Aguiar, Cláudio. O comedor de sonhos: narrativas. Rio de Janeiro: Caliban, 2007. 175 p.

By prolific novelist, playwright, and essayist, "Dream Eater" offers excellent stories with erudite epigraphs, which evince psychological acumen, structural skill, and, last but not least, a sense of humor.

2996 Albuquerque, Pedro Wilson Carrano. Palavras cruzadas e descruzadas. Brasília: LGE Editora, 2006. 195 p.

With its title, a pun on "crossed and solved words" this collection offers competent stories, some of which are appropriately word games and jokes. There are a variety of topics, characters, and perspectives, such as the author's own funeral; supposedly his grandmother's life story told after her death; a priest against celibacy; a slave unable to marry a beloved; and a boy and his philosophical frog.

2997 Almeida, Maurício de. Beijando dentes: contos. Rio de Janeiro: Editora Record, 2008. 111 p.

"Kissing [Your] Teeth," the first published book by its author (an anthropologist and co-author of two plays), offers 13 disconcerting and poetic tales. The book won the prestigious São Paulo SESC Prize for 2007. The title refers to an incident in the eponymous story in which a lover thinks of kissing a woman's teeth before killing her and himself. Other stories share a surrealistic atmosphere and a precise use of language and deal with dysfunctional families, mysterious actions, and meditations, all in a highly imaginative and forceful style. An admirable book.

2998 Amaral, Tata. Hollywood: depois do terreno baldio. São Paulo: Nome da Rosa, 2007. 136 p.

The title, "Hollywood After the Empty Lot," relates to the author's profession as a film director and scriptwriter. Amaral is well-known and has won over 40 Brazilian and international prizes. *Hollywood* is Amaral's auspicious debut in another form of story-telling; its 56 masterful tales are very brief (sometimes one page or less), and their topics and approaches varied. Among the characters are old people, concerned relatives, dreamy children, murderers and their victims, and corrupt policemen. The stories are dialogues, snapshots, or meditations. An outstanding book.

2999 Aquarelas do Brasil: contos da nossa música popular. Seleção de Flávio Moreira da Costa. Rio de Janeiro: Agir, 2005. 311 p.: bibl.

Delightful and useful anthology reunites stories about popular Brazilian music by 20 of its best and most famous authors from Machado de Assis (1839–1908) to João Gilberto Noll (b. 1946). The sections of the book are: Before the samba; A country dance; Carnival; Samba's birth, agony, and death; "Cavaquinho" (in English, ukulele); and Bossa Nova.

3000 Braga, Roberto Saturnino. Os quatro contos do mundo. Rio de Janeiro: Editora Record, 2008. 173 p.

"The Four Tales of the World" presents stories that take place in each of Brazil's four corners: south, west, north, and east. The pun starts with the title. "Conto" means "tale," and "I count," while "canto" means "corner," "I sing," and "song," as well as "canto" in the Dantean sense. Each section of the book is introduced historically and geographically, and because of explanations and development, it is more akin to a novella than a short story. This intelligent, clever, and well-constructed book by the former Rio de Janeiro mayor and state senator makes for good reading. In the first story (South), the protagonist's (and narrator's) Argentinian bias is surprising.

3001 Carone Netto, Modesto. Por trás dos vidros. São Paulo: Companhia das Letras, 2007. 201 p.

A journalist and professor of literature in his own São Paulo state and in Austria, Carone received the prestigious Jabuti Prize twice: for *As marcas do real: stories* (1979) (see *HLAS 42:6122*), and for the novel *Resumo de Ana* (1998). *Por trás dos vidros* (Beyond the Glass), his fourth story collection, offers 11 pieces, which until now had only been published in periodicals, as well as many stories from previous collections. Oneiric, hermetic, and mysterious settings in which present, past, and memory are often undistinguishable in the male narrators' conveyance of feelings, thoughts, and actions, give these stories a Kafkian tinge. (Carone is the Brazilian Kafka translator "par excellence," having translated all of his fiction.) For him, the great Czech's work loses when interpreted through a fantastic lens, but gains through a realistic one. *Por trás dos vidros* is a remarkable collection, a generous anthology of Carone's short fiction.

3002 Cavalcanti, Geraldo Holanda. Encontro em Ouro Preto. Rio de Janeiro: Editora Record, 2007. 188 p.

Tzvetan Todorov's description of fantastic fiction is the epigraph for this collection by a prize-winning poet, translator, and essayist, who is also a career diplomat. This, his first story collection published in the author's late 70s, is a solid and admirable work. Varied and imaginative, well-developed stories create dreams, nightmares, coincidences, mistaken identities, and even a Martian Messiah. Some characters' realities are not the same as that of other characters'. Marco Lucchesi, a younger short-fiction writer, notices the healthy influence of Murilo Rubião, the dean of the Brazilian fantastic.

3003 Cocaína: literatura e outros companheiros de ilusão. Seleção e apresentação de Beatriz Resende. Prefácio de Luis Eduardo Soares. Rio de Janeiro: Casa da Palavra, 2006. 147 p.: bibl.

Carefully composed, this erudite and handsome volume organized by Beatriz Resende offers pieces by eminent writers (from Bilac's 1894 story "Haxixe" to João do Rio's 1933 "A mulher carioca aos 22 anos"). Resende's introductions and Luis E. Soares' preface present a historical, sociological, and literary analysis of the use of narcotics as an imported fashion introduced in Brazil during the Belle Epoque. Most of the pieces are essays and stories, except for three poems.

3004 Coelho, Fabiana. Encruzilhadas: encontros e oposições nos cordéis de Manoel Pereira Sobrinho. Recife, Brazil: Prefeitura do Recife, Secretaria de Cultura, Fundação de Cultura Cidade do Recife, 2005. 219 p.: bibl., ill.

"Crossroad" is the 2004 city of Recife prize-winning essay on Manoel Pereira Sobrinho's *cordel* (literature on a string). This handsome volume, which includes traditional *cordel* linocuts, examines the subgenre as seen by some readers (or listeners), for whom it is at a literary crossroad, thus belonging to "an exclusion zone," i.e., it is not literature but "paraliterature, infraliterature, subliterature" (p. 22). Coelho carefully and imaginatively shows why *cordel* is literature and "integrational literature."

3005 Conte, Naomi. A livraria da esquina: e outros contos de mulheres. São Paulo: Edições GLS, 2007. 94 p.

Competent and sensitive "women's stories" are, for the most part, about lesbian encounters and attachments. A moving story on transvestitism tells of a girl on her 21st birthday, as she reaches adulthood, leaving home and her parents dressed as a man in order to start a new life.

3006 Contos cruéis: as narrativas mais violentas da literatura brasileira contemporânea. Organização de Rinaldo de Fernandes. Nota introdutória e textos de apresentação dos autores de Rinaldo de Fernandes. Prefácio de Linaldo Guedes. São Paulo: Geração Editorial, 2006. 417 p.: ill.

Massive anthology covers half a century and almost 50 authors, 15 of whom had stories selected for Moriconi's *Os cem melhores contos brasileiros do século*, 2000. (The 15 authors are: Abreu, Angelo, Brandão, Denser, R. Drummond, Emediato, Fonseca, Moreira Campos, N. Oliveira, Pellegrini, Piñon, Santiago, Scliar, Telles, and Trevisan). For its organizer, the book is "a 'thriller' [sic] of Brazilian fiction being written now." These are indeed cruel tales mirroring part of Brazilian reality. Although the preface stresses cruelty as mainly an urban phenomenon, akin to the film *Cidade de Deus [City of God]*, a few stories have a country or small-town setting. Artistic quality varies.

3007 Contos sobre tela. Rio de Janeiro: Edições Pinakotheke, 2005. 142 p.: col. ill.

With a richly ambiguous title, these "Tales about Pictures" or "Tales on Canvas" compose an anthology in which 16 authors each create a story based on artwork by renowned Brazilian artists. High-quality reproductions of paintings, one print, and a sculpture accompany very good stories by predominantly Rio de Janeiro and São Paulo authors. A handsome book that is well-worth reading.

3008 Costa, Lustosa da. Contos de Sobral e de outros sítios. Fortaleza, Brazil: s.n, 2007. 101 p.

Competent stories about inhabitants of Sobral, in Northeastern Ceará, describe a group of regional characters and their customs.

3009 Engrácio, Arthur. Histórias de submundo. 2a. ed. Manaus, Brazil: Editora Valer: EDUA, 2005. 122 p.: ill. (Col. Resgate)

First published in 1960 by eminent Amazonas state fiction writer and critic, "Stories of the Underworld" is reprinted on its 50th anniversary as part of a collection of Clube da Madrugada (Dawn Club), a late Modernist association in Amazonia. Engracio was one of the club's founders in 1954. The collection's excellent pace and characterization match the stories' tragic endings: murder by cuckolded husband, exploited servants and children, deaths by snakebite and hunger. The tone seems to spring from the stereotypical 19th-century idea of Amazonia as a "green hell." The only exceptions are "Tigre," which is about a faithful dog, and another story about a charitable, curious judge. Handsomely illustrated with Amazonian motifs.

3010 Franklin, Jeová. Dupla face de pedra. Posfácio de Piero Eyben. Brasília: Thesaurus Editora, 2008. 109 p.: ill.

A collaboration between Franklin and 10 xylographers, whom he calls friends and co-authors, "Double Stone Face" is a product of the Brazilian Northeast (Bahia, Ceará, and Pernambuco). Franklin declares that he is following a model: "a popular image, the true pictorial expression of Brazilian culture." He is clearly referring to *cordel* (stories on a string), the medieval chapbook brought from Portugal and whose poems are still sung in street fairs in Northeastern Brazil. Indeed, the book's prints are faithful to *cordel* style as are the stories. Hermetic tales deal with dramatic, even monstrous incidents often within nuclear families, such as betrayal, incest, and adultery. A dark, impressive, and handsome book.

3011 Freire, Marcelino. Rasif: mar que arrebenta. Gravuras de Manu Maltez. Rio de Janeiro: Editora Record, 2008. 123 p.: ill.

Each story in this collection is a masterful internal monologue (except for one in dialogue format) by different characters such as a child in a slum, a mother who lost her son, an aging homosexual actor, a man who escaped a bomb attack in a bus, a blind man waiting for his blind date, a parent worrying about the predominance of negative Muslim news. With popular as well as erudite and always pertinent epigraphs, this dark and remarkable collection is an homage to the city of Recife ("reef," from the Arabic "rasif"). In the stories, love and peace are anything but, for example: "peace is disgraceful," "Children are sweet. A lie," and "love is a bite from a pitbull."

3012 Fuks, Julián. Fragmentos de Alberto, Ulisses, Carolina e eu. Rio de Janeiro: 7 Letras, 2004. 64 p. (Col. Rocinante; 25)

Well-constructed, elegant, and somewhat cryptic stories, which earned their 22-year old São Paulo author the 2003 Univ. de São Paulo and Editora Abril Nascente Prize. An imaginative writer, he explores "small interstices between prosaic reality and the world's 'insondável' mystery" (Marcos A. Moraes). Journalist Fuks is a talent to be watched.

3013 Fuks, Julián. Histórias de literatura e cegueira. Rio de Janeiro: Editora Record, 2007. 157 p.: bibl.

A splendid book that successfully re-unites fiction and scholarship as it narrates particular aspects of master writers' lives: Jorge Luis Borges, João Cabral de Melo Neto, and James Joyce (in that order). Includes a "Necessary Prologue" and bibliography. A delight to read.

3014 Monteiro, Túlio. Dois dedos de prosa com Graciliano Ramos. Fortaleza, Brazil: Imprensa Universitária, Univ. Federal do Ceará, 2006. 139 p.: ill.

"A Chat With Graciliano Ramos" proposes varied topics connected with the author's native Ceará state. Stories run the gamut from historical to contemporary, fantastic to real, comic to tragic. Celebrated literary figures are protagonists of some stories, such as Graciliano Ramos, the poets and artists of the Padaria Espiritual (Spiritual Bakery) Movement (1892), as well as Jean-Paul Sartre and Simone de Beauvoir whom the narrator meets in a dream. Other characters such as devils, street children dying tragically, a mad civil servant, and a "fan" of a losing soccer team are encountered. A solid and imaginative collection.

3015 Paiva, Fernando. Salvem os monstros. Rio de Janeiro: 7Letras, 2010. 123 p. (Col. Rocinante)

Extremely well-constructed Kafkian stories present a varied cast of characters and plots often including metamorphoses. In the story that bears the title of the book, the monsters to be saved are mutant chickens evolving into enormous predators. Other stories include plots such as a male sexual maniac turned into a frog by a woman dressed as a witch during Carnival; a young fortune teller with 123 moles who reads customers' futures according to any five moles they choose; a pond and an ocean temporarily orange colored; and an artist who only painted portraits of dead people brought to his own first exhibit in a coffin—as a corpse. Multi-talented Paiva is a journalist, guitar player, and composer. *Salvem os monstros* is his second published work and first story collection. His keen irony touches upon our own era's foibles and includes himself. In L. Lichote's words on the book jacket: "Monster myself; monsters they; monsters the rioting crowd. Save them."

3016 Pinheiro, Mauro. Os caminhantes e outras histórias. Rio de Janeiro: 7 Letras, 2008. 98 p.

Road Travelers is an appropriate title for these intelligent and well-structured stories focused on characters' thoughts, feelings, and actions from unsuspected angles. Here 'travel' is both figurative and metaphorical as it includes voyages, dreams, and even suicide. Unexpected incidents are developed into situations. The reader is suddenly aware that a character in one story becomes a narrator in another story. This book is by a novelist who is also an English and French translator; this is his second story collection. A must.

3017 15 cuentos brasileros. Compilação de Nelson de Oliveira. Traducción de Federico Lavezzo. Buenos Aires: Comunicarte, 2007. 170 p.

This anthology is another successful effort at strengthening Spanish-American and Brazilian cultural and literary ties. The organizer is an eminent short-story writer who avoids Brazilian stereotypes like carnival, soccer, Rio slums, the northeastern "Sertão", and "ecological mysticism." Most of the 16 authors included in this publication were born in the 1960s and 1970s, and less than one-third in the 1940s and 50s.

3018 Seminário A Literatura Latino-Americana do Século XXI, *Centro Cultural Banco do Brasil, 2005.* A literatura latino-americana do século XXI. Organização de Beatriz Resende. Rio de Janeiro: Aeroplano, 2005. 188 p.: bibl.

From a seminar in Rio de Janeiro's Banco do Brasil Cultural Center, this publication includes eight stories written by eminent Argentinian, Brazilian, Chilean, Colombian, and Cuban authors in their native Portuguese or Spanish. The stories are preceded by a scholarly preface on Latin American literature and followed by critical essays on the topic, which, of course, mention the authors published here. An important book.

3019 Silva, Carlos Nascimento. A menina de cá: contos. Rio de Janeiro: Agir, 2008. 180 p.

Although "The Girl from Here" is the author's first short-story collection, Nascimento is a seasoned novelist and winner of major literary prizes. Most of these stories deal with mysterious events occurring in dysfunctional families. Like mini-novels, the stories have different sections/chapters. "A menina de cá," the eponymous last story, is 35 pages long. A very good collection.

3020 Silva, Nereu Afonso da. Correio litorâneo: contos. Rio de Janeiro: Editora Record, 2007. 79 p.

This is Silva's first book and a recipient of the prestigious São Paulo state SESC Prize for 2006. Each of the short stories is based on a news item in the fictitious newspaper, the *Coastal Courier* (the title of the book): a con man, a shipwreck, etc. Varied perspectives and story-telling styles—many more akin to meditation than to narration—add to the collection's interest. Precise and elegant, *Correio litorâneo* is extremely well written and this author is a talent to watch.

3021 Souza, Assionara. Amanhã, com sorvete! Rio de Janeiro: 7Letras, 2010. 150 p.

The stories in "Tomorrow, With Ice Cream!" dwell more on sensations, feelings, discoveries, and memory fragments than on organized plots. Often hermetic, they succeed in focusing on moments without determining time boundaries. Souza is a skillful writer.

3022 Terriblemente felices: nueva narrativa brasileña. Selección, traducción y prólogo de Cristian de Nápoli. Buenos Aires: Emecé, 2007. 284 p. (Lingua franca)

Generous and impressive anthology reunites several literary generations from "the great contemporary authors born before 1940 (Rubem Fonseca, João Antonio, Hilda Hilst, Loyola Brandão, Dalton Trevisan, and Raduan Nassar) . . . to 15 others born between 1941 and 1971." "[The latter] started publishing after 'bossa nova,' futurist architecture, and 'soccer World Cup victories' had become part of the Brazilian ethos." Each group of writers is, not unexpectedly, representative of its era and geography. De Nápoli's careful and successful translations take stock of each author's style. The result is a balanced and important introduction to the Brazilan short story.

3023 Val, Vera do. Histórias do Rio Negro. São Paulo: WMF Martins Fontes, 2007. 176 p.

The preface to this award-winning collection shows São Paulo author's knowledge of Amazonian lore and psychological acumen as she creates a society along the large Amazon affluent. The Rio Negro's presence, common to every one of these stories, is stated in one of them, "Curuminha" [little Indian girl]: "The river. Always the river, sinuous, flowing lasciviously, in no hurry." As the reader gets deeper into the book, it becomes evident that it offers several angles and that the characters are all connected. A distinguished, poetic work of literature.

3024 Véras, Everaldo Moreira. Depois eu conto: estórias. Recife, Brazil: Edições Sarev, 2007. 146 p.

With its title as a pun ("conto" means "short story," "I tell," and "I count") "I'll Tell You Later" collects 32 very short stories with equally short titles. Both concise and incisive, the stories cover different emotions such as joy, pride, shame, and remorse. This is a collection with a personality. By a veteran author and recipient of numerous literary prizes who is also a poet and an essayist.

Crônicas

DÁRIO BORIM JR., *Associate Professor and Chairperson of Portuguese, University of Massachusetts, Dartmouth*

FOR OVER A CENTURY, the habit of writing and reading *crônicas* on a daily basis has been as deeply rooted in Brazilian society as *cafezinho*, rice-and-black beans, samba, and soccer. With origins going back to the late 1700s, following the lead of early French journalists and their *feuilleton*, *crônicas* have acquired a remarkable formalist and pragmatic development in Brazil. There, starting in the second half of the 1800s, a new literary category took shape, one of sophisticated esthetic value, or a specific and autonomous genre, according to Afrânio Coutinho (1911–2000). That new space in the French newspapers was a haven of "slack water in the rough seas of the daily news," argues Mario Higa (item **3029**). It constituted a getaway, an alternative trail open to a blander horizon—"more feminine, more personable, or else, less conflictive, less violent, less objective," adds Higa. Most of the texts examined in this section corroborate Coutinho's recognition of the *crônica's* growth in Brazil, Higa's account of the *feuilleton's* origins, and the newer trends and blends of the genre in the age of electronic social media.

One of the elements that has fueled the prolific writing of *crônicas brasileiras* has been the financial reality of a writer's life. Newspapers and magazines help professional writers by paying them in a faster, more assiduous, and more reliable manner than the book market. The pressure, though, is on the *cronistas* to produce their texts on a regular basis before each deadline, explains Vinicius de Moraes with great humor (item **3043**). The genre's tradition of commenting on linguistic issues or experimenting with its own language remains strong, most notably in items **3027**, **3028**, **3034**, **3043**, **3047**, **3050**, and **3051**. By using ethnic register, which is marvelously the case in "Foi sonho," Mário de Andrade (1893–1945) composes a *crônica* that reads like a crafted short story narrated by an uneducated African-Brazilian worker. Elsewhere, Andrade employs an innovative spelling method which, for him, better represents the language and oral contours of Brazilian Portuguese (item **3027**). Ruy Castro, in turn, discusses the 2007 bill attempting to ban the use of so-called foreign words in Brazilian printed and electronic media, commercial contracts, and official signage and documentation (item **3034**). In our day and age, argues Castro, that law would be clearly biased against words from English, for example, and tacitly in favor of keeping African words that have been incorporated into contemporary Brazilian Portuguese. Ironically, Castro ponders, if this law had been put into effect in the 19th century, it would have deprived Brazil's melodic idiom of the enormous linguistic legacy it inherited from African languages.

The topical emphasis on day-to-day deeds and the short temporal distance between events narrated and publication dates continue to characterize the *crônica*, especially in items **3029**, **3030**, **3036**, **3039**, and **3041**. A writer whose works are often forwarded from one email box to the next, the *gaúcha* Martha Medeiros adopts a posture of the friendly and wise commentator on matters that affect the common reader's everyday life, such as urban issues and romantic and family relationships (item **3041**). Language promoting a degree of intimacy between readers and authors continues to be a goal for the typical *cronista*. Here it appears nearly across the board, but most visibly in items **3030**, **3032**, **3036**, **3041**, **3043**, **3047**, and **3050**. It is indeed plausible to think that the fast and easy ways by which readers can contact writers today—by email, Facebook, Orkut, personal blogs, and other electronic services—have prompted *cronistas* to write even more "intimately." Loyal *crônica* followers often send their comments to their favorite writers. Readers may thus impact the writing of new *crônicas*. Apart from teaching college-level creative writing, Carpinejar, for example, maintains a personal blog that has received more than one million visitors (item **3033**).

The world depicted in *crônicas brasileiras* often conveys a historical description or a social mapping of the country at large or the cities and communities where their authors have lived. A special political concern, the dubious ethics of

Brazil's President Luiz Inácio Lula da Silva, inspires nearly all the texts in item **3039**. Collectively, the titles examined for *HLAS 66* display a diverse number of settings beyond Rio de Janeiro (the city featured in items **3029, 3030, 3034, 3037, 3042, 3043, 3046,** and **3048**), an aspect of the contemporary *crônica* which was discussed in the introduction to *HLAS 62* (p. 507–508).

One volume gathers texts written by various celebrated writers on São Paulo (item **3050**), a metropolis which is also the focus of items **3027, 3036,** and **3052**. Whereas Goiânia and the central plains of the country prevail in item **3045**, Porto Alegre takes the central stage in items **3029** and **3041**. Small-town Brazil reveals itself, too, through portraits of remote communities in Minas Gerais (items **3026** and **3038**) and Goiás (item **3045**). The peculiar milieu of specific *bairros* in Belo Horizonte (item **3026**), São Paulo (items **3045** and **3050**), and Rio de Janeiro (items **3030** and **3046**) also emerge. The "suspicious" *carioca* bar scene, in particular, frames most of the scenes in Luís Pimentels stories (item **3046**). Whether they are narrated in first- or third-person, his *crônicas* are short and fast, without much ado about nothing. Including brief dialogs, they build characters who often dwell on the fringes of society or visit the exotic side of the human condition. These people make us laugh as they get vexed and wonder about or ponder the clashes and bonds, differences and compatibilities of interpersonal relationships, especially those of lovers (ex-, temporary, or future) and watering-hole regulars.

There is a great deal of formalist excellence and innovation in these works, especially in Eliane Brum and João do Rio (1881–1921), creating, in different eras, a new journalistic *crônica* language (items **3031** and **3048**). Betty Milan and Vinicius de Moraes mix prose and poetry (items **3042** and **3043**). Gabriel Chalita, Eustáquio Gomes, and Lygia Fagundes Telles, on the other hand, blur the borders of fact and fiction (items **3035, 3038,** and **3053**). Contardo Calligaris also excels in his own way (item **3032**). One of the most noticeable and effective aspects of his writing is his creation of a smooth textual collage, which brings together a rich gathering of allusions to different sources of insight, such as a research project, a family case, a poem, or a movie, coalescing into a single *crônica*, often ending with a concise paragraph of two or three sentences that pull together the entire piece.

One last characteristic of many of the books of *crônica* is the long-lasting didactic aspect of the genre, expressing itself in recent works as a discursive form of self-help. In the 1930s, painter Tarsila do Amaral (1886–1973) published *crônicas* meant to instruct Brazilians in art history (item **3052**), and for at least half a century Austregésilo de Athayde (1898–1993) connected world literature to current affairs in order to educate his readers (item **3028**). The challenges of a postmodern society have become sources of confusion for many, and several authors respond with expertise and wisdom in their *crônicas*. Among those who seem to be addressing their readers' well being most directly are Carpinejar, Medeiros, and Prata (items **3033, 3041,** and **3047**).

While Rubem Fonseca, Oscar Niemeyer, and Bariani Ortêncio share their knowledge about literature, architecture, and folklore (items **3037, 3044,** and **3045,** respectively), four physicians and psychotherapists' good judgment and writing styles appeal to very wide audiences: Rubem Alves, Betty Milan, Contardo Calligaris, and Moacyr Scliar (items **3025, 3032, 3042,** and **3051**). Poets, like Milan and Sant'Anna, also contribute. Like most of Sant'Anna's other writings, his short prose pieces are serious discussions of artistic, sociopolitical, and psychological issues in which he shares stylistic and thematic traits with other authors from

Minas Gerais. He has the witty and economical tongue to depict the wonders, ironies, and coincidences of quotidian life. (Another Belo Horizonte native, Fernando Sabino (1923–2004), writes about similar themes.) Sant'Anna observes and feels the impulse to write metaphorically, but also objectively about injustices and absurdities, in the best tradition of Carlos Drummond de Andrade (1902–87), whose *crônica* column in *Jornal do Brasil* Sant'Anna inherited. Andrade's influence can likewise be detected in the writings of a good number of the authors featured in the following section.

3025 Alves, Rubem A. Ostra feliz não faz pérola. São Paulo: Planeta, 2008. 276 p.

The title of this poetic and thought-provoking book comes from its first text, which contains a simile. In order to develop a pearl, says the acclaimed author and lecturer, an oyster must have the unpleasant company of a grain of sand inside its shell. For the oyster, that pearl will be no adornment, but mere protection against the discomfort caused by the sand. So, a happy oyster yields no pearl, just as a happy human being will not create art. No art is created without pain, even if that pain is light, "like the itching provoked by curiosity" (p. 12). The short text that explains this idea is but one of hundreds gathered in this volume. Alves notes that when fragmentary thoughts came to him, he wrote them down, so that later they might grow into an essay. Those small thoughts were like birds that sat on his shoulder and remained "in the cages of his notebook." He never had enough time to allow them all to become full texts, and then he realized it was time to release them as they came: no matter how short or incipient. In the present volume, those fragments are divided into 11 topical sections. All of them but the first (Kaleidoscope) display thematic cohesion: Love, Beauty, Children, Education, Nature, Politics, Mental Health, Religion, Old Age, and Death. Born and raised until puberty in Boa Esperança, Minas Gerais, Alves moved with his family to Rio in 1945. With a Ph.D. from the Princeton Theological Seminary, he has been teaching college and living in Campinas, São Paulo, since 1973. Some of Alves' books are regarded as foundational texts for the Liberation Theology movement of the 1980s. Characterized by a poetic but unpretentious language, his *crônicas* confirm the breadth and depth of his intellect in pedagogy, psychology, philosophy, and theology, plus all the richness of his firsthand experiences through a long and multifaceted professional career as an unusually open-minded clergyman, social activist, and psychiatrist.

3026 Andrade, Jeferson de. Crônicas selecionadas para algumas emoções. Belo Horizonte, Brazil: Pagina Alberta, 2009. 103 p.

This is the 12th book by a Mineiro author who became nationally known for his nonfiction best-seller on Euclides da Cunha, *Anna de Assis: história de um trágico amor,* upon which a TV Globo mini-series was based. Also a novelist and short-story writer, Andrade had his political activism and career as editor boosted by working with the famous and influential humorists of the Rio de Janeiro tabloid *O Pasquim*. *Crônicas* gathers 42 short pieces previously published in *Folha do Padre Eustáquio*, the monthly newspaper from a mostly working-class *bairro* in northwestern Belo Horizonte, the capital of that state. The collection sheds light on the multifaceted day-to-day life of that neighborhood, including grassroots movement events, unusual bar scenes, and personal profiles of street artists and poets. Andrade also shares anecdotes of his private life and those of close friends whose thoughts and deeds have had a bearing on local development and the arts. He also chronicles stories of his small town, Paraguaçu, located in the south of his home state. His *crônicas* discuss social and political issues affecting other metropolitan areas, the state of Minas, the nation at large, and current affairs on a global scale, such as violence and unemployment.

3027 Andrade, Mário de. Os filhos da Candinha. Estabelecimento do texto e notas de João Francisco Franklin Gonçalves. Revisão do texto estabelecido de Aline

Nogueira Marques. Rio de Janeiro: Agir, 2008. 187 p.: bibl.

Like the vast majority of poets, novelists, and short-story writers, this outstanding author among Brazil's Modernists also wrote *crônicas* throughout his career. The 43 titles included in this volume were initially published among many others by Andrade in newspapers and magazines between 1929–39. Then the *cronista* himself selected his favorites for the first edition of this volume, which came out in 1942. He explained the title of the book as an expression of popular wisdom or public knowledge, a "trustworthy hearsay." He also declared in a letter to poet Manuel Bandeira that with that book he wanted to highlight his unpretentious, light-tone *crônicas*, rather than his "serious" short pieces. Whereas the former type represented a form of personal liberation for the author, the latter did not please him because of their "shortcomings and hurried thoughts." Despite that disclaimer, these light writings provide us with Andrade's typical abashing humor, unconventional wit, and other whimsical traits of an intellectual bound to break complacent expectations and esthetic traditions. He attacks totalitarian regimes, but he also shares his skepticism toward the redemptive power of democracy and the secret ballot. He makes fun of the obsessive and intoxicating ideologies for economic progress, while questioning the very pillars of Brazil's model of provincial modernization. His nationalism is clearly open to controversy. He heralds the enticement of Brazilian cuisine (still considered rather inferior to foreign ones), but wonders how people can be productive under such unpleasantly hot weather in the tropics. This is an authoritative edition with very informative footnotes and two critical essays by Universidade de São Paulo researchers João Francisco Gonçalves and Marco Antônio de Moraes.

3028 Athayde, Austregésilo de. Austregésilo de Athayde. Seleção e prefácio de Murilo Melo Filho. São Paulo: Global Editora, 2008. 359 p. (Col. Melhores crônicas)

In this posthumously gathered collection of undated *crônicas* spanning 60 years, the acclaimed Rio de Janeiro-based journalist covers a wide range of topics, most dealing with social, political, and cultural matters often addressed in newspaper editorials. Throughout his career, this Pernambuco-born member of the Academia Brasileira de Letras received a law degree, taught college, and published 10 books. All but one of them (a collection of short stories) are nonfiction volumes of either cultural essays, reports, or *crônicas*. Several of the topics discussed in this 2008 release arise from the author's eventful life as a newspaper reporter for *Correio da Manhã, O Jornal,* and *Diário da Noite* (which he directed), and the weekly magazine *O Cruzeiro*. Athayde translated for Associated Press and United Press. He interviewed and wrote about world celebrities such as Eleonor Roosevelt and President Herbert C. Hoover. Because of his political views and publications, the Vargas dictatorship sent him into exile in the early 1930s. He then lived in Argentina. Despite the folkloric rivalry between Brazilians and Argentinians in soccer matters, which he also wrote about, he was well received in that country. That was an experience of both humiliating expulsion and gratifying welcome that strengthened his belief in freedom (for him, a human need far greater than peace itself) and the honorable pursuit of one's ideals (at all costs and risks). An erudite and a proud Latinist, Athayde displays a remarkably consistent use of clear and objective language. By examining classic pieces of multicultural literature, especially Brazilian, French, North American, and Russian titles, he evidently seeks to raise awareness of world problems and to educate others about the importance of reading and thus enriching one's life. In some of his *crônicas*, Athayde evokes the negotiations that led to the writing of the Universal Declaration of Human Rights. In 1948 he was Brazil's official delegate to the UN, and his contribution to that groundbreaking document was praised by President Jimmy Carter in a speech delivered in 1978. Following two traditional themes in *crônica* writing, several pieces of this book discuss new book releases and pay tribute to famous writers and dignitaries after their deaths, including poet and playwright Frederico García Lorca and US Secretary of State John Foster Dulles.

3029 Barreto, Lima. Lima Barreto: antologia de crônicas. Edição de Mario Higa. Sao Paulo: Lazuli, 2010. 280 p.

Based on the texts edited for the two volumes of *Toda crônica* by Beatriz Resende and Rachel Valença (Agir, 2004), Mario Higa selects and organizes Barreto's *crônicas* into thematic sections. The Carioca author's late 19th-century and early 20th-century *crônica* style comprises various attributes found in his celebrated fiction: dramatic tension sparsely balanced by irony or satire, unpretentious skepticism paralleled by moralistic language, and occasional outbursts of idealism broken down but undisguised pessimism. Poignant and convincing, Afonso Henriques Lima Barreto (1881–1922) addresses issues which continue to affect Rio de Janeiro's population today, such as flooding, and defends causes that remain as open sores in society, like the killing of women by their husbands. The author offers a detailed map of the history of Rio and of Brazil as a whole, and their transformations between 1888, the year of the abolition of slavery, a celebration in which he participated as a seven-year-old child, and 1922, the year of the Modern Art Week in São Paulo, and of his own death at the age of 41. In a well informed essay, Higa introduces the texts while placing them in the context of the genre's history within world literature and, more specifically, within Brazil's sociopolitical dynamics.

3030 Blanc, Aldir. Rua dos artistas e transversais: crônicas. Rio de Janeiro: Agir, 2006. 428 p.

This volume gathers two whole books by the famous songwriter, *Rua dos Artistas e arredores* (1978) and *Porta de tinturaria* (1981), plus selected *crônicas* published by the magazine *Bundas* between 1999 and 2000, and others by the newspaper *Jornal do Brasil* between 2005 and 2006. One distinguished street in the Rio de Janeiro bohemian *bairro* of Vila Isabel is the setting of a good number of these *crônicas*. It is more than just a setting, of course. The reader becomes intimate with Blanc's friends and neighbors as if the reader him/herself were just another member of that Carioca community. The language of the people who hang around in the streets, dirty bars, small businesses, or backyards constitutes the medium by which Blanc explores human compassion, nostalgia, and tragedy. The comic side of life for the humble is present, as is those extravagant and yet unpretentious people's love for telling jokes and other stories. Blanc's characters actually have nothing to lose by sharing their lives in the form of dreams and fancy-free gab. His tone reflects his loyalty to those characters and the lifestyles he depicts. His writing abounds in colloquial terms, slang, and otherwise, some of which may be rendered obscene. As critic Luiz Horácio puts it, Blanc's *crônica* writing style is peculiar. It has much to do with the techniques of songwriting: the rhythm, syncopation, phrase, and beat of music. Some of the *crônicas* even take the form of burlesque lyrics on political matters or fake lyrical poems of amorous animosity. Others gather small fragments of plain and uncommitted humor, or bits of sardonic social criticism. The enormous variety of themes in Blanc's tapestry does not avoid the significant shades of the prosaic or unusual overtones of the dramatic, such as erotic dreams or the good humor of a failed suicide.

3031 Brum, Eliane. A vida que ninguém vê. Prefácio de Marcelo Rech. Posfácio de Ricardo Kotscho. Porto Alegre, Brazil: Arquipélago Editorial, 2006. 205 p.: ill.

The main body of this volume republishes texts which originally appeared in 1999 in the author's homonymous column in Porto Alegre's *Zero Hora*, arguably the most prestigious newspaper of Brazil outside the Rio de Janeiro-São Paulo axis. The editors of the book contend that "journalism is an art" and Brum confirms it with her fine mix of objectivity and subjectivity, *crônica* and report, realist description and metaphorical language, sharp criticism of the powers that be and endearing sympathy for the downtrodden. The book's title signals its main focus. By addressing *A vida que ninguém vê* ("The life that nobody sees"), the *cronista* and reporter seeks the marvelous and wondrous in the real-life stories of individuals often seen but constantly ignored in society, such as a paraplegic man who earns a living by keeping his belly and chest rubbing on the ground. He thus sustains the public posture of an exotic and pathetic man, which makes him look like a *sapo* (toad), his nickname in downtown Porto Alegre. When the day is over, he often enjoys the luxury of taking a taxi and going back to a normal life of drinking beer and barbecuing with family and friends. Israel is another person on the fringes of society. Mentally challenged, this 29-year old man was considered useless, and was abandoned by family. He was jeered, even stoned, by the neighborhood children. One elementary school teacher changes his family, and he, in turn, changes many other lives with learning and regains his dignity after being accepted in school. There is also Adail's compelling story. He was an illiterate African-Brazilian who had handled bags and dealt with racial slurs at the city's airport for over 26 years before he had an opportunity to fly. Most stories are not those of relative ease or success. In "Enterro de pobre" ("Poor people's funeral"), the death and burial of extremely poor children make the author see that the main difference between the funerals of the rich and those of the poor is how people, in the latter case, mourn much more for the hardship of the loved one's life than for the pain of his or her death. Brum's exceptional qualities in this book result from her clear language and from her sensibility and empathetic ability to express the complexity of apparently simple lives. Equally praiseworthy is the way she mingles dialogues and narration in a harmonious cohesion facilitated by a figurative language embedded, but often unnoticed, in day-to-day life. She also uses humor and irony to counterbalance staggering suffering.

3032 Calligaris, Contardo. Quinta-coluna. São Paulo: Publifolha, 2008. 381 p. (101 crônicas)

This collection of short texts originally published between January 2004 and December 2007 in *Ilustrada*, the arts and culture section of the newspaper *Folha de São Paulo*, is another valuable release in the series 101 Crônicas. The author utilizes his vast knowledge in various fields of study, including art history, cinema, literature, medical anthropology, religion, political science, psychiatry, social psychology, and theater in the writing of well-argued and structured *crônicas*. Calligaris is an astute and pragmatic critic of the modern and post-modern times. Some of his central issues are the rampant cynicism towards human dignity and respect, ecological disasters, unemployment, and violence. This Italian-born Brazilian, who was educated in France (his Ph.D. in clinical psychology is from the Université de Provance), might not have a parallel in the history of the *crônica* genre. With a sophisticated technique by which he manages to intertwine various illustrative points on the same issue, and with a language that makes his texts understood and appreciated by the common reader, Calligaris inspires the reader to think more comprehensively about intriguing topics, such as the impossible science of love, the beneficial sides to depression, the harms of living without affection, the difficulties of long-lasting marriage, and the pitfalls of passion and deceit.

3033 Carpinejar. Canalha!: retrato poético e divertido do homem contemporâneo: crônicas. Rio de Janeiro: Bertrand Brasil, 2007. 315 p.

This is a book remarkably complex, candid and convincing. It offers that which cannot be easily found in the market: an amusing and educational take on contemporary notions and expectations about sex and romance from the perspective afforded by a relatively young sensitive male who is also a highly dexterous writer. Born in Caxias do Sul, Rio Grande do Sul, this award-winning author keeps an intense writing schedule for various newspapers and magazines, including a column in *Crescer*. In *Canalha!* Carpinejar does not shy away from taboos or other sensitive matters. His short and fast-paced *crônicas* come out witty and cunning with their views on both men's and women's sexual needs and choices, as well as their different perceptions on work, friendship, dating, domestic life, and divorce. They carry the synergic power of those who feel and understand human behavior far beyond societal prejudices defined on gender lines. In "O orgasmo feminino e o quindim" (Woman's orgasm and coconut candy), Carpinejar creates an analogy between his grandmother's thoughts on the egg-based desert she adores and women's special timing in achieving orgasm. In "Boêmio de casa" (Domestic bohemian), the narrator wonders why married or unmarried couples sharing quarters tend not to dress up for each other, but only for others to see them when they go out to work or to have fun. He no longer acts that way. When Friday night comes, he has showered. He turns on the music, washes a couple of glasses and fetches the ice cubes for the whisky. Then he and his wife sit and chat on the patio of their house or dance for their own pleasure, without having to prove to each they are happy. He wears new shoes and a new shirt, and he is proud: "Now I get dressed up to be home too" (p. 83).

3034 Castro, Ruy. Ungáua! São Paulo: Publifolha, 2008. 217 p. (101 crônicas)

This is another release of the series 101 Crônicas, which has published several volumes gathering texts by regular columnists of the newspaper *Folha de São Paulo*. Born and raised in Caratinga, Minas Gerais, but otherwise a Carioca since 1948, Castro means to be humorous from the start, more precisely, from the mind-boggling excerpt on the book jacket of a volume that brings together pieces initially printed from February 2007 to March 2008. In the introduction, the author, best known for his book *Bossa Nova: The Story of the Brazilian Music that Seduced the World*, confesses that his aim is not to write serious pieces. The will to entertain and play around with his ideas is there, no doubt, but the majority of his *crônicas* do address serious issues without too much to laugh or even smirk about. Following one of the *crônica* traditions, the book carries pieces on linguistic matters. With his strong background in music, the author dedicates several texts to that topic, such as myths around the history of bossa nova, curious coincidences of deaths of musicians on carnaval, plus historical links among jazz, samba, and tango. Castro's writing style is both pleasant and captivating. One of the topics he approaches most often in these 101 *crônicas* is urban violence in Rio de Janeiro, an issue about which one can hardly pretend to be comical.

3035 Chalita, Gabriel. Mulheres de água. São Paulo: Editora ARX, 2007. 143 p.

This is a thematically and stylistically cohesive gathering of 21 stories about women of various ages, social status, and economic backgrounds. They blend the features commonly associated with the *crônica* or the short story. This present edition offers its readers a glimpse of that ambiguity even before they face the text itself. On the one hand, the book jacket calls these texts *contos* (fictional short stories). On the other hand, the cataloging data determine that the present volume is one of *crônicas brasileiras* (Brazilian *crônicas*). Reinforcing that ambivalence, a subsequent edition of the same book (Ediouro, 2009) has the same title but a new subtitle: *Contos sobre o universo feminine* (Short stories about the feminine universe). Following a certain tradition in *crônica* writing, these short texts evoke real-life characters and day-to-day events. The language is simple but exquisite, and it creates a degree of closeness between the narrators and the readers. Unlike the *crônica* conventions, however, there is not a line of identification between the author, a male, and each of the voices of narration, all of them female. The book's title, *Mulheres de água* (Water Women), points to the central metaphor in the volume as a whole. Water molds itself to its surroundings, fills in gaps, alters landscapes, and grows stronger if more water is added to it. Women are water: "fluids, blood, menses, sap," says Chalita (p. 9). With a rich educational background (doctoral degrees in law philosophy and semiotics), the author tells delicate, poetic and sensitive tales of pains and powers over crises of solitude, suicide, broken marriage, children's death, and abusive friendship. This book appeals to readers of various profiles, but, more specifically, those with great interest in cultural anthropology and gender issues.

3036 Diaféria, Lourenço. Mesmo a noite sem luar tem lua: crônicas. Organização e apresentação de Roniwalter Jatobá. São Paulo: Boitempo Editorial, 2008. 246 p.

Born to a couple of immigrants, a libertarian Italian father who spanked him just once and then cried, and a steadfast Portuguese mother who often resorted to her wooden clogs to teach her son a lesson, the author writes primarily about the city of São Paulo, his birthplace. His eyes and other senses capture the city's life and translate it in peculiar forms through *crônicas* originally published in *Folha de São Paulo* between 1973 and 1977. One of the 72 pieces gathered in this volume had a dramatic story of its own. It did not please a general and cost Diaféria a few nights in jail. Brazil was then ruled by draconian military dictators and their civilian cohorts.

In order to survive as a writer Diaféria had to apply what one might call "language in disguise," the same subterfuge by which songwriters saved their skin and, at the same time, dribbled the official censors to get their protest songs across on stage and airwaves. One of the means this *cronista* uses is to communicate with his readers through political fables. Among them is the story of a parrot whose litany has a single word, "cassação," the constant "impeach-ment" threat given to politicians who dared to speak against the government. In order to convey social criticism and pinpoint the troubles and injustices of São Paulo's daily life, Diaféria's language abounds in caustic humor, such as the hospital patient who is sick with an "institutional act" in his stom-ach, and allegorical metaphors, like those of a botanic garden where flowers, vegetables, and trees have a voice on sociopolitical matters. The settings vary enormously, from hilarious family scenes to crimes in the underworld of transvestites. Third-person narration and a short story type of tone and structure are not rare in these *crônicas*, which are subdivided thematically into four sections. Most concern the human heartbeat of a gigantic city that never stops growing.

3037 Fonseca, Rubem. O romance morreu: crônicas. São Paulo: Companhia das Letras, 2007. 198 p.

These *crônicas* by the widely translated, award-winning, quasi-Carioca writer born in Juiz de Fora, Minas Gerais, do not carry most of the elements which have made his fiction unique and famous. Fonseca's texts do not employ his typical language: straightforward, crude, and raw as it can be in literature, without reserva-tion or fear to shock, for example, when it depicts violent characters and their motiva-tions. His fiction's sharp and cunning nar-ratives, nearly always suggesting social and economic abuses, or psychological torment and helplessness, are replaced by an essay-like argumentation or the *crônica*-like tone of cordiality and intimacy. While the lan-guage of common people, where it applies, is gutsy in its purpose of making reality look and sound not only visible but also disturb-ing in his novels and short stories, these *crônicas* convey the voice of the educated

man, the expression of the intellectual who travels and who has the knowledge and sensibility to comment on poetry and other forms of reputable literature. Despite their different languages, these *crônicas* seem to do what Fonseca's fiction also does. Subdued and sober, authoritative and kind, they are, likewise, touching and thought-provoking, and, arguably, action-inducing, since the first step toward action is the feeling that leads an individual to pursue action. Most of Fonseca's texts in this volume are very light in tone and within the typical length of the modern *crônica*. They explore a wide variety of topics, such as the author's pres-ence in western Berlin when its wall was historically torn down, the continuous and ever-growing number of writers despite the rampant disappearance of readers, the most enjoyable ways of eating popcorn, and the contrasting elements of cinema and literature.

3038 Gomes, Eustáquio. Paisagem com ne-blina e buldôzeres ao fundo: cromos. São Paulo: Geração Editorial, 2007. 151 p.

Even though these *crônicas* had ap-peared separately in a magazine called *Metrópole*, here they are compiled and arranged in a way that results from the author's conception of lemniscates, "like a dog that seeks his own tail." Gomes, a Campinas-based journalist, focuses his writing on his coming of age and emo-tional ties to a remote village by the name of Campo Alegre, in northwestern Minas Gerais, where he was born and raised, but also where he did not set foot in 40 years. The author, a novelist with another 12 titles published, experiments with the *crônica* form, calling what he writes, "chromos." The volume is divided into four sections. In the first one, dedicated to his childhood memories, all 16 short pieces are comprised of one single paragraph each. The second section, with 12 pieces of varied topics and tones, narrates the author's adulthood years as a writer and family man. While the third part of the volume consists of 11 narrative fragments of an unpublished novel, the last section has only one long story that chron-icles in poetic dexterity and psychological depth the experience of revisiting the vil-lage of his childhood and youth. Through-out this book, Gomes' language is elegant, sophisticated, and exquisitely crafted in a way that captures the reader's imagination and stirs his or her esthetic sensibilities. Apart from an appealing graphic design, this book has much to offer. The narrator's sharp perceptions of his emotional encounters with people and places which have shaped his personality and life story, as well his objective descriptions of human motivations and adventures beyond the beaten track, make this volume unique and sheer reading delight.

3039 Mainardi, Diogo. Lula é minha anta. Rio de Janeiro: Editora Record, 2007. 238 p.: ill.

A constant feature in the authoritative and nationally distributed *Veja*, Mainardi's texts in this collection have appeared in 94 issues of that magazine between 2005 and 2007. Following the 2004 book publication of his *crônicas* from *Veja* issues of previous years, *A tapas e pontapés* (also by Record), this present gathering reflects a consistent concern with the deeds and deceits of politics, especially the bribery scandal known as Mensalão, or, for what it was, "the Big Monthly Paycheck Scheme." This historic case of multiple frauds is deeply associated with unscrupulous bankers, President Lula da Silva's party representatives in Congress, and his top administration as a whole. The president, however, has always claimed he knew nothing about the scandal. Many people, like Mainardi, were not convinced. So, the author becomes "the archeologist of the Mensalão" (p. 33). He attacks journalists who offer Lula an unquestionable cover-up, and he explicitly seeks and insists to predict Lula's impeachment. The book title itself suggests its leitmotif. Literally it translates as "Lula is my tapir." The Portuguese name for this hoofed, hoglike mammal is a slang term for the naïve who is taken advantage of by impresarios. With a zigzagging tone between those of a humorous but merciless satire and others of a straightforward denouncement of public culprits, these texts either entertain or irritate readers (perhaps according to their faith in the president). While carrying elements of sarcasm and irony, mockery and malediction, this type of journalistic inquiry through the poetically licensed voice of a *crônica* does not conceal bias or personal an-

imosity. Nonetheless, the rhetorical power of a subjective discourse, for better or worse, comes to fruition in just about every piece in this volume. Several original *crônicas* are introduced and/or followed by short remarks adding information either to the content or on the consequences of the original publication. One of those end remarks tells that the author was charged with libel (and found innocent) eight times in reaction to the accusations made by one single weekly article (p. 132). Dozens of other lawsuits applied, actually, and Mainardi claims he won them all. By mingling individuals and circumstances of his personal life with the paths and tales of his journalistic discoveries and revelations, this TV commentator, novelist, and cinematic scriptwriter undoubtedly knows how to produce *crônicas* with a bite. Peppery, sour or sweet, it is a distinctive and bold approach to national politics.

3040 Mambrini, Miriam. Maria Quitéria, 32: crônicas. Rio de Janeiro: Bom Texto, 2008. 206 p.

At the age of 70 this Carioca novelist and short story writer publishes a memoir that looks back into her childhood and adolescence in Rio de Janeiro's beach district of Ipanema in the 1940s and 1950s. Mambrini's 27 texts, written approximately 20 years prior to the book release, were not meant for publication, but as a form of family history preservation. With very little resemblance to the typical language of *crônicas* written for newspapers and magazines, they narrate coming-of-age anecdotes from the protagonist child's perspective mixed with that of the adult in an exercise of remembering and explaining her past dreams, fears, and adventures. The type of feminine narration voice one encounters throughout the volume matches the design of hand-painted flowers reproduced on the front cover and on some of the inside pages. That voice operates on a tone of delicate tenderness and affection for family members, as well as on an undisguised nostalgia for selected painless and conflict-free days of family harmony and tradition.

3041 Medeiros, Martha. Doidas e santas. Porto Alegre, Brazil: L&PM Editores, 2008. 231 p.

The 99 short pieces of this collection were originally published by the newspapers

O Globo and *Zero Hora* between October 2005 and July 2008. Dated and organized in chronological order, they display various features typically present in weekly *crônicas*: recurrent focus on day-to-day events, including those happening the day before the newspaper or magazine was published; themes which may be of interest to a large readership; gradual sense of familiarity between the writer and the readers; and colloquial language and light tone allowing for humor and modesty. The author is a celebrated *gaúcha* poet and an award-winning *cronista* who has published at least 26 books. Medeiros is interested in selecting and elaborating on pieces of news that come to her through other newspapers and magazines. Just about any topics may serve as motivation for her good-humored and thought-provoking *crônicas*, but she certainly prefers to discuss books, films, theatrical plays and, occasionally, TV shows as well. In her mid-40s the author reveals great sensitivity to emotional challenges such as solitude, divorce, depression, and death. Her attitude in general is very positive to all sorts of difficulties which she chooses to address in *crônicas* that resemble personal essays, stories, or movie reviews. Her voice is consistently pleasurable to read and nearly always sounds like that of a close friend full of earthly wisdom who has something interesting to confess or to discuss with us—without any fear of shocking us or any shame in showing us that we might need to reconsider some of our most deeply held convictions.

3042 Milan, Betty. Quando Paris cintila. Rio de Janeiro: Editora Record, 2008. 149 p.

Short *crônicas* in the form of unpunctuated prose poems make this book one of a kind. Novelist, playwright and psychiatrist, Milan makes her writing shine through a style that embodies the poetic license and the formalist freedom of expression which one sees in Modernist writing: no capital letters, no rhymes, no metric patterns, no consistent point-of-view, and no fixed setting. While the widespread use of aphorisms invites us to recall Oswald de Andrade, Milan's unabashed *crônicas* know no nationalistic impulse. Quite on the contrary, they urge us to think globally, to

travel in time and space through meditation and curiosity, magic and contemplation, art and risk taking, patience and willingness to change, adventure and awareness of the enigmatic sides to living and of the educational aspects of dying. Profoundly impacted by Eastern philosophy and folkways, Milan questions traditional medicine. While a Western physician appears to be the one who knows, the Eastern doctor tells us s/he is the one who studies continuously (p. 102). Spiritually motivated, the author advocates the redemptive clout of imagination and surprise in dealing with the mundane and the nonsensical appeal of stagnation, helplessness, and surrender. Reality can be perceived as a dream-like scene, she argues, while reflecting on the changes undergone by one single tree in Paris. That's how the world enchants us: "it's necessary not to succumb to the force of habit / not to be controlled by the natural tendency to wish things remained the same / and to look at them the same way" (26).

3043 Moraes, Vinicius de. Para viver um grande amor. Rio de Janeiro: MEDIAfashion, 2008. 205 p. (Col. Folha Grandes Escritores brasileiros; 9)

Among the 47 *crônicas* of this volume is a 1946 text entitled "A transfiguração pela poesia" (Transfiguration through poetry), the first the poet ever wrote or ever published. The author was 33 years old, a late start for someone who would write more than 1,000 *crônicas* within the next 16 years, a record stated in his own introductory note "Advertência" (Warning). The author also informs us that most of the selected prose pieces appeared first in *A Última Hora* between 1959 and 1962. Some of the titles, though, had "lost their tracks," adds Moraes, as he himself had no clue where they had first been published (p. 5). The important thing now was "to soften the impact of all of them" by interspersing them with 21 poems, explains the author. Such poems may offer "new balance" (p. 5). They were penned between his last days as a diplomat in Paris (1957) and his departure from Montevideo (1960), a period of his life marked by the experience of the "greatest love." This is a concept he hopes the reader will be capable of understanding by the end of the book. Love and poetry are undoubtedly the most recurrent themes of this collection. Highly eclectic, the book displays enormous stylistic variety with more than only the central concerns in Moraes' life and career. Among his prose statements on love and romance is the argumentative, well-known "Para viver um grande amor" (Recipes for living the greatest love), which gives the volume its title, and the anthological, exquisitely crafted reflection on death, "Mistério a bordo" (Mystery onboard). These are fine examples of the book's case of poetic prose. There are instances of prose poetry as well, such as "Poema de aniversário" (Birthday poem) and "O amor dos homens" (Men's love). Esthetically, Moraes also experiments with single-paragraph crônicas and others without periods. While the author is going through the last few years before reaching the age of 50 he dedicates some of his most poignant crônicas to aging: "A arte de ser velho" (The art of being old) and "O tempo sob o sol" (Time under the sun). Death is no stranger to a middle-aged person's circle of friends. It is his concern in one of the most dramatic pieces: "Morte de um pássaro" (A bird's death), a requiem to Frederico García Lorca. The tone in his crônicas is not always serious or somber, however. Quite on the contrary, there is plenty of room for humor and lightness of expression, such as those in the first text, "O exercício da crônica" (Writing the crônica) and "Feijoada à minha moda" (Feijoada a la myself). It is also noteworthy how intimately personal and deeply confessional Moraes' crônicas can be, as he depicts, for example, his love for and complex relationship with family members, including "O dia do meu pai" (My father's day) and "Pedro, meu filho . . ." (Pedro, my son . . .).

3044 Niemeyer, Oscar. Crônicas. Rio de Janeiro: Editora Revan, 2008. 113 p.
Brazil's world class architect has also left a distinguished written legacy. His 17th book by the publishing house Revan alone, this collection brings together Niemeyer's crônicas originally published in different magazines and newspapers, including *Folha de São Paulo, Jornal do Brasil,* and *Correio Brasiliense.* After turning 100 years old, he penned a few titles especially for this 2008 edition of his crônicas, a volume which

also displays black and white drawings by the designer of Brasília's Modernist architecture. Some of Niemeyer's pieces create images of sophisticated imagery and emotional candor. The opening crônica on the author's imaginative look on the shapes and meanings of cloud formations in the Brasília skies is undoubtedly precious. This crônica inspires us to understand the origin and role of the architect's penchant for curve forms in so many of his buildings. The second text of the collection alludes to a repetitive and trivial scene on the road to the capital, but the author closes that text with a philosophical spin that makes his writing anything but dry or trite. Though the simplicity of his linguistic style remains, there is no structural consistency, tone cohesion, or thematic organization to this collection. Several pieces praise politicians of the left and profess the author's staunch patriotism, profound sense of Latin American identity, and undaunted adherence to communism. On several occasions the internationally celebrated architect makes clear how he sees his own art: "architecture is unfair. It only serves the powerful people. For the less fortunate, it does not exist. In their cardboard shacks, people can only experience architecture from afar" (p. 110).

3045 Ortêncio, W. Bariani. Crônicas 2.
Goiânia, Brazil: Editora da UCG: Prefeitura Goiânia, 2007. 195 p. (Col. Goiânia em prosa e verso. Crônicas)
This Goiânia-based folklorist has worn many hats and his crônicas show it. Apart from publishing 33 books until 2007, he had been a tailor, a math teacher, a business manager, an industrialist, a farmer, and even a goalkeeper of his city's major league soccer team. Previously published in newspapers and magazines, his writings here cover a wide range of topics, from the lives of all saints celebrated in June throughout Brazil, to the teaching of folklore in public schools; to the thrills of central Brazil's legends, myths, and superstitions; and to the best ways of cooking native fish from the Araguaia River. Often using detailed descriptions of country objects and rural scenes, Ortêncio's language is unfailingly simple and direct, personal and friendly. His texts clearly aim to entertain and educate readers about multiple subjects related to

the fauna and flora of his region and to the values and intellectual interests of his community work and social activism.

3046 Pimentel, Luís. Noites de sábado e outras crônicas cariocas. Belo Horizonte, Brazil: Editora Leitura, 2007. 117 p.

These stories unveil a world of off-the-wall figures and lifestyles which are usually not seen or experienced except by those who humbly frequent the little dirty bars of Rio de Janeiro. Originally from southern Bahia, the author has published more than 30 books of various genres, including short stories, novels, humorist sketches, and biographies. He has worked in the Wonder City long enough to have absorbed the tricks and the tastes of the Carioca populace in order to write so movingly and convincingly about their humorous day-to-day encounters and dramatic strives off the beaten tracks of Ipanema and Copacabana beaches. In "Dissimulada é a vida" (Life is a sham), for instance, the narrator compares a woman at a bar in Lapa to Machado de Assis' character, Capitu. Her name is Sandroval. Born male, her parents combined their own names, Sandro and Valéria, into the son's name. After his 20th glass of beer, the narrator, a journalist, had been enthusiastically talking about injustices perpetrated against prostitutes. He was fully aware of their plight now, after interviewing one of their union representatives. That was when Sandroval approached him. She said she was moved by his speech, but she also invited him to think of all the suffering which transvestites went through in that city, and nobody seemed to care about them. She offered to tell him a sad story, her story, which runs in half a paragraph in that remarkable crônica. Sandroval was the father of two children. As a male, he was married to a woman who died right after giving birth to their two children. Sandroval, like Capitu, had deceiving eyes. She was not crying at that Lapa bar. It had been raining, that's all.

3047 Prata, Mário. Cem melhores crônicas (que, na verdade, são 129). São Paulo: Editora Planeta, 2007. 374 p.

Humor in this book gets started on its cover. Its title reads, "The Best 100 Crônicas (Which Are, In Truth, 129)." Not many people can pen stories as comically as Mário Prata. Born in Uberaba, Minas

Gerais, he lived in São Paulo for 30 years before moving to Florianópolis, where he has been living for nearly 10 years. He has written extensively for the theater, radio, and television and won more than 20 literary awards in Brazil and elsewhere. Prata's interest in linguistic issues, a common choice among cronistas, leads to some of the most entertaining texts. In "Coentro" (Cilantro), for instance, he elaborates on how certain words sound as if they were acronyms. His satirical verve verges on several sexual themes, including the need for a Cuckold Anonymous. Prata's short texts often carry a story in which he develops a sort of theory on a given issue. In "Ponto de vista masculino" (Male's Point of View), for instance, he narrates in third person the tale of a woman addicted to weight control spas. At a convenience store she buys a battery operated toy monkey which whistles nonstop in a flirting way. It becomes a companion for some private, self-indulged striptease fantasies of her own. Later, other spa women learn about the monkey's flirting. They start sharing his attention collectively, in dancing sessions, and soon develop an obsession about him. The problem arose when the monkey "got tired of so much distraction" and his batteries ran out late at night, when the stores were closed. Prata says even though the frustration was real, the whole spa slept well and happy that night because they knew they would buy new batteries in the morning. He concluded: "they all had fun because they realized that pleasure happens in one's mind, not in one's flesh" (p. 102).

3048 Rio, João do. A alma encantadora das ruas = The enchanting soul of the streets. Versão para o inglês = English translation by Mark Carlyon. Introdução = introduction by MV Serra and Antonio Edmilson Martins Rodrigues. Ilustrações = illustrations by Waltercio Caldas. Rio de Janeiro: Cidade Viva Editora, 2010. 487 p.: ill. (Col. River of January = River of January series)

This is an extraordinarily well done bilingual, annotated, and illustrated new edition of an old book of crônicas. The graphic design in black and dark blue has everything to do with the volume's title and content: *The Enchanting Soul of the Streets*. Journalist João do Rio's 1908 book release is the first of a series entitled River of January—Rio de Janeiro through the Eyes of its Writers. The editors could hardly have chosen a better book with which to launch a series aimed at republishing the most representative works on the Carioca life of the past 200 years. João do Rio's *crônicas* truly convey a fascinating, incredibly animated and in-depth report of a city undergoing rapid transformation in the first years of the 20th century. In Brazil at large his work as a journalist was groundbreaking because before penning his articles, he would conduct extensive, firsthand field research into the undesirable and unknown corners and alleys of the city. More remarkably, he would not write his pieces as others would. He preferred a subjective perspective, the light tone, the intimate register, and the esthetic concerns which few *crônica* literary writers, like Machado de Assis, were already applying. The combination of those traits was successfully coupled with João do Rio's wide intellectual background, undeniable talent for writing, and boldness to enter and to understand marginal enclaves, such as tattoo service providers or extremely overcrowded, rodent-infested hotels and abandoned colonial houses in downtown. The topics of his research and, therefore, of the *crônicas* he produced, extended far beyond his view of the city's exotic or misbegotten dwellers. His texts reveal other materials which may delight anthropologists, sociologists, and historians of various subfields. He, for example, collects and transcribes dozens of printed prayers sold in the streets, an impressive collection of poems written by inmates, a huge repertoire of lyrics which people sang during seasonal festivals, and a catalog of bands and other musical groups which performed in Belle Époque Rio de Janeiro. João do Rio also investigates the complex lives, power dynamics, and brutal exploitation behind the lives of women and children involved in the begging industry; the unusual lifestyle of high-profile prostitutes; the overbearing level of intimidation under which coal deckhands and stevedores fought for better working conditions; the intertwined web of amorous relations that provoked love crimes; and the connection between the literature of violence shared by inmates and the new ideas they arguably acquired from such readings.

3049 Sant'Anna, Affonso Romano de. Tempo de delicadeza. Floresta, Brazil: L&PM Editores, 2007. 158 p. (Col. L&PM pocket; 616)

These 47 *crônicas* explore a variety of themes and circumstances. As a renowned poet and journalist, Sant'Anna has been a dexterous and appealing *crônica* writer for many decades. He knows how to employly the sophisticated language of metaphors and subtle irony while keeping an eye on facts and forces in motion, whether they are the trepidations of society or the pains of their prediction. Collectively speaking, these texts configure multiple responses to the dilemmas of life in a city as violent as Rio de Janeiro, in a country with gigantic socioeconomic inequalities like Brazil, and in the world at large where everyone is self-absorbed, in a hurry, under stress, in fear of losing a job, through road-rage, on a divorce dispute, or simply feeling lonely, abandoned, or useless. If one of Sant'Anna's *crônica* assesses the role of linguistic vices in everyday conversations, another will make fun of the strange chic appeal of ragged clothing, and a third may even express nostalgia for the days when we did not receive dozens of emails every day. Sant'Anna is both elegant and charming. Resorting to an allegorical tale or quoting a poem by Robert Frost, he is likewise sensible and sensitive enough to make us appreciate life while we strive to understand it and work to make it better for ourselves and our various surrounding communities.

3050 São Paulo, 450 anos: histórias e crônicas da cidade na Folha. Organização e notas de Oscar Pilagallo. São Paulo: Publifolha, 2004. 209 p.: ill.

Organized by Oscar Pilagallo, this volume celebrates the city's 450th anniversary with articles published by the newspaper *Folha de São Paulo* or those dailies which joined forces in 1960, *Folha da Noite*, *Folha da Manhã*, and *Folha da Tarde*, and adopted that same name. There are 12 journalistic, historical, and sociological analyses penned by canonical or otherwise distinguished authors, such as Hermínia Brandão, Sérgio Buarque de Holanda, and Nicolau Sevcenko. Eight *crônicas* also focusing on the city complement the book. Manuel Bandeira's 1957 memoir reveals that it was there, in São Paulo, between 1903 and 1904, where he really fell for poetry. In his 1935 piece, Rubem Braga elaborates on his relationship with a personal shoeshine and the modus operandi of this class of immigrant workers. While Plínio Marcos compares, in 1977, the old carnaval traditions of Rio de Janeiro and São Paulo, Ignácio de Loyola Brandão's 1987 crônica chronicles the changes undergone by Perdizes, one of the best known bairros of the megalopolis by the Tietê River. The book closes with irreverent and unrestrained humor by José Simão, a columnist who continues to provoke critical thinking by his constant attacks on political figures, artists, and sports celebrities from around the world. In his 2000 contribution to São Paulo, 450 he makes fun of the chaotic sides to that city's rampant development, a catch-22 of modernity: "São Paulo cannot stop, because there is not enough parking space. It won't move, because of its traffic jams" (p. 193).

3051 Scliar, Moacyr. Do jeito que nós vivemos. Belo Horizonte, Brazil: Editora Leitura, 2007. 175 p.

With 16 undated texts originally published in Correio Brasiliense and another 39 in Zero Hora, this collection lives up to the high expectations raised in the book jacket introduction by Luís Fernando Veríssimo, for whom Scliar is the greatest Brazilian writer alive. Everything that distinguishes Scliar as an outstanding novelist has a place in his crônicas, argues Veríssimo: "humanism, intellectual audacity, penchant for the uncommon, and the sortilege of language." Scliar as a writer is a complete kit, adds Veríssimo, for his crônicas, in turn, bear a "shrewd eye on the historical and the quotidian, undiscriminating curiosity, and the art of being colloquial but not condescending." The collected texts by the gaúcho physician in this volume discuss a vast array of topics, such as family dynamics, psychological mechanisms, marriage issues, sex on the Internet, street children, and unemployment. Scliar's well-informed writings also comment on philosophy, literature, music, and religion, apart from themes of linguistic oddities and curiosities so often embraced by cronistas of all ages.

3052 Tarsila. Crônicas e outros escritos de Tarsila do Amaral. Pesquisa e organização de Laura Taddei Brandini. Campinas, Brazil: Editora Unicamp, 2008. 748 p.

This modernist painter of such high influence and visibility in Brazilian art history eventually found her way into the world of crônicas as a source of income, and as way of sharing life stories and professional expertise. Texts penned and first published from 1936 to 1956 in different newspapers and magazines of Rio de Janeiro and São Paulo display her storytelling and ability to convey information relevant to the visual and performing arts. Most of these 233 crônicas, gathered, annotated, and introduced by scholar Laura Brandini, had never appeared in book form. Though dozens of such texts show little creativity (and are evidently based on encyclopedic data regarding landscapers, musicians, novelists, painters, and other plastic artists), other texts are valuable in as much as they afford accounts of her face-to-face intellectual exchanges with canonical and vanguard figures in the European and Latin American art circuits. Amaral's crônicas intend to educate Brazilian readers about topics such as architecture, art philosophy, photography, sculpture, ceramics, and the press. Her didactic tone switches sometimes to self-aggrandizement when she discusses modernism in Brazil. That is the case in two or three pieces where she claims that the Antropofagia Movement originated from her painting Abaporu (p. 539). Some of her more compelling crônicas are pieces of memoir on her family and friends. The volume also includes a very well written short story of great dramatic tension and humor, apart from three sonnets on love, harmony, tedium, and other imperatives in an artist's life.

3053 Telles, Lygia Fagundes. Conspiração de nuvens. Rio de Janeiro: Rocco, 2007. 131 p.

Few women writers in Brazil have had the superb critical and commercial success which this Paulista novelist and short story writer has achieved nationally and internationally. Among several other awards, she has won four Jabutis and the Camões for her entire oeuvre. Curiously enough, not many Brazilian writers, male or female, have published crônicas as rarely as she has. Her writings very often mix and fuse fact and fiction, though, which is probably the case in this volume officially cataloged in Brazil as a collection of both short stories and *crônicas*. It might be up to each reader to decide which is which. It is quite possible that the genre that best applies to at least three of the 19 texts gathered here is memoir, for their length, language, and subject matter: "Elzira," about her great aunt who died at the age of 20 because of racial prejudice in the family; "Quermesse" (Church Bazaar), on her own adventures as a little girl; and "Fim de primavera" (End of Spring), recalling her conversations with high profile intellectuals at a bookshop during her college years in São Paulo. Though all texts are narrated in first-person (nearly all of which employ free indirect speech), the other 16 titles carry esthetic attributes more typically associated with the *crônica*: light tone, wit, humor, colloquial and economical language, focus on day-to-day deeds, plus a degree of intimacy and complicity with the reader. While the two most comical pieces discuss a bill to do away with cemeteries and contrast biographies of Brazilian romantic poets, one text describes the irony of a conversation with two humble and illiterate people at the Brazilian Academy of Letters and another reveals the narrator's anguish at trying to find something interesting on TV on a Carnaval evening. Loyal readers of Telles' fiction may find several *crônicas* insightful in regards to the genesis of her works.

3054 Werneck, Humberto. O espalhador de passarinhos e outras cronicas. Sabará, Brazil: Dubolsinho, 2010. 160 p.

Solid, witty, elegant, and compassionate, these *crônicas* (2007–2010) deal with usual matters of daily life, politics, journalism, literature, and art. The title, *The Bird Spreader*, is both a pun and an homage to "the Pope of modernism," Mario de Andrade, whose last book was *O Empalhador de Passarinhos* (The Bird Taxidermist) 1944. In Werneck's collection, "the bird spreader" is his father, who loved birds. The *cronista* Werneck is a connoisseur of the genre, having published a selection of Ivan Angelo's pieces as well as *Boa companhia* (see *HLAS 64:2354*), an anthology of illustrious *cronistas* ranging from Machado de Assis (1894) to Werneck's own contemporaries. Also renowned as a biographer of musicians and poets, Werneck's study of the life of Jayme Ovalle (*Santo sujo*, 2008) earned him the prestigious Jabuti award. [M.A.G. Lopes]

Poetry

CHARLES A. PERRONE, *Professor of Portuguese and Luso-Brazilian Literature and Culture, University of Florida*

A MOST THOUGHT-PROVOKING EVENT in the realm of Brazilian lyric in the last half of the first decade of the new century and millennium was the theatrical launch of "Os Desmandamentos" (The un-commandments, Aug. 1, 2009, *O Globo*), a self-declared manifesto against the "indiscriminate banalization of poetry" and "dedicated to those who hold that it is . . . a basic necessity." The 11-item proclamation by Geraldo Carneiro (b. 1952) (item **3079**) and Salgado Maranhão (b. 1953) (item **3105**) (re-)affirms the vitality and the plurality of the genre, which can offer its own brands of reality, truth, and sincerity. Essential features such as linguistic imagination, musicality, and paradox are pondered in the current conjuncture, when one can still appreciate the best legacies of the Western tradition. The diverse references in this at once playful and quite serious document are further reminders of the marked proliferation of different voices and approaches over the last 20 years. Indeed, as Domício Proença Filho (item **3087**) endeavors to demonstrate, multiplicity and dispersion above all characterize contemporary Brazilian lyric. The most important point in these two writings is that poetry, despite unrelenting worldwide instrumentalization, still matters. The increased role of technology in letters has resulted in the ever-increasing utilization of the Internet as a means of distribution and place for debate, discussion, and fora. Brazil has a remarkable lineup of art-oriented websites, some for literature in general, and a few exclusively for poetry of the past and/or the present (see especially, http://www.germinaliteratura.com.br, http://www.cronopios.com.br, and http://www.revistazunai.com). Despite this competition, print publication continues apace, thanks, beyond the enthusiasm of poets themselves, to the dedication of a select group of publishers (especially 7Letras, Azougue, Iluminuras, and Nankin), and to tax incentives that encourage sponsorship of cultural projects.

Among the many developments pertinent to the production of poetry in the last half-decade, there are historical commemorations, geographical points, biographical landmarks, and thematic clusters. The domain of criticism is marked by monographs by non-Brazilian scholars concerning *modernismo*, vanguards, the poetry of song, women's literature, and inter-American relations (items **3055**, **3102**, **3119**, **3121**, and **3122**). Brazilian authors released volumes about the history of national poetry (item **3073**), epic/neo-epic poetry over the centuries (items **3128** and **3131**), Parnassianism-Symbolism (item **3096**), great historical figures such as Cruz e Sousa (item **3056**) and Murilo Mendes (item **3061**), so-called marginal poetry (items **3075** and **3113**), and Afro-Brazilian genius (items **3056** and **3067**), about which a substantial edited volume (item **3137**) has made a notable contribution and additional anthologies were issued (items **3125** and **3138**). Useful conference proceedings also continue to appear (items **3126** and **3130**). History and criticism are further enhanced with anthologies or multi-author volumes with analytical presentation. Manuel Bandeira's classic account has a new luxury edition (item **3066**) and a gathering of currently active poets was expertly done (item **3123**). The Academia Brasileira de Letras promotes its own members (item **3083**), and the city of Belo Horizonte supports new poetry (items **3058** and **3059**). Rio de Janeiro was the flash point to illustrate heteroglossia in lyric (item **3087**), though two of the selected poets were born elsewhere. Academician Carlos Nejar pens a sequence about his home borough in Rio (item **3111**) and poet-diplomat Catunda sings of the city at large (item **3084**). Of all municipal considerations, the most timely are those of Brasília, which celebrated its 50th year in 2010. Nicolas Behr issued a flurry of publications (items **3068**, **3069** and **3070**), Francisco Kaq pursues formalism locally (item **3101**), and Antonio Miranda (item **3109**) brings together nature poems in a volume sponsored by the city's botanical garden. Horácio Costa brings together his poems about the city of São Paulo in a package with homoerotic verse as well (item **3089**). The body and sensuality are of particular concern to urbane urban poets (item **3092**). Eros is a prime concern of one female voice (item **3080**) clearly engaged with language too, while women's poetry includes a stunning debut (item **3107**), the continuation of a culturally rich repertory (item **3077**), another title by a venerable interpreter of the quotidian (item **3116**), and a novelty item (item **3132**). A stateside bilingual anthology (item **3136**) features selections by outstanding active women poets. Cecília Meireles was honored at the First Conference on Brazilian Women Writers in New York (Brazilian Endowment for the Arts, Oct. 15, 2009), and several studies of her work appeared in Brazil (items **3106**, **3114**, and **3128**) and abroad (items **3102** and **3119**).

A few items in the present report are relevant to the appreciation of concrete/ visual poetry of past decades, both in the creative realm, Affonso Ávila (item **3063**) and José Lino Grünewald (item **3097**), and in the critical arena (items **3055** and **3120**).

Of current names, Arnaldo Antunes continues to impress, even with reissues (items **3060** and **3112**). With respect to the best of popular poetry in print, the only items of note are new editions of known works (items **3117** and **3134**). New books by established poets at reputable publishing houses tend to appear every quarter. Whether in free verse or metered composition, contemporary poets continue what has been termed "the tradition of the image." They confront the perplexities of postmodern existence, and express ever-evolving subjectivities. Poets born before 1945 who have produced fresh offerings include Ivan Junqueira (item **3100**), Leonardo Fróes (item **3095**), and Carlos Felipe Moisés (item **3110**). The latter joins a cohort of poets who have been inspired by jazz and other popular musics. Recent collections displaying conceptual melodies, appealing harmonies, or complex diction include those of Nelson Ascher (item **3062**), Régis Bonvicino (item **3071**), Paulo Henriques Britto (item **3072**), Ricardo Corona (item **3088**), Adriano Espínola (item **3091**), and Marcos Siscar (item **3133**). As for historical appreciation, key edited volumes of select poetry are those of Sousândrade (item **3135**) and Cabral (item **3076**). A new compilation of all the poetry of the master of Brazilian letters Machado de Assis (item **3104**) is news unto itself; other items of academic interest are the collected works of Dante Milano (item **3108**) and the poems of Mário Pederneiras (item **3118**), both of the early 20th century. The complete poetry of recently deceased writers includes Paes in one volume (item **3115**) and Piva in several volumes (item **3124**). Living poets have organized new editions of their earlier work in multiple (items **3069**, **3093**, and **3094**) or single volumes, including such names as the cosmopolitan Moacir Amâncio (item **3057**), the academic Carlos Vogt (item **3139**), the surprising Chacal (item **3085**), and the relatively young Alberto Pucheu (item **3127**). The largest collection is that of Lêdo Ivo (item **3098**), as he has been prolific since 1940. To come full circle in this introduction, we note the hardcover editions of the complete poems, to date, of the two engaged poets who, born in other states, made their artistic careers in Rio de Janeiro and there launched a commanding manifesto calling for enterprise in poetry throughout the land.

3055 Aguilar, Gonzalo Moisés. Poesia concreta brasileira: as vanguardas na encruzilhada modernista. Tradução por Regina Aida Crespo, Rodolfo Mata e Gênese Andrade. São Paulo: Edusp, 2005. 404 p.: bibl., ill. (some col.).

Portuguese edition of Spanish original (2003) based on exhaustive doctoral dissertation. Single best monograph on Brazilian concrete poetry in wide perspective and subsequent poetry of Augusto de Campos and Haroldo de Campos. Insightful theorization includes reading of concretism within the realm of "museum culture." Nicely illustrated volume.

3056 Alves, Uelinton Farias. Cruz e Sousa: Dante Negro do Brasil. Rio de Janeiro: Pallas, 2008. 411 p.: bibl., ill.

Deservedly well-received biography of the leading symbolist poet of Brazil, who,

as the author stresses, was wholly African and not of mixed blood. Ethnic and existential factors concern the specialist writer throughout as he intertwines historical and textual analyses.

3057 Amâncio, Moacir. Ata. Rio de Janeiro: Editora Record, 2007. 584 p.

Collected poetry of active São Paulo poet, professor, and journalist. Eight sections composed of seven books from 1990–2004 and a previously unpublished sequence, each with distinctive international substance, including divisions written in English, Spanish, and Hebrew. Lacks satisfactory bibliographical information on the source volumes.

3058 Antologia Dezfaces. Edição de Camilo Lara. Belo Horizonte, Brazil: s.n., 2008. 100 p.

In this short anthology, the editors present the best of 10 authors in 10 publication projects backed by the municipality from 2006–08. The selections, generally of good quality, range from postmodern free verse to neovanguardist arrangements and visual poems.

3059 Antologia Vacamarela. Edição de Andrea Catropa. São Paulo: s.n., 2007. 80 p.

Selections of 17 very young poets, some having already published a first book. Emphasis is on fresh perspective and inter-American outreach, as the material is all translated into Spanish and English.

3060 Antunes, Arnaldo. Como é que chama o nome disso: antologia. São Paulo: Publifolha, 2006. 391 p.: ill.

Excellent anthology of the poetical work of the stellar multimedia artist, complemented with a few creative essays. Covering 1983–2006, the volume includes concrete/visual poems, calligraphies, minimalist microtexts, playful prose, song lyrics, and a penetrating interview.

3061 Araújo, Laís Corrêa de. Murilo Mendes: ensaio crítico, antologia, correspondência. Reed. rev. e ampliada. São Paulo: Editora Perspectiva, 2000. 398 p.: bibl., ill. (Signos; 29)

Originally released in 1973, this comprehensive and iconographically rich study of an essential Modernist author was reissued in the prestigious Signos series to celebrate the centenary of his birth in 1901; inclusion here further recognizes the passing of the critic in 2006, whose legacy in Minas Gerais embraces original poetry and criticism alike.

3062 Ascher, Nelson. Parte alguma: poesia, 1997–2004. São Paulo: Companhia das Letras, 2005. 117 p.

Fourth book of poetry since 1983 by this São Paulo poet-critic whose constructive rigor distinguishes him as one of the nation's most skillful contemporary verse makers. This markedly informed collection is at once subtly humorous and intellectually challenging.

3063 Ávila, Affonso. Homem ao termo: poesia reunida, 1949–2005. Introdução de Benedito Nunes. Carta-posfácio de Antonio Candido. Belo Horizonte, Brazil: Editora UFMG, 2008. 669 p.: ill. (Inéditos & esparços)

Magnificent volume containing six decades of poetical work by an original and persistent artist of the word who often applies his renowned Baroque scholarship to the creative realm. Each of the 12 sequences included is constructed over some sort of conceit of form (e.g., architecture, photography), genre (e.g., sonnet, cantiga) or specific discourse (e.g., traffic code, oracle). Ludismo (gamesomeness, playfulness) and social irony are constants in this sui generis oeuvre.

3064 Ayala, Walmir. Walmir Ayala: melhores poemas. Seleção de Marco Lucchesi. São Paulo: Global Editora, 2008. 277 p. (Melhores poemas)

The author (1933–91) always showed a concern with being and elevated poetic space. Here his selected work is presented in reverse chronological order (1986–55) and balance is sought between "document and monument," signs of the times and the highest quality verse.

3065 Azevedo, Carlito. Monodrama. Rio de Janeiro: 7Letras, 2009. 152 p.

After more than a decade of absence, this involved poet of the 1990s returns with a modest volume of prosaic prose poetry and sentimental lyric, not anti-normative or sharp in image as in the past. Despite the title, not a dramatic monologue.

3066 Bandeira, Manuel. Manuel Bandeira: apresentação da poesia brasileira. Posfácio de Otto Maria Carpeaux. São Paulo: Cosac Naify, 2009. 501 p.

Designed (1946) to introduce Brazilian poetry to foreign audiences in the Good Neighbor decade, this classic consists of a superb critical presentation and an anthology (125 poems by 55 poets, including Ferreira Gullar and Augusto de Campos in a 1950s upgrade). This best ever single volume account of the genre is made even better in this brand new edition with an afterword by Otto Maria Carpeaux and illustrations from the renowned José Mindlin Library.

3067 Barbosa, Maria José Somerlate. Recitação da passagem: a obra poética de Edimilson de Almeida Pereira. Belo Horizonte, Brazil: Mazza Edições, 2009. 269 p.: bibl., ill., index.

Solid academic study of formal and ideological aspects of the poetry of the brilliant poet-anthropologist, one of the principal voices of the active group of writers in the historically significant city of Juiz de Fora, Minas Gerais.

3068 Behr, Nicolas. Braxília revisitada. 2a ed. Brasília: Entre Livros Livraria: Pau-Brasília, 2005. 1 v.

The modernistic capital city of Brazil, with all its bureaucratic foibles, is the main character of this amusing collection of aphorisms, flashes, fragments, and brief lyrical commentaries. Reminiscent of the telegraphic Oswald de Andrade and the zen reductionist Paulo Leminski.

3069 Behr, Nicolas. Laranja seleta: poesia escolhida, 1977–2007. Rio de Janeiro: Língua Geral, 2007. 170 p. (Col. Língua real)

Inaugural volume of the pan-Lusophone collection Língua Geral (the Jesuits' term for the pan-Tupi language they formulated during colonial times), which aims to present a personal selection of a poet's best material over four decades.

3070 Behr, Nicolas. Poesília: poesia pau-brasília. Brasilia: N. Behr, 2005. 88 p.: ill.

In this droll volume, the poet brings together all the poems in which the capital city figures from his some two dozen chapbooks, 1977–2001, beginning during the so-called mimeograph generation. Alongside serial apostrophes to the city, or some aspect of it, there are constant allusions to landmarks of modern Luso-Brazilian lyric.

3071 Bonvicino, Régis R. Página órfã: 2004–2006. São Paulo: Martins Fontes, 2007. 133 p.

Tenth book of verse by the accomplished São Paulo poet-editor-jurist. The title is somewhat ironic since the author so endeavors to articulate international relations in Latin America, Europe, and North America, the present volume even includes a four-handed piece with noted language poet Charles Bernstein. High-quality production values evident, with sharp critical afterword.

3072 Britto, Paulo Henriques. Tarde: poemas. São Paulo: Companhia das Letras, 2007. 92 p.

Fifth book of poetry by this award-winning poet and translator. Robust verse incorporating sensibilities as wide ranging as early modern lyricism and postmodern irony. The mid-volume "Art poétique" includes a symptomatic image of a fan opening and closing.

3073 Bueno, Alexei. Uma história da poesia brasileira. Rio de Janeiro: G. Ermakoff, 2007. 454 p.: bibl., ill., index.

In this controversial history of lyric in Brazil, the poet-critic follows the conventional chronological progression from colonial letters to the present, with additional segments on popular poetry and translation (a welcome addition). While the readings of 19th century and early 20th century verse are consistently valuable, the interpretations of experimental modernism, the neo-avantgarde and late modernism betray a very problematic unwillingness to accept the evolution of esthetic ideas or to engage with inventive new constructs.

3074 Buss, Alcides. Olhar a vida. Florianópolis, Brazil: Editora Insular, 2007. 108 p.

In his fourth decade of activity, the poet-professor, known as an advocate for literacy and reading, maintains his primary concern with the expression of experience. His humanistic approach never diminishes literary interest per se.

3075 Cabañas M., Teresa. Que poesia é essa?: poesia marginal: sujeitos instáveis, estética desajustada. Goiânia, Brazil: Univ. Federal de Goiás, 2009. 215 p.: bibl., ill.

Thirty years after the decline of so-called marginal poetry, an academic study as concerned with subject positions of the writers as with esthetic results.

3076 Cabral de Melo Neto, João. O artista inconfessável. Rio de Janeiro: Alfaguara, 2007. 198 p.: ill.

Custom compilation of the leading late 20th century poet (1920–99) comprising a sort of artistic memorial or autobiography with origins in rural Pernambuco, long stays in Spain, and encounters with admired authors. No new primary texts but a useful critical bibliography as appendix.

3077 Caiafa, Janice. Estúdio. Rio de Janeiro: 7Letras, 2009. 80 p.

Fifth collection by accomplished poet-anthropologist as keen to artistic and intellectual legacies of Western civilization as to personal experience and moments of perceptual impact. Fine press edition with hard cover, color string binding, and ribbon fasteners.

3078 Calixto, Fabiano. Sangüínea: 2005–2007. São Paulo: Editora 34, 2007. 124 p.

Third book of poetry by poet-editor (1973) unafraid to display affection, admiration, friendship, intimate moments, and "circumstantial verse."

3079 Carneiro, Geraldo. Poemas reunidos. Rio de Janeiro: Nova Fronteira/Fundação Biblioteca Nacional, 2010. 462 p.

Collection of seven previous books, each of which, in turn, is subdivided under imaginative rubrics. From sophisticatedly alternative publications of the 1970s to gamesome contemporary contemplations of self and civilizational legacies, the poet-lyricist-screenwriter (b. 1952) moves between applications of popular registers (slang, rock, tango, television) and offbeat invocations of the high Western canon (Homer, Orpheus, Plato, Dante, Camões, and especially Shakespeare). Over the decades, his unique free/metered verse has been favorably reminiscent of such Portuguese language greats as Olavo Bilac, Manuel Bandeira, Fernando Pessoa, and Vinícius de Moraes. The volume has an honest and insightful introduction by Nelson Ascher.

3080 Carneiro, Rosane. Corpo estranho. Rio de Janeiro: Editor da Palavra, 2009. 91 p.

In the author's third short book, she poeticizes the body, encounter, and possibilities for rebirth under the sign of eros.

3081 Carpinejar. Meu filho, minha filha. Rio de Janeiro: Bertrand Brasil, 2007. 141 p.

In this thematically driven title, the active poet of diverse interests seeks to resignify the father figure in a conjuncture of unrelenting change, when traditional family relations and stability are no longer a given. Unavoidable sentimental tones can be distracting.

3082 Castro, Nei Leandro de. Autobiografia poemas. Natal, Brazil: Offset, 2008. 118 p.

In his tenth book of verse since 1961, the poet (re)imagines his late adolescence, young adulthood, affairs, and travels in Brazil and abroad. Characteristically wry observations abound.

3083 Castro, Sílvio. Modernização, modernidade: 7 poetas contemporâneos da Academia Brasileira de Letras. Rio de Janeiro: Edições Galo Branco, 2006. 266 p.: bibl.

A volume highlighting the poetry of current members of Brazil's National Academy of Letters, some of whom are bonafide leading voices in the field in terms of conventional lyrical production.

3084 Catunda, Márcio. Emoção Atlântica. Rio de Janeiro: Oficina, 2010. 116 p.

Poems about persons and places of the "marvelous city" of Rio de Janeiro, especially the nice beachfront districts. Recurring concerns are to write chronicles of urban experience and to express an environmentally friendly consciousness.

3085 Chacal. Belvedere: 1971–2007. São Paulo: Cosac Naify; Rio de Janeiro: 7Letras, 2007. 371 p. (Col. Ás de colete)

Collected poetry, 13 books/chapbooks, 1971–2007, from the beginnings of *poesia marginal*, of which the author is one of the foundational voices, to new millennium free verse, successful in its informality.

3086 Cisneros, Odile. Novos olhos sobre a poesia: Brazilian poetry journals of the 21st century. (*Aufgabe*, 6, 2007, p. 13–21)

Very useful brief account of key periodicals for poetry as the transition to web-based presence takes place.

3087 Concerto a quatro vozes. Organização de Domício Proença Filho. Rio de Janiero: Editora Record, 2006. 190 p.

In this special anthology, the editor wishes to show "multiplicity and dispersion" in contemporary Brazilian lyric. For this demonstration, he chooses four distinguished voices and outlooks: Adriano Espínola, the voice of the urb; Antonio Cicero, the voice of Eros; Marco Lucchesi, the voice of the desert; and Salgado Maranhão, the voice of the sun. Includes carefully selected excerpts of the critical reception of the poets.

3088 Corona, Ricardo. Corpo sutil. São Paulo: Iluminuras, 2005. 92 p.: port.

Second substantial collection by this sophisticated cultural activist whose poetic sources are varied, ranging from indigenous oral traditions and symbolism to Russian constructivism and Beat poetry. A critical yet generous inter-American thread runs through the three parts of the book.

3089 Costa, Horácio. Paulistanas. Homo-eróticas. São Paulo: Lumme Editor, 2007. 2 v., 1 folded pamphlet, 6 p. (Série Caixa preta: poesia)

Three-item box with front matter, poems inspired in Brazil's megalopolis, and homoerotic (very broadly understood) verse. Fine press production.

3090 Costa, Horácio. Ravenalas: po-emas, 2004–2008. 2a ed. São Paulo: Demônio Negro, 2009. 145 p.

Ninth book of poetry since 1981 by the effusive poet-professor, creator of a multifaceted and open-ended lyrical universe blending personal experience and sophisticated cosmopolitanism.

3091 Espínola, Adriano. Praia provisória. Rio de Janeiro: Topbooks, 2006. 116 p.

Sixth book of poetry by the versatile poet-professor whose present day verse, here most often contained and synthetic, echoes or recalls in original fashion myriad moments of the great Western tradition, especially Orphism. Highlights of five centuries of Brazilian lyric, especially modernism and late-century reformulations.

3092 Ferraz, Eucanaã. Cinemateca. São Paulo: Companhia das Letras, 2008. 167 p.

This fifth book of verse by the poet-editor manifests interests in physical and psychic phenomena alike. Material is experiential, from the feeling of the tactile to the abstraction of sound. The sometimes colloquial tone never affects textual confidence.

3093 Freitas, Iacyr Anderson. Primeiras le-tras. São Paulo: Nankin Editorial; Juiz de Fora, Brazil: FUNALFA Edições, 2007. 214 p.: bibl., ill. (Col. Janela do caos. Poesia brasileira; 26)

Third and final volume of the complete poems, composed of six books of the 1980s, with some revisions. Generally terse lines express both colloquial and dense inner experience. Good documentation as back matter. Excellent examples of the lively poetry scene in the college town of Juiz de Fora in the 1980s.

3094 Freitas, Iacyr Anderson. Quaradouro. São Paulo: Nankin Editorial; Brazil: Funalfa Edições, 2007. 218 p. (Janela do caos. Poesia brasileira; 25)

Second volume of the award-winning author's complete poems, composed of four books of the early 1990s, with some revisions. History, temporality, and mythical heritage inform the carefully crafted verses.

3095 Fróes, Leonardo. Chinês com sono: seguido de Clones do inglês. Rio de Janeiro: Rocco, 2005. 157 p.: ill.

The poet-translator (b. 1941) here offers a dozen translations from the English to complement the mature vision of his fabular poems that embody explorations of the natural world.

3096 Gil, Fernando Cerisara. Do encanta-mento à apostasia: a poesia brasileira de 1880–1919: antologia e estudo. Curitiba, Brazil: Editora UFPR, 2006. 405 p.: bibl. (Série Letras do Brasil; 6)

Academic study and anthology of verse in the late romantic, Parnassian, symbolist and premodernist phases of Brazilian letters.

3097 Grünewald, José Lino. Escreviver. Organização de José Guilherme Correa. Revisão de Augusto de Campos. São Paulo: Perspectiva; Rio de Janeiro: Fundação Biblioteca Nacional, 2008. 269 p.: ill. (Col. Signos; 47)

Collected poems including early discursive personal lyric, canonical concrete poems of the heroic phase of the movement, later experimental word constructs, and some previously unpublished items. Selection of critical appreciations of his contribution to the Brazilian arts.

3098 Ivo, Lêdo. Poesia completa, 1940–2004. Estudo introdutório de Ivan Junqueira. Rio de Janeiro: Topbooks, 2004. 1099 p.: index.

The sheer size of this volume indicates how prolific this enduring poet has been since his debut under the sign of the neo-Parnassian Generation of '45. In seven decades of production, rigor and control have always been evident in his verse, almost always measured, rarely free or speech-based. Useful introduction by poet-critic Ivan Junqueira, who shares esthetic positions.

3099 Junqueira, Ivan. O outro lado: 1998–2006. Rio de Janeiro: Editora Record, 2007. 111 p.

Technical dominion, linguistic polish, and meditative approach characterize this veteran verse maker, who has lost no expressive vigor late in his five decade career.

3100 Junqueira, Ivan. O tempo além do tempo: antologia. Organização e prefácio de Arnaldo Saraiva. Vila Nova de Famalicão, Portugal: Quasi Edições, 2007. 139 p.: ill. (Biblioteca Arranjos para assobio)

With six books since 1964, the author (poet, critic, translator, editor) has a well-established reputation as a serious voice, bolstered by his election to the Academia Brasileira de Letras. The volume editor is the leading authority on Brazilian letters in the mother country and understands well the poet's aversion to modernist excess, colloquialism, and indiscipline. The selection illustrates his lyrical dexterity.

3101 Kaq, Francisco. Diz. Brasília: Casa das Musas, 2007. 49 p.

Fifth very brief collection of this adventurous minimalist poet with evident debts to concrete poetry (which invoked the pilot plan of Brasília) and such modernist endeavors as calligramme and invention à la William Carlos Williams.

3102 Latin American women writers: an encyclopedia. Edited by María Claudia André and Eva Paulino Bueno. New York: Routledge, 2008. 612 p.: bibl., index.

This reference work has nine valuable entries on Brazilian women poets, most notably Cecília Meireles.

3103 Machado, Nauro. Pátria do exílio. São Luís, Brazil: Lume Edições, 2006. 93 p.

The author (b. 1935) has been prolific for decades, with some three dozen books of verse. This third and final canto of "Trindade Dantesca," begun in 2003, comprises conventional six-line stanzas celebrating a voyage to Portugal.

3104 Machado de Assis. Toda poesia de Machado de Assis. Organização de Cláudio Murilo Leal. Rio de Janeiro: Editora Record, 2008. 750 p.

The most complete set of poems by the master of Brazilian letters, as it includes texts left out of other collections and "complete" works. Not extensive, but good introduction and critical bibliography.

3105 Maranhão, Salgado. A cor da palavra. Rio de Janeiro: Imago: Biblioteca Nacional, 2009. 421 p.

Collected poems (1978–2009) of one of the nation's most beloved and admired poets. While ever aware of conjuncture and relevant collective experience, the poet consistently contemplates words themselves in his multichromatic clusters.

3106 Mello, Ana Maria Lisboa de and Francis Utéza. Oriente e ocidente na poesia de Cecília Meireles. Porto Alegre, Brazil: Libretos: FAPA; Montpellier, France: Univ. Paul Valery/Études Ibériques Latino-Américaines et Lusophones, 2006. 310 p.: bibl., ill.

Not a coauthored monograph, but two discreet academic studies in one volume. The first part is conventional textual analysis concerned with transcendence, especially via India, while the second part examines hermetic codes in the neo-epical Romanceiro da Inconfidência.

3107 Mello, Simone Homem de. Périplos: 31 poemas. Cotia, Brazil: Ateliê Editorial, 2005. 93 p.

Startling debut book (31 poems written from 1994 to 2003) by São Paulo poet-translator residing in Berlin. At times arresting imagery in an elegant lyrical periplus, or periplum in a Poundian sense.

3108 Milano, Dante. Obra reunida. Apresentação e biobibliografia de Ivan Junqueira. Organização e estabelecimento do texto de Sérgio Martagão Gesteira. Rio de Janeiro: Academia Brasileira de Letras, 2004. 529 p.: ill. (Col. Austregésilo de Athayde; 21)

Author of a single volume of poetry, numerous translations of classics, and plentiful prose pieces, mostly about literature, this author (1899–1991) was unusual for eschewing recognition as a writer. This smart volume allows for deserved appreciation of his dry, contemplative verse and of his discerning critical eye, which organized the first anthology of modernismo in the 1930s.

3109 Miranda, Antonio. De ornatu mundi. Ecopoemas de Antonio Miranda. Ilustrações de Álvaro Nunes. Brasília: LGE Editora, 2010. 89 p.: col. ill.

Ecologically conscious lyric written in the course of the last five decades and inspired in diverse regions of the country, especially the Amazon, where the author (director of the capital city national library) was born. Very attractive square volume with color botanical plates by the nation's most highly regarded scientific illustrator.

3110 Moisés, Carlos Felipe. Noite nula. São Paulo: Nankin, 2008. 95 p.: ill.

Latest sequence by established and respected poet-professor of São Paulo. Subjectivity expressed through longish lyrics (just 20 all told) mostly addressed to great figures in music (Leadbelly, Coltrane, Carlos Gardel, Billie Holiday), thus participating in a surprisingly common inter-American vein of national poetry inspired in music-making of the US and Spanish America.

3111 Nejar, Carlos. O inquilino da Urca: sonetos em chamas. Rio de Janeiro: Edicões Galo Branco, 2008. 117 p.

Latest title by the member of the Academy of Letters regarded as one the most significant voices of lyric since 1960. A series of flawlessly executed traditional sonnets dedicated to the celebrated neighborhood of the "Marvelous City."

3112 NOME. DVD realizado por Arnaldo Antunes *et al.* Produzido e distribuído no Pólo Industrial de Manaus por Sonopress Rimo da Amazónia Industría e Comércio Fotográfica. Direção de produção (som) realizado por Leonardo Netto. Manaus, Brazil: Sony BMG Entertainment: RCA, 2005. 1 DVD, 1 CD, 1 booklet (12 p.).

Welcome reissue of the artist's first solo work (BMG 1993), with 23 animated/kinetic visual poems, experimental poetic narratives, and illustrated songs, some coauthored. Remarkable verbivocovisual undertaking.

3113 Nuvem Cigana: poesia & delírio no Rio dos anos 70. Organização de Sergio Cohn. Rio de Janeiro: Azougue, 2007. 221 p.: ill.

History, criticism, and interviews with principal figures of the days of "marginal poetry," featuring poet-lyricist Ronaldo Bastos.

3114 Oliveira, Fernanda Ribeiro Queiroz de. Canto e corte: a épica e o drama nas vozes de Cecília Meireles e João Cabral de Melo Neto. Goiânia, Brazil: Editora UFG, 2006. 150 p.: bibl. (Col. Hórus)

Academic study of the epical and dramatic elements in the repertories of two of Brazil's leading 20th-century poets.

3115 Paes, José Paulo. Poesia completa. Apresentação de Rodrigo Naves. São Paulo: Companhia das Letras, 2008. 514 p.

Complete poetical work (1947–2001) of the admirable São Paulo poet-translator (1926–98) noted for his aphorisms, epigrams, faux proverbs, poetic capsules, and "minimal odes." Economical sarcasm and mordant experimentalism characterize his work over the course of five decades.

3116 Pallottini, Renata. Um calafrio diário. São Paulo: Editora Perspectiva, 2002. 211, 4 p.: ill.

Poetry comprises about 40 percent of the author's extensive list of published works. As the present title suggests, it contains poems about daily life (confessional lyric), but there is also a section on poetic art itself. In addition, the contents include letters from Carlos Drummond de Andrade to the poet (b. 1931) and reprints of select books of her poetry, which add worth to the nicely produced volume.

3117 Patativa, do Assaré. Inspiração nordestina. São Paulo: Hedra, 2003. 351 p. (Col. de literatura popular)

Third edition, with some additions, of the renowned poet's inaugural publication (1956). His work, all based on inherited forms of popular poetry (quadras, sextilhas, décimas) includes oral lyrics, narrative chapbooks, and simulations of verbal duels. An institution in the largely rural culture of the Northeast region.

3118 Pederneiras, Mário. Poesia reunida. Estudo introdutório, organização e estabelecimento de texto de Antonio Carlos Secchin. Rio de Janeiro: Academia Brasileira de Letras, 2004. 316 p.: ill. (Col. Austregésilo de Athayde; 22)

Superbly prepared volume in the Academia's own publication series. The author (1867–1915) lived a literary transition from pompous neoromanticism and symbolism to an unconflicted premodernist personal lyricism.

3119 Peña, Karen Patricia. Poetry and the realm of the public intellectual: the alternative destinies of Gabriela Mistral, Cecília Meireles, and Rosario Castellanos. Leeds, UK: Legenda, 2007. 231 p.: bibl., index.

Two of the six chapters in this well-researched and admirably well-written monograph concern the leading female modernist poet of Brazil. One describes poetic explorations of the (feminine) self and the other examines sociocultural critiques, with inter-American episodes.

3120 Perrone, Charles A. ABC of AdeC: reading Augusto de Campos. (*Review/ New York*, 73, Jan./June 2006, p. 236–244)

A synthesis of the ever ingenious poetic universe of the originator of concrete poetry, elegant translator of poetry of invention from the troubadors to the postmoderns, and electronic bard.

3121 Perrone, Charles A. Brazil, lyric, and the Americas. Gainesville, Fla.: Univ. Press of Florida, 2010. 250 p.: bibl., index.

Critical monograph concerning inter-relations of Brazilian lyric since the mid-1980s. Considers uses of English by poets of Brazil, varied intertextualities, utilizations of nonliterary input (comics, film, popular music, tourism), connections with Spanish America, and new applications of Tropicália. Guiding analytical tropes are interface, insularity (plus deterritorialization), and invention (contrivance and discovery alike). Further bibliography on repertories considered in the present volume (*HLAS 66*).

3122 Perrone, Charles A. Letras e letras da MPB. 2a. ed. histórica comemorativa do 200 aniversário. Revisada pelo autor. Rio de Janeiro: Booklink, 2008. 274 p. (Col. A letra do som)

A second "historical edition" of this pioneer study of the poetry of song (1960s-80s) with new prefaces by Augusto de Campos and Amador Ribeiro Neto.

3123 Pinto, Manuel da Costa. Antologia comentada da poesia brasileira do século 21. São Paulo: Publifolha, 2006. 382 p.: bibl.

An extremely valuable anthology of 205 poems by 70 poets active in the new millennium, with concise and perceptive critical commentary by the editor. Single most important source for recent Brazilian poetry.

3124 Piva, Roberto. Mala na mão & asas pretas. São Paulo: Editora Globo, 2006. 171 p. (Obras reunidas; 2)

Volume two of the collected works of the polemical author (1937–2010) with four books between 1976–83, plus reprints of manifesti of 1983–84. Since many consider this period to be the poet's most fertile, the present title gains importance to understand a mostly discursive writer who has been called marginal, transgressive, hardcore, experimental, and unorthodox.

3125 Poemas afro-brasileiros. Organização de Esmeralda Ribeiro e Márcio Barbosa. São Paulo: Quilombhoje, 2006. 263 p.: bibl., ports. (Cadernos negros; 29)

Continuation of a well-established project to promote Afro-Brazilian poetry.

3126 Poéticas do olhar e outras leituras de poesia. Organização de Celia Pedrosa e Maria Lucia de Barros Camargo. Rio de Janeiro: 7 Letras, 2006. 252 p.: bibl.

This edited multi-author volume includes both general theoretical essays on the current state of lyric in the Western world and studies on specific contemporary Brazilian poets. The coeditors have been active in the organization of events and publication about lyric for years, and this project may well be the best fruit of their efforts.

3127 Pucheu, Alberto. A fronteira desguarnecida: poesia reunida, 1993–2007. Rio de Janeiro: Azougue Editorial, 2007. 285 p.

Reunion of nine collections plus selections of interviews. The title image—of breaking down/ desupplying borders—suggests the governing poetics, which oscillates between contemplation of private life and urban existence, and extends to genre, challenging boundaries between modern verse and prose poem, philosophy and literature.

3128 Ramalho, Christina. Elas escrevem o épico. Prefácio de Simone Caputo Gomes. Ilha de Santa Catarina, Brazil:

Editora Mulheres; Santa Cruz do Sul, Brazil: EDUNISC, 2005. 194 p.: bibl.

Unique study of (neo-)epic poetry by 10 women, nine Brazilians and Chilean Gabriela Mistral, who acted as cultural attaché in Rio in the 1940s. Feminist perspective and recovery of relevant texts prove to be more significant than the adopted semiotic method.

3129 Salgueiro, Wilberth Claython Ferreira. Lira à brasileira: erótica, poética, política. Vitória, Brazil: EDUFES, 2007. 203 p.: bibl., ill.

Small university press monograph specifically concerned with different aspects of the genre of lyric in the 20th century in Brazil.

3130 Seminário Internacional Poesia Contemporânea: Identidades e Subjectividades em Devir, *Universidade Federal Fluminense*, 2007. Subjetividades em devir: estudos de poesia moderna e contemporânea. Organização de Celia Pedrosa e Ida Alves. Rio de Janeiro: 7Letras, 2008. 332 p.: bibl.

Conference proceedings of a 2007 international seminar on identities and developing subjectivities in modern and contemporary poetry, thus a very wide-angle orientation. No specifically Brazilian imperative in the charge of the project, but about one-half of the essays concern poets/poetry of Brazil. The second main focus is Portugal.

3131 Silva, Anazildo Vasconcelos da and Christina Ramalho. História da epopéia brasileira: teoria, crítica e percurso. Rio de Janeiro: Garamond, 2007. 1 v.: bibl. (Garamond universitária)

This is the first volume (of a projected three) of the most extensive study ever done of the epic genre in Brazil. Here, sequential sections treat the epical subject, myth, uses of history, and literary portraiture. The point of departure is a rearticulation of the lead author's 1980s study of the "semioticization" of epic discourse.

3132 Silva, Dora Ferreira da. O leque. Rio de Janeiro: Instituto Moreira Salles, 2007. 1 v. (unpaged).

First posthumous book by the poet (d. 2006), who published 12 collections in her lifetime. The title refers both literally to the format of the slim volume, a continuous unfolding series of cards instead of separate cut pages, as well as textually to the contents, 10 lyrical variations on the theme/image of the fan.

3133 Siscar, Marcos. O roubo do silêncio. Rio de Janeiro: 7Letras, 2006. 66 p. (Col. Guizos)

One-page pieces of prose poetry that play with notions of self, genre, history, and memory. Instigating interplay of intellectual and emotive planes.

3134 Soares, José. José Soares. Introdução e seleção de Mark Dinneen. São Paulo: Hedra, 2007. 158 p.: bibl., ill. (Biblioteca de cordel)

This title represents the 21st addition to the series Biblioteca de cordel. This enterprise—directed by Joseph Luyten (1941–2006)—documents the work of authors of nonindustrial chapbooks of popular narrative poetry, estimated at 2000 writers and 30,000 items. Each book has reprints of 10 to 12 folhetos and critical appreciation.

3135 Sousândrade. Melhores poemas. Seleção e notas de Adriano Espínola. São Paulo: Global, 2009. 189 p.: bibl. (Melhores poemas)

The most assiduously prepared volume in this best poems series, with careful selection, insightful introduction, and extensive notes.

3136 Tigertail: a south Florida poetry annual. v. VI, Brazil issue. Edited and with introductions by Horácio Costa and Charles A. Perrone. Miami, Fla.: Tigertail Productions, 2008. 54 p.

Bilingual anthology of very recent voices including a trio of stellar women poets, Virna Teixeira, Simone Homem de Mello, and Adriana Zapparolli.

3137 Um tigre na floresta de signos: estudos sobre poesia e demandas sociais no Brasil. Organização de Edimilson de Almeida Pereira. Belo Horizonte, Brazil: Mazza, 2010. 748 p. (Col. Setefalas)

Besides the project coordinator, who launched his complete poems in four volumes in 2003, 32 authors contribute studies to this substantial and very useful volume, divided into six clusters: Afro-Brazilian literature in general, poetic models of Afro-

Brazilian-ness, divergent models, women's voices, liberty/transgression, and oral poetry/performance, where anthropological approaches enter. The essays concern a wide range of topics related to poetry in different ways, from collective consciousness to individual repertories, notably those of Ricardo Aleixo and Salgado Maranhão.

3138 Trindade, Solano. Poemas antológicos de Solano Trindade. Seleção e introdução de Zenir Campos Reis. São Paulo: Nova Alexandria, 2008. 167 p.: ill. (Obras antológicas. Poemas)

This series of "anthological poems" selects and presents clusters of representative poems of established names. The author (1908–74), a pioneer of Afro-Brazilian poetry, wrote texts for declamation or theatrical performance more than for silent book reading.

3139 Vogt, Carlos. Poesia reunida. São Paulo: Landy Editora, 2008. 511 p.

Reunion of seven books by a poet-linguist who reached the president's office at Unicamp. His verse ranges from the very contained (epigrammatic, curt, incisive) to the more extended (discursive, evocative, meditative). Ironic or melancholic depending on the situation, the poet demonstrates both wide historical awareness and intimacy.

3140 Weintraub, Fabio. Baque. São Paulo: Editora 34, 2007. 67 p. (Poesia)

Third short book by this off-center observer of urban malaise and human figures in extreme situations.

Drama

SEVERINO J. ALBUQUERQUE, *Professor of Portuguese, University of Wisconsin-Madison*

BRAZILIAN THEATER HISTORY has been well served by the recent publication of several volumes from commercial as well as government publishers. Particularly noteworthy is the continuation of the Coleção Dramaturgos do Brasil (under the general direction of João Roberto Faria of the Universidade de São Paulo (USP)) and the Martins Fontes series reviving the dramatic works of major 19th-century authors, this time with the publication of Gonçalves de Magalhães' tragedies (item **3151**; see also *HLAS 64:2434*). Professor Faria has also edited a 680-page edition of Machado de Assis' theater criticism entitled *Do teatro: textos críticos e escritos diversos* (2008; item **3177**). An indispensable research tool for students of 19th-century Brazilian theater, the work is a logical companion to *Teatro de Machado de Assis* (2003) (see *HLAS 64:2427*). Another important aspect of the critical attention being paid to the 19th century is the research on leading directors, impresarios, and actors of the time, as for example, Correa Vasques (item **3180**). Equally important is the continued critical attention to the theater of the fascinating if controversial figure of Qorpo-Santo (items **3160** and **3178**). The influence of 19th-century foreign dramatists has also received recent attention, as witnessed by the publication of Karl Erik Schollhammer's collection of essays on Ibsen and the Brazilian stage (item **3174**).

Despite occasional instances of political theater—for the most part anarchist theater by Italian immigrants, well represented in another Martins Fontes edition (item **3141**)—the early part of the 20th century was dominated by a form of light comedy known in Brazil as *teatro ligeiro*. The form has received critical scrutiny, as for example, in Beti Rabetti's book on two leading names of the genre, Gastão Tojeiro and Armando Gonzaga (item **3189**). The revolutionary staging of Nelson Rodrigues' *Vestido de noiva* in 1943 signaled the disappearance of the *teatro* *ligeiro* and ushered in a new period. One of the most accomplished critics of this new period was Barbara Heliodora, whose writings from 1944–94 have been compiled by Cláudia Braga in a carefully edited 950-page volume (item **3173**).

The theater of Nelson Rodrigues continues to receive considerable scholarly attention in Brazil and elsewhere, and his plays remain among the most staged in theaters around the nation. Critical works include David George's overview of Nelson's theater with emphasis on his role in the creation of a truly Brazilian theater (item **3170**) and Petra Souto's study of women and society in Nelson's drama (item **3191**). Efforts to make Nelson's theater more easily available to foreign directors and groups include the publication of translations of his plays. An essential part of such efforts is Joffre Rodrigues' project to make his father's entire dramatic output available in English; two volumes have appeared so far (item **3158**). In addition, a trilingual edition (English, French, and Portuguese) of Nelson's *Beijo no asfalto* has been published (item **3155**), as have the English translations of his works used for the US stage adaptations of *A vida como ela é—Life as it is* (item **3156**) and *Pornographic angel* (item **3157**).

New memoirs and biographies of key theater practitioners provide a wealth of information for students of the Brazilian theater. Particularly auspicious are the memoirs of Sérgio Britto (item **3164**) and Gianni Ratto (item **3190**) and critical biographies of playwrights Oduvaldo Vianna Filho (Vianinha) (item **3184**), Plínio Marcos (item **3181**), and Leilah Assumpção (item **3182**). English translations of plays by Marcos and Assumpção are found in a paperback anthology of Brazilian theater now available in the US (item **3152**).

Marcos, Vianinha, Assumpção, and scores of other playwrights and theater practitioners were the victims of official censorship during most of the 19th and 20th centuries in Brazil, as documented in Cristina Costa's remarkable book (item **3167**). Equally remarkable and relevant to censorship (and collective creation theater) are the diaries of Judith Malina (who with Julian Beck led the Living Theater during a harrowing sojourn in Brazil in the early 1970s) now available in a carefully edited publication of the Arquivo Público of the state of Minas Gerais (item **3179**). Historical and literary figures and events have been the frequent subjects of original plays in the period under consideration. Examples of historical drama have focused on the figures of Domingos Fernandes Calabar, a Brazilian who fought with the Dutch in Pernambuco (item **3147**); former president Getúlio Vargas (item **3150**); journalist and educator Anália Franco (item **3154**); and João Cândido, leader of the 1910 naval mutiny, the Revolta da Chibata (item **3159**). Transition periods in the recent history of Brazil have inspired widely different plays ranging from the comedies of Flávio Marinho as well as those by the duo Jandira Martini and Marcos Caruso in works such as *Sua Excelência, o Candidato* (included in item **3153**) to the more serious drama of Bosco Brasil, whose excellent *Novas diretrizes em tempos de paz* is presented in a bilingual (French and Portuguese) edition (included in item **3144**). Among the plays focusing on literary figures, those on Elizabeth Bishop (item **3148**) and Jorge Luis Borges (item **3143**) are noteworthy. Another major literary figure, Clarice Lispector, is the subject of a scholarly study, André Luís Gomes' important analysis of Clarice's relationship with the theater, including documentation on the several stage adaptations of her life and works (item **3171**).

Regional drama continues to be the topic of several publications, with the theater of Northeast Brazil receiving the most attention in the last few years. Relevant examples include, from Maranhão, a study of puppet theater (item **3162**) and a history of the theater in that state (item **3175**); and from Pernambuco, a three-volume edition of the plays of a distinguished man of the theater, Hermilo Borba Filho (item **3142**).

Key 20th-century drama critics and theater professors have been the focus of important scholarly books. Foremost among these are Silvana Garcia's edition of a collection of essays on Alfredo Mesquita and his Escola de Arte Dramática (item **3176**) and Ana Bernstein's study of the career and contributions of Décio de Almeida Prado (item **3161**).

Theater groups have also received considerable critical attention. A number of these publications have an historical orientation, such as Tânia Brandão's study of the Companhia Maria Della Costa (item **3163**), editor Christiane Tricerri's coffee-table volume tracing the activities of the Teatro do Ornitorrinco troupe (item **3192**), Kátia Paranhos' study of labor union-sponsored groups (item **3183**), and Rosângela Patriota's essay on the historiography of theater groups in Brazil, with a focus on the writing of the history of the seminal Teatro de Arena de São Paulo (item **3185**). Numerous groups are featured in photographer Lenise Pinheiro's visual documentation of the Brazilian stage in the last quarter-century (item **3187**). Some of the volumes are collections of documents from a group's archives, such as the ones compiled by Jorge Figueira for the first decade of Folias (item **3169**) and by Reginaldo Nascimento for Cadernos do Kaus (item **3165**). In addition, in a valuable contribution to theater research, some groups have made their scripts available in print, in some cases for the first time: Galpão (item **3149**), Latão (item **3146**), Satyros (item **3145**), and Asdrúbal trouxe o trombone (item **3186**). The Latão volume has an excellent preface by Iná Camargo Costa, and Asdrúbal's includes short introductory texts by its three best-known members: Hamilton Vaz Pereira, Regina Casé, and Luiz Fernando Guimarães. Most of the troupes have ongoing study groups and acting workshops with a strong emphasis on the study of the body and movement; the results of some of these workshops are now appearing in print (item **3166**). Finally, a deeper involvement of playwrights with the craft of the theater has lead to the return of the *dramaturgo*, as for example in the case of Bernardo Carvalho and Teatro da Vertigem's production of *BR-3* (see *HLAS 64:2435*). Daniel Wajnberg explains this trend, with numerous examples, in his article, "A escrita contaminada pela cena" (item **3193**).

The publications reviewed here illustrate a few trends. First, the works of new, outstanding playwrights (e.g., Bosco Brasil) and groups (e.g., Latão, Folias, Satyros) are beginning to appear in print. These are paralleled by excellent scholarly studies of contemporary theater such as that by Sílvia Fernandes (item **3168**) and Fátima Saadi and Silvana Garcia's edited collection of scholarly explorations of contemporary theatricality (item **3188**). Another trend is the recent availability in English and French of texts by some of the most important playwrights. Also notable is the primacy of the theater scene of the city of São Paulo. To a large extent, the energy and talent that characterize its current theater scene (with typically over 150 productions on stage every week) can be traced to government subsidies via the successful Programa Municipal de Fomento ao Teatro. Government support for the dramatic arts also appears in the form of the state of São Paulo's official printing house (Imprensa Oficial) and two of its remarkable series, Coleção Aplauso-Teatro (critical studies and biographies) and Coleção Primeiras Obras (featuring the work of new playwrights). For free online access to the e-book versions of the works in the Coleção Aplauso-Teatro series, consult the website of the Imprensa Oficial: http://www.imprensaoficial.com.br/colecaoaplauso.

ORIGINAL PLAYS

3141 Antologia do teatro anarquista.
Edição preparada por Maria Thereza Vargas. São Paulo: WMF Martins Fontes, 2009. 316 p.: bibl., ill. (Col. "Dramaturgos do Brasil"; 18)

Part of the carefully edited series featuring out-of-print or never-published important plays from the 19th and early 20th centuries. This volume is dedicated to the theater of immigrant workers, mostly Italians, with a strong commitment to the anarchist movement. The three plays ("O semeador" by Avelino Fóscolo, a self-taught pharmacist; "A bandeira proletária" by Marino Spagnolo, a tailor; and "Uma mulher diferente" by Pedro Catallo, a shoemaker) reflect the struggle for the rights of women and factory workers.

3142 Borba Filho, Hermilo. Hermilo Borba Filho: Teatro selecionado. Organização de Leda Alves e Luis Augusto Reis. Rio de Janeiro: Funarte, 2007. 3 v.: ill.

Twelve plays by the prolific, multifaceted theater practitioner. Borba Filho was a playwright, stage director, translator, critic, and researcher of the theater of Northeast Brazil. Along with his companion and co-worker, Leda Alves, Ariano Suassuna, and several others, he founded the Teatro Popular do Nordeste (Recife, 1961) and for more than three decades was instrumental in fostering dramatic arts and encouraging the careers of young actors and playwrights.

3143 Brandão, Ignácio de Loyola. A última viagem de Borges: duas possibilidades de encenação. São Paulo: Global Editora, 2005. 171 p.: bibl., ill.

This one-act play is best described as an evocation of the Argentinian master who, about to embark on his last trip, interacts with characters like Sheherazade and historical figures like Sir Richard Burton, the translator of *The One Thousand and One Nights* and *The Lusiads*. Book includes two different versions of the play, a faster-paced one (the version that was staged) and a slower, more meditative text.

3144 Brasil, Bosco. Cheiro de chuva; Novas diretrizes em tempos de paz. Edição bilíngüe português-francês. São Paulo: Aliança Francesa: Consulado Geral da França: Imprensa Oficial do Estado de São Paulo, 2007. 111 p. (Col. Palco sur scène; BR 02)

Bilingual edition (Portuguese/French) of the best plays by one of the most important playwrights of the 1990s and 2000s. Short introductions by Sábato Magaldi, Thomas Quillardet, and others.

3145 Cabral, Ivam. Quatro textos para um teatro veloz: o teatro de Ivam Cabral. São Paulo: Imprensa Oficial do Estado de São Paulo, 2006. 276 p.: ill., ports. (Col. Aplauso teatro Brasil)

Two of the texts are adaptations of works by Lautréamont ("Os cantos de Maldoror") and Oscar Wilde ("De Profundis"), while the other two are originals by Cabral, who cofounded (with Rodolfo García Márquez) the important group Os Satyros in 1989. The volume has introductory texts by Alberto Guzik and Jefferson del Rios. (See also Alberto Guzik, *Os Satyros: um palco visceral*, another part of the Coleção Aplauso, reviewed in *HLAS 64:2437*.)

3146 Carvalho, Sérgio de and **Márcio Marciano.** Companhia do Latão: 7 peças. Prefácio de Iná Camargo Costa. São Paulo: CosacNaify, 2008. 410 p.: ill.

This important volume includes the texts of seven of the plays staged by the key São Paulo-based group, Companhia do Latão, since its beginnings in 1996. The plays (which Carvalho calls "peças autorais") divided into three groups, Imagens do Brasil, Cenas da mercantilização, and Releituras. Includes a learned introduction by Iná Camargo Costa and important background information about the group's creative process (a combination of "dramaturgia coletiva" and epic or critical experimentation), culled from serious historical and political research, group discussion, and debates with intellectuals and theater practitioners.

3147 Cavalcante, Homero. Liberdade e sonho em cena: dois textos de Homero Cavalcante. Organização de Antônio José Rodrigues Xavier. Maceió, Brazil: EdUFAL: CESMAC-Centro de Estudos Superiores de Maceió, 2009. 126 p.: bibl., ill.

Two plays by the multitalented actor, director, and theater professor Homero Cavalcante. The first, "Calabar: Sonho e liberdade," is a historical play that focuses on the controversial figure of Domingos Fernandes Calabar during the Dutch occupation of Northeast Brazil in the 17th century. The second, "Eira, beira e ramo de figueira, ou Dona Moça Solteira," is a comedy that draws heavily on types and myths of his native Alagoas.

3148 Góes, Marta. Um porto para Elizabeth Bishop. São Paulo: Editora Terceiro Nome, 2001. 64 p.: ill.

This monologue addresses different periods of Elizabeth Bishop's sojourn in Rio de Janeiro and Ouro Preto, with a focus on her 15-year relationship with the Brazilian architect, Lota de Macedo Soares. Written especially for the actor Regina Braga, the play, directed by José Possi Neto, was premiered in Curitiba's Festival Internacional de Teatro in 2001.

3149 Grupo Galpão. Textos de rua. Organização de Eduardo Moreira. Belo Horizonte, Brazil: Autêntica: Editora PUC Minas, 2007. 84 p.: ill. (Espetáculos do Galpão; 1)

Compilation of the texts of three of the plays ("A comédia da esposa muda"; "Foi por amor"; "Corra enquanto é tempo") by the best street theater group in Brazil, Belo Horizonte's Galpão. Includes photos and a short introduction by the volume editor.

3150 Louzeiro, José and Denise Andrade. O poder e a glória. Rio de Janeiro: Editora Museu da República, 2004. 40 p. (Dramaturgias republicanas)

First in a projected series of texts that dramatize key moments in Brazil's Republic (1889 to date), this play focuses on the last day in the life of President Getúlio Vargas, who killed himself in the presidential palace on August 24, 1954.

3151 Magalhães, Domingos José Gonçalves de. Tragédias. Organização de Mariângela Alves de Lima e João Roberto Faria. São Paulo: Martins Fontes, 2005. 268 p. (Dramaturgos do Brasil; 9)

Part of the outstanding series of critical editions of 19th-century Brazilian drama being published by Martins Fontes under the general editorship of João Roberto Faria of the Univ. de São Paulo. Edited and with an introduction by the important critic Mariângela Alves de Lima, this volume contains the two tragedies by the man credited with initiating both Brazilian Romanticism

(with his book of poetry, Suspiros poéticos e saudades, 1836) and Brazilian theater (with Antônio José ou O poeta e a Inquisição, 1838, included in this volume).

3152 Marcos, Plínio; Leilah Assunção; and Consuelo de Castro. Three contemporary Brazilian plays. Edited by Elzbieta Szoka and Joe W. Bratcher. 2nd ed. Austin, N.Y.: Host Publications, Inc., 2006. 476 p.: bibl.

Three important plays from the 1960s-80s, Plínio Marcos's Dois perdidos numa noite suja, Leilah Assunção's Boca molhada de paixão calada, and Consuelo de Castro's Aviso prévio, appear here in English translation followed by the Portuguese original. With an introduction by Margo Milleret. Each play is prefaced by critical texts. The bibliography on pages vii–viii is carelessly done and none of the quotes in the back cover is by a Brazilian theater specialist.

3153 Martini, Jandira and Marcos Caruso. Comédias de Jandira Martini e Marcos Caruso. São Paulo: Panda Books, 2005. 383 p.: ill.

Three of the biggest box-office hits by the most accomplished comedy writing duo in Brazil. Their award-winning play Sua Excelência, o Candidato (1985) had a four-year run while Porca miséria was staged for six consecutive seasons. (A solo by Caruso, Trair e coçar é só começar, has been showing for over 20 years.) Volume has short introductory texts by Aimar Labaki, Alberto Guzik, and Ilka Marinho Zanotto.

3154 Medeiros, Marcelo. Anália Franco: um candeeiro sobre o alqueire. São Paulo: Sindicato dos Jornalistas: Imprensa Oficial, 2001. 91 p.

Winner of the 2001 Herzog Award for plays that expose past or present human rights violations in Brazil, Medeiros' play focuses on the groundbreaking figure of journalist and educator Anália Franco in early 20th-century Brazil.

3155 Rodrigues, Nelson. O beijo no asfalto. Edição trilíngüe. Rio de Janeiro: Editora Nova Fronteira, 2007. 104 p.

This trilingual edition of one of Nelson's best plays fits in with several other translations of his theater now appearing in the US and Europe. O beijo no asfalto, which premiered in 1961, addresses for the first time in Brazilian theater the issue of death as the ultimate moment of revelation of homosexual feelings as it contrasts Aprígio's outburst to Arandir's supreme humanitarian gesture.

3156 Rodrigues, Nelson. Life as it is. Translated from the Portuguese by Alex Ladd. Austin, Tex.: Host Publications, 2008. 314 p.

More English translations of the work of Brazil's top playwright. This short volume and item **3157** include the stories that were transposed to the stage as the plays *Life as it is* and *Pornographic angel,* both produced in the US in the last decade. For comment by translation specialist, see item **3287.**

3157 Rodrigues, Nelson. Pornographic angel: the short stories that inspired the play. Translated by Alex Ladd. Austin, Tex.: Host Publications, 2007. 64 p.

For annotation, see item **3156.**

3158 Rodrigues, Nelson. The theater of Nelson Rodrigues. Text selected and arranged by Joffre Rodrigues. Vol. 1 translated by Joffre Rodrigues and Toby Coe. Vol. 2 translated by Joffre Rodrigues, Toby Coe, and Flávia Carvalho. Rio de Janeiro: Ministério da Cultura, FUNARTE, 2001. 2 v. (369, 550 p.).

These translations are important for a better understanding of Nelson's work, particularly as his plays begin to draw the attention of theater directors and groups in the English-speaking world. The second volume has fewer of the translation and edition problems found in the first, and it boasts excellent introductory texts by the distinguished critic, Sábato Magaldi. Vol. 1 includes: *The Wedding Dress (Vestido de noiva); All Nudity Shall Be Punished (Toda nudez será castigada); Lady of the Drowned (Senhora dos Afogados); Waltz #6 (Valsa número 6);* and *The Deceased Woman (A falecida).* Vol. 2 includes: *The Woman Without Sin (A mulher sem pecado); Family Album (Album de família); Black Angel (Anjo negro); Doroteia; A Widow but Chaste (Viúva porém honesta); Forgive Me For You Betraying Me (Perdoa-me por me traíres);* and *The Seven Kittens (Os sete gatinhos).*

3159 Vieira, César. João Cândido do Brasil: a Revolta da Chibata. São Paulo: Casa Amarela, 2003. 170 p.: bibl.

César Vieira (Idibal Pivetta), founder of the group Teatro União e Olho Vivo (TUOV), has been a leading name in activist political theater in Brazil for almost 50 years. This historical musical focuses on the Revolta da Chibata, a 1910 mutiny against harsh corporal punishment of sailors. Introductory texts by Antonio Candido, Clóvis Moura, Ilka Marinho Zanotto, and Iná Camargo Costa.

THEATER CRITICISM AND HISTORY

3160 Arantes, Marco Antonio. Qorpo-Santo: Inovação e conservação. São Paulo: Editora da Univ. de São Paulo, 2010. 224 p.

A comprehensive study of the works of one of the most creative and controversial writers in 19th-century Brazil, José Joaquim de Campos Leão [Qorpo-Santo] (1829–83). Using the Foucauldian notion of the place of the author within his work, Arantes examines Qorpo-Santo's groundbreaking plays at the same time that he exposes the playwright's retrograde politics and petty morality.

3161 Bernstein, Ana. A crítica cúmplice: Décio de Almeida Prado e a formação do teatro brasileiro moderno. São Paulo: Instituto Moreira Salles, 2005. 378 p.: bibl., ill., index.

The definitive study of the career of the influential critic and professor Décio de Almeida Prado (1917–2000). Extremely well researched and documented. Preface by the distinguished critic, Flora Sussekind.

3162 Borralho, Tácito Freire. O boneco: do imaginário popular maranhense ao teatro: uma análise de O Cavaleiro do Destino. São Luís, Brazil: SESC, 2005. 180 p.: bibl., ill.

Study of puppetry in the state of Maranhão, from its deep roots in popular mythology and dramatic dances ("bumba-meu-boi") to the artisans who create the "bonecos" to the interaction of actors and puppets in street performances or on the more traditional stages. Volume includes a history of LABORARTE, the workshop responsible for preserving and fostering this art form, as well as a detailed study of one of the plays of the repertoire.

3163 Brandão, Tânia. Uma empresa e seus segredos: Companhia Maria Della Costa. São Paulo: Perspectiva, 2009. 455 p.: bibl., ill.

A seminal work that is important not only for understanding the careers of Maria Della Costa, her husband Sandro Polonio, and their theater groups (Teatro Popular de Arte and, later, Companhia Maria Della Costa), but also for studying the history of theater in Brazil. Book questions the canonical narrative of a (conservative) modernization of the Brazilian theater put forth by an elite group led by Décio de Almeida Prado and others.

3164 Britto, Sérgio. O teatro e eu: memórias. Rio de Janeiro: Tinta Negra Bazar Editorial, 2010. 416 p. bibl.

Memoirs of one of the most important actors in contemporary Brazilian theater. Abundant information on Britto's career and also on theater groups since the 1940s. Britto, whose stage career spans over six decades, won in 2009, at age 85, the most coveted acting award in the nation.

3165 Cadernos do Kaus: o teatro na América Latina. Organização de Reginaldo Nascimento. São Paulo: Scortecci Editora, 2007. 199 p.: bibl., ill.

Publication of this volume was the final step in the Latin American theater outreach project by the group, Teatro Kaus Companhia Experimental, based originally in São José dos Campos and more recently in São Paulo. The group is heavily invested in the study of acting and performance. One of many projects funded by the City of São Paulo's Programa Municipal de Fomento ao Teatro.

3166 Corpos em fuga, corpos em arte. Organização de Renato Ferracini. São Paulo: Aderaldo & Rothschild Editores: Hucitec, 2006. 319 p.: bibl., ill. (Teatro; 56)

Relevant compilation of essays on theoretical and practical aspects of the uses of the body on stage, written by members of the Lume group. Table of contents does not credit authors of individual chapters.

3167 Costa, Maria Cristina Castilho. Censura em cena: teatro e censura no Brasil. São Paulo: EDUSP: FAPESP: Imprensa Oficial, 2006. 282 p.: bibl., ill.

Based on the author's long-term research in the Miroel Siveira Archives of the Escola de Comunicação e Artes of the Univ. de São Paulo, the book traces the history of theater censorship in Brazil from the colonial period to the military regime of the 1960s and 1970s. Includes abundant documentation, historic photos, and previously unreleased materials.

3168 Fernandes, Sílvia. Teatralidades contemporâneas. São Paulo: Perspectiva: FAPESP, 2010. 243 p.: bibl., ill. (Estudos; 277)

Major study by a leading scholar of Brazilian theater. Examines the most important trends and groundbreaking stagings of the last three decades. Attention is paid to commercial theater as well as avantgarde groups and experimental troupes. Book includes numerous photos of recent productions.

3169 Figueira, Jorge Louraço. Verás que tudo é verdade: uma década de folias, 1997–2007. São Paulo: Galpão do Folias, 2008. 303 p.: bibl., ill.

A history of the prestigious group's first decade. Provides detailed information on each of the group's stagings, as well as scholarly articles by critics such as Valmir Santos, Iná Camargo Costa, Maria Sílvia Betti, and Beth Néspoli.

3170 George, David Sanderson. Nelson Rodrigues and the invention of Brazilian drama. Lawrence: LATR Books: Univ. of Kansas, 2010. 160 p.: bibl., ill., index. (Col. José Juan Arrom)

Solid study of the life and career of the most important Brazilian playwright of the 20th century. Looks at Nelson's 17 plays as explorations of the subconscious and denunciations of social hypocrisy and sexual repression. Considerable attention is given to the posthumous recovery of Nelson's theatrical legacy, with focus on the stagings of Antunes Filho.

3171 Gomes, André Luís. Clarice em cena: as relações entre Clarice Lispector e o teatro. Brasília: Editora UnB: Finatec, 2007. 292 p.: bibl., ill.

Originally presented as the author's doctoral dissertation at the Univ. de São Paulo in 2004, this publication fills a gap in the vast criticism on Clarice Lispector; at long last we have a monograph on the important place of the theater in Clarice's writing. A key component of Gomes' research is his study and documentation of the many stage adaptations of Clarice's texts and life.

3172 Guimarães, Carmelinda. Teatro brasileiro: tradição e ruptura. Goiânia, Brazil: Editora Alternativa, 2005. 141 p.: bibl.

Brief survey of the Brazilian theater. Although published in 2005, book seems to have been written two decades earlier. Names described as new playwrights were active in the 1970s and what is referred to as the new theater scene was that of the early 1980s.

3173 Heliodora, Barbara. Escritos sobre teatro. Organização de Cláudia Braga. São Paulo: Perspectiva, 2007. 947 p.: ill., index. (Col. Textos; 20)

Hefty collection of articles by the distinguished critic and foremost Shakespeare scholar in Brazil. Most of these pieces appeared originally in the arts section of leading newspapers spanning half a century (1944–94). The sections in this collection reflect different facets of Heliodora's interests (theory of drama and theater; relationship of the theater and the state; and staging of plays, as illustrated in hundreds of production reviews).

3174 Henrik Ibsen no Brasil. Organização de Karl Erik Schollhammer. Rio de Janeiro: Editora PUC Rio: 7Letras, 2008. 129 p.: bibl., ill.

A collection of texts written in connection with Brazilian celebrations of Ibsen's centennial. Of special importance are Jane Pessoa's historical overview of Ibsen's presence in Brazilian theater and Fátima Saadi's reflections on her company's (Teatro do Pequeno Gesto) stagings of two of Ibsen's plays.

3175 Leite, Aldo. Memória do teatro maranhense. São Luís, Brazil: EdFUNC, 2007. 340 p.: bibl., ill.

Volume is simultaneously a history of the theater in the state of Maranhão and the memoirs of a key theater practitioner in that state. Includes several interviews as well as abundant information about the region's most important productions, groups, stage directors, and actors.

3176 Lição de palco: EAD-USP, 1969–2009. Organização de Silvana Garcia. São Paulo: EDUSP, 2009. 281 p.: bibl., ill.

Founded by Alfredo Mesquita in 1948 and incorporated 20 years later into the drama department of the Univ. de São Paulo, the Escola de Arte Dramática spawned numerous groups and careers. Its history is told in three long essays by Nanci Fernandes, Silvana Garcia, and Monica Montenegro. Volume includes a memoir by Yolanda Amadei, detailed information on the EAD's productions, and a vast iconography.

3177 Machado de Assis. Do teatro: textos críticos e escritos diversos. Organização, estabelecimento de texto, introdução e notas de João Roberto Faria. São Paulo: Editora Perspectiva, 2008. 679 p.: bibl., ill., index. (Col. Textos; 23)

This outstanding contribution to the history of 19th-century Brazilian theater and to the study of Machado de Assis' drama criticism gathers for the first time all of Machado's writings on the theater. For his compilation, the volume editor used the first edition of these essays in a painstaking job of textual criticism. Preceded by an indispensable 82-page introductory text by Faria. (See also *Teatro de Machado de Assis* in *HLAS 64:2428*; and *Idéias teatrais* by João Roberto Faria reviewed in *HLAS 60:4223*.)

3178 Magaldi, Sábato. Teatro sempre. São Paulo: Perspectiva, 2006. 230 p.: bibl. (Col. Estudos; 232. Teatro)

In many ways this is a continuation of Magaldi's *Depois do espetáculo* (2003) and other compilations of short pieces by the doyen of Brazilian theater criticism. Includes essays on classic dramatists like Artur Azevedo, Ariano Suassuna, and Jorge Andrade, as well as on innovators like Qorpo-Santo, Oswald de Andrade, and Plínio Marcos.

3179 Malina, Judith. Diário de Judith Malina: o Living Theatre em Minas Gerais. Organização de Heloísa Maria Murgel Starling e Adyr Assumpção. Belo Horizonte, Brazil: Secretaria de Estado de

Cultura de Minas Gerais: Arquivo Público Mineiro, 2008. 269 p.: bibl., ill.

Meticulously edited and abundantly documented, this volume includes Malina's prison diaries and provides a fascinating account of the experimental theater group's visit to and incarceration in Minas Gerais in 1971, during the most repressive period of the military dictatorship. Book is a vindication of the work of Judith Malina, Julian Beck, the Living Theater collaborative, and their Brazilian friends in the teatro coletivo and counterculture communities.

3180 Marzano, Andrea. Cidade em cena: o ator Vasques, o teatro e o Rio de Janeiro, 1839–1892. Rio de Janeiro: FAPERJ: Folha Seca, 2008. 236 p.: bibl., ill.

Revised version of the author's doctoral dissertation at the Univ. Federal Fluminense in Niterói in 2005, under the title *Respeitável público*. Important contribution to the history of 19th-century Brazilian theater, a time when key actors like Francisco Correa Vasques (1839–92) ruled the scene.

3181 Mendes, Oswaldo. Bendito maldito: uma biografia de Plínio Marcos. São Paulo: Leya, 2009. 497 p.: bibl., ill.

Exhaustive biography of the seminal playwright of the 1960s and 1970s. Marcos' plays are powerful depictions of an underclass trapped in crass, violent exploitation and extreme disaffection. This volume is expected to be for many years the definitive study of the man whose works speak so eloquently about how the self-destructive behavior of the oppressed reveals the ampler societal forces that dictate it.

3182 Pace, Eliana. Leilah Assumpção: a consciência da mulher. São Paulo: Imprensa Oficial, 2007. 146 p.: ill. (Col. Aplauso teatro Brasil)

Survey of the life and career of one of the most important women playwrights in 20th-century Brazil.

3183 Paranhos, Kátia Rodrigues. Do palco à praça: teatro engajado no ABC. (*in* Escritas da história: narrativa, arte e nação. Organização de Elio Cantalicio Serpa e Marcos Antonio de Menezes. Uberlândia, Brazil: EDUFU, 2007, p. 311–329)

A study of engaged theater during a key period of the labor movement in Brazil. Research focuses on the activities (on stage and off) of two labor union theater groups, Ferramenta (1975) and Forja (1979–91).

3184 Patriota, Rosângela. A crítica de um teatro crítico. São Paulo: Perspectiva, 2007. 224 p.: bibl., ill. (Col. Estudos; 240)

Important new critical work on the key playwright, actor, and director of the 1960s and 1970s, Oduvaldo Vianna Filho, known as Vianinha (1936–74). Emphasizes his belief that a revolutionary theater must be so in both content and form. Complements previous book-length studies of Vianinha by Leslie Damasceno and Carmelinda Guimarães.

3185 Patriota, Rosângela. A escrita da história do teatro no Brasil: questões temáticas e aspectos metodológicos. (*História/São Paulo*, 24:2, 2005, p. 79–110)

Important research on the writing of theater history in Brazil. Discusses relevant methodology and historiography issues. Author focuses her research on how the history of the seminal group, Teatro de Arena de São Paulo, is being written.

3186 Pereira, Hamilton Vaz. Trate-me leão. Rio de Janeiro: Objetiva, 2004. 179 p.: ill.

Volume contains a short history of the groundbreaking, Rio de Janeiro-based theater group, Asdrúbal trouxe o trombone (1974–84), and the text of their best-known work, *Trate-me leão*, which premiered in 1977. Although the text is credited to one of the members of the group (Hamilton Vaz Pereira), their theater is a good example of "criação coletiva," a type of theater prominent in Brazil during the bleakest years of the military dictatorship.

3187 Pinheiro, Lenise. Fotografia de palco. São Paulo: Editora SENAC São Paulo: Edições SESC SP, 2008. 456 p.: ill.

Outstanding work by an accomplished photographer. Superb visual documentation of the Brazilian stage in the last 25 years.

3188 Próximo Ato: questões da teatralidade contemporânea. Organização de Fátima Saadi e Silvana Garcia. São Paulo: Itaú Cultural, 2008. 148 p.: bibl., ill.

Collection of key texts by Brazilian and foreign critics on the theory and practice of contemporary theatricality. Includes important material on group theater and interviews with prominent directors.

3189 Rabetti, Maria de Lourdes. Teatro e
comicidades 2: modos de produção do
teatro ligeiro carioca. Rio de Janeiro: 7Letras, 2007. 170 p.: bibl., ill.

While the first volume of *Teatro e
comicidades*, published in 2005, focused on
the plays of Ariano Suassuna, this second
volume examines the mode of light theater
("comédia ligeira") associated with Rio de
Janeiro stages in the early years of the 20th
century, particularly two key playwrights
of the genre, Gastão Tojeiro (1880–1965) and
Armando Gonzaga (1884–1953).

3190 Ratto, Gianni. Hipocritando: fragmentos e páginas soltas. Prefácio de
Plínio Marcos. Rio de Janeiro: Bem-Te-Vi
Produções Literárias, 2004. 142 p.: bibl., ill.

Ratto was one of many Italian theater
practitioners who emigrated to Brazil after
WWII. This beautifully designed book is a
combination of memoirs, short fiction, art
criticism, and ruminations about the meaning of the theater. Special attention is given
to the central role of the actor in the theatrical event. Preface by a key figure of the
1960s and 1970s, Plínio Marcos.

3191 Souto, Petra Ramalho. As mulheres
de Nelson: representações sociais das
mulheres em *Os sete gatinhos* de Nelson
Rodrigues. João Pessoa, Brazil: Idéia, 2005.
134 p.: bibl.

Short study of the representation of
women in a 1958 play by the Brazilian master. Part of Nelson's extended denunciation
of sexual repression and social hypocrisy,
Os sete gatinhos focuses on the patriarch
Noronha and his hope that his youngest
daughter's virginity and eventual marriage
rescue the family from economic decline
and moral corruption.

3192 O Teatro do Ornitorrinco: 30 anos.
Organização de Christiane Tricerri.
São Paulo: Imprensa Oficial do Estado de
São Paulo, 2009. 524 p.: bibl., ill.

Created in 1977, the irreverent troupe
lead by Cacá Rosset is celebrated in this
luxurious volume. Special attention is given
to each of the group's productions, with
photos, stage maps, sketches of settings and
wardrobe, interviews with group members,
and reviews by media critics.

3193 Wajnberg, Daniel Schenker. A escrita
contaminada pela cena. (*Rev. Teatro/
Rio de Janeiro*, 519, julho/agosto 2008, p. 4–
18, photos)

A survey of the Brazilian stage in the
last decade or so. Article points to a stronger
connection between play writing and stage
production, with several new playwrights
and plays as examples. Includes photos of
the more relevant stagings.

TRANSLATIONS INTO ENGLISH FROM THE SPANISH AND THE PORTUGUESE

CAROL MAIER, *Professor of Spanish, Kent State University*
DAPHNE PATAI, *Professor of Portuguese, University of Massachusetts, Amherst*
MAUREEN AHERN, *Professor of Spanish, Ohio State University*
STEVEN WHITE, *Professor of Spanish and Portuguese, St. Lawrence University*

TRANSLATIONS FROM THE SPANISH

MANY NEW TRANSLATIONS of high quality saw publication during the years
under review (2008–mid 2010). Even areas in which few new titles were published
included outstanding work.

As was the case in the last biennial period, there was a wide variety of excellent anthologies, which makes it difficult to single out only a few. Examples,
however, would have to include two collections of work from Mexico—*Best of*

Contemporary Mexican Fiction (item **3242**) and *Mexico City Noir* (item **3248**); Mark Weiss' *The Whole Island* (item **3203**), a bilingual volume that includes six decades of poetry from Cuba; and the bilingual *Oxford Book of Latin American Poetry* (item **3230**). The last collection is particularly notable in that it successfully delineates the ethnic and linguistic diversity of the region by including poets across the centuries who write in Spanish, Portuguese, and several indigenous languages. Too often, the literary histories of Brazil and Hispanic America are studied separately, even though they have a great deal in common. This anthology is a refreshing attempt to portray Mesoamerica and South America as a whole, while highlighting the pieces of the complex mosaic of voices. A final example that should be included here, although it is not an anthology per se, is *Zoetrope: Short Stories*, a special, bilingual Latin American issue of the literary journal featuring 10 stories by Latin American writers under the age of 40 (item **3204**). Each of the above-mentioned titles contains work by numerous translators, thus both introducing new talent and drawing on contributions by well-established names in the field. Despite the fact that, by definition, anthologies can offer only limited selections of work by any given author, their role in research, reading, and teaching cannot be overestimated.

Poetry in this biennium saw a wealth of exceptional work. Several independent publishing houses were particularly active in promoting poetry from Hispanic America in bilingual editions. Host Publications from Austin, Texas offers titles by Noni Benegas (item **3209**), Enrique Fierro (item **3216**), Miguel Gonzalez-Gerth (item **3217**), Óscar Hahn (item **3218**), María Rosa Lojo de Beuter (item **3222**), Nicanor Parra (item **3231**), Ida Vitale (item **3238**), and Oliver Welden (item **3239**). The small, attractive books by Green Integer, based in Los Angeles, California, include *Aphorisms* by César Vallejo (item **3237**), a comprehensive anthology edited and translated by John Oliver Simon of work by Chilean Gonzalo Rojas (item **3234**), and an important volume of the selected poetry of Reina María Rodríguez, born in Cuba in 1952 (item **3233**). Shearsman Books in the UK brought out a collection of work by Mexican poet Elsa Cross (item **3214**) as well as additional titles by Latin American writers;[1] and, in a joint effort, Counterpath Press and Kenning Editions published Jen Hofer's outstanding translations of work by Dolores Dorantes (item **3215**). From City Lights Books, there was the intriguing and moving collaboration between Cristina Peri Rossi and the late Marilyn Buck, who translated *State of Exile* while serving time in her own exile of imprisonment (item **3232**).[2] The university presses were also responsible for several essential publications by individual writers: Randall Couch's edition and translation of *Madwomen* by Gabriela Mistral for the University of Chicago Press (item **3227**), the retranslation of Raúl Zurita's *Purgatory* for the University of California Press (item **3241**), and Daniel Shapiro's translation of Tomás Harris' *Cipango* for Bucknell University Press (item **3219**).

New translations in brief fiction and theater continued to be scarce, but there were noteworthy publications in both areas. Examples include the stories in Carlos Fuentes' *Happy Families: Stories* (item **3244**); *Monkey Business Theatre*, an important anthology of 12 Mayan language scripts from a Tzotzil and Tzeltal writing cooperative based in Chiapas (item **3246**); and Chilean playwright Juan Radrigán's *Finished from the Start and Other Plays* (item **3249**).

As in other periods, fiction was the area that saw the greatest amount of new work; in fact, in this category there were more titles than could be reviewed here. The high quality of many of the novels and some outstanding translations make it hard to single out several as exemplary. Gloria Lisé's *Departing at Dawn* (item **3260**) and Alicia Kozameh's *259 Leaps: The Last Immortal* (item **3245**), two novels of Argentina's "dirty war," must be mentioned, though. The same is true of several "big novels" published this biennium: Fernando del Paso's *News from the Empire* (item **3263**); Ignacio Solares' *Yankee Invasion* (item **3268**); Jorge Volpi's *Season of Ash*; and Roberto Bolaño's *2666* blockbuster, rendered in Natasha Wimmer's luminous translation (items **3274** and **3254**). Despite its length and challenging subject matter, Bolaño's novel was received with acclaim by both readers and critics; an additional four new translations of his work also appeared during the review period: *Nazi Literature in the Americas, The Skating Rink, Monsieur Pain,* and *Antwerp.*[3]

There was also work in translation from 2010 Nobel Prize winning Mario Vargas Llosa—*The Bad Girl* (item **3272**)—and from his younger compatriot Santiago Roncagliolo, whose *Red April* won the Alfaguara Novel Prize (item **3265**). Other award-winning titles included Anne McLean's outstanding translations of Evelio Rosero Diago's *The Armies* (item **3266**) and Juan Gabriel Vásquez's *The Informers* (item **3273**) and Katherine Silvers' *Senselessness* (item **3255**). The novels in Leonardo Padura's Havana Quartet also merit special mention (item **3262**). Given the growing readership of international detective fiction in English translation, one hopes that North American readers soon discover Padura's Lieutenant Mario Conde—along with other engaging noir figures from south of the border.

In the area of Essays, Interviews, and Reportage, entries were not numerous. However, Electa Arenal and Amanda Powell's expanded edition of *The Answer/ La Respuesta* (item **3195**), which in this new version includes a number of additional poems and villancicos and an extensive, updated bibliography, makes an important contribution to Colonial Studies and deserves recognition as do author Diamela Eltit and photographer Paz Errázuriz's moving collaboration on *Soul's Infarct* (item **3277**); Eduardo Galeano's brief but encompassing history of the world in *Mirrors: Stories of Almost Everyone* (item **3278**); and Gaby Brimmer and Elena Poniatowska's multi-voiced *Gaby Brimmer: An Autobiography in Three Voices* (item **3276**). Unfortunately, the very welcome attention paid in the last biennium to primary texts in cultural history and indigenous literatures was not repeated.

In the area of Bibliography, Theory, and Practice, however, it is a pleasure to note that the increase discussed in *HLAS 64* in work on the history of translation as realized and published in both Latin America and the US has continued.

Here the focus is two-fold. Studies such as those by Edwin Gentzler (item **3310**), Molly Metherd (item **3314**), and Sarah Pollack, and much of Jeremy Munday's book (item **3316**) examine the circulation and reception of literature from Latin America in English translations, with an eye to the policies and politics of publishing in the US. Scholars such as Rosemary Arrojo (item **3307**), Georges L. Bastin (item **3308**), Fiona MacIntosh (item **3313**), and Munday when he looks at the work of Harriet De Onís, mentioned above, devote their attention to the work of specific figures, whether as individual "agents" of translation or as cultural workers in a larger context. As one would expect, that context is primarily North America in the work on translations into English; in much of the work on individual translators, though, it is Latin America. As Bastin notes in his essay about Francisco de Miranda, "Latin America as a whole is a translation continent" in which there have been "many important figures who have translated, encouraged translations . . . or reflected on the ways of translating and its impact on the construction of a genuine culture and identity" (p. 19). That there is such an increase of this primary research is encouraging because it indicates the growing strength of Translation Studies as a discipline and a deepened understanding of multiple aspects of translation itself.

Although not limited to the translation of Latin American literature, two encouraging new trends can be noted in this biennium. The first is a significantly increased attention to the reading and teaching of literature in translation. Scholars, teachers, and, in some cases, critics, have noted that to appreciate fully a work in translation it is useful to read in an informed way. Indeed, David Damrosch has referred to reading work in translation as an actual "mode of reading."[4] He devotes an entire chapter to that mode in *How to Read World Literature*; and *Teaching World Literature*, his edited collection of essays, includes Lawrence Venuti's "Teaching in Translation."[5] Venuti's essay will be of particular interest to readers of Latin American literature, since he uses Paul Blackburn's translation of Julio Cortázar's short story "Las babas del diablo" as his primary example.

Two additional examples of this interest would be Santa Arias and Eyda M. Merediz's discussion in "Texts and Editions" in their *Approaches to Teaching the Writing of Bartolomé de Las Casas* (See p. 9–18, particularly p. 11–12) and Carol Maier's "English Translations" in Emilie L. Bergman and Stacey Schlau's *Approaches to Teaching the Works of Sor Juana Inés de la Cruz* (see p. 9–13 and *HLAS 64:1785*). *Literature in Translation: Teaching Issues and Reading Practices* should also be mentioned in this context.[6] A collection of essays devoted to pedagogical considerations specific to work with translated texts, it includes chapters that focus on work from Latin America, for example, Kelly Washbourne's discussion of the McOndo and Crack groups[7] and Kathleen Ross' comments about Claribel Alegría, Margo Glantz, and Pablo Neruda.[8]

The second new trend is the marked increase of online journals and sites that, like *Words Without Borders* (see http://wordswithoutborders.org/ and *HLAS 64:2470*), regularly feature bilingual writing and review literature in translation. The new quarterly *S/N: NewWorldPoetics*, for example, edited by American poets Charles Bernstein (North) and Uruguayan-born Eduardo Espina (South), publishes innovative creative work and commentary in both languages (http://www.snnewworldpoetics.com/index.html); and *Three Percent* (http://www.rochester.edu/College/translation/threepercent/), an online literary website published by Open Letter Press regularly reviews work in translation and offers a list of numerous links to websites, weblogs, publishers, and organizations related to literature in translation. Not a few print journals regularly publish supplementary material online—reviews and interviews, for example, in the case of *Rain Taxi*, (http://www.raintaxi.com/) or literary texts, in the case of *Two Lines* (http://www.catranslation.org/two-lines). Online reviewing has more and more significance in view of the demise of weekly book review supplements in the *Washington Post*, *Los Angeles Times*, and other newspapers across the country and the decrease in coverage of literature in general on the part of the print media. Consequently, readers of Latin American literature in translation will want to keep an eye on sites such as *Belleletrista* (http://www.belletrista.com/2010/issue8/index.php), which is devoted to work of women writers from around the world, *The Complete Review* (http://www.complete-review.com/main/main.html), which reviews a wide variety of work, often work in translation, or *ForeWord Reviews* (http://www.forewordreviews.com/) which focuses on books from independent and university presses. They will also want to consult the websites of individual publishers, many of which feature comprehensive information about their books, including interviews with authors and translators, reviews, and other information not available in the books themselves. This is particularly true of independent and university presses.

In closing the overview for this biennium, it is a pleasure to add a few words of thanks to Kathleen Ross, who served as a contributing editor for the Translations into English section for *HLAS 54–64*. Kathleen worked primarily with nonfiction titles, and her annotations and commentaries about essays, interviews, and reportage invariably made knowledgeable and perceptive contributions. We are grateful to have had the opportunity to work with her for over a decade. [CM with MA and SFW]

NOTES:

1. Branda, María, *Ficticia*, trans. Joshua Edwards (ISBN 9781848611238); Kozer, José, *Anima*, trans. Peter Boyle (ISBN 9781848611467); López-Columé, Pura, *Aurora*, trans. Jason Stumpf (ISBN 9781905700387); Mandiola, Victor Manuel, *Selected Poems*, trans. Ruth Fainlight, Jennifer Clement and others (ISBN 9781905700899

2. Margalit Fox. Obituary for Marilyn Buck. *New York Times*. 9 August, 2009, p. B9.

3. *Nazi Literature in the Americas; The Skating Rink, Monsieur Pain*, all translated by Chris Andrews, and *Antwerp*, translated by Natasha Wimmer.

4. "How to Read in Translation." In *How to Read World Literature*. Chichester, UK: Wiley-Blackwell, 2009, p. 281.

5. "Teaching in Translation." In *Teaching World Literature*. NY: MLA, 2009, p. 89–96.

6. *Teaching Literature in Translation: Teaching Issues and Reading Practices*. Edited by Carol Maier and Françoise Massardier-Kenney. Kent, OH: Kent State Univ. Press, 2010.

7. Washbourne, Kelly. "The North-South Translation Border: Transnationality in the New South American Writing," p. 188–201.

8. Ross, Kathleen, "Identity and Relationships in the Context of Latin America," p. 136–147.

TRANSLATIONS FROM THE PORTUGUESE

SOMETHING INTERESTING IS HAPPENING in the field of translation. Suddenly, a great deal of activity and attention is being devoted to translation, as indicated by the unusually broad range of publishers and translators who have contributed to the works under review here. Perhaps this is due in part to the enormous energy and easy accessibility of numerous internet sites devoted to publishing literature from around the world. It is possible that the Internet is also stimulating the publication of translations in print. Even the Modern Language Association (MLA) has noticed, as was evident in the selection of translation as the theme of its annual meeting in December 2009. MLA President Catherine Porter, professor emerita of French and herself a prolific translator, devoted her presidential address to "The Tasks of Translation in the Global Context" (see Jennifer Howard, "Translation Has Its Moment at MLA," at: http://chronicle.com/article/Translation-Has-Its-Moment-at/63275/). Famed scholars and translators took part in many panels about translation and its place in the academy. They included Jonathan Culler, Marjorie Perloff, Michael Holquist, Lawrence Venuti, Michael Henry Heim, Esther Allen, Elizabeth Lowe, Suzanne Jill Levine, Marilyn Gaddis Rose, and others. (See Susan Bernofsky's account of the presence of translation at the 2009 MLA in her essay in the *American Literary Translators Association [ALTA] News* of January 2010, at: http://archive.constantcontact.com/fs080/1102775044524/archive/1102936617282.html/.)

A detailed account of a fascinating panel at the MLA on literary translation was written as a guest post for *Inside Higher Ed* by Martin Riker, associate director of Dalkey Archive Press, who moderated the panel. Riker had expected the panel to be more divided than it actually was on the question of translation theory versus training in applied translation (the kind of practical program Dalkey established at the University of Illinois). After summarizing the contributions of key participants to the panel, Riker addressed one question to them. Noting that translation seemed to be present now in a way it had not been before, he asked: "If you could have one thing result from all this, what would it be?" Here are his paraphrases of the answers:

Catherine Porter: to encourage that translation become an ongoing focus of this conference and of other academic conferences so that it begins to take a greater place in the consciousness of those in the academic community.

Suzanne Jill Levine: more funding, whether it be from the schools, foundations, wherever.

Edwin Gentzler: to see students encouraged to bring their translations to publishers, including more experimental (his word) translation forms.

Benjamin Paloff: to encourage more widely knowledgeable translators stemming from greater interaction between departments.

Susan Bernofsky: that American universities all start to offer translation studies as a necessary component of a humanistic education.

Bill Johnston: that translation studies moves back toward the study of English and literature as the prerequisite knowledge for good translation.

Emmanuelle Ertel: that more programs are established seeking a balance of theory and practice.

Elizabeth Lowe: the integration of translation studies into other curriculum.

David Bellos: that of the 8,000 or so attendees at this year's MLA, perhaps 2,000 of them go back to their universities with a greater interest in translation as a discipline.

Michael Henry Heim: that of the 8,000 or so attendees at this year's MLA, all 8,000 of them go back to their universities with a greater interest in translation.

Riker then concludes: "As for myself, I agree with Suzanne Jill Levine's wish: increased funding! It seems that, more often than not, when anything radical happens within American culture, it's because somebody threw a whole bunch of money at it." (See http://www.insidehighered.com/blogs/the_education_of_oronte_churm/guest_post_martin_riker/.)

Not having been present at this panel, I cannot gauge whether the special case of Brazil ever came up. As I have noted before in *HLAS*, publishers often complain about the scant sales of their translations of Brazilian writers (always exempting Paulo Coelho, of course). Despite occupying nearly 50 percent of the land mass of South America and more than 50 percent of its population, Brazil does not lead either in literacy or in number of new books relative to its population that are published per year. And if one extends the comparison to the Americas in general, it is striking that in 2009 Brazil (which has about 2/3 the number of inhabitants as the US), published about 8 percent as many new titles as were published in the US that same year (22,000 vs. 275,000). Perhaps that situation has much to do with the unceasing comments by translators about the lack of interest in translation in the US book market.

Nonetheless, and despite the continuing difficulties faced by trade publishers who undertake translations from Brazilian literature, a great deal of creativity and initiative on the part of translators is in evidence as new translations from Brazilian literature appear in many venues. There are new anthologies of short stories, a genre in which Brazilians have always excelled; new and long-awaited translations of classics such as Eúclides da Cunha's *Os Sertões*; reprints of translations of important writers (Machado de Assis, Loyola Brandão, Osman Lins), as well as translations of writers young and old who have not, until now, appeared in English. And, of course, new work by currently popular authors such as Garcia-Roza, Patrícia Melo, Nélida Piñon, and Milton Hatoum these days appear quickly in translation into English. Trade publishers, university presses, and small independent presses all show signs of increasing interest in the translation of literary works, despite the frequent complaint of small press publishers that translation is a "niche market."

But beyond all this, a multiplicity of small-scale endeavors to promote translation generally is underway, and these efforts are creating a formidable network of access to writers young and old from around the world. Online journals, blogs, and websites are providing interested readers with an energetic and ever-renewed supply of work. And, in addition, those enterprises that manage to survive tend to enlarge the range of their activities and function in a variety of media. Thus, for example, gifted and prolific translators such as Alison Entrekin, Alexis Levitin, and Clifford Landers, who continue to produce translations of Brazilian literature that are published by trade and university presses, also contribute to online journals with new translations as well as excerpts from novels they have translated and published in print.

Among the most successful of these online venues is *Words Without Borders: The Online Magazine for International Literature*, which publishes international poetry and prose in translation. Their website, which can be searched by country (see http://wordswithoutborders.org/find/contributors-by-country/brazil/), indicates they have quite a roster of Brazilian writers, both famous and little known. These include Rubem Fonseca, Milton Hatoum, Carlos Machado, Paulo Henriques Britto, Augusta Faro, Manoel de Barros, Paulo Polzonoff Jr., João Anzanello Carrascoza, Millôr Fernandes, Sérgio Rodrigues, Paula Parisot, Carlos Eduardo de Magalhães, Machado de Assis, Cristovão Tezza, Laurentino Gomes, Pena Cabreira, and Angela Dutra de Menezes. For a sampling of Brazilian works and their translators, see http://www.wordswithoutborders.org/?sec=Brazil& sec2=Americas/.

A recent issue of *WWB* devoted to international science fiction included Clifford Landers' translation of Machado de Assis' story "A Visit from Alcibiades." Landers published another previously untranslated Machado story, "Justice Unbalanced," in an earlier issue, as well as a story by Pena Cabreira. Other Brazilian writers whose work has appeared online in *Words Without Borders* over the past few years include prize-winning author Cristovão Tezza, Angela Dutra de Menezes, and Laurentino Gomes—all in translations by the seemingly tireless Alison Entrekin. The work of poets Manoel de Barros and Paulo Henriques Britto also appears in *WWB*, in translations by poet Idra Novey. Novey has published other translations of Manoel de Barros' poetry in the online journal, *Guernica: A Magazine of Arts and Politics*, founded in 2004 (see their site: http://www.guernicamag.com/information/history/). She has also collaborated on translations with Brazilian poet Flávia Rocha, who is the editor of the new online poetry journal *Rattapallax* (see: http://rattapallax.com/blog/magazine/), produced by Rattapallax Press in New York.

In addition to its online magazine, *Words Without Borders* collaborates with publishing houses to release print anthologies. *WWB* editorial director Susan

Harris, in conjunction with poet Ilya Kaminsky, produced one of the most important anthologies to have appeared in recent years: the 600-page *Ecco Anthology of International Poetry* (item **3279**). The latter is a good example of the interesting synergy these days between online ventures such as *WWB* and traditional publishers such as HarperCollins, which published the volume under its Ecco imprint.

Words Without Borders is also engaged in building educational programs geared to the high school and college levels, and provides resources and content designed to foster the use of international literature in the classroom. As the *WWB* website states: "We hope that in reaching out to students we can create a passion for international literature, a curiosity about other cultures, and help cultivate true world citizens."

Another important site is *Three Percent*, founded by Chad Post in 2007, which is very assertively presenting a rich array of international writers in a number of venues. It describes itself in these terms:

> The motivating force behind the website is the view that reading literature from other countries is vital to maintaining a vibrant book culture and to increasing the exchange of ideas among cultures. In this age of globalization, one of the best ways to preserve the uniqueness of cultures is through the translation and appreciation of international literary works. To remain among the world's best educated readers, English speakers must have access to the world's great literatures. It is a historical truism and will always remain the case that some of the best books ever written were written in a language other than English.

Noting that few of the titles that do make their way into English are reviewed by the mainstream media, *Three Percent* aims to alter this situation by providing readers with information about international literature, along with reviews and samples of books available in translation or soon to appear. Affiliated with the University of Rochester's translation program and its translation press, Open Letter, *Three Percent* sees itself as nurturing the next generation of lovers of literature and encourages students to submit their translations and reviews. It also maintains a useful translation database, which can be searched in various ways, including by country, at: http://www.rochester.edu/College/translation/threepercent/index.php?s=database/. The latest success of *Three Percent* founder Chad Post concerns the Best Translated Book Awards that he initiated a few years ago. Amazon has agreed to provide 25,000 dollars for this prize, to be awarded at the 2011 American Literary Translators Association annual conference.

Of course, not all ventures make it. Some made significant contributions during the short time they existed, but are now defunct. This is the case, for example, with Aflame, ("African, Latin America and Middle East"), which, billing itself as "the library of the global village," began in London in 2005 and published its first book in 2006. This small press was started by Richard Bartlett, a South African with knowledge of Portuguese and Arabic, and Gavin O'Toole, an Irishman with a special interest in Latin America. Its mission was a lofty one (shared by almost all the small presses and online endeavors in this area): To provide readers "with the finest English translations of literature from across the world hitherto hidden by barriers of culture and language." To this end, Aflame published "fiction and poetry fired with the passion and originality that abounds in what was once called the 'Third World' and is now more positively referred to as the Warm World (see their website, http://www.aflamebooks.com/?page_id=10). Aflame published about six books a year during its short life; two were by Brazilian authors: Alberto Mussa's *The Riddle of Qaf* (item **3299**) and Edyr Augusto Proença's *Hornets' Nest* (item **3301**). Aflame's sales of works translated from Portuguese were never as strong as those from Spanish, Richard Bartlett wrote to me in the fall of 2010, despite such unusual items as the brilliantly named *Jaime Bunda, Secret Agent*, a satirical crime story by Angolan writer Artur Pestana (who writes as "Perpetla").

In mid-2009, Douglas Messerli, founder of Green Integer, began a new blog, called *Exploring Fictions*, which appears daily or weekly, as the spirit moves him. "The Green Integer Blog will continue to feature cultural events and information on new Green Integer titles, but most new fiction and many of the essays I write on fiction will appear on the blog, devoted only to fiction: http://exploringfictions .blogspot.com." Messerli, who began Sun & Moon Press in the 1970s, has long been associated with experimental writers. But he now feels that:

> American publishing aligned with tepidly written and rapidly disappearing critical commentary has left us instead with a seemingly endless series of dispirited personal narratives, flat-footed fantasies, and sentimentalized social statements.
>
> By exploratory writing I do not merely mean "experimental writing," but works that in their language and structures challenge our thinking, surprising and sometimes even mystifying readers, who are left not with simple comprehension but with wonderment.

In June, the site offered a sampling of Brazilian literature: an essay by Jorge Amado on Julio Jurentio and Ilya Ehrenburg; excerpts from Brazilian authors published in translation by Green Integer, such as: Domício Coutinho Tereza Albues, João Almino, Osman Lins, and others (see: http://exploringfictions.blogspot. com/2009/06/brazilian-sampler.html).

Messerli has an astonishing number of websites and blogs, and is also linked to several similarly motivated efforts to spread the word about international poetry and prose. One of the most interesting endeavors is called *PennSound*, which makes its mission instantaneously clear: *All the Free Poetry You Care to Download*. A project of the University of Pennsylvania's Center for Programs in Contemporary Writing, *PennSound* is an online archive of poetry readings, including poetry in English translation, which was launched in January 2005. It makes available, with as much documentation as possible and without charge, the largest collection of poetry sound files on the Internet, currently more than 1,500. It was founded and is directed by University of Pensylvania English professors Charles Bernstein (who directs the Center) and Al Filreis (see http://writing .upenn.edu/pennsound/).

Charles Bernstein at UPenn also co-directs an online magazine called *Sibila*, which appears in both English and Portuguese. His co-director is Régis Bonvicino in São Paulo (see http://sibila.com.br/index.php/about-sibila.) The English-language site, which has original pieces in English and translations, is at: http://sibila .com.br/index.php/sibila-english.

Another small journal, *Zoetrope: All-Story* (a quarterly literary publication founded by Francis Ford Coppola in 1997 "to explore the intersection of story and art, fiction and film"), has published many outstanding writers, both famous and newcomers. In 2001 *Zoetrope* won the National Magazine Award for Fiction. But only in the spring of 2009 did *Zoetrope* finally publish, in its "Latin American Issue," a Brazilian writer, Veronica Stigger. Her story, "The Dwarves," translated by Andrea Strane, can be sampled at the website http://www.all-story.com/issues.cgi?issue_id=48, but to read it all, one must purchase a copy online.

Host Publications in Austin and NY (see http://www.hostpublications.com) continues to include Brazilian works in their publishing program, this time with the volume of crônicas, by Nelson Rodrigues, *Life As It Is* (item **3287**), translated by Alex Ladd, whose earlier translations of Rodrigues' plays have been staged both in Brazil and in the US.

Scribe Publishers in Australia, winner of the 2006 prize for best Australian small publisher (though it publishes about 65 books a year), has published two works by Brazilians, Mario Sabino and Cristovão Tezza (items **3302** and **3303**), both translated by Alison Entrekin, the immensely talented Australian translator now living in Brazil (see http://www.publishersmarketplace.com/members/AlisonEntrekin/). Entrekin has many projects underway and takes full advantage of both print and online publishing, where her translations of work by Brazilian writers regularly appear. See, for example, the independent British quarterly *The Drawbridge* (www.thedrawbridge.org.uk), begun in 2006.

A most original series of print travel books has been appearing from Whereabouts Press, in Berkeley, California, founded and directed by David Peattie and premised on the conviction that "one of the best ways to get to know about a place is to read the best stories that have been written about it. Through these stories, we think, readers come to see not just a place but the soul of a place" (see http://www.whereaboutspress.com). In 2010, Whereabouts published a superb volume in this series, *Brazil: A Traveler's Literary Companion*, edited by Alexis Levitin, which will appeal as much to those who already know Brazil as to those who do not (item **3282**).

An unusual project that must be mentioned here—demonstrating how easily the Internet bypasses the problem of publishing print books in translation—is the recent Brazilian participation in Steampunk, a subgenre of science fiction rooted in the 19th-century world of steam and electricity, which began to develop in the 1990s in the US. In Brazil, where it is a much newer phenomenon, beginning in about 2007, it has grown rapidly. There are already seven Steampunk Lodges throughout the country, as well as a Steampunk Council that organizes the movement and its events (complete with 1880s costumes). In October 2010 the Brazilian anthology called *Vaporpunk: relatos steampunk publicados sob as ordens de suas majestades,* an original collection of steampunk fictions from Brazil and Portugal, edited by Gerson Lodi-Ribeiro and Luis Filipe Silva, along with three anthologies of Brazilian sci fi, fantasy, and horror, edited by Tibor Moricz, Saint-Clair Stockler, Eric Novello, and Erick Santos Cardoso, came to the attention of Larry Nolen at *ofblog* (see http://ofblog.blogspot.com/2010/10/more-brazilian-portuguese-fcvaporpunk.html). Because only a few individual sci-fi works from Brazil have been available online, and in volumes such as *Cosmos Latinos: An Anthology of Science Fiction from Latin America and Spain* (see *HLAS 62:3196*), *Shine,* and *Steampunk II: Steampunk Reloaded* (edited by Ann and Jeff VanderMeer), Larry Nolen quickly decided to start translating the work of these Brazilian Steamers, together with Fábio Fernandes, a writer and translator living in São Paulo, who has translated approximately 70 novels into Brazilian Portuguese, among them

A Clockwork Orange, Neuromancer, and *Snow Crash.* (See http://www.tor.com/blogs/2010/11/review-vaporpunk-relatos-steampunk-publicados-sob-as-ordens-de-suas-majestades/.)

The phenomenon is an interesting one, rapidly crossing national borders through the Internet. In Brazil, Steamers have been busy all year gaining attention for their movement. In March 2010, they had organized a SteamCamp day in São Paulo, which they called SteamPunk de Volta—a pun on the name of Alessandro Volta, the Italian physicist who in 1800 created the first electric cell, and whose name is enshrined in the word "volt." For more on Brazilian Steampunk, see http://www.steampunk.com.br/; and the website of the SteamPunkCouncil, http://aolimiar.com.br/. Also of interest is Bruno Accioly's description of the movement he helped found in Brazil, which is turning from a literary movement into a cultural one, at: http://www.steampunk.com.br/2010/09/02/steampunk-o-conselho-e-o-movimento/

No review of the state of translation from the work of Brazilian writers is complete without an update on Paulo Coelho, said to be one of the most widely translated living writers in the world today. Perhaps he stopped counting when, by 2008, sales of his books passed the hundred million mark worldwide. Now he is everywhere—still publishing books, energetically invested in electronic media, traveling to countries and bookfairs large and small, with his own websites, blogs, and constant new ventures. He is a passionate advocate of electronic media and even the free distribution of literary work, and has made some of his own books available in that format (see http://paulocoelhoblog.com/free-texts/), after what must have been interesting discussions with his publishers. He also maintains a website dedicated to a persona of his, called, "The Pirate Coelho" (http://paulo coelhoblog.com/pirate-coelho/).

Coelho has argued that free online access to his work has increased rather than decreased sales of his books—and substantially so. In his opening address at the Frankfurt Book Fair in October 2008, Coelho stressed his embrace of new technologies and the possibility they have opened of free distribution of texts, saying that new media make him seek out a new language. But Coelho's activities do not stop there. He also sells yearly agendas—attractively produced thematic "daily planners" illuminated by his thoughts on particular themes. These, too, are available in multiple languages.

The year 2009 also saw the publication of two hefty biographies of world-famous Brazilian writers. Paulo Coelho is the subject of Fernando Morais' *Paulo Coelho: A Warrior's Life. The Authorized Biography* (New York: HarperOne, 2009). And Clarice Lispector is currently the object of renewed interest thanks to a highly praised and widely reviewed book by Benjamin Moser (also a translator), *Why This World: A Biography of Clarice Lispector* (2009).

It is dismaying that despite all the publicity that Brazilian writers are now attracting, writers and critics still publish books ostensibly about "Latin America" without including Brazil. Consider, for example, the volume *Writing Toward Hope: The Literature of Human Rights in Latin America*, edited by Marjorie Agosin (2007). Weighing in at 645 pages, and with the term "Latin America" appearing prominently in and on the volume, the book nonetheless excludes Brazil. With texts in Spanish and introductions in English, it appears to be destined for adoption as a textbook, thus passing on the misnomer to young readers.

The same misrepresentation occurs in another new book. The Center for the Art of Translation, in San Francisco, since 1994 has published a yearly anthology of international fiction and poetry in translation. In 2007 it inaugurated a new series called Two Lines World Library, featuring "the most flavorful writing from around the globe." The first volume was *New World/ New Words: Recent Writing from the Americas*, edited by Thomas Christensen, with an introduction by Gregory Rabassa (see *HLAS 64:2460*). This is a bilingual anthology—in Spanish and English—yet descriptions of the book constantly refer to "Latin America." The University of Washington Press website advertising the book says the volume "makes the literature of Latin America available to those who want to sample its scope and depth, and includes works published for the first time in English." No wonder, then, that many people still do not realize that Portuguese, not Spanish, is spoken in Brazil.

To end on a positive note, however, readers should consult a useful website being compiled by Alok Yadav. Available at http://mason.gmu.edu/~ayadav/anthologies#latin-am/, the site offers a detailed listing of multicultural and world literature anthologies in English. Yadav's mission is an important one:

> The purpose of this list is to give interested individuals a sense of some of the primary texts available in English or in English translation for the teaching and study of world literature. (A very few anthologies consisting of translations into other languages are also included.) Wherever possible, I have listed the authors and/or works included in an anthology, so one can search for particular authors or works by name to check their availability in English.

Readers are urged to contact him to suggest corrections and additions.

ANTHOLOGIES

3194 Aravena de Herron, Sandra E. The changing faces of Chilean poetry: a translation of avant-garde, women's, and protest poetry. Foreword by Ana Maria Zurbuch. Lewiston, New York: Edwin Mellen Press, 2008. 135 p.: bibl., index.

This slim volume is divided into three sections, each with a very minimal critical framework to orient the reader: "Chilean Male Poets of the Avant-Garde Generation" (Huidobro, Neruda, Parra, Rojas and Lihn), "Chilean Women's Poetry" (Mistral, Rosabetty Muñoz, Carmen Orrego, and Heddy Navarro Harris), and "Chilean Protest Poetry" (Magdalena Fuentes Zurita, Aristóteles España, Víctor Jara, David Valjalo, Sergio Macías, and Jorge Etcheverry). In the introduction, the translator briefly discusses her understanding of the differences between intralingual, interlingual, and intersemiotic translations, offering different English versions of Neruda's "Antes de amarte" as an example of how she moves from theory to practice. [SFW]

3195 Juana Inés de la Cruz, Sor. The answer: expanded edition, including The letter to which it replies & new selected poems = La respuesta. Critical edition and translation by Electa Arenal and Amanda Powell. 2nd ed. New York: Feminist Press at the City Univ. of New York, 2009. 240 p.: bibl., index.

The much-awaited expanded edition of the original bilingual edition first published in 1994 that restores Sor Juana's own emphasis, diction, and humor in her awareness of gender. It combines new research and perspectives on this great poet, thinker, and defender of women's rights to education and scholarship. Responding to the enhanced interest in this extraordinary writer "whose work illuminates the thought of her world and may throw light on unsettled questions in our own," in the preface to the second edition, "What Does Sor Juana Mean?" Arenal and Powell bring new perspectives to bear on the nun's famous letter, "Answer to Sor Filotea," in which she defended women's learning. Added to the appendix of the new edition is a translation of the letter from "Sor Filotea" (actually a powerful bishop) that clarifies for readers "the opinions and chastisement that prompted Sor Juana's eloquent statement." The many additions to the bibliography give updated printed and online readings on relevant topics. The section on Sor Juana's poetry has been broadened to better reflect her engagement with women's intellectual ability, adding her parodic ballad, "Prologue to the Reader of These Poems," additional *villancicos*, two more sonnets, and another ballad, all of which inquire into the nature of love. The new preface also discusses new criticism, recent attention to her neglected works, and the "mystery" of her final years. Superb scholarship and translation combine to make this essential reading for understanding Sor Juana and her world. For translation specialist's comment on 1st ed. (1994), see *HLAS 56:4611*. For literary specialist's comment on 1st ed., see *HLAS 58:3460*. [MA]

3196 Lugones, Leopoldo. Leopoldo Lugones: selected writings. Translated from the Spanish by Sergio Waisman. Edited with an introduction by Gwen Kirkpatrick. Oxford, England; New York: Oxford Univ. Press, 2008. 111 p.: bibl. (Library of Latin America)

Selected Writings represents the first time that Leopoldo Lugones' work has been translated into English, but the selections included here offer readers both fiction (six stories) and nonfiction (for example, the prologue to the first edition of *Lunaria sentimental*, "The Ayacucho Address," and "The Morality of Art," among others). Multiple examples of a writer of Lugones' importance are always welcome, and Gwen Kirkpatrick's introduction provides information about his work and its context, as does Lisa Rose Bradford's comprehensive review in *Translation Review* (Vol. 77/78, 2009, p. 181–185). [CM]

3197 Nuestra cama es de flores = Our bed is made of flowers: antología de poesía erótica femenina. Textos de Gloria Ortiz *et al.* Compilación de Roberto Castillo Udiarte. Tijuana, Mexico: Consejo Nacional para la Cultura y las Artes, Centro Cultural Tijuana, 2007. 118 p.: bibl. (Col. Literatura)

According to the editor, this anthology of 42 women writers from Baja California seeks to combat a "panoramic prejudice" on the part of regional literary critics (and others) against female authors who dare to write on erotic themes. In her preface to this volume, Teresa Vicencio Álvarez states that these are "voices that refuse to bow down to the traditions and rituals which society previously sought to impose on them." A bibliography shows that the books from which the poems are taken were published from the 1980s to the present. [SFW]

3198 Ortega, Julio. The art of reading: stories and poems. San Antonio, Tex.: Wings Press, 2007. 121 p.

Peruvian writer, literary critic, and professor of Latin American literature at Brown Univ. offers a sample of his short stories, poems, conversations, and a play that have appeared in international journals over the years in English language versions by various translators. [MA]

3199 Our Caribbean: a gathering of lesbian and gay writing from the Antilles. Edited and with an introduction by Thomas Glave. Durham, N.C.: Duke Univ. Press, 2008. 405 p.: bibl.

Important for both the Social Sciences (see *HLAS 65:2623*) and the Humanities, *Our Caribbean* includes selections of work by 37 authors, quite a few of them translated into English for the first time. Readers will be familiar with names such as Reinaldo Arenas, but other names will be new to them. As Glave explains in his introduction, his goal was to present "Caribbean lesbian and gay voices in conversation" (p. 5) about "issues that still have neither been completely confronted nor fully understood" not only outside of Cuba but within the Caribbean itself (p. 7). Numerous translators. [CM]

3200 Praises and offenses: three women poets from the Dominican Republic. Poems by Aída Cartagena Portalatín, Angela Hernández Núñez, and Ylonka Nacidit-Perdomo. Translated by Judith Kerman. Rochester, N.Y.: BOA Editions, 2009. 160 p.: bibl., index.

An introduction provides the necessary sociohistorical context for a more informed reading of these three important,

though relatively unknown, women writers, who, in the case of Aída Cartagena
Portalatín (1918–94), began publishing in
the Dominican Republic in the 1940s.
Her generation was marked by political
activism against the dictatorship of Rafael
Trujillo. Contemporary authors Ángela
Hernández Núñez (b. 1954) and Ylonka
Nacidit-Perdomo (b. 1965) grew up during the repressive military government
of Joaquín Balaguer. According to the introduction, both of these younger writers
"are active in literary circles promoting
the work of women writers and freedom of
expression in the Caribbean." For Cartagena Portalatín, "Our national history has
nothing in common/with the history of
happiness./Almost all Dominican rulers/
were gestated with material from the toilet
or from Hell." [SFW]

**3201 Tapestry of the sun: an anthology
of Ecuadorian poetry.** Edited and
translated by Alexis Levitin and Fernando
Iturburu. San Francisco, Calif.: Coimbra
Editions, 2009. 329 p.

This volume includes the work of
18 poets from Ecuador born between 1931
and 1987: Fernando Cazón, Carlos E. Jaramillo, David Ledesma, Hipólito Alvarado,
Agustín Vulgarín, Antonio Preciado, Sonia Manzano, Fernando Nieto, Hernán
Zúñiga, Maritza Cino, Eduardo Morán, Roy
Sigüenza, Fernando Balseca, Edwin Madrid,
Siomara España, Augusto Rodríguez, Ana
Minga, and Carolina Patiño. The work is
presented in a bilingual format and each
poet is introduced with two paragraphs of
bio-bibliographical information. The editors, due to support they received from the
Centro Ecuatoriano Norteamericano de
Guayaquil, have given preference to authors
from the major coastal city of Guayaquil.
Preciado, Ecuador's leading black poet
writes of his mother, "She,/with simplicity,/embroidered hundreds of times my
two names/on a chunk of flesh/torn from
her body." Sonia Manzano, an important
voice among women writers, says, "The
day when I will drown forever/I will have
my pockets filled/with the tiny corpses of
flowers." Sigüenza, who, according to the
editors, "focuses principally on the experience of dissident sexuality," says in a poem
"the waltz goes well for Mr. Whitman./He

dances peacefully in Jack's arms,/his final
comrade." [SFW]

3202 Vallejo, César. "Spain, take this
chalice from me" (and other poems).
Translated by Margaret Sayers Peden. Edited
with an introduction by Ilan Stavans. New
York: Penguin Books, 2008. 294 p.: bibl.,
index. (Penguin classics)

Given the many translations of César
Vallejo's work available in English, in particular, the highly praised work by Clayton
Eshleman in the US (see *HLAS 64:2491*)
and Michael Smith Valentino Gianuzzi in
the UK (see *HLAS 64:2489; 2490; 2492;
and 2493*), one might be tempted to ask why
Margaret Sayers Peden has produced yet
another version. She answers that question
succinctly with what she refers to as the
"cardinal rule of translation: Somewhere
among the many drafts and versions, somewhere deep between the lines, lies the authentic poem" (p. xviii). In the same context,
she suggests that the reader's experience is
enriched by reading multiple translations,
noting that "correct" and "definitive" are
adjectives appropriate only when used with
"factual material" (p. xiii). Ilan Stavans, in
his introduction, explains that his "editorial criterion follows personal taste." He has
tried to be "eclectic and ecumenical," giving
preference to the poems he considers "most
lucid and inspired, where form and content
are in harmony" (p. xl). [CM]

**3203 The whole island: six decades of
Cuban poetry, a bilingual anthology.**
Edited by Mark Weiss. Berkeley: Univ. of
California Press, 2009. 602 p.: bibl., index.

A veritable compendium of contemporary Cuban poetry, *The Whole Island*
comprises bilingual selections of work by
55 authors from Nicolás Guillén (1902–89)
to Javier Marimón (1975-) in chronological
order according to date of birth. Editor Mark
Weiss provides a comprehensive introductory essay, whose title ("Cuban Tightrope:
Public and Private Lives of the Poets") suggests the difficulties implicit in any attempt to present a wealth of creative work
written in a period as highly charged both
politically and esthetically as that of 20th-
century Cuban history. He acknowledges
both those difficulties and the possible over-
simplification of his comments, but readers
will find his essay informative and agree

with John Palatella that he has "effectively broadened the sense of poetic terrain outside the United States." ("Shelf Life," *The Nation*. Feb. 15, 2010). [CM]

3204 Zoetrope: Short Stories. Vol. 13, No. 1, Spring 2009. Guest-edited by Daniel Alarcón and Diego Trelles Paz. New York: AZX Publications.

Guest-editors Alarcón and Trelles Paz have assembled an outstanding collection of 10 stories by young Latin American writers under 40 from nine Latin American countries, accompanied by the spectacular drawings of filmmaker Guillermo del Toro. With the exception of the late Aura Estrada (whose story is translated by Francisco Goldman), the authors will no doubt be new to readers in English. Their work is well worth knowing, though, and the guest-editors' desire to propose a "reevaluation of Latin American letters" in English (similar to Alberto Fuguet and Sergio Gómez's 1996 *McOndo* or Hay Festival Bogotá39 in 2007) is timely and welcome. All of the stories are published in both English and Spanish. [CM]

TRANSLATIONS FROM THE SPANISH

Poetry

3205 Agosín, Marjorie. Among the angels of memory = Entre los ángeles de la memoria. English translation by Laura Rocha Nakazawa. Introduction by Robert Bonazzi. San Antonio, Tex.: Wings Press, 2006. 197 p.

For Agosín, poetry is a "map of memory," in this case a way to recall the life of her great-grandmother Helena Broder, who fled Nazi persecution as a Jew and emigrated from Vienna to Valparaíso, Chile. The book, with a bilingual presentation, is divided into two sections: the Old World retains "traces of pillaged suitcases and plundered souls,/traces of a blue suitcase"; in the New World, "Vienna is a far away memory./You have left your words behind/in the forest of ashes." [SFW]

3206 Agustini, Delmira. Selected poetry of Delmira Agustini: poetics of Eros. Edited and translated by Alejandro Cáceres, with a foreword by Willis Barnstone. Car-

bondale: Southern Illinois Univ. Press, 2003. 191 p.: bibl.

Major Uruguayan-born poet Delmira Agustini (1886–1914) was murdered by her husband, who then shot himself. As Willis Barnstone has written, all we have from her consists of "her fragile white book, her morning songs, her empty chalices and her stars in the abyss." The editor-translator of this volume includes half of the 130 poems Agustini wrote and orders them chronologically in keeping with their date of publication. Agustini's verse is by turns sacrilegious and transgressive. The introduction discusses how Agustini follows *modernista* traditions and also includes an overview of critical approaches to her poetry. [SFW]

3207 Ambroggio, Luis Alberto. Difficult beauty: selected poems, 1987–2006. Edited by Yvette Neisser Moreno. Translated by Xavier I. Ambroggio *et al.* Merrick, N.Y.: Cross-Cultural Communications, 2009. 167 p.: ill.

More than 50 poems drawn from eight books represent the oeuvre of this Argentine-born writer who has lived in the Washington, DC area since 1967. As the editor of the volume states in her introduction, "Our goal in preparing *Difficult Beauty* was to present a range of Ambroggio's work, both in terms of theme and style, and to span his career, with an emphasis on his more recent poetry." In "US Landscapes," Ambroggio discusses the reality of being Hispanic in the US: "If each brick could speak;/if each bridge could speak;/if the parks, plants, flowers could speak;/if each piece of pavement could speak,/they would speak Spanish . . . /But they cannot speak./ They are hands, works, scars,/that for now keep silent." [SFW]

3208 Aridjis, Homero. Solar poems. Translated from the Spanish by George McWhirter. San Francisco, Calif.: City Lights Books, 2010. 289 p.

Born in Mexico in 1940, Aridjis has served his country as ambassador to the Netherlands and Switzerland and currently is Mexico's ambassador to UNESCO. Internationally known as an environmental activist, Aridjis writes poetry that invokes Mesoamerican myth and religion to understand and combat the world's current ecological crisis. As the poet says in "The

Hunt for the Red Jaguar," "He called upon his ancestral gods in the savannah,/howling at the death of the Jungle,/the Animals and Trees/in the Era of Extinction." [SFW]

3209 Benegas, Noni. Burning cartography. Translated and with an introduction by Noël Valis. Austin, Tex.: Host Publications, Inc., 2007. 99 p.

Noni Benegas and her translator selected poems for this volume from the author's five published books and one unpublished manuscript. Although born in Argentina, Benegas has lived in Spain since 1977, which explains why all her books are from Spanish publishing houses, beginning with *Argonáutica* (Barcelona, 1984). Some readers may be familiar with her work as an anthologist of contemporary women poets from Spain in *Ellas tienen la palabra* (1997). The poems by Benegas contain references to Greek mythology, the painting "The Raft of the Medusa" by Géricault, and avoid overt references to recognizable contemporary events, preferring instead to search for inner worlds such as she does in "Another Light": "Groping through the house, blind steps/of chalk/with the light of dreams/suddenly opaque or radiant/Who shimmers that screen/in the darkened brain?/Like skin withering on the inside/the mystery of that glow persists." [SFW]

3210 Bolaño, Roberto. The romantic dogs: 1980–1998. Translated by Laura Healy. New York: New Directions Pub., 2008. 143 p.

Best known as the author of novels such as *2666* and *The Savage Detectives*, Chilean Roberto Bolaño (1953–2003) also wrote the 44 poems offered in this bilingual edition. Bolaño's poems are always full of edgy surprises and arresting imagery: "Poetry slips into dreams/like a diver who's dead/in the eyes of God." In "The Worm," it is clear that Bolaño looks at the world like a tough detective, "walking into Café la Habana/and checking out a blonde girl/seated in the back/in the evicted Mind." For some reason, perhaps because Bolaño writes so well, the lack of introductory materials on the author makes absolutely no difference at all. [SFW]

3211 Borinsky, Alicia. Frivolous women and other sinners = Frívolas y pecadoras. Translated by Cola Franzen with the author. Chicago, Ill.: Swan Isle Press, 2009. 209 p.: ill.

It is commendable that the texts are presented in a bilingual format, but many readers will need more introductory material for a fuller understanding of this Argentine poet who teaches at Boston University. Illustrations by Julio Silva accompany an ample selection of nearly 100 poems. Reconnecting with her city of birth, Borinsky says: "Of your voice I recall certain words/evenings in a Buenos Aires street/the overlay of a tango/a cadence in the speech and the embrace." The politically engaged literature of exile has transformed itself here into: "right in the middle of the revolution he was struck by pain and, blinded by the need of a dentist, fell into the arms of a woman with no scruples who demanded more and more money . . ." Also missing in this book is a biographical note on Cola Franzen and her many accomplishments as the translator of Jorge Guillén, Juan Cameron, Saúl Yurkievich, and other works by Borinsky. [SFW]

3212 Bracho, Coral. Firefly under the tongue: selected poems of Coral Bracho. Translated by Forrest Gander. New York: New Directions Book, 2008. 133 p.

"The poems made me think of Gaudí architecture, but underwater," translator Forrest Gander writes in his introduction to *Firefly under the Tongue* as he recalls his first reading of Coral Bracho's work (p. xii). His description is apt, as are his brief but informative comments about the six volumes and additional new poems from which he has drawn his selections. Bracho's poetry leads the reader to "discover a world of uncanny interrelationships" (p. xii), and there is nothing quite like it in English, as Steven White argues in an extensive review that addresses both Bracho's poems and Gander's fine translations (*Review 80*, Vol. 43, No. 1, May 2010, p. 131–133). For comment by poetry specialist, see item **2628**. [CM]

3213 Cardenal, Ernesto. Pluriverse: new and selected poems. Edited by Jonathan Cohen, with a foreword by Lawrence Ferlinghetti. Translations from the Spanish by Jonathan Cohen *et al.* New York: New Directions Pub., 2009. 249 p.: bibl., index.

It must have been a daunting task to select the poems for this anthology of poetry by the prolific Nicaraguan author Ernesto Cardenal, born in 1925. *Pluriverse* is a monolingual offering since, as Cohen points out in his introduction, "Cardenal himself preferred just translations, rather than a bilingual format, in order to allow for the inclusion of more poems." Cohen, in his introduction, synthesizes the poet's technique for composing his earlier pieces: "Cardenal used the eye of explorers, travelers, journalists, and adventurers for recovering the wonderment and otherness of his world. And, like Pound, he adapted documentary sources, crosscutting from source to source, making a kind of verse montage that attains a lyric or epic movement of energy and whose grace lies in the cuts and seams of the poems." The later poems in this well-selected and expertly translated anthology are written in keeping with an Epicurean tradition under the aegis of Marx and Darwin. Throughout, the poetry reflects the ongoing hardship of the Nicaraguan people as well as the deepest desires of human beings as a species. [SFW]

3214 Cross, Elsa. Elsa Cross, selected poems. Translated by Anamaría Crowe Serrano *et al.* Edited by Tony Frazer. Exeter, England: Shearsman Books, 2009. 125 p.: bibl.

Although readers have previously had access to Elsa Cross' work (for example, in *Reversible Monuments: Contemporary Mexican Poetry* (see *HLAS 62:2730*) or the work of John Oliver Simon), *Selected Poems* is the first volume that spans her production as a whole. The poems selected here have been drawn from 11 books written over some four decades. As editor Tony Frazer explains in his brief introduction, their often metaphysical nature (which reflects Cross' work as a scholar and professor of philosophy who specializes in religion and comparative mythology) is "nevertheless rooted in an empirical reality." The translations are the work of multiple translators, but the majority of them are by Spanish translator Luis Ingelmo and Irish poet Michael Smith. [CM]

3215 Dorantes, Dolores. sexoPURO-sexoVELOZ; Septiembre: una edición bilingüe de libros dos y tres de Dolores Dorantes = Puresexswiftsex: September: a bilingual edition of books two and three of Dolores Dorantes. Traducción de Jen Hofer. Introducción de Jorge Solás Arenasas. Denver, Colo.: Counterpath Press; Chicago, Ill.: Kenning Editions, 2008. 127 p.: bibl.

Jen Hofer's translations of Books Two and Three of *Dolores Dorantes* (which she describes in her Translator's Note as "a lifelong series of interconnected books begun nearly a decade ago" (p. 107)), comprise an exemplary collection. Dorantes (b. 1973), a Mexican poet, activist, and journalist (founder, for example, of the border arts collective Compañía Frugal), explains that each of her books is "an 'I' in motion" and that the structure of the poems "has to do with a thought structure . . . the formal occurrence of the author's thoughts" (p. ix). Hofer has participated totally in that moving 'I.' Making her work as exciting and innovative as Dorantes'. Her extensive Translator's Note provides an excellent introduction to both Dorantes' esthetics and her own. A totally bilingual volume. [CM]

3216 Fierro, Enrique. Natural selection. Translated by Miguel Gonzalez-Gerth. Austin, Tex.: Host Publications, Inc., 2005. 89 p.

This volume of selected poems is drawn from more than a dozen books published between 1972 and 1997 as well as from unpublished material. Fierro, born in Uruguay in 1942, has taught at the University of Texas, Austin, along with his emeritus colleague Gonzalez-Gerth, the translator of these poems that sometimes echo William Carlos Williams: "I want to see a red-colored cow/at three in the afternoon/on a February day/in a green field." [SFW]

3217 Gonzalez-Gerth, Miguel. Looking for the horse latitudes. Austin, Tex.: Host Publications, 2007. 159 p.

Gonzalez-Gerth, born in Mexico City in 1926, considers himself an "ambilingual poet," who conceived some of the poems in this collection in English first. As he states in his Author's Note, "I have purposely refrained from referring to these texts as translations, although they may be such to some extent. Their peculiar character is that of something like mirror-images somewhat distorted when not the originals." The title poem, written in an English that sounds like Wallace Stevens, begins: "Something unseen weighs heavy/on the resilience of the mind./The usual apparitions/have all been exorcised./The sea that seemed at first/ to hesitate has come/at last into the rooms/ leaving in the dark a wedge of light." [SFW]

3218 Hahn, Óscar. Ashes in love. Translated from the Spanish by James Hoggard. Austin, Tex.: Host Publications, 2008. 169 p.

As one of Hispanic America's most important living poets, Óscar Hahn (b. 1938) is still producing verse at a rate that should keep his translators busy. The Chilean poet continues to write with his cunning, innovative, trademark combination of colloquial and formal literary language that requires creative solutions outside the parameters of Spanish. James Hoggard is clearly in it for the long haul. *Ashes in Love* is his fourth published effort to bring Hahn's poetry to English-speaking readers. This new volume, presented in a bilingual format, includes two recent collections: *Apariciones profanas* (*Profane Apparitions*) (2002) as well as *En un abrir y cerrar de ojos* (*In the Blink of an Eye*) (2006), which won Spain's prestigious Casa de América Award. Hahn does the barely imaginable even in his shortest poems, such as "Domino": "Like dominoes set upright/ Manhattan skyscrapers/To the right the Empire State/To the left the Chrysler Building/In the center the Twin Towers/The devil comes and blows." [SFW]

3219 Harris, Tomás. Cipango. Translated by Daniel Shapiro. Lewisburg, Pa.: Bucknell Univ. Press, 2010. 321 p.: bibl.

Cipango comprises a complete translation of important Chilean poet Tomás Harris' four-volume epic-like journey through Chilean history in a bilingual edition (*Cipango*, 1992; 1996, see *HLAS 54:4370*). Poet, translator, and *Review* editor Daniel Shapiro also includes an informative introduction, a series of detailed notes, and a bibliography of Harris' work. [CM]

3220 Huerta, David. Before saying any of the great words: selected poems. Translated by Mark Schafer. Port Townsend, Wash.: Copper Canyon Press, 2009. 261 p.: bibl.

This selection of more than 80 poems comes from 15 books by Huerta, all published in Mexico between 1972–2006.

It includes the neo-Baroque language of Huerta's *Cuaderno de noviembre* (1976), which Schafer calls a "milestone in late-twentieth-century Mexican letters." The selection also has 15 fragments from *Incurable*, "the longest poem in Mexican history." Chp. 1 of this poem begins: "The world is a stain on the mirror./Everything fits in the bag of the day, even when drops of quicksilver/capsize in the mouth, make one fall silent, crush/the words of the human soul with fine insect feet." The edition is bilingual and has an introduction which is less than five pages, inadequate for such a major figure. The reader should be prepared for the abstract: "Sparks eclipse/the face of the haruspex." [SFW]

3221 Lamat, Estela. The worst of all. Translated by Michael Leong. Buffalo, NY: BlazeVOX, 2009 112 p.

BlazeVOX bills itself as a "publisher of weird little books." According to a press release to announce the publication of this volume, "Estela Lamat is a Chilean poet associated with the so-called 'Novísima' Generation, a group of various writers that redeploys and extends the difficulty of dictatorship-era writing in response to the more diffuse and unofficial 'dictatorships' that continue to police and control the social body." The title of the book, which offers only the English translation and not the original Spanish, obliges the reader to consider Lamat's poetry in relation to Sor Juana Inés de la Cruz. The translator is careful to identify certain landmarks such as the Mapocho River and the Alameda Boulevard that link the poems to Chile's capital city Santiago as well as a handful of literary allusions. In his introduction, Leong says that "numerous voices populate and haunt this wild, fugue-like work," including Panic (the Greek god Pan), Sor Juana, and La Llorona. Recalling the poetry of Ginsberg, Lamat knows how to set words free: "He measures himself/he sketches himself between the planes/like a naked and infinite line/he mutates/he shapes himself like a tooth in the mouth/and gobbles the celestial platforms of the ships/he slips away/he turns into a scream and throws himself/from the tongue to the ground/from the window to a howl/and sleeps/imprisoned by a tidal wave of ants." [SFW]

3222 Lojo de Beuter, María Rosa. Awaiting the green morning. Translated and with an introduction by Brett Alan Sanders. Austin, Tex.: Host Pub., 2008. 115 p.

This Argentine poet, born in 1954, is the daughter of exiled Spaniards from Galicia. According to the translator's introduction, the poems describe "a small world, in which both time and space—like reality and illusion—are compressed, confused, and juxtaposed against each other." Thematically, they address the Galician diaspora as well as the tragedy of Argentina's Dirty War, which is portrayed as a microcosm "of the nation's larger history." In "The Disappearing Woman," Lojo writes of a female figure, throwing her "roses of acid against the closed doors of paradise." [SFW]

3223 Manzano Díaz, Roberto. Synergos: selected poems of Roberto Manzano. Translated by Steven Reese. Wilkes-Barre, Pa.: Etruscan Press, 2009. 237 p.

Manzano, born in Ciego de Ávila, Cuba, in 1949, has selected poems for this volume written from 1970–99. According to the author, "any sample is a cruel mutilation . . . Integrity of discourse is the lyric material's inalienable condition." There is an ecstatic energy linked to a Caribbean landscape in many of the poems from *Synergos*, which won Cuba's prestigious Nicolás Guillén Prize: "and the great kingfishers cross the air while the convalescing sun/rises over the polished waters of the ocean." Other poems invoke the spirit of Whitman: "I am, as well, the shaped and crazy travel/of space and time, and under this almond tree/where I sit alone now to sing my song . . . ." In an interview included in this bilingual edition, Manzanos says, "I love the monumental, the great frescoes, the great murals . . . where over the space of meters and meters an artist outlines a whole world." [SFW]

3224 Martí, José. Ismaelillo. In the original Spanish and with a translation into English by Tyler Fisher. San Antonio, Tex.: Wings Press, 2007. 76 p.: bibl.

A complete translation of José Martí's collection of 15 poems written for his young son and published as his first book of poetry (1882). Tyler Fisher also includes an introduction (in both English and Spanish), in which he presents background on the poems and his approach to their translation. [CM]

3225 Martín, Kathleen Rock. Discarded pages: Araceli Cab Cumí, Maya poet and politician. Albuquerque: Univ. of New Mexico Press, 2007. 312 p.: bibl., ill., index.

The subject of this book, Araceli Cab Cumí, is an indigenous woman in her late 70s from Yucatán, Mexico, where she is an elected representative in the Yucatecan State Congress and is also an essayist and poet. Kathleen Rock Martín teaches in the Anthropology Dept. at Florida International Univ. and has compiled a study of Araceli's life and work with reproductions of handwritten manuscripts and commentary on her diverse writings that include the following: "If the memory of these hours so dear/Erased the torments from your life/Like a beautiful flowering rain/whose drops are these thoughts." [SFW]

3226 Mistral, Gabriela. Gabriela Mistral: selected poems. Translated by Paul Burns and Salvador Ortiz-Carboneres, with an introduction by Paul Burns. Oxford, England: Oxbow Books, 2006. 168 p.: bibl., ill. (Aris & Phillips Hispanic Classics)

The selection is taken from the poet's major works that include: *Desolación, Ternura, Tala, Lagar,* and *Poema de Chile.* The introduction may strike some readers as unusual in that it includes the geological history of Chile, beginning with the Ice Age. Lucila Godoy Alcayaga, the birth name of Gabriela Mistral, appears in the volume in many photographs that document her life and travels. The Elqui Valley, where the poet was born, is reflected in "My Mountains": "I was raised among mountains,/with three dozen ranged around./It seems that never, never,/wherever my steps may be heard,/ have I forgotten them, neither by day/nor by starlit night,/and even now, when pools reflect/my snow-white hair,/I never left them, nor they me/like a cast-off daughter." In addition to presenting the poems bilingually, the volume also has a good bibliography. [SFW]

3227 Mistral, Gabriela. Madwomen: the Locas mujeres poems of Gabriela Mistral. Edited and translated by Randall Couch. A bilingual ed. Chicago, Ill.: Univ. of Chicago Press, 2008. 168 p.: bibl., index.

This volume includes poems from *Lagar* (Winepress) I, II. In the introduction, Couch says these "are poems of the self *in extremis*, marked by the wound of blazing catastrophe and its aftermath of mourning." Born in northern Chile in 1889, Mistral died in 1957 in Hempstead, N.Y. She received a great deal of recognition in her life, including the 1945 Nobel Prize for Literature, the first Latin American to be honored this way. Couch also says that "in the dramatic monologues of the 'madwomen,' the poet plays the part of prophet or sibyl speaking through the masks of personae." These are self-portraits, or the self as witnessed in the other: the Ballerina, Antigone, the Storyteller, the Cross-Eyed Mother, Clytemnestra, and many others. The book has an excellent section on texts and sources, as well as explanatory notes on the poems and a very useful selected bibliography. [SFW]

3228 Neruda, Pablo. The hands of day. Translated by William O'Daly. Port Townsend, Wash.: Copper Canyon Press, 2008. 193 p.

O'Daly says that in *The Hands of the Day*, originally published in Spanish in 1968, "the beloved Chilean poet celebrates the transformative powers of others' hands, of those who build with wood or metal or who harvest the grain or the fish, of those who make the wine, and of the powerful hands he entreats to help him change the profile of the planets, to shape the triangular stars the traveler needs." These ideas come from "The Gift," a good example of Neruda's late poetry and his lifelong gift with words. This is O'Daly's seventh translation of the late and posthumous poetry by Neruda, which he began with *Still Another Day*. [SFW]

3229 Neruda, Pablo. World's end. Translated by William O'Daly. Port Townsend, Wash.: Copper Canyon Press, 2009. 303 p.

World's End is the eighth and final translation by O'Daly of the late and posthumous poetry by this legendary Chilean poet published by Copper Canyon. In his introduction, the translator says that this book-length poem, composed from 1968–69, "is an often startling historical journey through social and political disillusionment." The edition is bilingual with translations on facing pages. Thematically, the poems treat 1968 in Prague, memories of the Spanish Civil War, and images of 20th-century destruction. As he moved toward the end of his own life, Neruda seems to be stripping himself clean: "And if I leave on the roads/I turn to the forgotten aroma/of an uninhabited rose,/of a fragrance that I lost/like a shadow loses its way:/I remained with no love at all,/naked in the middle of the street." These are poems in which Neruda is obsessed with the apocalyptic end of the century. The poet would appear to be writing fast in this collection, anchoring himself in the news and certain known landscapes to counteract the velocity of life, especially his own life. He mentions other writers such as Oliverio Girondo, Julio Cortázar, César Vallejo, Juan Rulfo, Carlos Fuentes, Ernesto Sábato, and Gabriel García Márquez. He also presents a well-known political figure: "In Cuba, Fidel roared/ with indisputable grandeur." [SFW]

3230 The Oxford book of Latin American poetry: a bilingual anthology. Edited by Cecilia Vicuña and Ernesto Livon-Grosman. New York: Oxford Univ. Press, 2009. 561 p.: bibl.

This essential anthology covers the region of Latin America from precolumbian times to the present with the work of nearly 150 poets from Hispanic America as well as Brazil. The Maya, Aztec, and Inca cultures are represented through works by anonymous Amerindian authors, some of whom are identified as female scribes. Contemporary Quiché culture from Guatemala (Humberto Ak'abal) and Mapuche culture from Chile (Elicura Chihuialaf Nahuelpan) are also included with the original texts in their indigenous languages. Gloria Gervitz, an important Mexican writer of Eastern European Jewish descent, also appears with a fragment from her *Migrations*. The expertly chosen Brazilian authors are an especially welcome addition since, too often, the Spanish- and Portuguese-speaking parts of the Americas are studied separately despite the fact that they have a great deal in common in terms of shared colonial histories and connections to influential 20th-century European avant-garde cultural movements. The editors recognize the monumentally complex nature of their project. They decided to present two introductions: "The first, on mestizo poetics, offers background to the creative principles underlying the poetic ideas of the ancient Americas and how they influenced later works. This is followed by a historical account of Latin America's poetry that connects the vernacular experimental tradition with its international context." For comment by Portuguese translation specialist, see item **3280**. [SFW]

3231 Parra, Nicanor. After-dinner declarations. Translated and with an introduction by Dave Oliphant. Austin, Tex.: Host Publications, 2009. 513 p.

This collection by Chilean poet Nicanor Parra, born in 1914, contains five "verse" speeches delivered during the 1990s on different occasions. According to Oliphant in his introduction, these highly colloquial poems with a definite Chilean twist contain Parra's "antipoetic pronouncements, his diatribes and eulogies, his quipping challenges to those satisfied with the status quo or even, through graft and greed, bent on the destruction of the environment and life on earth as we know it." [SFW]

3232 Peri Rossi, Cristina. State of exile. Translated from the Spanish by Marilyn Buck. San Francisco, Calif.: City Lights Books, 2008. 149 p. (Pocket poets series; 58)

In this volume, Peri Rossi establishes links between translation conceived as a "Dialogue of Exile" and the Uruguayan author's own experience as a writer whose works were banned by the military in her country in 1972. At that time, she was forced to give up her teaching position and ended up in Spain. These poems correspond to those years of exile, during which she received many honors, including the Rafael Alberti International Prize, named after the Spanish poet and friend of Lorca who also spent years living outside Spain after the Civil War. Each exiled person is different, says Peri Rossi, but they all have one thing in common: nostalgia. At the beginning of the volume, the poet speaks of a journey then asks a poignant question: "I dreamed that I was going far from here/on a wind-crested sea/waves black and white/a wolf dead on the beach/a raft floating/lights fiery-red on high seas/Did a city named Montevideo once exist?" [SFW]

3233 Rodríguez, Reina María. Violet Island and other poems. Translated from the Spanish by Kristin Dykstra and Nancy Gates Madsen. København, Denmark; Los Angeles, Calif.: Green Integer, 2004. 204 p. (The Marjorie G. Perloff series of international poetry) (Green Integer; 119)

These bilingually presented poems by Cuban Reina María Rodríguez (b. Havana, 1952) were selected from five books published in Cuba between 1982 and 1998. Kristin Dykstra writes in an Afterword that the Cuban Revolution shaped the world in which Rodríguez was raised: "her education, her career as a writer, the institutions that have supported artistic dialogue and exchange central to her experience, the books available for her to read." Dykstra wants it to be clear, however, that Rodríguez "consistently resists heavy-handed polemics" in her poetry, preferring "to create delicate disruptions in the fabrics of personal and social experience." Dozens of poets regularly gather at her home in Havana to talk and to read poetry on her rooftop. The final essay in this volume, "The Making of the Writer," provides an excellent critical overview of Rodriguez's poetry in the context of Cuban history during the author's life with all its controversies. As Rodríguez says in her poem "—at least that's how he looked, backlit": "a simple click of the shutter/and history returns like a declaration of love (Michelet)/but empty and dry. Like the fountain in Central Park/or the ghost of fallen leaves that was once its protective tree./she has been trapped by light (history, truth)." [SFW]

3234 Rojas, Gonzalo. From the lightning: selected poems. Translated from the Spanish by John Oliver Simon. København, Denmark; Los Angeles, Calif.: Green Integer; Saint Paul, Minn.: Consortium Book Sales and Distribution, 2008. 377 p. (The Marjorie G. Perloff series of international poetry)

Green Integer is admirable in the way it gets so much into the little package of its books. Gonzalo Rojas, born in 1917 and still going strong, is one of Latin America's greatest living poets, and another treasure from Chile. This selection artfully covers his life's work, drawn from almost a dozen books, many of which are themselves conceived as constantly evolving anthologies of new and selected poetry. Translator John Oliver Simon even includes five poems from Rojas' first book, *La miseria del hombre* (1948), which the poet usually does not allow, since he enjoys starting his readings and his career with the crowd-pleasing "What Do You Love When You Love?" from *Contra la muerte* (1964). Simon's Translator's Foreword is full of personal and heartfelt insights: "Gonzalo Rojas's poems begin with that instantaneous blast that separates the verbal from the material, charging language with spirit, making the words buzz like angry bees." Also included are two fine introductions by Rojas to his own readings in Valparaíso and Buenos Aires in 1997 and 1998. [SFW]

3235 Sabines, Jaime. Pieces of shadow: selected poems. Translated by W.S. Merwin. México: Fondo de Cultura Económica, Fundación para las Letras Mexicanas, 2007. 131 p.

Current US Poet Laureate W.S. Merwin originally published these poems by Mexican Jaime Sabines (1926–99) in 1996 (see *HLAS 58:4597*). They have been reissued in this volume by a major Mexican publisher, but, surprisingly, in an English-only edition. In writing about the translated poems, Merwin says that he especially appreciates "the jarring authenticity of passion in their tone, a great cracked bell note of craving and frustration, irony and anger, outrage and black humor all jangled at once, unabashed, unsweetened, unappeased, and all of it essential to the rest." All of this is true, as Sabines proves when he writes: "Someone spoke to me every day of my life,/into my ear, slowly, taking their time./Said to me: live, live, live!/It was death." [SFW]

3236 Sepúlveda, Jesús. Hotel Marconi. 2. ed. bilingue. Santiago: Editorial Cuarto Propio, 2006. 116 p. (Col. Uvas de la ira. Poesía)

Sepúlveda (b. Santiago, Chile, 1967) has lived in Eugene, Oregon, since 1995, where he teaches at the Univ. of Oregon. It was there, "on a porch at a party in the rain" that Sepúlveda met the translator Paul Dresman. Together, they also co-edited the large-format literary journal *Helicóptero*. Dresman characterizes *Hotel Marconi* as

"a season in hell, Picasso in 1904 among the acrobats, a time of danger and transformation." Published in Chile, this bilingual edition does not observe the conventional format and has the original Spanish texts on the right-hand page. These poems often describe an urban world of self-destructive behavior: "Reality spins/like a merry-go-round that never stops and makes you nauseous/ Sometimes I want to leap from the eleventh floor/And smash my stash on the concrete/ Smoke streams over the chessboard/Silhouettes of edifices under construction/catch the reflections of our faces/upon a table spread with white crystals." [SFW]

3237 Vallejo, César. Aphorisms. Translated from the Spanish by Stephen Kessler. Los Angeles, Calif.: Green Integer; London: Turnaround, 2007. 83 p.

About these aphorisms by Peruvian César Vallejo (1892–1938), Stephen Kessler writes in his preface that "these fragments, jottings, notes, and pungent zingers offer illuminating glimpses into the working mind of a writer considered by many to be one of the greatest and most original voices of twentieth century poetry." The gathering here is drawn from notebooks (kept by the poet during a crucial trip to Moscow in 1929) that remained unpublished until 1992. Some of the aphorisms, unsurprisingly, sound like the poetry Vallejo wrote during the Spanish Civil War: "Pity and compassion of people for other people. If at the hour of someone's death everyone else's pity were joined together to keep him from dying, that person wouldn't die." [SFW]

3238 Vitale, Ida. Reason enough. Translated by Sarah Pollack. Austin, Tex.: Host Publications, 2006. 77 p.

Born in Uruguay's capital Montevideo in 1923, Vitale is associated with her country's "Generation of 1945," a talented group of writers and intellectuals that included Mario Benedetti, Emir Rodríguez Monegal, and Ángel Rama. Like so many of her compatriots, Vitale was forced into exile after the military coup of 1973 in her country and lived in Mexico for a decade, where she collaborated with Octavio Paz on the renowned journal *Vuelta*. *Reason Enough* was originally published as *Oidor andante* in Montevideo in 1972. Although Vitale has published more than a dozen books, the translator chose this work to introduce English-speaking readers to her poetry because of its "sociopolitical overtones" and the way that "Vitale confronts the world as it is, exacting a critical and ethical response to human behavior in it." Be that as it may, Vitale's poems are as dense, subtle, and complex as the psychological realities she describes: "I see suicidal storm clouds./ Kings of sorrow, apexes of a dream/submerged, the still-lyrical,/the always hopeful,/the fishermen of other magic seas,/with each step taken we brush aside the glass/and fear." [SFW]

3239 Welden, Oliver. Love hound. Translated from the Spanish and with an introduction by Dave Oliphant. Austin, Tex.: Host Publications, 2006. 59 p.: ill.

The incessant tracker of Chilean poetry, Dave Oliphant, has resurrected this lost gem originally published as *Perro del amor* in 1970 by Oliver Welden (b. 1946). Welden was part of the cultural renaissance in pre-coup Chile as editor of the journal *Tebaida* (1968–73) in the northern desert city Arica. After Sept. 1973, Welden settled in Alabama, where he still lives and writes, though publishes little. Photographs figure prominently in Welden's violent moribund world: "These days if we had to gather again in that way/some afternoon, we would find ourselves with more/than one corpse combing itself for the camera." [SFW]

3240 Zeller, Ludwig. The eye on fire: poems, September 1998–March 1999 = Imágenes en el ojo llameante: septiembre 1998-marzo 1999. Translated by A.F. Moritz. Victoria, Canada: Ekstasis Editions, 2007. 70 p.

Born in 1927 in northern Chile, Zeller is considered one of Latin America's foremost Surrealist poets. This book was published on his 80th birthday. Zeller is also an artist who went into exile in Canada and remained there after the fall of the Allende government in Chile in 1973. Unfortunately, the book does not have an introduction to the poet's long and productive life as a writer and artist. According to material on the back cover, Zeller "combines eroticism and spirituality in poems where reality shines with the light of mystery and imagination." There are 27 poems in *The Eye on Fire*, but no indication as to why the seven

months indicated in the book's subtitle are significant. Often there is a dialogue with other painters and their work. For example, Zeller mentions Paul Delvaux and writes: "Night's great secret is silence, shadows of a ghost/Drag themselves toward you, gentlemen of dream, who leave/The stones to meet you finally at the bottom of the garden." [SFW]

3241 Zurita, Raúl. Purgatory. Translated from the Spanish and with an afterword by Anna Deeny. Foreword by C.D. Wright. Bilingual ed. Berkeley: Univ. of California Press, 2009. 117 p.: bibl., ill.

This retranslation of a new edition of a seminal work of contemporary Chilean poetry insists too much on a causal relationship to the 1973 military coup. It is clear that something else is going on in *Purgatory*, especially considering that certain poems in the books were composed *before* the tragic events that led to the overthrow of Salvador Allende, a fact that is not indicated in the introductory materials. Nor is this avant-garde poetry of self-mortification and trauma considered in relation to experimental body performance artists of the 1970s in the US such as Chris Burden. Despite the myth-making at work here and Zurita's immodest retrospective comment in his preface that "when faced with horror, we had to respond with art that was stronger and more vast than the pain and damage inflicted upon us," *Purgatory* is a literary landmark that retains its disconcerting, enigmatic, and controversial force decades after it was first published in Chile. [SFW]

Brief Fiction and Theater

3242 Best of contemporary Mexican fiction. Edited by Álvaro Uribe. Translation edited by Olivia Sears. 1st U.S. ed. Champaign, Ill.: Dalkey Archive Press, 2009. 529 p. (Latin American literature series)

Sixteen authors prototypical of the generation born since 1945 offer a variety of distinctive voices, represented by stories submitted by the authors themselves. Spanning several generations, the anthology is organized in chronological order with half born in the 1960s, another five in the 50s, three from the 40s, and one author born in the 70s. Contributors are Vivian Abens-hushan, Álvaro Enrique, Eduardo Antonio Parra, Cristina Ribera-Garza, Guillermo Fadanelli, Jorge F. Hernández, Ana García Bergua, Rosa Beltrán, Enrique Serna, Juan Villoro, Fabio Morábito, Francisco Hinojosa, Daniel Sada, Guillermo Samperi, Hernán Lara Zavala, and Héctor Manjarrez with English versions by 16 experienced translators. Uribe's Introduction discusses the stories included in the context of modern Mexican narrative. Biographies of the authors, translators, and editors conclude the volume. The bilingual format printed on facing pages allows readers who know Spanish to judge the translations for themselves and gives those who are not bilingual a chance to see the original texts. The volume is part of a two-way publishing exchange project sponsored by the National Endowment for the Arts, to coincide with a collection of American writers translated into Spanish and published by UNAM Press in 2009. Highly recommended for courses in literature and translation studies. For comment by specialist in Mexican literature, see item **2149**. [MA]

3243 Blum, Liliana V. The curse of Eve and other stories. Translated from the Spanish by Toshiya Kamei. Austin, Tex.: Host Publications, 2008. 159 p.

Brings together 28 stories set in Durango and Tampico that explore the lives of Mexican women from diverse backgrounds, and the violence and oppression in their lives. The Translator's Note lacks useful information about the author and her original Spanish language publications. [MA]

3244 Fuentes, Carlos. Happy families: stories. Translated by Edith Grossman. 1st U.S. ed. New York: Random House, 2008. 331 p.

In these 16 stories, the celebrated Mexican narrator take a hard look at kinship conflicts in tales of fathers and sons, mothers and daughters, sisters and brothers, and spouses through themes of nostalgia, aging, infidelity, and loss of beauty. Each story is paired with a brutal free form poem that contrasts the lives of poor Mexicans with the turbulence of gangs, drugs, rape, incest, and death. Grossman's translation flows nicely. The Spanish original was published in 2006 as *Todas las familias felices* (see item **2173**). [MA]

3245 Kozameh, Alicia. 259 leaps, the last immortal. Translated from the Spanish by Clare E. Sullivan. Introduction by Gwendolyn Díaz. San Antonio, Tex.: Wings Press, 2007. 167 p.

Originally published as *259 saltos, uno inmortal* by Narvaja Editor, Cordoba, Argentina (2001). This author from Rosario was apprehended by police in 1975, shortly before the onset of the infamous Dirty War, imprisoned for more than 3 years, and then released due to pressure from Amnesty International. Her narrative of life in exile in California and Mexico is written in fragments or "leaps" that appear to be disconnected but a thread of continuity runs throughout: the common denominator of the experience of exile. The translator worked closely with the author to render the many word plays, punning, and poem-like sonoral constructions that challenge meaning. [MA]

3246 Laughlin, Robert M. and **Sna Jtz'ibajom.** Monkey Business Theatre. Austin: Univ. of Texas Press, 2008. 315 p.: bibl., ill., index, map. (The Linda Schele Series in Maya and pre-Columbian studies)

Anthropologist Robert Laughlin presents his translation of 12 plays created by Sna Jtz'ibajom, an internationally acclaimed Maya-language writer's cooperative based in San Cristobal de las Casas, Chiapas, Mexico, that has been producing creative performance and writing for more than 20 years. Laughlin's translation from Tzotzil and Tzeltal of each play is accompanied by an introduction for each piece. Six are based on cultural myths while social, political, and economic issues are topics for the others. The Foreword by Carter Wilson and Preface by Ralph Lee offer valuable context. Highly recommended for English-language theater groups as well as classroom study in cultural anthropology and indigenous Mexican cultures. [MA]

3247 Martiatu, Inés María. Over the waves and other stories = Sobre las olas y otros cuentos. Translated by Emmanuel Harris II, with a critical essay by Tànit Fernández de la Reguera Tayà. Chicago, Ill.: Swan Isle Press, 2008. 204 p.: bibl.

Although Martiatu is known as a critic of Caribbean theater, contemporary Afro-Cuban theater in particular, this volume is a bilingual collection of short stories. The significance of Martiatu's work as both critic and author is well described by Tànit Fernández de la Reguera Tayà's "critical assessment," which concludes the book. As she explains, the book's "ideological framework and the principal esthetic interests" are "the recovery of collective memory, the processes of forming Caribbean culture and identity, and the role of black women as transmitters of culture in all of this" (p. 195). [CM]

3248 Mexico City noir. Edited by Paco Ignacio Taibo. Translated by Achy Obejas. New York, NY: Akashic Books, 2010. 170 p.: map. (Akashic noir series; AKB179)

Who better than Taibo, the internationally acclaimed crime novelist, to set the stage for this entry in Akashic's noir series set in a variety of neighborhoods across one of the largest and most violent cities in the world. His compelling introduction, "Snow White vs. Dr. Frankenstein," gives us real-life examples of this "infinite city's" culture of crime and corruption that mirrors the daily news: a chief of the state anti-drug force who was one of the most notorious drug traffickers; kidnappers and killer rapists who go free; undercover agents steal cars; throwaway kids sniff glue. The 12 writers in this volume "use very different narrative styles to speak about a city they love . . . Almost all of them take refuge in humor, a very dark humor, acidic, which allow us enough distance to laugh at Lucifer. Another shared element is the interest in experimentation, in crossing narrative planes, points of view. The neodetective story born in Mexico is not only a social literature but also one with an appetite for moving outside the traditional boundaries of the genre" (Taibo, p. 19). Contributors include Taibo himself, Eduardo Antonio Parra; Bernardo Fernández, F.G. Haghenbeck, Julia Rodríguez, Juan Hernández Luna, Eugenio Aguirre, Myriam Laurini, Oscar de la Borbella, Rolo Diez, Edcuadro Monteverde, and Victor Luis González. Highly recommended sampler of Mexico's noir narrative for students and fans of the genre alike. [MA]

3249 Radrigán, Juan. Finished from the start and other plays. Translated from the Spanish by Ana Elena Puga with Mónica Núñez-Parra. Evanston, Ill.: Northwestern Univ. Press, 2007. 193 p.: bibl., ill.

Ana Elena Puga and Mónica Núñez-Parra's contribution to this volume is two-fold. They make available in English four works from Chilean playwright Juan Radrigán's *Teatro de Juan Radrigán: 11 obras* (1984)—*Testimony to the Deaths of Sabrina; The Beasts;* the trilogy *Funeral Drums for Lambs and Wolves;* and *Finished from the Start.* In addition, Puga provides a comprehensive commentary on the work as a translator, Radrigán's theatrical *testimonio,* and Pinochet's dictatorship, in which all the plays are set. Her extensive translator's note is of particular interest because of her candid discussion of the translation challenges she encountered and because her approach to the translations was linked closely to an actual staging of *Isabel Banished in Isabel* (from the trilogy) and *Finished from the Start.* For a detailed review of this volume, see Carys Evans-Corrales' essay in *Translation Review,* 77/78, 2009, p. 191–197. [CM]

3250 Shua, Ana Maria. Quick fix: sudden fiction. Edited by Rhonda Dahl Buchanan and Luci Mistratov. Buffalo, N.Y.: White Pine Press, 2008. 203 p. (Secret weavers series; 21)

A bilingual illustrated anthology that collects microfictions from all four of Shua's books of short fiction. Rhonda Dahl Buchanan's exquisite translations are enhanced by the whimsical line drawings of Luci Mistratov, bringing these "funny, fanciful, disturbing and insightful" miniatures by one of Argentina's most gifted writers to English language readers. The brief narratives in Spanish and English are an excellent choice for language and literature classrooms. [MA]

3251 Sun, stone, and shadows: 20 great Mexican short stories. Edited by Jorge F. Hernández. 1st ed. in English (FCE). Mexico: Fondo de Cultura Económica/Fundación para las Letras Mexicanas, 2008. 243 p. (Tezontle)

A collection of 20 classic short stories by Mexico's most distinguished writers born during the first half of the 20th century in versions by distinguished translators. Five thematic sections are The Fantastic Unreal that includes Carlos Fuentes' "Chac-Mool"; Mexican Reality, Elena Garro's "Blame the Tlaxcaltecs"; The Tangible Past; Juan

Rulfo's "Tell them not to Kill Me"; Urban Life, Rosario Castellanos' "Cooking Lesson"; Intimate Imagination, Juan José Arreola's "The Switch Man." Among other authors featured are José Emilio Pacheco, Jorge Ibargüengoitia, Martín Luis Guzmán, Inés Arredondo, and Salvador Elizondo. Hernández's introduction outlines Mexico's vibrant tradition of short literary fiction. A useful brief biography for each author concludes the volume. The original version was *Sol, piedra y sombras: veinte cuentistas mexicanos de la primera mitad del siglo XX* (2008). This English language version is the first in The Big Read Program created by The National Endowment for the Arts in partnership with the Institute of Museum and Library Services and in cooperation with Arts Midwest. Highly recommended for students and readers of modern Mexican literature. [MA]

Novels

3252 Aguilar, Eduardo García. The triumphant voyage. Translated by Jay Miskowiec. Minneapolis, Minn.: Aliform Pub., 2009. 272 p.

Originally published in Colombia as *El viaje triunfal* (1989), this picaresque novel relates the sentimental journeys of the fictional poet Arnaldo Faría Ultrillo during the early 20th century as he goes from the San Francisco earthquake to Paris between the wars, from his mother's youth in Veracruz, Mexico, to his death in Colombia at the start of *la violencia*. Miskowiec's translation easily follows the wanderings of "a professional foreigner." [MA]

3253 Aira, César. Ghosts. Translated from the Spanish by Chris Andrews. New York: New Directions, 2008. 139 p.

César Aira's fiction invariably captivates, and it just as invariably defies neat summaries. The rather fantastical *Los fantasmas* (1999), published as *Ghosts* in Chris Andrews' excellent translation, is no exception. Scott Bryan Wilson has offered an appropriate description, however, commenting that the novel is "[u]ltimately . . . about the mechanics within families and the ways in which they create expectations for our lives, expectations which perhaps we can't or don't always want to meet" (*The Quarterly Con-*

versation: http://quarterlyconversation.com/ghosts-by-cesar-aira). For comments about *Los fantasmas*, see *HLAS* 54:4079. [CM]

3254 Bolaño, Roberto. 2666. Translated from the Spanish by Natasha Wimmer. 1st American ed. New York: Farrar, Straus and Giroux, 2008. 898 p.

Wimmer's luminous translation offers access to this powerful enigmatic novel of 898 pages of rhythmic sentences and tangential plot lines by the Chilean narrator who spent most of his erratic life in Mexico and Spain where he died in 2003 at age 50. Published posthumously in 2004, the release in 2008 of the English-language edition was hailed "as an event in its own right" by a "writer of globalization," considered by many to be the most important Latin American novelist since García Márquez. Five loosely related sections and scores of characters wander across continents and nearly a century of history. At the core, all strands converge in the horrific serial murders in the mythic Mexican border city of Santa Teresa, a fictionalized version of Ciudad Juárez, where since 1993, more than 430 women and girls have died in unsolved serial killings. "Part 4 is a ruthlessly precise forensic catalog of those killings . . . along with the stories of the victims and the investigating detectives. It is a police procedural straight from the precinct of hell. It is also as bravura a displacement of novelistic mastery and as devastating a reading experience as you are likely ever to encounter" (Lev Grossman, *Time*, 24 Nov. 2008). Marcela Valdes' penetrating analysis in *The Nation* (12/8/2008) points out, "The great subject of his oeuvre is the relationship between art and infamy, craft and crime, the writer and the totalitarian state . . . It isn't for the faint hearted . . . . 2666, like all of Bolaño's work, is a graveyard. His previous novels memorialized the dead of the 1960s and 70s. His ambitions for 2666 were greater: to write a postmortem for the dead of the past, the present and the future." [MA]

3255 Castellanos Moya, Horacio. Senselessness. Translated from the Spanish by Katherine Silver. New York: New Directions, 2008. 142 p.

Senselessness (*Insensatez*, 2004) is not the first novel by Salvadoran Horacio Castellanos Moya (b. Honduras, 1957), but it was the first to be published in English translation. Two earlier works have also appeared in English during the present biennium: Katherine Silver's translation of *Diabola en el espejo* (2000) as *The She-Devil in the Mirror* (2009), and Lee Paula Springer's translation of *Baile con serpientes* (1996) as *Dance with Snakes* (2009). Each of the novels is set in the context of El Salvador's civil war and all have received considerable (positive) critical attention. *Senselessness*, for example, won a Rainmaker Translation Grant. The two translators have also been praised, in particular by expert (Bolaño) translator Natasha Wimmer, who notes that "the plainness and slang" of Castellanos Moya's novels, which are characterized by "a pleasingly jittery, caffeinated rhythm . . . also cleverness and the sharpness of their bite"—, present a definite challenge to a translator. However, in an extensive review article she finds that both translators "acquit themselves eloquently" ("Novelist from another planet," *The Nation*, 14 Dec. 2009, p. 11–15). Her comments provide a good introduction to Castellanos Moya and his work in the absence of introductory material in all three of the translations. [CM]

3256 Clavel, Ana. Shipwrecked body. Translated from the Spanish by Jay Miskowiec. Translation edited by Juan Arciniega. 1st ed. of the English translation. Minneapolis, Minn.: Aliform Pub., 2008. 151 p.: ill.

First published in Mexico as *Cuerpo naúfrago* by Alfaguara in 2005. In Mexico City a female narrator relates the out-of-body experiences of a woman in the body of a man. [MA]

3257 Fernández, Macedonio. The museum of eterna's novel: the first good novel. Translated from the Spanish by Margaret Schwartz. Rochester, N.Y.: Open Letter, 2010. 238 p.

Macedonio Fernández (Argentina, 1874–1952) is far less well known than his famous pupil, Jorge Luis Borges. However, as translator Margaret Schwartz explains, he was the mentor who prompted what Adam Thirwell has aptly described "the still unstably active" consequences of the fictional experimentation that flourished in Buenos Aries during the first decades of the 20th century (p. v). Schwartz's transla-

tion makes *Museo de la novela de la eterna* available in its entirety, and her informative translator's introduction provides the reader with a sound orientation to a challenging but necessary writer. For commentary on the Spanish version of this novel, see *HLAS* 50:3449. [CM]

3258 Filloy, Juan. Op Oloop. Translated by Lisa Dillman. Champaign, Ill.: Dalkey Archive Press, 2009. 251 p. (Latin American literature series)

As presented in the brief author's note, Argentine author Juan Filloy (1894–2000) "used only seven letters in the titles of all his works," was a world-champion palindromist, and had a penchant for the dictionary and for neologisms. The few lines about Filloy and the intriguing nature of *Op Oloop* (1934) make the reader wish there had been more background information about him and his work. The novel has been summarized, however, in *HLAS* 32:3984. [CM]

3259 Ibargüengoitia, Jorge. Kill the lion! Translated by Helen Lane and Ronald Christ. 1st ed. in English. México: FCE: F,L,M, 2008. 206 p. (Tezontle)

The original title was *Maten al león* (1969). This "near slapstick tale of attempts to assassinate an aging dictator" achieves comedy in its setting in the fictional Caribbean island of Arepa. "Shortly before her death, Helen Lane . . . rendered this novel mentally, noting certain choices, queries and observations between the lines of her copy. Ronald Christ has followed her penciled lead." Yet, no introductory note about the author or the translation process was included. [MA]

3260 Lisé, Gloria. Departing at dawn: a novel of Argentina's dirty war. Translated by Alice Weldon. New York: Feminist Press at the City Univ. of New York, 2009. 175 p.

Originally published as *Viene clareando* in 2005, this first novel was hailed by critics and chosen by the Argentine National Public Library to be placed in libraries throughout the country. The author uses her personal memories of life under the 1976 military junta to weave a compelling narrative set in Tucumán during "the pact of silence that shrouded an entire country" and traumatized the daily life of innocent citizens. Weldon's skillful translation captures the climate of terror produced by the dirty war as well as the lexicon of regional popular culture. Highly recommended for classroom topics in Latin American culture and women's studies. [MA]

3261 Muñoz, Braulio. Alejandro and the fishermen of Tancay. Translated from the Spanish by Nancy K. Muñoz. Tucson: Univ. of Arizona Press, 2008. 148 p. (Camino del sol)

Set in Chimbote, the Peruvian coastal boomtown of the 1960s, Don Morales tells stories about the town and changes the fishermen of Tancay experienced during the war between the Shining Path movement and the Peruvian army during the 1980s into the 1990s. Muñoz, also author of *The Peruvian Notebooks* (2006), is a sociologist who lived in Chimbote and witnessed many of the events in his narrative. The skillful translation of the regional *Alejandro y los pescadores de Tancay* is smooth and natural. Don Morales' message is: "When the natural order is disrupted, it is not only fish that die. When nature dies, so might we all." A glossary of Peruvian terms is helpful. Recommended for students and scholars, ecology issues, and for local interest in Peru. [MA]

3262 Padura, Leonardo. Havana gold. Translated by Peter Bush. London: Bitter Lemon, 2008. 286 p.

Vientos de cuaresma (1994), translated by Peter Bush as *Havana Gold*, was the second of the four novels identified with a particular season in 1989 and known in English as the Havana quartet. Its protagonist Lieutenant Mario Conde (the Count) was introduced to English readers in *Havana Red*, Bush's 2005 translation of *Máscaras* (1997). This might be the best novel with which to begin one's acquaintance with the four. An excellent example of Padura's incisive social and cultural criticism, it is a novel of "poetic license," to quote Leonardo Padura in the opening "Author's Note," and a subversive homage of sorts to Virgilio Piñera and other writers, particularly gay writers, marginalized and persecuted by the Cuban government. Padura explains that his characters and the events in the novel are "the work of my imagination, even if they are pretty close to reality." Mario Conde, he

says, "is a metaphor, not a policeman, and his life unfolds in the possible space that is literature" (p. vii). *Havana Red* was followed in English by *Havana Black* (2006) and *Havana Blue* (2007), Bush's translations of *Pasaje de ontono* (1998), and *Pasado perfecto* (1991), repectively. *Havana Fever*, Peter Bush's translation of *La neblina del ayer* (2009), was also published during the biennium; it continues the tale of Mario Conde. Readers interested in Padura's highly creative work with the detective novel will find it informative to read Clemens A. Franken K.'s "Leonardo Padura Fuentes y su detective nostálgico," *Revista Chilena de Literatura*, 74, 2009, p. 29–56. [CM]

3263 Paso, Fernando del. News from the Empire. Translation by Alfonso Gonzalez and Stella T. Clark. Champaign, Ill.: Dalkey Archive Press, 2009. 704 p.

Noticias del Imperio was widely acclaimed when it was published in 1987 by the author of *Palinuro of Mexico* and winner of the prestigious Juan Rulfo and Xavier Villaurrutia literary prizes. In 1861, when Mexico defaulted on its foreign debt, Napoleon III of France sent an army of occupation to Mexico to create an empire headed by Ferdinand Maximilian of Habsburg and his wife, Princess Charlotte of Belgium, from 1863–67. The first, last, and off-numbered chapters are the memories and rantings of the mad ex-empress addressing the dead Maximilian. Even-numbered chapters are a polyphony of dialogue, testimony, stream of consciousness, letters, and conversations of "multiple and conflicting accounts: of a vast cast of characters who bore witness to the turbulent events from the final years of Maximilian's life to the early days of the 20th century." The translators skillfully meet the challenges of this "microscopic historiography" and its vast range of genres and registers. [MA]

3264 Recacoechea S., Juan. Andean express: a novel. Translated by Adrian Althoff. New York: Akashic Books, 2009. 172 p.: map.

First published as *Altiplano express* in 2000, this Bolivian take on the noir tradition plays out in sex, poker, and murder on an overnight train from La Paz to Arica. A large cast of characters mirrors a political scene that is now rather dated given the dramatic political changes in Bolivia during the past decade. [MA]

3265 Roncagliolo, Santiago. Red April. Translated from Spanish by Edith Grossman. 1st American ed. New York: Pantheon Books, 2009. 271 p.

When originally published as *Abril rojo* in 2006, the Peruvian author became the youngest writer to win Alfaguara's Premio de Novela. Set in the frame of a whodunit in the Andean city of Ayacucho, a public prosecutor pursues a murder case that might be linked to the brutal terrorist group, Shining Path. It becomes a riveting political novel about the brutality of Peruvian society in the 1990s, caught between indiscriminate slaughter by Shining Path and the equally savage counterinsurgency waged by the Fujimori government and the army. [MA]

3266 Rosero Diago, Evelio. The armies. Translated from the Spanish by Anne McLean. New York: New Directions, 2009. 199 p.

Winner of the 2009 Independent Foreign Fiction Prize, *The Armies* (*Los ejércitos*, 2007) by Colombian Evelio Rosero (b. 1958) also received the Tusquets Prize and has been highly praised in both Spanish and English. Anne McLean, Rosero's accomplished translator, explains that the novel, which takes place in the context of Colombia's ongoing civil war, "is beautifully told . . . It's not a comfortable read, but it is a page-turner and he [Rosero] somehow makes it universal even though it's so Colombian" (*The Guardian*, 14 May 2009, http://www.guardian.co.uk/books/2009/may/14/colombian-independent-foreign-fiction-prize). [CM]

3267 Ruy Sánchez, Alberto and **Rhonda Dahl Buchanan.** The secret gardens of Mogador: voices of the earth. Buffalo, N.Y.: White Pine Press, 2008. 188 p. (Companions for the journey; 17)

Los jardines secretos de Mogador: voces de tierra is the third novel of a tetralogy that uses the four basic elements of air, water, earth, and fire to "explore the nature of feminine and masculine desire." It is comprised of four spirals, divided into nine sections in which the narrator takes on the role of "a new Scherazade" as he transforms himself into a voice so that he may once again inhabit the body of his beloved, in this poetic meditation on Arabian culture that has fascinated the author since he first visited the Sahara desert in 1975. Brief information on the author is lacking. [MA]

3268 Solares, Ignacio. Yankee invasion: a novel of Mexico City. Translated by Timothy G. Compton. Introduction by Carlos Fuentes. Minneapolis, Minn.: Scarletta Press: Aliform Pub., 2009. 237 p.

The original novel *La invasión* was a best-seller when it was published in Mexico in 2005 as it evoked "the trauma of the shared history of Mexico and the United States" in the invasion and occupation of Mexico City by US forces during The Mexican War (1846–47), when Mexico lost half its territory to the US. Cast as a memoir of a soldier in the dramatic conflict in Mexico City occupied by the army of Gen. Winfield Scott, the novel opens on Sept. 14, 1847, the day the US flag was raised in the heart of the city. Fuentes notes: "Solares gives us a very rich tale of history relived, the past as present, the wholeness of experience as an act of the imagination directed not only at the past, but also at the future of the final warrior, the reader" (p. xiii). Timothy Compton's lucid translation conserves the tone and flow of events and characters. Maps and a timeline of Mexican history from 1838–48 are very useful for the general reader. Highly recommended for students of Mexican history, border studies, and the general reader interested in the other side of the story. [MA]

3269 Szperling, Cecilia. Natural selection. Translated by Oscar Luna. Laverstock, U.K.: Aflame Books, 2009. 161 p.

First published as *Selección natural* in 2006. A novel in four parts viewed through the eyes of young urbanites in the drug and crime scene of contemporary Buenos Aires. [MA]

3270 Tejera, Nivaria. The ravine: (El barranco). Translation and with an afterword by Carol Maier. Albany: State Univ. of New York Press, 2008. 165 p.: bibl., index. (SUNY series, women writers in translation)

First published in French in 1958 as *Le ravin*; in Spanish in Cuba in 1959 as *El barranco*; and subsequently in editions in

Spain in 1982, 1989, and 2005. A seven-year-old girl narrates her experience of the early days of the Spanish Civil War in the Canary Islands when her father is taken prisoner and sent to forced labor in a concentration camp, facing fear of death before the firing squad and burial in the ravine. A glossary of Spanish terms, the author's revisit to her novel; "About *El barranco*, After Many Year's;" and the translator's "Afterword: Reading *El barranco*, Writing *The Ravine*" make this a model first English edition. Maier notes that since Tejera was born in Cuba in 1929 and has lived nearly all her life in Tenerife and Paris, her work has been "absent from most discussions of both Cuban and Latin America writers," although Joseph Schraibman's essay in Pérez and Aycock's *The Spanish Civil War in Literature* (1990) offers an excellent introduction to this novel. Maier's superb translation strikes a delicate balance between the "complex sensitivity" of the child-narrator and the presence of her adult author. Her "Afterword" traces the process of coming to grips with the vitality of the double-voiced text. [MA]

3271 Urbina, Cecilia. A Tuesday like today. Translated from the Spanish by Clare Sullivan. San Antonio, Tex.: Wings Press, 2008. 162 p.

The original publication of *Un martes como hoy* in 2004 won the prestigious Mexican literary Premio Coatlicue. Interwoven stories of three Mexican travelers come together in Angkor, in the heart of a ruined Cambodia that becomes a place of magical realism and shared fantasies. Sullivan worked with the author to meet "the challenge of translating Urbina's 'literal snapshots' of the human consequences of the Vietnam War and the bombing of Cambodia" as well as the connections between nature and humanity in a village on the Tonle Sap river. [MA]

3272 Vargas Llosa, Mario. The bad girl. Translated from the Spanish by Edith Grossman. 1st American ed. New York: Farrar, Straus and Giroux, 2007. 276 p.

Fluid, crisp translation of *Travesuras de la niña mala* (see *HLAS 64:1975*). The story of a grand passion between Peruvian expatriates played out in Lima of the 1950s, Paris of the 60s, London in the 70s, Tokyo

in the 80s, and ending in Paris and Madrid in the 1990s. "Sexy, romantic and sad," with an autobiographical feel to the scenarios and cultures in which the winner of the Nobel Prize for Literature 2010 "came of intellectual age." [MA]

3273 Vásquez, Juan Gabriel. The informers. Translated from the Spanish by Anne McLean. New York: Riverhead Books, 2009. 351 p.

Praised by *Washington Post* reviewer and critic Jonathan Yardley as "unquestionably the best new novel he had read in 2009," Colombian Juan Gabriel Vásquez's *The Informers* (*Informantes*, 2004) has received unqualified praise; the same has been true for translator Anne McLean. As Yardley notes, the many Germans in post-WWII Latin America "were under strong pressure to deny any sympathy for Nazi Germany. This led to a tangled web of alliance and betrayals" (*Washington Post, Book World*, "Our Critics' Favorite Books of 2009", 15 Dec. 2009, p. 8). The web Yardley describes is precisely what provides the charged context of *The Informers*. [CM]

3274 Volpi Escalante, Jorge. Season of ash: a novel in three acts. Translated from the Spanish by Alfred Mac Adam. Rochester, N.Y.: Open Letter, 2009. 413 p.

Mexican novelist Volpi, a founder of the "Crack" group, sets his *No será la tierra* (2006) in cycles of crisis, violence, and destruction in 20th-century history: the Chernobyl disaster, the fall of the Berlin Wall and the Soviet Union, and the scientific advances of the Human Genome Project as told through the eyes of three women. Volpi has arranged his text like a play, with a prelude and three acts, each covering a broad time period from 1929 to 2000. Multiple plots and characters weave murder, scientific investigation, and journalistic exposé that converge into a dark love story. Mac Adams' translation that omits quotation marks or line breaks within dialogue at times is confusing for the reader. [MA]

3275 Zapata Olivella, Manuel. Changó, the biggest badass. Translated from the Spanish by Jonathan Tittler. Introduction by William Luis. Lubbock, Tex.: Texas Tech Univ. Press, 2010. 463 p. (The Americas series)

"To the Fellow Traveler," the salutation by Manuel Zapata Olivella (Colombia, 1920–2004) found on the opening page of *Changó*, sums up the breadth and challenge of the experience that awaits the reader: "Climb aboard this novel like so many African prisoners on the slave ships . . . Forget about academics, verb tenses, the boundaries between life and death . . . confront this truth: the history of the black man in America is as much yours as that of the Indian or the white man" (p. xxxv). Exaggerated though Zapata Olivella's words may sound at first, he is in fact not overstating the scope of his novel, seeing that, as translator Jonathan Tittler explains, its "alien [to a Western reader] Afro-centric cosmos . . . ranged over five centuries and spanned three continents" (p. x). Both Tittler's notes and William Luis' comprehensive introduction, in addition to the extensive glossary (which in his opening remarks Zapata Olivella urges the reader to ignore) provide an excellent guide. And one hopes that there will be readers. The novel is formidable for its length and dimension, but even a brief glance indicates that Luis is accurate when he affirms that Zapata Olivella is "the most significant Afro-Spanish-American narrator of the twentieth century" (p. xiv). [CM]

Essays, Interviews, and Reportage

3276 **Brimmer, Gabriela** and **Elena Poniatowska.** Gaby Brimmer: an autobiography in three voices. Translated by Trudy Balch. Foreword by Judith E. Heumann & Jorge Pineda. Introduction by Laura Umansky. Afterword by Avital Bloch. English language ed. Waltham, Mass.: Brandeis Univ. Press; Hanover, N.H.: Univ. Press of New England, 2009. 200 p.: bibl. (HBI series on Jewish women)

Originally published in Spanish as *Gaby Brimmer* in 1979, this multi-voiced memoir alternates the voices of Gaby Brimmer, 1947–2000, born with cerebral palsy and who learned to type with her left foot, with those of her mother and her caretaker in a text structured by foremost Mexican writer, Elena Poniatowska. The testimony of an extraordinary woman, who became a key activist in launching the disability rights movement in Mexico, records "a pivotal moment in disability history, when

the disability rights and Independent Living movements gained momentum around the world, and international alliances began to take shape." Umanski's Introduction, the Afterword by Bloch, and a Time Line for Disability Rights History and Reading List offer a valuable frame for our reading 30 years later, now well within the disability studies movement. Highly recommended for general readers as well as disability studies courses. [MA]

3277 **Eltit, Diamela** and **Paz Errázuriz.** Soul's infarct. Translated by Ronald Christ. Sante Fe, N.M.: Lumen Books; Minneapolis, Minn.: Consortium Books Sales 2009. 87 p.: ill. (Helen Lane editions)

In *El infarto del alma* (1994), Chile's celebrated experimental writer joined a renowned photographer of the marginalized to record and interpret the mysteries and magic of the discourse of love in couples living in a Chilean psychiatric institution for the poor and insane. Eltit's text and Errázuriz's lens confront society's most abject and vulnerable human beings—face to face and lens to lens. Christ's translation brings out the power of the searing prose and images. [MA]

3278 **Galeano, Eduardo H.** Mirrors: stories of almost everyone. English translation by Mark Fried. New York: Nation Books, 2009. 391 p.: ill., index.

A translation of *Espejos*—a brief history of the world told in hundreds of vignettes—*Mirrors* speaks for itself without the need for an introduction or an afterword. Eduardo Galeano is well known to (and acclaimed by) English-language readers for his brief, story-like incisive narratives and for "offering as effective an act of political dissent as exists anywhere in contemporary literature" (Neil Gordon, "A History of Us," *New York Times Book Review*, 23 Aug. 2009, p. 14). [CM]

TRANSLATIONS FROM THE PORTUGUESE

Poetry

3279 **The Ecco anthology of international poetry.** Edited by Ilya Kaminsky and Susan Harris. New York: Ecco, 2010. 540 p.: index.

Poet Kaminsky and *Words Without Borders* editorial director Harris have compiled an outstanding volume of 20th-century poetry from around the world, in some cases providing the first translations of significant international figures. Includes Brazilian poets Jorge de Lima, Carlos Drummond de Andrade, João Cabral de Melo Neto, and Adélia Prado, all represented by skilled previously published translations. [DP]

3280 The Oxford book of Latin American poetry: a bilingual anthology. Edited by Cecilia Vicuña and Ernesto Livon-Grosman. New York: Oxford Univ. Press, 2009. 561 p.: bibl.

A superb and beautifully illustrated bilingual anthology presenting outstanding selections and translations. With a rich representation of 20 Brazilian poets, ranging from Gregório de Matos—some of whose most infamous satiric poems about Bahia are brilliantly translated by Mark A. Lokensgard—through major 19th- and 20th-century figures, ending with Josely Vianna Baptista (b. 1957). A diverse group of translators contributes to the success of this volume, among them Elizabeth Bishop, Michael Palmer, and Richard Zenith. Particularly noteworthy, in addition to the translations by Lokensgard, are the many poems excellently translated by Odile Cisneros. For comment by Spanish translation specialist, see item **3230**. [DP]

3281 Pereira, Edimilson de Almeida. Livro de falas = Books of voices. Imagens de Antônio Sérgio Moreira. Tradução de Steven White. Juiz de Fora, Brazil: Funalfa; Belo Horizonte, Brazil: Mazza Edições, 2008. 129 p.: ill., index.

A fascinating bilingual volume presenting verse and prose poems inspired by the Afro-Brazilian religious practice, *candomblé* . First published in 1987, and then in English in 1996 in *Callaloo: A Journal of African Diaspora Arts and Letters* (Vol. 19, No. 1). The present volume includes valuable additional material. In the book's first part, each poem is preceded by an epigraph recounting the original myth, with which the poem then dialogues. The lengthy final essay analyzes White's translation of the poems in the context of contemporary translation theory. [DP]

Brief Fiction and Theater

3282 Brazil: a traveler's literary companion. Edited by Alexis Levitin. Foreward by Gregory Rabassa. Berkeley, Calif.: Whereabouts Press, 2010. 243 p.: map.

A wonderful and inventive collection of over 30 stories by Brazilian writers old and new, urban and rural, organized by geographic region and designed to whet the appetite of travelers to Brazil. Selections, preceded by Levitin's brief introduction to each writer, range from Machado de Assis' "The Wallet," passing through figures such as Simões Lopes Neto, Jorge Amado, Clarice Lispector, Guimarães Rosa, Dalton Trevisan, and Rubem Fonseca, and including an outstanding representation of lesser-known and younger writers. New stories by Moacyr Scliar, Pena Cabreira, and Paula Parisot were written especially for this volume. The translations are by nearly 20 different translators, with Levitin, Landers, and Entrekin particularly well represented. [DP]

3283 The Brazilian short story in the late twentieth century: a selection from nineteen authors. Edited by M. Angélica Lopes. Preface by Mary L. Daniel. Lewiston, N.Y.: Edwin Mellen Press, 2009. 164 p.: bibl., index.

An unusual selection of 19 short stories originally published in Brazil in the 1970s and 1980s, ably translated by Lopes and six others. Many of these authors are not known in the English-speaking world and the collection is thus a welcome addition to the increasingly diverse body of work by Brazilians appearing in English translation. [DP]

3284 Contemporary Jewish writing in Brazil: an anthology. Edited and translated by Nelson H. Vieira. Lincoln: Univ. of Nebraska Press, 2009. 287 p.: bibl. (Jewish writing in the contemporary world)

Despite their very small numbers (approximately 120,000 by current estimates), Jews in Brazil have had a significant literary presence. This invaluable anthology brings together for the first time a large body of work by contemporary Jewish writers, famous and less known, in a variety of narrative genres. Includes 21 writers. Vieira provides an excellent and detailed introductory essay, an illuminating interview with

Moacyr Scliar, and brief introductions to each writer. An ambitious and much-needed project demonstrating Vieira's exceptional skill as both translator and scholar. [DP]

3285 Fonseca, Rubem. The taker and other stories. Translated from the Portuguese by Clifford Landers. Rochester, N.Y.: Open Letter, 2008. 166 p.

Fifteen stories, some of them previously published separately in English, make up this volume, the first in English to bring together a sampling of Fonseca's short (and a few longer) stories. Selected from various of Fonseca's short story collections, these tales demonstrate why Fonseca is a master of this genre, which he has cultivated for decades. Thematically familiar (violence, obsession, grim humor, skepticism–with an occasional startling departure), they offer an intense display of Fonseca's skills. Ably and gracefully translated so that even the most macabre of these tales can be enjoyed. [DP]

3286 Machado de Assis. A chapter of hats: selected stories. Translated from the Portuguese and with an introduction by John Gledson. London: Bloomsbury, 2008. 275 p.

In addition to being a prolific translator, Gledson has become a crucial mediator between Brazil's greatest writer and the English-language world (and also continues to publish critical analyses of Machado in Portuguese). Here he translates, carefully and with great respect, 20 stories by Machado, most of them not hitherto available in English in one volume or in an enticing translation. Gledson's excellent introduction includes important reflections on Machado's status in English. [DP]

3287 Rodrigues, Nelson. Life as it is. Translated from the Portuguese by Alex Ladd. Austin, Tex.: Host Publications, 2008. 314 p.

From 1951 to 1961, famed playwright Nelson Rodrigues wrote a column, six days a week, for the Rio newspaper *Ultima Hora.* Starting as *crônicas,* the column quickly turned into short fiction on Rodrigues' usual themes: sex, violence, and urban life. From the 2,000-plus short pieces thus produced, this volume gathers about 60 short stories, mini-dramas heavy on dialogue, often culminating in a revelatory and ironic one-liner. Translator Alex Ladd comments in his introduction that Rodrigues is perhaps "too Brazilian" to be translated, especially since he often uses contemporaneous Rio slang (but never vulgarity). Nonetheless, Ladd has successfully conveyed the characteristic Rodrigues tone. For comment by drama specialist, see item **3156.** [DP]

Rodrigues, Nelson. Pornographic angel: the short stories that inspired the play. See item **3157.**

3288 Stages of conflict: a critical anthology of Latin American theater and performance. Edited by Diana Taylor and Sarah J. Townsend. Translation coordination by Margaret Carson. Ann Arbor: Univ. of Michigan Press, 2008. 325 p.: bibl., ill.

Spanning more than five centuries and 10 Latin American countries, the editors of this important volume have selected 19 works (from 10 countries) intended for performance in a variety of languages: Spanish, Portuguese, Quiché, Quechua, and Nahuatl. More than half the works are translated here for the first time. They represent indigenous, colonial, and postcolonial perspectives, and justify the pun in the volume's title. With excellent introductions and bibliographies. Three Brazilian writers are included: Martins Pena (*The Jealous Officer, or The Fearsome Slave Catcher,* trans. by Sarah J. Townsend); Oswald de Andrade (*The Candle King,* trans. by Ana Bernstein and Sarah J. Townsend); and Denise Stoklos (*Denise Stoklos in Mary Stuart,* trans. by Denise Stoklos and Marlène Ramírez-Cancio). For comment by theater specialist, see item **2961.** [DP]

3289 Women righting: Afro-Brazilian women's short fiction = Mulheres escre-vendo: uma antologia bilingüe de escritoras Afro-Brasileiras contemporâneas. Edited by Miriam Alves and Maria Helena Lima. Preface by M. Alves. Introduction by M.H. Lima. Translated by M.H. Lima with Kevin Meehan. Bilingual ed. London: Mango Pub., 2005. 100 p.

The first bilingual edition of Afro-Brazilian women's short fiction, this volume claims space for their voices in a hostile society. Includes eight pieces by six writers (Esmeralda Ribeiro, Lia Vieira, Sônia Fátima da Conceição, Geni Guimarães, Miriam

Alves, and Conceição Evaristo). The translations are only occasionally successful; more often they are too literal and explanatory, thus lacking in evocative power. [DP]

Novels

3290 Brandão, Ignácio de Loyola. Anonymous celebrity. Translated by Nelson H. Vieira. Champaign, Ill.: Dalkey Archive Press, 2009. 389 p. (Latin American literature series)

Brandão's fascinating and kaleidoscopic novel (the fourth of his books to be translated into English), with its echoes of Machado's famous stories "O Espelho" and "Teoria da Medalhão," is a parable of our time in which celebrity itself, dispersed through the media, has become a central life goal. Brandão handles the theme with irony, humor, and gall, using short titled chapters, a variety of typefaces and sizes, and narrative voices. Vieira's expert translation energetically conveys the inventiveness and weirdness of the original. [DP]

3291 Coelho, Paulo. The winner stands alone. Translated from the Portuguese by Margaret Jull Costa. New York: Harper-Collins Publishers, 2009. 343 p.

Coelho's 12th novel veers considerably from his usual inspirational style. It is set during 24 hours at the Cannes Film Festival, in the glitzy world of the "super-class," as Coelho terms the powerful who congregate there. A somewhat strained philosophical-thriller, the book, Coelho says in his introduction, is intended as "a snapshot of my own time." Thematically akin to Brandão's *Anonymous Celebrity* (see item **3290**) (in this respect alone), the novel skewers the drive for glamour and fortune and the obsessive pursuit of fame. Costa's translation is highly skilled and fluent. [DP]

3292 Coutinho, José Domício. Duke, the dog priest. Translated by Clifford E. Landers. 1st Green Integer ed. København; Los Angeles, Calif.: Green Integer; Saint Paul, Minn.: Consortium Book Sales and Distribution, 2009. 495 p. (Masterworks of fiction (1998))

For decades, the Pernambucano Domício Coutinho has lived in New York, where he has become a major force in pro-

moting Brazilian culture, including through his activities as co-founder and president of the Brazilian Cultural Center (and its Brazilian public library) in Manhattan. Landers has produced a brilliant translation of Coutinho's inventive and endlessly entertaining 1998 novel that revolves around the lives of parishioners in a Manhattan Catholic Church. The world as understood by Duke, a dog eager to become a priest, is a quirky and fascinating novel, a worthy companion to Machado's *Quincas Borba*. [DP]

3293 Garcia-Roza, Luiz Alfredo. Alone in the crowd: an Inspector Espinosa mystery. Translated by Benjamin Moser. 1st U.S. ed. New York: Henry Holt and Co., 2009. 225 p.

The popularity among English-language mystery buffs of Garcia-Roza's melancholy and philosophical Inspector Espinosa continues with the publication of the seventh of this series to appear in English. This time, in a translation of Garcia-Roza's 2007 novel *Na multidão*, the inspector investigates the murder of an elderly woman, and in the process becomes embroiled in aspects of his own past. Moser's generally fluent translation is occasionally stilted, becoming overly literal and explanatory at times. [DP]

3294 Garcia-Roza, Luiz Alfredo. Blackout: an Inspector Espinosa mystery. Translated by Benjamin Moser. 1st U.S. ed. New York: Henry Holt and Co., 2008. 243 p.

Garcia-Roza by now has a loyal following for his Inspector Espinosa series, psychological thrillers set in Rio de Janeiro and featuring an intelligent and book-loving protagonist. The series is the object of glowing reviews in the English-language press. Originally published in Brazil as *Espinosa sem saída* in 2006, this sixth Espinosa novel revolves around the murder of a one-legged homeless man. Benjamin Moser, who has become Garcia-Roza's translator of choice, again produces a readable and faithful translation. For comment on Portuguese original, see item **2973**. [DP]

3295 Hatoum, Milton. Ashes of the Amazon. Translated by John Gledson. London: Bloomsbury, 2008. 278 p.

First published in Brazil in 2005, with the title *Cinzas do Norte* (see *HLAS 64:2284*), this is Hatoum's third novel

634 / Handbook of Latin American Studies v. 66

(and the third to win the prestigious Jabuti award). Set in Manaus, it tells the story of two boys, one rich (the rebellious protagonist, an artist seeking to escape his father's world), and one poor (the narrator, an orphan), against the backdrop of the military dictatorship. Gledson's translation is competent and faithful, yet on occasion is too formal. [DP]

3296 Hatoum, Milton. Orphans of Eldorado. Translated by John Gledson. Melbourne, Australia: Text Publishing Company, 2010. 164 p.

First published in Brazil in 2008, this is the 13th book in Canongate's much-admired Myths series. Hatoum creates a first-person narrative set in the heart of the Amazon and drawing on its rich lore. In a simple and engaging style, he combines a love story with local legends of the Enchanted City and other magical events. In an Afterword, Hatoum recounts how, as a child, he first heard this story from his grandfather, and only later realized it was a version of the fabled Eldorado, the much-sought-after city of gold. Gledson's translation is fluent and evocative. For comment on Portuguese original, see item **2975**. [DP]

3297 Lisboa, Adriana. Symphony in white. Translated from the Portuguese by Sarah Green. Edited by Irene Vilar. Lubbock, Tex.: Texas Tech Univ. Press, 2010. 192 p. (The Americas)

The recipient of numerous literary awards, Lisboa won the José Saramago Prize in 2003 for this novel, originally published in Brazil in 2001. It is a subtle, lyrical, and multivocal work, in which time is fragmented and memories clash, unfolding the story of two sisters who move between the rural Brazil of their childhood in the 1960s, and their later lives in Rio de Janeiro in the 1970s, carrying with them a secret that only slowly is revealed. Beautifully translated with a touch that maintains the delicacy and indirection of the original. [DP]

3298 Melo, Patrícia. Lost world. Translated by Clifford Landers. London: Bloomsbury, 2009. 214 p.

In her 2006 novel *Mundo perdido*, Melo continues the story of Máiquel, 10 years after his first appearance as protagonist of her second novel, *O Matador* (1995)

(see *HLAS 64: 2292*) [in English: *The Killer*, made into a film titled *Man of the Year*]. In this sequel Máiquel is on a quest to find Erica and his missing daughter Samantha. Landers' translation is lively, capturing well the colloquial voice of Máiquel, with occasional lapses into a too-formal register. [DP]

3299 Mussa, Alberto. The riddle of Qaf. Translated by Lennie Larkin. Laverstock, U.K.: Aflame, 2008. 211 p.

In this prize-winning novel originally published in 2004, Mussa, a Brazilian of Lebanese descent who also translates Arabic poetry, turns to pre-Islamic Arab legend, myth, and poetry to spin a tale of a Brazilian poet seeking to solve an ancient literary mystery. With 28 chapters representing the 28 letters of the Arabic alphabet, interspersed with "parameters" and "excursions," the novel is a mixed-genre work that is both fabulous and poetic. A love story as well as a meditation on language and history, this immensely challenging and erudite novel is competently, if somewhat too literally, translated by Larkin. [DP]

3300 Piñon, Nélida. Voices of the desert: a novel. Translated from Brazilian Portuguese by Clifford E. Landers. 1st American ed. New York: Alfred A. Knopf, 2009. 254 p.

Arabic literature is making a comeback in Brazil. Piñon's 2004 novel defends the art of storytelling by refocusing on the 14th-century Arabic classic *One Thousand and One Nights*, placing Scheherazade and her sisters at the center of the tale. In lush and dramatic prose, Piñon explores the inner and outer worlds of the brave and imaginative Scheherazade. Landers' translation is elegant and fluent, conveying effectively the tone and style of the original. At times, however, he seems to ignore Piñon's careful choice of words, leading to some anachronistic passages. [DP]

3301 Proença, Edyr Augusto. Hornets' nest. Translated by Richard Bartlett. Laverstock, U.K.: Aflame Books, 2007. 85 p.

This third novel by Edyr Augusto, a poet, playwright, and journalist from Belém do Pará, was originally published in Brazil in 2004. It is the first of Augusto's novels to be translated into English, and is a disturbing thriller, written in a staccato style with constantly shifting points of view. As Eugene Carey writes in the *Latin American Review of Books*, "This is a deep-fried rib of revenge with a lusty hot sauce cooked in a steaming Amazonian boiler—then served up with blood" (1 June 2007). Bartlett's translation is biting, vivid, and intense. [DP]

3302 Sabino, Mario. The day I killed my father. Translated by Alison Entrekin. Melbourne, Australia: Scribe Publications, 2009. 183 p.

Originally published in Brazil in 2004, this first novel by prize-winning short story writer Mario Sabino (who is also editor-in-chief of the magazine *Veja*) presents a Portnoy-esque narrative, in which the narrator attempts to justify himself to his analyst. Entrekin's translation is outstanding, both faithful and fluent, conveying perfectly the unreliability and oddness of this narrator. [DP]

3303 Tezza, Cristovão. The eternal son. Translated by Alison Entrekin. Melbourne, Australia: Scribe, 2010. 218 p.

Tezza's autobiographical novel, first published in Brazil in 2007, won numerous prizes (including the Jabuti). It is a disturbing and even brutal work, in which Tezza perhaps distances himself from a too-familiar reality by creating a third-person narrative, covering several decades in the life of a father struggling with his sense of shame at having a son with Down syndrome. Beautifully translated by Alison Entrekin in a compelling and at times poetic tone. [DP]

Essays, Interviews, and Reportage

3304 Cunha, Euclides da. Backlands: the Canudos Campaign. Translated by Elizabeth Lowe. Introduction by Ilan Stavans. New York: Penguin Books, 2010. 513 p.: bibl., index. (Penguin classics)

Elizabeth Lowe has undertaken an ambitious and long overdue project: a new and more accessible translation of Eúclides da Cunha's classic *Os Sertões* (1902), an account of the Brazilian government's campaign in the 1890s against the messianic religious leader Antonio Conselheiro and his 30,000 followers, who had settled in Canudos, in the state of Bahia. Then a journalist from São Paulo, da Cunha went to Canudos to report on the campaign and produced a complex and challenging work long considered a masterpiece of Brazilian literature. The English translation by Samuel Putnam, published in 1944 as *Rebellion in the Backlands*, attempted to replicate the ornate and often convoluted prose of the original. By contrast, Lowe's aim, she tells us, is to "inject new life" into the text, and she has succeeded in this by modernizing the language and opting for a freer and more straightforward version of the original. Her translation will make da Cunha's book accessible to a new generation of readers. The Penguin edition includes an informative introduction by Ilan Stavans, who also compares Putnam's and Lowe's translation decisions. [DP]

3305 Sattamini, Lina Penna. A mother's cry: a memoir of politics, prison, and torture under the Brazilian military dictatorship. Edited and with an introduction by James N. Green. Translated by Rex P. Nielson and James N. Green. Epilogue by Marcos Penna Sattamini Arruda. Durham, N.C.: Duke Univ. Press, 2010. 188 p.: bibl., index.

Originally published in Portuguese in 2000, this memoir utilizes numerous contemporaneous letters written during and after the arrest of Marcos Arruda, Lina Sattamini's son, in 1970 during the most repressive phase of the Brazilian dictatorship. Following nine months of imprisonment and torture, Marcos Arruda was released, thanks to the untiring struggle waged by his family, which then went into exile. Sattamini's narrative is completed by a 35-page memoir written by the son, describing his imprisonment. An important contribution to the historical record of the dictatorship and its procedures, as well as an inspiring story of love and endurance. [DP]

3306 Staden, Hans. Hans Staden's true history: an account of cannibal captivity in Brazil. Edited and translated by Neil L. Whitehead and Michael Harbsmeier. Durham, N.C.: Duke Univ. Press, 2008. 206 p.: bibl., ill., index, maps. (The cultures and practice of violence series)

A key document in 16th-century European views of the New World, Staden's controversial first-person account of his nine months' captivity among the Tupi

Indians was originally published in Germany in 1557. This is the first new translation of this foundational text since 1928, and has an excellent and fully annotated critical introduction of over 100 pages stressing the work's importance for ethnographic, literary, and historical studies. The volume also restores the 56 woodcuts from the original 1557 German edition. A major contribution to colonial studies. For colonial historian's comment, see item 1957. [DP]

BIBLIOGRAPHY, THEORY, AND PRACTICE

3307 **Arrojo, Rosemary.** Translation, transference, and the attraction to otherness: Borges, Menard, Whitman. (*in* Conferencia Internacional Traducción e Intercambio Cultural en la Época de la Globalización, Barcelona, 2006. (Actas. Frankfurt am Main: P. Lang, 2008, p. 1–32)

In this major article on Borges as reader, translator, and writer, Arroja investigates Borges' view of translation "as a form of rewriting which is not in any way neutral or secondary to the original" (p. 1). To do that, and also to examine the significance of a translator's choice of texts with which to work, she looks at "the paradigmatic relationship" between Borges' interest in translation early in his career, his own first poem, and the translation of *Leaves of Grass*, produced half a century later. [CM]

3308 **Bastin, Georges L.** Francisco de Miranda: intercultural forerunner. (*in* Agents of translation. Edited by John Milton and Paul Bandia. Amsterdam; Philadelphia: John Benjamins Publishing Company, 2009, p. 19–42)

Georges L. Bastin's article about "the first universal criollo" and the "Intellectual Precursor of translation in Hispanic America" examines the life and thought of Venezuelan Francisco de Miranda (1750–1816); Miranda's translation of Juan Pablo Viscardo y Guzmán's *Lettre aux Espagnols-américains*; the extensive influence he exerted during the period he lived in London; and his collaboration with publicists as "an agent of propaganda through sponsoring newspapers and books." A comprehensive and fascinating essay about a man known

primarily for revolutionary activities of a different sort. [CM]

3309 **Bradford, Lisa Rose.** The agency of the poets and the influence of their translations: *Sur, Poesía Buenos Aires,* and *Diario de Poesía* as aesthetic arenas for twentieth-century Argentine letters. (*in* Agents of translation. Edited by John Milton and Paul Bandia. Amsterdam; Philadelphia: John Benjamins Publishing Company, 2009, p. 19–42)

Lisa Rose Bradford's interest lies in "the role of poetry translation in the development of Argentine twentieth-century literature," in particular the contributions of poet/translators to the three major literary journals in her title. She provides background discussion of the cultural and historical/political moment in Argentina, with an emphasis on translation production, and then discusses in depth the complex work of poet/translator "agents introducing and interweaving avant-garde aesthetics through relatively conservative techniques" to present and disseminate foreign work in Argentina but also to "fortify their own aesthetic stance." A difficult article to summarize but an excellent study of contemporary Argentine poetry; the role of literary magazines; and the efforts of poets and translators to bring attention to and incorporate new, international work and simultaneously maintain an individual voice. [CM]

3310 **Gentzler, Edwin.** Translation and identity in the Americas: new directions in translation theory. New York: Routledge, 2007. 214 p.: bibl., index.

Working from an understanding of translation in the Americas as "less something that happens between separate and distinct cultures and more something that is *constitutive* of those cultures" (p. 5), Gentzler has looked at translation activity by focusing on five geographical regions: the US, where he studies multiculturalism; Canada, where he looks at theater and feminist translation practice; Brazil, where his focus is the cannibalism of Haroldo and Augusto de Campos; Latin America, where he studies fiction; and the Caribbean, where his interest is border writing. His discussions of each and of what he terms "internationality" will interest all readers of Latin American literature in translation. [CM]

3311 Grossman, Edith. Why translation matters. New Haven, Conn.: Yale Univ. Press, 2010. 135 p.: bibl., index. (Why X matters)

Prompted by an invitation to give a series of lectures at Yale University about "Why X Matters"—and to define the 'X,' Edith Grossman quite naturally chose translation. Three of the four chapters in her book (in which she addresses both general questions of literary translation and, more specifically, her own work as a translator), are based on those lectures. The fourth is devoted to translating poetry. Grossman has translated many of the most influential contemporary Latin American writers, and readers will find her comments about translation and its role in literary relations to be interesting and often provocative. [CM]

3312 Leone, Leah. La novella cautiva: Borges y la traducción de *Orlando*. (*Var. Borges*, 25, 2008, p. 223–226)

As Leah Leone notes, Virginia Woolf could never have imagined the enormous impact that Borges' translation of *Orlando* would have on Latin American literature. That translation, given both its influence and the international importance of its translator, has received no small amount of critical study. Leone's essay, however, offers a commentary on what she defines as the translation's "popularidad inquietante," and "la neutralización o hasta el sabotaje . . . de precisamente estos elementos del género que han hecho de *Orlando* un texto fundamental de los studios feministos y queer" (p. 224). In a second article ("A Translation of His Own: Borges and A Room of One's Own," *Woolf Studies Annual*, Vol. 12, 2009, p. 48–66), she studies Borges' work from a similar perspective, not "to denounce a translator in 1935 for not adhering to standards of a feminist scholar in 2009," but in an effort to "highlight the aspects of Borges's translation strategy that have created undermining or contradictory meanings in the text" and their "consequences" for the book in Spanish (p. 48). [CM]

3313 MacIntosh, Fiona J. Alejandra Pizarnik as translator. (*Translator/Manchester*, 16:1, 2010, p. 43–44)

Alejandra Pizarnik's work has been widely read and translated in recent years, but her own translations have not yet received much study. In this article, MacIntosh goes a long way toward remedying that lack of attention by examining Pizarnik's "two major published translation projects": André Breton and Paul Éluard's *L'Immaculée conception* and Marguerite Duras' *La vie tranquille*. She also studies the close interrelation between Pizarnik's translations, "her own aesthetic convictions, and . . . the radically changed socioliterary context of the moment of translation" (p. 43). [CM]

3314 Metherd, Molly. Transnational book markets and literary reception in the Americas. (*CLC Web*, 10:3, 2008, http://docs .lib.purdue.edu/clcweb/vol10/iss3/3/)

Molly Metherd uses the work of Chilean author Alberto Fuguet as a case study in this in-depth exploration of transnational publishing and the activities of US-American and Spanish American writers who "are taking advantage of this shifting field to redefine the problematic and largely misunderstood relationships between nations in the Americas." She shows how, on the one hand, the mass media are a force of homogenization but, on the other hand, they open new opportunities for writers, in this instance, Fuguet, who exploits "these new modes of literary distribution and consumption and who negotiates the oppositional forces of corporate publishing and self-fashioning through the world wide web and the internet." Her incisive observations and comments will be of interest to all readers of work from Latin America. [CM]

3315 Millones Figueroa, Luis. Colonial Andean texts in English translation. (*LARR*, 44:2, 2009, p. 181–192)

An exemplary review article that examines in detail new editions and translations of six essential primary texts from the colonial period: Felipe Guaman Poma de Ayala's *The First New Chronicle and Good Government* (see *HLAS 64:2547*); Inca Garcilaso de la Vega's *Royal Commentaries of the Incas and the General History of Peru* (see *HLAS 64: 2557*); Pedro Sarmiento de Gamboa's *The History of the Incas* (see *HLAS 64:2554*); and Diego de Castro Titu Cusi Yupanqui's *An Inca Account of the History of Peru* (see *HLAS 64:2559*), *History of How the Spaniards Arrived in Peru* (see *HLAS 64:2558*), and

Titu Cusi: A 16th Century Account of the Conquest (see *HLAS 64:2560*). As Maureen Ahern remarked in an earlier volume of the *Handbook*, the publication of these texts has brought them the "significant and long-overdue attention they deserve" (see *HLAS 64*, p. 463). Her comments, together with Luis Millones Figueroa's thoughtful and thorough discussion of the decisions and contributions made by the volumes' translators and editors, provide students and scholars with an excellent evaluation and orientation. [CM]

3316 Munday, Jeremy. Style and ideology in translation: Latin American writing in English. New York: Routledge, 2008. 261 p.: bibl., index. (Routledge studies in linguistics; 8)

As Jeremy Munday explains, the focus of his study is two-fold: "how and why style differs in translation, how we might approach the subject of style and choice by centring on the translator and the compostion of the target text" (p. 1). In order to answer those questions, he offers six case studies in the context of two extensive theoretical chapters, in one of which he examines discursive presence, voice, and style in translation practice; the other looks at the "ideological macro-text" with respect to the translation of Latin America. In the case studies, he examines most specifically the work of Harriet de Onís and Gregory Rabassa; the "multiple voices" of Gabriel García Márquez; audiovisual translation, using Senel Paz's *Fresa y chocolate* as an example; political ideology; and identity. Munday knows that even as he answers the questions he has posed for himself, he will raise new questions (p. 7). That's the strength of a work like his, though, and

readers will welcome both his book and the questions it poses. [CM]

3317 Pollack, Sarah. Latin America translated (again): Roberto Bolaño's *The Savage Detectives* in the United States. (*Comp. Lit.*, 61:3, 2009, p. 346–365, bibl.)

Following an overview of the production and reception of Latin American literature in English translation in the US, Pollack offers a detailed case study of Roberto Bolaño's *The Savage Detectives* (see *HLAS 60:36290* and *HLAS 64:2513*). What she finds is that, despite its break with the esthetics of the "boom," in particular magical realism, Bolaño's novel has been received in the same reductive way that made possible the enormous success of *One Hundred Years of Solitude*. Thus, she argues, the novel "unintentionally feeds" an image of Latin America in the "US collective imagination" (p. 360) and "plays on a series of opposing characteristics that the United States has historically employed in defining itself [in a highly positive way] vis-à-vis its neighbors to the south" (p. 362). [CM]

3318 *Translation Review.* No. 77/78, 2009. Richardson, Tex.: Univ. of Texas at Dallas.

This special issue, guest-edited by Charles Hatfield, comprises a generous selection of essays by translators about specific translations; translated texts, accompanied by extensive translator's comments; and 11 book reviews that offer in-depth readings of recent translations. Essays include, for example, a discussion of Jorge Luis Borges (by Suzanne Jill Levine), Ricardo Piglio (by Sergio Waisman), and William Carlos Williams' work with Jorge Carrera Andrade (by Keith Ellis). [CM]

MUSIC

GENERAL

3319 Béhague, Gerard. La problemática de la identidad cultural en la música culta hispano-caribeña. (*Lat. Am. Music Rev.*, 27:1, Spring/Summer 2006, p. 38–46, bibl.)

Gerard Béhague (1937–2005), dedicated his life to the music of Latin America, especially ethnomusicology. He specialized in the music of the Andes, Brazil, and the influence of West Africa on the Caribbean and South America. Born in France and raised in Rio de Janeiro, he presented this essay originally at the Tercer Foro de Compositores del Caribe in San Juan, Puerto Rico in October, 1990. The editors of the *Latin American Music Review* are to be congratulated for dedicating this entire issue to the work of Béhague and for publishing this excellent essay which examines the musical philosophy of the region's composers of "música culta." The essay explores the influences of a European-centric music, nationalism, and the quest of composers to create and maintain their own appropriate "voice." [A. Lemmon]

3320 Pérez de Arce, José. Análisis de las cualidades sonoras de las botellas silbadoras prehispánicas de los Andes. (*Bol. Mus. Chil. Arte Precolomb.*, 9, 2004, p. 9–33, bibl., photos, ills.)

Organological and acoustic study of "whistling bottles," ceramic globular flutes that produce sound as a result of the movement of liquid within their chamber(s), which were found prominently among prehispanic cultures of the coastal Andean region. Based on direct examination of 28 bottles at the Museo Chileno de Arte Precolombino and data from other published sources, the author provides an overview of the instrument's diffusion, its structural characteristics, and probable uses. [J. Ritter]

3321 Tablante, Leopoldo. Los sabores de la salsa: de la rumba brava a la fiesta mansa, de Héctor Lavoe a Jennifer López. Catia, Venezuela: Museo Jacobo Borges, 2005. 288 p.: bibl., ill.

A genre study and social history of salsa music, written by a Venezuelan sociologist. After brief introductory chapters on the images and sounds of salsa, the author traces the genre's history through an analysis of its lyrics, opposing the "misogyny and resignation" of *salsa brava* in the 1970s to its "socially-conscious" counterparts, then following the rise of erotic, romantic, and ultimately "salsa pop" in the 1980s and 90s. Includes more than 20 full-color images of important salsa albums and figures. [J. Ritter]

3322 Tickner, Arlene B. Aquí en el ghetto: hip-hop in Colombia, Cuba, and Mexico. (*Lat. Am. Polit. Soc.*, 50:3, Fall 2008, p. 121–146, bibl.)

Comparative study of hip-hop reception and local production in three Latin American countries. The author argues that the homogenizing effects of hip-hop's commercialization and global market reach must be held in tension with the ways that the genre has been localized and adapted within particular contexts, drawing particularly on theoretical writings by Michel de Certeau, Paul Gilroy, and Nestor García Canclini in making the latter point. After a brief discussion of hip-hop's origins and commodification in the US, the bulk of the article traces the genre's development in Colombia, Cuba, and Mexico, focusing primarily on the social and political engagements of particular groups and songs through lyric analysis. [J. Ritter]

CENTRAL AMERICA AND THE CARIBBEAN

ALFRED E. LEMMON, *Director, Williams Research Center, The Historic New Orleans Collection*

THE ITEMS SELECTED for commentary invariably reflect the status of scholarship on the music of the Caribbean, Cuba, and Central America. The present selection is no exception. However, this volume provides us with the opportunity to recall critical publications that have had a resounding impact on the study of the region's music and to indicate emerging trends in available resources.

First and foremost among the critical works studying the region's music is Robert M. Stevenson's *A Guide to Caribbean Music History* (See *HLAS 38:9081*). Originally a typewritten, 103-page bibliographic supplement to a paper presented by Dr. Stevenson at the 1975 meeting of the Music Library Association meeting in San Juan, Puerto Rico, the guide was later expanded into "Caribbean Music History: A Selective Annotated Bibliography with Musical Supplement" and published in the *Inter-American Music Review* 4:1, 1985). Revised, expanded, and presented in a more luxurious format than the 1975 version, it remains (35 years after its initial appearance) indispensable. In 1970, Carroll Edward Mace published his *Two Spanish Quiché Dance-Dramas of Rabinal* (see *HLAS 36:3933* and *HLAS 36:4899*). Published as Number 3 (1970) of the Tulane Studies in Romance Languages and Literature, the 221-page work, along with Barbara Bode's "The Dance of the Conquest of Guatemala" (Middle American Research Institute, Tulane University, Publications 27, 1961, p. 203–298) revealed the wealth of material awaiting both linguists and ethnomusicologists in Guatemala. While Bode later focused her attention on other topics, Mace continued to study Guatemalan dance-drama and contributed articles to scholarly journals, such as his epochal "Algunos apuntes sobre los bailes de Guatemala y de Rabinal" (see *HLAS 60:4436*) and countless encyclopedia articles to the 10-volume *Diccionario Española e Hispano-Americana*. Now, decades later, he has produced another volume, *Los negritos de Rabinal y el juego del tun* (see item **3339**), and the Universidad Francisco Marroguin has announced the forthcoming publication of his *Los negritos de Rabinal: los otros juegos.*

Malena Kuss, a former student of Stevenson and now Professor Emeritus of the University of North Texas, Denton, actively represented Latin America in numerous international dictionary projects during the course of her 25 years (1976–99) at North Texas. In her capacity as Secretary of the Bibliography Commission of the International Association of Music Libraries, Archives, and Documentation Centers for two terms (1984–90), she advanced the status of Latin American music through her bibliographical contributions. More recently, she edited the four-volume *Music in Latin America and the Caribbean*. Volume 2, *Performing the Caribbean experience*, is a remarkably scholarly, panoramic view of the musical development of the Caribbean (item **3330**).

The Music Library Association journal, *Notes*, (34, 1977 p. 27–38) included Catherine A. Dower's article, "Libraries with Music Collections in the Caribbean Islands" on doing research on Caribbean musicology. Fortunately, the researcher's task is easier today as one can easily access information via the internet on significant Caribbean manuscript and sound recording collections. Kenneth M. Bilby's Jamaican Maroon Collection is available at the Library of Congress (http://hdl.loc.gov/loc.afc/eadafc.afoo2001). The collection includes his audio field recordings made in various Caribbean locations from 1974 to 2008. Likewise, the University of Pennsylvania's Folklore and Folklife archives website (http://www.sas.upenn

.edu/folklore/center/archive.html) presents descriptions and inventories of the Roger D. Abrahams Caribbean Recorded Sound and Manuscript Collection, the Jane and Horace Beck West Indies Recordings Collection, the Jacob Elder Recorded Sound and Manuscript Collection (West Indies), and the Mac Edward Leach Recorded Sound and Manuscript Collection. Florida International University is home to the Diaz-Ayala Cuban and Latin American Popular Music Collection and has developed an impressive website for the collection (http://latinpop.fiu.edu/).With more than 100,000 items (including recordings, books, music, and other media), the site spans the vast history of popular music of the region. The collection's website boasts an online version of Diaz-Ayala's *Encyclopedic Discography of Cuban Music* that covers the years 1898–1960. In addition, the collections are searchable online.

In *HLAS 62*, this section began to include commentaries of sound recordings, particularly of the colonial period. In this offering, attention must be drawn to the appearance of *Music and Politics* (http://www.music.ucsb.edu/projects/musicandpolitics/index.html) a peer-reviewed, inter-disciplinary electronic journal established in 2007. Undoubtedly this emerging media will become ever more critical for scholars of the region's music. At the same time, it is noteworthy that traditional musicological journals have taken more notice of Latin America and the Caribbean during the past two years. *The Musical Quarterly*, a premier US scholarly journal dedicated to music founded in 1915, presented its first theme issue devoted to Latin American music (92/3–4, 2009). The issue includes Rebecca Bodenheimer's essay on regionalism in Cuban dance music (item **3345**). The University of Toulouse's *Musicorum* dedicated an issue to the St. Domingue violinist, composer, and the first musician member of France's Academie Française, Michel Paul Guy de Chabanon (item **3331**).

Lastly, we note with sadness that Dr. Donald Thompson, a long-time advocate of music in Puerto Rico, died. Thompson (February 28, 1928–February 23, 2010) was a founding member of the University of Puerto Rico's music department. The organizer and director of the institution's major music ensembles, he taught courses of music history and research methods. In addition, he served as musical director for zarzuelas, musical comedy, and opera. He is primarily known to users of the *Handbook of Latin American Studies* as an author of books and scholarly articles concerning Puerto Rico. He was editor of several journals and the editor for Puerto Rico of the *Diccionario Española e Hispano-Americana*. His contributions were critical in bridging the divide between English and Spanish scholarship. Particularly noteworthy was his *Music and Dance in Puerto Rico from the Age of Columbus to Modern Times: An Annotated Bibliography*, a work co-authored in 1991 with his wife Dr. Annie Thompson and containing more than 900 bibliographic references (see *HLAS 58:1839*).

THE CARIBBEAN (EXCEPT CUBA)

Creolizing contradance in the Caribbean. See *HLAS 65:1544*.

3323 Díaz Ayala, Cristóbal. San Juan-New York: discografía de la música puertorriqueña, 1900–1942. Río Piedras, Puerto Rico: Publicaciones Gaviota, 2009. 327 p.

In 1994, Cristóbal Díaz Ayala published *Cuba Canta y Baila: Discografía de la Música Cubana, 1898–1925*. It documented some 3800 recordings of that particular period when acoustical commercial recordings, as opposed to electrical recordings, were done. Florida International University Libraries, which houses Díaz Ayala's extensive collection of Cuban music, has maintained an electronic database of the

1994 publication, as well as for the subsequent period of 1925–60 (http://latinpop.fiu .edu/discography.html). Díaz Ayala's publication devoted to Puerto Rican music is a similarly monumental discography. Robert Stevenson in "The Latin American Music Educator's Best Ally: the Latin American Musicologist" (*Inter-American Music Review*, 2:2, 1980, p. 120–122) observed that while efforts were needed to document the classical music tradition, "another musicological task that sorely needs attention is the conscientious appraisal of popular music purveyed everywhere in Latin America . . . ." The efforts of Díaz Ayala have done much to promote such study. It is hoped that his scientific efforts will be emulated.

3324 Díaz Díaz, Edgardo. Danza antillana, conjuntos militares, nacionalismo musical e identidad dominicana: retomando los pasos perididos del merengue. (*Lat. Am. Music Rev.*, 29:2, Fall/Winter 2008, p. 232–262, bibl.)

Employing a bibliography spanning more than 140 years, Díaz Díaz explores the common threads of the danza and the merengue. Focusing on the period from the late 1860s to late 1920s, the present article should be read in conjunction with the same author's "El merengue dominicano: una prehistoria musical en diez pasos" (*El Merengue en la cultura dominicana y del Caribe*. Edited by Darío Tejeda and Rafael Emilio Yunen, Santiago: Centro León, 2006; p. 179–209.) Employing printed sources from as early as 1848, manuscript materials from Spain's Archivo General Militar (Segovia), to the most current publications, he examines the links between the danza and merengue, the role of Puerto Rican military musicians in the Dominican Republic, the repertoire of the same musicians, and a host of varying factors musical and nonmusical. The role of music in Santo Domingo national identity and the musical interaction between Puerto Rico, Santo Domingo, and Cuba are clearly outlined.

3325 Dudley, Shannon. Carnival music in Trinidad: experiencing music, expressing culture. New York: Oxford Univ. Press, 2004. 114 p.: bibl., discography, ill., index, 1 sound disc. (Global music series)

Intended for classroom use, it serves as an excellent introduction to Trinidad life and culture for the lay reader. Three themes prevail throughout the contribution: tradition, social identity, and performance. With chapters focusing on calypso texts, the actual music, and the steelband, Dudley traces the evolution of Trinidad music in the 20th century. Particularly important is the emergence of the steelband in the 1950s as the principal musical ensemble of Carnival and how it impacted calypso music. The volume concludes with a discussion of recently emerging Trinidad popular music.

Guadeloupe, Francio. Chanting down the new Jerusalem: calypso, Christianity, and capitalism in the Caribbean. See *HLAS 65:2619.*

3326 Guilbault, Jocelyne. Governing sound: the cultural politics of Trinidad's Carnival musics. Chicago: Univ. of Chicago Press, 2007. 343 p., 16 p. of plates: bibl., ill., index, music, 1 CD (4 3/4 in.). (Chicago studies in ethnomusicology)

Since the appearance of her PhD dissertation in 1984, Guilbault has focused on the music of the Caribbean. With four books to her credit, edited collections, 19 chapters in books, and more than 15 articles, she has firmly established a solid reputation in the field of Caribbean musical studies. Exploring the emergence of the carnival music industry, she successfully studies the tradition not only in Trinidad but with reference to other islands, as well as North American cities. The major problem facing so many scholars examining "popular" music is the lack of a well-organized archive. As a result, interviews were conducted not only with performers, but with a wide variety of participants ranging from audience members to sound technicians. In turn, the interviews were supplemented by newspaper articles. The study is well organized into two parts: the emergence of calypso in light of the political and cultural reality and how it contribution to the overall musical vocabulary. The second part of the volume, similarly focuses on the exchange between calypso and the political and cultural realities of Trinidad, this time looking at the post-independent era (beginning in 1962). An understanding of both pre- and post-1962 is necessary to understand the changes occurring after 1990, ranging from the development of musical forms to the participation of women and the evolving roles of government and the music industry. Of particular value is the inclusion of the criteria used for the various national competitions held during Carnival. The volume appropriately includes a CD with musical samples.

3327 Hernández, Alberto. Jesús María Sanromá: an American twentieth-century pianist. Lanham, Md.: Scarecrow Press, 2008. 339 p.: bibl., ill., index.

Jesús María Sanromá (1902–84) career is documented through more than 150 boxes of annotated books, scores, recordings, contracts, reviews, correspondence, interviews, and travel receipts. The result of eight years of researching these papers, Hernández's contribution shows how Sanromá's life is a reflection of the integration of Puerto Rican life into the US. For example, Sanromá served as orchestral pianist for the Boston Symphony Orchestra, and developed strong working relations with conductors Pierre Monteaux and Serge Koussevitsky and composer Paul Hindemith. As seen in the description of Sanromá's 112 day, 18 state, 48 city, US transcontinental tour in 1949, there is a wealth of information available on the impact of this pianist in the US. Unfortunately, the English is marred, on occasion, by a translation lacking in subtlety (for example: the Spanish term for "audition" being inaccurately translated as "performance"). Nonetheless, this is an important contribution that illustrates the developing musical relationship between Puerto Rico and the US.

3328 Howard, Dennis. Punching for recognition: the jukebox as a key instrument in the development of popular Jamaican music. (*Caribb. Q./Mona,* 53:4, Dec. 2007, p. 32–46, bibl., photo)

After a highly informative history of the jukebox, a late 19th-century invention, the essay traces the development of the jukebox in Jamaica. While a definite date of introduction is not absolute, all evidence indicates that it became common in the early 1950s. It actually followed the same trend as Great Britain, which in the 1930s had only a few, while by 1955 records indicate there were over 500. Noting the proximity to the US, an examination of the repertoire of the early jukeboxes in Jamaica reveals the popularity of such American rhythm and blues musicians such as Fats Domino,

Roscoe Garden, and Lloyd Price. However, the jukebox would soon emerge as a means of promoting Jamaican music. Likewise, the economic impact of jukeboxes was significant. Jukebox operators owned as many as 2000 boxes. They operated on a percentage basis with the bar and shop owners. Relating the importance of the jukebox in Jamaica the realms economic, social life and musical education, it is clearly evident that the role of the role of the jukebox in Jamaica music development was critical.

3329 Menéndez Maysonet, Guillermo. Francisco Pedro Cortés González: músico puertorriqueño de la Belle époque. Ponce, Puerto Rico: SIIM, Casa Paoli, 2007. 1 v. [multiple pagings]: bibl., ill., music (Col. Pájaro carpintero)

Francisco Pedro Cortés González (b. Ponce, Puerto Rico, 31 January 1873; d. New York, 20 July 1950) was a pianist and composer. Beginning a successful career at an early age, he continued his studies at the Liceo in Barcelona and later in Paris. Established as a conductor, he appeared at the Exposition Universelle of Paris in 1900. Remaining in France, he developed a successful career as a conductor with orchestras in Monte Carlo and Nice, as well as a ten-year period as conductor of the Casino Houlgate orchestra. Situated on the English Channel in Normandy, the casino boasted its own theater company and regularly hosted touring companies. The casino orchestra, which presented a daily concert from 11 am to 5 pm, was a major feature of the social acitivities. After returning to Puerto Rico, he eventually relocated to New York in 1914 where he established himself as a music teacher. The present volume covers his years in France and contains 10 compositions published by him between 1901 and 1905. The compositions selected for inclusion are all found in the Bibliotheque nationale de France. They stand as testimony to that particular institution as an important source of music for all of Latin America.

3330 Music in Latin America and the Caribbean: an encyclopedic history. v. 2, Performing the Caribbean experience. Edited by Malena Kuss. Austin: University of Texas Press, 2004. 1 v.: bibl., ill., index (Joe R. and Teresa Lozano Long series in Latin American and Latino art and culture)

This magnificent contribution is part of the Joe R. and Teresa Lozano Long Series in Latin American and Latino Art and Culture. With some 37 books published to date, it stands as testimony to the philanthropy of the individuals for whom the series is named. The philanthropic contributions of the Longs are substantial and have advanced both educational and cultural activities. This excellent assemblage by Malena Kuss, who gathered together 27 writers, is testimony of the Longs' philosophy that persistence and hard work offers unlimited opportunities. The scholars assembled represent some of the finest in the field. They represent both the healthy development of musicology in the region in American and European circles, but also within the Caribbean itself. While Cuba remains the most sophisticated Caribbean island in the realm of musicology, it is particularly gratifying to see the growth of trained musicologists in the region. A work that should be on every Latin Americanists' bookshelf, it illustrates the historically fluid, evolving nature of Caribbean culture and music. Cultural historians, sociologists, students of religion, linguistics, and a wide variety of disciplines will find much of value in this assemblage by Malena Kuss. The success of the present volume will only be appreciated in the future: when future authors acknowledge the innumerable doors opened by this particularly well designed compilation. The challenges of presenting lengthy essays of so many different scholars are enormous. The volume is a tribute not only to Malena Kuss, and the numerous individuals she thanked for their invaluable assistance, but to the editorial skills of the University of Texas Press staff. The various peoples (African, Chinese, Dutch, French, Spanish and indigenous peoples, to mention only a few) of the Caribbean found a highly creative voice in music that reflected their evolving history and identity. The contributors have successfully illustrated the resulting creativity of the region.

3331 *Musicorum:* 6, Michel Paul Guy de Chabanon et ses contemporains. Tours, France: Université François Rabelais.

A theme issue of *Musicorum*, a journal based at the University of Toulouse, explores the world of Michel Paul Guy de Chabanon and his contemporaries. A native of St. Domingue, de Chabanon (1703–92) achieved distinction as a violinist, composer, and writer on music theory. His prominence in French musical and intellectual circles is attested to by his election to the Académie des inscriptions et belles-lettres (1760) and the Académie Française (1779). He was a violinist in the Concert des Amateurs, which was under the direction of another musician of Caribbean origin, Joseph Boulgne, chevalier de Saint-Georges (1745–99). The current volume, indisciplinary in nature, examines de Chabanon's importance in literary, theatrical, and musical practice in 18th-century France. Bernard Camier's contribution, "Musicque et sociíeté colonial Saint-Domingue à l'époque de Chabanon," is typical of the highly researched and well-written articles on the topic of St. Domingue music that one expects of Camier. Camier's article on de Chabanon should be written in conjunction with the article of Laurent Dubois and Camier entitled "Volaire et Zaïre, ou le théâtre des lumières dans l'aire atlantique française," which appeared in *Revue d'histoire modern et contemporaine* (4, 2007). It is an examination of theaters and theatrical productions in Saint-Domingue, Martinique, Guadalupe, and Louisiana, and the role of both slaves and free people of color as actors, musicians, and audience.

3332 Neely, Daniel T. Calling all singers, musicians and speechmakers: mento aesthetics and Jamaica's early recording industry. (*Caribb. Q./Mona*, 53:4, Dec. 2007, p. 1–15, bibl., photo)

In the current contribution, Neely draws attention to several aspects of the early recording history of Jamaica. By examining the pioneers of the country's recording industry and their decisions, he is able to illustrate their impact on Jamaican music industry and identity. This work is based to a large degree upon oral history interviews conducted by the author with music industry pioneers Ken Khouri and Stanley Motta, and on sound scholarship. While other countries such as Cuba and Trinidad seized upon the possibilities of the recording industry significantly earlier, it was not until after WWII, in 1947 that Ken Khouri, an energetic and enterprising individual, launched the

Jamaican recording industry. The author's reference to a 1948 tourist lament that Jamaica did not have recordings "of all the native calypsos" clearly demonstrates the impact of foreign interest on the Jamaican music industry's success. Indeed, nearly all of the recordings of Khouri and Motta were destined for the tourist industry. As a result, a direct link between the tourism industry and the developing recording industry firmly established.

3333 Reggaeton. Edited by Raquel Z. Rivera, Wayne Marshall, and Deborah Pacini Hernandez. Durham, N.C.: Duke Univ. Press, 2009. 371 p.: bibl., ill., index. (Refiguring American music)

Reggaeton brings together critical assessments of this wildly popular genre. Journalists, scholars, and artists delve into reggaeton's local roots and its transnational dissemination; they parse the genre's aesthetics, particularly in relation to those of hip-hop; and they explore the debates about race, nation, gender, and sexuality generated by the music and its associated cultural practices, from dance to fashion. [CEG]

3334 Rommen, Timothy. "Come back home": regional travels, global encounters, and local nostalgias in Bahamian popular music. (*Lat. Am. Music Rev.*, 30:2, Fall/Winter 2009, p. 159–183, bibl., ill., music)

Outlining three major influences on the music of the Bahamas: (1) the relation of the Bahamas to the US, (2) tourism, and (3) colonial and post-colonial history, Rommen examines "rake-n-scrape" music in the light of the above. Performed on an accordion, a construction saw and a goatskin drum, "rake-n-scrape" music has, at times, been central to the musical experience of the Bahamas and, at other times, has dwelt on the periphery. The proximity to the US (as well as to other larger Anglo islands) has made the music of the Bahamas particularly vulnerable to the fashions of those regions. The impact of tourism has been critical. Cruise ships were not allowed to have onboard entertainment until a 1968–69 change in government regulations. Other tourism developments to impact local music were the rise of casinos during the 1960s and 70s, and the establishment of large, self-contained resorts. The impact on local

night clubs was tremendous. The music scene shifted from night club dance music to entertainment spectacles. Colonial vs. post-colonial history has manifested itself musically through myth, nostalgia, and a search for identity.

3335 Whylie, Marjorie. Ernest Ranglin, creative activist, initiator, innovator, living legend. (*Caribb. Q./Mona*, 53:4, Dec. 2007, p. 75–80, photo)

Born on June 19, 1932, Ranglin was raised in the small town of Robin's Hall, Manchester, Jamaica. Raised in that rural community, his musical initiation was in the hands of two uncles who were guitarists. Noting his natural musical ability, they gave him a ukele. The development of him as a self-taught musician parallels the leisure industry in Jamaica. Indeed, this contribution should be read together with the articles by Daniel Neely on the development of the recording industry (p. 1–14) and Howard Dennis' study of the jukebox (p. 32–46) as they provide tremendous insight into critical, interacting factors of Jamaican music. The essay, originally presented at a symposium at the University of the West Indies on May 21, 2001, examines his rhythmic and harmonic vocabulary, technical prowess, and the influence of African vs. European forms.

CENTRAL AMERICA

3336 Anderson, Guillermo. En busca de la música de la Mosquitia hondureña. (*Yaxkin/Tegucigalpa*, 24:2, 2008, p. 195–203, photos)

Based in La Ceiba, Anderson and his band Ceibana are known for the use of rhythms and folklore representative of the coastal regions of Honduras. He uses his music to draw attention to environmental, literacy, and health issues. This article is a personal narrative of his visits to the region in preparation for the CD "El Tesoro que tenés"; in it, he draws attention to the ethnic components of La Mosquitia, as well as the natural, tropical riches of the region. The essay is wonderfully illustrated by photographs, and the equally appealing video documenting the trips throughout the region may be viewed at http://es.youtube.com/watch?v=JHiHq_Abg2M. The availability of such resources is invaluable to a wide variety of teachers. At the same time, it poses the all-important question of preserving such resources for the future.

3337 Brenner, Helmut. Marimbas in Lateinamerika: historische Fakten und Status quo der Marimbatraditionen in Mexiko, Guatemala, Belize, Honduras, El Salvador, Nicaragua, Costa Rica, Kolumbien, Ecuador und Brasilien. Hildesheim; New York: Olms, 2007. 501 p.: bibl., discography, ill., index, maps. (Studien und Materialien zur Musikwissenschaft, 43)

Probably the first "global," as opposed to regional, study of marimbas, this comparative study, richly enhanced by a wide variety of photographs, drawings, and engravings, demonstrates the regional and historical variations of the instrument. It is a history of the instrument greatly influenced by the Sachs-Hornbostel system of classification of musical instruments, first published by Curt Sachs and Erich Moritz von Hornbostel in the *Zeitschrift für Ethnologie* (1914). It is an exhaustive study of the variety of marimbas based on both historical sources and actual observation of contemporary practice.

3338 Casasa Núñez, Laura. Malpaís: identidad y memoria en una propuesta musical costarricense. (*Cuad. Am./México*, 122:4, oct./dic. 2007, p. 139–150,)

An analysis of the songs presented to the public by the group Malpaís (organized in 1999) in Costa Rica. Noting particularly the role of nostalgia in the group's vocabulary, the author explores the lyrics which elaborate on themes such as "love," "youthful infancy," and "neighbors." The role of nostalgia is further strengthened by the use of historical photographs in the CD packaging. The author observes that the texts do not necessarily advocate a return to the past; rather, they are a response to the globalization and subsequent loss of identity.

3339 Mace, Carroll Edward. Los negritos de Rabinal y el juego del tun. Guatemala: Academia de Geografía e Historia de Guatemala, 2008. 352 p.: bibl., ill., index, maps. (Publicación Especial; 44)

Special publication number 44 of the Academia de Geografía e Historia de Guatemala, this is a continuation of the author's work on Quiché drama as practiced by the Achí Indians in and near Rabinal. Having begun to collect materials for this volume in 1958, Mace is able to focus both on the ancient origins of these plays, and also on their evolution. As it is virtually impossible to separate the literary from the music and dance aspects of these dramas, Mace, as a literary historian and musician, is in a unique position to evaluate and examine the history and modern practices of these incredibly rich manifestations of indigenous life. Mace presents comical parodies that chronicle the most routine of village occurrences, ranging from merchant life to marriages. Musically, the dances can be linked to western Spain as they are accompanied by a "Su" (a small flute) and "tamborcito" performed by one musician.

3340 Neustadt, Robert. Reading indigenous and mestizo musical instruments the negotiation of political and cultural identities in Latin America. (*Music Polit.*, 1:2, 2007, http://www.music.ucsb.edu/projects/musicandpolitics)

In his introduction to this fine essay, the author notes that he intends to explore "diverse examples of indigenous and mestizo musical instruments in order to underscore the manner in which these instruments can help us to comprehend the political negotiation and location of culture." Using examples primarily from Guatemala, Costa Rica, and southern Mexico, he illustrates his point in an exemplary fashion. He begins by citing how the Guatemalan *son* is representative of how the Hispanic, indigenous, and African cultures have merged to create a "local" music. He continues by stressing how musical instruments (ranging from the marimba, chirimia to violin) are manifestations of transculutural routes. A superb example is the chirimia. Of Islamic origins, it was brought to the Americas by Spanish missionaries. Indigenous peoples then transformed it into their own instrument. The author astutely illustrates how the instruments continue to evolve in the hands of modern composers. For example, Joaquín Orellana's *imbaluna* and *Ciclo Im* (of marimba derivation) enable him to develop new classical compositions inspired by the marimba tradition. This article is available on the e-journal's site in html and pdf versions.

3341 Pieper, Jim. Guatemala's masks &
drama. Torrance, Calif.: Pieper and
Associates; Albuquerque: Univ. of New
Mexico Press, 2006. 283 p.: bibl., col. ill.,
1 col. map.

The role of masks in Guatemalan
folk dances is fundamental. Pieper has
assembled a visually stunning volume
dedicated to the art of mask making, which
is a vital part of the native dance-dramas.
The volume fills a critical void in the understanding of such dance dramas. Most of
the bibliography on this found within the
pages of the periodical literature. While the
work does not rise to the level of Donald
Cordry's *Mexican Masks* (1980), it does fill
a void in understanding the Guatemalan
dance-dramas.

3342 Shátskaya, Ekaterina. Estudio del
contenido musical en las cinco misas
del compositor Julio Fonseca. (*Bol. Música/
Habana*, 22, 2008, p. 25–28)

Costa Rican composer Julio Fonseca
(May 22, 1885-June 22, 1950) studied at the
Milan and Brussels conservatories. After
completion of his studies he returned to
Costa Rica in 1906 and became one of the
country's most prolific composers. The
essay focuses attention on his five masses
written between 1920–40 and the use of can-
tus firmus, settings of text, and tonality vs.
modality. The author notes that while the
works are not necessarily of international
significance, they are important for understanding the musical vocabulary of Costa
Rica in the first half of the 20th century.

CUBA

3343 Alén Rodríguez, Olavo. Pensamiento
musicológico. La Habana: Letras
Cubanas, 2006 363 p.: bibl., ill. (Ensayo/Edi-
torial Letras Cubanas)

Olavo Alén Rodríguez's extensive
work as Director of the Centro de investigación y Desarrollo de la Música Cubana
(CIDMUC) allows him to offer a unique
perspective on Cuban music trends. The
present volume conveniently reunites a
wide variety of writings by Alén Rodriguez,
which would be difficult for a scholar to
locate. Particularly important are the essays
gathered together in the following sections:
"Apuntes para una historia de la musi-

cología" and "Reflexiones sobre la política
cutlral en el desarrollo de la música." In
those two sections, he outlines the needs for
the ongoing development of Cuban musicology and surveys the actual state of Cuban
music (ranging from musical education,
concert activity, and music as an industry).

**3344 Antología de la musica afrocubana =
Anthology of Afro-Cuban music.**
v. 1, Viejos cantos afrocubanos. v. 2, Oru
de lgbodu. v. 3, Música Iyesá. v. 4, Música
Arará. v. 5, Tambor yuka. v. 6, Fiesta de
Bembé. v. 7, Tumba Francesa. v. 8, Toque de
Güiros. v. 9, Congos. v. 10, Abakuá. Habana:
EGREM, 2005. 10 sound discs: digital;

María Teresa Linares is one of the
great musical legends of Cuba. As a researcher in the fields of ethnology and folklore at Academia de Ciencias de Cuba, as
director of the Museo Nacional de Música,
as a vice president of the Fondation Fernando Ortiz, and numerous other capacities
she has sought to document and promote
Cuba's vast musical legacy. Still working at
an age when less enthusiastic individuals
would have retired, Linares presents a 10
CD collection devoted to the diversity and
multi-faceted Afro-Cuban musical legacy.
Invaluable for any number of disciplines,
ranging from religious studies to music and
linguistics, the selected examples clearly
represent the breadth of the topic.

3345 Bodenheimer, Rebecca. "La Habana
no aguanta más": regionalism in
contemporary Cuban society and dance
music. (*Music Q.*, 92:3/4, Fall/Winter 2009,
p. 210–220)

In this special issue of the *Musical
Quarterly*, devoted entirely to Latin America, Bodenheimer examines how music
reflects the ongoing issues of regionalism
within Cuba. After an extensive analysis of
three selected compositions, she is able to
demonstrate that regional loyalties remain.
The compositions examined are "La Habana
no aguanta más," "Soy Cubano y soy de
Oriente," and "Un pariente en el campo."
She ably demonstrates by textual analysis
of these popular dance pieces that Cubans
remain faithful to their provincial identify, while the official government policy
stresses egalitarianism.

3346 García, David F. Arsenio Rodríguez and the transnational flows of Latin popular music. Philadelphia, Penn.: Temple University Press, 2006. 210 p.: bibl., discography, ill., index, music. (Studies in Latin American and Caribbean music)

Based on fieldwork and interviews in California, Havana and New York, as well as transcripts of interviews by other researchers and archival investigations, the life and musical career of Aresnio Rodrígues is traced from his days as a young musician in Cuba to his North American career in cities such as Chicago, Los Angeles, and New York. In this study of the self-proclaimed "originator" of the mambo, the author carefully notes that in many cases the racial identification of the music is not that of the performers, but in the intended audience.

3347 Giro, Radamés. Diccionario enciclopédico de la música en Cuba. La Habana: Letras Cubanas, 2007. 4 v.: bibl., ill., ports.

Containing approximately 2,800 entries, each with bibliography and many with multiple illustrations, this *Diccionario Enciclopédico* of Cuban music is the result of nearly four decades of work on the part of Radamés Giro. Not limited to one particular aspect of Cuban music, the work includes articles on composers, dances, musical instruments, musical forms, performers, venues, and a wide variety of incidental articles. Each article has an ample bibliography and illustrations (including both modern and historic photographs). along with musical examples and discography where appropriate. Particularly valuable are lists of compositions organized by composer. The work, apparently developed independently of *Diccionario de la Música Española e Hispanoamericana* published by the Sociedad General de Autores y Editores (2000), is free of the confines of space inherent in such massive international undertakings. As a result, it included far more articles on Cuban music and was able to include lengthy articles on other topics. In addition to focusing on Cuban composers, the encyclopedia includes information on foreign composers and performers, such as Nicholas Slonimsky and Bruno Walter, who either had careers in

Cuba or gave significant performances on the island. The dictionary is one of Cuba's most sweeping efforts to document the musical history of the island, building and enlarging upon the efforts of Helio Orovio's *Diccionario de la Musica Cubana* (see *HLAS 46:89a* and *HLAS 58:4809*; published in English as *Cuban Music from A to Z*, (2003)) and Alicia Valdés Cantero's studies on Cuban women in music. The work clearly reveals Giro's work as both an editor (Instituto Cubano del Libro) and music educator (assistant director of the Escuela Nacional de Música en Cubanacán).

3348 Manuel, Peter. From contradanza to son: new perspectives on the prehistory of Cuban popular music. (*Lat. Am. Music Rev.*, 30:2, Fall/Winter 2009, p. 184–212, ill.)

In this essay the author reviews the belief that the Cuban son emerged from Oriente and became popular in Havana in the early 20th century. It is now known that the musical form was "consolidated" in Havana between 1910 and 1920. Manuel, based upon the study of editions of Havana contradanzas from the 1850s-60s, shows the presence of several features of the son such as: the structure of melodies as duets, distinctive syncopations, and the reliance on a bi-partite structure. Comparing the printed material with early recordings Manuel demonstrates that certain rhythmic features of the son existed only in a very early stage in Oriente, but were developed in Havana.

3349 Moore, Robin. Music and revolution: cultural change in socialist Cuba. Berkeley: Univ. of California Press, 2006. 350 p.: ill., index, music. (Music of the African diaspora; 9)

Focusing on the development of Cuba's music since 1959, the author traces two particular themes: the musical genres that have been dominant since the Revolution and an examination of the forces that have shaped Cuban musical life during the same time period. Well known as an excellent scholar, Moore describes the lavish musical live of the 1950s, a musical period which could explain the Revolution. However, at the same time many remember it with great nostalgia. The complexities of the revolution are reflected in Cuba's response to the growth of the samba, in particular in the US and Puerto Rico. Yet, Cuba responded to the welcoming of the salsa in foreign lands with the songo and timba. The ongoing musical developments of the island are also reflected in nueva trova. Originally associated with highly individualistic singer-song writers—not necessarily in tune with the government—it was eventually accommodated by state musical institutions. The Afro-Cuban musical experience is testified to both as a sign of the unprejudiced view of the government, but also as process of tourist development through government funded folklore performing organizations. Moore has assembled a tremendous amount of data concerning the economy of music and musicians over the life of the revolution.

3350 Ruiz Pérez, Miviam. Archivística, musicología y redes en la creación de un archive personal de musica. (*Bol. Música/Habana*, 22, 2008, p. 25–28)

Employing the example of the papers of Cuban composer Carlo Borbolla (1902–90), examines techniques for exploring the organization of a composer's personal archive. Based largely on two recently published works—the *Biblioteca básica del archivero cubano* (2003) and Mayra Mena Mugica's *Gestión documental y organizacíon de archives* (2005), provides an excellent exposition of how to handle the papers of composers. Borbolla's output included more than 450 compositions and given the wealth of media involved, it is an ideal case study. The author effectively demonstrates that when the cataloging a manuscript collection, the relevance of the various items within the collection must be demonstrated, as well as their connection to the wider holdings of the institution, in this case the Museo Nacional de la Música.

3351 Thomas, Susan. Cuban zarzuela: performing race and gender on Havana's lyric stage. Urbana: Univ. of Illinois Press, 2008. 250 p.: bibl., ill., index, music.

Thomas' work reflects the long hours of solitude required of excellent scholarship. Using a wide variety of sources, she places the development of the Cuban zarzuela in the broader social context by astutely observing the impact of Cuban independence on shifts of population, the desire for appropriate entertainment for women, and the economic realities of the Cuban music industry of the 1920s and 30s. Such topics, seemingly easy to examine, challenge the scholar. The lack of published scores, a result of composers jealously guarding their work for necessary economic gain, has a tremendous impact on the present-day researcher. The analysis of text, for both social and musical exploration, requires an intimate knowledge of language, both spoken and written. In order to place the "social constructs" of race, class, and gender" of the Havana zarzuela in proper context, the author displays a strong knowledge of the physical differences of the city during the time period of the study and the present day, and is very sensitive to the nuances of Spanish as employed in Cuba. The documentary effort of this work is critical. The author's reliance upon private collections of generous individuals is an indication of challenges awaiting musicologists throughout Latin America. The efforts to document scores, libretti, and recordings will prove to be of great value to future scholars.

ANDEAN COUNTRIES

JONATHAN RITTER, *Assistant Professor of Ethnomusicology, University of California, Riverside*

SURVEYING THE LITERATURE published on music in and from the Andean region over the last several years, I am reminded of the ongoing debate and critique of "area studies" paradigms, particularly by Latin American scholars and others in the Global South, as an inherently confining and neo-colonial enterprise privileging North American scholarly views. Writing for the quintessential "area studies" publication, and focused on the topic of music, this may seem an odd and risky reference with which to begin a bibliographic essay, but I recall the critique for two reasons. First, a number of music scholars working in the Andes have begun to grapple with issues of cultural policy, neoliberalism, and the history of colonialism in ways that engage, both directly and indirectly, with this debate (see particularly items 3355 and 3360; also 3352, 3358, and 3376). These articles resurrect and refine issues also addressed a decade ago by Javier León ("Peruvian Musical Scholarship and the Construction of an Academic Other," *Latin American Music Review*, 20:2, Autumn/Winter 1999, p. 168–183, bibl.), and by Raúl Romero ("Tragedies and Celebrations: Imagining Foreign and Local Scholarships," *Latin American Music Review*, 22:1, Spring/Summer 2001, p. 48–62, bibl.). With the recent establishment of both a School of Music and a cultural studies graduate program at the Pontificia Universidad Católica del Peru in Lima, and a similar critical mass of young music scholars in Bogotá and elsewhere in Colombia, this sort of postcolonial critical perspective will likely be a regular feature of musical scholarship from the Andes for some time.

Second, multiple entries here highlight the ways in which categorizing or delimiting music scholarship (or music itself) by "area"—whether region or nation—is increasingly untenable in an era of rapid globalization and instantaneous digital communications. José Olvera's ethnography of Colombian music in Monterrey, Mexico (item 3359), offers a perfect illustration of the sort of transnational flows and categorical conundrums marking most music production and reception today, as does Arlene Tickner's comparative analysis of hip-hop in New York, Cuba, Colombia, and Mexico (item 3322). Some of the most compelling recent work done on "Andean music" complicates the matter even further. Fernando Rios' early history of Andean folkloric music presentations in Europe traces the development of the quintessential Andean ensemble from the folk music clubs of Buenos Aires to the Left Bank clubs of Paris in the mid-20th century, effectively placing the most influential years in the development of this style outside of the Andean region altogether, amidst a global reshuffling of political alliances and cultural influences (item 3420).

Though transnational scholarship and the study of musical migrations certainly constitute major trends, much scholarship on music in the Andes continues to hew to national and stylistic boundaries. In terms of the latter, popular music studies again dominate output, from monographs and articles on pan-Latin genres like *salsa* and *bolero* (items 3321 and 3352), to studies of national(ist) genres like the Ecuadorian *pasillo* and *música rocolera* (items 3363 and 3365). One promising development within Andean popular music studies is the growing focus on media circulation, technology, and the recording industry, a trend best represented here in the works by Pereira et.al. on the culture industry in Colombia (item 3356), Stobart on piracy and new media in Bolivia (item 3353), Tucker's analysis of recording studio and radio DJ practices in "Andean Lima" (item 3383), and Llorens' and Chocano's emphasis on the role of the recording industry in their history of the Peruvian *vals* (item 3370).

Curiously, recent years have witnessed a notable downturn in ethnographic studies of indigenous and/or other forms of folkloric or traditional music, once the mainstay of ethnomusicological work in the region. Among the exceptions,

Michelle Wibblesman's ethnography of ritual festival practices in Otavalo, Ecuador (item 3367), and Zoila Mendoza's ethnographically informed history of folkloric music and dance in early 20th-century Cuzco stand out for their clarity of writing and depth of research (item 3378). Other notable titles include Swiss ethnomusicologist Claude Ferrier's two volumes on harp-related traditions in Peru (items 3372 and 3373), Raúl Romero's edited, beautifully illustrated, coffeetable-sized volume on festival music, dance, and theater in highland Peru (item 3374), and a new edition of Daniel Castro's ethnography of indigenous musics in the Lake Maracaibo area, winner of the Casa de las Americas musicology prize in 1995 (item 3388). Research on prehispanic music continues as well; recent articles include technical studies of ceramic flutes and other instruments held in archeological museums in Arequipa (item 3385) and Chile (item 3320), as well as extraordinary ethnohistorical work on Inca vocal genres and performance at the time of the Spanish conquest (item 3382).

In contrast to the relative paucity of ethnographic work, the last few years yielded an unexpected burst of publications on Western art music in the Andes. Among works on music during the colonial era, British ethnomusicologist Geoffrey Baker's impressive new monograph on sacred music and social life in colonial Cuzco stands out as a major achievement (item 3369), while Louise Stein's lengthy article (item 3380) on the social and cultural context in which the first opera was written in the Americas—Tomás de Torrejón's *La Púrpura de la Rosa*, in 1701—will surely be a frequent reference source for students and teachers of this oft-mentioned but little-studied work.

Contemporary Western art music institutions in the Andes were also subject to scholarly attention, though at times wistfully so. As recent Nobel laureate Mario Vargas Llosa notes in his prologue to a commemorative volume celebrating the centennial of Lima's Philharmonic Society (item 3371), the Western classical tradition holds a relatively marginal place in the cultural life of contemporary Peru. Without subscribing to Vargas Llosa's ethnocentrism—he refers to the Philharmonic Society as "an oasis in the great desert of Peruvian musical culture. . . a solitary raft where one could take refuge from the shipwreck of our cultural life"—other contributors to the volume, while tracing the history of both the orchestra and major figures in its musical life, also acknowledge the embattled position occupied by art music institutions in the country.

The situation does not appear as dire elsewhere in the Andes. As reflected in Nancy Yañez' history of opera and musical theater in Quito (item 3368) and Pablo Guerrero's biography of Ecuadorian composer Juan Pablo Muñoz Sanz (item 3362), both the Conservatorio Nacional de Música and the Orquesta Sinfónica Nacional are thriving in that country. José Jaramillo's history of the Orquesta Filarmónica de Bogotá (item 3357), though focused unfortunately more on administrative organization than creative activity, also demonstrates the steady presence and growth of classical music in Colombia in recent decades. The greatest success story lies in Venezuela, thanks almost entirely to Jose Abreu's famed *sistema* of music education and youth orchestras, which has survived and thrived despite seismic shifts in the political and cultural landscape of the country over the past four decades. And due to the international career of its most famous graduate, Gustavo Dudamel (now music director of the Los Angeles Philharmonic), the story of Venezuela's support of Western art music is now also receiving attention in the US (item 3389).

BOLIVIA

3352 Rios, Fernando. Bolero trios, mestizo panpipe ensembles, and Bolivia's 1952 revolution: urban La Paz musicians and the Nationalist Revolutionary Movement. (*Ethnomusicology*, 54:2, spring-summer 2010, p. 281–317, bibl.)

Discusses the popularity of the bolero and the rise of folkloric panpipe ensembles in La Paz in the 1950s and early 1960s within the context of Bolivia's 1952 revolution and policies of the Nationalist Revolutionary Movement government. Based on a close reading of period documents and extensive interviews, Rios arrives at surprising conclusions regarding the nationalist sentiments evoked (and not) by these disparate genres.

3353 Stobart, Henry. Rampant reproduction and digital democracy: shifting landscapes of music production and piracy in Bolivia. (*Ethnomusic. Forum*, 19:1, June 2010, p. 27–56, bibl.)

Important study of the changing dynamics of the recording industry in Bolivia as a result of digital piracy, the rise of new media such as video compact discs, and the proliferation of small-scale producers catering largely to working class audiences. Stobart balances the democratizing effects of localized production and cheap costs with the deleterious effects of piracy on musicians' ability to make a living, also noting the ambiguous position of the state vis-à-vis cultural policy and copyright.

COLOMBIA

3354 Castiblanco Lemus, Gladys. Rap y prácticas de resistencia: una forma de ser joven, reflexiones preliminares a partir de la interacción con algunas agrupaciones bogotanas. (*Tabula Rasa*, 3, 2004, p. 253–270, bibl., photo)

Theoretical and ethnographic exploration of "resistance" as a mode of social practice and self understanding among rap groups in Bogotá, based on interviews with young rap artists.

3355 Hernández, Salgar, Oscar. Colonialidad y poscolonialidad musical en Colombia. (*Lat. Am. Music Rev.*, 29:2, Fall/Winter 2008, p. 242–270, bibl.)

A compelling postcolonial critique of what the author identifies as "colonial imaginaries" governing attitudes about music in Colombia, particularly the ideology of "whitening" (*blanqueamiento*) and scientific discourses on the rationality of (European) tonal harmony. Hernández positions these colonial imaginaries within new discourses on multiculturalism and "world music" that emerged in the 1990s, including an insightful comparison with notions about biodiversity. The latter portion of the article analyzes the complex resurgence of Afro-Colombian marimba music from the Pacific Coast within this postcolonial framework.

3356 Industrias culturales, músicas e identidades: una mirada a las interdependencias entre medios de comunicación, sociedad y cultura. Edición académico de José Miguel Pereira González *et al.* Contribuciones de Ángela Garcés Montoya *et al.* Bogotá: Editorial Pontificia Univ. Javeriana, 2008. 394 p.: bibl., ill.

Edited collection of essays by Colombian scholars on the culture industry in Colombia. Two of the five sections of the book deal explicitly with music, with essays on genres as varied as salsa, techno, *vallenato*, religious music, and hip-hop, as well as the industries that cater to and support them. Other sections of the book offer critical analyses of radio, television, and mass communication industries in the country.

3357 Jaramillo Giraldo, José Manuel. Historia institucional de la Orquesta Filarmónica de Bogotá, 1967–2004. Bogotá: Secretaría General, Alcaldia Mayor de Bogotá, Archivo de Bogotá, 2006. 114 p.: bibl., ill. (Historia de la administración distrital de Bogotá)

Institutional history of the Philharmonic Orchestra of Bogotá, focused almost exclusively on the administrative development of the organization.

3358 Nieves Oviedo, Jorge. De los sonidos del patio a la música mundo: semiosis nómadas en el Caribe. Bogotá: Convenio Andrés Bello; Cartagena de Indias: Observatorio del Caribe Colombiano, 2008. 426 p.: bibl., discography, ill., index.

An excellent history and analysis of the changing styles, presence, and importance of Caribbean music in Colombia in the 20th and early 21st centuries. Drawing on perspectives from Latin American cultural studies, semiotic analysis, and the sociology of culture, the author offers a richly theoretical critique of the discourses of tradition, folklore, hybridity, and "world music" that collectively mark Colombian music and the way it is discussed and understood. With a prologue by ethnomusicologist Ana María Ochoa. Highly recommended.

3359 Olvera Gudiño, José Juan. Colombianos en Monterrey: origen de un gusto musical y su papel en la construcción de una identidad social. México: Consejo para la Cultura y las Artes de Nuevo León, 2005. 238 p.: bibl., ill., maps (Investigación/Fondo Estatal para la Cultura y las Artes)

Innovative study of the popularity of Colombian music, particularly *cumbia*, *vallenato*, and *porro*, in Monterrey, Mexico, and the ramifications of that popularity for constructing social identity in the city. Includes a brief discussion of the development of "tropical" music in Colombia, and multiple appendices listing media outlets and prominent musical groups in Monterrey.

3360 Santamaría Delgado, Carolina. El bambuco, los saberes mestizos y la academia: un análisis histórico de la persistencia de la colonialidad en los estudios musicales latinoamericanos. (*Lat. Am. Music Rev.*, 28:1, Spring/Summer 2007, p. 1–23, bibl.)

Drawing on Latin American postcolonial theory, Santamaría argues that the exclusion of folkloric and popular music from schools and conservatories in Latin America has taken place not only for political and social reasons, but due to epistemological barriers that block understanding of all types of musical knowledge that are not based on European models. She explores this hypothesis in relation to the Colombian *bambuco*, a mestizo musical genre at once lauded as the "national music" of the country and simultaneously excluded from the curriculum of higher education in music, which focused entirely on the Western European art music canon.

ECUADOR

3361 Guerrero Gutiérrez, Pablo. Fandangos o fandanguillos: bailes de la época colonial en el Ecuador. (*Rev. Arch. Hist.*

Guayas, 3–4, primer semestre 2008, p. 17–63, bibl., photos, appendix)

Historical study of the fandango—usually defined as a secular social gathering marked by music and dance—in Ecuador during the period of Spanish colonialism. The author argues that these gatherings were originally Spanish dances that, over time, adapted to local circumstances and tastes, taking on their own characteristics and featuring dance styles typical of Ecuadorian and other regional origins. Includes an extended appendix with a transcription of 18th- and 19th-century documents, largely letters conveying Catholic institutional disapproval of fandango.

3362 Guerrero Gutiérrez, Pablo. Voces en la sombra: Juan Pablo Muñoz Sanz. Quito: Banco Central del Ecuador, 2007. 381 p.: bibl., ill., index. (Biografías ecuatorianas, 8)

Biography of the Ecuadorian composer Juan Pablo Muñoz Sanz (1898–1964), including contextual chapters about music and Muñoz' life in Ecuador in the early 20th century, theoretical analyses of select works, a chronology of his life, and selected writings by the composer.

3363 Guerrero Gutiérrez, Pablo and **Juan Mullo Sandoval.** Memorias y reencuentro: el pasillo en la ciudad de Quito. Quito: Museo de la Ciudad, 2005. 146 p.: bibl., ill., photos.

A genre study of the Ecuadorian pasillo, including a social history of its origins in the 19th century as an adaptation of the European waltz, through its apogee in the mid-20th century as Ecuador's "national" music. Noting the influence of other genres on the *pasillo*, including the Andean *yaravi* and the romantic bolero, the authors trace the *pasillo's* development as a marker of social identity and differentiation. Appendices include an article on gender and the *pasillo* by Soledad Quintana Arroyo, a timeline, and a selection of notable song texts.

3364 Mullo Sandoval, Juan. La etnomusicología ecuatoriana: su aporte al conocimiento de la diversidad y la construcción de la identidad de los pueblos indígenas, negros y montubios del Ecuador. (*Rev. Arch. Hist. Guayas*, 3–4, primer semestre 2008, p. 9–16, bibl., photos)

Brief overview of Ecuadorian ethnomusicology in the 20th century, cataloging both prominent subjects as well as theoretical paradigms utilized by Ecuadorian scholars. Particular attention is given to the early work of Segundo Luis Moreno (1882–1972) and Pedro Traversari Salazar (1874–1956).

3365 Santillán C., Alfredo. Las representaciones sociales de la música popular: una mirada etnográfica a las prácticas de reconocimiento de las clases populares. (*Cuad. Sociol./Quito,* 3, 2005, p. 37–49, bibl.)

Ethnographic study of working-class *música rocolera* fans in Quito and the social values they associate with listening to this music. Written by an Ecuadorian sociologist, emphasis is placed on social interaction and self-identification with the genre as experienced at concerts and live events.

3366 Wamsley, Emily. "Bailando como negro": ritmo, raza y nación en Esmeraldas, Ecuador. (*Tabula Rasa,* 3, 2004, p. 179–195, bibl., photo)

Ethnographic study analyzing the discourses surrounding "black rhythm" in Esmeraldas, Ecuador, both as an essentialist, external stereotype of African and African diasporic peoples (who "have rhythm" and "can dance"), and as a valued marker of social identity and cultural practice for Afro-Esmeraldeñans themselves.

3367 Wibbelsman, Michelle. Ritual encounters: Otavalan modern and mythic community. Urbana: Univ. of Illinois Press, 2009. 208 p.: bibl., ill., index. (Interpretations of culture in the new millennium)

Ethnographic study of contemporary ritual, dance, and music in the Otavalo region of northern Ecuador. Through analysis of particular ritual events in Cotacachi, Peguche, and other towns of the region, Wibblesman positions ritual performance as simultaneously a link to the indigenous prehispanic past, a mode of working out social relations in the present, and a statement of identity in the face of transnational migration and the impact of globalization. Chapter 3, "Encuentros: Dances of the Inti Raymi," was previously published in the *Latin American Music Review,* see *HLAS 64:2722.*

3368 Yánez Cevallos, Nancy. Memorias de la lírica en Quito. Quito: Banco Central del Ecuador, 2005. 406 p.: ill.; (Col. Histórica; 28)

A history of opera and musical theater in Ecuador, focused primarily on the activities and repertoire of opera companies in the late 19th through late 20th century. The founding of the national conservatory and national symphony orchestra receive particular attention. Three useful appendices complete the volume, including biographies of notable singers and composers, interview transcripts, and a timeline of important musical events in Ecuador in the 20th century.

PERU

3369 Baker, Geoffrey. Imposing harmony: music and society in colonial Cuzco. Durham, N.C.: Duke Univ. Press, 2008. 308 p.: bibl, index

An important and in many ways groundbreaking study of musical life in Cuzco during the first centuries of Spanish colonial rule. Baker's novel methodology eschews traditional musicological methods for studying colonial Latin American music— examining scores in cathedral archives— and focuses instead on non-musical archival holdings within religious institutions and beyond. The result, though understandably short on discussion of the music itself, is a rich and detailed portrait of the institutions (cathedrals, seminaries, monasteries, convents, urban and rural parishes), social classes, and, in places, individual musicians who played a role in the performance of sacred music during the colonial era. Chapter 3 appeared previously in *Latin American Music Review* (see *HLAS 64:2724*).

3370 Celajes, florestas y secretos: una historia del vals popular limeño. Investigación y textos de José Antonio Lloréns Amico y Rodrigo Chocano Paredes. Lima: Instituto Nacional de Cultura: Qhapaq Ñan, 2009. 297 p.: bibl., ill. (Música popular peruana; 1)

History and genre study of the Peruvian *vals.* The authors trace the genre from its origins as an adaptation of the European waltz in the later 19th century, through its golden age in the mid-20th century as both a popular music and, symbolically, as the maximum expression of criollo identity in Peru, and finally, its slow attenuation as a popular form in recent decades. Picking up where Lloréns' influential earlier study left off (*Música popular en Lima: criollos y andinos*, 1983), the authors pay close attention to the role of radio, television, and the recording industry in the rise and sustained popularity of the genre.

3371 100 años, Sociedad Filarmónica de Lima. Edición de Heriberto Ascher *et al.* Coordinación general de Francisco Hernández Astete. Lima: Sociedad Filarmónica de Lima, 2006. 199 p.: bibl., ill.

A well-illustrated, large format book published to commemorate the 100th anniversary of the Philharmonic Society in Lima. The first quarter of the book, written by noted Peruvian musicologists Aurelio Tello, Enrique Iturriaga, and Juan Carlos Estenssoro, traces the history of Western art music in Peru from the early colonial period through the end of the 19th century. The second and longer section covers the history of the Philharmonic Society itself during its first century.

3372 Ferrier, Claude. El huayno con arpa: estilos globales en la nueva música popular andina. Lima: Instituto de Etnomusicología, Pontificia Univ. Católica del Perú: Instituto Francés de Estudios Andinos, 2010. 144 p.: bibl., ill., maps, music (Estudios etnográficos; 5) (Travaux de l'Institut français d'études andines, 278)

Musicological study of the "harp *wayno*," a new and popular variation of the Peruvian *wayno* incorporating amplified harp, electronic percussion, and voice. Ferrier begins and ends the book with brief chapters on the social significance of this musical style, including discussion of the role of mass media in its diffusion and the influence of globalization and transnational migration, but the bulk of the text offers a more narrowly focused analysis of musical style and instrumental technique, particularly for the harp. Eighty-seven recorded examples discussed in text are included on the accompanying MP3 CD, which listeners unfamiliar with this genre (and even those who are) will find invaluable.

3373 Ferrier, Claude. Navidad en los Andes: arpa, comparsas y zapeteo en San Francisco de Querco, Huancavelica. Lima:

Instituto de Etnomusicolgía, Pontificia Univ. Católica del Perú; Switzerland: Swiss Society for Ethnomusicology, 2008. 160 p.: ill., maps, music; (Estudios etnográficos; 3)

Detailed ethnographic study of Christmas music and dance traditions in the Huancavelica region of the southern Peruvian Andes. Arguing for continuity with the ancient past, the author interprets contemporary ritual traditions in the district of Querco as governed by similar relations of "complementary duality" as those that shaped the prehispanic Inca festival of Qhapaq Raymi. Latter chapters include extensive illustrative material, dance diagrams, musical transcriptions, and a DVD with nearly two hours of supporting footage.

3374 Fiesta en los Andes: ritos, musica y danzas del Perú. Edición de Raúl R. Romero. Textos de Juan M. Ossio *et al.* Lima: Instituto de Etnomusicología, Pontificia Universidad Católica del Perú: Fondo Editorial, Pontificia Universidad Católica del Perú, 2008. 199 p.: bibl., col. ill., col. ports.

Edited collection of articles on music, dance, and ritual in the Andes, with essays by many of Peru's leading cultural anthropologists. Published in a large format, the volume is beautifully illustrated with more than a hundred full-color photos drawn from the archive of the Instituto de Etnomusicología in Lima. Individual essays discuss themes as varied as space and time in Andean festivals, memory, identity, generational change, music and work, gender, and organology.

3375 Huamán, Carlos. El *wayno* ayacuchano y los movimientos sociales. (*Cuad. Am./México*, 4:122, oct./dic. 2007, p. 151–166,)

The author, himself a renowned songwriter from Ayacucho and now professor of literature in Mexico, traces a brief history of political developments and social movements in Ayacucho throughout the 20th century as they were represented in key *wayno* song texts.

3376 León, Javier F. National patrimony and cultural policy: the case of the Afro-Peruvian *cajón*. (*in* Music and Cultural Rights. Edited by Andrew Weintraub and Bell Yung. Chicago and Urbana: Univ. of Illinois Press, 2009, p. 110–139, bibl.)

Discusses the recent declaration of the Afro-Peruvian *cajón* (wooden box drum) as "cultural patrimony of the nation" in Peru. Positioning this declaration within both a transnational politics of neoliberal cultural policy and the complicated history of Afro-Peruvian music in the 20th century, including its relationship with state entities like the Instituto Nacional de Cultura, León traces the events and individual efforts that led to this declaration, and evaluates its impact on the Afro-Peruvian community itself.

3377 Limansky, Nicholas E. Yma Sumac: the art behind the legend. New York: YBK Publishers, 2008. 282 p.: index, ill.

Biography of the legendary Peruvian exotica singer Yma Sumac. Though informal in tone and non-academic in approach (problematically so in its inaccurate descriptions of Peruvian music and history), this first biography of Sumac nonetheless contains a wealth of previously unpublished information about the singer's life and career in the US.

3378 Mendoza, Zoila S. Creating our own: folklore, performance, and identity in Cuzco, Peru. English ed. Durham, N.C.: Duke Univ. Press, 2008. 234 p.: bibl., discography, ill., index.

A critical historical study of the development of folkloric music and dance in Cuzco in the early 20th century. Mendoza departs somewhat from her own earlier positions on folklore and indigenismo (see her *Shaping Society Through Dance*, 2000), arguing against interpretations that reduce early folkloric performance to an elite imposition of sanitized versions of local traditions. Instead, she advocates for understanding Cuzqueño folklore as a co-production between indigenista elites and indigenous or working-class mestizo performers who, she argues, also exerted some influence over the process of creating and defining a folkloric repertoire in the region. Individual chapters discuss: the Misión Peruana de Arte Incaico and their South American tour in the early 1920s; the Centro Qosqo de Arte Nativo, one of the first folkloric institutions in Peru; the growth of tourism to Cuzco at mid-century; the *Hora del Charango*, an hour-long early radio show in Cuzco that in the late 1930s featured local *charango* players; and the Instituto Americano de Arte de Cuzco.

3379 Robles Mendoza, Román. Los nuevos rostros de la música andina a través de los instrumentos musicales. (*Investig. Soc./San Marcos*, 18, junio 2007, p. 67–107, bibl., photos)

General overview of Peruvian organology, reconstructing the history of Peruvian musical instruments and representative regional ensembles, with a special emphasis on the Cajatambo border region between present-day Lima and Ancash departments. Drawing on his prior work on brass bands in southern Ancash, the author focuses in particular on the growth of large instrumental ensembles in the 20th century and their relationship to emerging notions of modernity in the Andean highlands.

3380 Stein, Louise K. "La música de dos orbes": a context for the first opera of the Americas. (*Opera Q.*, 22:3–4, p. 433–458, facsims.)

Long-overdue study of the sociopolitical context in which the "first opera of the Americas"—Tomás de Torrejon's *La púrpura de la rosa* (Lima, 1701)—was written and performed. As Stein rightly notes, the study of secular Spanish music during the colonial era in Latin America continues to lag far behind scholarship on sacred music, due in part to the church's own antipathy at the time to secular performance and the resulting paucity of data. Stein's achievement here is thus all the more notable.

3381 Toledo Brückmann, Ernesto. Mariátegui y la música de su tiempo: cuatro ensayos históricos sobre la influencia musical en el Amauta. Lima: San Marcos, 2008. 145 p.: bibl., ill.

Unusual and interesting study of music in the life of early-20th-century Peruvian intellectual and writer Jose Carlos Mariátegui. Includes chapters on music in Lima in the first decades of the century, the Italian, French, and German musical currents Mariátegui experienced during his sojourn in Europe in the early 1920s, music and indigenismo in the magazine Amauta, and Mariátegui's complex relationship with criollo popular culture in Peru at the end of his life.

3382 Tomlinson, Gary. The singing of the New World: indigenous voice in the era of European contact. Cambridge, UK; New York: Cambridge Univ. Press, 2007. 220 p.: bibl., ill., index. (New perspectives in music history and criticism)

One chapter in a longer book examining indigenous vocal music in the Americas at the dawn of the colonial era, Tomlinson here provides a nuanced account of the role of singing in the Inca court at Cuzco. Drawing on a close reading of early colonial sources and a deep understanding of contemporary anthropological and ethnohistorical debates over Inca cultural practices, the essay focuses on one particular Inca festival, celebrated in April of 1535, to explore broader concepts regarding the place of music and the perceived power of song among the Incas.

3383 Tucker, Joshua. Mediating sentiment and shaping publics: recording practice and the articulation of social chance in Andean Lima. (*Pop. Music Soc.*, 33:2, May 2010, p. 141–162, bibl.)

Study of the development and significance of *música ayacuchana* in the 1990s and 2000s, a popular Peruvian Andean musical style incorporating influences from the regional Ayacuchan *wayno*, transnational Andean folkloric music, and international pop. Through both reception analysis and ethnographic work in recording studios, Tucker argues that the new genre's success derived in part from the self-conscious manner in which it was crafted and disseminated by one particular music studio, Dolby J.R., which targeted the emergent Andean middle-class in Lima.

3384 Turino, Thomas. Music in the Andes: experiencing music, expressing culture. New York: Oxford Univ. Press, 2008. 154 p.: bibl., ill., index. (Global music series)

Part of Oxford's series of "world music" mini-textbooks, this short volume on the Andes focuses primarily on highland indigenous and mestizo musical traditions from Peru, and the ways they have been represented both nationally and internationally. Bringing together and updating some of the best work on Peruvian music by ethnomusicologist Tom Turino, individual chapters discuss panpipe ensembles of the altiplano, charango traditions, mestizo

dance dramas, urban popular music, and the transnational "Andean band" phenomenon. Written for an undergraduate classroom audience, the text also includes detailed "listening guides" for the recorded examples on the accompanying CD.

3385 Vega, Zoila S. Instrumentos y sistemas musicales de Arequipa prehispánica. (*Bol. Lima*, 28:147, set. 2007, p. 45–57, ill., photos, music)

Brief illustrated overview of prehispanic musical instruments and scales known to exist in the Chile River Valley of contemporary Arequipa, Peru, based on study of extant archeological collections in local museums and private collections.

3386 Vergara Figueroa, Abilio. La tierra que duele de Carlos Falconí: cultura, música, identidad y violencia en Ayacucho. Ayacucho, Peru: Sección de Postgrado de la Universidad Nacional de San Cristóbal de Huamanga, 2010. 222 p.: bibl., discography, photos.

A hybrid of biography, history, and cultural anthropology, this book examines the life and music of Ayacuchan musician and songwriter Carlos Falconí within the context of Ayacuchan folkloric music and, especially, the political violence that marked this region in the 1980s and 90s. The author, an Ayacuchan anthropologist now teaching in Mexico, witnessed much of this history personally while teaching at the local university in the 1980s, and was one of the primary chroniclers of the socially-committed song movement in which Falconí played an important role.

VENEZUELA

3387 Barreto, Sofia. Venezuelan carnival songs: singing calipso en El Callao. (*World Music (Wilhelmshaven)*, 50:1, 2008, p. 63–71)

Examines carnival performance traditions in the mining town of El Callao, in Venezuelan Guayana, where a majority of residents are descendants of Caribbean islanders who moved to the area in the mid-19th century. The author argues that contemporary carnival practices, including hybrid musical styles and multilingual lyrics, continue to reflect a diverse array of influences from various Caribbean islands and populations and thus form the basis for a distinctly "Venezuelan" version of calypso.

3388 Castro Aniyar, Daniel. El entendimiento: historia y significación de la música indígena del Lago de Maracaibo. 2a ed. corr. y aum. Zulia, Venezuela: Univ. del Zulia, Ediciones del Vice Rectorado Académico, 2008. 115 p.: bibl., 1 map (Col. Textos universitarios)

Historical and ethnographic study of music and ritual among indigenous groups of the Lake Maracaibo region. The first edition won the prestigious Casa de las Americas prize for musicology in 1995; this second edition is corrected and updated.

3389 Lubow, Arthur. Conductor of the people. (*N.Y. Times Mag.,* Oct. 28, 2007, p. 32–37)

Profile of young Venezuelan conductor Gustavo Dudamel, a prodigy trained in Venezuela's famed *sistema* of national youth orchestras and now artistic director of the Los Angeles Philharmonic as well as the Caracas-based Simón Bolivar Youth Orchestra. The article also probes the history of *el sistema* and its founder (and Dudamel's mentor) José Antonio Abreu.

SOUTHERN CONE AND BRAZIL

CRISTINA MAGALDI, *Associate Professor of Music, Towson University*

THE SCHOLARLY PRODUCTION ON MUSIC of the Southern Cone continues to increase exponentially with an abundance of high-level studies. A welcome trend during this review cycle has been the increasing output of important studies stemming from Chile, indicating a change in the pattern of uneven scholarly publications in the region, dominated in the past by studies on music in Brazil. A large number of important articles about Chilean music continue to be published in *Revista Musical Chilena*, the longest continuously running Latin American music periodical, created in 1945 and published by the Universidad de Chile. The periodical's website states that their publication aims at disseminating knowledge about music in Chile and Latin America. Although the articles are still predominantly about Chile and by Chilean scholars, the idea of expanding its scope to focus on Latin America as a whole is a positive move.

Musicological and ethnomusicological studies from local scholars have for too long remained encased in localized publications and are in much need of circulation outside Latin America. Thus, it is welcome news that since 2007, articles in *Revista Musical Chilena* are indexed in large international databases, permitting online access of its articles to a much wider readership, and since 2008 the periodical site also includes pages in English and Portuguese. A few Brazilian periodical publications already function this way, such as the *Revista Opus* and *Revista Eletrônica de Musicologia*, which continue to produce first-rate articles. Also good news on the Brazilian music front is the continuation of more recently established online academic periodicals, such as *Música & Cultura*, a publication of the Brazilian Society for Ethnomusicology (ABET), active since 2006. Another fortunate event has been the return of the *Revista Brasileira de Música*, which started in 1934 and included seminal articles by luminaries such as Mário de Andrade. The *RBM* ran until 1945 and returned in the 1980s, but only sporadically. In

2010, the School of Music of the Universidade Federal do Rio de Janeiro restarted the publication promising a more stable output.

A significant trend in the recent publications on the Southern Cone is the emergence of studies that offer fresh ways of looking at much-researched topics, identifying new directions for further studies. These tend to be short studies, rather than book-length publications. Rather than examining Spanish and Portuguese colonial music centered on the patronage of the Catholic Church, for example, Guerra Rojas' article examines music in Protestant churches in 19th-century Valparaiso (item **3413**), a study that will certainly inspire similar investigations in other regions of Latin America. Rondón and Vera's study offers new perspectives about the agency of the indigenous population in the process of colonization (item **3421**). Rios' study (item **3420**) also tackles a well-researched topic, *Nueva Canción*, and offers fresh insight into the politics of identity in Chile and Latin America. Rios shows that middle-class *Nueva Canción* musicians were attracted to *kenas* and *charangos*, rather than Mapuche music and culture, a choice that was consistent with the pan-Latin-American sentiments of the day. In Brazilian colonial music, Marcos Tadeu Holler's article (item **3446**) challenges the much accepted idea that music played an important role in Jesuit missions.

Another noteworthy area of musical investigation in Brazil has been the focus on religiosity and music-making in the 20th century. While Vicente (item **3469**) examines the growth of the market for recordings of Catholic and Evangelical musics in contemporary Brazil, Burdick and Oosterbaan (items **3435** and **3455**) focus on the role that music is playing in the present-day spread of Evangelical and Pentecostal religions in Brazil.

The large number of excellent studies on music and race during this review cycle highlight Brazilian musicology and ethnomusicology paths towards music criticism. The myth of racial democracy in Brazil has long been challenged in the social sciences, it is now time that music scholars start to confront the topic in a critical manner. The result of a 2010 conference on Brazilian music and race at the University of California at Riverside will be a volume devoted to the topic, although a book-length monograph challenging long-standing claims of race and musical identity in Brazil and that addresses the political debates about race and ethnicity in contemporary Brazil is still in order.

Paul Sneed's article (item **3464**) on Rio de Janeiro's *bailes funk* examines how funk music provides a collective space and a "utopian experience" in which participants rise above vulnerability, poverty, and social exclusion. Burdick's study on music, class, religion, and ethnicity (item **3434**) offers a different perspective, showing that soul music popularity among Afro-Brazilians in urban areas may serve to dilute, rather than to strengthen, the racial content of the subject's identity. Dantas' ethnographic study (item **3438**) uncovers yet another angle from which to analyze music making and ethnic representations. She shows that in traditional dances, Indians are portrayed as serious and courageous warriors, while blacks appear as happy individuals and good workers. She concludes that representations of Indians and blacks in traditional musical performances are similar to those found in classic literary and intellectual works that interpret Brazilian society from the standpoint of a tri-ethnic logic, a view the author believes has been transmitted orally to popular culture over time.

Although contemporary music is usually the preferred venue for analyzing gender and race in music making, an overview of the publications about music in Brazil reviewed in this cycle points to a different direction, as scholars start to scrutinize the music of the past. Budasz's examination of the activities of black guitar players during the colonial era (item **3433**) and Bittencourt-Sampaio's biography of two female black singers at the turn of the 19th and 20th centuries (item **3432**) opens the path for in-depth investigations on issues of race and gender in musical performances in Rio de Janeiro during 18th- and 19th-centuries. Hazan's perceptive study (item **3444**) examines a manuscript collection to show that a specific repertory can highlight class, race, and gender hierarchies in 19th-century Brazil.

The intersections between race and gender, and national and cosmopolitan identities have prompted scholars to look beyond national borders to find international connections in music. One such historical study is Seigel's excellent article (item **3461**) showing how the emergence and disappearance of the maxixe in the US was interwoven in the history of US internal social and racial relations. By focusing on intellectual property laws, Hertzman (item **3445**) shows that in early 20th-century Rio de Janeiro, black musicians adapted themselves and their music to international views about race, music, and property. Paulina Alberto focuses on the spread of soul music in Rio de Janeiro during the 1970s (item **3428**) to demonstrate that Afro-Brazilians used the music to analyze, communicate, and contest established folkloric representations of race, blackness, and national identity in 1970s Brazil.

Gender and race studies are also making advances as a major area of study in other countries of the Southern Cone. Excellent examples are Gustavo Blásquez's study about masculinity and the *cuarteto* in Cordoba (item **3390**) and Cecconi's examination of the gender politics in the rebirth of tango among a new generation of Argentineans (item **3391**). Daniel Party's article, "Placer culpable," also addresses gender and class in the revival of the *balada* in 1990s Chile (item **3419**) to conclude that the revival of *baladas* served to interpret the political, gender, and class ambivalences and tensions in post-authoritarian Chile.

The publications described above form a wonderful sample of the sophisticated scholarship in music stemming from the Southern Cone. However, these are short studies, restricted in scope that illuminate specific areas and should instigate further reading. Book-length studies were scarce during the period under review, although we can point out some excellent publications. Stroud's book *The Defence of Tradition in Brazilian Popular Music: Politcs, Culture and the Creation of Música Popular Brasileira* (item **3466**), elegantly investigates ideologies of music and national identity in Brazil. Dent's *River of Tears: Country Music, Memory, and Modernity in Brazil* (item **3440**) on Brazilian country music, on the other hand, brings a most welcome relief to the usual focus on MPB, as the work investigates a musical style not associated with representations of Brazilianidade or national identity.

Finally, it is worth highlighting here the exquisite coffee-table books that came out during this review cycle. Although a genre of publication that is usually classified as second-rank in academic circles, several recent publications about Brazilian traditional music came out in such a format, showing a successful blending of richly illustrated materials with first quality field research. The results were some wonderful volumes, worth having for informal browsing on your coffee table, while informative enough to catch the attention of the most refined reader. See for instance Pimentel et al. *Museu vivo do Fandango* (items **3454**), Risério, ed. *Os tambores da terra* (item **3460**), and Taubkin, (ed.)*Violões do Brasil* (item **3470**).

ARGENTINA

3390 Blázquez, Gustavo. Nosotros, vosotros y ellos: las poéticas de las masculinidades heterosexuales entre jóvenes cordobeses. *(Trans (online)*, 12, 2008, http://www.sibetrans.com/trans/trans12/art06.htm, bibl.)

Explores the politics of masculinity and the social experience of becoming a heterosexual man among the youths who dance cuarteto in Córdoba. Argues that gender and social classification are repetitions of a discriminatory discourse in a national, postcolonial context.

3391 Cecconi, Sofía. Tango queer: territorio y performance de una apropiación divergente. *(Trans (online)*, 12, 2008, http://www.sibetrans.com/trans/trans12/art06.htm, bibl.)

Describes the rebirth of tango in contemporary Buenos Aires and the innovations it has produced. Examines the "tango queer" trend as an urban tango micro-scene and shows how the gay/lesbian scene adapts and transforms traditional tango to redefine a novel territory that avoids identity ghettos.

3392 Donozo, Leandro. Diccionario bibliográfico de la música argentina: (y de la música en la Argentina). Buenos Aires: Gourmet Musical Ediciones, 2006. 534 p.

Dictionary of music and musicians in Argentina, covering traditional, popular, and art music. Summarizes established sources, and although dated and lacking organization, the volume might be useful for those looking for an initial and broad survey of Argentina's music.

3393 Fanjul, Adrián Pablo. Acúmulos e vazios de pesquisa sobre o rock argentino. *(Lat. Am. Music Rev.*, 29:2, Fall/Winter 2008, p. 121–144, bibl.)

Examines 40 years of literature on Argentine rock music. Shows that studies focusing on Argentine rock as a social phenomenon have predominated. Other areas privileged by the available literature are studies on national and generational identity and works on historical periodization of the style based on political changes in Argentina. Concludes that these approaches usually erase the music's esthetical aspects

and avoid addressing language as an element for understanding the Argentine rock phenomenon.

3394 Giacosa, Santiago Manuel. Carlos Vega, a cuarenta años de su muerte (1966–2006). *(Temas Hist. Argent. Am.*, 10, enero/junio 2007, p. 31–68, photo)

A tribute on the 40th anniversary of Argentine musicologist Carlos Vega's death, the article traces his career in musicology and his role in the organization of the Instituto Nacional de Musicologia; discusses two of Vega's unpublished works.

3395 Groussac, Paul. Críticas sobre música. Buenos Aires: Biblioteca Nacional, 2007. 346 p.: bibl. (Col. Libros de música)

Collection of critical texts about music written by the French critic active in Buenos Aires at the turn of the 20th century. Groussac's writings about music, dating from the 1880s to the second decade of the 20th century, address a wide range of topics, from analysis of the works of Beethoven, Meyerbeer, Bizet, Gounot, Verdi, and Wagner to reviews of local performances in the Argentine capital. In addition to its historical value, this collection offers a unique insight into the world of concert music in a European city like Buenos Aires and reveals its connection to Paris. Includes an introductory essay by Pola Suárez Urtubey.

3396 Heile, Björn. The music of Mauricio Kagel. Aldershot, England; Burlington, VT: Ashgate, 2006. 209 p.: bibl., ill., indexes, music.

Examines the music of Argentine born composer, conductor, and professor. Discusses Kagel's upbringing in Buenos Aires and the influence of Jorge Luis Borges on his musical aesthetics. Examines the composer's music after he settled in Germany and shows the social and cultural contexts that led to Kagel's musical eclecticism and satire. Describes the composer's varied approach to music, from serialism to aleatoric ideas of John Cage, to music theater and with film music.

3397 Kuri, Carlos. Piazzolla: la música límite. 3. ed. Buenos Aires: Corregidor, 2008. 318 p.: bibl., ill.

Revised and expanded 3rd edition, the work includes a chronology of Piazzolla's life, an overview and analysis of his style, and his connections to jazz and art music. Shows that Piazzolla's music is a result of the tension between popular and art music languages and esthetics present in Buenos Aires and Paris. Argues that Piazzolla works in zones of frontiers and borders (classical/popular, jazz, primitive/transcendence, tonal/atonal, etc). Includes discography and list of works.

3398 Matallana, Andrea. Qué saben los pitucos: la experiencia del tango entre 1910 y 1940. Buenos Aires: Prometeo Libros, 2008. 208 p.: bibl., ill. (Col. Comunicación y crítica cultural)

Social and cultural history of the Argentine tango in the first part of the 20th century; based on primary sources, this volume consists of six essays assessing and interpreting the dissemination of the tango in Europe and the US and examines the cultural and social outcomes of this diffusion for the porteño culture. Addresses the widespread popularity of tango in Hollywood as part of the Pan-American cultural politics after the 1930s crisis and as a result of technological development and expansion of mass culture during the first part of the 20th century.

3399 Ortiz Oderigo, Néstor R. Esquema de la música afroargentina. Edición de Norberto Pablo Cirio. Buenos Aires: EDUNTREF, 2008. 439 p.

Posthumous publication, this collection of essays covers a wide range of topics related to Afro-Argentine music and music making, including musical instruments, performers, description of dances, and notes of the rhythms of tango. The volume includes an introduction by Noberto Pablo Cirio, whose editorial notes are valuable aids to the collection.

3400 Priore, Oscar del. Osvaldo Pugliese: una vida en el tango. Buenos Aires: Editorial Losada, 2008. 226 p.: discography, ill.

Short biographical study on the life and works of the famous tango composer and performer; includes a list of compositions and recordings, but not citations or bibliography.

3401 Pujol, Sergio Alejandro. En nombre del folclore: biografia de Atahualpa Yupanqui. Buenos Aires: Emece Editores, 2008. 350 p., 16 p. of plates: bibl., discography, ill., ports., music. (Biografías y memorias)

Biographical study, documents the travels of Argentine folklorist, poet, singer, and composer Atahualpa Yupanqui in Argentina, as well as his trips to various Latin American countries, Europe, and the US. Describes his work in radio, his performances and recordings, and his participation in politics as a performer, writer, and activist. Through interviews and examination of publications, letters, and documents, the study also offers a panorama of Latin American culture and politics before, during, and after the Cold War. Includes lists of Yupanqui's writings and recordings, and an extensive bibliography.

3402 Sacchi de Ceriotto, María Antonieta. La profesión musical en el baúl: músicos españoles inmigrantes radicados en Mendoza a comienzos del siglo XX: música de Mendoza. Mendoza, Argentina: EDIUNC, 2007. 161, 1 p.: bibl. + 1 CD-ROM (4 3/4 in.) (Serie Documentos y testimonios; no. 14)

Through archival research and investigation of newspapers and magazines, this work documents the lives of a family of Spanish immigrant musicians and their activities in Mendoza at the turn of the 20th century. This welcome study offers a glimpse of the musical life in the city and the extent to which Spanish musicians dominated music making, music education, and the business of music. Argues that in turn-of-the-20th-century Mendoza, not only the Italian, but also the Spanish immigration influenced the local culture. Includes bibliography and a CD with documents and scores, illustrations, and music.

3403 Santos, Laura. Música y dictadura: por qué cantábamos. Buenos Aires: Capital Intelectual, 2008. 133 p.: facsims. (Claves para todos; 91)

Examines the participation of popular musicians in Argentine society during the military regime of the 1970s and 1980s; includes lists of censured songs and musicians and describes the control of radio and TV programming, the position of the musicians and their participation in peace concerts during the war with Great Britain (Malvinas). Reports on the political position of musicians of folk and protest song (Sosa), rock (Gieco), and tango (Osvaldo Pugliese and Piazzolla). Lacks citations and is therefore of limited use for research. Includes facsimiles of governmental documents.

3404 Vardaro, Arcángel Pascual. La censura radial del lunfardo, 1943–1949: con especial aplicación al tango. Buenos Aires: Editorial Dunken, 2007. 165 p.: bibl., ill.

Includes archival and primary sources and facsimile copies of documents to show the censorship of the *lunfardo* (language) on the radio during the revolution of 1943 in Argentina. Describes the political and historical moments when titles and lyrics of tangos were changed to comply with requirements to prohibit *lunfardo*.

3405 Vega, Carlos. Estudios para los orígenes del tango argentino. Edición de Coriún Aharonián. Buenos Aires: Editorial de la Univ. Católica Argentina, 2007. 222 p.: music (Serie Libros)

With the goal to rescue the unpublished work of Argentine musicologist Carlos Vega, this posthumous edition brings to life works written in a period of some three decades before his death in 1966. Edited carefully by Coriún Aharonián, this is a welcome publication that rescues an important body of work by one of the foremost Latin American musicologists of the 20th century.

3406 Veniard, Juan María. Juan Moreira: la transformación de un gaucho cuchillero en personaje de ópera italiana. (*Temas Hist. Argent. Am.*, 10, enero/junio 2007, p. 221–237)

Traces the path followed by a character (Juan Moreira) created by Eduardo Gutiérrez from a newspaper novel to the circus and the theater. As the story of Moreira was retold and recreated over the years, it was translated into Italian and eventually set as an operatic libretto that was put to music twice during the last decade of the 19th century. Argues that operas helped establish the figure of the 'gaucho,' now a mythical national character in the collective memory of Argentineans.

CHILE

3407 Bustos Valderrama, Raquel. Leni Alexander Pollack, 1924–2005. (*Rev. Music. Chil.*, 61:207, enero/junio 2007, p. 28–64, appendix, bibl., music)

Based on interviews with the Chilean composer, this study focuses on three works to show the styles, techniques, and evolution of her compositional output. Includes musical examples and bibliography.

3408 Course, Magnus. Why Mapuche sing. (*J. Royal Anthropol. Inst.*, 15:2, June 2009, p. 295–313)

Anthropological study, focuses on personal songs among rural Mapuche people in southern Chile. Describes personal songs, explains their role within Mapuche thinking, and suggests that for the Mapuche personal songs are not simply an expression of a person's life, but a part of it. Argues that Mapuche songs are isomorphic with a Mapuche theory of personhood and that through singing personal songs of others, one has the chance of inhabiting the author's personhood and of experiencing their subjectivities.

3409 Díaz-Inostroza, Patricia. El canto nuevo de Chile: un legado musical. Santiago: Univ. Bolivariana, 2007. 270 p.: bibl., discography (Col. Cultura popular)

Brief study, surveys 10 years (1974–84) of activities of selected poets, performers, and composers associated with the Nueva Canción and Canto Nuevo movements in Chile. Offers an overview of artists and songs and their relationships to other contemporary popular musics, like rock, punk, disco, and 'alternative' musics. Includes lyrics organized by topic, a discography, and a limited bibliography.

3410 Díaz S., Rafael. Poética musical mapuche: factor de dislocación de la música chilena contemporánea. El caso de "Cantos ceremoniales" de Eduardo Cáceres. (*Rev. Music. Chil.*, 62:210, julio/dic. 2008, p. 7–25, bibl., ill.)

Analysis of Eduardo Cáceres's "Cantos ceremonials" (2004) with Mapuche text by Elicura Chihuailaf. Shows that the composer recreated elements of the Mapuche culture within a unique musical context that is neither art (academic) music, nor traditional (indigenous, Mapuche) music.

Argues that his work is an example of a postmodern composition that has crossed traditional borders between academic/traditional musics and that it has modified notions of Chilean contemporary music.

3411 En busca de la música chilena: crónica y antología de una historia sonora. Edición de José Miguel Varas y Juan Pablo González. Santiago: Presidencia de la República, 2005. 518 p.: ill., indexes, music + 2 sound discs (4 3/4 in.) (Cuadernos bicentenario; 4)

Anthology of writings about music in Chile; includes musical criticism, articles, editorials, and interviews that document various aspects of music making during the 20th century. This welcome volume is organized chronologically, and includes an index, and 4 CDs with musical examples.

3412 González Rodríguez, Juan Pablo and Claudio Rolle. Escuchando el pasado: hacia una historia social de la música popular. (*Rev. Hist./São Paulo*, 157, segundo semestre 2007, p. 31–53, bibl.)

Based on the introduction to his book *Historia social de la música popular en Chile, 1890–1950* (see *HLAS 64:2771*) and his 2005 article (see *HLAS 64:2770*), the author discusses some historical approaches to the study of popular music in Chile.

3413 Guerra Rojas, Cristián. La música en los inicios de los cultos cristianos no católicos en Chile: el caso de la Union Church (Iglesia Unión) de Valparaíso, 1845–1890. (*Rev. Music. Chil.*, 60:206, julio/dic. 2006, p. 49–83, bibl., music) <http://www.scielo.cl/scielo.php?script=sci_arttext&pid=S0716-27902006000200003&lng=es&nrm=iso&tlng=es>

Excellent study, argues that the emergence of Protestantism in 19th-century Latin American countries reflects the authorities' ideals to modernize the Catholic Church to fit the newly independent society. In Valparaíso, the presence of British merchants favored tolerance for Protestantism. Describes the work of the missionary David Trumbull, who arrived in Chile in 1845, and examines the repertory borrowed from English collections of psalms and hymns used for congressional singing. Includes musical examples.

3414 Knudsen, Jan Sverre. Those that fly without wings: music and dance in a Chilean immigrant community. Oslo, Norway: Unipub AS, Oslo Academic Press, 2006. 234 p.: bibl., ill. (some col.). (Acta humaniora, 194)

An outgrowth of the author's PhD dissertation (Univ. of Oslo, 2004), this excellent book documents the activities and experiences of Chilean immigrants in Oslo. Reports on their use of music and dance to interact with their new surroundings and to articulate their changing views about their Chilean identity.

3415 Marchant E., Guillermo J. Acercándonos al Repertorio del Archivo Musical de la Catedral de Santiago de Chile en la primera mitad del siglos XIX. (*Rev. Music. Chil.*, 60:206, julio/dic. 2006, p. 28–48, bibl., music)

Describes the musical archive of the Santiago de Chile Cathedral and the process of cataloguing and editing the material for publication. Examines 28 works that show the transition from the colonial Baroque style of the 18th century to the 'modern' republican style that dominated the repertory after 1840. Includes musical examples.

3416 Merino Montero, Luis. La Sociedad Filarmónica de 1826 y los inicios de la actividad de conciertos públicos en la sociedad civil de Chile hacia 1830. (*Rev. Music. Chil.*, 60:206, julio/dic. 2006, p. 5–27, bibl., table)

Examines the emergence of public concerts in Santiago during the first part of the 19th century, emphasizing the activities of the Philharmonic Society. Shows that the repertory, consisting of symphonic, chamber, and operatic music, reflects the musical taste favored in aristocratic salons and that it included European art music, but not by composers born or living in Chile. Explains that Philharmonic concerts were social events with limited participation of professional musicians. Nonetheless, important performers and composers of 19th-century Chile started their careers in such concerts. Includes concert programs and describes the importance of music derived from the theater in shaping music making in Chile during the 19th century.

3417 Orrego Salas, Juan. Encuentros, visiones y repasos: capítulos en el camino de mi música y mi vida. Santiago: Ediciones Univ. Catolica de Chile, 2005. 453 p.: bibl., ill., index, ports. (Biografías)

Memoires of well-known Chilean composer and musicologist: looks back on his life in Chile and the US, reflects on his music and times, and describes his encounters and friendship with renowned composers and performers. Includes bibliography and index.

3418 Osorio Fernández, Javier. *Canto para una semilla*: Luis Advis, Violeta Parra y la modernización de la música popular chilena. (*Rev. Music. Chil.*, 60:205, enero/junio 2006, p. 34–43, bibl.)

Analysis of the song *Canto para una semilla*, with music by Luis Advis and lyrics by Violeta Parra, premiered in Chile by Inti-Illimani in 1972. Claims that the song is an example of a new, urban, and modern collective identity in the context of 1960s and 1970s Chile, and shows the transformation of traditional Chilean music into "authentic" expressions of urban popular music in the second part of the 20th century.

3419 Party, Daniel. "Placer culpable": shame and nostalgia in the Chilean 1990s *balada* revival. (*Lat. Am. Music Rev.*, 30:1, Spring/Summer 2009, p. 69–98)

Studies the revival of 1970s *baladas*, or popular romantic ballads, during the 1990s by middle class youth in Chile. Shows that, despite a general disfavor for the style in the 1970s, radio DJs and rock musicians in the 1990s saw them as a "guilty pleasure" and later as a form of nostalgic entertainment. Argues that interest in the style was also part of a process of reconfiguring old *baladas* and investing in them a sociopolitical connotation. Concludes that the revival of *baladas* serves to interpret the political, gender, class ambivalences, and tensions in post-authoritarian Chile.

3420 Rios, Fernando. *La flûte indienne*: the early history of Andean folkloric-popular music in France and its impact on *nueva canción*. (*Lat. Am. Music Rev.*, 29:2, Fall/Winter 2008, p. 145–189, bibl.)

Excellent study, examines the early history of *nueva canción* in Chile and the music's reliance on Andean musical instruments as a symbols of pan-Latin Americanism and leftism. Shows that highland instruments were rarely heard in Santiago before the 1960s and that they were brought to Europe by Argentine expatriates well before exiled Chilean *nueva canción* artists arrived in Paris. Describes Violetta Parra and her family's role in introducing Andean instruments and genres into the Chilean milieu. Rather than Mapuche music and culture, middle-class *nueva canción* musicians were attracted to *kenas* and *charangos*, "modernist-cosmopolitan" versions of rural indigenous instruments. Argues that the choice was consistent with the pan-Latin American sentiments of the day, because the music called to mind a precolonial unified Andean region that counteracted US political and cultural imperialism.

3421 Rondón, Víctor and Alejandro Vera. A propósito de nuevos sonidos para nuevos reinos: prescripciones y prácticas músico-rituales en el área surandina colonial. (*Lat. Am. Music Rev.*, 29:2, Fall/Winter 2008, p. 190–231, bibl., photo)

Surveys the literature about prehispanic music in Latin America and points to the need to widen our understanding of indigenous music making before the conquest. Argues that through ethnographic analogy one can create parallels between today's indigenous cultures and prehispanic musical cultures. Offers a reassessment of 16th-century historical accounts to conclude that early texts unify the indigenous repertories and diminish differences among musical cultures to privilege European religious practices.

3422 Schumacher Ratti, Federico. 50 años de música electroacústica en Chile. (*Rev. Music. Chil.*, 61:208, julio/dic. 2007, p. 66–81, bibl.)

Surveys the history of electroacoustic music in Chile from the 1950s on. Discusses the modes of composition and the technological resources available today and addresses the processes of change in the way people think about, perceive, and perform electro-acoustic music. Points to the need to create educational policies in Chile that will provide incentives to the education and production of electro-acoustic music.

3423 Vera, Alejandro. En torno a un nuevo corpus musical en la Iglesia de San Ignacio: música, religión y sociedad en Santiago, 1856–1925. (*Rev. Music. Chil.*, 61:208, julio/dic. 2007, p. 5–36, appendix, music, tables)

Describes the music (manuscript copies and early publications) extant in the church of San Ignacio in Santiago and the musical activities in the Jesuit school Colegio de San Ignacio from 1856 to 1920. Includes information on composers, performers, and teachers, some of whom played important roles in the musical life of turn of the 20th-century Santiago. Examines the repercussions of the sacred reforms of the turn of the 20th century. Includes musical examples and an appendix with a partial list of works in the collection, including pieces by composers active in Santiago at the turn of the 20th century.

3424 Vera A., Alejandro. Santiago de Murcia's *Cifras Selectas de Guitarra* (1722): a new source for the Baroque guitar. (*Early Music*, 35:2, May 2007, p. 251–269, music, tables)

Reports on the discovery in Santiago de Chile of a manuscript, copied in 1722, with music for the guitar by the Baroque composer Santiago de Murcia (1673–1739). The manuscript, acquired by the Universidad Católica de Chile, is the earliest source solely dedicated to the guitar preserved in Latin America. Well-documented study, describes the manuscript and the repertory, which includes a majority of Spanish dances. Includes a discussion of concordances with repertories of other known sources of Murcia's music. Shows that the manuscript was originally intended to be sent to America.

PARAGUAY

3425 Colman, Alfredo. El arpa diatónica paraguaya en la búsqueda del *tekorã*: representaciones de paraguayidad. (*Lat. Am. Music Rev.*, 28:1, Spring/Summer 2007, p. 125–149, bibl.)

Argues that the Paraguayan harp has transcended its function of traditional musical instrument to play a crucial role in the articulation of "Paraguayidad." Describes the harp as an agent of cultural transmission that links today's Paraguayans to the Guarani's precolonial society and their concept of *tekó*—a way of being and a collective feeling. Discusses the role played by musical festivals in promoting this idea and includes information about harpists and groups, and their repertory and performing styles.

3426 Gutiérrez Miglio, Roberto. El tango, el litoral y Paraguay: su relación con el chamamé, la polca paraguaya y la guarania. Buenos Aires: Ediciones Corregidor, 2007. 399 p.: bibl., ill.

The author traces parallels between tango, *chamamé*, and *polca*, including common musical instruments, types of ensembles, performers, and dance choreographies. Shows the musical and cultural connections between Buenos Aires and Paraguay and provides lists of compositions, including tangos with titles in the Guarani language.

URUGUAY

3427 Goldman, Gustavo. Lucamba: herencia africana en el tango, 1870–1890. Montevideo: Perro Andaluz Ediciones, 2008. 252 p.: bibl., ill. (Serie Orígenes)

Examines primary sources to show the extent of Afro-Uruguayans' participation in the musical cultures of Uruguay at the end to the 19th century. Reviews and reassesses a large literature on the topic; argues that Afro-Uruguayans reinterpreted cultural and musical marks of Africanism, and played a role in the formation of Rioplatense culture in general, and in tango in particular. Includes illustrations, musical examples, lyrics, list of published music, and bibliography.

BRAZIL

3428 Alberto, Paulina L. When Rio was *black*: soul music, national culture, and the politics of racial comparison in 1970s Brazil. (*HAHR*, 89:1, Feb. 2009, p. 3–39)

Examines the proliferation of soul dances in Rio de Janeiro during the 1970s. Shows that hundreds of thousands of young people of color participated in these gatherings with music, a phenomenon much criticized by commentators from across the political spectrum. Argues that soul dances created a "parallel city" to mainstream Rio de Janeiro, one that sought to analyze, communicate, and contest established folkloric representations of race, blackness, and national identity in 1970s Brazil.

3429 Albin, Ricardo Cravo. MPB mulher. Rio de Janeiro: Instituto Cultural Ricardo Cravo Albin, 2006. 193 p.: ill. (some col.), photos.

This exquisite coffee table book includes photographs by Mario Luiz Thompson of 150 women composers and singers who are part of the MPB movement. Includes a CD with 14 performances by well known Brazilian female singers.

3430 Almada, Carlos. A estrutura do choro: com aplicações na improvisação e no arranjo. Rio de Janeiro: Da Fonseca Comunicação, 2006. 87 p.: bibl.

Description and classification of various choro styles, performance techniques, and formulae for improvisation; includes musical examples and exercises.

3431 Bastos, Rafael José de Menezes. Brazil in France, 1922: an anthropological study of the congenital international nexus of popular music. (*Lat. Am. Music Rev.*, 29:1, Spring/Summer 2008, p. 1–28, bibl.)

Documents the 1922 Parisian performances by the Brazilian ensemble Os Oitos Batutas under the guidance of Pixinguinha (Alfredo da Rocha Viana Filho). The examination of Parisian newspapers and magazines adds valuable information about the reception of Os Oitos Batutas in Paris as well as about Parisians' views on the "exotic" popular music arriving from the New World.

3432 Bittencourt-Sampaio, Sérgio. Negras líricas: duas intérpretes negras brasileiras na música de concerto, séc. XVIII-XX. Rio de Janeiro: 7 Letras, 2008. 116 p.: bibl., ill.

Biography of two black singers active in Rio de Janeiro at the turn of the 19th and 20th centuries respectively, Joaquina Maria da Conceição Lapa and Camila Maria da Conceição. These women enjoyed relative success in the opera house and concert halls and their singing careers can serve as seeds for in-depth investigations on issues of race and gender in musical performances during that era in Rio de Janeiro.

3433 Budasz, Rogério. Black guitar-players and early African-Iberian music in Portugal and Brazil. (*Early Music,* 35:1, Feb. 2007, p. 3–22, ill., music)

Well-researched study documenting the activities of mulattos and black guitar performers in Brazil and Portugal during the colonial era. Places black and mulatto musicians as social mediators that brought popular music and dance, such as modinhas and lundus, to the Portuguese and Brazilian white elite. Includes musical examples, facsimiles of documents and manuscripts, and illustrations.

3434 Burdick, John. Class, place and blackness in São Paulo's gospel music scene. (*Lat. Am. Caribb. Ethn. Stud.,* 3:2, July 2008, p. 149–169, bibl.)

Insightful article, shows that black gospel and gospel rap play different roles within the political debates about race and ethnicity in Brazil. Argues that gospel rap articulates the artists' class experience and sense of place, more so than race and ethnicity.

3435 Burdick, John. The singing voice and racial politics on the Brazilian evangelical music scene. (*Lat. Am. Music Rev.,* 30:1, Spring/Summer 2009, p. 25–55, bibl., photo)

This ethnography examines the spread of evangelical Protestant black gospel music in São Paulo to show how religious songs, perceived as nonracial and with universal themes of redemption and salvation, can serve as a vehicle of black identity. Argues that vocal technique is central to articulating race in black gospel music, but less so in gospel rap.

3436 Chico Buarque: tantas palavras, todas as letras. Reportagem biográfica de Humberto Werneck. Projeto gráfico de João Baptista da Costa Aguiar. Edição revista e ampliada. São Paulo: Companhia das Letras, 2006. 477 p., 16 leaves of plates: bibl., ill., indexes, photos.

This revised and updated edition (1st ed., 1989; 2nd ed., 1994) includes a short biography of the leader of the MPB movement, the lyrics of Buarque's songs, a discography, and a filmography. The work lacks citations; includes archival photographs and an index.

3437 Comunicação & música popular massiva. Organização de João Freire Filho e Jeder Janotti Junior. Salvador: EDUFBA, 2006. 167 p.: bibl.

Collection of scholarly essays examining various styles of popular music at the turn of the 21st century, from samba to rock to hip-hop. The essays, from scholars working in communication studies, discuss ideologies of popular music, modes of production and consumption, processes of music circulation, reception, and identity.

3438 Dantas, Beatriz Góis. Representações sobre índios em danças e folguedos folclóricos. (*Rev. Inst. Hist. Geogr. Sergipe*, 35, 2006, p. 89–104, bibl., photo)

Brief but perceptive study, offers an analysis of the representations of Indians and blacks in folk dances of the Brazilian Northeast. Shows that in traditional dances Indians are portrayed as serious and courageous warriors, while blacks appear as happy individuals and good workers. Concludes that representations of Indians and blacks in traditional musical performances are similar to those found in classic literary and intellectual works that interpret Brazilian society from the standpoint of a tri-ethnic logic, a view the author believes has been transmitted orally to popular culture over time.

3439 Dent, Alexander Sebastian. Cross-cultural "countries": covers, conjuncture, and the whiff of Nashville in música sertaneja (Brazilian commercial country music). (*Pop. Music Soc.*, 28:2, May 2005, p. 207–227, bibl.)

Insightful study, examines a cover of the song "Achy Breaky Heart" by Brazilian singers of *música sertaneja* (country music). Argues that *sertaneja* musicians covering English-language songs create cross-cultural spaces, and that they cannot be simply understood as cases of cultural imperialism.

3440 Dent, Alexander Sebastian. River of tears: country music, memory, and modernity in Brazil. Durham, N.C.: Duke Univ. Press, 2009. 297 p.: bibl., ill., index.

An outgrowth of the author's doctoral work, this book is a welcome ethnographic study focusing on the production and reception of Brazilian country music. Addresses Brazilian *música sertaneja* musicians as mediators between rural and urban spaces, as their songs negotiate concepts of forward-looking and backwardness within the music industry.

3441 Dias, Adriana Albert. Mandinga, manha & malícia: uma história sobre os capoeiristas na capital da Bahia, 1910–1925. Salvador, Brazil: EDUFBA, 2006. 194 p.: appendixes, bibl., ill., photos.

The work, a revision of the author's masters thesis (Universidade Federal da Bahia, 2004), is supported by archival research and fieldwork (interviews) to reconstruct the early history of capoeira performances in Bahia. The author delineates the geographical spaces of performances and addresses the social ambiguities that permeated the daily lives of early 20th century capoeira masters. Includes photographs, appendices with names of early 20th century capoeiristas, and bibliography.

3442 Durão, Fabio Akcelrud and **José Adriano Fenerick.** Appropriation in reverse; or what happens when popular music goes dodecaphonic. (*Lat. Am. Music Rev.*, 30:1, Spring/Summer 2009, p. 56–68, bibl.)

Study of Brazilian composer Arrigo Barbabé's piece "Acapulco Drive-in" (1980). Offers a brief history of Brazilian popular music post-1964 and an analysis of the work's characteristics in terms of rhythm, melody, and vocal emission. Argues that the use of serialism in popular music results in highly elaborate compositions that can be used as commodities.

3443 Encontro de Musicologia Histórica, 6th, Juiz de Fora, Brazil, 2004. Anais. Juiz de Fora, Brazil: Centro Cultural Pró-Música, 2006. 527 p.: bibl., ill.

Annals of the 2004 national meeting of historical musicology in Juiz de Fora, state of Minas Gerais. This is the sixth in a series of biannual meetings (the first was held in 1994) gathering the most recent research by Brazilian scholars. The present volume showcases the healthy state of Brazilian musicology; edited by musicologist Paulo Castagna, it includes 37 scholarly articles on a wide array of topics and periods raging from colonial days to the 20th century. The volume includes a most useful index listing all the papers presented in the past meetings (1994–2002).

3444 Hazan, Marcelo Campos. Música e morte, diferença e poder no Rio de Janeiro oitocentista: o inventário post-mortem de José Batista Brasileiro. (*Inter-Am. Music Rev.*, 17:1/2, Summer 2007, p. 205–226, tables)

Excellent study, investigates a group of 300 manuscripts, sacred pieces left by José Batista Brasileiro, a musician active in Rio de Janeiro during the first part of the 19th century. The author examines documents, music manuscripts (by Portuguese and Brazilian composers), and the performance practices associated with the repertory to highlight class, race, and gender hierarchies in 19th century Brazil. Includes an inventory of all pieces.

3445 Hertzman, Marc Adam. A Brazilian counterweight: music, intellectual property and the African diaspora in Rio de Janeiro, 1910s-1930s. (*J. Lat. Am. Stud.*, 41:4, Nov. 2009, p. 695–722)

Insightful study, examines discussions about intellectual property laws in early 20th century Rio de Janeiro and shows how black musicians adapted themselves and their music to international views about race, music, and property. Using interviews and newspaper articles to track the activities of a local musician, Tio Faustino, and comparing him to the internationally known composer/performer, Pixinguinha, the author claims that both musicians were subjected to local and external forces in constructing their identities. Argues that Afro-Brazilians explored solidarity with the African diaspora to assert the authenticity of their own musical legacy and to claim the legitimacy of their culture.

3446 Holler, Marcos Tadeu. O mito da música nas atividades da Companhia de Jesus no Brasil colonial. (*Rev. Eletrôn. Musicol.*, 11, set. 2007, bibl.)

Based on documentary work done in Brazilian and European archives, the author offers a new perspective regarding the importance of music in the missionary work of Jesuit priests in colonial Brazil. Addresses the exclusion of women from music making and the restrictions on instruments and on singing in specific services. Shows that similar restrictions were in place in the Jesuit work in the missions in India. Argues

that music was not as important in the Jesuit missions as was previously thought.

3447 Leu, Lorraine. Brazilian popular music: Caetano Veloso and the regeneration of tradition. Aldershot, England; Burlington, VT: Ashgate, 2006. 180 p.: bibl., ill., index. (Ashgate popular and folk music series)

Focusing on the work of Brazilian popular music icon, singer, and composer Caetano Veloso, the author seeks to understand the multidimensional nature of popular song: vocal performance, music, and cultural expression. She undertakes this enormous task in a rather brief manner by using selected recordings as case studies. Provides analysis of song lyrics and vocal styles, and offers an interpretation of the artist's use of body, clothing, and gender bending. The author places the essence and meaning of the artist's output in the cultural and political context of 1960s Brazil. Reviewed in *Latin American Music Review*, Vol. 29, No. 2, Fall/Winter 2008, p. 279–282; *Notes*, Vol. 63, No. 4, June 2007, p. 870–872; *Ethnomusicology*, Vol. 51, No. 3, Fall 2007, p. 486–491; *Popular Music and Society*, Vol. 31, No. 1, Feb. 2010, p. 126–127.

3448 Machado, Cacá. O enigma do homem célebre: ambição e vocação de Ernesto Nazareth. São Paulo: Instituto Moreira Salles, 2007. 264 p.: bibl., ill., index.

An outgrowth of the author's doctoral dissertation (Universidade de São Paulo, 2005), this work offers a musical analysis of Nazareth's famous piano pieces and places them in the cultural context of early 20th century Rio de Janeiro. Richly illustrated, the work includes a chronology, index, and a CD with four works discussed in the book.

3449 Magaldi, Cristina. Cosmopolitanism and world music in Rio de Janeiro at the turn of the twentieth century. (*Music Q.*, 92:3/4, Fall/Winter 2009, p. 329–364, ills., music, photos)

The author of the pathbreaking work, *Music in Imperial Rio de Janeiro: European culture in a tropical milieu* (see *HLAS 62:3592*), Magaldi has gone on to bring the impact of several musical cultures and interpretations in that capital city at the dawn of the 20th century. With a solid basis in theoretical approaches, Magaldi's research led her to a number of archives such as the Divisão de Música and Arquivo Sonoro in the Biblioteca Nacional, the author demonstrates the impact of music from Iberia, Asia, Europe, and the US in the emergence of popular music in the city as part of a larger context of international urban cultures. Contemporaries such as Luiz Edmundo stated that in Rio one could be proud to have the highest number of the best music best music halls with companies and artists that performed in Europe and North America. Slowly but surely, given Brazil's own demographic roots, American cakewalk found its own audiences and composers in Rio. Brazilian nationalism, now more focused on the African element, became intertwined with all facets of Brazilian life, including music. One hopes that Magaldi will go on to focus on the later 20th century and Brazil's premier composer, Villa Lobos. [I. Wiarda]

3450 Marchi, Lia. Tocadores Portugal—Brasil: sons em movimento. Curitiba: Olaria Projetos de Arte e Educação, 2006. 127 p.: bibl., ill. (some col.), col. maps, photos.

The text supplements the video documentary *Tocadores* (2003) documenting performances and musical instruments of selected popular traditions in contemporary Portugal and Brazil. Coffee-table format with exquisite photographs by Zig Koch, the book includes a bibliography and a list of websites.

3451 Metz, Jerry D. Cultural geographies of Afro-Brazilian symbolic practice: tradition and change in Maracatu de Nação (Recife, Pernambuco, Brazil). (*Lat. Am. Music Rev.*, 29:1, Spring/Summer 2008, p. 64–95, bibl., music, photos)

Explores the transformations in performance practices in contemporary *maracatu de nação* groups that parade during carnival in Recife and Olinda, state of Pernambuco. Suggests that substitutions of material objects in the performance—trading the single bell *gonguȩ* for the double-bell *agogô*, and replacing the traditional symbol of the *calunga* doll with a plastic doll wearing an African style outfit—offer a renewed sense of Africanness to modern participants and indicate a dispute over symbols of Afro-Brazilian identity in Pernambuco.

3452 Moehn, Frederick. Music, mixing and modernity in Rio de Janeiro. (*Ethnomusic. Forum*, 17:2, Nov. 2008, p. 165–202)

Suggests that the discourses of mixture and hybridity postulated by modernist intellectuals in the 1920s and 1930s continue to shape the ways Brazilian music is represented locally and abroad. Focusing on the career of singer/composer Fernanda Abreu, the author argues that the musical production of middle and upper class musicians in Rio de Janeiro shows a cultural ambivalence, as they are caught between social and cultural flows and conflicting views of modernity. Proposes the use of the word "mixing" rather than "hybridity" to characterize the cultural dynamics of middle class artists in a Brazilian urban setting, one in which mixings and stirrings of old and new materials will leave the Brazilian element recognizable.

3453 Moore, Robin. Editor's note: a selection of works of Gerard Béhague. (*Lat. Am. Music Rev.*, 27:1, Spring/Summer 2006, p. 28–37, bibl.)

Introduction to the memorial edition of *Latin American Music Review* in homage of Gerard Béhague. The volume includes nine essays by the musicologist, several of which deal with Brazilian music: "Indianism in Latin American art-music composition of the 1920s to 1940s: case studies from Mexico, Peru, and Brazil" (p. 28–37), "Música 'erudita,' 'folclórico,' e 'popular' do Brasil: interações e inferências para a musicologia e etnomusicologia modernas" (p. 57–68), and "Perspectivas atuais na perquisa musical e estratégias analíticas da Música Popular Brasileira" (p. 69–78).

3454 Museu vivo do fandango. Organização de Alexandre Pimentel, Daniella Gramani e Joana Corrêa. Rio de Janeiro: Associação Cultural Caburé, 2006. 199 p.: bibl., ill. (chiefly col.), photos.

Subsidized by Petrobras and organized by the Museum of Fandango, this volume successfully presents ethnographical material in a coffee table book format to report on and document the fandango tradition which is alive and vibrant in the south coastal region of the state of São Paulo. Exquisite photographs and maps help illustrate dance and performing styles, instruments and techniques, and help put into context individuals' life narratives. The volume also includes an introduction by anthropologist Antonio Carlos Dieques, two CDs, and a bibliography.

3455 Oosterbaan, Martijn. Spiritual attunement: Pentecostal radio in the soundscape of a favela in Rio de Janeiro. (*Soc. Text*, 96:3, Fall 2008, p. 123–145)

Ethnography, examines the growth of Pentecostal churches in Brazil and the importance of evangelical broadcasts in the everyday lives of residents of Rio de Janeiro's favelas. Shows how sound is used to delineate social spaces in the favelas, to express identity or alterity, and to differentiate the "worldly" (samba and funk) from the "Godly" (gospel). Describes the heterogenous soundscape of the favelas, where Evangelical radio listening is believed to instill Christian values and separate Evangelicals from the rest of the favela residents.

3456 Ópera à brasileira. Organização de João Luiz Sampaio. São Paulo: Algol Editora, 2009. 199 p.: bibl., ill. (some col.), photos.

This collection of essays by journalists, musicians, and scholars focuses on the difficult task of opera production in contemporary Brazil. Authors address cultural and governmental policies, archival research, the staging of contemporary works, musical taste, and generational preferences. Includes photographs of recent opera productions.

3457 Packman, Jeff. Signifyin(g) Salvador: professional musicians and the sound of flexibility in Bahia, Brazil's popular music scenes. (*Black Music Res. J.*, 29:1, Spring 2009, p. 83–126)

Focuses on the activities of local musicians as part of a flexible workforce in contemporary Salvador, Bahia. Addresses the politics of music making and the everyday struggle for survival in a competitive employment market. Describes the specificities of Salvador's music market, a city viewed as the "heart of Afro-Brazil." Describes the stylistic versatility of local musicians able to adapt to the musical demands linked to a seasonal (religious) calendar while staying active in a variety of nonseasonal venues, where they perform a core repertory by canonic composers.

3458 Perpetuo, Irineu Franco. Cyro Pereira, maestro. Organização e texto de Irineu Franco Perpetuo. São Paulo: DBA, 2005. 118 p.: ill. (some col.)

Biography of the Brazilian composer and conductor whose career is intertwined with famous musicians of Brazilian popular music. This coffee table book is richly illustrated and includes information about the composer's activities with the Orquestra Jazz Sinfônica in São Paulo.

3459 Resgate. Campinas, Brazil: Centro de Memória UNICAMP, Ano 2007, Num 16. 1 v.: ill.

This volume of the periodical *Resgate* (Universidade de Campinas) includes five articles on samba and an interview with singer Ilcéi Miriam.

3460 Risério, Antonio. Os tambores da terra: PercPan. São Paulo: BYI Projetos Culturais, 2004. 264 p.: ill. (chiefly col.), photos.

This coffee table book documents with exquisite photographs, by Marcelo Kertész, the International Percussion Festivals (Panorama Percussivo Mundial or PercPan) that have taken place since 1994 in Salvador, Bahia. Includes text in Portuguese and English.

3461 Seigel, Micol. The disappearing dance: Maxixe's imperial erasure. (*Black Music Res. J.*, 25:1/2, Spring/Fall 2005, p. 93–117, bibl.)

Well-researched study, examines the emergence, popularity, and disappearance of the Brazilian song/dance maxixe in the US early in the 20th century. Shows that US audiences enjoyed the maxixe and other Latin American dances as the result of an "exoticist culture of empire", as a way of adding another touch of "spice" to the US melting pot of cultures. US audiences consumed the maxixe as exotic, while ascribing to the dance racial and national traits and hierarchies. Demonstrates that the emergence and disappearance of the maxixe in the US was interwoven in the history of US internal social and racial relations.

3462 Severiano, Jairo. Uma história da música popular brasileira: das origens à modernidade. São Paulo: Editora 34, 2008. 499 p.: bibl., ill., index.

This history of Brazilian popular music from the late 18th to 20th centuries offers a good survey with general information on composers and performers, especially on the canonic styles and artists of the 20th century. Includes illustration, bibliography, and an index, but lacks citations and is therefore of limited scholarly use.

3463 Simson, Olga Rodrigues de Moraes von. Carnaval em branco e negro: carnaval popular paulistano, 1914–1988. Campinas, Brazil: Editora UNICAMP; São Paulo: Edusp: Imprensa Oficial, 2007. 389 p.: bibl., ill.

This history of carnival in São Paulo relies on documents, archival photographs, and interviews with 15 people who lived through the transformations of carnival celebrations in the city. Describes the ethnic and racial components of these celebrations and maps different carnival styles in several São Paulo neighborhoods. The volume is richly illustrated and includes an extensive bibliography.

3464 Sneed, Paul. Favela utopias: the *bailes funk* in Rio's crisis of social exclusion and violence. (*LARR*, 43:2, 2008, p. 57–79, bibl.)

Ethnographic study, describes the musical scene and cultural context of the *bailes funk* in Rio de Janeiro's favelas. Discusses meanings of song lyrics and addresses gender and class relations among participants of *bailes*. Argues that *bailes* and funk music offer a temporary, collective space and a "utopian experience," in which participants rise above scarcity, vulnerability, and the dreariness of poverty and social exclusion.

3465 Sotuyo, Pablo. Damião Barbosa de Araújo, 1778–1856: novas achegas biográficas e musicais. Salvador, Brazil: Fundação Gregório de Mattos: EDUFBA, 2007. 162 p.: bibl., ill.

This archival study on the life and work of the composer from Bahia assigns dates and authorship to selected works and provides information on Araújo's activities in Rio de Janeiro and Salvador early in the 19th century.

3466 Stroud, Sean. The defence of tradition in Brazilian popular music: politics, culture, and the creation of música popular

brasileira. Aldershot, England; Burlington, VT: Ashgate, 2008. 215 p.: bibl., index. (Ashgate popular and folk music series)

Scholarly study relates the emergence, popularity, and canonical status of Música Popular Brasileira (MPB) to a surge of nationalistic sentiments in Brazil during the 1970s. Examines the debates about cultural imperialism, national culture, music authenticity, and globalization that helped shape the music. Concludes that MPB was bound up with the Brazilian middle class and that it has lost its appeal as a symbol of national identity for the wider public in contemporary Brazil. Reviewed in *Popular Music*, Vol. 29, No. 1, Jan. 2010, p. 173–176; *Journal of Latin American Studies*, Vol. 41, No. 1, Feb. 2009, p. 183–184.

3467 Travassos, Elizabeth. Tradição oral e história. (*Rev. Hist./São Paulo*, 157, segundo semestre 2007, p. 129–152, bibl.)

Examines the confluence between history and tradition in historical and anthropological studies and, by extension, in musicology and ethnomusicology. Shows that the performances of *caxambu* or *jongo* in the region of the Paraíba River valley (state of Rio de Janeiro) are examples of traditional styles shaped by history and that they challenge accepted views offered by historians and social scientists.

3468 Tyrrell, Sarah. M. Camargo Guarnieri and the influence of Mário de Andrade's modernism. (*Lat. Am. Music Rev.*, 29:1, Spring/Summer 2008, p. 44–63, bibl.)

Explores the relationship between Guarnieri's music and the nationalist and modernist ideologies put forward during the 1930s by Mário de Andrade. Describes Guarnieri's music as a successful marriage between a modern esthetic and a nationalistic ideology. Outlines the composer's musical language and the reception of his music.

3469 Vicente, Eduardo. Música e fé: a cena religiosa no mercado fonográfico brasileiro. (*Lat. Am. Music Rev.*, 29:1, Spring/Summer 2008, p. 29–42, bibl.)

Examines the growth of the market for recordings of religious music in Brazil, in particular for Catholic and Evangelist musics, and surveys the main recording labels and artists. Shows that this emergent market has not yet received the attention of the Brazilian major labels, and that it operates autonomously, separated from the mainstream recording industry.

3470 Violões do Brasil. Organização de Myriam Taubkin. 2a ed. revista e ampliada. São Paulo: Editora Senac: Edições Sesc-SP, 2007. 234 p.: bibl., col. ill., photos.

The volume accompanies a DVD, *Violões do Brasil*, which documents the performance of renowned Brazilian guitar performers. In coffee table format, the volume includes a brief history of the guitar in Brazil and a short essay on selected performers, a few of whom provided narratives themselves. It also includes exquisite photographs documenting the work of Brazilian luthiers and a list of performers and luthiers active today.

PHILOSOPHY:
LATIN AMERICAN THOUGHT

JUAN CARLOS TORCHIA ESTRADA, *Independent Consultant, Hispanic Division, Library of Congress, Washington, DC*
CLARA ALICIA JALIF DE BERTRANOU, *Professor, Facultad de Filosofía y Letras, Universidad Nacional de Cuyo, Mendoza, Argentina*

TANTO LOS MATERIALES de esta Sección como su orientación son similares a los de los años inmediatamente anteriores.[1]

No hay mucho estudio de la producción filosófica propiamente dicha, porque en este sentido la atención de los críticos latinoamericanos va más hacia la filosofía europea o norteamericana que hacia la propia. Pero sí se encuentra amplia contribución a la historia de las ideas de la región, la cual es más variada en temas y con frecuencia movida por el interés que siempre despierta en América Latina el pensamiento político y social. Hay un amplio desarrollo de la profesión filosófica en la región, al punto de que en ciertos casos se ha cancelado la distancia que antes separaba a la filosofía latinoamericana de la que se producía en los grandes centros culturares de Occidente; pero este aspecto no se cubre ahora en el *Handbook*, por decisión editorial y porque sería imposible cubrirlo sin desproporcionar la economía del volumen. Esto debe tenerse presente porque esa actividad existe, pero no se refleja en estas páginas. Lo que ocupa mucho del espacio disponible son las grandes vistas interpretativas de América Latina, tanto en lo que ella fue en su pasado como en los rumbos que se estima debería tomar en el futuro. Estas contribuciones, aun cuando proceden del ámbito académico, no son necesariamente siempre historia o filosofía en el sentido profesional de la palabra, y suelen adoptar el tono del ensayo interpretativo y responder a preferencias políticas o ideológicas. Sin embargo, su omisión restaría mucho a la visión general de las orientaciones de pensamiento en Latinoamérica. En este sentido, y desde hace algunos años, existe una abundante literatura que retoma las posiciones intelectuales de izquierda, que habían disminuido tras el fin del "socialismo realmente existente". La ocasión para su retorno la proporcionó lo que se ha considerado el fracaso de las medidas económicas neoliberales, aplicadas en algunos casos sin consideración a las condiciones específicas del país correspondiente y con serias consecuencias sociales. (Estas consecuencias han jugado un importante papel en el cambio). Esto explicaría, en la bibliografía aquí considerada, la omnipresente crítica al neoliberalismo, a la cual se suma la denuncia a la " globalización hegemónica" (es decir, la globalización entendida no sólo como fenómeno mundial, sino también como intención) y a veces la posible reconsideración de las ideas socialistas, bien que casi siempre éstas se postulan en términos muy generales. Hay también críticas a estas posiciones (especialmente cuando se muestran a favor de ciertos gobiernos latinoamericanos), pero no son mayoritarias. Como es habitual en esta Sección, los aspectos más salientes se indican en los distintos apartados de la Introducción.

GENERAL

Para mejor intelección del lector el material de esta subsección puede agruparse según determinados temas o en función de la naturaleza de las contribuciones. En materia de fuentes encontramos la continuación de la edición del *Thesaurus Indicus* de Diego de Avendaño, empresa llevada a cabo con gran propiedad (ítems **3476** y **3477**). (Ver también *HLAS 62:3621*). En cuanto a trabajos monográficos, vale destacar: un buen estudio sobre Ginés de Sepúlveda (item **3533**); el primer tomo de un amplio proyecto de *Historia de los intelectuales en América Latina* (item **3511**); un logrado libro sobre los hispanistas norteamericanos (item **3515**); y una valiosa obra sobre la universidad latinoamericana (item **3534**). Por la naturaleza de los trabajos que contiene entraría también en este grupo el item **3552**.

También es de particular interés para nosotros el material de estudio de la filosofía latinoamericana. La influencia de Heidegger está representada en el item **3488**. La hermenéutica en América Latina, en el item **3509**. Una obra fundamental y de amplias dimensiones, realizada en España, es *El legado filosófico español e hispanoamericano* (item **3517**). A ella se une *El pensamiento filosófico latinoamericano, del Caribe y "latino"* (item **3535**), un intento enciclopédico sobre la filosofía latinoamericana desde sus orígenes hasta la actualidad y en la que colaboraron numerosos autores. Son también panorámicos sobre la filosofía latinoamericana los trabajos de Pablo Guadarrama González (items **3505** y **3506**), especialmente el segundo, con dimensión de libro. Y nunca falta el reiterado tema de la posibilidad y naturaleza de la filosofía latinoamericana, como se advierte en el item **3525**.

Ya no específicamente sobre la filosofía latinoamericana, sino sobre aspectos generales de las ideas se encuentran, como siempre, varias contribuciones. Señalamos, como ejemplo, un excelente libro sobre pensadores latinoamericanos del siglo XX (item **3536**); un artículo sobre el liberalismo (item **3539**); un buen examen del marxismo en América Latina (item **3554**); un análisis de la idea de ciudadanía en la época colonial (item **3507**); y un volumen colectivo sobre la integración latinoamericana (item **3514**).

Una preocupación siempre presente es la de lo que podría denominarse la interpretación de América Latina. Al respecto encontramos: una comparación entre Helio Jaguaribe y Samuel Huntington (item **3482**); un libro sobre el llamado descubrimiento de América elaborado desde categorías no convencionales (item **3501**); el tema de América Latina como cultura o civilización (item **3526**); un artículo sobre el positivismo y el postmodernismo como enfoques de interpretación de la realidad latinoamericana (item **3531**); y un libro sobre identidad nacional y violencia (item **3538**).

Proclives a la defensa de un pensamiento socialista son los trabajos recogidos en los siguientes ítems: **3479**, **3484**, **3511**, **3540** y **3557**. Responden a la misma motivación general un libro sobre el pensamiento social en América Latina (item **3486**) y un diccionario del pensamiento alternativo, parte de una obra más amplia (item **3495**). La crítica más decantada a estas posiciones se encontrará en la publicación de los resultados de un seminario sobre la izquierda (item **3546**).

En otros casos es fácil reconocer la agrupación por temas. Así los siguientes: utopía, con frecuente mención de Fernando Aínsa (items **3481**, **3541**, **3542** y **3547**); redes intelectuales (items **3494**, **3510** y **3537**); feminismo y estudios de género (items **3502**, **3503**, **3555** y **3558**); multiculturalismo, con especial referencia a Raúl Fornet Betancourt (items **3498**, **3518** y **3545**). (Sobre filosofía intercultural puede verse *HLAS 64:2862* y *2864*.)

La preocupación por los estudios postcoloniales está presente en una obra importante dentro de esa literatura (item **3483**) y una visión de conjunto que realmente ilumina el tema (item **3530**).

Más difícil es dar cuenta con algún detalle de ciertos volúmenes colectivos, por la variedad de temas, que es independiente de la calidad de los artículos individuales. Pero no querríamos dejar de señalar números especiales de publicaciones periódicas, como, por ejemplo, tres de *Cuadernos Americanos*: ítems **3489**, **3490** y **3491**.

MÉXICO

Sobre el pensamiento mexicano hay dos buenas contribuciones de Mauricio Beuchot, filósofo y máxima autoridad sobre la filosofía colonial en el país: *Cartografía del pensamiento novohispano* (item **3562**) y *Ciencia y filosofía en México en el siglo XX* (item **3563**). Leopoldo Zea es objeto de varios trabajos: tres artículos (items **3564**, **3578** y **3579**) y un volumen de homenaje con motivo de su muerte (item **3570**). Una visión de conjunto sobre la estética en México fue realizada por María Rosa Palazón (item **3575**). Se destacan también: una buena antología de escritos de Pablo González Casanova (item **3569**), y artículos sobre: José Gaos (item **3565**); Fray Servando Teresa de Mier (item **3572**) y Adolfo Sánchez Vázquez (item **3582**). Se recoge también un buen conjunto de ensayos sobre historia intelectual mexicana (item **3577**).

AMÉRICA CENTRAL

Excepcionalmente se registra una sola entrada referente a esta región y el tema es la influencia de Ortega y Gasset en Honduras (item **3585**).

CARIBE INSULAR

Se encuentran aquí cuatro obras de índole general sobre el Caribe. Una sobre el autor jamaiquino Stuart Hall (item **3590**); otra que reúne escritos de autores de lengua inglesa, española y francesa (item **3586**); una tercera, muy bien realizada, sobre los autores caribeños y la tradición (item **3592**); y una última sobre la producción del saber en el Caribe (item **3600**). Dentro de sus características individuales, las cuatro son obras bien logradas.

Respecto de Cuba, Eduardo Torres Cuevas continúa su *Historia del pensamiento cubano*(item **3594**) y Rafael Rojas reitera la calidad de sus ensayos sobre la vida intelectual cubana (items **3598** y **3599**). Como siempre, está presente el interés por Martí (items **3595** y **3597**). Como Haití está generalmente escasamente representado, conviene señalar que se encuentra un artículo sobre el "indigenismo" haitiano (item **3596**).

VENEZUELA

Hay tres artículos que atienden a la filosofía en Venezuela: en el aspecto colonial (item **3608**); sobre fenomenología y existencialismo (item **3610**); y sobre el filósofo contemporáneo Ernesto Mayz Vallenilla (item **3617**). Entre otras entradas, Bolívar está representado por una "antología polémica" (item **3602**) y por su pensamiento sobre la unidad hispanoamericana (item **3614**). Son de interés también un artículo sobre la biblioteca personal de Francisco de Miranda (item **3606**) y otro que trata las ideas políticas y educativas de Simón Rodríguez, este último de Javier Ocampo López (item **3612**).

COLOMBIA

Se destacan dos amplios volúmenes sobre el pensamiento colombiano del siglo XX, representativos de una gran variedad de labor intelectual, y no sólo de la filosofía (items **3621** y **3622**). Otro serio esfuerzo, éste desde el punto de vista filosófico, es un coloquio sobre la filosofía y la crisis colombiana (item **3619**). También se recuerda al filósofo Estanislao Zuleta (item **3624**), y en el orden de los artículos vale mencionar uno sobre la idea de progreso en Colombia desde el siglo XVIII (item **3623**).

ECUADOR y PERÚ

Casi todos los materiales incluidos son de verdadero interés. Destacamos un libro sobre Gabriel García Moreno (item **3626**), una obra de autores que se reconocen como representantes de diferentes etnias y aplican esa condición a su trabajo profesional (item **3627**), y un buen libro sobre la influencia de Sartre (item **3630**).

La obra de mayor aliento es la que fue coordinada por María Luisa Rivara de Tuesta sobre la intelectualidad peruana del siglo XX (item **3642**). Artículos sobre filósofos se encuentran dos: uno sobre Augusto Salazar Bondy (item **3631**) y otro sobre Pedro Zulen (item **3647**). Haya de la Torre y el APRA tienen varias entradas: ítems **3636**, **3640** y **3654**. Como siempre, José Carlos Mariátegui sigue despertando interés, como se refleja en los ítems **3632**, **3635**, **3638**, **3641**, **3644**, **3651** y **3652**. Es destacable también un libro sobre la tradicional cultura andina, interpretada y defendida desde sus propias bases conceptuales (item **3653**).

CHILE

Dos entradas se refieren a la filosofía chilena: una a su historia (item **3658**), y la otra a las condiciones de su efectiva constitución (item **3662**). Un libro sobre Francisco Bilbao (item **3657**) recoge documentos y textos sobre este pensador chileno.

BRASIL

El número de entradas sobre Brasil es menor que en otras oportunidades. Desde el punto de vista estrictamente filosófico se destacan una investigación sobre la recepción de Kant en el país (item **3674**) y un libro sobre la filosofía en la universidad (item **3668**). En cuanto a figuras individuales, hay dos buenas obras sobre Celso Furtado (ítems **3665** y **3666**); una, también muy bien elaborada, sobre Joaquim Nabuco (item **3663**); una biografía intelectual de Caio Prado Jr., de buena factura académica (item **3671**), y una antología de este mismo autor (item **3680**). La literatura sobre Gilberto Freyre no da muestras de decrecer, y en esta entrega hay dos obras de buena calidad sobre él: ítems **3667** y **3673**). El cuarto centenario del jesuita Antonio Vieira ha dado lugar a varios trabajos: ítems **3675**, **3676**, **3678**, **3681**. Además del interés que presenta la recepción de Franz Fanon en Brasil (item **3670**), destacamos un ensayo bien logrado sobre las interpretaciones de la realidad brasileña, de Bernardo Ricupero (item **3682**).

PARAGUAY

Es afortunado recoger una publicación sobre el pensamiento paraguayo del siglo XX (item **3684**), dado lo infrecuente de ese tipo de estudios sobre Paraguay.

URUGUAY

De la no muy abundante representación de materiales de Uruguay, en esta entrega destacamos una apreciación general del país por el intelectual hispano–uruguayo Fernando Aínsa (item **3685**)

ARGENTINA

Entre monográficas y de síntesis, se destacan varias obras referentes a Argentina: un libro clásico sobre el krausismo en el país (item **3716**); un estudio del socialismo argentino en la primera mitad del siglo XX (item **3703**); y una clara síntesis de la historia de las ideas en la Argentina (item **3722**). En el orden de los volúmenes colectivos, es de particular interés *Argentina entre el optimismo y el desencanto* (item **3690**), y una obra que, bajo el rótulo general de 'pensamiento alternativo', estudia temas históricos en los que predomina la intención de reivindicación social (item **3709**). Se recuperan textos del filósofo Carlos Astrada (item **3691**) y de la recepción de Darwin en el país (item **3710**). Se ha enriquecido la serie de ediciones de textos de filosofía colonial, como lo muestran los ítems **3720**, **3721** y **3706**. Encontramos asimismo materiales sobre autores individuales: Alberdi (item **3689**), Eduardo Wilde (item **3698**), Arturo A. Roig (item **3702**), Alberto Rougès (item **3707**), Bernardo Monteagudo (item **3723**), y Sarmiento (item **3724**). Alberdi y Sarmiento, además de Eduardo Mallea y Víctor Massuh son estudiados, entre otros temas, por Lucía Piossek Prebisch (item **3711**). [JCTE]

NOTE:

1. Para una descripción de los temas que incluye esta Sección puede verse la Introducción del *HLAS 52*, p. 751. En el *HLAS 58*, p. 731–734, mostramos cómo los materiales incluidos y su tratamiento se fueron desarrollando a lo largo del tiempo, acompañando el proceso del pensamiento latinoamericano y el de la política editorial del *Handbook*.

GENERAL

3471 Abellán, José Luis. España—América Latina, 1900–1940: la consolidación de una solidaridad. (*Rev. Indias*, 67:239, enero/abril 2007, p. 15–32, bibl.)

Considera el período 1900–40 como una etapa de vigencia del modernismo literario, con el cual se habría producido un nuevo y fecundo acercamiento entre España e Hispanoamérica. Destaca los intelectuales de ambas regiones cuyas letras y amistades habrían propiciado ese hecho. Algunos de ellos son: Rafael Altamira, Miguel de Unamuno, Rubén Darío, Alfonso Reyes y Pedro Henríquez Ureña. [CJB]

3472 Acosta, Yamandú. Filosofía latinoamericana y sujeto. Caracas: Editorial El Perro y la Rana, 2008. 216 p.

Reunión de dos libros anteriores: *Sujeto y democratización en el contexto de la globalización* (2005) y *Filosofía latinoamericana y democracia en clave de derechos humanos* (2008). Dialoga con diversos autores, pero es apreciable la influencia de Arturo A. Roig y Franz Hinkelammert. El propósito es aportar a una universalidad concreta donde el horizonte futuro permitiría la convivencia sin exclusiones y la vigencia de los derechos humanos. El estilo expositivo no favorece la comprensión del lector. [CJB]

3473 Aguilar Camín, Héctor. Pensando en la izquierda. México: Fondo de Cultura Económica, 2008. 70 p. (Centzontle)

La socialdemocracia le parece al autor el modo de conciliar la producción de riqueza con el sentido de justicia social. El breve libro contiene duras críticas al pensamiento de izquierda en general, pero en particular al mexicano. [JCTE]

3474 Ainsa, Fernando. Matices del *otro* Occidente. (*Cuad. Am./México*, 121:3, julio/sept. 2007, p. 11–25)

Pasadas las discusiones y los acalorados debates originados por el V Centenario, el autor se pregunta qué quedó de ello y de los buenos propósitos entonces expresados, especialmente sobre las relaciones entre dos mundos "desencontrados". Sostiene que América no es el "extremo Occidente", sino "el otro Occidente" (según la expresión de José Guilherme Merquior), por herencia propia y por la europea. Pese a sus tensiones, se ofrecería como espacio para el diálogo plural e intercultural. [CJB]

3475 Astigueta, Bernardo P. Problemática filosófica del siglo XX: filosofía universal y filosofía latinoamericana. (*Iberoamericana/Tokyo*, 27:2, 2005, p. 39–51, bibl.)

Artículo de carácter general que, en lo que se refiere a la filosofía latinoamericana, abarca desde Juan Bautista Alberdi hasta la actualidad. Contiene algunas ideas cuestionables (por ejemplo, Alberdi sería un escéptico). También se encuentran ciertos errores: no fue Francisco Romero el precursor de dos corrientes que señala el autor (la histórica y la teórica) sino Alejandro Korn. [CJB]

3476 Avendaño, Diego de. Corregidores, encomenderos, cabildos y mercaderes: thesaurus indicus, vol. 1, Tít. VI-IX. Introducción, texto y traducción de Ángel Muñoz García. Pamplona, Spain: Ediciones Univ. de Navarra (EUNSA), 2007. 518 p.: bibl. (Col. de pensamiento medieval y renacentista; 93)

Esta parte de la valiosa edición del *Thesaurus* (1668) de Diego de Avendaño continúa la reseñada en *HLAS 62:3621*. La Introducción es de excelente calidad, y a pesar de su erudición resulta de agradable lectura. Aclara procedimientos de los corregidores y es de especial interés la parte correspondiente a la esclavitud. [JCTE]

3477 Avendaño, Diego de. Mineros de Indias y Protectores de Indios: Thesaurus Indicus, vol. I, Tít. X-XI y complementos. Introducción y traducción de Angel Muñoz García. Pamplona, Spain: Ediciones Univ. de Navarra (EUNSA), 2009. 335 p. (Col. de pensamiento medieval y renacentista; 103)

Se le aplican las mismas características del item anterior (item **3476**). Es una valiosa fuente de información para el historiador de las ideas. [JCTE]

3478 Barreto, Luz Marina. El socialismo del siglo XXI y los límites de las utopías en la racionalidad y la motivación humanas. (*Colomb. Int.*, 66, julio/dic. 2007, p. 52–69, bibl.)

Asume la defensa del modelo liberal clásico en las instituciones políticas, por apoyarse en el concepto de 'justicia' antes que en el de 'bienestar', característico de los "programas utópicos". Critica al llamado "socialismo del siglo XXI" del presidente venezolano Hugo Chávez. Este contribuiría, en aras de una justicia para todos, a negar la racionalidad de los individuos, del mismo modo que lo hacen las derechas en el marco de una economía neoclásica. [CJB]

3479 Borón, Atilio. Socialismo siglo XXI: ¿hay vida después del neoliberalismo? Buenos Aires: Ediciones Luxemburg: Badaraco Distribuidor, 2008. 143 p.: bibl.

Propuesta de socialismo para América Latina en el siglo XXI. Tesis básicas: el capitalismo no es el camino para el desarrollo de la región; las condiciones que permitían un desarrollo autónomo por la vía capitalista han desaparecido. No se limita a la crítica, y presenta alternativas al sistema actual. [JCTE]

3480 Bracho, Jorge. Estado y cultura: un acercamiento a su desenvolvimiento y percepciones letradas. (*Tierra Firme/Caracas*, 23:91, julio/sept. 2005, p. 299–310, bibl.)

Reflexión sobre el vínculo entre estado y cultura, examinado en el mundo moderno y en América Latina. Uno de los principales temas es el de desarrollo y cultura, conceptos que se vinculan a los de nación e identidad nacional. Una nueva relación entre estado y cultura recogería la expresión de los sectores subalternos, teniendo en cuenta que toda concepción de la cultura sería de "tenor político". [CJB]

3481 Celentano, Adrián. Utopía: historia, concepto y política. (*Utop. Prax. Latinoam.*, 10:31, oct./dic. 2005, p. 93–114)

Analiza el concepto de utopía, del cual dice que no ha sido objeto de una teoría crítica, y reconoce varias etapas en su historia. En el caso latinoamericano, se detiene en los escritos de Arturo A. Roig. Concluye que el pensamiento utópico debería incursionar en la relación entre cada posición política y los elementos utópicos contenidos. [CJB]

3482 Clemente Bolívar, José. Helio Jaguaribe y Samuel Huntington: dos visiones de América Latina. (*Tierra Firme/Caracas*, 28:62/63, 2007, p. 230–237)

Compara los puntos de vista de Helio Jaguaribe en *Un estudio crítico de la historia* y de Samuel Huntington en *The Clash of Civilizations*, en lo que se refiere a considerar América Latina como una civilización independiente o como parte de la cultura occidental. [JCTE]

Coello de la Rosa, Alexandre. Historias naturales y colonialismo: Gonzalo Fernández de Oviedo y José de Acosta. See item **404**.

3483 Coloniality at large: Latin America and the postcolonial debate. Edited by Mabel Moraña, Enrique Dussel, and Carlos Jáuregui. Durham, N.C.: Duke Univ. Press, 2008. 628 p.: bibl., index. (Latin America otherwise: languages, empires, nations)

Obra difícil de resumir por su extensión y el número de contribuyentes importantes dentro del tema. Algunos de los autores más representativos son Aníbal Quijano, Walter Mignolo, Santiago Castro Gómez, Enrique Dussel y Fernando Coronil. El objeto permanente de crítica es Occidente (que incluye a Estados Unidos) y su cultura, no sólo por su pasado colonialista, sino también por lo que su eurocentrismo ha significado para la incomprensión, negación y dominio de la periferia. No queda eximido del reproche de eurocentrismo el Sistema-Mundo de Wallerstein. Se reitera la defensa de la teoría de la dependencia, y se favorece la atención a los estudios subalternos. Se quieren explicar los efectos del colonialismo aún después de la descolonización política, situación que se prolongaría debido a la hegemonía de Occidente. Representa un movimiento académico en defensa del mundo colonizado, aunque en general los autores no quieren asumir una posición paternalista. El artículo de Santiago Castro Gómez es un buen mapa de la tendencia representada por el volumen. La exposición más comprensible para un público general es la de Aníbal Quijano. La de Dussel es una narración muy rica de los orígenes y el desarrollo de la filosofía de la liberación. Occidente, capitalismo y modernidad son temas resaltados en la exposición de Mignolo. Favorece el equilibrio del volumen la inclusión del artículo de Mario Roberto Morales, crítico de la academia norteamericana y que distingue entre la situación subalterna de América Latina y la de los otros países postcoloniales. Dentro del tema, cultivado por un grupo afín de autores, es uno de los volúmenes más significativos que se han escrito. [JCTE]

3484 El comunismo: otras miradas desde América Latina. Coordinación de Elvira Concheiro Bórquez, Massimo Modonesi y Horacio Crespo. México: UNAM; Centro de Investigaciones Interdisciplinarias en Ciencias y Humanidades, 2007. 683 p.: bibl. (Col. Debate y reflexión; 9)

Resultado de un coloquio realizado en México en 2005. Se intenta "una nueva conceptualización" del 'comunismo' después del derrumbe de la Unión Soviética. Además de contribuciones sobre el comunismo en general las hay también sobre marxismo y socialismo en América Latina, y casos especiales sobre el comunismo en Argentina, Brasil, Chile, Guatemala, Perú y México. [JCTE]

3485 Contemporary Latin American social and political thought: an anthology. Edited by Iván Márquez. Lanham, Md.: Rowman & Littlefield Publishers, 2008. 391 p.: bibl., ill., index. (Latin American perspectives in the classroom)

La selección de autores es muy amplia, pero todos representan un pensamiento directamente enfocado hacia la praxis. (En el prefacio se reconoce este hecho, diferenciado de las comunidades académicas que buscan una teoría y la argumentan.) Los grande temas y los correspondientes autores estudiados son: Resistencia y liberación (Rigoberta Menchú, Domitila Barrios de Chungara); Teología, filosofía y pedagogía de la liberación (Gutiérrez, Boff, Cardenal, Dussel, Paulo Freire); Teoría de la dependencia (Galeano, Prebisch, Faletto, Teotonio dos Santos y los autores del Manual del perfecto idiota latinoamericano); Guerrilla y socialismo (Guevara, Marighela, movimiento zapatista). También se consideran autores posteriores al fin de la Guerra fría (Evelina Dagnino, Jorge Castañeda, Salinas de Gortari, Roberto Mangabeira Unger, Hernando de Soto). [JCTE]

3486 Contribuciones al pensamiento social de América Latina. Coordinación del Centro Mexicano de Estudios Sociales, A.C. México: Centro de Investigaciones Interdisciplinarias en Ciencias y Humanidades, UNAM, 2007. 290 p.: bibl. (Col. Debate y reflexión)

"Pensamiento social" se entiende aquí más bien como pensamiento político, y éste, a veces, se toma en términos muy amplios, como lo muestra la inclusión de ocho hombres de letras, entre ellos Alejo Carpentier y Alfonso Reyes. También figura un filósofo como Leopoldo Zea. Otros son activistas políticos como Pedro Albizu

Campos; sociólogos como Sergio Bagú y Darcy Ribeiro; figuras revolucionarias como Ernesto Guevara y Camilo Torres, y algunos menos conocidos, como el marxista ecuatoriano Manuel Aguirre. Las mencionadas no son las únicas figuras incluidas. Un volumen, por lo tanto, muy variado. [JCTE]

3487 Cordero, Allen. El paradigma inconcluso: Kuhn y la sociología en América Latina. Guatemala: Postgrado Centroamericano, FLACSO-Costa Rica, FLACSO-El Salvador, FLACSO-Guatemala, 2008. 192 p.: bibl., ill. (Col. Lecturas de ciencias sociales; 2)

La obra de Kuhn, *The Structure of Scientific Revolutions* (especialmente en su 2a ed. de 1970), fue pensada para las ciencias naturales "duras", y aquí se aplica a las ciencias sociales en América Latina—una región donde el enfoque de estas últimas ciencias suele darse junto con la preocupación social y de reforma. Pero el propósito del autor— que el texto sirva para estudiantes—queda ampliamente logrado por la extensa y compleja discusión del asunto. [JCTE]

3488 Cortés-Boussac, Andrea. Heidegger en Latinoamérica. (*Humanitas/Monterrey*, 1:34, 2007, p. 75–97)

Ejemplifica la recepción y asimilación de Heidegger en América Latina con varios autores: Carlos Astrada, Alberto Wagner de Reyna, José Gaos, Emilio Uranga, Octavio Paz, Danilo Cruz Vélez, Rodolfo Kusch. Distingue tres etapas: lectura y traducción; explicación e interpretación (Astrada, Wagner de Reyna, Víctor Farias); y aplicación al pensar latinoamericano (Uranga, Cruz Vélez, Kusch). Este esquema es un tanto simplificado, pero expresa lo principal de la exposición del autor. [JCTE]

3489 *Cuadernos Americanos.* Vol. 22, No. 3, julio/sept. 2008. México: UNAM.

Son de interés en este número tres secciones: (1) Cultura e identidad: "Nuestra América: identidad y cultura" (Andrés Fábregas Puig); "Universidad, cultura y democracia en América Latina: la era neoliberal" (Rafael Cuevas Molina). (2) Bicentenario de la Independencia: "El mito de Garibaldi en las Américas" (Alberto Filippi); "Manuela Sáenz: 'mi patria es el continente de la América'" (Jenny Londoño López); "Laberintos de la independencia grancolom-

bina: polémica entre Constant y De Pradt" (Carolina Guerrero). (3) Estudios martianos: "Los Cuadernos de apuntes de José Martí o la legitimación de la escritura" (Caridad Atencio); "Las Escenas norteamericanas: su calidad polifónica" (Marlene Vázquez Pérez); "El guiño sonriente de José Martí en sus apuntes de viaje por Guatemala" (Egberto Almenas). [CJB]

3490 *Cuadernos Americanos.* Vol. 23, No. 1, enero/marzo 2009. México: UNAM.

Presenta dos secciones de interés: (1) Revistas culturales: "Cuadernos Americanos y el exilio español" (Ana González Neira); "Repertorio americano y el discurso cultural, 1919–1949" (Flora Ovares); "La revista académica" (Fernando Curiel). (2) Bicentenario de la Independencia: "Francisco de Miranda en la guerra de independencia de las trece colonias: ¿realidad o leyenda?" (Wilfredo Padrón Iglesias); "Simón Rodríguez y José Martí en las biografías de Alfonso Rumazo González" (Lupe Rumazo); "Manuela Sáenz: la insurrección, la nación y la patria" (Cecilia Méndez Mora). [CJB]

3491 *Cuadernos Americanos.* Vol. 24, No. 2, abril/junio 2008. México: UNAM.

Este número contiene colaboraciones en tres grandes temas: (1) Universidad e integración: "Educación, ciencia y desarrollo: el caso de América Latina" (José Narro Robles). (2) Bicentenario de la Independencia: "Miranda: el viaje ilustrado de un nómada" (Fernando Guzmán Toro); "Junta soberana de Quito (1809): el primer gobierno autónomo de Hispanoamérica" (Jorge Núñez Sánchez); "Confederación anfictiónica: orígenes del modelo bolivariano de unión hispanoamericana" (Germán A. de la Reza); "Repercusión de las ideas ilustradas en la Revolución de Independencia" (Alberto Saladino García). (3) Pensamiento social latinoamericano: "Hart y la revolución de las palabras" (Pablo González Casanova); "El hombre como ser social en Juan David García Bacca" (Carmen L. Bohórquez); "Vasconcelos y los debates sobre el indígena y la nación en Guatemala" (Marta Elena Casaús Arzú); "Reflexiones en torno al pensamiento marxista de Ludovico Silva" (Lino Morán Beltrán y Yohanka León del Río); "Salvador de la Plaza: clave para la historia del socialismo en Venezuela" (René Arias); "Imperialismo-antiimperialismo en el unionismo centroamericano, 1900–1930" (Teresa García Giráldez); "Sobre el concepto de identidad latinoamericana" (Herminio Núñez Villavicencio). [CJB]

3492 De La Vega V., Marta. Positivismo republicano y evolucionismo liberal: modernización y crisis en América Latina. (*Apunt. Filos.*, 16:31, dic. 2007, p. 185–196)

Además de señalar que el movimiento de Independencia no cambió la estructura social de la Colonia, uno de los principales temas que toca es la relación del positivismo (Comte) y el evolucionismo (Spencer) entre sí y en la forma en que se reflejaron en el orden económico-social. (Este tema lo trató la autora en su libro *Evolucionismo versus positivismo* [1998].) [JCTE]

3493 Devés V., Eduardo. La circulación de las ideas económico-sociales de Latinoamérica y El Caribe, en Asia y Africa: ¿cómo llegaron y cómo se diseminaron? (*Universum/Talca*, 23, 1998, p. 86–111, bibl.)

Da varios ejemplos, ilustrativos de ideas económico-sociales de América Latina y el Caribe que se difundieron en el resto del llamado Tercer Mundo. El caso más frecuente fue el de las ideas de la CEPAL, y fueron difundidas principalmente por los organismos internacionales. Ilustra el fenómeno con varios "modelos", en la descripción de los cuales llega a un considerable grado de detalle. [JCTE]

3494 Devés V., Eduardo. Redes intelectuales en América Latina: hacia la constitución de una comunidad intelectual. Santiago: Instituto de Estudios Avanzados, Univ. Santiago de Chile, 2007. 267 p.: bibl. (Col. Idea. Segunda época)

El tema de las redes intelectuales, de origen relativamente reciente, es cercano a la sociología de la cultura. Lo que se busca con él es averiguar qué relaciones han tenido entre sí intelectuales con algún tipo de afinidad y por cuáles medios se han mantenido en contacto y promovido intereses comunes. Este libro, además de fundamentar el asunto y dar ciertas pautas metodológicas, presenta varios "estudios de casos" y es sin duda muy buena contribución al tema. [JCTE]

3495 Diccionario del pensamiento alternativo. Dirección de Hugo E. Biagini y Arturo A. Roig. Buenos Aires: Editorial Biblos Lexicón; Partido de Lanús, Buenos Aires: Univ. Nacional de Lanús, 2008. 589 p.: bibl., indexes. (Lexicón)

Aunque fue concebido dentro de una trilogía del 'pensamiento alternativo' en la Argentina, este volumen tiene significación general. Se analizan términos contrahegemónicos, o bien modernos que han significado avances para la humanidad, por ejemplo 'seguridad social', 'salud pública', 'bioética', 'recursos renovables', etc. Más de 250 entradas ilustran sobre el arco conceptual que cubre el volumen y sobre la cantidad de colaboradores. Obra importante. [CJB]

3496 Dussel, Enrique D. Filosofía de la cultura y la liberación: ensayos. México: UACM, Univ. Autónoma de la Ciudad de México, 2006. 329 p.: bibl. (Col. Pensamiento Propio)

El libro es oportuno porque la posición del autor ha tenido un desarrollo en el tiempo y los trabajos aquí contenidos cubren un plazo de 40 años. La Introducción es una contribución más reciente, que en alguna medida muestra las etapas recorridas. El tema permanente es América Latina como cultura, y lo que podría llamarse su lugar en el mundo. [JCTE]

3497 Espacio público, conflictividad y participación: reflexiones desde América Latina. Coordinación académica de Adriana Arpini. Textos de Delia Albarracín *et al.* Mendoza, Argentina: Centro de Estudios Transandinos y Latinoamericanos, 2005. 192 p.: bibl.

Contiene estudios que, desde el punto de vista de la filosofía práctica, presentan una diversidad de enfoques críticos sobre el concepto de 'sociedad civil'. Algunos de los artículos y autores son: Adriana Arpini, "Espacio público, conflictividad y participación: de Jean Jacques Rousseau a José Martí"; María Cecilia Tosoni, "Del 'nosotras hablamos' al 'nosotras vivimos': una crítica desde la filosofía de la liberación al concepto de sociedad civil"; Paula Ripamondi, "Esfera pública, libertad y participación: un análisis desde los aportes políticos de Hannah Arendt"; Nicolás Lobos, "La cultura, el conflicto, el sujeto"; Marcos Olalla, "Modernismo y esfera pública en Argentina: socialismo y literatura en Leopoldo Lugones y Manuel Ugarte". [CJB]

3498 Etica, hermenéutica y multiculturalismo. Compilación de Pablo Lazo Briones. México: Univ. Iberoamericana, 2008. 268 p.

Aunque el libro se refiere al tema del título en general, hay materiales latinoamericanos. En un artículo sobre "Hermenéutica y multiculturalismo en América Latina" se discute, entre otros asuntos, la posición del filósofo mexicano Luis Villoro (además de haber otro artículo dedicado especialmente a este filósofo). [JCTE]

3499 Ferreira Gonçalves Jr., Arlindo. A pessoa humana como protagonista da "História Ética" na filosofia de María Zambrano. (*Utop. Prax. Latinoam.*, 12:37, abril/junio 2007, p. 69–77, bibl.)

Traza las líneas principales del pensamiento filosófico de María Zambrano (1904–91), perteneciente al ámbito filosófico madrileño que lideraba Ortega y Gasset. Zambrano pasó parte de su vida en Hispanoamérica, después de 1939. [JCTE]

3500 Filosofía actual: en perspectiva latinoamericana. Compilación de Jesús Antonio Serrano Sánchez. Bogotá: Univ. Pedagógica Nacional: San Pablo, 2007. 283 p.: bibl., index.

Es una especie de enciclopedia de movimientos filosóficos occidentales de la segunda mitad del siglo XX, pensada para lectores latinoamericanos. Los temas son: fenomenología, hermenéutica, filosofía analítica, filosofía de la ciencia, Escuela de Frankfurt, postestructuralismo, liberalismo, filosofía y cultura, y filosofía intercultural. Estas tendencias, de un modo u otro, han sido recibidas y adoptadas en América Latina, pero la idea del volumen es representar las tendencias filosóficas europeas o norteamericanas. [JCTE]

3501 Flores Morador, Fernando. Tierra firme anticipada: el descubrimiento de América y las raíces arcaicas de Occidente. Montevideo: Ediciones de la Banda Oriental, 2006. 318 p.: bibl., ill., index.

En general, predomina en el libro la intención de mostrar el efecto que el Nuevo Mundo tuvo sobre el pensamiento europeo. El autor declara que su posición es cercana a la del postmodernismo, que ha convertido los textos históricos en textos "casi literarios" y centrados en su propio discurso, por

falta de un criterio seguro para reconocer el conocimiento objetivo. Son conceptos clave en la obra los de 'arcaísmo' y 'modernidad', que dan lugar a dos concepciones del mundo: la arcaica americana y la moderna europea u occidental. Mucho del libro aprovecha los resultados de la antropología cultural. [JCTE]

3502 Fornet-Betancourt, Raúl. Mujer y filosofía en el pensamiento iberoamericano: momentos de una relación difícil. Barcelona: Anthropos, 2009. 206 p.: bibl. (Pensamiento crítico/pensamiento utópico; 178. Cultura y diferencia)

Analiza el aporte del pensamiento de mujeres en la filosofía latinoamericana, generalmente ignorado por la formación de un canon eminentemente masculino. Estudia antecedentes como el de Sor Juana, pasando por nombres emblemáticos del siglo XIX, hasta abordar el aporte de las feministas. Dentro de esta última línea considera a Rosario Castellanos, Graciela Hierro, Gloria Comesaña Santalices, Sara Beatriz Guardia, Urania Ungo, Diana de Vallescar Palanca, Ofelia Shutte, Alejandra Ciriza, María Luisa Femenías y Magali Méndez de Menezes. También se incluyen, más brevemente, otros nombres del siglo XX. Al final, recupera tres autores que contribuyeron al tema: Eugenio María de Hostos, José Martí y Francisco Romero. [CJB]

3503 Gargallo, Francesca. Ideas feministas latinoamericanas. 2. ed. México: UACM, 2006. 298 p.: bibl., index. (Historia de las ideas)

El tema constante es la crítica a la sociedad falocrática y patriarcal, pero el libro es muy útil para el reconocimiento de las variedades que ofrece el tema feminista en América Latina. Discusión especial merecen las filósofas, Ofelia Schutte y Graciela Hierro Perezcastro, entre otras. Además de representar una posición combativa con la cual coincidir o disentir, el lector hallará rica información sobre las muy variadas manifestaciones del movimiento, tanto actuales como históricas. [JCTE]

3504 González Ordosgoitti, Enrique Alí. Pensar América Latina desde las dimensiones de la realidad. (*Apunt. Filos.*, 16:31, dic. 2007, p. 115–162, bibl.)

Lineamientos más bien programáticos vinculados a la labor de la cátedra de Pensamiento Latinoamericano de la Universidad Central de Venezuela. Intenta constituir tres bloques de investigación: (1) la meditación que el hecho de América originó en Europa; (2) la adopción de doctrinas europeas en Latinoamérica; (3) el pensamiento original de América Latina sobre sí misma. Este esquema no refleja la variedad de opiniones y perspectivas que contiene el artículo. [JCTE]

3505 Guadarrama González, Pablo. Filosofía latinoamericana: momentos de su desarrollo. (*Cuad. Am./México*, 119:1, enero/marzo 2007, p. 11–45)

Artículo panorámico sobre el desarrollo de la filosofía latinoamericana desde el período precolombino hasta nuestros días. Contiene observaciones críticas, pero algunos juicios, al no estar avalados con pruebas, resultan ambiguos o de validez restringida, como la afirmación de que en el momento de la conquista algunas culturas indígenas estaban en el umbral de "un pensamiento propiamente filosófico", lo que, al no cumplirse, habría interrumpido su "desarrollo auténtico". [CJB]

3506 Guadarrama González, Pablo. Pensamiento filosófico latinoamericano: humanismo vs. alienación. Caracas: Fundación Editorial El Perro y la Rana, 2008. 3 v.: bibl. (Col. Heterodoxia. Serie Crítica emergente)

Coincide en parte con su libro *El humanismo en el pensamiento latinoamericano* (ver *HLAS 64:2868*), pero es una obra independiente, o en todo caso una continuación ampliada. Plantea el problema de la filosofía latinoamericana y los presupuestos para su estudio. Trata el tema del humanismo en una serie de pensadores, desde Varona hasta Francisco Romero, pasando por Rodó, Ingenieros, Vasconcelos, Caso, Henríquez Ureña, Korn, Vaz Ferreira, Mariátegui y el pensamiento socialista. Otra parte está dedicada al pensamiento latinoamericano de la segunda mitad del siglo XX, donde se incluyen José Gaos, Leopoldo Zea, la filosofía de la liberación, el marxismo, Ernesto Guevara, y Antonio García Nosa, culminando la exposición con un "Balance y perspectiva de la filosofía latinoamericana del siglo XX e inicios del siglo XXI". Contiene muchos elementos para una historia general. [JCTE]

3507 Guerrero, Carolina. Súbditos ciudadanos: antinomias en la ilustración de la América andina. Caracas: Fundación Centro de Estudios Latinoamericanos Rómulo Gallegos, 2006. 134 p.: bibl. (Col. cuadernos)

El objetivo del libro es comprender el sentido histórico de las ideas de ciudadanía en la "América andina" de fines del siglo XVIII. La condición de "súbdito ciudadano" refiere a la concepción de la ciudadanía hasta donde era posible dentro de un régimen monárquico y centralista. Se aplicaba, además, sólo a la clase social superior. [JCTE]

3508 Heredia, Edmundo A. La guerra de los congresos: el Pan-Hispanismo contra el Panamericanismo. Córdoba, Argentina: Junta Provincial de Historia, 2007. 189 p. (Cuadernos de historia; 73)

El tema central es la contraposición entre los esfuerzos de España por crear un pan-hispanismo con sus antiguas colonias, y el panamericanismo prohijado por Estados Unidos (última década del siglo XIX). Así hubo, hacia esas fechas, una Unión Panamericana (con sede en Washington, DC.), una Unión Iberoamericana (apoyada por España) y una Unión Latinoamericana (creada por Torres Caicedo en París). Quizás la mayor contribución del libro esté en el uso de fuentes diplomáticas españolas. También expone los intentos, menos conocidos, de Colombia y Venezuela para organizar un Congreso Hispanoamericano, fracasado sin embargo por diferencias de intereses nacionales entre varios países latinoamericanos. [JCTE]

3509 La hermenéutica en América Latina: analogía y barroco. Coordinación de Samuel Arriarán. México: Editorial Itaca, 2007. 177 p.: bibl.

Varias posiciones adoptadas en la obra son cercanas a la hermenéutica analógica de Mauricio Beuchot. Este último, en su contribución, vincula la posibilidad de la hermenéutica con lo que debiera ser una filosofía latinoamericana. El coordinador, en la introducción, pregunta si es posible desarrollar una hermenéutica latinoamericana que incluya las expresiones de las culturas originarias de América. Uno de los temas que interesan es el de superar la oposición entre "universalismo" y "particularismo", y en el caso especial de la filosofía latinoamericana, se busca insertarla en la "filosofía universal", aunque respetando su particularidad. [JCTE]

3510 Hilar ideas: travesías del pensamiento en América Latina. Coordinación de Adriana Arpini, Claudio Maíz y Silvana Montaruli. Mendoza, Argentina: Univ. Nacional de Cuyo: Centro de Estudios Trasandinos y Latinoamericanos, 2007. 295 p.

Conjunto de 24 contribuciones precedidas de una introducción general donde, entre otras cosas, se intenta determinar el concepto de red intelectual. Los trabajos se dividen en tres partes, de las cuales seleccionamos la tercera, precisamente dedicada al tema de redes. Entre otras ponencias, se encuentran allí las siguientes: Eugenia Molina, "La red literaria como espacio de legitimación intelectual: el caso de 'La Ilustración Argentina' (1849)"; Claudio Maíz, "Enlaces transatlánticos y comunidad imaginada"; Marcela Maciff, "Las revistas de fin de siglo en Argentina"; Laura Jara, "La construcción de la cultura de izquierda en Latinoamérica: 1959–1971". [CJB]

3511 Historia de las ideas: repensar la América Latina. Coordinación de Mario Magallón Anaya y Roberto Mora Martínez. México: UNAM, 2006. 252 p.: bibl.

El marco general es la contraposición, en la historia de América Latina, entre aspectos negativos como la conquista, la dominación y, más recientemente, el neoliberalismo y el armamentismo de Estados Unidos, por un lado, y gestas revolucionarias como la Independencia, la Revolución cubana y el socialismo chileno, por otro. Los temas son muy variados: aprismo y sindicalismo, el Partido Comunista de El Salvador, América Latina y Africa en relación con la democracia, la estrategia militar de los aztecas, Bolívar, la teología de la liberación, la religiosidad en México, entre otros. En general son trabajos breves y de no muy elaborada investigación. [JCTE]

3512 Historia de los intelectuales en América Latina. Vol. 1, La ciudad letrada, de la conquista al modernismo. Coordinación general de Carlos Altamirano. Recopilación del volumen de Jorge Myers. Buenos Aires: Katz, 2008. 1 v.: bibl., index. (Conocimiento; 3042)

El propósito no es dar una historia de la literatura, ni del pensamiento, ni de la historiografía, sino del tipo del intelectual como "letrado", aunque, si hubiera que atribuir un género a los trabajos, podría ser el de historia de las ideas. Las contribuciones, en su mayor parte, están bien logradas, y además de temas hispanoamericanos incluye autores de Brasil. Son particularmente útiles la introducción general, de Carlos Altamirano, y la correspondiente a este volumen, de Jorge Myers. [JCTE]

3513 Ilustración y emancipación en América Latina: materiales para la reflexión ético-política en el segundo centenario. Coordinación de Gustavo Ortiz y Nelson G. Specchia. Córdoba, Argentina: Editorial de la Univ. Católica de Córdoba, 2008. 383 p.: bibl.

Contiene varios artículos de interés sobre los siguientes temas: identidad y modernidad en América Latina; la emancipación latinoamericana en sus aspectos políticos y económicos; la modernidad del barroco latinoamericano en Bolívar Echeverría; Enrique Dussel en relación con Richard Rorty y Charles Taylor; y Octavio Paz. Además hay sendos artículos sobre el feminismo en Argentina y sobre la familia en el siglo XVIII iberoamericano. [JCTE]

3514 Integración latinoamericana: raíces y perspectivas. Coordinación de Rodrigo Páez Montalbán y Mario Vásquez Olivera. México: UNAM, Centro de Investigaciones sobre América Latina y el Caribe: Ediciones y Gráficos Eón, 2008. 299 p.: bibl. (Col. Miradas del centauro)

Las contribuciones se dividen en dos grandes campos: (1) de carácter histórico-cultural, referidas a las ideas de integración; y (2) aspectos económicos, políticos y sociales de la segunda mitad del siglo XX. Entre los autores se cuentan: Patricia Escandón, Clara Alicia Jalif de Bertranou, Dante Ramaglia, Carlos Guevara, Horacio Cerutti Guldberg, Tania García y Alfredo Guerra-Borges. Las reflexiones finales de los compiladores dan cuenta de los proyectos y acuerdos de integración de las últimas décadas, señalando la necesidad, para su éxito, de una cultura de la integración. [CJB]

3515 Jaksic, Ivan. Ven conmigo a la España lejana: los intelectuales norteamericanos ante el mundo hispano, 1820–1880. México: Fondo de Cultura Económica, 2007.

487 p.: bibl., index. (Sección de obras de historia)

Estudio realizado con la mejor calidad historiográfica, recurriendo a numerosas fuentes inéditas, característica que no impide el carácter evocativo de muchas de sus páginas y la viva representación de los autores estudiados. Analiza la obra de Washington Irving, George Ticknor, Henry W. Longfellow, William H. Prescott y Mary Peabody Mann, "los pioneros del hispanismo norteamericano". Estos autores, influidos por el romanticismo, habrían sido llevados al estudio de lo hispánico buscando evitar para Estados Unidos la decadencia y los errores españoles, especialmente el fanatismo religioso y la Inquisición. Afirma que la comparación no fue ajena a la preocupación por la propia identidad norteamericana, y que muchos hispanoamericanos leyeron a estos autores buscando justificación para su reacción contra España. [JCTE]

3516 Jochims Reichel, Heloisa. A identidade latino-americana na visão dos intelectuais da década de 1960. (*Estud. Ibero-Am./Porto Alegre*, 33:2, dez. 2007, p. 116–133, bibl.)

Investiga el tema de la identidad latinoamericana a través de las opiniones de izquierda vertidas en tres revistas (dos mexicanas y una argentina) durante los años 60: *Revista Mexicana de Sociología, Cuadernos Americanos* y *Desarrollo Económico*. Las tres reflejarían la identificación con la unidad de la "nación latinoamericana." [CJB]

3517 El legado filosófico español e hispanoamericano del siglo XX. Coordinación de Manuel Garrido et al. Madrid: Cátedra, 2009. 1328 p.: bibl., ill., index. (Teorema / Cátedra. Serie Mayor)

Posiblemente la obra de tipo enciclopédico más completa sobre el pensamiento filosófico español (pero atendiendo también a Hispanoamérica), que difícilmente sea reemplazada por otra semejante en un tiempo considerable. La mayor parte se dedica a la filosofía en España, donde se elaboró la obra. Es temáticamente muy amplia, al punto de hacer imposible la mención de los autores considerados. Del lado latinoamericano incluye los filósofos en el exilio: José Gaos, Joaquín Xirau, Eduardo Nicol, Ramón Xirau, Adolfo Sánchez Vázquez, Juan David García Bacca, María Zambrano, José Ferrater Mora.

En cuanto al pensamiento hispanoamericano en el siglo XX, hay una visión general, resaltando el valor de la filosofía analítica; capítulos por grandes corrientes: fenomenología y existencialismo, filosofía analítica, marxismo; y breves panoramas generales por país: México (Enrique Hurtado); Argentina (Nora Stigol); Colombia (Juan J. Botero C.); Chile (Eduardo Fernandois); Perú (Pablo Quintanilla); América Central (Gerardo Mora-Burgos); Caribe hispano (Pablo Guadarrama González). [JCTE]

Maíz, Claudio. Constelaciones unamunianas: enlaces entre España y América, 1898–1920. See item **442.**

3518 Márquez-Fernández, Álvaro B. and Doris Gutiérrez. Presencia de la filosofía intercultural de Raúl Fornet-Betancourt en América Latina. (*Apunt. Filos.*, 16:31, dic. 2007, p. 163–183)

Descripción y positiva valoración de la llamada filosofía intercultural. Como es habitual, se opone a la globalización y a la modernidad occidental. [JCTE]

3519 Maturo, Graciela. Fenomenología y hermenéutica: desde la transmodernidad latinoamericana. (*Utop. Prax. Latinoam.*, 12:37, abril/junio 2007, p. 35–50, bibl.)

Fenomenología y hermenéutica son utilizadas para la consideración de la obra literaria y estética en general. Después de una crítica a las corrientes nacidas del estructuralismo y de las tendencias formalistas, afirma la utilidad metodológica de ambas líneas, que mantendrían el valor del sujeto, su lugar en el mundo y las relaciones intersubjetivas. Toma como figura importante a Rodolfo Kusch. [CJB]

3520 Mejía Quintana, Oscar and Jacqueline Blanco Blanco. Democracia y filosofía de la historia en América Latina. Bogotá: Univ. Libre, Facultad de Filosofía, Especialización en Filosofía del Derecho y Teoría Jurídica: Ediciones Jurídicas Gustavo Ibañez, 2005. 153 p.: bibl.

El libro está de hecho compuesto de tres partes, unidas por cierta simpatía hispanista. Considera que América Latina no ha sido entendida porque se le han aplicado categorías extrañas o extranjerizantes, especialmente en el caso de la "metodología anglosajona". En otro aspecto del libro se intenta mostrar que el espíritu democrático latinoamericano proviene del pensamiento político español, incluyendo la Escuela de Salamanca en el siglo XVI. Todavía en otro se reconocen tres clases de humanismo en los siglos XVII y XVIII, culminando en un "humanismo ilustrado", que no debe confundirse con el "enciclopédico", el cual nunca habría arraigado en América. [JCTE]

3521 Memoria y autobiografía en Ibero-américa. Coordinación de Florencia Ferreira de Cassone. Buenos Aires: Editorial Dunken, 2008. 334 p.: bibl.

Se recogen textos en los que los autores explican su pensamiento o actuación política. La autobiografía serviría así para interpretar aspectos historiográficos o de historia de las ideas. Se analizan los casos de Julio Irazusta, Roberto Giusti, Clorinda Matto de Turner, Francisco A. Encina, Leopoldo Castedo, Ricardo Rojas, José Vasconcelos, y la autobiografía en la revista *Claridad*. Son autores: Enrique Zuleta Alvarez, Florencia Ferreira, María del Carmen Llano, Gloria Hintze, María Marcela Aranda, María Clara Varela y Walter Camargo. Interesante contribución. [CJB]

3522 Mendieta, Eduardo. Ni orientalismo ni occidentalismo: Edward W. Said y el latinoamericanismo. (*Tabula Rasa*, 5, julio/dic. 2006, p. 67–83, bibl., photo)

Tras apreciaciones elogiosas de la obra de Said en torno al concepto de "orientalismo", distingue cuatro clases de latinoamericanismo: (1) el de los arielistas; (2) el de los "estudios de área" en Estados Unidos; (3) el "latinoamericanismo crítico", representado por figuras latinoamericanas como Darcy Ribeiro, Leopoldo Zea, Augusto Salazar Bondy, Gustavo Gutiérrez (Teología de la Liberación) y Enrique Dussel; (4) el latinoamericanismo de los "latinos" de Estados Unidos. [JCTE]

3523 Monsiváis, Carlos. De los intelectuales en América Latina. (*Am. Lat. Hoy/Salamanca*, 47, dic. 2007, p. 15–38, bibl.)

Es una especie de libre crónica y comentario, cuya unidad no reside tanto en la estructura del libro como en las generalmente razonables apreciaciones del autor. Presenta situaciones en las que intervinieron (o fueron protagonistas) los intelectuales, como, por ejemplo, la defensa de la secularización en los liberales del siglo XIX;

los llamados "maestros de la juventud"; la "ciudad letrada"; importantes revistas literarias latinoamericanas; la izquierda y el estalinismo; la Revolución cubana, etc. Para el comentario del historiador, ver item **447**. [JCTE]

3524 Montiel, Edgar. Repensar el bicentenario de la Independencia de las Américas desde una visión geopolítica. (*Cuad. Am./México*, 122:4, oct./dic. 2007, p. 27–36)

La idea central es repensar el significado de la Independencia. Entre las sugerencias que ofrece están: (1) la conveniencia de hablar de procesos independentistas en toda América, desde Estados Unidos hasta Latinoamérica; y (2) tener una visión geopolítica que relacione lo acontecido en el Continente con lo sucedido en Europa, tomando en cuenta la participación de próceres americanos en ambos lados del Atlántico. El autor utiliza estos aspectos para confrontar ciertos desafíos de la actual globalización. [CJB]

3525 Morales, Gabriel. De la "conciencia inauténtica" a la "conciencia histórica" latinoamericana: apuntes para una historiología de nuestro ser histórico. (*Apunt. Filos.*, 16:31, dic. 2007, p. 89–113)

El tema es la frecuentadísima cuestión de la posibilidad, existencia y naturaleza de la filosofía latinoamericana. Expone las posiciones de los más reconocidos representantes (Salazar Bondy, Zea, Miró Quesada y varios otros), pero al final tiende a colocar el problema en el ámbito de América Latina como civilización, lo que ampliaría el asunto y lo colocaría mucho más atrás de la época colonial. [JCTE]

3526 Morales, Gabriel. ¿Qué es eso de una civilización latinoamericana?: una interpretación a partir del concepto de *rendimiento cultural* en Alfred Weber. (*Tierra Firme/Caracas*, 28:62/63, 2007, p. 182–200, bibl.)

El objetivo es aproximarse a lo que sería una caracterización de Latinoamérica como cultura o civilización. Toma en cuenta dos autores: Helio Jaguaribe, en *Un estudio crítico de la historia*, al cual critica, y Alfred Weber, en *Historia de la cultura*, que le resulta más aprovechable, especialmente en su concepto de "rendimiento cultural". [JCTE]

3527 Motta, Sara C. Old tools and new movements in Latin America: political science as gatekeeper or intellectual illuminator? (*Lat. Am. Polit. Soc.*, 51:1, Spring 2009, p. 31–56, bibl.)

Sostiene que hay una serie de movimientos populares (como los Sem Terra en Brasil, los zapatistas en México, los comités de tierra urbana en Venezuela y otros) que se salen de las formas de la acción política consagrada, y la autora sostiene que los abordajes tradicionales (la socialdemocracia o el marxismo, por ejemplo) no están preparados para comprender esos movimientos. Luego desarrolla con cierto detalle la estrategia interpretativa que correspondería. [JCTE]

3528 ¿Un mundo sin filosofía? Coordinación de Benjamín Panduro Muñoz y A. Xóchitl López Molina. Colima, Mexico: Univ. de Colima, 2007. 350 p.: bibl. (Dos siglos, dos milenios; 5)

La pregunta del título queda de hecho contestada en la Introducción, al afirmar la necesidad de la filosofía desde un sujeto histórico latinoamericano y superando las consecuencias negativas del postmodernismo y los efectos del "capitalismo globalizado". Siguen 17 trabajos, y algunos de los temas son: la identidad latinoamericana; la función social de la filosofía; educación y filosofía política; la enseñanza de la filosofía. Estos artículos parecen independientes de la fundamentación central del volumen y de un modo u otro reivindican la necesidad de la filosofía. [JCTE]

3529 Nineteenth-century nation building and the Latin American intellectual tradition: a reader. Edited and translated by Janet Burke and Ted Humphrey. Indianapolis, Ind.: Hackett Pub. Co., 2007. 366 p.: bibl.

Este *reader* sera muy útil como instrumento de enseñanza, aunque por su amplitud no pueda ser utilizado totalmente en un curso. Cada parte contiene una breve introducción con bibliografía básica. El número de autores es amplio, siendo todos representativos del pensamiento de la región en el siglo XIX. La introducción general señala los grandes problemas que inspiraron a los autores de los textos seleccionados, y al final una guía de temas vincula los asuntos con las obras representadas en la antología. Según los organizadores, 12 de los autores

incluidos nunca habían sido traducidos al inglés anteriormente. [JCTE]

3530 Omar, Sidi M. Los estudios postcoloniales: una introducción crítica. Castellón de la Plana, Spain: Univ. Jaume I, 2008. 243 p.: bibl. (Cooperació i solidaritat. Estudis; 3)

Si algo demuestra este libro es que el campo de los estudios postcoloniales manifiesta una considerable variedad de opiniones y enfoques, que provienen no sólo de los sujetos postcoloniales reales, sino en gran medida de los académicos occidentales que hacen de lo postcolonial su tema de trabajo. La obra es muy valiosa precisamente por su carácter clarificador. Esto lo logra el autor por diferentes medios: (1) el examen crítico de la bibliografía más reciente, lo cual es particularmente orientador; (2) examinando el concepto de *négritude* y las obras de Aimé Césaire y Frantz Fanon; (3) el análisis del discurso postcolonial en sus principales representantes, comenzando con la obra de Edward Said; (4) analizando el fenómeno de la "hibridez", que es una reelaboración de los conceptos de cultura e identidad, en la cual se centra la aportación del autor al problema estudiado. [JCTE]

3531 Osorio, Jaime. El estudio de América Latina frente al positivismo y al posmodernismo. (*Cuad. Am./México*, 118:4, oct./dic. 2006, p. 47–64, bibl.)

Es una crítica—en el sentido negativo—del positivismo y el posmodernismo como medios de interpretar a América Latina, y por su influencia en las ciencias sociales. Ambas posiciones, a juicio del autor, "terminan por desintegrar a América Latina como problema teórico". A esta conclusión se llega tras una argumentación mucho más compleja de lo que puede mostrase aquí. [CJB]

3532 Palti, Elías José. The problem of *Misplaced Ideas* revisited: beyond the *History of Ideas* in Latin America. (*J. Hist. Ideas*, 67:1, Jan. 2006, p. 149–179)

El artículo es una larga y compleja argumentación sobre la "teoría" de Roberto Schwarz referente a las "ideas fuera de lugar". Pero la más importante conclusión es que la tradicional 'historia de las ideas' en América Latina sería superada o reemplazada por una aplicación de la filosofía del lenguaje sugerida por J.G.A. Pocock en *Politics, Language and Time.* [JCTE]

3533 Patiño Palafox, Luis. Juan Ginés de Sepúlveda y su pensamiento imperialista. México: Libros de Homero, 2007. 296 p.: bibl. (Novohispania; 1)

Toma en consideración toda la obra de Sepúlveda y no sólo la famosa polémica con Las Casas. Después de presentar históricamente el problema de la esclavitud, examina la literatura sobre la conquista, especialmente—y en detalle—la obra de Francisco de Vitoria. Sepúlveda es visto como ideólogo del imperio español, y examinado en sus divergencias con Lutero y Erasmo, entre otros. Buena parte del libro se dedica a la posición de Sepúlveda frente a la "polémica indiana", polémica que— concluye el autor—se llevó a cabo cuando la conquista estaba desarrollada y no alteró la realidad del hecho americano. Es una buena pieza de investigación. [JCTE]

3534 Pensadores y forjadores de la universidad latinoamericana. Edición de Carmen García Guadilla. Textos de Agueda Rodríguez Cruz et al. Caracas: UNESCO-IESALC: Bid&Cco.editor: CENDES, 2008. 821 p.: bibl. (Col. Intramuros. Serie Académica)

Se trata de una obra valiosa, posiblemente sin precedente en su composición y alcance. Veintiséis contribuyentes cubren 20 países, entre aquellos que tuvieron universidad desde la época colonial y los que la tuvieron después de la Independencia. Entre los colaboradores con antecedentes en la investigación del tema se encuentran Agueda Rodríguez Cruz, Ildefonso Leal, Iván Jaksic y Carlos Tünerman. Precede a los textos un acertado panorama general por Carmen García Guadilla, que asimila bien los estudios nacionales del volumen. Los estudios de países se refieren a los aspectos históricos propios de cada caso, a los actores descollantes y a los intentos de reforma. [JCTE]

3535 El pensamiento filosófico latino-americano, del Caribe y "latino" (1300–2000): historia, corrientes, temas y filósofos. Edición de Enrique Dussel, Eduardo Mendieta y Carmen Bohórquez. México:

CREAL, Centro de Cooperación Regional para la Educación de Adultos en América Latina y el Caribe: Siglo Veintiuno Editores, 2009. 1111 p.: bibl., index, maps. (Filosofía)

Obra importante, única en su género por la extensión de su contenido. Se divide en cuatro grandes partes (y correspondientes subdivisiones internas): (1) Períodos (filosofía precolombina, modernidad temprana, modernidad madura); (2) Corrientes filosóficas del siglo XX (antipositivismo, fenomenología y existencialismo, filosofía cristiana, filosofía de las ciencias, filosofía analítica, filosofía de la revolución y marxista, filosofía latinoamericana, filosofía de la liberación, feminismo filosófico, filosofía política, filosofía del derecho, filosofía brasileña, filosofía de los 'latinos' en Estados Unidos, etc.); (3) Temas filosóficos (ética, estética, ontología y metafísica, filosofía de la historia, filosofía de la religión, filosofía intercultural, indigenismo, pensamiento del "giro descolonizador", etc.); (4) Filósofos y pensadores (pueblos originarios, siglo XVI, reacción crítica de los oprimidos, siglos XVII y XVIII, Independencia, conservadores y liberales, krausistas, positivistas, revolucionarios y marxistas, filósofos de Brasil, México, Argentina, Uruguay, Chile, Paraguay, Bolivia, Perú, Ecuador, Colombia, Venezuela, Centroamérica, Caribe, 'latinos' en Estados Unidos). Los filósofos representados suman 207. La nómina de colaboradores supera los 90. Elogiable esfuerzo colectivo. [CJB]

3536 Piñeiro Iñíguez, Carlos. Pensadores latinoamericanos del siglo XX: ideas, utopía y destino. Buenos Aires: Instituto Di Tella: Siglo XXI, 2006. 823 p.: bibl.

Con la modalidad del ensayo bien logrado y de inteligente comentario, tiene dos grandes méritos: transmitir al lector la obra de un alto número de autores (casi 50 intelectuales latinoamericanos, entre clásicos y destacados), y realizarse desde una eficaz compenetración con cada autor tratado. Participa del sentimiento que el intelectual latinoamericano con frecuencia tiene para su región y su cultura, y que lo lleva a que América Latina termine siendo el gran tema, no importa cuál sea su línea de averiguación o creación. De esa inquietud está hecha la sustancia de este bien logrado libro. [JCTE]

3537 Pita González, Alexandra. La Unión
Latino Americana y el Boletín Renovación: redes intelectuales y revistas culturales en la década de 1920. México: Colegio
de México; Colima, Mexico: Univ. de Colima, 2009. 386 p.: bibl., ill., index.
  Investigación bien elaborada sobre
una publicación de difícil acceso. El Boletín
Renovación fue órgano de la Unión Latino
Americana. Nació en 1923 y precedió en
dos años a la Unión Latino Americana,
que la adoptó como órgano de difusión.
Ambos desaparecieron en 1930. El libro
analiza la institución, sus representantes—
especialmente José Ingenieros—su condición antiimperialista en relación con
Estados Unidos, su vinculación con el movimiento de la Reforma Universitaria y, con
gran detalle, los artículos que aparecieron
en el Boletín. [JCTE]

**3538 Political violence and the construc-
tion of national identity in Latin
America.** Edited by Will Fowler and Peter
Lambert. New York: Palgrave Macmillian,
2006. 244 p.: bibl., index.
  Los organizadores reconocen que hay
muchos escritos sobre la identidad latinoamericana, pero estiman que no ha sido vista
en relación con la violencia. Y les interesa el
papel que la violencia ha tenido para afirmar
las identidades nacionales y, a la vez, el uso
de la identidad para justificar las formas de
violencia. El volumen se compone de "estudios de caso" de países como México, Cuba,
El Salvador, Colombia, Venezuela, Perú,
Chile, Paraguay y Argentina. Hay un capítulo que toca el tema más general de esta
obra, vinculando identidad y violencia con
el poder político. [JCTE]

3539 Pozas, Mario A. El liberalismo hispanoamericano en el siglo XIX. (*Reali-
dad/San Salvador*, 108, abril/junio 2006, p.
293–313, bibl.)
  Panorámico, pero señala variantes
internas del liberalismo, así como contrapo-
siciones, no sólo con el pensamiento conservador, sino también con el positivismo.
[JCTE]

3540 Raby, D.L. Democracy and revolution:
Latin America and socialism today.
London: Ann Arbor, Mich.: Pluto; Toronto:
Between the Lines, 2006. 280 p.: bibl., index.

  Sólo es posible reproducir algunas de
las afirmaciones que contiene el volumen,
a saber: debe haber una estrategia para
tomar el poder y un modelo económico-
social alternativo al actual; la democracia
representativa es una expresión liberal,
y debe ser sustituida por una democracia
directa o participativa; no es posible confiar
en los partidos socialdemócratas, por estar
demasiado incorporados al sistema; ciertos
movimientos, como el zapatista, son aus-
piciosos, pero no cambian la realidad; en la
actualidad Cuba y Venezuela representan la
alternativa revolucionaria real. A pesar del
carácter terminante de estas afirmaciones, a
lo largo del libro se presentan opiniones más
matizadas. [JCTE]

3541 Ramírez Ribes, María. Fernando
Ainsa: la seducción por la utopía
revolucionaria en América Latina. (*Utop.
Prax. Latinoam.*, 12:37, abril/junio 2007,
p. 91–97, bibl.)
  Análisis de la interacción de las ideas
utópicas entre Europa y América, como
formas imaginarias de una vida buena.
Algunas veces la realidad contradice esa
condición ideal. Tales serían los casos, en
la actualidad, de Cuba y Venezuela. Para la
autora, la verdadera utopía sería la que hable
de evolución, y no de revolución. [CJB]

**3542 Religión y política en América
Latina: la utopía como espacio de
resistencia social.** Coordinación de Horacio Cerutti Guldberg y Carlos Mondragón
González. México: UNAM, 2006. 182 p.:
bibl. (Col. Filosofía e historia de las ideas en
América Latina y el Caribe; 1)
  La utopía como aspiración y los movimientos religiosos como promotores del
cambio social son los temas básicos que
animan los artículos del libro. Asuntos
más específicos son, por ejemplo: la utopía
en América Latina; la religiosidad popular
en los procesos de construcción de nuevas
utopías; teología de la liberación; y utopía y
revolución. [JCTE]

**3543 Repensando el siglo XIX desde Amé-
rica Latina y Francia: homenaje al
filósofo Arturo A. Roig.** Compilación de
Marisa Muñoz y Patrice Vermeren. Textos
de Yamandú Acosta *et al.* Con la colaboración de Joséphine Delaporte, Louise Ferté y
Stéphan-Eloise Gras. Traducción del francés

de Isadora Aizenman. Buenos Aires: Colihue, 2009. 815 p.: bibl. (Colihue universidad. Filosofía)

Son casi 80 trabajos sobre muy variados temas relacionados con Francia y América Latina en el siglo XIX. De particular interés es el homenaje al filósofo argentino Arturo A. Roig, en el cual aparecen escritos de varios autores, entre ellos Elisabeth Roig, Horacio Cerutti Guldberg, Carlos Pérez Zavala, Ricardo Maliandi, Clara Jalif de Bertranou y Gerardo Oviedo. El volumen concluye con un trabajo de Roig sobre Amadeo Jacques y Étienne Vacherot. [JCTE]

3544 Salas Chacón, Álvaro. Espiritualidad, violencia y androcentrismo: retos prácticos de los feminismos para el siglo XXI en América Latina. (*Rev. Filos. Univ. Costa Rica*, 44:111/112, enero/agosto 2006, p. 65–71, bibl.)

Propone el cultivo de valores espirituales para el éxito del feminismo en América Latina. Distingue cuatro tipos de actitudes negativas que operarían (como en el marxismo, a juicio del autor) en detrimento del éxito: el resentimiento; el sentimiento de victimización acompañado de la demonización del opresor; el separatismo; y el dogmatismo. [CJB]

3545 Schramm, Christina. La filosofía intercultural latinoamericana de Raúl Fornet-Betancourt: una discusión de sus elementos principales. (*Rev. Filos. Univ. Costa Rica*, 45:114, enero/abril 2007, p. 77–84, bibl.)

Describe la filosofía intercultural, pero considera que ella debe incorporar la preocupación por el poder, la teoría feminista y los estudios postcoloniales. [JCTE]

3546 Seminario 'La Izquierda' en América Latina, *Madrid, 2005*. La "izquierda" en América Latina. Edición de Pedro Pérez Herrero. Madrid: Editorial Pablo Iglesias, 2006. 310 p.: bibl.

Es un examen académico de la situación política actual de América Latina, especialmente de la democracia liberal y la socialdemocracia, y las nuevas formas de populismo, en el contexto del fin de las propuestas neoliberales y la aparición de nuevos regímenes considerados de "izquierda". La colocación de este calificativo entre comillas, así utilizado en el libro, resulta de considerar a esos regímenes más bien como

populismos nacionalistas y no como continuación del viejo tronco socialista. Se considera en la obra que no se es de izquierda solamente por oponerse a la globalización, estar contra Estados Unidos y defender los derechos humanos, la igualdad de género, y los valores ecológicos. Hay artículos especiales sobre Argentina, Brasil, México y los países andinos. [JCTE]

3547 Simposio "La Concepción de la Utopía desde América Latina, en Homenaje a Fernando Ainsa", *Seville, Spain, 2006*. Utopía en marcha. Edición de Horacio Cerutti Guldberg y Jussi Pakkasvirta. Quito: Editorial Abya-Yala, Univ. Politécnica Salesiana; Finlandia: Instituto Renvall, Univ. de Helsinki, 2009. 449 p.: bibl., ill.

Son 27 trabajos, en homenaje a Fernando Ainsa, autor de origen español pero radicado en Uruguay, quien elaboró una extensa obra sobre el concepto de utopía. El homenajeado cierra el volumen con un "Alegato final por una nueva utopía", que en parte es reflexión sobre su propia obra, y que se refiere a la renovación del impulso utópico cuando ya no está presente la utopía de la revolución. [JCTE]

3548 Sobrevilla Alcázar, David. Una historia de la filosofía latinoamericana. (*Rev. Filos./Santiago*, 63, 2007, p. 87–97)

Comentario al libro del autor español Carlos Beorlegui, *Historia del pensamiento filosófico latinoamericano: una búsqueda incesante de identidad* (véase *HLAS 64: 2847*). Considera que, pese a sus méritos, el libro es una visión "sesgada" del pensamiento filosófico latinoamericano, especialmente por los aspectos de ese pensamiento (filósofos y corrientes) que no son atendidos por el autor. [CJB]

3549 Sujetos, discursos y memoria histórica en América Latina. Edición de Dante Ramaglia, Gloria Hintze y Florencia Ferreira. Mendoza, Argentina: Qellqasqa Editorial, 2006. 229 p.

Veintiún ensayos, de interés para el pensamiento latinoamericano. Los trabajos se agrupan en tres partes y señalamos algunos de ellos. (1) El espacio discursivo de la mujer (estudios sobre Clorinda Matto de Turner, Herminia Brumana y Victoria Ocampo, por Gloria Hintze, Herminia Solari y Liliana Vela, respectivamente).

(2) Figuras de la memoria en la historia de las ideas americanas (Florencia Ferreira sobre la revista *Clarté*, y Walter Camargo sobre José Vasconcelos desde la perspectiva autobiográfica. (3) Ideas, discursos y representaciones en torno al primer centenario de la Independencia (Dante Ramaglia sobre el disenso ideológico en la Argentina de 1910, y Marisa Muñoz sobre Macedonio Fernández y el humorismo). [CJB]

3550 Taboada, Hernán. Un mundo sin ellos: en torno al discurso criollo decimonónico. (*Cuad. Am./México*, 121:3, julio/sept. 2007, p. 27–39)

Desde lo que el autor llama "una antropología de la negación", analiza los distintos modos de rechazo, ocultamiento y sojuzgamiento de poblaciones indígenas, negras y de otros orígenes. Artículo rico en matices, señala las contradicciones de aquel proceso, hasta la necesidad de aceptación (nunca del todo definitiva) de esas "razas", bajo la idea del mestizaje con preponderancia de los valores criollos. [CJB]

3551 Tenenbaum, Ernesto Jorge. Movimientos populares en la historia de nuestra América. Buenos Aires: Conferencia Permanente de Partidos Políticos de América Latina y el Caribe: Editorial Sudamericana, 2006. 394 p.: bibl.

Expone, en términos relativamente breves en cada caso, los "movimientos populares" que se han dado en América Latina, pero incluyendo también Jamaica, Guyana, Belice y otros estados del Caribe. Para dar un ejemplo, en el caso de Perú, se incluyen: la rebelión de Túpac Amaru; el APRA; las ideas de Mariátegui; el gobierno del Gen. Velazco Alvarado; y la posición de Ollanta Humala. También hay capítulos sobre las relaciones de América Latina con Estados Unidos, Inglaterra y Francia. Aunque la forma de organizar el material lo acerca al carácter de inventario, el libro expresa opiniones políticas en cada página. [JCTE]

3552 Torchia Estrada, Juan Carlos. Filosofía y colonización en Hispanoamérica. México: UNAM, Instituto de Investigaciones Filosóficas: Centro de Investigaciones sobre América Latina y el Caribe, 2010. 194 p.: bibl. (Col. Cuadernos; 70)

Reúne estudios sobre los siguientes temas: los comienzos de la enseñanza de la filosofía en Hispanoamérica en el siglo XVI; representantes de la filosofía novohispana del mismo siglo: Fray Alonso de la Veracruz, el Padre Antonio Rubio y Fray Tomás de Mercado; y un examen de la apreciación de la filosofía escolástica desde su implantación hasta el siglo XX. [JCTE]

3553 Torchia Estrada, Juan Carlos. La querella de la escolástica hispanoamericana: crisis, polemica y normalización. (*Cuyo/Mendoza*, 27, 2007, p. 35–77, bibl.)

Revisa la visión que se tuvo en Hispanoamérica de la escolástica, desde su predominio en los siglos XVI y XVII, pasando por la crisis del XVIII y las polémicas del XIX, hasta llegar a la normalización del estudio de la filosofía colonial en el siglo XX. [JCTE]

3554 Twentieth-century Marxism: a global introduction. Edited by Daryl Glaser and David M. Walker. London: New York: Routledge, 2007. 260 p.: bibl., index.

El capítulo dedicado a América Latina ("Marxism in Latin America/Latin American marxism?", por Ronaldo Munck), es un lúcido, amplio y bien informado análisis de la cuestión del marxismo y el socialismo en la región, que llega hasta fechas muy recientes. Señala la presencia de una veta gramsciana a lo largo de ese proceso, pero recorre numerosos movimientos y autores, desde Mariátegui en adelante, y atiende a las varias transformaciones por las que ha pasado el pensamiento marxista en Latinoamérica. [JCTE]

3555 Vallescar Palanca, Diana de. El impacto del género en la filosofía latinoamericana. (*Utop. Prax. Latinoam.*, 10:31, oct./dic. 2005, p. 79–92)

Defensa del feminismo y de los estudios de género. Presenta los antecedentes europeos, norteamericanos y latinoamericanos en esta cuestión. Dedica especial atención al progreso de la conciencia feminista en la filosofía latinoamericana, y a las mujeres que ejercitan la filosofía en la región. [JCTE]

3556 Vergara Estévez, Jorge. La utopía neoliberal y sus críticos. (*Utop. Prax. Latinoam.*, 10:31, oct./dic. 2005, p. 37–62)

Sostiene que la teoría neoliberal, en sus clásicos representantes, pretende ser una interpretación de la realidad humana y social, más allá del orden económico. Las numerosas críticas que se le han efectuado mostrarían que el neoliberalismo actuaría como una especie de partido político que abarca diferentes grupos corporativos, asumiendo una supuesta universalidad, y que finalmente resultaría un modelo político excluyente. [CJB]

3557 Volver al futuro: la búsqueda de un socialismo latinoamericano. Compilación de Gustavo Ayala Cruz. Quito: Ediciones La Tierra, 2008. 255 p.: bibl. (Ediciones La Tierra; 39)

La perspectiva principal desde la cual se organizan los trabajos es la desaparición del socialismo en la Unión Soviética y el posterior "triunfo" del neoliberalismo. Luego, al "fracaso" de este último, siguió la renovación del programa socialista, que casi había desaparecido en los años 90. Aunque hay constantes referencias históricas al socialismo latinoamericano, la tónica de los autores es proyectiva: cómo debe ser el socialismo en el inmediato futuro. Esta nota general se matiza según los temas especiales: el nacionalismo, la necesidad de un gran debate dentro de la izquierda, la función de Ernesto Guevara, entre otros. [JCTE]

3558 Vuscovic, Sergio. La mujer en la filosofía. (*Cuad. Pensam. Latinoam.*, 16, 2008, p. 137–144)

Reflexión sobre el lugar de la mujer en la filosofía. Rastrea el tema en los diálogos platónicos y menciona casos de mujeres intelectuales europeas y latinoamericanas del pasado, incluyendo también algunos nombres actuales. Muestra que en los últimos tiempos las mujeres habrían acentuado su protagonismo. [CJB]

3559 Wingartz Plata, Oscar. Teología de la liberación latinoamericana: una construcción propia. (*Cuad. Am./México*, 128:2, abril/junio 2009, p. 39–52)

Considera que la teología de la liberación aparece como una necesidad eclesial compartida y surge de un contexto marcado por la pobreza y la marginación. Coincide con el análisis de Luis Gerardo Díaz Núñez en su libro *La teología de la liberación a treinta años de su surgimiento* (2005), que recomienda especialmente. [CJB]

MÉXICO

3560 Aguilar Rivera, José Antonio. The shadow of Ulysses: public intellectual exchange across the U.S.-Mexican border. Foreword by Russell Jacoby. Translated by Rose Hocker and Emiliano Corral. Lanham, Md.: Lexington Books, 2000. 136 p.: bibl., index.

Traducción de *La sombra de Ulises*. Ver *HLAS 60:4627*. [JCTE]

3561 Aguirre, Gabriela. La iglesia católica y la revolución mexicana, 1913–1920. (*Estud. Filos. Hist. Let.*, 84, primavera 2008, p. 43–62)

Analiza las conflictivas relaciones entre la Iglesia y el gobierno mexicano, desde Francisco Madero hasta el restablecimiento de la presencia eclesiástica durante la época de Victoriano Huerta. [CJB]

3562 Beuchot, Mauricio. Cartografía del pensamiento novohispano. México: Los Libros de Homero, 2008. 153 p. (Novohispania; 4)

Algunos temas del libro son: el estado de la cuestión de la filosofía novohispana de los siglos XVI y XVII; los centros de cultura en la Nueva España; el problema de la conquista; Fray Alonso de la Veracruz y el libro *Sobre el Cielo*; algunos teólogos dominicos (información poco conocida); Descartes en la Nueva España. Continúa la excelente obra del autor sobre la filosofía colonial en México. [JCTE]

3563 Beuchot, Mauricio. Ciencia y filosofía en México en el siglo XX. México: UNAM, 2006. 164 p.: bibl. (Col. Debate y reflexión; 8)

En tono sobrio y apreciativo rescata valores de la cultura mexicana del siglo XX y hace una verdadera aportación al tema. Los asuntos tratados son: la filosofía de la ciencia de Arturo Rosenblueth; el pensamiento de Antonio Gómez Robledo; Leopoldo Zea y el problema de la filosofía latinoamericana; la obra de Juan Hernández Luna y Bernabé Navarro sobre la historia de la filosofía en México; la filosofía poética de Ramón Xirau; el existencialismo de José Raúl Sanabria; el pensamiento filosófico de Fernando Salmerón, Adolfo García Díaz y Abelardo Villegas. [JCTE]

3564 Colonna, Roberto. Leopoldo Zea: originalidad y filosofía sin más. (*Cuad. Am./México*, 130:4, oct./dic. 2009, p. 181–194)

Expone los principales aspectos de la meditación de Leopoldo Zea sobre la relación entre la cultura latinoamericana y la occidental. Zea sostendría que la originalidad filosófica latinoamericana consistiría en responder a las cuestiones planteadas por las propias circunstancias, independientemente de la aspiración a la condición universal. [CJB]

3565 Cortés Rodríguez, Pedro. El sentido filosófico de la historia en José Gaos. (*Humanitas/Monterrey*, 1:34, 2007, p. 99–114)

Para Gaos la vida humana es histórica, como lo es la sociedad, por el hecho de crear cultura. Pero no todos los hechos culturales serían recuperados por la historiografía, sino aquellos que revelan grados crecientes de autorreflexión. La reconstrucción del historiador requeriría criterios de selección, que para Gaos serían: el de lo "influyente" (los hechos que hacen historia); el de lo "representativo" (los sucesos concomitantes): y el de lo "permanente" (la persistencia de lo histórico del pasado en el presente). [CJB]

3566 Crespo, Regina Aída. Itinerarios intelectuales: Vasconcelos, Lobato y sus proyectos para la nación. 2. ed. México: UNAM, 2004. 369 p.: bibl. (Serie Nuestra América; 61)

Paralelo entre José Vasconcelos (México) y Monteiro Lobato (Brasil). Además de la comparación entre los dos intelectuales, presenta mucho material de contexto: sobre los dos países y sobre las dos ciudades (México y San Pablo). Además de ser Lobato un admirador de Estados Unidos, ambas figuras divergen porque Vasconcelos hablaba, con criterio integrador y optimista, de la "raza cósmica", en tanto Lobato consideraba perjudicial la mezcla de razas. [JCTE]

3567 Gandler, Stefan. Marxismo crítico en México: Adolfo Sánchez Vázquez y Bolívar Echeverría. Prólogo de Michael Löwy. Versión en español de Stefan Gandler. Con la colaboración de Marco Aurelio García Barrios y Max Rojas. México: Fondo de Cultura Economica: UNAM, Facultad de

Filosofía y Letras; Querétaro, Mexico: Univ. Autónoma de Querétaro, 2007. 621 p.: bibl., ill. (Sección de obras de filosofía)

El autor, de origen alemán, rechaza con gran intensidad emocional toda forma de eurocentrismo. Precedido de extensas notas biográficas de los autores seleccionados, el libro es una extensa exposición, no carente de examen crítico, de la obra de Sánchez Vázquez (español "transterrado") y Bolívar Echeverría (ecuatoriano, residente en México). Muy abundante la parte bibliográfica del libro. Para el comentario sobre la versión original en alemán, ver *HLAS* 60:4636. [JCTE]

3568 Garciadiego Dantan, Javier. "Particularidades" históricas mexicanas. (*Estud. Filos. Hist. Let.*, 80, primavera 2007, p. 57–70)

Señala 16 "particularidades" en la historia de México. Entre las principales se encontrarían: la coexistencia de indígenas y conquistadores en la etapa colonial; la falta de un gobierno central y efectivo durante el siglo XIX; el mestizaje; la Revolución en el siglo XX; el catolicismo; el nacionalismo. [CJB]

3569 González Casanova Henríquez, Pablo. De la sociología del poder a la sociología de la explotación: pensar América Latina en el siglo XXI. Antología y presentación de Marcos Roitman Rosenmann. Bogotá: Siglo del Hombre Editores; Buenos Aires: CLACSO, 2009. 462 p.: bibl. (Biblioteca universitaria. Ciencias sociales y humanidades. Col. Pensamiento crítico latinoamericano)

Util antología de la extensa obra de González Casanova, que refleja también su acción intelectual y política. El estudio introductorio de Marcos Roitman Rosenmann es muy aprovechable, tomando en cuenta la riqueza de los materiales del libro. [JCTE]

3570 Homenaje a Leopoldo Zea. México: UNAM, 2006. 269 p.: bibl.

La multifacética personalidad de Leopoldo Zea se refleja en los trabajos de este homenaje con motivo de su muerte, en el que también hay testimonios y recordaciones personales. Se destacan las vinculaciones de Zea con: la filosofía; la circunstancia latinoamericana; las relaciones internacionales; y las revistas a las que estuvo vinculado. Algunos autores son: Estela Morales Campos, Porfirio Muñoz Ledo, Guillermo Hurtado, Joaquín Sánchez McGrégor, Liliana Weinberg, Margarita Vera Cuspinera, Alberto Saladino García, María Elena Rodríguez Ozán y Mario Magallón Anaya. [JCTE]

3571 Lértora Mendoza, Celina Ana. La enseñanza Jesuita de la física en Nueva España. Buenos Aires: Fundación para el Estudio del Pensamiento Argentino e Iberoamericano, 2006. 239 p.: bibl.

Utiliza manuscritos de cursos de 10 profesores jesuitas. Los cursos fueron dictados entre 1742 y 1767. Hay una introducción histórica general, pero luego para cada caso se presenta una descripción del texto, con comentarios de interpretación. Es obviamente una contribución muy valiosa. [JCTE]

3572 Méndez Reyes, Salvador. Fray Servando Teresa de Mier y la comunidad hispanoamericana en Londres. (*Cuad. Am./México*, 129:3, julio/sept. 2009, p. 95–107)

Estudia la significación de Mier para la independencia hispanoamericana, y en especial su actuación en las Cortes de Cádiz y en la Sociedad de los Caballeros Racionales de Londres (aparentemente parte de la red mirandina con miras a la Independencia). En esta última ciudad conoció al rioplatense Carlos de Alvear, a Andrés Bello y a Blanco White. Habría sido de tendencia moderada y antijacobina. [CJB]

3573 Monsiváis, Carlos. El estado laico y sus malquerientes: crónica/antología. México: UNAM: Random House Mondadori, 2008. 303 p. (Debate)

Apología de la secularización (la "laicidad"). Aunque es un ensayo (o serie de ensayos), utiliza mucho material de la historia de México y presenta numerosas manifestaciones, tanto de conservadores defensores de la religión como de librepensadores anticlericales. (Estos últimos defendían la concepción de un estado y una educación libres de la influencia de la Iglesia). Naturalmente, hay muchas referencias a la época de la Reforma en México. Tiene algo de manifiesto o de cruzada intelectual. [JCTE]

3574 Ortiz Castro, Ignacio. Acercamiento a la filosofía y la ética del mundo mixteco. Oaxaca, Mexico: Secretaría de Cultura del Gobierno de Oaxaca; México: CONACULTA, Culturas Populares e Indígenas, 2006. 179 p.: bibl., ill. (Col. Diálogos, pueblos originarios de Oaxaca; 1. Serie Veredas)

Explicación, en términos de pensamiento occidental, de la mentalidad mixteca, sus concepciones cosmogónicas y, en especial, su ética, que tiene un marcado sentido práctico, referida a un *nosotros* o representación de la comunidad. [JCTE]

3575 Palazón, María Rosa. La estética en México, siglo XX: diálogos entre filósofos. México: UNAM-Facultad de Filosofía y Letras: Fondo de Cultura Económica, 2006. 452 p.: bibl., index. (Filosofía)

La característica principal de la obra es que en lugar de estar organizada según las posiciones de los filósofos del caso, la autora traza un esquema (extenso y complejo) de temas estéticos, y va desarrollando esos temas al hilo de las opiniones y teorías de los distintos autores que toma en cuenta. Caso, Vasconcelos, Sánchez Vázquez y Ramón Xirau son los más reiterados. [JCTE]

3576 Rajo Serventich, Alfredo. Emilio Castelar en México: su influencia en la opinión pública mexicana a través de "El Monitor Republicano". México: Univ. Autónoma de la Ciudad de México, 2007. 281 p.: bibl. (Pensamiento propio)

Buena monografía. Castelar es visto como político, gobernante y periodista, y se examinan sus ideas republicanas (antimonárquicas), expresadas en el *Monitor Republicano*. Se muestran también sus relaciones con intelectuales y políticos mexicanos, que constituyeron una verdadera "red" intelectual, sobre el trasfondo de las relaciones entre España y México. [JCTE]

3577 Rionda Arreguín, Luis. México entre el sueño y la realidad: ensayos. Guanajuato, Mexico: Univ. de Guanajuato, Dirección General de Extensión, 2007. 215 p.: bibl. (Pliego historia)

Sin excesos, ni de teoría ni de expresión, se trata de buenos y acertados ensayos en los que se consideran figuras señeras de México, aunque debajo del tratamiento individual late siempre la preocupación por la interpretación general del país. Son temas del libro: la obra de Silvio Zavala; Juan Ruiz de Alarcón; Carlos de Sigüenza y Góngora; José Antonio Alzate; Fray Servando Teresa de Mier; Andrés Molina Enríquez; Alfonso Reyes; Antonio Caso; y Edmundo O'Gorman. [JCTE]

3578 Rojas Gómez, Miguel. La identidad integracionista en la filosofía de Leopoldo Zea. (*Cuad. Am./México*, 130:4, oct./dic. 2009, p. 195–217)

Después de examinar diversos aspectos del pensamiento de Zea, como la relación del hombre latinoamericano y su cultura con el conjunto del mundo y los demás hombres, concluye que la propuesta de Zea sobre la integración siguió la línea bolivariana de integración "horizontal" o de igualdad entre países, contrapuesta a la "vertical" o integración hegemónica. En esa posición la integración cultural jugaría el papel más importante. [CJB]

3579 Santana, Adalberto. Leopoldo Zea y el socialismo latinoamericano. (*Cuad. Am./México*, 122:4, oct./dic. 2007, p. 117–126)

Reflexión sobre la labor de Leopoldo Zea y la vigencia de su pensamiento, realizada desde la perspectiva del socialismo latinoamericano. Aunque Zea no adhirió al marxismo, recogió lo mejor de una tradición revolucionaria en busca de la equidad y la justicia para América Latina, con proyecciones universales. [CJB]

3580 Spenser, Daniela and **Rina Ortiz Peralta.** La Internacional Comunista en Mexico: los primeros tropiezos: documentos, 1919–1922. México: Instituto Nacional de Estudios Históricos de las Revoluciones de México, 2006. 417 p.: bibl., ill. (Fuentes y documentos)

Son casi 90 documentos, del Comintern (o relacionados con él). El Comintern fue creado para fomentar la revolución mundial y luego fue instrumento de la política exterior de la Unión Soviética. La etapa seleccionada corresponde a la primera época de la institución. Sus dirigentes no tenían gran conocimiento de los países no europeos, y por eso se enviaban misiones especiales, como fue el caso de México. Se muestran los esfuerzos para crear un Partido Comunista durante los gobiernos de la Revolución mexicana. La Presentación de Spenser es muy útil, y por supuesto los documentos reproducidos. [JCTE]

3581 Taboada, Hernán. Oriente y mundo clásico en José Vasconcelos. (*Cuyo/Mendoza*, 27, 2007, p. 103–119, bibl.)

Muestra el tránsito de Vasconcelos desde su admiración por el Oriente y su

opinión sobre las bondades del mestizaje a posiciones opuestas y extremas en la etapa final de su vida. Ensayo breve e inteligente. [JCTE]

3582 Vargas Lozano, Gabriel. El humanismo teórico-práctico de Adolfo Sánchez Vásquez. (*Utop. Prax. Latinoam.*, 11:34, julio/sept. 2006, p. 115–124, bibl.)

Expone aspectos biográficos y de acción política de Sánchez Vázquez, que fue parte de la emigración intelectual de España a México en el siglo XX. Pero sobre todo se ocupa de su pensamiento filosófico y su interpretación del marxismo. Muy buen artículo. [JCTE]

3583 Velasco Gómez, Ambrosio. Republicanismo y multiculturalismo. México: Siglo Veintiuno Editores, 2006. 152 p.: bibl. (Sociología y política)

Hace extensas consideraciones sobre la democracia liberal (representativa) y la democracia republicana (participativa). Estas consideraciones son aplicadas al "republicanismo novohispano", especialmente a Las Casas y Fray Alonso de la Veracruz, republicanismo que estaría más cerca del multiculturalismo que la democracia liberal. Esto es, en opinión del autor, importante para el caso de México, con sus diferentes etnias. El libro se prestará a discusiones, pero está seriamente elaborado. [JCTE]

3584 Yankelevich, Pablo. El exilio argentino de José Vasconcelos. (*Iberoamericana/Madrid*, 6:24, 2006, p. 27–42, bibl.)

Pese al título, aunque el mayor detalle se destina a su estancia en Argentina, se ocupa en realidad de todo el exilio de Vasconcelos después de 1929. Aunque escrito sin ninguna simpatía hacia el Vasconcelos que en su etapa final negó las condiciones de "maestro de juventudes" de su primera época, el artículo es muy rico en contenido y, consiguientemente, útil. [JCTE]

AMÉRICA CENTRAL

3585 Sierra Fonseca, Rolando. Ortega y Gasset en Honduras: la razón histórica vista por Ramón Oquelí. (*Cuad. Am./México*, 118:4, oct./dic. 2006, p. 67–77)

Oportuno artículo sobre el pensador hondureño Ramón Oquelí (1933–2004). Se vincula su visión de la realidad hondureña a varios filósofos españoles, pero especialmente a Ortega y Gasset. [CJB]

CARIBE INSULAR

3586 The birth of Caribbean civilisation: a century of ideas about culture and identity, nation and society. Compilation by O. Nigel Bolland. Kingston; Miami: Ian Randle Publishers; Oxford: J. Currey, 2004. 665 p.: bibl., index.

Contiene 45 textos de autores de habla española, francesa e inglesa, representantes del Caribe en términos amplios. Algunos de ellos son: José Martí, Fernando Ortiz, Luis Muñoz Marín, Fernández Retamar, Fidel Castro, Aimé Césaire, Frantz Fanon, René Depestre, Marcus Garvey, Eric Williams, Rex Nettleford, Walter Manley, Walter Rodney, Arthur Lewis, Orlando Paterson. Se aclara que 'civilización' se aplica a una específica cultura. Todos los textos son precedidos de una adecuada presentación. Es un volumen valioso y oportuno. [JCTE]

3587 Camino a lo alto: aproximaciones marxistas a José Martí. Compilación de Revista "Marx ahora". La Habana, Cuba: Editorial de Ciencias Sociales, 2006. 375 p.: bibl. (Col. ponencia; 01)

Antología de escritos sobre Martí de autores marxistas o simpatizantes del marxismo. Entre ellos: Julio Antonio Mella, Emilio Roig de Leuchsenring, Juan Marinello, Roberto Fernández Retamar, Carlos Rafael Rodríguez, Isabel Monal, Julio Le Riverend, Olivia Miranda. Tiene una breve presentación general. [JCTE]

3588 Carvalho, Eugênio Rezende de. El krausismo en Latinoamérica y Cuba. (*Cuad. Am./México*, 119:1, enero/marzo 2007, p. 77–88, bibl.)

Breve artículo que traza sucintamente las ideas de Karl Krause, y su recepción en España. Se refiere luego a las opiniones sobre los posibles vínculos de José Martí con el krausismo. [CJB]

3589 *Cuadernos Americanos*. Vol. 23, No. 3, julio/sept. 2009. México: UNAM.

Contiene varios artículos sobre el político y escritor dominicano Juan Bosch. Los de mayor interés para esta sección (p. 11–92) son: Pablo A. Maríñez, "Bosch ante Hostos: anticolonialismo y antiimperialismo en el Caribe" (influencia de Hostos sobre Bosch, antes de la etapa marxista del segundo [1969]); Angel R. Vilarino Jusino, "Los cuentos de Juan Bosch como textos de formación

ético-política democrática" (comentario a un libro sobre el tema del título); Graciela Leticia Raya Alonso, "Juan Bosch, un hombre del pueblo" (la dedicación de Bosch a la masa campesina que conoció en su niñez). [CJB]

3590 Culture, politics, race and diaspora: the thought of Stuart Hall. Edited by Brian Meeks. Kingston; Miami: I. Randle Publishers; London: Lawrence & Wishart, 2007. 316 p.: bibl., index. (Caribbean reasonings)

Stuart Hall, autor jamaiquino que desarrolló su obra en Londres, es uno de los impulsores de los Estudios Culturales. El libro está dedicado a su obra y a problemas del Caribe vinculados con su pensamiento. Se cierra con una reflexión del propio Hall sobre su obra, donde manifiesta que no se considera un *scholar* sino un intelectual, en el sentido gramsciano de la palabra, porque el intelectual puede usar el conocimiento para fines que van más allá de su condición, lo que no ocurre necesariamente con el productor de conocimiento o *scholar*. [JCTE]

3591 Díaz Infante, Duanel. Mañach o la República. La Habana: Letras Cubanas, 2003. 195 p.: bibl.

Mañach es estudiado con detalle en sus principales obras (*Estampas de San Cristóbal* (1926), *Indagación del choteo* (1928), y *Martí el apóstol* (1933)) y en el contexto de la vida cultural y las polémicas de su época. El autor destaca que en los años 70 y 80 no hubiera sido posible, en Cuba, publicar un libro expositivo, crítico y comprensivo de una figura que murió en el exilio. [JCTE]

3592 Díaz Quiñones, Arcadio. Sobre los principios: los intelectuales caribeños y la tradición. Bernal, Argentina: Univ. Nacional de Quilmes Editorial, 2006. 526 p.: bibl. (Col. Intersecciones)

Buen trabajo académico. Además de Menéndez y Pelayo, trata a Pedro Henríque Ureña, José Martí, Ramiro Guerra y Sánchez (Cuba), Tomás Blanco y Antonio S. Pedreira (Puerto Rico). Cada uno de estos temas es tratado con gran extensión y amplio conocimiento. [JCTE]

3593 En busca de una estrella: antología del pensamiento independentista puertorriqueño de Betances a Filiberto.

Compilación de Juan Mari Brás. Mayagüez, Puerto Rico: Editora Causa Común, 2007. 494 p.: bibl., ill.

Contiene numerosas declaraciones, escritos y discursos sobre la independencia de Puerto Rico, desde Ramón Emeterio Betances hasta los representantes más recientes, pasando por Hostos y Albizu Campos. [JCTE]

3594 Historia del pensamiento cubano.
v. 1, t. 2, Del liberalismo esclavista al liberalismo abolicionista. Compilación, introducciones, presentaciones y notas de Eduardo Torres-Cuevas. La Habana: Editorial de Ciencias Sociales, 2006. 418 p.: bibl. (Historia)

Es continuación de una obra anterior (ver *HLAS 64:2956*). Aunque contiene muchos textos, es más que una antología porque las introducciones a cada tema son muy extensas, de modo que resulta formalmente una historia, bien que con textos seleccionados como complemento. Algunos autores estudiados son: José Antonio Saco, José de la Luz y Caballero, Domingo del Monte, Felipe Poey, Francisco Arango y Parreño, Domingo André, Joaquín Gómez, Juan José Díaz de Estrada y Juan Bernardo Gaván. Buena parte del contenido se refiere a asuntos económicos y a la cuestión de la esclavitud. [JCTE]

3595 Martí, José. Crónicas. Prólogo de Javier Lasarte. Selección, notas e introducción de Susana Rotker. México: Debate; New York: Random House, 2007. 294 p.: bibl.

De las muy numerosas crónicas periodísticas que escribió Martí, Rotker ha seleccionado en este libro un grupo que merece permanecer, y que reflejan no sólo su prosa, sino también sus opiniones testimoniales de la vida en Estados Unidos, tema nunca ajeno al observador latinoamericano. Algunas están dedicadas a Longfellow, a Emerson, a Whitman, y naturalmente hay ideas en los temas menos esperados. La introducción de Rotker es un estudio sobre las variantes de la crónica modernista y su función literaria en el periodismo. Agudas son también sus breves introducciones a cada crónica. [JCTE]

3596 Mezilas, Glodel. ¿Qué es el indigenismo haitiano? (*Cuad. Am./México*, 126:4, oct./dic. 2008, p. 29–52)

El indigenismo haitiano es caracterizado como una liberación de la cultura popular, que acentuó vigorosamente la fuente africana de la identidad nacional. Coincidiría con el surgimiento del sentimiento nacionalista y antiimperialista con motivo de la ocupación norteamericana de 1915. No omite el autor, sin embargo, que hubo críticas a esta posición, las cuales tuvieron en cuenta también los elementos culturales europeos como parte integrante de la cultura nacional. El indigenismo habría sido el principal antecedente del movimiento de la negritud, y ambos serían complementarios. [CJB]

3597 Rivas Toll, Elena. Pensamiento filosófico de José Martí: un estudio desde las mediaciones político-axiológicas. La Habana, Cuba: Editorial de Ciencias Sociales, 2008. 216 p.: bibl.

Cuanta expresión cosmovisional, política, ética, religiosa o expresiva de valores que puede encontrarse en los textos de Martí (sean éstos periodísticos, poéticos o ensayísticos) se traslada a un cuadro sistemático que representaría la filosofía de Martí. En las conclusiones se elogia esta filosofía como alternativa al "afán de universalismos abstractos de sistemas filosóficos modernos impuestos desde los centros de poder". [JCTE]

3598 Rojas, Rafael. Anatomía del entusiasmo: la revolución como espectáculo de ideas. (*Am. Lat. Hoy/Salamanca*, 47, dic. 2007, p. 39–53, bibl.)

Explica la adhesión a la Revolución cubana—y posterior actitud crítica sobre ella—de intelectuales como Jean-Paul Sartre, Wright Mills, Pablo Neruda, Regis Debray, sin ser los únicos. Explica cómo la experiencia cubana se vio en un momento como un aspecto de la descolonización, por efecto de la obra de Franz Fanon, y en otros casos como un enfrentamiento con el problema del desarrollo. [JCTE]

3599 Rojas, Rafael. Essays in Cuban intellectual history. New York: Palgrave Macmillan, 2008. 197 p.: bibl., index. (New concepts in Latino American cultures)

Con ensayos que eluden la aridez de la prosa académica pero no por ello están menos bien informados, el libro es una contribución importante a la historia cultural de Cuba, y una muestra de que esa historia tiene una riqueza no siempre bien conocida. Algunos son medulosos, como el dedicado a Fernando Ortiz. Es aclaratorio y no trillado el que se refiere al republicanismo de Martí. Otro ofrece buenos elementos para conocer autores que se ocuparon de la interpretación general de Cuba. Precisamente, el tema que reaparece en casi todos los artículos es la identidad cubana, sea tratando de la Cuba tradicional, del efecto de la Revolución o de la cultura de la diáspora. [JCTE]

3600 San Miguel, Pedro Luis. Los desvaríos de Ti Noel: ensayos sobre la producción del saber en el Caribe. San Juan: Ediciones Vértigo, 2004. 227 p.: bibl. (Col. Caida libre)

Son reflexiones bien organizadas y bien apoyadas en la literatura pertinente. Posiblemente el trabajo más logrado sea "Visiones históricas del Caribe, entre la mirada imperial y la resistencia de los subalternos", que es una excelente síntesis de la historia caribeña (del Caribe de habla española, principalmente), de sus rasgos geopolíticos, económicos, de identidad y de reacción de las grandes masas subalternas. Algunos pueden ser ensayos breves y más libres, o pueden ser críticas de libros. [JCTE]

3601 Valdés García, Félix. El Caribe: integración, identidad y *choteo*. (*Utop. Prax. Latinoam.*, 9:27, oct./dic. 2004, p. 49–60)

Reflexiones sobre la posible integración latinoamericana (especialmente la del Caribe) y sobre la identidad y el "choteo" ("el no tomar las cosas en serio", o "relajo"). El choteo se toma como rasgo identitario y por lo tanto como posible alternativa a la globalización y la "homogeneización cultural". Precisamente, el aspecto cultural es considerado fundamental para todo proceso de integración. [CJB]

VENEZUELA

3602 Bolívar: antología polémica. Compilación de David Viñas y Gabriela García Cedro. Buenos Aires: Crónica General de América Latina, 2007. 382 p.: bibl.

Los organizadores dicen que la antología se elaboró especialmente para el público argentino, por su menor interés en los asuntos latinoamericanos. La idea de la

obra es presentar "una versión múltiple de Bolívar", con textos controvertibles, evitando la monotonía de las opiniones consagradas. Comienza y concluye con sendos textos de Carrera Damas. Incluye el famoso texto de Marx sobre Bolívar, y opiniones de Bartolomé Mitre, Juan Montalvo, José Martí, y Rufino Blanco Bombona, sin que esto agote la antología. A cada texto precede un comentario, en el tono no académico del volumen. [JCTE]

3603 Bracho Martínez, Jorge. Arturo Uslar Pietri y el Nuevo Mundo. (*Cuad. Am./México*, 122:4, oct./dic. 2007, p. 95–116, bibl.)

Analiza la concepción liberal de Uslar Pietri y la contribución que realizó en sus ensayos sobre el Nuevo Mundo. Sirve como herramienta de apoyo a posibles lecturas del ensayista venezolano y ofrece un panorama amplio de sus obras. [CJB]

3604 Da Silva, José Luis. El modo de escribir la historia o la importancia de los hechos en el pensamiento histórico de Andrés Bello. (*Apunt. Filos.*, 16:31, dic. 2007, p. 45–66)

Sobre la concepción de la ciencia histórica en Bello, basado en varios de sus escritos. Se destaca el valor que Bello atribuía a la documentación como base de la labor histórica, frente a la especulación filosófica de la historia con escasa base empírica. [JCTE]

3605 Da Silva, José Luis and Rafael García Torres. Revolución francesa y revolución americana: dos visiones desde Fermín Toro. (*Bol. Acad. Nac. Hist./Caracas*, 90:360, oct./dic. 2007, p. 71–91, bibl.)

Reflexiones de Fermín Toro sobre la Revolución francesa, a la que critica, en contraste con las virtudes que encontraba en las revoluciones de América. [JCTE]

3606 De Freitas Santos, Mayke. La hora de la biblioteca: los libros de Francisco de Miranda. (*Cuad. Am./México*, 126:4, oct./dic. 2008, p. 117–133)

Narración, muy personal y con algún dejo literario pero con numerosos datos históricos, sobre el desmantelamiento de la importante biblioteca de Francisco de Miranda en Londres, a partir de 1828. Incluye detalles personales de los libreros que compraron los libros en la subasta, y muestra cómo el contenido de la biblioteca representaba los intereses del Precursor. [CJB]

3607 Falcón, Fernando. El cadete de los valles de Aragua: el pensamiento político y militar de la ilustración y los conceptos de guerra y política en Simón Bolívar, 1797–1814. Caracas: Univ. Central de Venezuela, Facultad de Ciencias Jurídicas y Políticas, 2006. 246 p.: bibl.

Es un estudio muy pormenorizado de las ideas militares de Bolívar, pero consideradas en relación con el pensamiento político. Trabajo académico, elude los juicios ditirámbicos usuales en el tratamiento del Libertador. [JCTE]

3608 García Torres, Rafael. Apuntes sobre el pensamiento filosófico venezolano: de la escolástica colonial a la propuesta moderna. (*Apunt. Filos.*, 16:31, dic. 2007, p. 67–87)

Trata cuatro momentos del pensamiento filosófico en lo que es hoy Venezuela: lo que Silvio Zavala llamó "filosofía de la conquista" (que en realidad vale para toda Hispanoamérica); Alfonso Briceño (siglo XVII); Agustín de Quevedo y Villegas (siglo XVIII); y la Filosofía del entendimiento, de Andrés Bello (siglo XIX). El autor daría la impresión de pensar que son asuntos poco estudiados. [JCTE]

3609 Gavidia Montilla, Fernando Rafael. Propuesta de Unión Americana en los planteamientos políticos de Simón Bolívar y Andrés Bello. Caracas: Univ. Central de Venezuela, Facultad de Ciencias Jurídicas y Políticas, 2007. 196 p.: bibl. (Serie Trabajos de grado; 12)

Aunque profuso en su estructura y estilo de exposición, el trabajo señala con alto grado de detalle cuanta manifestación referente a la unidad de las repúblicas hispanoamericanas se encuentra en los escritos y declaraciones de Bolívar y Bello. [JCTE]

3610 Jalif de Bertranou, Clara Alicia. El devenir de las ideas filosóficas en Venezuela: la vertiente fenomenológico-existencial. (*Cuad. Pensam. Latinoam.*, 16, 2008, p. 41–50)

Sin excluir otras líneas de pensamiento, analiza el caso de la fenomenología y el existencialismo en Venezuela, previo realizar una contextualización histórica e ideológica. Estudia el aporte de emigrados

españoles y de especialistas del país que se situaron en este movimiento. [CJB]

3611 Meza Dorta, Giovanni. Miranda y Bolívar: dos visiones. Caracas: Comala.com, 2007. 255 p.: bibl.

Contraposición polémica de las respectivas ideas políticas y actuaciones personales de Miranda y Bolívar, en la cual, no sin cierta emotividad, el autor inclina la balanza a favor del Precursor. No debieran desestimarse, sin embargo, las comprobaciones que aporta en su defensa de Miranda. [JCTE]

3612 Ocampo López, Javier. El pensamiento hispanoamericano del maestro Simón Rodríguez. (*Cuad. Am./México*, 122:4, oct./dic. 2007, p. 11–26)

Presenta el pensamiento de Simón Rodríguez (1771–1854), sus propuestas políticas y sus ideas educativas, tomando en cuenta la situación posterior a las guerras de independencia en Hispanoamérica. Finaliza indicando la actualidad de las reflexiones del maestro venezolano a la luz del bicentenario de la revolución de 1810. [CJB]

3613 Reyes Duarte, Hernando. Las bestias negras del libertador: el Simón Bolívar de Karl Marx y los libros de sus inspiradores, La historia secreta de la independencia, según Ducoudrey-Holstein [y] La expedición de Hippisley, calumniador de Bolívar. Bogotá: Editorial Temis, 2004. 203 p.: bibl.

El libro trata del tantas veces recordado y criticado artículo que Marx escribiera sobre Bolívar para *The New American Cyclopedia* (1858). El autor lo coloca entre las "bestias negras" del Libertador. Es de utilidad que reproduzca el artículo en el original inglés y lo traduzca al español. (Afirma que no hay otra traducción española fidedigna.) En la bibliografía del artículo, Marx menciona tres obras, dos de las cuales tienen la misma tendencia desfavorable a Bolívar. Estas son: la *Histoire de Bolivar* de H.L.V. Ducoudray Holstein (1831) y *A Narrative of the Expedition to the Rivers Orinoco and Apuré* de G. Hippisley (1810). Ambas se reproducen en el presente libro, traducidas pero compendiadas. [JCTE]

3614 Rojas, Reinaldo. La unidad latinoamericana en el pensamiento de Bolívar. (*Cuad. Am./México*, 126:4, oct./dic. 2008, p. 75–96)

El pensamiento de Bolívar es considerado aquí especialmente en su "Carta de Jamaica". Según el autor, ese pensamiento tendría aún vigencia en los siguientes aportes al derecho internacional latinoamericano: el principio de solidaridad defensiva; la igualdad jurídica de los estados; la garantía de la integridad territorial; una reglamentación para la convivencia de las naciones de la región; y la conciliación como principio de las relaciones internacionales. [CJB]

3615 Rosales Sánchez, Juan. Razón y acción: reflexiones en torno al sujeto político en la filosofía de Simón Rodríguez. (*Apunt. Filos.*, 16:31, dic. 2007, p. 19–44)

Sobre las ideas de razón, opinión y educación en Simón Rodríguez. [JCTE]

3616 Urueña Cervera, Jaime. Bolívar republicano: fundamentos ideológicos e históricos de su pensamiento político. Bogotá: Ediciones Aurora, 2004. 267 p.: bibl.

Se opone a lo que considera erróneas apreciaciones del ideario de Bolívar, provenientes todas de no tener en cuenta su condición de republicano, en su acción y como legislador. Para ello realiza comparaciones muy minuciosas con numerosos autores de la época, mencionados o no mencionados por el propio Bolívar. Trabaja principalmente con el proyecto de *Constitución para Venezuela y el Discurso de Angostura* (1819). Discute otras interpretaciones latinoamericanas. [JCTE]

3617 Yoris-Villasana, Corina. El ejercicio filosófico de Ernesto Mayz Vallenilla a partir de su concepción del hombre del nuevo mundo. (*Apunt. Filos.*, 16:31, dic. 2007, p. 199–205)

Breve y acertada semblanza personal y filosófica del filósofo venezolano Ernesto Mayz Vallenilla. Hace especial referencia a su libro *El problema de América* (1959). [JCTE]

COLOMBIA

3618 Álvarez Hoyos, María Teresa. Élites intelectuales en el sur de Colombia, Pasto, 1904–1930: una generación decisiva. San Juan de Pasto, Colombia: RUDE-COLOMBIA: Univ. Pedagógica y Tecnológica de Colombia: Univ. de Nariño: ASCUN,

2007. 553 p.: bibl. (Col. Tesis doctorales RUDECOLOMBIA)

Examen de la acción de un grupo de intelectuales de las primeras décadas del siglo XX en el sur de Colombia (especialmente en la ciudad de Pasto). Dichos intelectuales representaron la modernización en medio de la visión tradicional de la Iglesia. Se denomina al grupo "generación de 1904" y su actuación llegó aproximadamente hasta 1930. Se expresó mediante el periodismo y las sociedades científicas. Es historia local, pero en el contexto de tendencias generales en Colombia y en América Latina. [JCTE]

3619 Coloquio La Filosofía y la Crisis Colombiana, 2nd, Bogotá, 2004. La crisis colombiana: reflexiones filosóficas. Edición de Rubén Sierra Mejía. Bogotá: Univ. Nacional de Colombia, Facultad de Ciencias Humanas/Depto. de Filosofía, 2008. 382 p.: bibl., indexes. (Biblioteca abierta; 353. Col. General. Filosofía)

Los enfoques son verdaderamente filosóficos (en ciertos casos, de filosofía política, teoría del estado, etc.), pero todos son movidos por las circunstancias de la vida política de Colombia en la actualidad y el pasado inmediato. En general no descienden a la polémica de partidos, aunque varían en la defensa o crítica de la estructura gubernamental. Uno de los temas recurrentes, como podía esperarse, es la existencia de la guerrilla y la violencia, juzgadas de modo diferente según los autores. No se percibe una conclusión generalizada o una perspectiva unitaria, excepto la motivación de origen. Es de presumir que por su naturaleza especulativa no incidirá directamente en la práctica política, pero los trabajos tienen el valor de una meditación seria, más allá de sus diferencias. [JCTE]

3620 Gómez García, Juan Guillermo. Colombia es una cosa impenetrable: raíces de la tolerancia y otros ensayos sobre historia política y vida intelectual. Bogotá: Diente de León, 2006. 454 p.: bibl., indexes.

Conjunto de artículos de variados temas, escritos a lo largo de 20 años, con abundantes opiniones muy personales del autor (aunque no por eso necesariamente arbitrarias). Hay textos sobre políticos y la política de Colombia, y sobre obras literarias expresivas de situaciones sociales. También los hay históricos: uno sobre el trotskismo y otro sobre la cultura alemana en el país (los viajeros Alfonso Stübel y Wilhelm Reiss, además de Humboldt). Un artículo se dedica a Rafael Gutiérrez Girardot. [JCTE]

3621 Pensamiento colombiano del siglo XX. v. 1. Edición de Santiago Castro-Gómez *et al.* Bogotá: Pontificia Univ. Javeriana, 2007. 1 v.: bibl., ill., index.

Es un volumen muy bien logrado. Se tratan numerosos autores, y no solamente filósofos. Algunos son nombres muy reconocidos, como Baldomero Sanín Cano, Carlos Arturo Torres o José María Vargas Vila. Pero también se encontrarán Camilo Torres, Estanislao Zuleta, Gonzalo Arango, Luis López de Mesa, Manuel Quintín Lame y Marta Traba, entre otros que omitimos. [JCTE]

3622 Pensamiento colombiano del siglo XX. v. 2. Edición de Santiago Castro-Gómez *et al.* Bogotá: Pontificia Univ. Javeriana, 2008. 1 v.: bibl., ill., index.

Como en el volumen anterior (item **3621**), 'pensamiento' está tomado en un sentido lato, lo que favorece la presentación de un cuadro más amplio de "intelectuales". Así se encontrarán figuras vinculadas a la pintura (Débora Arango); a la filosofía (Edgard Garavito, Fernando González Ochoa, Rafael Gutiérrez Girardot); a la antropología (Gerardo Reichel-Dulmatoff); a la literatura (José Eustaquio Rivera); a la arqueología (Luis Duque Gómez); y mujeres vinculadas a la vida política (María Cano Márquez). De ninguna manera son todos los incluidos. [JCTE]

3623 Sánchez Cabra, Efraín. Las ideas de progreso en Colombia en el siglo XIX. (*Bol. Hist. Antig.*, 94:839, oct./dic. 2007, p. 675–697)

Señala las vicisitudes y fracasos de los planes de progreso en el antiguo reino de Nueva Granada. Examina el asunto en cuatro aspectos: educación, industria, vías de comunicación e inmigración. Concluye que esos fracasos serían parte del "drama de Colombia". [CJB]

3624 Vallejo Morillo, Jorge. La rebelión de un burgués: Estanislao Zuleta, su vida. Bogotá: Grupo Editorial Norma, 2006. 276 p.: bibl. (Col. Biografías y documentos)

Es una biografía del filósofo colombiano Estanislao Zuleta, concebida muy libremente, y que expresa gran simpatía por el personaje. Zuleta fue autor de *Elogio de la dificultad* (1994), se ocupó de temas de historia de la filosofía e incursionó también en la historia económica de Colombia y en el psicoanálisis. [JCTE]

ECUADOR

3625 Granda Aguilar, Víctor. Manuel Agustín Aguirre y el socialismo hoy. Quito: Ediciones La Tierra, 2008. 208 p.: bibl., ill. (Debate; 40)

El libro resulta útil desde dos puntos de vista: (1) el conocimiento del pensamiento y la acción de Manuel Agustín Aguirre (1903–92)—objetivo principal del libro— en el contexto del socialismo ecuatoriano del siglo XX; y (2) como introducción muy aprovechable a la discusión actual sobre el llamado "socialismo del siglo XXI", el cual es visto desde diversos ángulos. Contiene una útil "ficha biográfica" del autor estudiado. [JCTE]

3626 Henderson, Peter V.N. Gabriel García Moreno and conservative state formation in the Andes. Austin: Univ. of Texas Press; Teresa Lozano Long Institute of Latin American Studies, 2008. 310 p.: bibl., ill., index, map. (LLILAS new interpretations of Latin America series)

Bien elaborada narración de la vida y la acción política de Gabriel García Moreno (1821–75), que contradice algunas interpretaciones tradicionales. Se destaca el papel de su extrema posición católica, tanto en su acción como dentro de las disputas entre conservadores y liberales, comunes, por otra parte, a toda la región. Para el comentario del historiador, ver item **1702**. [JCTE]

3627 Intelectuales indígenas piensan América Latina. Compilación de José Ancan Jara *et al.* Quito: Univ. Andina Simón Bolívar, Ecuador: Abya-Yala; Santiago, Chile: Centro de Estudios Culturales Latinoamericanos, 2007. 340 p.: bibl. (Col. Tinkuy; 2)

Caracteriza a la obra el hecho de que sus autores/as se reconocen como miembros de distintas etnias ("indígenas") que, por su preparación académica, pueden convertirse en estudiosos y críticos. Las contribuciones tratan temas como: identidad y memoria; escritura y oralidad; posibilidad de una educación intercultural; luchas y resistencias desde la Colonia a la actualidad; y el futuro de los pueblos indígenas. En este último aspecto representan una posición afirmativa frente a preconceptos tradicionales. Uno de los propósitos es "descolonizar" las disciplinas de que se ocupan estos investigadores. [JCTE]

3628 Paladines Escudero, Carlos. La odisea de la modernización en el Ecuador: dos momentos de su desarrollo. (*Estud. Filos. Práct. Hist. Ideas*, 8:9, dic. 2007, p. 125–149)

Los dos momentos referidos de la modernización en el Ecuador son: (1) las ideas de los ilustrados (siglo XVIII) y las de los liberales (siglo XIX); (2) los intentos del siglo XX y la actualidad. Para este último caso, se plantean las dificultades que surgen del choque entre el espíritu tradicionalista y las exigencias del mundo actual. También señala la necesidad de que el resultado modernizador sea un verdadero progreso para la sociedad ecuatoriana. [JCTE]

3629 Paredes Ramírez, Willington. El pensamiento político y social de Benjamín Carrión. (*Rev. Arch. Hist. Guayas*, 3/4, primer semestre 2008, p. 143–154, photos)

Emotiva apreciación de Benjamín Carrión (1897–1979), destacado intelectual ecuatoriano del siglo XX, en aquellos aspectos de su pensamiento que el autor considera válidos para la orientación de las nuevas generaciones del país. [JCTE]

3630 Sartre y nosotros. Edición de François Noudelmann *et al.* Quito: Univ. Andina Simón Bolívar: Editorial El Conejo, 2007. 331 p.: bibl.

El propósito del libro es mostrar la recepción de Sartre entre los intelectuales ecuatorianos, en lo literario, pero además en las posiciones políticas y de compromiso. Algunos artículos versan sobre Sartre en general, pero otros se refieren directamente a la influencia del autor francés en los años 60 y 70 en Ecuador. Es de particular valor la contribución de la editora: "Trayectorias y memorias del diálogo con Sartre en la escena cultural de Quito". [JCTE].

PERÚ

3631 Arpini, Adriana. Valor y experiencia valorativa en los escritos de Augusto Salazar Bondy: momentos de su reflexión axiológica. (*Solar*, 2:2, 2006, p. 157–203)

Extenso análisis del tema axiológico en Augusto Salazar Bondy (1925–74). Distingue tres etapas: (1) la fenomenológica (1958–64), con el valor entendido como realización ontológica de los entes valiosos, en la línea del tratamiento dado en la primera mitad del siglo XX; (2) la analítica (1965–69), caracterizada por la impronta de la filosofía del lenguaje; (3), la posterior a 1969, cuando maneja categorías como "dominación", "alienación", "dependencia", etc., y donde elaboraría el vínculo entre valor, cultura y praxis filosófica. En esta última etapa considera la autora que se darían las condiciones para una conciencia de las condiciones de opresión y por lo tanto de emancipación. [CJB]

3632 Becker, Marc. Mariátegui, the Comintern, and the indigenous question in Latin America. (*Sci. Soc.*, 70:4, Oct. 2006, p. 450–479, bibl.)

Versa sobre la posición de José Carlos Mariátegui frente al Primer Congreso de Partidos Comunistas de América Latina, celebrado en Buenos Aires en 1929. Mariátegui se opuso a la iniciativa del Congreso de crear naciones indígenas separadas de los estados nacionales, por considerar que el problema no residía en la condición racial sino en la situación de clases oprimidas que caracterizaba a esos grupos. Trabajo bien elaborado que aporta más de lo que aquí se consigna. [CJB]

3633 Castro Carpio, Augusto. El desafío de las diferencias: reflexiones sobre el estado moderno en el Perú. Lima: Centro de Estudios y Publicaciones: FONDO Editorial, Univ. Ruiz de Montoya: Instituto Bartolomé de Las Casas, 2008. 555 p.: bibl. (Serie Etica y desarrollo) (CEP-323)

En lo que podría considerarse la parte central de la obra, el tema es la constitución del estado en el Perú, que habría sido impuesto desde fuera y no tuvo en cuenta las grandes mayorías. Aquí se analiza "la comunidad política antigua en el Perú", y el pensamiento de Haya de la Torre, Mariátegui, Belaúnde, Alcides Arguedas y José

Matos Mar sobre propuestas para resolver el conflicto entre sociedad y estado. La obra responde a una motivación actual y ética, pero trata de aprovechar la historia política occidental. Uno de sus fines es comprender las sociedades andinas y de la selva para ver cómo pueden integrarse en una nueva forma de estado que no sea ajena a ellas. [JCTE]

3634 Cuesta Alonso, Marcelino. La relación estado e iglesia en la polémica Vigil-Gual. Zacatecas, Mexico: Univ. Autónoma de Zacatecas, 2008. 299 p.: bibl.

El tema es la polémica entre conservadores y liberales peruanos, a partir de la década de 1840, y en particular la relación Iglesia/ estado. Estudia principalmente dos autores: Francisco de Paula González Vigil (1792–1875) y Pedro Gual (1813–90), este último franciscano nacido en España. De cada autor hay una extensa noticia biográfica. La discusión que sostuvieron se desgranó en una serie de asuntos específicos: patronato, bienes de la Iglesia, defensa de los valores tradicionales, relaciones con Roma, tolerancia de cultos, matrimonio, divorcio, enseñanza religiosa, en forma muy similar a otros países hispanoamericanos. Monografía muy completa. [JCTE]

3635 Dancourt, Carlos. Pluralidad étnica y nación en el Perú en los ensayos de José Carlos Mariátegui. (*Allpanchis/Cuzco*, 37:68, segundo semestre 2006, p. 27–65, bibl.)

Traducción de un estudio publicado en francés en 1991. Se funda en tres obras de Mariátegui: *Peruanicemos al Perú*; *Siete ensayos de interpretación de la realidad peruana*; e *Ideología y política*. Señala los cambios que Mariátegui efectuó en sus ideas sobre la cuestión indígena, la lucha de clases, el imperialismo y la nación peruana. Sigue un hilo expositivo coherente y de ilustrativa lectura. [CJB]

3636 De la Fuente, José Alberto. Víctor Raúl Haya de la Torre, el APRA y el indoamericanismo. (*Cuyo/Mendoza*, 20, 2007, p. 79–101, bibl.)

Expone con cierta simpatía el pensamiento de Haya de la Torre y el APRA. Encuentra limitada la vigencia actual de este último movimiento. Tal vez lo más claro del artículo sea el señalamiento de la diferencia entre Haya y Mariátegui, y la referencia al tema del indigenismo. [JCTE]

3637 Ferreira de Cassone, Florencia. Magda Portal: una voz femenina en el aprismo. (*Cuad. Am./México*, 2:128, abril/junio 2009, p. 23–37)

Sitúa a la intelectual peruana Magda Portal (1900–89) en el marco de la historia de las ideas. Contextualiza su biografía e indaga en sus ensayos y escritos literarios. De ellos la autora del artículo extrae los puntos de vista políticos, más allá de su desilusión del aprismo y su rechazo. Destaca su antiimperialismo y su defensa de los derechos de la mujer y los seres humanos en general. [CJB]

3638 Filippi, Alberto. De Mariátegui a Bobbio: ensayos sobre socialismo y democracia. Lima: Viuda de Mariátegui e Hijos, 2008. 285 p.: bibl., index.

Hay trabajos sobre Mariátegui, Bobbio, Gramsci y el intelectual argentino Juan Carlos Portantiero (estudioso de Gramsci). Lo de mayor interés para nosotros es la comparación entre Mariátegui y Piero Gobetti (1901–26). En un apéndice documental de artículos de Mariátegui hay tres que se refieren a Gobetti. [JCTE]

3639 Flores Quelopana, Gustavo. Búsquedas actuales de la filosofía andina. Lima: IIPCIAL, Fondo Editorial, 2007. 120 p.: bibl. (Biblioteca IIPCIAL de filosofía)

El libro repasa, en capítulos breves, la contribución de un número de autores que tratan de la existencia de una filosofía andina, basada en el pensamiento precolombino y diferenciada de la filosofía occidental. Estos estudiosos no profesan, sin embargo, dicha filosofía andina, sino que la explican o interpretan, y además la defienden y lamentan su interrupción por la conquista. El libro representa algunas posiciones poco conocidas, y merece tomarse en cuenta junto con otras expresiones del indigenismo y de los estudios postcoloniales. [JCTE]

3640 García Salvattecci, Hugo. El Apra entre dos orillas: ochenta años de Aprismo. Lima: Univ. Alas Peruanas, 2009. 618, 9 p.: bibl.

No es una historia del APRA sino una extensa meditación política, filosófica y ética, que surge de los grandes problemas del mundo actual, y que quiere rescatar del APRA su intención original, aunque como movimiento político ya no se encuentre al día. La base del pensamiento del autor es una posición religiosa cristiana. Recorre una serie de temas: la dialéctica, el individuo, el marxismo, el socialismo, el liberalismo, el estado, el imperialismo y el anarquismo. [JCTE]

3641 Ibáñez, Alfonso. La utopía del "socialismo indoamericano" de Mariátegui. (*Social. Particip.*, 103, junio 2007, p. 103–116)

De los varios elementos del pensamiento de Mariátegui (marxismo abierto, pensamiento indígena, el mito soreliano) destaca especialmente la utopía como factor dinamizante para lograr un socialismo autóctono. [JCTE]

3642 La intelectualidad peruana del siglo XX ante la condición humana. Coordinación de María Luisa Rivara de Tuesta. Lima: Edit. Gráfica Euroamericana, 2004–2008. 2 v.: bibl.

Este conjunto de trabajos surgió de un proyecto cuyo título era el pensamiento latinoamericano ante la condición humana, razón por la cual todos los artículos que integran el volumen llevan esa expresión como parte del título. En realidad, son artículos independientes sobre diversos autores: Manuel González Prada, Alejandro Deustua, Jorge Polar, Mariano H. Cornejo, Manuel Vicente Villarán, Francisco García Calderón, Oscar Miró Quesada, Pedro Zulen, Francisco González Gamarra, Luis E. Valcárcel, Mariano Iberico, José Carlos Mariátegui y Augusto Salazar Bondy. El conjunto es una buena contribución, y representa el pensamiento peruano del positivismo y la etapa subsiguiente, aunque no sea exhaustivamente. Quizás podría decirse que entre los mejores trabajos se encuentren los dedicados a García Calderón y Salazar Bondy. [JCTE]

3643 Lego, Pablo. Fe y cultura: una aproximación filosófica a la relación entre naturaleza y cultura en el contexto de los estudios andinos. (*Allpanchis/Cuzco*, 38:69, primer semestre 2008, p. 219–244, bibl.)

Propone para los estudios andinos la perspectiva de una "filosofía realista", fundada en la tesis creacionista y contrapuesta a las posiciones "inmanentistas". Se apoya en E. Wilson, J. Maritain, O. N. Derisi y Juan Pablo II. [CJB]

3644 Mazzeo, Miguel. Invitación al descubrimiento: José Carlos Mariátegui y el socialismo de nuestra América. Buenos Aires: Editorial El Colectivo, 2009. 216 p.: bibl.

El autor afirma que el libro es una lectura de Mariátegui desde una posición de lucha social "y en el marco de tareas militantes". Se considera al pensador peruano como una fuente aprovechable para propósitos de construcción socialista. A esta última la distingue el autor no sólo de tendencias contrarias, sino también de posiciones "progresistas" que todavía defienden el desarrollo por "etapas". [JCTE]

3645 Neira Samanez, Hugo. Del pensar mestizo: ensayos. Lima: Editorial Herética, 2006. 446 p.: bibl.

Algunos temas de estos ensayos son: la generación española de 1898; América Latina en los comienzos del siglo XX y el novecentismo; y Octavio Paz. La segunda parte se ocupa de la inteligencia peruana también en los inicios del siglo XX, incluyendo a González Prada, Porras Barrenechea, Mariátegui, Haya de la Torre, y Jorge Basadre. A pesar del título, el autor dice que el libro no debe nada ni al concepto de "mestizo" ni al de "mestizaje", que "han perdido mucho de su valor legitimante". [JCTE]

3646 Neira Samanez, Hugo. El país de Montaigne y nosotros. (*Bull. Inst. fr. étud. andin.*, 36:1, 2007, p. 5–17, bibl.)

El tema es la relación—cultural en sentido amplio—entre Francia y Perú. Por lo tanto se detiene en lo asimilado por Perú de la cultura francesa y la difusión en Francia de los temas incaicos. Expresa escasa simpatía por la influencia angloparlante. No es tanto estudio como ensayo. [JCTE]

3647 No, Song. Entre el idealismo práctico y el activismo filosófico: la doble vida de Pedro Zulen. (*Solar*, 2:2, 2006, p. 73–88)

El filósofo peruano Pedro Zulen (1889–1925) es examinado en dos obras filosóficas: *La filosofía de lo inexpresable* (una crítica a Bergson) y *Del neohegelianismo al neorrealismo* (sobre filósofos de habla inglesa del siglo XX). El otro aspecto de lo que el autor llama "doble vida" de Zulen estaría representado por sus ideas políticas indigenistas y su adhesión al liberalismo inglés. [CJB]

3648 Quiroz Avila, Ruben. Hermenéutica de *El porvenir de las razas en el Perú.* (*Solar*, 2:2, 2006, p. 129–156)

Se refiere al texto del positivista Clemente Palma, *El porvenir de las razas en el Perú* (1897), expresión del racismo de fines del siglo XIX. Se analiza su discurso sobre los indios, españoles, chinos, negros, y mestizos criollos. Palma estimaba que los mestizos, mejorados con la inmigración germana, serían los llamados para regir el país. El autor del artículo opina que la misma ideología excluyente se mantiene en el país en la actualidad. [CJB]

3649 Rey de Castro Arena, Alejandro. El pensamiento político y la formación de la nacionalidad peruana, 1780–1820. Lima: Fondo Editorial de la Facultad de Ciencías Sociales, Unidad de Post-Grado, UNMSM, 2008. 317 p.: bibl.

En el fondo se trata del tema reiterado de la interpretación (o "las causas") de la Independencia hispanoamericana, en este caso aplicado al Perú. Se reconoce que la cuestión supone dos elementos: acciones e ideas, y el autor representa bien ambos factores en su interrelación. Uno de los principales—y razonables—énfasis del libro es que las ideas, tomadas del ambiente europeo, no hubieran ejercido influencia sin la existencia de una mentalidad local (denominada "criolla"). En la historia de las ideas se distinguen los ideólogos del siglo XVIII (Viscardo, Baquíjano y Carrillo, Rodríguez de Mendoza, Unanue) y los del siglo XIX (Vidaurre, José de la Riva Agüero). [JCTE]

3650 Rochabrún Silva, Guillermo. Batallas por la teoría: en torno a Marx y el Perú. Lima: IEP, Instituto de Estudios Peruanos, 2007. 565 p.: bibl. (Serie Ideología y política, 29)

Los trabajos son de buena calidad y muy variados. Algunos de sus temas: el marxismo adoptado de manera muy personal por el autor; los enfoques de la sociología general y de la sociología política; y variados asuntos de interpretación de la realidad social e histórica del país. Precede una larga introducción sobre el desarrollo intelectual del autor, que no deja de iluminar la marcha de las ideas en Perú en las últimas décadas del siglo XX. [JCTE]

3651 Simposio Internacional Amauta y su Epoca, 2nd, Lima, 2006. Amauta y su época. Lima: Viuda de Mariátegui e Hijos, 2007. 277 p.: bibl.

La revista *Amauta* fue fundada por Mariátegui en 1926. Algunos trabajos tratan de su contenido, y otros de temas relacionados con ella. Dos se refieren a la vida intelectual "de los años 20" (uno de ellos a la escritura femenina). Por último, un artículo tiene por tema, además de *Amauta*, otras dos revistas: el *Mercurio peruano* (1791–95) y la *Revista de Lima* (1859–73). [JCTE]

3652 Sosa Fuentes, Samuel. La vigencia del pensamiento de José Carlos Mariátegui en un mundo global: identidad, cultura y nación en América Latina. (*Rev. Mex. Cienc. Polít. Soc.*, 49:199, enero/abril 2007, p. 107–131, bibl.)

Elogiosa exposición de Mariátegui desde simpatías marxistas y socialistas, cuyos principales temas son: la cuestión indígena y la identidad en América Latina. Ambos asuntos son largamente desarrollados. [JCTE]

3653 Valenzuela Lovón, Armando. La civilización andina: nuevo enfoque científico, filosófico y tecnológico. Cusco, Peru: Academia Mayor de la Lengua Quechua: Asociación Mundial de Escritores Andinos Cusco, AMEA, 2006. 565 p.: bibl., ill. (some col.).

Es una explicación y defensa de la cultura incaica en todos sus aspectos, desde los filosóficos y de concepción del mundo hasta la técnica, pasando por los sociales y científicos. Lo que interesa en este caso no son los rasgos ya reconocidos por la etnología y la antropología, sino la actitud de reivindicación que el autor representa, y la explicación en términos propios de la cultura estudiada, distinguidos de la visión occidental. [JCTE]

3654 Vida y obra de Víctor Raúl Haya de la Torre. Textos de Raúl Chanamé *et al.* 2. ed. Lima: Instituto Víctor Raúl Haya de la Torre, 2006. 1 v.: bibl., ill.

Estos trabajos (21 en total) se originaron en varios concursos sobre el pensamiento y la acción de Haya de la Torre. Se cubren numerosos aspectos: biográficos, de pensamiento, de acción política y de contexto histórico del pensador peruano. [JCTE]

BOLIVIA

3655 Argueta, Arturo. El darwinismo en
Iberoamérica: Bolivia y México. Ma-
drid: Consejo Superior de Investigaciones
Científicas, 2009. 348 p.: bibl., ill.

De los dos países considerados, el
caso de Bolivia es el de mayor interés por
ser menos conocido y porque se encuentran
más elementos para el tema de lo que podría
imaginarse. Se refiere a la transmisión del
darwinismo tanto en el aspecto propiamente biológico como en el de otras ciencias
naturales y sociales. Es de gran valor la distinción entre las respectivas influencias de
Lamarck, Haeckel, Spencer y el darwinismo
social. Es un volumen de excelente calidad
y altamente aprovechable para la historia de
las ideas. [JCTE]

3656 Salmón, Josefa. Una historia del
pensamiento indianista *Ukhamawa
Jakawisaxa*. (*Rev. Indias*, 68:244, sept./dic.
2008, p. 115–138, bibl.)

El indianismo aquí estudiado está
representado por la autobiografía del líder
aimara Luciano Tapia, que es el tema central del artículo. Se busca su significado para
el pensamiento aimara en general, y para la
situación del indígena en su condición de
inferioridad social. Para el comentario sobre
Ukhamawa jakawisaxa, ver *HLAS 59:1078*.
[JCTE]

CHILE

3657 Bilbao, Francisco. El autor y la obra.
Edición y compilación de José Al-
berto Bravo de G. Santiago: Editorial Cuarto
Proprio, 2007. 764 p.: bibl., ill., ports. (Serie
Historia cultural)

Consta de una presentación del editor
y un preámbulo metodológico a cargo de
Miguel E. Orellana Benado. Incluye apuntes
cronológicos debidos a Francisco Bilbao; la
biografía de Francisco Bilbao realizada por
su hermano Manuel; el juicio al que fue
sometido por publicar *Sociabilidad chilena*;
textos de la edición de *Obras* de 1866; artículos periodísticos escritos por Bilbao en
Argentina y Perú, tomados de libros debidos
a Clara Alicia Jalif de Bertranou y David
Sobrevilla, respectivamente. [CJB]

3658 Escobar, Roberto. El vuelo de los
búhos: visión personal de la actividad
filosófica en Chile de 1810 a 2010. Presen-

tación de Ricardo Ortega Perrier. Santiago:
RiL Editores, 2008. 501 p.: bibl., indexes.
(Ensayos & estudios)

Amplio inventario comentado de
autores chilenos vinculados a la filosofía a
lo largo de dos siglos. Es una versión muy
ampliada de una obra anterior, *La filosofía
en Chile* (1975). [JCTE]

3659 Loyola T., Manuel. La felicidad y la
política en Luis Emilio Recabarren:
ensayo de interpretación de su pensamiento.
Santiago, Chile: Ariadna Ediciones, 2007.
129 p.: bibl.

Se exponen las ideas generales que
estaban en la base de la lucha socialista
de Recabarren (1876–1924), especialmente
el materialismo científico, el concepto de
igualdad de los hombres y la concepción del
trabajador como artífice de la civilización.
La exégesis posiblemente sea más compleja
de lo que requería el tema. [JCTE]

3660 Pinedo, Javier. El pensamiento de los
ensayistas y cientistas sociales en
los largos años 60 en Chile, 1958–1973: los
críticos al proyecto de Francisco A. Encina.
(*Atenea/Concepción*, 497, primer semestre
2008, p. 123–149, photos)

Se analizan las críticas realizadas a
la obra del historiador chileno Francisco A.
Encina desde diversas posiciones, representadas, entre otros, por Jorge Teillier, Julio
César Jobet, Felipe Herrera, Jaime Eizaguirre, Mario Góngora y Ricardo Donoso. [CJB]

3661 Salas, Ricardo. Para una reconstrucción intercultural de la historia
republicana. (*Universum/Talca*, 22:2, 2007,
p. 238–251)

Sobre la necesidad de una "reconstrucción intercultural de la historia", debido
a que las historias nacionales no han reconocido la presencia de las culturas indígenas, lo que no es sino parte de su exclusión
también social y política. Aquí se trata el
caso especial de las comunidades mapuches.
[JCTE]

3662 Silvas Rojas, Matías. Normalización
de la filosofía chilena: un camino de
clausura disciplinar. (*Universum/Talca*,
24:2, 2009, p. 172–191)

La filosofía no se caracterizaría tanto
por su contenido o definición como por el
modo (profesional) de hacerla. Partiendo
del concepto de "normalidad filosófica" de

Francisco Romero tiende a delimitar, para el caso de Chile, la relación entre la constitución de la disciplina filosófica y su soporte institucional. [JCTE]

BRASIL

3663 Alonso, Angela Maria. Joaquim Nabuco. Coordinação de Elio Gaspari e Lilia M. Schwarcz. São Paulo: Companhia das Letras, 2007. 379 p.: bibl., ill., index. (Perfis brasileiros)

Se trata de una biografía animada, bien informada y bien escrita, donde desfilan las actividades políticas y diplomáticas de Nabuco, y los rasgos personales que estuvieron detrás de su acción. Se reconoce que en los comienzos del panamericanismo (últimos años del siglo XIX) Nabuco intentó, sin éxito, una mayor cercanía de Brasil a Estados Unidos. En general, el libro puede ser una buena base para el estudio del pensamiento del diplomático brasileño. En lugar de la bibliografía habitual, la obra se cierra con un ensayo bibliográfico. También tiene una útil cronología. [JCTE]

3664 Amaral, Roberto. O papel do intelectual na política. Fortaleza, Brazil: Edições Demócrito Rocha, 2005. 162 p.: bibl.

Conjunto de ensayos que expresan una posición militante y de compromiso con la causa de la justicia. Dos de ellos son dedicados a Antônio Nouaiss y Florestan Fernándes, ambos intelectuales socialistas. Un tema reiterado es la función del intelectual (especialmente de izquierda) en el esfuerzo por modificar la realidad. Hay también presentaciones de libros, discursos y recordaciones. [JCTE]

3665 A atualidade do pensamento de Celso Furtado. Organização de Marcos Costa Lima e Maurício Dias David. Goiás, Brazil: Verbena Editora, 2008. 268 p.: bibl., ill.

Valiosa obra colectiva que examina el pensamiento político y las ideas económicas de Celso Furtado (1920–2004). Su extensa acción como economista e intérprete de Brasil es vista con simpatía, pero en general con buena calidad de las contribuciones. [JCTE]

3666 Berriel, Rosa Maria Vieira. Celso Furtado: reforma, política e ideologia (1950–1964). São Paulo: Educ, 2007. 432 p.: bibl. (Hipótese)

Una de las características de este libro es vincular la posición "cepalino-keynesiana" de Furtado con el pensamiento social brasileño anterior, y con autores como Sergio Buarque de Holanda, Caio Prado Júnior, y Oliveira Viana, entre otros. [JCTE]

3667 Burke, Peter and **Maria Lúcia G. Pallares-Burke.** Gilberto Freyre: social theory in the tropics. Oxford: Peter Lang, 2008. 261 p.: bibl., index. (The past in the present)

Aunque la intención haya sido presentar una imagen integral de Freyre al lector de habla inglesa, el resultado es una buena biografía intelectual del antropólogo brasileño y un análisis e interpretación de los variados aspectos de su obra. El libro culmina comparando a Freyre con historiadores e intelectuales de gran significación y señalando los aspectos todavia vigentes de esa obra. [JCTE]

Crespo, Regina Aída. Itinerarios intelectuales: Vasconcelos, Lobato y sus proyectos para la nación. See item **3566**.

Em família: a correspondência de Oliveira Lima e Gilberto Freyre. See item **2023**.

3668 Filosofia na universidade. Organização de Adriana Mattar Maamari, Antônio Tadeu Campos de Bairros e José Fernandes Weber. Ijuí, Brazil: Editora Unijuí, 2006. 328 p.: bibl. (Col. Filosofia e ensino; 9)

La relación de la filosofía con su enseñanza es examinada desde una variedad de perspectivas: la formación filosófica en la universidad; el estado y las instituciones de enseñanza; la investigación filosófica; el currículo; la relación de la filosofía con los otros saberes; el uso de las nuevas tecnologías. La elaboración de los temas está orientada a la situación de Brasil. [JCTE]

3669 Guimarães, Antonio Sérgio Alfredo. Africanism and racial democracy: the correspondence between Herskovits and Arthur Ramos, 1935–1949. (*Estud. Interdiscipl. Am. Lat. Carib.*, 19:1, enero/junio 2008)

Entre otros aspectos, se muestra la diferencia (en la época estudiada y según el autor) entre la asentada profesionalización de la antropología en Estados Unidos y el ejemplo particular de Arthur Ramos, con su amplio conocimiento directo de la población negra en Brasil, pero sin las técnicas de la investigación académica. [JCTE]

3670 Guimarães, Antonio Sérgio Alfredo. A recepção de Fanon no Brasil e a identidade negra. (*Novos Estud. CEBRAP*, 81, julho 2008, p. 99–114)

Estudia la lenta y progresiva recepción de Fanon en Brasil. Reconoce tres etapas: (1) los años 60, que contaron con la visita de Sartre; (2) el acogimiento de Fanon por la izquierda revolucionaria de fines de esa década; (3) las lecturas de los jóvenes negros entre 1970 y 1980. Señala que influye el hecho de que haya pocos académicos negros en las universidades. Artículo bien documentado y aprovechable. [CJB]

3671 Iumatti, Paulo Teixeira. Caio Prado Jr.: uma trajetória intelectual. São Paulo: Editora Brasilense, 2007. 248 p.: bibl., ill., index.

Biografía intelectual, bien elaborada, de estilo académico (se basa en una tesis doctoral). Caio Prado Jr. (1907–90), de orientación marxista y afiliación comunista, fue autor de *Formação do Brasil contemporâneo*, una de las grandes interpretaciones de Brasil de la primera mitad del siglo XX. [JCTE]

3672 Jardim, Eduardo. Mário de Andrade: a morte do poeta. Rio de Janeiro: Civilização Brasileira, 2005. 155 p.: bibl.

Es un ensayo sobre Mário de Andrade, pero que ilumina el movimiento modernista y la historia intelectual del periodo al que pertenece ese movimiento. El impulso inicial del modernismo habría sido el intento de colocar al país en el conjunto de la vida y la cultura modernas, o de los grandes países del momento. [JCTE]

3673 Jornada de Ciências Sociais, 7th, Universidade Estadual Paulista, Faculdade de Filosofia e Ciências, 2000. Gilberto Freyre em quatro tempos. Organização de Ethel Volfzon Kosminsky, Claude Lépine e Fernanda Arêas Peixoto. São Paulo: FAPESP: Editora UNESP Fundação; Bauru, Brazil: Editora da Univ. do Sagrado Coração, 2003. 379 p.: bibl. (Ciências sociais)

Por la calidad de sus trabajos, el libro es uno de los mejores sobre la obra del antropólogo brasileño. Muestra además que esa obra, mezcla de trabajo científico y gran ensayo, no termina de originar interés y estudio, más allá de acuerdos y desacuerdos, y que sigue contribuyendo a la cuestión de la realidad brasileña. Los temas son varios, comenzando por un excelente artículo de Thomas Skidmore sobre la recepción de *Casa-grande e senzala* en los años 30s y 40s.

3674 Kant no Brasil. Organização de Daniel Omar Perez. Textos de Valerio Rohden *et al.* São Paulo: Escuta, 2005. 316 p.: bibl. (Filosofia no Brasil)

El organizador del volumen presenta una reseña histórica de la recepción de Kant en Brasil desde comienzos del siglo XIX. El mayor énfasis se pone en las últimas décadas del siglo XX y los comienzos del XXI. La labor de esta última etapa evidencia un conocimiento técnico especializado muy superior a los momentos anteriores. No se presentan tanto filósofos brasileños que desarrollan su filosofía bajo la influencia de Kant como expresiones de detallada exégesis kantiana. [JCTE]

3675 Lopes, Marcos Antônio. Lógica e alegoria: argumentação e ação nos sermões de Vieira. (*Síntese/Belo Horizonte*, 35:112, maio/agosto 2008, p. 157–165)

Reconocimiento de los valores literarios y políticos del Padre Vieira, en los 400 años de su nacimiento. Principalmente destaca el valor de los sermones, donde se lo compara con Bossuet. [JCTE]

3676 Margutti Pinto, Paulo Roberto. O padre Antônio Vieira e o pensamento filosófico brasileiro. (*Síntese/Belo Horizonte*, 35:112, maio/agosto 2008, p. 167–188, bibl.)

Además de presentar las características filosóficas del Padre Vieira (1608–97), el autor sostiene que en la filosofía colonial brasileña, a diferencia de Portugal, no habría predominado Aristóteles, como habitualmente se considera. [JCTE]

3677 Mota, Carlos Guilherme. Ideologia da cultura brasileira (1933–1974): pontos de partida para uma revisão histórica. Prefácio de Alfredo Bosi. 3a ed. São Paulo: Editora 34, 2008. 421 p.: bibl., ill., index.

Este libro fue publicado en 1977, pero la presente edición agrega una historia de sus ediciones. Es una revisión de las interpretaciones que se dieron de la cultura brasileña entre 1933 y 1974, vistas desde el punto de vista político del autor. [JCTE]

3678 Muraro, Valmir Francisco. Padre Antônio Vieira: retórica e utopia. Florianópolis, Brazil: Editora Insular, 2003. 341 p.: bibl.

Los escritos del jesuita Antônio Vieira son numerosos y variados (dejó 700 cartas y 200 sermones) y por eso abundan los enfoques parciales. Aquí es visto en su aspecto mesiánico-profético, y el autor lo hace revisando la vasta obra en función de la idea del "Quinto imperio" que Vieira anunciaba después del persa, el asirio, el griego y el romano. [JCTE]

3679 Oliveira, Fabiane Costa. Helio Jaguaribe e o PSDB: possibilidades e limites da ação intelectual na política partidária. (*in* Escritas da história: narrativa, arte e nação. Organização de Elio Cantalicio Serpa e Marcos Antonio de Menezes. Uberlândia, Brazil: EDUFU, 2007, p. 221–256)

Recorre los diferentes momentos en que Helio Jaguaribe trató de vincular o aplicar sus ideas a instituciones de estudio—como el Instituto Superior de Estudios Brasileños—o a partidos políticos, como el Partido Social-Demócrata de Brasil. [JCTE]

3680 Prado Júnior, Caio. Caio Prado Jr.: dissertações sobre a revolução brasileira. Organização de Raimundo Santos. Brasília: Fundação Astrojildo Pereira; São Paulo: Editora Brasiliense, 2007. 273 p.

Es una antología de escritos de Caio Prado Jr. tomados de sus libros *Evolução política do Brasil* y *A revolução brasileira*; de artículos publicados en la Revista Brasiliense; y de otras fuentes. La introducción vincula el pensamiento de Prado Jr. con el Partido Comunista de Brasil y en particular con la cuestión agraria. [JCTE]

3681 Reflexão. Vol. 33, No. 93, jan./junho 2008. Campinas, Brazil: Pontificia Univ. Católica, 2008.

Este número contiene ocho artículos sobre el Padre António Vieira, cuatro de ellos sobre su idea del Quinto Imperio. Otros versan sobre el tema de la escatología y del libre arbitrio en su pensamiento. [JCTE]

3682 Ricupero, Bernardo. Sete lições sobre as interpretações do Brasil. São Paulo: Alameda, 2007. 220 p.: bibl., index.

Toma en cuenta las obras de seis autores: Oliveira Viana, Gilberto Fryre, Sergio Buarque de Holanda, Caio Prado Jr., Raymundo Faoro y Florestan Fernández. Las exposiciones son claras e inteligentes, sin ser muy extensas. Al comienzo plantea la cuestión de si existe un pensamiento

político brasileño, relacionando el asunto con las obras comentadas. Lúcido examen. [JCTE]

3683 Silva, Maurício. Tradição acadêmica no Brasil e formação do *homo academicus*: o caso da Academia Brasileira de Letras. (*Estud. Ibero-Am./Porto Alegre*, 34:2, dez. 2008, p. 187–203, bibl., graph)

Análisis de la Academia Brasileira de Letras durante la transición del siglo XIX al XX, que muestra su espíritu corporativo, más guiado por cuestiones sociales (prestigio de sus miembros) que estéticas o éticas. Así se conformó lo que el autor llama el *homo academicus*. [CJB]

PARAGUAY

3684 Pensamiento paraguayo del siglo XX. Compilación de Beatriz G. de Bosio y Eduardo Deves-Valdes. Asunción: Intercontinental Editora, 2006. 337 p.: bibl.

Este libro llena un vacío bibliográfico, porque es muy poco lo que se conoce de la historia de las ideas en Paraguay fuera del país. Contiene contribuciones previamente publicadas y otras nuevas. En el primer caso se encuentran textos de Justo Pastor Benítez sobre el positivismo en Paraguay; de Raúl Amaral sobre el novecentismo; de Francisco Corral sobre Barret; de Milda Rivarola Espinoza sobre el Partido Socialista; de Efraim Cardozo sobre el desarrollo cultural; de Juan S. Dávalos y Lorenzo Vivieres Banks sobre el problema de la historia paraguaya, entre otros. Otros temas cubiertos son: corrientes políticas y reforma universitaria. [JCTE]

URUGUAY

3685 Ainsa, Fernando. La utopía de la democracia en Uruguay: entre la nostalgia del pasado y el desmentido de la historia. (*Am. Lat. Hoy/Salamanca*, 47, dic. 2007, p. 87–99, bibl.)

Ensayo bien escrito que, apoyado en oportunas fuentes, muestra, para Uruguay, un ideal utópico regresivo o por lo menos quietista, donde el conformismo habría hallado sus límites precisos hacia los años 60 del siglo XX. Para el autor, un espejo que mire al pasado y no sirva como plataforma para futuros posibles, sería una lente empañada. [CJB]

3686 Mora Rodríguez, Arnoldo. El arielismo: de Rodó a García Monge. San José de Mayo, Uruguay: EUNED, Editorial Univ. Estatal a Distancia, 2008. 321 p.: bibl.

El tema principal es el modernismo, considerado como la primera "revolución cultural" en Hispanoamérica, que tuvo, según el autor, una expresión filosófica propia. Aunque estudia a Martí y a Darío, se concentra especialmente en Rodó, a quien considera la figura más importante desde el punto de vista filosófico. Una constante en el libro es considerar a Rodó como el anti-Sarmiento, por las simpatías norteamericanas de este último. Un apartado tiene el extraño título de: "Arturo Ardao y la reivindicación marxista de Rodó". Se ocupa también de los que escribieron sobre Rodó o habrían representado su herencia. [JCTE]

3687 Pierrotti, Nelson. El nacimiento de una forma de ser: una nueva visión sobre la construcción de las mentalidades en el Montevideo colonial, 1726–1814. (*Estud. Ibero-Am./Porto Alegre*, 33:2, dez. 2007, p. 35–50, bibl.)

Trata de determinar los elementos de mentalidad de la población de Montevideo en la época colonial, en función del grado de educación y de los contactos con los estratos indígenas y africanos. Interesa especialmente por lo que señala sobre la cultura oral frente a la menos difundida de la cultura letrada. [JCTE]

ARGENTINA

3688 Adamovsky, Ezequiel. Más allá de la vieja izquierda: seis ensayos para un nuevo anticapitalismo. Buenos Aires: Prometeo Libros, 2007. 155 p.: bibl.

Sobre la base de una posición anticapitalista pero distinguida en diversas formas de la izquierda tradicional, el autor reflexiona sobre ciertas experiencias deliberativas comunitarias (populares) de la Argentina durante la crisis de comienzos del siglo XXI. [JCTE]

3689 Adelman, Jeremy. Between order and liberty: Juan Bautista Alberdi and the intellectual origins of Argentine constitutionalism. (*LARR*, 42:2, 2007, p. 86–110)

De interés para el tema del constitucionalismo en Alberdi. Examina las ideas de este intelectual argentino desde su *Frag-mento preliminar al estudio del derecho* hasta sus *Bases y puntos de partida para la organización política de la República Argentina* (1852). La tesis central es que las ideas de Alberdi no conformarían una "doctrina", pues su constitucionalismo no se asentaría en fundamentos estables. Las causas de este hecho estarían en las múltiples tensiones dentro del liberalismo sostenido por Alberdi, afectado por el devenir de los acontecimientos históricos. [CJB]

3690 Argentina entre el optimismo y el desencanto. Edición de Clara Alicia Jalif de Bertranou. Mendoza, Argentina: Univ. Nacional de Cuyo, Facultad de Filosofía y Letras, Instituto de Filosofía Argentina y Americana, 2007. 281 p.: bibl. (Col. Cuadernos de Cuyo)

Sin poder atender a todos los trabajos, dos grupos de ellos se destacan claramente: (1) tres que se dedican a revistas argentinas: *Nosotros* (Clara Jalif de Bertranou); *Revista de Filosofía Latinoamericana* (Adriana Arpini); y *Punto de Vista* (Gloria Hintze), los tres muy aprovechables; 2) varios dedicados a autores individuales: Alejandro Korn (Dante Ramaglia); Raúl Scalabrini Ortiz (María Antonia Zandanel); Carlos Astrada (Gerardo Oviedo): Héctor Agosti (Marcos Olalla); José Aricó (Carlos Balmaceda). En su conjunto es una inteligente contribución al tema de la interpretación de la realidad argentina. [JCTE]

3691 Astrada, Carlos. Metafísica de la pampa. Compilación y apéndice de Guillermo David. Buenos Aires: Biblioteca Nacional, 2007. 174 p.: bibl. (Col. Reediciones y antologías; 3)

Publicación oportuna, que recoge escritos, en general breves y poco conocidos, del filósofo argentino Carlos Astrada. La mayoría son de la década de 1940, y varios se refieren al tema de la identidad argentina y sus símbolos más reconocidos, como el poema Martín Fierro, o ciertos escritos de Leopoldo Lugones, por ejemplo. Un apéndice del compilador trata de la relación entre Astrada y el filósofo italiano Ernesto Grassi, la cual importa principalmente para comprender la posición del primero frente a temas como lo telúrico, el paisaje y la sabiduría de las culturas precolombinas. [JCTE]

3692 Biagini, Hugo Edgardo. Cambiar el mundo: entre la reforma universitaria y el altermundismo. (*Utop. Prax. Latinoam.*, 11:33, abril/junio 2006, p. 109–119)

Rescata los postulados de la Reforma Universitaria de Argentina (1918) que aún tendrían vigencia, y los vincula a los movimientos actuales opuestos a la globalización y a formas diversas de dominación, dentro de lo que el autor llama "altermundismo". [CJB]

3693 Billi, Noelia. Pasiones nietzscheanas en las izquierdas argentinas del siglo XX: el caso Astrada. (*Nombres/Córdoba*, 17:21, dic. 2007, p. 205–226, bibl.)

Adopción e interpretación del pensamiento de Nietzsche por parte de Carlos Astrada. Lo relaciona con el acercamiento de este filósofo argentino al peronismo y al marxismo (maoísmo) de su última etapa. [JCTE]

3694 Campa, Ricardo. José Ingenieros y el reformismo social. (*Cuad. Am./México*, 128:2, abril/junio 2009, p. 11–22)

El pensamiento de José Ingenieros es visto desde la perspectiva político-social. En él, la modernización de las fuerzas de producción y la liberación del proletariado serían complementarias. El pensamiento de Ingenieros sería un anticipo de las circunstancias actuales: cuanto más el hombre se libere de los sufrimientos físicos por el apoyo de la técnica, tanto más será libre para tomar adecuadas decisiones políticas y económicas. (Ingenieros nació en Palermo, Italia, y no en Buenos Aires, como se lee en el artículo.) [CJB]

3695 Carsen, Maria Victoria. El significado de *La Rosa Blindada* en el ámbito intelectual argentino de la década de 1960. (*Temas Hist. Argent. Am.*, 12, enero/junio 2008, p. 67–83, bibl.)

Se refiere a la revista *La Rosa Blindada*, aparecida en Buenos Aires entre 1964 y 1966. Ante la intensificación ideológica de la década del 60, la producción de la revista reflejó la convicción de la necesidad y posibilidad inmediata de la Revolución, insertándose en la llamada "nueva izquierda" que adhirió a las tesis de Gramsci, Mariátegui, Ernesto Guevara y otros. Fue así anticipo de la vía armada propia del final de la década. [CJB]

3696 Comesaña, Manuel. ¿Qué debe hacer un filósofo argentino? (*Rev. Filos./Maracaibo*, 31:2, 2006, p. 59–66)

Ante la afirmación de que los filósofos latinoamericanos no deben ocuparse de temas "importados" y deben en cambio dedicarse a los de su propio ambiente, algunas de las tesis defendidas por el autor son: (1) los problemas de la filosofía no son nacionales, sino "universales"; (2) el filósofo no puede intervenir seriamente en asuntos de los cuales no es especialista, porque a lo sumo haría contribuciones de sentido común; (3) el filósofo tiene derecho a ocuparse de los asuntos a que lo llama su vocación, con independencia de la utilidad práctica o el "impacto social". [JCTE]

3697 Cuadernos Americanos. Vol. 1, No. 123, nueva época, enero/marzo 2008. Historia y ensayo en Argentina. México: UNAM.

Este número contiene una sección dedicada a Historia y Ensayo en Argentina, con los siguientes trabajos: Patricia A. Oribe, "En torno a 'montoneras' y 'montoneros': políticas y disputas por la imposición de sentidos en la historiografía argentina"; Paula Bruno, "Lecturas de Miguel Cané sobre la función de la prensa en las sociedades modernas"; Omar Acha, "Grande historia e historia normal en Paul Groussac"; Adriana Lombroso, "La emergencia de los debates político-culturales en los ensayos de Ezequiel Martínez Estrada"; María Celia Vázquez, "Etica, política y retórica: ¿Qué es esto?, de Ezequiel Martínez Estrada". [CJB]

3698 Ferraro, Liliana Juana. Eduardo Wilde: pensamiento y acción de un agnóstico argentino. Mendoza, Argentina: Univ. Nacional de Cuyo Facultad de Filosofía y Letras, 2007. 204 p.: bibl., ill. (Col. Jarilla)

Eduardo Wilde (1844–1913) fue miembro de la llamada "generación de 1880" en Argentina. Este libro repasa su obra periodística, literaria y política, pero sobre todo destaca su actuación en las polémicas parlamentarias referentes a las relaciones entre la iglesia y el estado, las cuales concluyeron con el triunfo de la posición liberal, que sostenía la separación de ambos, la educación laica, y el matrimonio civil. Contiene un apéndice documental. [JCTE]

3699 Ferreira, Florencia. Estados Unidos en las ideas políticas de *Argentina de Hoy.* (*Cuad. Am./México*, 120:2, abril/junio 2007, p. 127–141)

Se refiere al periódico político *Argentina de Hoy* (1951–55), editado por antiguos socialistas que adhirieron a la posición del Presidente Perón y su partido. Describe los artículos que aparecieron en el mencionado periódico sobre Estados Unidos, en general muy críticos. [CJB]

3700 Ferreira, Luis. El *a priori* en Arturo Roig y Michel Foucault: diferencias y coincidencias. (*Solar*, 2:2, 2006, p. 9–21)

Examen del concepto de *a priori histórico* en los dos autores estudiados, con el fin de señalar coincidencias y diferencias. Ambos coincidirían en dar a la expresión el significado de mentar la experiencia histórica como momento fundante, y en que no tendría carácter formal. En cuanto a las diferencias, para Roig el *a priori histórico* incluiría categorías afectivas y volitivas, de tipo social e ideológico, mientras en Foucault parecería limitarse al campo del lenguaje. Lo dicho resume mucho la argumentación del artículo. [CJB]

3701 Finchelstein, Federico. La Argentina fascista: los orígenes ideológicos de la dictadura. Buenos Aires: Editorial Sudamericana, 2008. 221 p.: bibl., ill. (Nudos de la historia argentina)

No es una historia formal, sino una narración, muy animada, de las diversas manifestaciones del nacionalismo y el fascismo en la Argentina, con claras opiniones del autor contrarias a esas posiciones. Un lector general tal vez se sorprenderá de las muchas y muy variadas expresiones de la ideología que se expone. De particular interés es el capítulo sobre el peronismo. [JCTE]

3702 García Angulo, Jorge Jesús. Aportes de Arturo A. Roig a la historia de las ideas. (*Cuad. Am./México*, 119:1, enero/marzo 2007, p. 47–75)

Expone de modo ordenado y efectivo la concepción que el filósofo argentino Arturo A. Roig tiene sobre la historia de las ideas en América Latina. [CJB]

3703 Graciano, Osvaldo Fabián. Entre la torre de marfil y el compromiso político: intelectuales de izquierda en la Argentina, 1918–1955. Bernal, Argentina: Univ. Nacional de Quilmes Editorial, 2008. 382 p.: bibl. (Col. Convergencia. Entre memoria y sociedad)

Los personajes y la acción que llenan la trama del libro, y donde se destacan como figuras protagónicas Alfredo Palacios, Alejandro Korn y Pedro Henríquez Ureña, corresponden principalmente a la ciudad de La Plata. Dentro de estas coordenadas es un libro muy rico y bien elaborado. Entre las actividades que expone se encuentra la repercusión de la Reforma Universitaria (1918) en la Universidad de La Plata, la función de revistas como *Valoraciones* y *Sagitario*, y la Unión Latinoamericana, creada en 1925 por Alfredo Palacios y José Ingenieros. Luego describe la vinculación de estos intelectuales reformistas con el Partido Socialista y el anarquismo de la época, para concluir con su desencuentro frente al primer peronismo. El Epílogo es un buen resumen del libro. [JCTE]

3704 Groussac, Paul. Del Plata al Niágara. Estudio preliminar de Hebe Clementi. Buenos Aires: Biblioteca Nacional: Colihue, 2006. 532 p.: bibl. (Col. Los raros (Biblioteca Nacional (Argentina)); 7)

Crónica de viaje publicada por primera vez en 1897, donde pueden apreciarse las ideas y las corrientes de pensamiento que están en la base de los comentarios de Groussac (1848–1929), intelectual de origen francés pero de gran actuación intelectual en Argentina. En referencia a Estados Unidos, anticipa ideas que luego expresaría José Enrique Rodó en su *Ariel*. La civilización de estilo europeo es su constante referencia de comparación. No desdeñable para la historia de las ideas. [CJB]

3705 Jalif de Bertranou, Clara Alicia. Alejandro Korn en la revista *Nosotros:* lecciones del pasado, aportes al presente. Homenaje en el 70 aniversario de su fallecimiento, 1869–1936. (*Estud. Filos. Práct. Hist. Ideas*, 8:9, dic. 2007, p. 89–104)

Oportuna recuperación de escritos de Alejandro Korn, publicados en la revista argentina *Nosotros*, algunos de los cuales no fueron recogidos en sus obras completas. Son de interés para la apreciación del filósofo argentino, pero también para la de la revista, importante y de larga duración en la primera mitad del siglo XX. [JCTE]

3706 Lértora Mendoza, Celina Ana. La enseñanza de la filosofía en tiempos de la colonia: análisis de cursos manuscritos. Buenos Aires: Fundación para la Educación, la Ciencia y la Cultura, 2007. 1 v.: bibl., index.

Los manuscritos de 11 cursos dictados en el Río de la Plata en la época colonial son descritos prolijamente en su contenido, dándose noticias del autor y de las fuentes utilizadas. En cada caso hay un *Index totius operae* y una apreciación crítica. La obra continúa otra de tipo semejante, de 1979 (*La enseñanza de la filosofía en tiempos de la Colonia. Análisis de cursos manuscritos.* Buenos Aires: Ediciones FEPAI), y es parte de una valiosa tarea de ediciones críticas de cursos llevada a cabo por la autora (véase, por ejemplo, *HLAS 64:3063, 3095 y 3100,* y en este volumen: items **3571, 3722,** y **3721**). [JCTE]

3707 Manso, Eduardo Oscar. Tiempo y nacimiento: responsabilidad y conciencia histórica en la obra filosófica de Alberto Rougès. Tucumán, Argentina: Centro Cultural Alberto Rougès, Fundación Miguel Lillo; Santa Fe, Argentina: Univ. Católica de Santa Fe, 2008. 367 p.: bibl., index.

Estudio minucioso del concepto de tiempo en el filósofo argentino Alberto Rougès (1880–1945). Se organiza en tres partes: (1) Estructura temporal del nacimiento y *coexistencia de lo sucesivo;* (2) Estructura ético-moral del nacimiento y configuraciones del tiempo; (3) Metafísica del nacimiento y conciencia histórica. Utiliza, además de *Las jerarquías del ser y la eternidad,* obra fundamental de Rougès, otros escritos, publicados e inéditos. El autor acuña categorías interpretativas que otorgan nuevo giro a la bibliografía existente, y su libro es un aporte valioso. [CJB]

3708 Norambuena Carrasco, Carmen. Imaginarios nacionales latinoamericanos en el tránsito del siglo XIX al XX. (*Estud. Filos. Práct. Hist. Ideas,* 8:9, dic. 2007, p. 117–128)

El imaginario a que se refiere el artículo no es sólo la visión que las élites dieron de su propia "comunidad imaginada", sino también la imagen del país que los nuevos estados elaboraron para presentarse ante (y atraer a) los posibles immigrantes y potenciales capitales de inversión. [JCTE]

3709 El pensamiento alternativo en la Argentina del siglo XX. v. 2, Obrerismo, vanguardia, justicia social, 1930–1960. Dirección de Hugo E. Biagini y Arturo A. Roig. Textos de Omar Acha *et al.* Buenos Aires: Editorial Biblos, 2006. 1 v.: bibl., indexes.

En el prólogo, Arturo Roig define al "pensamiento alternativo" como aquel que se erige, frente a un saber "único", como ejercicio crítico, de compromiso humanitario, caracterizado por la apertura y la inclusión social. Los grandes temas bajo los que se agrupan los más de 40 trabajos son: Filosofía e Ideología; Sociedad y Poder; Arte y Deporte; Ciencia y Educación; y Los Medios. Para referirnos sólo a la primera de las secciones mencionadas, se encontrarán artículos sobre: el pensamiento marxista de Aníbal Ponce y Héctor Agosti; la experiencia gramsciana en el Partido Comunista Argentino; la corriente nacionalista de izquierda; Arturo Jauretche en el movimiento denominado FORJA; la Escuela de Frankfurt en Argentina; y el tema de la libertad en el filósofo Carlos Astrada, sin agotar la lista. Para el primer volumen véase *HLAS 62:3905.* [CJB]

3710 La piedra del escándalo: Darwin en Argentina, 1845–1909. Edición de Leila Gómez. Buenos Aires: Simurg, 2008. 228 p.: bibl. (Testimonios)

Oportuna edición de textos de intelectuales argentinos que fueron testimonio de la recepción de Charles Darwin. Son ellos: Guillermo Enrique Hudson, Francisco Javier Muñiz, Domingo F. Sarmiento, Florentino Ameghino, Leopoldo Lugones, Germán Burmeister, Francisco P. Moreno, Eduardo L. Holmberg, José Manuel Estrada, José María Ramos Mejía, Carlos O. Bunge y José Ingenieros. Los textos van precedidos de un estudio introductorio de la compiladora. [CJB]

3711 Piossek Prebisch, Lucía. Argentina: identidad y utopía. Tucumán, Argentina: Univ. Nacional de Tucumán, 2008. 328 p.

Algunos de los temas tratados son: Alberdi y la filosofía; Sarmiento y su *Facundo;* la generación del 80 en la historia de las ideas; y autores como Alberto Rougès, Eduardo Mallea y Víctor Massuh. Pero lo que persigue la autora no es la simple exégesis, sino que esos temas son manejados en función de preguntas y problemas de la vida y la historia argentinas, y son utilizados para aproximarse a posibles respuestas, lo que da al libro a la vez profundidad y agilidad de lectura. [JCTE]

3712 Pro, Diego F. Juan Dalma: personalidad, pensamiento y acción. v. 1. Tucumán, Argentina: Centro Cultural Alberto Rougès, 2009. 300 p.

Edición póstuma sobre el médico ítalo-argentino Juan Dalma (1895–1977). Analiza el pensamiento político, diplomático, filosófico y médico de este autor, incluidos los aspectos psicológicos y psiquiátricos. Destacamos el capítulo titulado "Antropovisión filosófica". [CJB]

3713 Rajland, Beatriz. El pacto populista en la Argentina, 1945–1955: proyección teórico-política hacia la actualidad. Buenos Aires: Ediciones del Centro Cultural de la Cooperación Floreal Gorini, 2008. 171 p.: bibl.

Al referirse al peronismo lo interpreta como una forma de populismo, y no de "bonapartismo" o "cesarismo". Por su parte, el populismo es considerado en sus características generales, y en su presencia en América Latina y en Argentina en particular. Sostiene que el peronismo fue una forma de "welfare state", aunque lo distingue del modelo "keinesiano". Es finalmente una contribución a la interpretación del fenómeno peronista, cuyos rasgos ideológicos quedan bien representados. [JCTE]

3714 Ramaglia, Dante. Apropiación crítica de Hegel en la filosofía argentina contemporánea. (*Cuyo/Mendoza*, 24, 2007, p. 121–137)

Hegel visto por tres filósofos argentinos: Alejandro Korn, Carlos Astrada y Arturo A. Roig. [JCTE]

3715 *Revista Crisis*, 1973–1976: antología del intelectual comprometido al intelectual revolucionario. Presentación y selección de textos por María Sonderéguer. Bernal, Argentina: Univ. Nacional de Quilmes Editorial, 2008. 590 p. (Col. "La ideología argentina")

Edición oportuna, porque pone a disposición materiales poco accesibles, y además los organiza de modo de resaltar la función ideológica e histórica que cumplieron. La revista fue una de las varias

manifestaciones de izquierda de la época. La compiladora señala bien el contexto de la publicación, cuyos elementos fueron: el efecto de la Revolución cubana, las luchas sociales en la Argentina, el boom literario latinoamericano, y la modernización del estilo periodístico, todo confluyendo hacia "las luchas de liberación". Intelectuales involucrados: Arturo Jauretche, Raúl Scalabrini Ortiz, Ernesto Palacio, Homero Manzi, Elías Castelnuovo, Haroldo Conti. [JCTE]

3716 Roig, Arturo Andrés. Los krausistas argentinos. Ed. corr. y aum. Buenos Aires: Ediciones El Andariego, 2006. 211 p.: bibl., index. (Contracorriente)

Edición ampliada de un libro único sobre el tema, y difícil de superar por el detalle de su estudio. Aspectos de particular interés son las relaciones entre krausismo y positivismo. En uno de los capítulos el autor reflexiona sobre su propia e inicial interpretación del tema. [JCTE]

3717 Salvioni, Amanda. L'invenzione di un medioevo americano: rappresentazioni moderne del passato coloniale in Argentina. Reggio Emilia: Diabasis, 2003. 238 p.: bibl. (Passages. L'albero del cadirà; 6)

La "invención de un medioevo americano" alude a la consideración de los siglos coloniales en América Latina, y especialmente en Argentina, como una Edad Media que desemboca en la modernidad de la Independencia. Desde estas bases la autora presenta un rico cuadro de materiales, que incluye: la labor del historiador italiano Pedro de Angelis, residente en la Argentina en la época de Rosas; la obra de Juan María Gutiérrez en el siglo XIX; y otras contribuciones, inclusive literarias. De particular interés es el tratamiento del autor argentino Ricardo Rojas, considerado como el "creador" de la historia de la literatura argentina a comienzos del siglo XX. [JCTE]

3718 Santiago, Dulce Maria. El problema de la cultura. Buenos Aires: Educa— Editorial de la Univ. Católica Argentina, 2010. 106 p.

Trata el tema filosófico de la cultura, pero contiene un largo capítulo sobre la teoría de la cultura en el filósofo argentino Francisco Romero. [JCTE]

3719 Seghesso de López, M. Cristina.
El jurista Manuel Antonio Sáez,
1834–1887: voz crítica y pensamiento de su
tiempo. Mendoza, Argentina: EDIUNC—
Editorial de la Univ. Nacional de Cuyo,
2007. 280 p.
Biografía intelectual de Manuel A.
Sáez, a la que se agregan documentos, juicios críticos y datos sobre su actuación política. Es parte de su contenido un proyecto de
reforma constitucional para Mendoza. Sitúa
a Sáenz dentro de un pensamiento liberal
moderado, de tintes conservadores, amante
del "orden". [CJB]

3720 Suárez, Anastasio Mariano. Curso
de ética: segunda parte del Curso de
filosofía de 1793. Transcripción, traducción, introducción y notas de Celina A.
Lértora Mendoza. Buenos Aires: Ediciones
F.E.P.A.I., 2006. 51 p.: bibl. (Filosofía Colonial. Fuentes)
Lértora Mendoza indica que el Curso
refleja la adhesión de los franciscanos de la
época al regalismo de los borbones. Se dictó
en la Univ. de Córdoba. [JCTE]

3721 Suárez, Anastasio Mariano. Curso
de lógica: primera parte del Curso de
Filosofía de 1793. Transcripción, traducción,
introducción y notas de Celina A. Lértora
Mendoza. Buenos Aires: Fundación para el
Estudio del Pensamiento Argentino e Iberoamericano, 2006. 186 p.: bibl. (Filosofía colonial. Fuentes)
Curso dictado en la Univ. de Córdoba.
La editora dice que el escotismo de Suárez
es más declarado que real y que trató de elu-
dir las discusiones con los modernos. Véase
también item **3720.** [JCTE]

3722 Terán, Oscar. Historia de las ideas en
la Argentina: diez lecciones iniciales,
1810–1980. Buenos Aires: Siglo Veintiuno

Editores, 2008. 318 p.: bibl. (Biblioteca básica
de historia)
Muy eficaz desde el punto de vista di-
dáctico (aunque también aprovechable para
el estudioso), y con una razonable selección
de temas e interpretaciones plausibles. Es
un libro bien logrado. Cubre desde el siglo
XVIII hasta 1983. [JCTE]

3723 Vázquez Villanueva, Graciana. Revolución y discurso: un portavoz para
la integración hispanoamericana: Bernardo
Monteagudo, 1809–1825. Buenos Aires: Isla
de la Luna, 2006. 256 p.: bibl.
Basada en las doctrinas de los autores
franceses contemporáneos sobre teoría del
discurso, la autora proyecta esas ideas a los
escritos del patriota argentino Bernardo
Monteagudo. Resulta también una contribución al tema de la integración de los nuevos
países hispanoamericanos en los años inmediatamente posteriores a la Independencia.
Incluye un artículo de Elvira Narvaja de
Arnoux sobre Juan Bautista Alberdi y su
contribución de 1844 al pensamiento de la
mencionada integración. [JCTE]

3724 Villavicencio, Susana. Sarmiento y
la nación cívica: ciudadanía y filo-
sofías de la nación en Argentina. Buenos
Aires: Eudeba, 2008. 221 p.: bibl. (Temas.
Política)
El enfoque de la obra es conceptual (filosófico en un cierto sentido) y
son centrales para él las ideas de "nación
cívica" y de "república". Además, quiere
situar el pensamiento de Sarmiento (y el
de la revolución de Independencia) en las
circunstancias reales del país, donde la
teoría republicana se ha dado junto con la
ausencia del pueblo como su sujeto real.
[JCTE]

ABBREVIATIONS AND ACRONYMS

Except for journal abbreviations which are listed: 1) after each journal title in the *Title List of Journals Indexed* (p. 729); and 2) in the *Abbreviation List of Journals Indexed* (p. 737).

ALADI	Asociación Latinoamericana de Integración
a.	annual
ABC	Argentina, Brazil, Chile
A.C.	antes de Cristo
ACAR	Associação de Crédito e Assistência Rural, Brazil
AD	Anno Domini
A.D.	Acción Democrática, Venezuela
ADESG	Associação dos Diplomados de Escola Superior de Guerra, Brazil
AGI	Archivo General de Indias, Sevilla
AGN	Archivo General de la Nación
AID	Agency for International Development
a.k.a.	also known as
Ala.	Alabama
ALALC	Asociación Latinoamericana de Libre Comercio
ALEC	*Atlas lingüístico etnográfico de Colombia*
ANAPO	Alianza Nacional Popular, Colombia
ANCARSE	Associação Nordestina de Crédito e Assistência Rural de Sergipe, Brazil
ANCOM	Andean Common Market
ANDI	Asociación Nacional de Industriales, Colombia
ANPOCS	Associação Nacional de Pós-Graduação e Pesquisa em Ciências Sociais, São Paulo
ANUC	Asociación Nacional de Usuarios Campesinos, Colombia
ANUIES	Asociación Nacional de Universidades e Institutos de Enseñanza Superior, Mexico
AP	Acción Popular
APRA	Alianza Popular Revolucionaria Americana, Peru
ARENA	Aliança Renovadora Nacional, Brazil
Ariz.	Arizona
Ark.	Arkansas
ASA	Association of Social Anthropologists of the Commonwealth, London
ASSEPLAN	Assessoria de Planejamento e Acompanhamento, Recife
Assn.	Association
Aufl.	Auflage (edition, edición)
AUFS	American Universities Field Staff Reports, Hanover, N.H.
Aug.	August, Augustan
aum.	aumentada
b.	born (nació)
B.A.R.	British Archaeological Reports
BBE	Bibliografia Brasileira de Educação
b.c.	indicates dates obtained by radiocarbon methods
BC	Before Christ

bibl(s).	bibliography(ies)
BID	Banco Interamericano de Desarrollo
BNDE	Banco Nacional de Desenvolvimento Econômico, Brazil
BNH	Banco Nacional de Habitação, Brazil
BP	before present
b/w	black and white
C14	Carbon 14
ca.	*circa* (about)
CACM	Central American Common Market
CADE	Conferencia Anual de Ejecutivos de Empresas, Peru
CAEM	Centro de Altos Estudios Militares, Peru
Calif.	California
Cap.	Capítulo
CARC	Centro de Arte y Comunicación, Buenos Aires
CARICOM	Caribbean Common Market
CARIFTA	Caribbean Free Trade Association
CBC	Christian base communities
CBD	central business district
CBI	Caribbean Basin Initiative
CD	Christian Democrats, Chile
CDHES	Comisión de Derechos Humanos de El Salvador
CDI	Conselho de Desenvolvimento Industrial, Brasília
CEB	comunidades eclesiásticas de base
CEBRAP	Centro Brasileiro de Análise e Planejamento, São Paulo
CECORA	Centro de Cooperativas de la Reforma Agraria, Colombia
CEDAL	Centro de Estudios Democráticos de América Latina, Costa Rica
CEDE	Centro de Estudios sobre Desarrollo Económico, Univ. de los Andes, Bogotá
CEDEPLAR	Centro de Desenvolvimento e Planejamento Regional, Belo Horizonte
CEDES	Centro de Estudios de Estado y Sociedad, Buenos Aires; Centro de Estudos de Educação e Sociedade, São Paulo
CEDI	Centro Ecumênico de Documentos e Informação, São Paulo
CEDLA	Centro de Estudios y Documentación Latinoamericanos, Amsterdam
CEESTEM	Centro de Estudios Económicos y Sociales del Tercer Mundo, México
CELADE	Centro Latinoamericano de Demografía
CELADEC	Comisión Evangélica Latinoamericana de Educación Cristiana
CELAM	Consejo Episcopal Latinoamericano
CEMLA	Centro de Estudios Monetarios Latinoamericanos, Mexico
CENDES	Centro de Estudios del Desarrollo, Venezuela
CENIDIM	Centro Nacional de Información, Documentación e Investigación Musicales, Mexico
CENIET	Centro Nacional de Información y Estadísticas del Trabajo, Mexico
CEOSL	Confederación Ecuatoriana de Organizaciones Sindicales LIbres
CEPADE	Centro Paraguayo de Estudios de Desarrollo Económico y Social
CEPA-SE	Comissão Estadual de Planejamento Agrícola, Sergipe
CEPAL	Comisión Económica para América Latina y el Caribe
CEPLAES	Centro de Planificación y Estudios Sociales, Quito
CERES	Centro de Estudios de la Realidad Económica y Social, Bolivia
CES	constant elasticity of substitution
cf.	compare
CFI	Consejo Federal de Inversiones, Buenos Aires
CGE	Confederación General Económica, Argentina
CGTP	Confederación General de Trabajadores del Perú
chap(s).	chapter(s)
CHEAR	Council on Higher Education in the American Republics

Cía.	Compañía
CIA	Central Intelligence Agency
CIDA	Comité Interamericano de Desarrollo Agrícola
CIDE	Centro de Investigación y Desarrollo de la Educación, Chile; Centro de Investigación y Docencias Económicas, Mexico
CIDIAG	Centro de Información y Desarrollo Internacional de Autogestión, Lima
CIE	Centro de Investigaciones Económicas, Buenos Aires
CIEDLA	Centro Interdisciplinario de Estudios sobre el Desarrollo Latinoamericano, Buenos Aires
CIEDUR	Centro Interdisciplinario de Estudios sobre el Desarrollo Uruguay, Montevideo
CIEPLAN	Corporación de Investigaciones Económicas para América Latina, Santiago
CIESE	Centro de Investigaciones y Estudios Socioeconómicos, Quito
CIMI	Conselho Indigenista Missionário, Brazil
CINTERFOR	Centro Interamericano de Investigación y Documentación sobre Formación Profesional
CINVE	Centro de Investigaciones Económicas, Montevideo
CIP	Conselho Interministerial de Preços, Brazil
CIPCA	Centro de Investigación y Promoción del Campesinado, Bolivia
CIPEC	Consejo Intergubernamental de Países Exportadores de Cobre, Santiago
CLACSO	Consejo Latinoamericano de Ciencias Sociales, Secretaría Ejecutiva, Buenos Aires
CLASC	Confederación Latinoamericana Sindical Cristiana
CLE	Comunidad Latinoamericana de Escritores, Mexico
cm	centimeter
CNI	Confederação Nacional da Indústria, Brazil
CNPq	Conselho Nacional de Pesquisas, Brazil
Co.	Company
COB	Central Obrera Boliviana
COBAL	Companhia Brasileira de Alimentos
CODEHUCA	Comisión para la Defensa de los Derechos Humanos en Centroamérica
Col.	Collection, Colección, Coleção
col.	colored, coloured
Colo.	Colorado
COMCORDE	Comisión Coordinadora para el Desarrollo Económico, Uruguay
comp(s).	compiler(s), compilador(es)
CONCLAT	Congresso Nacional das Classes Trabalhadoras, Brazil
CONCYTEC	Consejo Nacional de Ciencia y Tecnología (Peru)
CONDESE	Conselho de Desenvolvimento Econômico de Sergipe
Conn.	Connecticut
COPEI	Comité Organizador Pro-Elecciones Independientes, Venezuela
CORFO	Corporación de Fomento de la Producción, Chile
CORP	Corporación para el Fomento de Investigaciones Económicas, Colombia
Corp.	Corporation, Corporación
corr.	corrected, corregida
CP	Communist Party
CPDOC	Centro de Pesquisa e Documentação, Brazil
CRIC	Consejo Regional Indígena del Cauca, Colombia
CSUTCB	Confederación Sindical Unica de Trabajadores Campesinos de Bolivia
CTM	Confederación de Trabajadores de México
CUNY	City University of New York
CUT	Central Unica de Trabajadores (Mexico); Central Unica dos Trabalhadores (Brazil); Central Unitaria de Trabajadores (Chile; Colombia); Unitaria de Trabajadores (Costa Rica)

CVG	Corporación Venezolana de Guayana
d.	died (murió)
DANE	Departamento Nacional de Estadística, Colombia
DC	developed country; Demócratas Cristianos, Chile
d.C.	después de Cristo
Dec./déc.	December, décembre
Del.	Delaware
dept.	department
depto.	departamento
DESCO	Centro de Estudios y Promoción del Desarrollo, Lima
Dez./dez.	Dezember, dezembro
dic.	diciembre, dicembre
disc.	discography
DNOCS	Departamento Nacional de Obras Contra as Secas, Brazil
doc.	document, documento
Dr.	Doctor
Dra.	Doctora
DRAE	*Diccionario de la Real Academia Española*
ECLAC	UN Economic Commision for Latin America and the Caribbean, New York and Santiago
ECOSOC	UN Economic and Social Council
ed./éd.(s)	edition(s), édition(s), edición(es), editor(s), redactor(es), director(es)
EDEME	Editora Emprendimentos Educacionais, Florianópolis
Edo.	Estado
EEC	European Economic Community
EE.UU.	Estados Unidos de América
EFTA	European Free Trade Association
e.g.	*exempio gratia* (for example, por ejemplo)
ELN	Ejército de Liberación Nacional, Colombia
ENDEF	Estudo Nacional da Despesa Familiar, Brazil
ERP	Ejército Revolucionario del Pueblo, El Salvador
ESG	Escola Superior de Guerra, Brazil
estr.	estrenado
et al.	*et alia* (and others)
ETENE	Escritório Técnico de Estudos Econômicos do Nordeste, Brazil
ETEPE	Escritório Técnico de Planejamento, Brazil
EUDEBA	Editorial Universitaria de Buenos Aires
EWG	Europaische Wirtschaftsgemeinschaft. *See* EEC.
facsim(s).	facsimile(s)
FAO	Food and Agriculture Organization of the United Nations
FDR	Frente Democrático Revolucionario, El Salvador
FEB	Força Expedicionária Brasileira
Feb./feb.	February, Februar, febrero, febbraio
FEDECAFE	Federación Nacional de Cafeteros, Colombia
FEDESARROLLO	Fundación para la Educación Superior y el Desarrollo
fev./fév.	fevereiro, février
ff.	following
FGTS	Fundo de Garantia do Tempo de Serviço, Brazil
FGV	Fundação Getúlio Vargas
FIEL	Fundación de Investigaciones Económicas Latinoamericanas, Argentina
film.	filmography
fl.	flourished
Fla.	Florida
FLACSO	Facultad Latinoamericana de Ciencias Sociales
FMI	Fondo Monetario Internacional

FMLN	Frente Farabundo Martí de Liberación Nacional, El Salvador
fold.	folded
fol(s).	folio(s)
FPL	Fuerzas Populares de Liberación Farabundo Marti, El Salvador
FRG	Federal Republic of Germany
FSLN	Frente Sandinista de Liberación Nacional, Nicaragua
ft.	foot, feet
FUAR	Frente Unido de Acción Revolucionaria, Colombia
FUCVAM	Federación Unificadora de Cooperativas de Vivienda por Ayuda Mutua, Uruguay
FUNAI	Fundação Nacional do Indio, Brazil
FUNARTE	Fundação Nacional de Arte, Brazil
FURN	Fundação Universidade Regional do Nordeste
Ga.	Georgia
GAO	General Accounting Office, Wahington
GATT	General Agreement on Tariffs and Trade
GDP	gross domestic product
GDR	German Democratic Republic
GEIDA	Grupo Executivo de Irrigação para o Desenvolvimento Agrícola, Brazil
gen.	gennaio
Gen.	General
GMT	Greenwich Mean Time
GPA	grade point average
GPO	Government Printing Office, Washington
h.	hijo
ha.	hectares, hectáreas
HLAS	Handbook of Latin American Studies
HMAI	Handbook of Middle American Indians
Hnos.	hermanos
HRAF	Human Relations Area Files, Inc., New Haven, Conn.
IBBD	Instituto Brasileiro de Bibliografia e Documentação
IBGE	Instituto Brasileiro de Geografia e Estatística, Rio de Janeiro
IBRD	International Bank for Reconstruction and Development (World Bank)
ICA	Instituto Colombiano Agropecuario
ICAIC	Instituto Cubano de Arte e Industria Cinematográfica
ICCE	Instituto Colombiano de Construcción Escolar
ICE	International Cultural Exchange
ICSS	Instituto Colombiano de Seguridad Social
ICT	Instituto de Crédito Territorial, Colombia
id.	idem (the same as previously mentioned or given)
IDB	Inter-American Development Bank
i.e.	id est (that is, o sea)
IEL	Instituto Euvaldo Lodi, Brazil
IEP	Instituto de Estudios Peruanos
IERAC	Instituto Ecuatoriano de Reforma Agraria y Colonización
IFAD	International Fund for Agricultural Development
IICA	Instituto Interamericano de Ciencias Agrícolas, San José
III	Instituto Indigenista Interamericana, Mexico
IIN	Instituto Indigenista Nacional, Guatemala
ILDIS	Instituto Latinoamericano de Investigaciones Sociales
ill.	illustration(s)
Ill.	Illinois
ILO	International Labour Organization, Geneva
IMES	Instituto Mexicano de Estudios Sociales
IMF	International Monetary Fund

Impr.	Imprenta, Imprimérie
in.	inches
INAH	Instituto Nacional de Antropología e Historia, Mexico
INBA	Instituto Nacional de Bellas Artes, Mexico
Inc.	Incorporated
INCORA	Instituto Colombiano de Reforma Agraria
Ind.	Indiana
INEP	Instituto Nacional de Estudios Pedagógicos, Brazil
INI	Instituto Nacional Indigenista, Mexico
INIT	Instituto Nacional de Industria Turística, Cuba
INPES/IPEA	Instituto de Planejamento Econômico e Social, Brazil
INTAL	Instituto para la Integración de América Latina
IPA	Instituto de Pastoral Andina, Univ. de San Antonio de Abad, Seminario de Antropología, Cusco, Peru
IPEA	Instituto de Pesquisa Econômica Aplicada, Brazil
IPES/GB	Instituto de Pesquisas e Estudos Sociais, Guanabara, Brazil
IPHAN	Instituto de Patrimônio Histórico e Artístico Nacional, Brazil
ir.	irregular
IS	Internacional Socialista
ITESM	Instituto Tecnológico y de Estudios Superiores de Monterrey
ITT	International Telephone and Telegraph
Jan./jan.	January, Januar, janeiro, janvier
JLP	Jamaican Labour Party
Jr.	Junior, Júnior
JUC	Juventude Universitária Católica, Brazil
JUCEPLAN	Junta Central de Planificación, Cuba
Kan.	Kansas
KITLV	Koninklijk Instituut voor Tall-, Land- en Volkenkunde (Royal Institute of Linguistics and Anthropology)
km	kilometers, kilómetros
Ky.	Kentucky
La.	Louisiana
LASA	Latin American Studies Association
LDC	less developed country(ies)
LP	long-playing record
Ltd(a).	Limited, Limitada
m	meters, metros
m.	murió (died)
M	mille, mil, thousand
M.A.	Master of Arts
MACLAS	Middle Atlantic Council of Latin American Studies
MAPU	Movimiento de Acción Popular Unitario, Chile
MARI	Middle American Research Institute, Tulane University, New Orleans
MAS	Movimiento al Socialismo, Venezuela
Mass.	Massachusetts
MCC	Mercado Común Centro-Americano
Md.	Maryland
MDB	Movimiento Democrático Brasileiro
MDC	more developed countries
Me.	Maine
MEC	Ministério de Educação e Cultura, Brazil
Mich.	Michigan
mimeo	mimeographed, mimeografiado
min.	minutes, minutos
Minn.	Minnesota

MIR	Movimiento de Izquierda Revolucionaria, Chile and Venezuela
Miss.	Mississippi
MIT	Massachusetts Institute of Technology
ml	milliliter
MLN	Movimiento de Liberación Nacional
mm.	millimeter
MNC	multinational corporation
MNI	minimum number of individuals
MNR	Movimiento Nacionalista Revolucionario, Bolivia
Mo.	Missouri
MOBRAL	Movimento Brasileiro de Alfabetização
MOIR	Movimiento Obrero Independiente y Revolucionario, Colombia
Mont.	Montana
MRL	Movimiento Revolucionario Liberal, Colombia
ms.	manuscript
M.S.	Master of Science
msl	mean sea level
n.	nació (born)
NBER	National Bureau of Economic Research, Cambridge, Massachusetts
N.C.	North Carolina
N.D.	North Dakota
NE	Northeast
Neb.	Nebraska
neubearb.	neubearbeitet (revised, corregida)
Nev.	Nevada
n.f.	neue Folge (new series)
NGO	nongovernmental organization
NGDO	nongovernmental development organization
N.H.	New Hampshire
NIEO	New International Economic Order
NIH	National Institutes of Health, Washington
N.J.	New Jersey
NJM	New Jewel Movement, Grenada
N.M.	New Mexico
no(s).	number(s), número(s)
NOEI	Nuevo Orden Económico Internacional
NOSALF	Scandinavian Committee for Research in Latin America
Nov./nov.	November, noviembre, novembre, novembro
NSF	National Science Foundation
NW	Northwest
N.Y.	New York
OAB	Ordem dos Advogados do Brasil
OAS	Organization of American States
OCLC	Online Computer Library Center
Oct./oct.	October, octubre, octobre
ODEPLAN	Oficina de Planificación Nacional, Chile
OEA	Organización de los Estados Americanos
OECD	Organisation for Economic Cooperation and Development
OIT	Organización Internacional del Trabajo
Okla.	Oklahoma
Okt.	Oktober
ONUSAL	United Nations Observer Mission in El Salvador
op.	opus
OPANAL	Organismo para la Proscripción de las Armas Nucleares en América Latina

OPEC	Organization of Petroleum Exporting Countries
OPEP	Organización de Países Exportadores de Petróleo
OPIC	Overseas Private Investment Corporation, Washington
Or.	Oregon
OREALC	Oficina Regional de Educación para América Latina y el Caribe
ORIT	Organización Regional Interamericana del Trabajo
ORSTOM	Office de la recherche scientifique et technique outre-mer (France)
ott.	ottobre
out.	outubro
p.	page(s)
Pa.	Pennsylvania
PAN	Partido Acción Nacional, Mexico
PC	Partido Comunista
PCCLAS	Pacific Coast Council on Latin American Studies
PCN	Partido de Conciliación Nacional, El Salvador
PCP	Partido Comunista del Perú
PCR	Partido Comunista Revolucionario, Chile and Argentina
PCV	Partido Comunista de Venezuela
PD	Partido Democrático
PDC	Partido Demócrata Cristiano, Chile
PDS	Partido Democrático Social, Brazil
PDT	Partido Democrático Trabalhista, Brazil
PDVSA	Petróleos de Venezuela S.A.
PEMEX	Petróleos Mexicanos
PETROBRAS	Petróleo Brasileiro
PIMES	Programa Integrado de Mestrado em Economia e Sociologia, Brazil
PIP	Partido Independiente de Puerto Rico
PLN	Partido Liberación Nacional, Costa Rica
PMDB	Partido do Movimento Democrático Brasileiro
PNAD	Pesquisa Nacional por Amostra Domiciliar, Brazil
PNC	People's National Congress, Guyana
PNM	People's National Movement, Trinidad and Tobago
PNP	People's National Party, Jamaica
pop.	population
port(s).	portrait(s)
PPP	purchasing power parities; People's Progressive Party of Guyana
PRD	Partido Revolucionario Dominicano
PREALC	Programa Regional del Empleo para América Latina y el Caribe, Organización Internacional del Trabajo, Santiago
PRI	Partido Revolucionario Institucional, Mexico
Prof.	Professor, Profesor(a)
PRONAPA	Programa Nacional de Pesquisas Arqueológicas, Brazil
PRONASOL	Programa Nacional de Solidaridad, Mexico
prov.	province, provincia
PS	Partido Socialista, Chile
PSD	Partido Social Democrático, Brazil
pseud.	pseudonym, pseudónimo
PT	Partido dos Trabalhadores, Brazil
pt(s).	part(s), parte(s)
PTB	Partido Trabalhista Brasileiro
pub.	published, publisher
PUC	Pontifícia Universidade Católica
PURSC	Partido Unido de la Revolución Socialista de Cuba
q.	quarterly
rev.	revisada, revista, revised

R.I.	Rhode Island
s.a.	semiannual
SALALM	Seminar on the Acquisition of Latin American Library Materials
SATB	soprano, alto, tenor, bass
sd.	sound
s.d.	*sine datum* (no date, sin fecha)
S.D.	South Dakota
SDR	special drawing rights
SE	Southeast
SELA	Sistema Económico Latinoamericano
SEMARNAP	Secretaria de Medio Ambiente, Recursos Naturales y Pesca, Mexico
SENAC	Serviço Nacional de Aprendizagem Comercial, Rio de Janeiro
SENAI	Serviço Nacional de Aprendizagem Industrial, São Paulo
SEP	Secretaría de Educación Pública, Mexico
SEPLA	Seminario Permanente sobre Latinoamérica, Mexico
Sept./sept.	September, septiembre, septembre
SES	socioeconomic status
SESI	Serviço Social da Indústria, Brazil
set.	setembro, settembre
SI	Socialist International
SIECA	Secretaría Permanente del Tratado General de Integración Económica Centroamericana
SIL	Summer Institute of Linguistics (Instituto Lingüístico de Verano)
SINAMOS	Sistema Nacional de Apoyo a la Movilización Social, Peru
S.J.	Society of Jesus
s.l.	*sine loco* (place of publication unknown)
s.n.	*sine nomine* (publisher unknown)
SNA	Sociedad Nacional de Agricultura, Chile
SPP	Secretaría de Programación y Presupuesto, Mexico
SPVEA	Superintendência do Plano de Valorização Econômica da Amazônia, Brazil
sq.	square
SSRC	Social Sciences Research Council, New York
STENEE	Empresa Nacional de Energía Eléctrica. Sindicato de Trabajadores, Honduras
SUDAM	Superintendência de Desenvolvimento da Amazônia, Brazil
SUDENE	Superintendência de Desenvolvimento do Nordeste, Brazil
SUFRAMA	Superintendência da Zona Franca de Manaus, Brazil
SUNY	State University of New York
SW	Southwest
t.	tomo(s), tome(s)
TAT	Thematic Apperception Test
TB	tuberculosis
Tenn.	Tennessee
Tex.	Texas
TG	transformational generative
TL	Thermoluminescent
TNE	Transnational enterprise
TNP	Tratado de No Proliferación
trans.	translator
UABC	Universidad Autónoma de Baja California
UCA	Universidad Centroamericana José Simeón Cañas, San Salvador
UCLA	University of California, Los Angeles
UDN	União Democrática Nacional, Brazil
UFG	Universidade Federal de Goiás

UFPb	Universidade Federal de Paraíba
UFSC	Universidade Federal de Santa Catarina
UK	United Kingdom
UN	United Nations
UNAM	Universidad Nacional Autónoma de México
UNCTAD	United Nations Conference on Trade and Development
UNDP	United Nations Development Programme
UNEAC	Unión de Escritores y Artistas de Cuba
UNESCO	United Nations Educational, Scientific and Cultural Organization
UNI/UNIND	União das Nações Indígenas
UNICEF	United Nations International Children's Emergency Fund
Univ(s).	university(ies), universidad(es), universidade(s), université(s), universität(s), universitá(s)
uniw.	uniwersytet (university)
Unltd.	Unlimited
UP	Unidad Popular, Chile
URD	Unidad Revolucionaria Democrática
URSS	Unión de Repúblicas Soviéticas Socialistas
UNISA	University of South Africa
US	United States
USAID	*See* AID.
USIA	United States Information Agency
USSR	Union of Soviet Socialist Republics
UTM	Universal Transverse Mercator
UWI	Univ. of the West Indies
v.	volume(s), volumen (volúmenes)
Va.	Virginia
V.I.	Virgin Islands
viz.	*videlicet* (that is, namely)
vol(s).	volume(s), volumen (volúmenes)
vs.	versus
Vt.	Vermont
W.Va.	West Virginia
Wash.	Washington
Wis.	Wisconsin
WPA	Working People's Alliance, Guyana
WWI	World War I
WWII	World War II
Wyo.	Wyoming
yr(s).	year(s)

TITLE LIST OF JOURNALS INDEXED

For journal titles listed by abbreviation, see *Abbreviation List of Journals Indexed*, p. 737.

Actual. Univ. de Los Andes, Dirección General de Cultura y Extensión. Mérida, Venezuela (Actual/Mérida)

Aisthesis. Instituto de Estética, Facultad de Filosofia, Pontificia Univ. Católica de Chile. Santiago (Aisthesis/Santiago)

Allpanchis. Instituto de Pastoral Andina. Cuzco, Peru (Allpanchis/Cuzco)

América Latina Hoy: Revista de Ciencias Sociales. Univ. de Salamanca, Instituto de Estudios de Iberoamérica y Portugal. Salamanca, Spain (Am. Lat. Hoy/Salamanca)

The American Historical Review. Indiana Univ. at Bloomington. Bloomington, Ind (Am. Hist. Rev.)

American Indian Quarterly. Univ. of Nebraska Press. Lincoln, Neb (Am. Indian Q.)

The Americas: A Quarterly Review of Inter-American Cultural History. Catholic Univ. of America, Academy of American Franciscan History; Catholic Univ. of America Press. Washington, D.C (Americas/Washington)

Anais do Museu Histórico Nacional. Museu Histórico Nacional, Instituto do Patrimônio Histórico e Artístico Nacional, Ministério da Cultura. Rio de Janeiro (An. Mus. Hist. Nac.)

Anais do Museu Paulista: História e Cultura Material. Museu Paulista. São Paulo (An. Mus. Paul.)

Anales del Instituto de Investigaciones Estéticas. UNAM, Instituto de Investigaciones Estéticas. México (An. Inst. Invest. Estét.)

Ancient Mesoamerica. Cambridge Univ. Press. Cambridge, England; New York (Anc. Mesoam.)

ANDES: Antropología e Historia. Univ. Nacional de Salta, Facultad de Humanidades, Centro Promocional de las Investigaciones en Historia y Antropología. Salta, Argentina (ANDES Antropol. Hist.)

Annales: histoire, sciences sociales. L'École des Hautes Études en Sciences Sociales. Paris (Ann. hist. sci. soc.)

Annales historiques de la Révolution française. Société des Études Robespierristes. Paris (Ann. hist. Révolut. fr.)

Anthropologica del Departamento de Ciencias Sociales. Pontificia Univ. Católica del Perú, Depto. de Ciencias Sociales. Lima (Anthropol. Dep. Cienc. Soc.)

Antiquity. Antiquity Publications Ltd. Cambridge, England (Antiquity/Cambridge)

Antropología e Historia de Guatemala. Instituto de Antropología e Historia de Guatemala. Guatemala (Antropol. Hist. Guatem.)

Anuario de Estudios Americanos. Consejo Superior de Investigaciones Científicas, Escuela de Estudios Hispano-Americanos. Sevilla, Spain (Anu. Estud. Am.)

Anuario de Estudios Bolivianos, Archivísticos y Bibliográficos. Ediciones Archivo y Biblioteca Nacionales de Bolivia. Sucre, Bolivia (Anu. Estud. Boliv. Arch. Bibliogr.)

Anuario de Estudios Centroamericanos. Univ. de Costa Rica. San José (Anu. Estud. Centroam.)

Anuario del Instituto de Historia Argentina. Editorial de la Univ. Nacional de La Plata. La Plata, Argentina (Anu. Inst. Hist. Argent.)

Anuario IEHS. Univ. Nacional del Centro de la Provincia de Buenos Aires, Facultad de Ciencias Humanas, Instituto de Estudios Histórico-Sociales. Tandil, Argentina (Anu. IEHS)

Apuntes de Investigación del CECYP. Centro de Estudios en Cultura y Política, Fundación del Sur. Buenos Aires (Apunt. Invest. CECYP)

Apuntes Filosóficos. Univ. Central de Venezuela, Escuela de Filosofía. Caracas (Apunt. Filos.)

The Art Bulletin. College Art Assn. of America. New York (Art Bull.)

Art Journal. The College Art Assn. New York (Art J.)

Atenea. Univ. de Concepción. Concepción, Chile (Atenea/Concepción)

Aufgabe. Litmus Press. Provincetown, Mass (Aufgabe)

Black Music Research Journal. Fisk Univ., Institute for Research in Black American Music. Nashville, Tenn (Black Music Res. J.)

Boletín de Historia y Antigüedades. Academia Colombiana de Historia. Bogotá (Bol. Hist. Antig.)

Boletín de la Academia Nacional de la Historia. Caracas (Bol. Acad. Nac. Hist./Caracas)

Boletín de Lima: Revista Cultural Científica. Asociación Cultural Boletín de Lima A.C. Lima (Bol. Lima)

Boletín del Fideicomiso Archivos Plutarco Elías Calles y Fernando Torreblanca. México (Boletín/México)

Boletín del Museo Chileno de Arte Precolombino. Santiago, Chile (Bol. Mus. Chil. Arte Precolomb.)

Boletín Música. Casa de las Américas. La Habana (Bol. Música/Habana)

Bulletin de l'Institut français d'études andines. Lima (Bull. Inst. fr. étud. andin.)

Bulletin of Latin American Research. Blackwell Publishers. Oxford, England; Malden, Mass (Bull. Lat. Am. Res.)

Business History Review. Harvard Univ., Graduate School of Business Administration. Boston, Mass (Bus. Hist. Rev./Boston)

Cahiers des Amériques latines. Univ. de la Sorbonne nouvelle—Paris III, Institut des haute études de l'Amérique latine. Paris (Cah. Am. lat.)

Caribbean Quarterly: CQ. Univ. of the West Indies, Vice Chancellery, Cultural Studies Initiative. Mona, Jamaica (Caribb. Q./Mona)

Caribbean Studies. Univ. of Puerto Rico, Institute of Caribbean Studies. Río Piedras, Puerto Rico (Caribb. Stud.)

CLC Web: Comparative Literature and Culture. Purdue Unversity Press, Purdue University, West Lafayette, IN (CLC Web)

Colombia Internacional. Univ. de los Andes, Centro de Estudios Internacionales. Bogotá (Colomb. Int.)

Colonial Latin American Historical Review. Univ. of New Mexico, Spanish Colonial Research Center. Albuquerque (CLAHR)

Colonial Latin American Review. City Univ. of New York (CUNY), City College, Dept. of Foreign Languages and Literatures, Simon H. Rifkind Center for the Humanities. New York; Carfax Publishing, Taylor & Francis, Ltd. Abingdon, England (Colon. Lat. Am. Rev.)

Comparative Literature. Univ. of Oregon. Eugene, Ore (Comp. Lit.)

Comparative Studies in Society and History. Society for the Comparative Study of Society and History; Cambridge Univ. Press. London (Comp. Stud. Soc. Hist.)

Cuadernos Americanos. UNAM. México (Cuad. Am./México)

Cuadernos de Antropología. Univ. de Costa Rica, Depto. de Antropología, Laboratorio de Etnología. San José (Cuad. Antropol./San José)

Cuadernos de Economía. Univ. Nacional de Colombia, Facultad de Ciencias Económicas, Centro de Investigaciones para el Desarrollo. Bogotá (Cuad. Econ./Bogotá)

Cuadernos del Pensamiento Latinoamericano. Univ. de Playa Ancha de Ciencias de la Educación. Centro de Estudios del Pensamiento Latinoamericano (CEPLA). Valparaíso, Chile (Cuad. Pensam. Latinoam.)

Cuadernos Sociológicos. Depto. de Sociología y Ciencias Políticas, Pontificia Univ. Católica del Ecuador. Quito (Cuad. Sociol./Quito)

Current Anthropology. Univ. of Chicago Press. Chicago, Ill (Curr. Anthropol.)

Cuyo: Anuario de Filosofía Argentina y Americana. Univ. Nacional de Cuyo, Instituto de Filosofía, Sección de Historia del Pensamiento Argentino. Mendoza, Argentina (Cuyo/Mendoza)

Desacatos. CIESAS, Centro de Investigaciones y Estudios Superiores en Antropología Social. México (Desacatos)

Early American Studies. McNeil Center for Early American Studies. Philadelphia, Pa (Early Amer. Stud.)

Early Music. Oxford Univ. Press. London (Early Music)

Ecuador Debate. Centro Andino de Acción Popular. Quito (Ecuad. Debate)

Eighteenth-Century Studies. Johns Hopkins Univ. Press for the American Society for Eighteenth-Century Studies. Baltimore, Md (Eighteenth-Century Stud.)

Encuentro de la Cultura Cubana. Asociación Encuentro de la Cultura Cubana. Madrid (Encuentro Cult. Cuba.)

Entrepasados: Revista de Historia. Buenos Aires (Entrepasados/Buenos Aires)

Environment and Planning: D, Society & Space. Pion Ltd. London (Environ. Plann. D Soc. Space)

EspacioTiempo: Revista Latinoamericana de Ciencias Sociales y Humanidades. Univ. Autónoma de San Luis Potosi. San Luis Potosi, Mexico (EspacioTiempo)

Estudios, Filosofía Práctica e Historia de las Ideas. Instituto de Ciencias Humanas, Sociales y Ambientales (INCIHUSA), CRICYT. Mendoza, Argentina (Estud. Filos. Práct. Hist. Ideas)

Estudios Atacameños. Univ. del Norte, Museo de Arqueología. San Pedro de Atacama, Chile (Estud. Atacameños)

Estudios de Cultura Maya. UNAM, Instituto de Investigaciones Filológicas, Centro de Estudios Mayas. México (Estud. Cult. Maya)

Estudios de Cultura Náhuatl. UNAM, Instituto de Investigaciones Históricas. México (Estud. Cult. Náhuatl)

Estudios de Historia Moderna y Contemporánea de México. UNAM, Instituto de Investigaciones Históricas. México (Estud. Hist. Mod. Contemp. Méx.)

Estudios de Historia Novohispana. UNAM, Instituto de Investigaciones Históricas. México (Estud. Hist. Novohisp.)

Estudios: Filosofía, Historia, Letras. Instituto Tecnológico Autónomo de México, División Académica de Estudios Generales y Estudios Internacionales, Depto. Académico de Estudios Generales. México (Estud. Filos. Hist. Let.)

Estudios Interdisciplinarios de América Latina y el Caribe: E.I.A.L. Univ. de Tel Aviv, Escuela de Historia. Tel Aviv (Estud. Interdiscipl. Am. Lat. Carib.)

Estudios Migratorios Latinoamericanos. Centro de Estudios Migratorios Latinoamericanos. Buenos Aires (Estud. Migr. Latinoam.)

Estudios Paraguayos. Univ. Católica Nuestra Señora de la Asunción. Asunción (Estud. Parag.)

Estudios Políticos: Revista de Ciencias Políticas y Administración Pública. UNAM, Facultad de Ciencias Políticas y Sociales. México (Estud. Polít./México)

Estudios Sociales: Revista Universitaria Semestral. Univ. Nacional del Litoral, Secretaría de Extensión, Centro de Publicaciones. Santa Fe, Argentina (Estud. Soc./Santa Fe)

Estudios Sociológicos. El Colegio de México, Centro de Estudios Sociológicos. México (Estud. Sociol./México)

Estudos Avançados. Univ. de São Paulo, Instituto de Estudos Avançados. São Paulo (Estud. Av.)

Estudos Históricos. Fundação Getulio Vargas, Centro de Pesquisa e Documentação de História Contemporânea do Brasil. Rio de Janeiro (Estud. Hist./Rio de Janeiro)

Estudos Ibero-Americanos. Pontificia Univ. Católica do Rio Grande do Sul, Faculdade de Filosofia e Ciências Humanas, Depto. de História, Programa Pós-Graduação em História. Porto Alegre, Brazil (Estud. Ibero-Am./Porto Alegre)

Ethnohistory: The Bulletin of the Ohio Valley Historic Indian Conference. American Society for Ethnohistory. Columbus, Ohio (Ethnohistory/Columbus)

Ethnomusicology. Univ. of Illinois Press. Champaign, Ill (Ethnomusicology)

Ethnomusicology Forum. Routledge Taylor & Francis Group. Basingstoke, England (Ethnomusic. Forum)

Explorations in Renaissance Culture. South Central Renaissance Conference. Memphis, Tenn (Explor. Renaissance Cult.)

Foro Internacional. El Colegio de México, Centro de Estudios Internacionales. México (Foro Int./México)

French Historical Studies. Society for French Historical Studies. Raleigh, N.C (Fr. Hist. Stud.)

Frontera Norte. El Colegio de la Frontera Norte. Tijuana, Mexico (Front. Norte)

Gender & History. Blackwell Publishers. Abingdon, England; Williston, Vt (Gend. Hist.)

Guaraguao: Revista de Cultura Latinoamericano. Univ. Autónoma de Barcelona, Centro de Estudios y Cooperación para América Latina. Barcelona (Guaraguao/Barcelona)

Harper's. Harper's Magazine Foundation, New York, NY (Harper's)

Hispania. Consejo Superior de Investigaciones Científicas, Instituto de Historia, Depto. de Medieval Moderna y Contemporánea. Madrid (Hispania/Madrid)

Hispanic American Historical Review. Duke Univ. Press. Durham, N.C (HAHR)

Histoire, économie et sociéte. Editions C.D.U. et S.E.D.E.S. Paris (Hist. écon. soc.)

Historia. Pontificia Univ. Católica de Chile, Facultad de Historia, Geografia y Ciencia Política, Instituto de Historia. Santiago (Historia/Santiago)

História. Univ. Estadual Paulista, Fundação para o Desenvolvimento, Instituto de Letras, História e Psicologia. São Paulo (História/São Paulo)

História Ciências Saúde: Manguinhos. Fundação Oswaldo Cruz, Casa de Oswaldo Cruz. Rio de Janeiro (Hist. Ciênc. Saúde Manguinhos)

Historia Contemporánea. Univ. del País Vasco, Depto. de Historia Contemporánea. Bilbao, Spain (Hist. Contemp.)

Historia Crítica. Univ. de los Andes, Facultad de Ciencias Sociales, Depto. de Historia. Bogotá (Hist. Crít./Bogotá)

Historia Mexicana. El Colegio de México, Centro de Estudios Históricos. México (Hist. Mex./México)

História: Questões e Debates. Univ. Federal do Paraná, Programa de Pós-Graduação em História, Associação Paraense de História. Curitiba, Brazil (Hist. Quest. Debates)

Historia y Grafía. Univ. Iberoamericana, Depto. de Historia. México (Hist. Graf./México)

Historia y Política. Univ. Complutense de Madrid, Depto. de Historia del Pensamiento y de los Movimientos Sociales y Políticos; Univ. Nacional de Educación a Distancia, Depto. de Historia Social y del Pensamiento Político. Madrid (Hist. Polít.)

Historia y Sociedad. Univ. Nacional de Colombia—Sede Medellín, Facultad de Ciencias Humanas y Económicas, Depto. de Historia. Medellín, Colombia (Hist. Soc./Medellín)

History of Religions. Univ. of Chicago. Chicago, Ill (Hist. Relig./Chicago)

The History of the Family: An International Quarterly. JAI Press Inc. Greenwich, Conn (Hist. Fam.)

History Workshop Journal. Oxford Univ. Press. Oxford, England (Hist. Workshop J.)

Humanitas: Anuario del Centro de Estudios Humanísticos. Univ. Autónoma de Nuevo León, Secretaría de Extensión y Cultura, Centro de Estudios Humanísticos. Monterrey, Mexico (Humanitas/Monterrey)

Iberoamericana. Madrid (Iberoamericana/Madrid)

Iberoamericana = Ibero Amerika Kenkyu. Univ. Sofia, Instituto Iberoamericano. Tokyo (Iberoamericana/Tokyo)

Illes i imperis = Islas e imperios = Islands and empires. Univ. Pompeu Fabra, Dept. d'Humanitats, Institut Universitari d'Història Jaume Vicens Vives. Barcelona (Illes Imp.)

Inter-American Music Review. Theodore Front Musical Literature, Inc. Van Nuys, Calif (Inter-Am. Music Rev.)

The International History Review. Simon Fraser Univ., Dept. of History. Burnaby, British Columbia (Int. Hist. Rev./Burnaby)

Investigaciones Sociales: Revista del Instituto de Investigaciones Histórico Sociales. Univ. Nacional Mayor de San Marcos, Facultad de Ciencias Sociales. Lima (Investig. Soc./San Marcos)

Iztapalapa. Univ. Autónoma Metropolitana—Unidad Iztapalapa, División de Ciencias Sociales y Humanidades. México (Iztapalapa/México)

Journal of Anthropological Archaeology. Academic Press. New York (J. Anthropol. Archaeol.)

Journal of Archaeological Science. Academic Press. New York (J. Archaeol. Sci.)

The Journal of Caribbean History. Univ. of the West Indies Press; Univ. of the West Indies, Dept. of History. Mona, Jamaica (J. Caribb. Hist.)

Journal of Church and State. Baylor Univ., J.M. Dawson Studies in Church and State. Waco, Tex (J. Church State)

The Journal of Economic History. Economic History Assn.; Univ. of Arizona. Tucson (J. Econ. Hist.)

The Journal of Interdisciplinary History. The MIT Press. Cambridge, Mass (J. Interdiscip. Hist.)

Journal of Latin American Cultural Studies. Carfax Publishing. Abingdon, England (J. Lat. Am. Cult. Stud.)

Journal of Latin American Geography. Conference of Latin Americanist Geographers. Tucson, Ariz (J. Lat. Am. Geogr.)

Journal of Latin American Studies. Cambridge Univ. Press. Cambridge, England (J. Lat. Am. Stud.)

Journal of Social History. George Mason Univ. Press. Fairfax, Va (J. Soc. Hist.)

Journal of the Bahamas Historical Society. Bahamas Historical Society. Nassau, Bahamas (J. Bahamas Hist. Soc.)

Journal of the History of Ideas. Johns Hopkins Univ. Press. Baltimore, Md (J. Hist. Ideas)

Journal of the History of Sexuality. Univ. of Chicago Press. Chicago, Ill (J. Hist. Sex.)

The Journal of the Royal Anthropological Institute. London (J. Royal Anthropol. Inst.)

Journal of the Southwest. Univ. of Arizona, Southwest Center. Tucson (J. Southwest)

Journal of World History. World History Assn.; Univ. of Hawaii Press. Honolulu (J. World Hist.)

Latin American and Caribbean Ethnic Studies. Taylor & Francis. Colchester, England (Lat. Am. Caribb. Ethn. Stud.)

Latin American Antiquity. Society for American Archaeology. Washington, D.C (Lat. Am. Antiq.)

Latin American Music Review. Revista de Música Latinoamericana. Univ. of Texas Press. Austin (Lat. Am. Music Rev.)

Latin American Perspectives. Sage Publications, Inc. Thousand Oaks, Calif (Lat. Am. Perspect.)

Latin American Politics and Society. Univ. of Miami, School of Interamerican Studies. Coral Gables, Fla (Lat. Am. Polit. Soc.)

Latin American Research Review. Latin American Studies Assn.; Univ. of Texas Press. Austin (LARR)

Lecturas de Economía. Univ. de Antioquia, Facultad de Ciencias Económicas, Depto. de Economía, Centro de Investigaciones Económicas. Medellín, Colombia (Lect. Econ.)

Literatura Mexicana. UNAM, Instituto de Investigaciones Filológicas, Centro de Estudios Literarios. México (Lit. Mex.)

Luso-Brazilian Review. Univ. of Wisconsin Press. Madison (Luso-Braz. Rev.)

Maguaré. Univ. Nacional de Colombia, Depto. de Antropología. Bogotá (Maguaré/Bogotá)

Memorias: Revista Digital de Historia y Arqueología desde el Caribe. Univ. del Norte. Colombia (Memorias)

Mesoamérica. Plumsock Mesoamerican Studies. South Woodstock, Vt.; Centro de Investigaciones Regionales de Mesoamérica. Antigua, Guatemala (Mesoamérica/Antigua)

Mexican Studies/Estudios Mexicanos. Univ. of California Press. Berkeley (Mex. Stud.)

Music & Politics. Univ. of California, Santa Barbara. Santa Barbara, Calif (Music Polit.)

The Musical Quarterly. G. Schirmer. New York (Music Q.)

Musicorum. Universitaire François-Rabelais. Tours, France (Musicorum)

New Mexico Historical Review. Univ. of New Mexico; Historical Society of New Mexico. Albuquerque (N.M. Hist. Rev.)

The New York Times Magazine. New York (N.Y. Times Mag.)

Nombres. Univ. Nacional de Córdoba, Facultad de Filosofia y Humanidades, Centro de Investigaciones, Area de Filosofia. Córdoba, Argentina (Nombres/Córdoba)

Nova Economia. Univ. Federal de Minas Gerais, Faculdade de Ciências Econômicas, Depto. de Ciências Econômicas. Belo Horizonte, Brazil (Nova Econ./Belo Horizonte)

Novos Estudos CEBRAP. Centro Brasileiro de Análise e Planejamento. São Paulo (Novos Estud. CEBRAP)

NWIG: New West Indian Guide/Nieuwe West Indische Gids. Royal Institute of Linguistics and Anthropology, KITLV Press. Leiden, The Netherlands (NWIG)

Outre-mers: revue d'histoire. Société française d'histoire d'outre-mer. Paris (Outre-mers)

Pesquisas Antropologia. Instituto Anchietano de Pesquisas. São Leopoldo, Brazil (Pesqui. Antropol.)

Politeia. Univ. Central de Venezuela, Instituto de Estudios Políticos. Caracas (Politeia/Caracas)

Popular Music and Society. Taylor & Francis Group, Routledge Press. London; New York (Pop. Music Soc.)

Population and Development Review. Population Council. New York (Popul. Dev. Rev.)

Procesos. Corporación Editora Nacional. Quito (Procesos/Quito)

Procesos Históricos. Univ. de los Andes. Merida, Venezuela (Procesos Hist.)

Prohistoria. Manuel Suárez Editor. Rosario, Argentina (Prohistoria/Rosario)

Radical History Review. Duke Univ. Press. Durham, N.C (Radic. Hist. Rev.)

Realidad: Revista de Ciencias Sociales y Humanidades. Univ. Centroamericana José Simeón Cañas. San Salvador (Realidad/San Salvador)

Reflexão. Instituto de Filosofia, Pontifícia Univ. Católica de Campinas. Campinas, Brazil (Reflexão/Campinas)

Relaciones Internacionales. UNAM, Facultad de Ciencias Políticas y Sociales, Coordinación de Relaciones Internacionales. México (Relac. Int./México)

Res. Harvard Univ., Peabody Museum of Archaeology and Ethnology. Cambridge, Mass (Res/Cambridge)

Resumen, Pintores y Pintura Mexicana. Promoción de Arte Mexicano. México (Resumen)

Review: Latin American Literature and Arts. The Americas Society. New York (Review/New York)

Revista Brasileira de História. Associação Nacional de História. São Paulo (Rev. Bras. Hist./São Paulo)

Revista Centroamericana de Economía. Univ. Nacional Autónoma de Honduras, Programa de Postgrado Centroamericano en Economía y Planificación del Desarrollo. Tegucigalpa (Rev. Centroam. Econ.)

Revista Chilena de Historia y Geografía. Sociedad Chilena de Historia y Geografía. Santiago (Rev. Chil. Hist. Geogr.)

Revista Complutense de Historia de América. Univ. Complutense de Madrid, Facultad de Geografía e Historia, Depto. de Historia de América I. Madrid (Rev. Complut. Hist. Am.)

Revista de Antropologia. Univ. de São Paulo, Faculdade de Filosofia, Letras e Ciências Humanas, Depto. de Antropologia. São Paulo (Rev. Antropol./São Paulo)

Revista de Dialectología y Tradiciones Populares. Consejo Superior de Investigaciones Científicas, Instituto de Filología. Madrid (Rev. Dialectolog. Tradic. Pop.)

Revista de Estudios Políticos. Centro de Estudios Políticos y Constitucionales. Madrid (Rev. Estud. Polít.)

Revista de Filosofía. Univ. de Chile, Depto. de Filosofía y Humanidades. Santiago (Rev. Filos./Santiago)

Revista de Filosofía. Univ. de Zulia, Facultad de Humanidades y Educación. Maracaibo, Venezuela (Rev. Filos./Maracaibo)

Revista de Filosofía de la Universidad de Costa Rica. Editorial de la Univ. de Costa Rica. San José (Rev. Filos. Univ. Costa Rica)

Revista de Historia. Univ. Nacional, Escuela de Historia. Heredia, Costa Rica; Univ. de Costa Rica, Centro de Investigaciones Históricas de América Central. San José (Rev. Hist./Heredia)

Revista de História. Univ. de São Paulo, Faculdade de Filosofia, Letras e Ciências Humanas, Depto. de História. São Paulo (Rev. Hist./São Paulo)

Revista de Historia Americana y Argentina. Univ. Nacional de Cuyo, Instituto de Historia. Mendoza, Argentina (Rev. Hist. Am. Argent.)

Revista de Historia de América. Instituto Panamericano de Geografía e Historia. Comisión de Historia. México (Rev. Hist. Am./México)

Revista de Historia Militar. Servicio Histórico Militar. Madrid (Rev. Hist. Mil.)

Revista de Historia Naval. Ministerio de Defensa, Armada Española, Instituto de Historia y Cultura Naval. Madrid (Rev. Hist. Nav.)

Revista de Humanidades: Tecnológico de Monterrey. Depto. de Humanidades, División de Ciencias y Humanidades, Instituto Tecnológico y de Estudios Superiores de Monterrey. Monterrey, Mexico (Rev. Humanid./Monterrey)

Revista de Indias. Consejo Superior de Investigaciones Científicas, Instituto de Historia, Depto. de Historia de América. Madrid (Rev. Indias)

Revista de Teatro. Sociedade Brasileira de Autores Teatrais. Rio de Janeiro (Rev. Teatro/Rio de Janeiro)

Revista del Archivo Histórico del Guayas.
Archivo Histórico del Guayas. Guayaquil,
Ecuador (Rev. Arch. Hist. Guayas)
Revista del Archivo Nacional. San José (Rev.
Arch. Nac./San José)
**Revista do Instituto Histórico e Geográfico
de Sergipe.** Instituto Histórico e Geográ-
fico de Sergipe. Aracajú, Brazil (Rev. Inst.
Hist. Geogr. Sergipe)
**Revista do Instituto Histórico e Geográfico
do Rio Grande do Sul.** Instituto Histórico
e Geográfico do Rio Grande do Sul. Porto
Alegre, Brazil (Rev. Inst. Hist. Geogr. Rio
Gd. Sul)
Revista Eletrônica de Musicologia. Univ.
Federal do Paraná, Depto. de Artes. Curi-
tiba, Brazil [http://www.humanas.ufpr
.br/rem/] (Rev. Eletrôn. Musicol.)
**Revista Española de Antropología Ame-
ricana.** Univ. Complutense de Madrid,
Facultad de Geografia e Historia, Depto.
de Historia de América II (Antropología
de América). Madrid (Rev. Esp. Antropol.
Am.)
**Revista Europea de Estudios Latinoameri-
canos y del Caribe = European Review of
Latin American and Caribbean Studies.**
Center for Latin American Research and
Documentation = Centro de Estudios
y Documentación Latinoamericanos.
Amsterdam (Rev. Eur. Estud. Latinoam.
Caribe)
**Revista Mexicana de Ciencias Políticas y
Sociales.** UNAM, Facultad de Ciencias
Políticas y Sociales. México (Rev. Mex.
Cienc. Polít. Soc.)
Revista Mexicana de Sociología. UNAM,
Instituto de Investigaciones Sociales.
México (Rev. Mex. Sociol.)
Revista Musical Chilena. Univ. de Chile,
Facultad de Artes, Sección de Musicolo-
gía. Santiago (Rev. Music. Chil.)
**Revue d'histoire moderne et contempora-
ine.** Société d'histoire moderne. Paris
(Rev. hist. mod. contemp.)
Science & Society. S & S Quarterly, Inc.;
Guildford Publications. New York (Sci.
Soc.)
**Secuencia: Revista de Historia y Ciencias
Sociales.** Instituto de Investigacio-
nes Dr. José María Luis Mora. México
(Secuencia/México)
Signos Históricos. Univ. Autónoma Metro-
politana, División de Ciencias Sociales

y Humanidades, Depto. de Filosofía.
México (Signos Hist.)
Síntese: Revista de Filosofia. Companhia
de Jesus, Centro de Estudios Superiores,
Faculdade de Filosofia. Belo Horizonte,
Brazil (Síntese/Belo Horizonte)
Slavery and Abolition. Taylor and Francis.
Oxon, England (Slavery Abolit.)
Social Text. Duke Univ. Press. Durham,
N.C (Soc. Text)
Socialismo y Participación. Centro de Es-
tudios para el Desarrollo y Participación.
Lima (Social. Particip.)
Solar: Revista de Filosofía Iberoamericana.
Fondo Editorial de la Univ. Nacional
Mayor de San Marcos: Fondo Editorial
de la Univ. Científica del Sur: Embajada
de España en el Perú, Centro Cultural de
España. Lima (Solar)
Southern Quarterly. Univ. of Southern Mis-
sissippi. Hattiesburg, Miss (South. Q.)
Tabula Rasa. Univ. Colegio Mayor de Cun-
dinamarca. Bogotá (Tabula Rasa)
Tareas. Centro de Estudios Latinoamerica-
nos. Panamá (Tareas)
Td: Temas y Debates. Univ. Nacional de
Rosario, Facultad de Ciencia Política
y Relaciones Internacionales. Rosario,
Argentina (Td Temas Debates)
Temas de Historia Argentina y Americana.
Pontificia Univ. Católica Argentina,
Facultad de Filosof ía y Letras, Centro de
Historia Argentina y Americana. Buenos
Aires (Temas Hist. Argent. Am.)
Tempo Social: Revista de Sociologia da USP.
Univ. de São Paulo, Faculdade de Filosofia,
Letras e Ciências Humanas, Depto. de So-
ciologia. São Paulo (Tempo Soc./São Paulo)
Tierra Firme. Editorial Tierra Firme. Cara-
cas (Tierra Firme/Caracas)
**T'inkazos: Revista Boliviana de Ciencias
Sociales.** Programa de Investigación
Estratégica en Bolivia. La Paz (T'inkazos)
Trans. Sociedad de Etnomusicología. Barce-
lona; www.sibetrans.com/trans/ (Trans
(online))
Translation Review. Univ. of Texas at Dal-
las, Center for Translation Studies. Rich-
ardson (Transl. Rev.)
Translator. St. Jerome Pub. Manchester,
England (Translator/Manchester)
Tzintzun: Revista de Estudios Históricos.
Univ. de Michoacán de San Nicolas de
Hidalgo. Morelia, Mexico (Tzintzun)

Ultramarines: bulletin des Amis del archives d'outre-mer. Univ. de Provence, Institut d'histoire del pays d'outre-mer; Amis des archives d'outre-mer. Aix-en-Provence, France (Ultramarines/Aix-en-Provence)

Universum. Univ. de Talca. Talca, Chile (Universum/Talca)

Utopía y Praxis Latinoamericana. Univ. de Zulia, Facultad de Ciencias Económicas y Sociales. Maracaibo, Venezuela (Utop. Prax. Latinoam.)

Variaciones Borges. Aarhus Univ., Borges Center, Romansk institut. Aarhus, Denmark (Var. Borges)

The Western Historical Quarterly. Western History Assn.; Utah State Univ. Logan, Utah (West. Hist. Q.)

The William and Mary Quarterly. College of William and Mary. Williamsburg, Va (William Mary Q.)

World of Music. Department of Ethnomusicology, Otto-Friedrich-University of Bamberg, Germany (World Music (Wilhelmshaven))

Yaxkin. Instituto Hondureño de Antropología e Historia. Tegucigalpa (Yaxkin/Tegucigalpa)

Zoetrope: Short Stories. AZX Publications. New York (Zoetrope)

ABBREVIATION LIST OF JOURNALS INDEXED

For journal titles listed by full title, see *Title List of Journals Indexed*, p. 729.

Actual/Mérida. Actual. Univ. de Los Andes, Dirección General de Cultura y Extensión. Mérida, Venezuela

Aisthesis/Santiago. Aisthesis. Instituto de Estética, Facultad de Filosofía, Pontificia Univ. Católica de Chile. Santiago

Allpanchis/Cuzco. Allpanchis. Instituto de Pastoral Andina. Cuzco, Peru

Am. Hist. Rev. The American Historical Review. Indiana Univ. at Bloomington. Bloomington, Ind

Am. Indian Q. American Indian Quarterly. Univ. of Nebraska Press. Lincoln, Neb

Am. Lat. Hoy/Salamanca. América Latina Hoy: Revista de Ciencias Sociales. Univ. de Salamanca, Instituto de Estudios de Iberoamérica y Portugal. Salamanca, Spain

Americas/Washington. The Americas: A Quarterly Review of Inter-American Cultural History. Catholic Univ. of America, Academy of American Franciscan History; Catholic Univ. of America Press. Washington, D.C

An. Inst. Invest. Estét. Anales del Instituto de Investigaciones Estéticas. UNAM, Instituto de Investigaciones Estéticas. México

An. Mus. Hist. Nac. Anais do Museu Histórico Nacional. Museu Histórico Nacional, Instituto do Patrimônio Histórico e Artístico Nacional, Ministério da Cultura. Rio de Janeiro

An. Mus. Paul. Anais do Museu Paulista: História e Cultura Material. Museu Paulista. São Paulo

Anc. Mesoam. Ancient Mesoamerica. Cambridge Univ. Press. Cambridge, England; New York

ANDES Antropol. Hist. ANDES: Antropología e Historia. Univ. Nacional de Salta, Facultad de Humanidades, Centro Promocional de las Investigaciones en Historia y Antropología. Salta, Argentina

Ann. hist. Révolut. fr. Annales historiques de la Révolution française. Société des Études Robespierristes. Paris

Ann. hist. sci. soc. Annales: histoire, sciences sociales. L'École des Hautes Études en Sciences Sociales. Paris

Anthropol. Dep. Cienc. Soc. Anthropologica del Departamento de Ciencias Sociales. Pontificia Univ. Católica del Perú, Depto. de Ciencias Sociales. Lima

Antiquity/Cambridge. Antiquity. Antiquity Publications Ltd. Cambridge, England

Antropol. Hist. Guatem. Antropología e Historia de Guatemala. Instituto de Antropología e Historia de Guatemala. Guatemala

Anu. Estud. Am. Anuario de Estudios Americanos. Consejo Superior de Investigaciones Científicas, Escuela de Estudios Hispano-Americanos. Sevilla, Spain

Anu. Estud. Boliv. Arch. Bibliogr. Anuario de Estudios Bolivianos, Archivísticos y Bibliográficos. Ediciones Archivo y Biblioteca Nacionales de Bolivia. Sucre, Bolivia

Anu. Estud. Centroam. Anuario de Estudios Centroamericanos. Univ. de Costa Rica. San José

Anu. IEHS. Anuario IEHS. Univ. Nacional del Centro de la Provincia de Buenos Aires, Facultad de Ciencias Humanas, Instituto de Estudios Histórico-Sociales. Tandil, Argentina

Anu. Inst. Hist. Argent. Anuario del Instituto de Historia Argentina. Editorial de la Univ. Nacional de La Plata. La Plata, Argentina

Apunt. Filos. Apuntes Filosóficos. Univ. Central de Venezuela, Escuela de Filosofía. Caracas

Apunt. Invest. CECYP. Apuntes de Investigación del CECYP. Centro de Estudios en Cultura y Política, Fundación del Sur. Buenos Aires

Art Bull. The Art Bulletin. College Art Assn. of America. New York

Art J. Art Journal. The College Art Assn. New York

Atenea/Concepción. Atenea. Univ. de Concepción. Concepción, Chile

Aufgabe. Aufgabe. Litmus Press. Provincetown, Mass

Black Music Res. J. Black Music Research Journal. Fisk Univ., Institute for Research in Black American Music. Nashville, Tenn

Bol. Acad. Nac. Hist./Caracas. Boletín de la Academia Nacional de la Historia. Caracas

Bol. Hist. Antig. Boletín de Historia y Antigüedades. Academia Colombiana de Historia. Bogotá

Bol. Lima. Boletín de Lima: Revista Cultural Científica. Asociación Cultural Boletín de Lima A.C. Lima

Bol. Mus. Chil. Arte Precolomb. Boletín del Museo Chileno de Arte Precolombino. Santiago, Chile

Bol. Música/Habana. Boletín Música. Casa de las Américas. La Habana

Boletín/México. Boletín del Fideicomiso Archivos Plutarco Elías Calles y Fernando Torreblanca. México

Bull. Inst. fr. étud. andin. Bulletin de l'Institut français d'études andines. Lima

Bull. Lat. Am. Res. Bulletin of Latin American Research. Blackwell Publishers. Oxford, England; Malden, Mass

Bus. Hist. Rev./Boston. Business History Review. Harvard Univ., Graduate School of Business Administration. Boston, Mass

Cah. Am. lat. Cahiers des Amériques latines. Univ. de la Sorbonne nouvelle—Paris III, Institut des haute études de l'Amérique latine. Paris

Caribb. Q./Mona. Caribbean Quarterly: CQ. Univ. of the West Indies, Vice Chancellery, Cultural Studies Initiative. Mona, Jamaica

Caribb. Stud. Caribbean Studies. Univ. of Puerto Rico, Institute of Caribbean Studies. Río Piedras, Puerto Rico

CLAHR. Colonial Latin American Historical Review. Univ. of New Mexico, Spanish Colonial Research Center. Albuquerque

CLC Web. CLC Web: Comparative Literature and Culture. Purdue Unversity Press, Purdue University, West Lafayette, IN

Colomb. Int. Colombia Internacional. Univ. de los Andes, Centro de Estudios Internacionales. Bogotá

Colon. Lat. Am. Rev. Colonial Latin American Review. City Univ. of New York (CUNY), City College, Dept. of Foreign Languages and Literatures, Simon H. Rifkind Center for the Humanities. New York; Carfax Publishing, Taylor & Francis, Ltd. Abingdon, England

Comp. Lit. Comparative Literature. Univ. of Oregon. Eugene, Ore

Comp. Stud. Soc. Hist. Comparative Studies in Society and History. Society for the

Comparative Study of Society and History; Cambridge Univ. Press. London

Cuad. Am./México. Cuadernos Americanos. UNAM. México

Cuad. Antropol./San José. Cuadernos de Antropología. Univ. de Costa Rica, Depto. de Antropología, Laboratorio de Etnología. San José

Cuad. Econ./Bogotá. Cuadernos de Economía. Univ. Nacional de Colombia, Facultad de Ciencias Económicas, Centro de Investigaciones para el Desarrollo. Bogotá

Cuad. Pensam. Latinoam. Cuadernos del Pensamiento Latinoamericano. Univ. de Playa Ancha de Ciencias de la Educación. Centro de Estudios del Pensamiento Latinoamericano (CEPLA). Valparaíso, Chile

Cuad. Sociol./Quito. Cuadernos Sociológicos. Depto. de Sociología y Ciencias Políticas, Pontificia Univ. Católica del Ecuador. Quito

Curr. Anthropol. Current Anthropology. Univ. of Chicago Press. Chicago, Ill

Cuyo/Mendoza. Cuyo: Anuario de Filosofía Argentina y Americana. Univ. Nacional de Cuyo, Instituto de Filosofía, Sección de Historia del Pensamiento Argentino. Mendoza, Argentina

Desacatos. Desacatos. CIESAS, Centro de Investigaciones y Estudios Superiores en Antropología Social. México

Early Amer. Stud. Early American Studies. McNeil Center for Early American Studies. Philadelphia, Pa

Early Music. Early Music. Oxford Univ. Press. London

Ecuad. Debate. Ecuador Debate. Centro Andino de Acción Popular. Quito

Eighteenth-Century Stud. Eighteenth-Century Studies. Johns Hopkins Univ. Press for the American Society for Eighteenth-Century Studies. Baltimore, Md

Encuentro Cult. Cuba. Encuentro de la Cultura Cubana. Asociación Encuentro de la Cultura Cubana. Madrid

Entrepasados/Buenos Aires. Entrepasados: Revista de Historia. Buenos Aires

Environ. Plann. D Soc. Space. Environment and Planning: D, Society & Space. Pion Ltd. London

EspacioTiempo. EspacioTiempo: Revista Latinoamericana de Ciencias Sociales y Humanidades. Univ. Autónoma de San Luis Potosi. San Luis Potosi, Mexico

Estud. Atacameños. Estudios Atacameños. Univ. del Norte, Museo de Arqueología. San Pedro de Atacama, Chile

Estud. Av. Estudos Avançados. Univ. de São Paulo, Instituto de Estudos Avançados. São Paulo

Estud. Cult. Maya. Estudios de Cultura Maya. UNAM, Instituto de Investigaciones Filológicas, Centro de Estudios Mayas. México

Estud. Cult. Náhuatl. Estudios de Cultura Náhuatl. UNAM, Instituto de Investigaciones Históricas. México

Estud. Filos. Hist. Let. Estudios: Filosofía, Historia, Letras. Instituto Tecnológico Autónomo de México, División Académica de Estudios Generales y Estudios Internacionales, Depto. Académico de Estudios Generales. México

Estud. Filos. Práct. Hist. Ideas. Estudios, Filosofía Práctica e Historia de las Ideas. Instituto de Ciencias Humanas, Sociales y Ambientales (INCIHUSA), CRICYT. Mendoza, Argentina

Estud. Hist. Mod. Contemp. Méx. Estudios de Historia Moderna y Contemporánea de México. UNAM, Instituto de Investigaciones Históricas. México

Estud. Hist. Novohisp. Estudios de Historia Novohispana. UNAM, Instituto de Investigaciones Históricas. México

Estud. Hist./Rio de Janeiro. Estudos Históricos. Fundação Getulio Vargas, Centro de Pesquisa e Documentação de História Contemporânea do Brasil. Rio de Janeiro

Estud. Ibero-Am./Porto Alegre. Estudos Ibero-Americanos. Pontificia Univ. Católica do Rio Grande do Sul, Faculdade de Filosofia e Ciências Humanas, Depto. de História, Programa Pós-Graduação em História. Porto Alegre, Brazil

Estud. Interdiscipl. Am. Lat. Carib. Estudios Interdisciplinarios de América Latina y el Caribe: E.I.A.L. Univ. de Tel Aviv, Escuela de Historia. Tel Aviv

Estud. Migr. Latinoam. Estudios Migratorios Latinoamericanos. Centro de Estudios Migratorios Latinoamericanos. Buenos Aires

Estud. Parag. Estudios Paraguayos. Univ. Católica Nuestra Señora de la Asunción. Asunción

Estud. Polít./México. Estudios Políticos: Revista de Ciencias Políticas y Administración Pública. UNAM, Facultad de Ciencias Políticas y Sociales. México

Estud. Soc./Santa Fe. Estudios Sociales: Revista Universitaria Semestral. Univ. Nacional del Litoral, Secretaría de Extensión, Centro de Publicaciones. Santa Fe, Argentina

Estud. Sociol./México. Estudios Sociológicos. El Colegio de México, Centro de Estudios Sociológicos. México

Ethnohistory/Columbus. Ethnohistory: The Bulletin of the Ohio Valley Historic Indian Conference. American Society for Ethnohistory. Columbus, Ohio

Ethnomusic. Forum. Ethnomusicology Forum. Routledge Taylor & Francis Group. Basingstoke, England

Ethnomusicology. Ethnomusicology. Univ. of Illinois Press. Champaign, Ill

Explor. Renaissance Cult. Explorations in Renaissance Culture. South Central Renaissance Conference. Memphis, Tenn

Foro Int./México. Foro Internacional. El Colegio de México, Centro de Estudios Internacionales. México

Fr. Hist. Stud. French Historical Studies. Society for French Historical Studies. Raleigh, N.C

Front. Norte. Frontera Norte. El Colegio de la Frontera Norte. Tijuana, Mexico

Gend. Hist. Gender & History. Blackwell Publishers. Abingdon, England; Williston, Vt

Guaraguao/Barcelona. Guaraguao: Revista de Cultura Latinoamericano. Univ. Autónoma de Barcelona, Centro de Estudios y Cooperación para América Latina. Barcelona

HAHR. Hispanic American Historical Review. Duke Univ. Press. Durham, N.C

Harper's. Harper's. Harper's Magazine Foundation, New York, NY

Hispania/Madrid. Hispania. Consejo Superior de Investigaciones Científicas, Instituto de Historia, Depto. de Medieval Moderna y Contemporánea. Madrid

Hist. Ciênc. Saúde Manguinhos. História Ciências Saúde: Manguinhos. Fundação Oswaldo Cruz, Casa de Oswaldo Cruz. Rio de Janeiro

Hist. Contemp. Historia Contemporánea. Univ. del País Vasco, Depto. de Historia Contemporánea. Bilbao, Spain

Hist. Crít./Bogotá. Historia Crítica. Univ. de los Andes, Facultad de Ciencias Sociales, Depto. de Historia. Bogotá

Hist. écon. soc. Histoire, économie et sociéte. Editions C.D.U. et S.E.D.E.S. Paris

Hist. Fam. The History of the Family: An International Quarterly. JAI Press Inc. Greenwich, Conn

Hist. Graf./México. Historia y Grafía. Univ. Iberoamericana, Depto. de Historia. México

Hist. Mex./México. Historia Mexicana. El Colegio de México, Centro de Estudios Históricos. México

Hist. Polít. Historia y Política. Univ. Complutense de Madrid, Depto. de Historia del Pensamiento y de los Movimientos Sociales y Políticos; Univ. Nacional de Educación a Distancia, Depto. de Historia Social y del Pensamiento Político. Madrid

Hist. Quest. Debates. História: Questões e Debates. Univ. Federal do Paraná, Programa de Pós-Graduação em História, Associação Paraense de História. Curitiba, Brazil

Hist. Relig./Chicago. History of Religions. Univ. of Chicago. Chicago, Ill

Hist. Soc./Medellín. Historia y Sociedad. Univ. Nacional de Colombia—Sede Medellín, Facultad de Ciencias Humanas y Económicas, Depto. de Historia. Medellín, Colombia

Hist. Workshop J. History Workshop Journal. Oxford Univ. Press. Oxford, England

Historia/Santiago. Historia. Pontificia Univ. Católica de Chile, Facultad de Historia, Geografia y Ciencia Política, Instituto de Historia. Santiago

História/São Paulo. História. Univ. Estadual Paulista, Fundação para o Desenvolvimento, Instituto de Letras, História e Psicologia. São Paulo

Humanitas/Monterrey. Humanitas: Anuario del Centro de Estudios Humanísticos. Univ. Autónoma de Nuevo León, Secretaría de Extensión y Cultura, Centro de Estudios Humanísticos. Monterrey, Mexico

Iberoamericana/Madrid. Iberoamericana. Madrid

Iberoamericana/Tokyo. Iberoamericana = Ibero Amerika Kenkyu. Univ. Sofia, Instituto Iberoamericano. Tokyo

Illes Imp. Illes i imperis = Islas e imperios = Islands and empires. Univ. Pompeu Fabra, Dept. d'Humanitats, Institut Universitari d'Història Jaume Vicens Vives. Barcelona

Int. Hist. Rev./Burnaby. The International History Review. Simon Fraser Univ., Dept. of History. Burnaby, British Columbia

Inter-Am. Music Rev. Inter-American Music Review. Theodore Front Musical Literature, Inc. Van Nuys, Calif

Investig. Soc./San Marcos. Investigaciones Sociales: Revista del Instituto de Investigaciones Histórico Sociales. Univ. Nacional Mayor de San Marcos, Facultad de Ciencias Sociales. Lima

Iztapalapa/México. Iztapalapa. Univ. Autónoma Metropolitana—Unidad Iztapalapa, División de Ciencias Sociales y Humanidades. México

J. Anthropol. Archaeol. Journal of Anthropological Archaeology. Academic Press. New York

J. Archaeol. Sci. Journal of Archaeological Science. Academic Press. New York

J. Bahamas Hist. Soc. Journal of the Bahamas Historical Society. Bahamas Historical Society. Nassau, Bahamas

J. Caribb. Hist. The Journal of Caribbean History. Univ. of the West Indies Press; Univ. of the West Indies, Dept. of History. Mona, Jamaica

J. Church State. Journal of Church and State. Baylor Univ., J.M. Dawson Studies in Church and State. Waco, Tex

J. Econ. Hist. The Journal of Economic History. Economic History Assn.; Univ. of Arizona. Tucson

J. Hist. Ideas. Journal of the History of Ideas. Johns Hopkins Univ. Press. Baltimore, Md

J. Hist. Sex. Journal of the History of Sexuality. Univ. of Chicago Press. Chicago, Ill

J. Interdiscip. Hist. The Journal of Interdisciplinary History. The MIT Press. Cambridge, Mass

J. Lat. Am. Cult. Stud. Journal of Latin American Cultural Studies. Carfax Publishing. Abingdon, England

J. Lat. Am. Geogr. Journal of Latin American Geography. Conference of Latin Americanist Geographers. Tucson, Ariz

J. Lat. Am. Stud. Journal of Latin American Studies. Cambridge Univ. Press. Cambridge, England

J. Royal Anthropol. Inst. The Journal of the Royal Anthropological Institute. London

J. Soc. Hist. Journal of Social History. George Mason Univ. Press. Fairfax, Va

J. Southwest. Journal of the Southwest. Univ. of Arizona, Southwest Center. Tucson

J. World Hist. Journal of World History. World History Assn.; Univ. of Hawaii Press. Honolulu

LARR. Latin American Research Review. Latin American Studies Assn.; Univ. of Texas Press. Austin

Lat. Am. Antiq. Latin American Antiquity. Society for American Archaeology. Washington, D.C

Lat. Am. Caribb. Ethn. Stud. Latin American and Caribbean Ethnic Studies. Taylor & Francis. Colchester, England

Lat. Am. Music Rev. Latin American Music Review. Revista de Música Latinoamericana. Univ. of Texas Press. Austin

Lat. Am. Perspect. Latin American Perspectives. Sage Publications, Inc. Thousand Oaks, Calif

Lat. Am. Polit. Soc. Latin American Politics and Society. Univ. of Miami, School of Interamerican Studies. Coral Gables, Fla

Lect. Econ. Lecturas de Economía. Univ. de Antioquia, Facultad de Ciencias Económicas, Depto. de Economía, Centro de Investigaciones Económicas. Medellín, Colombia

Lit. Mex. Literatura Mexicana. UNAM, Instituto de Investigaciones Filológicas, Centro de Estudios Literarios. México

Luso-Braz. Rev. Luso-Brazilian Review. Univ. of Wisconsin Press. Madison

Maguaré/Bogotá. Maguaré. Univ. Nacional de Colombia, Depto. de Antropología. Bogotá

Memorias. Memorias: Revista Digital de Historia y Arqueología desde el Caribe. Univ. del Norte. Colombia

Mesoamérica/Antigua. Mesoamérica. Plumsock Mesoamerican Studies. South Woodstock, Vt.; Centro de Investigaciones Regionales de Mesoamérica. Antigua, Guatemala

Mex. Stud. Mexican Studies/Estudios Mexicanos. Univ. of California Press. Berkeley

Music Polit. Music & Politics. Univ. of California, Santa Barbara. Santa Barbara, Calif

Music Q. The Musical Quarterly. G. Schirmer. New York

Musicorum. Musicorum. Universitaire François-Rabelais. Tours, France

N.M. Hist. Rev. New Mexico Historical Review. Univ. of New Mexico; Historical Society of New Mexico. Albuquerque

Nombres/Córdoba. Nombres. Univ. Nacional de Córdoba, Facultad de Filosofia y Humanidades, Centro de Investigaciones, Area de Filosofia. Córdoba, Argentina

Nova Econ./Belo Horizonte. Nova Economia. Univ. Federal de Minas Gerais, Faculdade de Ciências Econômicas, Depto. de Ciências Econômicas. Belo Horizonte, Brazil

Novos Estud. CEBRAP. Novos Estudos CEBRAP. Centro Brasileiro de Análise e Planejamento. São Paulo

NWIG. NWIG: New West Indian Guide/ Nieuwe West Indische Gids. Royal Institute of Linguistics and Anthropology, KITLV Press. Leiden, The Netherlands

N.Y. Times Mag. The New York Times Magazine. New York

Outre-mers. Outre-mers: revue d'histoire. Société française d'histoire d'outre-mer. Paris

Pesqui. Antropol. Pesquisas Antropologia. Instituto Anchietano de Pesquisas. São Leopoldo, Brazil

Politeia/Caracas. Politeia. Univ. Central de Venezuela, Instituto de Estudios Políticos. Caracas

Pop. Music Soc. Popular Music and Society. Taylor & Francis Group, Routledge Press. London; New York

Popul. Dev. Rev. Population and Development Review. Population Council. New York

Procesos Hist. Procesos Históricos. Univ. de los Andes. Merida, Venezuela

Procesos/Quito. Procesos. Corporación Editora Nacional. Quito

Prohistoria/Rosario. Prohistoria. Manuel Suárez Editor. Rosario, Argentina

Radic. Hist. Rev. Radical History Review. Duke Univ. Press. Durham, N.C

Realidad/San Salvador. Realidad: Revista de Ciencias Sociales y Humanidades. Univ. Centroamericana José Simeón Cañas. San Salvador

Reflexão/Campinas. Reflexão. Instituto de Filosofia, Pontifícia Univ. Católica de Campinas. Campinas, Brazil

Relac. Int./México. Relaciones Internacionales. UNAM, Facultad de Ciencias Políticas y Sociales, Coordinación de Relaciones Internacionales. México

Res/Cambridge. Res. Harvard Univ., Peabody Museum of Archaeology and Ethnology. Cambridge, Mass

Resumen. Resumen, Pintores y Pintura Mexicana. Promoción de Arte Mexicano. México

Rev. Antropol./São Paulo. Revista de Antropologia. Univ. de São Paulo, Faculdade de Filosofia, Letras e Ciências Humanas, Depto. de Antropologia. São Paulo

Rev. Arch. Hist. Guayas. Revista del Archivo Histórico del Guayas. Archivo Histórico del Guayas. Guayaquil, Ecuador

Rev. Arch. Nac./San José. Revista del Archivo Nacional. San José

Rev. Bras. Hist./São Paulo. Revista Brasileira de História. Associação Nacional de História. São Paulo

Rev. Centroam. Econ. Revista Centroamericana de Economía. Univ. Nacional Autónoma de Honduras, Programa de Postgrado Centroamericano en Economía y Planificación del Desarrollo. Tegucigalpa

Rev. Chil. Hist. Geogr. Revista Chilena de Historia y Geografía. Sociedad Chilena de Historia y Geografía. Santiago

Rev. Complut. Hist. Am. Revista Complutense de Historia de América. Univ. Complutense de Madrid, Facultad de Geografía e Historia, Depto. de Historia de América I. Madrid

Rev. Dialectolog. Tradic. Pop. Revista de Dialectología y Tradiciones Populares. Consejo Superior de Investigaciones Científicas, Instituto de Filología. Madrid

Rev. Eletrôn. Musicol. Revista Eletrônica de Musicologia. Univ. Federal do Paraná, Depto. de Artes. Curitiba, Brazil [http://www.humanas.ufpr.br/rem/]

Rev. Esp. Antropol. Am. Revista Española de Antropología Americana. Univ. Complutense de Madrid, Facultad de Geografía e Historia, Depto. de Historia de América II (Antropología de América). Madrid

Rev. Estud. Polít. Revista de Estudios Políticos. Centro de Estudios Políticos y Constitucionales. Madrid

Rev. Eur. Estud. Latinoam. Caribe. Revista Europea de Estudios Latinoamericanos y del Caribe = European Review of Latin American and Caribbean Studies. Center for Latin American Research and Documentation = Centro de Estudios y Documentación Latinoamericanos. Amsterdam

Rev. Filos./Maracaibo. Revista de Filosofía. Univ. de Zulia, Facultad de Humanidades y Educación. Maracaibo, Venezuela

Rev. Filos./Santiago. Revista de Filosofía. Univ. de Chile, Depto. de Filosofía y Humanidades. Santiago

Rev. Filos. Univ. Costa Rica. Revista de Filosofía de la Universidad de Costa Rica. Editorial de la Univ. de Costa Rica. San José

Rev. Hist. Am. Argent. Revista de Historia Americana y Argentina. Univ. Nacional de Cuyo, Instituto de Historia. Mendoza, Argentina

Rev. Hist. Am./México. Revista de Historia de América. Instituto Panamericano de Geografía e Historia. Comisión de Historia. México

Rev. Hist./Heredia. Revista de Historia. Univ. Nacional, Escuela de Historia. Heredia, Costa Rica; Univ. de Costa Rica, Centro de Investigaciones Históricas de América Central. San José

Rev. Hist. Mil. Revista de Historia Militar. Servicio Histórico Militar. Madrid

Rev. hist. mod. contemp. Revue d'histoire moderne et contemporaine. Société d'histoire moderne. Paris

Rev. Hist. Nav. Revista de Historia Naval. Ministerio de Defensa, Armada Española, Instituto de Historia y Cultura Naval. Madrid

Rev. Hist./São Paulo. Revista de História. Univ. de São Paulo, Faculdade de Filosofia, Letras e Ciências Humanas, Depto. de História. São Paulo

Rev. Humanid./Monterrey. Revista de Humanidades: Tecnológico de Monterrey. Depto. de Humanidades, División de Cien-

cias y Humanidades, Instituto Tecnológico y de Estudios Superiores de Monterrey. Monterrey, Mexico

Rev. Indias. Revista de Indias. Consejo Superior de Investigaciones Científicas, Instituto de Historia, Depto. de Historia de América. Madrid

Rev. Inst. Hist. Geogr. Rio Gd. Sul. Revista do Instituto Histórico e Geográfico do Rio Grande do Sul. Instituto Histórico e Geográfico do Rio Grande do Sul. Porto Alegre, Brazil

Rev. Inst. Hist. Geogr. Sergipe. Revista do Instituto Histórico e Geográfico de Sergipe. Instituto Histórico e Geográfico de Sergipe. Aracajú, Brazil

Rev. Mex. Cienc. Polít. Soc. Revista Mexicana de Ciencias Políticas y Sociales. UNAM, Facultad de Ciencias Políticas y Sociales. México

Rev. Mex. Sociol. Revista Mexicana de Sociología. UNAM, Instituto de Investigaciones Sociales. México

Rev. Music. Chil. Revista Musical Chilena. Univ. de Chile, Facultad de Artes, Sección de Musicología. Santiago

Rev. Teatro/Rio de Janeiro. Revista de Teatro. Sociedade Brasileira de Autores Teatrais. Rio de Janeiro

Review/New York. Review: Latin American Literature and Arts. The Americas Society. New York

Sci. Soc. Science & Society. S & S Quarterly, Inc.; Guildford Publications. New York

Secuencia/México. Secuencia: Revista de Historia y Ciencias Sociales. Instituto de Investigaciones Dr. José María Luis Mora. México

Signos Hist. Signos Históricos. Univ. Autónoma Metropolitana, División de Ciencias Sociales y Humanidades, Depto. de Filosofía. México

Síntese/Belo Horizonte. Síntese: Revista de Filosofia. Companhia de Jesus, Centro de Estudios Superiores, Faculdade de Filosofia. Belo Horizonte, Brazil

Slavery Abolit. Slavery and Abolition. Taylor and Francis. Oxon, England

Soc. Text. Social Text. Duke Univ. Press. Durham, N.C

Social. Particip. Socialismo y Participación. Centro de Estudios para el Desarrollo y Participación. Lima

Solar. Solar: Revista de Filosofía Iberoamericana. Fondo Editorial de la Univ. Nacional Mayor de San Marcos: Fondo Editorial de la Univ. Científica del Sur: Embajada de España en el Perú, Centro Cultural de España. Lima

South. Q. Southern Quarterly. Univ. of Southern Mississippi. Hattiesburg, Miss

Tabula Rasa. Tabula Rasa. Univ. Colegio Mayor de Cundinamarca. Bogotá

Tareas. Tareas. Centro de Estudios Latinoamericanos. Panamá

Td Temas Debates. Td: Temas y Debates. Univ. Nacional de Rosario, Facultad de Ciencia Política y Relaciones Internacionales. Rosario, Argentina

Temas Hist. Argent. Am. Temas de Historia Argentina y Americana. Pontificia Univ. Católica Argentina, Facultad de Filosofía y Letras, Centro de Historia Argentina y Americana. Buenos Aires

Tempo Soc./São Paulo. Tempo Social: Revista de Sociologia da USP. Univ. de São Paulo, Faculdade de Filosofia, Letras e Ciências Humanas, Depto. de Sociologia. São Paulo

Tierra Firme/Caracas. Tierra Firme. Editorial Tierra Firme. Caracas

T'inkazos. T'inkazos: Revista Boliviana de Ciencias Sociales. Programa de Investigación Estratégica en Bolivia. La Paz

Trans (online). Trans. Sociedad de Etnomusicología. Barcelona; www.sibetrans.com/trans/

Transl. Rev. Translation Review. Univ. of Texas at Dallas, Center for Translation Studies. Richardson

Translator/Manchester. Translator. St. Jerome Pub. Manchester, England

Tzintzun. Tzintzun: Revista de Estudios Históricos. Univ. de Michoacán de San Nicolas de Hidalgo. Morelia, Mexico

Ultramarines/Aix-en-Provence. Ultramarines: bulletin des Amis del archives d'outre-mer. Univ. de Provence, Institut d'histoire del pays d'outre-mer; Amis des archives d'outre-mer. Aix-en-Provence, France

Universum/Talca. Universum. Univ. de Talca. Talca, Chile

Utop. Prax. Latinoam. Utopía y Praxis Latinoamericana. Univ. de Zulia, Facultad de Ciencias Económicas y Sociales. Maracaibo, Venezuela

Var. Borges. Variaciones Borges. Aarhus Univ., Borges Center, Romansk institut. Aarhus, Denmark

West. Hist. Q. The Western Historical Quarterly. Western History Assn.; Utah State Univ. Logan, Utah

William Mary Q. The William and Mary Quarterly. College of William and Mary. Williamsburg, Va

World Music (Wilhelmshaven). World of Music. Department of Ethnomusicology, Otto-Friedrich-University of Bamberg, Germany

Yaxkin/Tegucigalpa. Yaxkin. Instituto Hondureño de Antropología e Historia. Tegucigalpa

Zoetrope. Zoetrope: Short Stories. AZX Publications. New York

SUBJECT INDEX

Abolition (slavery), 411, 1227. Brazil, 2010, 2013, 2057, 2096, 3663. British Caribbean, 1246. Chile, 1479. France, 1240. French Caribbean, 1166, 1295. Haiti, 1243. Jamaica, 1246, 1282, 1297. Philosophy, 3631. Viceroyalty of New Spain, 766. *See Also* Freedmen; Slaves and Slavery.

Aboliton (slavery) Brazil, 2068.

Abortion Mexico, 669.

Abramo, Lívio, 142.

Abreu, Fernanda, 3452.

Abreu, José Antonio, 3389.

Academia Brasileira de Letras, 3683.

Academia de Guerra (Chile), 1799.

Acadians Colonial Administration, 1192. *See Also* Ethnic Groups and Ethnicity.

Ação Integralista Brasileira (political party), 2066.

Acapulco, Mexico (city) Tourism, 969.

Acción Democrática (Venezuela), 1578.

Acculturation, 64. Argentina, 1495, 1525. Colonial History, 360, 471, 477. French Guiana, 1165. Mexico, 212, 251. Viceroyalty of New Spain, 32, 221.

Achi (indigenous group) Guatemala, 3339.

Acosta Solís Misael, 1697.

Acre, Brazil (state) History, 2078.

Adolescents. *See* Youth.

African-Americans. *See* Blacks.

African Influences, 1912. Brazil, 3451. Colombia, 1387. Music, 3399. Uruguay, 3427. *See Also* Africans.

Africans, 444, 495, 1191, 1912. Brazil, 185, 1958. Colonial History, 769, 1405, 1435. Cuba, 1259. Cultural Identity, 1337. France, 1240. Historiography, 465. Medicine, 501. Mexico, 670. Peru, 1405. Relations with Europeans, 490. Sources, 468.

Afro-Americans. *See* Blacks.

Agrarian Reform. *See* Land Reform.

Agricultural Colonization, 670. Colombia, 1642. Paraguay, 1899. *See Also* Land Settlement.

Agricultural Development, 450. Chile, 1837. Mexico, 889, 922, 933. *See Also* Development Projects; Economic Development; Rural Development.

Agricultural Development Projects. *See* Development Projects.

Agricultural Industries. *See* Agroindustry.

Agricultural Labor Brazil, 2010. Costa Rica, 1138. French Caribbean, 1192. Mexican-American Border Region, 965.

Agricultural Policy Argentina, 409. Brazil, 409. Viceroyalty of New Spain, 790. *See Also* Land Reform.

Agriculture Brazil, 2009. Chile, 1828. Colonial History, 450. Mexico, 889.

Agripino, João, 2002.

Agroindustry, 615.

Aguascalientes, Mexico (state) Economic Development, 645. Railroads, 645.

Aguirre, Erick, 2264.

Aguirre, Juan Francisco, 1504.

Aguirre, Manuel Agustín, 3625.

Ahuacatlán, Mexico (city) Local History, 191.

Ainsa, Fernando, 3541, 3547.

Alberdi, Juan Bautista, 3689.

Alcohol and Alcoholism Argentina, 1509. Colonial History, 1509.

Alcoholism. *See* Alcohol and Alcoholism.

Alemão, Francisco Freire, 1962.

Alencar, José Martiniano de, 1979.

Alexis, Nord, 1260.

Alfaro, Ricardo Joaquín, 1134.

Alianza Popular Revolucionaria Americana. *See* APRA (Peru).

Allende Gossens, Salvador, 1829. Chile, 1832, 1854.

Almeida, Guilherme Pompeu de, 1924.

Alpha, 1674.

Alvarado Tezozómoc, Fernando, 252.

Amaral, Braz do, 1965.

Amazon Basin Colonization, 1753. Ecuador, 1699. Ethnic Groups and Ethnicity, 1911. Expeditions, 2018. History, 1911. Travel, 329.

Amazonas, Brazil (state) Description and Travel, 1928. History, 2063.

Atlántico, Colombia (dept.) Political History, 1630.
Audiencia of Charcas Archives, 1466. Independence Movements, 1474. Political Culture, 1461, 1471. Social Structure, 1465. State-Building, 1469.
Audiencia of Lima Literacy and Illiteracy, 312.
Audiencia of Nueva Granada Catholic Church, 1381. Colonial Administration, 1375. Indigenous/Non-Indigenous Relations, 1375. Indigenous Peoples, 1383. Slaves and Slavery, 1369, 1377–1378.
Audiencia of Quito Blacks, 1398. Boundaries, 1393. Cabildos, 1391. Discovery and Exploration, 1393–1394. Elites, 1393. Poverty, 1396. Race and Race Relations, 1396. Social Classes, 1396. Social Structure, 1396.
Augustinians Mexico, 39.
Authoritarianism Brazil, 2117. Venezuela, 1593. See Also Dictatorships.
Authors, 2351, 2947. Cuba, 1283. Nicaragua, 2239.
Autobiography, 3521.
Automobile Industry and Trade Brazil, 2135. See Also Transportation.
Autonomy Mexico, 1007. Paraguay, 1512. Puerto Rico, 3593. See Also Sovereignty.
Avendaño, Diego de, 3476–3477.
Aviation, 425. Mexico, 1012.
Ayllus Bolivia, 1790.
Aymara Indians. See Aymara (indigenous group).
Aymara (indigenous group) Biography, 3656. Bolivia, 355, 376. Colonial History, 1406. Ethnohistory, 1467.
Azevedo, Militão Augusto de, 168.
Azoreans Uruguay, 1501. See Also Portuguese Influences.
Aztecs Ceramics, 709. Codices, 240. Gender Relations, 216. Iconography, 41. Imperialism, 197, 257. Inter-Tribal Relations, 197. Kings and Rulers, 271. Land Settlement, 709. Manuscripts, 220. Migration, 2, 258. Nobility, 252. Obsidian, 709. Origins, 258. Philosophy, 201. Political Anthropology, 709. Political Conditions, 10. Political Systems, 709. Relations with Spaniards, 721. Religion, 10, 230. Rites and Ceremonies, 5. Warfare, 201. Women, 216.
Bahia, Brazil (state) Colonial History, 1953. Discovery and Exploration, 320. History,

1965. Newspapers, 1953. Race and Race Relations, 2104. Social Change, 2014.
Baja California, Mexico (region), 662. Colonial History, 662. Cultural History, 632. Education, 608. Indigenous Peoples, 251. Modernization, 666. Political History, 608, 632, 960, 989–990. Regionalism, 666. Revolutionaries, 989–990. Rural Development, 662. Social History, 608, 632. Water Rights, 990.
Balzan, Luigi, 522, 1759.
Banana Trade Colombia, 1623.
Banco Central del Ecuador, 1707.
Bandeira, Antônio, 143.
Bandits. See Brigands and Robbers.
Banking and Financial Institutions, 1707. Chile, 1826. Mexico, 867. Nicaragua, 1125.
Banks and Banking. See Banking and Financial Institutions.
Barbabé, Arrigo, 3442.
Baroque Art Ecuador, 48. Peru, 49. See Also Art History.
Baroque Music Chile, 3415, 3424.
Barquisimeto, Venezuela (city) History, 1605.
Baseball Venezuela, 1586.
Basques, 503. Colonial History, 748.
Beaches Brazil, 1969.
Bearden, Romare, 103.
Bechis, Martha, 280.
Béhague, Gerard, 3319, 3453.
Belgrano, Manuel, 1503.
Beliefs and Customs. See Religious Life and Customs. See Social Life and Customs.
Bello, Andrés, 542, 3604, 3609.
Beni, Bolivia (dept.). See El Beni, Bolivia (dept.).
Benítez, Cipriano, 1871.
Biassou, George, 1254.
Bilbao, Francisco, 3657.
Binda, Ramnarine, 1302.
Bioarcheology Mexico, 223, 741.
Biography, 597, 671. Argentina, 1494, 1503, 1507, 1513, 1538, 1549. Bolivia, 1795. Brazil, 1941, 2065. Chile, 1839. Mexico, 995. See Also Literature.
Biology Mexico, 952.
Birds Brazil, 2021. Symbolism (art), 9.
Birth Control Chile, 1833.
Bishop, Elizabeth, 3148.
Black Legend, 452, 560, 1293. See Also Colonial History; Indigenous Policy.
Blacks, 393, 1191. Argentina, 1888. Bolivia,

Dias, Cícero, 149.
Díaz, Porfirio, 813, 848.
Díaz Vargas, Miguel, 122.
Dictatorships, 458, 580. Argentina,
1891. Venezuela, 1596. *See Also*
Authoritarianism.
Dictionaries Social Sciences, 3495.
Diplomatic History, 431, 551, 1333. Brazil,
2032. Haiti, 1264. Panama, 1134. Spain,
564. US, 449, 521.
Diplomats Brazil, 1970, 2023, 3663.
Martinique, 1210. National Indentity,
1158.
Dirty War (Argentina, 1976–1983) Music,
3403.
Disappeared Persons Brazil, 2020.
Discography Puerto Rico, 3323.
Discovery and Exploration, 404, 445, 456,
475, 487, 522. Bolivia, 1759. Brazil, 136,
1921, 1944, 1947–1948. Chile, 1485.
Colombia, 333. Ecuador, 340, 1394. Me-
soamerica, 705. Mexico, 225. Painters,
134. Peru, 1404, 1421. Puerto Rico, 1182.
Venezuela, 1362.
Diseases Brazil, 2011, 2120. Colombia, 1688.
Colonial History, 497, 703. Panama, 1148.
See Also Epidemics.
Divorce Venezuela, 1582.
Doctors. *See* Physicians.
Documentaries Brazil, 3450.
Documentation Centers. *See* Libraries.
Domestics Brazil, 2012.
Dominican Revolution (1965), 1305, 1344,
1355.
Dominicans Viceroyalty of New Spain, 33.
Dominicans (religious order) Chile, 1486.
Colonial History, 1486.
Dowry Colonial History, 480. Viceroyalty of
New Spain, 714.
Drama Venezuela, 2948.
Dress. *See* Clothing and Dress.
Drug Enforcement, 422, 584.
Drug Traffic, 584. Mexico, 967. Peru, 422.
Drugs and Drug Trade. *See* Drug Enforce-
ment. *See* Drug Traffic.
Duarte, Juan Pablo, 1267.
Duchamp, Marcel, 112.
Dudamel, Gustavo, 3389.
Duportail Hermanos (firm), 1883.
Durango, Mexico (state) Land Reform, 988.
Dutch Conquest Brazil, 1941.
Earthquakes, 391. Chile, 1812. Colonial His-
tory, 1433, 1456. Mexico, 391. Peru, 391,
1433, 1456–1457.
Easter Island Archeology, 20.

Echeverría, Bolívar, 3567.
Ecological Crisis. *See* Environmental
Protection.
Economic Conditions, 600. Bolivia, 1762.
Coffee Industry and Trade, 1131. Colom-
bia, 1653, 1666. Costa Rica, 1081. Cuba,
1351. Ecuador, 1709. Guadeloupe, 1346.
Honduras, 1110. Viceroyalty of New
Spain, 718, 740.
Economic Development, 403, 417, 590–591,
605. Amazon Basin, 1753. Brazil, 2083,
3666. Chile, 1837, 1846. Colombia, 1677.
Colonial History, 485. Mexico, 610, 618,
670, 953. Tamaulipas, Mexico, 654.
Economic Development Projects. *See* Devel-
opment Projects.
Economic Growth. *See* Economic
Development.
Economic History, 390, 403, 405, 413, 430,
449, 462, 516, 562, 591, 598, 600. Argen-
tina, 437, 530, 1497, 1524. Barbados, 1201.
Bolivia, 530. Brazil, 2005. Chile, 1814,
1827, 1830–1831, 1836, 1851. Colombia,
1637, 1646. Cuba, 1185, 1294, 1318, 3594.
Dominican Republic, 1338. Mexico, 530,
610–611, 615–616, 637, 641–642, 670, 824,
828, 834, 844, 860, 867, 874, 876, 882, 957,
1015. Peru, 530, 1422–1423, 1455. Puerto
Rico, 1168.
Economic Integration, 556, 586, 3514. *See
Also* Free Trade.
Economic Planning. *See* Economic Policy.
Economic Policy, 562, 588. Colonial History, 479. Great Britain, 568.
Economic Theory, 579, 588–589, 598, 3479,
3493.
Education, 453, 3489–3491. Argentina,
3720–3721. Brazil, 1989, 2049. Chile,
1841. Colombia, 1626, 1628, 1640, 1673.
Colonial History, 500, 1399. Ecuador,
1696. Haiti, 1336. History, 548. Jesuits,
1365. Mexico, 623, 890. Nicaragua, 1136–
1137. Venezuela, 1591. Women, 1595,
1700. *See Also* Elementary Education.
Education and State. *See* Educational Policy.
Educational Policy Argentina, 409. Brazil,
409. Mexico, 880, 984, 997. Peru, 1444.
Educational Reform Argentina, 3692, 3703.
Chile, 1841. Colombia, 1668. Mexico,
880.
Educational Research, 634. History, 573.
Educators Brazil, 2042.
Eeckhout, Albert van der, 134.
Egaña, Mariano, 1802.
Einstein, Albert, 2928, 2988.

Literary Criticism, 3519, 3547. Cuba, 3599.
Mexico, 3577.
Literatura de Cordel Brazil, 2991. *See Also*
Popular Literature.
Literature Argentina, 112, 3717. Cuba,
1347, 2350, 2358–2359. Haiti, 2359. History, 536. Philosophy, 3519. *See Also*
Biography.
Lithuanians Brazil, 2136.
Loayza, Luis, 2366.
Lobato, José Bento Monteiro, 3566.
Lobato, Monteiro, 2116.
Local Elections Mexico, 877, 1000.
Local Government. *See* Municipal
Government.
Local History Bolivia, 1792. Colombia, 1618,
1647. Dominican Republic, 1306. Mexico,
767, 811. Paraguay, 1520. Peru, 1409, 1725,
1737.
Lockouts. *See* Strikes and Lockouts.
Logic Argentina, 3720–3721.
López, Estanislao, 1862.
López Obrador, Andrés Manuel, 977.
Louisiana, US (state) Freedmen, 1296. Race
and Race Relations, 1296.
Louverture, Toussaint, 1208, 1230, 1258.
Lutz, Bertha, 2119.
Mac Gregor, Gregor, *Sir*, 1146.
Machado de Assis, 3177.
Machismo. *See* Sex Roles.
Madero, Francisco I., 855, 948, 989, 2918.
Madero, Gustavo A., 948.
Magalhães, Domingos José Gonçalves de,
3151.
Magalhães, Roberto, 156.
Magallanes, Chile (prov.) Economic History,
1836. History, 1824.
Magón, Ricardo Flores. *See* Flores Magón,
Ricardo.
Maids. *See* Domestics.
Maldonado Sández, Braulio, 960.
Malina, Judith, 3179.
Malinche. *See* Marina.
Malnutrition. *See* Nutrition.
Mañach, Jorge, 3591.
Manilla, Manuel, 70, 77.
Mann, Erika, 2060.
Mann, Heinrich, 2060.
Mann, Thomas, 2060.
Mann family, 2060.
Manso de Noronha, Juana, 1885.
Mantilla Jácome, Carlos, 1713.
Manufactures Mexico, 824.
Manufacturing. *See* Manufactures.
Manuscripts Argentina, 3706. Aztecs, 2.

Brazil, 3444. Colonial History, 241. Mesoamerica, 196, 241, 256. Peru, 1431.
Manzon, Jean, 169.
Mapa de Otumba, 32, 221.
Mapa de Sigüenza, 2.
Maps and Cartography, 283, 546. Mexico,
218. Viceroyalty of New Spain, 32, 221.
Mapuche (indigenous group) Chile, 281, 364,
1800, 1806, 1810, 1822, 3408, 3410. Colonial History, 1477, 1527. History, 3661.
Indigenous/Non-Indigenous Relations,
1490.
Maracaibo, Venezuela (city) Insurrections,
1590. Mortuary Customs, 1604. Nationalism, 1576.
Maranhão, Brazil (state) Theater, 3175.
Marcos, Plínio, 3181.
Marcos, *subcomandante*, 946.
Marginalization. *See* Social Marginality.
María de Jesús, *de Agreda, sor*, 702.
Mariátegui, José Carlos, 3381, 3632, 3635,
3638, 3641, 3644, 3651–3652.
Marihuana. *See* Marijuana.
Marijuana Colombia, 1676.
Marimba, 3337. Colombia, 3355.
Marín, Javier, 68.
Marina, 234, 706.
Marine Resources, 427.
Maritime History Argentina, 1547. Barbados, 1255. Brazil, 1913. Caribbean Area,
833. Cuba, 1185. Mexico, 833. *See Also*
Naval History.
Markets Viceroyalty of Río de la Plata, 1509.
Mármol, Miguel, 1115.
Maroons Colombia, 1378. Dominica, 1236.
Márquez Montoya, Judith, 120.
Marranos, 481.
Marriage Argentina, 1565. Colonial History,
480, 515, 713, 1360. French Caribbean,
1239. Haiti, 1214, 1224. History, 531.
Indigenous Peoples, 381. Mesoamerica,
198. Mexico, 818.
Martí, José, 100, 3587–3588, 3595, 3597,
3686.
Martin de Moussy, Victor, 1879.
Martínez Compañón y Bujanda, Baltasar
Jaime, 1401.
Marx, Karl, 3613.
Marxism, 3484, 3506, 3554. Mexico, 3567,
3582. Peru, 3650. Philosophy, 3587.
Masks Guatemala, 3341. Painting, 126.
Masons. *See* Freemasonry.
Mass Media, 594, 635, 664. Argentina,
3697. Chile, 1804, 1829, 1842. Colombia,
1662, 1687, 3356. Colonial History, 1448.

Texas, US (state) Colonial History, 784. History, 614. Military History, 784.
Texas Rangers, 945.
Textbooks, 639. Colombia, 1626.
Textiles and Textile Industry Colonial History, 1186. Indigenous Peoples, 1419. Mexico, 951. Peru, 1419.
Theater, 2955. Argentina, 2949, 2952. Brazil, 3168. Censorship, 3167. Chile, 2958. Cuba, 2959. El Salvador, 1150. History, 3185. Mexico, 2954. Pictorial Works, 3187. Political Thought, 1217.
Thesaurus Indicus, 3476–3477.
Thistlewood, Thomas, 1180, 1188.
Ticuna (indigenous group). *See* Tucuna (indigenous group).
Time Indigenous Peoples, 378.
Tira de Tepechpan, 216.
Tiwanaku Culture, 21.
Tlapanec (indigenous group) Rites and Ceremonies, 214.
Tlaxcala, Mexico (state) Education, 890, 984.
Tobacco Industry and Trade Argentina, 1497. Colonial History, 1455. Costa Rica, 1105. History, 502. Peru, 1455.
Tobacco Use History, 502.
Tocantins, Brazil (state) Historiography, 2089. Indigenous Peoples, 1917.
Tojolabal (indigenous group) Social Conditions, 931.
Tolima, Colombia (dept.) History, 1663.
Toluca, Mexico (city) Colonial History, 696.
Toluca de Lerdo, Mexico (region) History, 726.
Topa Amaro, 341.
Tornel y Mendívil, José María, 797.
Toro, Fermín, 3605.
Torre, Manuel Antonio de la, 1494.
Torre, Víctor Raúl Haya de la. *See* Haya de la Torre, Víctor Raúl.
Torreón, Mexico (city) Economic History, 640. Railroads, 640.
Torres, Camilo, 1388.
Totalitarianism. *See* Authoritarianism.
Totonicapán, Guatemala (dept.) Insurrections, 1061.
Tourism, 1333. Jamaica, 1202. Mexico, 949, 969, 1011, 1021. Music Industry, 3332, 3334. Puerto Rico, 1011.
Towns. *See* Cities and Towns.
Traba, Marta, 116.
Trade. *See* Commerce.
Trade Unions, 625, 645. Bolivia, 1757. Brazil, 1963, 2043, 2130, 3183. Jamaica, 1322. Theater, 3183. Women, 1675.
Traditional Medicine Peru, 334.

Transatlantic Trade Mexico/Spain, 28.
Translating and Interpreting, 3310–3313, 3318. Colonial Literature, 3315. Spanish Conquest, 706.
Translation. *See* Translating and Interpreting.
Transportation Panama, 1123.
Tratado de Quilín (1641), 281.
Travel. *See* Description and Travel.
Travelers, 549. Brazil, 1973, 2107. Colombia, 1661. French Caribbean, 1176. Honduras, 1099. Viceroyalty of New Spain, 26.
Traversari Salazar, Pedro, 3364.
Treaties Brazil/Bolivia, 2078. Indigenous/Non-Indigenous Relations, 281. Mexican-American Border Region, 565.
Trees Brazil, 180. Myths and Mythology, 236.
Trials Argentina, 1859.
Trinidadians Cultural Identity, 3326.
Triple Alliance War (1865–1870). *See* Paraguayan War (1865–1870).
Trujillo, Peru (prov.) History, 334.
Trujillo Molina, Rafael Leónidas, 1300, 1308, 1324.
Tucumán, Argentina (city) Indigenous Peoples, 1528. Social History, 1528.
Tucumán, Argentina (prov.) Colonial History, 1525, 1542. Social Conflict, 1884.
Tucuna (indigenous group) Social Control, 380.
Tulancingo, Mexico (city) Historical Geography, 218.
Tumaco, Colombia (city) Urbanization, 1651.
Tunja, Colombia (city) Colonial History, 1389.
Túpac Amaru, José Gabriel, 374.
Tupi-Guarani (indigenous group) Indigenous Languages, 1921.
Tupiguarani (indigenous group). *See* Tupi-Guarani (indigenous group).
Tupinamba (indigenous group) Relations with Europeans, 1957.
Txeltal (indigenous group) Land Tenure, 265.
Uicab, María, 872.
Unamuno, Miguel de, 442.
Underwater Archeology, 427.
Unión Latino Americana, 3537.
Unión Nacional Sinarquista (Mexico), 947.
United Brands Company. *See* United Fruit Company.
United Fruit Company, 1623.
United States. Army, 826.
United States. Central Intelligence Agency, 1321.

AUTHOR INDEX

Marzano, Andrea, 3180
Mascareño, Pablo, 2944
Masetti, Jorge Ricardo, 1331
Masetto, Antonio dal, 2589
Mason, Peter, 20
Massardo, Jaime, 1825
Massimi, Marina, 1939
Masterson, Daniel M., 1740
Mata, Sara Emilia, 534
Matallana, Andrea, 3398
Mateo Palmer, Margarita, 2313, 2354
Materiales para la historia de Sonora, 744
Matesco, Viviane, 146
Mathis, Sophia, 342
Matos, Ramiro, 18, 310
Matos Paoli, Francisco, 2314–2315
Matthews, Mariana, 1839
Matto, Francisco, 129
Mattoni, Silvio, 2774
Mattos, Hebe Maria, 1940
Mattos, Marcelo Badaró, 2073
Matul, Daniel, 209
Maturana, Andrea, 2533
Maturo, Graciela, 3519
Mauleón Isla, Mercedes, 1038
Mavila, José Enrique, 2912
Mayer, Alicia, 648, 768
Mayer Center Symposium, *Denver Art Museum, 2006*, 22
Mayo Santana, Raúl, 1285
Mazín Gómez, Oscar, 445, 762
Mazzei de Grazia, Leonardo, 1826
Mazzeo, Miguel, 3644
Mazzoco, Maria Inês Dias, 2074
Mazzuca, Sebastián, 1654
Mc Evoy, Carmen, 555, 1741
McBeth, Brian Stuart, 1596
McClellan III, James E., 1237
McFarlane, Anthony, 499, 745
McGee, R. Jon, 231
McGuinness, Aims, 1117
McKnight, Kathryn Joy, 468
McLean, Anne, 3266, 3273
McNamara, Patrick J., 848
McPhee, Kit, 2075
McPherson, Alan L., 603
McWhirter, George, 3208
Mecánica política: para una relectura del siglo XIX mexicano: antología de correspondencia política, 849
Medeiros, Marcelo, 3154
Medeiros, Martha, 3041
Medina, Celso, 2647
Medina, Dante, 2913
Medina, Eden, 1827

Medina Carrero, Alberto, 2316
Medina Onrubia, Salvadora, 2914
Medina Vidal, D. Xavier, 962
Medinaceli, Ximena, 1463
Medrano de Luna, Gabriel, 645
Meeks, Brian, 3590
Megged, Amos, 746
Meier, Johannes, 1379
Meireles, Cecília, 3106
Mejía, José Luis, 2615
Mejía, Manuel Esteban, 2425
Mejía Lequerica, José, 1395
Mejía Macía, Sergio Andrés, 1655
Mejía P., Germán, 1656
Mejía, portavoz de América (1775–1813), 1395
Mejía Quintana, Oscar, 3520
Mejía Restrepo, Isabela, 1657
Mejía Sánchez, Ernesto, 2246
Meléndez, Mariselle, 1426
Meléndez Obando, Mauricio, 1026
Melgar-Palacios, Lucía, 656, 2177
Meliá, Bartomeu, 1558
Mellado, Marcelo, 2534
Mello, Amílcar d'Avila de, 343
Mello, Ana Maria Lisboa de, 3106
Mello, Evaldo Cabral de, 1941
Mello, Frederico Pernambucano de, 2076
Mello, Maria Tereza Chaves de, 2077
Mello, Simone Homem de, 3107
Melo, Patrícia, 2978, 3298
Melvin, Karen, 747
Memoria y autobiografía en Iberoamérica, 3521
Mencía, Mario, 1332
Mendes, Murilo, 3061
Mendes, Oswaldo, 3181
Méndez, Francisco Alejandro, 2259
Méndez, Helena, 2317
Méndez, Luz María, 1828
Méndez, Roberto, 2355
Méndez J., Mauricio, 2885
Méndez Paz, Carlos A., 1546
Méndez Reyes, Salvador, 3572
Méndez Vides, 2253
Mendieta, Eduardo, 3522, 3535
Mendieta, Eva, 748
Mendieta Parada, Pilar, 1785–1786
Mendieta Paz, Pablo, 2378
Mendonça, Sonia Regina de, 409
Mendoza, Irma, 1603
Mendoza, Zoila S., 3378
Mendoza L., Gunnar, 1795
Mendoza Muñoz, Jesús, 646, 749
Meneghetti, Sylvia Bojunga, 2112

Montañez, Carmen L., 2320
Montañez, Gustavo, 1090
Montani, Andrés, 130
Montaño Balderrama, Celso, 2379
Montaruli, Silvana, 3510
Montealegre, Jorge, 2780–2781
Montecino Aguirre, Sonia, 1835
Monteiro, Peter Ribon, 181
Monteiro, Túlio, 3014
Montello, Josué, 2018
Montemayor, Carlos, 2205
Montenegro, Silvia, 2782
Montero Méndez, Hortensia, 101
Montes, Aníbal, 345
Montes, José Wolfango, 2380
Montes Huidobro, Matías, 2916
Montiel, Edgar, 3524
Montoya, Ramón Alejandro, 965
Montreal Museum of Fine Arts, 98
Monzant Gavidia, J.L., 1597
Mooney, Jadwiga E. Pieper, 1833
Moore, Robin, 3349, 3453
Mora, Genoveva, 2869
Mora, Mariana, 966
Mora Covarrubias, Guadalupe de la, 2882
Mora Martínez, Roberto, 3511
Mora Queipo, Ernesto, 1363
Mora Rodríguez, Arnoldo, 3686
Morado Macías, César, 613
Moraes, Vinicius de, 3043
Morais, Taís, 2080
Moral Roncal, Antonio Manuel, 1334
Morales, Gabriel, 3525–3526
Morales, Gary, 2783
Morales Alemañy, Suyín, 2863
Morales Damián, Manuel Alberto, 236–237
Morales Guinaldo, Lucía, 1375
Morales Moreno, Humberto, 853
Morales Reynoso, María de Lourdes, 875
Morales Santos, Francisco, 2674
Morán Ramos, Luis Daniel, 1428
Moraña, Mabel, 510, 3483
Morasan, J.A., 2271
Moreira, Eduardo, 3149
Moreira da Costa, Flávio, 2999
Moreno, Gabriel René, 1466
Moreno, Norberto, 936
Moreno, Yvette Neisser, 3207
Moreno Cebrián, Alfredo, 1429–1430
Moreno Heredia, Eugenio, 2784
Moreno Jeria, Rodrigo, 1484
Moreno Pérez, Edgardo, 652
Moreno Sandoval, Armando, 1376
Morettin, Eduardo Victorio, 2081
Morgade, Pablo, 3403

Moritz, Albert Frank, 3240
Moro Junior, Enio, 182
Morong, Germán, 308
Morris, Mark, 238, 854
Morrison, Mateo, 2321, 2785
Mosca, Stefania, 2502
Moscona, Myriam, 2786
Moscoso, Martha, 346
Moser, Benjamin, 3293–3294
Mota, Carlos Guilherme, 3677
Mott, Maria Lucia, 2082
Motta, Sara C., 3527
Mottier, Nicole, 967
Moulian, Tomás, 1834
Moura, Denise Aparecida Soares de, 2083
Moura, Esmeralda Blanco Bolsonaro de, 2005
Moura, Rodrigo, 153
Movimientos armados en México, siglo XX, 968
Movimientos universitarios: América Latina siglo XX, 592
Moya, José C., 448
Moya, Pastor de, 2787
Mraz, John, 80
Muchnik, José, 2591
Mudarra Montoya, Américo, 2366
La mujer en la historia del Perú: siglos XV al XX, 1742
La mujer frente al espejo: antología anotada de dramaturgas dominicanas contemporáneas, 2917
Mujeres chilenas: fragmentos de una historia, 1835
Mujica, Wilfredo, 2788
Mujica Pinilla, Ramón, 54
Mukerjee, Anil, 347
Muleiro, Vicente, 2592
Mullo Sandoval, Juan, 3364
Munday, Jeremy, 3316
El mundo ranchero, 653
¿Un mundo sin filosofía?, 3528
Munduruku, Daniel, 2981
Múnera, Alfonso, 1658
Munive, Manual, 128
Muñiz, Francisco Javier, 2645
Muñoz, Braulio, 3261
Muñoz, Marisa, 3543
Muñoz, Nancy K., 3261
Muñoz, Willy Oscar, 2254, 2871
Muñoz Cordero, Lydia Inés, 1659
Muñoz García, Angel, 3476–3477
Muñoz Pini, Laura María, 617
Muñoz Pinzón, Armando, 1123
Munro, Arlene, 1335
Munteal Filho, Oswaldo, 1982

Piña, Juan Andrés, 2958
Piña Chán, Beatriz Barba de, 6
Pinedo, Javier, 3660
Piñeiro Iñíguez, Carlos, 3536
Piñera, Virgilio, 2329
Pinheiro, Lenise, 3187
Pinheiro, Mauro, 3016
Pino, Amado del, 2959
Pino Iturrieta, Elías, 1600
Piñon, Nélida, 3300
Pinto, António Costa, 2114
Pinto, Manuel da Costa, 3123
Pinto Herrera, Honorio Sabino, 1744
Pinto Huaracha, Miguel, 1440
Pinto Soria, Julio César, 1077
Pinto Vallejos, Julio, 1838
Los Pioneros Valck: un siglo de fotografía en el sur de Chile, 1839
Piossek Prebisch, Lucía, 3711
Piqueras Arenas, José Antonio, 1213
Pires, Mário Jorge, 183
Piroli, Wander, 2984
Pita González, Alexandra, 3537
Piva, Roberto, 3124
Pïneres de la Ossa, Dora, 1668
Plascencia Ñol, León, 2801
Platt, Tristán, 355, 1790
Plaza, Ramón, 2802
Pleguezuelo Hernández, Alfonso, 28
Pobreza e historia en Costa Rica: determinantes estructurales y representantes sociales del siglo XVII a 1950, 1041
Poemas afro-brasileiros, 3125
Poemas de amor y rebeldía social: poetas del mundo, antiguos y contemporáneos, 2652
Poesía ecuatoriana: antología esencial, 2653
Poesía mística del interiorismo: antología de la lírica teopoética y protomística, 2654
Poetas argentinas, 1961–1980, 2655
Los poetas interiores: una muestra de la nueva poesía argentina, 2656
Poéticas do olhar e outras leituras de poesia, 3126
Pohl, John M. D., 10
Pol, Julio César, 2659
Polhamer, Eric, 2803
Policastro, Cristina, 2503
Political violence and the construction of national identity in Latin America, 3538
Políticas y estéticas del cuerpo en América Latina, 451
Pollack, Aaron, 1061
Pollack, Sarah, 3238, 3317
Poloni-Simard, Jacques, 354
Pomareda, Fernando, 2442

Pompejano, Daniele, 1062
Pompeu, Renato, 2985
Ponce, Víctor Andrés, 2479
Ponemos tu obra en escena: Los número seis; El arca de Noé; Efímero, 2920
Poniatowska, Elena, 977, 3276
Pons, André, 551
Pontificia Universidad Católica de Valparaíso, 413, 536
Pontificia Universidad Católica del Perú, 2365
Pontificia Universidad Católica del Perú. Instituto de Etnomusicología, 3372–3374
Pontificia Universidad Javeriana. Facultad de Comunicación y Lenguaje, 3356
Popkin, Jeremy D., 1219, 1242–1243
Por la salud del cuerpo: historia y políticas sanitarias en Chile, 1840
Portela, Ena Lucía, 2330
Portinari, Cândido, 152, 155
Portinari, João Candido, 152
Portuondo Zúñiga, Olga, 1198, 1288
Posada, José Guadalupe, 90
Posgrado Centroamericano en Historia (Universidad de Costa Rica), 1041
Possamai, Zita Rosane, 170
Powell, Amanda, 3195
Powell, Philip Wayne, 452
Power, culture, and violence in the Andes, 1791
Pozas, Mario A., 3539
Pozzi, Edna, 2804
Prada Prada, Jorge, 2936
Prado, Maria Lígia Coelho, 2051
Prado Júnior, Caio, 3680
Praises and offenses: three women poets from the Dominican Republic, 3200
Prata, Mário, 3047
A pre-Columbian world, 247
Preciado, Antonio, 2657
Premat, Julio, 2563
Premio Nacional de Literatura Efraín Huerta, 2848
Premo, Bianca, 507
La prensa como fuente para la historia, 657
Prenz, Juan Octavio, 2596
Pretorianismo venezolano del siglo XXI: ensayos sobre las relaciones civiles y militares venezolanas, 1601
Price, Richard, 103
Price, Sally, 103
Priego Martínez, Natalia, 864
Prieto, Jenaro, 2536
El primer Sínodo del Paraguay y Río de la Plata en Asunción en el año de 1603, 1558

Rodríguez Vásconez, Byron, 2431
Roemer, Andrés, 2928
Rogers, Dominique, 1172, 1245
Rohden, Valério, 3674
Roig, Arturo Andrés, 3495, 3543, 3709, 3716
Roig, Elisabeth, 2802
Roitman, Marcos, 3569
Rojas, Ángel F., 2421–2422
Rojas, Beatriz, 775, 849
Rojas, Gonzalo, 3234
Rojas, Mauricio F., 1843
Rojas, Rafael, 2356, 3598–3599
Rojas, Reinaldo, 1605, 3614
Rojas Díaz, Wilder, 2816
Rojas Flores, Jorge, 1844
Rojas Gómez, Miguel, 3578
Rojas Jiménez, Miguel, 2929
Rojas-Mix, Miguel, 458
Rojo Redolés, Rolando, 2540
Rokha, Winétt de, 2817
Rolland, Denis, 1983
Rolle, Claudio, 1829, 3412
Román, Reinaldo L., 1343
Román Jáquez, Juana Gabriela, 614
Romano García, Martín, 1526
Romeiro, Adriana, 1945
Romero, Alexis, 2818
Romero, Jilma, 1043
Romero, Raúl R., 3374
Romero de Solís, José Miguel, 986
Romero de Vázquez, Natividad, 1562
Romero Galván, José Rubén, 252, 634
Rommen, Timothy, 3334
Romo, Anadelia A., 2104
Rompecabezas de papel: la prensa y el periodismo desde las regiones de México, siglos XIX y XX, 871
Ron, Alex, 2432
Ronald Flores, 2269
Roncagliolo, Santiago, 3265
Rondón, Víctor, 3421
Ronquillo, Víctor, 2216
Rood, Daniel, 560, 1293
Rosa, Jesús de la, 1344
Rosa Izaguirre, Ramón, 1099
Rosado, Georgina Rosado, 872
Rosal, Miguel Á, 1888
Rosales Ayala, Silvano Héctor, 75
Rosales Sánchez, Juan, 3615
Rosario, Emilio, 1731
Rosario Candelier, Bruno, 2654
Rosario Esobar, María del, 125
Rosas, Alejandro, 659, 671
Rosas Lauro, Claudia, 1427, 1447–1448
Rosas Ledezma, Enrique, 561

Rosas Moscoso, Fernando, 1449
Rose, Sonia V., 482
Roselló Soberón, Estela, 776
Rosenberg, Mirta, 2819
Rosenmann Taub, David, 2820–2821
Rosenmüller, Christoph, 777–778
Rosero Diago, Evelio, 3266
Rossell, Cecilia, 253
Rossi, Anacristina, 2257
Rossignol, Jacques, 364
Los rostros de la Hidra: antología de revistas y poetas del siglo XXI, 2659
Los rostros de la modernidad: vías de transición al capitalismo: Europa y América Latina, siglos XIX–XX, 562
Rostworowski de Diez Canseco, María, 365–366
Rotker, Susana, 3595
Roulet, Florencia, 367
Roux, Jean-Claude, 1794
Roux López, Rodolfo de, 459
Royo Aspa, Antoni, 1138
Rubial García, Antonio, 779
Rubiano Caballero, Germán, 118
Rubiano Vargas, Roberto, 2407
Rubinsky, Sonia, 3448
Rubio Hernández, Alfonso, 1383
Rueda Enciso, José Eduardo, 368
Rugeley, Terry, 873
Ruisánchez, José Ramón, 2217
Ruiz, Iván, 63
Ruiz Medrano, Carlos Rubén, 254, 621, 780–781
Ruiz Medrano, Ethelia, 782
Ruiz Montealegre, Manuel, 2394
Ruiz Pérez, Miviam, 3350
Ruiz Rosas, Teresa, 2483
Rupke, Nicolaas A., 563
Rustán, María E., 1563
Rutman, Jacques, 156
Ruy Sánchez, Alberto, 2218, 3267
Ruz, Mario Humberto, 213
Ruz Barrio, Miguel Ángel, 255–256
Ryden, David B., 1246

Saadi, Fátima, 3188
Saavedra Inaraja, María, 511
Saavedra Restrepo, María Claudia, 1675
Saavedra Villarroel, Oscar, 2822
Sábato, Hilda, 1889
Sábato, Mario, 2600
Sabines, Jaime, 3235
Sabino, Carlos A., 1139–1140
Sabino, Mario, 3302
Sabsay, Fernando L., 597